THE DARKEST SIDES OF POLITICS, I

This book examines a wide array of phenomena that arguably constitute the most noxious, extreme, terrifying, murderous, secretive, authoritarian, and/or anti-democratic aspects of national and international politics. Scholars should not ignore these "dark sides" of politics, however unpleasant they may be, since they influence the world in a multitude of harmful ways.

The first volume in this two-volume collection focuses on the history of underground neo-fascist networks in the post-World War II era; neo-fascist paramilitary and terrorist groups operating in Europe and Latin America in the 1960s and 1970s; and the manipulation of those and other terrorist organizations by the security forces of various states, both authoritarian and democratic. A range of global case studies are included, all of which focus on the lesser known activities of certain secular extremist milieus.

This collection should prove to be essential reading for students and researchers interested in understanding seemingly arcane but nonetheless important dimensions of recent historical and contemporary politics.

Jeffrey M. Bale is Professor in the Nonproliferation and Terrorism Studies Program at the Middlebury Institute of International Studies at Monterey, USA.

Routledge Studies in Extremism and Democracy
Series Editors: Roger Eatwell, *University of Bath*, and
Matthew Goodwin, *University of Kent*.
Founding Series Editors: Roger Eatwell, *University of Bath*, and
Cas Mudde, *University of Antwerp-UFSIA*.

www.routledge.com/politics/series/ED

This new series encompasses academic studies within the broad fields of 'extremism' and 'democracy'. These topics have traditionally been considered largely in isolation by academics. A key focus of the series, therefore, is the (inter-)*relation* between extremism and democracy. Works will seek to answer questions such as to what extent 'extremist' groups pose a major threat to democratic parties, or how democracy can respond to extremism without undermining its own democratic credentials.

The books encompass two strands:

Routledge Research in Extremism and Democracy offers a forum for innovative new research intended for a more specialist readership. These books will be in hardback only. Titles include:

36. **Understanding the Populist Shift**
    Othering in a Europe in Crisis
    Edited by Gabriella Lazaridis and Giovanna Campani

37. **The Darkest Sides of Politics, I**
    Postwar Fascism, Covert Operations, and Terrorism
    Jeffrey M. Bale

38. **The Darkest Sides of Politics, II**
    State Terrorism, "Weapons of Mass Destruction," Religious Extremism, and Organized Crime
    Jeffrey M. Bale

THE DARKEST SIDES OF POLITICS, I

Postwar Fascism, Covert Operations, and Terrorism

Jeffrey M. Bale

Routledge
Taylor & Francis Group
LONDON AND NEW YORK

First published 2018
by Routledge
2 Park Square, Milton Park, Abingdon, Oxon OX14 4RN

and by Routledge
711 Third Avenue, New York, NY 10017

Routledge is an imprint of the Taylor & Francis Group, an informa business

© 2018 Jeffrey M. Bale

The right of Jeffrey M. Bale to be identified as author of this work has been asserted by him in accordance with sections 77 and 78 of the Copyright, Designs and Patents Act 1988.

All rights reserved. No part of this book may be reprinted or reproduced or utilised in any form or by any electronic, mechanical, or other means, now known or hereafter invented, including photocopying and recording, or in any information storage or retrieval system, without permission in writing from the publishers.

Trademark notice: Product or corporate names may be trademarks or registered trademarks, and are used only for identification and explanation without intent to infringe.

British Library Cataloguing-in-Publication Data
A catalogue record for this book is available from the British Library

Library of Congress Cataloging-in-Publication Data
A catalog record for this book has been requested

ISBN: 978-1-138-78560-1 (hbk)
ISBN: 978-1-138-78561-8 (pbk)
ISBN: 978-1-315-76611-9 (ebk)

Typeset in Bembo
by Apex CoVantage, LLC

CONTENTS

Notes on the materials included in these volumes — vii
Acknowledgements — xi

1 Introduction: ideologies, extremist ideologies, and terrorist violence — 1

2 Political paranoia versus political realism: on distinguishing between bogus conspiracy theories and genuine conspiratorial politics — 46

3 Postwar neo-fascist internationals, part 1: Nazi escape networks, the Mouvement Social Européenne, Europäische Neu-Ordnung, and Jeune Europe — 60

4 Postwar "neo-fascist" internationals, part 2: Aginter Presse and the "strategy of tension" in Italy — 136

5 The December 1970 "Borghese coup" in Rome — 212

6 The May 1973 terrorist attack at Milan police HQ: anarchist 'propaganda of the deed' or 'false-flag' provocation? — 364

7 Concluding thoughts on the terrorist "strategy of tension" in Italy — 399

8 The ultranationalist right in Turkey and the attempted
   assassination of Pope John Paul II   411

9 'National revolutionary' groupuscules and the resurgence
   of 'left-wing' fascism: the case of France's Nouvelle Résistance 466

Contents of volume II   *491*
Index   *493*

NOTES ON THE MATERIALS INCLUDED IN THESE VOLUMES

The materials collected in the two volumes of this book derive from a variety of sources. Most have already been published in academic works or journalistic magazines devoted to extremism, terrorism, and covert politics, whereas others originated as chapters from my doctoral dissertation at the University of California at Berkeley, two were especially prepared for contractors for agencies of the U.S. government and have not yet been published, and one was written initially for another book. The reader should be warned, however, that most of the materials herein are examples of "old school" historical scholarship, which means that they are densely packed with rich, empirical details, are based as much as possible on a careful evaluation of the existing corpus of primary sources, and contain very extensive reference notes. Thus those who have become accustomed to reading modern "social science" literature, with its excessive emphasis on theories and models, obsession with quantification, and embarrassingly limited use of primary sources, may find some of them rough going. On the other hand, traditional historians should feel themselves right at home. That is entirely intentional.

Volume I

The introductory chapter was mostly prepared for a separate book-length study (provisionally titled *Where the Anti-democratic Extremes Touch: Patterns of Interaction and Collaboration between Islamist Networks and Western Left- and Right-Wing Extremists*) that I had planned and begun to write. However, the emotional fallout from the sudden death of my longtime girlfriend interrupted the process of writing that book, which therefore may never be written. Hence I have added some new prefatory paragraphs to a chapter focusing on the nature and importance of extremist ideologies.

The second chapter was first published in the 1990s in *Lobster: A Journal of Parapolitics*, and then expanded and republished in the academic journal *Patterns of Prejudice*.

Chapters 3 through 7 were all originally prepared in the early 1990s for my doctoral dissertation in Late Modern European History at the University of California at Berkeley. Although several academic publishers expressed an interest in publishing a book version of that six-hundred-plus-page dissertation, I instead moved on to work on other research topics because I felt that I would have had to add a very large chapter on the 12 December 1969 Piazza Fontana massacre, an extraordinarily complicated case. As a result, only Chapter 6 on the May 1973 attack on Milan police headquarters was subsequently published, in the journal *Terrorism and Political Violence*. For this collection, I have slightly augmented Chapter 3, significantly updated sections of Chapters 4 and 5 (because a wealth of new sources has since appeared on those topics), and added a brief paragraph addendum to Chapter 6. I am very pleased and proud to say that my detailed reconstructions and close analyses of these murky events over three decades ago proved to be extremely accurate and indeed prescient, because the new information that has subsequently appeared has not only confirmed, but further reinforced, virtually all of my narrative accounts and conclusions. This goes to show, yet again, that comprehensive scholarly research generally stands the test of time, unlike the trendy, fashionable theoretical drivel that too many people in the humanities and "social sciences" have been peddling in recent decades.

Chapter 8 was originally published in the *Bulletin of the Turkish Studies Association*, and then republished sometime later in *Lobster* so that it would reach a specialized non-academic audience. It has been slightly amended.

Chapter 9 was previously published in *Patterns of Prejudice*. It has not been altered.

Volume II

Chapter 1 originally appeared in an edited volume titled *Making Sense of Proxy Wars*, edited by Michael Innes. It has not been altered.

Chapter 2 was published in the journal *Democracy and Security*. I am happy to say that the fears of many analysts (myself included) that some toxic chemical or biological agents produced in connection with "Project Coast" may have been smuggled out of South Africa appear not to have materialized. The reconstruction of the actual details of this covert program, including special operations assassinations carried out with the use of these agents, has proven to be accurate. It has not been altered.

Chapter 3 was originally written for a graduate seminar course at the University of California at Berkeley and then published in *Lobster*. It has been slightly amended and updated.

Chapter 4 is an unpublished report that I prepared under contract for a U.S. government entity. It contains no classified information.

Chapter 5 was first published as a chapter in a book titled *Jihadists and Weapons of Mass Destruction*, edited by Gary Ackerman and Jeremy Tamsett. It has been slightly altered.

Here I would like to emphasize that I would have preferred to devote most of my research efforts in recent years to reconstructing particular jihadist terrorist plots and attacks, on the basis of an in-depth examination of judicial materials and other primary sources, which is the same methodology I employed for many years while doing research on neo-fascist terrorism. I did indeed adopt those tried-and-true methods in connection with both the 1999 Ahmad Rassam "Millennium" bomb plot (see Chapter 9 in this volume) and the 2004 Madrid train bombings (in a monograph titled *Jihādist Cells and I.E.D. Capabilities in Europe: Assessing the Present and Future Threat to the West*, which was published by the United States Army War College's Strategic Studies Institute in 2012). Unfortunately, given the proliferation of ill-informed nonsense being peddled after 9/11 by so many newly minted "terrorism experts," most of whom had no prior academic background in the study of terrorism, Islamic history, Islamic religious and legal doctrines, or Islamist ideologies and movements, I increasingly felt compelled to try to promote more conceptual clarity about these broader issues. This seemed all the more necessary because naïve and erroneous ideas about Islam and Islamism were exerting an ever-growing influence on the counterterrorism policies adopted by the United States and other Western nations, with predictably disastrous real-world consequences.

The next three articles included herein were therefore designed to counter widespread but misleading claims that (a) Islam is inherently a "religion of peace" (despite numerous Qur'anic *sura*s that explicitly enjoin warfare against non-believers, Muhammad's own "exemplary" behavior as a warlord, and centuries of brutal Muslim conquests of "infidel" territory); that (b) Islamism, an intrinsically literalist, strict, and puritanical but in most respects orthodox interpretation of core Islamic doctrines, can be "moderate" with respect to its goals (as opposed to its methods); that (c) jihadist terrorism has "nothing to do with Islam" despite the fact that its Islamist sponsors and perpetrators correctly insist otherwise (and, indeed, obsessively cite canonical Islamic sources in order to justify every action they take); and that (d) Western counterterrorist policies should be based on promoting these absurd revisionist fictions instead of acknowledging reality. In these three chapters, my growing exasperation about the West's stubborn refusal to recognize or acknowledge the nature of our Islamist adversaries is at times on display. Then again, this sort of denial of reality is rarely if ever a problem when one writes about fascism and neo-fascism. Although Islamist apologists are currently omnipresent in academia (and the media), as are communist apologists and cult apologists, fascist apologists have fortunately not been common there since the 1920s and 1930s. How does one explain the seemingly never-ending willingness of supposedly educated people to engage in such embarrassing apologetics for totalitarian ideologies and movements? As George Orwell once wryly noted, "[t]here are some ideas so absurd that only an intellectual could believe them." American literary critic Lionel Trilling helped to explain why when he observed that "[t]hose members of the intellectual class who prided themselves upon their political commitment were committed not to the fact but to the abstraction." Sadly, this is no less true today.

Chapter 6 was published in a special issue, devoted to Islamism, of the journal *Totalitarian Movements and Political Religions* (now *Politics, Religion, and Ideology*), which was edited by myself and my colleague Bassam Tibi.

Chapter 7 was published in the leading online Terrorism Studies journal, *Perspectives on Terrorism*. It is now being republished, as I always prefer, in a hard copy format.

A shorter version of Chapter 8 was published as a special report for the Investigative Project on Terrorism (IPT) website. The longer, slightly updated version appears here for the first time.

Chapter 9 is a previously unpublished segment that I originally prepared for a larger research report for a U.S. government agency. It has been slightly modified.

Chapter 10 was first published in a 2014 McGraw-Hill e-book edited by Russell E. Howard, *The Terrorism-Trafficking Nexus: A Clear and Present Danger?*, and is now being republished in a hard copy format. It has not been altered.

ACKNOWLEDGEMENTS

The author would like to thank the following persons and organizations for inspiration or assistance that has resulted in the publication of this volume: Craig Fowlie from Taylor & Francis, who shared my interests in the dark but arcane subjects covered in this volume, and thus encouraged me to prepare a collection of some of my scholarly publications and unpublished materials; Matthew Twigg from Taylor & Francis and both Chris Mathews and Autumn Spalding from Apex CoVantage for logistical assistance throughout the publishing process; Zsofia Baumann, my Graduate Student Researcher and editorial and technical assistant at the Middlebury Institute of International Studies at Monterey (MIIS), who aided me in the preparation of the final manuscript; my colleagues, inside and outside of academia, who I have collaborated with off and on over the decades in the study of "parapolitics" and covert operations, including Professor Peter Dale Scott, Kevin Coogan, Jonathan Marshall, Robin Ramsay, Jim Hougan, Professor Stephen Dorril, Professor Jeffrey Burds, Bernard Fensterwald (RIP), and "David Teacher"; other academic historians and mentors (and/or friends), including Professors Rudi P. Lindner, Andrew Ehrenkreutz (RIP), John V. A. Fine, John Masson Smith, Grace Smith, Richard Webster (RIP), Harold Nicholson (RIP), William Hoisington, and Gerald Feldman (RIP); academic colleagues who study the radical right, fascism, and/or terrorism, including Walter Laqueur, Brigadier General Russell Howard (ret.), Jean-Yves Camus, Fernando Reinares, Angel Rabasa, Olivier Guitta, Guido Olimpio, and Professors Roger Griffin, Alex P. Schmid, Martha Crenshaw, Robert Paxton, Stanley Payne, Graham Macklin, David Rapoport, Anton Shekhovtsov, Nicolas Lebourg, Andreas Umland, George Michael, Jeffrey Herf, Adam Dolnik, and Leonard Weinberg; colleagues who study "weapons of mass destruction" in relation to terrorism, including Gary Ackerman, Raymond Zilinskas, Milton Leitenberg, Sharad Joshi, Markus Binder, Eric Croddy, Chandre Gould, Glenn Cross, Adam Dolnik, and Jonathan Tucker (RIP); colleagues who study religious extremism, cults, Islam, Islamism, and/or jihadism, including Timothy Furnish, Gordon Hahn, John Rosenthal,

Robert Reilly, Steven Emerson, Matthias Küntzel, Jamal Hasan, Alexandre del Valle, and Professors Bassam Tibi, Lorenzo Vidino, David Cook, Nelly Lahoud, Ana Belén Soage, Richard Landes, Richard Ofshe, Janja Lalich, Benjamin Zablocki, and Benjamin Beit-Hallahmi; Professor Phil Williams, a colleague specializing in organized crime and other *sub rosa* groups; Professors Raimondo Catanzaro, Piergiorgio Corbetta, Arturo Parisi, and Gianfranco Pasquino of the Istituto di Studi e Ricerche "Carlo Cattaneo" in Bologna, as well as the unfailingly helpful staff there (in particular, Giovanni Cocchi, Anna Galetti, and Mirella Mirani), who kindly allowed me to examine several thousand pages of judicial sentences on the premises; the library staffs at the University of Michigan, University of California at Berkeley, Stanford University, the Hoover Institution, Columbia University, the Biblioteca della Camera dei Deputati, the Biblioteca Nazionale, and the Library of Congress, for putting up with innumerable requests for obscure books; the archival staffs at the U.S. National Archives (especially John Taylor [RIP]), and the Archivio Centrale dello Stato in Rome; Professor Franco Ferraresi (RIP), Professor Piero Ignazi, Professor Aldo Giannuli, Giuseppe De Lutiis, Paolo Cucchiarelli, and Gianni Flamini, who provided me with useful information and/or materials; other faculty colleagues or staff at MIIS, who have – at least most of the time, LOL – made my extended sojourn there congenial (William Potter, Jeffrey Knopf, Avner Cohen, Anna Vassilieva, Mike Gillen, Philipp Bleek, Barbara Burke, Ann Flower, Edith Bursac, Jan Dahlstrom, Phil Murphy, Fernando De Paolis, Bob McCleery, Moyara Ruehsen, Kent Glenzer, Jeff Dayton-Johnson, Robert Rogowsky, Jason Scorse, Dan Pinkston, Clay Moltz, Amy Sands, Viktor Mizin, and Tim McCarthy); the intellectuals from assorted extremist milieus who have shared their often fascinating ideas with me during in-person and email interviews over the decades; Jean-Gilles Malliarakis, Peter Sebastian, and Marco Battara, at whose bookstores in Paris, Rome, and Milan, respectively, I obtained many obscure but crucially important primary and secondary sources concerning the history of neo-fascism and the postwar radical right; the most intellectually inquisitive, thoughtful, and dedicated students at the academic institutions where I have taught, who have forced me to augment my own knowledge and refine my own arguments; all of my countercultural hippie and punk rock friends from the 1960s to the present day (especially Terry Nelson, who has been an obsessive underground rock 'n' roll fanatic for as long as I have; needless to say, "we're never, ever gonna stop," even though "the Pistols quit, the Clash slowed down, and Gen X are in a [J]am!"), who have made my life infinitely more fun than any one individual has a right to experience; my close long-term friends, Chris Burns (RIP) and Robert Doner (RIP), both of whom died prematurely and whom I miss very much; and, above all, Mimi Harary (RIP), the stunningly beautiful and remarkably brilliant woman I loved for thirty-three years prior to her premature death in September 2012, a tragic event that I will never, ever get over – if I could turn back the clock, knowing what I do now, I would have spent more quality time with you, Mimi, and less time in musty libraries and at underground rock 'n' roll gigs.

I only wish I could blame my mentors and colleagues listed above for any shortcomings found herein, but unfortunately I cannot.

1

INTRODUCTION

Ideologies, extremist ideologies, and terrorist violence

The title of this two-volume collection of scholarly materials, *The Darkest Sides of Politics*, should be more or less self-explanatory given the addition of the subtitles to those volumes. The first volume is subtitled *Postwar Fascism, Covert Operations, and Terrorism*, and the second is subtitled *State Terrorism, "Weapons of Mass Destruction," Religious Extremism, and Organized Crime*. Individually and collectively, these subjects arguably constitute the most noxious, extreme, terrifying, murderous, secretive, authoritarian, and/or anti-democratic aspects of national and international politics. For better or worse, it is precisely these grim but relatively arcane areas of politics and religion that have been the primary focus of my scholarly research for nearly four decades, long before some of them became increasingly "fashionable" in the wake of the spectacular and devastating jihadist terrorist attacks on 11 September 2001. Throughout those decades, faculty colleagues, students, and acquaintances have often asked me how I managed to cope psychologically with devoting so much time and effort studying the most horrific aspects of human political behavior. One of my glib responses has been that "it's a dirty job, but someone has to do it." Yet those who know me better realize that for me it has never been a "dirty" or unpleasant task, but rather an endless source of intellectual fascination, irrespective of whether such subjects happen to be considered important within the halls of academe. In fact, I personally find it much more difficult to understand how so many people in academia can spend their entire lives studying the far more mundane, conventional, and mainstream aspects of politics, most of which I consider to be deadly dull.

In order to explain my obsession with the nastier and less conventional topics that are the focus of these volumes, perhaps a brief personal introduction is called for. I am a very unconventional person who has also had an unusual academic trajectory. It seems that nowadays most people who end up on university faculties go straight from high school into college, then straight from college into graduate school, and then – if they are fortunate, well-connected, brilliant, or sufficiently servile and conformist – straight into junior academic jobs, which means that they usually begin their academic careers in their late twenties or very early thirties. In marked contrast, I did not obtain my Ph.D. in modern European history from the University of California at Berkeley until I was forty-three. The reason for this long delay is directly related to the reasons why I am attracted to studying the aforementioned subjects. Far from being a "normal" academician from a comfortable upper middle class background, I came from a poor, dysfunctional single-family household, and only managed to escape from these difficult, unpleasant childhood circumstances by reading huge numbers of books, especially horror novels and volumes on military history, and listening obsessively to primitive rock 'n' roll. As a teenager I was a countercultural, authority-hating, rock 'n' roll rebel who soon became one of the first hippies, and thus "dropped out, turned on, and tuned in" as soon as I graduated from my depressing public high school. A few years later, as the '60s counterculture increasingly degenerated into a parody of itself, I entered college and obtained my B.A. in Middle Eastern, Islamic, and Central Asian history from the University of Michigan. Meanwhile, in 1977 I became one of the first punk rockers and again "dropped out, turned on, and tuned in" for several years, which once again interrupted and delayed the completion of my academic career. Even after I completed my doctorate and spent some years teaching, I withdrew from the academic world for a few more years in order to publish and edit an underground rock 'n' roll magazine. Indeed, it was only after 9/11 that I decided to return once and for all to academic life, because everyone else suddenly became interested in certain types of extremist groups that I had already increasingly been examining. As one of the professors on my dissertation committee wryly remarked after 9/11, "the rest of the world has finally caught up with your arcane interests." In short, I have always been psychologically attracted to and intellectually interested in "extreme" phenomena, whether literary, aesthetic, musical, cultural, social, or political. To use the phrase coined in a science fiction/horror novel, I am an "extremophile," someone who loves immersing myself in extreme phenomena.[1]

This peculiar background is important for three reasons. First, it eventually caused me to gradually shift my focus from ancient and medieval to modern history, and to direct my scholarly attention to the post–World War II history of sectarian extremist political and religious groups, in particular violent paramilitary and terrorist organizations. Second, given my rebellious, anti-establishment personality, I have never shied away from bucking academic orthodoxies, rejecting "hegemonic" but often ridiculous academic fads, or openly challenging the views of influential academicians that I regarded as seriously mistaken – for which I make no apologies whatsoever. Third, and perhaps most importantly, because I myself have long been a profoundly alienated, disgruntled person, this has arguably enabled me to better understand, relate to, and empathize with – albeit, nota bene, *not* sympathize with – various types of ideological extremists. These extremists, almost by definition, likewise tend to be disgruntled individuals, very often from higher socio-economic classes and with more rather than less educational training, who are profoundly alienated from key aspects of the social and political status quo, so much so that they are willing to formulate utopian, world-transformative agendas, create or join insurgent organizations that advocate the violent overthrow of that status quo, kill people whom they designate as societal villains, and even sacrifice their own lives for what they believe to be a higher cause. Having spent decades reading the ideological treatises and communiques issued by a vast array of ideological extremists, studying their actions in detail on the basis of judicial and parliamentary investigative or archival materials, personally interacting with or interviewing quite a number of them, and also sharing their own psychological alienation from the status quo, I feel that I may have developed a clearer perspective on how their anti-establishment beliefs animate their actions than many of today's terrorism experts, who seem to spend far more time devising fanciful "social science" theories or crunching irrelevant numbers than they do conducting actual qualitative research based on the extensive use of primary sources. Of course, this admittedly partisan hypothesis will be up to readers to evaluate after examining selections from this volume.

As the table of contents indicates, this anthology will cover the following subjects. Volume 1 will concentrate on the history of underground neo-fascist networks in the post–World War II era, neo-fascist paramilitary and terrorist groups operating in Europe and Latin America in the 1960s and 1970s, and the manipulation of those and other terrorist organizations by the security forces of various states, both authoritarian and democratic. Volume 2 will instead focus on state terrorism and assorted religious extremists, including apocalyptic cults, Islamism, and jihadist terrorist networks, as well as on CBRN (chemical, biological, radiological, and nuclear) terrorism and the supposedly new "nexus" between organized criminal and extremist groups employing terrorist operational techniques. One might say, then, that the first volume is dedicated to the darkest, most unsavory dimensions of certain secular political milieus, whereas the second is dedicated largely to the darkest, most unsavory dimensions of particular religious milieus.

Some problems with the analysis of terrorism and "violent extremism"

Definitional problems

As with all broad political concepts (e.g., democracy), it has proven impossible to define the term "terrorism" to everyone's satisfaction despite the existence of tens of thousands of studies devoted to the subject. No unambiguous and universally accepted definition of terrorism yet exists, and its exact relationship to other, related concepts like political violence, guerrilla warfare, and political assassinations also remains a matter of contention. This situation is unlikely to change any time soon. Moreover, both the dramatic nature of the topic and the pejorative connotations of the term contribute to conceptual confusion by lending themselves to overly emotional assessments and political polemics. Scholars have complained for decades that no unanimously accepted definition of terrorism exists, even among specialists, and indeed some have become so frustrated by this that they have advocated abandoning the use of the word altogether. However, it seems unwise to stop using the term simply because not everyone can agree about its definition, just as the fact that specialists cannot fully agree on the definitions of other terms in the humanities and social sciences has not led to their wholesale abandonment. Even if not everyone can be expected to concur, it is not that difficult to identify the unique characteristics of terrorism that serve to distinguish it from other forms of collective violence.

In order to avoid the temptation of ascribing the label "terrorist" to every group which resorts to violence whom one does not like, as is all too common, it is necessary to define the term precisely and in a neutral fashion. All such formal definitions are bound to be awkward, but in this volume the word terrorism applies to *the use (or threatened imminent use) of violence, directed against victims selected for their symbolic or representative value, as a means of instilling anxiety in, transmitting one or more messages to, and thereby manipulating the perceptions and behavior of, a wider target audience (or audiences)*. Terrorist acts are thus by nature triadic rather than dyadic, in contrast to normal acts of violence. They invariably involve three parties or protagonists – the perpetrator(s), the victim(s), and the wider target audience(s) whose behavior the perpetrators hope to influence. Hence the key relationship in an act of terrorism is between the perpetrator and the target audience. Paradoxically, the persons who suffer the actual physical harm from such acts have the least intrinsic importance, and are simply the hapless instruments used by the perpetrators to send messages to wider audiences. It is precisely this feature that differentiates acts of terrorism from simple violent assaults upon political enemies. To constitute terrorism, an act of violence has to be specifically intended *by the perpetrator* to manipulate the perceptions or behavior of a wider target audience (i.e., persons beyond the actual victims of the attack). From this it follows that neither violent actions which inadvertently terrorize or alter the behavior patterns of people beyond the victims (for example, a sequence of rapes in a given neighborhood), nor those aimed merely at physically eliminating a specific enemy (for example, assassinations) are examples of terrorism in the strict sense of the term – unless, of course, the perpetrators mainly intended to deliver some sort of message to a larger audience. A certain group might, of course, try to fulfill two or more objectives at once, such as eliminating a particular police official and transmitting a warning to other such officials and/or the public, but the latter would have to take precedence for this action to be interpreted primarily as an act of terrorism.

Viewed in this way, terrorism is nothing more than a violent operational technique, specifically a violent technique of psychological manipulation. Like any other technique or tool, it can be used by anyone, whatever their ideological orientation or relationship to the state. It can be – and indeed has been – employed by a vast array of actors: by states and non-state groups; on behalf of state power and in opposition to state power; by left-wingers, right-wingers, and centrists; by the religious, the non-religious, and the anti-religious; and for an almost infinite variety of causes. It is for this reason that pithy phrases such as "one man's terrorist is another man's freedom fighter" are misleading, if not entirely mistaken, except insofar as they reflect the generally partisan and unsystematic way that such labels are applied. First, they confuse *means*, in this case terrorism, with *ends*, in this case "freedom fighting," ignoring the possibility that one might employ terrorist techniques in a fight for freedom. Second, they imply that the term terrorism has no objective meaning, that it is something subjective which is purely in the "eye of the beholder," like idiosyncratic personal tastes in food or women. On the contrary, terrorism is an objectively identifiable operational technique. From a technical point of view, "one man's terrorist" should invariably also be "another man's terrorist," because regardless of the cause involved a terrorist can be identified purely by the methods he or she chooses to employ. Whether or not one sympathizes with a given perpetrator's underlying motives, be they political, religio-political, or criminal, every individual who commits an act of violence which is specifically designed to influence or manipulate a wider audience is, strictly speaking, a terrorist. All other factors are superfluous, and indeed only serve to obscure this fundamental reality. To restrict the term solely to violence committed by one's enemies is thus an error of the first order, one which reflects either a great deal of confusion and ignorance or the thematic requirements of propaganda campaigns.

Methodological problems

In recent years, a number of important volumes have appeared highlighting several of the major methodological problems that afflict the academic literature in the field of Terrorism Studies, an interdisciplinary subfield that has metastasized – some would say like a malignant cancer – in the wake of the 9/11 attacks.[2] Many of the harsh recent criticisms aimed at much of that literature sadly echo criticisms that I myself made back in the early 1990s, in the introductory chapter of my doctoral dissertation. As I argued back then, from an historian's point of view, this literature exhibits the same basic shortcomings as the "social science" literature in general – a penchant for excessive theorizing and speculation, an overabundance of abstraction and schematization at the expense of description and qualitative empirical detail, and an embarrassingly limited use of the relevant primary sources.[3] To which one need only add that the obsessions with the use of quantitative methods, methods that arguably have only limited utility and applicability when one is dealing with the intangible aspects of human behavior, such as the highly important historical, cultural, and ideological factors contributing to terrorism, has only increased. These serious deficiencies are further compounded by a pronounced infusion of political bias, both unconscious and conscious. This sort of ideological contamination is perhaps to be expected, given the obvious public policy implications of the topic, but it is no less corrosive in its effects. Indeed, the terrorism literature is arguably among the least original and distinguished in all of academia, in part due to the vast influx of people without the requisite scholarly backgrounds who have entered the field in the wake of the 9/11 attacks. There is only a relatively small handful of studies that genuinely contributes to a greater conceptual understanding of the phenomenon, along with an ever-growing number of specialized works that provide valuable information about specific terrorist groups. Even so, many works dealing with terrorism still tend to uncritically recycle many of the same superficial or misguided notions that have held sway in this field for decades, albeit in a variety of new and different contexts. Although these are rather harsh criticisms that deserve further discussion and analysis, a thorough dissection of the methodological shortcomings of this vast literature would require another book-length study.

Disciplinary biases and "mirror imaging"

The phrase "mirror imaging" is used, both within and outside of the intelligence community, to refer to a phenomenon in which analysts unconsciously project their own ways of thinking, their own values, their own frames of reference, and their own fantasies onto their adversaries, including those emanating from very different cultures with very different histories and values, instead of trying to view the world from their adversaries' own perspectives and points of view. This sort of parochial approach is widely regarded – and rightly so – as problematic, counterproductive, harmful, and potentially catastrophic insofar as it can easily lead to serious misunderstandings of the nature of the adversary, which can in turn result in the adoption of misguided policies and ineffective responses. Sadly, this myopic, self-referential mirror imaging approach is nowadays practically the norm in the West, particularly in relation to the threat posed by jihadists, whose actions are undeniably and indeed explicitly animated primarily by their Islamist interpretations of core Islamic doctrines.

The following factors all contribute to the problem of analytical "mirror imaging" in this context:

- First, people who grow up in materialistic societies tend to ascribe materialistic motives to other people, even those from other and quite different foreign cultures – that is, they tend to believe that the "real" underlying motivations of human actors, which they identify as narrowly political goals, materialistic social or economic motives, a vulgar lust for power, and so forth, are either being intentionally concealed or unwittingly distorted in those actors' ideological statements and justifications.
- Second, "social scientists" normally prefer to highlight various tangible supposed causal factors that they believe can be measured, quantified, and "tested," as opposed to concerning themselves with intangible, messy, unquantifiable factors (such as the convoluted influence of beliefs, culture, and history – topics which, by the way, also require years of study to even begin to comprehend).
- Third, academicians from different disciplines not surprisingly tend to overemphasize the value of particular theories and methods deriving from their own disciplines, to minimize the importance of rival theories and methods from their own and other disciplines (especially supposedly "soft" disciplines in the humanities like political philosophy, history, and religious studies), and then to

apply their favored theories and methods, sometimes carelessly and uncritically, even to topics that are quite removed from their own areas of specialization. Here are some examples of this rather common phenomenon (albeit ones that often cite, as illustrations, some of the best rather than the worst of the existing terrorism literature):

1 Social scientists in general (and economists in particular) tend to promote hyper-rationalist interpretations of human behavior, as if human beings were little more than androids involved in mechanistically calculating or weighing "costs" and "benefits," even though human behavior is in fact the product of a complex combination of rational, semi-rational, and irrational motives undergirded by often subconscious emotional drivers;[4]
2 Mathematicians often employ models deriving from the natural sciences to explain human behavior in the social sphere, even though the application of those models to the social sphere is generally fraught with dangers, if not fundamentally ill-conceived;[5]
3 Sociologists typically prioritize the impact of large impersonal social structures or the material aspects of social movements such as "resource mobilization," in many cases without paying due attention to the beliefs and underlying emotions of social actors or the role played by influential individuals;
4 Economists (as well as many people on the left) tend to overemphasize the importance of economic factors (e.g., poverty, economic exploitation) and economic motives at the expense of non-material factors such as beliefs and values (which Marx erroneously characterized as epiphenomenal "superstructures" deriving from underlying "modes of production");[6]
5 Social psychologists tend to exaggerate the importance of the influence of social networks to the exclusion of other factors, including individual proclivities, beliefs, and values;[7]
6 Psychologists tend to focus too narrowly on individual psychology, and often attribute psychopathologies to violent human actors who behave in ways that they find incomprehensible or problematic;[8]
7 Strategic and military analysts pay special attention to the relatively pragmatic strategic, operational, and tactical methods used by adversaries, rather than to the underlying worldviews that serve to influence those adversaries (including their selection of particular types of targets and their use of certain methods in preference to others).[9]

In short, what many people from these various disciplinary backgrounds all have in common is that they tend to overemphasize the importance of tangible, ostensibly measurable and quantifiable (i.e., economic, psychological, social psychological, sociological, or narrowly political) factors and to ignore or minimize the importance of less tangible (historical, cultural, and ideological) factors, even though the latter are often of decisive importance, especially when one is trying to understand groups animated by extremist ideologies. Surely it is both analytically and methodologically unsound to ignore the influence or deny the importance of the fervently held beliefs of protagonists, all the more so when one is analyzing groups that *explicitly define themselves by their beliefs, generally act in accordance with those beliefs, and indeed feel compelled to justify all of their actions on the basis of those beliefs.*[10] And it is even more foolish to stubbornly dismiss what the actual protagonists keep telling everyone about their own motivations, and instead to ascribe other preferred motivations to them in the absence of any verifiable evidence.

I am not suggesting, of course, that ideology or any other single factor is alone responsible for the behavior of violent ideological extremists, because all monocausal explanations for complex social phenomena are oversimplifications inasmuch as a multiplicity of intersecting factors are always at play. But not all of those factors are equally important, no matter what the context, and *ideology is arguably the single most important factor in understanding the behavior of political and religious extremists.* That is why it is necessary at this point to undertake an extended discussion of both ideologies in general and extremist ideologies in particular.

The characteristics of ideological extremism

> Ideology – that is what gives evildoing its long-sought justification and gives the evildoer the necessary steadfastness and determination. That is the social theory which helps to make his acts seem good instead of bad in his own and others' eyes, so that he won't hear reproaches and curses but will receive praise and honours.[11]
>
> Aleksandr Solzhenitsyn

> What persuades men and women to mistake each other from time to time for gods or vermin is ideology.[12]
>
> Terry Eagleton

> One can say that what the priest is to religion, the intellectual is to ideology.[13]
>
> Daniel Bell

> Any examination of ideology makes it difficult to avoid the rueful conclusion that all views about ideology are themselves ideological. But avoided it must be – or at least modified by saying that some views are more ideological than others.[14]
>
> David McLellan

Many commentators appear to believe that the terms "extremism" and "extremists" have no substantive meaning, but are simply pejorative labels used by centrist, conventional, consensus thinkers or by supporters of the existing political, social, economic, and cultural status quo as a means of delegitimizing various "anti-Establishment" political and religious groups that they view as disreputable or morally "beyond the pale" in one way or another. Emblematic of this perspective is the oft-cited comment, reportedly made by Jerome L. Himmelstein in 1998 at the American Sociological Association (ASA) convention, that "[a]t best this characterization [extremist] tells us nothing substantive about the people it labels; at worst it paints a false picture."[15] There is certainly no denying that the terms "extremism" and "extremist" have pejorative connotations inasmuch as the members of groups that others characterize as "extremist" neither accept that characterization nor employ that term to designate themselves. Therefore, in this and other respects, these two terms are more akin to the terms "fanatic" or "terrorist," which are also rejected even by individuals and groups that are characterized – no matter how justifiably – as fanatical or as terrorists, than they are to terms like "fascist," "Nazi," "racist," or "radical," because genuine fascists, Nazis, racists, and assorted radicals not only accept those labels but typically regard them as badges of honor.[16] Indeed, it is an indisputable fact that the terms "fascist" and "Nazi" were originally created by those who enthusiastically espoused those particular ideologies, and were later adopted but given a pejorative meaning by their enemies. The terms "radicalism" and "radical" – appellations that are typically preferred and even embraced by many extremists – tend to have broadly positive connotations, because etymologically they signify that the individual or group in question is striving to understand, confront, and ultimately resolve the deeper "root causes" of existing political and social problems.

A more serious criticism of the appellation "extremist" is that the term is essentially relational – that is, that one can only be considered "extreme" in relation to something that is considered "not extreme," as opposed to one that refers to a concrete, observable socio-political phenomenon with certain intrinsic, identifiable characteristics. For example, Peter T. Coleman and Andrea Bartoli define extremism as "activities (beliefs, attitudes, feelings, actions, strategies) of a character *far removed from the ordinary*."[17] To some extent the term "extremist" is indeed relational, because almost by definition it tends to be contrasted with terms like "mainstream," "moderate," or "centrist," which are ipso facto regarded as normal, legitimate, and acceptable rather than politically, socially, or morally illegitimate. This is why radicals of various stripes have frequently criticized and condemned the label "extremist," especially when it is applied to themselves, and why they have so often insisted that it is a loaded term with a built-in pro-Establishment bias. It follows from this perspective that people who regularly employ the term are basically endeavoring to support and defend the status quo by delegitimizing and perhaps even justifying the repression of its most fervent, intransigent opponents.[18] Nevertheless, simply because a term has a built-in relational dimension does not mean that it has no substantive meaning or that it does not refer to a "really existing" phenomenon.

For that very reason, even though many pundits have employed the terms "extremism" and "extremist" in a biased, partisan fashion so as to discredit or delegitimize groups they vehemently oppose or find morally distasteful – in the same way that others apply terms like "communist," "fascist," "racist," "sexist," "homophobe," or "Islamophobe" in similarly imprecise, inappropriate, slanderous, or propagandistic ways – a number of scholars have rightly insisted that those terms, while pejorative, have a substantive and objective meaning. Perhaps not surprisingly, however, they have not been able to agree among themselves about exactly what the defining characteristics of extremism are. For example, decades ago Eric Hoffer provided an essentially psychological analysis of extremists, one that overemphasized the purported psychopathologies of "true believers" and arguably underestimated the crucial importance of the actual contents of their ideological beliefs, even though he was quite right to emphasize that alienated individuals who are attracted to one form of ideological extremism are also likely to find other types appealing.[19] More recently, Laird Wilcox (and his collaborators) has made efforts to describe the characteristics of extremist behavior in a variety of publications dealing with American left- and right-wing extremists.[20] According to his analysis, those characteristics included character assassination, name-calling and labeling, making sweeping and irresponsible generalizations, providing inadequate proof for assertions, advocacy of double standards, viewing their opponents and critics as irremediably evil, a Manichean worldview, advocacy of censorship or repression, identification of themselves in terms of who they hate, a tendency toward argument by intimidation, use of slogans and buzzwords, assumption of moral superiority, doomsday thinking, the use of disreputable means is warranted to achieve noble ends, emphasis on emotions rather than reason, hypersensitivity, intolerance of ambiguity and uncertainty, an inclination toward "groupthink," and the personalization of hostility.[21] American sociologist Neil Smelser has also recently listed some of the traits associated with ideological extremism: the vilification of enemies, the drawing of an absolutist distinction between oneself and one's enemies (i.e., Manicheanism), the exaggeration of the "agency" (i.e., the intentionality and strategic rationality) of enemies, and the reliance on rhetorical excesses to reaffirm one's own legitimacy.[22] In a much more limited context, economist Ronald Wintrobe has argued that the extremists in HAMĀS and Jewish fundamentalist groups share various common traits, including an unwillingness to compromise, the promotion of maximalist goals, complete certainty, a willingness to utilize violence, an intolerance of dissent within their groups, and the demonization of enemies.[23] Finally, Maxwell Taylor has enumerated what he considers to be the ten primary descriptive characteristics of fanaticism, many of which overlap with the aforementioned traits ascribed to extremism, such as "excessive and all-absorbing focusing," "personalisation" of the world (or an "exclusive concern with his own ideological construction of the world"), insensitivity to others and accepted standards of behavior, loss of critical judgment, logical inconsistency and tolerance of incompatibility, single-minded certainty, Manichean oversimplification of the world's complexity, stubborn resistance to altering views, disdain for outsiders and enemies, and ideological filtering of outside information.[24]

Even so, important differences in their emphases, theoretical approaches, methodologies, and de facto knowledge of actual extremist milieus have made it impossible for the aforementioned scholars to agree completely. Furthermore, much of the current conceptual confusion about the nature of extremism is attributable to a basic failure to distinguish between, or a misleading attempt to conflate or commingle, two distinct types of extremism. The first is *extremism of goals*, which is almost entirely the product of a group's political or religious ideology. The second is *extremism of means*, which may or may not be linked to ideological extremism. Extremism of means refers to the employment of methods, means, or techniques that are regarded as extraordinary, disproportionate, unnecessary under the circumstances, or morally beyond the pale within particular social and cultural contexts, such as the use of unconstrained, indiscriminate violence or the carrying out of otherwise violent, destructive, and harmful actions that explicitly or implicitly violate existing cultural taboos (as opposed to similar actions that do not violate such taboos because they are widely regarded as legitimate, such as committing acts of violence in self-defense, executing violent criminals, or carrying out military actions considered vital to national security). Among the types of means that might be considered extreme, at least in the West, would be the commission of war crimes or other atrocities in wartime, the use of torture involving severe physical mutilation (although not necessarily less damaging but nonetheless unpleasant and potentially humiliating "enhanced" interrogation techniques), the deliberate targeting of civilians, depriving people of their constitutional rights without justification, killing family members who are regarded as weak or without economic value, "honor killings," involuntary clitoradectomies, cannibalism, physically or sexually abusing children, and carrying out mass casualty attacks in non-wartime contexts. Note, however, that what is regarded as extreme can vary significantly in different cultural contexts – not that this should ever make such actions immune from criticism, as radical cultural relativists and hypocritical "multiculturalists" have all too often argued – and that these types of "extreme" methods need not be employed by people who have embraced an extremist ideology, although in practice they frequently are. For example, democratic governments have all too often sanctioned the creation of paramilitary "death squads" as well as their employment of terrorist techniques against perceived "enemies of the state," sometimes in their own homelands but much more often in other countries.[25] In such cases, "extreme means" are essentially authorized or utilized by political "centrists" rather than by ideological extremists.

However, the primary concern at this juncture is to identify the common characteristics of ideological extremism, which in turn often leads to the stubborn and destructive pursuit of delusional (in the non-clinical sense), utopian agendas or goals, rather than focusing on the use of extreme means to achieve those goals. Hence the first desideratum is to clarify what ideologies are, then to enumerate the fundamental questions that all political ideologies, extremist or otherwise, address and purport to provide an answer for.[26] Many scholars have argued that ideology is a particularly difficult term or concept to define, in part because of its radically varying historical interpretations. Thus David McLellan insisted that ideology was "the most elusive concept in the whole of the social sciences," whereas Michael Freeden stated, rather more circumspectly, that "the concept of ideology has emerged as one of the most complex and debatable political ideas," one which has been "remarkable . . . for causing confusion among scholars and political commentators."[27]

Despite these claims, the term has nowadays, after a very convoluted history, acquired a broadly accepted basic meaning. In popular parlance, the word ideology remains "a vague term [that] seems to denote a world-view or belief-system or creeds held by a social group about the social arrangements in society, which is morally justified as being right."[28] Similarly, among most scholars the term ideology has eventually come to refer, more or less neutrally, to *systematic, relatively coherent, well-articulated, and often all-encompassing sets of ideas about the nature of social reality, whether or not those ideas have a solid factual basis.*[29] Thus according to John B. Thompson, in a neutral sense ideologies are best characterized as "systems of thought" or "systems of belief" or "symbolic systems" pertaining to social thought and action, whereas Lyman Tower Sargent describes them simply as "organized or patterned beliefs.... that present a coherent, understandable picture of the world."[30] This means that ideologies per se – contrary to the views of some analysts – are *not* equivalent to or synonymous with the vague, unarticulated, impressionistic, and often incoherent presuppositions that most people have unconsciously acquired, as a result of their socialization processes and life experiences, about the way the wider social world operates.[31] Nor should these two very different phenomena be conflated, as some have done in their definitions of ideology.[32] If they are mistakenly conflated, then virtually any thoughts about the external world, no matter how simple-minded, formless, inconsistent, incomprehensible, delusional (in the clinical sense), or absurd, would constitute a bona fide ideology, which would effectively deprive the term of any specificity, conceptual precision, or defining criteria that could serve to distinguish it from other modes of perception, understanding, and explanation. As British historian Roger Eatwell has emphasized, "there are dangers in inflating the term 'ideology' to cover what might be better termed 'propaganda', 'socialization', and 'culture'."[33] Terms other than ideology should therefore be employed to refer to the barely conscious, taken-for-granted values and attitudes that are inculcated, as if by osmosis, in members of all social groups as a result of normal processes of cultural transmission and socialization.[34]

Others have instead tried to have their cake and eat it too by distinguishing between "forensic" ideologies, "the articulated, differentiated, well-developed political arguments put forward by informed and conscious Marxists and Fascists or liberal democrats," and "latent" ideologies, "the loosely structured, unreflective statements of the common men."[35] This is certainly an improvement, in that it avoids the aforementioned danger of complete conflation, but the real issue is whether the latter should be designated as ideologies at all. In this study, the term ideology refers essentially to Robert E. Lane's so-called forensic ideologies, that is the ideas consciously formulated by self-styled intellectuals or political leaders, even though these ideas are then often subsequently embraced, at times uncritically or unreflectively, in an oversimplified, schematic, bastardized, or distorted form by less educated or intellectually inclined people. Indeed, the widespread diffusion of ideological concepts also tends to influence, at least in an indirect way, the unarticulated sentiments and beliefs of many others, even those who do not consciously adopt them or who have little familiarity with their explicit intellectual contents and arguments, much less with the historical contexts in which they emerged, their complex processes of elaboration, or their diverse internal currents and subcurrents.[36] That is why Kenneth Minogue has cleverly opined that "[l]ike sand at a picnic, [ideology] gets in everything."[37]

Clearly, political ideologies form one very important subset of the systematic sets of ideas that fall within the broader category of ideology, so much so that most of the intellectual debates about ideology have been concerned mainly with political ideologies.[38] In the words of Andrew Heywood, the author of one of the better introductory books on the subject, a political ideology is "a more or less coherent set of ideas that provides the basis for organized political action, whether this is intended to preserve, modify or overthrow the existing system of power."[39] He adds that "the complexity of [political] ideology derives from the fact that it straddles the conventional boundaries between descriptive and normative thought, and between political theory and political action."[40] Concerning the first combination, political ideologies

> are descriptive in that . . . they provide individuals and groups with an intellectual map of how their society works and, more broadly, with a general view of the world . . . However, such descriptive understanding is deeply embedded within a set of normative or prescriptive beliefs, both about the adequacy of present social arrangements and about the nature of any alternative of future society.[41]

With respect to the second, political "ideologies resemble political philosophies in that they deal with abstract ideas and theories, and their proponents may at times seem to be engaged in dispassionate enquiry . . . At an operative level, however, ideologies . . . may be expressed in sloganizing, political rhetoric, party manifestos and government policies."[42] Furthermore, whereas political philosophizing tends to encourage deeper intellectual introspection, political ideologies instead heighten emotions in order to promote the taking of action.[43] Finally, ideologies are directed toward mobilizing the masses, or at least certain segments of society whose interests the ideologues claim to represent.[44] Several of these points will be discussed further later.

That notions approximating the preceding definition of ideology have now become the standard academic view can be seen in many of the introductory textbooks devoted to political ideologies, all of which include sections on the most historically important and/or currently influential political ideologies, rather than only those that have been characterized in more restrictive, negative ways by, say, Marxists or theorists of totalitarianism. A few examples, either from other scholarly works or from those textbooks, should suffice to illustrate this point. For Eatwell, a political ideology is "a relatively coherent set of empirical and normative beliefs and thought, focusing on the problems of human nature, the process of history, and socio-political arrangements."[45] For American political theorists Carl J. Friedrich (1901–1984) and Zbigniew Brzezinski (1928–2017), an ideology is

> a set of *literate* ideas – a reasonably coherent body of ideas concerning practical means of how to change and reform a society, based upon a more or less elaborate criticism of what is wrong with the existing or antecedent society.[46]

For British political theorist Andrew Vincent, ideologies are

> bodies of concepts, values and symbols which incorporate conceptions of human nature . . .; critical reflections on the nature of human interaction; the values which humans ought either to reject or aspire to; and the correct technical arrangements for social, economic and political life.[47]

For Roy C. Macridis, an ideology is a "set of ideas and beliefs through which we perceive the outside world and *act* upon our information."[48] Finally, the American social scientist Robert E. Lane reportedly described political ideologies as "organized, articulated, and consciously held systems of political ideas incorporating beliefs, attitudes, and opinions."[49] For most mainstream liberal and conservative academicians, then, the term ideology is no longer reserved exclusively for intellectual worldviews or visions – political or otherwise – that are regarded as intrinsically irrational or otherwise unsavory, which constitutes a significant conceptual advance in relation to the many previous partial, restrictive, and wholly pejorative interpretations of the word. It is now accepted by many that not all ideologies are narrowly political, and that not all political ideologies are inherently or equally problematic. It is precisely for this reason that it is necessary to distinguish conceptually between (1) political ideologies in the general sense of the term and (2) extremist political (and religious) ideologies.

However, before surveying some of the most influential interpretations of the term ideology, it is necessary to counter certain notions that have long encouraged academicians and policy analysts to ignore or underestimate the role and significance of ideas in motivating human behavior. For example, some social scientists have falsely claimed that human beliefs in general are unimportant in terms of their tangible effects on behavior, such as "radical" behaviorists like B. F. Skinner (1904–1990),[50] whereas far too many others have foolishly concluded that political conflicts are simply the product of naked struggles for power and wealth, and consequently that ideological doctrines and beliefs are little more than propaganda ploys or "window dressing" used by political actors to conceal their vulgar appetites for power behind justificatory moralistic verbiage.[51] It is this widespread underlying assumption, one that is all the more appealing to some given the inherent difficulties involved in "scientifically" (i.e., quantitatively) measuring intangible causal factors like ideological beliefs, which especially accounts for the tendency of Western political analysts to ascribe political behavior mainly, if not exclusively, to the pursuit of concrete material interests. Yet such a hopelessly narrow, reductionist, and one-sided interpretation cannot even be justified when one is trying to comprehend mainstream political behavior in modern Western societies where materialist worldviews – in both senses of that term – are widely held, much less in pre-modern Western societies or non-Western societies, past and present. Stubbornly or unwittingly attempting to project one's own frames of reference onto others instead of endeavoring to see the world from their perspective, the "mirror imaging" phenomenon discussed earlier, is usually a recipe for error if not disaster. Indeed, the adoption of restrictive, intellectually impoverished notions of this sort has in general led to the serious neglect of, failure to understand, and ongoing underestimation of the importance of the ideological beliefs of a wide array of political and religious extremists, including those who rely heavily or primarily on the operational technique of terrorism.[52] This has in turn seriously interfered with the West's ability to comprehend the worldviews, motives, and agendas of its terrorist adversaries, as well as to respond effectively to the threats that they pose.[53]

In marked contrast, a case will be made herein that strongly held ideological beliefs generally exert a significant if not a decisive impact on political behavior. Anyone who has seriously studied or personally witnessed the power of ideas to inspire and mobilize people in particular historical and political contexts, such as specialists on apocalyptic millenarianism, communism, or fascism (not to mention the leaders of successful movements of these types), is very well aware of this. As American Catholic theologian George Weigel has rightly emphasized, "[i]deas have consequences, and bad ideas can have lethal consequences."[54] American political scientist Max Lerner (1902–1999) went even further by proclaiming that "ideas are weapons."[55] This may be an overstatement, but at the very least, ideas can potentially be used as weapons, both in personal disputes and in larger collective socio-political struggles. It should be apparent that if ideas in general so often have observable and indeed demonstrable behavioral consequences, so too must political ideologies, whose primary functions are, among other things, to inspire and provide guides for political action.[56] Indeed, Eatwell and Anthony Wright insist, quite properly, that ideologies "are major motive forces in history."[57] This is all the more true when one is dealing with political and religious extremists, fanatics, or "true believers," who by definition are obsessed with ideological matters, even if many of those matters seem inexplicable, picayune, or hopelessly arcane to outsiders. In short, far from espousing ideological worldviews as a mere stratagem to disguise the pursuit of narrowly materialistic interests or an atavistic hunger for power (although that phenomenon too is at times observable), an individual's or a social group's "commitment to ideology – the yearning for a cause, or the satisfaction of deep moral feelings – is *not* necessarily [even] the reflection of interests in the shape of ideas": on the contrary, the ideology in question typically transcends or at least attenuates vulgar material interests and often constitutes something that is far more all-consuming and all-encompassing, that is "a secular religion."[58] This is why Terry Eagleton rightly emphasizes that, while struggling for material reasons is readily comprehensible, it is "much harder to grasp how [people] may come to do so in the name of something as abstract as ideas. Yet ideas are what men live by, and will occasionally die for."[59]

Despite this, the bulk of the recent and current work in various social science fields, driven as it is by predetermined and often problematic theoretical or methodological concerns, studiously ignores the actual ideas expressed by political and social actors, and instead vainly searches for ostensibly "deeper" psychological, economic, or structural "root causes" to explain their behavior.[60] For example, how many people nowadays take the bitter and often arcane ideological disputes between various sectarian communist groups seriously, even though such disputes once had tremendous historical importance? And how many people are currently taking the ongoing ideological disputes between different types of Islamists sufficiently seriously, despite their overriding importance and tangible influence on Islamist behavior?[61] This neglect is all the more inexplicable given that *ideology is arguably the main behavioral driver of individuals who have enthusiastically embraced extremist worldviews, whatever their specific beliefs may be.* This is true even though in practice both their behavior and even some of their less fixed ideas are often modified in response to changing circumstances, at least to some extent, and there are usually many other factors that likewise influence their actions.[62] Hence one should not mistakenly go to the opposite extreme by asserting that ideas alone are the sole drivers of behavior, political or otherwise, even for ideological fanatics, if only because – as noted earlier – monocausal explanations for observable human behavior are always inadequate, if not completely false. Given the extraordinary complexity of the world we live in, our behavior will always be affected by a multiplicity of factors, many of them imperceptible, both to ourselves and to others.

It is now time to outline some of the more influential conceptions of ideology, from the time when the term was first introduced into political discourse up to the present. However, at the very outset it would be useful to highlight the important distinction, with respect to ideas about ideology, that political scientist Martin Seliger (1914–2001) made in his outstanding work, *Ideology and Politics*. Therein he rightly differentiated between what he termed "restrictive conceptions" of ideology and "inclusive conceptions" of ideology.[63] A very similar bipartite division has been proffered by J. B. Thompson, who refers, respectively, to "critical conceptions" and "neutral conceptions" of ideology.[64] Those who promoted the "restrictive" or "critical" conceptions characterized ideologies in essentially negative terms and therefore applied the term only to certain types of ideas that they viewed as problematic or dangerous for various reasons, as opposed to other ideas that they favored. In contrast, those who adopted the "inclusive" or "neutral" conceptions sought to define ideologies in more or less non-normative terms and hence applied the term in a less selective, partial, and partisan fashion. As noted earlier, the common tendency today, at least among most academicians and intellectuals who are not Marxists, critical theorists, or postmodernists, is to adopt an inclusive, relatively neutral conception of the term, although some of the older restrictive or critical conceptions still influence the views of certain analysts.

However that may be, the English word "ideology" is derived from the French term *idéologie*, which was first used in 1796, in the context of heated debates surrounding the French Revolution and its aftermath, by French Enlightenment philosopher Antoine Destutt de Tracy (1754–1836).[65] The latter term literally means "the science of ideas," and De Tracy viewed it in precisely that positivist way, as a means of disaggregating and analyzing sensations and the ideas they gave rise to in a rigorous, scientific manner. The relatively recent date of the term's first employment has led some analysts of ideology to suggest that not just the term, but ideologies themselves, first appeared in the latter half of the eighteenth century. Briefly, their argument is that ideological conflicts of the modern type could only have emerged during a historical period in which traditional beliefs, based on widely accepted historical and religious "myths" that had an integrative socio-political function and helped to buttress the authority of existing elites, were breaking down.[66] However, others have rightly noted that this is a very ahistorical view given that periods marked by the breakdown of traditional beliefs and intensified ideological conflict are quite common, even though each individual historical case inevitably has many unique features. As such, although the substantive contents of ideologies in different historical periods and geographical regions are bound to differ, ideologies themselves are certainly not new phenomena that first appeared in modern times. On the contrary, the only "new" thing has been the coining of the term and the ongoing efforts by Western intellectuals to "conceptualize" the term ideology since the late eighteenth century.[67]

In any event, De Tracy's idiosyncratic and ostensibly scientific interpretation of the concept was never even widely understood, much less widely accepted, either by his contemporaries or by later intellectuals who wrote about ideology. Although he viewed ideology as something positive and even characterized it as the queen of the sciences, many subsequent adopters of the term instead conceptualized it in very negative terms. For example, after falling out with them as a result of his adoption of increasingly autocratic policies and his arranging of a Concordat in 1801 with the Catholic Church, Napoleon Bonaparte (1769–1821) contemptuously referred to "the ideologues" – De Tracy and other positivist, secular liberal republican philosophers – as "windbags," by which he meant that their opinions were overly abstract, pompous, and impractical even if their goal was ultimately to undermine political authority.[68] Indeed, the French emperor subsequently adopted an even harsher and bitterer view of ideologies in the wake of his costly and humiliating retreat from Russia:

> It is to ideology, this cloudy metaphysics which, by subtly searching for first causes, wishes to establish on this basis the legislation of peoples, instead of obtaining its laws from knowledge of the human heart and from the lessons of history, that we must attribute all the misfortunes of our fair France.[69]

Meanwhile, the counterrevolutionary right in France likewise explicitly portrayed the very same liberal republican ideologues as potential subversives.

Yet it was the main use of the term by Karl Marx (1818–1883) and Friedrich Engels (1820–1895) that made it increasingly common in modern political discourse.[70] Ironically, they began by characterizing the Young Hegelians in Germany in much the same way as Napoleon had characterized the ideologues in France, that is as armchair metaphysicians peddling unrealistic ideas.[71] However, they soon radically altered the meaning of the word ideology itself by explicitly linking it to their views on class struggle and class consciousness, specifically by identifying it with the dominant ideas promoted by the ruling classes. According to their famous formulation,

> [t]he ideas of the ruling class are in every epoch the ruling ideas, i.e., the class which is the ruling material force of society, is at the same time the ruling

intellectual force. The class which has the means of *material* production at its disposal, has control at the same time over the means of mental production, so that thereby, generally speaking, the ideas of those who lack the means of mental production are subject to it.[72]

In short, the basic notion here was that ideologies were in actuality mechanisms of mystification through which the ruling classes promoted a false, deceptive view of the world that both reflected and benefited their class interests. As a result, the proletariat was being indoctrinated by bourgeois ideologists with what Engels later referred to as a "false consciousness" that prevented them from recognizing their "objectively" revolutionary class interests. Far from agreeing with De Tracy that ideologies were scientific, then, Marx and Engels in the end argued that they were actually distorted, partisan worldviews – which only their own ostensibly "scientific socialist" analyses could unmask.

Given the ongoing failure of the proletariat to rise up and launch a successful revolution against the bourgeoisie in the most advanced capitalist countries, which belied Marx's optimistic, teleological predictions about the looming transition to communism, his ideas were thence adopted and further elaborated upon by subsequent generations of Marxist thinkers. In contrast to Marx, Vladimir Lenin insisted that other social classes, not simply the ruling classes, possessed ideologies designed to advance their interests, including the proletariat in capitalist societies. That meant that there was nothing inherently negative about class-based ideologies, as long as they were "progressive." Indeed, communist ideology was explicitly viewed as a weapon in the class struggle.[73] Alas, because Lenin also apparently believed that the proletariat was currently "enslaved" by bourgeois ideology, he argued that it could never fully achieve class consciousness or mobilize for revolution without the help of so-called vanguard parties composed of professional revolutionaries, people such as himself and his Bolshevik "comrades," one of whose primary tasks would be to develop and disseminate an effectively combative socialist ideology.[74] Hungarian Marxist philosopher György Lukács (1885–1971) agreed with Lenin that the working class possessed an ideology, historical materialism, which he argued was different from other ideologies that embodied "false consciousness" because it was the "ideological expression of the proletariat in its effort to liberate itself."[75] But although Lukács also saw the communist party as the representative of the proletariat's supposed class interests, he explained the existing dominance of bourgeois ideology as being a result of the basic socio-economic organization of capitalist society. Later, French "structural Marxist" philosopher Louis Althusser (1918–1990) argued that ideology, which he thought had a quasi-material existence because it was rooted in "ideological state apparatuses" despite being antithetical to science, was nonetheless both omnipresent and indispensable for promoting social cohesion, even in communist societies.[76]

However, it was Italian communist Antonio Gramsci (1891–1937) who especially refined and elaborated upon these Marxist notions of ideology.[77] In the first place, like Lukács he challenged the "vulgar Marxist" overemphasis on material factors by emphasizing the importance of what Marx had labeled "superstructural" forces, that is the political, legal, and cultural institutions that supposedly emanated from and functioned to justify particular modes of production,[78] and indeed insisted that ideologies "must be analysed historically, in the terms of the philosophy of praxis, as a superstructure."[79] Second, he argued that the capitalist bourgeoisie had thus far managed to maintain its dominant position and prevent proletarian revolution not primarily by using the coercive powers of the state, but rather mainly by attaining and maintaining what he referred to as ideological and cultural "hegemony" via subtler mechanisms of socialization and indoctrination operating within civil society, which in turn generated the seemingly " 'spontaneous' consent given by the great masses of the population to the general direction imposed on social life by the dominant functional group [i.e., class]."[80] Thus, in the words of Andrew Vincent, for Gramsci

> [t]he ideology of the ruling class becomes vulgarized into the common sense of the average citizen. Power is not just crude legal or physical coercion but domination of language, morality, culture and common sense. The masses are quelled and co-opted by their internalization of ideational domination.[81]

As such, Gramsci concluded that the "organic intellectuals" emerging from the proletariat had to win over segments of the "traditional intellectuals," who fancied themselves to be above the interests of specific social classes but in fact functioned as ideologists and functionaries who buttressed the increasingly moribund status quo, which would then enable the former to contest bourgeois hegemony in the ideological and cultural spheres by waging a "war of position" and, ultimately, to replace it with "proletarian counter-hegemony" as a necessary precursor to revolution.[82] Hence Gramsci's conception of the term ideology, unlike those of Lenin and Lukács, was a broad one that encompassed not only the coherent doctrines developed by intellectuals, but also their indirect manifestations in the forms of popular culture, religion, folklore, and whatever passes for "common sense."[83]

After World War II, certain left-wing philosophers associated with the so-called Frankfurt School, such as Herbert Marcuse, made even more extravagant claims about the influence and pervasiveness of bourgeois ideology in democratic societies which, under the guise of promoting freedom and tolerance, had instead allegedly facilitated the establishment of an even more insidious form of totalitarian control.[84] Indeed, even early critics of Marxist notions nevertheless ended up accepting some of the same problematic premises despite their efforts to develop new social science interpretations of ideology. For example, although Hungarian sociologist Karl Mannheim (1893–1947) attempted to distinguish between wholly partisan "particular conceptions" and more inclusive "total conceptions" of ideology, and to transform the latter into a new "sociology of knowledge" by means of "purely empirical investigation[s] through description and structural analysis of the ways in which social relationships . . . influence thought," he nonetheless could not fully abandon the quasi-materialist and somewhat deterministic Marxian notion that ideologies were invariably formulated by concrete social groups enmeshed in particular historical, political, and socio-economic contexts.[85]

Nor was it only Marxist thinkers who formulated negative characterizations of what ideologies were. For example, French sociologist Émile Durkheim (1858–1917) criticized what he called the "ideological method" for "the use of notions to govern the collation of facts rather than deriving notions from them," an approach he viewed as an inversion of the proper scientific method.[86] No less pejorative views of ideologies were also produced by researchers from other academic disciplines. Thus, according to psychologist Abram Kardiner and his colleagues, ideologies were essentially "compounds of projective systems, in the interest of which empirical evidence is mobilized, and have therefore the same structure as rationalizations."[87] From this perspective, ideologies were developed to provide more or less elaborate intellectual and moral justifications for the potentially problematic or illegitimate behavior of collectivities, that is to conceal their baser, more reprehensible underlying motives. In the words of political scientist David E. Apter, some analysts appeared to regard ideologies as little more than "a cloak for shabby motives and appearances."[88] For American sociologist Lewis S. Feuer (1912–2002), instead, ideologies had a quasi-Freudian functional interpretation:

> the ideological fanatic is repressing tremendous segments of his personality. . . . Ideology thus helps provide the internal energy for the repression of human impulses and external energy for aggression against others. Ideology is the instrument whereby men repress their humane responses, and shape their behavior to a political mandate.[89]

However, some of the most influential negative characterizations of ideologies were produced by other Western social scientists and philosophers after World War II. Taking a new and different tack, several postwar theorists of totalitarianism tended to restrict the term "ideology" exclusively to extremist ideologies that they characterized as totalitarian, like fascism and communism. They viewed such ideologies as "closed," dogmatic systems of thought that claimed a monopoly on truth and therefore sought to suppress all rival ideas, in contrast to "open" systems of thought like liberalism.[90] Hence totalitarian ideologies, and the movements and states they gave rise to, effectively constituted "secular religions" that aspired to achieve total control not only over the external behavior of people but, even more importantly, over their innermost thoughts. From this perspective, the Fascist regime in Italy, the Nazi regime in Germany, and the Bolshevik regime in the Soviet Union were all examples of a terrible new type of ideologically based totalitarian state. For German-American political theorist Hannah Arendt (1906–1975), "the trouble with totalitarian regimes is not that they play power politics in an especially ruthless way, but that behind their politics is. . . . their unswerving faith in an ideological fictitious world."[91] Indeed, the core of her argument was that

> ideological thinking becomes emancipated from the reality that we perceive with our five senses, and insists on a "truer" reality concealed behind all perceptible things, dominating them from this place of concealment and

requiring a sixth sense that enables us to become aware of it. This sixth sense is provided by precisely the ideology . . . [which] provides a consistency that exists nowhere in the realm of reality. . . . Once it has established its premise, its point of departure, experiences no longer interfere with ideological thinking, nor can it be taught by reality.[92]

Hence irrespective of their degree of elaboration and sophistication, totalitarian ideologies were fundamentally if not intrinsically irrational. For their part, Friedrich and Brzezinski – who did make a distinction between ideologies in general and totalitarian ideologies, even though they focused their attention exclusively on the latter in their famous work *Totalitarian Dictatorship and Autocracy* – defined a totalitarian ideology as "a reasonably coherent body of ideas concerning practical means of how totally to change and reconstruct a society by force, or violence, based upon an all-inclusive or total criticism of what is wrong with the existing or antecedent society."[93] In that sense such ideologies were always utopian, because they combined "moral indignation against the Today with a fiercely fanatical conviction that the Tomorrow, which is bound to come, will be a higher, indeed a near perfect, state of society."[94] And like Arendt, they too criticized totalitarian ideologies for being based on pseudo-scientific "myths."[95]

In short, for the theorists of totalitarianism, these sorts of ideologies were not only said to represent the antithesis of liberal democratic politics, which are typically characterized by the promotion of individual freedom, pluralism, toleration of dissent, and a pragmatic willingness to compromise, but also the antithesis of rational scientific thinking. They were not alone in drawing such a sharp dichotomy. For example, in 1959 American sociologist Talcott Parsons (1902–1979) opined that "deviations from [social] scientific objectivity" constituted the "essential criteria of an ideology."[96] Meanwhile, a number of other distinguished Western social scientists, above all sociologists, went so far as to suggest that ideologies, which they too identified with extremist ideologies and hence characterized in similarly negative ways, were becoming increasingly attenuated, unattractive, and irrelevant in Western democratic consumer societies.[97] This notion was perhaps best expressed by American political sociologist Seymour Martin Lipset (1922–2006) in his famous book, *Political Man*:

> The fundamental political problems of the industrial revolution have been solved. The workers have achieved industrial and political citizenship; the conservatives have accepted the welfare state; and the democratic left has recognized that an increase in over-all state power carries with it more dangers to freedom than solutions for economic problems. This very triumph of the democratic social revolution in the West ends domestic politics for those intellectuals who must have ideologies or utopias to motivate them to political action.[98]

For his part, Daniel Bell (1919–2011) argued that for radical intellectuals, these developments "meant an end to chiliastic hopes, to millenarianism, to apocalyptic thinking – and to ideology," which he understood as "an all-inclusive system of comprehensive reality . . . a set of beliefs, infused with passion, [that] seeks to transform the whole of a way of life."[99] In sum, "[t]oday, these ideologies are exhausted. . . . [and] the old passions are spent."[100] Likewise, for French sociologist Raymond Aron (1905–1983), "[s]uch fanaticism is not for us."[101] Similar notions were promoted for a time by Edward Shils and Lewis Feuer. Yet this so-called end of ideology thesis was very soon undermined, if not entirely disconfirmed, by the dramatic rise of the New Left(s) in the United States and Western Europe and Third World revolutionary movements, which was marked by the enthusiastic resumption of ideological politics, above all by alienated youths from relatively privileged socio-economic strata. The same embarrassing fate later befell the naïve beliefs of Francis Fukuyama and others in the 1990s that the collapse of the Soviet Union had ushered in the "end of history," because the Western liberal democratic model had seemingly triumphed and allegedly no longer had any significant challengers.[102]

Similarly, several moderately conservative thinkers in Britain likewise consigned the term ideology exclusively to political doctrines and practices that they found objectionable. For example, political philosopher Michael Oakeshott (1901–1990) sought to draw a clear distinction between political ideas and projects stemming from an arrogant faith in "rationalism," which he portrayed as distorted, misdirected, exquisitely ideological abstractions that grossly oversimplified the complexities of the real world, and those linked to "traditional knowledge," that is more pragmatic, non-ideological political philosophies and practices, which had appropriately limited objectives and were supposedly grounded in reality.[103] For Minogue, ideologies were doctrines that claimed to reveal "the hidden and saving truth about the evils of the world in the form of social analysis," and were specifically premised on the belief that "modern European civilization, beneath its cleverly contrived appearances, is the most systematically oppressive despotism the world has ever known," because only there has oppression "begun to hide itself behind a façade of freedom."[104] He therefore argued that ideology, in this narrowly specific sense, is "incompatible with the activity of politics," first because it "assumes that mankind is enslaved" whereas politics is an activity of the free, and second because the majority of citizens cannot participate actively in politics in equal measure because "the understanding of most people has [supposedly] been fatally clouded by the experience of domination."[105]

Having surveyed some of the main conceptions of ideology proffered by various intellectuals, past and present, it can be seen that they are divided broadly into two contrasting camps. In the first camp, thinkers like Destutt de Tracy argued that "ideology," the study of ideas, was itself a science, whereas most actual ideologues have been convinced that their own doctrinal tenets were intrinsically correct or even scientific, whether or not they referred to them as "ideologies."[106] In the second camp, most theorists have (up until recently) argued that ideologies were worldviews that were intrinsically false, distorted, illusory, and fundamentally unscientific. Those varying interpretations of ideology also clearly illustrate the distinctions that were delineated earlier between "restrictive" or "critical" conceptions on the one hand, and "inclusive" or "neutral" conceptions on the other.[107] However, further potentially significant differences are also noticeable, which has caused French sociologist Raymond Boudon to develop a more sophisticated scheme for categorizing

the various historical interpretations of the term ideology.[108] In his scheme, conceptions of ideology are not based explicitly on the distinction between "partisan" and "neutral" conceptions, but rather on other criteria. He begins by distinguishing between "traditional" *definitions* of ideology, both Marxist and non-Marxist, which portray ideologies as beliefs that are inherently false in some sense, and "modern" definitions, also both Marxist and non-Marxist, which instead insist that they are not intrinsically false, that is that ideologies can be false, true, or embody a mixture of truth and falsity. His second division is between *explanations*, both Marxist and non-Marxist, that either characterize ideologies as intrinsically irrational and as the product of forces beyond the individual's control, or as rational in the sense that they "can be analysed as *meaningful* behavior in the [Max] Weberian sense," without necessarily being "deliberate or calculated."[109] If one combines those definitional and explanatory criteria, one ends up with four possible combinations:

- *Traditional* definition (ideology is falsehood) and *irrational* explanation (adherence to ideology is because of forces beyond the control of the subject);
- *Traditional* definition (ideology is falsehood) and *rational* explanation (adherence to ideology is meaningful);
- *Modern* definition (ideology does not derive from the criterion of true or false) and *irrational* explanation (adherence to ideology is because of forces beyond the control of the subject);
- *Modern* definition (ideology does not derive from the criterion of true or false) and *rational* explanation (adherence to ideology is meaningful).[110]

Whether this more elaborate scheme represents a significant improvement vis-à-vis the simpler division between "partisan" and "neutral" conceptions of ideology is likely to remain a matter of opinion. However, it should be noted that the first three of Raymond's categories would all reflect "partisan" conceptions of ideology, for one reason or another, whereas only his fourth category corresponds roughly to "neutral" conceptions of ideology.

In any event, although all of the aforementioned "restrictive" notions of ideology have been widely criticized for their partial and partisan definitions of ideologies, there is much to be said for some of these critical interpretations of ideologies – provided that one qualifies them by *limiting them to extremist ideologies* rather than wrongly ascribing them to political ideologies in general. After all, liberalism and conservatism are themselves both political ideologies, albeit ones that most non-Marxist analysts would view in much more neutral, less pejorative senses of that term. However, if one restricted such negative criticisms solely to extremist ideologies, they would arguably be all too applicable, as will soon become clearer.

However that may be, all political ideologies, extremist or otherwise, perform various intellectual and social functions. First, and virtually by definition, they provide a more or less coherent explanation of how the world works, regardless of the accuracy of that explanation. In other words, they provide an *explanatory* framework for interpreting and understanding human socio-political interaction. And like all intellectual constructs, including social science theories, mathematical models, and conspiracy theories, political ideologies invariably present only a partial picture of – and thereby inevitably oversimplify – reality, which is in fact one of the reasons for their appeal: they make the inordinately complex, extraordinarily fluid, seemingly incomprehensible, and often frightening external world seem more understandable, and thus potentially more manageable. As American sociologist Neil Smelser puts it, ideologies "structure the complex world of reality for the believer and potential believer," and thereby "crystallize confusion and vagueness into structure and certainty."[111] Some analysts have argued further that the explanatory frameworks provided by ideologies contain both elements of knowledge, which are subject to the rules of logic and empirical verification, and elements of belief, which are not necessarily either logical or verifiable but instead may be "accepted or adhered to on the basis of socialization, or habit, or repetition," that is for other than rational reasons.[112] If that is indeed the case – and the claim is somewhat problematic, both because it reflects a positivist view that there is a clear demarcation between that which is "rational" and that which is "irrational," and because it arguably does not differentiate political ideologies from most other human beliefs – then "all ideologies have certain elements of distortion, illusion, or myth."[113] Be that as it may, it is important to emphasize that once one intellectually (and emotionally) embraces particular sets of ideas or worldviews – narrowly political or not, extremist or not – they thenceforth function as de facto filters through which all information emanating from the outside world is not only screened but also filtered and even distorted to a lesser or greater degree. That is one of the most important tangible effects of the enthusiastic adoption of ideologies, and one which inevitably affects both the perceptions and the behavior of their adherents.

Second, political ideologies inevitably contain *normative* elements. They are not only formulated in such a way as to describe the world, but also in such a way as to evaluate, judge, and perhaps criticize it, implicitly if not explicitly. Thus Mostafa Rejai argues that political ideologies "make value judgments in two ways: negatively, by denouncing an existing system of social and political relationships; positively, by putting forth a set of norms according to which social and political reconstruction is to take place."[114] From this perspective, ideologies invariably

> denounce the existing society as corrupt, immoral, and beyond reform – and they do so by appealing to high-sounding moral principles. . . . The attack against society is presented, rationalized, justified, and dignified in the light of an appeal to "higher" principles.[115]

This is not necessarily the case, however, because we have already seen in discussing interpretations of the term "ideology" – especially those of Marx, Gramsci, and Marcuse – that the goal of many political ideologies is to justify and rationalize the *maintenance of the existing socio-political arrangements in particular societies*, as opposed to transforming or overthrowing them. As examples, one can note the various counterrevolutionary ideologies that emerged in the course and immediate wake of the

French Revolution whose purposes were to justify defending or restoring the power and authority of throne and altar.[116] Indeed, several authors have usefully divided political ideologies into (1) status quo ideologies, "which seek to conserve the existing order"; (2) reform ideologies, "which seek change within the existing order"; and (3) revolutionary ideologies, "which seek to replace the existing order."[117]

Third, it follows that all political ideologies have an important *affective* dimension. Whether an ideology is seeking to promote the maintenance of the status quo or to justify its overthrow and replacement, it must appeal to the emotions of the individuals or social groups its exponents hope to influence, convince, or mobilize the support of. As Rejai notes, "a most distinctive feature of all ideologies is an appeal to human passion, an eliciting of emotive response."[118] According to Smelser, ideologies provide "a structure for the affects of anxiety, despair, indignation, hope, anticipation, and elation, and [wed] them to its selective existential picture of the world."[119] Indeed, some analysts have gone so far as to claim that ideologies appeal mainly to the emotions rather than to the intellect.[120] However that may be, politically influential ideologies, past and present, are both psychologically seductive and emotionally resonant, which explains why they have so often been capable of inducing certain segments of particular communities to make extraordinary sacrifices on behalf of the causes they espouse. Indeed, even scholars who have characterized ideologies in a negative, restrictive way have often recognized their tremendous emotional appeal. For example, Aron argued that such political ideologies embody

> the longing for a purpose, for communion with the people, for something controlled by an idea or a will. The feeling of belonging to the elect, the security provided by a closed system in which the whole of history as well as one's own person find their place and their meaning, the pride of joining the past to the future in present action – all this inspires and sustains the believer.[121]

In what ways, then, are ideologies emotionally appealing? As Aron suggests, they provide the individuals who embrace them – rich or poor, educated or illiterate, fortunate or disadvantaged, young or old, from whatever social strata or life circumstances – with a comforting degree of intellectual certainty, a higher sense of purpose in life, a conviction of their own moral superiority, a feeling of belonging to a special community with a grand historical mission and destiny, and a sense of emotional stability and security in an otherwise inhospitable, chaotic, and seemingly meaningless world.

Fourth, political and religious ideologies function as a powerful source of *social solidarity*, because they effectively divide – intellectually, psychologically, and perhaps also socially and organizationally – the "righteous" group members from all of the "dark" or "alien" forces operating outside of and allegedly against the interests of the group. They therefore help to provide both a sense of collective identity to individual group members and to bond them socially and emotionally to each other, thus offering them a profound feeling of fellowship as "comrades" or "brothers" who are all ostensibly working together harmoniously and making common (and perhaps even at time extraordinary) sacrifices for a great and noble cause. Hence unlike most other people, such ideologically bonded group members are no longer suffering psychologically from loneliness and anomie or engaged in selfishly pursuing their own individual material interests. Indeed, one might say that the enthusiastic adherence to a common ideology constitutes the intellectual "glue" which holds socio-political organizations and movements together, and which in turn welds their members into a purposeful collectivity working toward the realization of what they regard as a glorious higher cause. Moreover, once a person embraces such an ideology and joins a particular group, especially one that espouses an extremist ideology, he or she is then typically subjected to further ideological indoctrination, authoritarian forms of charismatic leadership, intense peer group pressure, and severe sanctions for dissenting, refusing to obey, or otherwise violating the group's norms.[122] In the case of clandestine insurgent organizations relying on violence and terrorism, groups which are usually being actively hunted by the security forces of the incumbent regime, these processes become even more intensified, and the result is the development of a kind of insular "hothouse" environment marked by collective paranoia in which the significance and potential danger of every group member's thoughts and actions are magnified.[123] In such a strained micro-social context, what were originally perceived as socially and emotionally attractive elements of belonging to the group can eventually become terribly oppressive.

Be that as it may, all political ideologies, extremist or otherwise, claim to provide the answers to three interrelated questions:

- First, what is wrong with the world?
- Second, who is responsible for those wrongs?
- Third, what needs to be done to correct those wrongs?

This means, effectively, that political ideologies all contain both *diagnostic* elements – the answers they provide to the first and second questions – and *prescriptive* elements that are intended to serve as a guide for action – the answer they provide to the third question.[124] The foregoing is a shorthand way of formulating ideas that many other scholars have discussed at greater length. For example, Smelser emphasizes these same three aspects of ideologies, among others. First, ideologies claim to "identify and explain what is wrong or threatened in the world of believers and hoped-for believers," thereby structuring and making concrete "the more diffuse dissatisfactions experienced by a group and [lumping] the diverse reasons for these dissatisfactions into a single explanation."[125] Second, they typically "identify one or more target groups who are responsible for the dangers to and suffering in a given group," that is they tend to ascribe both the world's and their own group's problems to the actions supposedly initiated by certain designated villains.[126] Third, and more optimistically, they provide "an ideal vision of a better society and a better life."[127]

The argument herein is that all forms of ideological extremism, irrespective of their specific, variable, and unique doctrinal contents, share certain common characteristics or features that are both identifiable and easily recognizable. Some of those specific features are of course applicable, in varying degrees, to many other kinds of beliefs and attitudes. However, it is the combination, interaction, and mutually reinforcing nature of all of these problematic individual characteristics that together serve to mark ideological extremism. These characteristics include the following:

- Manicheanism – named after a dualistic, syncretistic, gnostic Near Eastern religion founded by Mānī (216–276) in Sassanid-era Iran, this term refers more broadly to a belief that everything in the world falls into one of two clearly distinct and opposed categories: that which is good and righteous and that which is evil and immoral.[128] It is a very moralistic, black-and-white view of the world, one that fails to acknowledge the extent to which most human behavior falls along a broad moral continuum between the hypothesized poles of light (goodness) and darkness (evil), that is that human morality is better viewed in terms of shades of gray than in absolute terms of black and white, even though some shades of gray are clearly lighter or darker than others. Those who perceive the world in this stark, dualistic fashion invariably characterize themselves as representatives of the forces of righteousness who are struggling valiantly against the powerful dark forces that surround and threaten to overwhelm them. The common phrase "you are either with us or against us" epitomizes the Manichean attitude, because from this perspective no one is viewed as a neutral party or an innocent bystander.
- Monism – a term with multiple technical meanings in philosophy, but referring in this context to an attitude that is the antithesis or opposite of political pluralism.[129] According to Jaroslaw Piekalkiewicz and Alfred Wayne Penn, monism "is the doctrine that reality may be understood as one unitary, indivisible whole; thus a monistic ideology posits that this reality can be interpreted by a universally true and exhaustive system of ideas."[130] In practice, this translates into the conviction that there is one, and only one, correct belief system, set of moral values, and/or appropriate course of action, whether this is decided upon by recognized group leaders or derived from ostensibly "eternal" theological or intrinsically "correct" political doctrines.[131] The phrase "my way or the highway" epitomizes this attitude, which is extremely intolerant of alternative, contrary, or dissenting views.
- Utopianism – a term referring to the promotion of a political or religious vision, agenda, or plan for a better society that is very unlikely to be achieved, if not impossible to achieve, in the real world (as well as to fictional societies portrayed in literature).[132] The term "utopia" derives from the Greek phrase *oú* ("not") and *tópos* ("place"), which therefore literally means "no place" or "nowhere," and was the title of a famous novel written in 1516 by Sir Thomas More (1478–1535). Hence in political parlance it is typically applied, pejoratively, to world transformative visions concerning the creation of an idealized society, in which all existing social problems can and will be surmounted or eradicated, visions that are viewed by critics as absurdly impractical because they are premised on false ideas about human nature or about its potential malleability.[133] Among the many extremist ideologies that have been characterized as utopian are communism (which postulates the creation of an ostensibly just, harmonious international classless society

free of want, hardship, and exploitation), fascism (which postulates the creation of an ostensibly just, harmonious organic national community free of internal conflict and debilitating divisions), anarchism (which postulates the creation of an ostensibly just, harmonious non-hierarchical, non-authoritarian decentralized socio-political system, also free of exploitation, where decisions are made and collectively acted upon from the bottom up), and Islamism (which postulates the creation of an ostensibly just, harmonious theocratic state and society that is free of want, hardship, and strife because everyone will behave in accordance with a strict, puritanical interpretation of Muslim divine law, the *sharīʿa*).

- Collectivism – a term referring to beliefs that the interests of the group as a whole, however that group is defined, must invariably take precedence over the rights of the individuals who make up the group. It is antithetical to individualism insofar as the individual is regarded as having no "natural rights" whatsoever that are distinct from his or her membership in the group, much less any intrinsic rights that cannot be abridged by the group, whose needs and interests are always granted priority. In that sense, modern collectivist ideologies have provided new intellectual justifications for suppressing individual rights, which in the West have replaced the unreflective communitarian beliefs commonly held and accepted in pre-modern or non-Western traditional societies, before certain natural rights doctrines had evolved and spread which proclaimed that individuals had certain inalienable rights of a moral, spiritual, or legal nature.[134]
- Hyper-moralism – a word that refers to excessive, uncompromising moralism or self-righteousness, if not outright moral puritanism. Although their opponents have often characterized extremists as either lacking any discernable morality or being unconcerned about moral strictures, the truth is precisely the opposite. Far from consciously ignoring morality (although they may well repudiate and intentionally violate existing moral standards) or lacking a moral compass, if anything they are "moral to a fault," in the sense that they both demand that everyone adhere to moral standards that are so strict that it is virtually impossible to achieve them and also often act to punish those who cannot meet such standards. Even when they cannot personally live up to their own unrealistic moral standards, which is all too common, they nonetheless try to impose them forcibly on everyone else. Extremists invariably believe that they are acting in the service of a higher morality, which is why they tend to be so morally rigid and intolerant of the perceived moral flaws of others and so brutal in dealing with their supposedly "immoral" opponents. Hence the horrendous atrocities and crimes against humanity that have often been committed by extremists are not generally attributable to immorality, amorality, or outright cruelty and sadism, but rather to their excessive moralism and fanatical conviction that they are struggling righteously against overwhelming odds to create a better world. In such contexts, the proverb incorrectly attributed to famed English author Samuel Johnson (1709–1784) – "the road to Hell is paved with good intentions" – is all too applicable, as is British historian Herbert Butterfield's statement that the "greatest menace to our civilization is the conflict between giant organized systems of self-righteousness. . . ."

- Authoritarianism or Totalitarianism – terms referring to the efforts by the leaders of extremist movements and organizations (1) to tightly control the external behavior of their followers (authoritarianism), or (2) to tightly control the external behavior *and* to transform and dominate, via a combination of systematic ideological indoctrination, psychological manipulation, and the creation of all-encompassing and confining organizational webs, the very thoughts and consciousness of their followers (totalitarianism). The aim of totalitarian leaders is to get inside their followers' heads and thereby create obedient, enthusiastic, disciplined, deployable "new men" who are willing to sacrifice themselves by struggling, heroically if necessary, in order to achieve their movements' ostensibly higher, noble causes. As the name itself implies, totalitarian leaders and movements aspire to achieve *total* control over their own followers and, ultimately, their entire societies, even though in practice they are never actually able to achieve such a thoroughgoing level of control.[135]
- Dehumanization or Demonization of Designated Enemies – terms referring to the characterization of opponents as intrinsically and irremediably evil or, in the case of religious extremists, as literally "satanic" or "demonic." Given this simplistic mindset, designated enemies are never viewed as garden variety political rivals or as people who simply have contrasting perspectives or different ideas, but rather as veritable "evildoers" who are consciously doing everything in their power to prevent extremist organizations from achieving their righteous goals. After all, why would anyone who was not thoroughly evil or inhuman intentionally stand in the way of such noble goals? Of course, different types of extremist groups designate different enemies based on the specific contents of their ideological belief systems: for communists, it is "class enemies"; for anarchists, all illegitimate "authorities" and "hierarchies"; for fascists, "anti-national" elements; for Nazis (and other racial supremacists), "racial enemies"; and for Islamists, "infidels," "hypocrites," and "apostates." Yet irrespective of how their enemies are actually defined, such a dehumanizing perspective easily serves as an intellectual and moral justification for the harsh persecution and physical elimination of real and imagined "enemies." Indeed, the achievement of proclaimed utopian agendas necessitates the suppression and merciless eradication – or, at the very least, the enforced ideological conversion by means of systematic re-education – of any and all opponents.
- Conspiratorial Paranoia – this phrase refers not to clinical forms of paranoia or actual psychopathologies, but to the penchant of extremists for believing that their enemies are utterly malicious, frightfully powerful, omnipresent, and incessantly engaged in sinister plotting to destroy their own group and thereby prevent the realization of its noble goals. Indeed, from their perspective there is not only a vast array of declared enemies operating *outside* of the movement who must be vanquished, but also "subversive," traitorous enemies operating secretly *within* the movement itself who must be ruthlessly purged lest they fatally weaken it. Such convictions easily lend themselves to the elaboration or adoption of all-encompassing conspiracy theories, which postulate that sinister cabals of evildoers are working constantly behind the scenes so as to manipulate or control the

course of events, invariably in detrimental if not catastrophic ways. Alas, because it is never possible for extremist movements to totally defeat or completely eliminate all opposition, group members are urged to remain perpetually vigilant and aggressively wage "continuous," never-ending life-and-death struggles against a host of real or imagined external and internal enemies.

These, then, are the common characteristics of virtually all forms of ideological extremism, and it would be easy enough for anyone who was sufficiently motivated to find innumerable quotations from a diverse array of extremist ideologues or ideological treatises that would perfectly illustrate all of those characteristics.

The ultimate goal of most political and religio-political extremists is to establish some form or system of "political rule in the name of a monistic ideology," that is an "ideocracy."[136] This term, which combines the ancient Greek root terms *kratía* ("[political] rule") and *idéa* ("idea"), refers to a polity or society that is in theory ruled in accordance with various ideological tenets, in this context those that embody extremist characteristics, albeit in practice one that is actually ruled by particular leaders who claim to adhere to those tenets. In the words of the American esoteric historian Arthur Versluis,

> [a]n ideocracy is a form of government characterized by an inflexible adherence to a set of doctrines, or ideas, typically enforced by criminal penalties. . . . An ideocracy is monistic and totalistic; it insists on the total application of ideology to every aspect of life, and in it, pluralism is anathema. . . . In an ideocracy, the greatest criminal is imagined by ideocrats to be the dissenter, the one who by his very existence reveals the totalistic construct imposed on society to be a lie.[137]

The proponents of such aims can thus be referred to generically as ideocrats, and the political systems they hope to establish can be referred to as ideocracies. Although most ideological extremists fortunately fail either to mobilize mass movements or to seize political power, those who do so typically endeavor to establish ideocratic political systems. That is precisely why one must always take the political or religio-political ideologies they espouse seriously, because those worldviews normally provide a blueprint, however vague and inconsistent it may be, for the regimes and societies they hope to establish should they succeed in coming to power.

Notes

1 Tess Gerritsen, *Gravity* (London: HarperCollins, 2000), p. 241, although the term is defined therein, in reference to a single-celled organism known as an *Archaeon*, as a "lover of extreme conditions."
2 See, e.g., Andrew Silke, ed., *Research on Terrorism: Trends, Achievements and Failures* (New York: Routledge, 2003); and Magnus Ranstorp, ed., *Mapping Terrorism Research: State of the Art, Gaps, and Future Direction* (New York: Routledge, 2006). Compare also Adam Dolnik, *Conducting Terrorism Field Research: A Guide* (New York: Routledge, 2013), for an

extended discussion of conducting field research in this area. For "critical terrorism studies" approaches adopted by unabashed leftist academicians, see Richard Jackson and Marie Breen Smith, eds., *Critical Terrorism Studies: A New Research Agenda* (New York: Routledge, 2009).
3 Jeffrey M. Bale, "The 'Black' Terrorist International: Neo-Fascist Paramilitary Networks and the 'Strategy of Tension' in Italy, 1968–1974," (Unpublished Ph.D. Dissertation: University of California at Berkeley, 1994), p. 26.
4 See, e.g., Eric van Um, *Evaluating the Political Rationality of Terrorist Groups* (Wiesbaden: Springer, 2016).
5 See, e.g., Nasrullah Memon et al., eds., *Mathematical Methods in Counterterrorism* (Vienna and New York: Springer, 2009); Alexander Gutfraind, *Mathematical Terrorism: Quantitative Modeling of Sub-State Conflicts* (Saarbrücken: Lambert, 2010); Sean F. Everton, *Disrupting Dark Networks* (New York: Cambridge University, 2012); and Daniel Cunningham, Sean F. Everton, and Philip Murphy, *Dark Networks: A Strategic Framework for the Use of Social Network Analysis* (Lanham, MD: Rowman & Littlefield, 2016).
6 See, e.g., Walter Enders and Todd Sandler, *The Political Economy of Terrorism* (New York: Cambridge University, 2011); and Eli Berman, *Radical, Religious, and Violent: The New Economics of Terrorism* (Cambridge, MA: MIT, 2011), wherein Berman argues that religious terrorists are not primarily motivated by religious ideas or the promise of rewards in the afterlife. One wonders, then, why they are even called "religious terrorists."
7 See, e.g., the works of forensic psychologist Marc Sageman, *Understanding Terror Networks* (Philadelphia: University of Pennsylvania, 2004); and Marc Sageman, *Leaderless Jihad: Terror Networks in the Twenty-First Century* (Philadelphia: University of Pennsylvania, 2008).
8 See, e.g., Bruce Bongar et al., *Psychology of Terrorism* (New York: Oxford University, 2006), especially chapters 1–5; James Jones, *Blood That Cries Out from the Earth: The Psychology of Religious Terrorism* (New York: Oxford University, 2008); and Jerrold M. Post, *The Mind of the Terrorist: The Psychology of Terrorism from the IRA to al-Qaeda* (New York: St. Martin's, 2008).
9 See, e.g., Andrew H. Kydd and Barbara F. Walter, "The Strategies of Terrorism," *International Security* 31:1 (Summer 2006), pp. 49–80, wherein there is not a single reference to ideology (except, inadvertently, in the title of an article cited in note 80). Indeed, in many articles dealing with terrorism and terrorists in academic social scientist journals, a word search yields *not a single reference to ideology*, which is an indication of how commonly this important aspect of terrorism has been ignored or neglected. Part of the problem, of course, is that "social science" and military analysts who have little or no prior knowledge of political philosophy or extremist ideologies, much less of the history of past revolutionary movements, simply lack the expertise necessary to understand the core beliefs of radical political or religio-political groups and regimes. Unfortunately, just as it was impossible during the Cold War to understand and effectively counteract the behavior of communist guerrillas and terrorists without understanding their ideologies, it is currently impossible to understand and effectively counteract the behavior of jihadist terrorists without understanding Islamist ideological currents. That is one key reason why so many Western counterinsurgency and counterterrorist operations have ended in failure.
10 Here is an illustrative example found in an article written by Christopher Massie, "Is ISIS a Faith-Based Terrorist Group?" *Columbia Journalism Review* (17 September 2014), available at www.cjr.org/behind_the_news/is_isis_a_faith-based_terroris.php?page=all:

> When I asked Marc Sageman, a senior fellow at the Foreign Policy Research Institute, if he thought it was worthwhile to debate whether the causes of Islamic extremism were ideological, he said, "I do not. I really do not. And I stress that." Sageman argues that political violence, from the French Revolution to modern jihad, is essentially the same: a kind of "ritual," *not dependent on ideology* [italics added], that people act out to earn "a sense of legitimacy within the 'in' group."

So it is that Sageman cavalierly dismissed, on the basis of his own preferred social network-centric psychological theories, the conclusions derived from decades, nay centuries, of serious historical scholarship on a multitude of extremist, revolutionary, and insurgent movements. Of course, there are innumerable other examples of this tendency to ignore or downplay ideological factors, such as assorted sociological, Marxist, and "world systems" theories of revolution that overemphasize impersonal structural forces and inexplicably minimize the importance of the articulated beliefs of the participants in these movements. Note that these structural approaches rely almost entirely on theoretical abstractions rather than the disconfirmatory evidence found in masses of primary sources.

11 Aleksandr Solzhenitsyn, *The Gulag Archipelago, 1918–1956: An Experiment in Literary Investigation* (New York: HarperCollins, 1991), volume 1, pp. 173–4.
12 Terry Eagleton, *Ideology* (London: Verso, 1991), p. xiii.
13 Daniel Bell, "The End of Ideology in the West: An Epilogue," in *The End of Ideology: On the Exhaustion of Political Ideas in the Fifties*, ed. by Daniel Bell (New York: Free Press, 1962), p. 394.
14 David McLellen, *Ideology* (Minneapolis: University of Minnesota, 1995), p. 2.
15 Himmelstein's remark has been cited on many websites that provide definitions of extremism. They were apparently made at a special session of the 1998 ASA convention devoted to right-wing social movements, at which he presented the findings of a paper titled "All But Sleeping with the Enemy: Studying the Radical Right Up Close." The author would like to thank Himmelstein for providing him with a copy of the actual paper, which is quite insightful.
16 For the pejorative connotations of the terms "fanatic" and "fanaticism," as well as the term "terrorism," see Maxwell Taylor, *The Fanatics: A Behavioural Approach to Political Violence* (London: Brassey's UK, 1991), pp. 12–14, 16. The term "fanaticism" originally had the connotation of excessive enthusiasm in religious belief – in literary contexts, the Latin word *fanaticus* means "to be put into a raging enthusiasm by a deity" – but its meaning has since been expanded to apply to similarly excessive enthusiasm in other, non-religious contexts, including political contexts. See ibid., p. 13.
17 Peter T. Coleman and Andrea Bartoli, *Addressing Extremism* (New York and Washington, DC: International Center for Cooperation and Conflict Resolution/Institute for Conflict Analysis and Resolution, undated), p. 2 (emphasis added), available at www.tc.columbia.edu/i/a/document/9386_WhitePaper_2_Extremism_030809.pdf. Exactly how far removed something has to be to fall into the "extremist" category remains unclear. Note, however, that Coleman and Bartoli do not claim that extremism is not a real phenomenon, even though they acknowledge the difficulties in defining it and the biased way the term can be applied.
18 See, e.g., Chip Berlet, "Time to Rethink Using the Term 'Extremism'," Huffington Post blog, 28 December 2010, available at www.huffingtonpost.com/chip-berlet/time-to-rethink-using-the_b_802001.html. Therein Berlet argues that

> [e]very time the government uses the term "extremist" it helps justify political repression against political opponents. . . . Every time the term "extremist" is used to describe a political opponent, it marginalizes political dissent across the political spectrum. . . . Every time liberals and leftists use the term "extremist" it undermines the movement for progressive social change. . . . The term "extremist" is often used by those in the political center to demonize dissidents on the political left and right.

While Berlet, the lead analyst in an "anti-fascist" watchdog organization known as Political Research Associates, is to be commended for opposing the use of the term for both right-wing radicals and left-wing radicals, he mainly opposes its use because it is so "elastic" that it has often been abusively applied against the left. It is unclear whether he believes that the term has no substantive meaning, although that is certainly the implication. Compare also William F. Jasper, "Media Jump to Smear Right with Extremist Label," *The New American*, 1 April 2010, available at www.thenewamerican.com/usnews/

politics/3238-media-jump-to-smear-right-with-extremist-label. *The New American* is a publication of the right-wing John Birch Society.
19 Eric Hoffer, *The True Believer: Thoughts on the Nature of Mass Movements* (New York: Harper Perennial, 2002 [1951]).
20 See, e.g., John George and Laird Wilcox, *American Extremists: Militias, Supremacists, Klansmen, Communists, and Others* (Amherst, NY: Prometheus Books, 1996), especially chapter 2.
21 Laird Wilcox, *The Hoaxer Project Report: Racist and Anti-Semitic Graffiti, Harassment and Violence: An Essay on Hoaxes and Fabricated Incidents* (Olathe, KS: Laird Wilcox Editorial Research Service, 1990), pp. 39–41. This study was later updated as *Crying Wolf: Hate Crime Hoaxes in America* (Olathe, KS: Laird Wilcox Editorial Research Service, 1995). Needless to say, many of those specific characteristics appear in other contexts as well, but it is their combination with each other that allegedly marks extremism.
22 Neil J. Smelser, *The Faces of Terrorism: Social and Psychological Dimensions* (Princeton: Princeton University, 2007), pp. 80–6. Ironically, in this section he is highlighting the dangers of adopting a post-9/11 counterterrorist ideology that has "manifested a point-by-point structural correspondence with the Islamic fundamentalist ideology in the name of which the attacks were made," although he also emphasizes that pointing out these parallels does not in any sense "connote a moral equivalence." See ibid., pp. 82, 86.
23 Ronald Wintrobe, *Rational Extremism: The Political Economy of Radicalism* (New York: Cambridge University, 2006), p. 5. However, his overall argument is severely problematic inasmuch as he argues that extremism is a rational strategy in struggles for power. Therein lies yet another egregious absurdity associated with fashionable "rational choice" approaches: the claim that even non-rational human beliefs and behavior, in this case ideological fanaticism and the actions it engenders, are nonetheless somehow "rational." Compare also the unconvincing "rationalist," "materialist," and "economist" explanations of extremist behavior by Eli Berman and various colleagues, for example Eli Berman, *Radical, Religious, and Violent: The New Economics of Terrorism* (Cambridge, MA: MIT, 2009); Eli Berman, Jacob N. Shapiro, and Joseph H. Felter, "Can Hearts and Minds Be Bought? The Economics of Counterinsurgency in Iraq," *Journal of Political Economy* 119:4 (August 2011), pp. 766–819; and Laurence R. Iannacone and Eli Berman, "Religious Extremism: The Good, the Bad, and the Deadly," an article prepared for a special issue of *Public Choice*. Frankly, anyone who believes that, say, Islamists, including jihadist terrorists, are not motivated primarily by puritanical religious beliefs and literalist theological interpretations has clearly never read what they have written or interacted with them. Other factors also undoubtedly affect their behavior, but they are usually of less central importance.
24 Taylor, *The Fanatics*, pp. 37–56. Compare also Josef Rudin, *Fanaticism: A Psychological Analysis*, trans. by Elisabeth Reinecke and Paul C. Bailey (Notre Dame, IN: University of Notre Dame, 1969).
25 For more on "death squads," see Bruce B. Campbell and Arthur D. Brenner, eds., *Death Squads in Comparative Perspective: Murder with Deniability* (New York: Palgrave Macmillan, 2002); Jeffrey A. Sluka, ed., *Death Squad: The Anthropology of State Terror* (Philadelphia: University of Pennsylvania, 2000); Marie-Monique Robin, *Escadrons de la mort, l'école française* (Paris: Découverte, 2004); Cecilia Menjívar and Néstor Rodríguez, eds., *When States Kill: Latin America, the U.S., and Technologies of Terror* (Austin: University of Texas, 2005); Paddy Woodworth, *Dirty War, Clean Hands: ETA, the GAL and Spanish Democracy* (New Haven: Yale University, 2003); and Scott Anderson and Jon Lee Anderson, *Inside the League: The Shocking Exposé of How Terrorists, Nazis, and Latin American Death Squads Have Infiltrated the World Anti-Communist League* (New York: Dodd Mead, 1986).
26 For a brief introduction to the concept of ideology, see Michael Freeden, *Ideology: A Very Short Introduction* (New York: Oxford University, 2003). Compare also McLellen, *Ideology*; and David Hawkes, *Ideology* (New York: Routledge, 2003), although the latter adopts a literary and cultural studies approach that many will find uncongenial.

27 See, respectively, McLellan, *Ideology*, p. 1; and Michael Freeden, *Ideologies and Political Theory: A Conceptual Approach* (Oxford: Clarendon Press, 1996), p. 13. To say that the concept of ideology itself is "essentially contested" is an understatement. Yet ironically, one of the chief aims of particular ideologies is "to end the inevitable contention over concepts by *decontesting* them, by removing their meanings from contest." See Freeden, *Ideology*, p. 54.

28 Bell, "End of Ideology in the West," p. 399. Here Bell suggests that the common understanding of the term is rather neutral. In contrast, Terry Eagleton argues that "to claim in ordinary conversation that someone is speaking ideologically is surely to hold that they are judging a particular issue through some rigid framework of preconceived ideas which distorts their understanding." See Eagleton, *Ideology*, p. 3. Compare also Roger Eatwell and Anthony Wright, eds., *Contemporary Political Ideologies* (London and New York: Pinter, 1999), p. vi: "In everyday usage, 'ideology' tends to be a pejorative term, synonymous with deceitful and fanatical. As such, it is often contrasted with pragmatism and truth." No doubt this would depend upon whom one was talking to.

29 Compare Manfred B. Steger, *Globalism: Market Ideology Meets Terrorism* (Lanham, MD: Rowman & Littlefield, 2005), p. 5:

> Most social and political theorists define *ideology* as a system of widely shared ideas, patterned beliefs, guiding norms and values, and lofty ideals accepted as "fact" or "truth" by some group. Ideologies offer individuals a more or less coherent picture of the world, not only as it is, but also as it should be.

30 See, respectively, John B. Thompson, *Ideology and Modern Culture: Critical Social Theory in the Era of Mass Communication* (Cambridge, UK: Polity Press, 1990), p. 5; and Lyman Tower Sargent, *Contemporary Political Ideologies: A Comparative Analysis* (Belmont, CA: Wadsworth, 2008), pp. 2–3. Like Thompson, American anthropologist Clifford Geertz (1926–2006) highlighted the symbolic dimensions of ideologies by defining them, neutrally, as "systems of interacting symbols" and "patterns of interworking meanings" that were necessary due to the human need for "symbolic templates" to make sense of the external world. See his "Ideology as a Cultural System," in *Ideology and Discontent*, ed. by David E. Apter (New York: Free Press of Glencoe, 1964), pp. 56, 63. Compare also the more pithy but generic formulation of Raymond Boudon, *The Analysis of Ideology*, trans. by Malcolm Slater (Cambridge, UK: Polity Press, 1986), p. 71: "ideologies are systems of ideas which relate to society." They are also "socially shared ideas," at least insofar as they aspire to have any historical or political importance. See Teun A. van Dijk, *Ideology: A Multidisciplinary Approach* (London: Sage, 1998), p. 15.

31 Thus American sociologist Edward Shils (1910–1995) insisted that ideologies "are characterized by *a high degree of explicitness of formulation* over a very wide range of objects with which they deal." See Edward Shils, "The Concept and Function of Ideology," in *International Encyclopedia of the Social Sciences*, ed. by David L. Sills (New York: Macmillan, 1968), volume 7, p. 66 (italics added). Compare the views of numerous other academicians, such as Noël O'Sullivan, *Conservatism* (London: Dent, 1976), p. 9: "An ideology, unlike an attitude, requires a self-conscious attempt to provide an explicit and coherent theory of man, society, and the world." For his part, Raymond Williams, *Marxism and Literature* (New York: Oxford University, 1978), p. 109, refers to ideologies as both the "fully articulate and systematic forms" of ideas and, in contrast to hegemony writ large, as an "articulate formal system" of ideas.

32 For example, Willie Thompson argues that if the "taken-for-granted framework of assumptions, habits, [and] metaphysical, social, and political beliefs" falls into the category of ideology, in which case it would be "a mode of consciousness ... which is all pervasive [that] none of us can escape," then the term could be "applied to anyone anywhere at any time in all history." As a result, he defines ideology as "an interconnected system or structure of basic belief applicable to particular social or cultural collectives – one which incorporates conscious beliefs, assumptions, and unthinking modes of perception – through which its adherents view the world around them." See his *Ideologies in the Age of*

Extremes: Liberalism, Conservatism, Communism, Fascism 1914–91 (New York: Pluto Press, 2011), pp. 1–2. Thus, by including everything but the kitchen sink under the same rubric, such an approach collapses the crucial distinction between coherent doctrines and impressionistic feelings about the world.

33 Roger Eatwell, "Introduction," in *Contemporary Political Ideologies*, ed. by Roger Eatwell and Anthony Wright, p. 3, and further on pp. 15–16.

34 Or, in the words of Canadian philosopher Charles Taylor, the "taken-for-granted shape of things, too obvious to mention." See Charles Taylor, *A Secular Age* (Cambridge, MA: Harvard University, 2007), p. 176. One such possible term is the annoyingly postmodern phrase "the social imaginary." Although this concept has been defined and employed in different ways, some of them unbearably pretentious, Manfred Steger has described it as "the micromappings of social and political space through which we perceive, judge, and act in the world." Thus the social imaginary is neither a theory nor an ideology, but rather

> an implicit "background" that makes possible communal practices and a widely shared sense of their legitimacy. It offers explanations of how "we" – the members of the community – fit together, how things go on between us, the expectations we have of each other, and the deeper normative notions and images that underlie those expectations.

See Manfred B. Steger, *The Rise of the Global Imaginary: Political Ideologies from the French Revolution to the Global War on Terror* (New York: Oxford University, 2008), p. 6.

35 See Robert E. Lane, *Political Ideology: Why the American Common Man Believes What He Does* (New York: Free Press, 1962), p. 16. Compare also George Rudé, *Ideology and Popular Protest* (New York: Pantheon, 1980), p. 27, who similarly draws a distinction between two types of ideologies, "a structured, or relatively structured type of ideology (the only 'ideology' worthy of the name, according to some) and one of more simple attitudes, *mentalités* or outlooks." Of course, given that his book is a study of "popular ideology," it would have been impossible for him to limit himself to structured, coherent doctrines developed by intellectuals. But that does not mean that "simple attitudes" necessarily fall into the category of ideologies.

36 This distinction between consciously embracing ideologies and being unconsciously affected by them has been emphasized by Boudon, *Analysis of Ideology*, p. 71 (italics in original):

> received ideas which go to make up ideologies can emerge *normally* in the subject's mind, rather than being the result of arbitrary or unclear forces over which the subject has no control. In other words, we can very often analyse adherence to received ideas as a *meaningful* act in the Weberian sense of the word.

37 Kenneth Minogue, *Alien Powers: The Pure Theory of Ideology* (New York: St. Martin's, 1985), p. 1.

38 Some analysts have even argued that *all* ideologies are political ideologies. For example, Martin Seliger claims that ideologies are always linked to politics, and that all politics are linked to ideology. See Martin Seliger, *Ideology and Politics* (London: George Allen & Unwin, 1976), p. 15. However, not all ideologies are focused on narrowly political matters, even if they have certain implicit political connotations, and a good deal of garden variety political behavior is not motivated primarily or explicitly by conscious adherence to political ideologies. After all, naked struggles for power between human groups or political candidates, democratic or otherwise, do not necessarily stem from concrete ideological differences. Thus, according to Steger, "[w]hat makes an ideology 'political' is that its concepts and claims select, privilege, or constrict social meanings related to the exercise of power in society." See Steger, *Globalism*, p. 5.

39 Andrew Heywood, *Political Ideologies: An Introduction* (New York: Palgrave Macmillan, 2003), p. 12.

40 Ibid.

41 Ibid.
42 Ibid., p. 13.
43 Leon P. Baradat, *Political Ideologies: Their Origins and Impact* (Boston: Longman, 2012), p. 12. But compare the cautionary remarks of Andrew Vincent, who argues that ideologies are not so easily distinguishable, either from political philosophies or from scientific theories, as many suppose. See Andrew Vincent, *Modern Political Ideologies* (Malden, MA: Wiley-Blackwell, 2009), pp. 13–17.
44 Baradat, *Political Ideologies*, p. 10.
45 Eatwell, "Introduction," p. 17.
46 Carl J. Friedrich and Zbigniew Brzezinski, *Totalitarian Dictatorship and Autocracy* (Cambridge, MA: Harvard University, 1965), p. 88 (italics in original).
47 Vincent, *Modern Political Ideologies*, p. 16.
48 Roy C. Macridis, *Contemporary Political Ideologies: Movements and Regimes* (Boston: Little, Brown, 1983), p. 4 (emphasis in original). He reformulated his definition in later editions, but in all of the iterations there is an emphasis on the action-oriented nature of ideologies. For example, in the sixth edition of this textbook, Macridis and Mark L. Hulliung argue that, in contrast to philosophy and theory, "ideology shapes beliefs that incite people into action." See *Contemporary Political Ideologies: Movements and Regimes* (New York: HarperCollins, 1996), p. 3.
49 According to Michael Freeden, *Ideologies and Political Theory: A Conceptual Approach* (Oxford: Clarendon Press, 1996), p. 15, citing Lane, *Political Ideology*, pp. 3, 14–16. However, that particular quote does not in fact appear on the cited pages of Lane's book, at least not in the edition that I examined.
50 Skinner's core argument against what he called "mentalism" was that "what is felt or introspectively observed is not some nonphysical world of consciousness, mind, or mental life but the observer's own body." Hence these thoughts, beliefs, and feelings are not "the causes of the behavior. An organism behaves as it does because of its current structure, but most of this is out of reach of introspection." See B. F. Skinner, *About Behaviorism* (New York: Knopf, 1974), pp. 18–19.
51 Compare Heywood, *Political Ideologies*, pp. 1–2. For example, the "classical realist" school postulates that political conflicts ultimately derive from basic human nature, specifically the various protagonists' allegedly innate drive for power and their will to dominate. "Power politics" are thus prioritized, whereas the roles of ideology and morality are minimized.
52 See, e.g., Andrej Zwitter, "The Anatomy of Ideology: An Analysis of the Structure of Ideology and the Mobilisation of Terrorists," *HUMSEC Journal* 1 (2007), pp. 30–46, available at www.humsec.eu/cms/fileadmin/user_upload/humsec/Journal/Zwitter_The_Anatomy_of_Ideology.pdf. As he puts it, "ideology is overlooked and therefore underestimated and under-researched" (p. 31) in the field of terrorism studies, even though "[t]errorism exists by the [sic] virtue of the ideologies adhered to by its perpetrators" (p. 30) – unless, of course, one is talking about acts of terrorism carried out for mercenary reasons by criminal organizations. However, it is not only foolish but dangerous to neglect the ideologies of extremist groups that rely heavily on violence and terrorism, since those ideologies, by explicitly identifying who the groups' enemies are, play a decisive role in determining their initial target selection and in providing them with the moral justifications they need for attacking their designated enemies. See C.J.M. Drake, "The Role of Ideology in Terrorists' Target Selection," *Terrorism and Political Violence* 10:2 (Summer 1998), pp. 53–85.
53 A particularly egregious example of this myopic attitude is evident in the influential works of Robert Pape, who continues to insist – against all evidence to the contrary – that there is no link between the disproportionate number of suicide attacks that have been carried out by jihadists (which they themselves refer to as "martyrdom operations"), explicitly on behalf of Allāh (*fī sabīl Allāh*), and their particular theological interpretations of Islamic doctrine. See Robert A. Pape, *Dying to Win: The Strategic Logic of Suicide Terrorism*

Introduction **37**

(New York: Random House, 2006); and Robert A. Pape and James K. Feldman, *Cutting the Fuse: The Explosion of Global Suicide Terrorism and How to Stop It* (Chicago: University of Chicago, 2010). This interpretation is manifestly absurd, as anyone familiar with the extraordinary efforts made by Islamists to justify such attacks by reference to the Qur'ān and the collections of *hadīth* (reports of what Muhammad allegedly said and did) can attest. See, e.g., Ayman al-Zawahiri, "Jihad, Martyrdom, and the Killing of Innocents," in *The Al Qaeda Reader*, ed. and trans. by Raymond Ibrahim (New York: Broadway Books, 2007), pp. 137–71. Compare the analysis of David Cook and Olivia Alison, *Understanding and Addressing Suicide Attacks: The Faith and Tactics of Martyrdom Operations* (Westport, CT: Praeger Security International, 2007). See further David Cook, *Martyrdom in Islam* (New York: Cambridge University, 2007); and David Cook, ed., *Jihad and Martyrdom* (New York: Routledge, 2010), a four-volume collection of previously published articles on these subjects (including Pape's original article). This is not to claim, of course, that there are not also strategic, operational, or tactical "logics" involved in employing suicide terrorism, only that religious beliefs and cultural values are crucially important as motivating factors and should therefore not be ignored in this context.

54 George Weigel, *Letters to a Young Catholic* (New York: Basic Books, 2005), p. 44.
55 Max Lerner, *Ideas Are Weapons: The History and Uses of Ideas* (New York: Viking, 1939), a collection of essays.
56 Hence the pithy conclusion of Lane in *Political Ideology*, p. 439: "Ideologies have consequences." The key functions of ideologies will be further clarified later.
57 Eatwell and Wright, *Contemporary Political Ideologies*, p. vii.
58 Bell, "End of Ideology in the West," p. 400. Compare the views of the many scholars who have analyzed and elaborated the concept of sacralized secular ideologies or "political religions," e.g., Emilio Gentile, *Politics as Religion*, trans. by George Staunton (Princeton: Princeton University, 2006); Emilio Gentile, *The Sacralization of Politics in Fascist Italy*, trans. by Keith Botsford (Cambridge, MA: Harvard University, 1996); and A. James Gregor, *Totalitarianism and Political Religion: An Intellectual History* (Stanford: Stanford University, 2012); the three-volume collective work edited by Hans Meier and his colleagues, *Totalitarianism and Political Religions: Concepts for the Comparison of Dictatorships* (New York: Routledge, 2005–2008); Michael Burleigh, *Earthly Powers: The Clash of Religion and Politics in Europe, from the French Revolution to the Great War* (New York: Harper Perennial, 2007); Michael Burleigh, *Sacred Causes: The Clash of Religion and Politics, from the Great War to the War on Terror* (New York: Harper Perennial, 2008); Roger Griffin, ed., *Fascism, Totalitarianism and Political Religion* (New York: Routledge, 2006); Rainer Bucher, *Hitler's Theology: A Study in Political Religion* (London and New York: Continuum, 2011); and Walter Skya, *Japan's Holy War: The Ideology of Radical Shinto Ultranationalism* (Durham, NC: Duke University, 2009); and many articles and special issues of the former journal *Totalitarian Movements and Political Religions* (which was recently renamed *Politics, Religion and Ideology*), some of which were later reissued in book format.
59 Eagleton, *Ideology*, p. xiii.
60 For critical analyses of such approaches in the context of terrorism, see Tore Bjørgo, ed., *Root Causes of Terrorism: Myths, Reality and Ways Forward* (London and New York: Routledge, 2005).
61 Here, of course, I am excluding the relative handful of serious scholars who have studied important aspects of Islamist ideology in an appropriately critical and non-apologetic fashion, such as David Cook, Jean-Pierre Filiu, Hillel Fradkin, Timothy Furnish, Thomas Hegghammer, Johannes J. G. Jansen, Gilles Kepel, Farhad Khosrokhavar, Nelly Lahoud, Brynjar Lia, Will McCants, Rolf Meijer, Reuven Paz, Kumar Ramakrishna, Ana Belén Soage, Anne Stenersen, Suha Taji-Farouki, Bassam Tibi, Joas Wagemakers, and Quintan Wiktorowicz.
62 In this context, it is worth noting Seliger's attempt to draw an analytical distinction between the "fundamental" dimensions of ideologies and their "operative" dimensions. See Seliger, *Ideology and Politics*, pp. 108–21, 175–208, and passim. He points out that

loyalty to a group's fundamental ideological principles is often tested by its need to confront and cope effectively with practical realities, and that those principles can be compromised in the process. As he puts it (ibid., p. 120),

> [c]ompromises cause ideology to bifurcate into the purer, and hence more dogmatic, fundamental dimensions of argumentation and the more diluted, and hence more pragmatic, operative dimension. In the latter, morally based prescriptions are often attenuated . . . by technical prescriptions. The tension between the two dimensions gives rise to the question of the sincerity of the valuations which are advanced, whereas out of the interaction between the two dimensions, which normally signifies an increase of ideological pluralism, arises the challenge of ideological change.

However, Seliger's focus in the preceding passage on a group's "argumentation," i.e., how it articulates its doctrines and agendas in public or in private, rather than on its core beliefs per se is misleading, and he fails to acknowledge that the more radical, utopian, and inflexible an ideology is, content-wise, the less willing and able its exponents usually are to compromise it in order to gain short-term political advantages. And if they do compromise it in noticeable ways, then they are likely to alienate their more purist, intransigent followers. Indeed, that is the norm, or at least the most common observable pattern, with respect to the historical evolution or trajectory of socio-political movements inspired by extremist ideologies.

63 Seliger, *Ideology and Politics*, p. 14 and passim.
64 See Thompson, *Ideology and Modern Culture*, pp. 53–4. These neutral conceptions do not assume that ideologies are "necessarily misleading, illusory or aligned with the interests of any particular group" and instead recognize that they can be revolutionary, reformist, or restorationist, that they can aim for the transformation or preservation of the social order, and that they are as useful to subordinate as they are to dominant groups. Unfortunately, Thompson himself ends up adopting a quasi-Marxist "critical conception." See ibid., pp. 56–67.
65 Although he had first introduced and discussed this concept in earlier books, De Tracy published a multi-volume work on ideology in 1817–1818 titled *Eléments d'idéologie*. All of those volumes are available in hard copy format from the Parisian publisher Hachette. Perhaps the most important of those volumes is the first, which is now accessible for free from Amazon France in Kindle format as Antoine Destutt de Tracy, *Eléments d'idéologie, I: Idéologie*. For more on De Tracy and his ideas, see Brian W. Head, ed., *Ideology and Social Science: Destutt de Tracy and French Liberalism* (Dordrecht and Boston: M. Nijhoff, 1985); Emmet Kennedy, *A Philosophe in the Age of Revolution: Destutt de Tracy and the Origins of Ideology* (Philadelphia: American Philosophical Society, 1978); Ulrich Lorenz, *Das Projekt der Ideologie: Studien zur Konzeption einer ersten Philosophie bei Destrutt de Tracy* (Stuttgart: Frommann-Holzboog, 1994); and Steger, *Rise of the Global Imaginary*, pp. 24–32.
66 For the distinction between traditional "myths" and modern "ideologies," see Ben Halpern, " 'Myth' and 'Ideology' in Modern Usage," *History and Theory* 1:2 (1961), pp. 129–49. For the view that ideologies are modern phenomena, see Jürgen Habermas, *Towards a Rational Society: Student Protest, Science, and Politics*, trans. by Jeremy J. Shapiro (Boston: Beacon Press, 1970), p. 99, who argued that ideologies "replace traditional legitimations of power by appearing in the mantle of modern science and by [paradoxically] deriving their justification from the critique of ideology. Ideologies are coeval with the critique of ideology. In this sense there are no pre-bourgeois ideologies." Compare also Michael Oakeshott, "Rationalism in Politics," in *Rationalism in Politics and Other Essays*, ed. Michael Oakeshott (London and New York: Methuen, 1962 [1947]), p. 21.
67 As per Alex Roberto Hybel, *The Power of Ideology: From the Roman Empire to Al-Qaeda* (New York: Routledge, 2009), p. 9.
68 George Lichtheim, *The Concept of Ideology, and Other Essays* (New York: Random House, 1967), pp. 5–6. Compare also the excellent short summaries in Steger, *Rise of the Global Imaginary*, pp. 33–7; and Vincent, *Modern Political Ideologies*, pp. 2–3. For more on these so-called *idéologues* and their ideas, see Charles Hunter van Duzer, *Contributions of the*

Idéologues to French Revolutionary Thought (Baltimore: Johns Hopkins University, 1935); and Cheryl Welch, *Liberty and Unity: The French Ideologues and the Transformation of Liberalism* (New York: Columbia University, 1984).
69 Cited by Hans Barth, *Wahrheit und Ideologie* (Zurich: Rentsch, 1961), p. 27. Compare Henry D. Aiken, *The Age of Ideology: The 19th Century Philosophers* (New York: New American Library, 1956), pp. 16–17: "During the Napoleonic Era . . . 'ideology' came to mean virtually any belief of a republican or revolutionary sort, that is to say, any belief hostile to Napoleon himself." Similar negative views of ideologies were later made by Michael Oakeshott and others, although it was their supposed rationality rather than their metaphysical nature that was the bone of contention.
70 On Marxist views of ideology, compare Martin Seliger, *The Marxist Conception of Ideology: A Critical Essay* (Cambridge, UK and New York: Cambridge University, 1977); Jorge Larraín, *Marxism and Ideology* (Atlantic Highlands, NJ: Humanities Press, 1983); and Walter Carlsnaes, *The Concept of Ideology and Political Analysis: A Critical Examination of Its Usage by Marx, Lenin, and Mannheim* (Westport, CT: Greenwood Press, 1981).
71 On the Young Hegelians and their disputes with Marx, see Warren Breckman, *Marx, the Young Hegelians, and the Origins of Radical Social Theory: Dethroning the Self* (New York: Cambridge University, 1999); David McLellan, *The Young Hegelians and Karl Marx* (New York: Praeger, 1969); Harold Mah, *The End of Philosophy, the Origin of Ideology: Karl Marx and the Crisis of the Young Hegelians* (Berkeley: University of California, 1987). For a collection of Young Hegelian writings, see Lawrence S. Stepelevich, ed., *The Young Hegelians: An Anthology* (Atlantic Highlands, NJ: Humanities Press, 1997). The most prominent of the Young Hegelians was German philosopher Ludwig Feuerbach (1804–1872).
72 Karl Marx and Friedrich Engels, *The German Ideology* (London: Lawrence & Wishart, 1970), p. 64.
73 Vladimir Lenin, *What Is To Be Done? Burning Questions of Our Movement* (New York: International, 1960 [1902]), pp. 40–1:

> Since there can be no talk of an independent ideology being developed by the masses of the workers in the process of their movement then *the only choice is*: Either bourgeois, or Socialist ideology. There is no middle course (for humanity has not created a "third" ideology, and, moreover, in a society torn by class antagonisms there can never be a non-class or above-class ideology). Hence, to belittle Socialist ideology *in any way*, to *deviate from it in the slightest degree* means strengthening bourgeois ideology.

74 Ibid., pp. 32–33, 76–90, 105–33. Recently an extreme revisionist interpretation of Lenin's attitudes with respect to the potential development of a revolutionary class consciousness by the workers has appeared, one which contests the standard interpretation of this notoriously polemical text: Lars P. Lih, *Lenin Rediscovered: What Is To Be Done? In Context* (Chicago: Haymarket Books, 2008).
75 Georg Lukács, *History and Class Consciousness: Studies in Marxist Dialectics*, trans. by Rodney Livingstone (Cambridge, MA: MIT, 1972 [1923]), p. 258. See further Roisin McDonough, "Ideology and False Consciousness: Lukacs," in *On Ideology*, ed. by the Centre for Contemporary Cultural Studies (New York: Routledge, 2006 [1978]), pp. 33–44.
76 Compare Louis Althusser, *On Ideology*, trans. by Ben Brewster (London: Verso, 2008), especially "Ideology and Ideological State Apparatuses: Notes toward an Investigation" (which is also available online at www.marx2mao.com/Other/LPOE70ii.html#s5); and Louis Althusser, *For Marx* (London: Verso, 2006), p. 232. See further Paul Q. Hirst, "Althusser and the Theory of Ideology," *Economy and Society* 5:4 (1976), pp. 385–412.
77 Compare Antonio Gramsci, *Prison Notebooks, Volumes 1–3*, trans. by Joseph A. Buttigieg (New York: Columbia University, 2010); Antonio Gramsci, *Selections from the Prison Notebooks*, ed. by Quintin Hoare and Geoffrey Nowell Smith (New York: International Publishers, 1971 [1935]); and Antonio Gramsci, *The Antonio Gramsci Reader: Selected Writings, 1916–1935*, ed. by David Forgacs (New York: New York University, 2000). For more on Gramsci and his ideas, see John M. Cammett, *Antonio Gramsci and the Origins of Italian*

Communism (Stanford: Stanford University, 1967); Alastair Davidson, *Antonio Gramsci: Towards an Intellectual Biography* (Atlantic Highlands, NJ: Humanities Press, 1977); Chantal Mouffe, "Hegemony and Ideology in Gramsci," *Research in Political Economy* 2 (1979), pp. 1–31 Joseph V. Femia, *Gramsci's Political Thought: Hegemony, Consciousness, and the Revolutionary Process* (New York: Oxford University, 1987); and – for a cultural studies approach – Stephen J. Jones, *Antonio Gramsci* (New York: Routledge, 2006).

78 According to Marx's famous formulation, "[i]t is not the consciousness of men that determines their existence, but, on the contrary, their social existence [that] determines their consciousness." See Karl Marx, *A Contribution to the Critique of Political Economy* (Charleston, SC: Forgotten Books, 2010 [1859]), pp. 11–12.

79 Gramsci, *Selections from the Prison Notebooks*, p. 376.

80 Ibid., p. 12.

81 Vincent, *Modern Political Ideologies*, p. 7.

82 Note that Gramsci's notions, sophisticated as they were in many respects, were also fragmented, occasionally rambling, and at times equivocal or contradictory, in large part due to his difficult and stressful living conditions in Fascist prisons as well as to his increasingly ill health, and that his arguments concerning hegemony are scattered throughout the *Quaderni del carcere*, but can be found especially in Part 1, in Part 2, the section on "State and Civil Society," and in Part 3, the section "The Study of Philosophy." See, e.g., Gramsci, *Selections from the Prison Notebooks*, pp. 5–14 (intellectuals), 210–14 (crisis of hegemony), 229–39 (war of position, etc.), 258–64 (the state and civil society), 323–43 (philosophy and praxis), 375–7 (ideology).

83 Compare McLellan, *Ideology*, p. 31.

84 Herbert Marcuse, *One-Dimensional Man: Studies in the Ideology of Advanced Industrial Society* (Boston: Beacon Press, 1991 [1964]), introduction and chapter 1, which summarize his main arguments. Note also his bizarre and frankly Orwellian notion of "repressive tolerance" in Herbert Marcuse, "Repressive Tolerance," in the volume *A Critique of Pure Tolerance* (Boston: Beacon Press, 1997 [1969]), pp. 81–117, which also contains contributions by Robert Paul Wolff and Barrington Moore Jr. Such sophistic ideas became even more elaborate and pronounced, and arguably even more divorced from reality, in the works of Michel Foucault and many postmodernists.

85 See Karl Mannheim, *Ideology and Utopia: An Introduction to the Sociology of Knowledge*, trans. by Louis Wirth and Edward Shils (New York: Harcourt, Brace, 1953 [1936]), chapters 2–5 (quote from p. 239). Indeed, his arguments carried the implication that most individuals were simply unable to transcend the historical contexts and interests of the social groups they were enmeshed by and socialized within. The only exceptions were members of what Alfred Weber called the "socially unattached intelligentsia" [*freischwebende Intelligenz*], who constituted a "relatively classless stratum" that was not "too firmly situated in the social order." Ibid., pp. 137–8. This is the same sort of spurious, elitist notion that was subsequently embraced wholeheartedly by many postmodern theorists, who fancied that they alone were somehow able to see through and "deconstruct" the mystifying veils of the hegemonic ideologies that purportedly kept lesser mortals in the thrall of the powerful. For an interesting short analysis touching upon these and other issues, see Anthony Arblaster, "Ideology and Intellectuals," in *Knowledge and Belief in Politics: The Problem of Ideology*, ed. by Robert Benewick et al. (London: George Allen & Unwin, 1973), pp. 115–29. Therein he rightly criticizes Mannheim's notion but also argues (p. 126) that intellectuals, whatever their commitments, must maintain both a "degree of detachment *from* ideology" and at least minimal levels of "honesty, accuracy and objectivity."

86 Émile Durkheim, *The Rules of Sociological Method*, ed. by Stephen Lukes (New York: Free Press, 1982 [1895]), p. 86. Alas, the "ideological methods" he justly castigated, when defined in this limited way, have arguably become the norm nowadays in both the "social sciences" and some humanities. The sustained attacks on the Enlightenment intellectual tradition, including its promotion of rationalism, positivism, and the notion of objectivity – from all sides of the political spectrum – have predictably resulted in the

widespread abandonment of serious scholarly standards, the conscious or unwitting neglect of open-ended factual research in the interests of promoting pre-selected and often faddish theoretical paradigms or narrow methodological preferences, and the increasingly blatant promotion of favored social and political agendas in academic publications. It is one thing to argue that no individual can be completely objective or disinterested, which is correct, but quite another to throw out the baby with the bathwater by advocating the abandonment of efforts to be as objective as humanly possible and/or enthusiastically embracing an unabashed activist posture oneself. Compare Eatwell and Wright, *Contemporary Political Ideologies*, p. vii. For diverse critics of the Enlightenment, compare Graeme Garrard, *Counter-Enlightenments: From the Eighteenth Century to the Present* (New York: Routledge, 2005); Zeev Sternhell, *The Anti-Enlightenment Tradition*, trans. by David Maisel (New Haven: Yale University, 2009); and – an excellent short survey and critique of left, right, and centrist anti-Enlightenment arguments – Dennis C. Rasmussen, "Contemporary Political Theory as an Anti-Enlightenment Project," undated, available at www.brown.edu/Research/ppw/files/Rasmussen_PPW.pdf. For an impassioned but erudite defense of the Enlightenment against its many critics, see Jonathan Israel, *A Revolution of the Mind: Radical Enlightenment and the Intellectual Origins of Modern Democracy* (Princeton: Princeton University, 2009); for a long overdue critique of certain negative, distorted postmodern views of the Enlightenment, see Daniel Gordon, ed., *Postmodernism and the Enlightenment: New Perspectives in Eighteenth-Century French Intellectual History* (New York: Routledge, 2000).

87 Abram Kardiner et al., *The Pscyhological Frontiers of Society* (New York: Columbia University, 1945), p. 34. In the context of psychology and psychiatry, the term "rationalization" has a somewhat more specific meaning than in normal discourse, where it signifies a post-facto attempt to explain and justify one's actions, with the implication that the explanation being proffered serves to conceal one's true motives or otherwise excuse those actions. According to the second edition (1968) of the *Diagnostic and Statistical Manual of Mental Disorders* (*DSM-II*), a handbook of mental disorders published in successive editions by the American Psychiatric Association, rationalization occurs "when the individual deals with emotional conflict or internal or external stressors by concealing the true motivations for his or her own thoughts, actions, or feelings through the elaboration of reassuring or self serving but incorrect explanations." For Sigmund Freud, such rationalizations served to conceal the true causes of obsessional neuroses.

88 David E. Apter, "Introduction: Ideology and Discontent," in *Ideology and Discontent*, ed. by David E. Apter, p. 16. Although it is surely the case that individuals sometimes cloak their sordid underlying motives behind high-sounding ideological principles, such a reductionist overall interpretation reflects egregious ignorance about the essential nature and function of ideology. In contrast, Apter himself rightly emphasizes (ibid.) that the term ideology "refers to more than doctrine. It links particular actions and mundane practices with a wider set of meanings and, by doing so, leads a more honorable and dignified complexion to social conduct."

89 Lewis S. Feuer, "Beyond Ideology," reprinted in *The End of Ideology Debate*, ed. by Chaim I. Waxman (New York: Clarion, 1969), p. 66.

90 Compare Karl R. Popper, *The Open Society and Its Enemies* (Princeton, NJ: Princeton University, 1971 [1962]), volume 1, especially the Introduction and Chapter 10; and Milton Rokeach, *The Open and the Closed Mind: Investigations into the Nature of Belief Systems and Personality Systems* (New York: Basic Books, 1960). For an analysis of Popper's famous work, see Ian Jarvie and Sandra Pralong, eds., *Popper's Open Society After Fifty Years: The Continuing Relevance of Karl Popper* (New York: Routledge, 2003).

91 Hannah Arendt, *The Origins of Totalitarianism* (New York: Harvest, 1973 [1951]), p. 417. For her, an "ideology is quite literally what its name indicates: it is the logic of an idea." But she then expanded upon this simple notion by associating the term solely with totalitarian ideologies, whose "subject matter is history, to which the 'idea' is applied. Ideologies pretend to know the mysteries of the whole historical process – the secret of the past, the intricacies of the present, the uncertainties of the future – because of the logic inherent in their respective ideas." Ibid., p. 469.

92 Ibid., pp. 470–1.
93 Friedrich and Brzezinski, *Totalitarian Dictatorship and Autocracy*, pp. 88–9.
94 Ibid., pp. 87 (quote), 89. In the quoted passage, the authors are specifically referring to communism, but the same undercurrent of apocalyptic millenarianism is also characteristic of other totalitarian ideologies (and, as will become clearer, of many extremist ideologies).
95 Ibid., pp. 90–4, referring to French political philosopher Georges Sorel's (1847–1922) somewhat idiosyncratic but influential conception of that term.
96 Talcott Parsons, "An Approach to the Sociology of Knowledge," *Transactions of the Fourth World Congress of Sociology, Milan and Stresa, 8–15 September 1959* (London: International Sociological Association, 1959), cited by Geertz, "Ideology as a Cultural System," p. 50.
97 Compare Raymond Aron, *The Opium of the Intellectuals* (London: Secker & Warburg, 1957), in the concluding chapter titled "The End of the Ideological Age?," pp. 305–24; Daniel Bell, *The End of Ideology: On the Exhaustion of Political Ideas in the Fifties* (New York: Free Press, 1962), especially "The End of Ideology in the West: An Epilogue," pp. 393–407.
98 Seymour Martin Lipset, *Political Man: The Social Bases of Politics* (Baltimore: Johns Hopkins University, 1981 [1960]), pp. 442–3. Furthermore, although he recognized that "the democratic class struggle will continue," he argued that it would be "a fight without ideologies, without red flags, without May Day parades." Ibid., p. 445. Fifty years on, it is painfully clear that such confident conclusions were decidedly premature. Nevertheless, some analysts have not been so quick to dismiss the "end of ideology" theorists. For example, Boudon has argued that, although ideologies have surely not disappeared, they have become increasingly less "general" or all-encompassing, and are instead increaasingly "local" or narrowly focused. See his "Local vs General Ideologies: A Normal Ingredient of Modern Political Life," *Journal of Political Ideologies* 4:2 (1999), pp. 141–61. But that is certainly not the case with Islamism, to name only one such "general" ideology. Indeed, a number of other grand political ideologies have also made comebacks in recent years, including anarchism, fascism, and communism, albeit at times in revised forms.
99 Bell, *End of Ideology*, pp. 393, 399–400. Note that in this passage he was describing what he called (following Mannheim) a "*total* ideology," in contradistinction to a "particular ideology." And Bell did acknowledge that the "need for utopia" will not disappear. But henceforth it would allegedly need to built on a foundation of empirical reality, not ideological faith. Ibid., p. 405.
100 Ibid., pp. 402, 404.
101 Aron, *Opium of the Intellectuals*, p. 323.
102 See Francis Fukuyama, *The End of History and the Last Man* (New York: Avon Books, 2006).
103 Perhaps not surprisingly, Oakeshott associated such "traditional" or "philosophical" politics," which were supposedly non-ideological, with his own conservative worldviews. See Oakeshott, "Rationalism in Politics," pp. 5–42. Martin Seliger rightly points out that Oakeshott essentially equated "rationalism," which he characterized in very negative terms, with ideology. See Seliger, *Ideology and Politics*, p. 31. For similar criticisms of ideology, compare David J. Manning, ed., *The Form of Ideology: Investigations into the Sense of Ideological Reasoning with a View to Giving an Account of Its Place in Political Life* (London and Boston: Allen & Unwin, 1980).
104 Minogue, *Alien Powers*, pp. 2, 221. Therein he also opined, sardonically, that "[i]t is a feature of all such doctrines to incorporate a general theory of the mistakes of everyone else" (p. 2), and that "[i]deology is the purest possible expression of European civilization's capacity for self-loathing" (p. 221).
105 Ibid., p. 167.
106 For example, Marx and Engels believed that their own materialistic conceptions of historical change, and their predictions concerning the transition from capitalism to socialism as a result of the growing contradictions of the former, amounted to "scientific

socialism" (in contrast to the unscientific "utopian socialism" espoused by thinkers such as Henri de Saint-Simon, Charles Fourier, and Robert Owen), whereas they used the term "ideology" to refer to false doctrines that served to mask the class interests of the dominant social class in order to justify and facilitate its exploitation of subordinate classes.

107 Note that I have intentionally ignored the input of postmodernists to the academic debates about ideology, mainly because their pretentious arguments are – as per usual – largely incomprehensible and at best only tenuously related to the real world. For an illustrative example, see Slavoj Žižek, *The Sublime Object of Ideology* (London: Verso, 2009), p. 140:

> But the case of so-called "totalitarianism" demonstrates what applies to every ideology, to ideology as such: the last support of the ideological effect (of the way an ideological network of signifiers "holds" us) is the non-sensical, pre-ideological kernel of enjoyment. In ideology "all is not ideology (that is, ideological meaning)," but it is this very surplus which is the last support of ideology.

To which the baffled reader can only respond in one of two ways, either "that is really heavy, maaaan," or "whatever, dude" (which in this case seems far more appropriate). If truth be told, this book reads like it was written by someone who has taken far too much blotter acid. Hence I make no apologies whatsoever for neglecting pomo "discourses" of this ilk.

108 Boudon, *Analysis of Ideology*, chapters 2–4. Compare p. 23, Table 1.
109 Ibid., pp. 22–33, 50–7 (quote on p. 53). Compare p. 52, Table 2.
110 Ibid., p. 54. Compare p. 55, Table 3, and especially p. 57, Table 4.
111 Smelser, *Faces of Terrorism*, p. 88. Why is this necessary? Because

> [i]t is an existential fact of life that everyone is exposed to a vast array of personal experiences, influences from others, orally presented and written materials, the media, and, through all these, an inconsistent if not chaotic view of the world, morality, and oneself.

112 Mostafa Rejai, *Political Ideologies: A Comparative Approach* (Armonk, NY and London: M. E. Sharpe, 1995), p. 4. Some of the discussion herein concerning the functions of political ideologies have been borrowed from Rejai.
113 Ibid.
114 Ibid., p. 7.
115 Ibid., pp. 7–8.
116 Compare Darrin M. McMahon, *Enemies of the Enlightenment: The French Counter-Enlightenment and the Making of Modernity* (New York: Oxford University, 2002); and Christopher Olaf Blum, ed. and trans., *Critics of the Enlightenment: Readings in the French Counter-Revolutionary Tradition* (Wilmington, DE: Intercollegiate Studies Institute, 2003). For selections from several French counterrevolutionary thinkers, see David McClelland, ed., *The French Right from De Maistre to Maurras* (New York: Harper Torchbooks, 1971). Note, however, that if these authors were writing in the aftermath of the Revolution, then they would no longer be defending an existing political system but rather seeking to restore one that had collapsed and been replaced by a new system.
117 Compare Max J. Skidmore, *Ideologies: Politics in Action* (Fort Worth, TX: Harcourt Brace Jovanovich, 1993), p. 8 (quotes); and Roy C. Macridis, *Contemporary Political Ideologies: Movements and Regimes* (New York: HarperCollins, 1992), pp. 16–17.
118 Rejai, *Political Ideologies*, p. 7. However, he also emphasizes (ibid., pp. 6–7) that, although "[i]n any ideology there are elements of emotionality alongside elements of rationality," "the balance between the two . . . varies from ideology to ideology." For his part, Freeden makes a more interesting point in *Ideology: A Very Short Introduction*, p. 120:

> On a more profound level, ideologies are the main form of political thought to accept passion and sentiment as legitimate, indeed ineliminable, forms of political

expression. Ideologies reflect the fact that socio-political conduct is not wholly or merely rational or calculating, but highly, centrally, and often healthily emotional.

Or, one must insist in many cases, *unhealthily* emotional.
119 Smelser, *Faces of Terrorism*, pp. 88–9.
120 Compare Bell, *End of Ideology*, p. 400: "What gives ideology its force is its passion.... One might say, in fact, that the most important, latent, function of ideology is to tap emotion."
121 Aron, *Opium of the Intellectuals*, p. 323, who wrote almost longingly about the supposedly disappearing qualities of ideological extremists:

> We can admire the somber grandeur of these armies of believers. We can admire their devotion, their discipline and self-sacrifice: such warrior virtues are of the kind that lead to victory. But what will remain tomorrow of the motives that led them to fight?

122 Not nearly enough research has been carried out on the intragroup dynamics, socialization processes, and peer pressures to which members of extremist groups are normally subjected. See, e.g., Donatella della Porta, *Social Movements, Political Violence, and the State: A Comparative Analysis of Italy and Germany* (Cambridge, UK and New York: Cambridge University, 1995), chapter 4; and Jerrold M. Post, "The Socio-Cultural Underpinnings of Terrorist Psychology," in *Root Causes of Terrorism*, ed. by Bjørgo, pp. 64–6. For more on the socio-psychological effects of these processes, particularly the relationship between charismatic leaders and their followers, see Jerrold M. Post and Alexander George, *Leaders and Their Followers in a Dangerous World: The Psychology of Political Behavior* (Ithaca: Cornell University, 2004), especially chapter 9. Much more has been written about the psychology of violent extremists than about the socio-psychological dimensions of membership in violent extremist groups. But see, e.g., the excellent study by John Horgan, *The Psychology of Terrorism* (New York: Routledge, 2014), which deals less with the alleged "psychopathology" of individual terrorists, for which there is generally no evidence, and instead develops a "process model" – "becoming" a terrorist, "being" a terrorist, and (sometimes) "disengaging" from terrorism. In his discussion of the "being" phase, he rightly emphasizes the effects on the individual of the social psychological dynamics operating within terrorist groups (especially in chapter 5).
123 For a horrifying illustration of the human impact of this combination of external pressures, ideological fanaticism, and intense intragroup social control processes, see "United Red Army," Kōji Wakamatsu's extraordinary 2007 film on the Rengō Sekigun (United Red Army), an ultra-left Japanese terrorist group. Compare also the analysis of Della Porta, *Social Movements, Political Violence, and the State*, chapter 5.
124 A slightly different formulation is that of Haywood, *Political Ideologies*, p. 12:

> All ideologies . . . (a) offer an account of the existing order, usually in the form of a "world view," (b) advance a model of a desired future, a vision of the "good society," and (c) explain how political change can and should be brought about.

125 Smelser, *Faces of Terrorism*, p. 65.
126 Ibid., p. 65.
127 Ibid., p. 70.
128 Frederick M. Watkins, *The Age of Ideology: Political Thought, 1750 to the Present* (Englewood Cliffs, NJ: Prentice-Hall, 1964), pp. 7–8.
129 Compare Seymour Martin Lipset and Earl Raab, *The Politics of Unreason: Right-Wing Extremism in America, 1790–1977* (Chicago: University of Chicago, 1978), p. 6: "Extremism *is* antipluralism or . . . monism," whose "operational heart" is "the repression of difference and dissent, the closing down of the market place of ideas. . . . the tendency to treat cleavage and ambivalence as *illegitimate*." Here Lipset and Raab essentially equate extremism with monism, whereas I prefer to identify the latter as one of several core characteristics of extremism.

130 Jaroslaw Piekalkiewicz and Alfred Wayne Penn, *Politics of Ideocracy* (Albany, NY: SUNY, 1995), p. 26.
131 Compare Oakeshott, "Rationalism in Politics," pp. 9–10, on the problematic combination of perfectionism and uniformity in "rationalist" (i.e., ideological) politics. However, Oakeshott ascribes negative characteristics to political ideologies in general, whereas I apply them solely to extremist ideologies.
132 For more on utopianism, compare Krishan Kumar, *Utopianism* (Minneapolis: University of Minnesota, 1991); Krishan Kumar, *Utopia and Anti-Utopia in Modern Times* (Oxford: Blackwell, 1987); Frank E. Manual and Fritzie P. Manuel, *Utopian Thought in the Western World* (Cambridge, MA: Belknap Press, 1979); Lyman Tower Sargent, *Utopianism: A Very Short Introduction* (New York: Oxford University, 2010); and Gregory Claeys and Lyman Tower Sargent, eds., *The Utopia Reader* (New York: New York University, 1999). There is a vast literature on diverse examples of utopian thought as well as case studies of utopian movements, past and present, religious and secular.
133 Watkins, *Age of Ideology*, p. 7.
134 Here some readers might object that individualism can also take radically unenlightened or philosophically extreme forms, which is true, and thence conclude that collectivism is not a necessary characteristic of ideological extremism. Perhaps so. However, even the most radical forms of individualism (psychopaths and sociopaths excepted) – e.g., callous selfishness, certain interpretations of Ayn Rand's "Objectivist" philosophies, individualist anarchism of the Max Stirner variety, or extreme "do what thou will" currents of Satanism – only rarely result in the carrying out of serious acts of violence or terrorism, and they have not yet led to the horrific levels of violence that various collectivistic mass movements have repeatedly carried out.
135 Here the reader may again object that this is not the case with anarchists who profess to hate authority and hierarchy. However, it should be pointed out that even the exponents of radically anti-authoritarian ideologies like anarchism, in particular its more collectivist forms, have all too often behaved in ways that are no less intolerant, authoritarian, and at times violent than the authoritarians they claim to hate. This has been true not only in relation to their designated authoritarian enemies, who they frequently tried to murder in the late nineteenth and early twentieth centuries, but also in relation to people who obstinately promoted dissenting or contrary views, especially former "comrades" who had supposedly "betrayed" the cause. The same is true of many of today's "alter-globalization" and "anti-fascist" activists, who despite constantly insisting upon the right of dissent and freedom of speech for themselves – and justifiably so – are typically unwilling to extend those same rights and freedoms to anyone they regard as "capitalist" or "right-wing" enemies, whom they frequently try to shout down, interrupt, intimidate, or even assault in public fora. In short, one can be a fanatically intolerant, self-righteous *anti-authoritarian* ideological extremist, just as one can be a fanatically intolerant, self-righteous authoritarian or totalitarian ideological extremist.
136 Piekalkiewicz and Penn, *Politics of Ideocracy*, p. 25.
137 Arthur Versluis, *The New Inquisitions: Heretic-Hunting and the Intellectual Origins of Modern Totalitarianism* (New York: Oxford University, 2006), pp. 7–8. Herein he specifically refers to both Italian Fascism and communist China and also favorably cites Lithuanian-Polish defector Czeslaw Milosz's (1911–2004) classic anti-Stalinist book *The Captive Mind*, but argues that the origins of this kind of ideocratic thinking in the West can be traced to the institutionalization of the Catholic Church's intolerant, orthodox view of heretics in the late ancient, medieval, and early modern periods.

2

POLITICAL PARANOIA VERSUS POLITICAL REALISM

On distinguishing between bogus conspiracy theories and genuine conspiratorial politics[1]

We live in a credulous age, despite the unprecedented scientific and technological progress of the past half-century. As the new millennium begins, millions apparently continue to believe in the existence and terrestrial intervention of angels and daemons, alien abductions, murderous Satanist undergrounds, sinister cattle mutilations, mind control devices embedded in televisions, the Chupacabra, ritual Jewish baby-killing and blood-drinking, Vatican-sponsored 'crusades' against Islam and elaborate conspiracies of the most fantastic sort. In reaction to the ongoing proliferation of such bizarre and unfounded 'conspiracy theories', which has only increased in the wake of the terrorist attacks of 11 September 2001,[2] more skeptical individuals have unfortunately sometimes moved too far in the other direction, so much so that they often deny the importance – if not the actual existence – of real clandestine and covert political activities.[3] If someone were to claim, for example, that it was necessary to counter 'an alien organization that uses conspiratorial methods', most educated people would probably raise their eyebrows and assume that they were in the presence of a nutty 'conspiracy theorist'. In this instance, however, the phrase can be found in an official definition of counter-espionage provided by the Office of Special Operations (OSO) of the U.S. Central Intelligence Agency (CIA), and was cited in a 1976 article by CIA counter-intelligence specialist William R. Johnson that appeared in the agency's classified inhouse journal, *Studies in Intelligence*.[4] Why should such a straightforward characterization automatically provoke so much skepticism among the intelligentsia?

Very few notions nowadays generate as much intellectual resistance, hostility and derision within academic circles as a belief in the historical importance or efficacy of political conspiracies. Even when this belief is expressed in a very cautious manner, limited to specific and restricted contexts, supported by reliable evidence and hedged about with all sorts of qualifications, apparently it still manages to transcend the boundaries of acceptable discourse and to violate unspoken academic taboos.

The idea that particular groups of people meet together secretly or in private to plan various courses of action, and that some of these plans actually exert a significant influence on particular historical developments, is typically rejected out of hand and assumed to be the figment of a paranoid imagination. The mere mention of the word 'conspiracy' seems to set off an internal alarm bell that causes scholars to close their minds in order to avoid cognitive dissonance and possible unpleasantness, since the popular image of conspiracy both fundamentally challenges the conception most educated, sophisticated people have about how the world operates and reminds them of the horrible persecutions that absurd and unfounded conspiracy theories have precipitated or sustained in the past. So strong is this prejudice among academicians that, even when clear evidence of a plot is inadvertently discovered in the course of their own research, they frequently feel compelled, either out of a sense of embarrassment or a desire to defuse anticipated criticism, to preface their account of it by ostentatiously disclaiming a belief in conspiracies.[5] They then often attempt to downplay the significance of the plotting they have uncovered. To do otherwise, that is, to make a serious effort to incorporate the documented activities of conspiratorial groups into their general political or historical analyses, would force them to stretch their mental horizons beyond customary bounds and, not infrequently, delve even further into certain sordid and politically sensitive topics. Most academic researchers clearly prefer to ignore the implications of conspiratorial politics altogether rather than deal directly with such controversial matters.

A number of complex cultural and historical factors contribute to this reflexive and unwarranted reaction, but it is perhaps most often the direct result of a simple failure to distinguish between 'conspiracy theories' in the strict sense of the term, which are essentially elaborate fables even though they may well be based on kernels of truth, and the activities of actual clandestine and covert political groups, which are a common feature of modern politics. For this and other reasons, serious research into genuine conspiratorial networks has at worst been suppressed, as a rule discouraged, and at best looked on with condescension by the academic community. An entire dimension of political history and contemporary politics has thus been consistently neglected.[6] For decades scholars interested in politics have directed their attention towards explicating and evaluating the merits of various political theories, or analysing the more conventional, formal and overt aspects of practical politics. Even a cursory examination of standard social science bibliographies reveals that tens of thousands of books and articles have been written about staple subjects such as the structure and functioning of government bureaucracies, voting patterns and electoral results, parliamentary procedures and activities, party organizations and factions, the impact of constitutional provisions or laws, and the like. In marked contrast, only a handful of scholarly publications have been devoted to the general theme of political conspiracies – as opposed to popular anti-conspiracy treatises, which are numerous, and specific case studies of events in which conspiratorial groups have played some role – and virtually all of these concern themselves with the deleterious social impact of the 'paranoid style' of thought manifested in classic conspiracy theories rather than the characteristic features of real conspiratorial politics.[7] Only the academic literature dealing with specialized topics like espionage, covert action, political corruption, organized crime, terrorism and revolutionary warfare touches on clandestine and covert political activities on a more or less regular basis, probably because such activities cannot be avoided when dealing with these topics. But the analyses and information contained therein are rarely incorporated into standard works of history and social science, and much of that specialized literature is itself unsatisfactory.[8] Hence there is an obvious need to place the study of conspiratorial politics on a sound theoretical, methodological and empirical footing, since ignoring the influence of such politics can lead to severe errors of historical interpretation.

This situation can only be remedied when a clear-cut analytical distinction has been made between classic conspiracy theories and the more limited conspiratorial activities that are a regular feature of politics. 'Conspiracy theories' share a number of distinguishing characteristics, but in all of them the essential element is a belief in the existence of a 'vast, insidious, preternaturally effective international conspiratorial network designed to perpetrate acts of the most fiendish character', acts that aim to 'undermine and destroy a way of life'.[9] Although this type of apocalyptic conception is nowadays generally peddled by political extremists, religious millenarians, technophobes and UFO buffs and is therefore regarded by respectable, 'right-thinking' people as the fantastic product of a paranoid mindset, in the past it was often accepted as an accurate description of reality by large numbers of people from all social strata, including intellectuals and heads of state.[10] The fact that a belief in sinister, all-powerful conspiratorial forces has not typically been restricted to small groups of clinical paranoids and mental defectives suggests that it fulfils certain important social functions and psychological needs.[11] First of all, like many other intellectual constructs, conspiracy theories help to make complex patterns of cause and effect in human affairs more comprehensible by means of reductionism and oversimplification. Second, they purport to identify the underlying source of misery and injustice in the world, thereby accounting for current crises and upheavals and explaining why bad things are happening to good people or vice versa. Third, by personifying that source they paradoxically help people to reaffirm their own potential ability to control the course of future historical developments. After all, if evil conspirators are consciously causing undesirable changes, the implication is that others, perhaps through the adoption of similar techniques, may also consciously intervene to protect a threatened way of life or otherwise alter the historical process in positive ways. In short, a belief in conspiracy theories helps people to make sense out of a confusing, inhospitable reality, rationalize their present difficulties and partially assuage their feelings of powerlessness. In this sense, it is no different than any number of religious, social or political beliefs, and is deserving of the same serious study.

The image of conspiracies promoted by conspiracy theorists needs to be further illuminated before it can be contrasted with genuine conspiratorial politics. In the first place, conspiracy theorists consider the alleged conspirators to be Evil Incarnate. They are not simply people with differing values or run-of-the-mill political opponents, but inhuman, superhuman and/or anti-human beings who regularly commit abominable acts and are implacably attempting to subvert and destroy everything that is decent and worth preserving in the existing world. Thus, according to John Robison, the Bavarian Illuminati were formed 'for the express purpose of ROOTING OUT ALL THE RELIGIOUS ESTABLISHMENTS, AND OVERTURNING ALL THE EXISTING GOVERNMENTS IN EUROPE'.[12] This grandiose claim is fairly representative, in the sense that most conspiracy theorists view the world in similarly Manichaean and apocalyptic terms.

Second, conspiracy theorists perceive the conspiratorial group as both monolithic and unerring in the pursuit of its goals. This group is directed from a single conspiratorial centre, acting as a sort of general staff, which plans and coordinates all of its activities down to the last detail. Note, for example, Prince Clemens von Metternich's claim that a 'directing committee' of radicals from all over Europe had been established in Paris to pursue insidious plotting against established governments.[13] Given that presumption, it is no accident that many conspiracy theorists refer to 'the Conspiracy' rather than (lower-case) conspiracies or conspiratorial factions, since they perceive no internal divisions among the conspirators. Rather, as a group, the conspirators are believed to possess an extraordinary degree of internal solidarity, which produces a corresponding degree of counter solidarity *vis-à-vis* society at large. Indeed, it is this very cohesion and singleness of purpose that enables them to execute effectively their plans to destroy existing institutions, seize power and eliminate all opposition.

Third, conspiracy theorists believe that the conspiratorial group is omnipresent, at least within its own sphere of operations. While some conspiracy theories postulate a relatively localized group of conspirators, most depict this group as both international in its spatial dimensions and continuous in its temporal dimensions: 'the conspirators planned and carried out evil in the past, they are successfully active in the present, and they will triumph in the future if they are not disturbed in their plans by those with information about their sinister designs'.[14] The conspiratorial group is therefore capable of operating virtually everywhere. As a consequence of this ubiquity, anything that occurs that has a broadly negative impact or seems in any way related to the purported aims of the conspirators can be plausibly attributed to them.

Fourth, the conspiratorial group is viewed by conspiracy theorists as virtually omnipotent. In the past this group has successfully overthrown empires and nations, corrupted whole societies and destroyed entire civilizations and cultures, and it is said to be in the process of accomplishing the same thing at this very moment. Its members are secretly working in every nook and cranny of society, and are making use of every subversive technique known to mankind to achieve their nefarious purposes. Nothing appears to be able to stand in their way – *unless* the warnings of the conspiracy theorists are heeded and acted upon at once. Even then there is no guarantee of ultimate victory against such powerful forces, but a failure to recognize the danger and take immediate countervailing action assures the success of those forces in the near future.

Finally, for conspiracy theorists, conspiracies are not simply a regular feature of politics whose importance varies in different historical contexts, but rather the motive force of all historical change and development. The conspiratorial group can and does continually alter the course of history, invariably in negative and destructive ways, through conscious planning and direct intervention. Its members are not buffeted about by structural forces beyond their control and understanding, like everyone else, but are themselves capable of controlling events more or less at will. This supposed ability is usually attributed to some combination of daemonic influence or sponsorship, the possession of arcane knowledge, the mastery of sinister techniques and/or the creation of a preternaturally effective clandestine organization. As a result, unpleasant occurrences that are perceived by others to be the products of coincidence or chance are viewed by conspiracy theorists as further evidence of the secret workings of the conspiratorial group. For them, nothing that happens occurs by accident. Everything is the result of secret plotting in accordance with some sinister design.

This central characteristic of conspiracy theories has been aptly summed up by Donna Kossy in a popular book on fringe ideas:

> Conspiracy theories are like black holes – they suck in everything that comes their way, regardless of content or origin . . . Everything you've ever known or experienced, no matter how 'meaningless,' once it contacts the conspiratorial universe, is enveloped by and cloaked in sinister significance. Once inside, the vortex gains in size and strength, sucking in everything you touch.[15]

As an example of this sort of mechanism, one has only to mention the so-called 'umbrella man', a man who opened up an umbrella on a sunny day in Dealey Plaza just as President John F. Kennedy's motorcade was passing. A number of 'conspiracy theorists' have assumed that this man was signalling to the assassins, thus tying a seemingly trivial and inconsequential act into the alleged plot to kill Kennedy.[16] It is precisely this totalistic, all-encompassing quality that distinguishes 'conspiracy theories' from the secret but often mundane political planning that is carried out on a daily basis by all sorts of groups, both within and outside of government.

Thus real conspiratorial politics, although by definition hidden or disguised and often deleterious in their impact, simply do not correspond to the bleak, simplistic image propounded by conspiracy theorists. Far from embodying metaphysical evil, it is perfectly and recognizably human, with all the positive and negative characteristics and potentialities that this implies. At the most basic level, all the efforts of individuals to plan in private and initiate secret actions for their own perceived mutual benefit – insofar as these are intentionally withheld from outsiders and require the maintenance of secrecy for their success – are conspiracies.[17] The Latin word *conspirare* literally means 'to breathe together', and need not suggest anything more sinister than people getting together to hold a private meeting. Thus, every time officers of a company participate in a board meeting to plan a marketing strategy they are 'conspiring', and in this sense there are thousands of conspiracies occurring every single day.

Moreover, in contrast to the claims of conspiracy theorists, conspiratorial politics are anything but monolithic. At any given point in time, there are dozens if not hundreds of competitive political and economic groups engaging in secret planning and activities, and most are doing so in an effort to gain some advantage over their rivals. Such behind-the-scene operations are present on every level, from the mundane efforts of small-scale retailers to gain competitive advantage by being the first to develop new product lines to the crucially important attempts by rival secret services to penetrate and manipulate each other. Sometimes the patterns of these covert rivalries and struggles are relatively stable over time, whereas at other times they appear fluid and kaleidoscopic, as different groups secretly shift alliances and change tactics in accordance with their perceived interests. Even internally, within particular groups operating secretly, there are typically bitter disagreements between various factions over the specific courses of action to be adopted. Total uniformity of opinion and complete intragroup solidarity cannot be maintained perpetually in any human social organization, though the carrying out of ruthless periodic purges may temporarily contribute to that impression.

Furthermore, the operational sphere of particular conspiratorial groups is invariably restricted in time and space, though the precise extent of those temporal and spatial boundaries can vary quite widely. There is probably not a single secret organization anywhere that has existed continuously from antiquity to the present, and only a small number could have had a continuous existence for more than a century. And, with the possible exception of those that have been created and sponsored by the governments of major nations and the world's most powerful business and religious institutions, the range of activity of specific conspiratorial groups is invariably limited to particular geographic or sectoral arenas.

Given these great disparities and divergences in range and power, it is obvious that actual conspiracies operate at varying levels of effectiveness. Although they are a typical facet of social and political life, in the overall scheme of things most conspiracies are narrow in scope, restricted in their effects and of limited historical significance. But this is not always the case. It should be obvious that, whenever powerful political figures engage in secret planning, the impact of their decisions on others will be correspondingly greater and more difficult to counteract. Therefore, when such influential figures meet to hatch and coordinate plots, these plots may well have a disproportionate impact on the course of events, and hence a broader historical significance. There is nothing mysterious about this, however. It is simply a covert reflection of existing and sometimes readily visible power relations, and should be recognized as such.

Perhaps the easiest and quickest way to clarify the distinction between 'conspiracy theories' and genuine conspiracies is by reference to the notorious antisemitic tract, the *Protocols of the Elders of Zion*. This document, which purported to record the secret meetings of a conspiratorial Jewish leadership group whose aim was to take control over the world, has played a major role in stirring up fears of a Jewish conspiracy and catalysing repressive actions against Jewish communities throughout Europe and beyond since its appearance in the late nineteenth century. Even today, it continues to be cited by conspiracy mongers and antisemites of all stripes as proof that there is a secret Jewish cabal that is carefully planning and directing worldwide efforts to subvert and destroy all that is good or decent in the world. As such, it provides a perfect example of classic conspiracy theory literature, one that further exacerbated the 'paranoid style' of thinking already characteristic of many of its readers. Of course, as Norman Cohn and others have conclusively demonstrated, the text of the *Protocols* is not really what it purports to be. Yet, even though it is not ascribable to a hidden group of Jewish plotters, it is nonetheless the product of real conspiratorial politics, since it was forged by persons affiliated with the Tsarist secret police, the Okhrana. In short, it was produced at the behest of a genuine clandestine agency in order to fan antisemitism and otherwise exploit and manipulate popular fears.[18]

It is clear, then, that there are fundamental differences between 'conspiracy theories' and actual covert and clandestine politics, differences that must be taken into account if one wishes to avoid serious errors of historical interpretation. The problem is that most people, amateurs and professionals alike, consistently fail to distinguish between them. On the one hand, the overwhelming majority of the self-appointed 'experts' who concern themselves with alleged conspiracies *are* in fact 'conspiracy theorists' in the negative sense outlined earlier. They seriously and passionately believe in the existence of vast, preternaturally effective conspiracies that successfully manipulate and control historical events behind the scenes, though they typically disagree vehemently with one another about exactly who is behind those conspiracies. This vocal lunatic fringe tends to discourage serious researchers from even investigating such matters, in part because the latter do not wish, understandably, to be tarred by the same soiled brush. In the process, however, most have unfortunately failed to heed the important qualification that Richard Hofstadter made in his analysis of the 'paranoid style' of political thinking, namely, that real conspiracies do exist, even though they do not conform to the elaborate and often bizarre scenarios concocted by conspiracy theorists.[19] How, indeed, could it be otherwise in a world full of intelligence agencies, national security bureaucracies, clandestine revolutionary organizations, economic pressure groups, criminal cartels, secret societies with hidden agendas, deceptive religious cults, political front groups and the like?

There has never been, to be sure, a single, monolithic Communist Conspiracy of the sort postulated by the American John Birch Society in the 1950s and 1960s. Nor has there ever been an all-encompassing International Capitalist Conspiracy, a Jewish World Conspiracy, a Masonic Conspiracy or a Universal Vatican Conspiracy. And nowadays, contrary to the apparent belief of millions, neither a vast Underground Satanist Conspiracy nor an Alien Abduction Conspiracy exists. This reassuring knowledge should not, however, prompt anyone to throw out the baby with the bathwater, as many academicians have been wont to do. For just as surely as none of the aforementioned Grand Conspiracies has ever existed, diverse groups of communists, capitalists, Zionists, Freemasons and Catholics have in fact secretly plotted, often against one another, to accomplish various specific but limited political objectives. No sensible person would claim, for example, that the Soviet secret police was not involved in a vast array of covert operations throughout the decades-long existence of the Soviet Union, or that international front groups controlled by the Russian Communist Party did not systematically engage in worldwide penetration operations and propaganda campaigns. It is nonetheless true that scholars have often hastened to deny the existence of genuine conspiratorial plots, without making any effort whatsoever to investigate them, simply because such schemes fall outside their own realm of knowledge and experience or – even worse – directly challenge their sometimes naïve conceptions about how the world functions.

If certain parties were to say, for example, that a secret Masonic lodge in Italy had infiltrated all of the state's security agencies and was involved in promoting or at least exploiting acts of neo-fascist terrorism in order to help condition the political system and strengthen its own influence in the corridors of government, most readers would probably assume that that they were joking or accuse them of having taken leave of their senses. Twenty-five years ago this author might have had the very same reaction. Nevertheless, although the preceding statement greatly oversimplifies a far more complex pattern of interaction between the public and private spheres, not to mention between visible political institutions ('the overground' or 'the Establishment') and covert political groups ('the underground'), such a lodge did in fact exist. It was known as Loggia Massonica Propaganda Due (P2), was affiliated with the Grand Orient branch of Italian Freemasonry, and was headed by a former Fascist militiaman named Licio Gelli.[20] In all probability smaller entities similar to P2 still exist today in an altered form, albeit not always promoting an authoritarian or rightist political agenda, even though that particular 'covered' lodge in Italy was officially outlawed in 1982. Likewise, if someone were to claim that an Afrikaner secret society founded in the early decades of this century had played a key role in promoting the system of apartheid in South Africa, and in the process helped to ensure the preservation of ultraconservative Afrikaner cultural values and Afrikaner political dominance until the early 1990s, some readers would undoubtedly believe that that person was exaggerating. Yet this organization also existed. It was known as the Afrikaner Broederbond (AB), and it formed a powerful 'state within a state' in that country by virtue, among other things, of its exercise of covert influence over elements of the security services.[21] There is no doubt that specialists in late twentieth-century Italian politics who fail to take account of the activities of P2, like experts on South Africa during the period of Afrikaner domination who ignore the AB, are missing an important dimension of political life in those countries at particular historical junctures. Nevertheless, neither of these two important organizations has been thoroughly investigated by academicians. In these instances, as is so often the case, investigative journalists have done most of the truly groundbreaking preliminary research.

The preceding remarks should not be misconstrued. They are in no way meant to suggest that conspiratorial groups are the propulsive force of most historical change or that they alone are capable of controlling our destiny, as legions of 'conspiracy theorists' would have us believe. For one thing, no group of individuals has that capability, no matter how powerful they are. Fortunately for the rest of us, even powerful human beings are inherently flawed creatures who regularly commit errors of judgement and other sorts of blunders. They have not only to cope with the formidable problem of unforeseen and unintended consequences, but also to contend with other powerful groups that are likewise vying for influence, broader social forces that are difficult if not impossible to control and deep-rooted structural and cultural constraints that place limits on how much they are able to accomplish. Moreover, to attribute that degree of power and influence to secret conspirators would be to commit what David Hackett Fischer has dubbed the 'furtive fallacy', that is, to embrace the idea that everything that is truly significant happens behind the scenes. On the other hand, Fischer may go too far in the other direction by inadvertently implying that only that which is above board is worth considering and that nothing that happens in the shadows has real significance.[22] To accept those unstated propositions uncritically could induce a person, among other things, to overlook the bitter nineteenth-century struggle between political secret societies (or, at least, between revolutionaries using non-political secret societies as a 'cover') and the political police of powerful states like Austria and Russia, to minimize the role played by revolutionary vanguard parties in the Russian, Nazi and Communist Chinese revolutions, or to deny that powerful intelligence services like the CIA and the Komitet Gosudarstvennoi Bezopasnosti (KGB) fomented coups and otherwise intervened extensively in the internal affairs of other sovereign states during the Cold War. In short, it might well lead to the misinterpretation or falsification of history on a grand scale.

It is easier to recognize such dangers when relatively well-known historical developments like these are used as illustrative examples, but problems often arise when the possible role played by conspiratorial groups in more obscure events is brought up. It is above all in these cases, as well as in high-profile cases where a comforting 'official' version of events has been widely diffused, that commonplace academic prejudices against taking conspiratorial politics seriously come into play and can exert a potentially detrimental effect on historical judgements. There is probably no way to prevent this sort of unconscious reaction in the current intellectual climate, but the least that can be expected of serious scholars is that they carefully examine the available evidence before dismissing these matters out of hand. Just because a host of bizarre, all-encompassing conspiracy theories continue to be peddled by political and religious extremists, ranging from the far right across the entire political spectrum to the far left, does not mean that academicians can afford to blithely ignore or systematically minimize the importance of certain 'really existing' covert and clandestine operations.

Researchers do, of course, face certain peculiarly difficult methodological problems when they attempt to study such operations, which by definition are meant to be concealed from public scrutiny. Most of these problems derive from a lack of adequate documentation and/or the profusion of biased, sensationalistic sources of uncertain or obviously contaminated provenance. Yet these problems are not necessarily insurmountable. For one thing, a fortuitous combination of human blunders, factional infighting that generates information leaks and the onset of unanticipated historical events – for example, the leftist military coup in Portugal in 1974 that led to the discovery of the archives of the Portuguese secret police, the revolution in Iran that led to the seizure of documents at the American embassy in Tehran, and the collapse of Communism in Russia and Eastern Europe that resulted in the opening of various Soviet-era archives[23] – sometimes leads to the unearthing of previously unknown or untapped source materials that belatedly permit outsiders to examine illustrative cases of such activities. For another, the rigorous techniques of primary and secondary source criticism that have long been employed with success by serious historians are in fact very well suited for analysing the sort of fragmentary bits of information that periodically surface in connection with actual cases of conspiratorial politics.

Notes

1 Reprinted with permission from: Jeffrey M. Bale, "Political Paranoia v. Political Realism: On Distinguishing between Bogus Conspiracy Theories and Genuine Conspiratorial Politics," *Patterns of Prejudice* 41:1 (2007), 45–60, www.tandfonline.com/10.1080/00313220601118751.

2 For representative examples from what has become a veritable cottage industry of recent books suggesting that someone other than al-Qāʻida was behind the 9/11 attacks – most often the Bush administration itself and Israeli intelligence – or at least that Usāma b. Lādin's network was aided and abetted by more powerful and sinister forces operating behind the scenes, see: Thierry Meyssan, *L'effroyable imposture: 11 September 2001* (Chatou: Carnot, 2002); Thierry Meyssan, *Le Pentagate* (Chatou: Carnot, 2003); Eric Hufschmid, *Painful Questions: An Analysis of the September 11th Attack* (Laporte, CO: Ink and Scribe, 2002); Jim Marrs, *Inside Job: The Shocking Case for a 9/11 Conspiracy* (San Rafael, CA: Origin, 2005); David Icke, *Alice in Wonderland and the World Trade Center Disaster: Why the Official Story of 9/11 Is a Monumental Lie* (Wildwood, MO: Bridge of Love, 2002); Arnold Schölzel, ed., *Das Schweigekartell: Fragen und Widersprüche zum 11. September* (Berlin: Homilius, 2002); Andreas von Bülow, *Die CIA und der 11. September* (Munich: Piper, 2004); Maurizio Blondet, *11 settembre: colpo di stato in USA* (Milan: Effedieffe, 2002); Maurizio Blondet, *Osama bin Mossad* (Milan: Effedieffe, 2003); Bruno Cardeñosa, *11-S, historia de una infamia: las mentiras de la 'versión oficial'* (Madrid: Corona Borealis, 2003); and Robin de Ruiter, *11 settembre: il Reichstag di Bush* (Frankfurt: Zambon, 2003). Recently, books have even appeared blaming the 11 March 2004 train bombings in Madrid on American machinations rather than on the jihadist cell that actually carried them out, even though the attack served to precipitate changes in Spanish government policy that were clearly unwelcome to the current U.S. administration. See, for example, Bruno Cardeñosa, *11-M: claves de una conspiración* (Madrid: Espejo de Tinta, 2004). What is surprising about all this is not that individual conspiracy theorists would rush forward to promote such nonsense, but that several of their books have subsequently become bestsellers. In part this is no doubt a reflection of the rampant anti-American and anti-Israeli attitudes that are so characteristic of the present era – concerning the latter, see Tobias Jaecker, *Antisemitische Verschwörungstheorien nach dem 11. September: Neue Varianten eines alten Deutungsmusters* (Munster: Lit, 2005) – but it also indicates that all too many of today's politically motivated readers are incapable of exercising sufficient critical judgement when it comes to assessing sources of information, no matter how controversial or flawed, that serve to reinforce their preexisting biases and delusions. This is not meant to suggest, of course, that serious researchers should refrain from independently investigating and, if necessary,

challenging problematic aspects of the 'official' version, either of the 9/11 operation or other recent terrorist attacks. For a standard, quasi-official account of the events leading up to the former, see *The 9/11 Commission Report: Final Report of the National Commission on Terrorist Attacks upon the United States* (Washington, DC: GPO, 2004).

3 Although the terms 'clandestine' and 'covert' are often used interchangeably, technically they refer to different types of operations. According to former Office of Strategic Services and Central Intelligence Agency officer James McCargar, clandestine operations are 'hidden but not disguised', whereas covert operations are 'disguised but not hidden'. See the very useful discussion in his pseudonymous book: Christopher Felix, *A Short Course in the Secret War* (New York: E. P. Dutton, 1963), pp. 27–9 (later editions of this classic work have recently been published). In this article the term 'conspiratorial politics' will be used to refer to secretive political activities in general, and might therefore encompass both clandestine and covert operations.

4 See William R. Johnson, "Clandestinity and Current Intelligence," reprinted in *Inside CIA's Private World: Declassified Articles from the Agency's Internal Journal, 1955–1992*, ed. H. Bradford Westerfield (New Haven: Yale University Press, 1995), p. 131. Compare also the OSO's definition of counterintelligence (CI), which indicates that CI techniques 'all have as their objective the frustration of the *active* efforts of alien conspiratorial organizations to acquire secret or sensitive information belonging to our government' (ibid., pp. 131–2).

5 Compare Robin Ramsay, "Conspiracy, Conspiracy Theories and Conspiracy Research," *Lobster* 19 (1990), p. 25: 'In intellectually respectable company it is necessary to preface any reference to actual political, economic, military or paramilitary conspiracies with the disclaimer that the speaker "doesn't believe in the conspiracy theory of history (or politics)." ' This type of disclaimer itself reveals that such speakers are unable to distinguish between bona fide conspiracy theories and actual conspiratorial politics.

6 Complaints about this general academic neglect have often been made by those few scholars who have done research on key aspects of covert and clandestine politics that are directly relevant to this study. See, for example, Gary Marx, "Thoughts on a Neglected Category of Social Movement Participant: The Agent Provocateur and the Informant," *American Journal of Sociology* 80:2 (September 1974), esp. 402–3. One of the few dissertations dealing directly with this topic, albeit in a somewhat oversimplified and overly polemical fashion, is Frederick A. Hoffman, "Secret Roles and Provocation: Covert Operations in Movements for Social Change," (Ph.D. Dissertation: University of California, Los Angeles, 1979). There are, of course, some excellent academic studies that have likewise given due weight to these matters – for example, Nurit Schleifman, *Undercover Agents in the Russian Revolutionary Movement: The SR Party, 1902–1914* (Basingstoke: Macmillan/ St Anthony's College, 1988); and Jean-Paul Brunet, *La Police de l'ombre: indicateurs et provocateurs dans la France contemporaine* (Paris: Seuil, 1990) – but they are unfortunately still few and far between.

7 Some standard historically oriented academic treatments of conspiracy theories are Richard Hofstadter, "The Paranoid Style in American Politics," in *The Paranoid Style in American Politics and Other Essays*, ed. by Richard Hofstadter (New York: Knopf, 1966), pp. 3–40; Norman Cohn, *Warrant for Genocide: The Myth of the Jewish World-Conspiracy and the Protocols of the Elders of Zion* (Chico, CA: Scholars, 1981 [1969]); Olivier Dard, *La Synarchie: le mythe du complot permanent* (Paris: Perrin, 1998); David Brion Davis, ed., *The Fear of Conspiracy: Images of Un-American Subversion from the Revolution to the Present* (Ithaca, NY: Cornell University Press, 1971); J. M. Roberts, *The Mythology of the Secret Societies* (London: Secker & Warburg, 1972); Johannes Rogalla von Bieberstein, *Die These von der Verschwörung, 1776–1945: Philosophen, Freimaurer, Juden, Liberale und Sozialisten als Verschwörer gegen die Sozialordnung* (Frankfurt on Main: Peter Lang, 1976); Carl F. Graumann and Serge Moscovici, eds., *Changing Conceptions of Conspiracy* (New York: Springer, 1987); Gerd-Klaus Kaltenbrunner, ed., *Geheimgesellschaften und der Mythos der Weltverschwörung* (Munich: Herder, 1987); Daniel Pipes, *The Hidden Hand: Middle East Fears of*

Conspiracy (New York: St. Martin's, 1995); Daniel Pipes, *Conspiracy: How the Paranoid Style Flourishes and Where It Comes From* (New York: Free Press, 1997); Eduard Gugenberger et al., *Weltverschwörungstheorien: die neue Gefahr von rechts* (Vienna: Deuticke, 1998); Ute Caumanns and Mathias Niendorf, *Verschwörungstheorien: Anthropologische Konstanten, historische Varianten* (Osnabrück: Fibre, 2001); Helmut Reinalter, ed., *Verschwörungstheorien: Theorie – Geschichte – Wirkung* (Innsbruck: Studien, 2002); and Michael Barkun, *A Culture of Conspiracy: Apocalyptic Visions in Contemporary America* (Berkeley: University of California Press, 2003). Compare the currently fashionable 'cultural studies' analyses by Mark Fenster, *Conspiracy Theories: Secrecy and Power in American Culture* (Minneapolis: University of Minnesota Press, 1999); Peter Knight, *Conspiracy Culture: American Paranoia from Kennedy to the X-Files* (New York: Routledge, 2001); Peter Knight, ed., *Conspiracy Nation: The Politics of Paranoia in Postwar America* (New York: New York University Press, 2002); and Jodi Dean, *Aliens in America: Conspiracy Cultures from Outerspace to Cyberspace* (Ithaca, NY: Cornell University Press, 1998), which shed little or no light on real covert and clandestine operations. Works that straddle the preceding two categories (but are unfortunately much closer to the latter than the former) are George E. Marcus, ed., *Paranoia within Reason: A Casebook on Conspiracy as Explanation* (Chicago: University of Chicago Press, 1999); and Harry G. West and Todd Sanders, eds., *Transparency and Conspiracy: Ethnographies of Suspicion in the New World Order* (Durham, NC: Duke University Press, 2003). Finally, there are journalistic studies: two insightful sober works by George Johnson, *Architects of Fear: Conspiracy Theories and Paranoia in American Politics* (Los Angeles: Tarcher, 1983); and Ron Rosenbaum, *Travels with Dr Death and Other Unusual Investigations* (New York: Penguin, 1991); as well as works by Jonathan Vankin, *Conspiracies, Cover-Ups, and Crimes: Political Manipulation and Mind Control in America* (New York: Paragon House, 1992); Jonathan Vankin and John Whalen, *The 80 Greatest Conspiracies of All Time: History's Biggest Mysteries, Coverups, and Cabals* (New York: Citadel, 2004); Al Hidell and Joan d'Arc, eds., *The New Conspiracy Reader: From Planet X to the War on Terrorism: What You Really Don't Know* (New York: Citadel, 2004) ('Al Hidell' was, not coincidentally, one of the aliases allegedly used by Lee Harvey Oswald); and Jon Ronson, *Them: Adventures with Extremists* (New York: Simon & Schuster, 2003), which are more popular in their orientation, sensationalistic and/or condescending toward their subjects.

8 One of the few historical overviews of revolutionary ideas and movements in modern Europe that has devoted sufficient attention to the important role played by secret societies, above all as a model for clandestine revolutionary organizations, is James H. Billington, *Fire in the Minds of Men: Origins of the Revolutionary Faith* (New York: Basic Books, 1980), esp. pp. 86–123.

9 See Hofstadter, "The Paranoid Style," pp. 14, 29.

10 Although conspiracy theories have been widely accepted in the most disparate eras and parts of the world, and thus probably have a certain universality as explanatory models, at certain points in time they have taken on an added salience due to particular historical circumstances. Their development and diffusion seems to be broadly correlated with the level of social, economic and political upheaval or change, although indigenous cultural values and intellectual traditions determine their specific form and condition their level of popularity.

11 As many scholars have pointed out, if such ideas were restricted to clinical paranoids, they would have little or no historical importance. What makes the conspiratorial or paranoid style of thought interesting and historically significant is that it frequently tempts more or less normal people and has often been diffused among broad sections of the population in certain periods. Conspiracy theories are important as collective delusions, delusions that nevertheless reflect real fears and real social problems, rather than as evidence of individual pathology. See, for example, Hofstadter, "The Paranoid Style," pp. 3–4.

12 See his *Proofs of a Conspiracy against All the Religions and Governments of Europe, Carried On in the Secret Meetings of Free Masons, Illuminati, and Reading Societies, Collected from Good Authorities* (New York: G. Forman, 1798), p. 14. This extract exhibits yet another

characteristic of 'conspiracy theorists': the tendency to over-dramatize by using capital letters with reckless abandon.
13 See his "Geheime Denkschrift über die Grundung eines Central-Comites der nordischen Mächte in Wien," in *Aus Metternichs nachgelassenen Papieren*, ed. by Richard Metternich-Winneburg (Vienna: W. Braumüller, 1881), volume 1, p. 595, quoted in Rogalla von Bieberstein, *Die These von der Verschwörung*, pp. 139–40.
14 Dieter Groh, "Temptation of Conspiracy Theory, Part I," in *Changing Conceptions of Conspiracy*, ed. by Graumann and Moscovici, p. 3. A classic example of conspiratorial works that view modern revolutionary movements as little more than the latest manifestations of subversive forces with a very long historical pedigree is the influential book by Nesta H. Webster, *Secret Societies and Subversive Movements* (London: Boswell, 1924). For more on Webster's background, see the biographical study by Richard M. Gilman, *Behind World Revolution: The Strange Career of Nesta H. Webster* (Ann Arbor, MI: Insight, 1982), of which only one volume has so far appeared; and Markku Ruotsila, "Mrs Webster's Religion: Conspiracist Extremism on the Christian Far Right," *Patterns of Prejudice* 38:2 (June 2004), p. 109–26.
15 Donna Kossy, *Kooks: A Guide to the Outer Limits of Human Belief* (Portland, OR: Feral House, 1994), p. 191.
16 It should, however, be pointed out that even if the 'umbrella man' was wholly innocent of any involvement in a plot, as he almost certainly was, this does not necessarily mean that the Warren Commission's comforting official reconstruction of the Kennedy assassination is accurate. As always, the fact that certain parties continue to promote unfounded and absurd conspiratorial scenarios should not lead serious researchers to neglect problematic issues that have been ignored or glossed over in official accounts.
17 Compare Hofstadter, "The Paranoid Style," 19: 'All political behavior requires strategy, many strategic acts depend for their effect upon a period of secrecy, and anything that is secret may be described, often with little exaggeration, as conspiratorial'.
18 For an English translation of the actual text, see *Protocols of the Meetings of the Learned Elders of Zion*, trans. from the Russian by Victor E. Marsden (London: Britons Publishing Society, 1933). For exposés and scholarly analyses, compare Binjamin W. Segal, *A Lie and a Libel: The History of the Protocols of the Elders of Zion* (Lincoln: University of Nebraska Press, 1995), which was originally published in Germany in 1926; Cohn, *Warrant for Genocide*; Pierre-André Taguieff, *Les Protocoles des sages de Sion: faux et usages d'un faux* (Paris: Berg Interantional/Fayard, 2004); Pierre-André Taguieff, *Les Protocoles des sages de Sion, 2: études et documents* (Paris: Berg International, 1992); and Stephen Eric Bronner, *A Rumor about the Jews: Antisemitism, Conspiracy, and the Protocols of Zion* (Oxford: Oxford University, 2003).
19 Hofstadter, "The Paranoid Style," 19: 'there *are* conspiratorial acts in history, and there is nothing paranoid about taking note of them' (emphasis in the original).
20 For more on P2, see, above all, the materials published by the Italian parliamentary commission investigating the organization, which are divided into the majority (Anselmi) report, five dissenting minority reports and over one hundred thick volumes full of documents or verbatim testimony before the commission. See Parlamento, IX Legislatura, *Commissione d'inchiesta sulla loggia massonica P2* (Rome: Camera dei Deputati, 1984–7). Compare also Martín Berger, *Historia de la lógia masonica P2* (Buenos Aires: El Cid, 1983); Andrea Barbieri et al., *L'Italia della P2* (Milan: Mondadori, 1981); Alberto Cecchi, *Storia della P2* (Rome: Riuniti, 1985); Roberto Fabiani, *I massoni in Italia* (Milan: L'Espresso, 1978); Gianfranco Piazzesi, *Gelli: la carriere di un eroe di questa Italia* (Milan: Garzanti, 1983); Marco Ramat et al., *La resistabile ascesa della P2: poteri occulti e stato democratico* (Bari: De Donato, 1983); Renato Risaliti, *Licio Gelli, a carte scoperte* (Florence: Fernando Brancato, 1991); and Gianni Rossi and Franceso Lombrassa, *In nome della 'loggia': le prove di come la massoneria segreta ha tentato di impadronarsi dello stato italiano. I retroscena della P2* (Rome: Napoleone, 1981). Pro-P2 works include those by Gelli supporter Pier Carpi, *Il caso Gelli: la verità sulla loggia P2* (Bologna: INEI, 1982), and the truly Orwellian work

by Gelli himself, *La verità* (Lugano: Demetra, 1989), which in spite of its title bears little resemblance to the truth.
21 For the AB, see Ivor Wilkins and Hans Strydom, *The Super-Afrikaners: Inside the Afrikaner Broederbond* (Johannesburg: Jonathan Ball, 1978); and J. H. P. Serfontein, *Brotherhood of Power: An Exposé of the Secret Afrikaner Broederbond* (Bloomington and London: Indiana University Press, 1978). Compare also B. M. Schoeman, *Die Broederbond in die Afrikanerpolitiek* (Pretoria: Aktuele, 1982); and Adrien Pelzer, *Die Afrikaner-Broederbond: Eerste 50 jaar* (Cape Town: Tafelberg, 1979). More generally, see T. Dunbar Moodie, *The Rise of Afrikanerdom: Power, Apartheid, and the Afrikaner Civil Religion* (Berkeley: University of California Press, 1975).
22 See David Hackett Fischer, *Historians' Fallacies: Toward a Logic of Historical Thought* (New York: Harper and Row, 1970), pp. 74–8.
23 For the discovery of a wealth of important materials in the Portuguese secret police archives, including documents concerning Aginter Presse, an international right-wing intelligence and paramilitary network involved in terrorist actions that operated under the cover of a seemingly innocuous press agency, see Frédéric Laurent, *L'Orchestre noir* (Paris: Stock, 1978); María José Tíscar Santiago, *A contra-revolução no 25 de abril: Os "Relatórios António Graça" sobre o ELP e Aginter Presse* (Lisbon: Colibri, 2014), pp. 69–149; and Fabrizio Calvi and Frederic Laurent, *Piazza Fontana: la verità su una strage* (Milan: Mondadori, 1997), pp. 60–121. For the corpus of secret documents found at the American embassy in Tehran, many of which were later published by the Iranian revolutionary regime, see the multi-volume series titled *Asnād-i lānah-i jāsūsī-i Amrīkā* (Documents from the U.S. Espionage Den) (Qum: Daftar-i Intishārāt-i Islāmī, 1981 –). For the analysis of various materials found in the newly opened Soviet archives, see the ongoing series of publications produced by the Cold War International History Project (CWIHP) at the Woodrow Wilson International Center for Scholars; see the Wilson Center's website at www.wilsoncenter.org/index.cfm?topic_id=1409&fuseaction=topics.home (viewed 26 October 2006).

3

POSTWAR NEO-FASCIST INTERNATIONALS, PART 1

Nazi escape networks, the Mouvement Social Européenne, Europäische Neu-Ordnung, and Jeune Europe

It is impossible to grasp the political impact or historical significance of the terrorist "strategy of tension" without recognizing the extent to which those who carried it out in Italy and elsewhere were linked in various ways to a number of clandestine international networks. Up until now this transnational dimension has generally been dealt with in a superficial fashion. On the one hand, mainstream commentators have tended to focus more on the indigenous causes and sources of this particular right-wing campaign of terrorism, and in the process have failed to attach sufficient weight to international factors. On the other hand, radical leftist journalists have tended to reduce the overall complexity of the phenomenon by viewing it simply as a sinister local manifestation of the worldwide efforts by the United States to wage the Cold War and extend its sphere of political and economic influence. These two contrasting analytical approaches are not so much incorrect as they are monodimensional and incomplete. While it would be foolish to ignore the powerful national political forces that secretly sponsored or exploited the "strategy of tension" for their own ends, it would be equally simplistic to divorce those forces entirely from the postwar East-West conflict, which exercised a great deal of influence on the course of domestic politics in nations throughout the world. However, the complex relationship between the various international and national forces behind this campaign of violence in Italy cannot be clarified until the international forces are themselves delineated more precisely.

What needs to be recognized is that these overlapping transnational networks were far more diverse than they have hitherto been depicted, and that each operated in accordance with its own particular political agenda. These agendas converged in certain fundamental respects, most notably around a vehement opposition to communism, but in other ways they were incompatible if not antithetical. The networks themselves fell into one of two basic categories. First, there were "internationals" created by neo-fascist and neo-Nazi extremists. These included Nazi escape organizations and "mutual aid" societies set up in the immediate postwar era, international neo-fascist liaison and support groups founded in the early 1950s, and clandestine operational and paramilitary networks established in the 1960s and 1970s. Second, there was a vast array of ostensibly "private" anti-communist organizations that were either created or used instrumentally by the secret services of the United States and other NATO countries, which Scott Lucas has termed a "state-private" network.[1] These included paramilitary stay/behind networks, "countersubversion" training centers, propaganda and psychological warfare agencies, cultural associations, labor unions, policy-oriented "think tanks," investigative firms, secret societies, press agencies, export-import companies or other sorts of financial fronts, and lay religious organizations. Although such diverse organizations clearly had their own specific interests and different spheres of operation, in practice they played distinct but complementary roles in a more or less coordinated overall Western strategy. On this complex subject, historian Aldo Giannuli – who was hired by Italian judicial authorities to examine documentary materials related to cases of neo-fascist terrorism and their links to covert anti-communist networks – has distinguished conceptually between (1) "moderate" Cold War–era anti-communist networks that promoted a "containment" strategy and (2) "radical" anti-communist networks that advocated a "rollback" strategy. Within the latter camp, he also made an important distinction between "white" (i.e., non-fascist, mainly liberal, social democratic, and monarchist) and "black" (i.e., fascist or radical right) elements.[2] However, the reality was that elements from all of these types of networks – transnational neo-fascist groupings, moderate and radical but "white" anti-communist networks, and Atlanticist intelligence fronts – commingled with each other and were frequently interconnected, if not interdependent. As will soon be documented, neo-fascist ultras often collaborated with other hard-line anti-communists, were quietly recruited into various covert secret service-linked networks, and were thence typically employed to carry out particularly unsavory and "plausibly deniable" jobs for their new sponsors and funders. Despite these operational linkages, the diverse elements in the Cold War struggle against communism need to be examined separately. In this chapter, the focus will be primarily on transnational neo-fascist networks, except where these directly intersect with their less radical anti-communist and secret service counterparts.

There are two salient characteristics of postwar fascism that at first glance may seem to be paradoxical. On the one hand, there was an extraordinary proliferation of small neo-fascist groups within every country of western and southern Europe after World War II. At the national level the omnipresence of divisive ideological conflicts, profound disagreements over political tactics, and contentious personal disputes between competing *Führers* made it virtually impossible for these sectarian and often insular groups to coordinate their activities in any meaningful way. The history of neo-fascism is therefore replete with a kaleidoscopic array and bewildering variety of organizations, personalities, and doctrines, many of which were the direct or indirect outgrowths of a complex process of fission and fusion precipitated by bitter internal struggles and rivalries.[3] On the other hand, some of the very same groups that could not manage to find a basis for cooperation with similarly minded organizations inside their own countries made strenuous efforts to "internationalize" and link up with their counterparts in other nations, both throughout Europe and elsewhere in the world.[4] Unfortunately, the significance of these frequent attempts to develop pan-European and international coordination, whether on an organizational, operational, or ideological basis, has not always been properly assessed by observers of the neo-fascist scene.

A certain degree of confusion, for example, is reflected in the following comments by Giuseppe Gaddi, author of a book on neo-fascism in Europe:

> One of the principal elements of differentiation between the old and the new fascism consists of the abandonment, or at least the attenuation, of traditional ultranationalist positions. Most of the current European neo-fascist movements have in fact substituted a "European" conception for the old concept of the nation.[5]

Although Gaddi correctly notes that the majority of post–World War II fascists have nourished a pan-European vision, he is wrong to suggest that this represented the abandonment of radical nationalism, which along with a voluntarist, elitist, and anti-materialistic form of "socialism" constituted one of the two key ideological components of classical fascism. The apparent contradiction is resolved if one recognizes that neo-fascist internationalism represented an *extension* rather than a rejection of nationalism, an attempt to transplant romantic radical nationalism onto the European plane. As neo-fascist theorists have repeatedly emphasized, however, their pan-European "international of nationalism" concept has nothing in common with the "anti-national" Europeanism advocated by social democratic and liberal proponents of a European Community.[6]

The conscious effort by many neo-fascists to repudiate or attenuate parochial forms of "national chauvinism" can be viewed as a perfectly rational response to the unfavorable political conditions in which the fascist diehards operated after 1945. For one thing, the vulnerability and weakness of neo-fascist radicals within their respective national milieus in the immediate postwar period caused them to establish links with like-minded groups abroad and attempt to create new "internationals" in order to augment their meager political influence.[7] For another, "no European, however megalomaniacal, could even dream [that] his nation . . . [was] strong enough to challenge successfully the two giants of the contemporary world," the United States and the Soviet Union. This "inescapable geopolitical fact" led the more perceptive neo-fascists to promote the idea of "a united nationalist Europe, a Nation Europa," which would oppose the imperialist designs of the triumphant and much-hated superpowers.[8] On this level, too, overall political and military weaknesses compelled them to advocate a consolidation of Europe-wide forces.

In addition to these compelling practical reasons for adopting a pan-European perspective, neo-fascists believed – not without justification – that similar notions had been propounded by classical fascist and Nazi ideologues. A representative example is provided by the notorious Norwegian collaborator Vidkun Quisling:

> We are living at a time when the countries of the world are uniting to form world empires. In the struggle for supremacy now being waged the smaller States have no prospect of continuing to live alone. Even Europe, with its impotence and divisions, is in danger of being crushed by the great powers which have grown up on either side. This danger has been averted thanks to the intervention of Germany, and with Germany as its pivot Europe is fast becoming the fifth great power in the world.[9]

Moreover, even before the Nazi seizure of power, certain "conservative revolutionary" theorists in Germany had adopted analogous geopolitical conceptions that placed Germany at the center of a continental European *Ordnungsmacht* which could hold its own against the rising power of the Russian and Anglo-American peripheries.[10] A number of other attempts to transcend nationalism by setting up "anti-Bolshevik" or fascist internationals were also made, such as the Anti-Komintern (Anti-Comintern) and the Ligue Internationale Anticommuniste (International Anti-Communist League). Even Mussolini, who had initially claimed that fascism was not something that could be exported, was later persuaded to sanction the efforts of radical fascist youngbloods to create a multinational "universal fascist" movement.[11]

But it was the Nazi conception of a new European order that really captured the imagination of fascist radicals throughout the continent, both during and after the war. Although Hitler's "new order" was based upon a racial (*völkisch*) rather than a strictly national or genuinely pan-European conception, and both he and SS Reichsführer Heinrich Himmler ultimately envisioned the establishment of an *Abendländische Reich Germanischen Blutes*, that is, a European empire under the absolute hegemony of the Teutonic peoples,[12] many fascist intellectuals from other countries, including even non-Germanic left-wing fascists, managed to persuade themselves that the Nazis were leading a European social revolution that would guarantee a place in the sun to all the faithful, irrespective of their nationalities.[13] Not surprisingly, Hitler and other Nazi leaders shamelessly exploited these romantic pan-European visions for propaganda purposes, to the chagrin of certain circles of chauvinistic ultranationalists and fanatical racists among their followers. Nevertheless, by an ironic twist of fate the Nazis were later compelled by adversity to adopt certain policies consonant with their own manipulative demagogic pronouncements. This will become clearer later, in connection with the development of the Waffen-SS.

The Nation Europa concept thus represented a postwar revival and adaptation of certain ideas that had been promoted, however naïvely or cynically, by various fascist and Nazi leaders during the 1930s and 1940s. It should be pointed out, however, that the European radical right adopted two distinct and in many ways incompatible geopolitical perspectives in the period between the early 1950s and the collapse of communism, one Western-oriented and the other Euro-centered.[14] Some fascists and elements of numerous non-fascist far right currents, including Catholic integralists, monarchists, and certain types of ultranationalists, were politically wedded to the Atlantic Alliance and its major sponsor, the United States. This was because these latter entities, despite their manifest shortcomings, were viewed as the bulwarks of a Western civilization that was locked in a life-or-death struggle against an implacable communist adversary. In contrast to the more or less pro-American orientation of this numerically dominant segment of the extreme right, various revolutionary neo-fascist factions advocated the establishment of a strong, united Nation Europa, which would constitute a "third force" opposed to the twin "imperialisms" of international communism and international finance capitalism, both of which they perceived as being materialistic, exploitative, dehumanizing, and – according to pro-Nazi elements – controlled by parasitic Jews. Variations on this theme appear in most neo-fascist ideological pronouncements, where bitter attacks on Anglo-American capitalism appear as frequently as attacks on communism. With this background, the early attempts to establish fascist-inspired transnational organizations can now be outlined.

Underground Nazi escape and action organizations

The first "internationals" set up by fascists in the postwar era were underground networks designed to provide assistance to wanted Nazi fugitives who were seeking to elude Allied dragnets and escape, either into anonymity in their own homelands or to safe havens elsewhere. Unfortunately, it is extremely difficult to reconstruct the history of these shadowy networks, even in a summary fashion, because a plethora of sensationalistic and rather speculative journalistic works has filled the void left by the current dearth of reliable documentary evidence. The brief overview that follows should therefore be regarded as tentative until such time as the relevant Allied intelligence archives are opened up to public scrutiny, a process that is already underway in the United States.

It appears, however, that many leading Nazi officials began planning for their postwar survival as soon as it became apparent that the Third Reich's days were numbered. A number of exiled anti-Nazi refugees and Allied propagandists began issuing warnings to this effect in popular works that were published as early as 1943.[15] Although it is clear that the authors of these works often exaggerated for political effect, and that certain of their alarming claims owed more to personal paranoia or a feverish imagination than to reliable information, certain evidence subsequently surfaced which suggested that some of their general concerns about Nazi plans for the postwar world were quite justified. Among the documents later unearthed that supposedly provided details of such planning were handwritten minutes allegedly prepared at a 10 August 1944 meeting held at the Hôtel Maison Rouge in Strasbourg.[16] Almost all of the relevant secondary sources have accepted these details more or less at face value, but there are good reasons to be cautious, both on evidentiary and intuitive grounds. There is no guarantee that the minutes are genuine, the firsthand testimony reported in certain secondary sources is suspect, and the information in various intelligence reports remains difficult to substantiate. Beyond this, in the vengeful atmosphere following the 20 July assassination attempt on Hitler, it would have been foolhardy for Nazi hierarchs and businessmen to adopt a "defeatist" attitude by meeting to devise plans for their postwar survival.

According to the available accounts, however, such a top secret meeting was in fact organized. Some sources claim that this was done at the behest of Nationalsozialistische Deutsche Arbeiterpartei (NSDAP: National-Socialist German Workers' Party) Secretary Martin Bormann, and that it was organized personally by the head of the Reichssicherheitshauptamt (RSHA: Reich Central Security Office), Obergruppenführer Ernst Kaltenbrunner, but this has not been verified. What seems certain is that the meeting, presumably unbeknownst to Hitler, brought certain Schutzstaffel (SS: Protection Squadron) officers and government ministry officials together with leading industrialists in order to develop or refine concrete plans for protecting Nazi functionaries and German economic assets following the now inevitable Allied victory. The civilian attendees reportedly included representatives from several firms that were heavily involved in key aspects of military production, such as I. G. Farben, Krupp, Thyssen, Rheinmetall, Volkswagenwerk, and Messerschmidt, as well as – according to some accounts – leading financial institutions like the Deutsche Bank and the Dresdner Bank. On the first day of the gathering, it was reportedly agreed that these German firms would accelerate the process of surreptitiously but systematically transferring large portions of their assets into secret bank accounts and businesses in friendly or neutral countries, utilizing dummy firms and foreign "front men" to conceal the ultimate source of the funds. The goal was not only to make it difficult for the Allies to trace and confiscate these assets once the war was over, but also to establish profitable business ventures abroad and thereby facilitate the provision of financial support to wanted Nazi officials who sought to take refuge overseas.[17] A portion of the money was likewise to be used to offer legal assistance to less fortunate *Kameraden* who were captured and put on trial, to form mutual aid associations for veterans and former prisoners-of-war, and to launch campaigns to rehabilitate the Waffen-SS and challenge the theory of German war guilt.[18] Although some of these funds may also have been earmarked for financing the creation of new fascist groups or covertly influencing the political affairs of postwar Germany, only a handful of starry-eyed fanatics could have dreamed of using them to subsidize the establishment of an actual Fourth Reich.

Be that as it may, not long after the conference date classified U.S. intelligence reports began signalling that German businesses were shifting vast sums of money out of the "fatherland" and into countries throughout the world.[19] Indeed, a 1946 Treasury Department analysis revealed that they had already transferred five hundred million dollars to bank accounts in Switzerland, Liechtenstein, Austria, Portugal, Spain, and various South American nations, and that they had purchased a controlling interest in 214 firms in Switzerland, 158 in Portugal, 112 in Spain, 98 in Argentina, 35 in Turkey, and 233 elsewhere.[20] In the first quarter of 1945, moreover, a large portion of the vast holdings accumulated by the state-owned Reichsbank and various Nazi bureaucracies, including looted treasure from all over Europe, was transported south and hidden in the mountainous region where the so-called *Alpenfestung* was supposed to be prepared for the Third Reich's last stand. A good deal of this wealth was later recovered by the Allies, but nearly twenty million dollars' worth was never found. As will soon become clear, considerable sums apparently ended up in the hands of key organizers of the postwar Nazi underground.[21]

Some of the money that had been invested overseas or hastily hidden in the Altaussee area was subsequently used to help set up and maintain underground escape and support organizations, which thence served as conduits for providing logistical and financial assistance to high-ranking party officials and SS men who were subject to arrest and stiff penalties. Unfortunately, so many sensationalistic and contradictory claims have been made about various clandestine Nazi networks – Die Organisation der ehemaligen SS-Angehörigen (ODESSA: Organization of Former SS Members), Die Spinne (the Spider), Die Stille Hilfe für Kriegsgefangene und Internierte (Silent Help for Prisoners-of-War and Internees), Die Schleuse (the Lock-Gate), Das Kameradenwerk (Comrades' Alliance), and Die Bruderschaft (the Brotherhood) – that to this day it remains difficult to distinguish between fact and fantasy, reconstruct their actual activities, and clarify the nature of the seemingly complex relationships between them. Some sort of SS underground undoubtedly existed in the postwar era, and it appears that some of the aforementioned organizations had a more or less important function within that underground. But there remain several unanswered questions about these organizations. One is whether the preceding rubrics all referred to different components of a single network, whether they applied to separate but parallel networks which in part overlapped with one another, or whether they were sometimes little more than the phantasmagoric products of disinformation campaigns designed to mislead and distract investigators. A second question has to do with just how extensive, powerful, and dangerous these networks really were. Alas, the sketchy and often contradictory descriptions of particular networks that appear in the available secondary sources make it impossible to resolve these central issues definitively.

The most notorious of these secretive SS organizations was undoubtedly ODESSA, about which novelist Frederick Forsyth even wrote a best-selling political thriller.[22] Nevertheless, there is little consensus about its historical role and significance. Some observers claim that ODESSA was an elaborate, highly efficient, and powerful clandestine organization that provided wanted Nazis with false identity papers and carefully arranged their flight from the ruins of the Reich to havens in Spain, Latin America, and the Middle East, whereas others assert that it was never a single coherent network, but rather a loose collection of small congeries of SS men who engaged in such activities.[23] Nor is there any general agreement about the relationship between ODESSA and other groups like Spinne and Schleuse. Thus Spinne has been variously referred to as the immediate forerunner of ODESSA, the parent body from which ODESSA broke away as a splinter group, the "escape arm" of ODESSA (which was itself an outgrowth of the "Skorzeny Organization"), a more sophisticated version of ODESSA which was used solely for large-scale operations, a separate and relatively small network which originated as a "Werwolf" commando unit, a loose association of imprisoned SS officers who secretly maintained regular contacts with one another to plan breakouts, and a different name for the ODESSA organization.[24] Not surprisingly, these authors cannot even agree about the date when Spinne was supposedly established. Two place its creation in the period just before the end of World War II and thus prior to the 1947 founding of ODESSA, another puts it in 1946 at Karlsfeld hospital, and still others put in 1948 at the Glasenbach POW camp in Austria.[25] According to former OSS operative Ladislas Farago, Spinne was the only Nazi network that attained real importance after the war, and then mainly in South America.[26] Die Schleuse, meanwhile, has been described by Michael Bar-Zohar as a Gestapo-created network that established escape routes similar to those Wiesenthal ascribed to ODESSA, whereas other authorities say little or nothing about such an organization.[27]

Fortunately, more reliable information is available about the Kameradenwerk, Stille Hilfe, and the Bruderschaft. According to former Luftwaffe ace Hans-Ulrich Rudel, a key figure in various postwar Nazi activities, the Kameradenwerk was a network set up by himself and other "patriotic" exiles in Buenos Aires. Its ostensible purpose was to raise money from German communities in Argentina, Brazil, and Chile for comrades in Europe who were having legal and financial problems, and it regularly sent clothing and goods it collected or purchased to Nazi fugitives and prisoners in West Germany, using a host of secretive far right organizations and "aid societies" for veterans and refugees as intermediaries. Rudel specifically noted that one such intermediary was "Mother" Helene Elisabeth, Princess von Isenburg, the official founder of the Stille Hilfe organization, upon which the Kameradenwerk was itself supposedly modeled.[28] In addition to carrying out their "humanitarian" work, however, the leading members of Rudel's South American network also maintained close political relationships with unregenerate Nazi activists throughout Europe, so much so that at least one investigator has claimed that the Kameradenwerk was actually the organization that ODESSA purported to be.[29]

For its part, Stille Hilfe was officially founded in 1951, and was perhaps modeled on the Soziale Friedenswerk (Establishment of Social Peace) association that had already been created in Austria. It helped several wanted Nazis to escape overseas in its earliest days, including SS Dr. Hans Eisele, formerly chief medical officer at the Buchenwald concentration camp, but later oriented its efforts toward providing logistical support to comrades who were in prison and legal aid to those who were on trial for various crimes. Among the latter were several SS guards who had been stationed at the Majdanak camp in Poland. Even as late as 1981, Stille Hilfe was looking after fifty imprisoned war criminals. More worrisome, perhaps, was the support granted to the organization by high-ranking government officials, both during the Allied occupation and after the establishment of the Federal Republic. Thus Princess Elisabeth supposedly established excellent relations with U.S. High Commissioner John J. McCloy, the group was granted tax-exempt status in December 1951 by the Munich tax office, and its later president, Dr. Rudolf Aschenauer, had influential connections within the Ministry of Justice. And, as if to belie their claims to have constituted an apolitical "non-profit association," members of Stille Hilfe increasingly developed links with a number of neo-fascist and far right groups not only in West Germany but also in other parts of the world. Among others, these reportedly included the Wiking-Jugend (Viking Youth), the Deutsches Kulturwerk Europäischen Geistes (DKEG: German Cultural Association for the European Spirit), the Nationaldemokratische Partei Deutschlands (NPD: National Democratic Party of Germany), Dr. Gerhard Frey's Deutsche Volksunion (DVU: German Peoples' Union), the Hilfsgemeinschaft Freiheit für Rudolf Hess ("Freedom for Rudolf Hess" Support Association), Thies Christophersen and his Bürger- und Bauerninitiative (BBI: Townsman and Countryman Initiative), Flemish fascists, South Tyrolean ultras, and the pro-Nazi Friends of Germany group in the United States. The funds used by Stille Hilfe to sustain and support imprisoned Nazis came from a variety of sources, including individual contributors, profits from a book on Adolf Eichmann published by Christophersen, other "aid" associations such as the Kameradenwerk, and – in all probability – portions of the Nazi treasure that were never accounted for.[30]

The Bruderschaft, on the other hand, was not an escape and support network at all, but rather a covert cadre organization operating in West Germany that aimed to infiltrate its members into established political parties and the state apparatus. Such an organization was first conceived in 1945 or 1946 by Major Helmut Beck-Broichsitter at a British POW camp where members of the Wehrmacht's elite "Grossdeutschland" division were being held. However, it was not actually established until July 1949, a couple of years after Beck had joined forces with Alfred Franke-Gricksch, a former SS Standartenführer in the RSHA who was said to have worked for British intelligence in the immediate aftermath of the war.[31] At its head was a so-called Council of Brethren (*Bruderrat*) consisting of six men, around which were arrayed – in a fashion reminiscent of classical secret societies – an "inner circle" and an "outer circle." The former consisted not only of former Nazi Gauleiters like Karl Kaufmann and Dr. Gustav Adolf Scheel, but also of high-ranking ex-military officers, including Wehrmacht generals Heinz Guderian, Hasso von Manteuffel, and Kurt Student, as well as Waffen-SS generals Paul Hausser, Herbert O. Gille, Felix Steiner, and Otto Kumm. The association of such prestigious figures with the Bruderschaft enabled the organization to establish a vast network of *sub rosa* contacts, both with influential figures associated with the West German political and economic establishments and with key activists from several very important right-wing or nationalist groups in Germany. Among these latter were the Deutsche Union (DU: German Union), a sort of elitist "gentlemens' club" which August Haussleiter established in January 1949 as a rallying point for "homeless" nationalist intellectuals; the Deutsche Gemeinschaft (DG: German Association), which succeeded the DU; the Deutsche Reichspartei (DRP: German Reich Party); the Bund Heimattreuer Deutscher (BHD: Federation of Patriotic Germans), which gathered together former members of the neo-Nazi Sozialistische Reichspartei (SRP: Socialist Reich Party) after the German government outlawed the latter in October 1952; the underground *Scheinwerfer* publishing circle, whose bitterly anti-Western leader, former SS Hauptsturmführer Joachim Nehring, was later tried and sentenced to four years hard labor for forging secret links with communist agents behind the "Iron Curtain"; and the Arbeitsgemeinschaft Nationaler Gruppen (ANG: Syndicate of National Groups), an umbrella organization. More significantly, it has been reported that the Bruderschaft established a network of clandestine cells in all four zones of occupied Germany, that it – improbably – gathered together enough former military personnel to staff both an infantry division and an armored division; that Beck secretly proposed to set up anti-communist shock troops in cooperation with the American military authorities (despite the Franke wing's philo-Soviet "nationalist-neutralist" public stance and the contacts initiated by elements from both factions with East Bloc officials); that it sponsored the creation of the paramilitary Freikorps Deutschland (Free Corps Germany); and that it sought, apparently with some degree of success, to facilitate the passage of anti-democratic far rightists into mainstream conservative parties.[32]

Of greater relevance in this context, leading members of the Bruderschaft were closely linked to various clandestine SS escape networks and to neo-fascist activists elsewhere in Europe. Franke had appointed Wilhelm Kiefer and Colonel Gottlob Gehret as his foreign liaison men, and they in turn relied upon Jean-Maurice Bauverd, a Swiss expatriate who lived in Madrid and had formerly worked for both Radio Damascus and the Egyptian government's press office in Cairo, to develop some of the Bruderschaft's overseas contacts. Bauverd, who was then responsible for organizing Islamic press centers in Rome, Paris, and Buenos Aires, was in regular contact with neo-fascist circles, and through him the Bruderschaft established connections with Maurice Bardèche and René Binet in Paris, Gaston-Armand ("Guy") Amaudruz in Lausanne, former SS officers like Erich Kernmayer and Max Prantl in Austria, several unidentified members of the Movimento Sociale Italiano (MSI: Italian Social Movement) in Italy, former employees of the NSDAP's Auslandsorganisation (AO: Foreign Organization) who still lived abroad, and pro-Nazi Austrian bishop Alois Hudal, rector of the Collegium Teutonicum Pontificum in Rome.[33] As will soon become clear, these particular individuals were almost all stars in the firmament of the postwar radical right. Some played key roles in the creation of early "fascist internationals," whereas at least one among them assiduously helped to spirit hundreds of wanted Nazi war criminals to safety. Other Bruderschaft-linked figures, such as the notorious Major Waldemar Pabst, engaged in arms trafficking after World War II in order to finance the Bruderschaft's underground apparatus or new anti-Komintern schemes. In Pabst's case this trafficking was apparently legal, because after 1951 he served as a representative of the Swiss armaments firm Oerlikon.[34]

In the middle of 1951, the ever-growing hostility between Beck's increasingly pro-Western faction and Franke's overtly Russophile faction, coupled with adverse media publicity about the organization's role as a Nazi secret society, led first to the formal expulsion of the Franke faction and then, shortly thereafter, to the formal dissolution of the Bruderschaft. This, however, did not mean that all of its leading members suddenly became quiescent and abandoned political scheming. Rather, they entered into several smaller but equally elitist groups, the most important of which was the so-called Naumann-Kreis (Naumann Circle) – otherwise known as the Gauleiter-Kreis (Gauleiter Circle) – which was named after Dr. Werner Naumann, a former top official of Joseph Goebbel's Propaganda Ministry, SD man, and SS Brigadeführer. In order to expand their range of influence behind the scenes, Naumann and his associates immediately began strengthening their links with top military circles and veterans organizations (including the Verband Deutscher Soldaten [VdS: German Soldiers' Association]), youth groups, the DKEG and other "cultural" associations, interest groups of all sorts, right-wing publishing houses (like ex-SS man Waldemar Schütz's Plesse-Verlag in Göttingen and the international backers of the monthly *Nation Europa* journal), conservative industrialists such as textile manufacturer Gerd Spindler, and radical fascist rabble-rousers like former Hitler Jugend (HJ: Hitler Youth) member Karl-Heinz Priester.[35] Perhaps most significantly, Naumann was in contact with Dr. Eberhard Taubert of the Volksbund für Frieden und Freiheit (VFF: People's League for Peace and Freedom), and entries in the former's diary specifically related his own political plotting to that of some of the most important figures within the international SS underground, including SS commando leader Otto Skorzeny, Rudel, and Wilfred von Oven, formerly Goebbels's personal adjutant.[36] More will soon be said about the clandestine activities of Skorzeny.

But the circle's chief efforts were devoted to infiltrating bourgeois rightist parties – especially the "liberal" Freie Demokratische Partei (FDP: Free Democratic Party), the Block der Heimatvertriebenen und Entrechteten (BHE: Bloc of the Expellees and Disenfranchised), and the Deutsche Partei (DP: German Party) – with a view toward eventually penetrating the entire state apparatus. Although apologists for the Naumann-Kreis later claimed that it constituted nothing more than a political "discussion group" which had been unjustly persecuted by the "victors," Naumann's diary entries and secret speeches – which explicitly advocated the infiltration and takeover of respectable rightist parties – demonstrate the spuriousness of that claim.[37] As it happens, members of Naumann's entourage almost ended up controlling the North Rhine-Westphalia and Lower Saxony branches of the FDP by placing unrepentent former Nazi officials in all the key party positions. Had Naumann and other circle leaders not been arrested in January 1953 by the British authorities for anti-democratic plotting, it is likely that this process of acquiring clandestine control over other party branches and organizations would have proceeded apace. The cases against the defendants were later discreetly dropped by the Justice Ministry, but the sensationalistic publicity surrounding the arrests and trial undermined their ability to reconstitute covert cadres and continue to manipulate other groups from inside.[38]

In any event, despite lingering confusion about the exact nature of ODESSA, Spinne, and Schleuse, it is clear that certain postwar SS underground organizations facilitated the escape of wanted Nazi war criminals. Several routes were used to exfiltrate these fugitives, most of which were patterned on routes that had earlier been used by the OSS and certain Zionist organizations to exfiltrate their own agents and refugees from Axis-occupied Central and Eastern Europe. Many of these routes have been identified, at least in their general outlines. One led from Flensburg in Schleswig-Holstein northwards across the Danish border, whence submarines, surface vessels, or aircraft could, with a modicum of luck, be surreptitiously boarded for Spain and Italy. One of the fugitives who escaped from the Allied dragnet in this way was Belgian Rexist and Waffen-SS leader Léon Degrelle, who first made his way to Oslo and thence commandeered a plane and flew to Spain. Some authors have also claimed that Bormann himself escaped by means of this route, but physical evidence seems to indicate that he was killed trying to make his way out of the ruins of Berlin. In any event, the more important and widely used routes led southwards from the Memmingen or Aussee areas. From the former town they branched out in one of two main directions, either southwest to Lindau or Bregenz on Lake Constance and then into Switzerland, or southeast into the Allgäu, across the Austrian border to Innsbruck, and then on through the Brenner Pass into Italy. Another starting point leading to this latter escape route lay in the Altaussee region, where Hitler had originally hoped to establish his impregnable redoubt and where many Nazi officials and their families had taken temporary refuge. Along these border regions in the midst of the Alps, with their intricate web of mountain pathways, clandestine SS escape organizations apparently set up and maintained an elaborate network consisting of "safe houses" every fifty or so miles. Fugitives were provided with false papers, sheltered in safe houses, and thence led over those pathways by knowledgeable mountain guides until, at a certain point, they were passed along to experienced personnel associated with the well-organized exfiltration networks run by the Vatican or Allied intelligence.

Among the estimated thousands of wanted Nazis and East European collaborators who made their escapes along these southern routes were reportedly SS Obergruppenführer Karl Wolff, one of Himmler's chief subordinates who had earlier negotiated a "secret surrender" with Allen Dulles, then an OSS officer in Switzerland and a future head of the U.S. Central Intelligence Agency (CIA); SS Dr. Josef Mengele, who conducted horrific "scientific" experiments on prisoners at Auschwitz; SS Hauptsturmführer Klaus Barbie, the Gestapo "butcher" of Lyon; SS Sturmbannführer Friedrich Schwend, who helped launder forged British bank notes in connection with "Unternehmen Bernhard"; SS Standartenführer Walther Rauff, inventor of the mobile gas chamber; SS Obersturmbannführer Adolph Eichmann, head of the Jewish Affairs section of the Gestapo and a bureaucratic architect of the logistical aspects of the *Endlösung*; SS Hauptsturmführer Franz Stangl, commander of the concentration camp at Treblinka; SS Hauptsturmführer Alois Brunner, one of Eichmann's key subordinates; Croatian *Poglavnik* Ante Pavelić, who was responsible for launching genocidal Ustaša anti-Serbian campaigns whose brutality even shocked the Nazis; and Horia Sima, leader of the fanatical Garda de Fier in Rumania following the death of Corneliu Codreanu. Once in Italy, under the protection of the Vatican's refugee bureaus, it was relatively easy for these high-profile criminals to escape overseas. Ships regularly departed for the Iberian Peninsula and Latin America from Genoa, Rome, and Naples, whereas from Bari they set sail to Middle

Eastern countries like Egypt or Syria. All of these destinations provided relatively secure havens for Nazi fugitives. Spain and Portugal were still ruled by right-wing dictators despite their official maintenance of neutrality throughout World War II and their behind-the-scenes attempts to ingratiate themselves with the victorious Allies toward the end of the conflict. Furthermore, the Germans were widely admired throughout Latin America for their discipline, efficiency, and technical skills, and certain Arab nationalist regimes had no hesitation about welcoming and secretly employing unrepentant anti-Semites in various capacities.[39]

Three major qualifications nonetheless have to be made about the preceding sketch of the various components of the postwar SS underground. First of all, the reach and power of these Nazi networks seem to have been greatly exaggerated, both by vengeful Nazi hunters seeking to bring war criminals to justice and by journalists hoping to sell books and articles by adopting a sensationalistic approach to the topic. It may be true, as Werner Brockdorff suggests, that ODESSA and Spinne were not functional escape networks at all, but rather elaborate fantasies concocted by paranoids, conspiracy theorists, or tellers of tall tales.[40] On the other hand, it would be a serious mistake to view all of these reported SS escape networks as mere figments of someone's overactive imagination, for it is apparent that a number of underground organizations were engaged in financing, sheltering, or protecting high-profile Nazi war criminals in various parts of the world.

Second, the postwar Nazi networks that actually existed and remained active soon became involved in a wide variety of clandestine political and paramilitary operations, most of which had an anti-democratic stamp. This can best be illustrated by sketching the postwar careers of Otto Skorzeny and certain members of the Kameradenwerk, although in these cases, too, heroic legends and disinformation are often difficult to separate from historical fact. Skorzeny was a colorful and important figure in the history of the Third Reich. Having established a close friendship with Ernst Kaltenbrunner in the late 1920s, joined the Austrian Nazi party in the mid-1930s, and displayed considerable initiative and boldness at the time of the 1938 *Anschluss*, he was recruited into the Waffen-SS and thence participated in the French, Yugoslav, and Russian campaigns before being wounded in the winter of 1941. In April 1943 Kaltenbrunner, who had in the meantime succeeded Reinhard Heydrich as head of the RSHA, put Skorzeny in charge of the top secret SS schools – located in Neustrelitz and, later, The Hague and Heinrichsburg (near Belgrade) – where selected personnel were to be trained to carry out sabotage and other types of clandestine operations. These schools were officially under the organizational jurisdiction of Amt VI, the foreign intelligence section of the RSHA headed by SS Brigadeführer Walter Schellenberg, but the VI/S "sabotage" subsection under Skorzeny's command also received direct orders from Hitler himself. Skorzeny established his headquarters at Friedenthal, converted the nearby Oranienberg SS battalion into Jagdverband 502, created a number of other battalion-strength Jagdverbände, and had the elite SS Kampfgeschwader 200 aerial group placed at his disposal by Himmler. After taking espionage courses from an Abwehr officer in Holland, Skorzeny took control over the German military intelligence service's "Zeppelin" networks, which had been established behind the lines on the eastern front, and commenced his extraordinary career as a leader of "special operations." Among his more notorious exploits were the daring rescue of Mussolini in September 1943; the recruitment of Dutch "double agents" to obtain information about British secret weapons; the 1944 kidnapping of the double-dealing Hungarian regent, Admiral Miklós Horthy; and "Unternehmen Greif," the generally unsuccessful attempt to pass infiltration teams through American lines during the December 1944 Ardennes offensive, some of which allegedly had been given the task of assassinating General Dwight D. Eisenhower, the supreme Allied commander on the Western front.[41]

Of more direct relevance in this context were the activities undertaken by Skorzeny at the close of and after World War II. Admiring biographers of the huge Austrian with the prominent dueling scars on his face have tended to dismiss stories about secret SS undergrounds as fanciful rumors or examples of Soviet disinformation, as well as to accept the former commando's own claims to have withdrawn from politics after 1945 in order to resume a normal life and establish a lucrative but "respectable" career as a businessman.[42] In marked contrast, self-appointed "Nazi hunters" and communist-linked sources have portrayed him as the central figure in a vast international organization of unreconstructed Nazis who sought to profit, promote their ideals, rehabilitate themselves, and lay the groundwork for their own return to the corridors of power in a new bipolar world.[43] As usual, the truth lies somewhere in the middle, although it is certainly closer to the latter interpretation than the former. This will become obvious when certain aspects of Skorzeny's postwar career are further elucidated.

First of all, it seems clear that "Scarface" helped to create and thereafter played a leading role in the postwar SS underground, whether or not he was the leader of ODESSA. Long before the war ended he had established close links with the special unit set up within Amt VI to produce forged documents, section F under SS Sturmbannführer Hermann Dörner. Among these documents were false identification papers and counterfeit bank notes that were circulated abroad to help undermine the Allied economies and exchanged for genuine foreign currency.[44] Due to his connections with the officials responsible for this latter operation, codenamed "Bernhard," Skorzeny was purportedly later consigned a portion of the forged currency and the materials used to produce it and asked to sequester them in the Alps for possible future use.[45] Kaltenbrunner, Bormann, and Eichmann also may have relied upon Skorzeny to bury valuable materials for them.[46] In addition, after allegedly helping German industrialists transfer money overseas in the wake of the August 1944 Strasbourg meeting, he was later reportedly given the important task of hiding a portion of the Reichsbank's Nazi treasure and various documentary records in the Toplitzsee area.[47] Finally, because Hitler officially entrusted him with training the "Werwolf" stay/behind commando units, recruiting "sleeper" agents in France and Italy, and creating an SS Schutzkorps Alpenland (SS Alps Region Protection Corps) for a last stand in the Alpine redoubt, he apparently arranged for the burial of large stockpiles of weapons in that remote region.[48] Access to these important materials and resources, as well as to complete lists of SD and Abwehr agents overseas, provided Skorzeny with the wherewithal to organize escape routes and logistical support networks that were then used by many of his SS comrades and other wanted Nazis.

Elements associated with these underground networks appear to have been directly or indirectly involved in almost all of his subsequent social, political, and financial activities. To cite only a few examples, it should be noted that Skorzeny escaped from Darmstadt prison on 27 July 1948 with the help of a relatively extensive Nazi support network that operated both inside and outside of various prisons and detention centers.[49] He then made his way to Argentina, where he seems to have renewed old contacts with Rudel and other key members of the Kameradenwerk. He was, after all, reputed to be in charge of underground networks in Germany and Austria that were in some way linked to their comrades in South America.[50] According to U.S. intelligence reports, he later returned to Europe and secretly visited a number of German cities in order to recruit additional SS men into his existing clandestine networks, which apparently sought to make use of legal organizations like veterans' associations and right-wing parties as a "cover" for infiltrating Nazi sympathizers into the new West German state.[51] As part of this effort, he maintained close contact with Werner Naumann and other leaders of the Bruderschaft, who may have been in the process of carrying out some sort of "plan" Skorzeny devised prior to the exposure and formal dissolution of the group.

When he settled in Spain in the early 1950s, he was welcomed with open arms by activist members of the more than fifteen thousand–strong fascist colony that had already been established there, including his old Belgian comrade-in-arms, SS Obersturmbannführer Léon Degrelle.[52] Shortly thereafter, he held a series of meetings in Madrid with the banker Hjalmar Schacht, Hitler's former financial advisor, with whom he had perhaps previously cooperated in efforts to transfer German assets abroad and whose daughter he later married. He then founded an engineering firm whose offices were located on the luxurious Avenida Gran Vía in the center of the Spanish capital, as well an export-import firm at Calle de Montera 25–27. Through the good graces of Schacht, as well as the contacts with other German businessmen he had forged before the collapse of the Third Reich and thence while awaiting trial in prison, he became the Spanish representative for several leading industrial firms, including Klöckner AG, the [Otto] Wolff-Trust, the Feldmühle paper company, the Messerschmidt-Werke, Krupp, the H. S. Lucht company, and the Vereinigte Österreichische Eisen- und Stahlwerke (VÖESt), formerly an integral component of the Hermann Göring-Werke. In this capacity, he engaged in a variety of business transactions, perhaps including worldwide arms trafficking, which netted him considerable profits. These more or less "legitimate" funds were in turn reportedly supplemented by the interest he collected from German overseas investments that he had earlier helped to arrange, the money he extracted from compromised German businessmen by means of blackmail, and portions of the secret Nazi treasure that he had helped to bury and now purportedly managed.[53] With these multiple sources of wealth, Skorzeny was not only able to maintain a lavish lifestyle, but also to help subsidize underground SS networks, the Bruderschaft, factions within Waffen-SS veterans' associations, ex-Nazi politicians, and other right-wing political groups. Although many of the specific details remain unclear or controversial to this day, the overall pattern of Skorzeny's associations and activities is scarcely in doubt.

To these persistent connections with unrepentant and activist Nazi circles must be added Skorzeny's apparent links to various Western intelligence agencies. His wartime activities necessarily brought him into contact with key secret service personnel in Nazi Germany. The most important of these intelligence officers was undoubtedly General Reinhard Gehlen, head of the Oberkommando des Heeres' Fremde Heere Ost (FHO: Foreign Armies East) organization, which was responsible for intelligence gathering and other types of special operations on the eastern front.[54] Skorzeny and Gehlen probably began coordinating the launching of various ventures behind Soviet lines as early as the summer of 1943, by which time "Scarface" had been put in charge of Amt VI's Zeppelin saboteur groups. This pattern of collusion was intensified after the disbanding of the Abwehr as an autonomous organization and the incorporation of much of its operational apparatus into other security organs. The bulk of it was absorbed into the RSHA as the Militäramt (Military Bureau), but Gehlen's FHO managed to obtain control over the Abwehr's "WALLI" intelligence networks in exchange for his agreement to assist the Zeppelin units. Toward the end of the war, Gehlen and Skorzeny worked closely together in an effort to combine the Zeppelin stay/behind resistance groups and the WALLI networks into a combined espionage organization behind the Soviet front. Thus, although personal rivalries between the two highly ambitious and headstrong men sometimes led to serious friction, especially after Hitler had a falling out with Gehlen over his pessimistic situation reports, their relationship survived the collapse of the Third Reich.[55] Some of Gehlen's intelligence files may have been consigned to Skorzeny for burial during the last days of the war. Later, Gehlen intervened on behalf of the imprisoned SS man, and then apparently recruited him as a contract agent for the West German intelligence service he had by then been appointed to head, the so-called Gehlen Org, which later evolved into the Bundesnachrichtendienst (BND: Federal Intelligence Service).[56]

Both his wartime role in Nazi intelligence and his subsequent efforts to set up clandestine SS support networks for wanted fugitives initially made Skorzeny the target of a massive Allied dragnet. But it was not long before his erstwhile enemies in American intelligence sought to enlist his services in the covert war against communism. As early as May of 1945, General Edwin Sibert, Chief of Intelligence for the U.S. Twelfth Army Group, was actively searching for Skorzeny and other German intelligence specialists, including Gehlen and Kaltenbrunner, who could provide him with valuable information about the Russians.[57] That same month "Hitler's commando" surrendered to the Americans and volunteered to participate in the impending struggle against the Soviet Bloc, after which he was interrogated at length by the U.S. Counter-Intelligence Corps (CIC). However, because he was wanted for war crimes by other Allied agencies, he was transferred back and forth from one prison to another and belatedly brought to trial in the late summer of 1947. As the trial wore on the predicament of Skorzeny and his co-defendants seemed to be worsening, but at the last minute a British intelligence officer appeared out of nowhere and unexpectedly came to his rescue. This was the famous "White Rabbit," Wing Commander Forest Yeo-Thomas, a special operations expert who had fought in occupied France with members of the Resistance before being captured and escaping from Buchenwald concentration camp. At the trial he testified – allegedly on his own initiative – that British commandos regularly carried out the same type of clandestine actions for which Skorzeny and his comrades were being tried, thereby destroying the prosecution's case in a single blow.[58]

From this point on, certain factions within U.S. intelligence appear to have secretly protected Skorzeny in order to make use of his specialized abilities, unbeknownst to other Allied security personnel without a "need to know," who tried to track his movements and prevent him from engaging in anti-democratic actions. This was a general pattern that has now been amply documented in the cases of many other high-profile Nazi figures, such as Barbie, Brunner, and Schwend. In this case the protective group issued a warning to their famous prisoner, who was then supposed to be writing an account of Mussolini's rescue for the U.S. Army's Historical Division, to the effect that continued Czech demands for his extradition could not be ignored or delayed indefinitely. In all probability they then facilitated his escape from the Darmstadt detention center by providing American military police uniforms for three former SS men, who were thereby able to dupe the German camp guards into releasing him into their custody. After a period of general confusion in which his whereabouts were known only to those who were actively involved in sheltering him, unsubstantiated stories appeared in the press which claimed that Skorzeny had been flown to an American base in Georgia to help train U.S. paratroopers. In 1950 he was definitely spotted in Paris, where politically motivated rumors were circulated that he was engaged in gathering information about the Parti Communiste Français (PCF: French Communist Party).[59]

However propagandistic these specific claims may appear, a report prepared by the 66th CIC group admitted that he might have been working for U.S. intelligence since his escape from prison, and another by the 7970th CIC group suggested that he may have been aided by the Americans during his subsequent flight from France and his secret re-entry into West Germany. There is no doubt, moreover, that Anglo-American intelligence personnel kept him under regular observation after he settled in Spain, because those outside the information loop did not know that he was working with certain other factions within their own organizations, and those affiliated with the latter were not yet entirely certain that he could be trusted. Indeed, in 1951 Skorzeny approached an American military attaché in Madrid and offered to recruit German veterans into anti-communist guerrilla units capable of fighting behind enemy lines should the Soviets invade Western Europe.[60] Although this particular proposal was turned down – perhaps because the United States was already setting up such stay/behind groups throughout non-communist Europe – Skorzeny was at some point recruited as a contract agent by Gehlen, a convenient arrangement that provided the Americans with a degree of "plausible deniability" had anyone asked if they were making use of his services themselves. It was in part due to these very intelligence contacts that Skorzeny became actively involved in a number of terrorist and covert operations over the course of the next twenty years.

Some of these operations deserve to be highlighted, because they provide a good illustration of the postwar utilization of European right-wing extremists by elements of Western intelligence. Among other things, Skorzeny purportedly trained personnel from the Argentine secret police and the Buenos Aires police in torture and interrogation techniques during his periodic stays with Juan and Eva Perón prior to the dictator's 1955 ouster and flight to Spain.[61] In late 1952, in response to a request from Jamāl 'Abd al-Nāsir, CIA chief Allen Dulles turned to Gehlen for help in recruiting personnel to train the Egyptian intelligence and security services. With Schacht's help, Gehlen persuaded Skorzeny to take the job after assuring him that the salary paid by al-Nāsir would be supplemented by CIA funds laundered through the Org. So it was that the Austrian spent a total of eighteen months recruiting one hundred German advisors from the SS underground and neo-fascist outfits, and more suspect sources claim that he also trained Arab guerrillas in commando tactics and protected some of the ex-Nazi technicians working for al-Nāsir from retaliation by Israeli "hit" teams.[62] Furthermore, "Scarface" may have secretly met with three CIA officials, two West Germans, a Spaniard, and three French military officers in Madrid on 12 April 1961. Among these Frenchmen were two experienced soldiers who were later to play a key role in the Organisation de l'Armée Secrète (OAS: Secret Army Organization), General Paul Gardy, formerly Inspector General of the Légion Étrangère (LE: Foreign Legion), and *guerre révolutionnaire* Colonel Jean Gardes, the most highly decorated officer in the French Army between 1944 and 1945 and eventually the head of its 5th (Psychological Warfare) Bureau in Algiers. Whether Skorzeny thereafter kept in contact with and provided operational or logistical assistance to elements of the OAS, as communist sources claim, is a controversial issue that deserves further study.[63] In this connection, it should be pointed out that Waffen-SS and Wehrmacht veterans made up a substantial portion of the rank-and-file within the elite paratroop regiments of the Légion, the very units that were actively involved in the military revolts in Algeria.

It is also worth noting the existence of various direct and indirect personal links between "Hitler's commando" and elements implicated in later acts of neo-fascist terrorist violence. For one thing, one of the key activists working for Aginter Presse, a press agency in Lisbon that served to disguise the activities of an international center of right-wing subversion, was Robert Leroy, formerly an instructor at Skorzeny's school for saboteurs.[64] For another, one of Skorzeny's chief patrons and associates in Spain, the Duke of Valencia, was the principal shareholder in the bank which owned a company that was used to "cover" the activities of the Exército de Libertação Português (ELP: Portuguese Liberation Army), a clandestine right-wing paramilitary group that sought to overthrow the post-1974 regime set up by leftist elements within the Portuguese armed forces.[65] In this context, it may also be significant that General António de Spínola, the titular leader of the Portuguese counterrevolutionary forces that had created the ELP, received a visit from a representative of the arms-trading company Merex during a July 1975 trip he took to Paris to develop a European support network. Merex, some of whose profits allegedly went into the coffers of certain neo-fascist organizations, exhibited other unusual characteristics. It had been founded in Bonn in 1963 by former SS man and wartime Skorzeny collaborator Gerhard Mertins, was thereafter represented by some of "Scarface's" Nazi associates in various Latin American countries, and was reportedly a proprietary of Gehlen's BND.[66] Last but not least, Skorzeny may have been one of the key figures in Gerhard Hartmut von Schubert's Paladin Group, which specialized in recruiting mercenaries and counterguerrilla specialists to undertake anti-communist operations in every part of the globe.[67]

In 1970, after collaborating with his old Nazi Propaganda Ministry associate Johannes von Leers, first in assisting Perón's secret police and then in disseminating anti-Western and anti-Semitic propaganda for al-Nāsir's Egypt, von Schubert moved to Spain and set up the Paladin Group, reportedly with Skorzeny's help. Within a surprisingly short time they managed to recruit a cadre of experienced operatives with military and intelligence skills, in particular ex-Nazis, OAS veterans, members of the Service d'Action Civique (SAC: Civic Action Service) who had been purged from that notorious Gaullist parallel police organization by President Georges Pompidou, and younger ultras from various European and Latin American neo-fascist groups. Paladin's headquarters and base of operations were located at Calle Albuferete 9 in Alicante, but the organization also opened branch offices in Zurich, Geneva, Paris, Brussels, Rome, and London.[68] Over the years von Schubert had apparently developed close relations with a number of Western secret services, and according to a former OAS "Delta" commando who worked for the Spanish secret service, the unreconstructed Nazi placed his prodigious talent for unconventional warfare at the disposal of the Dirección General de Seguridad (DGS: General Security Directorate), which in turn fully "covered" all the actions his agency undertook in Spain. At first Paladin's secret operations, like those of Aginter Presse in Lisbon, were directed primarily against "national liberation" movements in Africa and Maoist organizations in Europe, but the Madrid center's sphere of action was soon greatly expanded. So it was that Paladin, which the very same OAS veteran described as "undoubtedly the most serious" of all the parallel intelligence and "action" services then in operation, carried out a series of covert, "plausibly deniable" tasks for clients as varied as the DGS, the Colonels' Kentrike Yperesia Plerophorion (KYP: Central Intelligence Service) in Greece, the South Vietnamese government, and multinational firms like Rheinmetall and Cadbury's.[69] Some of these manipulative, violent operations were temporarily hamstrung or derailed in the spring of 1974, when a series of exposés appeared in the leftist French daily *Libération* and forced von Schubert to close all of Paladin's existing offices and dismantle the formal structure of the organization. Even so, many Paladin personnel simply joined other clandestine right-wing networks and continued the struggle.

Nor, alas, was Skorzeny the only former SS man with links to intelligence or security agencies and groups of neo-fascist ultras. Other key figures in the postwar SS underground were also discovered to be engaging in arms- and drug trafficking, gathering intelligence, and training the secret police in various South American countries. These included several high-profile Nazis and war criminals who, despite being on Allied arrest lists, managed to escape overseas and establish themselves in countries that provided them with a safe haven. Among those who were able to find refuge and begin a new life abroad were Klaus Barbie in Bolivia, Friedrich Schwend in Peru, Walter Rauff in Chile, Josef Mengele in Paraguay, Dutch SS officer Willem ("Alfons") Sassen in Ecuador, Alois Brunner in Syria, and Hans-Ulrich Rudel in Argentina, as well as a number of East European collaborators. Unlike most wanted Nazis who managed to elude capture, such as Adolf Eichmann until his 1961 seizure by Israeli commandos in Buenos Aires, these men were not satisfied to hide out and lead boring, unchallenging lives. They remained arrogant, unrepentant, manipulative, and opportunistic, and therefore engaged in a pattern of criminality that only differed from their former practices in terms of its scale and intensity.[70]

The third and final qualification that needs to be made about these postwar Nazi undergrounds is that a considerable number of the escape and evasion operations they supposedly organized were in fact carried out secretly by the Catholic Church, the International Red Cross, and various Allied intelligence agencies. It seems probable, in fact, that many of the sensationalistic claims made about ODESSA and the others were primarily designed to distract attention from, and provide a cover for, clandestine operations that were being carried out by these more "respectable" institutions.[71] This is a subject about which a good deal is now known. For example, virtually all of the major Allied powers, including the Soviet Union, secretly set in motion elaborate operations to recruit Axis personnel who possessed skills that were considered to be particularly valuable in the new postwar environment. It is hardly surprising to learn that both the Americans and Russians actively sought to locate and enlist the support of German physicists who were involved in the Nazi nuclear program, because tapping the knowledge of these experts offered each side enormous potential military advantages. Similar programs were soon activated to recruit other scientific experts, including Japanese biological warfare researchers and German rocketry specialists.[72]

Not long afterward hard-liners in various Western government agencies, who rightly foresaw that the Soviet Union was about to become the new main enemy, began making strenuous efforts to attract Axis intelligence and military personnel, especially those with expertise on eastern Europe or extensive experience in unconventional warfare. So it was that many Abwehr, SD, and Waffen-SS veterans, as well as Nazi collaborators from eastern Europe, were secretly recruited and incorporated into U.S., British, Canadian, Australian, and French structures that were entrusted with carrying out intelligence, psychological, and paramilitary operations against domestic communists and their masters in Moscow. In the process, many wanted war criminals were offered protection and employment, unbeknownst to other Allied agencies whose mission was to hunt down such criminals and bring them to justice. The recruitment of high-profile criminals like Klaus Barbie was only the tip of the iceberg, whose submerged portions were made up of dozens of SS men, senior personnel from Goebbels's Propaganda Ministry, top collaborators from Nazi puppet states in Croatia, Hungary, Rumania, the Ukraine, and Byelorussia, and Japanese ultranationalists. To facilitate this difficult task in a devastated postwar environment, American intelligence had recourse to the Vatican, whose refugee associations and network of monasteries were ideally suited to providing "humanitarian assistance" to refugees of all nationalities. High-ranking Vatican officials, including Pope Pius XII, thus played a significant role in helping Axis war criminals to elude their pursuers and thereby avoid punishment for their terrible human rights violations. Although SS underground networks undoubtedly facilitated the escapes of more than a few of these men, their efforts were clearly overshadowed by the top secret exfiltration operations mounted and run by elements of Western governments and the Vatican.[73]

Nevertheless, in the final analysis this large-scale recruitment of Axis war criminals and military specialists by rival Allied coalition partners proved to be something of a double-edged sword. As several informed observers have recognized, many of these "former" fascists and collaborators were neither loyal allies nor docile tools of the victorious powers that had recruited them, but rather manipulative *Schaukelpolitiker* who played one superpower-dominated bloc off the other in order to advance nationalist or fascist political schemes of their own, not to mention protect or enrich themselves. In the process, they facilitated the penetration operations of rival secret services, exacerbated Soviet-American tensions, and perhaps even hastened the onset of the Cold War. Skorzeny himself may be emblematic of this complex phenomenon. Although he ostensibly worked on behalf of the Americans and the Western Bloc, he rarely if ever subordinated his own personal or Nazi-inspired political interests to those of his ostensible patrons in connection with the "struggle against Bolshevism," and things only operated smoothly when their respective interests happened to coincide. Nor were he and many of his close associates averse to collaborating with the Eastern Bloc in order to advance what they perceived to be German interests, as the political activities of the Bruderschaft, the commercial links established by the H. S. Lucht Company, and the public pronouncements of Schacht, Rudel, and Remer clearly demonstrate. Indeed, the Soviet intelligence services also made repeated efforts to recruit "Scarface" and make use of his not inconsiderable talents, and at least one former Waffen-SS veteran (code-named "Kluf") identified Skorzeny as an important figure in "a secret international organization composed of former SS officers and partially funded by the Soviets" that allegedly worked with the Russians "against the Western orbit."[74] Whether or not this particular claim is true, the fact that so many fascists and Nazis were courted by their erstwhile enemies created an immensely convoluted pattern of political alliances, within which frequent transfers of loyalty were common and perhaps inevitable.

The international Waffen-SS support network

Alongside these clandestine networks, Waffen-SS veterans also organized themselves into a loose association of relatively undisguised "mutual aid" societies in countries throughout Europe. This image of fanatical German SS men forming an extensive international network with their "non-Aryan" comrades may seem incongruous to those unfamiliar with the earlier historical development of the organization. After all, Hitler and Himmler originally conceived of the Waffen-SS as an elite corps of Aryan "political soldiers" that would constitute both the guardians of the Nazi state (*Staatstruppenpolizei*) and a microcosmic model of the ruling racial caste in the *Gross-Germanisches Reich deutsches Nation* that they planned to create.[75]

However, as Robert Koehl has pointed out, this exclusively "Germanic idea merged in 1942 with a pan-European concept of antibolshevism which survived the war."[76] As early as 1938, Hitler had in principle authorized the acceptance of "non-Germans of Nordic blood" into the ranks of the Waffen-SS, but the large-scale recruitment of Germanic northern and western Europeans and ethnic Germans from eastern Europe (*Volksdeutsche*) was not undertaken until late 1940 and early 1941. Although certain idealistic German SS officers were initially quite enthusiastic about extending Waffen-SS membership to foreigners and became even more so later, the main reason for this development was much more prosaic – manpower shortages.[77] It was thus imperative for the imaginative SS officials attached to the newly formed Germanische-Freiwillige Leitstelle (Germanic Volunteer Head Office) to attract new sources of recruits. They resolved this problem in part by successfully creating a new myth about the nature of the Waffen-SS. Henceforth it was not so much a Germanic racial elite as a multinational "community of arms" (*Waffengemeinschaft*), that is, a new pan-European warrior elite whose solidarity would be forged on the battlefield. Later, as brilliant German victories gave way to bloody defeats, it was this myth that provided the justification for opening up the ranks of the Waffen-SS to non-Germanic West Europeans (Walloons and Frenchmen), East European *Untermenschen* (Balts and Slavs), and finally even Muslims (Bosnians, Turks). By the end of the war, the Waffen-SS contained over half a million troops from more than thirty countries, and afterwards the most active veterans from this corps formed an international network of more or less legal "mutual aid" societies.[78]

The flagship group and organizational hub of this postwar transnational network was the Hilfsgemeinschaft auf Gegenseitigkeit der ehemaligen Soldaten der Waffen-SS (HIAG: Mutual Aid Support Group for Former Waffen-SS Soldiers).[79] Local Waffen-SS support groups were first secretly set up in late 1949 or 1950, if not earlier, but HIAG itself was officially founded in Hamburg in the spring of 1951 by SS General Otto Kumm and others. Within a few months, hundreds of HIAG branches had been established throughout West Germany and Austria, and in October 1951 it joined the aforementioned Verband Deutscher Soldaten (VdS), an umbrella association for military veterans' groups.[80] HIAG originally consisted of a decentralized network of relatively autonomous local groups, but as time wore on the structure of the organization gradually solidified on the national level around high-profile "moderates" like Kumm and his fellow SS generals, Hausser, Gille, and Steiner. From the beginning, leading HIAG spokesmen declared that the group's primary tasks were to promote camaraderie, provide social services to its imprisoned or destitute members and their families, help locate or otherwise account for missing Waffen-SS men, oppose the government's discriminatory legal and economic policies against SS veterans (which were embodied in Article 131 of the Grundgesetz [Basic Law]), and rehabilitate the tarnished image of their elite fighting corps. In order to reassure Bonn, Hausser and the others publicly professed loyalty to the postwar democratic order, repudiated the most horrendous crimes of the Hitler regime, and refused to associate openly with neo-Nazi militants. They also incessantly campaigned to restore the reputation of the Waffen-SS, both at rallies and through HIAG's successive publications, first *Der Wiking-Ruf*, which was founded by Gille in 1951, and later *Der Freiwillige*, which was edited by Austrian hard-liner Erich Kernmayer from 1956 on.

Among other things, this campaign involved distorting history by falsely claiming that the Waffen-SS had been a "fourth arm" of the Wehrmacht, that it had no connection with the Allgemeine-SS (General SS), that it had not committed systematic atrocities, and that its ranks were filled with soldiers "like all the others." The Waffen-SS was also depicted, with somewhat more justification, as a multinational pan-European army united in the fight against "Asiatic" Bolshevism, and thus as a forerunner of the proposed European Defense Community, an image that appealed to Cold Warriors in the government and the mainstream political parties.[81] The aim of this campaign was to gain a measure of respectability and thereby attract political support for their demands to be granted pensions, full legal rights, and – once that was accomplished – commissions in the newly created and rearmed Bundeswehr. This strategy, coupled with the periodic threats issued by HIAG spokesmen to withhold members' electoral votes or to turn to the East Bloc for tangible support, soon persuaded Bundestag deputies and local politicians to appear publicly and express solidarity, however limited, at HIAG's periodic "search service meetings" (*Suchdiensttreffen*).

Even this degree of compromise with the Allied-imposed system was too much for the radicals within the organization, however.[82] Although they too were authoritarian nationalists, Hausser and the other moderates were increasingly attacked for betraying their fundamental principles, besmirching the Waffen-SS's elite status by equating its volunteers with conscripts in regular military units, and accepting, albeit only after certain conditions were met, the rearmament of West Germany within the "mercenary" framework of the Atlantic Alliance. In the face of this agitation from vocal elements of the rank and file, SS General Kurt ("Panzer") Meyer adopted a more aggressive public posture when he assumed a leadership position in HIAG following his 1954 release from prison. His more circumspect rivals, meanwhile, were pressured into resigning at an October 1955 meeting at Coblenz. Although Meyer made more fiery and belligerent public statements and was in general very popular, he too was considered a "sell-out" by the radicals for trying to solicit support from untrustworthy bourgeois parties, especially the Sozialdemokratische Partei Deutschlands (SPD: Social Democratic Party of Germany), as well as for making other opportunistic "tactical" compromises. In 1958, some of the leading radicals resigned in disgust from the organization's executive committee. Through intensive lobbying efforts Meyer ultimately managed to secure pensions and other rights for former SS men in a July 1961 Bundestag vote. Yet he and his successors nonetheless adopted an increasingly anti-democratic, right-wing, and unrepentant posture. Indeed, sections of HIAG tried to ally with the NPD and other rightist parties during the 1960s, and the Bundesamt für Verfassungsschutz (BfV: Federal Office for the Protection of the Constitution) listed HIAG as a right-extremist organization in each of its annual reports between 1972 and 1983.[83]

This brief sketch of the factional infighting within HIAG during its formative years in and of itself demonstrates that the portrayal of the organization as the legal arm of ODESSA or Spinne is a gross oversimplification of the real situation.[84] HIAG only represented 20,000 of the 250,000 surviving Waffen-SS members in postwar Germany, and of those only a minority were political extremists who actively opposed the new government; fewer still dreamed of restoring the Third Reich's former glory. Like the bulk of the membership in most of Europe's veterans associations after 1945, the majority of HIAG's members sought above all to reestablish themselves in civilian life and obtain the basic rights and privileges they felt they were entitled to after having honorably served their country.[85] However, the more intransigent, radical factions within HIAG were undoubtedly linked in various ways to the SS underground. It is known, for example, that selected HIAG members were specifically recruited to form a "shuttle service" for Stille Hilfe, and HIAG personnel also reportedly made use of contacts with ODESSA and Spinne in order to keep in touch with ex-SS men overseas.[86] In all likelihood, then, key Nazi activists like Skorzeny and Rudel attempted to penetrate HIAG, secretly manipulate its political activities, and utilize it as a legal "cover" for some of their own clandestine and illicit operations.

What is true of HIAG likewise applies, at least in part, to many of its European branches or sister organizations, which were established in Austria, Holland, Belgium, Denmark, Norway, Finland, and Spain. In order to strengthen this international network, the German parent group assigned "liaison men" to maintain regular contacts with its foreign counterparts. The HIAG affiliate in Austria, whose liaison man was Karl Gherbetz, was known as Kameradschaft IV (Fellowship IV). It was founded in 1957 by Dr. Felix Rinner, Kaltenbrunner's former chief of staff in the RSHA. Rinner was later succeeded by Anton Bergermayer, who was also the sales representative in Vienna for the Austrian Nationaldemokratische Partei's (National Democratic Party) publication, *Die Wochenzeitung*. The Kameradschaft IV group espoused a militant right-wing ideology, published a newsletter called *Die Kameradschaft*, and was linked to a number of far right and neo-Nazi organizations in Austria, including the paramilitary Kameradschaft Babenberg (Babenberg Fellowship), the Ulrichsberggemeinschaft (Ulrichsberg Community), the Verband Österreichischer Kameradschaften (Federation of Austrian Fellowships), Aktion Neue Rechte (ANR: New Right Action), and the Freiheitliche Partei Österreich (FPÖ: Austrian Freedom Party), as well as the German NPD and HIAG. Of particular interest here is the fact that Rinner allegedly worked together with Erich Kernmayer and former SS Standartenführer Pesendorfer in the clandestine Spinne network after the war, that members of the Salzburg branch of Kameradschaft IV later transported Skorzeny's remains from Spain to the Lehener Hof in their hometown for a ceremony before bringing it to Vienna for burial, and that Bergermayer presented Kernmayer with a silver medal of honor on the latter's seventieth birthday in order to thank him for his efforts to rehabilitate the honor of the Waffen-SS. It also appears that former SS men affiliated with Kameradschaft IV have periodically provided paramilitary training to young neo-Nazis.[87]

In the Netherlands, the HIAG branch was the association Hulp aan Invalide Oud-Oostfrontstrijders, Nabestaanden, [en] Politieke Gevangenen (HINAG: Help for Invalid Former East Front Fighters, Next of Kin, and Political Prisoners), many of whose members had earlier been in the "political" faction of the satirically named Stichting Oud Politieke Delinquenten (SOPD: Foundation for Former Political Delinquents), a broader association of Nazi sympathizers, collaborators, and East Front veterans. HINAG was founded on 27 April 1955, three weeks after the dissolution of the Nationaal Europese Sociale Beweging (NESB: National-European Social Movement), the Dutch branch of the (soon to be discussed) international Mouvement Social Européen/Europäische Sozialbewegung (MSE/ESB: European Social Movement). HIAG's official liaison man to HINAG was Heinz Mellinthin. The leading figures in the latter organization were Jan A. Wolthius and Paul van Tienen, who had been active in both the SOPD and the NESB, as well as practically every other neo-fascist group in early postwar Holland.[88]

In Belgium, the comparable group was the Sint-Maartensfonds (SMF: Saint Martin's Fund), which was established in 1953 to succeed the outlawed Vlaams Verbond van Oud-Oostfrontstrijders (Flemish Association of Former East Front Fighters). Peter de Vuyst was its HIAG-appointed liaison man. The SMF published the monthly *Berkenkruis*, whose animator was Toon van Overstraeten, and almost all of its sections were in Flanders, although after 1968 a Walloon section was created. The association established a social service fund and a search service, and maintained regular contacts with HIAG, as well as with groups of Flemish political refugees. Although the SMF claimed to eschew political action, it lent its electoral support to the rightist Volksunie (VU: People's Union) and *Berkenkruis* was filled with radical right and Nazi-inspired "social racist" perspectives. Moreover, some of the personnel associated with the SMF later became notorious for their right-extremist activities. One important member of the SMF who broke away in 1969 and formed a rival publication aimed at East Front veterans, Piet Peeters, went on to become a leader of the reconstituted version of the Vlaamse Militanten Orde (VMO: Flemish Militant Order), an active neo-fascist paramilitary group with extensive connections to international fascist circles. Another breakaway faction, upset over the presence of members who were not East Front veterans and over the irregular financing of the SMF's social service, formed a new group called the Hertog Jan Van Brabant (Duke John [I] of Brabant [a Belgian folk hero]), which had its own publication (*Periodiek Contact*) and its own youth group, the Jonge Wacht (Young Guard). In 1979, elements of the latter attended a conference held by the "new right" Groupement de Recherche et d'Études sur la Civilisation Européenne (GRECE: Research and Study Group for European Civilization) in Paris.[89]

In Denmark, the HIAG affiliate was the Dansk Frontkämpfer Forbund (Danish Front Fighters' Association). Over six thousand Danes had served in the Waffen-SS under Christian Frederick von Schalburg, who headed the Frikorps Danmarks (Free Corps Denmark) until his death in 1942, and many of the survivors were later found in the ranks of the Frontkämpfer Forbund. The latter worked closely with certain neo-fascists involved in paramilitary and terrorist activities, for example Konrad Melsen, a member of the Danish branch of the Stockholm-based neo-Nazi Nordiska Rikspartiet (NRP: Nordic Empire Party).[90] In Norway, HIAG's counterpart was the Hjelpeorganisasjonen for Krigsskadede (Aid Organization for War Wounded), which was composed of some of the eight thousand Norwegian veterans who had served in Waffen-SS units (like the "Norge" ski battalion and the "Nordland" division) and their supporters. Some members of the Hjelpeorganisasjonen later created the Institutt for Norsk Okkupasjonhistorie (Institute for Norwegian Occupation History) in Oslo, which glorified the Waffen-SS and sought to rehabilitate the memory of Vidkun Quisling. The Institutt was supported by *Folk og Land*, the monthly publication of Rolf Christiansen's neo-fascist Nordisk Front (Nordic Front), which itself regularly lauded Quisling and Knut Hamsun, another leading collaborator.[91] Franz Krause was HIAG's liaison man to both Denmark and Norway. In Finland, the HIAG branch was known as Veljesapu, and its HIAG liaison man was a certain Henrikson in Helsinki.[92] Further information about this group is practically non-existent in non-Finnish sources.

As for Spain, Patrice Chairoff mentions an "Association of Volunteers for the Crusade," which supposedly comprised members of the División Azul (Blue Division) who had fought on the Eastern Front and later in the SS. However, an association with this exact name does not appear in Spanish sources, so it is possible that either the División Azul veterans group or some other entity that formed part of José Antonio Girón's Confederación Nacional de Ex-Combatientes (National Federation of Former Soldiers) – an umbrella organization for anti-Republican Civil War and World War II veterans – was the HIAG affiliate in Spain.[93] On the other hand, it may be that the Spanish branch was made up of German or East European SS veterans who had taken refuge in Spain rather than native Spaniards. This was certainly true of the HIAG branches allegedly founded in Argentina, South Africa, and Australia.[94] Be that as it may, there is no doubt that certain members of this extensive HIAG network were in contact with a considerable array of international and local neo-fascist groups, even though it remains unclear how often they were involved in outright acts of subversion or terrorism.

The European Social Movement

It is now time to turn to some of the early postwar neo-fascist "internationals," transnational networks that made little or no attempt to disguise their pro-fascist or pro-Nazi sympathies. The initial impetus for re-establishing international fascist "fronts" came from the Movimento Sociale Italiano (MSI: Italian Social Movement), one of the largest and best organized neo-fascist electoral parties in Europe by the end of the 1940s. Certain elements within the MSI were assiduously working to establish contacts with former Nazi functionaries and neo-fascist groupings throughout Europe, and to this end they had founded the internationally oriented Centro Studi Europei (European Studies Center) in Trieste, which then began publishing the *Europa Unità* journal. In March 1950, a preliminary meeting was held in Rome between MSI representatives, British fascist leader Sir Oswald Mosley of the Union Movement, Falange observers from Spain, associates of Swiss neo-Nazi Guy Amaudruz, members of the Bruderschaft, and French collaborationist politicians like Georges Albertini and Guy Lemonnier. There it was decided to organize another gathering in the autumn, to which various far right European organizations would be invited to send delegates.[95]

Between 22 and 25 October 1950, this projected second meeting took place in the Italian capital, although it did so in the guise of a "youth conference" and under the formal auspices of the MSI's university student group, the Fronte Universitario di Azione Nazionale (FUAN: University Front for National Action). Several notorious fascists and collaborators who were soon to play a key role in the "internationalization" of postwar neo-fascism attended this meeting, including Per Engdahl, leader of the Nysvenska Rörelsen (NSR: New Swedish Movement); Maurice Bardèche of the Comité Français National (CNF: French National Committee); Erwin Vollenweider, a Swiss Nazi who later co-founded the Volkspartei der Schweiz/Parti Populaire Suisse (VPS/PPS: Swiss People's Party); Horia Sima of the Rumanian Garda de Fier (Iron Guard); and Karl-Heinz Priester, at that time a leader of the radical wing of the NPD. These veteran activists were also joined and encouraged by a number of idealistic youthful sympathizers, including a contingent of FUAN members, as well as by Benito Mussolini's youngest daughter, Anna Maria, and Pierre Péan of the French Cercle International de Relations Culturelles (International Circle for Cultural Relations).[96] At that meeting, the participants agreed to organize a major conference in southern Sweden the following spring, and in the process proceeded to lay the groundwork for the first openly pro-fascist international in the period after World War II.[97]

In May 1951, between sixty and one hundred delegates from all over Europe gathered at Malmö, Sweden, for three days. Among the participants were Swedes like Engdahl and his chief NSR lieutenants, including Bengt Olov Ljungberg and Yngve Nordborg; Frenchmen like Bardèche, René Binet, Odette Moreau, *Gringoire* editor Henri Bernard, and Henri Bonifacio, chairman of the Front d'Action Communautaire (Communitarian Action Front) and editor of *La Victoire*; Danes such as Arthur Kielsen of the Dansk Reform Bewegelse (Danish Reform Movement), *Faedrelandet* editor Frede Jordan, and Jens Kudsk; Norwegians like Franklin Knudsen and former Quisling associates Einar Jöntvedt and Hroar Hovden; Italians like MSI Deputy Secretary Arturo Michelini and FUAN activists Fabio Lonciari and Giuseppe Ciammarucconi; Mosley and some of his Union Movement comrades from England; Fritz Rössler (using the alias "Franz Richter") of the German DRP; the Swiss anti-Semite Theodor Fischer of the Verband Nationalsozialistischer Eidgenossen (Association of National Socialist Confederates); and the Belgian art historian Johann van Dyck, who represented the Vlaams Blok (VB: Flemish Bloc).[98] Their immediate practical goals were to rehabilitate the public image of fascism, devise an acceptable common program for all of the participating neo-fascist groups, determine an agreed-upon framework of action, and prepare a list of candidates for the upcoming elections that were planned – but later cancelled – for the European Parliament.[99] After deliberating, they formally gave birth to the Mouvement Social Européen/Europäische Soziale Bewegung (MSE/ESB: European Social Movement).

Engdahl was elected as the head of the MSE/ESB's governing "four-man council," which also originally included Bardèche, Priester, and moderate MSI leader Augusto De Marsanich. Later, this body was transformed into a "study commission," to which were appointed the same four council members, Ernesto Massi from the MSI's left wing, Manuel Ballesteros of Spain, Dr. Roland Timmel and Wilhelm Landig of Austria, Karel Dillen from Belgium, and Lieutenant Colonel Robert Gayre of Gayre and Nigg, a Scottish nobleman and Knight of Malta.[100] MSE/ESB activists then went about the business of establishing various national branches for their pan-European umbrella organization. These eventually included Priester's Deutsche Soziale Bewegung (DSB) for Germany, Engdahl's NSR for Sweden, the Comité National Français for France, Landig's Österreichische Soziale Bewegung (Austrian Social Movement) for Austria, the Nederlandse Sociale Beweging (Dutch Social Movement), successor of the Werkgemeenschap Europa in de Lage Landen [European Working Group in the Low Countries] for Holland, the Norsk Reform Bevaegelse (Norwegian Reform Movement) for Norway, the Dansk Reform Bewegelse for Denmark, the NESB for Flanders, the Mouvement Social pour les Provinces Romanes en Belgique (Social Movement for the Roman Provinces in Belgium) for Wallonia, and the Suomen Sociallinen Liike (SSL: Finnish Social Movement) for Finland. The MSI, in contrast, was only represented by individual members because the party leadership did not want to become officially entangled with a high-profile and potentially compromising international movement.[101] Finally, the MSE/ESB established contacts with over forty non-affiliated extreme right organizations, including representatives of the Falange, various groups of East European refugees, the Asociación Argentina-Europea under the direction of Kameradenwerk chief Rudel, and Edward A. Fleckenstein's minuscule New Jersey-based Voter's Alliance for Americans of German Ancestry. Despite this wide range of associations, the number of MSE/ESB activists in Western Europe never surpassed one thousand, and the organization laid no material foundations for the initiation of international action.[102]

What, then, was the new movement's political orientation? Like most postwar neo-fascist formations, it adopted a pan-European "third force" perspective. In practice, this meant advocating the formation of a federated, independent, and self-sufficient Europe freed from the domination of the two extra-European superpowers, the unification and rearmament of Germany, the establishment of a united European army under European command in place of the Atlantic Alliance, the integration of Spain into this projected European federation, and the creation of a new regime that would promote social justice throughout the continent.[103] That this regime would have had little in common with parliamentary democracy can be gleaned from the contemptuous dismissal of the latter by Engdahl: "democracy is that majority principle which holds that 51 idiots can get their way in relation to 49 others."[104] In addition to formulating these general propositions, at Malmö the MSE/ESB approved a 10-point manifesto that advocated the defense of Western culture against communism, the creation of a Europe-wide empire, the establishment of standardized salaries throughout the continent, the submission of all national military forces to a centralized command structure, the restriction of immigration to those who had already attained "a certain economic and cultural level," the election of government leaders every seven years by means of a plebiscite, the creation of a corporatist state which would regulate economic and social life, the promotion of "strong" men and women through education, the enlisting of the cooperation of all the "idealists" who had fought on opposite sides of the barricades during World War II, and the spiritual regeneration of man, society, and the state.[105] Aside from its characteristic Nation Europa elements, this somewhat vague manifesto reflected the ideals of Mussolini or Salazar far more than it did those of Hitler.

Given the intention of the MSE/ESB to field candidates in the forthcoming elections for the European Parliament, it is not surprising that its programmatic statements were specifically moderated in order to attract a measure of popular support. To this end, controversial themes that could be expected to alienate the general European public were intentionally downplayed. The leaders of the new movement not only refused to invoke Mussolini and Hitler as their spiritual forefathers, but also sought to distance themselves from and partially disavow crucial aspects of the policies and criminal activities associated with the two dictators. As regards fascism and Nazism in general, Bardèche had this to say:

> The MSE believes that fascism and national-socialism belong to the past. It refuses to bring upon them a judgement of condemnation, but it also refuses to revive or imitate political forms that are today superseded. Our ideal is the achievement of social justice and the construction of a social order founded on work: our doctrine can make use of all the experiments of the past, but our ideal is a new one which is only inspired by the present.

On the subject of racism, the judgment was more severe but no less ambiguous:

> The MSE condemns theories of racial persecution, but it desires that each race should be reintegrated into its own historic territory.[106]

Most outside observers have interpreted these quasi-"respectable" public pronouncements as little more than cynical, opportunistic ploys designed to alleviate legitimate public concerns, a view that is to some extent confirmed by the less diplomatic phraseology employed by many of the same MSE/ESB spokesmen in overtly neo-fascist or neo-Nazi publications with relatively restricted circulations.[107]

It can be argued, however, that the intellectuals at the helm of this particular "international" were faced with an insoluble political dilemma. It may be that they genuinely sought to divorce themselves from certain elements of classical Nazism which they believed had brought disaster upon the fascist cause, most notably biological racism and the genocidal policies it fueled, but were prevented from doing so because they could not afford to completely alienate their cadres of intransigent followers. It is nevertheless noteworthy that they stubbornly refused to abandon their moderate public stance, despite the fact that this very stance played a key role in precipitating subsequent schisms and the ultimate collapse of their movement.[108]

Indeed, although the debut conference proved to be a great success on the symbolic level and thus fanned the initial hopes of many participants, the MSE/ESB soon lost the support of much of its own base. In a recent interview, Bardèche attributed the rapid decline of the organization to the failure of its component groups to develop as anticipated, the decision to cancel the elections for the European Parliament, which vitiated its electoral strategy, and the repressive actions and surveillance to which its members were subjected in various European states.[109] These factors may well have played some peripheral role in the process, but it seems clear that the essential reasons for the failure of the MSE/ESB lay elsewhere. One problem was that not all the members were happy with the authority assumed by the four-man council, which in theory had the ability to override opposition within the national sections. Another had to do with the usual personality conflicts and petty bickering among would-be *Führers*, a constant feature of the postwar neo-fascist milieu. Still another had to do with the formally "democratic" and legalistic methods adopted by the organization, which provoked dissatisfaction among groups of youthful ultras who longed to engage in direct revolutionary action. But the chief problem, which quickly became intermingled with and served to exacerbate all the others, was an irreconcilable ideological dispute over racial matters.

As noted earlier, the leaders of the MSE/ESB purposely downplayed racism and anti-Semitism in their efforts to obtain a newfound respectability. These tactical compromises were bitterly opposed by radical neo-Nazi or "social racist" elements within the rank and file. So it was that a few months after the Malmö conference the racists, led by French neo-Nazi Binet and Swiss neo-Nazi Amaudruz, broke away from the parent organization and decided to form their own rival "international," one that gave explicit priority to racial matters. Thus was born the Nouvelle Ordre Européen/Europäische Neu-Ordnung (NOE/ENO: New European Order), which soon completely overshadowed the MSE/ESB in practical importance.[110] With the passage of time, more and more ultras affiliated with the latter's component groups, who had previously had no qualms about using the parent body as a cover for their own anti-democratic plotting, became disillusioned with the legalistic and moderate approach adopted by Engdahl and Bardèche. After failing to radicalize the organization from within, these hotheads then followed the earlier schismatics out of the MSE/ESB and into more radical, activist-oriented international formations like the NOE/ENO, the Europäische Verbindungstelle (EVS: European Liaison Office), and Jeune Europe (Young Europe).

Although the MSE/ESB was increasingly riven by factional infighting, the movement did not immediately disappear. For several years it sought to recover from a succession of schisms and regain its earlier organizational influence. It continued the process of consolidating and coordinating the activities of its national branches, extended its network of international contacts further afield, and organized several international conferences in the wake of the successful Malmö gathering. Existing accounts provide contradictory information about the exact number and location of these conferences, but the last MSE/ESB gathering was held in Malmö in 1958. Despite the fact that it attracted five hundred attendees, an overtly racist speech by Landig – which was thence harshly criticized by Bardèche in *Défense de l'Occident* – brought the underlying tensions between the remnants of the movement to a head. Two years later Priester made strenuous efforts to organize a new conference in Wiesbaden, but his death in April 1960 doomed that project, and with it the fate of the MSE/ESB.[111] What, then, of its rivals and successors?

New European Order

In September 1951, a mere four months after the close of the Malmö conference, Amaudruz and Binet presided over an international gathering of unrepentant Nazis and neo-Nazis in Zurich. In the course of this three-day conference, which was ostensibly a meeting of the Fourth Plenary Session of the so-called national pioneers, the groundwork for a new fascist "international" was laid. Among the prominent attendees, other than Amaudruz and Binet, were a certain Berti from the Centro Studi Europei in Trieste, Vollenweider from the Volkspartei der Schweiz/Parti Populaire Suisse, and Fritz Rössler from the German SRP. A delegation from Portugal arrived to "observe" the proceedings, and messages of solidarity were sent to the participants by militants from Belgium (Wallonia), Austria, Norway, Ireland, and England.[112] At the conference, the various delegates worked to establish a rudimentary organizational structure and hammer out an ideological manifesto, and in the end both differed significantly from the approaches adopted by the MSE/ESB. Amaudruz was elected secretary general of the organization, and several "adjunct secretaries" responsible for different language regions were appointed to assist him, including former Belgian SS man Jean-Robert Debbaudt, ex-SS man Jean Baumann, and several Italians. Unlike the MSE/ESB, however, the NOE/ENO made no attempt to set up its own national sections in different countries. Because new organizations of this type could be viewed as unwelcome rivals by existing neo-Nazi groups in each nation, the leaders of the new international decided to establish close working relationships with the latter, which later chose "national correspondents" to serve as liaisons to the loosely structured parent body. By the early 1960s, these liaison men included Debbaudt in Belgium, Baumann in Germany, Van Tienen in the Netherlands, Clementi in France, Giuseppe ("Pino") Rauti in Italy, and Zarco Moniz Ferreira in Portugal.[113]

From an ideological point of view, the chief element in the NOE/ENO's program was an explicit and pronounced emphasis on biological racism. This is hardly surprising, given the views of Amaudruz and Binet, its two main theorists. Amaudruz was born in Lausanne in 1920 and later became both a professor of languages and the personal adjutant of Colonel Arthur Fonjallaz, an admirer of Mussolini's who had founded the Schweizerische Faschistische Bewegung (Swiss Fascist Movement) in 1933. However, Amaudruz himself was not so much an enthusiast of Italian fascism as a racial extremist and an admirer of Nazism, and after the war he actively propagated "social racist" doctrines in a series of publications.[114] Binet, whom his rival Bardèche later described as a "fascist of the puritan type," was born in Saint-Nazaire in 1914. He had been a militant in communist (Jeunesses Communistes [Young Communists]) and Trotskyist (Groupes d'Action Révolutionnaire [Revolutionary Action Groups]) circles during his youth, but between 1934 and 1939 he developed a bitter hostility toward both the Jews and the Soviet Union. After joining the French army and being captured by the Germans during the 1940 campaign, he voluntarily entered the ranks of the French 33rd SS "Charlemagne" Panzergrenadier Division. When the war ended, he was among the first of the diehards to form new fascist parties and publications, and even found the time to write three booklets outlining his biological racist viewpoints.[115] These men helped to draft the ideological pronouncements of the NOE/ENO, which were codified in the so-called Zurich Declaration and the Social-Racist Manifesto that emerged in the wake of the organization's first congress.

An examination of the last two documents reveals that "defense of the race" was the central element in the NOE/ENO's platform. It occupied pride of place in the 1951 "Declaration," where it was discussed prior to the other announced goals of the organization, "social justice" and "European unity."[116] Moreover, the preface of the "manifesto" began by insisting upon the fundamental importance of the racial struggle, which underlay all human conflict. Blood was viewed as a "primordial phenomenon" that not only served to link human communities "long before historical states," but also lay at the root of all civilizations.[117] Because "Aryans," who were glorified as the "creators of all culture" and the "builders of all civilization,"[118] were locked in an unceasing life-or-death racial struggle with other, more numerous racial groups, it was necessary for a new European counter-elite to launch a "racial revolution" against the existing "plutodemocratic" regimes whose servile leaders were promoting racial suicide. The goal was to replace these decadent regimes with strong, independent "national worker's states" that would join together in a pan-European federation and adopt an explicitly "biological politics" in order to restore the health of the Aryan racial community. Among other things, this latter would include the regulation of marriages between Europeans and non-whites, the promotion of general population growth, the prevention of interbreeding between mental or physical defectives and healthy specimens, the repatriation of non-white foreigners, the semi-segregation of resident "whites" who belonged to degenerate interbred groups (such as Jews and Turco-Tatars), and the application of various "scientific" techniques to increase the overall quality of Aryan racial stock.[119] Although there were some noteworthy differences, such as the inclusion of Slavs as an authentic branch of the Aryan race, this portion of the NOE/ENO's program nonetheless owed much to Hitler's race-based social Darwinist views.

All other social racist policies grew directly out of this overwhelming concern for the achievement of racial purity and the establishment of Aryan dominance within the confines of Europe, if not beyond. On the geopolitical plane, it led to the adoption of a militant "third force" perspective, in which a united and racially regenerated Europe would oppose the imperialistic designs of both the "Stalinist Mongol state" and "negroid" or "Judeo-American" capitalism.[120] Therefore, the NOE/ENO not only advocated the repudiation of the Atlantic Alliance, the overthrow of the pseudo-democratic regimes that were subservient to the interests of the Americans and Russians, and the creation of an independent and fully armed pan-European confederation that could serve as a powerful counterweight to the two "materialist" superpowers, but also – somewhat paradoxically – an alliance between this confederation and non-Aryan peoples of the Near East, the Indies, and South America who sought to free themselves from U.S. and Soviet domination.[121] In a bizarre effort to try and justify this latter policy, Amaudruz claimed that

> the hierarchy of races can only be founded on their comparison and consequently on the respect for the peculiarities and the traditions of each. The re-establishment of a certain world equilibrium is only possible if one radically breaks with colonialism, [which is] founded solely on the exploitation of the colored races.[122]

However, the overall flavor of the NOE/ENO's geopolitical appeals is perhaps better captured by Binet's following pronouncements:

> Down with the Europe of Strasbourg, down with the Europe of the federalists, down with the Europe of the lackeys of Russian or American imperialism! . . . Liberate yourselves from the influence of Moscow and Washington! . . . Join with us to fight the Jewish capitalist, our exploiter, and his accomplice the Bolshevik, the Judaized instrument of a Jewish politics![123]

It is therefore clear that the "third force" view of these social racists was characterized by a pronounced biological emphasis.

The same was true of its proposed domestic policies. From the NOE/ENO's point of view, "social justice" meant permitting each individual to develop his capacities fully – as long as these were subordinated to and applied in the interests of the "racial community." The achievement of this goal mandated the formation of new societal elites based upon talent and service to that community rather than ascriptive social status or wealth, the preservation of private property insofar as it was acquired legitimately and not at the expense of the needs of the community, the joint participation of workers and managers in the management of economic production, the provision of jobs to every European who was willing and able to work, the maintenance of healthy working conditions, and the elevation of the cultural standards of every productive member of the community.[124] Although these tenets reflected the general fascist ideal of creating a harmonious and mutually beneficial form of organic class collaboration, one that in theory curbed both capitalist abuses and worker agitation, they were infused throughout with Nazi-style racial themes. These latter were exemplified by Binet's emphasis on the organization of an authoritarian party that would serve as the "vanguard or general staff" of the race, the systematic inculcation of racist and socialist values, and the previously noted measures designed to preserve or restore racial purity and health. The ultimate goal was the creation of a "racist and socialist society" throughout Europe that would be capable of successfully waging the never-ending struggle with other races.[125] It was this brutal racial struggle, rather than the Marxist class struggle or the egocentric individualism promoted by capitalism, that was truly decisive. As Amaudruz put it, the "highest imperative is that of the race . . . not the current corrupt and degenerate race, but [the race] which we carry in our hearts and will forge in the course of struggle."[126]

These relatively crude biopolitical themes, which reflected efforts by the NOE/ENO's chief theorists to adjust earlier Nazi concepts to the far less propitious conditions that existed in a bipolar postwar world, nonetheless appealed to successive generations of neo-Nazi activists. That this was the case, at least on a symbolic level, is demonstrated by the organization's subsequent development and long-term survival. Despite being frequently subjected to political and legal harassment by various European governments, which resulted in several of its meetings being banned and some of its activists being jailed, it nevertheless held periodic meetings of its "technical committee" and sponsored congresses every other year until the later decades of the twentieth century. These were usually organized without fanfare, if not under "cover," and were only open to invited members because the organization achieved a certain level of notoriety and had begun to attract the sustained attention of both the authorities and private "anti-fascist" groups.

The NOE/ENO also created a series of less successful and relatively transitory satellite organizations that it vainly hoped would provide a rallying point for "third force" activists throughout Europe. Among these were the aforementioned EVS, which was founded in January 1953 after Binet provoked a schism within the CNF. Once Bardèche and his more moderate followers had been driven out of the CNF, which was not a single organization but rather an umbrella outfit that encompassed a plethora of far right French groups, Binet and Amaudruz sought to establish the EVS as a new coordinating body for "social racists" dissatisfied with the pusillanimity of the MSE/ESB. The EVS held its own conferences between 1953 and 1955, which did in fact succeed in attracting the support of several groups that had previously been affiliated with the Malmö international, including the CNF itself, the Mouvement Révolutionnaire Fasciste Belge (the Belgian Fascist Revolutionary Movement, a renamed version of the Mouvement Social Belge), and Vollenweider's VPS/PPS. But an irreconcilable dispute over the Alto Adige/Süd Tirol conflict, in which the Italian and French groups opposed the German and Austrian groups, led to the dissolution of the organization in 1955.[127] Still another NOE/ENO project was the Junge Europäische Legion (JEL: Young European Legion), established in 1958, which sought to unite nationalist youth groups throughout western

Europe in the struggle against communism and Americanism, but this particular initiative failed to attract widespread support and soon died with a whimper.[128] Finally, the neo-Nazi international founded a "think tank" and publishing house in Montreal, the Institut Supérieur des Sciences Psychosomatiques, Biologiques et Raciales (Higher Institute of Psychosomatic, Biological, and Racial Sciences). This organization, which was headed by Dr. Jacques Baugé-Prévost, specialized in publishing "scientific racist" treatises by the Count Joseph Arthur de Gobineau, Houston Stewart Chamberlain, Alfred Rosenberg, Georges Vacher de Lapouge, and French collaborator Father Georges Montandon, as well as the works by Binet and Amaudruz.[129]

The real importance of the NOE/ENO did not lie within its own initiatives or organizational structure, however. Instead, it served as a convenient "umbrella" under which extremists affiliated with paramilitary groups from various nations could meet to plot subversive, violent actions aimed at undermining democratic regimes and eradicating their political opponents. As will become clearer, many leading NOE/ENO officers or "correspondants" were themselves members of such extremist groups, including Amaudruz, Rauti, and Moniz Ferreira. Three examples of this sort of secret operational planning can be used to illustrate what was in all probability a far more widespread practice. In March 1967, at the ninth NOE/ENO meeting held just outside Milan, there was open talk of instigating a military coup in Italy.[130] In April 1969, at the tenth NOE/ENO Congress in Barcelona, Ordine Nuovo (New Order) representatives advocated the operational unification (*unione operante*) of European national-revolutionary groups and discussed subversive strategies with pro-Ustaša Croatian exiles.[131] And in March 1975, at an international neo-fascist meeting in Lyon attended by Amaudruz and representatives of Ordine Nuovo, Avanguardia Nazionale (National Vangaurd), and Lotta di Popolo (People's Struggle), a discussion about the tangible measures to be taken in response to a recent crackdown on right-wing ultras by the Italian authorities took place.[132] This sort of practical plotting appears all the more ominous, given the fact that NOE/ENO-linked circles in Italy were directly involved in the "strategy of tension" and the likelihood that its supposedly secret gatherings were riddled with infiltrators manipulated by various Western secret services.[133] The alleged involvement of Amaudruz, François Genoud, Bauverd, and Hubert de Bergard in arms trafficking, whether on behalf of the Algerian FLN, South Tyrolean terrorists, or other parties, should also be noted in this context.[134] Thus, even if the NOE/ENO's earlier notoriety was in fact disproportionate to its "skeletal forces," it would be unwise to view it as an insignificant network made up entirely of harmless fascist nostalgics until further research has been conducted on these lesser-known clandestine dimensions of its activities.[135]

Young Europe and its offshoots

Perhaps even more important in this regard was Jeune Europe (JE), an international neo-fascist network created by Belgian optician Jean-François Thiriart, one of the most interesting and intriguing figures associated with the postwar radical right. He began his political activism before the war in liberal left circles, specifically the Jeune Garde Socialiste (Young Socialist Guard), but later embraced nationalism and joined the rightist Légion Nationale (National Legion). During World War II, Thiriart – like so many other misguided left-leaning fascists – had become a member of the collaborationist Amis du Grand Reich Allemand (AGRA: Friends of the Great German Empire) organization, and as a result he was imprisoned and deprived of his civil rights for a number of years after 1945.[136] Later, seeking to capitalize politically on the growing resentment in Belgium over the threatened loss of its Congolese colony, he joined an ultra-nationalist pro-colonial group that had been founded by respected but patriotic anti-Nazis, the Comité d'Action et de Défense des Belges en Afrique (CADBA: Committee for Action and Defense of the Belgians in Africa). CADBA had been hastily organized in the wake of the 8 July 1960 mutiny of the colonial Force Publique (Public Force) in Leopoldville, the Congolese capital, and its headquarters were thence established at the "Tanganyka" café in Etterbeek. On 10 July it distributed thousands of leaflets to returning colonists at the Melsbroek aerodrome and sponsored a demonstration in support of military intervention together with an ad hoc Rassemblement pour la Défense de l'Oeuvre Belge au Congo (Rally for the Defense of the Belgian Project in the Congo), an offshoot of the Association des Fonctionnaires et Agents de la Colonie (Association of Colonial Officials and Agents). Eleven days later the first edition of CADBA's new *Belgique-Congo* publication appeared, which mixed an intransigent pro-colonial stance with an anti-parliamentary and Poujadist-style domestic program. This populist but essentially conservative program did not satisfy the political longings of Thiriart and his cadre of radical supporters, including Paul Teichmann and Émile Lecerf, who then decided to recreate the movement in their own image. After a brief period of infiltration and behind-the-scenes manipulation, Thiriart and his faction skillfully managed to assume control over CADBA, which they then renamed the Mouvement d'Action Civique (MAC: Civic Action Movement).[137]

This revamped organization soon took on a number of overtly "fascist" trappings and characteristics. For example, MAC-Jeunes (MAC Youth) sections composed of university and high school students were formed and then outfitted with blue shirts bearing Celtic cross armbands, a symbol made popular in the postwar era by the Mouvement Jeune Nation (Young Nation Movement) in France and then adopted by the OAS. Special MAC shock troops were also recruited, largely from right-wing members of various paratrooper associations, such as the official Amicale des Parachutistes (Paratrooper Association) for post–World War II military veterans and the "private" Club National de Parachutisme (National Parachutist Club), which also received funds from the Defense Ministry.[138] Weapons were illegally hoarded, karate training was provided to the MAC-Jeunes, and paramilitary training camps were set up. Given the movement's involvement in these bellicose activities, it should come as no surprise to learn that the MAC increasingly had recourse to direct action. Its militants carried out a series of dramatic and spectacular protest actions, including one against the June 1961 summit meeting in Vienna between John F. Kennedy and Nikita Khrushchev and several in support of the OAS and the Katangese succesionist movement of Moise Tshombé.[139] As a result of its initial demands for the retention of European colonies in Africa, the MAC received funds from the Union Minière du Haut-Katanga, Tshombé's forces, and later the OAS, along with unspecified "material assistance" from the Portuguese secret police.[140] The MAC's shock troops also engaged in a number of violent confrontations with left-wing demonstrators and counterdemonstrators, during one of which Thiriart himself was wounded. Finally, the MAC established links with a wide variety of right-wing groups, both nationally and internationally. In Belgium these included authoritarian corporatist groups like the Parti National Belge (Belgian National Party), ultra-royalist outfits like the Organisation de Salut Public (Public Salvation Organization), the ultra-conservative Rassemblement National (National Rally), the pro-colonial Amitiés Belgo-Katangaises (Belgian-Katangan Friendship), and Pierre Joly's subversive Jeunesses Nationales (National Youth).[141] Although the total number of hardcore MAC militants inside Belgium probably never exceeded 350, approximately half of whom were former colonists or paratroopers, the extensive support network and dynamic leadership of the MAC made it more influential than it would have otherwise been.

Indeed, it was the transnational contacts which the MAC fostered that accounted for the organization's larger historical significance, especially in connection with the transmission of unconventional warfare techniques to new generations of neo-fascist extremists in western and southern Europe. Among the many organizations with which the MAC was linked were the Mouvement Jeune Nation, the Étudiants Nationalistes Français (French Nationalist Students), Robert Martel's Mouvement Populaire du 13 Mai (MP13: May 13th Popular Movement)), and Jean-Marie Le Pen's Front National pour l'Algérie Français in France (National Front for Algeria in France), Mosley's Union Movement in Britain, the anti-communist John Birch Society in the United States, diverse groups of ultras in Spain and Portugal, and above all the Organisation de l'Armée Secrète.[142] Indeed, Thiriart went out of his way to forge intimate personal connections not only to influential Nazi activists like Otto Skorzeny and Hans-Ulrich Rudel, but also to the most radical elements of the pro-*Algérie Française* movement in France, including OAS leaders like Colonel Antoine Argoud, Captain Pierre Sergent, and Captain Jean-Marie Curutchet, and in the process turned the MAC into the "principal agent" of the OAS in Belgium.[143] The support which the MAC offered to the OAS took a number of different forms, ranging from the relatively innocuous to the truly subversive. Thus the MAC's journal *Nation-Belgique* – the successor to CADBA's *Belgique-Congo* – regularly published the OAS's bulletin, *Appel de la France*, as a supplement. On a more sinister note, it also published secret coded messages for clandestine OAS networks in Algeria.[144] Thiriart's friend Teichmann and Raoul Bauwens, one of the leaders of MAC-Jeunes, were apparently the operational chiefs of the MAC's OAS support networks. In February 1962, growing indications that the MAC was providing tangible assistance to the OAS prompted the Belgian authorities to authorize a police raid on the former's headquarters, its post office box, its bank accounts, and the homes of several of its leaders. The following month Thiriart and two other MAC members, Willy Godeau and Claude Dumont, were arrested along with an OAS agent named Maduché for stealing municipal employee identification cards from the town of Asse and passports from the Foreign Affairs Ministry. Although Thiriart was later released due to lack of evidence, the other three spent time in jail.[145]

Moreover, the MAC did not only aid the OAS directly, but also provided logistical aid to OAS fugitives through the intermediary of other organizations or fronts. One of these was the Centre d'Études et de Formation Contre-Révolutionnaire (Counter-Revolutionary Studies and Training Center), which had been founded at Tournai on 1 February 1961 by José Delplace and Jean-Claude Absil, two MAC activists. Not coincidentally, Tournai was one of the Belgian towns near the French border, along with Mons, Namur, and Profondeville, where the OAS had established bases and safe houses. The leaders of the center sought to establish a network of "religious" priories and claimed to be inspired by counterrevolutionary Catholic integralist doctrines, not only those of long dead traditionalists like Joseph de Maistre and current dictators like Salazar, but also the modern, totalistic, activist variants promoted by Frenchmen such as Georges Sauge of the Centre d'Études Supérieures de Psychologie Sociale (CESPS: Social Psychology Higher Studies Center) and Jean Ousset of Cité Catholique (Catholic City).[146] It later emerged that one of the main Belgian supporters of the Centre at Tournai was General Émile Janssens, former commander of the Congolese Force Publique and an open sympathizer of the OAS, that the center was used to smuggle OAS commandos across the Belgian border, or that on one occasion Delplace's girlfriend was stopped at the wheel of an automobile filled with OAS tracts printed in Belgium. Furthermore, according to leftist press accounts the Centre housed a radio transmitter that was used to send messages to OAS leader Joseph Ortiz in the Balearic Islands.[147]

Perhaps even more important was the role played by Pierre Joly's Jeunesses Nationales.[148] Joly began his political career as a member of the left-wing Étudiants Progressistes (Progressive Students) at the University of Liege in 1949 and 1950, but then quit and began actively collaborating with the Belgian branch of the Union Démocratique pour la Paix et la Liberté (Peace and Freedom Democratic Union) organization, an international CIA-funded anti-communist front created in Paris in March 1949.[149] In 1952, he founded a short-lived École Internationale de Cadres Anti-Communistes (International School for Anti-Communist Cadres) and published a pamphlet praising Franco and Salazar. Later that same year he appeared in Algiers right around the time of the notorious bazooka attack on General Raoul Salan. Five years later he published an anonymous treatise on counterrevolutionary warfare that synthesized the writings of some of the most influential *guerre révolutionnaire* specialists within the French Army, such as Commandant Jacques Hogard and Colonels Gabriel Bonnet, Charles Lacheroy, and Roger Trinquier, which soon became a sort of *vademecum* for right-wing subversives in Algeria and Europe.[150] In May 1958, he participated in the Algiers demonstration which precipitated the collapse of the Fourth Republic alongside Pierre Lagaillarde, a right-wing student activist and future leader of the OAS. He then worked closely with the Mouvement Populaire 13 (MP13: Popular Movement 13 [May], commemorating the

13 May 1958 military coup in Algeria), and became the Belgian spokesman for Joseph Ortiz upon his return home. Indeed, up until September 1961, Joly collected money for Ortiz using the Aide Mutuelle Européenne (European Mutual Aid) organization as a cover. Between 1960 and 1961, he helped sponsor and contributed to the monthly publication *Réac*, the organ of the Étudiants Nationales. His own Jeunesses Nationales organization was the first Belgian group to establish a close relation with French activists, and after the assassinations of FLN activist Akli Aïssou and pro-FLN professor René-Georges Laperches in Belgium by the so-called Main Rouge (Red Hand), a front group created by the French secret service that was used to carry out politically sensitive *opérations ponctuelles*, Joly's organization was suspected of having lent its support to the killers.[151] In January 1962, Joly and René Boussart were accused of sheltering General Salan in Liege, although this was never actually proven. Shortly thereafter, the MAC denounced Joly as a traitor to the OAS, a police informant, and a crook, but this did not prevent Teichmann from restoring and thence maintaining close personal relations with him.

Even so, Belgian journalist Serge Dumont is probably wrong to characterize the Jeunesses Nationales as little more than a convenient screen behind which the MAC carried out illegal or subversive actions.[152] What appears more likely is that Joly was seeking to manipulate various neo-fascist groups, including Thiriart's organization, on behalf of certain intelligence agencies or parallel security services. His earlier connection to the Paix et Liberté organization certainly suggests this, as do his links to figures such as Roger Cosyns-Verhaegen and Suzanne Labin. Cosyns-Verhaegen, who was in contact with Joly in 1960, was the owner of the Les Ours publishing house in Brussels, which he used as a vehicle to publish a series of studies on communist subversion and counterrevolutionary warfare doctrine. In the mid-1960s, he appeared as an editor of Thiriart's *Nation Européenne* publication, the organ of Jeune Europe's successor organization, and together with Thiriart and Gérard Bordes he organized an international "work camp" at Torices in Spain in January 1966, whose participants placed flowers on the grave of martyred Falange chief José Antonio Primo de Rivera. A few years later, Cosyns-Verhaegen became a regular contributor and technical advisor to the Centre de Défense National (Center for National Defence), a right-wing "think tank" funded by the Ligue Internationale de la Liberté (LIL: International Freedom League), the Belgian branch of the intelligence-linked World Anti-Communist League (WACL).[153] Moreover, due to his connections with the Étudiants Nationales through *Réac*, Joly inevitably came into contact with Labin, an indefatigable anti-communist propagandist who was one of the founders of the Ligue Internationale de la Liberté organization – which was also known as the Union pour la Défense des Peuples Opprimés (Union for the Defense of Oppressed Peoples) – and subsequently a leading LIL activist. She apparently served as the main liaison person between the latter and the Anti-Bolshevik Bloc of Nations (ABN), a key member of WACL that received funds from the CIA and other Western intelligence agencies.[154]

Yet despite this intensive pattern of political activism, all was not well with the MAC. Aside from being periodically subjected to harassment or crackdowns by the authorities, the movement was bitterly divided into a Belgian nationalist (*belgiciste*) faction and a pan-European "third force" faction. Thiriart was the animator and chief representative of the latter, and as time wore on he adopted an increasingly radical, left-leaning fascist position, largely due to the influence exerted by syndicalist Henri Moreau and René Dastier. As a result of these developments, the more conservative members of the MAC began drifting away and joining more moderate organizations like the Parti National Belge, which had long been denounced by the MAC for being too "soft." In April 1962, as if to symbolize his organization's ever-growing radicalism, Thiriart renamed it Jeune Europe (JE: Young Europe) and reorganized it into a clandestine network of localized communist-style cells.[155] One month earlier, he had met in Venice with leaders of the MSI, Adolf von Thadden of the German NPD, and Oswald Mosley of the Union Movment in an attempt to organize a continent-wide National Party of Europe (NPE), but this effort was quickly derailed because the leaders of the German and Italian parties clearly had no real intention of subordinating the autonomy of their own organizations to a larger entity under someone else's control.[156] In the meantime, Thiriart made contact with a number of smaller and more radical neo-fascist groups, as well as with famous World War II figures like Kameradenwerk chief Rudel, in an effort to enlist their support for the creation of local branches of JE in every European country. This effort met with considerable success, because JE soon founded branches in countries all over the world, including Jong Europa in Flanders, Jong Europa in Holland, Jovem Europa in Portugal, Joven Europa in Spain, Giovane Europa in Italy, Junges Europa in Austria, Junges Europa in Germany, Young Europe in Britain, Eurafrika in South Africa, Jeune Europe in Switzerland, Europan in Brazil, Unga Europa in Sweden, the exile Rumanian Europa Tanara, and Joven América groups in Argentina, Colombia, Uruguay, and Ecuador. It could be, however, that in some cases these foreign affiliates consisted of little more than a handful of individuals who had set up a post office box, as opposed to a *bona fide* branch with a well-organized structure.[157]

Ideologically, Thiriart was one of the first fascist leaders to attempt to jettison and replace the nostalgic Nazi-inspired concepts that served to rally so many neo-fascist extremists in the early postwar period. As early as August 1961, in an editorial he wrote for the MAC's weekly, *Nation-Belgique*, he declared that fascism had perished in 1945 and insisted that "the members of the MAC are not Fascists, if for no other reason because we have not the slightest desire to have any contact with a corpse, however skilfully it may have been embalmed."[158] But this was merely the opening salvo in a succession of increasingly radical and original assaults on conventional neo-fascist views, a developmental process that was uneven and not always consistent. Take, for example, the "Manifeste à la Nation Européenne," a document prepared by Thiriart and other would-be leaders of the National Party of Europe in the wake of the aforementioned 4 March 1962 meeting in Venice. Therein it was argued that the Frenchmen who were fighting to maintain control over Algeria were fighting on behalf of all Europeans, a standard right-wing view that clashed sharply with Thiriart's later expressions of sympathy for anti-colonialist struggles and "national liberation" movements. Nevertheless, some themes that appeared in this manifesto prefigured his subsequent ideological formulations, and undoubtedly reflected his own unique contribution. The document began with the now familiar "third force" slogan, "neither Moscow nor Washington," and went on to promote the establishment of a united "communitarian" Europe armed with its own nuclear weapons and capable of liberating eastern Europe from the grip of the "Bolshevik dictatorship." In contrast to the decadent, subservient Europe that then existed, a virile new Europe would "carry on the struggle against both Communist and American imperialism," replace "chattering and corrupt parliamentarianism" with a "direct, hierarchical, stable, and LIVING democracy," abolish the class struggle, and tolerate capitalism only it were "civic, disciplined and controlled by the nation."[159] Thiriart's advocacy of a Nation Europa, like that of Mosley and other, more far-sighted fascist leaders, was based upon the recognition that older, parochial forms of nationalism could only provide a "cardboard barrier" against Soviet and U.S. power in the post-1945 world.[160]

These increasingly frequent attacks on national chauvinism and Nazi-style racism, which reflected Thiriart's adoption of various left-leaning geopolitical and syndicalist concepts, helped to bring the underlying conflicts between different factions of JE to the surface. This process was exacerbated by other, more prosaic factors, such as the drying up of sources of external funding following the "loss" of Algeria, the bitter disagreements between different JE sections over the Alto Adige/Süd Tirol question, Thiriart's decision to run electoral candidates in 1964, and the growing personal friction between the vainglorious and authoritarian Thiriart and other leading JE figures like Teichmann. The result of all these stresses and strains was a series of expulsions and schisms that frittered away the numerical strength, internal cohesion, and overall influence of this activist "international." For example, the Flemish Jong Europa section was expelled by Thiriart in May 1963 for exhibiting "neo-Nazi" tendencies, prompting its leaders to create the rival Europafront (Europe Front) organization with some German and Austrian comrades. In November, former MAC-Jeunes leader Bauwens quit and went on to form the Belgian branch of the German Stahlhelm organization. In 1964 Teichmann, Moreau, and Lecerf broke away, together with the Fédération Général des Étudiants Européens (General Federation of European Students), JE's student wing, and thence established a succession of rival entities, including Révolution Européenne (European Revolution) and the Front National-Européen du Travail (National European Labor Front), which incorporated some of Thiriart's social and economic themes. That same year, in September, the racist and philo-German extreme right wing of JE in Wallonia was expelled. Thirteen months later Jean Van den Broeck, who was then serving as the head of JE's labor union, the Syndicat Communautaire Européen (European Communitarian Labor Union), quit and founded the Union des Syndicats Communautaires Européens (Confederation of European Communitarian Labor Unions).[161] These major breakaways were emblematic of a more diffuse process of fission that increasingly afflicted JE. Although this process severely undermined the organizational integrity and effectiveness of JE, it did not deter Thiriart from moving further and further to the left. This was reflected not only in a process of continued ideological radicalization, but also in a pattern of apparent tangible collusion with certain far left regimes and groups.

In October 1965, Thiriart dissolved JE and incorporated the rest of his loyal followers into a new organization, the Parti Communautaire Européen (PCE: European Communitarian Party). The PCE in turn gave birth to a new publication in January 1966, *La Nation Européenne*. But the key works delineating Thiriart's increasingly radical ideology were *Un empire de 400 millions d'hommes*, which offered an elaborate extension of many of the positions he had already set forth in the 1962 "manifesto," and *La grande nation*, a more concise version arranged in programmatic form.[162] The essential purpose of these works was to generate a new myth, in the Sorelian sense of the term, capable of galvanizing all those Europeans who felt frustrated by the prevailing weakness and humiliation of their own nations in relation to the two superpowers. Thiriart hoped to create a new European consciousness by promoting the revolutionary myth of a greater Europe united by its traditions, its culture, its history, its current circumstances, and above all its future destiny. His Europe had nothing in common with the Europe of the "conventional nationalists [who] are against Europe . . . [or] the democratic Europeanists [who] are for a Europe without nationalism" – it was "a Europe with a pan-European nationalism," one that ranged from Brest to Bucharest.[163] This would be a well-armed, powerful, and neutral Europe that would develop a mutually beneficial symbiotic relationship with Africa, an alliance with Latin American countries that were struggling against both "Yankee imperialism" and "communist subversion," a friendship with the Arab world on the basis of vaguely defined "parallel interests," a relationship of equality with the United States once Europe had been freed from "Yankee economic and military tutelage," and "neighborly" relations with the Soviet Union *after* the Red Army had withdrawn from eastern Europe and agreed to re-establish the frontiers of 1938.[164] Thiriart felt that Europe should be prepared to take any steps necessary to accomplish these grandiose schemes, even if it meant "allying itself with the Devil."[165] In the end, he had no qualms about urging an alliance with communist China so as to enable Europe to "settle accounts with America and its accomplices from Moscow."[166] This pro-Beijing and Third World orientation represented quite an innovation within neo-fascist circles at the time.

The internal institutional arrangements Thiriart envisioned for his Nation Europa were naturally geared toward achieving and maintaining these geopolitical aims. His proposed "communitarian" alternative evoked the standard "neither communism nor plutocracy" slogan and presented itself as a "third way" that would transcend the manifest shortcomings of those twin materialist evils. However, the creation of such an alternative depended upon a "radical transformation of [Europe's] political and social structure."[167] The first step would be the building of a European "combat party" with a "centralized, [highly] structured, and hierarchical" clandestine apparatus, which would foment, organize, and eventually lead a series of popular revolts all over Europe.[168] This revolutionary vanguard party would then form the nucleus of an authoritarian state ruled by an "authentic chief" with foresight, decisiveness, and charisma. Only such a powerful pan-European regime would be capable of protecting the new "national-communitarian" society, and once established it would embark upon its economic and social program.

This program was predicated upon the absolute subordination of economic activity to greater Europe's poltical aims. The scheme to be adopted was a corporatist structure characterized by class collaboration, private ownership of light or service industries, joint worker-owner management of the less important heavy industries, and direct government management of critical large-scale industries. Activities that would be forbidden included the exploitation of workers by bosses, strikes, the extraction of wealth for speculative rather than direct use, business interference in politics, collusion with foreign capitalists, and anything else that might weaken the state or the solidarity of the national community. Thiriart was insistent that the only way for nationally oriented socialists on the continent to avoid being dominated by U.S. multinationals was to create an autarchic and highly productive economic unit on a Europe-wide scale. In the wake of Yalta, he felt that it was no longer possible to build and sustain "true socialism" in smaller, traditional nation-states.[169] Finally, racism of all sorts was downplayed, although not entirely suppressed, in Thiriart's convoluted and grandiloquent schemes.[170]

The PCE carried the left-wing elements of this program to their logical conclusions, and its anti-Americanism began to overshadow even its anti-communist sentiments. One very important reflection of this was the establishment of tangible links between the group and the People's Republic of China. Thiriart had begun promoting the idea of a European alliance with communist China as a counterweight to U.S. and Soviet power even before the transformation of JE into the PCE,[171] but, perhaps taking to heart his own admonition that allying with the Devil would be preferable to remaining under the yoke of American and Soviet imperialism, he began trying to translate these abstract geopolitical notions into reality. In 1966, after making contact with the Beijing government through the intermediary of the Rumanian Departamentul de Informatii Externe (DIE: External Intelligence Department), Thiriart traveled to Bucharest to meet with Zhou Enlai. Shortly thereafter, he allegedly began exchanging information about the Supreme Headquarters, Allied Powers Europe (SHAPE), and NATO installations in Belgium with Yang Xiaonong, chief of the Parisian bureau of the Xinhua news agency, and Wang Yujiang in Brussels, both of whom were operatives of the Chinese secret service (Tewu).[172] Needless to say, this created consternation among many of his followers, a growing number of whom decided to abandon the movement. In late 1968 the PCE was officially dissolved, after which Thiriart seems to have withdrawn from politics altogether for a number of years.

In the early 1980s he resurfaced, without having tempered his iconoclastic approaches to political action in the intervening years. During this period, Thiriart began openly praising features of the Soviet Union. In the July 1984 issue of *Conscience Européenne*, a new Thiriart-inspired publication, he expressed his preference for the Komitet Gosudarst'vennoi Bezopasnosti (KGB) over both the Catholic Church and Lech Walesa of Solidarnosc, and then went on to make these equally provocative remarks:

> The USSR displays other very positive facets: its centralism, its size, its totalitarianism [and] its army . . . If Moscow wanted to create a Russian Europe, I would be first to recommend resistance to the occupier. [But if] Moscow wanted to build a European Europe, I would promote total collaboration with the Russian venture. In that case I would be the first to place a red star on my helmet. A Soviet Europe, yes, without hesitation . . . We have the temperament of Stalinists, but of Stalinists who are familiar with Hobbes, Machiavelli, and Pareto. We want to open up the way for a new Stalin. A European Stalin.[173]

Besides revealing that Thiriart was foolishly repeating the very same errors he had earlier committed when he had naïvely supported the creation of a united, Nazi-dominated Europe, these statements represented a complete reversal of his previous views about the optimum pattern of geopolitical alliances for his beloved Nation Europa. Taking cognizance of the immense, geometrically expanding population of communist China, as well as its opportunistic improvement of relations with the United States, he now argued that Europe needed to ally with the Soviet Union in order to free itself from continued American domination and defend itself against the Asian masses that ultimately threatened to swamp the continent's ethnic integrity. His new European empire would extend from Reykjavik to Vladivostok, not merely from Brest to Bucharest![174]

Even more interestingly, he began to express open solidarity with left-wing terrorist groups, in particular the Belgian Cellules Communistes Combattantes (CCC: Fighting Communist Cells), whose chief fault, in his eyes, lay in the fact that they had initiated armed struggle against NATO and its American backers prematurely. He also chided them for their lack of a pan-European ideology and their failure to adopt a Leninist-style method for seizing power. Nor did he refrain from lauding the Libya of Mu'ammar al-Qadhdhāfī and other anti-American regimes in the Third World.[175] French journalist René Monzat has expressed doubts about whether these attempts to display solidarity and promote joint actions with the far left were genuine. He suggests that the apparent lack of interest displayed by Western security agencies in Thiriart's recent pro-communist and anti-Atlantic activities would be inexplicable – unless he was working as some sort of double agent on their behalf.[176] Such neglect is all the more peculiar given Thiriart's earlier "collusion" with communist Chinese intelligence operatives and his subsequently acknowledged links with certain East Bloc secret services, especially because it contrasted markedly with the attention the Belgian police had paid to the MAC's earlier activities in support of the OAS. There are thus some legitimate grounds for suspicion, and if it could be shown that Thiriart's espousal of leftist ideas and establishment of links to leftist groups or regimes represented an attempt to infiltrate that milieu and launch provocations, a large portion of the history of neo-fascism and postwar right-wing terrorism might have to be rewritten.

However, this sinister interpretation fails to give sufficient weight to the flowering of genuine left-leaning tendencies within a number of radical neo-fascist groups in the late 1960s and 1970s. Although this development occurred during the very same period in which Western intelligence agencies began to make extensive use of right-wing *agents provocateurs*, especially in the period after the dramatic events of 1968, these parallel trends need to be separated analytically and distinguished from each other in order to grasp the complexity of the history of neo-fascism in that era. It is all too easy to conflate or confound the two processes, particularly in the absence of clear evidence, an error that is even easier to commit because in practice the former development greatly facilitated the success of the latter. In other words, the fact that a number of neo-fascist grouplets existed whose political views had honestly been influenced by some of the ideas associated with the New Left made it easier for right-wing provocateurs working for the state to penetrate and manipulate both left fascist groups and actual left-wing organizations.[177] It would be hasty, then, to claim that the promotion of certain leftist notions by the leaders of Jeune Europe and the PCE was not genuine, especially because their stubborn adherence to these notions precipitated major internal divisions, schisms, and defections that seriously weakened their own organizations. Indeed, to argue that Thiriart had been serving as a double agent or provocateur all along would be to deny that he was a genuine iconoclast and a pioneer in the postwar ideological development of fascism, an assessment that is certainly not warranted given the current state of the evidence.

There can be no doubt at all, however, that JE played a crucial role as an intermediary in the process of transmitting various unconventional warfare techniques, specifically French counterinsurgency doctrines and methods, to neo-fascist activists throughout the European continent. To some extent this was an organic process that stemmed naturally from two interrelated characteristics of the organizations under Thiriart's control. On the one hand, the MAC had developed close operational linkages with various clandestine OAS networks, especially those operating in Europe. On the other, JE served as the chief organizational hub around which radical neo-fascist activists from all over the world gravitated during the mid-1960s. Some cross-fertilization of ideas and techniques between disaffected military personnel and their right-wing civilian supporters was therefore probably inevitable. But it was the willingness of Thiriart to experiment with novel left-leaning concepts, coupled with his enthusiasm for aspects of the revolutionary methods employed by experts such as Lenin, Hitler, Mao, and the OAS, which really accounted for Jeune Europe's importance in connection with the subsequent evolution of right-wing subversion and terrorism. Had he not argued, at one point, that "plastic explosives will be the megaphone of anti-Communism in the latter half of the twentieth century"?[178] Indeed, in addition to serving as a cadre training school for militants who exerted an enormous influence on the later development of almost every Belgian far right organization, it was precisely this predilection for clandestine operations that gave Jeune Europe its historical significance and differentiated it from the largely symbolic, talk-oriented "internationals" like the MSE/ESB. In this sense JE was a sort of forerunner of Aginter Presse, the front organization that functioned as a key transmission belt for *guerre révolutionnaire* techniques to Italian extremists who were later implicated directly in the "strategy of tension."

Notes

1 Scott Lucas, "Mobilizing Culture: The State-Private Network and the CIA in the Early Cold War," in *War and Cold War in American Foreign Policy, 1942–1962*, ed. by Dale Carter (New York: Palgrave Macmillan, 2002), pp. 83–107.
2 Aldo Giannuli, *Relazione di perizia*, Tribunale di Milano, Ufficio Istruzione, Procedimento penale n. 2/92F, 12 marzo 1997 [hereinafter Giannuli, *Relazione 12 III 97*], p. 24. Some recent academic studies have also helped to shed further light on these diverse but intersecting networks, e.g., Margaret Power and Martin Durham, eds., *New Perspectives on the Transnational Right* (New York: Palgrave Macmillan, 2010); Luc van Dongen, Stéphanie Roulin, and Giles Scott-Smith, eds., *Transnational Anti-Communism and the Cold War: Agents, Activities and Networks* (New York: Palgrave Macmillan, 2014); and Andrea Mammone, *Transnational Neofascism in France and Italy* (New York: Cambridge University, 2015).
3 Compare the astute observations of neo-fascist theorist Maurice Bardèche, *Qu'est-ce que le fascisme?* (Paris: Sept Couleurs, 1961), pp. 97–8, 101.
4 For the seeming paradox between these two characteristics of European neo-fascism, see Joseph Algazy, *La tentation néo-fasciste en France, 1944–1965* (Paris: Fayard, 1984), pp. 289–91.
5 See *Neofascismo in Europa* (Milan: La Pietra, 1974), p. 188.
6 See, for example, the speech made by former Hitler Jugend member Karl-Heinz Priester at an October 1950 conference of veteran fascist and neo-fascist activists in Rome, quoted in the magisterial work by Kurt P. Tauber, *Beyond Eagle and Swastika: German Nationalism since 1945* (Middletown, CT: Wesleyan University, 1967), volume 1, pp. 208–9.
7 Algazy, *Tentation néo-fasciste en France*, pp. 290–1.
8 Tauber, *Beyond Eagle and Swastika*, volume 1, pp. 206–7.
9 Cited in Angelo Del Boca and Mario Giovana, *Fascism Today: A World Survey* (New York: Pantheon, 1969), p. 59. This is an English translation of *I figli del sole*.
10 Tauber, *Beyond Eagle and Swastika*, volume 1, p. 209. For more on the "conservative revolutionaries," see Armin Mohler, *Die Konservative Revolution in Deutschland, 1918–1932: Ein Handbuch* (Darmstadt: Wissenschaftliche, 1972); Louis Dupeux, *La révolution conservatrice allemagne sur la république de Weimar* (Paris: Kimé, 1992); Stefan Breuer, *Anatomie der Konservativen Revolution* (Darmstadt: Wissenschaftliche, 1995); Roger Woods, *The Conservative Revolution in the Weimar Republic* (New York: St. Martin's, 1996); Kurt Sontheimer, *Antidemokratisches Denken in der Weimarer Republik* (Munich: dtv, 2000 [1962]); and Martin Travers, *Critics of Modernity: The Literature of the Conservative Revolution in Germany, 1890-1933* (New York: Peter Lang, 2001). For its influence on the later German right, see Armin Pfahl-Traughber, *Konservative Revolution und Neue Rechte. Rechtsextremistische Intellektuelle gegen den demokratischen Verfassungsstaat* (Opladen: Leske & Budrich, 1998).
11 Compare Gaddi, *Neofascismo in Europa*, p. 188; and Michael A. Ledeen, *Universal Fascism: The Theory and Practice of the Fascist International, 1928–1936* (New York: Fertig, 1972).
12 For more on Nazi ideas about Europe, see Paul Kluke, "Nationalsozialistische Europaideologie," *Vierteljahrshefte für Zeitgeschichte* 3:3 (July 1955), pp. 240–75; and Hans-Dietrich Loock, "Zur 'Grossgermanischen Politik' des Dritten Reiches," *Vierteljahrshefte für Zeitgeschichte* 8:1 (January 1960), pp. 37–63. Compare Hitler's revealing remarks about the "meaninglessness" of the conception of the nation, quoted in Herman Rauschning's book, *The Voice of Destruction* (New York: Putnam, 1940), p. 231.
13 See, for example, Marcel Déat's hopeful but naïve remarks shortly after the crushing defeat of the French army in 1940:

> We [French fascists] are not going to construct a new kind of France; we are going to build up a France which will be integrated into the new Europe and will have its own important and legitimate role . . . Is not the Nazi *Weltanschauung* anti-capitalist, anticlerical and Socialist?

Cited by Jean Plumyène and Raymond Lasierra, *Les fascismes français, 1923–1963* (Paris: Seuil, 1963), p. 155. For other such examples, see Del Boca and Giovana, *Fascism Today*, pp. 56–61. In marked contrast, among conservatives and right-wingers,

> rambling talk of a "new order" had never aroused much enthusiasm, or even qualified approval. For them the "new order" was just a barricade against the Communists, a form of political authoritarianism under which the iron fist of the police state would crush all opposition and popular demands, and at the same time safeguard the capitalist system and the hegemony of the traditional castes.

See ibid., p. 62.

14 See, in particular, Giorgio Galli, *La crisi italiana e la destra internazionale* (Milan: Mondadori, 1974), p. 60. There were also "national Bolshevik" and "nationalist neutralist" groups in postwar Germany that promoted an alliance *with* the Soviet Union against the West, but these were less numerous – although not necessarily less significant from an operational point of view. For the latter, see especially Tauber, *Beyond Eagle and Swastika*, volume 1, pp. 147–203. See also Martin A. Lee, *The Beast Reawakens: Fascism's Resurgence from Hitler's Spymasters to Today's Neo-Nazi Groups and Right-Wing Extremists* (New York: Routledge, 2000), pp. 3–5, 47–51, 58, 73–5, 82–4, 127–8, 141–3, 193–5, 229–31, 259–61, 385–6, who devotes considerable space to one of the most high-profile and important "nationalist neutralists," former Hitler bodyguard Otto Ernst Remer.

15 See, for example, Kurt Riess, *The Nazis Go Underground* (New York: Doubleday, 1944). For an interesting case study of the propagandistic manipulation of public fears about possible postwar Nazi subversion in Latin America, see Ronald C. Newton, *The 'Nazi Menace' in Argentina, 1931–1947* (Stanford: Stanford University, 1992), especially pp. 343–59.

16 The Maison Rouge meeting was first publicized by postwar Nazi-hunter Simon Wiesenthal, a former concentration camp inmate who was employed for several months by U.S. Army intelligence and the Office of Strategic Services (OSS) following his liberation in 1945. Shortly thereafter, he set up his famous Documentationszentrum (Information Center) in Austria – first in Linz and then in Vienna – for the express purpose of gathering information about Nazi crimes and, in the process, helping to bring escaped war criminals to justice. See his *The Murderers among Us: The Simon Wiesenthal Memoirs*, ed. by Joseph Wechsberg (New York: McGraw Hill, 1967), pp. 83–7; and Simon Wiesenthal, *Justice Not Vengeance* (London: Weidenfeld and Nicolson, 1989), pp. 50–1. According to Wiesenthal, these minutes were among a packet of documents given to him in 1946 by an American officer, who told him they had been confiscated from a Colonel Keitel at the SS internment camp at Ebensee, near Bad Ischl. See the latter work, p. 50. It should be pointed out, however, that certain well-informed journalists have long entertained suspicions about Wiesenthal's real agenda and honesty, and a recent book has openly called his credibility into account in connection with the Kurt Waldheim scandal and other matters. See Eli M. Rosenbaum with William Hoffer, *Betrayal: The Untold Story of the Kurt Waldheim Investigation and Cover-Up* (New York: St. Martin's, 1993), pp. 46–8, 92–4, 144–9, 298–313, 371–2. Compare Wiesenthal's own account of the Waldheim case in *Justice Not Vengeance*, pp. 310–22.

17 Among the attendees, according to Wiesenthal, were coal baron Emil Kirdorf, steel magnate Fritz Thyssen, Georg von Schnitzler of I. G. Farben, Gustav Krupp von Bohlen und Halbach, and Cologne banker Kurt von Schroeder. He notes, not without irony, that these men were all among the first businessmen who had turned to Hitler in 1933. See Wiesenthal, *Justice Not Vengeance*, p. 50. Therein he also quotes a statement allegedly made by the chairman of the conference:

The battle of France is lost for Germany; henceforth German industry must adjust to the fact that the war can no longer be won and that, in consequence, steps have to be taken for a postwar economic campaign. To this end every industrialist must seek and establish contact and links with foreign firms; but each one for himself and without attracting suspicion to himself. In the sphere of financial policy, moreover, the ground will have to be prepared for taking up large-scale credits after the war. On top of all this, however, industrialists must also be prepared to finance the party, which will be compelled to go underground.

See ibid. Compare also the recent interviews conducted with Wiesenthal by Maria Sporrer and Herbert Steiner, eds., *Simon Wiesenthal: Ein unbequemer Zeitgenosse* (Vienna: Orac, 1992), pp. 77–8, 81–5. His list of participants does not entirely conform to that found in a recently declassified 7 November 1944 intelligence report prepared by the intelligence section of Supreme Headquarters, Allied Expeditionary Force (SHAEF), which makes no mention of bankers, Kirdorf, or representatives from Thyssen or I. G. Farben, much less Kaltenbrunner and other top SS leaders. Yet this report (#RW-Pa 128), which was based on the testimony of a "reliable" agent of the French Army's 2nd (Intelligence) Bureau, acknowledges that all the participants at the meeting were not included in its listing. For further details about the meeting, based upon the unconfirmed account provided to U.S. Counter-Intelligence Corps (CIC) personnel by an alleged Sûreté double agent and RSHA collaborator who participated, Manfred Uhrig, see ex-Allied intelligence operative Victor Alexandrov, *La Mafia des SS* (Paris: Stock, 1978), pp. 45–61, 77–80. Therein it is claimed that additional secret discussions were held at the hotel on 11 August between Kaltenbrunner and several of his top Sicherheitsdienst (SD) subordinates. Like the meeting supposedly organized to safeguard German industrial secrets the day before, this may have been designed as a "cover" to satisfy Himmler that they were getting together to discuss future SD-coordinated guerrilla operations in Allied-occupied France and Belgium, the ostensible reason for organizing the second meeting, rather than their own survival in the wake of the impending Nazi defeat. In any event, the importance of this 1944 meeting is almost invariably emphasized in journalistic accounts of postwar Nazi activities. Compare Philippe Aziz, *Les criminels de guerre* (Paris: Denoël, 1974), pp. 114–16 (who denies, somewhat unconvincingly, that Himmler was kept in the dark); Michael Bar-Zohar, *The Avengers* (New York: Hawthorn, 1967), pp. 92–5; Rena Giefer and Thomas Giefer, *Die Rattenlinie: Fluchtwege der Nazis. Eine Dokumentation* (Frankfurt: Hain, 1991), pp. 25–6; Del Boca and Giovana, *Fascism Today*, p. 78; Glenn B. Infield, *Skorzeny: Hitler's Commando* (New York: St. Martin's, 1981), p. 179; Lee, *Beast Reawakens*, pp. 21–2; Jürgen Pomorin et al., *Blutige Spuren: Der zweite Aufstieg der SS* (Dortmund: Weltkreis, 1980), pp. 60–7; Jürgen Pomorin et al., *Geheime Kanäle: Der Nazi-Mafia auf der Spur* (Dortmund: Weltkreis, 1981), pp. 72–5; Jorge Camarasa, *ODESSA al sur: La Argentina como refugio de nazis y criminales de guerra* (Buenos Aires: Planeta, 1995), pp. 25–8; and "Patrice Chiaroff" (pseudonym for Dominique-Ivan Calzi), *Dossier néo-nazisme* (Paris: Ramsay, 1977), pp. 4, 465–6. According to the latter source, the RSHA spent over two years preparing escape and evasion networks in anticipation of Germany's ultimate defeat. This task was supposedly assigned to Walter Schellenberg, head of SD-Ausland, the section responsible for foreign intelligence. To carry out this enormous task, Schellenberg in turn relied upon a number of other RSHA officials, including SS Standartenführer Walter Huppenkothen of Amt IV/A; Humbert Achaner-Pifrader of Amt IV/B, who furnished a portion of the necessary false identity documents; W. Götsch; Herbert Rossner; Hermann Bielstein; Otto Skorzeny, chief of Amt VI/S, which handled special operations and sabotage (about whom much more will soon be said); Heiko Oetker, a colleague of Skorzeny's and a future leader of the postwar Wiking-Jugend; and SS Hauptsturmführer [Alfred] Ziedler, the head of Amt VI/WI, which was responsible for maintaining links with the top economic circles of the Third Reich. Between January and September of 1943, over 1.1 million Reichsmarks were allegedly placed at the disposal of the Freundeskreis der Reichsführer SS (a group created in 1938 to solicit financial support for the Nazi security apparatus) – for "special tasks" – by leading industrial firms. See Chairoff, *Dossier néo-nazisme*, pp. 3–4. It should be noted, however, that Calzi was apparently an intelligence operative linked to various Western secret services who was posing as a left-wing journalist, perhaps to gather intelligence on both fascists and "anti-fascists" and/or to disseminate disinformation, which means that his specific claims should probably not be accepted at face value unless they are corroborated by other sources.

18 Compare Del Boca and Giovana, *Fascism Today*, p. 79.

19 Four such documents have been cited in the secondary sources, a November 1944 Army intelligence report, an early 1945 State Department report, a March 1945 OSS report, and a 1946 Treasury Department report. All of these claimed that German industrial firms were buying up foreign companies, transferring money to secret accounts in "neutral" financial havens, and/or employing "front men" to launder money overseas to forestall the Allied seizure of their holdings. See, for example, Bar-Zohar, *Avengers*, pp. 93–4; William Stevenson, *The Bormann Brotherhood* (New York: Bantam, 1974), pp. 81–5; and Wiesenthal, *Murderers among Us*, pp. 84–6. It is difficult to be certain whether or not the information contained in those reports was accurate, because intelligence reports are generally only as reliable as the informants and sources upon which they are based. For examples of problematic Allied intelligence reports about purported Nazi plots in Argentina, see Newton, *"Nazi Menace" in Argentina*, passim. Note also that some observers have claimed that Nazi preparations for postwar survival went back to 1943, following the German defeat at Stalingrad. See Stevenson, *Bormann Brotherhood*, p. 66.

20 Cited by Wiesenthal, *Murderers among Us*, p. 84. Compare the figures cited by William Slang, Historian, Department of State, *U.S. and Allied Efforts to Recover and Restore Gold and Other Assets Stolen or Hidden during World War II: Preliminary Report, May 1997* [hereinafter *Nazi Gold Report*] (Washington, DC: GPO, 1997), p. 49, on the basis of a late July 1945 State Department report. The Argentine companies allegedly involved in this Nazi assets transfer scheme are listed in Jorge Camarasa, *Los nazis en la Argentina* (Buenos Aires: Legasa, 1992), pp. 23–4, note 10; and in Camarasa, *ODESSA al sur*, pp. 38–40, note 12. This latter work is an updated, expanded, and corrected version of the former.

21 Important details about aspects of the elaborate attempt to hide and thereby prevent the Allies from seizing control of Germany's wealth, including the Third Reich's ill-gotten gains, can be found in Ian Sayer and Douglas Botting, *Nazi Gold: The Story of the World's Greatest Robbery – and Its Aftermath* (London: Panther, 1984), a well-researched journalistic account. For the listing of unrecovered funds, which would nowadays be worth over ten times that amount, see pp. 291–2. Compare the account of East German propagandist Julius Mader, *Der Banditenschatz: Ein Dokumentarbericht über Hitlers geheimen Gold- und Waffenschatz* ([East] Berlin: Deutscher Militär, 1965), passim, although like all of his works it should be used with a great degree of caution and supplemented with less partisan sources.

22 See *The Odessa File* (New York: Viking, 1972). Before writing his novel, Forsyth apparently flew to Austria and consulted with Wiesenthal in order to obtain information about the historical context, as well as about various details. See Wiesenthal, *Justice Not Vengeance*, pp. 96–9.

23 For the idea that ODESSA constituted a vast underground network, see Wiesenthal, *Murderers among Us*, pp. 78–83; Wiesenthal, *Justice Not Vengeance*, pp. 54–6; Bar-Zohar, *Avengers*, pp. 122–3; Stevenson, *Bormann Brotherhood*, pp. 69–70; Pomorin et al., *Geheime Kanäle*, pp. 57, 66–7; Del Boca and Giovana, *Fascism Today*, pp. 79–80; and Chairoff, *Dossier néo-nazisme*, pp. 6–16. Those who think it was largely a mythical entity include ex-OSS officer Ladislas Farago, *Aftermath: Martin Bormann and the Fourth Reich* (New York: Avon, 1975), p. 185; "Werner Brockdorff" (pseudonym for former Hitler Jugend leader Alfred Jarschel), *Flucht vor Nürnberg: Pläne und Organisation der Fluchtwege der NS-Prominenz im "Römischen Weg"* (Munich and Wels: Welsermühl, 1969), p. 20; and Magnus Linklater, Isabel Hilton, and Neal Ascherson, *The Fourth Reich: Klaus Barbie and the Neo-Fascist Connection* (London: Coronet, 1985), pp. 174–5. The relative importance of ODESSA as an underground Nazi organization is highlighted by certain American intelligence reports,

such as a 27 January 1947 report prepared under the auspices of "Operation Brandy," which identified the imprisoned Otto Skorzeny as the leader of ODESSA, an organization that in turn supposedly lay behind both Spinne and the Bruderschaft. See Giefer and Giefer, *Rattenlinie*, pp. 27–8, 131–2. Compare also the documents cited by Lee, *Beast Reawakens*, pp. 40–1. However, after examining a wider corpus of CIC intelligence reports found in the U.S. National Archives, it seems clear to me that much of the information gathered by CIC field agents about the purported activities of ODESSA was based upon unreliable hearsay that subsequent investigations were unable to verify. See, e.g., "ODESSA Organization," File #ZFO15116, Box 64, Investigative Records Repository-Impersonal [IRR-Imp], Record Group [RG] 319, National Archives [NA]; "ODESSA Movement, Coburg Movement," File #XE180023, Box 39, IRR-Imp, RG 319, NA; and "Operation BRANDY" File #ZFO11666, Box 50, IRR-Imp, NA. Nevertheless, these files are anything but comprehensive, and it remains possible that other reports on ODESSA are either located elsewhere in the archives or still remain classified, so the verdict is not yet in concerning the true scope of the organization.

24 See, respectively, Pomorin et al., *Geheime Kanäle*, p. 60; Bar-Zohar, *Avengers*, p. 122; Infield, *Skorzeny*, p. 182; Stevenson, *Bormann Brotherhood*, p. 70; Chairoff, *Dossier néo-nazisme*, pp. 12–13; Brockdorff, *Flucht vor Nürnberg*, p. 19; and Michael Schmidt, *The New Reich: Violent Extremism in Unified Germany and Beyond* (New York: Pantheon, 1993), p. 42. According to Chairoff, the "Werwolf" unit that later developed into Spinne had earlier been responsible for the 18–19 May 1945 surprise attack on the Weihmulen internment camp, which resulted in the escape of seventeen Flemish SS officers and NCOs, as well as other commando actions at Lüneburg and Ehrenfeld. In January 1946, after its local logistical base was dismantled by the Allies, the group decided to give up direct action tactics and transform itself into an escape network. Among the leading figures in Spinne – assuming that this account of Spinne is accurate, which is by no means certain – were former SA men Ernst Löcke and Rudolf Maikowski, Klaus Imberger of the Abwehr, and three ex-SD officials, Böhmke, Henkel, and Langue.

25 Pomorin et al., *Geheime Kanäle*, pp. 57, 60; Chairoff, *Dossier néo-nazisme*, p. 12; Infield, *Skorzeny*, p. 181; Bar-Zohar, *Avengers*, p. 120; and Brockdorff, *Flucht vor Nürnberg*, p. 19.

26 Stevenson, *Bormann Brotherhood*, p. 185. Here Stevenson seems to be confusing Spinne with the Kameradenwerk. But compare also Claudio Díaz and Antonio Zucco, *La ultraderecha argentina y su conexión internacional* (Buenos Aires: Contrapunto, 1987), p. 68, who claim that both Spinne and the Kameradenwerk were Latin American affiliates of ODESSA. Note, however, that the latter work is filled with errors, both minor and major.

27 Bar-Zohar, *Avengers*, pp. 113–19, 122–3. According to Chairoff, Schleuse was especially active in Austria, and its last action involved helping ex-Nyilaskeresztes Párt – Hungarista Mozgalom (Arrow Cross Party – Hungarianist Movement) members to flee from Hungary in the wake of the 1956 Soviet invasion. See *Dossier néo-nazisme*, p. 12. I have not found any references to this particular organization in the U.S. National Archives.

28 For Rudel's own account of the activities of the Kameradenwerk, and of its links to Stille Hilfe, see *Zwischen Deutschland und Argentinien: Fünf Jahre in Übersee* (Göttingen: Plesse, no date), pp. 147–51, 159–61. Compare the more critical version of "Michael Frank" (pseudonym), *Die letzte Bastion: Nazis in Argentinien* (Hamburg: Rütten & Loening, 1962), pp. 116–21, 141. Wiesenthal later claimed that the Kameradenwerk enjoyed close contacts with the Argentine government – especially prior to Perón's ouster in 1955 – and with sympathetic personnel in the Buenos Aires embassies of West Germany, Austria, and Italy. See *Murderers among Us*, p. 306. This seems entirely believable, given the later history of the Rudel network.

29 See Stevenson, *Bormann Brotherhood*, p. 185. There is no doubt whatsoever that Rudel maintained close contacts with a wide assortment of unregenerate Nazis and right-wing organizations after World War II, and for a time he even considered trying to bring together groups of nationalist German war veterans under his own leadership. Many details about his varied postwar political activities can be found in "Ruedel, Hans," File

#XE153440, Box 308, IRR-Personal, RG 319, NA; and in "Operation SKYLARK," File #ZFO11652, Box 75, IRR-Imp, NA, which monitored the activities of former Luftwaffe personnel.

30 For these and other details about Stille Hilfe, see Oliver Schröm and Andrea Röpke, *Stille Hilfe für braune Kameraden: Das geheime Netzwerk der Alt- und Neonazis* (Berlin: Ch. Links, 2001), passim; and Pomorin et al., *Geheime Kanäle*, pp. 7–56. For further information about the BBI and Christophersen, see Kurt Hirsch, *Rechts von der Union: Personen, Organisationen, Parteien seit 1945. Ein Lexikon* (Munich: Knesebeck & Schuler, 1989), pp. 36–7, 361–3. For the Wiking-Jugend, a neo-Nazi youth group founded in 1952 that established "sister" organizations in Belgium, Holland, France, and Spain, not to mention links to a wide range of far right parties, see Hirsch, *Rechts von der Union*, pp. 147–50; and especially Peter Dudek, *Jugendliche Rechtsextremisten: Zwischen Hakenkreuz und Odalsrune, 1945 bis heute* (Cologne: Bund, 1985), pp. 127–39. For the DKEG, a right-wing cultural association, see Peter Dudek and Hans-Gerd Jaschke, *Entstehung und Entwicklung des Rechtsextremismus in der Bundesrepublik: Zur Tradition einer besonderen politischen Kultur* (Opladen: Westdeutscher, 1984), volume 1, pp. 44–7; and the Antifaschismus-Kommission des K[ommunistische]B[und], ed., *Wer mit wem?: Braunzone zwischen CDU/CSU und Neonazis* (Hamburg: Buntbuch, 1981), pp. 19–20. For the NPD, the most significant extreme right electoral party in postwar West Germany prior to the recent rise of the Republikaner, see Hans Frederick, *NPD: Gefahr von Rechts?* (Munich: Politisches Archiv, 1967); Reinhard Kühnl, Rainer Rilling, and Christine Sager, *Die NPD: Struktur, Ideologie und Funktion einer neofaschistischen Partei* (Frankfurt: Suhrkamp, 1969); Hans Maier and Hermann Bott, *NPD: Struktur und Ideologie einer "nationalen Rechtspartei"* (Munich: Piper, 1968); John David Nagle, *The National Democratic Party: Right Radicalism in the Federal Republic of Germany* (Berkeley: University of California, 1970); Lutz Niethammer, *Angepasster Faschismus: Politische Praxis der NPD* (Frankfurt: Fischer, 1969); Adolf Noll, Werner Plitt, and Winfried Ridder, *Die NPD: Programmatik und politisches Verhalten* (Bonn and Bad Godesberg: Neue Gesellschaft, 1970); Fred H. Richards, *Die NPD: Alternative oder Widerkehr?* (Munich: Olzog, 1967); Werner Smoydzin, *NPD: Geschichte und Umwelt einer Partei. Analyse und Kritik* (Pfaffenhofen: Ilmgau, 1967); and the excellent overviews by Horst W. Schmollinger, "Die Nationaldemokratische Partei Deutschlands," in *Parteien-Handbuch: Die Parteien der Bundesrepublik Deutschland, 1945–1980*, ed. by Richard Stöss (Opladen: Westdeutscher, 1983), volume 2, pp. 1922–94; and Dudek and Jaschke, *Entstehung und Entwicklung des Rechtsextremismus*, pp. 280–355. For the DVU, a far right party that attracted many former NPD supporters following the disintegration of the latter, see Dudek and Jaschke, *Entwicklung und Entstehung des Rechtsextremismus*, pp. 52–4; *Wer mit wem?*, pp. 20–1; and especially Annette Linke, *Der multimillionär Frey und die DVU: Daten, Fakten, Hintergründe* (Essen: Klartext, 1994).

31 For Franke's alleged work for British intelligence, see Tauber, *Beyond Eagle and Swastika*, volume 1, p. 123. Franke's prewar and wartime activities were equally suggestive. He had earlier been a member of the left wing of the NSDAP, and had followed Strasser and other uncompromising "socialists" out of the party and into exile, first to Vienna and then to Prague, where he edited newspapers published by the Schwarze Front (Black Front). At some point during this period, he was apparently recruited as a double agent by the Gestapo. In June 1934, he returned to Germany and divulged detailed inside information that enabled the Gestapo to penetrate and liquidate Strasser's underground network of anti-Hitler cells. Franke thereafter experienced a meteoric rise through the ranks of the SS. See the 3 November 1950 report of American Consul General in Bremen, LaVerne Baldwin, "History and aims of the Bruderschaft, with brief notes on 'Chancellor' Franke-Gricksch," Lot File #762A.00/11–350, RG 59, NA, p. 2; Tauber, *Beyond Eagle and Swastika*, volume 1, pp. 122–3; and Reinhard Opitz, *Faschismus und Neofaschismus 2: Neofaschismus in der Bundesrepublik* (Cologne: Pahl-Rugenstein, 1988), pp. 20–1. This last author and his publishing house were both closely linked to the outlawed Deutsche Kommunistische Partei (DKP: German Communist Party).

32 For further details about the Bruderschaft, see "History and Aims of the Bruderschaft"; 22 September 1950 Frankfurt HICOG report, "The Bruderschaft and the BHE," Lot File #762A.00/9–2250; 12 October 1950 report by American Consul General in Hamburg, Robert T. Cowan, "Interview with Beck-Broichsitter and Dr. Aschenbach of the Brotherhood," Lot File 762A.00/10–1250; 17 November 1950 report by Hamburg consular official Halleck L. Rose, "Conversation [with] Helmut Beck-Broichsitter, Bruderschaft leader," Lot File 762A.00/11–1750; and 2 March 1951 report by Cowan, "Resignation of Helmut Beck-Broichsitter from the Bruderschaft," Lot File #762A.00/3–251 – all in RG 59, NA; and Tauber, *Beyond Eagle and Swastika*, volume 1, pp. 122–32, 160–71, 272–4, and volume 2, p. 1116, note 181. Compare Opitz, *Faschismus und Neofaschismus 2*, pp. 17, 21–9; Hirsch, *Rechts von der Union*, pp. 198–200; and Manfred Jenke, *Verschwörung von rechts?: Ein Bericht über den Rechtsradikalismus in Deutschland nach 1945* (Berlin: Colloquium, 1961), pp. 285–8. The extent to which the Bruderschaft was engaged in outright subversive activities – and for whom – remains a matter of debate, but there is no doubt that some of its members were involved in covert political operations and linked in unclear ways to various security agencies. Leftists claim that the Bruderschaft worked in cooperation with Western intelligence organizations, whereas Jenke suggests that it was a vehicle for Soviet penetration of the West. My own view is that the organization contained agents from both sides within its ranks. For additional information about the DU, see Richard Stöss, "Die Deutsche Gemeinschaft," in *Parteien-Handbuch*, ed. by Richard Stöss, volume 1, pp. 879–81. For the DG, see ibid., pp. 877–900; and especially Richard Stöss, *Vom Nationalismus zum Umweltschutz: Die Deutsche Gemeinschaft/Aktionsgemeinschaft Unabhängiger Deutscher im Parteisystem der Bundesrepublik* (Opladen: Westdeutscher, 1980). For the DRP, see Horst W. Schmollinger, "Die Deutsche Reichspartei," in *Parteien-Handbuch*, ed. by Richard Stöss, volume 1, pp. 1112–91; and Dudek and Jaschke, *Entstehung und Entwicklung des Rechtsextremismus*, volume 1, pp. 181–279. For the *Scheinwerfer* group, see especially Ewald Hippe, ed., *Joachim Nehring – Neo-Nazismus? Der "Scheinwerfer" Prozess vor der Hauptspruchkammer München* (Munich: Hippe, 1950), a partisan defense of Nehring; and Tauber, *Beyond Eagle and Swastika*, volume 1, p. 200, and volume 2, pp. 1081–2, note 220. For the ANG, see the latter source, pp. 771–8.
33 See Tauber, *Beyond Eagle and Swastika*, p. 240.
34 Ibid., pp. 240–1.
35 For the alleged links between Naumann's group and other far right organizations, see especially the undated top secret report prepared by the British High Commissioner's office that sought to justify the arrest and prosecution of leading members of the Naumann-Kreis, "The Naumann Circle: The Study of a Technique of Political Subversion," File #XE246725: Naumann, Werner, Box 160A, IRR-Personal, RG 319, NA, pp. 10–16, 27–9, and appendixes A, E, F, G, H, and I. For more on the *Nation Europa* and Plesse publishing groups, see Jenke, *Verschwörung von rechts?*, pp. 370–3, 377–80. Priester was an important figure, both in the German and international radical right after World War II. See Tauber, *Beyond Eagle and Swastika*, passim.
36 See especially Opitz, *Faschismus und Neofaschismus 2*, pp. 41–3. In one of Naumann's diary entries the following notation appeared: "He has a liking for Skorzeny's plan. He will support it." See ibid., p. 156, note 969. Compare also East German propagandist Julius Mader, *Jagd nach dem Narbengesicht: Ein Dokumentarbericht über Hitlers Geheimdienstchef Otto Skorzeny* ([East] Berlin: Deutscher Militär, 1963), pp. 241–5, for the Skorzeny-Naumann link. Taubert was a former official in Goebbels' Propaganda Ministry who was entrusted with promoting Nazi propaganda in the occupied territories on the Eastern Front. In 1950 he created the VFF, the German affiliate of the international Paix et Liberté association, which received funding from the Central Intelligence Agency (CIA). In the case of the VFF, this was probably disbursed through the intermediary of the Bundesministerium für gesamtdeutsche Fragen (Federal Ministry for All-German Affairs). For more on Taubert and the VFF, see Matthias Friedel, *Der Volksbund für Frieden und Freiheit (VFF): Eine Teiluntersuchung über westdeutsche antikommunistische Propaganda im Kalten Krieg und*

deren Wurzeln im Nationalsozialismus (St. Augustin: Gardez!, 2001); Klaus Körner, "Von der antibolschewistischen zur antisowjetischen Propaganda, Dr. Eberhard Taubert," in *Der Kalte Krieg – Vorspiel zum Frieden?*, ed. by Arnold Sywottek (Munster: Lit, 1994), pp. 54–68; Bernard Ludwig, "La propagande anticommuniste en Allemagne Fédérale: Le VFF pendant Allemand de Paix et Liberté?," *Vingtième Siècle: Revue d'Histoire* 80 (October–December 2003), pp. 33–42; and Hirsch, *Rechts von der Union*, pp. 218–22, 453. For more on the VFF's Paix et Liberté French counterpart, see infra, note 149.

37 For the group's efforts to infiltrate rightist electoral parties, see "Naumann Circle," pp. 29–36; T. H. Tetens, *The New Germany and the Old Nazis* (New York: Random House, 1961), pp. 24–33, 64, 68–9, 112–15; and Lord Russell of Liverpool, *Return of the Swastika?* (London: Robert Hale, 1968), pp. 38–47. Compare the Naumann quotes cited by Tauber, *Beyond Eagle and Swastika*, volume 1, pp. 134, 136, 140–1, which directly conflict with the partisan accounts of the case by Nauman himself – see *Nau-Nau, gefährdet das Empire?* (Göttingen: Plesse, 1953) – and one of Naumann's lawyers, reported Nazi sympathizer Friedrich Grimm, *Unrecht im Rechtsstaat: Tatsachen und Dokumente zur politischen Justiz, dargestellt am Fall Naumann* (Tübingen: Deutsche Hochschullehrer-Zeitung, 1957). Therein (pp. 217–18), Grimm approves of Naumann's description of the Naumann-Kreis as an innocuous *Stammtisch*. In this connection it is interesting to note that West German neo-Nazi leader Michael Kühnen later openly bragged about the subversive plots and infiltration operations initiated by the Naumann-Kreis, thereby directly repudiating – whether justifiably or not – earlier Nazi efforts to downplay its anti-democratic activities and overall political significance. See *Die zweite Revolution, Band I: Glaube und Kampf* (Lincoln, NE: NSDAP/AO, 1987), pp. 58–9.

38 For more details about the Naumann-Kreis, see "Naumann Circle," passim; Tauber, *Beyond Eagle and Swastika*, pp. 132–46, 274–5; Opitz, *Faschismus und Neofaschismus 2*, pp. 37–52; Jenke, *Verschwörung von rechts?*, pp. 161–79; and Beate Baldow, "Episode oder Gefahr?: Die Naumann-Affäre" (Unpublished Ph.D. Dissertation: Freie Universität Berlin, 2012). For the legal actions taken (and not taken) against Naumann and other members of his circle, see the English translations of two reports prepared by Professor Kurt Rheindorf, "The case of Dr. Werner Naumann and company" and "Memorandum Concerning the Naumann case," forwarded to HICOG on 16 September 1954 by Bundesamt für Verfassungsschutz (BfV) officer Günter Nollau; the 18 January 1955 report by the American Consul General in Dusseldorf, Patrick Mallon, "The End of the Naumann Affair"; and the summary of the Karlsruhe Federal Supreme Court's 3 December 1954 sentence against Naumann and seven of his associates, all in File #XE246725: Naumann, Werner, Box 160A, IRR-Personal, RG 319, NA. Compare Naumann, *Nau-Nau*; Grimm, *Unrecht im Rechtsstaat*; and Hans Kruse, *Besatzungsmacht und Freiheitsrechte: Rechtsgutachten [zum Naumann Fall] nebst Anhang* (Göttingen: Musterschmidt, 1953). Although Rheindorf and Mallon agreed with the German judges that the British had not provided sufficient evidence of concrete violations of key articles of the German penal law code by Naumann and his colleagues, specifically articles 90a (forming an anti-constitutional association), 94 (endangering the state), 73 (conspiracy), and 128 (establishing connections with illegal secret societies), Mallon added that the British should have gathered additional evidence and let the German authorities handle the case instead of prematurely arresting the plotters themselves, which only fueled anti-British sentiment and made Naumann appear as a sort of martyr. See Mallon, "End of the Naumann Affair," p. 3.

39 For the details enumerated in the previous two paragraphs, compare the relevant sections of the sources listed in notes 16 and 23.

40 See Brockdorff, *Flucht vor Nürnberg*, pp. 19–20. Compare Linklater, Hilton, and Ascherson, *Fourth Reich*, pp. 174–5; and Gitta Sereny, *Into That Darkness: An Examination of Conscience* (New York: Vintage, 1983 [1974]), p. 276. The latter work deals with the Franz Stangl case.

41 For Skorzeny's prewar and wartime exploits, see his own account in *Secret Missions: War Memoirs of the Most Dangerous Man in Europe* (New York: Dutton, 1950), a translation of the

original German version, *Geheimkommando Skorzeny*; idem, *Lebe gefährlich: Wir kämpften, wir verloren* (Konigswinter: H. Cramer, 1973); Charles Foley, *Commando Extraordinary: The Incredible Exploits of SS Col. Skorzeny* (New York: Bantam, 1979 [1954]), pp. 12–158; Charles Whiting, *Skorzeny* (New York: Ballantine, 1972), passim; Jean Mabire, *Skorzeny: "L'Homme le plus dangereux d'Europe"* (Paris: Grancher, 1990), pp. 7–296; Infield, *Skorzeny*, pp. 9–117; and Mader, *Jagd nach dem Narbengesicht*, pp. 9–155.

42 See, for example, Foley, *Commando Extraordinary*, pp. 6–11, 183–9. Foley's contemptuous dismissals of reports of SS undergrounds should be taken with a grain of salt, given the numerous mistakes that can be found elsewhere in his brief account of Skorzeny's postwar actvities. After all, Foley likewise dismissed claims about the Austrian's provision of training to the Egyptian security services, claims which were later found – as we shall soon see – to be accurate, and gave an entirely misleading account of his 1948 escape from Darmstadt prison, one that omitted the role of elements of the SS underground and also, perhaps, certain U.S. authorities in the affair. This may have had something to do with the fact that for pertinent information Foley relied upon CIA director Allen Dulles and various Allied military personnel who had personally intervened to save Skorzeny from being convicted at his war crimes trial. See ibid., pp. i–ii (author's note). Whether he did so disingenuously or was part of a planned, intelligence-linked "cover-up" is unknown. Another author who dismisses accounts of Skorzeny's involvement in postwar undergrounds or subversion is the philo-fascist amateur historian Jean Mabire, who for years has specialized in writing books glorifying the wartime exploits of the various Waffen-SS formations, especially those made up of French and Belgian volunteers. See his *Skorzeny*, pp. 315–33.

43 See especially the book by East German propagandist Mader, *Jagd nach dem Narbengesicht*, passim. Although this work contains some very interesting material about Skorzeny's career, it adopts the usual uncritical "Stamokap" interpretation regarding Nazi-Big Business links and is filled with minor errors and tendentious, unsubstantiated claims. To provide just one salient example, Mader confuses – intentionally or not – the U.S. Army officer who testified on behalf of Skorzeny at the latter's trial, Lieutenant Colonel Donald McClure of the War Crimes Group, with Brigadier General Robert McClure, head of psychological warfare operations in the European theater during World War II and future head of the U.S. Army's Office of the Chief of Psychological Warfare. See ibid., pp. 165–9. For more on Robert McClure's postwar activities, which played a key role in legitimizing and laying the groundwork for American special operations, see Alfred H. Paddock, *U.S. Army Special Warfare: Its Origins* (Washington, DC: National Defense University, 1982), passim. Mader's ulterior motives for accusing this particular McClure of aiding Skorzeny are thus transparent. Ironically, the "anti-fascist" Mader was himself apparently a former leader of the Hitler Jugend who later offered his services to the communists. He was also supposedly a "personal enemy" of Skorzeny's. See Mabire, *Skorzeny*, p. 314. However, Mader is not the only writer who places Skorzeny at the hub of an international fascist network in the postwar era. See, for example, Federico Pérez-Galdós, *Extrema derecha S.A.: Nombres, conexiones y finanzas* (Madrid: España Crítica, 1982), p. 46, who claims that from his Madrid base Skorzeny helped establish such a network in over sixty countries; and Lee, *Beast Reawakens*, pp. 6–7 and passim.

44 The false money was actually produced by special sections under the jurisdiction of Amt VI/F, in particular subsection 4 under Sturmbannführer Bernhard Krüger, after whom the operation was named; the misleadingly named Sonderstab 3rd Germanische Panzerkorps (Special Staff, Third German Tank Corps) under Sturmbannführer Friedrich Schwend, which also reported directly to Obersturmbannführer Wilhelm Höttl, then head of the Balkan SD station; and the SD's production facility located at Friedenthal, which was under the supervision of Krüger and Skorzeny. For the complicated chain of command behind "Bernhard," see Pomorin et al., *Blutige Spuren*, pp. 27–49, especially the chart on p. 25. Compare the chart in Mader, *Banditenschatz*, p. 81. For more on "Bernhard," see Wilhelm Höttl, *Hitler's Paper Weapon* (London: Hart-Davis, 1955), a translation of his

Unternehmen Bernhard; Eberhard Frowein, *Wunderwaffe Falschgeld* (Kreuzlingen: Neptun, 1954); and Anthony Pirie, *Operation Bernhard: The Greatest Forgery of All Time* (New York: Morrow, 1962). Most of these sensationalistic works cannot be relied upon. After the war, in 1947, Höttl was recruited by the CIC. Years later, he claimed that the United States had recruited, armed, supplied, and trained former SS personnel and neo-Nazis, among whose many clandestine tasks were to maintain secret arms caches established in Austria after World War II by the Allies for the anti-communist "stay/behind" networks. See, e.g., "Britain Has Arms in Cold War Austria: Allies Relied on Former Waffen SS Personnel to Repel Potential Soviet Invasion," [London] *Guardian*, 27 January 1996; and Elizabeth Olson, "Documents Show U.S. Relationship with Nazis during Cold War," *New York Times*, 14 May 2004.

45 Mader, *Jagd nach dem Narbengesicht*, pp. 149–52, 239–41.
46 Ibid., pp. 149–54; Infield, *Skorzeny*, pp. 97–9.
47 Compare Infield, *Skorzeny*, pp. 100–1, 116, 122, 179; Lee, *Beast Reawakens*, p. 22; and especially Sayer and Botting, *Nazi Gold*, pp. 42–7, 291. The key figure involved in arranging for these last minute Reichsbank transfers and burials was SS Brigadeführer Josef Spacil, head of Amt II of the RSHA, the section responsible for economic affairs. On 22 April 1945, acting on Kaltenbrunner's orders even as the Russians were closing in on Berlin, Spacil and a contingent of SS troops had stolen what remained of the Reichsbank's funds – valued at over nine million dollars' worth – at gunpoint. They then rapidly made their way south toward the Alpine redoubt area, near Rauris, where Spacil buried some of the loot and distributed a portion to other SS men. On 27 April, he met with Skorzeny's chief subordinate, SS Hauptsturmführer Karl Radl, and provided him with over 8.5 million dollars' worth of gold and securities. Shortly thereafter, Skorzeny and Radl buried this treasure at an unknown location near Radstadt.
48 Infield, *Skorzeny*, pp. 110–13. Compare Mader, *Jagd nach dem Narbengesicht*, p. 147. For more on "Unternehmen Werwolf," see Arno Rose, *Werwolf, 1944–1945: Eine Dokumentation* (Stuttgart: Motorbuch, 1989); Charles Whiting, *Hitler's Werewolves: The Story of the Nazi Resistance Movement, 1944–1945* (New York: Stein & Day, 1972); and especially the well-documented recent study by Perry Biddiscombe, *Werwolf! The History of the National Socialist Guerrilla Movement, 1944–1946* (Toronto: University of Toronto, 1998). Compare "Werwolf Activities, February 1945–March 1947," File #XE049888, Box 37, IRR-Impersonal, RG 319, NA, volume 1. Note, however, that Skorzeny reportedly played very little role in the actual organization of the Werwolf groups, an operational task that had been entrusted to SS Obergruppenführer Hans-Adolf Prützmann, formerly the Höhere SS- und Polizeiführer for Southern Russia. Under his seemingly less than energetic direction, the organization did not develop into a truly formidable guerrilla force on the national level. Skorzeny's role was apparently limited to allowing selected Werwolf recruits to obtain training at his specialized training facilities and to providing Prützmann with a certain quantity of arcane weaponry and logistical support. Compare Rose, *Werwolf*, pp. 28–9; Whiting, *Hitler's Werewolves*, pp. 67–70; and the July 1945 British intelligence report published in A. D. Harvey, "Research Note: 'Werwolf' in Germany in 1945," *Terrorism and Political Violence* 6:3 (Autumn 1994), especially p. 395. This does not jibe with the extravagant claims made by some journalists, who argue that the five-man Werwolf stay/behind teams that Skorzeny purportedly set up formed "the nucleus of a committed, postwar Nazi underground." See Lee, *Beast Reawakens*, p. 25, referring to Danish journalist Henrik Krüger as a source. For exaggerated Allied reports about the imminent creation of a fortified Nazi redoubt, see Timothy Naftali, "Creating the Myth of the *Alpenfestung*: Allied Intelligence and the Collapse of the Nazi Police State," in *Austrian Historical Memory and National Identity*, ed. by Günter Bischof and Anton Pelinka (London: Transaction, 1997), pp. 203–46.
49 For Skorzeny's escape from Darmstadt with SS help, see Infield, *Skorzeny*, pp. 130–2, 150–3. Compare Mader, *Jagd nach dem Narbengesicht*, pp. 173–7.

50 For Skorzeny's intermittent visits and activities in Argentina between 1949 and 1955, see Infield, *Skorzeny*, pp. 191–204. Infield claims that most of the Austrian's efforts were directed at recovering the remnants of the Nazi treasure deposited by Bormann in Argentine banks and later confiscated by Perón and his ambitious wife, Evita. After several years of playing a cat-and-mouse game, especially with Evita, Skorzeny won their confidence and thereby managed to recover the bulk of the treasure for the use of his SS comrades. But there is a variety of circumstantial evidence which, when combined with logic, suggests that the commando leader strengthened his connections with Nazi networks while in South America. Note, for example, his reported contacts with Georg Mapusch, a former NSDAP Auslandsorganisation (AO: Foreign Country Organization) official who became the leader of a postwar Nazi underground group in Chile. See Dennis Eisenberg, *The Re-Emergence of Fascism* (New York: A. S. Barnes, 1967), pp. 273–4. Compare Chairoff, *Dossier néo-nazisme*, p. 403.

51 For this recruitment, see Infield, *Skorzeny*, pp. 161–3. For his connections in Germany and support of efforts to rehabilitate the Waffen-SS and infiltrate the Bonn government with Nazi sympathizers, see ibid., pp. 170–1, 189–90, 238. Compare Mader, *Jagd nach dem Narbengesicht*, pp. 213–17, 230–6, 269–81; and Lee, *Beast Reawakens*, pp. 63–4.

52 For an excellent recent study of Degrelle's activities during the German occupation of Belgium, see Martin Conway, *Collaboration in Belgium: Léon Degrelle and the Rexist Movement, 1940–1944* (New Haven and London: Yale University, 1993). For the earlier history of Rexism, see especially the bibliography compiled by Jean-Michel Étienne, *Le Mouvement rexiste jusqu'en 1940* (Paris: Colin, 1968). It is interesting to note that Degrelle, despite being sought by the Belgian government for war crimes, set up a construction company in Spain that was later hired to help build housing at U.S. Air Force bases in the Iberian Peninsula. According to Degrelle, the American airmen treated him like a hero and avidly sought to have their pictures taken with him, preferably decked out in his medals and swastika emblems. Groups of airmen even attended the weddings of two of his daughters. See *Léon Degrelle: Persiste et signe. Interviews recueillies pour la télévision française par Jean-Michel Charlier* (Paris: Jean Picollec, 1985), pp. 395–6. Compare Jean-Marie Frérotte, *Léon Degrelle, le dernier fasciste* (Brussels: P. Legrain, 1987), pp. 220–3.

53 For details about Skorzeny's economic transactions and sources of funds, see Infield, *Skorzeny*, pp. 163, 169–75, 183–4, 202–4, 209–10, 213–15. Compare Mader, *Jagd nach dem Narbengesicht*, pp. 209–12, 236–9, 241, 247–59; Lee, *Beast Reawakens*, pp. 58–63, 183–4; and Mariano Sánchez Soler, *Los hijos del 20-N: Historia violenta del fascismo español* (Madrid: Temas de Hoy, 1993), p. 151, who reveals that the offices of Skorzeny's export-import firm were occasionally used by Spanish fascists to publish their journals. Note also that the H. S. Lucht export-import company in Düsseldorf, owned by Degrelle's cousin Lea Lucht, was directed by Werner Naumann of the Bruderschaft, which provides further evidence of a connection between Skorzeny and the titular head of that anti-democratic cadre organization. According to a U.S. intelligence report, the company itself served as a "cover" for Skorzeny's contacts and movements throughout the world. It also had contacts with the Wolff-Trust, which engaged in extensive trading with the East Bloc, and had an office in the East German city of Leipzig, which Skorzeny allegedly used to recruit technicians and military experts for various Middle Eastern projects. See Infield, *Skorzeny*, pp. 210–11; and Lee, *Beast Reawakens*, p. 134, citing a 23 July 1954 U.S. State Department report.

54 For the FHO, see David Thomas, "Foreign Armies East and German Military Intelligence in Russia, 1941–45," *Journal of Contemporary History* 22:2 (April 1987), pp. 261–301. For more on Gehlen's career, see Reinhard Gehlen, *The Service: The Memoirs of General Reinhard Gehlen* (New York: World, 1972), a translation of the original German version, *Der Dienst*; E. H. Cookridge, *Gehlen: Spy of the Century* (New York: Random House, 1971); Heinz Höhne and Hermann Zolling, *Network: The Truth about General Gehlen and his Spy Ring* (London: Secker & Warburg, 1971), a translation of *Pullach intern*; Charles Whiting, *Gehlen: Germany's Master Spy* (New York: Ballantine, 1972); Mary Ellen Reese, *General*

Reinhard Gehlen: The CIA Connection (Fairfax, VA: George Mason University, 1990); and Jens Wegener, *Die Organisation Gehlen und die USA: Deutsch-amerikanische Geheimdienstbeziehungen, 1945–1949* (Berlin and Vienna: Lit, 2008). Compare also the following communist-linked sources: Alain Guérin, *Le général gris* (Paris: Julliard, 1968); and Julius Mader, *Die graue Hand* ([East] Berlin: Kongress, 1960).

55 According to Burton Hersh, the result was that Gehlen "figured prominently in Skorzeny's postwar Nazi machinations." See *The Old Boys: The American Elite and the Origins of the CIA* (New York: Scribner's, 1992), p. 162. For more details about the wartime interaction between Skorzeny and Gehlen, see Cookridge, *Gehlen*, pp. 72, 79, 93–5, 107–10; Höhne and Zolling, *Network*, pp. 41–4; and Rose, *Werwolf*, p. 205. Amt VI's Zeppelin units were made up of selected Russian POWs who had been trained as saboteurs and infiltrated behind Soviet lines. The recruitment for these units was dependent upon the Abwehr's WALLI units, front line reconnaissance detachments that were responsible for intelligence gathering, including the interrogation of Russian prisoners before they were sent on to POW camps. Once Gehlen was placed in charge of the WALLI units, then, he determined which Russian prisoners were transferred from Army control to that of the SD. Furthermore, the Zeppelin groups were forced to consult FHO for intelligence before undertaking particular actions, since their own intelligence-gathering capacities were limited. For more on the original division of labor between the Zeppelin and WALLI groups, see Höhne and Zolling, *Network*, pp. 15–21, 39–41.

56 For the burial of some of Gehlen's files by Skorzeny, see Infield, *Skorzeny*, pp. 96–7. However, Gehlen seems to have personally arranged for the burial of most of his valuable material. For Gehlen's efforts to get Skorzeny out of jail between 1946 and 1948, see ibid., pp. 155–6. His recruitment of the former commando as a contract agent will be discussed later.

57 See Reese, *General Reinhard Gehlen*, p. 43. Sibert was the senior officer responsible for the operation of Camp King, near Oberusel, an interrogation center used to house the highest ranking enemy prisoners, including Gehlen and Skorzeny. Along with Captain John Bokor, the CIC officer who was assigned to be Gehlen's interrogator, Sibert knowingly but surreptitiously defied official Allied policy for dealing with captured Nazis, and in the process played a key role in recruiting ex-Nazis who were interested in working for the Americans. It was he who arranged for Gehlen's later transfer to the United States, which was carried out with the knowledge of future CIA chief General Walter Bedell Smith, then chief of staff of the supreme allied command; future CIA head Allen Dulles, then working in Switzerland for the OSS; and General William J. ("Wild Bill") Donovan, then head of OSS. See Christopher Simpson, *Blowback: America's Recruitment of Nazis and Its Effects on the Cold War* (New York: Weidenfeld and Nicolson, 1988), pp. 41–3, 71–3. Indeed, according to one East Bloc source of dubious reliability, Donovan had already tried to contact Skorzeny in 1944, using intermediaries in Spain, and had then personally visited him in prison. See Mader, *Jagd nach dem Narbengesicht*, pp. 162–3.

58 For Yeo-Thomas's testimony, see Foley, *Commando Extraordinary*, pp. 178–83. An American army officer, Lieutenant Colonel Donald McClure, also testified on behalf of Skorzeny, saying that he would be proud to have had the Austrian and his co-defendants under his own command. See ibid., p. 169. For Yeo-Thomas's own exploits, see Bruce Marshall, *The White Rabbit* (New York: Evans Brothers, 1952). William Stevenson implies that British military intelligence intervened intentionally to save Skorzeny, as they also supposedly did later to protect Schacht. See Stevenson, *Bormann Brotherhood*, p. 151.

59 The role of the Americans in secretly facilitating Skorzeny's escape from Darmstadt prison was later confirmed by "Scarface" himself, his wife Ilse, and his close friend Degrelle. See Lee, *Beast Reawakens*, pp. 42–3, 404 (note 58), 61. For Skorzeny's alleged training of paratroopers in the United States, see Mader, *Jagd nach dem Narbengesicht*, pp. 180–1, citing a 3 September 1948 Associated Press story. His subsequent presence in Paris is more certain, since it was inadvertently confirmed by a photograph that appeared in the 13 February 1950 edition of the communist daily, *Ce Soir*. Nevertheless, even though the extreme left

sought to create a scandal and exploit it politically, it remains unclear just what Skorzeny was actually doing in France. See further ibid., pp. 183–4; Infield, *Skorzeny*, pp. 157, 159.

60 Compare Infield, *Skorzeny*, pp. 157–8, 160, who notes that the author of the 66th CIC group report knew that there was more than a "possibility" that the Austrian was being used by American intelligence, since a team of agents from his own unit had monitored a Bavarian meeting between Skorzeny and a Captain from the U.S. Military Attaché's office in Madrid only a few days earlier; and Lee, *Beast Reawakens*, pp. 61–2, who cites a 17 October 1951 report from Madrid apprising the director of the Federal Bureau of Investigation (FBI) about Skorzeny's offer.

61 See Infield, *Skorzeny*, pp. 197–200.

62 For Skorzeny's activities in Egypt, see ibid., pp. 206–9, 213, 215–17; Cookridge, *Gehlen*, p. 353; Stevenson, *Bormann Brotherhood*, pp. 151–61; Lee, *Beast Reawakens*, pp. 124–6, 128–32, 135; former high-ranking CIA officer Miles Copeland, *The Game of Nations* (New York: Simon & Schuster, 1970), p. 104 (who offers some interesting insights into American rationalizations for recruiting ex-Nazis); and especially Simpson, *Blowback*, pp. 249–52, who provides the most reliable details based upon primary U.S. documents he obtained via the Freedom of Information Act. Simpson considers this material to be merely the "tip of a much larger iceberg." See ibid., p. 347, note 10. Less reliable information can be found concerning the large-scale recruitment of former Nazis by King Farūq, General Muhammad Najīb, and al-Nāsir in Chairoff, *Dossier néo-nazisme*, pp. 449–60, who notes that several leading members of the Egyptian al-Dubbāt al-Ahrār (Free Officers') society had earlier been associated with the Misr al-Fatāt (Young Egypt, also known as the "Green Shirts" [Qāmis al-Akhdar]) movement and were Nazi sympathizers or agents, that several ex-SS men had participated at a January 1952 meeting with the future coup leaders to plan the operation beforehand, and that some wanted war criminals and high-ranking Nazi officials were among those hired to perform important tasks in the new government. The most important of these were former Goebbels adjutant Johannes von Leers, alias " 'Umar 'Amīn," who directed the Egyptian Propaganda Ministry and the "Voice of the Arabs" radio broadcasts, which he used to disseminate anti-Jewish materials of the most vulgar sort, as well as to establish a worldwide web of contacts; Gerhard Hartmut von Schubert, another ex-Goebbels subordinate who was put in charge of the Mukhābarāt, the Egyptian intelligence service; Franz Bünsch, a third propagandist from Goebbels' ministry who thence served as Gehlen's chief of station in Cairo and directly assisted Skorzeny; Alois Brunner, a notorious war criminal responsible for hundreds of thousands of deaths who became Gehlen's chief of station in Damascus and was temporarily assigned to work for the Egyptian Army's psychological services section; former paratroop General Wilhelm Fahrmbacher, an advisor to the Egyptian armed forces who played the key role in recruiting Nazi scientists and technicians to help develop al-Nāsir's rocketry weapons; and an unidentified ex-SS man using the alias "Mahmud Salīh," who founded an Anti-Zionist Society that linked up with affiliated groups all over the world, including the Comité Europe-Islam (Europe-Islam Committee) in France, the Deutsche-Arabische Gemeinschaft (German-Arab Association) in Germany, the Society for Combatting Zionism in Great Britain, two anti-Zionist organizations in the United States, and the Centre Eurafricaine d'Études et de Réalisations (CEDER: Euro-African Center for Work and Study). The key figures associated with CEDER were Jean-Maurice Bauverd, a former collaborator of the Grand Mufti's and later a counselor at the Saudi Arabian embassy in Madrid; Hubert de Bergard, CEDER's founder and editor of *La Documentation de Tanger*; Paul-Yves Rio, an ex-member of the French section of the Abwehr and Jacques Doriot's Parti Populaire Français (PPF: French Popular Party); and Otto-Karl Düpow, at various times a member of Otto Strasser's postwar Deutsche Soziale Union (DSU: German Social Union), the Europäische Verbindungstelle (EVS: European Liaison Office), and Theodor Souček's Sozialorganische Ordnungsbewegung Europas (SORBE: Social-Organic Movement for European Order) in Austria, which simultaneously promoted both "Eurafrica" conceptions and Nordic racism. Chairoff

claims – without providing any hard evidence – that Rio and Düpow later played a role in the abduction of Moroccan leftist leader Mahdi ibn Barka, that both men had close links to the CIA, and that Rio also worked for various Arab secret services and the Israelis. See Chairoff, *Dossier B . . . comme barbouzes: Une France parallèle, celle des basses-oeuvres du pouvoir* (Paris: Albin Michel, 1975), pp. 320–3. For more on these CEDER activists, who became actively involved in arming the Algerian Front de Libération Nationale (FLN: National Liberation Front) and who maintained regular contacts with Skorzeny, see especially Roger Faligot and Rémi Kauffer, *Le croissant et la croix gammée: Les secrets de l'alliance entre l'Islam et le nazisme d'Hitler à nos jours* (Paris: Albin Michel, 1990), pp. 161, 196–7, 221–2; and Tauber, *Beyond Eagle and Swastika*, volume 1, pp. 234–5; volume 2, pp. 1104–6, notes 135 and 143. Ironically enough, Chairoff does not even mention Skorzeny in connection with the Egyptian affair, which can only be intentional since he names so many other infamous Nazis and Nazi collaborators who were supposedly recruited to work there. Among these were SS Hauptsturmführer Hans Eisele, a doctor who conducted medical experiments at Buchenwald; SS Sturmbannführer Eugen Eichberger, a battalion commander in the "Dirlewanger" penal brigade; Willi Berner, an SS officer at the Mauthausen concentration camp; SS Obersturmbannführer Leopold Gleim, previously head of the Gestapo in Warsaw; SS Gruppenführer Alois Moser (alias "Hasan Sulaymān"), a war criminal involved in the extermination of Ukrainian Jewry; and a host of others (including several non-Germans). Compare ibid., volume 2, pp. 1113–16, notes 178–9, and a number of European newspaper articles that appeared in the first half of the 1950s. To these relatively sober treatments one can add sensationalistic conspiratorial accounts, such as that by Irving Sedar and Harold J. Greenburg, *Behind the Egyptian Sphinx: Nasser's Strange Bedfellows: Prelude to World War III?* (Philadelphia and New York: Chilton, 1960), pp. 57–79. More recently, some startling revelations were made in the Israeli media about Skorzeny. According to intelligence sources, "Scarface" had supposedly been "turned" in 1963 by Israeli Mossad Letafkidim Meyouchadim (MOSSAD: Central Institute for Intelligence and Special Duties) agents in Madrid. Then, with the help of NATO officers and some of the commando leader's former subordinates living in Cairo, they allegedly carried out a successful operation to infiltrate Nazi circles around al-Nāsir. Compare Giefer and Giefer, *Rattenlinie*, p. 135; Lee, *Beast Reawakens*, p. 152; and Faligot and Kauffer, *Croissant et la croix gammée*, p. 197, who cites September 1989 issues of *Matara* and *Yediot Aharonot*. Whether these claims are accurate or were instead part and parcel of a complex disinformation campaign designed to "snitch-jacket" Skorzeny remains to be seen. If true, they suggest that Skorzeny may have become an opportunist of the most shameless and unprincipled sort, one who might even willingly betray his former comrades. And if his subsequent clandestine activities really were "controlled" by Israeli and Western intelligence operatives, their political and historical significance would have to be newly assessed and revised.

63 For this April 1961 meeting in Madrid, see the account of Mader, *Jagd nach dem Narbengesicht*, pp. 285–6. Not surprisingly, the East German polemicist argues that Skorzeny later provided tangible assistance to the French military plotters. It would appear, moreover, that the Austrian's close associate Degrelle was an avid supporter of the OAS. See his remarks in the neo-fascist journal, *L'Europe Réelle*, quoted by Jean-Raymond Tournoux, *L'Histoire secrète: La Cagoule, le Front populaire, Vichy, Londres, Deuxième Bureau, l'Algérie française, l'OAS* (Paris: Plon, 1962), p. 291. But as yet no actual evidence that Skorzeny aided the OAS has surfaced, and there are some good reasons to doubt it. For one thing, more reliable researchers who place Skorzeny at that same meeting indicate that he was skeptical of the putschist's plans because he did not trust generals in the regular army – in this case Gardy and Raoul Salan – after his experiences rooting out the anti-Hitler conspirators in 1944. See Paul Henissart, *Wolves in the City: The Death of French Algeria* (New York: Simon & Schuster, 1970), p. 69. More importantly, like many of his old Nazi comrades Skorzeny was apparently philo-Arab due to feelings of antipathy toward Jews. Several of the men he worked with during his stint in al-Nāsir's Egypt, including Gerhard Harmut von Schubert

and Johannes von Leers, were active supporters of the sort of Arab nationalism being espoused by the FLN. (Von Leers was a longtime anti-Semite, as indicated by the titles of some of his primary publications, including *Vierzehn Jahre Judenrepublik: Die Geschichte eines Rassenkampfes* [Berlin: National-Sozialistische, 1933], 2 volumes; and *Juden sehen dich an* [Berlin: National-Sozialistische, 1933].) The same was true of certain of Skorzeny's probable business associates, such as François Genoud in Switzerland. According to one less than trustworthy source, while in Egypt Skorzeny trained bands of FLN terrorists to fight against the French Army in Algeria. See Seder and Greenburg, *Behind the Egyptian Sphinx*, p. 63. More reliable researchers have sought to reconcile these conflicting claims. According to journalistic intelligence specialists Roger Faligot and Rémi Kauffer, for example, Skorzeny not only placed his arms trading company Atlantica, located at Calle Jorge 28 in Madrid, at the service of the FLN, he also developed close associations with OAS activists operating in Spain due to his far right sympathies and hatred for De Gaulle. See Faligot and Kauffer, *Croissant et la croix gammée*, p. 197. Compare Lee, *Beast Reawakens*, pp. 144, 146. However that may be, the alleged presence of CIA representatives at this Madrid meeting, and the possibility that they encouraged and offered to support the conspirators, was a well-circulated story at the time. See, for example, *Le Procès des généraux Challe et Zeller: Textes complets des débats, réquisitoires, plaidoiries, annexes* (Paris: Nouvelles Editions Latines, 1961), p. 95; Alexander Werth, "The CIA in Algeria," *The Nation* 192 (13 May 1961), pp. 433–5; Orville D. Menard, *The Army and the Fifth Republic* (Lincoln: University of Nebraska, 1967), p. 216, note 109; and Edgar S. Furniss Jr., *De Gaulle and the French Army: A Crisis in Civil-Military Relations* (New York: Twentieth Century Fund, 1964), pp. 53–4. Despite a lack of documentary evidence and the possibility of communist-inspired disinformation, there is nothing inherently implausible about CIA participation in a secret meeting at which conspiratorial French officers and Skorzeny were present. After all, they had already allegedly been involved in hiring the latter to help train the Egyptian security forces. The crucial question concerning the April 1961 meeting is whether the CIA operatives – if actually present – were feigning support for the French putschists in order to gather additional information, supporting them on their own initiative, or carrying out policies formulated by higher ranking members of the Kennedy administration, a question that no one can hope to answer until the relevant U.S. archives are opened up to public scrutiny.

64 See Frédéric Laurent, *L'Orchestre noir* (Paris: Stock, 1978), p. 154, for this important bit of information. Both Leroy and Aginter Presse will be discussed in much greater detail in the next chapter. One Belgian journalist goes so far as to claim that Skorzeny was one of the founders, along with Yves Guillou, of Aginter Presse, but he provides no evidence at all for this assertion. See Hugo Gijsels, *L'Enquête: 20 années de déstabilisation en Belgique* (Brussels: Longue Vue, 1990), p. 261.

65 For these connections, see Laurent, *Orchestre noir*, pp. 317–18. The bank in question was the Banco de Avila, the company Technomotor, which was located in Madrid. According to an article in the 26 March 1975 issue of Lisbon's *A Capital*, Skorzeny himself was an "advisor" (*mentor*) for Technomotor. See Mariano Sánchez Soler, *Los hijos del 20-N: Historia violenta del fascismo español* (Madrid: Temas de Hoy, 1993), p. 155. Note also that another company that served as a legal "cover" for the ELP – the Sociedade Mariano Lana Villacampa, also in Madrid – was owned by Mariano Sánchez Covisa, a former member of the División Azul (Blue Division) and leader of the Guerrilleros de Cristo Rey (GCR: Guerrillas of Christ the King), a right-wing paramilitary organization founded in 1968 that was thereafter involved in periodic acts of anti-leftist violence, especially against reformist clergymen and "Marxist" bookstores. Furthermore, this very same Duke of Valencia served as the patron and host for other leading fascist-era exiles in Spain, including Degrelle and Italian prince Junio Valerio Borghese, who had been forced to take refuge there after his unsuccessful 1970 attempt to organize and launch a coup in Rome had come to light. This coup will be discussed at great length in another chapter of this volume. Not coincidentally, the Duke's wife was involved in the preparation

of a book glorifying Degrelle and whitewashing his ideas. See the Duquesa de Valencia, *Degrelle m'à dit* (Paris: Morel, 1961). For more on the ELP, see Günter Walraff, *Die Aufdeckung einer Verschwörung* (Cologne: Kiepenheuer & Witsch, 1976), which appeared after left-wing investigative journalist Walraff had successfully infiltrated the organization; former Spanish intelligence agent Luis González-Mata, *Terrorismo international: La extrema derecha, la extrema izquierda, y los crimenes de estado* (Barcelona: Argos, 1978), pp. 139–52; Laurent, *Orchestre noir*, pp. 315–37; "Ernesto Cadena" (pseudonym for radical Partido Español Nacional Sindicalista [PENS: Spanish National Syndicalist Party] leader Ernesto Milá Rodríguez), *La ofensiva neo-fascista: Un informe sensacional* (Barcelona: Acervo, 1978), pp. 253–9; Sánchez Soler, *Hijos del 20-N*, pp. 154–5; and Carlos Dugos, *M.D.L.P.-E.L.P.: O que são? A Verdade sobre os dois movimentos clandestinos* (Alfragides: Acrópole, 1976), especially pp. 91–113. For a listing of the violent actions reputedly carried out by the ELP and other ultra-rightist groups in Portugal up until March of 1977, see Partido Comunista Português, ed., *Dossier terrorismo* (Lisbon: Avante, 1977), passim. For more on the GCR, the "*brigadistas* of the truncheon" who emerged out of the rightist Defensa Universitaria (University Defense) group and were covertly linked to the intelligence service of the Guardia Civil (Civil Guard), see Sánchez Soler, *Hijos del 20-N*, pp. 144–5; Paul Preston, *The Politics of Revenge: Fascism and the Military in Twentieth-Century Spain* (London: Unwin Hyman, 1990), pp. 166–70; Cadena, *Ofensiva neo-fascista*, pp. 173–4; Laurent, *Orchestre noir*, pp. 311, 356–66; José Luis Rodríguez Jiménez, *Reaccionarios y golpistas: La extrema derecha en España del tardofranquismo a la consolidación de la democracia, 1967–1982* (Madrid: Consejo Superior de Investigaciones Científicas, 1994), pp. 221–2; Alejandro Muñoz Alonso, *El terrorismo en España: El terror frente a la convivencia pluralista en libertad* (Madrid: Planeta/Instituto de Estudios Económicos, 1982), pp. 37–8; Chairoff, *Dossier néo-nazisme*, pp. 169–70; and Gerardo Duelo, *Diccionario de grupos, fuerzas y partidos políticos españoles* (Barcelona: Gaya Ciencia, 1977), p. 71.

66 For more information about Merex, see Heinz Vielain, *Waffenschmuggel im Staatsauftrag: Was lange in Bonn geheim bleiben musste?* (Herford: Busse Seewald, 1986); Lee, *Beast Reawakens*, pp. 183–4, who claims that Skorzeny helped found the company (in addition to doing business with ex-CIA officer Sam Cummings' Interarms Company and becoming a "major weapons broker" for the Salazar regime); and González-Mata, *Terrorismo international*, pp. 146–51, who quotes a 13 September 1975 telegram prepared by an official at the Portuguese embassy in Paris for the details concerning Spínola's contacts. Among the other persons with whom Spínola supposedly met during his summer visits to several European countries were Franz-Josef Strauss of the Bavarian Christlich-Soziale Union (CSU: Christian Social Union); Sánchez Covisa of the GCR; billionaire Jorge Jardim, an ex-Secretary of State appointed by Salazar and a key financial backer of anti-independence organizations in Mozambique and other Portuguese colonies; Hermann Josef Abs of Krupp, previously head of the Deutsche Bank under the Nazi regime; leaders of the ELP; John McCone, formerly CIA director and at that time head of International Telephone and Telegraph (ITT), which had previously played a key role in anti-Allende subversion in Chile; several CIA officials, including an adjutant of Lieutenant General Vernon A. Walters, then Deputy Director of the agency; and representatives from a number of other multinational companies and arms trafficking firms, including Belgium's Société Général, Petrofina, ELF (a French oil company that was deeply implicated in the so-called sniffer planes scandal), MGM (an arms trading company in Modena that Italian judge Luciano Violante believed was linked to individuals associated with the Fronte Nazionale (National Front), the organizational backbone of the December 1970 Borghese Coup and later plots), and Permindex (an alleged Swiss-based CIA proprietary company that had earlier been implicated, almost certainly without justification, in the November 1963 assassination of President John F. Kennedy). This latter claim was originally made in the independent but philo-communist Italian newspaper *Paese Sera* in its 4 and 6 March 1967 editions, and was subsequently given extensive publicity by Soviet and other leftist sources. For a detailed summary of that claim, see Paris Flammonde, *The Kennedy*

Conspiracy: An Uncommissioned Report on the Jim Garrison Investigation (New York: Meredith, 1969), pp. 40, 214–24, 281. After investigating the matter in more depth, Stephen Dorril concluded that the assertions about Permindex and its parent company, the Centro Mondiale Commerciale (CMC: World Commercial Center) in Rome, were the products of a communist disinformation campaign, even though both companies did in fact exist and were involved in various shady business affairs. See "Permindex: The International Trade in Disinformation," *The Third Decade: A Journal of Research on the John F. Kennedy Assassination* 2:1 (September 1985), pp. 11–18. For the MGM export-import company, see Flamini, *Partito del golpe*, volume 3, part 2, pp. 604–5; and volume 4, part 1, pp. 7–8. For the "sniffer planes" scandal in France, see Service de presse du Premier Ministre Pierre Mauroy, *Livre blanc sur l'affaire dite des "avions renifleurs"* (Paris: Documentation Française, 1984); and Pierre Péan, *V: Enquête sur l'affaire des "avions renifleurs" et ses ramifications proches et lointaines* (Paris: Fayard, 1984). For more on Jorge Jardim, who was a covert intelligence operative and organizer of counterinsurgency operations as well as a government minister and financier, see the detailed study by José Freire Antunes, *Jorge Jardim: Agente secreto* (Lisbon: Bertrand, 1996).

67 However, the exact nature of Skorzeny's role in Paladin – which was named after the protagonist in *Have Gun Will Travel*, a popular American Western television series – is difficult to clarify. Some authors do not even mention his name at all in connection with Paladin, whereas others claim that it was "Scarface" rather than von Schubert who was the real leader of the organization. See, for example, Sánchez Soler, *Hijos del 20-N*, p. 157; Henrik Krüger, *The Great Heroin Coup: Drugs, Intelligence, and International Fascism* (Boston: South End, 1980), pp. 113–14, 209; Lee, *Beast Reawakens*, pp. 185–6; British anarchist Stuart Christie, *Stefano Delle Chiaie: Portrait of a Black Terrorist* (London: Anarchy/Refract, 1984), p. 73, who claims that Paladin was set up with the authorization of the Spanish Interior Ministry; and the study by communist propagandist Wilfred Burchett and Derek Roebuck, *The Whores of War: Mercenaries Today* (Harmondsworth: Penguin, 1977), p. 158. Although not every sinister activity in Spain during this period should be attributed to Skorzeny, it is impossible to believe that he had no connection with the activities of Paladin given the nature of its personnel, its clients, and it activities. In any event, the first public notice of Paladin's existence lay in the periodic advertisements that the organization took out in various European newspapers between the summer of 1971 and 1974. These ads, which were written in poor quality English, were provocatively worded:

> Danger no Objection [sic]! The Paladin Group carries out YOUR orders on National and International scale, including behind the Iron and Bamboo curtains, with complete confidence guaranteed. Fully trained experts in many fields are at YOUR disposal and willing to go anywhere in the world to bring YOUR order to a successful end. All replies and orders will remain fully confidential and will never be available to third parties. Reply to: The Paladin Group, c/o Dr. G.H. v. Schubert, "El Panorama," De Albuferete, Alicante, Spain.

A copy of this ad is reproduced in Sandro Ottolenghi, "I rapporti tra Giannettini e la CIA," *L'Europeo* 30:36 (5 September 1974), p. 21. Another Paladin ad placed a request for a pilot with a commercial license, a ship captain, a navigator, two explosives experts, two electronics experts, three photographers, six sailors, two camouflage experts, two experts in the Chinese language, two experts in the Vietnamese language, one psychologist, and four others with open specialties. The monthly pay was listed as over 3,000 dollars. It should also be noted that several key Paladin personnel were also affiliated with Aginter Presse, which has led a number of observers to conclude that there was an organic relationship between the two organizations. See González-Mata, *Terrorismo international*, pp. 129, 162; José Goulão, *O labirinto da conspiração: P2, Mafia, Opus Dei* (Lisbon: Caminho, 1986), p. 107; and Sánchez Soler, *Hijos del 20-N*, p. 156 (who claims that Aginter transferred its headquarters to Alicante, the seat of Paladin, in the wake of the 1974 Portuguese revolution). If so, this would further suggest that Skorzeny maintained close connections with Aginter, especially since it has been claimed that representatives from the Portuguese secret police – Aginter's immediate organizational patron – frequently visited Paladin's offices in Spain, along with Italian intelligence personnel and an assortment of fascists. Compare Guido Gerosa, "Ecco i documenti," *L'Europeo* 30:36 (5 September 1974), p. 24, citing a Spanish secret service document; González-Mata, *Terrorismo international*, p. 162.

68 For more information on the Paladin Group, which Skorzeny supposedly envisioned as "an international directorship of strategic assault personnel [that would] straddle the watershed between paramilitary operations carried out by troops in uniforms and the political warfare conducted by civilian agents" (Christie, *Stefano Delle Chiaie*, p. 74), see Laurent, *Orchestre noir*, pp. 326–9; Krüger, *Great Heroin Coup*, especially pp. 209–10; and González-Mata, *Terrorismo international*, especially pp. 164–7. Note that Paladin's Zurich office was shared with – and "covered" by – the arms trading company Worldarmco (which was registered in von Schubert's name), that its Paris office was shared with the International Business Offices Service (an umbrella group that sheltered several companies controlled by the networks of Jacques Foccart, a central figure in the creation of SAC-linked parallel apparatuses, which were then carrying out a vast range of covert operations in every corner of the world), that its London affiliate was none other than the "private" Watchguard organization headed by Colonel David Stirling, the former commander of Britain's elite Special Air Service (SAS) commando regiment, and that the individual in charge of its Brussels office was ex-SS man Jean-Robert Debbaudt, the well-known fascist activist who headed the Belgian branches of the MSE/ESB and, later, of the NOE/ENO, on which see further later. For more on the multifaceted activities of Foccart, see the recent study by Pierre Péan, *L'Homme de l'ombre: Éléments d'enquête autour de Jacques Foccart, l'homme le plus mystérieux et le plus puissant de la Vème République* (Paris: Fayard, 1990). For the SAC, see Chairoff, *Dossier B . . . comme barbouzes*; Serge Ferrand and Gilbert Lecavelier, *Aux ordres du S.A.C.* (Paris: Albin Michel, 1982); and especially Assemblée Nationale, Commission d'enquête sur les activités du Service d'Action Civique, *Rapport [le 17 juin 1982]* (Paris: Alain Moreau, 1982), 2 volumes. There is a large popular literature on the SAS. See, for example, Anthony Kemp, *The SAS: The Savage Wars of Peace, 1947 to the Present* (London: J. Murray, 1994); John Strawson, *A History of the SAS Regiment* (London: Secker & Warburg, 1984); and Tony Geraghty, *Who Dares Wins: The Story of the Special Air Service* (London: Arms and Armour, 1980).

69 Laurent, *Orchestre noir*, pp. 328–9. Paladin personnel were purportedly involved in "counterterrorist" campaigns against the ETA in Spain and France, special interventions in support of pro-Western forces in the Congo, Benin, Angola, Guinea, Cabinda, Mozambique, and Algeria, terrorist actions in Italy, and attempts to overthrow the new Portuguese regime. See González-Mata, *Terrorismo international*, pp. 166–7. Some of these anti-ETA campaigns, which were carried out by right-wing paramilitary groups using a variety of different cover names, were allegedly coordinated by Paladin operatives at the behest of the DGS during the 1970s. Compare Faligot and Kauffer, *Croissant et la croix gammée*, p. 231; and Christie, *Stefano Delle Chiaie*, p. 74. (It should be noted, however, that the anarchist Christie was himself arrested by the Spanish authorities, supposedly with explosives in his possession, and that his book contains both factual errors and unsubstantiated claims.) Paladin also did business with and carried out operations for the Libyan government and other Arab regimes, provided logistical support to Jūrj Habāsh's Front Populaire pour la Libération de Palestine (FPLP: Popular Front for the Liberation of Palestine), and made its facilities available for the planning of Arab terrorist attacks. For the Habāsh connection, see Faligot and Kauffer, *Croissant et la croix gammée*, p. 230. For examples involving the 17 December 1973 massacre at Fiumicino airport and the kidnapping of a Libyan exile in Liège, see Gerosa, "Ecco i documenti," pp. 22–4. Compare Giuseppe De Lutiis, *Storia dei servizi segreti in Italia* (Rome: Riuniti, 1984), pp. 170–3, where the foreknowledge and seemingly scandalous inactivity of the Italian secret service in the former case is summarized.

70 See, for example, Linklater et al., *Fourth Reich*, pp. 274–411; Didier Epelbaum, *Alois Brunner: La haine irréductible* (Paris: Calmann-Lévy, 1990), pp. 14–23, 253–319; Faligot and Kauffer, *Croissant et la croix gammée*, pp. 15–18, 174–5, 257–71 (Brunner); Stevenson, *Bormann Brotherhood*, passim; Peter Dale Scott, "How Allen Dulles and the SS Preserved Each Other," *Covert Action Information Bulletin* 25 (Winter 1986), pp. 4–14; and Farago, *Aftermath*, passim. It scarcely needs to be pointed out that many of the secondary sources dealing with purported Nazi activities since 1945 have proven to be untrustworthy, in part because the entire subject was exceptionally difficult to obtain accurate information about until various European governments began to request extradition in certain high-profile cases. Nevertheless, the reasonably well-documented postwar careers of Barbie, Schwend, and Brunner alone demonstrate that a number of unrepentant ex-Nazis engaged in covert political operations and highly profitable illegal activities after reaching secure havens abroad.

71 See, for example, Chairoff's characterization of Ustaša prelate Krunoslav Draganović as ODESSA's chief representative in Genoa until 1960. *Dossier néo-nazisme*, pp. 7–8. While this is by no means unlikely, leaving the matter at that obscures the fact that the Croatian cleric's success in spiriting thousands of wanted Nazis and Nazi collaborators out of harm's way derived primarily from his key position in the Vatican's refugee relief administration and his close ties to U.S. intelligence. Likewise, Brockdorff's portrayal of Rauff as the mastermind of the "Roman" escape route, albeit with the help of pro-Nazi prelates and American Catholic refugee organizations, minimizes the decisive role played by the Vatican hierarchy and secret American intelligence networks. See *Flucht vor Nürnberg*, pp. 68–92. Note also that the organizational and financial role of the most important Nazi activists is almost entirely ignored in the latter book. Skorzeny is not even mentioned, and Rudel barely makes an appearance. A similarly distorted account, with many of the very same lacunae, can also be found in Wiesenthal, *Justice Not Vengeance*, pp. 58–65. For more on the crucial behind-the-scenes role played by the Vatican and various intelligence agencies in helping wanted Nazis and fascists to escape, see the well-documented studies of Gerald Steinacher, *Nazis on the Run: How Hitler's Henchmen Fled Justice* (Oxford and New York: Oxford University, 2011); and, in the case of Argentina, Uki Goñi, *The Real ODESSA: How Peron Brought the Nazi War Criminals to Argentina* (London and New York: Granta UK, 2003).

72 For the scramble to recruit or shelter Axis scientists, see Linda Hunt, *Secret Agenda: The United States Government, Nazi Scientists, and Project Paperclip, 1944–1990* (New York: St. Martin's, 1991); Annie Jacobsen, *Operation Paperclip: The Secret Intelligence Program that Brought Nazi Scientists to America* (New York: Little, Brown, 2014); Tom Bower, *The Paperclip Conspiracy: The Hunt for Nazi Scientists* (Boston: Little, Brown, 1987); Clarence G. Lasby, *Project Paperclip: German Scientists and the Cold War* (New York: Atheneum, 1971); Peter Williams and David Wallace, *Unit 731: Japan's Secret Biological Warfare in World War II* (New York: Free Press, 1989); and Sheldon H. Harris, *Factories of Death: Japanese Biological Warfare, 1932–45, and the American Cover-Up* (London and New York: Routledge, 1994), which also deals with Unit 731.

73 For the protection and recruitment of Axis intelligence and military personnel, see Simpson, *Blowback*; John Loftus, *The Belarus Secret: The Nazi Connection in America* (New York: Paragon House, 1989); Tom Bower, *The Pledge Betrayed: America and Britain and the Denazification of Postwar Germany* (Garden City, NY: Doubleday, 1982); Tom Bower, *The Red Web: MI6 and the KGB Master Coup* (London: Aurum, 1989); David Matas, *Justice Delayed: Nazi War Criminals in Canada* (Toronto: Summerhill, 1987); Mark Aarons, *Sanctuary: Nazi Fugitives in Australia* (Melbourne: Heinemann, 1989); Mark Aarons and John Loftus, *Unholy Trinity: How the Vatican's Nazi Networks betrayed Western Intelligence to the Soviets* (New York: St. Martin's, 1991); David Cesarani, *Justice Delayed: How Britain became a Refuge for Nazi War Criminals* (London: Heinemann, 1992); and Alain Guérin, *Les commandos de la guerre froide* (Paris: Julliard, 1967). Aside from the latter book, which depends largely on Soviet and communist sources, the preceding studies all are based upon the results

of parliamentary investigations and declassified documents obtained in their respective nations. Loftus and Cesarani actually helped to prepare official government legal cases and/or reports.
74 Lee, *Beast Reawakens*, pp. 40 (Soviet recruitment effort) and 133–4 ("Kluf" testimony, citing a 2 March 1953 State Department report).
75 See George H. Stein, *The Waffen SS: Hitler's Elite Guard at War, 1939–1945* (Ithaca: Cornell University, 1966), pp. 123–4, 179. Compare the articles listed in note 10, *supra*.
76 Robert L. Koehl, *The Black Corps: The Structure and Power Struggles of the Nazi SS* (Madison: University of Wisconsin, 1983), p. 201.
77 See Stein, *Waffen SS*, pp. 94–100, 146–8; Heinz Höhne, *The Order of the Death's Head: The Story of Hitler's SS* (New York: Ballantine, 1971), pp. 517–19, 569–71; and Compare Tauber, *Beyond Eagle and Swastika*, volume 2, p. 1084, note 5.
78 Stein, *Waffen SS*, pp. 144–5, 163–96, 286; Koehl, *Black Corps*, pp. 201–2. Compare [former SS General] Paul Hausser, *Waffen-SS im Einsatz* (Göttingen: Schutz, 1953), pp. 231–2.
79 For the details about HIAG that appear in the next three paragraphs, see Jenke, *Verschwörung von rechts?*, pp. 311–20; Tauber, *Beyond Eagle and Swastika*, volume 1, pp. 332–62; Dudek and Jaschke, *Entstehung und Entwicklung des Rechtsextremismus*, volume 1, pp. 106–15; and David Clay Large, "Reckoning without the Past: The HIAG of the Waffen-SS and the Politics of Rehabilitation in the Bonn Republic, 1950–1961," *Journal of Modern History* 59 (March 1987), pp. 79–113.
80 For more on the VdS, its components, and its organizational rivals, see Dudek and Jaschke, *Entstehung und Entwicklung des Rechtsextremismus*, volume 1, especially pp. 83–9; and Tauber, *Beyond Eagle and Swastika*, volume 1, pp. 291–8.
81 Tauber, *Beyond Eagle and Swastika*, volume 1, pp. 354–6.
82 Among these HIAG radicals were Erich Kernmayer, Lothar Greil, Otto Weidinger, and Bernd Linn. See ibid., pp. 360–2.
83 See, for example, Bundesministerium des Innern, *Verfassungsschutz[bericht] 1980* (Bonn: BMI, 1981), p. 38; and Bundesministerium des Innern, *Verfassungsschutz[bericht] 1981* (Bonn: BMI, 1982), p. 45. Here it is perhaps worth noting that when Indonesian president Achmed Sukarno sought to acquire the services of a skilled German military advisor in the mid-1950s, Skorzeny recommended HIAG spokesman Kurt Meyer for the job. See Faligot and Kauffer, *Croissant et la croix gammée*, p. 180.
84 For these reductionist claims, see Infield, *Skorzeny*, pp. 182–3; and Schmidt, *New Reich*, p. 42.
85 See Large, "Reckoning without the Past," pp. 83–4; Tauber, *Beyond Eagle and Swastika*, pp. 347–8.
86 For the Stille Hilfe connection, see Jenke, *Verschwörung von rechts?*, p. 313. Compare Dudek and Jaschke, *Entstehung und Entwicklung des Rechtsextremismus*, volume 1, p. 109. For the connection to ODESSA and Spinne, see Dokumentationsarchiv des österreichischen Widerstandes, ed., *Rechtsextremismus in Österreich nach 1945* (Vienna: Österreichischer Bundesverlag, 1980), p. 204.
87 For Kameradschaft IV, see Chairoff, *Dossier néo-nazisme*, p. 100; and Dokumentationsarchiv, ed., *Rechtsextremismus in Österreich*, pp. 145, 204. The latter is still the most complete survey of right-wing extremism in Austria after World War II. For the Kameradschaft Babenberg, see ibid., pp. 144–5. For the Nationaldemokratische Partei, see ibid., pp. 149–52. For ANR, see ibid., pp. 134–5; and Alexander Mensdorf, *Im Namen der Republik: Rechtsextremismus und Justiz in Österreich* (Vienna: Löcker, 1990), pp. 50–68, 73–9.
88 For HINAG, see especially Jaap van Donselaar, *Fout na de oorlog: Fascistische en racistische organisaties in Nederland, 1950–1990* (Amsterdam: Bert Bakker, 1991), pp. 80–92. For the SOPD, see ibid., pp. 28–50. For the NESB, see ibid., pp. 51–79.
89 For the SMF, see Etienne Verhoeyen, *L'Extrême-droite en Belgique* (Brussels: Centre de Recherche et d'Information Socio-Politiques, 1974), volume 2, p. 44; Etienne Verhoeyen and Frank Uytterhaegen, *De kreeft met de zwarte scharen: 50 jaar rechts en uiterst rechts in België* (Ghent: Masereelfonds, 1981), pp. 86–7, an updated and modified Dutch version of the former.

90 Chairoff, *Dossier néo-nazisme*, pp. 269–70. For the NRP, see ibid., pp. 275, 280–1; Hans Lindquist, *Fascism i dag: Förtrupper eller eftersläntrare?* (Stockholm: Federativs, 1979), pp. 24–30; and Eisenberg, *Re-Emergence of Fascism*, pp. 224–5. The NRP was founded in 1956 by Göran Assar Oredsson, originally as the Sveriges Nationalsocialistiska Kampförbund (Swedish National-Socialist Fighting Alliance), but the name was later changed and branches were established in other Scandinavian countries.
91 Chairoff, *Dossier néo-nazisme*, pp. 274–5.
92 For Veljesapu, see Del Boca and Giovana, *Fascism Today*, p. 453, note 5. For Henrikson, see Dokumentationsarchiv, *Rechtsextremismus in Österreich*, p. 204.
93 Compare Chairoff, *Dossier néo-nazisme*, p. 167; and Duelo, *Diccionario de grupos*, p. 52. For the Confederación Nacional de Ex-Combatientes, see Rodríguez Jiménez, *Reaccionarios y golpistas*, pp. 105–9. More information on Girón will be provided later.
94 For an indication that these branches existed, see the list in Del Boca and Giovana, *Fascism Today*, p. 453, note 5.
95 For this initial March meeting in Rome, see especially Tauber, *Beyond Eagle and Swastika*, volume 1, p. 208. Compare Hans Jaeger, *The Reappearance of the Swastika: Neo-Nazism and Fascist International: Comprehensive Survey of all Organisations, Leaders, Cross-Connexions and Their Ideological Background* (London: Gamma, 1960), p. 27, for a list of the Rome attendees. It should be pointed out that some secondary sources containing information about the so-called Malmö international either telescope the two 1950 prepatory meetings or reverse their temporal sequence. Thus, for example, Jaeger (and, following his lead, Algazy) make it seem as though the March meeting attracted the older fascists, not the October "youth" meeting. See ibid., p. 27; Algazy, *Tentation néo-fasciste en France*, p. 294. However, this conflicts with other, more complete accounts.
96 The background of some of these activists is worth noting. Engdahl, who was fifty-seven in 1951, had been in a succession of far right organizations in Sweden since age seventeen, including the Sveriges Nationella Förbund (Swedish National Alliance). He had earlier been a rabid anti-Semite who had publicly applauded the Nazi persecution of the Jews, and during the 1930s he began his lifelong working relationship with Carl Enfrid Carlberg, the anti-Semitic millionaire who played a key role in bankrolling fascist organizations in Sweden, both before and after World War II. After the Axis defeat, Engdahl wrote that Nazism would live again, but in a different form. In 1946, perhaps in an effort to make good on his own prediction, he publicly repudiated anti-Semitism, which he now argued was responsible for the disasters which had befallen the fascist cause. In 1950 he founded the NSR. For more on Engdahl, see Lindquist, *Fascism i dag*, pp. 31–3; Armas Sastamoinen, *Ny-nazismen: Tillägnas alla bortglömda antinazistiska kämpar* (Stockholm: Federativs, 1962), pp. 53–62, 102–31; and Werner Smoydzin, *Hitler lebt!: Vom internationalen Faschismus zur Internationale des Hakenkreuzes* (Pfaffenhofen: Ilmgau, 1966), pp. 70–3. Bardèche was a self-described "fascist writer" who had befriended Robert Brasillach and other fascist intellectuals at the École Normale Superieure in the 1930s and had become a supporter of the Vichy government following the French defeat. After the liberation of Paris he was arrested for collaborationism and imprisoned for several months, and was traumatized both by the arbitrary brutality of the purge and the February 1945 execution of Brasillach (whose brother-in-law he had become in 1936). Upon his release he began publishing books defending Vichy and criticizing the "justice" of the victors, including *Lettre à François Mauriac* (Paris: Pensée Libre, 1947) and *Nuremberg ou la terre promise* (Paris: Sept Couleurs, 1948), one of the first works to argue that the *Endlösung* (Final Solution) was not a plan to exterminate the Jews. He later became the first editor to publish the "revisionist" books of Paul Rassinier, who denied that the Holocaust had taken place. Thus acquiring a position of authority in neo-fascist circles, Bardéche was asked to head the French delegation at Malmö, and thereafter took a great interest in these attempts to form an "international of nationalism." His views concerning Nation Europa and other matters were regularly outlined in a monthly publication he founded in 1951, *Defense de l'Occident*, as well as in the fascinating book he wrote a

decade later, *Qu'est-ce que le fascisme?*. For an excellent overview of his postwar activities and attitudes, see Algazy, *Tentation néo-fasciste en France*, pp. 199–221. Priester authored the pamphlet *Deutschland, Ost-West Kolonie oder gleichberechtigt in einem freien Europa?* (Wiesbaden: Europäische Nationale, 1951), which provides a clear indication of his radical "third force," Nation Europa perspective.

97 For the October 1950 meeting, see Smoydzin, *Hitler lebt!*, pp. 58–60; Tauber, *Beyond Eagle and Swastika*, volume 1, pp. 208–10. The vast gulf between the conservative leaders of the MSI, who sought to organize an "international" under their own direction, and the radical youths, who sought, without success, to produce a manifesto which would rally their foreign counterparts and simultaneously satisfy both the "socialist" leftist and the aristocratic and philo-Nazi rightist factions, is described by Mario Giovana, *Le nuove camicie nere* (Turin: Albero, 1966), pp. 79–84.

98 For a listing of these participants, see Jaeger, *Reappearance of the Swastika*, p. 28; Sastamoinen, *Nynazismen*, pp. 109–10. Note that Priester and members of his entourage were denied visas by the Swedish authorities. For the Vlaams Blok, see Hugo Gijsels and Jos Vander Velpen, *Het Vlaams Blok, 1938–1988: Het verdriet van Vlaanderen* (Berchem: EPO/Halt, 1989), although no mention of Van Dyck is made therein. For Fischer, who sought vainly to get the delegates to adopt his radical anti-Semitic program, see Tauber, *Beyond Eagle and Swastika*, volume 2, p. 1089, note 30. According to the May–June 1956 issue of *Signes*, the publication of the French section of the World Jewish Congress, Skorzeny and Mosley were expected to attend the conference, but did not. Cited in ibid., volume 2, p. 1088, note 19.

99 See Algazy, *Tentation néo-fasciste en France*, p. 295.

100 For this list of "study commission" members, see Chairoff, *Dossier néo-nazisme*, p. 437. Massi was a key leader of the MSI's left-wing who later broke away from the party when the moderates led by Michelini and De Marsanich seized control over it. For a clearer idea of his notions, see the collection of his articles in *Nazione sociale: Scritti politici, 1948–1976*, ed. by Gianni S. Rossi (Rome: Istituto di Studi Corporativi, 1990), pp. 87–609. Also of interest is the MSI left's motion at the party's Fourth Congress at Viareggio, reprinted in ibid., pp. 713–25. Timmel was an early member of the Austrian Nazi Party and a former SS Sturmbannführer who was associated with various right-wing groups after the war, including the Ring Vertrauer Verbände (RVV: Circle of Faithful Organizations), the Arbeitsgemeinschaft der Freiheitlichen Akademikerverbände Österreichs (Working Association of Free Austrian Academic Organizations), and the Union für Südtirol (South Tyrol Union). He has been described as "one of the most important activists in the radical right scene in Austria," and was awarded the "Freedom Prize" by the rightist *Deutsche National-Zeitung* in 1976. See *Rechtsextremismus in Österreich*, pp. 137, 157, 182, 202, 346, 380 (quote). Dillen was the founder of the [Belgian] Jong-Nederlandse Gemeenschap (Young Netherlands Society) in 1949, a member of the Volksunie (People's Union) party's council, and later the president of the [Belgian] Verbond van Nederlandse Werkgemeenschappen (Were Di: Confederation of Netherlands Action Groups), an extremist pan-Netherlands group established in 1962. He later went on to play an important role in the paramilitary VMO and the Vlaams Blok. See Verhoeyen, *Extrême droite en Belgique*, volume 2, pp. 32–7; and Gijsels and Vander Velpen, *Vlaams Blok*, passim. Gayre, an expert on heraldry, served as a military intelligence officer during World War II and subsequently became a vociferous proponent of hereditarian notions that are nowadays widely characterized as pseudo-scientific and racist. Because of this, he became involved with a variety of extremist organizations and publications, including the Northern League. See further Kevin Coogan, "The Importance of Robert Gayre," *Parapolitics U.S.A.* 2 (May 1981), pp. 44–51. Landig was an ex-SS officer who was also linked to the Northern League. He subsequently authored a bizarre anti-Semitic book reflecting the "Aryanization" of the myth of an Eden-like Hyperboria from whence "superior" specimens of humanity emerged – *Götzen gegen Thule: Ein Roman voller Wirklichkeiten* (Hanover: Hans Pfeiffer, 1971) – and in 1978 he attended the World Anti-Communist League conference in

Washington, DC. See, respectively, Joscelyn Godwin, *Arktos: The Polar Myth in Science, Symbolism, and Nazi Survival* (Grand Rapids, MI: Phanes, 1993), pp. 62–70; and Scott Anderson and Jon Lee Anderson, *Inside the League: The Shocking Exposé of How Terrorists, Nazis, and Latin American Death Squads Have Infiltrated the World Anti-Communist League* (New York: Dodd Mead, 1986), pp. 94, 97–8. Finally, it would be most interesting to ascertain whether the Manuel Ballesteros named by Chairoff is the same individual who later became head of the "anti-terrorist" section of the Spanish police, the Mando Unico de la Lucha Contraterrorista (MULC: United Command for the Counterterrorist Struggle), who was thence accused of participating in the launching and coordinating of a "dirty war" against separatist Basque terrorists as well as various other improprieties. His tender age of sixteen in 1951 certainly suggests otherwise, but if by some fluke it was the same individual, the important question in this context is whether he was a genuine neo-fascist extremist in the early 1950s, whether he had infiltrated the MSE/ESB organization on behalf of the Spanish security forces, or both. For Ballesteros the policeman's later career, see Melchor Miralles and Ricardo Arques, *Amedo: El estado contra ETA* (Barcelona: Plaza & Janes/Cambio 16, 1989), especially pp. 98–102, 769; and Manuel Cerdán and Antonio Rubio, *El "caso Interior": GAL, Roldán y fondos reservados: El triángulo negro de un ministerio* (Madrid: Temas de Hoy, 1995), especially pp. 222–3, 236–41.

101 Compare Smoydzin, *Hitler lebt!*, pp. 61–2; and Sastamoinen, *Nynazismen*, pp. 109–10, for the list of MSE/ESB branches.
102 Chairoff, *Dossier néo-nazisme*, p. 438.
103 See the summary in Bardèche's publication, *Défense de l'Occident* (May 1954), pp. 37–8.
104 Cited by Smoydzin, *Hitler lebt!*, p. 82.
105 See Algazy, *Tentation néo-fasciste en France*, p. 297, citing the 2 June 1951 edition of *Droit et Liberté*.
106 See *Défense de l'Occident* (May 1954), pp. 36–9. Compare his remarks in a special 1969 edition of that publication, cited by Bernard Brigouleix, *L'Extrême droite en France: Les "fachos"* (Paris: Fayolle, 1977), p. 220.
107 Compare, for example, Carlberg's "Dreizehn Thesen," in *Nation Europa* 12 (1954), pp. 42–3, as well as some of Engdahl's articles in various Swedish publications cited by Sastamoinen, *Nynazismen*, pp. 55–7, 126–30.
108 For the MSE/ESB's repudiation of racism and anti-Semitism as a self-serving political ruse, see Smoydzin, *Hitler lebt!*, pp. 68–9; Algazy, *Tentation néo-fasciste en France*, pp. 295–6. Chairoff, *Dossier néo-nazisme*, p. 437 disagrees.
109 See Algazy, *Tentation néo-fasciste en France*, p. 301, citing interviews he conducted with the fascist intellectual on 7 December 1980 and 31 January 1981.
110 For the overshadowing of the MSE/ESB by the NOE/ENO, see Brigouleix, *Extrême droite en France*, pp. 220–1.
111 For the gradual dissolution of the MSE/ESB, compare Smoydzin, *Hitler lebt!*, pp. 81–4; and Algazy, *Tentation néo-fasciste en France*, pp. 301–2. Note, however, that the DSB continued to exist until 1977, and some of its other branches may have outlived the parent body as well.
112 For the participants and well-wishers, see Chairoff, *Dossier néo-nazisme*, p. 439.
113 For the organizational structure and leaders of the NOE/ENO, see ibid., p. 439; Verhoeyen, *Extrême droite en Belgique*, volume 1, pp. 42–3.
114 For more on Amaudruz, see Jürg Frischknecht, Peter Haffner, Ueli Haldimann, and Peter Niggli, *Die unheimlichen Patrioten: Politische Reaktion in der Schweiz. Ein aktuelles Handbuch mit Nachtrag 1979–84* (Zurich: Limmat, 1987), pp. 468–9, 472–4, 478–82, 738–41; and Chairoff, *Dossier néo-nazisme*, pp. 245–6. Among his book-length publications are *Ubu-justicier au premier procès de Nuremberg* (Paris: Actes des Apôtres, 1949); *Nous autres racistes: Le manifeste social-raciste* (Montreal: Celtiques, 1971); and *Les peuples blancs survivront-ils? Les travaux du NOE de 1967 à 1985* (Montreal: Celtiques, 1987).
115 For more on Binet and his activities, see Algazy, *Tentation néo-fasciste en France*, pp. 72–3, 77–90 (especially 83–4); and François Duprat, *Les mouvements d'extrême droite en France*

depuis 1944 (Paris: Albatros, 1972), pp. 22–4, 33–7. His three main publications are *Théorie du racisme* (Paris: Wiking, 1950); *Contribution à une éthique raciste* (Montreal: Celtiques, 1975 [1946]); and *Socialisme national contre Marxisme* (Montreal: Celtiques, 1978 [1950]).

116 See the declaration, reprinted in Smoydzin, *Hitler lebt!*, pp. 179–81.
117 See the "manifesto," reprinted in ibid., pp. 188–206. Compare also the French edition reprinted (with glosses) in Amaudruz, *Nous autres racistes*, pp. 57–77. Hereinafter, the latter version of the "manifesto" will be cited. The quotes appear, respectively, on pp. 193 and 63.
118 By Binet in *Contribution à une ethique raciste*, p. 25. Compare also the "manifesto," quoted in Amaudruz, *Nous autre racistes*, pp. 64–6.
119 For the need to carry out a "racial revolution," unite the nations of Europe, and initiate a continent-wide "biological politics," see the "declaration," quoted in Smoydzin, *Hitler lebt!*, pp. 179–84.
120 See Binet, *Contribution à une ethique raciste*, pp. 82–3. Compare Algazy, *Tentation néo-fasciste en France*, p. 302; and Tauber, *Beyond Eagle and Swastika*, volume 1, p. 212.
121 See the "declaration," quoted in Smoydzin, *Hitler lebt!*, pp. 180–1.
122 Cited by Chairoff, *Dossier néo-nazisme*, p. 440. This seems to be a loose translation of one portion of the Zurich "declaration," reprinted in Smoydzin, *Hitler lebt!*, pp. 183–4.
123 See the March 1951 and September 1953 issues of *La Sentinelle*, cited by Algazy, *Tentation néo-fasciste en France*, pp. 80, 89. The Europe of "the federalists" or "Strasbourg" refers to the efforts by social democratic leaders to create a federal European system that would eventually supplant old-fashioned nation-states.
124 Compare the "manifesto" in Amaudruz, *Nous autre racistes*, p. 69; and the "declaration" in Smoydzin, *Hitler lebt!*, p. 180.
125 See his *Théorie du racisme*, p. 38.
126 See the 24 January 1959 issue of *La Legione*, cited by Gianni Flamini, *Il partito del golpe: Le strategie della tensione e del terrore dal primo centrosinistra organico al sequestro Moro, 1964–1978* (Ferrara: Bovolenta, 1981–85), volume 1, p. 23, note 43.
127 For more on the EVS, see Smoydzin, *Hitler lebt!*, pp. 82–6; Tauber, *Beyond Eagle and Swastika*, volume 1, pp. 212–14. The NOE/ENO was in fact the parent organization of the EVS, with whom it shared most of its own personnel, but the former long outlived its ephemeral offspring.
128 See Smoydzin, *Hitler lebt!*, p. 96. The JEL's rather convoluted slogan was "Neither War nor Peace, Revolution! The JEL, A Bomb-Proof Shelter for the Europe of Tommorrow!" Even so, the organization established contacts with a wide array of neo-fascist youth groups. In Germany alone, members of the JEL were linked to the Bund Heimattreuer Jugend (League of Youths Loyal to their Homeland), the Bund Nationaler Studenten (Federation of National Students), the Jugendbund Adler (Adler Youth League), the Deutsch-Wandervogel (German Rovers, literally Migratory Birds), the KDJ, and the Wiking-Jugend.
129 For this particular Institut, see Chairoff, *Dossier néo-nazisme*, p. 441. The decision to create it was made in 1969, following a suggestion to that effect by representatives of the Mouvement Celtique (Celtic Movement), at the Tenth NOE/ENO gathering in Barcelona. See Amaudruz, *Nous autre racistes*, p. 11.
130 See "Che cosa hanno detto i neofascisti all'*Europeo*," *L'Europeo* 30:33 (15 August 1974), p. 26. Compare Flamini, *Partito del golpe*, volume 2, pp. 143–4. See further later.
131 Flamini, *Partito del golpe*, volume 2, pp. 25–6.
132 Compare ibid., volume 4:1, p. 50; and Brigouleix, *Extrême droite en France*, pp. 222–3. Later, Amaudruz and Pierre Clementi both denied that this meeting was sponsored by the NOE/ENO, whether the parent body or its French branch, claiming instead that France was represented by members of the radical Peuple et Nation (People and Nation) organization. But the members of the latter group, which published a "national revolutionary" monthly bulletin and were purportedly linked to pro-Ustaša Croatian exile organizations, the West German Aktion Oder Neisse (AKON: Oder Neisse Action), and the World Union of National Socialists (WUNS), may also have been joined at the

conference by adherents of the "national populist" wing of the NOE/ENO. For the AKON and WUNS connections, see Joseph Algazy, *L'Extrême droite en France, 1965 à 1984* (Paris: Harmattan, 1989), p. 150.

133 See Chairoff, *Dossier néo-nazisme*, pp. 245, 442. He specifically mentions the CIA, the BND, the French Service de Documentation Extérieure et de Contre-Espionnage (SDECE: Foreign Documentation and Counterespionage Service), and the Italian Servizio Informazioni Difesa (SID: Defense Intelligence Service) as being among those services.

134 Ibid., pp. 245, 440. It should be recalled that Bauverd was the international liaison man for HIAG. For the involvement of Amaudruz and Genoud, both residents of Lausanne, in arms trafficking, see idem, *Dossier B . . . comme barbouzes* (Paris: Alain Moreau, 1975), pp. 403–4, 409. Genoud was a Swiss financier whose role as an intermediary between factions of the European extreme right, Arab nationalists, international criminal organizations, and several Western secret services has yet to be fully elucidated. He was born in 1915, and was personally introduced to Hitler while matriculating in Germany during the early 1930s. He then joined the pro-Nazi Front National (National Front) upon his return to Switzerland, and – like Bauverd – became a close associate of al-Hajj 'Amīn al-Ḥusaynī, the Grand Mufti of Jerusalem, while on an excursion to Palestine. In 1941 he was recruited into Abteilung III (Espionage and Counterespionage) of the Abwehr by SD officer Paul Dickopf (later a collaborator of Allen Dulles, the head of the West German Bundeskriminalamt [BKA: Federal Crime Office], and president of Interpol, the international police organization), and was thereby brought into contact with important Nazi leaders, including SS Obergruppenführer Karl Wolff, who together with Dulles secretly negotiated the surrender of German forces in Italy at the end of World War II. After the war, Genoud seems to have managed a portion of the Nazi funds deposited in Swiss banks by elements of the SS underground, which he used to provide assistance to Germans who were being held in Allied prisons and to help Nazi fugitives who sought to escape to the Middle East. He also acquired the posthumous publication rights to Hitler's "political testament" (which had supposedly been dictated to Bormann) and Josef Goebbels' diary, and undoubtedly made use of the money he obtained by selling those rights in the service of his Nazi and Arab associates. In the mid-1950s he began working for al-Nāsir's Egyptian intelligence service, established the Munich-based Arabo-Afrika export-import company (together with former Nazi Economics Ministry officer and paratrooper Hans Rechenberg, who shortly thereafter became the BND's station chief in Algiers) in order to disseminate anti-Semitic propaganda and sell weapons, co-founded the Banque Commerciale Arabe in Geneva in 1958 (along with the Syrian, Zuhayr Mardam Bey), became a key member of the Association Internationale des Amis du Monde Arabe (International Association of the Friends of the Arab World), which was established in 1959 in Lausanne, secretly used the aforementioned bank to manage the Algerian FLN's funds and thereby facilitate the financing of their war against the French (although after independence was achieved he was accused of stealing fifteen million dollars from the FLN's coffers), and made financial investments for friends like Dr. Hjalmar Schacht, Hitler's former finance minister who – as noted earlier – was himself linked to other key figures in the SS underground, including Skorzeny. Later, Genoud subsidized the defense of a number of Arab terrorists, and ended up doing the same for Klaus Barbie when the latter was arrested in Bolivia and extradicted to France in the 1983. For more on Genoud's background, see Karl Laske, *Le banquier noir: François Genoud* (Paris: Seuil, 1996); Pierre Péan, *L'Extrémiste: François Genoud de Hitler à Carlos* (Paris: Fayard, 1996); Edna Paris, *Unhealed Wounds: France and the Klaus Barbie Affair* (New York: Grove, 1985), pp. 139–45; and Faligot and Kauffer, *Croissant et la croix gammée*, pp. 159–62, 201–3, 250–3.

135 There is some difference of opinion about just how "skeletal" those forces were, however. According to Chairoff, the total number of NOE/ENO activists was around one hundred, but others claim that it could rely on several thousand activists throughout the world. Compare *Dossier néo-nazisme*, p. 442, citing Amaudruz himself; and Laurent,

Orchestre noir, p. 88, note 1. This apparent discrepancy can be reconciled if the first estimate is taken to apply solely to the NOE/ENO's own militants, whereas the latter applied to members of other right-wing groups who were also associated or affiliated with the neo-Nazi international.

136 For Thiriart's earlier career, see Verhoeyen, *Extrême droite en Belgique*, volume 1, p. 21; Chairoff, *Dossier néo-nazisme*, pp. 442–3; Del Boca and Giovana, *Fascism Today*, p. 87. According to Thiriart's associate Marcel Ponthier, the future JE leader was born into a wealthy Liegeois family but was early on influenced by the ideas of Bertrand De Jouvenal, Vilfredo Pareto, Gaetano Mosca, Roberto Michels, James Burnham, José Ortega y Gasset, José Antonio Primo de Rivera, and Vladimir Lenin. See Thiriart, *La grande nation: L'Europe unitaire de Brest à Bucharest* (Brussels: Parti Communautaire Européenne, 1965), p. 73.

137 For CADBA, see Michel Géoris-Reitshof, *L'Extrême droite et le néo-fascisme en Belgique* (Brussels and Paris: Pierre de Meyere, 1962), pp. 55–6; Verhoeyen, *Extrême droite en Belgique*, volume 1, pp. 20–1. There are a number of excellent studies of the movement created by Pierre Poujade in France in 1953, the Union de Défense des Commerçants et des Artisans (UDCA: Union for the Defense of Shopkeepers and Craftsmen), including Henri Bonnaud, *L'Aventure Poujade* (Montpellier: no publisher, 1955); Dominique Borne, *Petits bourgeois en revolte? Le mouvement Poujade* (Paris: Flammarion, 1977); Christian Guy, *Le cas Poujade* (Givors: André Martel, 1955); and especially Stanley Hoffmann, *Le mouvement Poujade* (Paris: A. Colin, 1956).

138 Géoris-Reitshof, *Extrême droite et néo-fascisme en Belgique*, pp. 71–2. Among the MAC's main supporters within the Club Nationale de Parachutisme was Colonel Cassart, who had been involved in the struggle for the Congo as a trainer of Tshombé's paratroopers.

139 Verhoeyen, *Extrême droite en Belgique*, volume 1, pp. 21–2.

140 Géoris-Reitshof, *Extrême droite et néo-fascisme en Belgique*, p. 57; Serge Dumont, *Les brigades noires: L'Extrême droite en France et en Belgique francophone de 1944 à nos jours* (Berchem: EPO, 1983), p. 101.

141 For the MAC's connections with other right-wing groups in Belgium, see Géoris-Reitshof, *Extrême droite et néo-fascisme en Belgique*, pp. 29–30, 33–4, 39–40, 42, 64–6. However, the MAC also considered the more conservative groups too "soft." See Dumont, *Brigades noires*, p. 100.

142 For these international links, see Géoris-Reitshof, *Extrême droite et néo-fascisme en Belgique*, p. 62.

143 See ibid., pp. 57, 59. For the contacts with Skorzeny, Rudel, and the OAS leaders, as well as Otto Strasser and Bardèche, see Verhoeyen, *Extrême droite en Belgique*, volume 1, p. 21. Curutchet himself provides detailed information on the OAS infrastructure in Belgium in his book, *Je veux la tourmente* (Paris: Robert Laffont, 1973), pp. 138–54, as well as the map at the bottom of the fourth page of photos. Note that Curutchet explicitly thanks some of his "Belgian friends," including "Jean-François Thiriart's lads," José Delplace and his girlfriend, Christian Absil (Delplace's brother-in-law), and *La Dernière Heure* editor Maurice Brébart, for their support. See ibid., p. 148.

144 Dumont, *Brigades noires*, pp. 95–6, 100; Géoris-Reitshof, *Extrême droite et néo-fascisme en Belgique*, pp. 57, 62. After July 1962, Jeune Europe continued publishing the bulletins of the OAS's successor, Argoud's Armée National Secrète (ANS: Secret National Army). See the latter work, pp. 61–2.

145 For these police crackdowns and arrests, see Dumont, *Brigades noires*, pp. 100–1; Géoris-Reitshof, *Extrême droite et néo-fascisme en Belgique*, pp. 57, 59.

146 For Sauge, Ousset, and other militant Catholic integralist organizations, see Madeleine Garrigou-Lagrange, "Intégrisme et National-Catholicisme," *Esprit* 27:278 (November 1959), pp. 515–43; and Jacques Maître, "Le catholicisme d'extrême droite et la croisade anti-subversive," *Revue Français de Sociologie* 2:2 (April–June 1961), pp. 106–17. Compare Algazy, *Tentation néo-fasciste en France*, pp. 182–92; Gregory Pons, *Les rats noirs* (Paris: Simoën, 1977), pp. 115–46; John Stewart Ambler, *The French Army in Politics, 1945–1962*

(Columbus: Ohio State University, 1966), pp. 319–23; George A. Kelly, *Lost Soldiers: The French Army and Empire in Crisis, 1947–1962* (Cambridge: MIT, 1965), pp. 243–7; and Marie-Monique Robin, *Escadrons de la mort, l'école française* (Paris: Découverte, 2004), pp. 151–64. For excellent examples of the practical "this-worldly" orientation of these groups, see Georges Sauge, *L'Armée face à la guerre psychologique* (Paris: CEPC, 1959); and the *guerre révolutionnaire* treatise published in Belgium by Pierre Joly, *Contre-Révolution: Stratégie et tactique*, for which see immediately below.

147 For the Tournai center, see Dumont, *Brigades noires*, p. 96; Géoris-Reitshof, *Extrême droite et néo-fascisme en Belgique*, pp. 69–70. For Janssens' views on the Congo affair, see his *J'etais le général Janssens* (Brussels: Charles Dessart, 1961). For the smuggling of fugitive OAS men, see the account by the former head of OAS-Métro's "action service," Gilles Buscia, *Au nom de l'O.A.S.: Requiem pour un cause perdue* (Paris: Alain Lefeuvre, 1981), p. 118.

148 For the information in the following paragraph dealing with the background and activities of Joly and the nature of the Jeunesses Nationales, see Géoris-Reitshof, *Extrême droite et néo-fascisme en Belgique*, pp. 64–6; and Dumont, *Brigades noires*, pp. 96–7.

149 For the origins and history of Paix et Liberté, see Irwin M. Wall, *The United States and the Making of Postwar France, 1945–1954* (Cambridge: Cambridge University, 1991), pp. 150–1, 293; Eric Duhamel, "Jean-Paul David et le Mouvement Paix et Liberté, un anticommuniste radical," in *Renseignement et propagande pendant la Guerre Froide, 1947–1953: Actes de un colloque international, 5–7 février 1998*, ed. by Jean Delmas and Jean Kessler (Brussels: Complexe, 1999), pp. 195–216; Philippe Régnier, "La propagande anticommuniste de Paix et Liberté, France, 1950–1956" (Unpublished Ph.D. Dissertation: Université Libre de Bruxelles, 1987); and René Sommer, "Paix et Liberté? La Quatrième Republique contre le PC[F]," *L'Histoire* 40 (December 1981), pp. 26–35. Paix et Liberté was not a centralized transnational organization whose "branches" took orders from Paris, but rather a loose network of affiliated groupings that maintained their own autonomy. For the broader network, see Bernard Ludwig, "Paix et Liberté: A Transnational Anti-Communist Network," in *Transnational Anti-Communism and the Cold War*, ed. by van Dongen et al., pp. 81–95. Under the leadership of Jean-Paul David, the French group engaged in both extensive anti-communist propaganda activities and in various lesser-known covert operations. The same was also apparently true of some of its affiliated organizations, including the German Volksbund für Frieden und Freiheit (People's League for Peace and Freedom) headed by Eberhard Taubert, a former high-ranking official in the Nazi Propaganda Ministry, and the Italian Pace e Libertà (Peace and Freedom) organization, headed by Edgardo Sogno and Luigi Cavallo, both of whom were later implicated in violent provocations and abortive coups. For more on the Italian affiliate of Paix et Liberté, see Gianni Flamini, *I pretoriani di Pace e Libertà: Storie di guerra fredda in Italia* (Rome: Riuniti, 2001); Aldo Giannuli, *Il Noto servizio, Giulio Andreotti e il caso Moro: La clamorosa scoperta di un servizio segreto che riscrive la recente storia d'Italia* (Milan: Tropea, 2011), pp. 74–80; and Andrea Pannocchia and Franco Tosolino, *Gladio: Storia di finti complotti e di veri patrioti* (Venice: Gino Rossato, 2009), pp. 24–8.

150 See *Contre Révolution: Stratégie et tactique. De la "guerre révolutionnaire" à la "guerre de libération nationale"* (Liege: Pierre Joly, 1957), which appeared in at least two editions.

151 For more on the Main Rouge organization, see Antoine Méléro, with Jean-Émile Néaumet, *La Main rouge: L'Armée secrète de la République* (Monaco: Rochet, 1997); Mathilde von Bülow, "Myth or Reality?: The Red Hand and French Covert Action in Federal Germany during the Algerian War, 1956–61," *Intelligence and National Security* 22 (2007), pp. 787–820; "Pierre Genève" (pseudonym for Kurt-Émile Schweizer, a spy novelist born in Monaco), *La Main Rouge: Reportage* (Paris: Nord-Sud, 1960), a work filled with SDECE disinformation; and Joachim Joesten, *The Red Hand: The Sinister Account of the Terrorist Arm of the French Right-Wing 'Ultras' – in Algeria and on the Continent* (London: Abelard-Schuman, 1962). For the organization's Belgian operations, see ibid., pp. 166–92; and Genève, *Main Rouge*, pp. 159–66. There was also a Main Rouge assassination attempt against another pro-FLN professor in Belgium, Pierre Legrève, but it

failed due to his wife's alertness. All of the intended victims were apparently activists in a secret group opposed to French rule in Algeria, known as the Jeanson Network to its supporters and La Jeune Résistance to the public. Along with Joly, a member of the Algiers Sûreté who had been seconded to the French Army's 5th (Psychological Action) Bureau – Jean-Louis Bovagnet – was implicated in these operations, and it may also be that personnel from the Belgian Sûreté provided some assistance to the killers. Compare Laurent, *Orchestre noir*, p. 74; and Joesten, *Red Hand*, p. 190. For more on Joly's subversive activities in Algeria, see Pierre Péan, *Le mystérieux Docteur Martin, 1895–1969: Action Française, Février 34, la Cagoule, le N.K.V.D., le Komintern, Vichy, la Synarchie, l'O.S.S., la lutte anti-communiste, les complots du 13 mai 58, l'O.A.S . . .* (Paris: Fayard, 1993), pp. 403–12, 427–30, 441–2.

152 Dumont, *Brigades noires*, p. 97.
153 For Cosyns-Verhaegen, see ibid., p. 26; Verhoeyen, *Extrême droite en Belgique*, volume 1, p. 23; Géoris-Reitshof, *Extrême droite et néo-fascisme en Belgique*, p. 73. His publications include *La guerre subversive, de l'approche indirecte à la résistance totale* (Brussels: Ponant, 1963); *Guerres révolutionnaires et subversives: Selection bibliographique* (Brussels: Ours, 1967); *Guerres subversives et questions connexes: Selection bibliographique compilée et commentée* (Wavre: Centre d'Information et de Documentation, 1972); and *Théorie de l'action subversive, au dela de la legalité et en deça de la violence* (Brussels: Ponant, 1963). For the Torices "work camp," which was to include cultural activities, ideological discussions, and "sports activities," see the announcement from an issue of *Vrij Europa*, reproduced in P.R.A. van Iddekinge and A. H. Paape, *Ze zijn er nog . . . : Een documentatie over fascistische, nazistische en andere rechtsradicale denkbeelden en activiteiten na 1945* (Amsterdam: Bezige Bij, 1970), p. 292.
154 For Labin's role in the Étudiants Nationales, see Géoris-Reitshof, *Extrême droite et néo-fascisme en Belgique*, p. 67. For her other activities, see Verhoeyen, *Extrême droite en Belgique*, volume 1, p. 11 and note 2; Olivier Dard, "Suzanne Labin: Fifty Years of Anti-Communist Agitation," in *Transnational Anti-Communism and the Cold War*, ed. by van Dongen et al., pp. 189–200; and Pierre Abramovici, "The World Anti-Communist League: Origins, Structures, and Activities," in *Transnational Anti-Communism and the Cold War*, ed. by van Dongen et al., pp. 119–20. The ABN was an umbrella group that coordinated the activities of various anti-communist émigré organizations from Eastern Europe and other "Captive Nations" of the Soviet Union, but it was dominated by former Ukrainian Nazi collaborators. For more on the ABN, see Anderson and Anderson, *Inside the League*, pp. 20–5, 33–8; Chairoff, *Dossier néo-nazisme*, pp. 420–1; and Simpson, *Blowback*, pp. 269–70. For a related, "non-fascist, non-communist" umbrella organization for Eastern European "Captive Nations" activists, the Assembly of Captive European Nations (ACEN), which was in part managed and funded through the CIA-sponsored Free Europe Committee (FEC), see Martin Nekola, "The Assembly of Captive European Nations: A Transnational Organization and Tool of Anti-Communist Propaganda," in *Transnational Anti-Communism and the Cold War*, ed. by van Dongen et al., pp. 96–112.
155 For the internal divisions in the MAC, which continued even after it was reorganized and renamed JE, see Dumont, *Brigades noires*, p. 98. For the communist-like cellular structure, see Géoris-Reitshof, *Extrême droite et néo-fascisme en Belgique*, p. 58. Note that although the MAC was officially renamed JE in the spring of 1962, JE sections began to be constructed in other countries in late 1961, which suggests that Thiriart was already drawing together a network of international support for a new pan-European organization. Oddly enough, some JE sections were also established abroad even after the main Wallonian branch of JE had again been officially renamed in 1965.
156 For this abortive NPE effort, see Smoydzin, *Hitler lebt!*, pp. 111–14.
157 For lists of JE's branches, see Dumont, *Brigades noires*, pp. 98–9; and Del Boca and Giovana, *Fascism Today*, pp. 454–5, note 20. Note that are some minor discrepancies in the two lists, but that the latter is more complete. Some of the organizations listed were

not actual branches of JE, but rather autonomous but interlinked neo-fascist movements: among these were Ordine Nuovo, Giovane Nazione (Young Nation), and the Centro Quaderni Neri (Black Lesson Books Center) in Italy, Fiatal Europa in Colombia, SAC in Canada, and the Runebevaegelse (Rune Movment) in Denmark. The latter authors also claim that JE was in touch with organizations of Bulgarian, Slovak, and Ukrainian refugees with headquarters in West Germany, the United States, and South America. It would be interesting to determine whether or not the Munich-based Anti-Bolshevik Bloc of Nations (ABN) was among these refugee groups, since it was directly or indirectly involved in a number of intelligence-linked ventures and covert operations. In any event, the major branches of JE were those in continental Europe. For Flanders, where the branch was established in December 1961 by Fred Rossaert, Karl Van Marcke, Werner Caluwe, and future *nouvelle droite* luminary Luc Pauwels, all of whom – together with Debbaudt – went on to found the Europafront after their expulsion from JE, see Verhoeyen, *Extrême droite en Belgique*, volume 2, pp. 47–8. For Holland, where a group of fifty militants led by ex-Nationaal Socialistische Beweging man Tijmon Balk existed until Balk broke with Thiriart in 1963 and joined the Europafront, see van Donselaar, *Fout na de oorlog*, pp. 135–6. For Italy, where the ostentatiously anti-American branch grew directly out of an October 1963 fusion between Giovane Nazione, the Perugia branch of Ordine Nuovo, the Formazioni Nazionali Giovanili (or Federazione Nazionale Giovanile) from La Spezia, and the "traditionalist" Gruppo Catullo (Catullus Group) from the Veneto, and was headed by Pierfrancesco Bruschi (former chief of Giovane Nazione) with the help of Claudio Mutti and Claudio Orsi, two future "Nazi-Maoists" linked closely to Franco Freda, see Giovana, *Nuove camicie nere*, pp. 112–13; Flamini, *Partito del golpe*, volume 1, pp. 181–4; and especially Orazio Ferrara, *Il mito negato: Da Giovane Europa ad Avanguardia di Popolo. La destra eretica negli anni settanta* (Sarno: Centro Studi I Diòscuri, 1996), pp. 19–41. It is worth noting here that many Giovane Europa militants were affiliated, before, during, or after their involvement with JE, with Ordine Nuovo, Avanguardia Nazionale, the Organizzazione Lotta di Popolo, or the MSI, and that in the audience at a 26 January 1968 Giovane Europa conference in Ferrara, where Thiriart himself made a presentation, was Dr. Giorgio Vitangeli, a member of Randolfo Pacciardi's unabashedly pro-American and Atlanticist Nuova Repubblica (New Republic) movement. For France, where groups of "national-European" militants from Europe-Action and the Fédération des Étudiants Nationalistes created a fifty-man branch, compare the sketchy and largely contradictory accounts of Francis Bergeron and Philippe Vilgier, *De Le Pen à Le Pen: Une histoire des nationaux et des nationalistes sou la Vème République* (Bouère: Dominique Martin Morin, 1985), pp. 96–7; and François Duprat, *Les mouvements d'extrême-droite en France depuis 1945* (Paris: Albatros, 1972), pp. 125–6, 176. As in Italy, certain members of the JE branch were later associated with the Organisation Lutte du Peuple, Lotta di Popolo's counterpart in France.

158 See Del Boca and Giovana, *Fascism Today*, p. 226, citing the 11 August 1961 edition of *Nation-Belgique*.
159 Ibid., pp. 88, 228, citing *La Révolution nationale européenne* (Brussels: Jeune Europe, no date), wherein the "manifesto" was reprinted.
160 See Dumont, *Brigades noires*, p. 102, note 140.
161 See ibid., pp. 117–19; Verhoeyen, *Extrême droite en Belgique*, volume 1, pp. 22–3. For the Europafront, see Smoydzin, *Hitler lebt!*, pp. 108–11; and Verhoeyen, *Extrême droite en Belgique*, volume 2, pp. 47–8. For the Stahlhelm, a right-wing veterans association centered in West Germany, see Dudek and Jaschke, *Entstehung und Entwicklung des Rechtsextremismus*, volume 1, pp. 115–24; and Jenke, *Verschwörung von rechts?*, pp. 308–11.
162 See *Un empire de 400 millions d'hommes: L'Europe* (Brussels: Jeune Europe, 1964); and Thiriart, *La grande nation*.
163 See Tauber, *Beyond Eagle and Swastika*, volume 1, p. 221, citing a speech by Thiriart. Compare Thiriart, *Empire de 400 millions*, pp. 19–20, 37–54; and Thiriart, *Grande nation*, pp. 7–10, 25–36.

164 See Thiriart, *Empire de 400 millions*, pp. 22–6. Later, Thiriart apparently tried to form an operational alliance with elements of certain Middle Eastern regimes. In 1967 and 1968 he contacted Arab leaders in Algeria, Egypt, Iraq, and Palestine with an offer to launch future direct actions against the Americans in Europe, help create a transcontinental intelligence service in order to carry out clandestine operations in both European and Arab countries, and organize paramilitary formations made up of European volunteers that would directly participate in the Palestinian resistance struggle. See René Monzat, *Enquêtes sur la droite extrême* (Paris: Le Monde, 1992), p. 55, citing an April 1968 "Mémorandum à l'intention du gouvernement de la République Algérienne" and the November 1968 issue of *Nation Européenne*. Compare Faligot and Kauffer, *Croissant et la croix gammée*, pp. 246–7, who note that Thiriart was especially sympathetic to the Libyan regime of Muʻammar al-Qadhdhāfī and that one of his followers, Belgian Waffen-SS veteran Roger Coudroy, was killed on 3 June 1968 while participating in operations with an al-Fatah commando group. Moreover, the files of Aginter Presse, a Lisbon-based press agency that was used as a front for a radical rightist countersubversive and counterterrorist center, indicated that Thiriart was linked to the intelligence services of several Arab countries. See Laurent, *Orchestre noir*, p. 133.

165 Chairoff, *Dossier néo-nazisme*, p. 444.

166 Thiriart, *Empire de 400 millions*, pp. 29–30. Chairoff views this as the forerunner of Italian "Nazi-Maoism," an ideology espoused by Franco Freda and other neo-fascist activists in Italy during the late 1960s and the early 1970s. See *Dossier néo-nazisme*, p. 444. But Thiriart's pro-Chinese statements were essentially a product of his geopolitical concerns, whereas the so-called Nazi-Maoists – assuming that they were not mere provocateurs attempting to disrupt and discredit genuine Maoists with slogans such as "Hitler and Mao united in the struggle" – appreciated Mao for his alleged advocacy and successful creation of an ascetic warrior mystique among his followers.

167 Thiriart, *Grande nation*, p. 16. For the "third way" emphasis, see Thiriart, *Empire de 400 millions*, pp. 99–104.

168 Thiriart, *Empire de 400 millions*, pp. 207–13, 223–63. His ideas about organizing a revolutionary vanguard owed much to both Lenin and the OAS.

169 For the most thorough discussion of Thiriart's proposed domestic programs, see ibid., pp. 99–153. Compare Thiriart, *Grande nation*, pp. 37–8, 41, 48, 50–1, for the specific points emphasized in my summary.

170 Both Tauber, *Beyond Eagle and Swastika*, volume 2, pp. 1098–9, note 9; and Del Boca and Giovana, *Fascism Today*, p. 230 claim that Thiriart's public criticism of racism was "tactical," and there is indeed some clear evidence of barely disguised antipathy toward "inferior" races and the promotion of pro-white policies. See, for example, Thiriart, *Empire de 400 millions*, pp. 56–9, 225–6. Compare Dumont, *Brigades noires*, p. 116; Monzat, *Enquêtes sur la droite extrême*, pp. 56–7. Nevertheless, Thiriart was certainly not overly concerned with racial issues and may have even included these offhand remarks in order to attract or maintain the support of other neo-fascists.

171 Indeed, paeans to communist China appeared with increasing frequency in the pages of JE's publications. See, for example, the 15 October 1964 issue of *Jeune Europe: Organisation Européenne pour la Formation d'un Cadre Politique* – the internal bulletin of JE that was sent exclusively to the organization's militants – that attacked the idea of an "Atlantic Europe" and argued that Europe had to support Chinese imperialism against Russian and American imperialism. In the 27 October 1964 issue of the same bulletin, he went so far as to praise the development of an atomic bomb by China, presumably as a counterweight to the nuclear monopoly of the United States and the Soviet Union. A selection of JE publications can be consulted at the Hoover Institution library on the Stanford University campus.

172 Compare Chairoff, *Dossier néo-nazisme*, pp. 444–5; and Monzat, *Enquêtes sur la droite extrême*, p. 56, citing another issue of *Conscience Européenne*. Note, however, that Thiriart's former secretary, Luc Michel, claims that these efforts to establish a tactical but

nonetheless operational anti-American alliance between the PCE and the communist Chinese secret service never bore fruit. See Lee, *Beast Reawakens*, p. 175. In any event, Thiriart was much impressed with the "national communist" doctrines promoted by Rumanian leader Nicolae Ceausescu, so much so that he persuaded Ceausescu to submit an article to *La Nation Européenne*.
173 Quoted in Monzat, *Enquêtes sur la droite extrême*, pp. 51–2.
174 Ibid., pp. 55–6, in part citing *L'Empire euro-soviétique de Vladivostok à Dublin: L'après-Yalta* (Charleroi: Machiavel, [1985 or 1986?]).
175 Ibid., p. 52, citing the March 1985 issue of *Conscience Européenne*. For more on the CCC, which began to launch terrorist attacks against NATO bases and other targets in 1984, see Jacques Offergeld and Christian Souris, *La Belgique etranglée: Euroterrorisme* (Montigny-le-Tilleul: Scaillet, 1985); and Jos Vander Velpen, *Les CCC: L'État et le terrorisme* (Anvers: EPO, 1988). For a collection of CCC communiques and documents, see *Cellules communistes combattantes: Textes de lutte, 1984–1985* (Brussels: Ligne Rouge, 1988); and (for English translations) Yonah Alexander and Dennis Pluchinsky, eds., *Europe's Red Terrorists: The Fighting Communist Organizations* (London: Frank Cass, 1992), pp. 148–93. Note that certain journalists suspect, albeit on the basis of sketchy and circumstantial evidence, that the ostensibly ultraleft CCC was manipulated and used as an instrument for provocations by elements of the far right and the state security apparatus. If so, Thiriart's efforts may have played some as yet unclear role in this process.
176 This is clearly the implication in Monzat, *Enquêtes sur la droite extreme*, pp. 55–6, although Monzat never actually claims that Thiriart was an agent.
177 One of the first to emphasize this crucial point was Galli in his pioneering study, *Crisi italiana e la destra internazionale*, pp. 25–6.
178 Quoted by Del Boca and Giovana, *Fascism Today*, p. 225.

4

POSTWAR "NEO-FASCIST" INTERNATIONALS, PART 2

Aginter Presse and the "strategy of tension" in Italy

Of all of the postwar right-wing "internationals," none was as important as the decentralized network of "action" groups established by former members of the Organisation de l'Armée Secrète (OAS: Secret Army Organization), most of whom had taken refuge in foreign lands following the failure of their efforts to preserve French control over Algeria and topple the Fifth Republic. This OAS diaspora had an enormous impact on the subsequent campaigns of violence carried out by extreme right paramilitary groups not only in Europe but also throughout areas of the Third World where bitter colonial and anti-communist struggles were being waged. Between 1966 and 1974, the Lisbon-based Aginter Presse was the primary vehicle through which intransigent OAS veterans and their neo-fascist supporters launched counterrevolutionary and counterguerrilla operations. The personnel who carried out these operations more or less consciously sought to apply certain techniques that were associated with the politicized French counterinsurgency doctrines subsumed under the name *guerre révolutionnaire*. Therefore, a brief summary of the development of these doctrines needs to be provided before Aginter Presse can be considered.

Following the traumatic defeat of the French expeditionary corps in Indo-China at the hands of the Vietminh, certain of France's most brilliant and battle-hardened junior officers became obsessed with trying to understand how a relatively ill-equipped peasant army had overcome one of the most experienced and professional fighting forces in the world. As a result, they immersed themselves in the military writings of Mao Zedong and other communist theorists in order to acquaint themselves further with the enemy's techniques of revolutionary guerrilla warfare.[1] On the basis of these studies and their own firsthand experiences in Southeast Asia, they developed a potent counterrevolutionary doctrine that eventually came to dominate French military thought in the late 1950s.[2]

Put simply, *guerre révolutionnaire* wedded a simplistic and Manichean geopolitical conception to a fairly sophisticated array of operational techniques. In regard to the former, it held that World War III between the West and its intransigent communist foe had already begun, but under a new guise. Nuclear weapons had made large-scale conventional war impractical and potentially suicidal, so the communists had devised and launched a new type of "subversive warfare" to destroy Western civilization. Rather than engaging in a direct confrontation, the Soviet Union was waging "remote control" or "surrogate" war by stirring up discontent in the Third World, particularly within the territories of colonial empires. The ultimate goal was to strip the West of its resources and isolate Europe geopolitically, thereby creating the preconditions for its total defeat. From this perspective, all so-called decolonization or national liberation struggles were seen as being communist-inspired and serving Soviet ends.[3] Moreover, this Third World War was viewed as a *total* war being waged on all fronts. It was no longer possible for Western nations to concern themselves solely with military measures, for in communist subversive warfare such measures were inextricably linked with political, social, psychological, and especially ideological elements.[4] To protect itself from this multidimensional assault, the West had to rally behind a coherent, monolithic doctrine that could successfully oppose the totalitarian doctrine of the communists on equal terms.

From an operational standpoint, the *guerre révolutionnaire* theorists described communist revolutionary strategy as a combination of partisan (guerrilla) warfare and psychological warfare.[5] According to their analysis, its primary objective was to "conquer" the population, not to seize strategic territory as in conventional war.[6] They had been amazed at the extent to which the Vietminh had retained the support of the population of Vietnam, but rather than examining the underlying historical and social *causes* of this allegiance, they focused on the organizational and psychological *techniques* used by the guerrillas to assert their control.[7] These were identified as the creation of "parallel hierarchies," clandestine cross-cutting vertical and horizontal organizational networks that tightly enmeshed each person in an elaborate, all-encompassing infrastructure geared toward exerting social control, as well as providing an alternative to existing governmental institutions;[8] the skillful and systematic application of *action psychologique*, which included both mass propaganda directed at groups and "thought reform" employed against particular invidividuals;[9] and the ruthless but controlled utilization of terrorism, whether selective or indiscriminate, to intimidate the population and complete its psychological separation from the incumbent regime. However, it is important to note that the French theorists did not see these as discrete or successive processes, but rather as different components of a single coordinated effort to gain control of the population; indeed, they felt that it was precisely this fusion of methods that made subversive war so dangerous and effective.

Having thus defined enemy techniques, the proponents of *guerre révolutionnaire* sought to devise ways of countering or neutralizing them. Most concluded that to gain the upper hand in the struggle against international communist subversion, it was necessary to adopt the enemy's totalitarian methods and turn them against its creators. Therefore, the young colonels experimented with varying combinations of these techniques to keep Algeria French and, in the process, avenge the army's earlier humiliations in Indo-China, Morocco, Tunisia, and at Suez.[10] But their zeal to apply totalitarian solutions throughout Algeria was not shared by the majority of the Army, the government, or the French population.[11] As a result, despite some notable successes achieved with *guerre révolutionnaire* methods, for example the destruction of the rebel Front de Libération Nationale (FLN: National Liberation Front) network in Algiers in 1957, the bitter war dragged on without definitive resolution, causing the government to waver in its commitment to *Algérie Française*.[12] This official vacillation completed the alienation of the *guerre révolutionnaire* officers, who had already become deeply estranged from the French public and regime due to the apathy and pusillanimity the latter groups had displayed during the Indo-China war.[13] Feelings of betrayal and abandonment again welled up inside them, and many decided that the only way to retain control of Algeria and recover their lost honor was to apply *guerre révolutionnaire* techniques against their own countrymen and thereby morally regenerate France itself, a subversive attitude fanned by extremist groups in both Algeria and the *métropole*.[14]

The stage was thus set for the fateful alliance between the disaffected practitioners of *guerre révolutionnaire*, especially those within the Army's 5th (Psychological Action) Bureau or commanding elite paratroop or Légion Etrangère units, and civilian *pied noir* ultras, an alliance that soon bore fruit in a series of insurrections in Algiers – the 13 May 1958 coup, "barricades" week in January 1960, and the "general's putsch" of late April 1961 – which brought down the Fourth Republic and threatened the political survival of its Gaullist successor.[15] Eventually, elements of the same forces joined together in the clandestine OAS, which applied numerous *guerre révolutionnaire* techniques, first to prevent France from abandoning Algeria and later to overthrow the Fifth Republic and replace it with an *état musclé* capable of rallying the nation behind its efforts to confront international communism.[16]

What needs to be emphasized here is how this alliance between anti-regime military personnel and civilian ultras affected both groups and thereby provided a foundation for subsequent right-wing terrorism. The rebellious colonels, who had been seeking to develop a powerful counterrevolutionary ideology capable of resisting communism on its own fertile terrain, were offered several by civilian extremists. The most important of these were "national Catholicism," which was promoted in slightly different versions by militant far right lay organizations like Ousset's Cité Catholique and Sauge's CESPS, and "national communism," a doctrine promoted by radical neo-fascist groups like the Mouvement Jeune Nation (JN). Both doctrines had their adherents within the armed forces and thence within the OAS, which was divided between an integralist wing led by Colonel Pierre Château-Jobert and a fascist wing dominated by Colonel Argoud.

On the other hand, right-wing extremists throughout the world were galvanized by the exploits of the seditious *guerre révolutionnaire* officers who led the military revolts in Algeria, and those in the superheated Algerian milieu were indoctrinated with the theory's tenets and more or less systematically trained in their application by elite, battle-hardened military personnel.[17] To be sure, many *pied noir* and even metropolitan ultras had already developed strong links with official security agencies. For example, some had been recruited into the Main Rouge (Red Hand) or its parent organization, the Service de Documentation Extérieure et de Contre-Espionnage (SDECE: Foreign Documentation and Counter-Espionage Service), in order to eliminate the FLN's support network in Europe and prevent supplies from reaching rebel forces in Algeria, whereas others had provided services for the Army's 2nd (Intelligence) Bureau or various police apparatuses.[18] Moreover, the Algerian *colons* had established several paramilitary "counterterrorist" groups on their own, most of which were later incorporated into the OAS.[19] But at that point they were directly exposed to the most advanced techniques of clandestine organization, *action psychologique*, and above all terrorism. OAS experts were even sent elsewhere to help European supporters of the organization accomplish various tasks.[20] In the end, however, the suppression of the OAS forced many of its members to flee abroad where, in return for asylum and other amenities, they offered their considerable skills to help train foreign counterinsurgency and parallel police units.[21] This is why many have viewed the OAS as the embryo out of which emerged a number of later right-wing terrorist internationals.

As noted earlier, Aginter Presse was itself a product of the OAS diaspora. Its founder Yves-Felix Marie Guillou, alias "Yves (or "Ralf") Guérin-Sérac," was a veritable prototype of the "lost soldier."[22] He was a French Army veteran who had fought in Korea, where he received a United Nations medal and the American Bronze Star and allegedly served as a liaison man between SDECE and the CIA, as well as in Indo-China, where he was wounded twice and awarded other medals for bravery. After being promoted to Captain in 1959, he was assigned to the 11th Demi-Brigade Parachutiste de Choc, a special "dirty tricks" unit under the direct control of SDECE, which was then stationed in Oran.[23] He subsequently deserted and became the leader of an OAS commando unit in the Oran area. Upon the declaration of Algerian independence in June 1962, he took refuge in Spain, where he helped Chateau-Jobert form the Mouvement de Combat Contre-Révolutionnaire (Counterrevolutionary Combat Movement) and then became a member of the directorate in Georges Bidault's Conseil National de la Résistance (National Resistance Council), an offshoot of OAS-Métro. At the end of 1962 he moved to Portugal, the last colonial empire that appeared to be willing to defend Western civilization, in order to continue the struggle against communist imperialism. Upon his arrival in Lisbon, he established contact with Vichy period exiles and other OAS fugitives, and was introduced to the Portuguese authorities by former Pétain supporter and ultranationalist pro-Salazar editorialist Jacques Ploncard d'Assac.[24] Guillou was thence hired as an instructor for the paramilitary Legião Portuguesa (Portuguese Legion), and later employed to train counterguerrilla units of the Portuguese Army.[25] Meanwhile, several of his former OAS comrades had made their way to Lisbon, and together they decided to form an international anti-communist organization of their own. Fortunately for them, the Polícia Internacional e de Defesa do Estado/Direcção Géral de Segurança (PIDE/DGS: International Police and Defense of the State/General Security Directorate) was then attempting to set up covert intelligence networks using foreign personnel in various African countries. So it was that this much-feared secret police agency, utilizing complicit officials within the Defense Ministry and the Foreign Affairs Ministry as intermediaries, began financing Guillou to the tune of two million escudos per month.[26] Thus was born Aginter Presse and its satellite organizations.

Most of our knowledge about Aginter Presse derives from one of those fortuitous accidents of history that periodically permits the general public to obtain a brief but tantalizing glimpse of the clandestine and covert operations which are an omnipresent feature of modern political life, in both authoritarian and democratic states. Indeed, had the leftist military personnel in the Movimento das Forças Armadas (MFA: Armed Forces Movement) not succeeded in overthrowing the Portuguese dictatorship in April of 1974, it is doubtful whether the operations of Aginter would ever have come to light. After seizing control of Lisbon and other key areas of Portugal, with the enthusiastic support of sections of the population in the central part of the country, one of the MFA's first goals was to dismantle the repressive apparatus of the former regime. On 26 April a contingent of MFA troops broke into the main PIDE/DGS headquarters on Rua António Maria Cardoso in the capital, where they found a vast archive chronicling fifty years of authoritarian rule. On 21 May, in the course of their interrogation of a PIDE/DGS agent, MFA soldiers learned about the existence of a certain press agency that had closely collaborated with the secret police. The following day they searched a recently abandoned office at Rua das Praças 13, where they discovered the archives and technical support section of Aginter, which allowed the agency to produce false identification papers and documents from different nations, radio equipment, explosives, and specialized weaponry.[27] Shortly thereafter, they raided its deserted headquarters at Rua de Campolide 27, also in Lisbon. The materials they found at these two offices provided them with an enormous amount of information about right-wing intelligence gathering, subversion, and terrorism in various parts of the world. A contingent of soldiers then transported this mass of documents to the fortress at Caxias, which had long been used to intern the political prisoners of the regime. A team of investigators, headed by Commander Abrantes Serra and a naval infantry captain named Costa Correia, was then entrusted with conducting a detailed examination of this material.[28] On this basis, a number of intelligence reports were prepared by the post-coup Portuguese security service, and copies of selected documents from the hoard at Caxias were provided to judicial authorities in Italy and a handful of journalists specializing in the study of neo-fascism.[29] It is on the basis of these documents, whether directly or indirectly, that the following account is based.

The Agence Internationale de Presse (International Press Agency), or Aginter Presse, was apparently named after a 1930's anti-Komintern organization headed by Armand Bernardini.[30] The new version was formally established in September 1966 and did in fact serve as an actual press agency. Among other things, it syndicated articles in various right-wing media outlets and published its own bimonthly bulletin called *Veritas Ubique*, which was originally printed in Lisbon but later published in Dieppe by ex-OAS man Jean Vannier. According to the header of this bulletin, whose motto was "It's better to light a candle than curse the darkness," Aginter had correspondents in Algiers, Bonn, Buenos Aires, Brussels, Geneva, La Haye, Lisbon, London, Madrid, Mexico City, Oslo, Ottawa, Paris, Pretoria, Rio de Janeiro, Rome, Saigon, Stockholm, Taipei, Tel Aviv, Tokyo, and Washington. Much of the "news" disseminated by its correspondents, however, contained a certain amount of intentionally misleading disinformation.[31] But the agency's main function was to camouflage the activities of what French journalist Frédéric Laurent has misleadingly referred to as a "center of international fascist subversion"[32] that was divided into several interlinked components, including:

- An espionage office "covered" by the PIDE/DGS and purportedly linked, through that agency, to the U.S. CIA, the West German Bundesnachrichtendienst (BND: Federal Intelligence Service), the Spanish Dirección General de Seguridad (DGS: General Security Directorate), the Greek Kentrike Ypseresia Plerophorion (KYP: Central Intelligence Service), and the South African Bureau of State Security (BOSS);[33]
- A unit that specialized in recruiting and training mercenaries in the arcane arts of modern unconventional warfare, in this case based upon *guerre révolutionnaire* concepts;
- A strategic center for coordinating "subversion and *intoxication* operations" that worked in conjunction with right-wing regimes and politicians on every continent;
- An international "action" organization called Ordre et Tradition (Order and Tradition), which had a clandestine paramilitary wing known as the Organisation d'Action contre le Communisme International (OACI: Action Organization Against International Communism).[34]

In his 1998 sentence, Milan Investigating Magistrate Guido Salvini aptly described Aginter Presse as not only a

> terrorist organization in the strict sense . . . but also a structure in a position to implant, wherever it operated, [mainly French *guerre révolutionnaire*] techniques of unconventional warfare . . . and to utilize instruments typical of . . . a true and proper unofficial secret service.[35]

Most of the personnel recruited for this organizational complex consisted of OAS veterans, former military officers, neo-fascist ultras, and rightist intellectuals.

Among these the most important, aside from Yves Guillou himself, was Robert-Henri Leroy, who had an extraordinarily lengthy career as both a right-wing political activist and a specialist in intelligence and covert operations. He had formerly been a member of Charles Maurras's Action Française (French Action), the prewar Cagoule terrorist underground, the Carlist Requeté militia forces during the Spanish Civil War, Vichy intelligence, the Waffen-SS's "Charlemagne" division (with the rank of Hauptsturmführer), and Otto Skorzeny's commando force, for which he served as an instructor. After the war he spent seven years in prison for collaborating with the enemy, but following his release he allegedly went to work for both NATO intelligence and the BND in the period between 1958 and 1968. From 1968 to 1970, according to his own admission, Leroy collaborated with Guillou at Aginter until his left-wing cover was "burned" by various journalists and he lost his ability to continue conducting "infiltration and *intoxication*" operations.[36] Others who formed the core group of the action-oriented Ordre et Tradition were Jay S. Sablonsky (alias "Castor," "Jay Salby," "Hugh Franklin," and several other pseudonyms) of Philadelphia, who apparently was affiliated in some way with American intelligence; ex-paratroopers Jean Vallentin (Aginter's legal director), Guy Mathieu, and Jeune Nation activist Jean-Marie Laurent (alias "Jean-Marie Lafitte"); Army veteran Guy d'Avezac de Castera (alias "the Baron" and "the Viscount"), Aginter's general administrator; former infantry officers Jean Denis Raingeard de la Bletière (alias "Jean Denis"), Alain Moreau, Jean Emmanuel Justin, and Pierre-Jean Surgeon; Alain Gauthier, who had been appointed by Pierre Sergent as the Conseil National de la Résistance's representative in Spain; Jean-Marie Guillou, Yves's brother; *pied noir* activists Georges Cot, an Army veteran, and Jean Brune, an ex-OAS man and author of several books; corporatist theoretician Henri Le Rouxel; Hugues Stéphane Hélie, a former activist in the Fédération des Étudiants Nationalistes (FEN) and the Comité Tixier-Vignancourt (Tixier-Vignancourt Committee); nationalist theoretician Jacques Ploncard d'Assac; mercenary chief Jacques Depret; José Vicente Pepper, former intelligence minister in the Dominican Republic under the dictator Rafael Trujillo; and four Portuguese ultras – José de Barcellos, José Valle de Figueirede, Armando Marques de Carvalho, and Zarco Moniz Ferreira, leader of the neo-fascist Jovem Portugal group.[37]

Moreover, shortly after the agency's creation, its operatives made extensive efforts to establish links with extreme right organizations and personalities throughout the world. In both January and April of 1967, Ordre et Tradition hosted meetings in Lisbon that were attended by representatives of neo-fascist organizations from various countries in Europe and South America, with the aim of enlisting their support for the creation of a worldwide network of "correspondents."[38] Close links were thereby solidified with extremist neo-fascist groups such as Ordine Nuovo and Avanguardia Nazionale in Italy, Ordre Nouveau (New Order) and the FEN in France, the Kinema tes 4 Augoustou (K4A: 4th of August Movement) in Greece, Jeune Europe and its successors in Belgium, Jovem Portugal and Ordem Novo (New Order) in Portugal, Fuerza Nueva (New Force) and the Círculo Español de Amigos de Europa (CEDADE: Spanish Circle of Friends of Europe) in Spain, and elements of both the NOE/NEO and the World Union of National Socialists (WUNS), another international neo-Nazi umbrella organization. But Aginter did not restrict its efforts to making contact with youthful neo-fascist ultras, it also established liaisons with Catholic integralist and ultraconservative forces, including some that were linked to various Western secret services. Among the agency's foreign contacts, for example, were Suzanne Labin and her husband Eduard, Belgian right-wing activist Florimond Damman, the editors of Rumanian and Ukrainian exile publications, and a number of right-wing Italian journalists connected to the Italian security and intelligence organizations, including Giano Accame of the Roman daily *Il Tempo* and Giorgio Torchia of Agenzia Oltremare (Overseas Agency).[39] Due to these far-reaching connections and the strength of its institutional base of support in Lisbon, Aginter exerted an influence far beyond its own limited numerical strength.

The history of Aginter Presse can be divided into two major phases. In the first, which began in 1966 and ended in 1969, the agency initiated a series of operations aimed at weakening and destroying guerrilla groups operating in Portuguese Africa.[40] These were undertaken at the behest and with the direct assistance of the PIDE/DGS and other organs of the Portuguese government. In the second phase, which lasted from 1969 until Aginter's formal dissolution in 1974, agency personnel offered their specialized *guerre révolutionnaire* training to a number of authoritarian regimes in Latin America, and were in fact hired to provide it in Guatemala and post-Allende Chile.[41] During this period, the organization was no longer subsidized by the Portuguese state, although its Lisbon apparatus was still "covered" by the PIDE/DGS. Following the April 1974 leftist coup and the dismantling of both the secret police and Aginter, many of the two services' former operatives later resurfaced in clandestine paramilitary organizations like the Exército de Libertação Português (ELP: Portuguese Liberation Army), the Frente de Libertaçao das Açores (FLA: Azores Liberation Front), Antiterrorismo ETA (ETA Anti-Terrorism), the Soldat de l'Opposition Algérienne (SOA: Soldiers of the Algerian Opposition), and the Organisation de l'Afrique Libre (Free Africa Organization).[42]

While it is beyond the scope of this study to delve into the entire history of Aginter Presse, it is necessary to focus attention on two of its activities that shed considerable light on features of the terrorist "strategy of tension" in Italy. As noted earlier, one branch of Aginter was charged with the training of mercenaries and terrorists. To accomplish this task, the agency set up facilities at specially designated Legião Portuguesa and PIDE/DGS training camps, and offered an intensive three-week course that included both theoretical instruction in the tradecraft of unconventional warfare (including methods of *action psychologique*, intelligence gathering, clandestine communication, and infiltration) and hands-on training in sabotage and urban terrorist techniques (including the use of explosives and other specialized weaponry).[43] For this purpose, Guillou prepared a mini-manual for the "perfect" terrorist, *Missions spéciales*. Among the key subjects covered in this manual were the purposes of subversion and terrorism, sabotage methods, the use of explosives, the handling of weapons, special operations, maintaining security, surveillance, liaison techniques, conducting and resisting interrogations, the administering of poisons, sedatives, and hallucinogenic drugs, and other sorts of lessons for secret agents. The following passages have particular relevance in connection with the types of terrorist actions that characterized the "strategy of tension":

- Subversion acts with appropriate means upon the minds and wills in order to induce them to act outside of all logic, against all rules, against all laws: in this way it conditions individuals and enables one to make use of them as one wishes.

- *Action psychologique* [is] a non-violent weapon [used] to condition public opinion through the use of the press, the radio, conferences, demonstrations, etc. . . . with the goal of uniting the masses against the authorities.
- Terrorism breaks the resistance of the population, obtains its submission, and provokes a rupture between the population and the authorities . . . There is a seizure of power over the masses through the creation of a climate of anxiety, insecurity, and danger.
- Selective terrorism . . . destroys the political and administrative apparatus by eliminating the cadres of those organs.
- Indiscriminate terrorism . . . destroys the confidence of the people by disorganizing the masses so as to manipulate them more effectively.[44]

According to Guillou, there was a logical progression of terrorist acts from the elimination of individuals in order to stun public opinion to the elimination of important officials in order to destabilize the administrative apparatus, the elimination of lesser officials and natural elites in order to disrupt society, the destruction of infrastructures in order to disorganize the economy, and, finally, the carrying out of attacks and general sabotage in order to provoke the paralysis of a given region. Not surprisingly, most of those who passed through Aginter's *guerre révolutionnaire* course were drawn from the ranks of European radical right and neo-fascist organizations, and some of these were later implicated in bloody terrorist actions.[45]

Perhaps even more importantly, "the infiltration of pro-Chinese [Maoist] organizations and the use of this [leftist] cover was one of the great specialties of Aginter."[46] Such methods were explicitly advocated by Guillou in his terrorist manual. In the section on violent demonstrations, for example, the former OAS man recommended that "the infiltrators at a demonstration should situate themselves strategically within the midst of it in order to cause it to disintegrate." From this choice position, "they can carry out violent provocations against the forces of order, thereby inciting the cycle of action-repression-reaction."[47] In the section on covert operations, he insisted that selected personnel should scrupulously observe the rules of "cover" by adopting false identities as journalists, identities that could be lent credence through the use of skillfully forged documents or genuine documents that had been surreptitiously acquired.[48] Although Guillou and Leroy both later denied – vehemently but seemingly falsely – that they had anything to do with terrorist atrocities, the latter openly bragged about the agency's success in carrying out infiltrations and provocations.[49] His evident pride in these accomplishments was hardly misplaced. At the end of 1965, even before the creation of Aginter, Guillou and his men commenced operations in Portuguese Africa with the objective of liquidating guerrilla leaders, installing informants and provocateurs in genuine resistance groups, and setting up *false* national liberation movements that were roughly analogous to the pseudo–Mau Mau "countergangs" that British Brigadier General Frank Kitson had earlier formed in Kenya.[50]

Somewhat later, Aginter found the perfect vehicle to use as a front for its operations – the Parti Communiste Suisse/Marxiste-Leniniste (PCS/ML: Swiss

Communist Party/Marxist-Leninist), an ostensibly Maoist organization headed by Gérard Bulliard. The Aginter man responsible for arranging this was Robert Leroy. With support from the communist Chinese embassy in Berne, which not coincidentally provided a convenient cover for the Tewu's main headquarters in Europe, he persuaded Bulliard to hire him and other Aginter personnel as correspondents for the PCS/ML's paper, *L'Étincelle*.[51] Armed with these credentials, Leroy and Jean-Marie Laurent were able to penetrate "liberated territory" in Angola, Guinea-Bissau, and Mozambique in order to "interview" several African guerrilla leaders. After doing so, they engaged in *intoxication* operations to provoke dissension within the resistance movements, and Leroy's machinations may have played some role in the bombing that killed Frente de Libertação de Moçambique (FRELIMO: Mozambique Liberation Front) leader Eduardo Mondlane. In addition to their African ventures, Aginter "correspondents" also infiltrated the Portuguese opposition in Western Europe by posing as Maoist journalists.[52] These examples, which could doubtless be multiplied, provide a general indication of the important role played by Aginter Presse in utilizing and thence in transmitting *guerre révolutionnaire* methods to the European extreme right. It now remains only to reveal the link between former OAS or Aginter personnel and leading members of the Italian neo-fascist organizations that carried out the "strategy of tension." These latter used many of those same techniques, including the employment of infiltration and "false flag" operations designed to implicate the radical left in terrorist actions.

The Italian components of the "Black International"

The three main neo-fascist groups that were repeatedly implicated in terrorist massacres in Italy in the late 1960s and early 1970s were Pino Rauti's Ordine Nuovo and its offshoots, Stefano Delle Chiaie's Avanguardia Nazionale, and the Padua cell headed by Franco Freda. In 1954, Ordine Nuovo was established as the organizational base of the ultra-rightist faction within the Movimento Sociale Italiano, which was then divided into a radical right inspired by the example of the Waffen-SS and the elitist ideas of Italian esoteric traditionalist philosopher Giulio Cesare ("Julius") Evola; a centrist, pro-Atlantic conservative majority which sought to obtain a much-needed legitimacy within the postwar parliamentary system; and a radical left which looked for its inspiration to "fascism of the first hour" and the quasi-socialist Verona Charter promulgated in 1944 by Mussolini's Salò rump regime.[53] In 1956, having been thoroughly disgusted and disillusioned by the close victory of the centrist "double-breasted suit" faction at the party's congress, the leading members of the Centro Studi Ordine Nuovo (CSON: New Order Study Center) officially broke with the MSI and transformed the center into an autonomous extraparliamentary cadre organization. From that point on, Ordine Nuovo served as a rallying point for intellectuals and youthful militants who received ideological indoctrination and paramilitary training and regularly engaged in direct actions against the radical left, disorderly protests against the "bourgeois" system, and – as would later become clear – terrorist provocations. The group's ideological views, which initially consisted of a relatively bastardized mixture of neo-Nazi "social racist" and elitist Evolan conceptions, were disseminated by a bimonthly journal, *Ordine Nuovo*, as well as other bulletins like *Noi Europa* and *Corrispondenza Europea*, which had a decidedly internationalist bent. Given the pronounced ideological influence of Evola, who argued in an issue of *Ordine Nuovo* for the creation "of an indestructible nucleus, of a small, ascetic, monastic-chivalric order, devoted to order and the elite, opposed to a [political] party, with a new conception of the fatherland," it is not surprising to discover that ON had three distinct levels of membership – "sympathizers," "adherents," and carefully selected and specially trained "militants" who formed a secretive, quasi-mystical elite within the organization – or that only the latter were relied upon to carry out the group's important and sensitive covert actions.[54] In the fall of 1969, Rauti's decision to bring Ordine Nuovo back within the fold of the MSI, then led by a sympathetic Giorgio Almirante, led to an apparent schism within the former and the creation of the Movimento Politico Ordine Nuovo (MPON: New Order Political Movement) by intransigent elements headed by Clemente Graziani. Several years later, in 1973, the MPON was belatedly banned by the government for attempting to "reconstitute the fascist party," a course of action which was in theory prohibited by the so-called Scelba Law.[55]

The founder and principal leader of Ordine Nuovo throughout most of its history was Pino Rauti. At the age of seventeen Rauti enlisted in the "M[ussolini]" battalion of the Guardia Nazionale Repubblicana (National Republican Guard), the militia of the Republic of Salò, and the following year was promoted to Second Lieutenant. After being captured in combat on the Po front, he was imprisoned in a series of Allied internment camps and ended up at POW Camp 211 at Algiers, where he made contact with former veterans of the "Giovani Fascisti" battalion of the Bir el Gobi unit. He subsequently managed to escape from the camp and enroll in the Falangist "El Tercio" unit in Spanish Morocco before being recaptured by the English and returned to Algiers. In February 1946 he was imprisoned in Camp S at Taranto, but was released at the end of the year. He then joined the newly created MSI and became a national youth leader and member of the party's Central Committee. This, however, was not enough to satisfy his craving for activism. In 1948, he helped Enzo Erra give birth, first to the fortnightly *La Sfida*, and later to the publication *Imperium*, both of which were inspired primarily by the doctrines of Evola. By the end of 1949, he was among the chief activists in the clandestine Fasci di Azione Rivoluzionaria (FAR: Revolutionary Action Fasci), a neo-fascist paramilitary group that was subsequently involved, sometimes beneath the façade of Legione Nera (the Black Legion), in a series of terrorist attacks in the early 1950s.[56] He was then arrested and tried, along with Evola himself, Clemente Graziani, Fausto Gianfranceschi, and several others for forming a criminal gang, trying to reconstitute the fascist party, and carrying out acts of violence. Following his release from prison ten months later, he returned to the ranks of the MSI. Shortly thereafter he helped to consolidate, with the encouragement of Evola and Almirante, the intransigent radical right *corrente* within the MSI by establishing the Centro Studi Ordine Nuovo. He was later implicated, along with many other Ordine Nuovo militants, in serious incidents of right-wing violence, the most important of which was the December 1969 Piazza Fontana bomb massacre.[57]

For its part, Avanguardia Nazionale Giovanile (National Youth Vanguard) was founded in 1959 by Stefano Delle Chiaie and other extremists who considered both the MSI and Ordine Nuovo to be too tame. Like ON, AN arrayed itself on the radical Evolan wing of the neo-fascist spectrum and bitterly denounced the moderate bourgeois elements at the helm of the MSI, although its ideological views were less sophisticated than those propounded by Rauti's group and it attracted more marginal social elements. It was, even more than ON, a group geared toward direct action rather than sterile philosophizing. As one early AN militant later claimed, "we didn't give a fuck for [the nuances of] ideology, we were just angry . . . and wanted to hit back."[58] A later AN pamphlet had this to say: "We are for man-to-man engagements. . . . Before setting out our men are morally prepared, so that they learn to break the bones, even of someone who gets down on his knees and cries."[59] From the very outset the organization was prominently involved in a series of street battles with the left, particularly when communist-sponsored events or workers' demonstrations were organized. As early as 1962, the judicial authorities nearly imprisoned and fined Delle Chiaie, but the sentence was overturned the following year. This omnipresent threat from the judiciary nonetheless prompted Delle Chiaie to dissolve the group in 1966 and return to the protective shelter provided by Almirante's faction within the MSI.

But AN's sudden disappearance was more *pro forma* than real, because its "former" members and cadres kept in regular clandestine contact with one another and continued to participate, ostensibly as isolated individuals, in political demonstrations, paramilitary training camps, and acts of political violence. In other words, the group merely went further underground in order to avoid being banned outright. As the 1960s wore on and political tension and polarization proceeded apace, however, personnel from AN became increasingly involved in infiltration and provocation operations designed to manipulate and discredit the far left. In late 1970 Adriano Tilgher formally revived AN at the behest of Delle Chiaie, who had been temporarily forced to take refuge in Spain so as to avoid being arrested in connection with the Piazza Fontana bombing, but six years later the group was officially banned by the Italian government after its members were found guilty of reconstituting the fascist party.[60]

Stefano Delle Chiaie, the charismatic founder of AN, was undoubtedly one of the world's most dangerous right-wing terrorist leaders during the 1960s and 1970s. In spite of being nicknamed "il Caccola," Roman slang for "shorty," his career was so much larger than life that a brief summary barely does it justice. He began his political career at a very young age as a militant in the local MSI Appio section in Rome, which he became the Secretary of in 1957. One year later, however, he had grown so disillusioned with the party's moderate orientation that he led some of his loyal followers out of the MSI and formed a short-lived group called the Gruppi di Azione Rivoluzionaria (Revolutionary Action Groups). When this effort failed to take off, he temporarily joined Ordine Nuovo and managed to lure several sympathizers away from Rauti's organization. Within a short time he broke away from ON and created AN, which quickly gained notoriety for launching brutal "punitive expeditions" and, toward the end of the 1960s, various sorts of covert operations against the extraparliamentary left.[61] After being implicated in the Piazza Fontana affair, he became a fugitive in Spain but continued to visit Italy at regular intervals even though he was wanted by the Italian police. In early 1971 he was directly implicated in Prince Junio Valerio Borghese's abortive December 1970 coup, after which he again fled to Spain along with Borghese and several Italian neo-fascists.

Delle Chiaie's original patrons in Iberia included the Duke of Valencia, the very same nobleman who had earlier welcomed and thereafter maintained close personal relationships with Degrelle and Skorzeny; Falangist ultra and former Labor Minister José Antonio Girón, who was later involved in overt and covert efforts to maintain "pure" Francoism before and after the Caudillo's death; Mariano Sánchez Covisa, head of the paramilitary Guerrilleros de Cristo Rey (GCR: Guerrillas of Christ the King); Hermandad de la Guardia de Franco (Guard of Franco Brotherhood) Secretary General Alberto Royuela; and Skorzeny himself.[62] Royuela later admitted putting up around ninety Italians, many in his own home, and during the late 1960s and early 1970s a regularized transit route for Italian neo-fascist fugitives had been set up in Barcelona. In exchange for serving as "bouncers" (*vigilantes*) at billiards parlors run by Royuela's lieutenant, Miguel Gómez Benet, they were provided with lodging by Royuela himself or his principal Guardia de Franco collaborators, especially Luis Antonio García-Rodríguez, whose Madrid-based Eniesa import-export company at Calle Núñez de Balboa 37 also provided them with "cover," means of subsistence, and weapons. Between late 1974 and early 1975 most of these Italians moved on to Madrid, where in November 1975 Delle Chiaie opened a pizzeria called El Appuntamento near the Avenida Gran Vía at Calle Marqués de Leganés 6, which provided employment for several of his countrymen and served as a gathering place for assorted European and Latin American right-wing extremists. This phase of Delle Chiaie's career was interrupted when a Spanish journalist writing for *Interviú* exposed his association with the restaurant in 1976. The following year, around the time of a February 1977 police raid on a neo-fascist weapons factory run by Italian fugitives and owned by Sánchez Covisa on Calle Pelayo 39 in Madrid, Delle Chiaie left Spain and spent several years living in various South American countries before being captured and extradited to Italy from Venezuela in 1987. Throughout much of this period in exile, however, he traveled to and from Europe with relative impunity and seems to have masterminded certain terrorist operations in the Italian peninsula.[63]

As for Giorgio ("Franco") Freda, the young lawyer began his political activities in the 1950s as an MSI member and local Fronte Universitario di Azione Nazionale (FUAN: University Front for National Action) leader in Padua. In 1963 he abandoned the overly tepid MSI, then joined ON and went on to form his own study circle and publishing house, the Gruppo di Ar (Ar[yan] Group), which held regular gatherings, published a number of anti-Semitic and fascist tomes, and from 1965 on served to provide cover for a loosely organized "action group" that carried out acts of political violence. Given his activist orientation, it was only a matter of time before Freda gravitated toward other like-minded extremists, including Giovanni Ventura, who edited the journal *Reazione*. Freda was formally introduced to Delle Chiaie in 1965, and by August of the following year had become Ordine Nuovo's representative in Padua.[64] These links with AN and ON were further strengthened in subsequent years, and in the process Freda became increasingly involved in acts of violence and outright terrorism. Throughout the course of 1969, his Padua cell carried out a series of operations aimed at manipulating Maoist groups, as well as an ever-growing number of terrorist bombings that culminated in the terrible 12 December massacre at a bank in Milan's Piazza Fontana. After initially focusing their attention almost exclusively on a number of anarchist bands, the police arrested Freda in 1970 for his involvement in these bombings after a friend of Ventura's made some startling revelations to the authorities.[65]

In addition to being extremely active and linked to one another in myriad ways, each of these key neo-fascist groups shared three important characteristics. First, they established an extensive network of contacts with neo-fascist paramilitary groups and far right organizations throughout the world. Second, they worked in close cooperation with hard-line elements from a number of Western secret services. Third, as a result of these contacts they indirectly or directly exposed to the full spectrum of techniques associated with French counterrevolutionary warfare doctrine, including the use of systematic terrorism, psychological warfare, and different types of "false flag" operations, techniques which they later applied with varying degrees of success during several phases of the "strategy of tension" in Italy. Indeed, it was precisely these *sub rosa* institutional connections and their familiarity with sophisticated unconventional warfare methods that differentiated such groups from garden-variety neo-Nazi street brawlers and lent them a degree of real historical importance.

Ordine Nuovo was undoubtedly the most assiduous of the three organizations in seeking to establish links with right-wing extremists abroad. Rauti began making contact with neo-fascist groups in other countries even before the official creation of ON, and by the end of the 1950s his organization served as the contact point in Italy for radical neo-fascists from all over the world. He was among those ultras who supported the activities of Amaudruz's Lausanne-based "international," the Nouvelle Ordre Européen/Europäische Neu-Ordnung (NOE/ENO: New European Order), and by the early 1960s – if not earlier – he became its "national correspondent" for Italy. In addition to attending or sending representatives to virtually every NOE/ENO Congress from the mid-1950s on, Rauti made certain that the NOE/ENO's pronouncements were regularly reprinted in *Ordine Nuovo* and *Noi Europa* and also arranged for ON to host Amaudruz's 1958 and 1967 Congresses in Milan. In this way, ON's leaders were able to establish closer connections with other extremist groups affiliated with the NOE/ENO, including the Portuguese organizations headed by Zarco Moniz Ferreira and similar groups in Spain, West Germany, France, Belgium, and Holland, as well as various associations of pro-fascist East

European refugees. It is thus not surprising to discover that Rauti periodically wrote articles for the Coburg-based *Nation Europa* journal, which served as an important forum for diverse neo-fascist and neo-Nazi groups throughout the European continent, many of which were affiliated with the NOE/ENO.[66]

But it was not until the renewed outbreak of anti-colonial strife in Africa, the seditious French military revolts in Algeria, and the formation of the OAS that these contacts took on real operational importance, because at that point ON and other Italian neo-fascist groups began actively supporting the OAS's desperate struggles against both Algerian nationalists and the government of the Fifth Republic. Indeed, Rauti personally organized public demonstrations on behalf of the OAS, and certain key ON personnel were identified by the Italian secret service as being among the principal agents of the OAS in Italy. For example, Rauti's ON co-leader Clemente Graziani later proudly admitted that he had carried an OAS membership card and had helped procure large quantities of weapons for the organization.[67] It was through these activities, and the shelter ON ultras secretly provided to OAS fugitives in Italy, that they came into contact with other activist groups like Jeune Europe. ON was undoubtedly in close touch with the succession of Belgian neo-fascist groups headed by Thiriart, because articles by key figures associated with JE appeared regularly in its main publication, *Ordine Nuovo*.[68] Moreover, in return for promoting the maintenance of Belgian control over the Congo, ON allegedly received funds from Thiriart and various powerful financial institutions, including the Union Minière de Haut-Katanga, which still had extensive economic interests in that vast, mineral-rich country. Even more significantly, groups of young ultras from ON and the Italian section of JE, which was itself composed of elements from Giovane Nazione and ON, visited special training camps in Belgium and West Germany to "learn techniques of OAS and Nazi propaganda," and the OAS also set up bases in Italy in order to give them "refresher courses."[69] In this way, members of Rauti's organization were exposed early on to *guerre révolutionnaire* techniques, whether directly by OAS personnel or indirectly through the intermediary of JE.

The OAS connection also accounted for the later development of links between ON and Aginter Presse, about which there is much reliable documentary evidence. Among other things, a file card for Rauti was found in the section of the Aginter archives that contained materials relating to the agency's Italian "correspondents."[70] Moreover, numerous letters were found therein that had been written to Yves Guillou, apparently on Rauti's behalf, by Armando Mortilla, director of the FIEL Italiana-Notizie Latine press agency in Rome. Despite Rauti's later denials, these letters provided evidence not only of collaboration on the informational and moral levels, but also in the operational sphere.[71] In 1967, for example, Mortilla wrote a letter to Guillou concerning the organization of "recreational and instructional camps" designed to facilitate a vast collaboration between like-minded European groups, a letter he closed by asking for suggestions about what sorts of actions to undertake. And at the end of 1968, Rauti and his organization allegedly cooperated with Aginter operatives in a joint project to recruit several Italian neo-fascists into the Portuguese Army. Most importantly of all, it was in the midst of the materials submitted to Aginter by Mortilla that a vitally important document was found that appeared to be a veritable blueprint for the forthcoming "strategy of tension," "Notre action politique," whose contents will be divulged and assessed later.[72] Nor did ON look only to Western Europe for such international allies. Rauti also developed very close contacts with Plevris's K4A after the 1967 coup in Greece, so much so that he subsequently became one of the key intermediaries between Italian and Greek ultras.[73]

Initially, Delle Chiaie seems to have been less interested in making contacts with neo-fascist groups abroad, but his attitude must have changed around the time that he joined ON. During the early 1960s, he made several visits to Spain, Austria, and West Germany in order to solidify his international connections, and in 1962 he may have attended the neo-Nazi conference in the Cotswolds, where British National Socialist Movement (NSM) chief Colin Jordan and American Nazi Party (ANP) leader George Lincoln Rockwell signed an agreement setting up the World Union of National Socialists (WUNS). It was also around this time that AN personnel began making regular appearances at NOE/ENO Congresses.[74] But, as in the case of ON, it was the OAS that acted as the medium through which AN attained a greater degree of operational significance. In the early 1960s one of Avanguardia Nazionale's key militants, Serafino Di Luia, risked his own safety to shelter OAS fugitives in his home.[75] Nor, in all probability, was he the only AN member who offered tangible support to the OAS at this time. Later, following the formal dissolution of AN in 1966, Delle Chiaie and his lieutenant Mario Merlino were often seen in the company of an ex-OAS man named "Jean" – apparently Jean-Marie Laurent of Aginter Presse – who described himself as a military instructor and an explosives expert. From at least that point on, Delle Chiaie remained in close contact with Aginter, a relationship that must have grown closer when he took refuge in the Iberian Peninsula.[76] Indeed, in 1973 Delle Chiaie traveled to different countries in Latin America, including Colombia, Panama, and Costa Rica, relying upon his credentials as an Aginter "correspondent." Hence it is not surprising that when Guillou was forced to flee from Portugal in the wake of the 1974 revolution, Delle Chiaie put him up temporarily in his Madrid apartment. That same year, a Banco de Panama check for 1,000 dollars signed by Guillou was found made out to AN member Fausto Fabruzzi, which the latter indicated was to be used to set up a branch of Aginter in Italy. Their formal association was confirmed in September 1977, when an Aginter press identification card in the name of "Giovanni Martelli," but with Delle Chiaie's picture on it, was discovered in the Roman apartment of a couple who had temporarily put up the "black bombadier."[77] That same year he attempted to set up an Aginter-style press agency in Chile.

In April 1968, several AN members were among the Italian neo-fascists who participated in a "tour" of Greece organized under the auspices of the Ethnikos Syndesmos Ellenon Spudaston Italias (ESESI: League of Greek Nationalist Students in Italy), which also brought them into contact with the K4A's Plevris.[78] And after settling in Spain, Delle Chiaie quickly fell in with militants from Ernesto Milá's Frente Nacional de Juventud (FNJ: National Youth Front) and Jorge Mota's CEDADE, operatives of the GCR and the Paladin Group, pro-fascist East European émigrés, right-wing followers of Perón who had taken refuge in Spain, anti-Castro Cubans, and other elements of the "Black International" with whom he subsequently collaborated in launching anti-Euskadi ta Askatasuna (ETA: Basque Fatherland and Freedom) operations. Later, during his many visits or sojourns in South and Central America, he invariably made contact with neo-fascist paramilitary groups, such as the Frente Nacional Patria y Libertad (Fatherland and Freedom National Front) in Chile, the Milicia (Militia) group in Argentina, the Frente Bolivia Joven (Bolivia Youth Front, also known as the Novios de la Muerte) in Bolivia, the Movimiento de Liberación Nacional (MLN: National Liberation Movement) in Guatemala, and militant factions of the Alianza Republicana Nacionalista (ARENA: Nationalist Republican Alliance) in El Salvador.[79]

Freda likewise developed links with various international neo-fascist groups, although these were by no means as extensive as those established by ON and AN. His roomate was Claudio Orsi, one of the founders of Giovane Europa, which probably brought him into peripheral contact with elements from the central Belgian branch of Jeune Europe, especially given his keen interest in both action and the fascist intellectual tradition. Nor was it an accident that a report of the proceedings at the NOE/ENO's April 1969 Barcelona Congress was found during a 1971 search of his home. Four months later, on 17 August 1969, Freda presented an initial draft of his famous booklet, *La disintegrazione del sistema*, at a Fronte Europeo Rivoluzionario (European Revolutionary Front) meeting in the Bavarian city of Regensburg.[80] It remains to be determined whether the strikingly innovative concepts he expressed at that conference, which included advocating an operational alliance between right- and left-wing revolutionaries, exerted any significant influence on the ideas or behavior of those in attendance who were not Italian. Finally, his close working relationship with Guido Giannettini during the whole of 1969 must have brought him, however tangentially, into the latter's extensive web of international right-wing connections. This will become clearer later.

Even more disturbing is the extent to which leading personnel from these three radical neo-fascist groups collaborated with factions within a variety of Western security and intelligence services. This certainly applies to Rauti and other Ordine Nuovo leaders. According to Italian secret service reports, he and Clemente Graziani traveled to Portugal and Spain in March 1963 in order to enlist political support for the establishment of "intelligence centers" (*centri informativi*) in Rome and other Italian cities. In Portugal they met with "high-ranking officials" of PIDE to negotiate the possible acquisition of weapons. They then went on to Madrid, supposedly to attend the national congress of Falangist corporations, but really to meet with officials of the Spanish political police and PIDE (who had in the meantime arrived from Lisbon) to discuss the neutralizing of anti-Franco and anti-Salazar propaganda disseminated by the communists in Italy. After meeting with Moniz Ferreira and General Agustín Muñoz Grandes, a powerful Franco confidant, they were assured of a "major financial contribution" so that ON could develop these various initiatives. The result may have been the establishment of an export-import firm in Italy that specialized in arms trafficking.[81] ON's subsequent connections to Aginter Presse could only have strengthened the group's contacts, whether directly or indirectly, with the Portuguese and Spanish security services. And there is no doubt that wanted ON and MPON militants who later took refuge in Spain, such as Elio Massagrande and Pierluigi Concutelli, were recruited by the Spanish police and secret services to carry out "counterterrorist" operations against the ETA. It is also noteworthy that even though the authors of the two Servizio Informazioni Forze Armate (SIFAR: Armed Forces Intelligence Service) reports expressed some concern about Rauti's 1963 meetings in Spain, within three years he was placed, if only temporarily, on the payroll of the Servizio Informazioni Difesa (SID: Defense Intelligence Service), SIFAR's immediate successor.

It is difficult to say exactly when Rauti began actively collaborating with elements of the Italian security services. Some left-wing commentators have suggested that he was recruited by the special operations section within the Ministry of the Interior, the Ufficio Affari Riservati (UAR: Secret Affairs Office), but little or no evidence has emerged to substantiate this claim.[82] There is no doubt, however, that Rauti became a minor protagonist in the bitter internecine quarrel within the armed forces general staff between General Giovanni De Lorenzo and General Giuseppe Aloja, which beyond the usual personal rivalries concerned practical matters such as the desirability of establishing elite special forces units to counter subversion and the best type of main battle tank to purchase.[83] It seems that Rauti and Guido Giannettini, an important ON member and author specializing in military affairs who contributed off and on to the official *Rivista Militare* journal, jointly directed Agenzia D, a press agency linked to the "private" Istituto di Studi Storici e Militari "Alberto Pollio" ("Alberto Pollio" Institute for Historical and Military Studies) and financed in part by Colonel Renzo Rocca, head of SIFAR's Ricerche Economiche e Industriali (REI: Industrial and Economic Research) section. Agenzia D vociferously backed Aloja's plans for the armed forces, and may even have been created to serve as his mouthpiece. Both ON militants were also among the speakers at the Istituto's SIFAR-funded conference on "revolutionary war" in May of 1965.[84]

A little over one year later, Aloja approached right-wing journalist and military intelligence service collaborator Eggardo Beltrametti – one of the organizers of the 1965 conference – to obtain some advice about how to counteract the De Lorenzo–sponsored campaign against him. Beltrametti suggested that Aloja respond to these attacks in the form of a book. After Aloja assented, Beltrametti asked his friend Rauti, a journalist for the rightist daily *Il Tempo* and a very fast writer as well as a co-director of Agenzia D, to produce such a work together with his associate Giannettini. The latter was to prepare the quasi-technical chapter in support of the German "Leopard" battle tank, which Aloja favored purchasing instead of the American M-60, and Rauti was to compose the rest, including a chapter promoting the creation of "politicized" military units capable of defending the nation against communist subversion. The resulting book, *Le mani rosse sulle Forze armate*, was completed in just over one week. After a few copies were distributed to military commands, Aloja was persuaded that it would be better to recall the book, which accused De Lorenzo of being a virtual communist, so as not to create an irreparable schism within the armed forces. He duly asked Rauti to suspend the diffusion of the book, which the ON leader agreed to do provided that he was adequately compensated. Ultimately, Aloja paid Beltrametti between three million and five million lire for his efforts, and Rauti and Giannettini both received some financial compensation. Shortly thereafter, the latter became a paid operative of SID.[85]

Rauti, meanwhile, established close links with members of the Greek military junta in the wake of the 1967 coup. According to KYP operative Plevris, Rauti came to Greece in his capacity as a journalist to interview him shortly after that coup. During the course of that visit Rauti also met officially with representatives of the new Greek government, including Interior Minister Stylianos Pattakos.[86] From that point on, the ON leader became a vocal supporter of the junta in Italy and a key liaison man between right-wing radicals from the two countries. So it was that he helped to organize a "tour" of Greece in April 1968 for fifty-one "students" affiliated with ON, AN, Nuova Caravella (New Caravel [a type of rigged sailing ship]), and Europa Civiltà (European Civilization), all of whose expenses were paid for by the Greek military regime. On 16 April, along with fifty-nine members of ESESI and the cultural attaché at the Greek embassy in Rome, Mikhalis (Michael) Poulantzas, the Italians embarked from Brindisi on the motorboat *Egnatia* and landed in Epirus the following morning. After a brief visit to some tourist sites they arrived in Athens, where they were put up in housing placed at their disposal by the student federation in that city. Officially, this trip was made to celebrate the Orthodox Church's Easter ceremony, but the dates likewise coincided with the celebrations surrounding the one-year anniversary of the 21 April 1967 seizure of power by the junta. The Italian "students" subsequently held meetings with their Greek counterparts, and on 21 April they were formally wined and dined at two military barracks, together with numerous high-ranking Army officers. Later in the evening, Pattakos made a public presentation and then personally welcomed his foreign guests. A few days later, they returned to Italy.[87]

The participants on this "tour" later testified that they had engaged in no political discussions or activities while in Greece, but there are good reasons to doubt this innocent version of events. Indeed, it seems probable that the neo-fascists met with their Greek *camerati* and official security personnel for a very specific purpose – to receive instruction in the techniques of infiltration and provocation, which the Colonels had applied to good effect as a pretext for launching their own coup.[88] The chief instruments used by the armed forces to precipitate the activation of the anti-subversive "Prometheus Plan" were various right-wing paramilitary groups, including Plevris's K4A, which carried out a series of bombings during and after the so-called night of fire, terrorist actions that were then blamed on the radical left.[89] The Greek military had already had extensive firsthand experience in applying the arcane techniques of unconventional warfare, including "false flag" operations, during the 1944–1947 civil war against communist guerrillas, and these techniques were further refined in the course of the anti-British revolts on Cyprus. Many Greek Army officers therefore developed a keen interest in *guerre révolutionnaire* doctrine, and Colonel Giorgios Papadopoulos was himself apparently an avid reader of works by leading French counterinsurgency theorists.[90] Furthermore, Papadopoulos was reportedly the KYP's chief liaison man to the CIA, which had played an integral role in organizing, financing, and training personnel for the KYP.[91] Given this background, and the junta's apparent desire to export its "revolution" to Italy and certain other nearby countries, it should come as no surprise to discover that after their trip to Greece many of the Italian "tourists" abandoned their reliance on traditional squadrist tactics and embarked upon a series of subtler covert operations designed to infiltrate and manipulate Maoist and anarchist groups.[92]

Moreover, Rauti and three MSI officials followed up this 1968 tour by arranging to shuttle groups of Italian neo-fascists to the island of Corfu, ostensibly for a series of "camping trips" but in all probability – if similar outings in Italy provide any indication – to receive paramilitary or unconventional warfare training.[93] All this is suggestive enough, but looming over the entire matter of Rauti's relationship to the Colonels is the so-called Signor P affair. On 7 December 1969 – only five days before the Piazza Fontana massacre – the English journalist Leslie Finer published an article in the *London Observer* that summarized the contents of an ostensibly top secret 15 May 1969 letter, to which was attached a report purportedly prepared by Greek government informants in Italy. This report, which allegedly outlined Greek plans to promote covert anti-constitutional actions in Italy, had then supposedly been forwarded to the Greek ambassador in Rome, Antoine Poumpouras, by the foreign affairs minister in Athens, Mikhalis Kottakis. Some of the information that was included in this document concerned the role that was being played by an agent of the junta in Italy, identified only as "Signor P," who was said to be the liaison man between the Greek government leaders and representatives of the Italian Army and the Carabinieri. On the basis of the numerous references to this person in the document, leftist journalists in Italy quickly concluded that "Signor P" was probably a reference to Pino Rauti, an identification that was also accepted by SID in an 8 April 1975 report.[94] If this was in fact the case, it would have confirmed that the ON leader was actively working on behalf of a dictatorial foreign power in order to subvert democracy in Italy, which in turn would have offered more fuel for the "anti-fascist" press campaign against Rauti and his organization.

Alas, it now seems that the document published by Finer was a forgery, whether or not he was aware of this from the outset. For one thing, all of the post-junta Greek officials questioned by the Italian judicial authorities insisted that it was not genuine.[95] In and of themselves, such denials are meaningless, because government officials typically engage in "damage control" to preserve the image and prestige of their own bureaucratic institutions. But there are other, more serious objections to accepting the *bona fides* of the document and the guilt of Rauti. As the rightist press hastened to point out, it was premature if not absurd to jump to the conclusion that the "P" referred to "Pino," especially in lieu of any hard evidence, and indeed that designation could just as easily have referred to a number of other individuals, such as right-wing journalist Guido Paglia. Be that as it may, the burden of proof that the document is genuine and that the "P" stands for "Pino" is – as always in such cases – on those who are making positive claims, and in the end Finer was unable to provide any evidence verifying its authenticity.[96] If it was an outright forgery or a clever piece of disinformation, it was probably produced and disseminated by the far left in order to cast suspicion on the Greek regime and its Italian supporters, such as Rauti. Alternatively, the right could have done so in order to increase the general level of political tension and/or destroy the credibility of left-wing journalists who could be expected to accept it as genuine and publish it for political reasons.[97] These considerations do not, however, alter the fact that ON's chief was closely linked to the Colonels' regime, or that their documented collusion likely had an operational dimension.

But if Rauti and other ON bigwigs had relations with a number of secret services and can legitimately be suspected of acting as their agents in certain contexts, there is little doubt that Delle Chiaie reportedly carried out "plausibly deniable" covert operations at the behest of such services for at least ten years. He has frequently been accused, both by left-wing and neo-fascist sources, of having been recruited as an informant and provocateur for the UAR, in all probability by Federico Umberto D'Amato at some point during the first half of the 1960s.[98] The "black bombardier" has always vehemently denied these charges in public forums, and has gone so far as to challenge one of his chief accusers, MSI Senator Giorgio Pisanò, to a duel. Given the lack of hard evidence, it remains possible that over the years such charges have been disseminated primarily by certain factions within the security forces, the left-wing opposition, or rival elements within the contentious neo-fascist milieu.[99]

Nevertheless, there is a considerable amount of circumstantial evidence that tends to buttress these accusations. Shortly before the abortive De Lorenzo "coup" in 1964, Delle Chiaie bragged to some of his *avanguardisti* that contacts inside SIFAR had alerted him that something big was brewing and that they should prepare themselves for action. It is also undeniable that heavily armed AN militants often attacked left-wing demonstrators under the benevolent gaze of the riot police. On one occasion in 1963, after being armed with official-issue police truncheons, they fought side by side with the non-uniformed Squadre Speciali (Special Squadrons) of the police against students protesting Moise Tshombé's meeting with the pope. Even more tellingly, an AN radical who threatened to expose Delle Chiaie's links to the Interior Ministry, Antonio Aliotti, was first threatened and later found dead in a car laden with explosives.[100] It is also the case, as will be amply documented in the next article, that one of D'Amato's deputies secretly admitted Delle Chiaie and a contingent of his men into the armory of the Interior Ministry in connection with the December 1970 Borghese coup.

Indeed, during a 1 December 1972 meeting in Barcelona, Delle Chiaie explicitly told an officer of SID, Captain Antonio Labruna, that in return for protection and funding he could "ruin the heads of the UAR and some functionaries of the Interior Ministry" within ten days if SID wanted him to, thereby implying that he could prove that the UAR was complicit in at least some of his anti-constitutional activities. When Labruna reported this to his Ufficio D superior, General Gianadelio Maletti, and proposed establishing a working relationship between SID and Delle

Chiaie, Maletti told him to forget it, apparently feeling that it was too dangerous to use the AN leader as a "double informant" given his group's existing contacts with the UAR.[101] Finally, the alleged protection provided by high-ranking Interior Ministry officials, regardless of whether this stemmed from genuine feelings of loyalty or fears about being blackmailed or publicly implicated in terrorist crimes, could help to explain why Delle Chiaie was able to enter and leave Italy almost at will despite having several warrants out for his arrest.

The best argument in favor of the thesis that Delle Chiaie was collaborating with or working for elements of the Italian secret services is provided by his *modus operandi* in other countries. Like Rauti, Delle Chiaie and his lieutenants had established links to the Greek secret services through Plevris. For example, Merlino and several ON ultras reportedly met with Colonel Ioannis Ladas, the minister of public order, on more than one occasion in 1968, and three years later Delle Chiaie and other key AN figures were reportedly provided with training in guerrilla warfare and sabotage techniques in courses organized in Greece by Ethnike Stratiotike Astinomia (ESA: National Military Police) chief Dimitrios Ioannides through the intermediary of Plevris and World Service.[102] Later, AN militant Roman Coltellacci helped to set up two export-import companies that traded with Greece, Mondial Import-Export in December 1969 and the Centro Italiano di Sviluppo Economico e Sociale (CISES: Italian Center for Economic and Social Development) in September 1972. Finally, one of Delle Chiaie's main collaborators, Elio Massagrande of the MPON, fled to Greece in 1974 to evade arrest with funds provided by the Greek government.[103]

Nor was Greece the only country where AN militants established links with foreign governments and secret services. Soon after his arrival in Spain, Delle Chiaie was reportedly contacted by Admiral Luis Carrero Blanco's anti-terrorism chief, José Ignacio San Martín, through the intermediary of several influential right-wingers who were already collaborating with the Spanish intelligence and security agencies. These included militants affiliated with the sector of the Falange Española (Spanish Phalanx) headed by former government minister Raimundo Fernández Cuesta, Fuerza Nueva leader Blas Piñar, and GCR head Mariano Sánchez Covisa, who is said to have personally introduced the AN leader to San Martín.[104] Together they supposedly worked to create the aforementioned underground support network, first in Barcelona and later in Madrid, whose purpose was to welcome, shelter, and provide subsistence to fugitive Italian neo-fascists. On 12 September 1973 Delle Chiaie and Prince Junio Valerio Borghese met together privately with Carrero Blanco, who offered them the added protection and support of the naval intelligence service in exchange for collaborating with San Martín's Servicio Central de Documentación de la Presidencia de Gobierno (SECED: Central Documentation Service of the President of the Government).[105] In concrete terms, this meant that Delle Chiaie would select suitable Italian exiles for recruitment into paramilitary bands, and then place them at the disposal of SECED and other security agencies. In return, those very same agencies would provide his men with funding, logistical support, advanced weapons, false documents, and other sorts of institutional protection. "Il Caccola" himself subsequently admitted that he had been granted a personal audience with Franco, an extraordinary privilege that would hardly have been granted to a garden-variety fugitive from Italian justice.[106] Nor was this the only "privilege" he was offered by the Spanish authorities. Among other things, he did not have to apply for a residence permit, his name did not appear on the Spanish police's list of resident foreigners, and his Madrid restaurant was not entered on the commercial register, as required by law.[107]

It was not long afterwards that Delle Chiaie and his action-oriented countrymen were secretly incorporated into various parastate commando groups that were used by hard-line elements of the police and secret services to conduct covert, "plausibly deniable" operations against domestic *aperturistas* and Basque terrorists. Among the cover names adopted by these ostensibly autonomous paramilitary squads – the forerunners of the now infamous Grupos Antiterroristas de Liberación (GAL: Anti-Terrorist Liberation Groups) – were the Batallón Vasco-Español (BE: Spanish-Basque Battalion), Antiterrorismo ETA (ATE: ETA Anti-Terrorism), and a number of more ephemeral groups such as Acción Nacional Española (ANE: Spanish National Action), the Grupos Antiterroristas Españoles (GAE: Spanish Anti-Terrorist Groups), Delta Sur (Delta South), Lucha Española Antimarxista (LEA: Spanish Anti-Marxist Struggle), the Organización de Voluntarios Antiterroristas (OVA: Organization of Anti-Terrorist Volunteers), the Grupos Armados Revolucionarios (GAR: Armed Revolutionary Groups), and the Alianza Apostólica Anticomunista (Apostolic Anti-Communist Alliance), which was modeled on the notorious Argentine parallel police apparatus, the Alianza Anticomunista Argentina (AAA or Triple A). Despite this plethora of fronts, the personnel in these ad hoc bands were all drawn from the same sources, including former OAS men, anti-communist émigrés from eastern Europe, disgruntled military veterans, off-duty policemen, neo-fascists from all over Europe, anti-Castro Cubans from the United States, mercenaries, adventurers of all sorts, and members of various Latin American "death squads" who had taken refuge in Spain.[108] Over the years these groups were collectively responsible for many violent assaults on Spanish leftists and dozens of clandestine "counterterrorist" operations in the Basque country, both inside Spanish territory and across the border in southern France.[109]

Although there is no evidence that Delle Chiaie personally engaged in actual anti-ETA field operations, he continually worked behind the scenes and did not hesitate to assign this grisly work to several of his exiled neo-fascist countrymen.[110] Among those who participated in actual "hit teams" were Giuseppe Calzona, Augusto Cauchi (Fronte Nazionale Rivoluzionario [FNR: National Revolutionary Front]), Roberto Nanni, Mario Ricci (AN), Carlo Cicuttini (ON), and Pierluigi Concutelli (MPON), whereas Salvatore Francia (MPON), MPON leader Clemente Graziani, Elio Massagrande, Eliodoro Pomar (ON and Fronte Nazionale [National Front]), Freda associate Giancarlo Rognoni (La Fenice), and Bruno Luciano Stefano (Europa Civiltà and AN) appear to have confined themselves to organizational and logistical roles. Many of the Italians were originally involved in actions carried out by BVE or ATE commando units, and several thence continued to wage a *guerra sucia* under the rubric of GAL. Usually they operated in multinational groups together with Spaniards (such as José Fernández del Barrio), Frenchmen (such as former paratrooper and OAS militant Jean-Pierre Cherid), Argentines (such as ex-AAA man Justo Alemán), and individuals of other nationalities (including the Czech Vladimir Vit and the Algerian Muhammad Khiyar), but on a few occasions they carried out operations against Basque separatists exclusively with fellow Italians. One such operation, carried out by Calzona, Nanni, and others, was the attempted 6 May 1976 assassination of "historic" ETA leader Tomás Perez Revilla in Bayonne, which left the target, his wife, and their son wounded.[111]

Italian neo-fascists also played key roles in certain high-profile acts of political violence directed against the Spanish left. Indeed, as time wore on, their leader Delle Chiaie found himself increasingly unable to resist the lure of direct action. On 9 May 1976 he participated, together with right-wing Carlists under the direction of Sixto Enrique de Borbón-Parma, ex-PIDE/DGS officers from Portugal, and members of the GCR and the Argentine Triple A, in a brutal attack on left-leaning Carlists at the movement's holy site at Montejurra, which left two people dead and three gravely wounded. There is no doubt about his presence, because photographers on the scene managed to snap pictures of him along with several other Italian *squadristi*, including Augusto Cauchi. In that incident, officers of the Guardia Civil (Civil Guard) who were present on the scene failed to prevent the attack and then belatedly intervened to protect the *sixtinos* from reprisals. Later, it was learned that rightist Interior Minister Manuel Fraga had ordered the Guardia not to intervene, that other members of the Arias government had urged Sixto and his chief associates to go to Montejurra, and that someone from Sixto's squad accidentally dropped a clip of 9 mm ammunition at the scene – the very same type regularly issued to the Army and Guardia Civil for use in their submachine guns.[112]

Several months later, on 23 January 1977, Delle Chiaie was among the ultras involved in an assault on a leftist pro-political amnesty demonstration in Madrid's Plaza de España that led to the fatal wounding of Arturo Ruiz García, a member of the communist-dominated labor union, the Comisiones Obreras (Workers' Commissions). It was later discovered that the AN leader (using the alias "Alfredo") was one of the principal culprits, along with Jorge Cesarsky, a member of the Argentine Triple A and an operative of SECED, and two Spaniards affiliated with the paramilitary ATE, José Ignacio Fernández Guaza (a collaborator of the SIGC who was also implicated in the Montejurra attack) and Angel Sierra.[113] The very next night, a neo-fascist commando squad forced its way into the offices of the Comisiones Obreras at Calle Atocha 55 and opened fire on its occupants with automatic weapons. This massacre, which resulted in the deaths of four labor lawyers and a union official as well as the serious wounding of four other lawyers, was the most dramatic and bloody single act of rightist violence – outside of Basque country – in the history of postwar Spain.[114] Whether Delle Chiaie had a hand in planning it is unclear, but such an operation would certainly not have been out of character for him.

Several Italian neo-fascists later testified that many of these terrorist activities in Iberia were carried out at the behest of high-ranking personnel within various Spanish intelligence and police agencies, and once again a significant amount of circumstantial evidence exists that lends support to their claims.[115] For one thing, members of the Brigada Político-Social (Political-Social Brigade) of the Madrid police often hung out at El Appuntamento, not to keep an eye on potential troublemakers but rather to recruit them for various "dirty" jobs.[116] For another, the Spanish authorities systematically sheltered and protected wanted Italian terrorists who were collaborating in these state-sponsored acts of violence. This protection took many forms. They repeatedly failed to cooperate with requests for assistance from their Italian counterparts, first by refusing to provide information about the whereabouts of Italian fugitives living in Spain, and then by denying extradition requests from the Italian judiciary. These efforts were obviously motivated by a desire to shelter their covert assets and thereby protect themselves by maintaining secrecy about their clandestine operations against the ETA.[117] The purpose of this obstructive behavior was perfectly clear to investigating magistrates in Italy, who rightly concluded that the Spanish secret services had regularly employed Delle Chiaie and other neo-fascist fugitives in such operations.

Most significantly, there is one piece of unimpeachable material evidence that bears mute witness to Delle Chiaie's intimate association with the Spanish security forces. It turned out that the Ingram MAC-10 9 mm machine pistol (serial #2/2000981) and silencer (serial #2/200527) used by Delle Chiaie's lieutenant Pierluigi Concutelli to assassinate Judge Vittorio Occorsio, an attack carried out in Rome on 10 July 1976, had previously been consigned to the AN leader by Spanish intelligence officers. Indeed, by tracing the precise movement of this and several other MAC-10s that ended up in the hands of Italian neo-fascists, elements of the clandestine command structure charged with waging the anti-ETA war can be identified. In February 1975 a shipment of MAC-10s and their silencers arrived in Spain. They had been sent together with an export permit (#86079) from the Military Armaments Corporation factory in Marietta, Georgia, a company run by CIA contract agent and alleged drug trafficker Mitchell WerBell III. These weapons were originally shipped to Madrid's Jefatura Superior de Policía (Police Headquarters), then headed by Colonel Federico Quintero Morente, but were thence transferred to the División de Armamento y Material of the Comisaría General de Información (CGI: General Intelligence Commisariat). With CGI chief Roberto Conesa's authorization, the arms were sent on to SECED for use in "special operations" in February 1976, and the following month certain unidentified SECED officers provided four of them to Delle Chiaie. These were loaned to the Italians specifically for use in operations against the Basques (and perhaps also Spanish leftists), and were in fact used in the attack on Perez Revilla, but "il Caccola" apparently had his own plans. He ordered Concutelli to bring two of the advanced machine pistols to Italy, where they were slated to be used to kill magistrates who were allegedly guilty of "persecuting" members of AN and ON. Although this decision sealed the fate of Judge Occorsio, it also led to the arrest of Concutelli and his fellow conspirators and to the confiscation of both weapons. However, in early 1977 Elio Massagrande told fellow neo-fascist Sergio Calore that he could procure two other MAC-10s for comrades in Italy, and added that they had been among those used previously in the Calle Atocha assassinations. The following year Carlo Cicuttini gave two MAC-10s – probably the same ones to which Massagrande had been referring – to Spanish fascist and Delle Chiaie collaborator Alfredo Blas Alemany. In the summer of 1980 Spanish police found these weapons in the possession of a group of Barcelona ultras, from whom they were confiscated. It is also worth noting that the serial numbers had been filed off of the weapons found in the neo-fascist Calle Pelayo arms factory, presumably in order to prevent them from being traced back to the Spanish security forces, but those on the inside of the barrels had accidentally not been removed. Finally, a number of Spanish police and military personnel were found listed in Concutelli's address book after his arrest, including General Tomás García Rebull, Air Force colonel Antonio Clavero, and CGI officer Ramón Lillo. Although these facts confirm that Delle Chiaie and other Italian fugitives worked in close operational collaboration with various Spanish secret services, they nonetheless reveal that at times he stubbornly pursued his own political agenda.[118]

The "black bombardier" was in any case compelled to leave post-Franco Spain shortly after the Calle de Atocha massacre, in the wake of the discovery of the elaborate Calle Pelayo arms factory run by Sánchez Covisa and fugitive Italian terrorists with whom he was closely associated. His destination was Chile. In April 1974, a few months after the coup that brought General Augusto Pinochet to power, Delle Chiaie and Prince Borghese had visited that country in order to propose the establishment, in Spain, of an import-export agency that would exchange Chilean for European goods and provide other, non-economic services to the junta. This proposal was made directly to Pinochet and Lieutenant Colonel Jorge Carrasco of the Brigada de Inteligencia Civil (Civil Intelligence Brigade), and in diary entries dated 29 April and 5 May 1974, the AN leader revealed that he was very impressed with both men and anticipated working with them in the future. Although this export-import scheme apparently never got beyond the planning stages, in late 1974 Colonel Juan Manuel Contreras, head of the Chilean Dirección de Inteligencia Nacional (DINA: National Intelligence Directorate), sent Army Major Hugo Prado Contreras (no relation) to Madrid to establish contacts with Avanguardia Nazionale and various other European far right organizations, including Ordine Nuovo in Italy, Nouvelle École (New School) in France, and the Falange Española, the GCR, Fuerza Nueva, and CEDADE in Spain. This was merely the opening phase of DINA's transatlantic operations.[119]

In the spring of 1975 an American-born "special operations" officer for DINA named Michael Townley (alias "Andrés Wilson") was sent to Europe in order to recruit right-wing ultras and arrange for the "neutralization" of high-profile Chilean exiles who opposed the junta. Having already picked up Virgilio Paz (alias "Javier Romero") of the violently anti-Castro Movimiento Nacionalista Cubana (MNC: Cuban Nationalist Movement) in Miami, Townley first made stops in Lisbon and Madrid, where he established contacts with Iberian ultras, intelligence officers from various secret services, Aginter Presse personnel, and other ex-OAS operatives, including Corsican gangster and future Nice bank robber Albert Spaggiari (alias "Daniel"). The American then returned briefy to Chile to obtain further instructions, while Paz traveled to Northern Ireland to photograph British camps where Irish Republican Army (IRA) members were interned in order to help DINA neutralize criticism of the Chilean junta by European governments and human rights groups. In July the two men rendezvoused in Frankfurt, where they met with LAN-Chile employee Wolf von Arnswaldt to fabricate explosives and plan an attack on Chilean socialist leader Carlos Altamirano, who lived under heavy guard in East Germany. Although Altamirano was then the agency's number one target, carrying out such a "hit" proved to be impossible. Thus, after being joined by Townley's wife Inés Mariana Callejas (alias "Ana Pizarro"), the trio flew on to Rome and conferred with "DINA's most enthusiastic Italian contact," Delle Chiaie (code name "Alfa"). The latter agreed to put his network at the disposal of the Chilean secret police by collecting intelligence on anti-Pinochet exiles and providing DINA operatives in Europe with weapons. After learning of the difficulties involved in eliminating Altamirano, the neo-fascist leader instead recommended the assassination of Chilean Partido Demócrata Cristiano (Christian Democratic Party) leader Bernardo Leighton, who was actively working to organize political opposition to Pinochet's regime and lived in an unprotected residence in Rome.[120] As soon as Townley received the go-ahead from Santiago, the operation was contracted out to Delle Chiaie and his men. Shortly after 8 PM on 6 October 1975, Pierluigi Concutelli gunned down Leighton and his wife Anita outside their Via Aurelia apartment and wounded them so severely that he mistakenly left them for dead without finishing the job. Because of this error, which Concutelli later described as the worst blunder he ever committed, DINA paid Delle Chiaie 100,000 U.S. dollars but refused to provide him with previously agreed-upon weaponry.[121]

Yet the survival of the Leightons, although a source of temporary annoyance to DINA hard-liners, did not cause them to abandon their working relationship with Delle Chiaie. Indeed, on the occasion of Franco's funeral in November 1975, the AN leader supposedly secretly conferred with DINA chief General Juan Manuel Contreras and Pinochet in the latter's hotel room. At that meeting it was reportedly agreed that Delle Chiaie's network would continue both to gather information about Chilean exiles in Europe and carry out covert, "plausibly deniable" assignments for the junta.[122] Given these circumstances it was perfectly natural for him to flee to Chile, where he had been promised refuge, when he was suddenly compelled to leave Spain in January 1977. Once in Santiago, with the financial and logistical support of DINA, he set up the Agencia Internacional de la Prensa (AIP: International Press Agency), which was named after and clearly modeled on Aginter Presse. The AIP, which only operated for a relatively brief period of time, occupied a large apartment equipped with a telex machine and other communications equipment. In return for this official protection and support, Delle Chiaie and his Italian associates carried out covert intelligence missions in Peru and possibly also in Argentina at the behest of Major Raúl Eduardo Iturriaga Neumann, then head of the "external affairs" section of DINA, in conjunction with Townley and his men. However, Delle Chiaie's activities on behalf of the Pinochet regime were officially brought to a close in 1978 due to the political fallout from the DINA-backed assassination of

Orlando Letelier, Salvador Allende's former foreign minister, which had been carried out in Washington, DC, on 21 September 1976. In the face of heavy pressure from the United States government, Pinochet was ultimately forced to extradite Townley, the organizer of the Letelier "hit," and transform the increasingly discredited DINA into the ostensibly less brutal Central Nacional de Informaciones (CNI: National Intelligence Center), which in practice led to the replacement of Contreras and the fall from favor of his murderous retinue within the service. Thereby deprived of his chief institutional protectors, Delle Chiaie was constrained to leave Chile for good and move to Buenos Aires.[123]

This, too, was hardly inexplicable. While residing in Spain, Delle Chiaie had already established contacts with right-wing elements inside the exiled dictator Perón's circle. Among these ultras was Perón's personal secretary José López Rega, a sinister figure who was soon to acquire the nickname "El Brujo." When the dictator made his triumphal return to Argentina in June 1973, López Rega was appointed social welfare minister and went on to establish the dreaded Triple A paramilitary squad. Some have even suggested that the brutal terrorist actions carried out by the AAA reflected the application of the *guerre révolutionnaire* techniques which "El Brujo" had been introduced to in Spain by Delle Chiaie or other personnel associated with the "Black International."[124] Although this cannot be conclusively demonstrated, López Rega could hardly have avoided being exposed to the cross-fertilization of various countersubversion doctrines in the hothouse of Madrid, which three generations of specialists in the anti-communist struggle had made their home. Be that as it may, Delle Chiaie had forged close links with exponents of the Argentine paramilitary right, links which survived the death of Perón and the subsequent ouster of López Rega from positions of power. The latter then returned to Spain with several members of the AAA in tow, including Eduardo Almirón, who afterwards became a bodyguard for Alianza Popular (Popular Alliance) leader Manuel Fraga. In this connection, it is worth recalling that some of these AAA "specialists" later participated in both anti-ETA campaigns and the 1976 assault at Montejurra.

When the Argentine military junta headed by General Roberto Viola seized power in March 1976, many civilian extremists were incorporated into parallel security apparatuses and used as assassins, torturers, kidnappers, and provocateurs in the regime's *guerra sucia* against the domestic opposition. Delle Chiaie and other fugitive Italians had resided in Argentina at various times during the mid-1970s, and had collaborated there with Townley and the Milicia, a pro-Nazi offshoot of the Triple A which received funding from the Argentine Secretaría de Inteligencia de Estado (SIDE: State Intelligence Secretariat).[125] Through this connection the Italians were themselves later recruited as contract agents by SIDE, initially to monitor the activities of Argentine exiles in Europe. After being equipped with Argentine passports and American dollars provided by that service, he and Pierluigi Pagliai returned to Europe and recruited neo-fascists for this purpose. During this period Delle Chiaie also visited other parts of Latin America, probably on behalf of the Argentine military, to help coordinate transcontinental right-wing collaboration.

He made a number of trips to Central America, where he advised right-wing leaders such as Roberto D'Aubuisson of El Salvador's ARENA party about the best techniques to employ in order to defeat communist subversives. In this sense, too, he and his associates were following in the footsteps of Aginter's operatives. Not long afterwards the "death squads" in Central America stepped up their grisly work, with the help of indigenous Argentine- or U.S.-trained security personnel.[126]

This intensification of hemisphere-wide countersubversive operations was also facilitated by a series of meetings between right-wing military and civilian personnel. Among the vehicles that helped to generate improved operational coordination were the conferences held under the auspices of ostensibly "private" anti-communist organizations, in particular the World Anti-Communist League (WACL) and its offshoots. One of the most noteworthy features of WACL was the extent to which various Asian and Western secret services were covertly involved in sponsoring its activities. Another was the degree to which the organization's European and Latin American affiliates had been infiltrated by extremist neo-fascist circles.[127] In 1979 Delle Chiaie may have accompanied MPON ideologist Elio Massagrande to the Twelfth Congress of the World Anti-Communist League in Asunción, Paraguay, which was hosted by President Alfredo Stroessner, and in September 1980 he definitely attended the annual conference of the extremist Confederación Anticomunista Latinoamérica (CAL: Latin American Anti-Communist Confederation), a regional WACL subgroup, in Buenos Aires.[128] Perhaps most importantly, in November 1979 Delle Chiaie allegedly attended a top secret meeting of high-ranking South American military and intelligence officers in Bogotá, Colombia, which was probably linked to "Operación Cóndor," the cooperative arrangement between their respective services to crush "Marxist" subversion throughout the continent. It may be that the Bolivian coup was agreed upon at this meeting.[129]

In November 1979 SIDE sent the AN leader and his lieutenant Pagliai to Bolivia to supplement a group of seventy Argentine intelligence officers whose mission was to overthrow the interim civilian government of Lidya Gueiler and install Army chief General Luis García Mesa and his crony Colonel Luis Arce Gómez, then head of Army intelligence, in power. This, however, was not Delle Chiaie's first contact with right-wing elements in Bolivia. For example, he had previously met with ousted General Alfredo Ovando Candía in Spain, and in 1978 he and Pagliai had visited La Paz to consult with Klaus Barbie, the Kameradenwerk representative in Bolivia and later a key operative within the Bolivian Army's 2nd (Military Intelligence) Department.[130] Shortly before the coup, he met with former military strongman Hugo Bánzer Suárez and other Bolivians in the Buenos Aires apartment of Argentine Major Hugo Raúl Miori Pereyra. Miori, not coincidentally chief of the Argentine branch of CAL, was the liaison man between the Argentine operatives in Bolivia, most of whom were veterans of the "dirty war," and one of their key sponsors, General Alberto Valín, the head of SIDE.[131] After their arrival in Bolivia, the "black bombardier" (alias "Alfredo Modugno") organized an efficient civilian intelligence network and perhaps also a paramilitary group at his operational base in La Paz, whereas Pagliai (alias "Roberto Costa Bruno") became an "advisor" for the intelligence section of the Bolivian Army's 8th Division in Santa Cruz de la Sierra. Both worked for Arce Gómez under the aegis of Department 2, where Barbie occupied an important position and was apparently entrusted with supervising their activities, and in conjunction with the paramilitary Novios de la Muerte (Bridegrooms of Death) mercenary group headed by West German neo-Nazi Joachim Fiebelkorn.[132]

On 17 July, the day when the so-called Cocaine Coup was launched, Delle Chiaie was reportedly one of the organizers of a Department 2–sponsored attack on the Central Obrera Boliviana (COB: Bolivian Workers' Center) headquarters in La Paz, where leaders of the opposition had gathered to discuss how to respond to the military coup. During this action three unarmed but uncooperative labor leaders were murdered in cold blood, and the others present were then arrested, imprisoned, and brutally tortured. Whether or not the Italian terrorist was involved, this assault was only the beginning of a wave of Argentine-style repression in Bolivia, in which the civilian paramilitary squads played a particularly vicious role. To the chagrin of less bloodthirsty Bolivian Army officers, Delle Chiaie himself reportedly advocated using the pitiless, fear-inducing methods perfected by the Argentine security forces, including the systematic carrying out of kidnappings, torture, and executions by hooded civilian gangs using unmarked vehicles or – irony of ironies – ambulances marked with the Red Cross symbol. In the wake of the coup, such actions commenced in earnest, and within a few weeks dozens of people had been "disappeared" and thousands had been arrested and herded into sports stadiums, a policy previously employed by the Chilean junta after its own 1973 coup. Newly appointed Interior Minister Arce Gómez sounded an appropriately ominous tone when he announced that any "subversives, extremists, and rumor mongers" who dared to violate the new National Security laws should "walk around with their last will and testament under their arm."[133]

Once resistance had been broken, Delle Chiaie and his men assumed positions of authority within the state's security apparatus. The "black bombardier" was himself entrusted with undertaking international propaganda activities designed to improve the public image of the junta, an extraordinarily difficult if not impossible task considering that only Argentina and South Africa officially recognized the new regime. To this end he was provided with an advance of 50,000 dollars and sent to Europe to set up Europe-Bolivia Associations in Lausanne, Madrid, Paris, and Rome. He also planned to establish a newspaper and a radio transmitter, apparently in an effort to create a Bolivian branch of Aginter, in La Paz.[134] Pagliai, meanwhile, became an enthusiastic torturer for the new regime and, on 20 September 1982, was appointed chief of the misnamed Bolivian drug control agency, whose real mission was to eliminate the small producers of coca in order to help concentrate the entire cocaine trade in the hands of the five major drug trafficking *padrinos*, including Roberto Suárez, the chief financial backer of García Meza and Arce Gómez. Neofascist *pentito* Aldo Tisei later told an Italian judge that Delle Chiaie was the primary intermediary between these South American "Godfathers" and the Sicilian Mafia, and both he and Pagliai were monitored for months by the U.S. Drug Enforcement

Agency (DEA) because of their purported participation in drug-trafficking activities.[135] In the end it was the documented participation of the new government in the international drug trade, coupled with its blatant violations of human rights inside Bolivia, that prompted the international community to apply sanctions and otherwise work to get rid of the new junta. In response to international pressure, García Meza forcibly disbanded the Novios in April 1981, but its members were allowed to depart quietly to Brazil – with a large quantity of cocaine – despite the havoc they had joyfully wreaked. The general himself was forced to cede power to military "moderates" the following month.

On 10 October 1982, shortly before this reorganized Bolivian military junta was compelled to transfer power to a new civilian government, the Italian and American secret services oversaw an incredibly inefficient operation designed to capture Pagliai in Santa Cruz and, ostensibly, Delle Chiaie in La Paz. Both neo-fascists were warned ahead of time by friends that something was in the works, and the latter wisely took these warnings seriously and thereby managed to avoid capture. But the arrogant Pagliai ignored the rumors and was caught in a daytime ambush in the streets of Santa Cruz, in the course of which he was shot and severely wounded by Italian or Bolivian policemen. Due to a bizarre combination of circumstances, which were either the result of a series of blunders or a complex plan designed to ensure that the victim would never talk, Pagliai's condition worsened and he never came out of the coma he fell into after briefly showing signs of a recovery. He died in Rome on 5 November 1982, approximately three weeks after his forcible repatriation.[136]

Delle Chiaie, meanwhile, had escaped to Argentina the day before Pagliai was ambushed. For several years he apparently hid out in various areas of South America, where he was probably sheltered at a fascist colony in the hinterlands or by some parallel security apparatus, but was eventually captured by the Venezuelan police in 1987. However, even his arrest and extradition to Italy did not result in any real punishment for "il Caccola." He was extended special judicial privileges and, perhaps in exchange for keeping quiet about his links to various high-ranking intelligence personnel, was eventually cleared of all criminal charges.[137] Such a lenient fate provides mute evidence, if any were still needed, of that continued "untouchability" for which he had already become justly famous.

The nature of Freda's relationship to the secret services, in contrast to those entertained by Rauti and Delle Chiaie, is more difficult to clarify. Recently published materials suggest that in the mid-1960s he was among the right-wing civilians who were employed by the 4th Alpine Army Corps, a unit stationed in the Alto Adige/Süd Tirol region that was specifically responsible for conducting counterguerrilla operations in conjunction with NATO. To carry out this task the Corps was organized as a mixed force consisting of personnel from the Army, SIFAR, the Carabinieri, and the Pubblica Sicurezza (Public Security) organization, to which were attached parallel structures made up of civilians. A few years later, two close associates of Freda were identified by Benito Zappulla as having served, respectively, as the director and instructor at a camp near Bolzano where neo-fascists and members of

U.S.-sponsored paramilitary "stay/behind" networks and other parallel apparatuses received training in guerrilla warfare and sabotage techniques.[138] If Freda was in fact involved in these activities, the case for viewing him as a government provocateur is certainly strengthened. And there is little doubt that by the late 1960s he had established a close working relationship with SID operative and fellow ON activist Guido Giannettini, or that he played an important role in the campaign of violence and provocation that culminated in the Piazza Fontana massacre.

Yet all along Freda's behavior was characterized by a host of ambiguities, and his true motives remain difficult to disentangle even today, almost fifty years after that bloody act of terrorism. The basic question is whether he sought to exploit the protection and logistical support offered by Giannettini in order to carry out a revolutionary design of his own, whether he was being manipulated by Giannettini in ways he was not aware of, or whether he was knowingly acting as the agent of conservative political forces whose interests were in most ways antithetical to his own proclaimed goals. This issue may be elucidated somewhat by outlining the career of Giannettini, in connection with which all of the international fascist and secret service strands enumerated earlier intersected.[139]

Like Rauti and Delle Chiaie, Giannettini had both extensive contacts with the international far right and close links to a number of Western secret services. He never made any secret of his pro-fascist and pro-Nazi views, and in his personal diary many dates with significance for the history of fascism were specially marked. He himself admitted having fascist associates and friends all over Europe, including Skorzeny and many other ex-Nazis.[140] These associations were by no means purely social in nature. In 1961 Giannettini reportedly met with OAS leader Pierre Lagaillarde in Madrid, and upon his return to Italy became one of the "principal agents" of the OAS in the peninsula. Because he was suspected of supporting or undertaking subversive anti-Gaullist activities, using the cover provided by the Formazione Nazionale Giovanile (National Youth Training), an organization he founded for this purpose, the UAR felt it necessary to keep him under surveillance for several years.[141] After the defeat and dispersal of the OAS, he began to write regularly for several right-wing publications in Italy, including *Roma*, the MSI's *Secolo d'Italia*, and Pino Romualdi's *L'Italiano*, and by 1965 he had joined Ordine Nuovo and become a national leader of the MSI.

Giannettini was also later identified by the police as a member of Avanguardia Nazionale's "national directorate," but he emphatically denied being a member of AN or ever meeting Delle Chiaie, accusations he attributed to disinformation promoted by the UAR. These claims are scarcely believable, as are his denials about having links to Aginter Presse or the Paladin Group, which he himself admitted was an "espionage and terrorist organization made up of ex-Nazis."[142] It now appears that Giannettini was first introduced to Guillou in 1964, before the establishment of Aginter, and that the invididual who made the introduction was former French Army Captain and OAS operative Jean-René Souètre.[143] Furthermore, according to former Spanish intelligence operative González-Mata, Giannettini visited Spain three times during June and October of 1973, and met there with von Schubert,

Skorzeny, and Guillou. Later, he was forced to return to Italy from Argentina after some former Nazis attempted to kidnap him in Buenos Aires in an effort to keep him from revealing any sensitive information about their activities.[144] He did, however, admit to being a close friend of Franco Freda's, along with whom he was later indicted for sponsoring the 1969 campaign of terrorism, but claimed he first entered into direct association with Freda three years after their probable initial contact.[145] He also acknowledged, with some degree of pride, that he had created an elaborate international intelligence network with branches in Italy and several other countries.[146]

Giannettini's connections with various security services were no less extensive. He first became associated with the armed forces when he served in a mechanized artillery unit in the aftermath of World War II, and – according to his own testimony – he initiated his long career as an intelligence agent in 1947. Between this period and the early 1960s, almost nothing is known about his activities, *sub rosa* or otherwise. However, his file card found in Aginter's Lisbon archives indicates that in 1962–1963 he entered into contact with the intelligence chief of the Legião Portuguesa, Gomes Lopes.[147] Also in 1962, apparently at the invitation of the commander of the U.S. Marine Corps training school, a fundamentalist Christian general named Pedro Del Valle, he is said to have offered a three-day course at Annapolis on "Opportunities [*possibilità*] and Techniques for Coups d'Etat in Europe." Shortly thereafter, he began publishing specialized articles for the official journal of the Italian Army's general staff, *Rivista Militare*.[148] During this same period he allegedly attended various NATO conferences and manuevers, perhaps as General Aloja's representative, including the second "Corazza Alata" exercise conducted in August 1964 by the Italian 3rd Army Corps.[149] That same year, he and certain unidentified Frenchmen founded the Appareil Mondial Secret d'Action Révolutionnaire (AMSAR: Secret World Apparatus for Revolutionary Action), an international fascist network supposedly funded by the Spanish and Portuguese secret services, which may be identical to the international intelligence organization mentioned earlier. In any event, it is likely that two of the Frenchmen involved in AMSAR were the representatives of the "international right" whom Giannettini later identified as recipients of all the information his network collected on the far left, Dominique De Roux and Jean Parvulesco. Both of these men seem to have worked for French intelligence agencies.[150]

There is no doubt, moreover, that Giannettini was a long-term operative of Italian intelligence. This was implied by his presence at various NATO affairs, his participation at the 1965 SIFAR-funded Istituto Pollio conference, his contribution to the *Mani rosse* project sponsored by Aloja, and his association with Agenzia Oltremare, which was linked to Aginter Presse and also received financial subsidies from the service. In June 1974 his presence on SID's payroll was revealed publicly by Defense Minister Giulio Andreotti, a revelation which constrained the heads of SID, however reluctantly, to acknowledge to the judicial authorities that Giannettini had in fact been employed by their agency. Officially, Giannettini had first been hired in October 1966 by Ufficio R (Ricerca) of SID at the request of General

Aloja, then chief of the Defense General Staff, but his association with military intelligence probably dated back at least to the period when Aloja was head of the more narrowly focused Servizio Informazioni Operative e Situazione (SIOS)-Esercito (Army Intelligence Service for Situational and Operational Intelligence). In August 1967, despite the replacement and transfer of Aloja during the interval, Giannettini was shifted to a higher-paying position under the jurisdiction of Ufficio D (Counterespionage), which was the SID section entrusted with protecting internal security. Although intelligence officials affiliated with that service tried to minimize his importance by testifying that all he did was submit a handful of useless reports based on information he obtained from open journalistic sources, this does not explain why they continued to employ him and later helped him escape arrest by aiding and abetting his April 1973 flight to Paris. Indeed, Giannettini continued receiving payments from the agency until April 1974, after which he felt it necessary to flee, first to Spain and then to Argentina.[151] This is why the state prosecutor concluded that from the beginning his work for the military intelligence service exhibited a number of "singular characteristics."[152]

Furthermore, Giannettini seems to have played a pivotal role in the transmission of *guerre révolutionnaire* doctrine to the Italian right. In a number of different forums, he explicitly advocated the adoption of the type of violent, manipulative, and provocative tactics that later became characteristic of the "strategy of tension." As was the case with many of the speakers, the views he expressed in his presentation at the 1965 Istituto Pollio conference were almost identical to those found in *La guerra non ortodossa*, a three-part SIFAR manual that had been prepared one year earlier.[153] He argued there that the West had to adopt communist methods of revolutionary warfare aimed at controlling the population, which in practice meant the application of scientifically devised techniques of propaganda, the establishment of a series of parallel and "camouflaged" organizations to infiltrate and manipulate the enemy's forces, and the possible recourse to guerrilla warfare and terrorism.[154] Yet his sources of information were certainly not restricted to Italian studies of unconventional warfare. His presentation at the conference was derived primarily from portions of a small manual he had just written himself, titled *Tecniche della guerra rivoluzionaria*, which contained some perspectives on terrorism that also conformed precisely to the ideas championed by Guillou in his mini-manual for the perfect terrorist. Among other things, Giannettini focused specifically on the uses of terrorism:

> As far as terrorism is concerned, it should be specified that it can be of two types: indiscriminate terrorism and selective terrorism. The first involves making bombs explode in public offices or locales, in the street, at the gatherings of crowds, or randomly shooting down people with firearms ... In contrast, selective terrorism is carried out by eliminating certain carefully selected persons, for a variety of reasons: either because they could be of use to the enemy; or because their death would paralyze (or impede) the adversary's organizational machine; or because, being moderates or moderators, they would inhibit the other side from intensifying the struggle; or, finally, because

their elimination would provoke harsh retaliations that would further increase tension, creating an irreversible phenomenon which could lead to civil war.[155]

In this connection, it is worth noting that AN militants who later took a series of guerrilla and psychological warfare training courses reportedly utilized Giannettini's manual as a sort of textbook.[156] Nor should it be surprising that the self-described "Nazifascist" was later accused of planning acts of indiscriminate terrorism designed to push political tensions past the breaking point. The judges at the Catanzaro trial concerning the Piazza Fontana bombing concluded that Giannettini served as the key intermediary between factions of SID and the Padua cell led by Freda, whose members may have actually planted the bombs in an effort to implicate and thereby scapegoat the extraparliamentary left.[157]

The preceding account should make it clear that leading Italian neo-fascists, the very ones who were repeatedly implicated in the terrorist operations associated with the "strategy of tension," were neither acting alone nor in an insular, parochial manner. They had forged close links not only with their activist-oriented comrades in other parts of the world, but also with other anti-communist operatives and hard-line factions within various secret services. In the process, they were exposed to a wide array of countersubversive techniques, especially those associated with French *guerre révolutionnaire* doctrine. To some extent this should already be clear, and it will be illustrated further in the Borghese Coup case study in the next chapter. But in addition to this documented web of connections, there is other evidence which explicitly reveals that these same Italian ultras had enthusiastically embraced the concepts developed by French counterinsurgency specialists. They then adapted those concepts to their own environment and began to have systematic recourse to them, thereby turning Italy into a terrorist killing ground.

The best indication of this doctrinal link is that Rauti, Giannettini, Delle Chiaie, and the latter's lieutenant Mario Merlino were all among the participants, either as speakers or members of the audience, at the infamous conference on *guerra rivoluzionaria* held at Rome's luxurious Parco dei Principi hotel in early May 1965. As noted earlier, this conference was officially sponsored by the newly formed but short-lived Istituto di Studi Storici e Militari "Alberto Pollio," which had been founded in 1964 by Enrico de Boccard and Gianfranco Finaldi, who were later joined as directors by Eggardo Beltrametti.[158] Behind the scenes, however, it was financed primarily by SIFAR, with the help of funds solicited by Rocca's REI from various defense-related firms for subscriptions to the news bulletin produced by Agenzia D, an offshoot of the institute.[159] On the surface the aim of the conference was simply to introduce those present to the ideas developed by French experts concerning the nature of communist revolutionary warfare, and for this purpose the speakers may have been granted access to restricted documentation prepared by the Defense Ministry's Centro Alti Studi Militari (Center for Higher Military Studies) and the Armed Forces General Staff.[160] Among the attendees were high-ranking politicians with close links to the security forces of NATO and the United States, top military officers, a bevy of right-wing journalists, twenty carefully selected "students," and some intransigent anti-communists from academia, the business world, and other influential sectors of Italian society. But behind this innocuous and purely "educational" façade the real goal was apparently to mobilize a coalition of influential military and civilian activists who would thenceforth combine forces to counter Marxist subversion, as well as to expose them to the most advanced methods for accomplishing that objective. Note, for example, that conference coordinator Finaldi specifically indicated that the Institute was in the process of forming "study groups" that would be given the task of conducting further research into revolutionary warfare techniques, and that one such group composed of the twenty students invited to the conference had already been set up under the direction of Dr. Dorrello Ferrari to carry out this sort of research.[161] The fact that Delle Chiaie and his lieutenant Merlino were among those students could easily lead one to suspect that such "research" may well have included practical training. Although it may be overstating the case to claim that this conference laid the theoretical and organizational groundwork for the terrorist "strategy of tension," there is no doubt that many of the concepts elaborated there were later put into practice by Italian neo-fascists and their secret sponsors within various security apparatuses of the state.[162]

It is not necessary to analyze the themes propounded by the speakers at this conference in detail, because the proceedings were later edited and published. A few that have particular relevance for the "strategy of tension" deserve further emphasis, however. The first basic idea was that World War III had already begun. The communists had long been successfully waging subversive warfare against the West, in accordance with the doctrines of Vladimir Lenin and Mao Zedong, and the situation had already reached the critical phase. The West supposedly had very little time left, so it had to respond collectively and energetically without further delay in order to avoid an otherwise imminent defeat.[163] Second, *guerra rivoluzionaria* was a total war being waged on all fronts – political, military, social, psychological, economic, and cultural – and hence could not be won by relying entirely on traditional, narrowly focused military action. In such a war, there were neither visible fronts nor any legal and moral limits. The enemy was slowly infiltrating and taking control over every sphere of human activity, and in this way it was undermining existing institutions and "conquering" the minds of the population, its central aim.[164] Third, from this it followed that revolutionary war could only be waged effectively by adopting and perfecting the very same methods devised and employed by the enemy, including psychological warfare, parallel hierarchies, infiltration, provocations, and terrorism. Indeed, the West had to abandon its hopelessly anachronistic humanitarian scruples, which provided the enemy with a great advantage, and begin to apply those methods as ruthlessly and instrumentally as the communists.[165] It scarcely needs to be pointed out that these basic tenets were all derived directly from French *guerre révolutionnaire* doctrine, and indeed the OAS was explicitly held up as a model to be emulated and improved upon by several of the speakers.[166]

Altogether more ominous were some of the concrete suggestions for countering communist aggression. Perhaps the most significant presentation from an operational point of view was that made by Count Pio Filippani Ronconi, who argued in favor of creating an elaborate counterrevolutionary organization, ideally on the international level, that would be capable of neutralizing communist initiatives and taking the offensive. According to Ronconi, a professor of Sanskrit and a translator for the Defense Ministry, what was needed was a three-tiered organization. The first level would consist of patriots who were only suited for "purely passive" actions that did not involve great risks. This category included, in his opinion, the majority of government officials and bureaucrats. Their tasks would be to impede enemy initiatives inside the administrative apparatus, build a network of reliable anti-communists who would assist each other, and serve as a "security screen" behind which elements from the other two levels could operate. The second level consisted of those forces, such as retired military personnel and members of nationalist, irredentist, or sporting associations, who were willing and able to take action by organizing demonstrations, pressure groups, and "civil defense" organizations that would assist the security forces should communist-inspired riots break out.[167]

However, it was the third level that was considered most important in Ronconi's general plan of "defense and counterattack." It was to consist of smaller but "much more qualified and professionally specialized" forces whose members would remain anonymous and be trained to carry out "counterterrorist" operations and other actions that would, if necessary, be capable of rupturing the existing political equilibrium and establishing a different constellation of forces in power. Their personnel would be recruited from among those brave youths – no doubt neo-fascists and assorted radical rightists – who were currently wasting their time, energy, and anonymity by carrying out "noble" symbolic gestures, gestures that generally fell on deaf ears in an Italy already poisoned by communist subversion. The activities of these cells, which were to be rigorously compartmentalized, would be coordinated with those of the other two levels by a mixed civilian-military general staff.[168] This projected third level corresponded, in its general outlines, to various organizations that were later implicated in political violence and abortive coups, such as the Rosa dei Venti (Compass Rose) group.

Nor was Ronconi the only presenter who made concrete suggestions of this type. Beltrametti likewise emphasized the need to create "civilian self-defense groups" and "commando groups" that would collaborate with the armed forces in periods of emergency, a theme that was even more pronounced in a paper prepared by ON leader Clemente Graziani for the Istituto Pollio conference.[169] According to Graziani, the counterrevolutionary movement must provide itself with an organization structured along the same lines as the enemy's. Counterrevolutionary cadres consisting of well-trained and morally prepared soldiers and civilians had to be formed, and their activities then needed to be coordinated by a central organism composed of counterterrorism specialists. Apparently, the kind of moral preparation advocated by Graziani was that which accepted that "every type of response [was] permissible and legitimate" in the life-or-death struggle against communism.[170] The ends of war could be evaluated in moral terms, but not war in and of itself, which might even help to develop a higher human type who was divorced from bourgeois sentimentalism and inspired by heroic values.

These carefully recruited cadres had, moreover, to adopt the very same techniques utilized by the communists, including the setting up of "small autonomous units" capable of living off the land and conducting unrestricted terrorism and guerrilla warfare in the enemy's rear, the formation of a network of parallel hierarchies and front groups, the systematic employment of psychological warfare with the goal of winning the support of the population, and the infiltration of left-wing organizations, especially unions, in order to manipulate or control them.[171] However, the success of such methods ultimately depended upon a direct intervention and the assumption of political responsibilities by the armed forces, and he urged the latter to act quickly in order to safeguard the nation's destiny and ensure Italy's continued participation in NATO and the Atlantic Alliance. Here that perverse logic ridiculed by Vinciguerra, the all too common neo-fascist tendency to view the Italian army and police as the guarantors of a revolutionary program, can be observed with all of its inherent contradictions.[172] However that may be, when Graziani's prescriptions were combined with De Boccard's advocacy of "preventative counterterrorism," the result was a volatile witches' brew that could easily catalyze the type of terrorism embodied in the "strategy of tension."[173]

The final link in this chain of documentary evidence is a November 1968 report that was found in the Lisbon archive containing materials sent in by Aginter Presse's Italian "correspondents." This report explicitly referred to the actual application in Italy of some of the key unconventional warfare techniques that were discussed at the Istituto Pollio conference and applied so consistently by Aginter's own operatives. It was written in French, probably by Leroy, and titled "Notre action politique," and deserves to be quoted at length:

> We think that the first phase of our political action should be to promote chaos in all the structures of the regime. . . . This will create a situation of great political tension, of fear in the world of industry, of antipathy toward the government and all the parties, with the goal of readying an efficient organization capable of rallying and restoring to us the malcontents of all social classes in order to gather this vast mass to make our revolution. In our opinion the first action that we should undertake is the destruction of the institutions of the state under the cover of communist and Maoist actions; we already have elements infiltrated into all these groups . . . and obviously we will have to adapt our actions to the ambience of that milieu (propaganda and forceful actions of the sort that seem to emanate from our communist adversaries). . . . This will create a feeling of hostility towards those that threaten the peace of each and every nation [the communists], and on the other hand will place a burden on the national economy. Along with this we should renew our action within the cadres of the Army, the judiciary, [and] the Church, [and] work on public opinion to demonstrate the failure and incapacity of the legally-constituted apparatus, making ourselves appear as the only ones who can furnish a social, political, and economic solution adapted to the moment. At the same time

> we should raise up a defender of the citizens against the disintegration provoked by subversion and terrorism. Hence a phase of infiltration, intelligence, and pressure by our elements on the vital nuclei of the state. Our political group should be extremely clever, [and] capable of intervening and displaying its force; it should form cadres and leaders and at the same time carry out a massive and intelligent propaganda operation. This propaganda should exert psychological pressure on both our friends and our enemies . . . attract international political and economic support, and persuade the Army, the judiciary, the Church, and the world of industry to act against subversion . . . To carry this action to its conclusion, it is clear that we need a lot of money. . . . The introduction of provocateur elements into the circles of the revolutionary left is merely a reflection of the wish to push this unstable situation to the breaking point and create a climate of chaos. . . . Maoist circles, characterized by their own impatience and zeal, are [especially] suitable for infiltration.[174]

Although it is not entirely clear who wrote or prepared this report, it is apparent from both the content and the context that it was from an Aginter correspondent in Italy with links to Ordine Nuovo or Avanguardia Nazionale, if not one or more secret services. It is therefore not surprising that Vincenzo Vinciguerra summarized the situation as follows:

> The secret and clandestine structures [of the U.S. and NATO] and an international espionage agency guided by Yves Marie Guillou [Aginter Presse] worked in harmony in a strategy of infiltration and instrumentalization of communist [Maoist] dissidents, utilizing men of the Italian extreme right with all of whom they had established close, collaborative relations in the political, intelligence, and operational spheres.[175]

In this chapter it has been demonstrated, beyond a shadow of a doubt, that the Italian neo-fascists who carried out the "strategy of tension" were linked to an extensive network of far right groups all over western Europe and Latin America. These linkages were both geographical and genealogical, in the sense that younger generations of ultras were able to "study" under past masters in the use of terrorism from both the Nazi period and the heyday of the OAS. More ominously, they were also supported behind the scenes by factions inside a number of Western intelligence and security agencies, as well as by the dictatorial regimes in southern Europe prior to their mid-1970s collapse. By means of these connections they were first introduced to and then trained to make use of the most sophisticated unconventional warfare techniques that existed at the time. It scarcely matters whether particular neo-fascists were exposed to such methods in Italy, Greece, Portugal, Spain, or Latin America. The essential point is that they *were* exposed to them, probably from several interconnected sources, and that they then sought to apply them more or less systematically in the Italian peninsula and beyond. This complex process will soon become even clearer, when certain emblematic operations associated with the "strategy of tension" are described in detail and analyzed.

Addendum

Since this chapter was originally prepared in the early 1990s, a vast amount of new primary and secondary source material has entered the public domain. Some of the rich information from those many new sources has been added to the relevant portions of the original chapter, but there was not sufficient time or space to incorporate all of the newly available factual details into the narrative. That would have required the writing of an entirely new book, separate from this collection of studies. In lieu of that, the following paragraphs will provide a summary overview of some of the key judicial and parliamentary investigative findings, based in large part on crucial inside information from some of the neo-fascist protagonists as well as documentary material, concerning the perpetrators and sponsors of major acts of terrorism associated with the "strategy of tension" in Italy.

First, it is now clear that all three of the Italian neo-fascist organizations discussed in the chapter – Ordine Nuovo, Avanguardia Nazionale, and Franco Freda's cell in Padua – were complementary components of a single organizational matrix, as well as dedicated *camerati* involved in the joint pursuit of a common, more or less coordinated strategy.[176] Despite the very different political ideologies and agendas of the "establishment" Atlanticist networks involved, that strategy was intended by both its national and international sponsors and its violent neo-fascist executors to block the efforts of the left wing of the Partito Socialista Italiano (PSI: Italian Socialist Party), the Partito Comunista Italiano (PCI: Italian Communist Party), and the extraparliamentary left to exert more political influence in Italy. As noted earlier, Ordine Nuovo had three separate levels of affiliation, and there is no longer any doubt that the most elite and committed cadres within ON were organized into a sophisticated militarized and compartmentalized structure capable of carrying out covert and clandestine operations, including acts of infiltration, provocation, and terrorism. At the top of this structure was Pino Rauti in Rome, who would give directives, orders, or instructions to his lieutenant in the capital, Paolo Signorelli. The latter would then transmit those orders to leaders of the separate, compartmentalized ON cells operating in different regions of Italy, in particular northeastern Italy.[177] Among the most important of those northeastern ON cells were the ones operating in the Triveneto (Veneto, Friuli-Venezia Giulia, and Trentino-Alto Adige) region, such as the Venice/Mestre cell headed by Carlo Maria Maggi (who was also ON's regional coordinator) and Delfo Zorzi; the Verona cell with Elio Massagrande and military officer Amos Spiazzi; the Trieste cell with Francesco Neami and Manlio Portolan; the Udine cell with the Vinciguerra brothers and Carlo Cicuttini; and – last but not least – the Padua cell headed by Freda and including Giovanni Ventura and Massimiliano Fachini, which became part of the secret ON structure. To these were added a Milanese group named La Fenice (The Phoenix, from 1971 on) headed by Giancarlo Rognoni and including Nico Azzi and Pierluigi Pagliai, smaller ON cells in other parts of Italy, and the ON elements based in Rome.[178] Members of these secret ON or ON-linked cells definitely carried out a long series of violent assaults in the late 1960s and early 1970s, the most important of which were – according to Italian investigating magistrates – mass casualty terrorist attacks such as the 12 December 1969 Piazza Fontana bank bombing (at first falsely attributed by the authorities to anarchist Pietro Valpreda and his *compagni*), the attack on Milan police headquarters on 17 May 1973 (carried out by a self-proclaimed "anarchist" who was apparently linked to and manipulated by ON), and the 28 May 1974 Piazza della Loggia bombing in Brescia.[179] For its part, AN reportedly provided materials to these ON cells, carried out bombings in Rome on the same day as the Piazza Fontana bombing (as well as numerous other attacks), and helped wanted ON militants take refuge overseas in Spain and Latin America, where they carried out other "dirty jobs" for assorted secret services.[180] Even if the terrorist campaigns that rocked Italy during this tense period were attributable only to small groups of right-wing extremists, they would still be historically significant. However, the reality was far worse, because their violent actions were alternately encouraged, manipulated, sponsored, and/or used instrumentally by much more powerful forces operating behind the scenes.

Second, as has been thoroughly documented in the chapter, the Italian neo-fascist groups involved in this terrorist "strategy of tension" received advanced training in the arcane techniques of *guerre révolutionnaire*, logistical aid, funding, and shelter from other more or less "private" anti-communist organizations, both at home and abroad, above all from OAS veterans affiliated with components of Aginter Presse. Moreover, as will become clearer in the following chapter, these neo-fascist groups also collaborated with other civilian organizations and networks that were involved in "coup" plots and actions that were ostensibly directed against the incumbent Italian government.

Third, the violent, provocative actions of ON and AN in Italy were linked in various ways to the activities of diverse parallel intelligence and paramilitary structures operating under the authority of components within the Italian military, the Carabinieri, and the UAR of the Interior Ministry. Much more information about these parallel structures has emerged since these chapters were first prepared, and these matters will be discussed at much greater length in connection with the 1970 "Borghese coup" in the next chapter. In the meantime, here is a summary overview of those overlapping clandestine parallel networks (drawn from that chapter). There were reportedly three main levels of such secret, parallel, anti-communist apparatuses within Italy. The highest level, linked to the NATO and U.S. secret services and nominally under the authority of reliable Italian statesmen, was a kind of "super" secret service within the secret services composed of "patriotic" elements (known, among other names, as "parallel SID" and as "Super SISMI") that only select pro-Atlantic politicians and officials were aware of. This level was apparently centered within Ufficio R of SIFAR, SID, and finally SISMI, and perhaps also the UAR. Beneath this was a second level composed of regular units of the military and Carabinieri that would form "stay/behind" or rapid response groups and would activate pre-planned operational protocols for resistance in the event of external invasion or internal civil disturbances. The third level was composed of the civilian "stay/behind" paramilitary groups that were mainly designated, in Italy, under the code name "Gladio." It was later discovered that these civilian groups, whose members were trained by special operations personnel and armed, equipped, and funded by the higher level parallel apparatuses, comprised some right-wing extremists along with a majority of law-abiding, pro-Atlanticist anti-communists. Elements from these parallel organizations were also at times allegedly involved in infiltrating, manipulating, and/or "collaborating with" seemingly autonomous political extremists, both neo-fascist and leftist, as well as in recruiting elements from criminal organizations, in order to carry out various illegal, "dirty," and plausibly deniable actions.[181] Furthermore, there were also "mixed" civilian-military groups ostensibly external to, but undoubtedly intersecting and actively collaborating with, the three *sub rosa* levels of quasi-official parallel organizations, such as the Nuclei di Difesa dello Stato (NDS: Nuclei for the Defense of the State, associated closely with the aforementioned covert and compartmentalized structures within Ordine Nuovo) and the "presidentialist" Rosa dei Venti (Compass Rose) groups.[182] Finally, there was apparently another secret entity involved in these convoluted covert activities, code-named "Anello" ("Ring"), about which more information is provided in the next chapter.[183]

Fourth, there is the no less important matter of the still murky covert relationships between those many parallel structures in Italy and the neo-fascist paramilitary groups that actually carried out the "strategy of tension," on the one hand, and the foreign intelligence apparatuses of the United States and NATO then operating in Italy (and beyond), on the other. In this context, we are truly entering into a "wilderness of mirrors" given the complexity of the situation and the difficulties of obtaining reliable information about such secretive activities. Nevertheless, there are many circumstantial indications that personnel from both the Italian parallel intelligence and paramilitary networks and from ON and other neo-fascist groups had links to, provided information to, and periodically collaborated with, components of both the CIA apparatus and the intelligence structures affiliated with NATO and the U.S. military that were operating in Italy. Of these, the most important were those based in Verona at the Headquarters of the Allied Land Forces in Southern Europe (HQ-LANDSOUTH), known in Italian as the Commando delle Forze Terrestri Alleate del Sud Europa (FTASE), and in Vicenza at the Southern European Task Force (SETAF) headquarters, where units from the U.S. Army's Counter Intelligence Corps (renamed U.S. Army Intelligence Corps in 1961, and then U.S. Army Intelligence Agency in 1967) and perhaps NATO intelligence were stationed.[184] Despite the claims of some overly conspiratorial analysts who see the "evil" hand of the CIA behind every unpleasant event in Italy and the rest of the world, it remains unclear whether these American and NATO networks actually sponsored various terrorist actions and "coup" plots initiated by components of the Italian military, the Carabinieri, the Italian secret services, and the radical paramilitary right. However, it is certain that they were aware of many of these actions and plots beforehand (because they had recruited assets and informants within both the parallel networks and the neo-fascist milieu), that they rarely acted to prevent them, and that they took various actions to protect some of their assets and informants afterwards.

In order to explain these convoluted covert operations and patterns of collaboration, one has to recall the tense Cold War context within which they were activated. Even before World War II ended, both the Western powers and the Soviet Union began recruiting individuals, including former enemy Axis unconventional warfare specialists and political extremists, into new covert structures in anticipation of future conflicts with their present wartime allies. Several of these secret networks were soon involved in carrying out secret political, espionage, and paramilitary operations against each other. When the Cold War heated up further, reciprocal tensions and fears grew. Among the many events that alarmed Western nations were the Berlin blockade in 1948 and 1949; the successful testing of a series of Soviet atomic bombs beginning in 1949; the intervention of Chinese troops in support of North Korea during the Korean War; the formation of the Warsaw Pact in 1955; the increasing assistance provided by the Soviet Union and China to communist "national liberation" movements in Southeast Asia and "anti-colonial" insurgencies elsewhere; the invasion of Hungary by Soviet troops in November 1956; the attempt by the Soviets to station nuclear missiles in Castro's Cuba in 1962; the withdrawal of the French from Algeria after a bitter nationalist war; the organization of the anti-Western, "third worldist" Tri-Continental Conference of Asian, African, and Latin American Peoples in 1965; the seditious and subversive post–World War II activities of Soviet front organizations operating in Western democracies; and the presence of the largest European communist electoral party in Italy, one which comprised a radical wing with a secret paramiliary apparatus. In this worrisome and threatening geopolitical context, it is hardly surprising that many governments and political forces in the West, ranging from anti-communist social democrats to liberals to the entire spectrum of the right, were alarmed about both a possible Soviet military invasion of Western Europe and the intensification of internal communist subversion and violence. After the rise of New Left student and worker militancy and the increase in violent street protests in the mid- to late 1960s, these concerns understandably became more acute. Although in retrospect the more alarmist portrayals of communist expansion and subversion may now seem exaggerated, because the worst fears of Western anti-communists did not materialize, at the time they appeared to be far more credible.

Given this context, it is hardly surprising that both moderate and radical anti-communists would endeavor to take actions to counter the threat of Soviet invasion and internal communist subversion. As such, the military establishments, intelligence agencies, and a host of private anti-communist organizations paid an ever-growing amount of attention to communist methods of agitation, propaganda, subversion, and revolutionary guerrilla warfare, which led to a proliferation of literature on anti-Western insurgencies and the most effective counterinsurgency techniques that should be employed against them. In continental Europe, French counterinsurgency doctrines – *guerre révolutionnaire* – arguably exerted more influence than American and British counterinsurgency doctrines, although there was in fact considerable overlap between them. As noted earlier, the key characteristic of *guerre révolutionnaire* doctrine was the conscious adoption and employment of ruthless communist guerrilla warfare techniques against the communists themselves. So it was that in the late 1950s and early 1960s, a series of official, quasi-official, and unofficial meetings were held in NATO countries in which the focus was on (1) explicating the nature of communist revolutionary warfare, and (2) developing covert, parallel structures and advocating the use of other proven operational techniques not only to resist but also to attack and destroy subversive communist and pro-communist networks operating in Western countries. It was precisely within that context that pro-Atlanticist forces – military and intelligence personnel, leading politicians, and private anti-communist activists – came together and began to forge closer links.[185] The result was that a new series of parallel intelligence and operational networks was created to augment those that had been established right after World War II. It was these organizations, together with radical anti-communist civilian groups, including neo-fascist ultras, that carried out the terrorist "strategy of tension" and participated in "coup" plots in order to "save" Western nations by reducing the political influence of communist parties and the extraparliamentary left.

Notes

1 See Peter Paret, *French Revolutionary Warfare from Indochina to Algeria: The Analysis of a Political and Military Doctrine* (New York: Praeger, 1964), pp. 6–7, 101; and John Stewart Ambler, *The French Army in Politics, 1945–1962* (Columbus: Ohio State University, 1966), pp. 170, 308–9.
2 The new doctrine's acceptance was not immediate, according to Paret, *French Revolutionary Warfare*, p. 8. Compare Ambler, *French Army in Politics*, p. 309; Orville D. Menard, *The Army and the Fifth Republic* (Lincoln: University of Nebraska, 1967), pp. 93–4; Paul Marie de la Gorce, *The French Army: A Military-Political History* (New York: Braziller, 1963), pp. 402–3.
3 Ambler, *French Army in Politics*, pp. 309, 311–13; and Menard, *Army and the Fifth Republic*, pp. 87–8.
4 Paret, *French Revolutionary Warfare*, p. 17; and Menard, *Army and the Fifth Republic*, p. 91.
5 For this formula, see Colonel Gabriel Bonnet, *Les guerres insurrectionnelles et révolutionnaires de l'Antiquité à nos jours* (Paris: Payot, 1958), p. 60.
6 This theme appears throughout all of the writings of the *guerre révolutionnaire* theorists. See, for example, ibid., pp. 7–8, 266; "Ximenès" (pseudonym for a group of officers), "La guerre révolutionnaire et ses données fondamentales," *Revue Militaire d'Information* 281 (February–March 1957), pp. 17–19; [Colonel] Roger Trinquier, *Guerre, subversion, révolution* (Paris: Laffont, 1968), pp. 34–5; and Michel Déon, *L'Armée d'Algerie et la pacification* (Paris: Plon, 1959), pp. 16–20. Compare Paret, *French Revolutionary Warfare*, pp. 11–12; De la Gorce, *French Army*, p. 401; George A. Kelly, *Lost Soldiers: The French Army and Empire in Crisis, 1947–1962* (Cambridge: MIT, 1965), pp. 119–20; and Jean Planchais, *Une histoire politique de l'Armée, 1940–1967* (Paris: Seuil, 1967), p. 322.
7 Ambler, *French Army in Politics*, pp. 317–18; and De la Gorce, *French Army*, pp. 401–2.
8 This was especially emphasized by Colonel Charles Lacheroy in a series of published and unpublished articles. The best description of the system of "parallel hierarchies" in English is that of Douglas Pike, *Viet Cong: The Organization and Techniques of the National Liberation Front of South Vietnam* (Cambridge: MIT, 1966), especially pp. 109–231.
9 For more on "psychological action," see Maurice Megret, *L'Action psycholgique* (Paris: Fayard, 1959). This general term was further subdivided into *guerre psychologique*,

operations directed against the enemy, and *action psychologique* proper, operations directed against *elements of one's own population*. The techniques utilized were derived from different sources, including the direct experience of French troops captured and "brainwashed" by the Vietminh and the writings of various Pavlovian psychological theorists, particularly Serge Chakotin, author of *The Rape of the Masses: The Psychology of Totalitarian Political Propaganda* (New York: Alliance, 1940).

10 Ambler, *French Army in Politics*, pp. 301, 316–18. While Lacheroy focused his attention primarily on the establishment of parallel hierarchies, Colonels Argoud and Trinquier emphasized the employment of "adapted justice" – torture and terrorism – whereas others, particularly 5th Bureau personnel, concentrated on mass propaganda and individual re-education.

11 Ambler, *French Army in Politics*, p. 160; Menard, *Army and the Fifth Republic*, p. 97; and Paret, *French Revolutionary Warfare*, p. 57.

12 For good but self-interested descriptions of the battle of Algiers, see [General] Jacques Massu, *La vraie bataille d'Alger* (Paris: Plon, 1972), pp. 85–271; and Colonel Yves Godard, *Les trois batailles d'Alger. Volume 1: Les paras dans la ville* (Paris: Fayard, 1972). For the FLN organization in the city, see Roger Trinquier, *Modern Warfare: A French View of Counterinsurgency* (New York: Praeger, 1961), pp. 10–15.

13 Ambler, *French Army in Politics*, p. 113; and De la Gorce, *French Army*, pp. 390–3, 399–400.

14 For the OAS's plan to use *intoxication* in the *métropole*, see *OAS parle* (Paris: Julliard, 1964), document 48, pp. 225–6, wherein the organization's objectives were listed as (1) the "paralysis of Gaullist power," (2) the "creation of a climate of generalized insecurity," and (3) the "total paralysis of the country." Compare also the remarks attributed to General Salan in the course of his trial. As he expressed it to his fellow OAS conspirators, their mission was to create a "climate of generalized insecurity by spreading false news . . . We must inflame all sectors." See *Le procès de Raoul Salan: Compte rendu stenographique* (Paris: Albin Michel, 1962), p. 457. Naturally, systematic terrorism also played a major role in OAS operations, both in Algeria and France. See [Captain] Pierre Sergent, *Ma peau au bout des mes idées 2: La bataille* (Paris: Table Ronde, 1968), pp. 315–18, 328–37.

15 On these insurrections, see, respectively, Merry Bromberger and Serge Bromberger, *Les 13 complots du 13 Mai* (Paris: Fayard, 1959); Merry Bromberger et al., *Barricades et colonels: 24 Janvier 1960* (Paris: Fayard, 1960); and Henri Azeau, *Révolte militaire: Alger, 22 Avril 1961* (Paris: Plon, 1961). The term *pied noir*, which means "black foot," referred to persons of European descent who were born in Algeria, the bulk of whom were the offspring of French colonists. Because they desperately sought to remain in their North African homeland without turning over power to the Arab majority, they flocked to the ranks of right-wing organizations that actively fought to keep Algeria under French control.

16 There is a substantial literature on the OAS. Among the general works are Geoffrey Bocca, *The Secret Army* (Englewood Cliffs: Prentice Hall, 1968); Robert Buchard, *Organisation Armée Secrète* (Paris: Albin Michel, 1963), 2 volumes; Hennisart, *Wolves in the City*; Rémi Kauffer, *O.A.S.: Histoire d'une organisation secrète* (Paris: Fayard, 1986); "Morland, Barangé, Martinez" (pseudonym for three journalists), *Histoire de l'Organisation de l'Armée Secrète* (Paris: Julliard, 1964); Axel Nicol, *La bataille de l'OAS* (Paris: Sept Coleurs, 1962); Jean-Jacques Susini, *Histoire de l'OAS* (Paris: Table Ronde, 1963); Alexander Harrison, *Challenging De Gaulle: The OAS and the Counterrevolution in Algeria, 1954–1962* (New York: Praeger, 1989); Arnaud Déroulède, *OAS: Étude de une organization clandestine* (Helette: Curutchet, 1997); Anne-Marie Duranton-Crabol, *Le temps de l'OAS* (Brussels: Complexe, 1999); Vincent Quivy, *Les soldats perdus: Des anciens de l'OAS racontent* (Paris: Seuil, 2003); George Fleury, *Histoire de l'OAS* (Paris: Grasset, 2002); Clément Steuer, *Susini et l'OAS* (Paris: L'Harmattan, 2004); Pierre Meallier, *OAS, la guerre d'Algérie vue de Bône à travers les tracts OAS* (Nice: France Europe, 2004); Olivier Dard, *Voyage au coeur de l'OAS* (Paris: Perrin, 2011); and Bertrand Le Gendre, *Confessions du n 2 de l'OAS: Entretiens avec Jean-Jacques Susini* (Paris: Arènes, 2012). For later OAS operations in the *métropole*, see Buscia, *Au nom de l'O.A.S.: Requiem pour une cause perdue*, pp. 89–128; Pierre Démaret

and Christian Plume, *Target–De Gaulle: The True Story of the 31 Attempts on the Life of the French President* (New York: Dial, 1975); Jacques Delarue, *L'OAS contre De Gaulle* (Paris: Fayard, 1994 [1981]); George Fleury, *Tuez De Gaulle!: Histoire de l'attentat de Petit-Clamart* (Paris: Grasset, 1996); Paul Guerande, *OAS Métro, ou les enfants perdus* (Paris: Fuseau, 1964); and Sergent, *Ma peau . . . 2*, pp. 53–295.

17 For the impact of the military revolts on the international right, see Angelo Del Boca and Mario Giovana, *Fascism Today: A World Survey* (New York: Pantheon, 1969), p. 88; and Frédéric Laurent, *L'Orchestre noir* (Paris: Stock, 1978), p. 99.

18 Compare Joachim Joesten, *The Red Hand: The Sinister Account of the Terrorist Arm of the French Right-Wing 'Ultras' – in Algeria and on the Continent* (London: Abelard-Schuman, 1962), pp. 15, 62–3; and Roland Gaucher, *The Terrorists: From Tsarist Russia to the OAS* (London: Secker & Warburg, 1965), p. 252. The latter was a rightist OAS sympathizer.

19 See Joseph Algazy, *La tentation néo-fasciste en France, 1944–1965* (Paris: Fayard, 1984), pp. 228–30; François Duprat, *Les mouvements d'extrême droite en France depuis 1944* (Paris: Albatros, 1972), pp. 103–4; and Del Boca and Giovana, *Fascism Today*, pp. 194–6. One of the key figures in the establishment of right-wing paramilitary groups in Algeria was Robert Martel, a wine producer in the Mitidja region, who was one of the founders of the Union Français Nord-Africaine (French North African Union) and was later involved in the so-called Grand O plot of May 1958. For a better indication of Martel's ideas, see the book he authored under the pseudonym "Claude Mouton," *La contrerévolution en Algerie de l'Algérie Française à l'invasion sovietique* (Vouille: Pensée Français, 1973).

20 Laurent, *Orchestre noir*, pp. 102–3.

21 To provide only one example, former OAS operatives, including ex–Delta Commando François Chiappe and *guerre révolutionnaire* practitioner Colonel Jean Gardes – one of the officers who supposedly met with Skorzeny in 1962 – may have played an important role in the massacre of left-wing *peronistas* by their rightist Perónist counterparts at Argentina's Ezeiza airport on 20 June 1973. See Richard Gillespie, *Soldiers of Perón: Argentina's Montoneros* (Oxford: Clarendon, 1982), p. 153, note 69, citing the Perónist left publication *El Descamisado* 7 (3 July 1973). Compare Claudio Díaz and Antonio Zucco, *La ultraderecha argentina y su conexión internacional* (Buenos Aires: Contrapunto, 1987), pp. 105, 175, note 3. The Frenchmen were apparently employed as trainers and operatives in Argentine Social Welfare Minister and Propaganda Due (P2) brother José López Rega's Alianza Anticomunista Argentina (AAA: Argentine Anti-Communist Alliance), a particularly vicious right-wing "death squad" (a popular term for a parallel terrorist apparatus sponsored by one or more state security agencies). See Henrik Krüger, *The Great Heroin Coup: Drugs, Intelligence, and International Fascism* (Boston: South End, 1980), pp. 113, 165. Other OAS veterans served in similar capacities elsewhere in Latin America, Africa, and the Iberian Peninsula, a subject that remains to be investigated fully.

22 For the following biography of Guillou, compare Laurent, *Orchestre noir*, pp. 120–2; Patrice Chairoff, *Dossier néo-nazisme* (Paris: Ramsay, 1977), p. 158; and María José Tíscar Santiago, *A contra-revolução no 25 de abril: Os "Relatórios António Graça" sobre o ELP e Aginter Presse* (Lisbon: Colibri, 2014), pp. 207–8.

23 For the 11th Choc as SDECE's "special operations" unit, see Roger Faligot and Pascal Krop, *La Piscine: Les services secrets français, 1944–1984* (Paris: Seuil, 1985), pp. 165–70. Compare the account of Erwan Bergot, a former commando in the unit: *Le dossier rouge: Services secrets contre FLN* (Paris: Grasset, 1976).

24 For the role played by Ploncard d'Assac – a French-language broadcaster for the international "Voix de la Occident" program on Radio Portugal – as an intermediary between Salazar's entourage, the Portuguese government, and both Guillou and Aginter, see the *ELP Relatório, Número 2: Aginter Presse* prepared by the Serviço do Descobrimento e da Coordinação da Informações (SDCI: Service for the Discovery and Coordination of Intelligence) [hereinafter cited as SDCI, *Relatório 2*], the new intelligence service set up by leftist military officers who engineered the April 1974 overthrow of the Caetano dictatorship in Portugal, p. 22. Indeed, a note from Fernando Silva Pais, Director General of

the Portuguese secret police, to Alvaro Pereira de Carvalho, the intelligence director and number three man within the organization between 1962 and 1974, described Aginter as the "news agency (D'Assac)." The secret police identification cards for Silva Pais and Pereira de Carvalho are reproduced in "Repórter Sombra," *Dossier PIDE: Os horrores e crimes de uma "polícia"* (Lisbon: Agencia Portuguesa do Revistas, 1974), pp. 162, 184. Those interested in Ploncard d'Assac's political views can consult his numerous publications, among which are *Doctrines du nationalisme* (Meaux: Fuseau, 1965 [1959]); *L'État corporatif: L'Expérience portugaise. Doctrine et législation* (Paris: Librairie Française, 1960); *Manifeste nationaliste* (Paris: Plon, 1972); and, perhaps most relevantly, *Coexistence pacifique et guerre révolutionnaire* (Paris: Librairie Française, 1963).

25 For the Legião Portuguesa, see Luís Nuno Rodrigues, *A Legião Portuguesa: A Milícia do Estado Novo, 1936–1944* (Lisbon: Estampa, 1996); and Josué da Silva, *Legião Portuguesa: Força repressiva do fascismo* (Lisbon: Diabril, 1975). Compare the illustrated paean to the Legião, *Legião Portuguesa: Expressão da consciência moral da Nação* (Lisbon: Empresa Norte, 1966). The Legião, which was created by Salazar's 30 September 1936 Executive Decree, was divided into a number of different components, including a territorial militia; a mobile Força Automóvel de Choque (FAC: Automobile Shock Force); a commando unit later known as the Grupo de Intervenção Imediata (GII: Immediate Intervention Group); a naval infantry brigade; a previously established youth group known as Mocidade Portuguesa (Portuguese Youth), which was later incorporated into the Legião; a number of university and student organizations, including the Frente de Estudantes Nacionalistas (Nacionalist Students' Front); a civil defense group known as the Defesa Civil do Território (Territorial Civil Defense); and a social services auxiliary. Although the militia was not considered an effective military force, the Legião did create an efficient Serviço de Informações (Intelligence Service), which built up a large number of informants and exchanged intelligence with the secret police. See Da Silva, *Legião Portuguesa*, pp. 13–17, 45–52. But compare the more detailed account by the historian Nuno Rodrigues (*Legião Portuguesa*, pp. 71–102 and 204), which is not fully reconcilable with that of Da Silva concerning organizational matters. For the Mocidade Portuguesa, see Lopes Arriaga, *Mocidade Portuguesa: Breve história de uma organização salazarista* (Lisbon: Terra Livre, 1976).

26 For the PIDE/DGS's financing of Aginter, see SDCI, *Relatório 2*, pp. 1–2. The Defense Ministry officials involved were General Deslandes, General João Paiva de Faria Leite Brandão, Major António César Limão Gata, and Captain João Alves Martins; those from the Foreign Affairs Ministry were ambassadors João Hall Themido and Caldeira Coelho. Compare Laurent, *Orchestre noir*, pp. 123–4. For more on PIDE, which Caetano "reorganized" and renamed the DGS, see Associação de Ex-Presos Politicos Antifascistas, ed., *A PIDE e as impresas* (Lisbon: AEPPA, 1977); Tom Gallagher, "Controlled Repression in Salazar's Portugal," *Journal of Contemporary History* 14:3 (July 1979), pp. 385–403; Alexandre Manuel, Rogério Carapinha, and Dias Neves, eds., *PIDE: A história da repressão* (Fundao: Jornal do Fundão, 1974); Fernando Luso Soares, *PIDE/DGS: Um estado dentro do estado* (Lisbon: Portugália, no date); "Repórter Sombra," *Dossier PIDE*; and especially Nuno Vasco, *Vigiados e perseguidos: Documentos secretos da PIDE/DGS* (Lisbon: Bertrand, 1977). Themido later recounted his experiences as Portugal's ambassador to the United States in his *Dez anos em Washington, 1971–1981: As verdades e os mitos nas relações Luso-Americanos* (Lisbon: Dom Quixote, 1995).

27 See SDCI, *ELP Relatório 1 [29 March 1975]*, p. 10. Compare Fabrizio Calzi and Frédéric Laurent, *Piazza Fontana: La verità su una strage* (Milan: Mondadori, 1997), pp. 60–62; Laurent, *Orchestre noir*, pp. 137–8; and Luis González-Mata, *Terrorismo international: La extrema derecha, la extrema izquierda, y los crimenes de estado* (Barcelona: Argos, 1978), p. 154.

28 For more details concerning the discovery of the archives of PIDE/DGS and Aginter, see Tíscar, *Contra-revolução no 25 de abril*, pp. 113–49; and Laurent, *Orchestre noir*, pp. 117–18. For an informative interview with Abrantes Serra, an apparent admirer of Ernesto ("Che") Guevara, see Sandro Ottolenghi, "Anonima attentati," *L'Europeo* 30:37 (12 September 1974), pp. 30–33.

29 I managed to obtain copies of some of these reports and documents, but unfortunately this process of disseminating Aginter documents for public scrutiny was soon interrupted, allegedly in response to heavy behind-the-scenes pressure placed on the new Portuguese regime by the American government. If all of the extensive Aginter files had been made available, much more could undoubtedly be said about international right-wing subversion during the late 1960s and the early 1970s.
30 Compare Laurent, *Orchestre noir*, p. 120, note 1; González-Mata, *Terrorismo internacional*, p. 162.
31 For Aginter's press activities, see Laurent, *Orchestre noir*, p. 120; González-Mata, *Terrorismo internacional*, p. 154.
32 In fact, although Aginter was indeed a center of international subversion – in the anti-leftist "destabilize in order to stabilize" mode – it is a mischaracterization of its nature to characterize it as "fascist." Guillou and many other key Aginter personnel (such as Leroy) were not fascists, ideologically speaking, but rather anti-communist Catholic traditionalists with a pro-Western and pro-Atlanticist orientation. Like the OAS itself, Aginter comprised both Catholic integralist and fascist elements, and thus operated as an ideologically non-sectarian organization within which both hard-line "white" and "black" anti-communists could work together to aggressively fight against their joint communist and pro-communist enemies. See Aldo Giannuli, *Relazione di perizia*, Tribunale di Milano, Ufficio Istruzione, Procedimento penale n. 2/92F, 12 marzo 1997 [hereinafter Giannuli, *Relazione 12 III 97*], pp. 149–50. Compare the remarks of Italian neo-fascist *pentito* Vincenzo Vinciguerra, *Stato d'emergenza: Raccolta di scritti sulla strage di piazza Fontana* (No place: Lulu, no date), p. 198:

> It [was] not . . . a common ideological factor that made possible the alliance between the men of the OAS and, later, of Aginter Presse and the Italian "neo-fascists," but the awareness of being on the same anti-communist barricade, deployed on the political and operational front with the "free world" whose battle [was] directed by the American and Atlantic secret services.

Indeed, according to UAR informant Armando Mortilla, when Guillou met with Rauti in January 1968, one of his main concerns was to determine the latter's attitude toward American policies, and whether the ON leader was prepared to support those policies. See ibid., pp. 160–1.
33 The evidence of Aginter links to these foreign intelligence services is, quite naturally, sketchy. There are clear indications that the agency's personnel had contacts with personnel from the DGS, BOSS, and the KYP, although similar links to the BND and CIA are harder to document. Chairoff claims, not only that Guillou had been the liaison man between SDECE and the CIA during the Korean War, but also that he had established close relations with high-ranking American intelligence agents while assigned to the 11th Choc – including Lisbon Chief of Station Fred E. Hubbard, Robert H. Flenner, Charles Evan Higdon, Dr. William Howard Taft, and Dr. Wallace Walter Atwood Jr. – and that Aginter operatives helped the CIA to train counterguerrilla forces in Guatemala. See Chairoff, *Dossier néo-nazisme*, pp. 158–9. Moreover, a left-wing Portuguese author, citing the 20 November 1975 issue of *O Século*, states that Guillou and his associate Jay Salby were "deep cover" agents of the CIA who were entrusted with maintaining links between the ELP and the international far right, as well as with Mozambique financier Jorge Jardim and the governments of South Africa and Rhodesia. See João Paulo Guerra, *Os "Flechas" atacam de novo* (Lisbon: Caminho, 1988), p. 102. In contrast, Vinciguerra originally believed that Aginter was not operating directly within the ambit of the CIA, but rather was a structure linked to NATO, presumably its secret services. See Captain Paolo Scriccia, Raggruppamento Operativo Speciale Carabinieri, Reparto Eversione, *Annotazione sulle attività di guerra psicologica e non ortodossa compiute in Italia tra il 1969 e il 1974 attraverso l'Aginter Presse*, Procedimento penale nei confronti di Rognoni, Giancarlo ed altri, 23 luglio 1996 [hereinafter ROS, *Annotazione sulle . . . Aginter Presse*], pp. 109–10.

Later, however, he appears to have changed his mind. See Vinciguerra, *Stato d'emergenza*, pp. 198, 206, etc. To these contrasting but unsubstantiated claims one should perhaps add a documented fact of great potential significance. In 1957, logistical cooperation between PIDE and the CIA was formally initiated by means of a secret protocol that stipulated the responsibilities of each agency in connection with the global anti-communist struggle. As a result, the director of PIDE at the time, Captain António Neves Graça, went to Washington to discuss the details with Allen Dulles and other CIA officials. This led to an arrangement whereby selected personnel from PIDE would attend two-month or four-month courses in the United States to obtain advanced training in intelligence work. In the next two years alone, thirteen PIDE officers (including ten from the Investigation Department, which was in charge of political prisoners) received such training, and among them was the pro-American Pereira de Carvalho, who collaborated with CIA case officer Diego Cortes Asensio and later aided Aginter operatives in his capacity as intelligence chief. A few of these trainees, such as Abílio Pires, Ernesto Lopes Ramos, and Miguel da Silva, were even recruited as contract agents by the CIA. For example, it turned out that Pires, who later became known as the CIA's "man" inside PIDE, was paid a monthly stipend of 500 dollars. From 1958 to 1962, elements of the two services worked in close cooperation with one another. Thereafter, the Kennedy-initiated policy of official American support for decolonization in Africa strained relations between the agencies. But since this policy coexisted awkwardly with the *de facto* support offered by various CIA right-wingers to the Portuguese cause in Africa, factional infighting broke out between both hard-line and moderate CIA case officers and between pro-American and anti-American PIDE personnel. How the clandestine alliances between these shifting, interconnected factions worked themselves out in operational terms is impossible to determine on the basis of the currently available evidence. For details about the CIA-PIDE connection, see the thoroughly researched historical study by José Freire Antunes, *Os Americanos e Portugal: Os anos de Richard Nixon, 1969–1974* (Lisbon: Dom Quixote, 1986), especially pp. 52–8; and Vasco, *Vigiados e perseguidos*, pp. 115–18, which publishes an important 27 August 1974 document on this subject. For Pereira de Carvalho's provision of assistance to Aginter personnel operating in Angola during the spring of 1967, see Laurent, *Orchestre noir*, p. 141. Finally, although Guillou claimed that he was still being hunted by elements of the French secret service because of his role in the OAS, Vinciguerra, who had temporarily taken refuge in Lisbon, believed, after becoming acquainted with him, that Guillou was still working at times for the "destabilization" section of SDECE. See Vincenzo Vinciguerra, *Ergastolo per la libertà: Verso la verità sulla strategia della tensione* (Florence: Arnaud, 1989), p. 20. Compare ROS, *Annotazione sulle . . . Aginter Presse*, p. 107, for other indications of Guillou and Aginter links to SDECE. This would not be at all surprising given the reconciliation between the Gaullist security forces and former members of the OAS that took place in the wake of the events of May 1968, if not before.

34 Compare Laurent, *Orchestre noir*, p. 119; and Calzi and Laurent, *Piazza Fontana*, p. 70. OACI's stated purpose was to "intervene in any part of the globe to confront the most serious communist threats," and its members pledged to maintain absolute organizational loyalty and secrecy. For OACI's "missions," see González-Mata, *Terrorismo internacional*, pp. 154–6.

35 Tribunale di Milano, Guidice Istruttore Guido Salvino, *Sentenza-ordinanza n. 9/92A del 3 febraio 1998 nel procedimento penale contro Rognoni, Giancarlo + 32* [hereinafter *Sentenza 3 II 98 contro Rognoni*], p. 369. Among other things, Aginter operatives used an unusual cryptological system based on alpha-numeric code names, much like those utilized by regular military and intelligence organizations. See ibid., pp. 369–70.

36 For summaries of Leroy's checkered career, see SDCI, *Relatório 2*, p. 4; ROS, *Annotazione sulle . . . Aginter Presse*, pp. 6–11; Tíscar, *Contra-revolução no 25 de abril*, pp. 204–6; Laurent, *Orchestre noir*, pp. 154–6; and several interviews he provided to the press, including one with Sandro Ottolenghi, "L'uomo del rapporto segreto," *L'Europeo* 30:27 (4 July 1974),

pp. 28–31. For the Action Française, a Catholic integralist organization with "fascist" trappings in prewar and interwar France, see especially Eugen Weber, *Action Française: Royalism and Reaction in Twentieth Century France* (Stanford: Stanford University, 1962), which is still the standard work on the subject. For the Cagoule ("Hooded Ones") organization, which was officially known as the Comité Secret d'Action Révolutionnaire (Secret Committee for Revolutionary Action), see Philippe Bourdrel, *La Cagoule: Histoire d'une société secrète du Front populaire à la Vème République* (Paris: Albin Michel, 1992); and "Dagore" (pseudonym for Aristide Corre), *Les carnets secrets de la Cagoule* (Paris: France-Empire, 1977), a more sympathetic treatment by a former member. For the Requetés, which were merged with the Falangist militia in 1937, see Rafael Casas de la Vega, *Las milicias nacionales en la guerra de España* (Madrid: Nacional, 1974), passim. For the modern history of the Carlists, see Martin Blinkhorn, *Carlism and Crisis in Spain, 1931–1939* (Cambridge: Cambridge University, 1975); and José Carlos Clemente, *Historia del Carlismo contemporáneo, 1935–1972* (Barcelona: Grijalbo, 1977). The French term *intoxication*, which in general means "poisoning," is used by Leroy and other *guerre révolutionnaire* proponents to refer to the "poisoning" of the mind. Specifically, it signifies the manipulation of the political environment by means of the systematic dissemination of false or misleading information to a targeted group (or groups), the purpose of which is to paralyze or otherwise influence that group's subsequent actions. The targeted group can be relatively small or encompass an entire society. For further discussion, see Pierre Nord, *L'Intoxication: Arme absolue de la guerre subversive* (Paris: Fayard, 1971), especially pp. vii–x (from Gabriel Veraldi's preface) and pp. 5–7.

37 For the chief Aginter and Ordre et Tradition operatives, see SDCI, *Relatório 2*, pp. 13–21; Laurent, *Orchestre noir*, pp. 122–3, 126–7; González-Mata, *Terrorismo internacional*, p. 153, who also adds the names of André Fontaine, António Kilby, and the Italian Silvio Morani; and especially Tíscar, *Contra-revolução no 25 de abril*, pp. 191–208, who also lists many of those organizations' collaborators (pp. 208–10), contacts (pp. 210–18, 221–2), and paid mercenaries who were involved in their operations (pp. 218–21).

38 Laurent, *Orchestre noir*, p. 129; and Calzi and Laurent, *Piazza Fontana*, pp. 67–8.

39 For Aginter's links to the international right, see SDCI, *Relatório 2*, pp. 25–34; the list appended to SDCI, *ELP Relatório 3* titled "Aginter Presse e Ordre et Tradition," pp. 1–5; Laurent, *Orchestre noir*, pp. 128–34; Calzi and Laurent, *Piazza Fontana*, pp. 68–70; González-Mata, *Terrorismo internacional*, p. 154; and Chairoff, *Dossier néo-nazisme*, p. 159. For more on CEDADE, see Xavier Casals, *Neonazis en España: De los audiciones wagnerianas a los skinheads, 1966–1995* (Barcelona: Grijalbo, 1995), pp. 37–194; José Luis Rodríguez Jiménez, *Reaccionarios y golpistas: La extrema derecha en España del tardofranquismo a la consolidación de la democracia, 1967–1982* (Madrid: Consejo Superior de Investigaciones Científicas, 1994), pp. 117–21; Mariano Sánchez Soler, *Los hijos del 20-N: Historia violenta del fascismo español* (Madrid: Temas de Hoy, 1993), pp. 89–92, 94–9; and CEDADE, *Qué es CEDADE?* (Barcelona: Bau, 1978). Note that Otto Skorzeny has been described as one of the co-founders, a major subsidizer, and the "technical advisor" of CEDADE, a Barcelona-based pan-European cultural circle established in September 1966 by dissident Falangist Angel Ricote which was taken over in February 1970 by its pro-Hitler youth wing (led by Jorge Mota) and thence transformed into a Catholic-tinged [!] neo-Nazi liaison organization. From the outset this organization was closely linked to a vast array of European and Latin American neo-fascist groups (including the NOE/NEO), and it remains active to this day. Although some sources have claimed that former Hamburg Deutsche Arbeitsfront chief Friedrich Kuhfuss and Spanish Eastern Front veterans Miguel Ezquerra (ex-SS) and Tomás García Rebull (ex-División Azul) played decisive roles in the establishment of CEDADE – compare Chairoff, *Dossier néo-nazisme*, pp. 170–1; and Wolfgang Purtscheller, *Aufbruch der Völkischen: Das braune Netzwerk* (Vienna: Picus, 1993), p. 34 – more detailed and thoroughly researched accounts have to some extent downplayed the degree of influence allegedly exerted on the organization by foreign fascists. See Casals, *Neonazis en España*, pp. 37–73, 86–90. It is now known, however, that CEDADE received funding

from Arab sources, including Saudi Arabian embassy personnel and the former Grand Mufti of Jerusalem, and probably also – like several other groups of Spanish ultras – from the Servicio Central de Documentación de la Presidencia del Gobierno (SECED). See ibid., pp. 84–5, 97–9; and Rodríguez Jiménez, *Reaccionarios y golpistas*, pp. 119–20 (citing a 23 January 1989 interview with CEDADE militant Ramón Bau). As for Aginter Presse, according to a team of Swiss investigative journalists, Guy Amaudruz of the NOE/ENO was also a member of Ordre et Tradition, and Roland Gueissaz of the Swiss section of Jeune Europe was an Aginter correspondent. See Jürg Frischknecht, Peter Haffner, Ueli Haldimann, and Peter Niggli, *Die unheimlichen Patrioten: Politische Reaktion in der Schweiz. Ein aktuelles Handbuch mit Nachtrag 1979–84* (Zurich: Limmat, 1987), p. 475. Compare Laurent, *Orchestre noir*, p. 133. For more details concerning Aginter contacts in Belgium, see Serge Dumont, *Les mercenaires* (Berchem: EPO, no date), pp. 174–8. In this context, Aginter materials were regularly reprinted by Labin in the Ligue Internationale de la Liberté's bulletin, *Damocles*. As noted earlier, the LIL became the Belgian section of the World Anti-Communist League. Moreover, Labin apparently played an important role in disseminating *guerre révolutionnaire* concepts and advocating the creation of anti-communist resistance organizations and networks, composed of both civilians and military personnel, that would be trained to employ them. See Giannuli, *Relazione 12 III 97*, pp. 17–20, 43–4. No less importantly, Guillou established personal contacts in 1969 with Damman, who was a key intermediary in Belgium between activist but "respectable" elements of the pro-Atlantic right or center-right – including Otto von Habsburg's Paneuropa Union (Pan-European Union), Franz Josef Strauss's CDU, the Cercle Pinay (Pinay Circle), and several other international networks with overlapping personnel – and a number of radical neo-fascist groups (including Jeune Europe and its offshoots). For further information and source references concerning some of these influential anti-communist networks, see the conclusion to the next chapter. For more on Ordine Nuovo and Avanguardia Nazionale, see immediately below. For more on the WUNS, an offshoot of earlier pro-Nazi "pan-Nordic" organizations like the Northern League and the Northern European Ring, see Frederick J. Simonelli, "The World Union of National Socialists and Postwar Transatlantic Nazi Revival," in *Nation and Race: The Developing Euro-American Racist Subculture*, ed. by Jeffrey Kaplan and Tore Bjørgo (Boston: Northeastern University, 1998), pp. 34–57; Werner Smoydzin, *Hitler lebt!: Vom internationalen Faschismus zur Internationale des Hakenkreuzes* (Pfaffenhofen: Ilmgau, 1966), pp. 135–74; Chairoff, *Dossier néo-nazisme*, pp. 446–7; Algazy, *Tentation néo-fasciste en France*, pp. 312–21; and Ernesto Cadena, *La ofensiva neo-fascista: Un informe sensacional* (Barcelona: Acervo, 1978), pp. 231–44. For the funding of 81 right-wing Italian journalists, including Accame and Torchia, by the Italian secret service, see Giuseppe De Lutiis, *Storia dei servizi segreti in Italia* (Rome: Riuniti, 1984), pp. 189–90, note 99, citing a 1976 article by Lino Jannuzzi in *Il Tempo*. Aginter's file cards on these two Italian correspondents were also quite revelatory. Thus Accame, who for many years served as the editor of Randolfo Pacciardi's "presidentialist" *Nuova Repubblica* publication, was described as an informant for a branch of the BND in Rome, a regular correspondent to Franz Josef Strauss, and an admirer of Argoud and the OAS. For his part, Torchia was identified as an agent of the Italian secret service who also had close links to the American embassy and the Italian Army. Indeed, his Agenzia Oltremare was subsidized by the military intelligence service. See Tribunale di Catanzaro, Giudice Istruttore Gianfranco Migliaccio, *Sentenza-ordinanza n. 14/75 del 31 luglio 1976 nel procedimento penale contro Giannettini, Guido + 16* [hereinafter *Sentenza 31 VII 76 contro Giannettini*], p. 59. Their Aginter fiches are quoted in González-Mata, *Terrorismo internacional*, pp. 160–1. Last and certainly least, Aginter made an effort to contact former CIA employee and *National Review* editor William F. Buckley Jr., but nothing seems to have come of this. See Laurent, *Orchestre noir*, pp. 133–4. In the final analysis, setting off bombs and developing torture techniques, even for a "good" cause, apparently does not mix well with genteel pursuits like yachting.

40 See especially SDCI, *Relatório 2*, pp. 2–12; José Manuel Duarte de Jesus, *A guerra secreta de Salazar em África: Aginter Press, uma rede internacional de contra-subversão e espionagem sediada*

em *Lisboa* (Lisbon: Dom Quixote, 2012), pp. 125–91; Tíscar, *Contra-revolução no 25 de abril*, pp. 78–108; and Laurent, *Orchestre noir*, pp. 139–56. For one example, see Jacques Debreton, *Coup d'État à Brazzaville* (Brussels: Espace, 1976), passim. The role of Guillou is briefly noted therein on pp. 31–4, and Aginter operative Jean-Marie Laurent – who also writes the preface – makes frequent appearances throughout the narrative.

41 Laurent, *Orchestre noir*, pp. 156–65.
42 For more on the clandestine activities of these groups (except the ELP, which has already been discussed), see ibid., pp. 337–55; and González-Mata, *Terrorismo internacional*, pp. 175–89. For the abortive FLA plot, see especially the article by Fred Strasser and Brian McTigue, "The Fall River Conspiracy," *Boston Magazine* (November 1978), pp. 121–4, 175–84, in whose stateside planning and financing Victor Fediay, an aide to conservative Senator Strom Thurmond (R.-SC) and a former employee in a top secret Air Force intelligence program, was personally involved. A more complete version of this article appeared in the 4 November 1978 issue of Lisbon's *O Expresso*, "1975: Americanos, OAS e Almeida reúnen-se em Paris para negociar a independência dos Açores," pp. 1R–3R.
43 Laurent, *Orchestre noir*, pp. 135–6; and De Lutiis, *Storia dei servizi segreti in Italia*, p. 168.
44 These and other excerpts from Guillou's manual can be found in González-Mata, *Terrorismo internacional*, pp. 155–6; "Une 'OAS' internationale," *Libération* (12 December 1974), p. 8; and Roger-X. Lantéri, "L'Internationale noire," *L'Express International* 1337 (21 February 1977), p. 34. The apparent title of the manual is identified by Antonio Cipriani and Gianni Cipriani, *Sovranità limitata: Storia dell'eversione atlantica in Italia* (Rome: Associate, 1991), p. 109, although perhaps they are confusing the heading of a particular section of it with the general title.
45 Laurent, *Orchestre noir*, p. 135.
46 Ibid., p. 148.
47 Cited by González-Mata, *Terrorismo internacional*, p. 155.
48 Compare ibid., pp. 155–6; and "Une 'OAS internationale,'" p. 8.
49 See, for example, the interview with Leroy published by Sandro Ottolenghi, "L'uomo del rapporto secreto," *L'Europeo* 30:27 (4 July 1974), pp. 28–30.
50 Laurent, *Orchestre noir*, p. 139. For pseudo-Mau Mau guerrillas in Kenya, see the account of Frank Kitson, *Gangs and Counter-Gangs* (London: Barrie & Rockliff, 1960), passim.
51 For the Bulliard affair, see the 11 April 1975 letter from the SDCI investigators at Caxias to the Portuguese consulate in Paris, plus appended documents; Laurent, *Orchestre noir*, pp. 148–51; and Frischknecht et al., *Unheimlichen Patrioten*, pp. 475–7. The story here is a rather complex one. It has sometimes been suggested that Bulliard's party was a genuine Maoist organization that was manipulated by Leroy into providing Aginter operatives with legitimate left-wing credentials. This is what Bulliard himself claimed after the activities of Aginter were exposed. See his letter to the post-coup Portuguese authorities, which was appended to the 11 April 1975 letter. But it is now clear, as I myself suggested in a 1987 article, that Bulliard was himself a neo-fascist provocateur who had consciously established a phony Maoist party which could be used as a cover by the far right. See Jeffrey M. Bale, "Right-Wing Terrorists and the Extraparliamentary Left in Post–World War II Europe: Collusion or Manipulation?," *Berkeley Journal of Sociology* 32 (1987), pp. 205, 226–7, note 108. Among other things, he was in contact with Manuel Coelho da Silva (alias "Manuel Rios"), a PIDE/DGS informant within the major anti-Salazarist opposition group, the Comité Portugal Libre (Free Portugal Committee) in Paris. In other words, Bulliard was undoubtedly a "player" rather than a dupe. Note, for example, that a Swiss book provides evidence that he was working as a paid informant for Marc-Edmond Chantre's virulently anti-communist Aktion freier Staatsbürger (Free Citizens' Action) organization in 1964, the very same year he formed the PCS/M-L (which was renamed the Parti Populaire Suisse [Swiss Popular Party] in 1967). See Claude Cantini, *Les ultras: Extrême droite et droite extrême en Suisse. Les mouvements et la presse de 1921 à 1991* (Lausanne: En Bas, 1992), p. 161, note 136. For Chantre, a former member of the Action Nationale, and his postwar group, which compiled a large archive of files on

suspected leftists in Switzerland prior to its dissolution, see ibid., pp. 89–91; Frischknecht et al., *Unheimlichen Patrioten*, especially pp. 113–34; and Julien Sansonnens, *Le Comité suisse d'action civique (1948–1965): Contribution à une histoire de la répression anticommuniste en Suisse* (Vevey: Aire, 2012). Moreover, Buillard provided information on Maoist parties in Switzerland to SID between March and July of 1967, but these data were allegedly considered to be of little value by the Italian service [!]. See ROS, *Attività sulle . . . Aginter Presse*, p. 9; and Vinciguerra, *Stato d'emergenza*, pp. 200–1. The role of the Chinese embassy at Berne in this affair likewise remains unclear, although it was far from innocent. In the wake of the Sino-Soviet split, the government of communist China expended increasing efforts to neutralize Soviet influence in Africa, and as noted earlier the Tewu had also established collaborative relations with Thiriart and his organizations. Indeed, according to Swiss journalist Serge Niklaus of the *Nationalzeitung*, it was Thiriart himself who originally brought Leroy together with Bulliard. See Frischknecht et al., *Unheimlichen Patrioten*, p. 476. Since the Chinese must have known that Thiriart and his associates were neo-fascists, their efforts to help them establish a Maoist cover could hardly have been accidental. The only real question is whether they did so simply because they shared the same goal of resisting the extension of Soviet and American power, whether they sought to conceal their own initiatives behind a network of neo-fascists, or whether they sought to utilize and manipulate neo-fascist groups covertly for entirely different purposes. It may also be that Leroy and his comrades were seeking to discredit or gather information about the Chinese apparatus in Europe at the behest of NATO and other Western secret services. These are important questions that deserve further consideration.

52 For these African and European operations, see SDCI, *Relatório 1*, p. 8; SDCI, *Relatório 2*, pp. 2, 4–13, 23–4; and Laurent, *Orchestre noir*, pp. 148–9, 151–4.

53 One of the best analyses of the contending factions within the MSI during the late 1940s and 1950s is that of Piero Ignazi, *Il polo escluso: Profilo del Movimento sociale italiano* (Bologna: Mulino, 1989), especially pp. 37–88. Compare Giuliana de'Medici, *Le origini del MSI: Dal clandestinismo al primo Congresso, 1943–1948* (Rome: Istituto di Studi Corporativi, 1986), pp. 49–133. For more on Evola and his influence on the postwar Italian radical right, see Richard H. Drake, "Julius Evola and the Ideological Origins of the Radical Right in Contemporary Italy," in *Political Violence and Terror: Motifs and Motivations*, ed. by Peter Merkl (Berkeley: University of California, 1986), pp. 61–89; and Anna Jellamo, "J. Evola, il pensatore della tradizione," in *La destra radicale*, ed. by Franco Ferraresi (Milan: Feltrinelli, 1984), pp. 215–52.

54 The Evola quote is cited in Mario Caprara and Gianluca Semprini, *Neri!: La storia mai raccontata della destra radicale, eversiva e terrorista* (Rome: Newton Compton, 2009), p. 172. For the different levels of ON membership, see Vinciguerra, *Ergastolo per la libertà*, pp. 167–8.

55 For more on Ordine Nuovo, see Franco Ferraresi, "La destra eversiva," in *La destra radicale*, ed. by Franco Ferraresi, pp. 62–6; Rosario Minna, "Il terrorismo di destra," in *Terrorismi in Italia*, ed. by Donatella della Porta (Bologna: Mulino, 1984), pp. 33–5; Paolo Guzzanti, *Il neofascismo e le sue organizzazioni paramilitari* (Rome: Partito Socialista Italiano, 1972), pp. 14–19; Flamini, *Partito del golpe*, volume 1, pp. 21–5; Petra Rosenbaum, *Il nuovo fascismo: Da Salò ad Almirante. Storia del MSI* (Milan: Feltrinelli, 1974), pp. 79–81; Daniele Barbieri, *Agenda nera: Trent'anni di neo-fascismo in Italia* (Rome: Coines, 1976), pp. 62–4; Extraparliamentary Left Research Group, *La strage di stato: Vent'anni dopo*, ed. by Giancarlo De Palo and Aldo Giannuli (Rome: Associate, 1989), pp. 79–81; and Claudio Nunziata, "Il Movimento Politico Ordine Nuovo: Il processo di Roma del 1973," in *Eversione di destra, terrorismo, stragi: I fatti e l'intervento giudiziario*, ed. by Vittorio Borraccetti (Milan: Angeli, 1986), pp. 71–86.

56 For the various clandestine right-wing paramilitary groups in early postwar Italy, see Pier Giuseppe Murgia, *Il vento del nord: Storia e cronica del fascismo dopo la Resistenza, 1945–1950* (Milan: Sugar, 1975), pp. 257–94; Pier Giuseppe Murgia, *Ritorneremo! Storia e cronica del fascismo dopo la Resistenza, 1951–1953* (Milan: Sugar, 1976), pp. 120–30; Ferraresi, "Destra eversiva," pp. 55–7; Leonard Weinberg, *After Mussolini: Italian Neo-Fascism and the*

Nature of Fascism (Washington, DC: University Press of America, 1979), pp. 14–16; Del Boca and Giovana, *Fascism Today*, pp. 131–2; and Daniele Barbieri, *Agenda nera: Trent'anni di neo-fascismo in Italia* (Rome: Coines, 1976), pp. 18–23. For more on the FAR, the most important neo-fascist group of this type prior to the formation of Ordine Nuovo and Avanguardia Nazionale, see especially Archivio Centrale dello Stato, Ministero dell'Interno, Pubblica Sicurezza, 1951, Prima Sezione, busta 34, fascicolo K8/A: "Movimento FAR," passim; Mario Tedeschi, *Fascisti dopo Mussolini* (Rome: Arnia, 1950), passim; and the fascinating series of articles by P. F. Altomonte, "Fascisti dopo Mussolini: Storia del FAR," in the left fascist publication *Il Pensiero Nazionale* between February and August 1958, which adopt a harshly critical posture toward both Evola and Tedeschi, who is openly suspected of having intentionally "burned" the fascist radicals by publishing his historical exposé. There are good reasons to consider this possibility, given Tedeschi's later pro-Atlanticist, conservative, and "respectable" public stance, which was ostensibly anathema to both the national syndicalist left and the Evolan right within the MSI.

57 For biographical material on Rauti, see Marco Sassano, *La politica della strage* (Padua: Marsilio, 1972), pp. 41–2; and Marco Revelli, "La nuova destra," in *Destra radicale*, ed. by Ferraresi, pp. 189–90, note 5. More information about Rauti can be found throughout all the studies on the postwar Italian radical right. For updated information on the terrorist activities of ON, see the Addendum to this chapter.

58 Quoted in Magnus Linklater, Isabel Hilton, and Neal Ascherson, *The Fourth Reich: Klaus Barbie and the Neo-Fascist Connection* (London: Coronet, 1985), p. 261. This is no doubt an exaggeration, but it does certainly reflect the "action" orientation of AN. See, e.g., the reprint of the organization's booklet, *La lotta politica di Avanguardia nazionale* (Rome: Settimo Segillo, 2012 [1972]), pp. 13–61. Even so, much of the focus therein is on organization and action rather than philosophical or doctrinal elaboration.

59 Cited in Rosenbaum, *Nuovo fascismo*, p. 82, quoting a 1969 AN flyer.

60 For more on AN, see Minna, "Terrorismo di destra," pp. 33–5; Ferraresi, "Destra eversiva," pp. 66–71; *Neofascismo in Europa* (Milan: La Pietra, 1974), pp. 33–5; Gianni Flamini, *Il partito del golpe: Le strategie della tensione e del terrore dal primo centrosinistra organico al sequestro Moro, 1964–1978* (Ferrara: Bovolenta, 1981–85), volume 1, pp. 76–7 and passim; and Extraparliamentary Left Research Group, *Strage di stato:Vent'anni dopo*, pp. 37–9; Giannuli, *Relazione 12 III 97*, pp. 182–97.

61 For Delle Chiaie's early career, see Stuart Christie, *Stefano Delle Chiaie: Portrait of a Black Terrorist* (London: Anarchy/Refract, 1984), pp. 18–23, 33–4, 36–9, 43–55, 61–8; Extraparliamentary Left Research Group, *Strage di stato:Vent'anni dopo*, pp. 178–96; and Ferraresi, "Destra eversiva," pp. 66–8. Compare also *Lotta politica di Avanguardia nazionale*, pp. 5–12, for AN's own defense of its ideals, methods, and violent behavior.

62 Extraparliamentary Left Research Group, *Strage di stato: Vent'anni dopo*, p. 47 (editors' introduction). According to this source, after his arrival in Spain Delle Chiaie was put up for a time by Girón at his villa in Fuengirol. This claim is perfectly believable, since both were intransigent opponents of liberal democracy with no qualms about resorting to coercive measures. Girón had been one of the few Spanish officials (along with Manuel Fraga, Colonel Enrique Herrera Marín, and several Navy officers, as well as Franco's sister Pilar) who unhesitatingly offered their support to Juan Perón when the Argentine dictator and his entourage began a twelve-year period of exile in Madrid in 1961. See Raanan Rein, *The Franco-Perón Alliance: Relations between Spain and Argentina, 1946–1955* (Pittsburgh and London: University of Pittsburgh, 1993), pp. 245–9, 306, note 12. He was also among the most prominent and inveterate opponents of *aperturista* policies prior to his retirement from political life in the early 1980s. For insights into his political views, see José Antonio Girón de Velasco, *Reflexiones sobre España* (Barcelona: Planeta, 1975); and José Antonio Girón de Velasco, *Si la memoria no mi falla* (Barcelona: Planeta, 1994). Perhaps his most notorious public political action was his belligerent media attack on Carlos Arias Navarro, who had been compelled to undertake some minor democratic

reforms after succeeding hard-line Admiral Luis Carrero Blanco as prime minister. (Carrero Blanco, it will be recalled, had been assassinated by Basque terrorists at the end of 1973.) Not coincidentally, this bitter critique of Arias, which was published in the 28 April 1974 issue of the Falangist daily *Arriba* and became known as the *Gironazo*, took place three days after the 25 April revolution in Portugal, and was linked to parallel efforts by military hard-liners to secure key operational posts from which they could control developments following Franco's death. For the *Gironazo*, which was also known as the "Manifesto of Fuengirol," and Girón's subsequent links to pro-coup military circles, see Paul Preston, *The Politics of Revenge: Fascism and the Military in Twentieth-Century Spain* (London: Unwin Hyman, 1990), pp. 160–1, 172–3; and Rodríguez Jiménez, *Reaccionarios y golpistas*, pp. 170–2, 281–93. Note also that Delle Chiaie was personally introduced to both Degrelle and Skorzeny by Borghese, who characterized the AN leader as a "man of action," and that the Spanish attorney used by the "black bombadier," José Luis Jerez Riesco, was a close friend of Degrelle, Skorzeny, and Sánchez Covisa. See Linklater et al., *Fourth Reich*, p. 260; Lee, *Beast Reawakens*, p. 188; and Sánchez Soler, *Hijos del 20-N*, p. 167.

63 For details about the setting up of a rightist support network in Spain for fugitive Italian terrorists, see Sánchez Soler, *Hijos del 20-N*, pp. 157–67, citing firsthand testimony and intelligence reports. During a January 1977 interrogation, Delle Chiaie openly admitted having close relations with Sánchez Covisa, Girón, Milá, Blas Piñar, and numerous other influential Spanish rightists. See ibid., pp. 172–3. Note that the Hermandad de la Guardia de Franco was originally conceived as an armed militia group. As for El Appuntamento, its titular owner was Spanish ultra José Luis Clemente de Antonio, its manager was Andrea Mieville (future manager of another neo-fascist front company, the Transalpina travel agency), and its Italian employees included Giuseppe Calzona, who had a flair for cooking, and Piero Carmassi, who served as a waiter. Among those arrested in connection with the Calle Pelayo arms factory were Delle Chiaie collaborators Sánchez Covisa, Clemente de Antonio, Pietro Benvenuto, and MPON militants Elio Massagrande and Eliodoro Pomar, a nuclear engineer who had earlier been involved in a plot to contaminate Roman reservoirs with radioactive material. See ibid., pp. 197–200. In addition to this arms fabrication factory, a neo-fascist production facility for false identification papers was discovered in an apartment on Madrid's Calle del Barco, where stolen documents had been modified by attaching the photos of leading neo-fascist figures like Clemente Graziani (MPON), Pierluigi Concutelli (MPON), Salvatore Francia (MPON), Flavio Campo (AN), Mario Tedeschi (MSI), and others. See Corte d'Assise di Firenze, Presidente Pietro Cassano, Giudice Estensore Francesco Carvisiglia, *Sentenza n. 1/85 del 21 marzo 1985 nel procedimento penale contro Graziani, Clemente + 18* [hereinafter *Sentenza 21 III 85 contro Graziani*], pp. 19–20; and Flamini, *Partito del golpe*, volume 4:2, pp. 353–4. For the later phases of Delle Chiaie's checkered career, see Linklater et al., *Fourth Reich*, pp. 260–73; and Christie, *Stefano Delle Chiaie*, pp. 71–128. Further information will very soon be provided about its more sinister aspects.

64 Flamini, *Partito del golpe*, volume 1, pp. 79, 100–1, quoting directly from Italian secret service reports. Compare Sassano, *Politica della strage*, pp. 40–1.

65 These 1969 provocations and acts of terrorism are described in considerable detail in several judicial sentences and a host of mostly partisan secondary sources. There is now a large and ever-growing literature on the Piazza Fontana bombing. Apart from certain sources that I cite in this and the next two chapters, they include the following works that were released after the preparation of this chapter: Maurizio Dianese and Gianfranco Bettin, *La strage: Piazza Fontana, verità e memoria* (Milan: Feltrinelli, 2000); Paolo Barbieri and Paolo Cucchiarelli, *La strage con i capelli bianchi: La sentenza per Piazza Fontana* (Rome: Riuniti, 2003); Fulvio Bellini and Gianfranco Bellini, *Il segreto della Repubblica: Perché non si può essere la verità giudiziaria sulla strage di Piazza Fontana* (Milan: Selene, 2005); Mario Consani, *Foto di gruppo da Piazza Fontana* (Milan: Melampo, 2005); Carlo Lucarelli, *Piazza Fontana* (Turin: Einaudi, 2007); Mary Pace, *Piazza Fontana. L'inchiesta: Parla Giannettini* (Rome: Armando Curcio, 2008); Antonella Beccaria and Simona Mammano, *Attentato imminente: Piazza Fontana, una strage che si poteva evitare – Pasquale Juliano, il poliziotto che nel 1969*

tentò di bloccare la cellula neofascista veneta (Viterbo: Stampa Alternativa, 2009); Giorgio Boatti, *Piazza Fontana, 12 dicembre 1969: Il giorno dell'innocenza perduta* (Turin: Einaudi, 2009); Luciano Lanza, *Bombe e segreti: Piazza Fontana, una strage senza colpevoli* (Milan: Elèuthera, 2009); Carlo Maria Maggi, *L'ultima vittima di Piazza Fontana: Carlo Maria Maggi racconta la sua verità* (Tortona: Chiaravalle, 2010); Andrea Sceresini, Nicola Palma, and Maria Elena Scandaliato, *Piazza Fontana, noi sapevamo: Golpe e strage di stato, la verità del generale Maletti* (Reggio Emilia: Aliberti, 2010); Massimiliano Griner, *Piazza Fontana e il mito della strategia della tensione* (Turin: Lindau, 2011); Marco Nozza, *Il pistarolo: Da Piazza Fontana, trent'anni di storia raccontati da un grande cronista* (Milan: Il Saggiatore, 2011); Paolo Cucchiarelli, *Il segreto di Piazza Fontana: Finalmente la verità sulle strage . . .* (Milan: Adriano Salani, 2012); Franceso Barilli and Matteo Fanoglio, *Piazza Fontana* (Ponte di Pavie: Becco Giallo, 2012); Stefano Cardini, *Piazza Fontana, 43 anni dopo: Le verità di cui abbiamo bisogno* (Milan: Mimesis, 2012); and Mario Casaburi, *Il diritto all'impunità: Piazza Fontana 1969. Inchieste, processi e depistaggi. Una strage senza colpevoli* (Rome: Castelvecchi, 2014).

66 For the close links between Rauti and the NOE/ENO, see Mario Giovana, *Le nuove camicie nere* (Turin: Albero, 1966), pp. 106, 110; and Extraparliamentary Left Research Group, *Strage di stato: Vent'anni dopo*, pp. 80, 88. Further evidence of this can be found in the reciprocal publication of articles in each other's journals. Note, for example, that Rauti published an article in *Nation Europa* under his pseudonym "Flavio Messalla," "KPI gegen die Armee," *Nation Europa* 17:8 (August 1967), pp. 19–22. In the very same issue there are articles by Italian neo-fascist theoretician Adriano Romualdi on Italy's role in the Mediterranean and by "Julian Attikos," probably a pseudonym for the K4A's Plevris, on recent developments in the Colonels' Greece. See ibid., pp. 15–18 and 23–8. For ON's connections to other interlinked European neo-fascist groups, see Flamini, *Partito del golpe*, volume 1, p. 23.

67 See Laurent, *Orchestre noir*, pp. 103–4, 174. One of the "principal agents" of the OAS who was affiliated with ON was Guido Giannettini, who will be discussed in more detail shortly.

68 See, for example, the short notes by "Coriolano," *Ordine Nuovo* 10:1–2 (January–February 1964), p. 52; ON 10:3 (April 1964), p. 61; and *ON* 10:5–6 (June–July 1964), p. 75. "Coriolan" was the alias used by Émile Lecerf, one of Thiriart's key associates. See Serge Dumont, *Les brigades noires: L'Extrême droite en France et en Belgique francophone de 1944 à nos jours* (Berchem: EPO, 1983), pp. 116 and 179, note 161. According to one less than reliable left-wing journalist, Rauti was among the Italians who attended the 1962 Venice conference organized by Mosley and Thiriart. See Sassano, *Politica della strage*, p. 42.

69 Compare Del Boca and Giovana, *Fascism Today*, pp. 158–9; Barbieri, *Agenda nera*, p. 68; and Giovana, *Nuove camicie nere*, pp. 110, 112–13.

70 This is noted by a variety of Italian journalists, including some who had access to a larger sample of Aginter documents than I was able to obtain. See, for example, De Lutiis, *Storia dei servizi segreti in Italia*, p. 166. However, Rauti's name does not appear in the corpus of Aginter documents in my possession.

71 For additional information on ON links to Aginter, see *Sentenza 3 II 98 contro Rognoni*, pp. 393–401, 419–20.

72 Compare *Sentenza 31 VII 76 contro Giannettini*, pp. 95–8, 118–19; and Flamini, *Partito del golpe*, volume 1, pp. 171–2.

73 For Rauti's contacts with Plevris, see *Sentenza 31 VI 76 contro Giannettini*, pp. 132 (citing an 8 April 1975 SID report), 140 (citing a 7 May 1975 KYP report), 144 (testimony of Greek official Kalamakis, who also confirmed Rauti's links to former Interior Minister Stylianos Pattakos and ex–military police chief Ioannis Ladas). Only Giorgios Antonopoulos, head of the Ministry of Public Order's National Security Service, said he could find no evidence concerning the activities of Italian neo-fascists in Greece. See ibid., p. 141. Plevris himself noted that Rauti and other Italians actively sought out his aid and advice, but he considered ON to be the only truly "serious" Italian group. See his interview with Oriana Fallaci, "Si farà il colpo di stato in Italia?," *L'Europeo* 30:39 (26 September 1974), pp. 30–2. Many leftist secondary sources in Italy also emphasize Rauti's role as an

intermediary between Italian and Greek neo-fascists, for example, Extraparliamentary Left Research Group, *Strage di stato: Vent'anni dopo*, p. 245; Cesare De Simone, *La pista nera. Tattica dell'infiltrazione e strategia delle bombe: Il complotto fascista contro la Repubblica* (Rome: Riuniti, 1972), pp. 16–19. Specialists familiar with Greek sources, including some who are quite conservative (like former British MP C. M. Woodhouse), also note that Rauti had close links to the Colonels' regime, in particular its intelligence services through the intermediary of his neo-fascist counterpart Plevris. Compare Solon Gregoriades, *Historia tes diktatorias, 1967–1974* (Athens: Kapopoulos, 1975), volume 2, pp. 91–101; C. M. Woodhouse, *The Rise and Fall of the Greek Colonels* (New York: Franklin Watts, 1985), p. 61; and Turkish propagandist Cem Bašar, *The Terror Dossier and Greece* (Istanbul: International Affairs Agency, 1993), pp. 43–5. Vassilis Kapetanyannis also highlights the links between Italian and Greek neo-fascists (and, through the latter, between the Italians and the Greek security services) in his article "Neo-Fascism in Greece," in *Neo-Fascism in Europe*, ed. by Luciano Cheles, Ronnie Ferguson, and Michalina Vaughn (New York and London: Longman, 1991), pp. 199, 209, notes 33–5, citing the leftist Athenian biweekly, *Anti*. However, he does not specifically mention Rauti, but focuses instead on his ON lieutenants Clemente Graziani and Elio Massagrande. Nor does Andreas Lentakes mention Rauti by name, although he emphasizes Plevris's links to Italian neo-fascist groups. See *Parakratikes organoseis kai eikoste prote Apriliou* (Athens: Kastaniotes, 1975), p. 359.

74 For Delle Chiaie's travels and liaison work in different European countries, including Britain, see Extraparliamentary Left Research Group, *Strage di stato: Vent'anni dopo*, p. 187. He also made personal appearances at the 1965 Milan Congress and the 1969 Barcelona Congress of the NOE/ENO, in all probability together with other members of AN. See Flamini, *Partito del golpe*, volume 1, pp. 79–80, 82; and volume 2, p. 25.

75 Extraparliamentary Left Research Group, *Strage di stato: Vent'anni dopo*, p. 187. Note also that De Luia lived in Munich, a center of right-wing activity, between the fall of 1967 and the spring of 1968, and that afterwards he took a trip to the Colonels' Greece. See ibid., p. 238.

76 For further information about the contacts between Delle Chiaie and other AN militants with Aginter, see *Sentenza 3 II 98 contro Rognoni*, pp. 374–84, 398–401, 413–19.

77 For these AN contacts with Aginter, see ibid., pp. 186–7; Flamini, *Partito del golpe*, volume 3:2, pp. 498–9 (Guillou check to Fabruzzi) and volume 4:2, pp. 377–8, citing a 28 September 1977 intelligence report (documents found in Rome apartment); Linklater et al., *Fourth Reich*, pp. 263, 271. Flamini identifies the occupants of the Rome apartment, which was located in the Tuscolano neighborhood, as Silvio Paulon, his wife Antonella, and her brother Vincenzo Modugno, all three of whom were AN members. Among the other materials found there inside Delle Chiaie's briefcase were various airline tickets between Spain and Latin America, London, and Paris, a photograph of Ustaša general Luburić signed by Spanish secret service operative Luis García Antonio Rodríguez, and a Costa Rican Dirección de Seguridad Nacional (National Security Directorate) identification card in the name of "Francisco Alonzo," but with Delle Chiaie's picture on it. Note also that the Banco de Panama check made out to Fabruzzi was issued by a Spanish branch of the bank. Vjekoslav Luburić was a high-ranking official of the Ustaša general staff who was later nicknamed the "Croatian Eichmann" because of the massacres he and his units perpetrated at the Jasenovac concentration camp during World War II. In 1949, he managed to flee surreptitiously through Austria and Italy to Spain, where thanks to the support provided by former División Azul commander Agustín Muñoz Grandes he managed to establish himself and live undisturbed for many years under the alias of "Vicente García Perez." In the wake of the 28 December 1959 death of his former *Poglavnik* and postwar collaborator Pavelić, he strengthened his links to international neo-Nazi networks such as CEDADE and the NOE/ENO and struggled to consolidate his leadership over certain organizations of right-wing Croatian terrorists, especially the Hrvatski Narodni Odpor (HNO: Croatian Popular Resistance). However, on the evening of 21–22 April 1969 he was assassinated inside his home at Carcagente by three or four knife-wielding assailants, probably at the behest of either the Yugoslav secret service, the Uprava Državne

Bezbednosti Armije (UDBA: Army State Security Service), or one of the rival Croatian émigré leaders with whom he was contending for preeminence (Dr. Stjepan Hefer, the cleric Branko Marić, or Vjekoslav Vrančić). See further Bogdan Krizman, *Pavelić u bjekstvu* (Zagreb: Globus, 1986), especially pp. 48–52, 454–7; Chairoff, *Dossier néo-nazisme*, pp. 163, 434; and Alain Guérin, *Les commandos de la guerre froide* (Paris: Julliard, 1967), pp. 117–19, 136. For additional information concerning the various postwar Ustašainspired paramilitary organizations, see Stephen Clissold, *Croat Separatism: Nationalism, Dissidence and Terrorism* (London: Institute for the Study of Conflict, 1979). For more on García Rodríguez, see Laurent, *Orchestre noir*, pp. 292, 295, 356; Flamini, *Partito del golpe*, volume 3:2, pp. 741–2; and Alejandro Muñoz Alonso, *El terrorismo en España: El terror frente a la convivencia pluralista en libertad* (Madrid: Planeta/Instituto de Estudios Económicos, 1982), pp. 39, 246. Aside from working for the Spanish secret service, he was a leader of the Hermandad de la Guardia de Franco organization who attended several international neo-fascist meetings – including a December 1974 NOE/ENO gathering in Lyon (along with Guillou) and a March 1976 summit meeting in Barcelona (along with Sánchez Covisa of the GCR, Blas Piñar of Fuerza Nueva, some former PIDE/DGS officials, and assorted Frenchmen and Argentines) – and seems to have been linked behind the scenes to the 23–24 May 1981 assault on the Banco Central de Barcelona. He was in fact a key figure in the "Black International," as suggested earlier. In this connection, an arrest warrant was issued for him on 29 July 1974 by Turin judge Luciano Violante, who accused him of having furnished arms to a group of Italian neo-fascists who were planning an October coup, through the intermediary of the Europreminent exportimport company owned by Salvatore Francia, an MPON leader. Francia then took refuge in Spain, initially at García Rodríguez's home in Barcelona. See Flamini, *Partito del golpe*, volume 3:2, pp. 574, 603–4; Laurent, *Orchestre noir*, p. 309; and Sánchez Soler, *Hijos del 20-N*, pp. 165–6, 200–3, who notes that he was later implicated – probably without justification – in the 1980 Rue Copernic synagogue and Bologna train station bombings. In a 2 October 1974 interview in *La Stampa*, García Rodríguez proudly described himself as a Falangist, a fascist, and a Nazi, and stated that killing people could sometimes be justified for the right goals and ideals. Nevertheless, he characterized the terrorist *stragi* in Italy as unjustifiable "murders of innocent people" and denied any involvement in them.

78 For more on ESESI, see Extraparliamentary Left Research Group, *Strage di stato: Vent'anni dopo*, pp. 244–9. The "tour" itself will be described later.

79 Perhaps the most important Spanish neo-fascists with whom Delle Chiaie entered into relations were those associated with Ernesto Milá. The "black bombardier" was introduced to Milá, one of the most interesting "national revolutionary" thinkers in Spain, and other leaders of the Partido Español Nacional Sindicalista (PENS) by Luis Antonio García Rodríguez. Milá and his comrades were apparently greatly impressed by Delle Chiaie's charisma and extensive political experience, so much so that at his suggestion they reorganized the group into five sections – operations, intelligence, press and propaganda, universities and education, and "parallel organizations" – and thence created three parallel or front organizations: the Brigada de la Fe (Brigade of the Faith), the Agrupación Excursionista Jaime I (James I [of Aragon] Tourist Association), and the Círculo Cultural España-Occidente (Spain-West Cultural Circle). PENS also published flyers attributed to the non-existent Unión Nacional Socialista Obrera (National Socialist Workers' Union). In short, with Delle Chiaie's help PENS developed an elaborate clandestine structure suitable for covert operations, and he and other AN members apparently helped provide paramilitary and *guerre révolutionnaire* training to PENS militants. After the dissolution of PENS, Milá first infiltrated and tried unsuccessfully to alter the political orientation of Fuerza Nueva and then formed the FNJ, which was also heavily influenced by the AN leader. See Casals, *Neonazis en España*, pp. 97, 103–4, 112–13. Compare Ernesto Milá, *El Frente Nacional de la Juventud en su historia y sus documentos: Un nuevo estilo en las fuerzas nacionales* (Barcelona: Alternativa, 1985), p. 92. For Delle Chiaie's right-wing contacts in South America, see Taylor Branch and Eugene M. Propper, *Labyrinth: The Sensational Story of International Intrigue in the Search for the Assassins of Orlando Letelier* (New York: Penguin,

1983), p. 327 (Patria y Libertad); Edwin Harrington and Mónica González, *Bomba en una calle de Palermo* (Santiago de Chile: Emisión, 1987), p. 379 (the Milicia); Latin America Bureau, ed., *Narcotráfico y politica: Militarismo y mafia en Bolivia* (Madrid: Instituto de Estudios Políticos para América Latina y Africa, 1982), p. 117, 136–7 (Novios); and Linklater et al., *Fourth Reich*, pp. 359–60, citing a report prepared by "Alfa" that was found in the files of a group close to Major Roberto D'Aubuisson, an ARENA activist and a key "death squad" coordinator (El Salvador).

80 See Flamini, *Partito del golpe*, volume 2, pp. 27, 79–82. I have not been able to uncover any further information about an organization called the Fronte Europeo Rivoluzionario. Either the meeting was held under the auspices of another organization, or this Fronte was unusually ephemeral, even by neo-fascist standards. As for Freda's involvement with Giovane Europa, Claudio Mutti later testified that he first encountered Freda at the organization's Bologna headquarters in 1963–1964. See *Sentenza 31 VII 76 contro Giannettini*, p. 26. Orsi also presented themes from *La disintegrazione del sistema* at a Congress of Giovane Europa, and later was himself involved in infiltrating small leftist groups. See Procura di Catanzaro, Pubblico Ministero Mariano Lombardi, *Requisitoria del giugno 1976 nel procedimento penale contro Giannettini, Guido + 16* [hereinafter *Requisitoria VI 76 contro Giannettini*], p. 21.

81 These reports are directly quoted by Flamini, *Partito del golpe*, volume 1, pp. 20–1. See also Giannuli, *Relazione 12 III 1997*, p. 147, who cites a 25 November 1963 report sent to the Italian Interior Ministry by informant "Aristo" – the code name for MSI member Armando Mortilla, who soon became the main intermediary between Rauti and Guillou – to the effect that a French paratroop lieutenant who had deserted and joined the OAS first brought Rauti to the attention of the Portuguese authorities. For the creation of an ON export-import firm that specialized in arms trafficking, compare Sassano, *Politica della strage*, p. 43, who claims it was named Mondial Import Export and was set up in 1964; and Flamini, who identifies an ON-linked firm called Mondial Export Import which was not established until 1 December 1969, although it did in fact specialize in arms trafficking to the Portuguese colony of Angola, as well as to South Africa and Rhodesia. See *Partito del golpe*, volume 2, pp. 104–5. Whether Sassano is simply incorrect, which is probable given his general imprecision, or whether we are here dealing with two successive or separate ON firms with similar names and business partners, is unclear. In any event, the conspicuous presence of Moniz Ferreira at these secret high-level negotiations in Spain suggests that he was a PIDE operative rather than a mere neo-fascist leader. For more on Muñoz Grandes, who went on to create the potent Servicio de Información del Alto Estado Mayor (Intelligence Service of the General Staff) in 1968, and his role in postwar military politics, see Preston, *Politics of Revenge*, pp. 142–58. The general's political views can be gleaned from the fact that he sent a telegram expressing his support to the neo-fascists assembled at the April 1969 NOE/ENO Congress in Barcelona. See Flamini, *Partito del golpe*, volume 2, p. 25. Among the other noteworthy persons that Rauti and Graziani met with in Madrid was Leo Negrelli, head of the Italian section of the Asociación Cristiana Ecuménica (Christian Ecumenical Association) and ON's chief correspondent in the Spanish capital. Negrelli later moved to Lisbon and became an Italian-language broadcaster for "La Voix de l'Occident," the international program on the official Radio Portugal station, in which capacity he may have transmitted coded messages from Aginter's central headquarters in Madrid to its agents in Italy. In 1967 he wrote to Guillou, informing him that two Italian comrades would be arriving in Portugal "for an exchange of ideas that can lead to interesting results" and reminding him that his own goal was still to organize operational connections on a supranational level. Compare ibid., volume 1, p. 171, and volume 2, p. 27. For the possible transmission of coded messages, see De Lutiis, *Storia dei servizi segreti in Italia*, p. 166.

82 Nevertheless, even if Rauti himself did not work for the UAR, some of his men probably did. Thus Flamini indicates, without any equivocation, that Rauti's liaison man to Aginter, Armando Mortilla, was a "valued informant" of that organization. See *Partito del golpe*, volume 1, p. 171. This has since been confirmed by official investigators.

Compare *Sentenza 3 II 98 contro Rognoni*, pp. 419–21; and Giannuli, *Relazione 12 III 1997*, pp. 164–9, who adds that Mortilla was an informant between 1955 and 1975 for several Italian entities, including the Pubblica Sicurezza corps, the Ministry of Foreign Affairs, and especially the UAR. "Aristo" mainly focused on collecting and providing information on the right, but also at times on the left. For more on the role of the UAR in covert activities, see Giacomo Pacini, *Il cuore occulto del potere: Storia dell'Ufficio affari riservati del Viminale, 1919–1984* (Rome: Nutrimenti, 2010), pp. 115–230.

83 For this struggle between the two generals, see Virgilio Ilari, *Le Forze armate tra politica e potere, 1943–1976* (Florence: Vallecchi, 1979), pp. 67–78; De Lutiis, *Storia dei servizi segreti in Italia*, pp. 76–80; and the account by MSI journalist Mario Tedeschi, *La guerra dei generali* (Milan: Borghese, 1968), especially pp. 105–41.

84 For Agenzia D, see De Lutiis, *Storia dei servizi segreti in Italia*, pp. 77–8. The 1965 conference will be discussed later.

85 For the preparation and publication of *Le mani rosse*, compare *Sentenza 31 July 76 contro Giannettini*, pp. 56–62; Tedeschi, *Guerra dei generali*, pp. 110–11; and Guido Giannettini and "Flavio Messala" (pseudonym for Pino Rauti), *Le mani rosse sulle Forze armate* (Rome: Savelli, 1975), pp. 7–49 (introduction by far left Lotta Continua commission). Note that the latter work was published by the left in order to illustrate the extremist views of the Aloja faction within the armed forces, as well as to embarrass all the parties involved in sponsoring and producing that divisive and paranoid treatise.

86 For the meetings with Plevris and the Corfu training camps, compare the interview with Plevris by Fallaci, "Si farà il colpo di stato in Italia?," p. 32; and Bašar, *Terror Dossier and Greece*, pp. 45–6. For Rauti's reception by Pattakos, a Brigadier General and former head of the Armored Training Center (KET), see Extraparliamentary Left Research Group, *Strage di stato: Vent'anni dopo*, p. 179. It should be pointed out that Plevris, aside from being the leader of the neo-fascist K4A, was the private secretary of Colonel Ladas, the former head of the ESA who was appointed secretary-general of the Ministry of Public Order after the coup. See Woodhouse, *Rise and Fall of the Greek Colonels*, p. 61. Plevris was also affiliated with Calzi's ("Chairoff's") World Service press agency, a front organization for the KYP that was funded in part by the CIA, and was allegedly the head of the KYP's Italian desk. Compare Christie, *Stefano Delle Chiaie*, pp. 39, 42; Chairoff, *Dossier néo-nazisme*, pp. 293–8; and the interview with "Chiaroff" (Calzi) in Frédéric Laurent, "Un agente della CIA parla dal carcere," *L'Europeo* 32:21 (21 May 1976), p. 38. Calzi was himself the person selected to serve as the titular head of the World Service agency, in connection with which he decided to adopt another pseudonym, "Dr. Siegfried Schönenberg."

87 For a basic account of the neo-fascist "tour" of Greece, see De Simone, *Pista nera*, pp. 9–13. Compare Flamini, *Partito del golpe*, volume 1, pp. 187–90.

88 Compare Barbieri, *Agenda nera*, pp. 115–16; De Simone, *Pista nera*, pp. 15, 52–4; and Flamini, *Partito del golpe*, volume 1, pp. 189–90.

89 For the Greek "strategy of tension," see Lentakes, *Parakratikes orgonoseis kai eikoste prote apriliou*, pp. 46–68, 140–1; Laurent, *Orchestre noir*, pp. 236–8; Barbieri, *Agenda nera*, pp. 115–17; De Simone, *Pista nera*, p. 18; Flamini, *Partito del golpe*, volume 1, pp. 147–8; and Jean Meynaud, *Rapport sur l'abolition de la démocratie en Grèce* (Montreal: Bibliographie Nationale du Quebec, 1970), pp. 221–31. Some important Greek works are Gregoriades, *Historia tes diktatorias*, 3 volumes; Kyriakos I. Diakogiannes, *Giati pera meros ste synomosia tes chountas kai tes CIA kata tou Andreou Papandreou kai tes Hellenikes demokratias* (Montreal: Patris, 1968), written by a former KYP officer; and Giorgos Karagiorgas, *Apo ton IDEA ste chounta: He pos phtasame sten 21 apriliou* (Athens: Papazeses, 1975). Documentary material from the trials of government and military functionaries accused of crimes against the Greek people after the collapse of the Colonels' regime can be found in Perikles Rodakes, ed., *Oi dikes tes chountas* (Athens: Demokratikoi Kairoi, 1975–1976), 9 volumes.

90 Meynaud, *Rapport sur l'abolition de la démocratie en Grèce*, p. 240.

91 For the close links between the CIA and KYP and/or Papadopoulos, see "Athenian" (pseudonym), *Inside the Colonels' Greece* (London: Chatto & Windus, 1972), p. 73; Maurice Goldblum, "United States Policy in Postwar Greece," in *Greece under Military Rule*, ed. by

Richard Clogg and George Yannopoulos (New York: Basic, 1972), pp. 234–5; John Iatrides, "American Attitudes toward the Political System of Postwar Greece," in *Greek-American Relations: A Critical View*, ed. by Theodore A. Couloumbis and John Iatrides (New York: Pella, 1980), pp. 66–7; John A. Katris, *Eyewitness in Greece: The Colonels Come to Power* (St. Louis: New Critics, 1971), pp. 44–6; Meynaud, *Rapport sur la abolition de la démocratie en Grèce*, pp. 249–51, 312–14; Andreas Papandreou, *Democracy at Gunpoint: The Greek Front* (Garden City: Doubleday, 1970), pp. 221–2, 226–30; Laurence Stern, *The Wrong Horse: The Politics of Intervention and the Failure of American Diplomacy* (New York: New York Times, 1977), pp. 13, 18, 23–4, 35–46; and Lawrence S. Wittner, *American Intervention in Greece, 1943–1949* (New York: Columbia University, 1982), pp. 299–301, 305–6. Compare Chairoff, *Dossier néo-nazisme*, p. 292; Flamini, *Partito del golpe*, volume 1, pp. 147–8; and Laurent, *Orchestre noir*, pp. 238–41. Other experts express doubt about Papadopoulos's alleged links to the CIA and deny that the agency played any role at all in the coup or the anti-constitutional events leading up to it, for example David Holden, *Greece without Columns: The Making of the Modern Greeks* (Philadelphia and New York: Lippincott, 1972), pp. 244–50; and Woodhouse, *Rise and Fall of the Greek Colonels*, pp. 7, 9–10, 20, 23, 27–8. However, their cautious arguments seem rather strained, and even Woodhouse is forced to admit that the CIA helped to set up the KYP in the early 1950s, that it had a relationship of "great intimacy" with the KYP, and that it exerted a "powerful influence" on its Greek counterpart. See ibid., pp. 6–7. If that was in fact the case, which presupposes that the agency had some well-placed informants within the KYP, how can one honestly believe that American intelligence knew nothing whatsoever about the coup beforehand?

92 Flamini, *Partito del golpe*, volume 1, pp. 190–1; Extraparliamentary Left Research Group, *Strage di stato: Vent'anni dopo*, p. 156; De Simone, *Pista nera*, pp. 50, 55; and Laurent, *Orchestre noir*, p. 175.

93 Plevris interview in Fallaci, "Si farà un colpo di stato in Italia?," p. 32.

94 See, for example, De Simone, *Pista nera*, p. 26; and Sassano, *Politica della strage*, p. 44. Compare *Sentenza 31 VI 76 contro Giannettini*, p. 132, for SID's report supporting that conclusion. However, a subsequent SID report, dated 5 June 1975, claimed that the Finer document was not genuine on the basis of the Greek government's denials. Note, however, that Army officer Dimitrios Bikos claimed that if the secret report published by Finer had been genuine, it would not have been found in the archives. See ibid., p. 139. For the article itself, see Finer, "Greek Premier plots Army coup in Italy," *London Observer*, 7 December 1969, pp. 1–2.

95 *Sentenza 31 VI 76 contro Giannettini*, pp. 136–44.

96 Extraparliamentary Left Research Group, *Strage di stato: Vent'anni dopo*, p. 91 (editors' introduction).

97 The reason why some suspect a right-wing forgery is that the report had originally been provided to Finer by Elena Vlachos, editor of the conservative daily *Kathimerini*, who continued to insist that the document was genuine. Compare *Sentenza 31 VI 76 contro Giannettini*, pp. 141–2; and Laurent, *Orchestre noir*, p. 210. Yet Vlachos was herself bitterly anti-junta, having been placed under house arrest following the coup. She thence escaped and emigrated to London, from where she served as an outspoken critic of the Greek regime's press censorship. See, for example, Helen Vlachos, "The Colonels and the Press," in *Greece under Military Rule*, pp. 59–74; and Helen Vlachos, *House Arrest* (Boston: Gambit, 1970).

98 D'Amato was the son of a Naples police chief who followed in his father's footsteps and joined the Pubblica Sicurezza corps during World War II. In June 1944, he was among the police officers sent northwards by the Office of Strategic Services (OSS) to make contact with, and obtain the cooperation of, high-ranking police officials of the Republic of Salò, including Guido Leto, head of the Fascist secret police. Between 1945 and 1957 D'Amato worked at the Rome Questura, mainly in the Ufficio Politico (which he headed from 1950 on). In 1957 he was assigned to the UAR, and rose rapidly through the ranks until becoming its second-in-command in 1969 and its commander in 1972. In this capacity he directed various covert operations, served as the UAR's liaison to NATO's security services (and, allegedly, to the CIA), and later became a member of Licio Gelli's

Propaganda Due (P2) masonic lodge. For his early career, see De Lutiis, *Storia dei servizi segreti in Italia*, pp. 48–9 and 54, note 46. In the next chapter, he will reappear in connection with the Borghese "coup."

99 Many of these accusations against Delle Chiaie have come from within the ranks of his own neo-fascist milieu. Thus in 1972, after Delle Chiaie submitted supportive declarations by five MSI members on his behalf to investigating magistrates, party chief Giorgio Almirante said he was sick and tired of being continually burdened with people paid by the Interior Ministry's UAR. Later that same year Mario Tedeschi argued in the weekly *Il Borghese* that if fascists were involved in the Piazza Fontana bombing, certain interior ministers, chiefs of police, and prime ministers should be in the dock with them. See De Simone, *Pista nera*, pp. 50–1. Compare Extraparliamentary Left Research Group, *Strage di stato: Vent'anni dopo*, pp. 189–90 (editors' note), where it is noted that in 1976 former members of the neofascist Organizzazione Lotta di Popolo (People's Struggle Organization) in Naples accused both AN and ON leaders of being at the service of the *corpi separati* of the state, which in turn provided them with cover and financing. Therein it is also pointed out that in 1978 members of an international Freda solidarity committee referred to Delle Chiaie as a secret service provocateur, an adventurer, and a professional assassin. MSI Senator Giorgio Pisanò also levelled harsh criticisms against the AN leader. See, for example, "Stefano delle Chiaje: Una 'sfida' da baraccone," *Candido*, new series, 8:1 (9 January 1975), p. 7, and another article in the 13 February 1975 issue of that publication. For AN's vitriolic and vulgar responses to Pisanò, see Avanguardia Nazionale, Settore Stampa e Propaganda, ed., *Cronistoria di un'infamia* (Rome: Avanguardia Nazionale, no date), passim. For examples of Delle Chiaie's denials of these charges, see Sergio Zavoli, *La notte della Repubblica* (Rome and Milan: Nuova Eri/Mondadori, 1992), pp. 64–7; the January 1983 interview he granted to journalist Enzo Biagi, portions of which are quoted by Christie, *Stefano Delle Chiaie*, pp. 130–1; and especially Stefano Delle Chiaie and Adriano Tilgher, *Un meccanismo diabolico: Stragi, servizi segreti, magistrati* (Rome: Publicondor, 1994), pp. 5–7, 278–9, and passim. One of the few principled revolutionary rightists to defend Delle Chiaie was self-confessed Peteano bomber Vincenzo Vinciguerra. According to the latter, Delle Chiaie was the target of a state-sponsored disinformation campaign designed to attribute all of the massacres from 1969 through 1980 to him. To make this convincing, they persuaded certain younger left fascist proponents of "armed spontaneanism" that the older generation of neo-fascists, especially Delle Chiaie and AN, were not genuine revolutionaries but tools of the hated bourgeois state. These attacks on Delle Chiaie by the ultras from within his own milieu helped add credence to the state's case, particularly since it conformed closely to his image as a provocateur in the far left journalistic literature. See Vinciguerra, *Ergastolo per la libertà*, pp. 56, 63–4, 66–9. Although the latter author is a very intelligent and knowledgeable insider, his assessment of Delle Chiaie, although rightly highlighting certain partisan political machinations and secret service manipulations in the 1980s (for example, Elio Ciolini's bogus revelations about Delle Chiaie and the "Organizzazione Terrorista" supposedly sponsored by P2 chief Licio Gelli – see Delle Chiaie and Tilgher, *Meccanismo diabolico*, especially pp. 149–78; and Parlamento, Commissione parlamentare d'inchiesta sulla loggia massonica P2 [hereinafter CPI/P2], *Allegati alla relazione, Serie II: Documentazione raccolti dalla commissione*, volume 7, tome 9, pp. 141–3) does not appear to accord with the facts. In his bitter narrative virtually every neo-fascist *but* Delle Chiaie is portrayed as a squalid, unprincipled lout who willingly sold his services to the security forces. Vinciguerra fails to note that radical members of AN had angrily complained about Delle Chiaie's links to the state apparatus as early as the mid-1960s – long before the government sought to discredit him and use him as a scapegoat for the yet to be launched "strategy of tension" – and he completely glosses over masses of evidence about the AN leader's work at the behest of foreign secret services, as will soon become clear. Later, however, Vinciguerra acknowledged the reality of the situation: "Avanguardia Nazionale [was] not a group opposed to the system. It [was] clearly [*perfettamente*] inserted into the battle conducted by the Italian and allied secret services against the Communist Party." See Vinciguerra, *Stato d'emergenza*, p. 200.

100 Extraparliamentary Left Research Group, *Strage di stato: Vent'anni dopo*, pp. 182–5, 189–91.
101 Norberto Valentini, *La notte della Madonna: L'Italia tragicomica dei golpe nei documenti inediti dei servizi segreti* . . . (Rome: Le Monde, 1978), pp. 22–3.
102 See, respectively, De Simone, *Pista nera*, p. 54, citing a 6 April 1972 article in *Panorama*; and Chairoff, *Dossier néo-nazisme*, p. 296. The latter author also emphasizes the close links between Guillou and these same Greek security agencies. See ibid., pp. 296–7.
103 Flamini, *Partito del golpe*, volume 1, p. 191. For CISES, see ibid., p. 178. Mondial was apparently the same company, discussed earlier, that engaged in arms trafficking with Portugal.
104 For the operational collaboration between Delle Chiaie and Colonel San Martín, see Melchor Miralles and Ricardo Arques, *Amedo: El estado contra ETA* (Barcelona: Plaza & Janes/Cambio 16, 1989), pp. 116–17; and Comite de Encuesta sobre las Violaciones de los Derechos Humanos en Europa, *El GAL: El terrorismo de estado en la Europa de las democracias. Informe de la encuesta, febrero-junio 1989* (Navarre: Txalaparta, 1990), p. 34. For the different branches of the Spanish intelligence and security services, see Luis González-Mata, *Cygne: Mémoires d'un agent secret* (Paris: Grasset, 1976), annex 2, pp. 362–9. Compare Roger Faligot and Rémi Kauffer, *Histoire mondiale du renseignement, tome 2: De la guerre froide à nos jours. Les maîtres espions* (Paris: Robert Laffont, 1994), pp. 282–8; and Sánchez Soler, *Hijos del 20-N*, pp. 148–50 (citing a 1975 report by the leftist Unión Militar Democrática), which do not always conform to the scheme in *Cygne*. The most important of these branches were the Servicio Central de Documentación de la Presidencia del Gobierno (SECED: Central Information Service of the President) and its attached Servicio de Coordinación Organización y Enlace (SCOE: Liaison, Organization, and Coordination Service), the DGS, the Brigada Central de Información (BCI: Central Intelligence Brigade) of the Police, the Servicio de Información de la Guardia Civil (SIGC: Civil Guard Intelligence Service, also known as "La Brigadilla"), Muñoz Grandes' Servicio de Información del Alto Estado Mayor (SIAEM: Intelligence Service of the General Staff), the Servicio de Información del Ejército de Tierra (SIE: Army Intelligence Service, also known as Segunda bis), and the more narrowly focused Navy and Air Force intelligence services. The Falange also had its own intelligence service, the Servicio de Información del Movimiento (Movement Intelligence Service), as did the influential Hermandad de Alféreces Provisionales (Brotherhood of the Provisional Sub-Lieutenants). Aside from the controversial work by González-Mata, only a few books deal specifically with the activities of the Spanish intelligence services, including Francisco Medina, *Las sombras del poder: Los servicios secretos de Carrero a Roldán* (Madrid: Espasa Calpe, 1995); José Ignacio San Martín, *Servicio especial: A las órdenes de Carrero Blanco, de Castellana a El Aaiún* (Barcelona: Planeta, 1983), authored by the original chief of SECED who was subsequently involved in both anti-ETA operations and the rightist "23F" coup of 23 February 1981; Manuel Cerdán and Antonio Rubio, *El "caso Interior": GAL, Roldán y fondos reservados: El triángulo negro de un ministerio* (Madrid: Temas de Hoy, 1995); Fernando Rueda and Manuel Cerdán, *La Casa. El CESID: Agentes, operaciones secretas y actividades de los espias españoles* (Madrid: Temas de Hoy, 1993); and Pilar Urbano, *Yo entré en el CESID* (Barcelona: Plaza y Janés, 1997). The last three works deal primarily with more recent activities. According to Chairoff, the head of the SIGC was none other than Salvador Bujanda, a high-ranking member of the far right Guerrilleros de Cristo Rey, whose paramilitary training camps at Onteniente (near Alicante), Mairena, Piedralaves (Madrid), and Iscar (near Valladolid) therefore operated without being disturbed by the security forces. See *Dossier néo-nazisme*, p. 170. As noted earlier, the GCR was one of the Spanish paramilitary groups that established links with the clandestine ELP and thus, however indirectly, with the Paladin Group.
105 See Miralles and Arques, *Amedo*, p. 117; and Sánchez Soler, *Hijos del 20-N*, pp. 168–9. SECED was officially established on 3 March 1972 by Carrero Blanco, at the instigation of San Martín, who was then appointed as its first chief. Previously, San Martín had

been in charge of the Organización Contrasubversiva Nacional (OCN: National Countersubversive Organization), which had been created in the spring of 1968 by General Muñoz Grandes, head of the armed forces general staff, to suppress domestic dissent. For the early history and organization of SECED, see Medina, *Sombras del poder*, pp. 21–36; and San Martín, *Servicio especial*, pp. 17–70.

106 See his interview with Sergio Zavoli, published in *Notte della Repubblica*, pp. 66–7. Compare Sánchez Soler, *Hijos del 20-N*, p. 169.

107 Linklater et al., *Fourth Reich*, p. 267.

108 For this host of Spanish paramilitary squads, see Muñoz Alonso, *Terrorismo en España*, pp. 75–6, 80–1, 241–4, etc.; Cadena, *Ofensiva neo-fascista*, pp. 173–4; Miralles and Arques, *Amedo*, p. 74 and passim chapters 2–10; and numerous articles in the Spanish newsweekly *Cambio 16* from the latter half of 1976 on up through the 1980s.

109 A partial listing of these right-wing terrorist actions can be found in Miralles and Arques, *Amedo*, pp. 763–7; and José Luis Piñuel, *El terrorismo en la transición española, 1972–1982* (Madrid: Fundamentos, 1986), pp. 142–52. It is also possible, however, that some terrorist actions attributed to Basque separatists or extreme left groups, particularly the Grupos de Resistencia Antifascistas Primero de Octubre (GRAPO: 1st of October Anti-Fascist Resistance Groups), were rightist provocations. For details concerning the anti-ETA actions carried out by the GAL and its predecessors, typically at the behest of the security services, see Miralles and Arques, *Amedo*; Alvaro Baeza López, *GAL, crimen del estado, 1982–1995* (Madrid: ABC, 1996); Eliseo Bayo, *GAL, punto final: Un testimonio inolvidable de lo que hay al otro lado del terror y de la esperanza* (Barcelona: Plaza y Janés, 1997); Cerdán and Rubio, *"Caso Interior"*; Javier García, *Los GAL al descubierto: La trama de la "guerra sucia" contra ETA* (Madrid: El País/Aguilar, 1988); José Luis Morales, *La trama del G.A.L.* (Madrid: Revolución, 1988); Comite de Encuesta, *GAL*; Antonio Rubio and Manuel Cerdán, *El origen del GAL: Guerra sucia y crimen de estado* (Madrid: Temas de Hoy, 1997); Rafael Torres Mulas, *La mirada en la nuca* (Madrid: Libertarias, 1991); Paddy Woodworth, *Dirty War, Clean Hands: ETA, the GAL and Spanish Democracy* (Cork, Ireland: Cork University Press, 2001); and a number of revelations in *Cambio 16*, for example the series of articles in "Caso GAL: El laberinto," *Cambio 16* 1209 (23 January 1995), pp. 14–37. For the political and terrorist activities of the Basques living in southern France, see Jean-François Moruzzi and Emmanuel Boulaert, *Iparretarrak: Séparatisme et terrorisme en pays basque français* (Paris: Plon, 1988). In this connection note that members of GAL were also accused, apparently falsely, of assassinating General René-Pierre Audran, the French Director of Industrial Affairs, an action originally attributed to – and claimed by – the left-wing terrorist group Action Directe. This murky tale is told by Jean-Marc Dufourg, *Section manipulation: De l'antiterrorisme à l'affaire Doucé* (Paris: Michel Lafon, 1991), pp. 75–102. For the possible manipulation of elements of GRAPO by the Spanish security forces, compare González-Mata, *Terrorismo internacional*, pp. 266–74; Muñoz Alonso, *Terrorismo en España*, pp. 77–87; and "GRAPO y CIA," *Cambio 16* 271 (20 February 1977), pp. 8–13. These claims are disputed by Rafael Gómez Parra, *GRAPO: Los hijos de Mao* (Madrid: Fundamentos, 1991), especially pp. 27–41, even though he himself provides evidence that several police agents succeeded in infiltrating GRAPO, at least temporarily.

110 For the nature of the role played by Delle Chiaie in the anti-ETA struggle, see especially Sánchez Soler, *Hijos del 20-N*, pp. 170–2. According to the 1984 testimony of neo-fascist Marco Pozzan, the AN leader organized his operational group in Spain into various sections, as was his custom. For example, Giancarlo Rognoni was put in charge of press and propaganda activities, whereas Carlo Cicuttini was assigned the task of maintaining links with key Spanish rightists. Pozzan added that the "black bombardier" sometimes pressured potential Italian "recruits" into joining parastate anti-ETA bands by using carrot-and-stick techniques. Those who failed to succumb to flattery and the lure of monetary rewards were threatened with extradition to Italy and, if necessary, denounced to the Spanish police. See Miralles and Arques, *Amedo*, p. 125. In the wake

of the 1974 Portuguese revolution, Delle Chiaie apparently placed some of the Italians he had recruited at the disposal of the Exército de Libertaçao Português (ELP). Here it should be recalled that Guillou, other Aginter Presse personnel, and a number of distressed Portuguese ultras (including many former members of the secret police) had gone underground, formed the paramilitary ELP, and established operational bases across the border in neighboring Spain.

111 For more on BVE and GAL personnel, as well as other terrorists residing in Spain who were linked to the "Black International" (including the Italian neo-fascists), see the listings in Sánchez Soler, *Hijos del 20-N*, pp. 296–324; and Miralles and Arques, *Amedo*, pp. 768–83, 786. Note that Vit (alias "André Pervins") was a former French Army officer of Czech origin who later worked as a translator for the DGS. As for Perez Revilla, he did not survive a second assassination attempt. On 15 June 1984 he was murdered in Biarritz by a mixed Franco-Portuguese GAL squad. See the latter work, pp. 79, 134, 182, 271.

112 For the assault of the *sixtinos* at Montejurra, see Sánchez Soler, *Hijos del 20-N*, pp. 176–82; Rodríguez Jiménez, *Reaccionarios y golpistas*, pp. 271–2; and especially Josep Carles Clemente and Carles S. Costa, *Montejurra 76: Encrucijada política* (Barcelona: Gaya Ciencia, 1976), pp. 101–30, which provides both a detailed account of the events and photographic evidence of the presence of ex-OAS man Jean-Pierre Cherid, Cauchi, Calzona, and other members of the BVE alongside Sixto and his closest collaborators. Among those later arrested for the resulting deaths and injuries were Sixto supporters José Arturo Márquez del Prado, former infantry commander José Luis Marín García-Verde ("the man with the gabardine raincoat" who fired the pistol shots that killed the first follower of Carlos Hugo), Alfonso Carlos Fal Macías, Domingo Fal Macías, Carlos Ferrando Sales, and José Ignacio Fernández Guaza, one of Fuerza Nueva chief Blas Piñar's bodyguards. The last named managed to take refuge abroad, the other Spaniards were released in the wake of the passage of a political amnesty law, and Sixto himself, a French citizen, was repatriated to France. Delle Chiaie not only participated directly in the Montejurra assault, but also apparently played a significant role in providing for its logistical and organizational support. See Miralles and Arques, *Amedo*, p. 123.

113 See Muñoz Alonso, *Terrorismo en España*, p. 80; and Sánchez Soler, *Hijos del 20-N*, p. 191. Compare Rodríguez Jiménez, *Reaccionarios y golpistas*, pp. 273–4, who notes that the day before the demonstration General Jaime Milans del Bosch (a right-wing ultra and close collaborator of Girón's) apparently ordered the commander of the 1st "Brunete" Armored Division to prepare a "special operations" unit for intervention in case the forces of order proved unable to control the crowd. During the actual demonstration, fascist squads pursued and assaulted left-wing marchers who had been driven away from the main body of the crowd as a result of police charges. Among those attacked in this manner was Ruiz, who was shot in the head at the corner of Calle de Silva and Calle La Estrella during a confrontation with a group of ultras that included Cesarsky, Fernández Guaza, Sierra, and the Italian "Alfredo." As in Italy, these actions seem to have been designed to create chaos and thereby provoke a military intervention and crackdown, if not an outright coup.

114 For the Atocha massacre, see Muñoz Alonso, *Terrorismo en España*, pp. 80–1; Sánchez Soler, *Hijos del 20-N*, pp. 192–6; and *La matanza de Atocha* (Madrid: Akal, 1980), which provides an abundance of details drawn from trial documents and testimony. Those who were actually brought to trial for having carried out the attack included the two assassins, José Fernández Cerrá (an ATE member who was also implicated in the murder of Arturo Ruiz) and Carlos García Juliá, a Fuerza Nueva dissident; and three of their accomplices, Fernando Lerdo de Tejada (the son of an ex-secretary of Blas Piñar), Gloria Herguedas, and Leocadio Jiménez Caravaca, a weapons expert and División Azul veteran. All had connections with Fuerza Nueva, the Hermandad de la Guardia de Franco, and Raimundo Fernández Cuesta. According to the February 1980 judicial sentence the attack stemmed from a dispute between right- and left-wing unionists, since the

presumed sponsor was the secretary of the Sindicato de Transportes (Transportation Union) in Madrid, Francisco Albadalejo Corredera. However, articles in the Italian and Spanish media on 24 and 25 March 1984 later reported, on the basis of testimony provided by an unnamed Italian *pentito* whose account was considered credible by Italian judges Pier Luigi Vigna and Alberto Macchia, that an Italian who was "well-known for his actions of criminal violence" was actually the first to open fire on the victims. This initially seemed to be an allusion to Delle Chiaie himself, but in a 13 March 1989 interview that appeared in *Tiempo*, he angrily denied being involved and accused the Spanish police – specifically police inspector Antonio González Pacheco (nicknamed "Billy el Niño," that is, "Billy the Kid"), a key organizer of the clandestine war against the ETA within the Interior Ministry – of manipulating rightist militants and instigating the attack in an effort to stabilize state power in a tense period of political transition. On 3 March 1987, a classified intelligence report prepared by the Italian Comitato Esecutivo per i Servizi di Informazione e di Sicurezza (CESIS: Executive Committee for the Security and Intelligence Services) identified Carlo Cicuttini (a member of ON, associate of Delle Chiaie, and BVE operative who was implicated along with Vincenzo Vinciguerra in the 1972 Peteano bombing in Italy) as the Italian who participated in the massacre. See Sánchez Soler, *Hijos del 20-N*, pp. 193–6.

115 For Delle Chiaie as an operative for the Spanish security services, see the testimonies of Aldo Tisei, Paolo Bianchi, Giorgio Cozi, and Sergio Calore, summarized in *Sentenza 21 III 85 contro Graziani*, pp. 270–80. Compare the revelations of some of the same individuals, plus Marco Pozzan, Vincenzo Vinciguerra, Marco Affatigato, Angelo Izzo, Valerio Viccei, Mario Ricci, Carlo Cicuttini, and Eliodoro Pomar, as well as information from Spanish intelligence reports, cited in Sánchez Soler, *Hijos del 20-N*, pp. 171–2, 186–7; and Miralles and Arques, *Amedo*, pp. 125–7.

116 See Sánchez Soler, *Hijos del 20-N*, pp. 167–8.

117 For evidence of official Spanish obstructionism, see ibid., pp. 158–9, 173–4; and Miralles and Arques, *Amedo*, pp. 128–32, who also note that those few Spanish policemen who made an honest effort to acquire information about the Italians found themselves the targets of bogus criminal prosecutions and had their careers destroyed.

118 For the trail of the MAC-10 used to murder Judge Occorsio, as well as others in the same shipment, compare Miralles and Arques, *Amedo*, pp. 118, 123, 131–5; Sánchez Soler, *Hijos del 20-N*, pp. 183–7; Linklater et al., *Fourth Reich*, pp. 269–70; and Laurent, *Orchestre noir*, p. 366. Note that Conesa and Quintero were key figures in the "dirty war" against both the ETA and the Spanish left, as the most reliable works on GAL indicate. For Calore's revelations, see *Sentenza 21 III 85 contro Graziani*, p. 274. For additional details about the Occorsio murder, see ibid.; and Tribunale di Firenze, Giudice Istruttore Alberto Corrieri, *Sentenza-ordinanza n. 337/77 nel procedimento penale contro Graziani, Clemente + 10*. For more on WerBell and his activities, see Jim Hougan, *Spooks: The Haunting of America: The Private Use of Secret Agents* (New York: Morrow, 1978), pp. 25–48 and passim; and Krüger, *Great Heroin Coup*, especially pp. 181–7.

119 For the 1974 visit of Delle Chiaie and Borghese to Chile, see Flamini, *Partito del golpe*, volume 3:2, pp. 559–60. For Major Prado's subsequent activities in Spain, see Manuel Salazar, *Contreras: Historia de un intocable* (Santiago: Grijalbo, 1995), pp. 66–70.

120 For these activities, see especially Branch and Propper, *Labyrinth*, pp. 303–5; John Dinges and Saul Landau, *Assassination on Embassy Row: The Shocking Story of the Letelier-Moffitt Murders* (New York: McGraw-Hill, 1980), pp. 154–5, 157–60; and Eugenio Ahumada and others, *Chile: La memoria prohibida. Las violaciones a los derechos humanos en Chile, 1973–1983* (Santiago: Pehuén, 1989), volume 2, pp. 150–3, 391–8.

121 For the Leighton assassination attempt and its results, see Flamini, *Partito del golpe*, volume 4:1, pp. 145–6; Dinges and Landau, *Assassination on Embassy Row*, pp. 158–63; Branch and Propper, *Labyrinth*, pp. 307–9; Linklater et al., *Fourth Reich*, pp. 272–3; and Ahumada et al., *Chile: La memoria prohibida*, volume 2, pp. 154–60; and Patricia Mayorga Marcos, *El cóndor negro: El atentado a Bernardo Leighton* (Santiago: El Mercurio/Aguilar, 2003).

According to Ahumada et al, citing the relevant Italian judicial sentence, suspicion first fell on Chilean ultras who were said to have visited Rome, including Juan Luis Bulnes Ossa, a key member of the right-wing paramilitary group Patria y Libertad. This line of inquiry, instigated by exiled Chilean leftists, failed to bear fruit. Later, the MNC's clandestine terrorist wing, known as Cero (Zero), falsely claimed responsibility for the attack in a series of communiques, making use of inside information provided to Townley and Paz by Delle Chiaie, in order to throw investigators off the track. For these details, see Ahumada et al., *Chile: La memoria prohibida*, volume 2, pp. 159–60, 400–2.

122 Branch and Propper, *Labyrinth*, p. 314; and Linklater et al., *Fourth Reich*, p. 273. This was later confirmed by Townley himself, in two 1979 (26 April and 23 August) letters he wrote from prison in the United States to his Chilean "contact," Gustavo Etchepare. Cited in Ahumada et al., *Chile: La memoria prohibida*, volume 2, p. 392. In the wake of this high-level meeting in Madrid, Delle Chiaie made two more visits to Chile, one in December 1975 together with Major Prado and two other Italians, and another in the fall of 1976, when he met with Chilean fascists from the Movimiento Revolucionario Nacional Sindicalista (MRNS: National Syndicalist Revolutionary Movement), the Partido Obrero Nacional Socialista Chileno (National Socialist Chilean Workers' Party), the Acción Nacionalista Revolucionaria (ANR: Revolutionary Nationalist Action), Patria y Libertad, Tacna, and others. At one such meeting, Delle Chiaie was put on the spot by various radical Chilean fascists, who viewed Pinochet as a representative of "one of the most dirty forms of capitalism," but in spite of this the Italian continued to express cautious support for the dictator. See Salazar, *Contreras*, pp. 72–5. In the end this unanticipated dispute prevented Delle Chiaie from collaborating with his Chilean counterparts (other than MRNS factional leader Misael Galleguillos), and made him so angry that he later urged Contreras to eliminate dissident neo-fascist elements, starting with ANR chief Erwin Robertson Rodríguez. Although Contreras decided not to follow this unsolicited advice, the fact that "il Caccola" even recommended the adoption of such repressive measures against his erstwhile comrades surely undercuts his claim to be a genuine revolutionary.

123 After his flight to Santiago in 1977, Delle Chiaie took temporary refuge in a house on Calle Via Naranja in the city's Lo Curro barrio, where DINA had established an operational base and interrogation center. Among those who frequented this locale were Townley and Chilean Army intelligence officer Eugenio Berríos, who was entrusted with manufacturing quantities of the deadly chemical warfare agent sarin. See Samuel Blixen, *El vientre del Cóndor: Del archivio del terror al caso Berríos* (Montevideo: Brecha, 1994), p. 25. For the AIP and/or some glimpses of Delle Chiaie's work for DINA in Latin America, see Branch and Propper, *Labyrinth*, p. 314; Linklater et al., *Fourth Reich*, pp. 348, 358; Harrington and González, *Bomba en una calle de Palermo*, pp. 380, 383–4; Dinges and Landau, *Assassination on Embassy Row*, p. 177 and note; Salazar, *Contreras*, p. 75; Ahumada et al., *Chile: La memoria prohibida*, volume 2, pp. 392 (citing a 26 April 1979 Townley letter to Etchepare); and Gerardo Irusta Medrano, *Espionaje y servicios secretos en Bolivia, 1930–1980: "Operación Condor" en acción* (La Paz: Self-published, 1995), pp. 374–6. After arriving in Buenos Aires, Delle Chiaie and his countrymen worked under the supervision of DINA officer Jorge Werner (nicknamed "El Pelao"), who had already recruited Roberto Eladio Acuña and other Argentine ultras associated with the Milicia group. In late January 1977 Delle Chiaie (alias "Alfredo Supo"), Pierluigi Pagliai (alias "Marcos"), a Belgian named Jean-Pierre and his wife Teresa, a Spaniard named Carlos or Luis, and Acuña traveled to Lima and gathered intelligence on Peruvian geographical features and military installations. The Italians were well paid for this work, and after returning to Argentina may have continued to spy for Chile.

124 Ignacio González Janzen, *La Triple-A* (Buenos Aires: Contrapunto, 1986), pp. 93–106, although he also identifies one of those who exerted a baleful influence on López Rega as former Ustaše secret service official Mile Ravlić (alias "Milosz de Bogetich"), who settled in Argentina after World War II and later formed part of Perón's inner circle in

Spain. See ibid., pp. 77–85. Compare Rogelio García Lupo, *Paraguay de Stroessner* (Buenos Aires: Zeta, 1989), pp. 212–13.
125 For the Milicia, see Dinges and Landau, *Assassination on Embassy Row*, pp. 140, 184; and Martin Edwin Anderson, *Dossier Secreto: Argentina's Desaparecidos and the Myth of the "Dirty War"* (Boulder: Westview, 1993), pp. 146, 241–3, 353–4, note 16. For Delle Chiaie's collusion with elements of this group, in particular Martín Ciga Correia, see Dinges and Landau, *Assassination on Embassy Row*, p. 177; and Harrington and González, *Bomba en una calle de Palermo*, pp. 379, 384–94.
126 Linklater et al., *Fourth Reich*, pp. 358–60. Note, however, that French military officers taught *guerre révolutionnaire* techniques directly to their South American counterparts, including in Argentina and Chile. See Marie-Monique Robin, *Escadrons de la mort, l'école française* (Paris: Découverte, 2004), part 2. Hence one should probably not overestimate the impact of former OAS operatives or European neo-fascists in this context. For Argentina's key role in the subsequent hemisphere-wide diffusion of "dirty war" techniques and the training of other Latin American security forces, see Ariel C. Armony, *Argentina, the United States, and the Anti-Communist Crusade in Central America, 1977–1984* (Miami: Ohio University Center for International Studies, 1996).
127 For more on WACL, see especially Scott Anderson and Jon Lee Anderson, *Inside the League: The Shocking Exposé of How Terrorists, Nazis, and Latin American Death Squads Have Infiltrated the World Anti-Communist League* (New York: Dodd Mead, 1986), the only full-length study of this important international organization.
128 For the participation of Massagrande and Delle Chiaie, respectively, at the 1979 WACL and 1980 CAL gatherings, see ibid., pp. 101, 147. Others have claimed that Delle Chiaie also made an appearance at the WACL conference, although this remains uncertain.
129 Christie, *Stefano Delle Chiaie*, p. 97. For "Operación Cóndor," see Blixen, *Vientre del Cóndor*; Stella Calloni, *Los años del lobo: Operación Cóndor* (Buenos Aires: Continente, 1999); Alejandro Carrio, *Los crímenes del Cóndor: El caso Prats y la trama de conspiraciones entre los servicios de inteligencia del Cono Sur* (Buenos Aires: Sudamericana, 2005); Alfonso Lessa, *Los espías de la basura* (Montevideo: Monte Sexto, 1988); Nilson Mariano, *Operación Cóndor: Terrorismo de estado en el Cono Sur* (Buenos Aires: Lohlé Lumen, 1998); Gladys Marín, *Regreso a la esperanza: Derrota de la Operación Cóndor* (Santiago: ICAL, 1999); Francisco Martorell, *Operación Cóndor: El vuelo de la muerte. La coordinación represiva en el Cono Sur* (Santiago: Lom, 1999); J. Patrice McSherry, *Predatory States: Operation Condor and Covert War in Latin America* (Lanham, MD: Rowman & Littlefield, 2005), a partisan scholarly work; Gladys Meilinger de Sannemann, *Paraguay y la "Operación Cóndor" en los "Archivios del Terror"* (Asunción: n.p., 1994); Irusta Medrano, *Espionaje y servicios secretos en Bolivia*, pp. 261–384; Alfredo Boccia Paz, Myrian Angélica González, and Rosa Palau Aguilar, *Es mi informe: Los archivios secretos de la Polícia de Stroessner* (Asunción: Centro de Documentación y Estudios, 1994), pp. 249–336; Andersen, *Dossier Secreto*, pp. 228–30; Edward S. Herman, *The Real Terror Network: Terrorism in Fact and Propaganda* (Boston: South End, 1982), pp. 69–73; and Soviet propagandist Valentin K. Mashkin, *Operación Cóndor: Su rastro sangriento* (Buenos Aires: Cartago, 1985), which should be used with the degree of caution befitting such polemical works. See also the growing collection of documents concerning "Operación Cóndor" housed at the National Security Archive in Washington, DC, many of which can be accessed on the organization's useful website: www.gwu.edu/~nsarchiv. In his discussion of the origins of the Condor "system," Irusta enumerates seven different theories concerning the primary sponsors of the operation: (1) clandestine neo-Nazi networks; (2) the Argentine military; (3) Chilean military circles; (4) Paraguayan police agencies; (5) the CIA; (6) Latin American army chiefs in the course of one of their annual meetings between 1969 (at Fort Bragg) and 1973 (in Caracas); and (7) the leaders of Colonia Dignidad, a cult-like religious colony established by ex-Nazis in Chile that collaborated actively with military hard-liners in that country. See Irusta Medrano, *Espionaje y servicios secretos en Bolivia*, pp. 279–88. It is now clear, however, that the Chilean secret service first proposed this scheme in early

1974. Although U.S. intelligence agencies apparently facilitated the development of some of its precursors, provided those services with advanced communications equipment, soon became aware of Condor itself, and sometimes appear to have supported its activities tacitly, there is no clear evidence as yet that they actually instigated them. For more on Colonia Dignidad, see Bruce Falconer, "Torture Colony," *The American Scholar* (Autumn 2008), available at http://theamericanscholar.org/the-torture-colony/; Carlos Basso Prieto, *El último secreto de Colonia Dignidad* (Santiago: Mare Nostrum, 2002); Friedrich Paul Heller, ed., *Colonia Dignidad: Von der Psychosecte zum Folterlager* (Stuttgart: Schmetterling, 1993); Friedrich Paul Heller, *Lederhosen, Dutt und Giftgas: Die Hintergründe der Colonia Dignidad* (Stuttgart: Schmetterling, 2006); Maria Poblete and Frédéric Ploquin, *La colonie du docteur Schaefer: Une secte nazie au pays de Pinochet* (Paris: Fayard, 2004); Claudio R. Salinas and Hans Stange, *Los amigos del "Dr." Schäfer: La complicidad entre el estado chileno y Colonia Dignidad* (Santiago: Debate, 2006); Dieter Maier, *"Äusserste Zurückhaltung" – die Colonia Dignidad und die deutsche Diplomatie, 1961–1978. Eine Akteneinsicht im Auswärtigen Amt, Berlin* (Nurenberg: Nürnburger Menschenrechtszentrum, 2008); and Gero Gemballa, *Colonia Dignidad: Ein Reporter auf den Spuren eines deutschen Skandals* (Frankfurt: Campus, 1998).

130 Linklater et al., *Fourth Reich*, p. 271. Note also that Ovando Candía had formerly been involved in Barbie's abortive Transmarítima Boliviana project. See ibid., p. 289. It is also worth emphasizing that Argentine "advisors" had already become influential in Bolivia, and had worked especially closely with the military hard-liners headed by García Mesa, after the November 1979 putsch of Colonel Alberto Natusch Busch. See Irusta Medrano, *Espionaje y servicios secretos en Bolivia*, p. 358.

131 See Andersen, *Dossier Secreto*, p. 290. Aspects of the careers of Valín and Moiri are worth noting. Valín had earlier served as an advisor for Nicaraguan dictator Anastasio Somoza's notorious Guardia Nacional (National Guard), and later helped organize and direct the Frente Democratico Nicaraguense's (FDN: Nicaraguan Democratic Front) anti-Sandinista campaign. Perhaps even more ominously, he was purportedly the "handler" of Montonero guerrilla leader Mario Firmenich, a possible double agent affiliated with the Argentine Army's Batallón 601. For his part, Moiri was a member of the right-wing Unification Church of Sun Myung Moon and served as Secretary of the CAL conference attended by Delle Chiaie in Buenos Aires. Later on, he was involved in several major corruption scandals. See Armony, *Argentina, the United States, and the Anti-Communist Crusade*, pp. 23, 82, 129–30, 162, 257 (note 84), and 259 (note 98). For the Argentine role in the Bolivian coup, see ibid., pp. 29–32; Asociación de Familiares de Detenidos, Desaparecidos y Martires por la Liberación Nacional (ASOFAMD), *Acusación a la dictadura del narcotráfico* (La Paz: Gráficas, 1993), pp. 85–6; Latin America Bureau, ed., *Narcotráfico y politica*, pp. 105–7.

132 For the Novios de la Muerte, see Latin America Bureau, ed., *Narcotráfico y politica*, pp. 112–25, 136–44; ASOFAMD, *Acusación a la dictadura*, pp. 90–5; Carlo Rossella, "Un uomo in vendita," *Panorama* 20:857 (27 September 1982), pp. 82–91; Linklater et al., *Fourth Reich*, pp. 350–7, 371–9; Jürgen Roth and Berndt Ender, *Geschäfte und Verbrechen der Politmafia: Eine kritische Bestandsaufnahme des internationalen Dunkelmännerwesen* (Berlin: IBDK, 1987), pp. 222–5; and Kai Hermann, "Eine Killer-Karriere [part 5]," *Der Stern* 37:24 (6 June 1984). Among the personnel in this undisciplined paramilitary squad were Fiebelkorn himself, a Bundeswehr deserter and ex-member of the Kampfbund Deutscher Soldaten who had also served for a time in the Legión Española (Spanish Legion); former Gestapo officer Hans Stellfeld; Adolfo Ustares Ferreira, a Bolivian lawyer linked to the drug barons; Fernando "Mosca" Monroy, an ex-Falange Socialista Boliviana (Bolivian Socialist Phalanx) militant; Waffen-SS veterans Herbert "Ike" Kopplin and Hans-Jürgen Lewandowski; Manfred Kuhlmann, a German from Rhodesia; Austrian mercenary Wolfgang Walterkirche; and ex-OAS man Jacques "Napoleon" Leclerc. A four-man Belgian paramilitary group headed by the famous mercenary Jean Schramme also may have been incorporated somewhere into the Bolivian security apparatus. See

Latin America Bureau, ed., *Narcotráfico y politica*, pp. 122–3; and ASOFAMD, *Acusación a la dictadura*, p. 84. It is very difficult to determine the precise organizational structure, not to mention the exact chain of command, of the various paramilitary groups involved in the 1980 Bolivian coup. Apparently, there were several different paramilitary bands operating under the aegis of the Interior Ministry and/or Department 2. The most important of these was the Servicio Especial de Seguridad (SES: Special Security Service), headed by Colonel Fernando ("Freddy") Quiroga, which seems to have been a parallel "special operations" unit staffed (at least in part) by active-duty Bolivian military officers. It was officially under the command of the Interior Ministry's Comando de Operaciones Conjuntas (COC: Combined Operations Command) – or, according to others, Department 2 – and collaborated closely on an operational level with the same ministry's Departamento de Orden Social (DOS: Department of Social Order). Under the loose supervision of Department 2 were several exclusively civilian paramilitary groups, including the Grupos Operacionales Especiales (GOES: Special Operational Groups) and the Novios de la Muerte. The first of these was probably composed entirely of Bolivian nationals, whereas the latter was the aforementioned mixed international band of Latin American and European neo-fascists and mercenaries. Compare ibid., pp. 81–100 and 101–6 (organizational charts); Latin America Bureau, ed., *Narcotráfico y politica*, pp. 100–12, 126–35; Pablo Ramos Sanchez, *Radiografía de un golpe de Estado: Otra vez la democracia en peligro* (La Paz: Puerta del Sol, 1983); and Federico Aguiló, *"Nunca Mas" para Bolivia* (Cochabamba: Asamblea Permanente de los Derechos Humanos de Bolivia, 1993), pp. 261–4.

133 Quoted in Aguiló, *"Nunca mas" para Bolivia*, p. 295. For the coup and Delle Chiaie's role in it, see ibid., pp. 245–91; ASOFAMD, *Acusación a la dictadura*, pp. 66–173; Linklater et al., *Fourth Reich*, pp. 362–9; Christie, *Stefano Delle Chiaie*, pp. 97–107; Latin America Bureau, ed., *Narcotráfico y politica*, pp. 136–7; Irusta Medrano, *Espionaje y servicios secretos en Bolivia*, pp. 376–8; and Michael Levine, *The Big White Lie: The Deep Cover Operation that Exposed the CIA Sabotage of the Drug War: An Undercover Odyssey* (Emeryville, CA: Thunder's Mouth Press, 1993), pp. 55–60. The human costs of the coup and subsequent campaigns of repression are tallied in Aguiló, *"Nunca mas" para Bolivia*, pp. 326–52. According to this source, 3,426 Bolivians became political prisoners, 36 were assassinated, 160 were killed in massacres, 87 were "disappeared," 554 were wounded, and 221 were tortured by the *golpista* regime.

134 See, respectively, Linklater et al., *Fourth Reich*, pp. 369–71; and Irusta Medrano, *Espionaje y servicios secretos en Bolivia*, p. 378.

135 For the active role of the new Bolivian junta, and the Novios themselves, in drug trafficking, see Linklater et al., *Fourth Reich*, pp. 371–7; Latin America Bureau, ed., *Narcotráfico y politica*, pp. 46–100; and Irusta Medrano, *Espionaje y servicios secretos en Bolivia*, p. 380; and ASOFAMD, *Acusación a la dictadura*, passim.

136 For the fates of Pagliai and Delle Chiaie in Bolivia, see Linklater et al., *Fourth Reich*, pp. 383–98; Christie, *Stefano Delle Chiaie*, pp. 124–8; and Irusta Medrano, *Espionaje y servicios secretos en Bolivia*, pp. 378–80. Compare Delle Chiaie and Tilgher, *Meccanismo diabolico*, pp. 193–5.

137 For his judicial "privileges," see Sandro Acciari, "L'imputato speciale," *L'Espresso* 33:14 (12 April 1987), pp. 24–6.

138 Cipriani and Cipriani, *Sovranità limitata*, pp. 54–5, 65–6. Note that other rightists associated with the 4th Alpine Army Corps also became key protagonists in later acts of terrorism, for example Elio Massagrande (ON), Massimiliano Fachini (Freda cell), Sandro Rampazzo (Rosa dei Venti), Eugenio Rizzato (Rosa dei Venti), and former "white" partisan Carlo Fumagalli (Movimento di Azione Rivoluzionaria). The director of the Passo Pennes paramilitary camp near Bolzano was Fernando Petracca, a former MSI member who headed the Volontari Nazionali (National Volunteers); the instructor there was former paratrooper Giuseppe Brancato. It turned out that Zappulla was himself a member of the "Gladio" stay/behind network.

139 For an overly sympathetic overview of Giannettini's career by an author who described him as a "friend, a confidant, and above all a teacher" (p. 13), see Pace, *Piazza Fontana*, pp. 23–67. In addition to confirming some of the details discussed later in that overview, this work has additional value inasmuch as it reprints (on pp. 68–310) several of the reports that Giannettini prepared for SID, as well as letters he wrote to General Gianadelio Maletti and to Catanzaro Investigating Magistrate Gianfranco Migliaccio.

140 See, for example, the interview with him in Sandro Ottolenghi, "Il fascista Giannettini confessa," *L'Europeo* 30:26 (27 June 1974), pp. 40, 44. For the revealing diary, see *Sentenza 31 VII 76 contro Giannettini*, p. 299, note 1.

141 Compare François Duprat, *L'Ascension du MSI* (Paris: Sept Couleurs, 1972), pp. 78–9; Flamini, *Partito del golpe*, volume 1, p. 61; Laurent, *Orchestre noir*, pp. 104, 193, note 1; and González-Mata, *Terrorismo internacional*, p. 161.

142 Ottolenghi, "Il fascista Giannettini confessa," pp. 42, 44. There he claimed that he had conducted an investigation into Guillou on behalf of SID, but discovered that the latter was nothing more than the director of a press agency! This alone should make one leery about his testimony given the many reports concerning his prior personal interactions with Guillou.

143 ROS, *Attività sulle . . . Aginter Presse*, pp. 108–9; and *Sentenza 3 II 98 contro Rognoni*, pp. 373–4. Curiously, Souètre (alias "Michael Mertz" and "Michel Roux") has also been linked by various sources to the assassination of JFK. See, e.g., the non-scholarly book by Peter Kross, *JFK: The French Connection* (Kempton, IL: Adventures Unlimited, 2012), especially chapter 7 therein for more information on Souètre.

144 See the interview with González-Mata in Ottolenghi, "I rapporti tra Giannettini e la CIA," pp. 20–1. It should also be recalled that a file card on Giannettini was found in the Aginter archives.

145 Ottolenghi, "Il fascista Giannettini confessa," p. 41. But compare *Sentenza 31 VII 76 contro Giannettini*, pp. 74–5, where the judges conclude that Giannettini and Rauti probably entered into contact with Freda and the latter's associate Giovanni Ventura in 1966, since the two Padua-area residents were found to have distributed some anti-constitutional Nuclei di Difesa dello Stato flyers; and Flamini, *Partito del golpe*, volume 1, p. 60, wherein it is noted that Freda's name appeared in Giannettini's diary entry for 8 August 1964.

146 *Requisitoria VI 76 contro Giannettini*, p. 46.

147 Quoted in Flamini, *Partito del golpe*, volume 1, pp. 92–3; and González-Mata, *Terrorismo internacional*, p. 161.

148 Compare De Lutiis, *Storia dei servizi segreti in Italia*, pp. 160, 164; Sandro Ottolenghi, "Chi è l'agente Z?," *L'Europeo* 30:35 (29 August 1974), p. 24; René Monzat, *Enquêtes sur la droite extrême* (Paris: Le Monde, 1992), p. 91; and Cipriani and Cipriani, *Sovranità limitata*, p. 127, citing an unpublished manuscript written by former OSS officer Peter Tompkins. For more on Del Valle, see *Semper Fidelis: An Autobiography* (Hawthorne CA: Christian Book Club of America, 1976). Del Valle's personal papers are now housed in the archives of the University of Oregon library.

149 Flamini, *Partito del golpe*, volume 1, pp. 59–60. It should be noted that the 3rd Army Corps was charged, among other tasks, with conducting anti-subversive operations under the aegis of NATO. Some of its personnel were later implicated in various incidents of anti-constitutional right-wing violence, so much so that the corps was officially disbanded due to its growing notoriety. This is a topic worthy of further examination.

150 For AMSAR, see De Lutiis, *Storia dei servizi segreti in Italia*, p. 164. Giannettini specifically identified these two men in his testimony to the Italian judicial authorities. See *Requisitoria VI 76 contro Giannettini*, p. 47; and *Sentenza 31 VII 76 contro Giannettini*, pp. 35, 169 (an allusion to SDECE). Both De Roux and Parvulesco were fairly well-known literary figures in francophone and occultist circles. See, for example, *Présence de Dominique De Roux* (Lausanne: L'Age d'Homme, 1986), which provides a chronology of his life (pp. 7–14), a list of his publications (pp. 133–7), a self-portrait (pp. 17–21), and some interesting material on his political ideas (pp. 39–41, 67–73, 83–106, 117–19); and *Cahiers Jean Parvulesco* (Pamier: Nouvelles Litteratures Européennes, 1989), which also includes some insights

into his politics (pp. 114–16, 201–56) and a photograph of Parvulesco alongside Ezra Pound (p. 296). Perhaps their most famous books are De Roux's *Le cinquième empire: Roman* (Paris: Belfond, 1977), a fictional paean to Portugal and her empire, and Parvulesco's *Le soleil rouge de Raymond Abellio* (Paris: Guy Trédaniel, 1987), wherein he notes that Guido Giannettini urged him to focus on Abellio's *political* biography (p. 11). For more on Parvulesco's ideas, see Godwin, *Arktos*, pp. 73–6. From other sources, we learn that De Roux was the scion of an aristocratic family and a senior French intelligence officer who, among other things, served as Jonas Savimbi's chief advisor in his struggle against the Marxist regime in Angola. See Faligot and Krop, *La Piscine*, pp. 340–1; Gordon Winter, *Inside BOSS: South Africa's Secret Police* (Harmondsworth: Penguin, 1981), pp. 539–40; Monzat, *Enquêtes sur la droite extrême*, pp. 36–41. According to an "informed observer" quoted in the first of these sources, De Roux "took a wicked pleasure in carrying out covert agitation and devising clandestine operations." He was also closely linked to neo-fascist "solidarist" circles in France. For his own response to the embarrassing Giannettini revelations, see the interview in Ferdinando Scianna, "Un editore di destra," *L'Europeo* 31:4 (23 January 1975), pp. 26–7. Therein he expressed doubts that someone named "Guérin-Sérac" even existed, but acknowledged that Aginter Presse was a "section" (*ufficio*) of PIDE. Perhaps more importantly, he admitted that every country has "parallel espionage sections like that agency which are attached to the official secret services." See ibid., p. 27. As for Parvulesco, according to Giannettini, he worked not for SDECE, which was more pro-American and Atlanticist, but for the French internal security service, the Direction de la Surveillance du Territoire (DST: Territorial Surveillance Directorate), which was perhaps more nationalist and Gaullist. See ROS, *Annotazione sulle . . . Aginter Presse*, p. 107. Parvulesco's involvement in international anti-communist networks is also revealed in his own correspondence. For example, in a 10 May 1962 letter to James Burnham, the former American Trotskyist turned anti-communist who thereafter became involved in many covert projects during the Cold War, Parvulesco identified himself as the chief of the "external apparatus" of a Europe- and Latin America-based organization called the Organisation de l'Armée Secrète "Charlemagne," which (according to that same organization's 23 April 1962 intelligence report, also sent to Burnham by Parvulesco) claimed to represent the "European, Catholic, and social revolutionary current" within the OAS, the current opposed to the Salan/Gardy faction. In his letter, Parvulesco suggested that Burnham collaborate with the OAS Charlemagne group and urged the American to meet with him in Madrid – where Parvulesco then lived – the next time he was in Europe. After meeting with an American recommended by Burnham in Spain, Robert Minelli, Parvulesco (using the pseudonym "Pierre-André Manda") wrote Burnham another letter on 2 June 1962, in which he revealed that the OAS Charlemagne group was only the "visible tip" of another secret organization whose highest echelon was known as AMSAR, the very group later identified by Giannettini. AMSAR itself comprised an external apparatus, an internal apparatus, and an intelligence apparatus called the Direction Générale de la Conjoncture Atlantique (DGCA: Directorate General of the Atlantic Conjuncture), a name which clearly reveals its Atlanticist geopolitical orientation. Indeed, Parvulesco argued in this second letter that a united Atlantic Community was alone capable of saving the West at this moment of crisis. AMSAR therefore hoped to undertake intelligence and other types of operations in cooperation with NATO, including operations beyond the Iron Curtain. Finally, in a 3 June 1962 letter written to William F. Buckley Jr., editor of *The National Review*, "Manda" indicated that Giannettini was his organization's chief in Italy and that the Italian would henceforth be contacting Buckley using the pseudonym "Marjorie Levin." All of these French-language documents can be found in the Hoover Institution Archives, James Burnham collection, Box 10, folder (Subject File) 5: OAS "Charlemagne."

151 For details about Giannettini's employment by SID, see *Requisitoria VI 76 contro Giannettini*, pp. 28–81; *Sentenza 31 VII 76 contro Giannettini*, pp. 53–72; and Flamini, *Partito del golpe*, volume 1, pp. 125–6, 129, 132–3, 179, 185–6, 199. A number of things are worth noting here. First of all, Giannettini was first hired by Ufficio R, the branch of SID concerned with foreign intelligence analysis and related activities (which also

bureaucratically housed various secret intelligence and paramilitary apparatuses, including "Gladio"). This makes sense, given Giannettini's special interests in geopolitical affairs. His transfer to Ufficio D, the defensive action arm of SID that was primarily concerned with internal security, therefore suggests that the nature of his work for SID had shifted. In the earliest phases, he had essentially done public relations work by writing articles in the rightist press which Aloja's faction wanted published, but his later tasks seem to have involved not only the gathering of intelligence on the Italian far left – as he claimed – but also the manipulation of neo-fascist and Maoist formations in accordance with the tenets of unconventional warfare. Moreover, he claims to have submitted hundreds of reports to SID, whereas officials of the service insisted that he only provided them with a few reports of scarce intelligence value. Those that later became public are rather bizarre and seem to conform to the latter description, although they were probably designed for the purposes of infiltration and provocation rather than to provide serious information to SID itself, but it could well be that these were released precisely to substantiate the claim that Giannettini's work for SID was of little importance. However that may be, several later heads of SID and Ufficio D, including Admiral Henke, Colonel Viola, Colonel Gasca Queirazza, failed to terminate his employment. If they really believed that his work was shoddy and insignificant, why was this the case?

152 *Requisitoria VI 76 contro Giannettini*, p. 39.
153 For a summary of the contents of this important SIFAR study, which was only recently declassified in connection with the "Gladio" investigation, see Cipriani and Cipriani, *Sovranità limitata*, pp. 68–73; and Giannuli, *Relazione 12 III 97*, pp. 73–81. In fact, Giannettini was himself the author of Part 1 ("L'offesa") and Part 2 ("La parata e la risposta") of this manual; the author of Part 3 ("La guerriglia") was Lieutenant Colonel Tommaso Argiolas. See ibid., pp. 73–4.
154 Giannettini, "La varietà delle tecniche nella condotta della guerra rivoluzionaria," in *La guerra rivoluzionaria: Il terzo conflitto mondiale è già cominciato*, ed. by Eggardo Beltrametti (Rome: Volpe, 1965), especially pp. 152, 155–68.
155 Quoted by De Lutiis, *Storia dei servizi segreti in Italia*, p. 168.
156 Flamini, *Partito del golpe*, pp. 78–9, quoting the testimony of AN member Paolo Pecoriello, who also noted that AN's leaders were in close contact with elements of the Interior Ministry, SIFAR, and Luigi Gedda's Comitati Civici (Civic Committees), a vast organization of lay Catholics sponsored by right-wing factions within the Vatican.
157 *Sentenza 31 VII 76 contro Giannettini*, p. 258. However, the verdicts in this case were appealed over and over until all of the defendants were acquitted – decades after the events for which they had originally been brought to trial! – on the basis of the "insufficient evidence" formula.
158 The backgrounds of these directors of the institute are worth noting. De Boccard was a right-wing Catholic who sought to reconcile Christian doctrine with the traditionalist but essentially "pagan" views of Evola. He had been a GNR militiaman during the Salò period, had then drifted into various postwar neo-fascist groups, and reportedly became one of the intermediaries between the Vatican and U.S. ambassador Clare Booth Luce during the height of the Cold War. See Giovanni Tassani, *La cultura politica della destra cattolica* (Rome: Coines, 1976), pp. 115–16, note 33; and Barbieri, *Agenda nera*, p. 96, note 44. Beltrametti was a journalist who regularly contributed to right-wing publications like the illustrated weekly *Il Borghese* and the daily *Il Tempo*, and was also the author, among other works, of an interesting book on military strategy, *Contestazione e megatoni* (Rome: Volpe, 1971). Together with Rauti and Finaldi, he was implicated in the anti-constitutional Nuclei di Difesa dello Stato affair. For his part, Finaldi wrote for *Lo Specchio*. All three were among the eighty-one journalists listed as having been financed by SID (and its predecessor). See De Lutiis, *Storia dei servizi segreti in Italia*, pp. 177 and 189–90, note 99.
159 Flamini, *Partito del golpe*, volume 1, p. 84. Indeed, Giannuli rightly noted that similar themes had been promoted in other anti-communist conferences or fora, as well as in official military counterinsurgency materials, in the years prior to the Istituto Pollio conference. See Giannuli, *Relazione 12 III 97*, pp. 17–21.

160 Barbieri, *Agenda nera*, p. 94.
161 Finaldi, "Inaugurazione del Convegno," in *Guerra rivoluzionaria*, p. 16.
162 For this conference, whose significance every informed observer highlights, see Flamini, *Partito del golpe*, volume 1, pp. 83–93; Barbieri, *Agenda nera*, pp. 94–9; De Simone, *Pista nera*, pp. 29–34; Roberto Chiarini and Paolo Corsini, *Da Salò a Piazza della Loggia: Blocco d'ordine, neofascismo, radicalismo di destra a Brescia, 1945–1974* (Milan: Angeli, 1985), pp. 247–51; Tassani, *Cultura politica della destra cattolica*, pp. 112–18; and Laurent, *Orchestre noir*, pp. 201–8.
163 This was not only apparent from the subtitle of the proceedings – "the Third World War has already begun" – but was also repeatedly emphasized by the speakers. See, for example, Finaldi, "Inaugurazione del Convegno," pp. 12–13; Giannettini, "Varietà delle tecniche," p. 169 (citing Suzanne Labin!); Pio Filippani Ronconi, "Ipotesi per una controrivoluzione," p. 243; Eggardo Beltrametti, "Squardo riassuntivo," p. 259; and "Documento conclusivo," pp. 262–3.
164 Compare Enrico De Boccard, "Lineamenti ed interpretazione storica della guerra rivoluzionaria," pp. 21–2; Beltrametti, "La guerra rivoluzionaria: Filosofia, linguaggio e procedimenti. Accenni ad un prasseologia per la risposta," pp. 66–7; Giannettini, "Varietà della tecniche," pp. 152–3; Vanni Angeli, "L'azione comunista nel campo dell'informazione," pp. 190–1; Fausto Gianfranceschi, "L'arma della cultura nella guerra rivoluzionaria," p. 197; Ivan Matteo Lombardo, "Guerra comunista permanente contro l'occidente," pp. 205, 212–15; and "Documento conclusivo," pp. 262–3. Vittorio De Biasi, in particular, focused on the communist technique of setting up parallel hierarchies and front groups. See "Necessità di un'azione concreta contro la penetrazione comunista," pp. 222–9. Compare Giannettini, "Varietà delle tecniche," pp. 161–7.
165 Compare Beltrametti, "Guerra rivoluzionaria," pp. 69–82; Giorgio Pisanò, "Guerra rivoluzionaria in Italia, 1943–1945," p. 127; Alfredo Cattabiani, "Un'esperienza controrivoluzionaria dei cattolici francesi," pp. 143–7 (using the propaganda campaigns and cellular organization of the French integralists associated with Cité Catholique as a model); Gianfranceschi, "Arma della cultura," p. 201; and "Documento conclusivo," p. 264. And Giannettini, Rauti, and Clemente Graziani rightly pointed out that democratic juridical and constitutional systems themselves allowed the communists to *legally* penetrate, undermine, and subvert the state's administrative apparatus. See Giannettini, "Varietà delle tecniche," p. 164; Rauti, "La tattica della penetrazione comunista in Italia," pp. 93–4; and Graziani, "Appunti per una risposta alla guerra sovversiva," (which was written for the Istituto Pollio conference but appeared instead in) *Ordine Nuovo* 11:3–4 (May–June 1965), pp. 18–19. The obvious but unspoken corollary was that the establishment of a more authoritarian regime would be necessary to resist and ultimately defeat communism.
166 See especially De Boccard, "Lineamenti ed interpretazione storica," pp. 44–7. In addition to the numerous references to the OAS and the French Army's campaigns in Indo-China and Algeria, there were specific references to French *guerre révolutionnaire* theorists in many of the presentations. See, for example, ibid., pp. 39, 45 (Trinquier); and Beltrametti, "Guerra rivoluzionaria," pp. 58, 72–3 (Argoud, Trinquier, Bonnet, and Lacheroy). Rauti alluded to the works of the Belgian unconventional warfare specialist Roger Cosyns-Verhaegen in his presentation, and his close comrade Graziani explicitly did so. Compare Rauti, "Tattica della penetrazione comunista," p. 93; and Graziani, "Appunti per una risposta," pp. 9, 11, 21. The latter author also referred to Serge Chakotin, whose modified Pavlovian views were looked upon with favor by French psychological warfare experts. See ibid., p. 15.
167 Ronconi, "Ipotesi per una controrivoluzione," pp. 243–4.
168 Ibid., pp. 244–5.
169 For Beltrametti's "self-defense" groups, see "Guerra rivoluzionaria," pp. 75, 84–5.
170 See Graziani, "Appunti per una risposta," p. 20.
171 For Graziani's views on appropriate countermeasures, see ibid., especially pp. 10–11, 19–29.

172 See Vinciguerra, *Ergastolo per la libertà*, pp. 4–6. From this point of view, Vinciguerra's bitterly sarcastic remarks, for example, that the eagle insignia on ON's membership card bore a remarkable similarity to the American eagle, make perfect sense. See ibid., p. 2.
173 Tassani, *Cultura politica della destra cattolica*, p. 116.
174 This document is quoted, almost in full, by Laurent, *Orchestre noir*, pp. 169–71.
175 See Vinciguerra, *Stato d'emergenza*, p. 202.
176 This is apparent from various judicial sentences, given that the criminal and violent activities of all of these apparently separate groups, whose members often interacted and collaborated, are discussed in connection with each other. Compare *Sentenza 3 II 98 contro Rognoni*; and Tribunale di Milano, Giudice Istruttore Guido Salvini, *Sentenza-ordinanza n. 2643/84A del 18 marzo 1995 nel procedimento penale control Azzi, Nico + 25* [hereinafter *Sentenza 18 III 95 contro Azzi*].
177 For more on ON's secret, compartmentalized cell structure, see especially Stefania Limiti, *Doppio livello: Come si organizza la destabilizzazione in Italia* (Milan: Chiarelettere, 2013), pp. 81–5. Therein Limiti notes that this elaborate, secretive operational structure was articulated like a honeycomb, was based on the organizational scheme and methods used by the OAS, maintained considerable continuity between the second half of the 1960s up until the early 1980s, and had access to significant quantities of weapons and explosives, including military munitions. Moreover, according to several neo-fascist *pentiti*, even core cadres within this action-oriented structure were not privy to information concerning the other cells, since no one had complete knowledge of the entire cell structure and only the cell leaders were aware of the activities of other cells. She concludes (p. 76) that these elite ON "militants" effectively constituted more of a "clandestine secret service" than a political movement, since they only sporadically engaged in normal political activities. Further details about the ON structure and network can be found in various judicial sentences.
178 See Anna Cento Bull, *Italian Neofascism: The Strategy of Tension and the Politics of Nonreconciliation* (New York and Oxford: Berghahn, 2007), pp. 30–1. Another strange entity that may have been loosely within the ON orbit was the "Nazi" Gruppo Ludwig (Ludwig Group), consisting of two (or more) youngsters, Marco Furlan and Wolfgang Abel, who set fires and carried out a series of gruesome but seemingly random murders (e.g., of tramps, priests, prostitutes, homosexuals) that were apparently designed to disseminate fear in the Verona region. See Augusto Caneva, *Il caso Ludwig* (Trento: Reverdito, 1986); and Monica Zornetta, *Ludwig: Storie di sangue, fuoco, follia* (Milan: Baldini Castoldi, 2011). Limiti tries, unconvincingly, to suggest a link between the individuals in Ludwig, certain ON operatives, and military psyops specialist Adriano Magi Braschi to the esoteric, secretive, anti-communist Indian yoga cult created by Prabhat Ranjan Sarkar in 1955, Ánanda Márga Pracáraka Samgha (Organization for the Propagation of the Path of Bliss), which was implanted in Italy during this period. See *Doppio livello*, pp. 59, 86–7. Components of that cult – in particular, its alleged paramilitary wing, the Universal Proutist Revolutionary Federation – have reportedly been involved in serious acts of violence in many different parts of the world, both against members and outsiders (including Indian government officials because of the imprisonment of Sarkar), perhaps including the bombing of the Hilton Hotel in Sydney, Australia, on 13 February 1978, which was apparently targeting Indian Prime Minister Morarji Desai but instead killed three innocent Australians. Compare Tom Molomby, *Spies, Bombs and the Path of Bliss* (Sydney: Potoroo, 1986); Rachel Landers, *Who Bombed the Hilton?* (Sydney: New South, 2014); and Ben Hills, "The Hilton Fiasco," *Sydney Morning Herald*, 12 February 1998, available at http://benhills.com/articles/scams-scoundrels/the-hilton-fiasco/. For a firsthand account of life within the group by a former member, see Marsha Goluboff Low, *The Orange Robe: My Eighteen Years as a Yogic Nun* (Bloomington: iUniverse, 2010).
179 *Sentenza 3 II 98 contro Rognoni*, pp. 59–274.
180 *Sentenza 18 III 95 contro Azzi*, pp. 297–350. Note that AN, like ON, also had a compartmentalized, secret internal structure, which most of the group's regular members knew nothing about. Many of the elite cadres in that secret structure were also reportedly

not known to the police and Carabinieri. See Cucchiarelli, *Segreto di Piazza Fontana*, pp. 39–40.
181 See, for example, the analysis in Rita di Giovacchino, *Il libro nero della Prima Repubblica* (Rome: Fazi, 2005), at 19% (ebook).
182 See Giacomo Pacini, *Le altre Gladio: La lotta segreta anticomunista in Italia, 1943–1991* (Turin: Einaudi, 2014), pp. 255–73. For more on the NDS, see *Sentenza 18 III 95 contro Azzi*, pp. 351–82; Giannuli, *Relazione 12 III 97*, pp. 87–92.
183 For the information on "Anello" and/or the Noto Servizio compare Di Giovacchino, *Libro nero della Prima Repubblica*, at 20%; Pacini, *Cuore occulto del potere*, pp. 154–64; Barbieri and Cucchiarelli, *Strage con i capelli bianchi*, pp. 19–21; Aldo Giannuli, *Noto servizio*; and Stefania Limiti, *L'Anello della Repubblica: La scoperta di un nuovo servizio segreto, dal Fascismo alle Brigate Rosse* (Milan: Chiarelettere, 2014), in addition to the detailed material in several recent judicial sentences. See also the brief interview with former P2 lodge head Licio Gelli, "Licio Gelli: 'Berlusconi un debole, Andreotti a capo dell'Anello e Fini è senza carattere," *Oggi*, 15 February 2011, available at www.oggi.it/people/vip-e-star/2011/02/15/licio-gelli-berlusconi-un-debole-andreotti-a-capo-dellanello-e-fini-e-senza-carattere/?refresh_ce-cp. Therein Gelli stated, without equivocation, that "I had P2, Cossiga had Gladio, and Andreotti had Anello."
184 For more on these alleged links to U.S. and NATO intelligence personnel, see *Sentenza 3 II 98 contro Rognoni*, pp. 275–365. Compare also Limiti, *Doppio livello*, pp. 29–72, who also cites information from other judicial sentences.
185 For the growing focus on unconventional warfare and psychological operations in the context of anti-communist action, see Giannuli, *Relazione 12 III 97*, pp. 12–87; Giannuli, *Noto servizio*, pp. 95–125. This manifested itself not only in intellectual presentations and discussions at conferences (such as the Istituto Pollio conference covered earlier), but above all in the formation of special units, offices, or sections within military and intelligence structures that were devoted to these arcane subjects, as well as the creation of parallel organizations to utilize them against the communists and other leftists. Even neo-fascist groups, such as Ordine Nuovo, created special components devoted to these kinds of actions. One of the key Italians involved in promoting these ideas and organizing such units was Army officer Adriano Magi Braschi, who had fought on the Russian front, was awarded two Iron Crosses by the Germans, was assigned to SIFAR's Raggruppamento Unità Speciali (Special Units Command) in 1959, had reported links to OAS leader Jacques Soustelle, was appointed head of SIFAR's Ufficio per la Guerra Non Ortodossa (Office of Unconventional Warfare) in 1963, participated at the 1965 Istituto Pollio conference on *guerra rivoluzionaria*, offered a course on these subjects at the Università Internazionale per le Studi Sociali Pro Deo (founded in Rome by Dominican priest Felix Morlion in 1948), was a supporter of General Aloja in his mid-1960s rivalry with General De Lorenzo, was an active organizer of mixed military-civilian anti-communist resistance groups, had documented links to a number of ON militants, had a great interest in religious cults and mysticism, succeeded Eggardo Beltrametti as head of the Italian branch of WACL in 1981, and was reportedly a high-level CIA asset. See Limiti, *Doppio livello*, pp. 58–60, 88; Calvi and Laurent, *Piazza Fontana*, pp. 297–9, reprinting sections of a Carabinieri report written by Captain Massimo Giraudo, Raggruppamento Operativo Speciale, Reparto Eversione, *Annotazione sulle emergenze investigative relative al coinvolgimento di strutture di intelligence straniere nella cosidetta "strategia della tensione"*; and Maurizio Dianese and Gianfranco Bettin, *La strage: Piazza Fontana, verità e memoria* (Milan: Feltrinelli, 2002), pp. 65–8. For more on Pro Deo's university, which had many influential Americans on its Board of Trustees and branches outside Rome, see the 22 May 1957 report published by the American Jewish Committee at www.ajcarchives.org/AJC_DATA/Files/686.PDF.

5

THE DECEMBER 1970 "BORGHESE COUP" IN ROME

On the night of 7–8 December 1970, the second in a series of right-wing "coups" aimed at transforming or subverting Italy's parliamentary system was mounted in Rome by a World War II naval hero, Prince Junio Valerio Borghese. This series had been initiated in 1964 by General Giovanni De Lorenzo, then head of the Carabinieri, who had secretly developed an anti-leftist counterinsurgency contingency plan code-named "Solo," and came to an end with the exposure of a rash of interlinked "presidentialist" coup plots in 1973 and 1974. Although these other operations were either called off before being activated or unmasked following the launching of preliminary psychological and terrorist actions but prior to their actual initiation, the so-called Borghese coup was already underway when it was suddenly and unexpectedly terminated. In strategic terms it may not have been the most dangerous of these coup schemes, but it was the only one that actually managed to achieve some of its tangible operational objectives.

Not surprisingly, the action launched by Borghese became the subject of considerable speculation in journalistic and political circles following its belated public exposure in the spring of 1971. Given the high degree of political polarization characteristic of Italian society in general and the media in particular, it is only natural that the political and journalistic analyses which later appeared reflected the partisan political interests of the groups or parties that sponsored them. The political establishment and the right immediately sought to downplay the seriousness of the plot, either by claiming that no coup had really been launched or by dismissing it as a farcical, chimerical operation promoted by pathetic nostalgics and carried out by incompetent buffoons. In contrast, the left initially viewed it as a serious effort to destroy Italian democracy that was modeled on the Greek military coup of 1967. However, a close examination of what actually transpired reveals that neither of these interpretations is entirely accurate. To grasp the historical significance and political complexity of the operation, it is necessary to trace the career of Borghese and the development of his Fronte Nazionale (FN: National Front), the organizational structure around which the plotters gravitated.

The background

Junio Valerio Borghese was the restless scion of an aristocratic family whose Roman branch had attained great prestige, influence, wealth, and power through association, first with the papacy and then with Bonaparte's family during the Napoleonic Wars. Thirsting for adventure and inflamed by patriotism, he had joined the Italian Navy in the years before World War II and was then assigned to an elite naval sabotage unit that eventually became known as the Decima Flottiglia [Mezzi d'Assalto] MAS (10th Assault Vehicle Flotilla). This innovative force was specifically created to develop secret weapons and new tactics, and was later entrusted with carrying out "special operations" at sea. To facilitate these tasks, it was provided with a compartmentalized cell structure to guarantee maximum secrecy, and was divided into a surface section consisting of motorized torpedo boats and an underwater section comprising midget submarines and "human torpedoes." During the first three years of the war it carried out a series of unusually daring exploits, including the sinking of British capital warships in the protected harbors of Gibraltar and Alexandria. Indeed, the Decima MAS was one of the few Italian military units which operated at a high level of efficiency and consistently displayed real élan, so much so that Admiral Karl Dönitz and other top German Kriegsmarine officials personally arranged for its commander Borghese to visit German naval facilities and help train Nazi "special operations" personnel in the various techniques his unit had pioneered. This phase of Borghese's military career was abruptly brought to a close when Mussolini was ousted from power in July 1943.[1]

When the Wehrmacht occupied northern Italy and disarmed Italian forces in a lightning operation on 9 September 1943, the Decima MAS base at La Spezia was the only Italian military installation that was not seized by German troops. Borghese at once offered to continue fighting alongside the Germans, provided that his unit remained directly under his own command and was allowed to retain its Italian uniforms and insignia. Five days later – and thirteen days *before* the establishment of the Repubblica Sociale Italiana (RSI: Italian Social Republic) – the Germans agreed to these terms, and the Decima MAS was placed under the overall operational command of SS Obergruppenführer Karl Wolff, who granted it increasing autonomy as his respect and friendship for Borghese grew. The Decima MAS at once embarked on an aggressive and highly successful recruitment campaign, and it eventually consisted of a hodgepodge of units, including several well-trained infantry battalions, a small naval sabotage unit, a police company with its own intelligence and interrogation section, and various other ad hoc formations. It was employed primarily as an anti-partisan force in the "hottest" zones, and performed these difficult and unrewarding counterguerrilla tasks with a singular efficiency and that paradoxical mixture of utter ruthlessness and genuine chivalry which only elite units seem capable of displaying. But Borghese and his men were anxious to test their mettle against Allied troops, and in February 1944 the "Barbarigo" battalion acquitted itself well after being sent to the Anzio front and deployed against American Rangers and Canadian troops. Later, at Borghese's request, Wolff authorized the transfer of the bulk of the Decima MAS to Venezia Giulia to fight Yugoslav and communist partisans, where the combat was especially nasty and brutish. In effect, then, the Decima MAS operated as an SS Sonderverband (Special Group) rather than as a unit under the control of the RSI's military command, a fact that caused Mussolini great consternation.[2]

Indeed, there were several unique aspects of the Decima MAS that deserve to be highlighted. As noted earlier, it maintained an almost total autonomy with respect to both the *Duce* and the entire Salò regime. Decima MAS recruits did not swear oaths to the RSI, and its personnel received much better pay and training than those of any other Italian force. When the RSI Undersecretary of the Navy later tried to transfer over two thousand men from Borghese's unit to help form a naval infantry brigade under Mussolini's direct orders, the two officers he sent were arrested on the spot by Decima MAS troops. In January 1944 Borghese was himself arrested and accused of plotting a "reactionary coup" against Mussolini, but a Guardia Nazionale Repubblicana (GNR: National Republican Guard) investigation cleared him and he was released after Dönitz personally intervened on his behalf. Approximately one year later, the Decima MAS began publishing a newspaper that was critical of certain aspects of fascism, which set off a new round of conflict between Borghese and the RSI government. The insubordinate naval officer and his men again emerged relatively unscathed due to high-level German protection.[3]

Second, the Decima MAS used rather unorthodox, if not criminal, means to requisition equipment and supplies. According to both RSI and German intelligence reports, Borghese's troops employed all sorts of illegal methods to obtain provisions or enrich themselves, including outright thievery, unauthorized confiscations, intimidation, blackmail, trafficking in contraband, and trickery, and even went so far as to steal weapons from German supply depots. Its commander supplemented this activity by "pressuring" Milan businesses to offer his unit funding.[4]

Third, Borghese set up various Decima MAS intelligence structures, including an espionage headquarters in Switzerland, a police intelligence unit, and an intelligence-gathering network that had been established throughout RSI territory. He also sought to infiltrate spies and saboteurs into Allied-controlled Italy, and in general directed his agents to engage in espionage and intelligence activities in conjunction with elements of German counterintelligence. One of the important tasks assigned to the American Office of Strategic Services (OSS) was to neutralize the Decima MAS's stay/behind networks, a task undertaken, among others, by James Jesus Angleton of the OSS's counterespionage branch, X-2.[5]

Fourth, on several occasions Borghese sought to open up negotiations with "enemy" forces, ostensibly in an effort to form an alliance with all patriotic elements against anti-national or foreign communist guerrillas. He and his officers first attempted to negotiate such an arrangement with a communist partisan codenamed "Taras" against the Anglo-Americans, then with the Catholic partisans of the "Osoppo" brigade in order to forge an alliance against Yugoslav-backed guerrillas, and finally with representatives of British intelligence, to whom he offered to abandon the Germans and join an alliance against Tito. All of these proposals were eventually rebuffed, and some observers have accused Borghese of seeking to deceive and betray his interlocutors or, in the latter case, save his own skin prior to the imminent Axis defeat.[6] Although a considerable degree of opportunism was undoubtedly involved, these efforts were also consistent with Borghese's self-portrayal as a committed patriot and a military commander who was deeply concerned about the fate of his men.

Finally, in exchange for helping to prevent the retreating Germans from sabotaging ports and industrial plants, Borghese was rescued from certain partisan retribution by Angleton, who dressed him up as an American soldier and drove him southwards in a jeep to Rome. After extensive debriefing at the Combined Services Interrogation Centre, during which he provided information on the "backgrounds of various members of the Italian military and diplomatic elite," the Black Prince was turned over to the Italian authorities for trial.[7]

The war crimes trial that resulted proved to be somewhat anti-climactic. It was initiated in Milan, but on 17 May 1947 the Court of Cassation transferred the trial to a special court in Rome, because the atmosphere in the Lombard capital was considered to be too prejudicial for Borghese to obtain a fair trial. At the trial, which began on 15 October 1947, the Black Prince and sixteen others were accused of aiding and abetting the RSI and its Nazi overlords by sending his men to fight against Allied troops and carrying out brutal anti-partisan operations, which resulted in the torture and execution of captured partisans, the razing of villages, the deportation of prisoners to German camps, and the expropriation of goods for private gain. In his defense, Borghese claimed that he was compelled to act under German orders, that he was not personally responsible for the atrocities committed by some of his men, that his troops were apolitical patriots who helped defend Italian interests in Venezia Giulia, that he had aided wounded veterans and bombing victims, and that he helped to save Italian industries from being destroyed by the retreating Germans during the closing weeks of the war. In the end, on 17 February 1949, he received a twelve-year sentence instead of the life sentence requested by the prosecution, because there was no material evidence that he had ordered or directly participated in atrocities. This sentence was further reduced to eight years in accordance with the terms of the general pardons of 1946 and 1948, and the time he had already spent in prison was then subtracted from the remainder. The government upheld the court's decision, despite the protests of left-wing deputies in Parliament and widespread public outrage.[8]

In mid-1949 the Supreme Court of Appeals, after further limiting the already reduced February sentence handed down by the Rome court, ordered that he be released from Procida prison. At that time the political passions that had been fueled by civil strife in northern Italy during the last two years of the war still ran very high. The victory of Alcide De Gasperi and the Democrazia Cristiana (DC: Christian Democratic) party in the April 1948 elections had quashed lingering leftist hopes that a fundamental restructuring of the Italian social and political system would grow out of the influence of the Resistance movement, and also made any serious future efforts to root out Fascist elements within the various state agencies impossible. Indeed, the abject failure of the Resistance-inspired "wind from the north" to sweep away the detritus of Fascism was nowhere better symbolized than by the exceptional judicial leniency granted to Borghese and other RSI leaders accused of committing war crimes against Italian citizens.[9] Hence Borghese's premature release only added to the already elevated levels of political frustration and tension that existed throughout the peninsula. On the very day the Black Prince left prison, Roberto Mieville led a demonstration by the MSI's Raggruppamento Giovanile Studenti e Lavoratori (Workers and Students Youth Grouping) through the streets of the capital, exalting Borghese and vilifying partisan leader Ferruccio Parri.[10] These events created considerable outrage and consternation in anti-Fascist and leftist circles, which responded by initiating intense protests in Parliament, a virulent press campaign, and political demonstrations. In order to escape official crackdowns or unofficial vendettas in this overheated atmosphere, Borghese maintained a low profile and eschewed overt political activities for a time, although he could not resist filing successive legal claims for compensation for his years in prison, the resumption of his career in the Italian Navy, and the dismissal of the charge of murder.[11] This period of relative inactivity was not destined to last, however, because Borghese was a restless individual who chafed at the bit for action and a former military hero whose prestige other political forces sought to utilize for their own ends.

Between the time of his release from prison and his formal adhesion to the MSI two years later, Borghese was kept "under observation" by the government.[12] While this unwelcome official attention prevented him from engaging in any visible political activities of an anti-democratic nature, there are indications that during this period the Black Prince was approached by representatives of different groups who sought to coax him out of his seclusion and recruit his support for various political initiatives. The most important of such attempts were apparently connected to efforts by hard-line anti-communists within the right wing of the DC, the American Embassy, the Vatican, and the employers' association Confindustria to create a rightist, pro-Atlantic "national front" coalition, parallel to and independent of both the DC constellation and the MSI, which were perceived as insufficiently reliable guardians of the political and economic interests of the West. These elements considered the left-leaning "social" wing of the DC to be too hostile to private capitalist economic agendas and too willing to compromise or make common cause with the right wing of the Partito Socialista Italiano (PSI: Italian Socialist Party). At the same time, they viewed the MSI as a nostalgic party with embarrassing attachments to an unpopular Fascist past, and saw its left wing as a hotbed of anti-American and anti-Atlanticist sentiment that had the potential to hinder efforts to integrate Italy into a pro-Western alliance system unless the party's moderates were able to obtain control and enforce internal discipline. Several parallel operations were thus initiated, both to strengthen conservative forces within the two "suspect" parties and to create rival anti-communist organizational alternatives. If the two existing parties continued to be heavily influenced by their "unreliable" leftist factions, the plan was to detach their "trustworthy" conservative factions and gather them into newly established formations and coalitions.[13]

To this end U.S. Central Intelligence Agency (CIA) chief Allen Dulles is said to have entrusted two of his top operatives in Italy, Carmel Offie, a wartime intelligence officer who had been appointed to supervise the postwar activities of the Italian secret services, and James Jesus Angleton, by then head of CIA "special operations" in Italy, with the delicate mission of transforming restless nationalist youths and ex-military leaders of the RSI into the guardians of Atlanticism. American intelligence operatives purportedly began by approaching the leaders of various veterans associations that had been created in 1949 by former fascist fighters, including the Federazione Nazionale Combattenti Repubblicani (FNCR: Federation of Republican National Veterans), the Associazione Paracadutisti Italiani (API: Italian Paratrooper Association), the Associazione Nazionale Arditi d'Italia (National Special Forces Association of Italy), and the Associazione Nazionale Combattenti Italiani di Spagna (ANCIS: National Association of Italian Veterans in Spain), in an effort to enlist their aid. They then attempted to garner the support of certain *ventennio*-era Fascist hierarchs, who had been excluded from the MSI due to the bitter hostility of its leftist and Evolan wings toward the so-called traitors of 25 July 1943.[14] Some of the plans that grew out of these behind-the-scenes efforts to forge political alliances envisioned a role for Borghese. One was linked to the attempts after 1950 to create a "pact of unity" between the MSI and the Partito Nationale Monarchico (PNM: National Monarchist Party), a project backed by factions within the two parties themselves, monarchist agents, some former Servizio Informazioni Militare (SIM: Military Intelligence Service) officials, elements within the American Embassy, and emissaries from the Vatican. Borghese seems to have been at least tangentially involved in this sensitive initiative, the aim of which was to draw the MSI into a conservative alliance that would strengthen its moderate factions and thereby ensure its fidelity to Atlanticism, inasmuch as his name was mentioned as a possible future King of Italy! But this quixotic and ridiculous suggestion, whose proponents naïvely hoped would appeal to both monarchists and ex-Salò fighters, was vociferously opposed by loyalists of the House of Savoy and was therefore almost immediately abandoned.[15]

A more serious effort was then apparently made to draw Borghese into the CIA-backed "national front" project, one of whose main operational instruments was Luigi Gedda's Comitati Civici (Civic Committees) network.[16] The goal of this elaborate anti-communist maneuver was the creation of a broad "patriotic" coalition that would act to regenerate Italian national sentiments in such a way that they would not conflict with key American and North Atlantic Treaty Organization (NATO) geopolitical interests. Exploiting the theme of military glory was one of the techniques employed to try to wean national-minded Italians away from insular, parochial forms of patriotism and xenophobic integral nationalism, both of which at times threatened to undermine attempts to create a multinational Western bulwark against the Soviet Bloc. The main targets of these efforts were members of the new veterans associations and the combative elements that constituted the base of the MSI, and it was believed that a prominent medal of valor winner like Borghese could function as a symbol of military heroism around whom such elements might rally. If this plan was successful, these militants would be withdrawn from the orbit of an unsavory, "unreliable" neo-fascist party and brought under the aegis and control of conservative Atlanticist forces. With these objectives in mind, CIA operatives supposedly visited Borghese at his small castle in Artena in an effort to persuade him to head this "national front" coalition. When Borghese's old friend and savior Angleton went to Artena himself to make a personal appeal for his help, the Black Prince became enthusiastic about the project.[17] According to Pier Giuseppe Murgia, Borghese's establishment of his own Fronte Nazionale organization more than fifteen years later, again allegedly in the ambit of a "special operation directed by the CIA," essentially represented a revival of this earlier intelligence-backed project to unite all "patriotic" Italians.[18]

When the news of these efforts to recruit Borghese into a separate rightist movement reached the MSI, it generated great consternation. The leaders of the party immediately recognized that such efforts were in part aimed at weakening the MSI itself, and at once took action to counter this new threat. A number of young RSI veterans affiliated with the party were sent to visit Borghese at Artena. They warned him that reactionary forces behind the "national front" were seeking to make instrumental use of his prestige, and that MSI-linked nationalist youths would not recognize his leadership or join such a front because it was inimical to the interests of an independent neo-fascist party. This threat of abandonment by ex-soldiers and youths who had always lionized Borghese was followed up by intensive efforts to recruit the Black Prince into the MSI. After holding a series of meetings with his associates and getting their approval, MSI Secretary Augusto De Marsanich personally offered to make Borghese honorary president of the party if he would consent to join.[19] In this way the MSI leaders hoped to lure him away from the rival "national front" project and exploit his fame for their own political ends. For reasons which are still not entirely clear, Borghese ended up accepting this proposal. He may have simply been won over psychologically by all the attention he received from various MSI representatives, as well as by the party's evocation of certain RSI traditions with which he identified. It is also conceivable – although there is no actual evidence of this – that he was encouraged to accept this invitation by Angleton, who may have modified his original plan to make use of the Black Prince because he felt that a loyal ally within the leadership circles of the MSI could help assure the party's pro-Atlantic orientation. Whatever the precise reasons, Borghese joined the MSI in November of 1951, and with great fanfare was made honorary president on 2 December. This proved to be an enormous propaganda coup for the party. Borghese was one of the MSI's most important new recruits, and his well-publicized entry into the party was followed not only by that of many youths who were inspired by his wartime military exploits, but also by additional financial subsidies from certain industrial and agrarian circles.[20]

On 4 December 1951 Borghese made his first postwar public appeal, in which he urged the MSI's members and supporters to form a compact, disciplined bloc in order to "reestablish the country's spiritual and material order." He also appealed to veterans and fighting men to join the party and make sacrifices so that "honor, independence, and freedom" could be restored to Italy.[21] The Black Prince's entry into the MSI had been anxiously anticipated by the party's leftist and Evolan wings, which expected that he could be enlisted in their struggle against the "soft" bourgeois leaders who were compromising the movement's principles, pursuing a strategy of insertion into the corrupt democratic party system, and adopting a subservient attitude toward the materialistic Western powers that had defeated and humiliated Italy during and after the war. Although his combative personality and decision to write an introduction to Evola's *Gli uomini e le rovine* temporarily fueled such hopes,[22] the expectations of the radicals were soon dashed. As Piero Ignazi points out, the former Fascist war hero soon distinguished himself by his "unconditional adherence" to a pro-Western and philo-American foreign policy.[23] It is therefore uncertain just how much Borghese's shift to the MSI really put him at loggerheads with his alleged conservative and CIA backers. He was labeled as a "clown" by some proponents of the "national front" immediately after his defection from the project,[24] and his actions initially strengthened the MSI at a time when various pro-American forces were actively trying to create more "respectable" anti-communist alternatives. Yet he lent support to the Atlanticist faction within the party during a crucial phase in the struggle to define its basic geopolitical orientation.

By the time Borghese joined the party, the pro-Atlantic current within the MSI was already asserting its predominance. On 28 November De Marsanich held a press conference, timed to correspond with a meeting of the Atlantic Council in Rome, in which he acknowledged the need for American help in Europe's rearmament process and struggle against communism, without however renouncing national independence and the need to maintain separate national armies.[25] The party's shift toward a pro-Atlantic stance thence proceeded apace, in part in order to ward off any future attempt to make use of the Scelba Law to ban the MSI, and was signaled by the ideological or tactical conversion of former Atlantic Alliance opponents and the placing of Atlanticists in key positions within the various party organizations and publications. Indeed, in December of 1951 both Michelini and Almirante, previously an ostensible critic of Atlanticism, appear to have visited the Supreme Headquarters Allied Powers Europe (SHAPE) in Paris on a diplomatic mission.[26] Others who publicly came out in support of NATO included Filippo Anfuso, Ernesto Botto, Prince Valerio Pignatelli, who was linked by personal friendship to many top British and American officials, and Borghese himself.[27]

The Black Prince soon became involved in the project to create a new party-linked newspaper, which seems to have been initially designed to speed up the Atlanticization, if not the deradicalization, of the MSI. According to Murgia, this conservative initiative was backed by secret service elements, presumably the same ones that had earlier sought to recruit Borghese as head of the "national front." In any event, the decision to create such a newspaper was taken without the knowledge of much of the MSI's leadership, and it was first announced to the National Directorate in a letter sent by Borghese, who asked the members to recommend it to the various party organs. On 16 May 1952, the first edition of *Il Secolo d'Italia* duly appeared, with the lead editorial written by Borghese himself. Others who initially participated in the production of *Secolo* were the editor Bruno Spampanato, an ex-sailor who had been entrusted by Borghese with preparing Decima MAS propaganda in January 1945, and Franz Turchi, the last Prefect of La Spezia to be appointed by Mussolini. The immediate reactions of party leaders to these developments were far from enthusiastic. Members of the MSI Directorate held a meeting and secretly expressed their concerns about *Secolo's* sudden, unannounced appearance and its unknown sources of financing, and Mieville, then head of the party's Centro Stampa e Propaganda (Press and Propaganda Center), made the rounds of party-linked publications and warned them that Borghese's paper was not affiliated with the MSI and had "obscure origins and even more obscure objectives."[28] After 18 August 1952, *Secolo* passed into the hands of Almirante and Anfuso (although Turchi remained to handle financing),[29] and Mieville himself began to write regularly for the paper, which then began to move to the left.[30] Certain external publishing ventures aimed at weakening the MSI and building a "national front" separate from the party were also undertaken by conservative forces.

Meanwhile, Borghese's support for De Marsanich's moderate and Atlanticist positions was publicly reaffirmed in his introductory speech at the Third MSI Congress at L'Aquila in late July 1952. He appeared on the podium next to retired General Rodolfo Graziani, another prestigious new MSI recruit, and, after angrily denying that the party was totalitarian, stated that the tasks of the *missini* were to interpret the "common aspirations" of their countrymen and then resolve their basic economic problems.[31] In an interview he claimed that the party's current opposition to the DC was not immutable, and confirmed its loyalty to the Atlantic Alliance by insisting that party members would certainly not become conscientious objectors in the event of an East-West war.[32] Although this conservative stance disappointed the MSI's leftist and Evolan currents, Borghese remained extraordinarily popular. He took an active part in the party's campaigning before the administrative elections of 1953 and, like Graziani, drew huge crowds whenever he made public appearances. The triumphal mass rallies they held were of such concern to the authorities that frequent attempts were made to ban them. Interior Minister Mario Scelba banned a projected Borghese rally at the Colosseum on 24 May 1953, and similar bans were imposed by officials in Rovigo, Bolzano, Udine, and Pescara. Sometimes these actions provoked confrontations, and the Black Prince was actually detained by police at Rovigo and Padua.[33] Nevertheless, despite their continued public support for the moderate line pursued by party leaders, by the end of 1953 both Borghese and Graziani had already begun to manifest their impatience with the MSI's petty infighting.[34] Moreover, Borghese's imperious behavior had made him increasingly unpopular in MSI leadership circles, and as a soldier he remained contemptuous of politicians whom he regarded as corrupt and unprincipled.[35] For these very reasons, he remained a pole of attraction for the militants at the MSI's base. When the crisis over the unresolved status of Trieste escalated again in late 1953, the rallying cry of nationalist student groups mobilizing to protect the city was "to Trieste with Valerio Borghese."[36] They apparently sought to re-enact, under Borghese's leadership, Gabriele D'Annunzio's 1919 feat at Fiume, and according to some accounts the aristocratic warrior assembled one thousand of his ex-sailors near Treviso, who were armed and ready to march in the event that Italian national interests in Zone A were further violated by the Allied Military Government or threatened by Yugoslav forces.[37]

In January 1954 the two RSI military leaders jointly opened the Fourth Congress at Viareggio with a ritual appeal, in the name of the fighting men of Salò, to "the forces ready to defend order in the country."[38] This generic appeal failed to paper over the party's profound internal differences, which immediately made themselves felt. Although the centrist faction represented by De Marsanich and Arturo Michelini emerged with the largest number of votes, the left and right opposition both made strong showings, Almirante shifted back to a more radical position, and the resulting programmatic statement represented a compromise that failed to satisfy anyone and only postponed a future showdown. In the aftermath the Evolans, then nominally led by Pino Romualdi, rallied around Borghese, who was removed from the National Directorate but not deprived of his status as honorary president.[39] Michelini's assumption of control over the party in October 1954, in the wake of De Marsanich's illness, only exacerbated the already pronounced internal strife. The new secretary made extensive efforts to reduce the influence of the internal opposition in party organs and publications, efforts that proved quite successful. These manipulative, autocratic actions, coupled with a renewal of the tentative alliance with the PNM, finally brought matters to a head at the Fifth Congress, held at the end of November 1956 in Milan, the stronghold of the MSI left. Tension was so high that brawls broke out between the opposing factions, and the very identity of the party was called into question. Only Michelini's formal acceptance of almost all the "social" emendments proposed by Almirante, who had resigned from the Political Secretariat during the summer and resumed the leadership of the left, permitted programmatic agreement. Borghese himself supported the leftist-led opposition forces at the Congress.[40] However, in the ensuing Central Committee elections, the left's list of candidates was defeated 314 to 307 by that of Michelini, assuring the latter's de facto control over the party. This led to a schism of some extremist elements positioned on the MSI left and right, including Ernesto Massi, who formed the short-lived Partito Nazionale del Lavoro (National Labor Party) in 1957, and Evola's disciple Rauti, who restructured the Centro Studi Ordine Nuovo (New Order Study Center) as an independent organization.

On the day after the Congress ended, the leaders of the MSI left held a meeting in Rome. After a bitter debate, during which Borghese and others made harsh attacks on the direction taken by Michelini and his cronies, most of those present decided to remain in the party and continue their battle from within rather than breaking away and establishing an entirely new movement.[41] Nevertheless, the process of mutual estrangement between the Black Prince and the MSI's accommodationist leaders had become irreversible, and shortly afterwards he formally resigned from the party. At first glance his decision to resign, and indeed the entire course of his career in the MSI, may seem perplexing and difficult to explain. After allegedly displaying an interest in the anti-communist "national front" project backed by conservative and American circles, which was in large part designed to weaken and circumvent the unreliable MSI, Borghese suddenly joined the latter movement. Within the MSI he publicly supported the moderate, accommodationist line of De Marsanich and Michelini, at least until 1954, and never abandoned his support for the Atlantic Alliance. Yet he lauded Evola's critiques of modern bourgeois society in his introduction to the latter's 1953 book, and during the Congress of Viareggio the MSI right rallied behind him in opposition to aspects of the program presented by party moderates. Two years later, he joined with Almirante and the MSI left to try and defeat Michelini's slate at the Milan Congress, and was then invited to participate in the left's separate post-Congress meeting.

It seems clear that these seemingly contradictory flip-flops were not dictated primarily by ideological considerations, because Borghese was a man of action rather than an ideologue in the strict sense. Nor is it likely that he was merely carrying out the orders of other "reactionary" forces that were seeking to manipulate the internal affairs of the MSI, as Murgia sometimes seems to imply. The real explanation for his behavior – although it is always hazardous to resort to such simplistic and unverifiable explanations – is probably to be sought in the psychological sphere. Despite his frequent glorification of the principles of order and authority, the Black Prince was himself a restless, independent, and ambitious man who found it difficult to follow orders and accept advice, especially from those whom he held in contempt.[42] This rebellious streak had prompted him to ignore or defy some of the directives issued by Fascist hierarchs and bureaucrats, up to and including Mussolini and certain high-ranking German officers, and operate in a more or less autonomous fashion at various times between 1943 and 1945. After the war, feeling embittered and frustrated, he at once developed a hatred for the new parliamentary democratic regime. For one thing, it had placed him on trial as a war criminal. For another, he considered it a repository of venality and corruption which was unwilling to defend national values and unable to protect Italy from the threat posed by the Soviets and their domestic communist allies. Therefore, once it became clear to Borghese that the MSI leadership was jockeying to become a part of the degenerate bourgeois parliamentary system rather than seeking to create a genuine alternative to it, he began collaborating with the seditious elements on the party's right and left wings.[43]

Although Borghese's career in the MSI cannot be described in full detail given the current shortage of available documentation, it is even harder to trace his multifaceted activities during the period between his resignation from the party and his creation of the Fronte Nazionale in 1968. At the time he broke with the MSI his only remaining visible connection to an official rightist organization was to the FNCR veterans group, which he had assumed the leadership of following Graziani's death in 1955. In 1959 the FNCR split into two rival organizations, the MSI-controlled Unione Nazionale Combattenti della Repubblica Sociale Italiana

(UNCRSI: RSI National Veterans' Union) and the far more radical Federazione Nazionale Combattenti della Repubblica Sociale Italiana (FNCRSI: National Federation of RSI Veterans), linked to Ordine Nuovo (ON: New Order), which was openly critical of the MSI. Borghese's role in this schism, if any, is not at all clear, and not long afterwards he apparently divorced himself from both groups.[44] Yet this separation from the official organs of the legalist extreme right did not temper his restlessness or moderate his political alienation, and as time wore on he developed an increasing interest in insurrectionary projects aimed at replacing the existing parliamentary system with a strong state.[45] There are numerous indications that the Black Prince did not eschew political intriguing in the decade prior to founding the Fronte. Despite his disgust with the compromised policies pursued by the official neo-fascist party, he remained in contact with its more combative leaders like Almirante, Giulio Caradonna, and Luigi Turchi.[46] Moreover, before leaving the MSI he had already established links to radical elements within the party, some of which had then broken away and formed autonomous extraparliamentary groups. His close subsequent collaboration with leading members of those groups, which will be described shortly, suggests that he maintained at least sporadic contact with them all along. Finally, he was never long out of favor with certain circles of industrialists and the Roman aristocracy, of which he himself was a prestigious member, and it would appear that he also had contacts with key U.S. intelligence personnel and, within the hermetic and rarefied environment of the elite Roman salons, various Italian political and military figures.[47]

This is perhaps best demonstrated by his involvement in various international financial schemes. In the early 1960s Borghese, who evidently had need of money, obtained the cushy job of president of the Banca di Credito Commerciale e Industriale (BCCI), which had been given up, and perhaps transferred to him, by Sicilian financier Michele Sindona. The bank then became involved in an extremely complicated financial operation involving a "vast sector" of conservative economic interests, including Rafael ("Ramfis") Trujillo, son of the dictatorial *Jefe* of the Dominican Republic; José María Gil Robles and Opus Dei (The Works of God) in Spain, Vatican, and DC circles; renovated economic elites dating back to the Fascist period; and a series of companies, many of which were established by a lawyer named Ovidio Lefebvre d'Ovidio. This venture ended with a clamorous collapse, and Borghese and his partners were then charged with committing embezzlement and other illegal financial manipulations.[48] Borghese's penalty ended up being rather light, but his very involvement with some of these other groups is certainly significant. As will soon become clearer, Sindona was a key figure in a long succession of financial and political scandals involving, among others, Sicilian Mafia families, powerful conservative groups in the United States, elements of various secret services, the Vatican Bank, international financial interests, and Licio Gelli's Propaganda Due (P2) masonic lodge.[49] Gil Robles had long been an important fixture on the Spanish political scene, beginning his career as a member of the Catholic, authoritarian corporatist, and legalist but nonetheless anti-democratic Confederacion Española de Derechas Autónomas (CEDA: Spanish Confederation of Autonomous Right-Wing

Groups), and ending up as a moderate reformist within the Franco regime who helped to ease the transition to democracy and thereby sought to ensure himself a role in the post-Franco system.[50] Opus Dei is a conservative and very secretive lay religious organization that was officially established on 2 October 1928 by José María Escrivá de Balaguer. For decades its upper ranks have been filled with members of the technocratic economic and political elites in Spain and other countries, and it too has been involved in a number of serious financial scandals, the most notorious of which was the Matesa affair of the 1970s.[51] It is therefore very clear that by the early 1960s, if not sooner, Borghese had made a number of powerful, high-level contacts, both in Italy and in other countries. Several of these same people were themselves implicated in various behind-the-scene attempts to influence the course of political events.

The first indications of the Black Prince's possible involvement in subversive plots surfaced in relation to the De Lorenzo "coup" of 1964. The most explicit information was provided by his later right-hand man in the Fronte Nazionale, Remo Orlandini. At a 19 June 1973 meeting with Captain Antonio Labruna of the Servizio Informazioni Difesa (SID), whom he was trying to enlist as a co-conspirator in later plots, Orlandini claimed that in 1964 De Lorenzo had come to an agreement with Borghese regarding a coup d'etat, but that the general had lost his nerve at the last moment, when Giuseppe Saragat was about to replace the infirm Antonio Segni as president. According to Orlandini, he and Borghese personally alerted the various Carabinieri "legions" that the projected operation was to be launched the night before Saragat took office. De Lorenzo was then supposed to contact the plotters and give them the go-ahead signal, but failed to do so. When Carabinieri commanders began calling Borghese and demanding to know what was happening, he and Orlandini sought to find out by visiting De Lorenzo at Carabinieri headquarters. Once they arrived, they found that the general was waiting there in his dress uniform. After a chagrined Borghese insisted that De Lorenzo should be in his fighting gear instead of a dress uniform, the latter replied that everything had been halted and that he could do no more.[52] This extraordinary testimony, provided by an insider with variable credibility, has not been confirmed. However, it receives some circumstantial support from a variety of other sources.

For example, some of the testimony presented to the parliamentary commission investigating the De Lorenzo affair suggested that Colonel Renzo Rocca of the Servizio Informazioni Forze Armate's (SIFAR: Armed Forces Intelligence Service) Ufficio Ricerche Economiche e Industriali (REI: Industrial and Economic Research Section) had secretly recruited armed civilian support groups to work in conjunction with the active-duty Carabinieri units earmarked to carry out the "coup." Among those whom Rocca allegedly sought to recruit into these clandestine "civilian militias" were former RSI soldiers, sailors, paratroopers, and Decima MAS members. The key accounts of these efforts to enroll civilians – those of Carabinieri Colonels Ezio Taddei and Guglielmo Cerica, as told to Senator Raffaele Jannuzzi in the course of conversations later recounted by the latter – indicated that veterans of Borghese's old unit constituted a privileged source of recruits for

Rocca.[53] Even if true, this does not prove that Borghese himself played any tangible role in the project. Yet there is no doubt that his participation would have helped to attract and rally members of the groups targeted for recruitment by Rocca, and it seems likely that the Black Prince would have learned of whatever recruitment efforts were made, if not directly from Rocca, from one of his old comrades-in-arms or other contacts he had established in various political and economic circles. Therefore, whether or not Roberto Faenza is correct in linking Rocca's recruitment efforts to CIA station chief William Harvey's plan to employ "action squads" to mount attacks that could then be attributed to the left,[54] the De Lorenzo "coup" may have been the first postwar operation in which Borghese and some of his close associates were enlisted to carry out actual paramilitary actions. In this connection, it should be recalled that some recently declassified testimony by other Carabinieri officers highlighted the important role played in the 1964 "coup" plan by former anti-fascist exile Randolfo Pacciardi and his "presidentialist" Unione Populare e Democratica per una Nuova Repubblica (Popular and Democratic Union for a New Republic).[55]

This is of some interest here, because the next highly visible political action taken by Borghese was alongside Pacciardi two years later, in the midst of the crisis between Austria and Italy over the settlement of ethnic disputes in the Alto Adige/Süd Tirol region. Terrorist violence ostensibly committed by German-speaking extremists against Italian officials and citizens prompted the far right in Italy to form, in January 1966, a Comitato Tricolore per la Italianità dell'Alto Adige (Tricolor Committee to Keep the Alto Adige Italian), which organized a series of public demonstrations to rally support for the defense of Italian interests in the area. Among the leaders of the Comitato, in addition to the Black Prince and Pacciardi, were various MSI leaders and the heads of several irredentist and veterans associations. They set up a central office in Rome, and branch addresses in a number of other cities. A rally held by the Comitato at the Cinema Cristallo in Rome was presided over by Borghese himself. From the podium in front of the assembled crowd, which included his trusted comrade Remo Orlandini and UNCRSI president Aurelio Languasco, the Black Prince proclaimed that the time had come to act in defense of the nation and urged all fighting men (*combattenti*) to be disciplined, remain on the alert, and "be ready."[56] There is no evidence that this call to action had any concrete follow-up under the aegis of the Comitato Tricolore, later renamed the Comitato Nazionale per la Difesa dei Confini d'Italia (National Committee for the Defense of the Italian Frontiers), but it provides further evidence of Borghese's activist sentiments. It would not be long before he would seek to transform those sentiments into concrete action of a subversive nature.

The National Front

Although the available information is sketchy, Borghese seems to have begun to flirt with the idea of establishing his own Fronte Nazionale sometime in 1967. The organization was officially registered in Rome on 13 September 1968, but before that date a certain amount of preliminary planning had already been undertaken. It was probably in the course of his frenetic activities on behalf of the Comitato Tricolore, which dramatically displayed his ability to evoke the enthusiastic support of veterans, active-duty military personnel, and rightist youths, that the idea first came to Borghese of rallying masses of patriotic, anti-communist forces and gathering them into a broader political movement under his own leadership. According to one of his closest associates, Benito Guadagni, the Comitato Tricolore was itself later transformed into the Fronte Nazionale.[57] Although this is undoubtedly an oversimplification, it is probably true that elements from the Comitato were among the earliest recruits into the FN. However, its original cadres seem to have been drawn from among the members of a preexisting Circolo dei Selvatici (Circle of Feral Ones), a "cultural" association headquartered at Via dell'Anima 55 in Rome.[58] In any case, it is clear that the FN grew out of an intensive effort to attract and mobilize ex-RSI fighting men and youths, and that the Black Prince also made efforts to appeal to former non-communist ("white") partisans who were disposed to join with their wartime opponents in the face of the threat posed to postwar Italy by communism. This attempt to obtain a broad base of support in order to rescue the nation from the clutches of the *partitocrazia* accounts for many of the emphases in the organization's political pronouncements.

From an ideological standpoint, Borghese's FN was neither original nor sophisticated. It relied upon the sort of generic appeals to patriotism and anti-communism that formed the common currency of the conservative, pro-Atlantic right in Italy. Aside from some nostalgic and ritualistic references to more radical fascist themes, which were aimed at securing the allegiance of left-leaning RSI veterans and youthful neo-fascist revolutionaries, there was very little that differentiated the FN's rhetoric from that of dozens of other reactionary and authoritarian groups. In a preliminary proclamation dated 7 June 1968, only three months prior to the official registration of the FN, Borghese made a special appeal to attract alienated youths who were disgusted with the existing system. Therein he claimed to be "carrying the banner of honor into the most advanced social trenches" in order to rally all the Italians, including the fighting men, the laborers, the producers, the men of culture, and "the youths, all the youths." After attacking the parliamentary regime for its scandals and corruption, which only facilitated the threatening advance of Bolshevism, he appealed to those who desired an independent Italy "freed from the oppobrium of the diktat" imposed on the country after World War II by the Allies. He then promoted a unified Europe liberated from Eastern and Western domination, and a restoral of the unity of the Italians, who had been "artificially divided by an insipid *partitocrazia* which places its own interests apart from those of the nation." He promised to realize the aspirations of youths who were raising the cry of protest from the universities, factories, and shipyards by establishing an honest State "beyond the center, right, and left."[59] But the proclamation ended on an ominous note: "There is no more time for words, it is necessary to pass to action." The "Commander" then revealed that several concrete steps had been taken to provide an organization for those who wished to rally behind him. First, a committee had been established in Rome to develop and coordinate plans. Second, "action groups" were being formed in every region, province, and city, headed by highly qualified "delegates." Third, these groups were to enter into contact with the committee in Rome which, acting in Borghese's name, would issue orders that had to be faithfully executed. Fourth, a meeting of all the delegates would be convoked as soon as possible in Rome.[60] The committee's address was listed as Via Giovanni Lanza 130, which corresponded to that of the office of Mario Rosa, one of Borghese's closest associates.

A lengthier and more typical FN ideological statement was the organization's January 1969 *Orientamenti Programmatici*. In it the FN was defined as a "free association" of Italians, as opposed to a political party, which sought to achieve a "new political order." An appeal was then issued to all the Italians who shared its notions about European civilization, the nation, society, the party system, and the state. According to the FN, "materialism and massification were two principles contrary to Italian and European civilization," and "dedication to the fatherland was the highest and most concrete form of altruism." The existing political parties were described as "seeds of disintegration, hotbeds of public and private corruption, and cabals (*congreghe*) operating in favor of particular interests, often foreign, in contrast to national interests." Hence in a "rational" State designed to satisfy the general interests of the nation, they could not be active protagonists of political life. Given this view, it is not surprising to discover that primacy of place among the FN's plans was the creation of a strong and "authoritative" State that would be capable not only of defending national honor and territorial integrity, but also of creating social and political institutions corresponding to the best traditions of the Italian people rather than the exigencies of modern civilization. Political parties were to be excluded from participating in government activities or the union system. The old class subdivisions and antagonisms were to be replaced by a "realistic and healthy" collaboration between various employment categories, organized corporately and headed by freely elected leaders of proven professional competence. A National Legislative Assembly was to be established, made up of both representatives from the employment categories and specially appointed citizens of merit. The nation's political economy was to be based on the recognition of private initiative and ownership, as long as these did not conflict with the national interest, and the "responsible participation" of employees in the management of businesses. Domestic policy was to be geared toward ensuring national cohesion, the rigorous observance of the law, the defense of public order and morality, and the material and moral support of the citizens. "Qualified" criticism would be tolerated insofar as it was expressed in order to further national interests. Foreign policy would be centered on maintaining the integrity, independence, and dignity of the nation, a task that was to be entrusted to the armed forces.[61]

In this program Borghese combined the standard themes of the conservative right – appeals to nationalism, order, anti-communism, traditional morality, the sanctity of private property – with some fascist-inspired ideas regarding corporatism, worker participation in company management, and the need for a strong, interventionist state. This somewhat contradictory ideological brew was a regular feature of FN proclamations. Two other characteristics of these pronouncements need to be further highlighted. As noted earlier, Borghese not infrequently made appeals to forces that on the surface appeared to be his sworn enemies. He strengthened his contacts with former anti-fascists like Pacciardi, and cooperated tangibly with them in various joint political ventures. This was of course nothing new for the Black Prince, who in late 1944 had sought to form an alliance between his Decima MAS units and groups of "white" partisans in the Veneto against Yugoslav partisans and their Italian communist allies.[62] Likewise, he sought to elicit the support of alienated youths and workers, including those who were not associated with the right. In 1970 the "Commander" indicated that the FN understood "the objectives that motivated the struggles of youth and labor" and recognized the spiritual components which underpinned them. In an interview he gave to journalist Giampaolo Pansa four days before the 1970 coup, he went so far as to claim that the FN was "progressive" rather than conservative, and that its ideas could even be categorized as leftist given its promotion of RSI-style "socialization" and worker participation. He added that the FN would apply whatever scheme was best for the Italians, regardless of whether it was pseudo-communist, socialist, or liberal in orientation.[63] These kinds of rhetorical appeals have been viewed by some on the left as evidence that he was trying to initiate a sinister operation of infiltration and manipulation, a possibility reinforced by some of the purported activities of the FN. However, it seems clear that Borghese genuinely empathized with the frustration and alienation felt by youths, in part because he himself felt so psychologically estranged from the existing political system. Then too, there were practical reasons for adopting this approach. In the 1970 interview, he specifically indicated that Italian youths would be seduced by Mao Zedong's *Little Red Book* if they weren't provided with patriotic alternatives that could satisfy their legitimate aspirations and grievances.[64]

Second, the FN sought to present itself as a legalistic, and even a democratic, organization in its public proclamations, despite its clear expressions of hostility toward parliamentary democracy. During a December 1969 phone conversation, Borghese told Pansa that it would be "pure folly" for anyone to try and reconstruct the Fascist party, with its specific symbols and salutes. In this he was probably sincere, especially given the unlikelihood that such a chimerical venture could meet with success. In his interview a year later he also claimed to respect freedom and personal dignity. Furthermore, in the FN's program it was emphasized that a just state would rigorously respect the tripartite separation of power between the legislative, judicial, and executive branches, and that the people themselves had the right to modify the structure of the state as long as such a modification was historically necessary and carried out in accordance with legally sanctioned methods.[65] Yet this half-hearted promotion of democratic formulas, which was intended to make the FN seem less threatening – or perhaps to justify Borghese's own future plans to modify the existing political system – rather than to serve as a real safeguard for democracy in the "new" political order he sought to establish, was certainly not reflected in his other stated goals. For example, the projected limitation of party activities and the severe restrictions to be placed on expressions of dissent were incompatible with genuine democracy. It is also apparent that Borghese's "presidentialist" plan would have altered the existing balance of the three branches of government in such a way as to strengthen the executive, discipline the judicial, and subordinate the legislative.

The lip service Borghese sometimes paid to democratic themes was also contradicted by his increasingly apocalyptic rhetoric and frequent allusions to the need to take dramatic action. In a 1970 introduction to the FN's *Orientamenti Programmatici*, the Black Prince claimed that it was "no longer possible to remain passive spectators of the ideological, social, and political 'stoning' (*lapidazione*) of the Italian fatherland." It was necessary for the Italians to resist the "oligarchy of interests and the conditioning, domestic and foreign," to which they were being subjected, because the ruling class's total lack of principles was one of the primary causes of the "rampant chaos" afflicting the country. Still later, in the December 1970 interview, he said that the incapacity of that class and the absence of any principle of national unity had resulted in a delegitimation and degeneration of the state apparatus, which had already "surrendered totally" to the communists. Because the Partito Comunista Italiano (PCI: Italian Communist Party) functioned as the "long arm" of Russia rather than as a democratic party, loyal communists would have no qualms about dressing up as priests if they received the order to do so. At some point the assistance invoked by party members could therefore provide a pretext for the Soviet invasion of Italy, as it had earlier done in Czechoslovakia.[66]

This perceived situation of acute crisis led the Black Prince to suggest that a "little coup" (*colpetto*) might be necessary to bring down the existing state, although that state was currently so rotten that it might collapse on its own at any time. In either case the Italian people would then be forced to choose between communism and the nation. That was where the FN came into the picture. According to Borghese, his organization was already in the process of establishing a "shadow state" that would be capable of replacing the existing regime when the latter collapsed. He tried to make it seem as though this imminent substitution of the government by the FN's structure would occur naturally, without resort to clandestine subversion or violence. Thus he claimed that when the FN was sufficiently consolidated in organizational terms, it would constitute a natural "center of attraction" that could simply fill the resulting political vacuum. Borghese and Guadagni both compared the situation in 1970 to that of 1922, when a degenerate old political class ceded power to a group that was more vital – the Fascist movement which had just marched on Rome – almost without a struggle. This type of surrender was even more likely now, in their opinion, because allegedly there were already many FN supporters in mainstream political parties, and even a few FN "shadow" deputies and senators in Parliament who promoted the Fronte's agenda even though they were officially members of other parties. Borghese had not actively sought to recruit them, however, because the FN did not aspire to be a mass electoral party. Instead, influential political figures had approached the Black Prince to make known their concerns about the course the country was following and express their sympathy for his patriotic goals. Rather than asking them to quit the parties to which they belonged and join the FN, Borghese told them to remain at their government posts and as members of their parties, at least for the time being. All that he demanded was that they be willing to renounce their current affiliations and openly join the FN if he asked them to do so in the future. It was via this "fifth column" of secret supporters that the FN was managing to insert itself into the system without having to rely on drastic measures. The communists were using the same techniques to insert themselves into governmental organs, from the communal level on up, so Borghese felt there was no reason why his supporters should do less.[67]

Despite all these references to replacing the current government, the former Decima MAS leader insisted that he had not thought much about a traditional coup d'etat. He felt that such an extreme action would not be necessary and that, in any case, it would be "very difficult" to launch a Greek-style military coup in a country like Italy. Yet he applauded the Colonel's coup for having saved Greece from communism, the "worst of evils" that could befall a people, and said the FN might view a coup in Italy favorably if the groups launching it shared the movement's own basic goals. For example, if the military launched a coup and set up a government of technicians, the FN could justify it as long as it was a short-term arrangement aimed at reestablishing order or preventing the communists from entering the government. He was quick to add, however, that the result of such an action would be the establishment of a conservative, "anti-social" government that would be divided from the people. In the long term, this would not be desirable from the FN's point of view.[68] Yet these reassuring remarks were soon belied by the course of events, because three days later Borghese launched his own "little coup," making use of the very subversive and violent means he claimed to eschew. Investigating magistrate Filippo Fiore was therefore right to conclude that, beneath a facade of legality, the FN promoted a subversive, anti-democratic project that depended upon the use of force for its realization.[69]

Although Borghese was clearly preparing for a coup throughout 1969 and 1970, this does not necessarily mean that he originally created the FN with this specific goal in mind. Yet that is precisely what the Italian military intelligence service concluded. According to an SID report compiled by the staff of Ufficio D (Counterespionage), the FN was created in 1968 in order to "subvert the institutions of the state by means of a coup." Perhaps this is so, but that same report indicated that the Fronte was intended to be a mass anti-communist organization.[70] These two contentions do not entirely mesh, however, because the type of clandestine cell structure that is best suited for carrying out a coup is in many ways unsuitable for promoting the growth of a mass political organization. There are three likely explanations for this apparent discrepancy. First, the Black Prince and his associates might have initially planned to build both a broad-based patriotic movement and a "shadow state," which together would hopefully be able not only to compel the existing regime to cede power, but also to take its place. The enthusiastic public response to his appearances at Comitato Tricolore rallies may have led Borghese to believe that he could mobilize nationalist sentiments like Charles de Gaulle had done in France. Both Borghese and Guadagni referred explicitly to this cisalpine model during the 1970 interview. The former Decima MAS commander noted that over one million citizens had rallied and marched through the streets of Paris in response to De Gaulle's appeal concerning the dangers posed to France by the May 1968 revolt, then suggested that something similar was needed in Italy. Guadagni added that only Borghese himself was capable of rallying the Italian people in this manner. The latter then claimed that the FN was trying to create an organization that could take advantage of such a massive popular response.[71] By that time, obviously, the two FN leaders were attempting to provide a cover for their imminent coup, but it may be that these remarks honestly reflected their earlier conceptions. When it became clear that the FN was unable to attract sufficient popular support, however, they may have felt compelled to modify their strategy and place all their hopes for political success on subversive projects.

Second, SID may have been right to conclude that Borghese intended all along to make use of the FN to launch a coup. This interpretation was certainly shared by sectors of the Italian left, which considered the Black Prince to be a "silent, spectral" figure who operated "discreetly behind the scenes" and held the "strands of the complex spiderweb" linking the various forces and actions of the right in his own hands.[72] There is no doubt that the Commander viewed the Fronte as an activist vanguard under his command rather than a mass movement, a fact that he himself acknowledged in his 1970 talk with Pansa. Moreover, one must grant due weight to Borghese's psychological makeup and background as a military adventurer. There are also a number of circumstantial factors that tend to support the view that his pseudo-legalistic portrayal of the FN's goals had always been aimed at disguising its real nature. If, for example, Borghese had been a collaborator of De Lorenzo's in 1964, this would suggest that he had long nourished and been involved in subversive schemes aimed at transforming Italy's parliamentary democracy. It has also been claimed that the Black Prince was among those who were provided with a copy of the published proceedings of the 1965 Istituto Pollio *guerre révolutionnaire* conference by its editor, Eggardo Beltrametti.[73] In that event, Borghese would certainly have become acquainted with the theme of that conference – the need to wage an all-out war against the communists, employing the same covert methods that they favored. The presentations in that particular book, by supplementing the firsthand knowledge he had earlier gained in the course of conducting antipartisan operations and providing a quasi-official justification for using the most extreme methods, perhaps gave him more of an incentive to have recourse to such methods himself. Finally, as will be detailed later, he was in close contact with the leading figures of several national and international right-wing extraparliamentary groups, groups that were themselves well versed in subversive techniques and covert operations. Such interactions could scarcely have encouraged him to employ legal, democratic means to achieve his political goals.

There is also a third possibility. From mid-1969 on, if not sooner, Borghese may have been knowingly employing a two-track strategy combining legal mass agitation and clandestine subversion. In fact, the developmental history of the FN suggests just that. Three months before the FN was formally established, he claimed to have already initiated preliminary organizational work, which involved the establishment of a planning committee in Rome and "action groups" in various regions and cities. It may well be that the basic organizational structure of the FN was conceived and fashioned in some rudimentary way around that time, but it is unlikely that much progress had actually been made in developing and elaborating that structure by June 1968. In creating the organization, Borghese relied upon the assistance of several close collaborators, including the building contractor Benito Guadagni, a former Decima MAS sailor whose father was killed by partisans, who initially provided most of the financing; the shipbuilder Remo Orlandini, the only Italian army officer entrusted by a suspicious Oberkommando der Wehrmacht (OKW) with the command of a German company during the Salò period, who handled various operational matters and became the FN's chief liaison with representatives of the state apparatus; and Mario Rosa, a former major in the Milizia Volontaria per la Sicurezza Nazionale (MVSN: Volunteer Militia for National Security) and commander of the 3rd battalion of the RSI's Apennine light infantry regiment, who was appointed secretary.[74] Following the Fronte's formal founding in September, this leadership group transformed the planning committee into an executive body, set up official branches in several regions, and accelerated its efforts to rally supporters and recruit members.

The resulting FN structure consisted of a central headquarters in Rome and a series of provincial "delegations" throughout Italy. The FN leaders ("delegates") in each province, who were selected by Borghese and his key associates from among prestigious and influential local supporters who had displayed enthusiasm and initiative, were charged with disseminating the FN's ideas, recruiting personnel, obtaining financing, "networking," and devising plans to counteract communist activities in their areas. When political conditions became propitious, they were intended to assume administrative functions analogous to those of the incumbent government Prefects. These delegates were each to be assisted by a committee, in theory composed of qualified representatives from various local economic sectors, whose members were in turn supposed to act as intermediaries with the people in their respective spheres. Although having a certain amount of autonomy in the local sphere, the delegates were required to execute orders emanating from headquarters without question. Such an organizational arrangement was more or less compatible with Borghese's contention that the FN was intended to constitute a "shadow state" that would be capable of assuming governmental functions upon the collapse of the existing system.[75] However, this visible and ostensibly legalistic structure was subsequently transformed. Toward the end of 1969, a clandestine, parallel structure was created alongside – or rather beneath – the overt, formal structure. Groups belonging to the latter were thenceforth referred to by those in the know as "A groups," whereas the covert groups were denominated "B groups." Although the existence of these "B groups" was known only to the Fronte's national leaders and those who actually provided their personnel, presumably the most trusted and action-oriented members of the local "A groups," every "A group" seems to have had an affiliated "B group," for which it provided an effective legal cover. The "B groups" therefore constituted clandestine armed cells within the bosom of the FN's official organizational structure, cells that were entrusted with the key operational tasks and clearly designed to carry out *sub rosa* acts. The existence of this two-tiered structure explains why Judge Fiore emphasized that not every Fronte member should be viewed as a conspirator, because many of them had been attracted to the movement primarily on the basis of its patriotic appeals and were not cognizant of its behind-the-scenes drift toward violence and subversion.[76]

Regardless of what the Commander's previous intentions may have been, the year 1969 clearly marked a crucial watershed in the elaboration of the FN's organizational network and operational plans. In the spring of that year, Borghese and his associates organized a series of meetings with leading FN supporters in several regions of Italy. According to SID intelligence reports, the Black Prince outlined various plans with a clearly subversive thrust at high-level gatherings held at the engineer Tommaso Adami Rook's villa in Pisa, at Pietro Paoletti's villa in Nugola Nuova, and at different locations in and around Rome. At a 19 March 1969 meeting in the Hotel Royal at Viareggio, Borghese asserted that the armed forces would not lack FN support in the struggle against communism. At another in Genoa, he told supporters that he intended to form "groups of public safety" to oppose, if necessary by force, the accession of the PCI to power. Luigi Federlini, the Genoese "delegation" leader, then revealed that a countercoup was to be launched if the communists took power, even through legal means. The military was to occupy key cities and public offices, and their civilian supporters in the Fronte were to help enlist the public's support for the operation. Federlini concluded by saying that the FN's goal was to establish a "national regime of the Gaullist type," and claimed that the rightist weekly *Il Borghese* was slated to become the movement's official organ. Attempts were also made in this period to enlist the aid of other interests presumed to be sympathetic to Borghese's goals. Thus, during a meeting with various heads of the Società Metallurgica Italiana toward the middle of the year, an FN representative, in an unsuccessful appeal to obtain weaponry produced in the company's factories, indicated that the Fronte intended to launch a coup between June and September of 1969.[77] Yet these grandiose schemes revealed themselves to be premature given the still limited manpower and resources at the FN's disposal.

After establishing the Fronte in 1968, Borghese had traveled throughout Italy, especially to various crisis points, in an effort to proselytize and recruit new members.[78] He exploited both his prestige as a soldier and his extensive network of contacts in this effort, and was thus able to attract constituents from a variety of different social groups. Not surprisingly, the bulk of the FN's adherents consisted of RSI veterans who had never reconciled themselves to the postwar order and younger right-wing ultras searching for adventure and something to believe in. These were joined by retired and active-duty military officers, ex-paratroopers, members of athletic and sports associations, some former "white" partisans, and people from all walks of life who were concerned above all with the preservation of social order and the prevention of a communist takeover.[79] Among these latter were a number of professionals and wealthy businessmen, especially in Liguria, who provided the organization with much of its financing.[80] Nevertheless, the total number of FN adherents apparently never exceeded a few thousand. Although Guadagni gave exaggerated estimates of the number of FN supporters to Pansa, presumably in order to give the impression that the organization was far more powerful than it really was, Judge Fiore concluded that the Black Prince's success in recruiting active new members was surprisingly limited. Indeed, according to the Interior Ministry, several of the Fronte's branches only existed on paper.[81] It is probable that the divergent assessments of FN strength derive in large part from a confusion between the number of its official members and the number of its covert supporters, which must have been considerably larger, especially if Borghese's claims regarding the existence of an extensive FN "fifth column" are true.

Even so, it seems clear that an inability to attract enough recruits directly into his own movement was one of the factors that prompted Borghese to strengthen links with other rightist political organizations. As he himself admitted at the time of his 1970 interview, the FN had contacts with every extraparliamentary rightist group in Italy, contacts that were mainly organizational rather than federative. Although Borghese seemed reluctant to specifically name any of these organizations, Guadagni said that he personally maintained excellent and frequent contacts with the secretary general of the Costituente Nazionale Rivoluzionaria (CNR: Revolutionary National Constituent Assembly), Giacomo De Sario.[82] The FN was also affiliated with the Lega Italia Unità (United League of Italy), an ephemeral umbrella organization that sought to group fifteen separate right-wing movements into a broad anti-communist front with expressly "presidentialist" designs. Among the participants at the Lega's founding meeting at Giuseppe Gattai's home in Viareggio on 7 November 1969 were representatives from the Fronte, Pacciardi's Nuova Repubblica, and several other key organizations, including Gaetano Orlando and Carlo Fumagalli, the leaders of the Movimento d'Azione Rivoluzionaria (MAR: Revolutionary Action Movement), and the intransigent monarchist Adamo Degli Occhi, future president of the Maggioranza Silenziosa (Silent Majority).[83] Despite its relatively short life span, this Lega may have played a role of some significance in the history of rightist anti-democratic plots by bringing together a number of more or less subversive groups and providing a legal cover for some of their organizational activities. In addition, the Fronte remained in contact with Pacciardi and, via Adriano Monti, with Edgardo Sogno, another uncompromisingly anti-communist ex-partisan.[84] Other groups known to be linked to the FN were Europa Civiltà (European Civilization) and Fronte Delta (Delta Front), both of which were actually mobilized on the night of the coup.

However, the most important contacts with the radical right that the FN cultivated in the second half of 1969 were with the two most active neo-fascist paramilitary groups in Italy, Ordine Nuovo (ON: New Order) and Avanguardia Nazionale (AN: National Vanguard). According to an SID report dating from this period, "there exists a precise agreement for political collaboration between Commander Borghese and Pino Rauti, Secretary General of ON."[85] The close collaboration between the two organizations was later confirmed by Borghese himself, who admitted that ON leaders Rauti, Rutilio Sermonti, and Giulio Maceratini had, due to their considerable organizing experience, made a valuable contribution to the FN's own organizational work prior to Rauti's decision to bring ON back within the MSI's protective fold. Yet this unexpected November 1969 rapprochement between the majority in ON and a revitalized MSI, although perhaps disrupting the previous accords between Rauti and Borghese, by no means put an end to FN-ON cooperation. According to Guadagni, individual members of ON continued to lend the FN a hand even after Rauti had rejoined the MSI.[86] Moreover, Rauti's decision had provoked a bitter schism within ON itself, and various members of the more radical breakaway faction – the Movimento Politico Ordine Nuovo (MPON: New Order Political Movement) led by Clemente Graziani – established, maintained, or increased their contacts with the FN. For example, the ex-paratrooper Sandro Saccucci, who was appointed head of the MPON's "parallel organizations" at a 21 December 1969 MPON meeting in Rome, later assumed important operational responsibilities in connection with the FN's coup attempt.[87] Nor was he alone. Other extremists affiliated with ON and the MPON also participated in that action, as well as in subsequent FN plots. The intermediary between the Fronte and ON was Sandro Pisano.[88]

Yet it was with Avanguardia Nazionale that Borghese forged the closest links. The personal connections between Borghese and Stefano Delle Chiaie, AN's charismatic leader, date back to at least the mid-1960s. Both had participated at various gatherings of the European radical right, and the "black bombardier" and his men were allegedly regular visitors to the seat of the Circolo dei Selvatici.[89] According to SID, relations between the FN and AN became even closer in the fall of 1969, and at the end of that year Delle Chiaie and two of his chief lieutenants, Flavio Campo and Cesare Perri, were recruited into the Fronte's National Directorate. Serious discussions about a possible coup, initially projected for June 1970, were then undertaken. The notorious Delle Chiaie, who SID justly described as a "technician of mass agitation and conspiracy," was personally given the job of creating political and revolutionary cadres throughout Italy and coordinating their interaction with FN headquarters.[90] Given AN's previous experience in planning and carrying out covert operations, it seems very probable that Delle Chiaie's organizational activity was in some way related to the creation of the FN's clandestine "B groups," a task that Rauti and his ON associates may have already laid the groundwork for prior to reentering the MSI. In any event, the Black Prince and Delle Chiaie soon developed so much respect for one another that Borghese gave special consideration to the latter's advice and ended up appointing him as the FN's "national military leader." This decision provoked the disapproval of some FN leaders, who feared that Delle Chiaie was untrustworthy and resented his usurpation of certain operational responsibilities that they themselves had wished to assume. But the stubborn old war hero, recognizing that the determination, discipline, and unscrupulousness of AN's ultras made them ideally suited to act as "point men" in any subversive operation, ignored their protests. In fact, he relied more and more upon Delle Chiaie and his men as time went on, and authorized Orlandini to distribute conspicuous sums of money to Campo and Perri.[91]

Of no less importance, Borghese and others associated with the FN had established contacts with various international networks of right-wing extremists. Among the most active of these was the Nouvelle Ordre Européen/Europäische Neu-Ordnung (NOE/ENO: New European Order), headed by Swiss neo-Nazi Gaston-Armand Amaudruz. Since its creation on 28 September 1951, the NOE/ENO has held a series of international congresses at which representatives from a wide variety of neo-fascist groups – including, from the late 1950s till the mid-1970s, Ordine Nuovo and Avanguardia Nazionale – have gathered to extend each other solidarity and map out joint political programs. Like the gatherings of other such umbrella organizations, however, it is probable that these "official" congresses were used as a cover behind which certain subversive groups secretly sought to develop more tangible operational linkages and devise more specific strategies for action. For example, at the 9th NOE/ENO congress held in Milan on 25 March 1967, participant Robert Leroy of Aginter Presse revealed that a "seizure of power" in Italy and other countries had been discussed. According to Leroy, allegedly a close acquaintance of Borghese, Delle Chiaie, Clemente Graziani, and Europa Civiltà's Stefano Serpieri, it was felt that a military putsch could rescue Italy from its disastrous social and economic conditions, and that there were many good officers there who were in a position to seize power.[92] If the Black Prince in fact knew Leroy well, this must have brought him, at least tangentially, into the orbit of Aginter Presse, the notorious network of right-wing subversives and terrorists headquartered in Lisbon. Nor, perhaps, was this Borghese's only contact with external forces later implicated in the "strategy of tension." The Extraparliamentary Left Research Group claimed, without providing any documentary evidence, that Borghese was one of the Greek Colonels' most trusted men in Italy. In this capacity he supposedly developed links with both the Greek foreign minister at the Rome embassy and Kostas Plevris, a leader of the neo-fascist Kinema tes 4 Augoustou (K4A: 4th of August Movement).[93]

Moreover, Borghese's efforts to enlist external aid were apparently not confined exclusively to far right circles. According to the subsequent testimony of various persons linked to organized crime, the Black Prince also sought to recruit elements of the Mafia as participants in his projected coup. Thus Antonino Calderone, sibling of Mafia boss Giuseppe "Pippo" Calderone, revealed that Borghese personally made such a proposal to his brother during a secret meeting in Rome during the spring of 1970. In return for the Mafia's armed support, Borghese promised to "reconsider" the sentences of imprisoned *mafiosi*. Pippo must have been won over or at least intrigued, because shortly thereafter he approached Tomasso Buscetta, a key Sicilian *capo*, and outlined the scheme to him. Buscetta further claimed that it was the freemasons who had first alerted the Cosa Nostra to Borghese's coup preparations. The Black Prince's idea was at first enthusiastically supported by some of the bosses, especially Luciano Liggio and the three Rimi brothers, but objections later surfaced to his insistence that a full list of participating *mafiosi* be provided and that they wear, along with the rest of the conspirators, identifying armbands. Borghese subsequently agreed to forego this list and, in the wake of a successful coup, bring a halt to the trials of Liggio and Vincenzo and Filippo Rimi. Although in the end the bosses decided that it was too risky to accept Borghese's offer, Natale Rimi and some other *mafiosi* apparently participated in certain actions related to the coup.[94]

Nevertheless, in spite of the extensive links that Borghese developed with other extreme right and criminal groups, toward the end of 1969 it had become clear to him that the forces at the FN's disposal were "absolutely insufficient" to carry out his objectives. He therefore intensified his efforts to expand the number of FN supporters within the ranks of the official forces of order, in particular the armed forces.[95] His own attitude toward the military, like that of many fascists and fascist sympathizers, had been characterized by a certain amount of ambiguity ever since World War II. As a onetime supporter of the wartime alliance with Germany, he clearly retained a bitter hostility toward those military leaders who had failed to do their duty and "betrayed" Italy by offering their allegiance to the servile Badoglio government after July 1943. On the other hand, as a career military man who only asked that his epitaph read "this is a soldier who has served his country well," the Black Prince had always felt a sense of solidarity with those officers and common soldiers who had supposedly placed the needs of the nation above their own personal interests and partisan political allegiances.[96] For this reason, he had long maintained personal contacts with some of the more immoderate, hard-line elements inside the officer corps, especially those in his old service, the Navy. His links to members of the armed forces, both tangible and emotional, were further reinforced during his public appearances at various MSI, FNCRSI, and Comitato Tricolore rallies, where both veterans and active-duty military personnel repeatedly demonstrated that they reciprocated the former Decima MAS commander's esteem and affection. Finally, he was convinced that many soldiers would feel an affinity for the FN simply because it promoted patriotism, traditional values, and the rigorous defense of disputed Italian border territories.[97]

These sentiments and perceptions made it natural for Borghese to view the armed forces as a rich potential source of recruits and "fifth column" supporters in his hour of need. Although he denied that the FN made active attempts to recruit soldiers,[98] this disclaimer is contradicted by a variety of evidence. In 1973, for example, his right-hand man Orlandini confided to Captain Labruna of SID that the Fronte had spent years conducting penetration operations into the ranks of the military.[99] Two years later, Investigating Magistrate Fiore concluded that the FN's efforts to enroll adherents within the armed forces were further accelerated in the last quarter of 1969. This development may be reflected in one of the SID intelligence reports, which indicates that Borghese met with selected military leaders in Fiesole in October 1969, and again in Florence at the Circolo Forze Armate (Armed Forces Circle).[100] Yet even though both the Black Prince and Orlandini appear to have expended a lot of time and energy working on these penetration and recruitment activities, gaps in the available sources and contradictory claims make it difficult to determine just how successful they ultimately were. There are two separate issues involved here. First, how extensive was the FN's network of supporters and sympathizers within the armed services and other forces of order in Italy? Second, what role did these alleged supporters and sympathizers actually play in the 1970 coup and the Fronte's subsequent subversive activities? The first matter needs to be tackled at once, but the second must be deferred until the coup has been described in detail.

There were undoubtedly a significant number of more or less tacit FN supporters within the military, especially among officers and in elite units, but the vast majority of them seem to have been unwilling to seriously entertain or actively commit themselves to subversive schemes. Despite this, many observers believed that the FN's infiltration into military ranks had reached worrisome levels. Various leftist investigators claimed that officers and NCOs who were secretly members of the FN had for years monitored their colleagues in order to assess their ideological reliability and, presumably, to sound out what their reaction might be if direct action was taken to transform the government and prevent a communist takeover. Those deemed to be sufficiently trustworthy were then carefully approached for recruitment.[101] In this way, clandestine networks of FN sympathizers were supposedly set up within the various armed services. Some confirmation of this general scenario, as well as an indication of just how extensive such networks might have been, was subsequently provided by Orlandini himself. In the course of his many meetings with Labruna, Orlandini claimed that the plotters had established contacts above all with "high military circles," and that among the FN's active supporters in the armed forces were Air Force Chief of Staff Duilio Fanali; a group of admirals, including the Navy's chief of staff, Admiral Giuseppe Roselli Lorenzini; the commander of the Air Force in the Rome region, along with most of his men and all of the Air Force squadrons (*stormi*); various unit commanders; and General Giuseppe Barbasetti, commander of the parachute brigade. He also asserted that several top functionaries of the Ministry of the Interior, various police commissioners from the traditionally "black" neighborhoods of Rome (such as Parioli, EUR, and Trionfale), entire units of the national civilian police, and all of the Carabinieri (other than some high-ranking generals) had secretly backed the Fronte, if not the actual coup.[102] Perhaps even more ominously, Orlandini revealed that three thousand military officers in Italy were members of masonic lodges. He indicated that FN representatives had approached various masonic leaders in order to solicit their aid, and that several meetings were then held in Rome to discuss the proposal. In the end, important groups of freemasons supposedly voted, presumably in secret lodge assemblies, to support Borghese's planned action.[103]

However, these extravagant and eye-opening claims cannot all be accepted at face value. For example, although there were clearly subversive elements within the ranks of the Carabinieri, it is impossible to believe that all the members of such a conservative, legalistic corps would have sympathized with or supported the type of violent, unconstitutional schemes that Borghese was promoting.[104] Likewise it is improbable that entire police units backed the coup, unless those units were small squads from notoriously nostalgic or pro-fascist locales.[105] Orlandini thus exaggerated, at least in part, the extent to which FN plotters were receiving behind-the-scenes support from high-ranking military and police officials and their subordinates. He was clearly trying to impress Labruna by bragging about the Fronte's powerful contacts, because he sought to recruit the SID man into the far-flung subversive network which was actively engaged, throughout 1973 and much of 1974, in planning new coups. Moreover, the transcripts of these Orlandini-Labruna talks themselves reveal that many ostensibly sympathetic superior officers were hesitant and prone to drag their feet when pressed by Orlandini to initiate concrete actions against the government.[106] In the end, given the absence of enough hard evidence and the omnipresence of political pressure being exerted to limit the damage to the reputation of state institutions, Judge Fiore was induced to minimize the amount of covert assistance provided to Borghese before, during, and after the coup by elements within the forces of order. This tendency was carried to even more absurd lengths by various appellate judges in the course of subsequent trials.

But the baby should not be thrown out with the bathwater. For one thing, several ranking members of the armed forces and the police can be shown to have been active co-conspirators, although their ultimate aims were in some cases quite different than those of Borghese and his radical neo-fascist followers. For another, it is clear that long before the coup Borghese and other FN plotters had secretly established contact with key operatives of various secret services, both Italian and foreign. The most important of these within Italy were the military intelligence service and the Interior Ministry's Ufficio Affari Riservati (UAR: Secret Affairs Office). In 1973, Orlandini told Labruna that he had first made contact with General Vito Miceli when the latter was head of the Servizio Informazioni Operative e Situazione (SIOS: Operational and Situational Intelligence Service)-Esercito (Army) – that is, before Miceli was appointed head of SID in October 1970 – and that Miceli, who had met with Borghese in Orlandini's Montesacro home on more than one occasion, was in agreement with the plotters and did nothing to harm them. Miceli later confirmed that he met with Orlandini personally in the spring and summer of 1969, and that he sent a trusted underling – Colonel Cosimo Pace – to meet with the shipbuilder four more times, all ostensibly in order to gather information. At these get-togethers, Orlandini repeatedly emphasized his respect for the armed forces, and discussed aspects of the FN's activities and requirements.[107] Yet Miceli's efforts to portray these meetings as falling within the ambit of legitimate intelligence gathering activities are not entirely credible, because both during and after the coup he personally went out of his way to prevent the exposure of the operation and, in the process, protect the conspirators. These top-level cover-up efforts, which helped bring an ongoing but largely hidden power struggle between rival factions within the government and SID to a head in 1974, will be discussed at some length later.

Orlandini further claimed that Dr. Salvatore Drago, a police medical examiner and one of the key FN plotters, had close links to the UAR.[108] Drago served as an important intermediary between that powerful clandestine apparatus and Borghese's men prior to and after the coup, and provided crucial logistical assistance beforehand to the AN commando group charged with penetrating the Viminale on the night of 7–8 December 1970. A 26 June 1974 SID report later identified the doctor as a very close friend of Federico Umberto D'Amato, de facto second-in-command within the UAR from 1969 until 1972, when he became its chief.[109] Nor was Drago the only FN putschist with reputed connections to D'Amato. It should be recalled that many sources, both leftist and neo-fascist, have accused Delle Chiaie himself of secretly working with or for D'Amato. If these claims have any basis in fact, which seems very likely, it would suggest that influential elements within the Interior Ministry were not only kept abreast of the FN's plans, but also played a "supportive" background role in the projected coup, at least to the extent that they could exploit or instrumentalize it for their own purposes. Yet the complicity of the Italian secret services in the Fronte's pre-coup activities apparently did not end there. In 1976, an anonymous informant told a journalist from *L'Europeo* that militants from the FN, AN, and ON had received training in unconventional warfare and disinformation techniques at a top secret base at Alghero in Sardinia. At the time this testimony was naturally viewed with some skepticism, because practically nothing was known about the installation itself. However, recent investigations have conclusively demonstrated that from the mid-1960s on it functioned as the principal training base for personnel recruited into the Italian "stay/behind" networks, as well as for those of other state security organizations and, perhaps, certain "unofficial" terrorist groups.[110]

If it is true that select cadres from the FN and affiliated neo-fascist groups received training in unconventional warfare at the Sardinia base, it must have been done with the knowledge, if not the explicit sanctioning, of some high-ranking elements within the American security forces. It is now known that the Sardinia base played an important role in U.S. and NATO plans for the defense of the Mediterranean basin, that it was in part staffed and managed by American military and secret service personnel, and that it was specifically slated to be defended by American military forces in the event of an outbreak of hostilities between the superpowers.[111] Given these circumstances and the extreme sensitivity of the activities being conducted at the isolated facility, it is inconceivable that the security-conscious Americans would have permitted Italian civilians to be trained there who were not earmarked to play a role that furthered, however indirectly, certain perceived U.S. interests. Nor is it believable that U.S. intelligence personnel did not know precisely who was being trained at the base. Unless it is assumed that those entrusted with running the base were extraordinarily incompetent, which is hardly warranted given the effectiveness with which the operations at Alghero were concealed for a decade, there is no reason to doubt that they would have made careful checks into the backgrounds of all the individuals selected for such specialized and potentially dangerous training. It is also unlikely that they were misled about the trainees by Italian intelligence, because the SID men assigned to oversee activities at the base had themselves been carefully chosen by Italian secret service officials considered "friendly" by their American counterparts. Finally, there is no reason to think that the U.S. intelligence personnel in charge of the base would have had any qualms about training or making use of radical rightists. Since 1945 hard-line factions within the U.S. military and intelligence establishments have repeatedly recruited right-wing extremists, including both former fascists and younger neo-fascists, into anti-communist intelligence and paramilitary organizations throughout Europe and other parts of the world. They would have had even less reluctance to make use of elements linked to Borghese, who American intelligence operatives had earlier rescued from a partisan vendetta and perhaps sought to recruit as titular leader of a postwar anti-communist "national front" coalition. Nevertheless, although there is nothing improbable about the informant's claim that FN members were among those trained at the Sardinia base, no documentary evidence has yet been uncovered to corroborate it.

There are, however, other indications that Borghese and some of his key associates were in contact with American intelligence officials in the months leading up to the coup. Orlandini himself testified that he was in direct contact with Hugh Fenwich, an American engineer who worked for a highly specialized electronics firm in Italy, Selenia, many of whose products had military applications and were classified "top secret." The building constructor had been introduced to Fenwich by AN member Adriano Monti, an SID operative who had earlier been sent to Cairo on some sort of mission by the CIA. According to Orlandini, Fenwich worked covertly overseas to promote the interests of both President Richard Nixon and the Republican Party, but was not a regular member of the CIA. Fenwich appears to have had a private communications channel to Nixon, because he personally phoned the president on at least one occasion in Orlandini's presence. At meetings with Captain Labruna in 1973 and 1974, Orlandini specifically identified the well-connected American as the intermediary between Nixon's entourage, NATO military personnel, and Borghese's plotters prior to and during the coup.[112] In an effort to verify some of these claims, Labruna then conducted an investigation of Fenwich. His Ufficio D investigative team soon concluded that the engineer was considered an *éminence grise* of the CIA in Italy. Fenwich was apparently a CIA "resident" – an intelligence operative who conducted normal business activities abroad but secretly carried out delicate intelligence tasks – rather than an actual case officer; hence his name did not appear on the official list of U.S. secret service personnel. He had arrived in Italy after a long sojourn in two other intelligence "hot spots," Korea and Vietnam, and resided with his family at a villa in Grottaferrata. The sensitivity and importance of Fenwich's work were apparently so great that one of SID's regular informants inside the CIA refused, when asked, to provide any information about the engineer.[113]

To this direct but unconfirmed testimony must be added a good deal of circumstantial evidence indirectly linking the FN to various Western secret services. As noted earlier, Borghese and other FN leaders had personal contacts with key representatives of Aginter Presse and, perhaps, the Greek K4A. It has already been shown in the preceding article that Aginter personnel were closely connected to hard-line factions of Portuguese, French, Spanish, West German, and probably U.S. intelligence, and that they carried out various dirty, "plausibly deniable" jobs at the behest of those factions in return for the provision of material aid and "cover." If it is true that Borghese was in contact with K4A leader Plevris, this would have linked him at least indirectly to elements of the Greek security services, because Plevris was an operative for both the Kentrike Ypiresia Pliroforion (KYP: Central Intelligence Service) and the Ellenike Stratiotike Astunomia (ESA: Greek Military Police).[114] Yet there is still more. The apparent connections between leading FN plotters and intelligence personnel seemed to receive further confirmation when the lists of P2 masonic lodge members were discovered by the Polizia Giudiziaria (Judicial Police) in Licio Gelli's villa at Castiglion Fibocchi in 1981. The names of many important people who were earlier implicated in the Borghese coup appeared on those lists. Among them were Fronte adherents like Orlandini, Drago, Sandro Saccucci, and Giacomo Micalizio; alleged military plotters like Fanali, General Giuseppe Casero, and General Ugo Ricci; and high-ranking secret service officials like Miceli and D'Amato. Even the two SID officials who investigated and belatedly exposed the putschists, Captain Labruna and his boss, Ufficio D head Gianadelio Maletti, were on the lists.[115] The presence of all of these names in fact reveals something significant about the nature of P2 that has been glossed over by some commentators – the presence of members from *rival* secret service factions within its secretive ranks – but in this context what needs to be emphasized is that Gelli and his P2 lodge were clearly linked to powerful political circles in the United States and other Western nations, including influential groupings inside their secret services. The significance of this for the outcome of the Borghese coup will soon be considered.

In any event, the end of 1969 saw Borghese and his chief henchmen strengthening alliances with right-wing paramilitary groups and sympathetic elements within the military and security services, both domestic and foreign. According to SID, this was merely the prelude to further organizational and operational developments. As the months passed in 1970, the Fronte accelerated its efforts to consolidate its forces, elaborate a structure capable of carrying out clandestine actions, and lay the groundwork for an operation designed to precipitate a military coup. At various meetings held at Adami Rook's villa near the end of April, at which Pisa FN leader Ugo Mazzari and Pistoia FN chief Esperio Cappellini participated, the armed occupation of an objective in Rome was originally planned for 24 May 1970.[116] This plan was abandoned soon after, presumably because the Fronte lacked sufficient strength or external support to carry it out at that point. On 1 June, at a meeting in Rosa's office, Delle Chiaie was appointed as leader of the Fronte's "B groups."[117] By that time, the AN chief had already fled to Spain in order to avoid being indicted for giving false testimony in the Piazza Fontana case, but despite the issuance of a warrant for his arrest he was able to travel to and from Italy without difficulty. Then, on 4 July, the Fronte's national council was granted "unlimited deliberative and executive powers" in the course of a top-level meeting at the organization's headquarters in Rome, which Judge Fiore believed was related to the approach of an operational "D-Day," because normal administrative needs would not have required such an action.[118] This interpretation was buttressed by SID, whose investigators indicated that Borghese's preparations for a coup were finalized sometime in July. According to their reconstruction, Adami Rook was to furnish "B group" personnel for the occupation of the Interior Ministry. In preparation for this, about twenty FN men from La Spezia and Genoa, including MSI *federale* Gaetano Lunetta, came to Rome to reconnoiter the Viminale. Drago divided these men into cells of three or four men and personally conducted the operation. In early August another such survey was carried out for the head of the Genoese "B group," ex-paratrooper Stelio Frattini, and his adjutant Angelo Cagnoni, nicknamed "the Beast." Frattini himself testified that Drago, acting on Orlandini's orders, accompanied Cagnoni on a reconaissance of the area *inside* the Viminale that was slated to be occupied, devised a plan for the various phases of the projected occupation, and then consigned that plan to Frattini.[119] The surreptitious entry of FN personnel into the interior of the Viminale in late summer was undoubtedly facilitated by conspirators within the Interior Ministry, as it later was on the night of the coup. With the approach of the scheduled December "zero hour," a number of FN meetings were held to put the finishing touches on Borghese's operational plans.

Meanwhile, selected cadres from the FN, AN, and ON had participated in a series of paramilitary training exercises throughout the spring and summer of 1970. According to Paolo Guzzanti, Borghese entrusted the training of the FN's commando groups to Saccucci. Saccucci and other former paratroopers conducted this training during camping outings at Lago Turano (organized by Europa Civiltà), in Cascia, in the mountains that surround Palermo, and at the Ponticelli cemetery near Naples. At least three hundred people were allegedly trained in techniques of guerrilla warfare at the latter locale, without being disturbed at all by the forces of order. Indeed, the rightist weekly *Lo Specchio* later published excerpts from two official military documents, which revealed that Saccucci had received authorization and logistical support from the Army General Staff before providing this training.[120] Members of Ordine Nuovo were no less active in this sphere. Between 1 and 31 August, ON militants participated in four training camps held in the mountains of central Italy. Among the themes of the lessons were "Revolutionary War," "The Third World War has already begun," "The Organization of an Operational Revolutionary Group," and "Techniques for Finding the Financial Means necessary for a Revolutionary Group's Political Action," instruction that was supplemented by intensive practical training in karate and other gymnastic exercises. Other ON training camps were held in northern Italy. One was established by Salvatore Francia in the Piedmontese Alps, where participants were trained to use portable radios and fight with knives. Still another was in operation during August 1970 at Fort Foin, near Bardonecchia, at which forty ON "group leaders" conducted joint maneuvers and practiced shooting machine guns, automatic rifles, and pistols.[121] Around the same time, AN organized one of its own paramilitary training camps near Leonessa.[122] Finally, as noted earlier, selected members of all of these organizations may have secretly received training at the "Gladio" base in Sardinia. It seems that a certain number of weapons were also stockpiled by the FN throughout this period, because arms were found stashed at the organization's headquarters after the attempted coup was exposed in March 1971.

Nor, alas, did FN personnel restrict their activities to devising plans, organizing, and training for unconventional warfare before launching the December 1970 operation. Less than one year after the Fronte was created in the fall of 1968, various ultras associated with it began to be implicated in acts of political violence and provocation. The first of these incidents seems to have occurred in the last quarter of 1969, a period characterized by exceptional student and labor unrest. It was precisely during this "hot autumn" that the Fronte intensified its efforts to strengthen its links with action-oriented elements of other radical rightist organizations, the most important of which had been engaged in carrying out a terrorist "strategy of tension" since the spring of 1968, if not earlier. A series of high-level planning sessions between representatives of the FN, ON, AN, and Europa Civiltà were therefore held in the weeks preceding the Piazza Fontana bombing. In the course of these meetings, the merits of employing certain operational techniques and the coordination of projected future actions were undoubtedly among the subjects discussed. One such gathering, called to discuss what the response should be to the 19 November "general strike" organized by the trade unions, was held in Rome at an apartment near Piazza Tuscolo on 15 November 1969. At the meeting, a violent disagreement erupted between those who favored a more moderate "containment" strategy and the "heavies" who promoted the use of terrorist attacks and public bombings in order to provoke a leftist overreaction, which would in turn precipitate an intervention of the forces of order. Following a brief exchange of fisticuffs, an outraged FN "moderate" and former Decima MAS trooper named Armando Calzolari stormed out of the meeting. Far from bringing a halt to the drastic measures proposed by the ultras, the resulting breakaway of some other moderates seems to have removed all the remaining obstacles to the activation of those measures. Thus on 6 December, the ultras apparently decided to follow through with their plans during a secret meeting held in Rome at the Viale delle Milizie headquarters of the Associazione Nazionale Paracadutisti.[123] There was almost certainly some relationship between the bombings in Milan and Rome on 12 December and the decisions taken by influential right-wing extremists in the course of these and other meetings, although later efforts to determine the precise criminal responsibility of actual FN activists – as opposed to that of members of the other groups with whom the FN was collaborating – have not proven successful.

Be that as it may, the mysterious year-end death of the disgruntled Calzolari may have been directly linked to his decision to break ranks with other *camerati* over the issue of employing certain types of violence. The exact role that Calzolari played in the FN's activities prior to his disappearance was a matter of dispute, at least at the outset. According to leftist sources, Calzolari, ostensibly a public relations man for a bridge- and road-building firm, was in fact one of the Fronte's two chief money-handlers, along with Luciano Luberti. In this capacity, he helped to procure and administer the organization's funds, a task for which he was allegedly well-suited given his knowledge of several foreign languages and his establishment of numerous contacts abroad, especially in the United States. Calzolari's wife, Maria Piera Romano, added that her husband had participated in regular get-togethers with top politicians, industrialists, and clerics, usually at elaborately organized dinners at Rome's Ville Radieuse restaurant on Via Aurelia.[124] These assertions were vehemently denied by Borghese and Guadagni on the eve of the 1970 coup. They insisted that Calzolari was too young and lacked the "intellectual breadth" to have been enrolled in the Decima MAS, that he was a good lad who worked temporarily as a telephone operator and usher for the FN, that Borghese did not know him and only saw him once at FN headquarters, that it was hard to imagine him being the victim of a political crime, and that claims of his importance within the Fronte and closeness to Borghese were the products of a PSI-sponsored propaganda campaign.[125] However, Calzolari's presence at various high-level meetings of the extraparliamentary right during the winter of 1969, which was later attested to by some of the other participants, itself demonstrates that his role in the FN was anything but insignificant. His subsequent fate only strengthens this interpretation, because otherwise it would not have been felt necessary to eliminate him in order to prevent the secret projects of the conspirators from being exposed.

At 8 AM on Christmas Day, 1969, Calzolari went out to walk his English setter Paulette. Although he indicated that he would be back shortly, he was never again seen alive by his family and friends. Despite intensive police efforts to locate him, it was not until 28 January 1970 that the corpse of the forty-three-year-old "nationalist" was found, along with that of his dog, in a small pond of water in the Bravetta area, just southwest of Rome's Villa Doria Pamphili park and about two miles from his house. Most of the police investigators assigned to the case seemed very anxious to classify the death as accidental, and Calzolari's wife was initially quick to agree. Nevertheless, a considerable amount of evidence, both technical and circumstantial, suggested that foul play was involved. Friends of the victim later testified that on 15 December, three days after the Piazza Fontana massacre, Calzolari told them he was worried because he had been threatened. Then, a couple of days before his disappearance, he confessed to his mother, Maria Pia Calzolari, that he had had a violent quarrel after listening to a 19 December speech by Almirante concerning the bombings in Milan and Rome. She also indicated that her son was a "bundle of nerves" when she first arrived for a stay at his house over the Christmas holiday. Finally, one dubious source claimed that Calzolari became so angry at a post-*strage* meeting – perhaps the one at which Almirante spoke – that he had threatened to reveal everything he knew about the background of the bomb plot. This disconcerting testimony suggests that some of his former political associates at once began applying psychological pressure in order to ensure his continued silence. Perhaps ominously, the ultras apparently held another secret meeting on 20 December, the day *after* Calzolari had had a second dispute with them about the bombings.[126]

Moreover, the intervention of right-wing extremists in this affair by no means ended with Calzolari's death. Various "friends" of his from "the party" immediately began to try and influence the behavior of his stunned wife. On the very day her husband disappeared, she received a call from someone who suggested that he was safe in Corsica. The next day the same person phoned and admitted that this was not in fact the case, after which she received a visit from three of the aforementioned "friends," who advised her that in order to protect Calzolari it would be better if she did not talk to anyone about what had happened. At that point she began telling the press that her husband may have been picked up by some friends and brought to Israel, where he was scheduled to participate in a course on counterguerrilla warfare, a story very similar to one which had apparently been disseminated by a particular FN leader to some of his associates. This was clearly a smokescreen designed to throw investigators off the track, because Calzolari's wife then warned her mother-in-law to keep her mouth shut so as not to jeopardize her husband's life.[127] In spite of Maria Romano's seeming willingness to cooperate, those who sought to guarantee her continued silence soon added a "carrot" to their barely veiled threats. Two years later, she told Judge De Lillo that she would be hurt economically if the case was not closed. Because Calzolari was not insured, this suggests that someone else had promised to help his wife financially if the investigation into his death was discontinued. According to the Extraparliamentary Left Research Group, she had already received money from G. Bertone, a financial backer of the MSI.[128]

The initial verdict of accidental death can also be criticized on logical and technical grounds. Although anything is possible, it seems unlikely that a robust person in the peak of health, an expert skindiver, and a former sailor in the merchant marine could have accidentally drowned in a small pond of water whose greatest depth was less than his own height. Nor is there any evidence that Calzolari intended to commit suicide, a possibility vehemently rejected by all of his family members and close friends. Instead, there are indications that he actually lost his life several days *after* his disappearance. Thus the autopsy report placed his death fifteen to thirty days prior to the date his body was discovered, the body was found in an area that had previously been searched by police dogs, and his car was inexplicably missing from its parking space between 25 and 28 December.[129] None of these facts jibe with the official theory of an accidental death, an explanation that even failed to satisfy certain neo-fascist journalists. On 2 January, an article in *Il Tempo* concluded that Calzolari's work for the FN had made him knowledgeable about certain events whose particulars could interest "organized groups of political adversaries." Twelve days later Sergio Tè, a former member of AN and close associate of Delle Chiaie, wrote an article for *Il Secolo d'Italia* in which he claimed that Calzolari's disappearance was a "political crime" and accused the radical left of responsibility. Tè further suggested that the lack of results in the investigation might be attributable, if not to foot-dragging, to an "overly efficient organization interested in 'disappearing' certain persons after making use of them to obtain important information." The first of these revelations agitated Calzolari's wife, but before she was able to take any action to help her husband she received a visit from Carabinieri Captain Castino, who temporarily persuaded her to abandon the idea that a crime had been committed.[130]

In view of these growing discrepancies, both Judge Aldo Vitozzi and Calzolari's mother became more and more suspicious. Vitozzi decided to pursue the case against the will of the prosecutor, and eventually concluded that the FN man's death was a homicide designed to cover up another crime: the 12 December bombings. Using the pretext that confidential information had somehow leaked out, the case was then taken away from the judge, who was subjected to disciplinary action. In March 1972 this particular case of "accidental death" was formally closed by the assistant prosecutor, Salvatore Pallara. Eighteen months later it was reopened, in large part due to pressure exerted by Calzolari's mother, and in 1976 it was finally reclassified as a premeditated murder.[131] Although the actual perpetrators were never definitively identified, the pall of suspicion fell directly upon Calzolari's erstwhile comrades within the orbit of the FN. His mother was convinced that the Di Luia brothers or the sadistic Luberti had killed her son, but later Marco Pirina, the leader of Fronte Delta, testified that Mario Rosa told him that he and other FN members had eliminated a colleague who "talked too much," which prosecutor Claudio Vitalone assumed was a reference to Calzolari.[132] If either of these people was in fact the culprit, the death of Calzolari may have been among the first examples of the FN's employment of homicidal violence.

Another possible indication of the Fronte's transition from clandestine planning to the actual commission of acts of provocation and terrorism emerged from the testimony of Evelino Loi, an unemployed Sardinian in his twenties. In the middle of January 1970, Loi appeared at the Rome offices of *L'Espresso*, where he testified at length about various alleged incidents involving himself and certain right-wing militants. According to Loi, a few days before the planned "general strike" on 19 November 1969, he was approached by Commander Guido Bianchini and Deputy Commander Santino Viaggio, two former Decima MAS men who had collaborated with Borghese in the organization of the FN. They alluded to the possibility of carrying out simultaneous terrorist actions in Rome and Milan, and asked Loi if he was willing to take part in such actions in return for payment. Recognizing the dangers involved, the young Sardinian refused, but right after the metalworkers' demonstration at the end of November he was again contacted by Bianchini and Viaggio, who offered him even more money to participate in these "very important terrorist acts." Loi again refused. A couple of days later, he went to the Questura and recounted his story to a top official of the Ufficio Politico (Political Section), Dr. Umberto Improta, who continued to display skepticism until the day after the 12 December bombings in Milan and Rome. At that point, he contacted Loi and asked him to come down to the Questura and use the secondary entrance on Via Genova so that he would not be seen coming and going. When he arrived, Improta listened to his story again and advised him not to speak of these matters to anyone, saying "[i]t's better for you. Don't get yourself into trouble."[133]

Loi's testimony regarding this supposed FN-sponsored provocation was generally disregarded, not least because Loi himself was an unscrupulous, dishonest, and apparently unbalanced person with a checkered past. After associating himself with the leftist student movement in order to obtain a free place to sleep and subsequently stealing donations that had been collected to provide bail for imprisoned students, he was kicked out by its leaders.[134] Then, in exchange for 100,000 lire, he accused his erstwhile comrades of "hooliganism" and not caring about workers in an interview published by the rightist daily, *La Luna*. This brought him into the orbit of various radical right groups, according to both his own testimony and that of others. He claimed, for example, that he was approached at Stazione Termini, the central train station in Rome, by a policeman named "King," apparently a Celere (riot police) officer named Murino, shortly after the interview appeared. "King" complimented him on recognizing the true nature of the communists, suggested that he join Giovane Italia (Young Italy), brought him to the Via Firenze headquarters of the organization that same evening, and introduced him to its president, Franco De Marco. There he was treated very well, so much so that he stayed on, took part in operational planning, and was later entrusted with the task of recruiting jobless youth for violent actions, in exchange for which he was allegedly provided with considerable sums of money.

During this period Loi is said to have appeared in the front ranks at a number of neo-fascist demonstrations, and claims to have met Caradonna, Massimo Anderson, and – at a meeting of former veterans held at the Cinema Teatro – Santino Viaggio. Afterwards Viaggio brought him to FN headquarters and had him recount his political experiences to those present. On another occasion, Viaggio and Bianchini spoke of carrying out an attack on Parliament with sleeping gas, but later indicated that the plan was opposed by various MSI leaders. Still later, Viaggio supposedly paid Loi 50,000 lire to recruit people to cause trouble on the day of the "general strike," and subsequently confided to him that he had quarreled violently with Almirante that same evening at MSI headquarters. Finally, Loi claimed to have observed Greek, Spanish, and Portuguese visitors at the seat of the MSI on several occasions, and to have encountered various police and Carabinieri officials at either MSI or FN headquarters.[135]

It appears, however, that the general skepticism about Loi's startling assertions was largely justified. Even if one overlooks his unbalanced personality and bizarre antics, some of Loi's claims were explicitly challenged in the course of a later judicial inquiry into the Piazza Fontana massacre. Thus Improta and his superior both testified that when Loi first visited the Ufficio Politico he said nothing at all about the FN, but rather offered to uncover deposits of arms and explosives hidden by the Unione dei Comunisti Italiani Marxisti-Leninisti (Marxist-Leninist Union of Italian Communists); it was only *after* 12 December that he fingered the two FN leaders. Although Loi reaffirmed the veracity of his previous revelations about the proposals of Bianchini and Viaggio, he admitted that at police headquarters he had originally attributed actions that were then being prepared by the right to "left-wing extremists." Be that as it may, Loi also participated in another effort to implicate the FN, a scheme that further contributed to Judge Vittorio Occorsio's belief that his testimony was unreliable. At the end of August 1970, Loi brought two friends – Giulio Cossu and Pierino Rotilio – with him to the Trotskyist Savelli publishing house, one of the publishers of *La strage di stato*. There, prompted by Loi, Cossu and Rotilio told the journalist Marco Ligini that they had been hired as "mercenaries" by the FN and driven to Piazza Venezia on 12 December 1969, after which they disembarked and supposedly placed bombs at the Altare della Patria. No evidence was ever unearthed to substantiate their involvement in these bombings, and the falsity and manifestly ridiculous nature of some of their testimony to Ligini buttresses Occorsio's conclusion that the whole incident was a "stunt orchestrated by Evelino Loi."[136]

This seems very probable, but the incident nonetheless raises the question of what Loi's motives were for trying to implicate the FN. The Extraparliamentary Left Research Group suggested three possible explanations for Loi's peculiar behavior. First, he may have been a compulsive liar or an irresponsible lunatic, in which case none of his claims should be taken seriously. Second, he may have been a police informant who was being used instrumentally to make certain declarations that cast suspicion on people who were innocent. Third, he may have been a provocateur paid by someone to make false revelations that would thence be exploited to discredit the media sources which printed them.[137] To these hypotheses I would add a fourth – that Loi, in the hopes of obtaining financial recompense, sought to concoct "revelations" that he believed partisan political publications would be interested in printing. All of these hypothesized motives are believable, although the second makes little sense here unless elements within Italian intelligence were trying to divert attention from the real perpetrators or "burn" unsavory fascist extremists. The most intriguing possibility is perhaps the third. It is standard procedure for secret services and other clandestine groups to utilize persons, wittingly or not, to act as conduits for various types of disinformation. In this instance it has been suggested that Loi had been hired to prompt certain leftist publications to print false and slanderous information, for which they could later be sued and perhaps discredited in the eyes of the public. Although there is no actual evidence of this, on another occasion startling "revelations" were made by an ex-legionnaire about the supposed training of fascist squads in Corsica by the French Légion Étrangère, and shortly thereafter *L'Espresso*, the newsweekly that printed them, was sued (although later acquitted of wrongdoing in court).[138] In lieu of any corroborating evidence, it is best to treat Loi's claims with great skepticism.

Nevertheless, even if the FN was innocent of any involvement in the death of Calzolari or the recruitment of Loi for terrorist actions, members of the organization clearly participated in a series of violent incidents in Reggio Calabria. It has been well-documented that right-wing extremists played a key role in exploiting, if not actually fomenting, the series of popular local protests against the government's decision to shift the capital of Calabria from Reggio to Catanzaro. Neo-fascist publications boast about the actions of their comrades in guiding the uprising, and freely acknowledge that militants linked to AN and the Fronte formed the nucleus of the Comitato d'Azione per Reggio Capoluogo (Action Committee to Keep Reggio the Capital). The most important of these Reggian activists were undoubtedly Felice Genoese Zerbi and Francesco ("Ciccio") Franco, both of whom had broken with the MSI's initial official line, which they viewed as too compromised and supportive of the *partitocrazia*, and gravitated toward the hard-line anti-government positions adopted by Delle Chiaie and Borghese. Sometime in 1969 local AN leader Genoese Zerbi seems to have become the FN's "delegate" in Reggio, and three years later he and Franco purged the moderates on the Comitato d'Azione in the hopes of turning it into a revolutionary instrument.[139]

But the specific role played by Borghese and the directorate of the FN in the uprising is not so easy to determine. The Black Prince did make two trips to

Reggio, once on 25 October 1969, prior to the outbreak of the revolt, and once on 8 August 1970, after it had already broken out. On both occasions the government refused to let him hold a rally, which precipitated violent confrontations between his supporters, led by Genoese Zerbi, and the forces of order.[140] The issue is whether Borghese intended beforehand to precipitate an insurrectionary action, or whether his presence simply exacerbated an already tense situation. Some right-wing sources dismiss the idea that he and other neo-fascists had developed a precise insurrectional strategy for Reggio, and Borghese himself sought to legitimize his organization's activities there by claiming that the FN sought to prevent violence and transform the revolt from one focused exclusively on local issues into one representing a protest against the ruling political system. Although this latter point was in fact reflected in FN propaganda leaflets distributed in Reggio, his assertions about trying to prevent violence cannot be taken at face value.[141]

Indeed, they are belied by various acts of violence and terrorism carried out in Reggio during this period by ultras affiliated with the Fronte. At 11 PM on 7 December 1969 – one year to the day prior to Borghese's abortive 1970 coup – someone tossed a powerful bomb at a window of the Reggio Questura from a speeding automobile, causing a great deal of damage and seriously wounding a police corporal.[142] Although the police at first oriented their investigation mainly toward the Mafia and elements of the extraparliamentary left, within a few days police commissioner Emilio Santillo's investigation laid bare the outlines of a rightist attack. On 17 December four neo-fascists were arrested: Aldo Pardo and Giuseppe Schirinzi for being the material perpetrators, Giovandomenico Zoccoli and Demetrio Modafferi for aiding and abetting the crime. Pardo and Schirinzi were notorious for their right-wing extremism and criminal behavior. Both had taken part in the April 1968 "tour" to Greece organized by the Ethnikos Syndesmos Ellinon Spudaston Italias (ESESI: League of Nationalist Greek Students in Italy), the far right Greek student organization in Italy which was used as a front by the KYP, and both were active at various times in the MSI's youth organizations, Ordine Nuovo, and Avanguardia Nazionale before joining Borghese's FN.

During the investigation that followed, several witnesses provided significant details about the background of the crime. First, Ugo Serranò indicated that Pardo had been seen in the company of Genoese Zerbi in Piazza Italia on the night of the Questura bombing, and said certain people had told him that a series of bomb attacks initiated during a 30 November rally organized by Almirante had also been carried out by the "usual gang" – Schirinzi, Genoese Zerbi, Benito Sembianza, and Carmelo Dominici. Next, Paolo Marcianò claimed that Pardo confided to him that these actions were designed to create chaos and make the public think that left-wing extremists had carried them out. Schirinzi himself then revealed that in every Italian city, including Reggio, there existed a right-wing political organization headed by Borghese that was plotting the seizure of power by revolutionary means, and that in Reggio this organization was led by Genoese Zerbi and counted Sembianza, Dominici, Pardo, Francesco Ligato, Giuseppe Barletta, and a certain Paratore among its members. In spite of all this damaging testimony, Genoese Zerbi denied knowing about any of the bombings, and claimed that the FN intended to take power without relying upon dynamite attacks and terrorist methods. In their report the police concluded that there was insufficient evidence to indict Genoese Zerbi and most of the others for planning and carrying out the attacks, although they felt certain that they were behind them. Only Pardo and Schirinzi were brought to trial, two years later at Lecce. Although they were originally sentenced to four years in prison, in January 1975 this sentence was overturned and suspended by the Reggio appeals court.

Despite this judicial leniency, which was typical of the sort regularly meted out to right-wing ultras, extremists associated with the FN were involved in several acts of squadrist violence against the left. On 28 January 1970, for example, a group of Borghese "sympathizers" from AN and Fronte Delta, led respectively by Adriano Tilgher and Marco Pirina, launched an attack against leftist students at the University of Rome.[143] Such sorties were standard features of neo-fascist political action, and thus require no further comment. However, other actions committed by various FN members suggest that Borghese and the Fronte were also active participants in the terrorist "strategy of tension" then being waged in Italy by elements of the radical right. It has already been noted that several bomb attacks were carried out by FN members in Reggio, some of whom had earlier gone to Greece for instruction in how to conduct provocations, and that these actions were explicitly designed, according to the testimony of Marcianò, to make it appear that the left was responsible. It also seems likely that a number of unsolved terror bombings dating from this period, like the one that derailed the "Freccia del Sud" express train at Gioia Tauro on 22 July 1970, killing six people and wounding fifty-six others, were committed by neo-fascists who were linked in some way to the FN. As has been amply documented, this type of terrorist action, for which no person or group ever claimed responsibility, lay at the very root of the "strategy of tension." Indeed, in his November 1975 sentence Judge Fiore concluded that Borghese's overall strategy was to kindle hotbeds of disorder and provoke clamorous episodes of violence in order to reveal the impotence of the existing political system and precipitate an intervention of those forces still able to save the country from further degeneration and communist subversion, above all the military.[144] The failure of the forces of order to intervene directly in response to this wave of terrorist provocations ultimately convinced Borghese that only a coup sparked by his own organization would compel them to get off the fence and take action. After a series of postponements, continued displays of supposed government pusillanimity in the face of leftist agitation prompted him to select a new "zero hour" on the anniversary of the Japanese attack on Pearl Harbor. Hence the code name, "Tora Tora."

The "Tora Tora" operation

According to Investigating Magistrate Fiore, the Fronte's operational plan was arranged in the most minute particulars, and the actions of the various participating groups were meticulously timed. The initial objective of the conspirators was to gain control of the Interior and Defense Ministries, with the inside help of FN supporters in the police and military. The seizure of these primary security headquarters would then make it possible for Borghese's supporters to issue orders via official channels to military and police units throughout the country. The Foreign Ministry may also have been targeted in this way, although it seems to have been a less immediate objective. At around the same time, various communications centers and the main broadcasting station of RAI-TV were to be seized, which would enable Borghese to read the following proclamation to the Italian people:

> Italians! The hoped-for political shift, the long-awaited coup d'etat has taken place. The political formula that has reigned for twenty-five years, and has carried Italy to the brink of economic and moral collapse, has ceased to exist. In the next few hours, in successive bulletins, the most immediate and opportune steps to deal with the current disequilibrium of the nation will be indicated. The armed forces, the forces of order, the men most able and representative of the nation are with us; on the other hand, we can assure you that the most dangerous adversaries, those . . . who want to subjugate the country to a foreigner [i.e., the communists], have been rendered powerless. Italians! The state that we will create together will be an Italy without distinctions (*aggettivi*) or political coloration. It will have only one flag, our glorious tricolor. Soldiers of the Army, Navy, and Air Force, forces of order, to you we will entrust the defense of the homeland and the reestablishment of internal order. We will not promulgate special laws or institute special tribunals. We ask only that the existing laws be respected. From this moment on, no one will be able to laugh at you, offend you, wound your body or spirit, or kill you with impunity. In placing the glorious tricolor in your hands again, we invite you to raise your voices in our overwhelming (*prorompente*) chorus of love: Italy! Italy! Viva Italy![145]

After these attempts to seize crucial strategic points had made some headway, diversionary acts of violence were to be carried out elsewhere in Rome with the aim of provoking a spontaneous, large-scale intervention of the still uncommitted forces of order. In addition to these primary tasks, other groups of plotters were assigned to impede the progress of military units loyal to the existing government by blowing up roads, getting rid of Police Chief Angelo Vicari, kidnapping or otherwise neutralizing President Giuseppe Saragat, and carrying out a number of important minor actions.[146]

Once these main objectives were secured, the civilian plotters planned to turn authority and control over to sympathetic hard-liners within the armed forces and assume an auxiliary role by helping the Carabinieri and Celere police units quell resistance and arrest left-wing union and political leaders. The names of those to be arrested, as in the case of the counter-insurrectionary "Plan Solo" formulated by General De Lorenzo in 1964, had been drawn up well in advance by the conspirators, which must have required a good deal of prior intelligence gathering. The projected arrestees – who apparently numbered in the hundreds – would initially be transported to Civitavecchia in vehicles provided by police agencies and Pier Francesco Talenti's bus company. They would then be transferred to islands off the coast of Italy by ships placed at the FN's disposal by some of Orlandini's shipowner friends.[147]

The missions were allocated as follows. According to a report prepared for SID man Labruna by a rightist journalist close to some of the leading conspirators, members of AN had originally been assigned two tasks. Some were to blow up certain roads to prevent armored forces loyal to the current government from moving on Rome from the Nettuno-Anzio area. The bulk were to occupy the Foreign Ministry and, with the help of Carabinieri plotters and technical specialists, take control of the radio transmitters inside. However, this plan engendered disapproval and suspicion among Delle Chiaie's men, because it excluded them from the main Interior and Defense Ministry operations and exposed them to a possible trap. With Drago's support, Delle Chiaie then appealed to the FN's leaders to allow his followers to undertake a more important role in the operation and to provide some guarantees for their future security. In response, Borghese put him in charge of seizing control of the armory within the Interior Ministry, a task whose success depended upon the active participation of certain police officials assigned to guard the Viminale.[148] Another AN commando group was entrusted with the kidnapping of Chief Vicari, which provides further evidence of just how much faith the Black Prince put in Delle Chiaie's group. In the end, the job of taking control of the main RAI-TV transmission center near the Foreign Ministry (and perhaps, somewhat later, the Foreign Ministry itself) was assigned to the Inspector General of the Guardie Forestali (Forest Rangers) training center in Cittaducale, Major Luciano Berti, unbeknownst to the men under his command. It is not entirely clear just how the plotters intended to take control of the Defense Ministry, but Air Force General Giuseppe Casero and Air Force Colonel Giuseppe Lo Vecchio apparently assured Orlandini that Air Force Chief of Staff Fanali would play a key role in this particular operation.[149] Meanwhile, a sizable group of conspirators under the direction of ex-paratrooper Saccucci were to gather at the ANPDI gym on Via Eleniana, where they were to await the arrival of instructions and perhaps also a truckload of weapons. Along with the members of extreme right youth groups like Europa Civiltà and Fronte Delta, Saccucci's men were apparently supposed to create disorders and provocations in various parts of Rome in an effort to distract and precipitate an intervention of the forces of order. It was then up to the military conspirators to do their part, for without the full support of FN sympathizers within the armed forces and police the operation had no chance of ultimately succeeding.

After making their way to Rome from all over Italy, several hundred conspirators converged at various prearranged locations in the hours leading up to the scheduled launching time. By the afternoon of 7 December, FN headquarters had become the site of frenetic organizational activity. A group of leading Fronte members had gathered there to discuss last-minute arrangements, including how to maintain contact between the different groups taking part in the action. Among the discussants were Giovanni De Rosa, Gino Arista, and Francesco Lombardi, as well as three

MSI members who had sought to confirm rumors of an impending FN action and been incautiously admitted to the meeting on the strength of their party affiliation. These three – Central Committee member Gaetano La Morte, Alberto Pompei, and Adalberto Monti – later testified that they heard some disturbing things there as the night wore on, including talk that the FN's hour had arrived, that power was about to fall into their hands, and that the only thing they were still awaiting was the issuance of orders. On the evening of the same day, a "political headquarters" ("command post A") was established at Mario Rosa's Via Sant'Angela Merici office, from which the strategic planners of the operation, including Rosa himself, the Black Prince, General Casero, Colonel Lo Vecchio, and Carabinieri Major Salvatore Pecorella, kept in contact with the various action groups. Finally, an "operational command" ("command post B") was set up at Orlandini's shipyard in Montesacro, where several of the most diehard conspirators had assembled to direct the successive phases of the operation. The most important of these were Orlandini, the ON-linked nuclear engineer Eliodoro Pomar, Dante Ciabatti, and Drago. An AN contingent from Rieti consisting of Adriano Monti, Gennaro Ciolfi, and Angelo Cagnoni stopped by for a time on its way to the Viminale. Still later in the evening, Orlandini and his henchmen were joined by other forces. Among the most important was the group from Genoa, which included Frattini, Frattini's right-hand man Pietro Benvenuto, and SID informant Torquato Nicoli, who was dressed in a Carabinieri major's uniform and headed a troop of men who were likewise dressed as Carabinieri. Various materials crucial to the success of the coup had also been concentrated at the shipyard, including "Fronte Nazionale" armbands and auto decals, carbines and rifles obtained a few days earlier in Milan by a group of Ligurian youths at the behest of Frattini, and tour buses from Talenti's fleet of vehicles that were to transport the assembled men into the city at the opportune moment.[150]

These command centers were not the only concentration points for the plotters. Between fifty and one hundred local members of AN converged on the organization's Via dell'Arco della Ciambella headquarters at 6 PM on 7 December, ostensibly in order to ward off an expected communist attack. When they arrived, they were told the real reasons why they had been summoned and ordered to prepare for action. Another fifty non-Roman *avanguardisti* gathered at various apartments in different parts of the capital to await further instructions, and still others remained outside Rome but ready to intervene if necessary.[151] Later that same night, a handful of youths affiliated with the extreme right university group Fronte Delta were mobilized by their leader Marco Pirina, who was also the president of FUAN. Earlier that day Pirina had received a phone call from Mario Rosa, with whom he had been in contact since the spring of 1970, asking him to come to his Via Sant'Angelo Merici office. There he met Rosa's son Dalmazio, and together they went to meet Mario at a bar in Montesacro, where Pirina was told that disorders would soon break out in the city and that it would be necessary for rightist organizations to defend their headquarters. So it was that Pirina, Vincenzo D'Ambrosio, Giuseppe Garibaldi, and Guido Fiorani assembled in the evening outside the apartment of Antonio Reitano and Francesco Calcaterra near University City, awaiting further news.[152] Considerably more activity occurred at the Largo Brindisi headquarters of Europa Civiltà, where a number of that organization's supporters anxiously gathered to await developments, including Alberto Ribacchi, Alessandro Rossi, SID informant Stefano Serpieri (who had previously given information to the authorities in connection with the Piazza Fontana bombing), and Civiltà Cristiana (Christian Civilization) leader Franco Antico, yet another SID informant.[153] Once these various operational components were in place, a green light was given to the plan.

Of all the initial actions planned by Borghese and his associates, perhaps none was more important than taking control of the armory inside the Viminale. For one thing, doing so would provide the conspirators with considerable quantities of arms and ammunition. For another, it was a necessary first step in seizing control of the Interior Ministry's communications center, which would in turn help them convince many policemen to follow their orders and hinder the ability of loyalist elements to put up resistance. With the supposed authorization of General Domenico Barbieri, former head of the Pubblica Sicurezza (Public Security) police training school at Castro Pretorio, Celere Captain Enzo Capanna, then Chief Adjutant of the head of the Ministry's Reparto Autonomo Guardie (Autonomous Protection Unit), discreetly admitted at least two separate AN commando groups into the Viminale during the afternoon and evening of 7 December. Among the extremists Capanna let inside were Delle Chiaie himself, Adriano Monti, Alberto Mariantoni, Giulio Crescenzi, the so-called Quadraro group (Salvatore Ghiacci, Carmine Palladino, and Roberto Pallotto), and Flavio Campo. Once inside the armory, the plotters set about readying the nearly two hundred machine guns they found there, including six Beretta machine pistols, for transport. An important FN insider (and MSI provincial leader), Gaetano Lunetta, subsequently claimed that this group managed to secure complete control of the Viminale, including its extensive communications equipment, for two hours. However that may be, the bulk of the automatic weapons in the armory were loaded onto a truck, which was driven out of the Interior Ministry building just after midnight so that its lethal cargo could be delivered, among other places, to Orlandini's shipyard.[154]

The complicity of Capanna and other members of the security forces was later highlighted by several sources privy to inside information. According to the summary prepared by Guido Paglia, a former AN leader and a journalist with close links to Aginter Presse and SID, the *avanguardisti* were actively assisted by Capanna and three other policemen. These latter indicated that they supported the operation even though they were not fascists, but insisted that the AN members follow their orders without hesitation. The nature of their assistance was later described in greater detail by Orlandini during his 17 June 1974 meeting with Labruna and Romagnoli in Lugano: Capanna's job was not only to admit and arm members of AN, but also to arrange for the subsequent defense of the Interior Ministry. To facilitate these tasks, he had earlier used a microbus to transport members of the police unit assigned to guard the Viminale over to the barracks on Via Panisperna, where they remained throughout the duration of the operation. Orlandini also claimed that the plotters had a police battalion at their disposal in Rome, which was ready to intervene at any moment, and that at some point Capanna was to occupy, presumably with the help of this battalion, the Chamber of Deputies and Senate buildings.[155]

The original revelations about AN's occupation of the Viminale were met with widespread skepticism and blanket denials by the authorities, and a ridiculously inadequate in-house Interior Ministry "investigation" concluded that there was no evidence to substantiate them.[156] But such reassuring responses proved to be premature. A Beretta machine pistol had in fact been stolen by one of the AN members who had penetrated the armory, probably Ghiacci or Pallotto, a potentially incriminating deed that later compelled Drago and Orlandini to arrange to have a replacement put in the missing weapon's place. Subsequent investigations revealed that one of these six weapons (serial #Q/2041) was not the original, but rather a composite made up of parts from different machine pistols. This discovery not only confirmed that a group of conspirators had entered the Viminale on 7 December, but also that they had relied upon inside help, both to penetrate the building on that occasion and, later, to replace the weapon stolen from the armory.[157] There can thus be no doubt that certain members of the Italian security forces were active participants in facilitating and then covering up a key aspect of Borghese's coup.

Another AN commando group, led by Mario Bottari and comprising Sergio Cardellini, Remo Sturlese, and Pietro Carmassi, was given the delicate task of kidnapping Police Chief Vicari. According to Orlandini, Vicari was the "only man who could disturb" the plotters, and it was felt that putting him out of action might help prevent the forces of order from intervening against them at the first sign of a coup. But this mission met with total failure, both because Bottari and his men were unexpectedly trapped for hours between floors in a defective elevator in Vicari's building and because Vicari happened to be visiting Palermo on the night of the coup. The latter circumstance subsequently prompted Giacomo Micalizio to lament that, had the plotters known, it would have been easy to arrange to have the Mafia eliminate Vicari. Other FN leaders seem to have toyed with this idea beforehand, because various Mafia *pentiti* later testified that Borghese's men had tried to recruit them for this and other purposes.[158]

Another key objective was the main RAI-TV transmitter, located in the state-owned company's headquarters building on Via Teulada, not far from Piazzale Clodio. In the late evening of 7 December, Major Berti led a motorized contingent of 197 Guardie Forestali south from their school at Cittaducale, ostensibly on a training exercise to the Alban Hills. But there were several anomalous aspects of this exercise, anomalies that were not lost on the perplexed participants. First, another exercise in the Alban Hills had been conducted only three days earlier. Second, Berti's men were very heavily equipped with arms and ammunition – including pistols, rifles, fifty-three M.A.B. machine guns, a flame-thrower, and 7,700 rounds of ammunition – a conspicuous array of armaments far beyond what could conceivably be of use on a normal Guardie training exercise. Finally, a fully equipped ambulance accompanied the thirteen-vehicle column, which was hardly warranted given the type of injuries one might expect to incur on such an exercise. The confusion of Berti's men was only increased when they reached Raccordo Annulare, where the vehicles, battered by heavy rain, veered toward Rome along Via Olimpia rather than toward the Alban Hills. When the column reached the Ponte Milvio bridge over the Tiber, Berti brought it to a halt while he stopped to talk to two men in a car parked along the side of the roadway. The march was then resumed until the large plaza adjacent to the Foreign Ministry was reached. After remaining there a few minutes and without offering any explanation, Berti wheeled the column around and led his forces back to Cittaducale, which they reached a little after 3 AM. Before dismissing his men for the evening, he complimented them on their efficiency and claimed that it had been noted by two functionaries of the Forestry and Agriculture Ministry, thus implying that the two men he had spoken to had been sent by the Ministry to assess their skills.[159]

Berti's later explanations of the purposes of this exercise were not at all credible. The Forestry and Agriculture Ministry denied that any such evaluation or encounter had taken place, and added that his "exercise" had been carried out without official authorization. The Ministry also disputed his claim that he was authorized to view classified documents. Moreover, in the fall of 1970 Berti had placed an order for a very large number of handcuffs, likewise without the authorization of his regular administrative superiors. Because there was no logical reason to order such items for the Guardie, it seems clear that they were to be used to secure the leftist political and union officials scheduled to be arrested after the FN and its allies had seized control of Rome, a view that is strengthened by Saccucci's parallel efforts to obtain handcuffs. Follow-up investigations seemed to indicate that Berti had taken all these actions on his own initiative, and had only made efforts to obtain authorization for them after the coup was aborted. Although Judge Fiore acknowledged that there was no material proof that Berti's movements on the night of 7–8 December were linked to Borghese's coup, several bits of circumstantial evidence suggested just that. Among other things, the supposed Alban Hills exercise was carried out in absolute secrecy and inexplicably ended up in the center of Rome, the route taken led directly from Salaria to Via Teulada, the participating Guardie were heavily armed without any justification, the column stopped several hundred meters away from the RAI-TV center, and Berti changed his original story, claiming that the two men he had spoken to were nothing more than indiscreet gay lovers. Furthermore, it emerged that Berti was a good friend of ANPDI vice president Umberto Poltronieri (who was in turn very close to Saccucci), and that he maintained links with some of the leading FN conspirators, including Borghese, Ciolfi, and Adriano Monti. Finally, Orlandini told several associates that over two hundred Guardie Forestali had been ready to intervene near RAI-TV on the night of the coup.[160]

Saccucci was one of the most dedicated FN conspirators, and as such assumed a good deal of responsibility for certain phases of the operation. On 10 March 1971, following the issuance of a search warrant by the judicial authorities, the Polizia Giudiziaria found an appointment book in Saccucci's home. This book contained numerous annotations, many of which shed light on his role as an organizer of the gathering at the ANPDI gym on the night of 7 December 1970. For example, the entry for 28 June refers to the delivery of a radio and 300,000 lire worth of handcuffs, the entry for 30 June indicates the concentration points and objectives of various groups of men under his direction, presumably for the projected coup, and the 7 March entry alludes to the Guardie Forestali for no appreciable reason. Most damning of all were his notations in the entry for 6–7 December, which listed the names of trusted associates who were to attend the meeting scheduled for the following evening at the ANPDI gym, including those he designated as "group leaders," along with the number of "certain" and "probable" persons each was to bring and the times and locations where they were supposed to meet before heading to the gym. Although the meeting there was billed as a "cultural event," at which the film *Berlin, Drama of a People* was to be shown, the mention of the number of "arms" and "autos" that different participants were to bring suggested that he planned to assemble them for purposes other than simple entertainment.[161]

Indeed, the ANPDI gym on Via Eleniana was the site of intense activity on the evening of 7 December. The movie was scheduled to be shown at 8 PM, and was supposed to be followed by a discussion. A large crowd eventually gathered, but according to a number of witnesses many of the attendees were neither members of ANPDI nor regular visitors to the gym. Among those present were its sponsor Saccucci and several of his chosen "group leaders," including Corrado Biazzo, Massimo Bozzini, Alessandro De Angelis, and Vito Pace, as well as members of other extremist groups like Bruno Stefàno (Movimento Integralista: Integralist Movement) and Fabio Di Martino (AN). A phalanx of young ultras was stationed at the doorway to monitor the admittance of guests, and once inside these latter were prevented from leaving. Testimony differs about whether the announced film was actually shown, but as time wore on the topic of conversation increasingly turned to the projected action. Various attendees overheard remarks like "the operation is in progress" and "the moment has arrived," and Saccucci and others spoke openly of a "demonstration action" or a coup. This is hardly surprising, because the chief function assigned to the group leaders and their men was probably to foment disorder at various points, although perhaps some were earmarked for other operational tasks. Inside the gym the general levels of anticipation and agitation steadily rose, reaching a crescendo as midnight approached. At that point Saccucci and Stefàno departed for Orlandini's shipyard, saying that they would return soon with precise operational orders. By then, the expected truckload of weapons should have arrived. But neither the truck nor Saccucci appeared at the gym at the allotted time, and as the minutes ticked by the crowd became more and more exasperated as its members argued about what to do.[162]

By midnight, then, the situation was as follows. A truck had just been driven out of the garage at the Viminale by members of AN, bearing automatic weapons for other groups of plotters. Aside from Orlandini's shipyard it is not clear exactly where all these weapons were to be delivered, but it is fair to assume that some of them were destined for the ANPDI gym or various locations where Delle Chiaie's followers were concentrated, including AN headquarters. Other *avanguardisti*, together with their police accomplices, remained inside the Interior Ministry and perhaps took control of its communications center. Still another AN commando group was by then trapped inside the elevator in Vicari's building. The Guardie Forestali column led by Berti was closing in on the center of Rome, on its way to RAI-TV headquarters. A sizable contingent of armed men at Orlandini's shipyard waited to move into action, while several right-wing ultras awaited further instructions in Largo Brindisi and University City. Groups of ex-paratroopers and their youthful supporters anxiously anticipated the arrival of more weapons and orders at the gym on Via Eleniana. Some of these civilian plotters, perhaps from the gym or the shipyard, probably intended to rendezvous with military conspirators near the Defense Ministry, because – as will be explained later – certain Army, Carabinieri, and police units seem to have been mobilized and/or deployed in Rome and various other cities. In short, after months of careful planning and preparation, not to mention delays, the operation was now about to enter its decisive phase.

It was precisely at this critical juncture that everything was abruptly and unexpectedly called off. Not long after midnight, Borghese apparently received a phone call at "command post A." After a brief exchange, he turned to his assembled confidants and announced that external support would not be forthcoming. Someone then telephoned Orlandini at "command post B," urging him to come to Rosa's office at once. Orlandini and Ciabatti immediately rushed to the scene, where they encountered General Casero leaving at the front gate. Casero invited them in but, to their consternation, refused to provide them with any information. Once inside, Borghese told the newcomers that everyone had to be recalled, news which Orlandini later said was so psychologically devastating that it would have prompted him to commit suicide had he brought along a gun. The Black Prince indicated that it was necessary to withdraw because a group of officers inside the Defense Ministry who were to open the doors for one of the key military plotters – General Duilio Fanali – was not in place, information that was later said to be false. According to Orlandini, Casero had been entrusted with the task of bringing Fanali to Palazzo Baracchini, from where the latter had volunteered to issue orders to the entire military apparatus. The conspiratorial shipbuilder further claimed that he had stationed Dalmazio Rosa and Colonel Lo Vecchio at "command post A" precisely in order to prevent any attempt to call off the operation, but that these two were unable to decide what to do because Borghese and the others present insisted that the action would only be postponed for a few days, not cancelled entirely. In any event, the issuance of the counterorder compelled Orlandini and others to make frantic efforts to recall the groups of plotters who had already deployed for action, including Berti's men, the AN contingent inside the Viminale, and perhaps various Carabinieri units, as well as notify those elements that were still awaiting orders of the need to withdraw. This proved to be a rather difficult task, both logistically and psychologically.[163]

Although it is not at all clear how the military and police units that allegedly participated in the operation were recalled, because their supposed involvement was systematically minimized in the successive judicial investigations, more is known about the recall of the FN-linked action groups. It appears that Francesco Lombardi and Saccucci were dispatched to halt Berti's column, and that they were the two mystery men with whom Berti talked shortly before returning with his men to Cittaducale.[164] Before embarking on this mission, Saccucci apparently instructed Bruno Stefàno to return to the ANPDI gym, tell the people who had gathered there that the operation had been cancelled, and send them home. Shortly after 2 AM, Stefàno arrived and informed the assembled crowd about the counterorder issued by Borghese, which produced enormous consternation and precipitated verbal protests, exchanges of insults, and bitter recriminations. The situation became so chaotic that Stefàno told his friend Tizzoni that they should get out of there before everyone was arrested, something that might well have happened had not Captain Pecorella arrived and, after removing his pistol from its holster and brandishing it in a threatening manner, ordered everyone inside to go home.[165] From a logistical standpoint, the most difficult task was intercepting the truck that had left the Viminale laden with arms.[166] Somehow this was accomplished, after which Capanna and the *avanguardisti* spent some time unloading the weapons and replacing them in the Interior Ministry's armory. Everyone who had concentrated at Orlandini's shipyard, AN headquarters, and the seat of Europa Civiltà was ordered to go home; the members of Fronte Delta got tired of waiting for something to happen, and dispersed on their own initiative. By the time dawn arrived, everything had apparently returned to normal. The operation had ended as quickly as it had been launched, and the only material evidence that it had taken place was a missing Beretta that would not be discovered for several years.

However, the frustrations and mutual recriminations of the conspirators did not end with the termination of the operation. In its aftermath a great deal of bitter reflection and angry discussion took place, on all levels, and many of the key participants blamed each other for the halting of the coup. Orlandini held Borghese personally responsible, Saccucci harshly criticized the Black Prince, Orlandini, and Rosa, and elements of AN accused several participants of purposely sabotaging the operation. Borghese remained reticent about this particular matter, and when asked he limited himself to saying that he had "obeyed superior orders."[167] This explanation raised more questions than it answered, and certainly did not satisfy the curiosity or lessen the disappointment of the ultras. When the FN organized a secret high-level meeting at its headquarters in Rome on 17 January 1971 in order to assess the situation, a number of serious disagreements arose. Some of the less extreme "A group" members who had not been informed of the action beforehand protested, either because they had been left out of the deliberations or because they opposed paramilitary adventurism, whereas ultras such as Orlandini, Frattini, Pomar, Micalizio, Rosa, Lo Vecchio, and De Rosa expressed anger that the action had been aborted. The latter group openly and heavily criticized Borghese, and demanded to know what had gone wrong. His half-hearted efforts to justify issuing the counterorder failed to satisfy his interlocutors, and in the end he stormed out of the meeting, leaving everyone unhappy except his most loyal followers. Although

Genoese lawyer Giancarlo De Marchi offered to procure large-scale financial support for serious future actions in which the intervention of high-ranking military personnel (or "eagles") could be counted on, the internal divisions that surfaced during this meeting threatened to destroy the cohesion of the entire organization.[168]

A second FN meeting was then held in February at the Montesacro home of the De Felice brothers, but again the December actions of the Black Prince, who was not present this time, came under heavy attack, and the existing factional disputes could not be resolved. This state of organizational turmoil persisted until the sudden arrest of Orlandini and other key plotters between 17 and 19 March, after which Borghese fled to Spain and in the process loosened his hold over the political movement he had created. Following a short-lived period of panic and confusion, the stage was set for a major restructuring of the Fronte, a resumption of its anti-democratic plotting, and an intensification of its collaboration with other subversive forces willing to employ violence to achieve their objectives. The extent of this activity would not fully emerge until a series of "presidentialist" coup plots involving FN ultras was uncovered by investigating magistrates in the course of 1973 and 1974.

Unfortunately, the very question that proved to be so divisive for disgruntled participants in the "Tora Tora" operation – who was really responsible for interrupting and terminating the action? – has yet to be satisfactorily answered. Nor can it be until the ultimate sponsors and real purposes of the operation have been identified with greater precision. Although these matters are no less difficult to assess, enough circumstantial evidence and firsthand testimony have been accumulated to enable the attentive researcher to hazard some educated guesses.

The exposure and investigation of the coup

Despite the fact that the coup was successfully aborted at the last minute, rumors that some sort of rightist action had taken place on the night of 7–8 December immediately began to circulate. Most of these were undoubtedly generated by careless tongue-waggers among the conspirators and within neo-fascist circles, but more than a few may have been disseminated by factions within the security services seeking to embarrass rival factions that were deeply compromised in the operation. These rumors and leaks, which quickly took on a life of their own, prompted the police to initiate an investigation of Borghese's organization. On 15 February 1971, the Ufficio Politico of the Rome Questura obtained permission from the Public Prosecutor's office to tap the phones of Orlandini, Rosa, Saccucci, and Giuseppe Garibaldi, inasmuch as they were FN members suspected of committing terrorist acts. It soon became evident that key members of the Fronte were planning new illegal activities, and that a number of them possessed weapons and explosives. On 8 March, the police were issued warrants authorizing them to search the homes and offices of Borghese, Rosa, Orlandini, Saccucci, Massimo Bozzini, and Flavio Campo. In the course of these searches, material evidence was discovered that provided significant details about the "Tora Tora" operation, including Saccucci's address book and copies of both a foreign policy position paper and the proclamation that the Black Prince intended to read over the radio after the main FN objectives had been seized. These revealed, according to Judge Fiore, that the plotters had developed a subversive plan "to attack the democratic institutions of the state." On 18 March the Ufficio Politico prepared a report outlining the structure and goals of the FN, with particular reference to "movements" that had apparently taken place in Rome on the night of 7–8 December 1970. Arrest warrants were then issued for Borghese, Orlandini, Rosa, Saccucci, De Rosa, and Lo Vecchio, but the Black Prince took refuge in Spain before he could be taken into custody.[169]

The arrest of several key figures in the FN and the initial revelations about the subversive actions they carried out on the anniversary of Pearl Harbor fell like a bombshell on the contentious Italian political scene. Every political group at once sought to exploit this information for its own partisan purposes. Groups on the left, which had grown increasingly concerned about the possibility of a right-wing military coup, portrayed Borghese's actions as evidence that their fears had been justified. This interpretation was contemptuously dismissed by both government spokesmen and rightist journalists, who characterized the Black Prince and his men as incompetent buffoons who hastened to abandon their comic opera as soon as it began to rain.[170] Although several plotters provided the police with details about the operation and documents were found that supported important aspects of their testimony, the interests of the political establishment were apparently best served by minimizing the significance of the whole affair. So it was that on 25 February 1972 the Court of Cassation overturned the Rome Court of Appeals' decision not to free the defendants, who were duly released, ostensibly because there was not enough evidence to prove their guilt. This situation persisted until 15 September 1974, when Andreotti sent an SID report on the Borghese coup and later FN plots to the Rome public prosecutor, thereby opening the way for a new judicial investigation of the events of 7–8 December.[171] The main results of that investigation, which were described in Vitalone's *Requisitoria* and especially in Judge Fiore's sentence, have already been summarized.

Yet this was by no means the end of the story. In his 1975 sentence, Fiore had indicted many of the conspirators for serious crimes and clearly revealed the seriousness of various phases of the operation. Not surprisingly, this verdict was appealed, and at a second trial in 1978 the "political conspiracy" and "armed insurrection" charges were dropped. To accomplish this remarkable feat, the appellate judges were compelled to resort to tortuous arguments that in some cases directly contradicted the evidence collected during the instruction phase. For example, as a way of discounting the evidence that FN plotters had penetrated the Viminale and stolen an automatic weapon, they suggested that Orlandini might have learned from his contacts ahead of time that one of the machine pistols in the Interior Ministry armory was a composite. Not only did this bizarre reconstruction go against all the participant testimony, it also ignored the revealing remarks made by Orlandini, in the course of a phone conversation tapped by SID ten days after the coup, concerning the need to replace the stolen weapon.[172] Likewise, testimony about the support offered to the plotters by elements within the Italian security forces and Nixon's coterie was generally dismissed as baseless hearsay or – when that proved impossible – attributed to acts of individual disloyalty and perfidy. This made it possible for the judicial authorities to attest to the "absolute fidelity" of the armed forces as an institution, as well as to conclude that the movements on 7–8 December constituted nothing more than a "muster of forces" (*adunata*) or "seditious demonstration."[173] If that conclusion were not ridiculous enough, on 27 November 1984 a second Rome Court of Appeals dropped the charges against all the remaining defendants and concluded that no armed subversion or serious anti-constitutional actions had taken place.[174] The logic of this judicial finding, especially given the vast amount of information that had surfaced about rightist plots during the intervening years, confounded virtually every informed observer.[175] In short, in all of these sentences the unwritten rule seems to have been to try to limit potential political embarrassment or damage by preventing the incrimination of the state apparatus, high-ranking political and military officials, and Italy's American allies.

Nevertheless, certain aspects of the coup contributed to the comforting illusion that it did not represent a serious threat and that its participants were nothing more than nostalgic bunglers. There was, after all, something rather comical about the march of a band of heavily armed but unwitting Guardie Forestali – the Italian equivalent of U.S. Forest Rangers – toward a key political and military objective. And the unexpected entrapment of Bottari's AN contingent in an elevator in Police Chief Vicari's building was worthy of a Three Stooges skit. Features such as these prompted the filming of a 1973 black comedy, *Vogliamo i Colonelli* (*We Want the Colonels*), which satirized the entire affair. However, it would be a major error to consider the Black Prince and his men apart from the far more powerful political forces that they claimed had promised to lend support to their action. Whatever else Borghese may have been, he was not an operational novice when it came to military affairs. No one with significant experience in military and paramilitary activities would have been foolish enough to believe that a total force consisting of a few thousand civilian activists would be able to carry out a successful coup d'etat in Rome without the support of elements from the regular security forces. Many of the plotters later testified that high-ranking military, Carabinieri, and police officers, as well as leading politicians and freemasons, had indicated their willingness to back the planned FN action. Even if one makes allowance for exaggeration and self-serving distortions, these converging claims should have been taken seriously and thoroughly investigated by the authorities.

The involvement of the security forces

Given the absence of an in-depth official inquiry into these claims, the best an outsider can do is examine the evidence that emerged during the trials about supposed links between the civilian conspirators and representatives of the security forces. The best place to begin is with the military intelligence service, whose task it was to monitor and neutralize threats to the security of the postwar democratic state. It has already been noted that General Miceli, head of SID from October 1970 to July 1974, had established contacts with Borghese and Orlandini as early as the spring of 1969, when he was still chief of SIOS-Esercito. He claimed that these contacts were undertaken in relation to his intelligence-gathering activities. However, this innocuous explanation directly conflicted with Orlandini's characterizations of those same meetings, and Miceli's superior at the time, General Francesco Mereu, later testified that such investigative methods were abnormal and dubious.[176] Perhaps more importantly, it is belied by Miceli's subsequent failure to take action against the plotters, even though he was regularly kept abreast of their intentions and subversive activities by means of intelligence reports in the months leading up to the coup.[177]

According to Judge Fiore, SID had begun to collect information on the FN, its leaders, and its links to other extraparliamentary rightist groups as early as the fall of 1968. As a result of this preliminary work, Borghese's contacts with various disparate political groups, including ON and AN, had come to light. During the first week of December 1970, SID's Raggruppamento Centri Controspionaggio (CS: Grouping of Counterespionage Centers) had obtained authorization from the public prosecutor's office to tap the telephones of Orlandini, Rosa, De Rosa, and Saccucci, a sign that leading FN conspirators were engendering more and more suspicion.[178] But the situation came to a head even before these taps had the opportunity to yield their secrets.

On the evening of 7 December, Lieutenant Colonel Giorgio Genovesi at Centro CS I in Rome received an alarming message from SID informant Franco Antico, a member of both Civiltà Cristiana and Europa Civiltà, who told him that groups of youths belonging to the latter organization, the FN, and ON intended to launch a coup later that very night. Antico listed the Interior Ministry as one of their possible targets, and indicated that their goal was to spark some sort of response to the recent wave of leftist demonstrations. Genovesi immediately informed his superior, Colonel Antonio Cacciuttolo, head of the Raggruppamento Centri CS, who suggested that he pass by the Viminale to see if anything appeared out of the ordinary. From the plaza in front of the building everything seemed normal, so Genovesi made his way back to his office on Via Quintino Sella. Meanwhile, Cacciuttolo transmitted the explosive news to the head of Ufficio D, General Federico Gasca Queirazza, who in turn informed Miceli sometime between midnight and 1:10 AM. Miceli ordered his subordinate to stand by and see what developed. It was not until 2:10 AM that Genovesi was given the green light, presumably by Cacciuttolo, to pass Antico's information along to the Carabinieri and the Ufficio Politico of the Rome Questura. After doing so, Genovesi returned to the Interior Ministry and remained on guard outside the building until 5 AM. Some three hours later he personally visited Antico, who provided him with further details about the Via Eleniana gym meeting.[179]

By the wee hours of 8 December, then, Miceli had already been made aware of the general outlines of the subversive actions initiated by Borghese, actions that the plotters were at that very moment desperately trying to abort and conceal.

But instead of launching an immediate counteraction to prevent the various FN contingents from withdrawing, undertaking a thorough official investigation, and providing the authorities with all the details which SID had gathered up to that point, as duty demanded, he appears to have done everything he could to protect the conspirators.[180] First, as noted earlier, he delayed taking any action until after 2 AM. Second, several hours later he limited himself to making a few vague allusions about the coup to General Enzo Marchesi, chief of the armed forces general staff, allusions which had little substance or probative value.[181] Third, over the next two and a half months he allegedly failed to provide additional information that had been gathered by Centro CS I to his superiors and colleagues in the security apparatus, even though he met with them on several occasions during that period. In the first half of December 1974, both Interior Minister Franco Restivo and police chief Vicari testified that Miceli had consistently minimized the significance of the coup on these occasions and that their first indication of its seriousness was gleaned from the newspapers and police investigations. Restivo claimed that the head of SID had said his Ufficio D investigators had been been unable to confirm Antico's revelations and had said nothing at all about a possible FN occupation of the Viminale. Moreover, on more than one occasion Miceli had referred to the meeting at the ANPDI gym as a "university student gathering." For his part, Vicari categorically denied that Miceli or anyone else at SID had provided the police with useful information about the coup.[182]

This latter failure is especially noteworthy, because Miceli's subordinates in Ufficio D had in the meantime managed to accumulate a significant amount of information about the operation. The wiretaps that had recently been installed in the phones of various FN leaders had immediately borne fruit. As indicated earlier, Orlandini made a number of incriminating phone calls, including one to Miceli loyalist Cosimo Pace, in the wake of the aborted coup. Saccucci also recounted some details of the operation over the phone on 8 December, and the following morning Rosa made a call and lamented that the action would have been successful if it had not been recalled. Yet none of these recorded conversations was made available to investigating magistrates until January of 1975.[183] Even more tellingly, Ufficio D prepared two initial reports on the plot, dated 15 and 23 December, both of which Miceli withheld from other investigative bodies until his hand was forced by the march of events.

This process began at the end of February 1971, after the Rome Questura had renewed its investigation of the FN and managed to obtain further information and compromising documents related to the coup. The police informed the judicial authorities of their findings, and as noted earlier the first arrest warrants were issued for some of the key conspirators in mid-March. Miceli was thence constrained to make Ufficio D's initial reports on the coup available to Judge Marcello De Lillo in order to avoid being accused of negligence or incompetence. Nevertheless, he rejected Ufficio D's suggestion that a newly prepared summary report of its findings be submitted to all the higher political authorities, in accordance with the normal bureaucratic practice. The SID chief instead recommended, presumably in order to delay the release of sensitive and compromising information without incriminating himself, that another report be prepared using somewhat different analytical criteria. Ufficio D then drew up a new report on the basis of these suggested criteria, but this too was filed away in SID's archives at Fort Braschi, at Miceli's orders, until the summer of 1974. Finally, Ufficio D proposed that SID prepare an "official" version of the events in response to a July 1971 request for information by the judicial authorities, but again Miceli blocked the initiative by insisting that all branches of SID await his orders before taking any further action. Needless to say, these orders never arrived.[184]

It was precisely during this highly sensitive phase of the investigation that Miceli allegedly took another significant action. According to Orlandini, in mid-1971 the general made a personal visit to Villa Margherita, the luxurious Roman clinic where Orlandini was being held under house arrest. They encountered each other briefly in the crowded hallway of the clinic, at which point Miceli supposedly put his finger alongside his nose, a gesture indicating that he was protecting the shipbuilder and that the latter should be patient and hold his tongue. Miceli later admitted that he had visited the clinic around that time, but denied seeing Orlandini or giving any such signal, an explanation the judges found unbelievable.[185] Be that as it may, the military intelligence chief's initial efforts to derail the judicial investigations continued up until 13 August 1971, when he responded in writing to the judges' request for information. In his letter, he claimed that SID was unable to confirm Antico's information about the launching of a subversive right-wing action on the night of 7–8 December, and insisted that no evidence had been found of any "collusion, connivance, or participation" in such an action by active-duty military personnel or military circles.[186] The progress of the investigation was thereby stalled, and toward the end of February 1972 those FN members who had been arrested for plotting subversion were released from prison.

It is likely that the case against Borghese and his supporters would have collapsed right then, had it not been for the personal initiative taken by Miceli's rival, General Gianadelio Maletti, who had replaced Gasca Queirazza as head of Ufficio D in June 1971. Maletti discreetly reactivated Ufficio D's investigation of Fronte Nazionale activities, a delicate task that he assigned to the Nucleo Operativo Diretto (NOD: Directed Operational Cell), a small operational group he established under his own direct personal authority, outside SID's normal chain of command. Captain Labruna was put in charge of the NOD, and was assisted in his tasks by Colonel Sandro Romagnoli, head of Ufficio D's security section. After learning about Orlandini's key role in the coup from one of the latter's friends and business associates toward the end of 1972, Labruna made personal contact with the shipbuilder in early 1973 and, after a few meetings, managed to convince him that he was an FN sympathizer within the secret services. Once reassured, Orlandini began making a series of increasingly important revelations to Labruna about aspects of the "Tora Tora" operation, as well as about details of new FN plots against the government. Almost all of these revelations, which culminated in the confessions made by Orlandini during the 17 June 1974 meeting at Lugano, were duly recorded by Labruna.[187]

Along with the convergent testimony of other key witnesses and various material evidence, the details revealed by Orlandini soon made it possible to reopen the judicial investigation and bring Borghese's supporters to trial.

In mid-1973, Maletti informed Miceli that he had resumed his investigation of the FN and the rightist movements with which it was associated. Miceli replied that in the absence of concrete facts, no information should be provided to the judicial authorities "in order to avoid scandals detrimental to the institutions of the state."[188] Once again, the head of SID succeeded in delaying the exposure of compromising information that his own subordinates had gathered. But this stonewalling could not be continued indefinitely, and the following summer the chickens finally came home to roost. After learning of the explosive revelations made by Orlandini at the Lugano meeting, Maletti ordered Labruna and Romagnoli to prepare a new report incorporating the shipbuilder's recorded testimony. This report, known as the "Malloppone" ("big file" in slang) and dated 24 June 1974, was presented to Miceli on 3 July. The latter was visibly surprised and unable to hide his consternation, especially because he had recently been caught lying to the political and judicial authorities about Guido Giannettini's links to SID. Now he was being confronted with embarrassing information about "collusion between subversive forces and high-ranking military and civilian officials," information he had long gone out of his way to conceal, and was no longer in a position to prevent its release because he was soon to be replaced as head of SID by Admiral Mario Casardi.[189]

Miceli's only remaining option was to try to prevent the dissemination of the report by means of a normal bureaucratic evaluation process rather than a unilateral personal action, which would be certain to engender suspicion. In the hopes of diverting attention from his prior obstructionist role, he convoked a meeting at Palazzo Baracchini to discuss the contents of the report with his chief Ufficio D subordinates: Maletti, Marzollo, Genovesi, and Major Agostino D'Orsi. At the meeting he sought to discredit Orlandini's testimony – which, it should be recalled, directly implicated Miceli himself – by repeatedly emphasizing that the FN plotter's revelations had not been substantiated by any evidence. His goal was to persuade his colleagues that it would be preferable to either verify or revise the controversial claims in the report before actually releasing it, but the majority agreed that, whatever its possible deficiencies, it should nonetheless be transmitted to the judges entrusted with investigating various FN-linked plots. In desperation, Miceli then appealed to Admiral Eugenio Henke, who had by then become chief of the armed forces general staff, for help. The latter, not wishing to jeopardize his own position by colluding with or covering up for his departing intelligence chief, advised him to transmit the report to Andreotti without further delay. Thus deprived of further institutional support and protection, Miceli reluctantly did so on 7 July 1974. Shortly thereafter, Andreotti arranged a meeting between himself, Miceli, Casardi, Henke, General Enrico Mino of the Carabinieri, and General Vittorio Emmanuele Borsi di Parma of the Guardia di Finanza (Finance Guard). Miceli again emphasized the absence of material evidence in support of Orlandini's claims, which inadvertently buttressed the defense minister's decision to investigate the alleged links between high-ranking military officers and Borghese's civilian plotters.[190]

In the first week of August, Casardi transmitted an investigative report prepared by Borsi di Parma to Andreotti. This report absolved General Roselli Lorenzini and five other military officers of the charges of colluding with the FN, a politically convenient conclusion that Andreotti blithely accepted. In response, he ordered Casardi to reorganize the Labruna-Romagnoli report and excise the unverified allegations about military plotters and U.S. involvement. The revised report (known as the "Malloppino" or "small file" in slang) was returned to Andreotti, who in turn transmitted it on 15 September to Chief Prosecutor Elio Siotto, along with a letter warning him that not all the information contained therein had been confirmed. Siotto seems to have tried to consign the report to a prosecutor other than Vitalone, but Andreotti hastily intervened and the report was then sent on to Vitalone and Fiore. At that point Miceli played his last card. On 26 September he sent an unsolicited letter directly to Fiore. In that letter he acknowledged that he had met with Borghese and Orlandini in 1969 and 1970 in connection with his legitimate intelligence-gathering duties, as noted earlier, and referred to the original Labruna intelligence reports which had *not* been sent to the judges by Andreotti. Apparently, his aim was to cast suspicion on the defense minister by suggesting that he was purposely withholding information from the judicial authorities. In response to an 18 October request for clarification from Fiore, Andreotti claimed that he had not sent the originals – with the full support of Miceli himself and certain other security chiefs – because they contained unverified information and might therefore cast suspicion on innocent people. But Andreotti's hand was now forced. On 24 October, he addressed the Defense Committee of the Chamber of Deputies and explained his reasons for withholding the original reports. Immediately afterwards, he ordered Casardi to send all of Labruna's reports to the judicial authorities.[191]

Any respite or sense of satisfaction that Miceli may have derived from the defense minister's discomfiture was short-lived, however. On 31 October Judge Tamburino, then in the midst of investigating the Rosa dei Venti (Compass Rose) organization, issued an arrest warrant for Miceli. The charge was "political conspiracy," because the SID chief had been identified by insiders as a key figure in "parallel SID," a top secret structure within the military intelligence service whose personnel overlapped with those of the subversive Rosa group, which in turn was actively conspiring with FN activists in Rome and Liguria. He was taken into custody in the waiting room of Achille Gallucci, head of the Ufficio Istruzione, by Carabinieri Colonel Ruggero Placidi, placed in a waiting automobile, and immediately whisked toward Padua. Miceli had no illusions about the trouble he was now in, and decided to make every effort to avoid being interrogated as a defendent by Tamburino. Just outside the Rome city limits the general claimed that he had fallen ill, so Placidi had no choice but to turn around and bring him to the Celio military hospital. The next day Tamburino dispatched a Paduan medical examiner to the capital with the task of determining whether or not Miceli was really too ill to be transported to Padua. Despite the latter's protestations, Dr. Paolo Cortivo authorized his transfer to the Paduan military hospital, which took place on the same day. Unfortunately, it was this very action that precipitated the jurisdictional struggle that resulted in the Court of Cassation's decision to combine both Tamburino's investigation and Judge Luciano Violante's Milan investigation of Edgardo Sogno's "white" coup with Fiore's Rome investigation of the FN. This occurred officially on 30 December, before Tamburino had had the opportunity to question Miceli.[192]

These transfers of jurisdictional competence prevented the more dogged magistrates from fully exposing the parallel, quasi-official networks that were making instrumental use of various right-wing coup plots and terrorist actions, but they did not let Miceli completely off the hook. On 4 January 1975, in the first of three appearances he was to make as a defendant before judges Fiore and Vitalone, Miceli angrily contested Andreotti's claims that prior to July 1974 he had ignored rightist violence and refused to acknowledge that a coup had taken place. He pointed out that he himself had later ordered Ufficio D to form an operational group to investigate subversive right-wing movements, and had only suggested that Maletti dissolve it and reassign Labruna after the latter's "cover" had been blown by the press in connection with the Giannettini affair. He further insisted that he had carried out his duties by informing other security agencies and his political superiors – Restivo, Defense Minister Tanassi, and President Giuseppe Saragat around the time of the coup – about the basic information gathered by his service concerning the "clamorous" FN action on the night of 7–8 December 1970.[193] Indeed, he accused all three of the aforementioned government officials of knowingly withholding information that he had provided them from the judicial authorities.

Given the overall pattern of uncooperativeness displayed by Miceli, however, these claims failed to convince the investigating magistrates that his superiors were ultimately to blame or that he had properly performed his duties as head of the military intelligence service. As a result, public prosecutor Vitalone and Judge Fiore both ended up severely criticizing Miceli's half-hearted efforts to investigate the Borghese coup and subsequent FN plots. According to Vitalone, Miceli had "shamelessly lied, clearly violating the fundamental duties of his office . . . [e]ither he had artfully disinformed his superiors or he lacked some of the essential qualities to undertake the highly delicate functions conferred upon him."[194] For his part, Fiore accused Miceli of intentionally and repeatedly trying to impede the investigation of the judicial authorities by withholding crucial information that his agency had accumulated on the plotters, and attributed this "unlawful conduct" not only to his general tendency to say "as little as possible," but also to his feelings of "reciprocal sympathy and consideration" for Borghese.[195] There is no doubt whatsoever that Miceli's duplicitous and obstructionist actions, by delaying and then sabotaging the prosecution of the leading FN conspirators, effectively made it possible for them to continue hatching seditious plots for another three and a half years. Even so, the judicial officials in Rome were clearly unwilling to charge the SID chief with anything other than aiding and abetting a crime, a far less serious offense than actively conspiring to commit one. Although Miceli was in this way absolved of serious wrongdoing and ultimately spared from serving a prison sentence, his professional career was destroyed by his bureaucratic rivals in order to protect higher ranking members within the Italian political establishment and, in all probability, their American allies.

Nonetheless a considerable body of diverse evidence, both circumstantial and material, demonstrates that Miceli was far from the only top security official who had actively sought to aid and abet Borghese's plotters. To believe that the general and his coterie of loyalists inside SID were acting solely on their own initiative, one would have to completely discount the links that they had forged with other powerful groups implicated in the coup. Among these were elements within the Carabinieri, the UAR and Pubblica Sicurezza corps, the armed forces, the NATO security apparatus, the U.S. national security establishment, freemasonry, and the Italian political class. Each of these must be discussed in turn, although the reader should keep in mind that they are all closely intertwined.

Any operational assistance or cover-up orchestrated by SID on behalf of Borghese's plotters would have inevitably involved the participation of Carabinieri officers, because much of the military intelligence service's personnel has long been regularly drawn from that very corps. In 1974 one specialist estimated that the bulk of the two thousand men employed by SID's Ufficio D were members of the Carabinieri, a proportion which was by no means abnormal.[196] The traditionally close links between the service and the corps were further strengthened during the 1960s by General De Lorenzo, who had been appointed as commander of the Carabinieri after spending several years at the helm of SIFAR. During his controversial tenure at Viale Romania, De Lorenzo transferred several of his loyal subordinates from the military intelligence service and appointed them to fill important positions within the corps, a process that created considerable resentment among high-ranking Carabinieri officers who had not been previously seconded to SIFAR. At the same time he ensured that his own cadre of loyalists, headed first by General Egidio Viggiani and after 1965 by General Giovanni Allavena, maintained control over the latter organization. In this way, he solidified his power base within the Carabinieri and established much closer operational linkages, both formal and informal, between that corps and the military intelligence service, linkages that undoubtedly persisted in an attenuated form even after his own forced retirement.

But these general institutional patterns are not the only factors that would lead one to suspect Carabinieri involvement in the coup. According to neo-fascist *pentito* Paolo Aleandri, the real purpose of Borghese's action was in fact to provide a pretext for the activation of emergency Carabinieri anti-insurrectional plans. Select elements within that corps were said to be fully aware of this plot in advance. Following the outbreak of disorders provoked by the Black Prince's men in the capital, these elements were to transmit a coded signal to the various Carabinieri commands, ordering them to carry out the actions delineated in certain top secret contingency plans that were stored in their secured areas. Among the tasks that these units had been assigned was the arrest of leftist politicians, union leaders, and "suspect" military officers, a plan about which many of the FN conspirators and their associates had already testified.[197] Aleandri indicated that he had gleaned this information from several sources, the most important of which was Fabio De Felice, with whom he was in close contact throughout the mid-1970s. Along with his brother Alfredo, Fabio De Felice played a role in the FN similar but subordinate to that of Filippo De Jorio.[198] More will be said about De Jorio's important political connections later, but Aleandri's unsettling testimony, although not yet definitively confirmed, has been buttressed by other evidence of Carabinieri involvement in the coup.

The reportedly direct operational participation of active-duty Carabinieri officials such as Pecorella has already been noted, as has the apparent wearing of Carabinieri uniforms by some of the civilian conspirators. But this was by no means the entire story. FN leader Gaetano Lunetta later claimed that a number of high-ranking Carabinieri officers, including some who were seconded to SID, had participated in various 1969 and 1970 Fronte meetings at which there was open talk of a coup. One of these men, a lieutenant who had come to a Florence meeting with Adami Rook, enabled Lunetta to buy hundreds of military uniforms, including camouflage outfits, by displaying his official identification card at Unione Militare stores during a fifteen-day shopping spree in northern Italy. Lunetta added that among the guards who admitted the plotters into the Viminale there were members of the same corps, and that after the issuance of the counterorder the FN commandos inside supposedly had to wait for the return of a complicit Carabinieri guard troop before retiring from the Ministry. Lunetta further claimed that Carabinieri units were placed on alert on the night of 7–8 December, and that he personally saw the Black Prince for the last time at a Carabinieri barracks in Florence, *after* an arrest warrant had been issued for him and just before he took flight to Portugal on a naval vessel.[199] This last assertion may not be at all far-fetched. Orlandini and Borghese were allegedly key players in the Carabinieri-centered De Lorenzo "coup" of 1964, and according to an April 1971 report sent in to Ufficio D from a regional SID office, the former Decima MAS leader had actually been a guest at the corps' main headquarters on Viale Romania in Rome.[200]

Perhaps most damningly, Brigadier Renato Olino later testified that at least one large contingent of Carabinieri was actually readied for action and deployed on the night of the coup. Olino claimed that General Dino Mingarelli, then commander of the corps' non-commissioned officers' training school in Florence, led a column of forty-five to fifty Army trucks carrying eight hundred heavily armed cadets south from the Tuscan capital to Cecchignola on the night of 8 December 1970. This force had ostensibly been mobilized to guarantee order during Tito's visit scheduled for the next day, yet the men were ordered to sleep with their clothes on and be ready to move at a moment's notice.[201] Other sources indicated that Olino's unit was not the only Carabinieri force to be deployed that night. For example, Giorgio Pisanò, an MSI senator with close ties to both neo-fascist and intelligence circles, later claimed that Rome had been encircled by a network of Carabinieri blockade posts on the afternoon of 7 December, but that these had been ordered *not* to impede any troop movements, no matter how suspicious these appeared, or confiscate any weapons they ran across.[202] Hence Orlandini, despite possible embellishments, seems to have been telling the truth when he confided to Labruna that the plotters had the support of certain Carabinieri units, some of which were allegedly moving into action before being recalled when the counterorder was issued.

There is also scattered evidence that Carabinieri officers participated in efforts to protect the plotters, both prior to and after the coup. For example, a revealing report was compiled on 16 June 1969 by Lieutenant Colonel Gian Maria Giudici, at the time commander of the Genoese Carabinieri legion, concerning an April FN meeting held in that city. On 17 June it was sent to General Luigi Forlenza, then chief of the corps, who filed it away and then failed to acknowledge its existence even after Vitalone began his judicial investigation of the Borghese coup.[203] Later, other personnel linked to the Carabinieri were accused of trying to interfere with that investigation. Thus Vitalone, defending himself from charges of being compromised by his political connections and revealing secret information to the press, noted that there *was* no secrecy as far as the trial materials were concerned. He claimed that members of SID with "NOS" status had open access to the most secret trial documents, and added, in this connection, that assistant prosecutor Raffaele Vessichelli, an ex-Carabinieri officer, was a close associate of Marzollo, Miceli's former right-hand man at the military intelligence service. Vitalone argued that it was impossible to prevent leaks under such conditions, an opinion shared by chief prosecutor Siotto.[204] Finally, Orlandini told Labruna a strange story in January 1973. He claimed that corrupt Carabinieri detachments had recently searched the homes of three or four FN plotters in La Spezia, ostensibly in search of arms and ammunition, even though they knew full well that these weapons had been stored elsewhere.[205]

If Borghese's 1970 "coup" was in fact meant to spark a Carabinieri anti-insurrectional action, there are obvious parallels between that operation and the plans developed by De Lorenzo in 1964, which according to some insiders called for the utilization of civilian paramilitary groups to foment disorders and thereby set in motion a similar Carabinieri contingency plan.[206] This in turn provides further indirect evidence that efforts to initiate and implement certain sorts of anti-leftist actions were not abandoned despite the exposure of earlier plots, and that there was a noticeable degree of continuity among the personnel involved in successive phases of this plotting.

The complicity of high-ranking officials of the Interior Ministry in the "Tora Tora" operation has also been attested to by a number of sources. The fact that Drago, whose close links with UAR official D'Amato worried many of the participating neo-fascists, prepared a floor plan of the Viminale and personally conducted groups of plotters on a tour *inside* the building is in itself significant. It is difficult to believe that a police medical examiner, however trusted and well-regarded, could have provided tours of such sensitive, high-security areas to unknown civilians without obtaining authorization from someone much higher up the chain of command. In this case, all the circumstantial evidence points to D'Amato as the official who provided such authorization. Aleandri later testified that the De Felice brothers had explicitly identified D'Amato as one of the people who had pledged to support the projected coup,[207] a claim that is surely strengthened by the actions taken by the Reparto Autonomo Guardie contingent entrusted with protecting the Interior Ministry on the night of 7–8 December. According to an April 1971 SID report, the AN conspirators were admitted into the Viminale that evening by Major Capanna, "on behalf of D'Amato's deputy [*vice*]."[208] This did not occur until after Capanna had facilitated their entry by transferring the bulk of the guard troops under his command to the Via Panisperna barracks. To rationalize ordering his men to abandon their regular posts without engendering suspicion, Capanna probably had – or at least pretended to have – some sort of authorization from above.

This also raises the issue of Pubblica Sicurezza involvement in the coup, because that corps is under the authority of the Interior Ministry and the guards at the Viminale are specially selected from among its personnel. In 1989, FN leader Lunetta asserted that police officials had participated in various FN planning sessions along with Carabinieri and military officers, that several police agencies were instructed not to interfere with the movement of thirty cars filled with weapons and Ligurian plotters, and that mobile battalions were ready to occupy strategic points in Rome.[209] As noted earlier, Orlandini and other plotters indicated that various police units were supposed to participate in the operation, and a high-ranking police official is said to have testified that some police barracks had been placed on alert on the afternoon of 7 December.[210] The shipbuilder further claimed that Capanna had General Barbieri's authorization for his actions that day. Although Barbieri himself denied making any efforts to facilitate or cover up the coup, he admitted to the judges that during the winter of 1970–1971 Vicari had warned him to be ready for a coup plot initiated by Borghese, an alert confirmed by other Pubblica Sicurezza officials.[211] Nevertheless, the precise nature of Barbieri's role remains uncertain, and no definitive evidence of the corps' direct participation in the operation – other than that of Capanna himself – has yet been uncovered.

Whatever the degree of actual Pubblica Sicurezza involvement, it would surely be naïve to imagine that an intelligence official as able and well-connected as D'Amato was unaware of the fact that Borghese's men had penetrated the Interior Ministry and stolen one of the prized Beretta machine pistols.[212] Here it is worth noting that these particular weapons had originally been consigned to the UAR in 1966, and had subsequently been transferred to the Reparto Autonomo armory.[213] It would be of great interest to know just when this transfer took place, for had it occurred immediately prior to the coup the possibility of official complicity would surely be strengthened. In any case, knowledge about key aspects of the plot at the highest levels of the UAR was perhaps reflected in the subsequent activities of Drago, who personally went out of his way to "acknowledge" SID's top-level cover-up efforts. At a meeting he arranged with an SID official in early 1971, Drago indicated that he and his associates appreciated and would not forget that SID had not exposed them by revealing details of the coup.[214] Whether the associates he was alluding to were members of the FN, officials of the UAR, or personnel from both entities is impossible to determine. At the very least, however, this thinly veiled "thank you" threat from a figure closely associated with D'Amato and the UAR seems to have reflected the traditional interservice rivalries – if not some degree of collusion or pattern of mutual blackmail – between the Interior Ministry's intelligence apparatus and the military intelligence service. These incidents, whatever their exact import, do nothing to undermine the testimony of Orlandini and other FN plotters about the UAR's supposed involvement in the operation.

Furthermore, the police and secret services were not the only state security forces implicated in the Borghese coup, and the Carabinieri were not the only military force that allegedly provided backup support for it. As several of the Black Prince's chief lieutenants readily acknowledged, the overall success of the operation depended above all on the active support and direct intervention of selected elements of the regular armed forces. To ensure the provision of such support when "X hour" finally arrived, Orlandini and other FN leaders had expended considerable effort over a period of years trying to set up clandestine cells within various military units. In the end, if the plotters had not been led to believe that some military backing would be forthcoming, it is very doubtful that they would have ever undertaken such a risky paramilitary venture. As noted earlier, Orlandini told Labruna on several occasions that various high-ranking military officers were among the conspirators not only in connection with the "Tora Tora" operation, but also in connection with subsequent anti-constitutional coup plots. Lunetta later claimed that representatives from all three armed services had attended various FN planning sessions in 1969 and 1970. Both testified that certain military units had been placed on alert in their barracks, mobilized, or actually deployed and then recalled on the night of the coup.[215] Throughout the evening, Borghese is said to have anxiously awaited information about whether armored forces stationed outside Rome and Naples were moving into action, and according to one source an armored column had actually headed toward the capital.[216]

In the end, Judge Fiore considered the eyewitness testimony about the active participation of General Casero and Colonel Lo Vecchio credible enough to recommend that the two Air Force officers be placed on trial for political conspiracy.[217] But neither he nor Vitalone made any effort to ascertain whether or not the alleged alerts and troop movements had actually taken place. Because at this point it is unlikely that an official investigation of this matter will ever be conducted, one must consider various types of indirect evidence in order to try and assess the degree of military participation on the night of 7–8 December 1970. There are, as it happens, some suggestive bits of information. First of all, lists of military officers, military departments (*uffici*), and arms factories were discovered in the residence of Giovanni De Rosa, one of Borghese's main collaborators. As Nunziata points out, it is reasonable to suspect that these materials contained the names of military personnel who were considered to be sympathetic to the Fronte's aims, if not those who had actually promised to support the coup. Unfortunately, no attempt was made by the prosecutor to carry out a follow-up investigation.[218] Second, in his sentence Fiore noted that ex-paratrooper Saccucci, another key FN operative, enjoyed the protection of "special military agencies (*enti*)," although the identity of those agencies was not further specified.[219] Third, it is possible that "Operation Triangle," an emergency intervention plan making use of select anti-communist cadres from regular military units, was activated on the night of 7–8 December 1970.[220] Finally, it is worth taking a closer look at the two highest ranking military officers identified as key co-conspirators by Orlandini: Air Force General Duilio Fanali and Admiral Giuseppe Roselli Lorenzini. Although both of these men were absolved of guilt by Guardia di Finanza head Borsi di Parma following a two-week investigation in late 1974, and they were never formally charged with complicity by the judges investigating the Borghese coup, there are a number of reasons to suspect them of having had some involvment in it.

The most important of the officers implicated by Orlandini was probably General Fanali, at the time Air Force chief of staff, who had allegedly agreed to accompany Casero and assist the plotters in taking control of the Defense Ministry and its communications network. Fanali has been aptly described by one researcher as a highly trained military man of "scarce democratic reliability."[221] Some time after 8 September 1943, the Badoglio government had entrusted the young colonel with the task of reorganizing the remnants of the Italian Air Force. Between 1947 and 1949, he was among that new generation of military theorists who contributed to various doctrinal debates concerning the nature and orientation of the postwar Italian armed forces. His sympathies were clearly aligned with the Italian right and the Atlantic Alliance, and for many years he was associated with Partito Socialdemocratico Italiano (PSDI: Italian Social Democratic Party) circles. Later, he served as the director of the Scuola dell'Aeronautica (Aeronautics School) and then became president of the prestigious Centro Alti Studi Militari (CASM: Center for Higher Military Studies), the school where selected officers of the Italian armed forces were sent to receive the most advanced and specialized military training. These assignments reflected not only his high professional qualifications, but also the amount of trust placed in him by top military and political authorities. In February 1968, following the establishment of a new cabinet headed by Aldo Moro, he was appointed as chief of the Air Force general staff.[222] From that point on, perhaps provoked by the public disturbances associated with growing worker and student agitation, he appears to have become involved, at least tangentially, in various right-wing plots. Although the only "evidence" of his supposed participation in the Borghese coup derives from the testimony of Orlandini and other plotters, his subsequent activities and associations are clearly indicative of authoritarian political proclivities.

After failing to become General Marchesi's successor as chief of the armed forces general staff when his DC supporters were unable to get the retirement age raised from sixty to sixty-one, Fanali officially retired from military service on 31 October 1971.[223] Yet he did not cease his involvement, now as a "private" citizen, in military and quasi-military affairs. According to FN leader Attilio Lercari's detailed memorandum, following the flight of Borghese and the arrest of leading Fronte plotters in early 1971, "the initiative in the operations for the overthrow of the regime passed into the hands of Admiral Roselli Lorenzini . . . with the collaboration of Generals Fanali and [Vincenzo] Lucertini."[224] Whatever the truth of this particular claim, there is no doubt that Fanali was in contact with various groups implicated in subsequent anti-parliamentary plots.

For example, Fanali maintained a close association with Filippo De Jorio – an intermediary, both before and after the coup, between Borghese's plotters and representatives of the political class – and other "respectable" proponents of authoritarian political solutions. This was exemplified by his participation in certain projects later sponsored by De Jorio, including the Istituto di Studi Strategici e per la Difesa (ISSED: Institute of Strategic and Defense Studies) and its triannual journal *Politica e Strategia*, the first issue of which appeared in December 1972. Fanali was named honorary president of ISSED and became a regular contributor to that particular publication, which investigative journalist Flamini has characterized as a mouthpiece for pro-coup elements within leading Italian political and military circles. Even the most cursory examination of its editorial staff and contributors lends credence to this assessment. To name only a few, De Jorio himself acted as the editor-in-chief, *guerre révolutionnaire* doctrine promoter Eggardo Beltrametti originally served as associate editor, and the contributors included FN conspirator Alfredo De Felice; Gaetano Rasi, head of the intellectually respectable but philo-fascist Istituto di Studi Corporativi (Institute of Corporate Studies) in Rome; General Corrado San Giorgio, head of the Carabinieri; French military officers like General Michel Garder and Colonel Marc Geneste; counterinsurgency theorist Brian Crozier; and two very important figures associated with the pro-Atlanticist European right, Ivan Matteo Lombardo and Leo Magnino.[225]

Yet Fanali also appears to have been in some sort of contact with intransigent "presidentialist" circles. For example, "white" coup proponent Edgardo Sogno boasted, at a private 29 March 1974 meeting in the home of Princess Elvina Pallavicini, that he had already contacted Fanali and other officers in connection with his plan to modify the constitution and alter the command hierarchy of the armed forces.[226] As if to illustrate that claim, Fanali was present in person at a February 1975 rally held by Pacciardi, Sogno, and Luigi Cavallo at the Cinema Adriano in Rome. Pacciardi initiated the proceedings by warning the assembled crowd that Italy was undergoing an institutional crisis, that Parliament was hopelessly ineffectual (*inconcludente*), that the judiciary was polluted by politics, and that even the police and armed forces had reached the point of disintegration. Sogno then took the stage and urged those present to respond to these debilitating crises by uniting under the direction of a temporary emergency government formed by men not compromised by association with the existing system. To the surprise of no one, he also indicated his willingness to assume a key role in such a government – as long as sufficient power was granted to the executive authority and there was an energetic liberalization of economic life.[227] It can be assumed, on the basis of Fanali's expressed views and activities in other contexts, that these sorts of extraconstitutional appeals were not at all alien to his thinking. Perhaps, then, it was no coincidence that the Lercari memorandum, an important source on post-1970 FN plots which explicitly implicated the former Air Force commander, was found in the home of Sogno's long-term political associate Luigi Cavallo.

Moreover, Fanali made one of seven keynote presentations at a May 1975 conference on western European security sponsored by the Centro Italiano Documentazione

Azione Studi (CIDAS: Italian Documentation Center for Studies of Action), one of the innumerable pseudo-scholarly institutes and study centers established by right-wing and ultraconservative groups all over Europe between the 1950s and the 1970s. CIDAS was founded in Turin at the beginning of 1973 by Alessandro Uboldi De Capei, head of IBM Italia, and was closely linked to the conservative MSI elements gravitating around former Marxist philsopher Armando Plebe. Its proclaimed goal was a very ambitious one – to mobilize intellectuals in a renewed effort to forge a respectable "culture of the right" and thereby oppose the dominance of the left in intellectual discourse. These efforts, which were initiated at CIDAS' first conference in January 1973, were lauded by the entire spectrum of conservative publications in Italy, even though Plebe himself acknowledged that the unfocused conference represented only a preliminary step in a long-term process of consolidation. A second CIDAS-sponsored conference, which again attracted rightist intellectuals from Europe and Latin America, was held in the fall of 1974 at Nice.[228]

In any event, at the 1975 CIDAS conference held in Florence, Fanali shared the speaker's platform with French General Garder of the Institut des Etudes Stratégiques (IES: Institute of Strategic Studies) in Paris, MSI journalist and Aginter Presse "correspondent" Piero Buscaroli, and Partito Liberale Italiano (PLI: Italian Liberal Party) Senator Manlio Brosio, a former secretary general of NATO, among others. The attendees included Colonel Geneste, also of the IES; Brigadier General Miguel Cuartero of the Instituto Español de Estudios Estratégicos (IEEE: Spanish Institute of Strategic Studies) in Madrid; Richard Foster, director of the Stanford Research Institute (SRI) in Washington, DC; Professor Werner Kaltefleiter, director of the Konrad-Adenauer-Stiftung, a foundation closely linked to the West German Christlich-Demokratische Union (CDU: Christian Democratic Union); several retired and active-duty Italian generals; a group of conservative intellectuals; and a number of other right-wing journalists, including Aginter "correspondent" and SID agent Giano Accame. Not surprisingly, a major theme of this particular conference was the threat posed to Europe by the Soviet Union and its communist party allies, and it may have been intentionally timed to exert political pressure on NATO leaders, who were scheduled to meet in Brussels later that month.[229]

Later still, Fanali adhered to the short-lived Partito Socialdemocratico Europeo (PSDE: European Social Democratic Party), a new political party founded in the fall of 1977 by anti-communist circles linked to Sicilian prince and P2 member Alliata di Montereale, who became its president. This party grew out of one of several parallel initiatives aimed at restructuring the Italian right so that it could effectively contest the advance of the PCI, which at that point seemed to be on the verge of superseding the DC as the dominant party in the Italian Parliament. Among the PSDE's other leading members were Bruno Zoratti and SID operative Lando Dell'Amico, and it was apparently supported by George Meany, head of the American AFL-CIO union, and Cardinal Giovanni Benelli, an influential conservative with close links to Montini and his Vatican network, traditionalist German prelates, and Franz Josef Strauss, head of the Bavarian Christlich-Soziale Union (CSU: Christian Social Union).[230]

As for Roselli Lorenzini, he had previously held a series of increasingly important and highly sensitive appointments within the Navy's command hierarchy. On 22 October 1970, just six weeks before the "Tora Tora" operation was launched, he replaced Admiral Virgilio Spigai as Chief of Staff of that branch of the service.[231] In the course of later meetings with Labruna, Orlandini gave the impression that Roselli Lorenzini had backed Borghese's December 1970 coup, but all of his specific comments about the admiral's actual role were made in relation to subsequent plots. The conspiratorial shipbuilder independently confirmed Lercari's claim that Roselli Lorenzini was slated to be the operational commander of the projected coup, and emphasized that the Fronte and its allies placed a great deal of faith in him, especially because they anticipated that he would eventually be appointed to replace Marchesi as armed forces chief of staff.[232] In December 1971, the admiral apparently conferred in Rome with De Jorio and Genoese industrialist Andrea Piaggio, one of several Ligurian financial backers of the renewed FN-linked coup preparations.[233] However, the plotters' hopes were temporarily dashed following the February 1972 elections, when the new Prime Minister Andreotti selected Admiral Henke instead of Roselli Lorenzini for the highest ranking military post. The latter was retired from the Navy that same month, at which point he assumed the presidency of the Società di Navigazione Italia, the Italian state's commercial fleet. According to Lercari, the admiral had wanted to "wipe out the political class by force" and, prior to his unanticipated dismissal, had ordered Fronte leaders to establish contact with the Colonels' regime in Greece and attempt to enlist its support for their forthcoming operation.[234] After a brief period of confusion and consternation following Roselli Lorenzini's forced retirement, the task of obtaining and directing military support for the planned coup was entrusted to less well-placed hard-liners like Generals Ugo Ricci and Francesco Nardella.

If Fanali and Roselli Lorenzini were in fact actively involved in the Borghese coup and/or susbsequent FN conspiracies, military and security forces above and beyond the national armed forces might well be implicated, at least indirectly, in acts of anti-democratic subversion in Italy. It turns out that both of these high-ranking officers were closely linked to circles within the NATO and American security establishments, as were Ricci and Nardella, who were indisputably protagonists in later plots. Prior to becoming Navy chief of staff, Roselli Lorenzini had commanded NATO's naval forces in southern Europe, one of the more sensitive and important of the alliance's naval assignments.[235] For his part, Fanali was no less intimately associated with the NATO hierarchy. In 1966, having already served a two-year stint as Italy's military representative at NATO headquarters in Paris, he was abruptly recalled at the insistence of the French government after publicly deriding De Gaulle's decision to pull France out of the defense organization's military structure. This undiplomatic gesture did no harm to his future career, however, because it only served to highlight his stubborn fidelity to the Atlantic Alliance and its American backers. Indeed, shortly thereafter he was appointed as director of the NATO Defense College, which had in the meantime been transferred from Paris to Rome.[236]

Yet all along Fanali seems to have been operating in the interests of certain defense-related groups within the United States rather than – except where these may have overlapped – in the interests of the European alliance per se. The Italian judicial authorities later discovered, for example, that he was deeply involved in the Lockheed bribery scandal, along with ex-Prime Minister Mariano Rumor, former Interior Minister Luigi Gui, Defense Minister Mario Tanassi, and the omnipresent D'Ovidio brothers. He apparently acted as the Lockheed Aircraft Corporation's chief agent within the Italian Air Force, and as such played an active role in manipulating that service's procurement policy so as to arrange for the purchase of fourteen Lockheed C-130 "Hercules" transports. Thus in February 1972, he wrote to General Wood, the U.S. Air Force's attaché at the American embassy in Rome, to ask him to facilitate the visit that two Italian Air Force colonels would soon make to Washington in order to discuss purchase terms, and a few days later sent Colonels Ciarlini and Terzani to meet with Lockheed representatives at the Pentagon. In July of that year, he urged Gui to buy the C-130s and criticized its competitor, the FIAT-made C-222. He persisted in these intensive lobbying efforts despite the opposition of both his own service's technical directorate, Costarmaereo, and that of his Army and Navy counterparts. After a sometimes acrimonious bureaucratic struggle, in October Fanali managed to persuade his opponents to vote for the "Hercules," a much larger and perhaps less appropriate long-range transport. As a result of these and other activities, he was subsequently found guilty of accepting bribes from European representatives of the Lockheed Corporation.[237] It should also be noted that in early 1975 the Americans backed Fanali's bid to succeed the recently deceased president of Panavia, General Gastone Valentini, but that this effort failed due to the Italian government's veto.[238]

Even if one attaches no importance at all to these links between supposed Italian military plotters and the Atlantic security organization, there are other possible indications of NATO involvement in the Borghese coup. For one thing, a complete file of top secret documents concerning Italian and NATO military dispositions was found in Orlandini's possession. These documents were said to be so sensitive that they would have been the envy of military high commands and hostile foreign intelligence services.[239] Moreover, both Lunetta and Orlandini testified that elements of NATO had backed the coup. According to the former, NATO ground forces stationed at the Southern Europe Task Force (SETAF) base in Verona had, at the orders of a certain general, moved south and surrounded half of Rome on the night of 7–8 December.[240] Orlandini provided still other details of NATO's supposed role in the operation. He explicitly claimed that NATO naval forces, acting at the behest of the highest ranking American political circles, were standing by to intervene. Although the judges decided not to pursue these politically sensitive matters, in part due to an absence of material evidence, the shipbuilder's testimony is so explosive that it deserves to be fully recounted here.

As noted earlier, Orlandini indicated that Fenwich served as the main liaison between the plotters and Nixon's entourage at the time of the coup. Indeed, the go-ahead signal for the operation was supposed to be transmitted to the plotters, via a series of intermediaries, by Nixon himself. Once Borghese's men were in position and had attained their initial objectives, Fenwich was to make a call from Rome, using unofficial channels, to one of his trusted associates at Allied Forces Southern Europe (AFSOUTH) headquarters in Naples. From there it was to be transferred first to NATO's southeast Mediterranean naval base on Malta, and then directly on to Nixon, who was to give the order to proceed with the operation. According to Orlandini, the scheduled call was actually made from Rome to Naples on the evening of 7 December 1970, but was then apparently blocked (*arenata*) at Malta. Although the resulting failure to obtain anticipated American authorization and support seems to have been a key factor in the subsequent issuance of the counter-order by Borghese, Orlandini insisted on more than one occasion that elements of the NATO fleet had been placed on alert and readied for any eventuality. Several naval vessels had already started their engines and been put in motion so as to be ready to sail, at a moment's notice, in support of the plotters. "That is why I tell you," the shipbuilder confided to Labruna, "that you don't have the slightest idea of the importance and seriousness of the thing."[241]

Nor was Orlandini the only leading FN conspirator who believed that Borghese's "coup" would be actively supported by senior U.S. government officials. The Black Prince himself seems to have been convinced of this, something that does not seem at all unreasonable when viewed in the context, outlined earlier, of his apparent collusion with elements of U.S. intelligence in the earlier postwar period. He must also have been aware, given the close links that several Italian right-wing extremists had forged with the Greek military junta, that factions within the American national security establishment had covertly supported the Colonels' 1967 coup, and that afterwards the U.S. government had formally recognized the new regime as soon as it became satisfied that this illegal seizure of power would not jeopardize American or NATO security interests. These perceptions may well have accounted, at least in part, for some of the positions outlined in the important foreign policy position paper that police later found in Borghese's office.

In this document the former war hero emphasized, first and foremost, that his projected post-coup regime would maintain the Italian government's current military and financial commitment to NATO. Indeed, it would develop a plan designed to *increase* Italian participation in the Atlantic Alliance. He also agreed to continue Italy's involvement, with certain important qualifications, in the European Economic Community and the United Nations. Finally, he planned to nominate a special envoy to establish direct contact with the U.S. president. The initial task of this envoy would be to arrange for the participation of Italian troops in Southeast Asia in exchange for an American loan.[242] All of these measures were clearly intended to reassure the U.S. government that the new Italian regime would act in such a way as to reinforce, not weaken, the existing Western system of collective security. For his part, General Maletti not only believed that "[t]he Americans, without a doubt, knew everything" about the Borghese operation, but that they were probably behind the coup.[243]

Are the claims of Orlandini and other FN plotters concerning American support for their coup "manifestly incredible," as Andreotti ally Vitalone argued in his *Requisitoria*?[244] To those unfamiliar with the details of the various clandestine operations sponsored by President Nixon and his closest political advisors, such claims *may* at first glance seem incredible. But when they are placed, as they should be, within the context of the American-backed overthrow of Chilean President Salvador Allende and the illegal domestic activities that precipitated the Watergate scandal, the possibility of American backing for a rightist coup in Italy cannot be so easily dismissed as fanciful. Taken together, the actions leading up to the 1973 Chilean coup and the creation of special investigative units under the president's direct control exhibit certain parallels with some of the contemporaneous activities, both confirmed and unconfirmed, which were said to have been undertaken by Nixon's appointees in Italy.

One of the key features of the Chilean operation was the utilization of right-wing paramilitary groups, the most important of which was Pablo Rodríguez's Frente Nacional Patria y Libertad (Fatherland and Freedom National Front) movement, to foment disorder and thereby provide a pretext for the direct intervention of the armed forces. To provoke such an intervention, Patria y Libertad commando units began carrying out a series of terrorist attacks in the fall of 1970 – that is, in the weeks immediately preceding the Borghese coup – which they then falsely attributed to nonexistent leftist organizations like the Brigada Obrero Campesina (Peasant and Worker Brigade).[245] According to pro-communist Chilean sources, members of right-wing paramilitary formations also infiltrated genuine leftist groups, then used them as a cover to commit crimes.[246] The parallels between this particular provocation campaign and the terrorist "strategy of tension" in Italy are self-evident. Nor was this the only disconcerting possible similarity between right-wing violence in the two countries. It was later discovered, for example, that leading members of Patria y Libertad had established close operational links with hard-liners in the Chilean armed forces and the Carabineros corps, including officers within their respective intelligence services. Even more suggestively, they had also been the recipients of covert CIA funding.[247] Finally, some sources claim that more than ten thousand members of Patria y Libertad and other civilian "independent units" had actively supported the military on the day of the coup, particularly in rounding up leftists who were targeted for arrest.[248] Note that this function was precisely that which Borghese and his men were supposed to carry out after they had succeeded in provoking the intervention of the Carabinieri and armed forces. Given these circumstances, it should come as no real surprise to learn that both the Black Prince and Delle Chiaie later established close links with the Chilean junta, from which they sought to obtain operational and logistical support.

Furthermore, Nixon's paranoia and willingness to run dirty tricks operations against putative domestic "enemies" should also be taken into consideration when the credibility of claims about his alleged backing of the "Tora Tora" operation is being evaluated. His decision to create a so-called Plumbers Unit that would be answerable only to himself grew out of his conviction that he could not fully depend upon the unswerving personal loyalty of elements within the regular American national security establishment, particularly the upper-class Ivy League "liberals" who were overrepresented in the highest levels of the CIA bureaucracy. Among other things, he apparently believed that the "clowns . . . out at Langley" had acted to sabotage his 1960 election bid, a transgression for which he had never forgiven them.[249] As a result, he ordered two of his key subordinates, Egil ("Bud") Krogh and Attorney General John Mitchell, to create autonomous intelligence units under direct White House control. These were staffed with presumed Nixon loyalists and entrusted with carrying out some of the president's most sensitive domestic operations. The most notorious of such operations was the illegal 1972 break-in at the Watergate Hotel, whose repercussions eventually forced Nixon to resign and thereby put an end to his efforts to establish an "imperial presidency."[250] But the creation of those units was by no means an isolated act. Nixon's tenure as president was in fact marked by continuous attempts to strengthen the executive office under his immediate control at the expense of other sections of the government bureaucracy. This was exemplified by his rapid reorganization of the structure and functioning of the committees affiliated with the National Security Council, which in practice concentrated real power in the hands of National Security Advisor Henry Kissinger's staff rather than those of Secretary of State William P. Rogers. The result was that Nixon and Kissinger were "able to use the NSC system to establish their own supremacy, not only over foreign policy decisions, but also over their planning and preparation in general – and even to some extent over their execution."[251] In Italy, the president seemingly adopted a similar strategy of relying primarily on hand-picked functionaries, rather than career State Department or CIA personnel, to carry out his policies.

On 26 September 1969 Nixon appointed one of his most trusted and "hawkish" diplomatic officials, Graham A. Martin, as ambassador to Italy. Martin was a former U.S. Army colonel and a forceful, manipulative diplomat who had recently finished a stint as ambassador to Thailand, where he had helped supervise the militarization of the country in connection with the Vietnam build-up. By the time he arrived in Rome at the end of October, right in the midst of the "hot autumn," American policy toward Italy appeared to be in a state of considerable confusion and disarray. In the May 1968 general elections, the moderate Partito Socialista Unificato (PSU: Unified Socialist Party), upon whose success U.S. support for the center-left experiment then chiefly depended, had won only 14.5 percent of the vote. In contrast, electoral support for the PCI had increased to 26.9 percent, which prompted some DC leaders to propose a nationwide "constitutional pact" with the communists at their April 1969 convention. Perhaps most importantly, from early 1968 on waves of student protest and growing worker agitation had combined to generate both a widespread sense of "moral panic" among the citizenry and serious problems of public order. These tumultuous developments, which apparently threatened to destabilize the conservative status quo and made it increasingly difficult to justify or sustain a policy of cautious support for the formation of a center-left government, prompted the launching of some seemingly contradictory American initiatives. On the one hand, personnel from both the embassy's political section and the CIA made some preliminary behind-the-scenes attempts to approach influential elements within the PCI, ostensibly with a view toward forging closer links with members who had grown disillusioned with the Soviets.[252] At first glance, these initiatives seem to have represented a new adaptation of the more flexible American policy, honed during World War II and resumed periodically thereafter by liberal elements within the State Department and CIA, which was predicated on supporting the relatively moderate and democratic factions of the left at the expense of pro-Soviet hard-liners.

In marked contrast, Martin's activities reflected a more rigid and less sophisticated American approach, that of intransigent opposition to any form of real or imagined socialism. On the surface, this appeared to be a sort of throwback to the era of ambassadors Clare Booth Luce and James David Zellerbach, who had vehemently opposed all initiatives aimed at covertly backing or publicly courting the democratic left. Martin was an aggressive and equally uncompromising anti-communist whose concerns about a worldwide Soviet conspiracy colored his evaluation of recent Italian political developments. Despite the objections raised by certain State Department and CIA officials with more experience in Italian affairs, he soon breathed fresh life into the policy of secretly enlisting the aid of the far right to contest, by whatever means necessary, the growing political influence of the communists and their sympathizers. He later admitted that he would not have ruled out the use of violence or the sponsorship of a military coup if all other methods had failed to prevent the PCI from coming to power, even if the latter had done so through legal means.[253]

To carry out these covert anti-communist policies, Martin sought to bypass the normal bureaucratic channels, which included both the CIA station and State Department intelligence officials. Instead of reporting to or relying upon CIA station chief Howard ("Rocky") Stone, for example, the ambassador sought to use non-CIA personnel to establish autonomous intelligence-gathering and operational networks. He relied first and foremost upon the embassy's military attaché, Colonel James D. Clavio, who acted as his liaison man to the armed forces, the military intelligence service, and Miceli in person, and its legal attaché, Thomas Biamonte, in reality the leading Federal Bureau of Investigation (FBI) operative in Italy, who acted as his intermediary with the Pubblica Sicurezza corps, the Carabinieri, and the Interior Ministry's UAR. In addition, he met regularly with certain "private" citizens who formed part of Nixon's network of supporters in Italy. Among these were scandal-ridden figures such as Sicilian financier Michele Sindona, a member of the P2 lodge, and Archbishop Paul Marcinkus of Chicago, who collaborated with Sindona in various economic affairs after becoming head of the Vatican Bank in 1971. Martin's unofficial helpers also included Pier Francesco Talenti and Hugh Fenwich, both of whom were later explicitly identified by Orlandini as the key intermediaries between the FN leadership and the Nixon administration.[254] Talenti had made his fleet of buses available to the conspirators on the night of 7–8 December 1970, and that same evening Fenwich had allegedly made the call to Nixon on behalf of the plotters. In short, Martin was merely following the president's own example in attempting to operate autonomously and outside the restrictive confines of the official CIA and State Department bureaucracies.

Although there are no specific indications that the ambassador provided any tangible support for the Borghese coup, some of the plotters later testified that Fenwich, another "Nixon man" in Italy, had personally kept Martin abreast of the FN's activities. Orlandini added that Clavio had monitored the actions of the conspirators and tried to sound out the views of Italian officers about a possible military intervention.[255] To these perfectly believable claims one must add another significant fact that was later revealed in the report of a congressional committee chaired by Representative Otis Pike. In February 1972, Martin ignored the protests of CIA station chief Stone and covertly funneled over 800,000 dollars to SID head Miceli, who was in regular contact with both the ambassador and Clavio. Although this sum represented only about 10 percent of the American funds that were supposedly earmarked for centrist parties during that period, and the money in question was ostensibly to be used to pay for propaganda activities on the eve of the general elections, Miceli was in fact given control over the distribution of a far greater percentage of the total funds being provided, and it is generally believed that he dispersed a good deal of it to various extreme right groups with which he had long been in contact.[256] Most of these groups did not cease their anti-democratic plotting or their participation in violent actions until 1975 – if they did so at all – and then only in the wake of a belated and half-hearted crackdown by the Italian government. Thus Martin not only took an active interest in the conspiratorial activities of the FN and its supporters, which is only to be expected given his position, but thence arranged for considerable sums of money to be distributed to an Italian secret service chief who was himself later implicated, to say the least, in a cover-up of the "Tora Tora" operation. It seems likely that the ambassador did so with the imprimatur of Nixon and Kissinger, both of whom were active proponents of coup plots against Allende during that same period.

However, although Nixon and his hand-picked emissaries are said to have encouraged rightist plots in Italy over the strenuous objections of the CIA station in Rome, one should not conclude that the agency was opposed in principle to such plots or that its personnel played no role at all in the Borghese coup. As we have seen, Fenwich was not just an influential businessman with close links to Nixon's entourage, but in all probability an important CIA operative. And several commentators have concluded that Clavio, who functioned as Martin's chief liaison to Miceli, was also a CIA man. This remains to be demonstrated, but there is no doubt that Clavio specialized in organizing various types of covert provocations or that he was using his position as military attaché at the American embassy as an intelligence cover.[257] Furthermore, Lunetta testified that the CIA station chief in Rome, "a small but very energetic man," had attended a series of FN preparatory meetings at which the launching of a coup had been discussed.[258] At first glance it seems highly improbable that Stone's predecessor, Seymour Russell, would have attended such potentially compromising meetings, and indeed the presence of any official CIA case officer would have violated the most elementary rules of tradecraft unless the meetings were held in total secrecy or arranged in such a way that the officers would have had a legitimate reason for attending. If Russell did personally participate at these meetings instead of employing a "cut-out," this would have constituted an exceptional circumstance whose attendant risks could only have been justified by the importance of the ensuing discussions.[259] Finally, yet another unconfirmed report indicates that CIA counterintelligence chief James Angleton – Borghese's angel of mercy in 1945 – visited the Black Prince some weeks before the coup, and that shortly thereafter he returned to the United States.[260]

Although it might be argued that very few things could be as important as plotting a coup, one must be skeptical of such claims in the absence of corroborating evidence, especially because the dangers and repercussions of exposure would be correspondingly greater. But regardless of whether these last two assertions have any basis in fact, which it is at present impossible to determine, there is little doubt that elements of the CIA were later involved, at least indirectly, in covertly promoting anti-communist violence in Italy. Thus Stone himself, who had earlier played an important role in the 1953 coup that brought the Shāh to power in Iran, is said to have urged Italian intelligence chiefs to use Vietnam-style counterinsurgency techniques to halt the advance of the communists. According to General Gerardo Serravalle, chief of the training component of the official Italian "Gladio" organization from 1971 to 1974, both Stone and his deputy station chief, Michael Sednaoui, visited the Sardinian training camp at Alghero in late 1972. This visit was ostensibly made in order to review the training exercises for the "gladiators," but its real purpose was to discuss future American funding for the base. The CIA had already decided to reduce its previously high levels of support for the "stay/behind" program, because the possibility of a Soviet invasion and occupation of the Italian peninsula seemed increasingly remote. But the two CIA men reportedly took Serravalle aside and told him that large-scale financing for the secret organization would only be restored provided that its role was expanded to encompass operations directed against "internal subversion."[261]

On the surface this offer seems downright bizarre, because countering internal subversion had always been one of the chief functions of the "Gladio" network. This task was specifically listed in a June 1959 report clarifying the organization's sphere of action, and was reaffirmed even more forcefully at a 26 January 1966 meeting, during which the Americans proposed that select elements of the Italian services take a course in "counterinsurgency operations" at the U.S. Army's Special Warfare School at Fort Bragg in North Carolina so that they would be better able to employ the "stay/behind" forces in these types of operations.[262] How, then, can one explain the peculiar offer made by Stone in December of 1972? One possibility is that it simply signified the abandonment of the network's earlier anti-invasion function and a full-scale shift toward its other chief task. However, both Serravalle and General Fausto Fortunato, then head of Ufficio R, the SID section under whose authority "Gladio" fell, supposedly turned down this offer. One can only wonder why, because by doing so they rejected increased American funding and repudiated one of the central functions of the organization they were entrusted with directing. Something is clearly fishy here, especially given the fact that a few months later Serravalle claimed to have discovered, to his chagrin, that many of the network's group leaders had a distorted and dangerous perception of it as an instrument for suppressing domestic leftists.[263] Be that as it may, Stone's offer itself suggests that his complaints about Martin's plan to fund Miceli, which supposedly caused Martin to threaten to have Marine guards throw him out of the embassy and put him on a plane back to Washington, were motivated more by his opposition to the ambassador's tactless encroachment upon his bureaucratic turf than by a sincere opposition to employing rightists in covert anti-communist operations. It also raises the question of whether contemporaneous CIA approaches to the PCI had been designed primarily to obtain inside intelligence information that could later be used to discredit or fracture the party, not to open serious discussions or establish some sort of genuine *modus vivendi* with party representatives.[264]

Although there is certainly not enough hard evidence to demonstrate that NATO or American officials directly sponsored or participated in Fronte Nazionale plots, including the Borghese coup, the evidence that they were involved indirectly, via intermediaries, is considerably more compelling. The most important of these intermediaries were the "parallel" intelligence networks headed by Miceli at SID and D'Amato at the UAR, and Gelli's P2 masonic lodge. These organizations have already been introduced in this chapter, and it would require additional book-length studies to describe everything that is now known about their history. But it is worth highlighting those features that might shed some light on the instrumental use and ultimate goals of the "Tora Tora" operation.

As has already been described, Judge Tamburino issued an arrest warrant for Miceli on 31 October 1974. The head of SID was accused of

> having promoted, formed, and organized, in conjunction with other persons, a secret association of military personnel and civilians in order to provoke an armed insurrection and, as a consequence of this, an illegal transformation of the constitution of the State and the form of government by means of the intervention of the armed forces, provoked by the actions of, and in part guided by, the very same association.

To achieve this objective, the association in turn made use of

> various armed groups with hierarchical structures, linked to each other at the base by "liaison officers" and linked to the summit by leaders spread out in various locales . . . [These groups were] financed to foment disorders, commit assaults, [and] carry out violent and threatening activities.[265]

In formally charging Miceli with these crimes, which primarily referred to his activities in the years after the Borghese coup, Tamburino sought to bring to light the links between neo-fascist paramilitary groups, an apparent intermediate civilian-military coordinating body known as the Rosa dei Venti, and the top secret structure within the armed forces intelligence services that later came to be known, somewhat inaccurately, as "parallel SID."

As it happens, a number of people who were privy to inside information had already revealed important details about this particular structure and certain other parallel apparatuses linked to the secret services. In order to provide a justification for some of his unconstitutional activities in the mid-1960s, for example, General Giovanni De Lorenzo had been compelled to acknowledge the existence of one such apparatus. He claimed that the compiling of extensive personal files on leading Italian political figures was part and parcel of the vetting responsibilities of the Ufficio Sicurezza Patto Atlantico (USPA: Atlantic Pact Security Office), which like SIFAR was attached to the Defense Ministry's general staff but was also linked, for intelligence gathering purposes, to the Carabinieri corps.[266] It was later discovered that separate USPAs had been set up within the Defense and Interior Ministries, and that both were directly linked to a central headquarters located in Brussels. At the time of the Borghese coup, control of the Defense Ministry's USPA had been entrusted by Miceli to Colonel Antonio Alemanno of SID, whereas the Interior Ministry's USPA was attached to the UAR and headed by D'Amato. But these secretive NATO security offices should not be confounded with other structures, including the more visible NATO secretariats in every Italian ministry, the clandestine "stay/behind" networks, "parallel SID" itself, or the Rosa dei Venti.[267]

The entity known as "parallel SID" was an even more secret organization which had responsibilities that were primarily operational rather than intelligence-oriented. Several of its members, most of whom had themselves been arrested for anti-democratic subversion, began to break their code of silence during the mid-1970s. The first member to spill the beans was right-wing trade unionist Roberto Cavallaro, who testified in 1974 that the parallel organization, which he called Organizzazione X (Organization X), included high-ranking elements from the Italian and American secret services, as well as from some leading multinational corporations, among its leaders. He traced its origins back the period right after De Lorenzo's "Plan Solo" was abandoned in 1964, and claimed that ever since it had manipulated, financed, and directed terrorist groups, via intermediaries, to undertake a strategy of destabilization. The goal, of course, was to provoke the security forces into activating emergency contingency plans designed to reestablish order. Cavallaro added that the organization aimed to alter the management of power in Italy, that NATO supported such an action, that the armed forces had been placed on alert, and that U.S. officials had taken part in operational meetings.[268] Finally, he indicated that Major Amos Spiazzi, an intelligence officer in an Army artillery unit stationed at Cremona and a key figure in later "coup" plots, was also associated with Organizzazione X.

Shortly thereafter, Judge Tamburino ordered Spiazzi's arrest. After remaining silent for several months, the latter realized that none of his military superiors would be interceding on his behalf and thence admitted that he was in fact a member of this "security organization," whose ostensible purpose was to defend Italian institutions against the threat posed by communism. In May 1974 he testified that the organization was not identical to SID, although it largely coincided with SID, and acknowledged that it consisted of civilians, industrialists, and politicians as well as military personnel. The following year he told Judge Fiore that it constituted the "alter ego" of the official Ufficio I chain of command within the three armed services. He further claimed that he received a coded telephone message in April 1973 from Major Mauro Venturi, the secretary of Miceli's right-hand man, Colonel Marzollo, which instructed him to make contact with Attilio Lercari and Giacomo Tubino, two Genoese industrialists who were providing funds for renewed FN coup plots.[269] Spiazzi soon put these Ligurian conspirators in contact with the representatives of right-wing paramilitary circles in the Veneto, including Eugenio Rizzato and General Nardella, and it was out of their collaborative efforts that the Rosa dei Venti organization congealed. Thus Spiazzi served as midwife in the birth and development of the Rosa network, within which he himself then assumed a very active role. But his real aim was to make instrumental use of this network in the interests of "parallel SID," that ultra-secret organization whose top leaders met with their Atlantic Alliance counterparts in Brussels at least once a year and were granted a NATO security clearance even higher than "cosmic." Among the members of this restricted elite, which amounted to a few dozen people at most, was the head of SID.

Miceli himself made no concerted effort to deny the existence of such an organization. On the contrary, when he was being questioned by Judge Fiore about "parallel SID" shortly after his October 1974 arrest, he responded as follows:

> To be able to defend myself adequately and collaborate in the ascertainment of the truth, as I think it is my duty to do, I must refer to facts and circumstances, investigative methods, and intelligence results that involve the security of the state and that I believe to be covered by political-military secrecy agreements. I have already asked three times to be released from the bonds of secrecy, but up till now I have not received the authorization . . . [Therefore,] I find myself constrained to avail myself of the right to abstain from responding.[270]

Newly elected Prime Minister Aldo Moro, who had played an important role in covering up the clandestine activities of De Lorenzo ten years before, refused to grant Miceli's request because, as he put it, he knew nothing about an organization within the secret services that had as its task the "subversion of the state."[271] This elusive response was a model of political doublespeak. For one thing, Moro refused to address Fiore's key question about why it was necessary to hold Miceli to secrecy agreements concerning things that supposedly did not even exist. For another, he referred exclusively to a parallel organization that aimed at undermining the state, which did not in fact exist within the services, and said nothing at all about the one that various witnesses claimed was designed to strengthen and protect the state from leftist subversion.

Miceli was therefore left to stew in his own juices, and he never forgave Andreotti and Moro for what he perceived to be their willingness to make him the "fall guy" and sacrifice his career. Three years later, after having been elected as an MSI deputy in 1976 and thereby obtaining parliamentary immunity, he finally had the opportunity to take a measure of revenge. In response to a precise question from Judge

Antonio Abate, who was then presiding over the second Borghese coup trial, the former SID chief seized the moment:

> In essence you want to know if a top secret organism exists within the framework (*ambito*) of SID. Up until now I have spoken of the twelve branches into which [the service] is divided. Each of these has, as an appendix, other organisms, other operational organizations, all of which have (*sempre con*) institutional aims. There is, and has always been, a particular top secret organization that the highest authorities of the state also know about. Seen from outside, by the profane, this organization could be interpreted as something alien to official policy. It is an organism inserted into the framework of SID, separated from the [regular] chain of officers belonging to Ufficio I, which undertakes fully institutional tasks, even if they concern activities that are far removed from intelligence gathering [!!!]. If you ask me about particular details, I tell you I cannot respond. Ask the highest authorities of the state about them so that you can obtain a definitive clarification.[272]

In this way, Miceli issued a direct challenge to the political establishment and implicated high-ranking politicians in the actions undertaken by "parallel SID." Unfortunately, Abate chose not to follow up on this suggestive firsthand testimony.

During the summer of 1984, further information about this organization was provided by yet another witness with firsthand knowledge of the neo-fascist milieu, convicted right-wing bomber Vincenzo Vinciguerra. Vinciguerra claimed that every terrorist massacre since 1969 – even, unbeknownst to him until later, the Peteano bombing for which he claimed personal responsibility – could be traced to a common organizational matrix. Indeed, the entire terrorist "strategy of tension," which was designed to reinforce the existing power structure and the Atlantic Alliance, was sponsored by a secret, parallel apparatus connected to the Interior Ministry's UAR and, via the Carabinieri, to SID. This strategy was not generally carried out by radical rightist organizations per se with the help of ideological sympathizers within those services, as Vinciguerra himself had originally believed, but rather by camouflaged elements of the security forces or their agents who operated inside those rightist organizations.[273] Once again, the existence of a secret structure resembling "parallel SID" was confirmed, this time by a political radical who had become convinced that the militants within his own milieu had been systematically manipulated by it.

Moreover, this particular parallel organization was explicitly linked to NATO "stay/behind" networks in the wake of recent revelations about the existence of the latter. The report on "Gladio" that Prime Minister Andreotti sent to Parliament in October 1990 was suggestively titled *Operazione Gladio – La cosidette "SID Parallelo,"* and a few months later Spiazzi proudly referred to himself as a "gladiator" and likewise (falsely) conflated the two organizations.[274] Since then, many commentators have attempted to attribute all the massacres and coup plots that afflicted Italy between 1964 and 1984 to these recently uncovered "stay/behind" networks, which undoubtedly represents a gross oversimplification and distortion of the real situation.

Indeed, much more has since been revealed about these secret structures within the security and intelligence services. The general situation was apparently as follows. There were reportedly three main levels of such secret, parallel, anti-communist apparatuses within Italy. The highest level, linked to the NATO and U.S. secret services and nominally under the authority of reliable Italian statesmen, was a kind of "super" secret service within the secret services composed of "patriotic" elements (known, among other names, as "parallel SID" and as "Super SISMI") that only select pro-Atlantic politicians and officials were aware of. This level was apparently centered within Ufficio R of SIFAR, SID, and finally SISMI. Beneath this was a second level composed of regular units of the military and the Carabinieri that would form "stay/behind" or rapid response units and would activate pre-planned operational protocols for resistance in the event of external invasion or internal civil disturbances. The third level was composed of the civilian "stay/behind" paramilitary groups that were designated, in Italy, under the code name "Gladio." It was later discovered that these civilian groups, whose members were trained by special operations personnel and armed and funded by the higher level parallel apparatuses, comprised some right-wing extremists along with a majority of law-abiding, pro-Atlanticist anti-communists. Elements from these parallel organizations were also at times allegedly involved in infiltrating, manipulating, and/or "collaborating with" seemingly autonomous political extremists, both neo-fascist and leftist, as well as in recruiting elements from criminal organizations, in order to carry out various illegal, "dirty," and plausibly deniable actions.[275] Furthermore, there were also "mixed" civilian-military groups ostensibly external to, but undoubtedly intersecting and actively collaborating with, the three *sub rosa* levels of quasi-official parallel organizations noted earlier, such as the Nuclei di Difesa dello Stato (NDS: Nuclei for the Defense of the State, associated closely with select covert and compartmentalized structures within Ordine Nuovo, especially in the Veneto region) and the "presidentialist" Rosa dei Venti groups.[276]

Finally, there was apparently another secret entity involved in these convoluted covert activities. On the basis of information found in a 4 April 1972 report and other materials compiled by *Corriere della Sera* journalist Alberto Grisolia (code-named "Fonte Giornalista"), an informant for the Milan section of the UAR, which was found in stashed UAR archives on Via Appia Antica that were discovered by historian and forensic judicial investigator Aldo Giannuli, previously unknown names for a secret structure linked to elements of SID and various other services were uncovered. One was the code name "Anello" ("Ring" or, perhaps more accurately, the circular "Link" in a chain), which suggested that the organization was a body that eventually functioned to link together and possibly coordinate the activities of the diverse levels of a more extensive and layered network of parallel organizational elements or components. Another name, apparently for this very same organization – one that was perhaps sardonic given that it was almost entirely unknown except to highly select cadres and influential politicians – was Il Noto Servizio (the Known Service).[277] This "civilian" organization, composed of ex-military personnel, ex-RSI operatives, entrepreneurs, journalists, and right-wing activists, had originally been created – with a different name – by General Mario Roatta (formerly head of the Servizio Informazioni Militari [SIM: Military Intelligence Service] during the Fascist era and thence Chief of the General Staff of the Army under the new government of Marshal Pietro Badoglio) in 1944. Later, apparently in exchange for assistance in taking refuge inside the Vatican and thence fleeing to Franco's Spain in March 1945 so as to escape prosecution for war crimes, Roatta transferred control of this secret organization to the new postwar Italian state (or perhaps, according to some observers, to its American backers), and it was thence headed for a time by a Polish officer in General Władysław Anders's Army named Solomon Hotimsky. The organization, which was headquartered in a palace in central Milan very near to the Carabinieri barracks on Via Moscova, thereafter intersected with many of the other secret structures discussed in this chapter, and it continued to operate until the mid-1980s. According to a member of the group, Michele Ristuccia, the name "Anello" was chosen for the organization by Andreotti himself after the SIFAR scandal erupted in the late 1960s.[278]

Throughout much of its history, "Anello" was informally dependent upon the prime minister, most often Andreotti during the 1970s, but its "dirty" operations to impede the left (perhaps including kidnappings and/or murders of "troublemakers" made to look like "accidents") were also reportedly "aided" by personnel from the Defense and Interior Ministries, and especially by Carabinieri seconded to SID and SISMI. By 1972, it was headed by Adalberto Titta, a former pilot in the RSI Air Force, and included key operatives such as businessman Felice Fulchignoni (head of the Roman branch), engineer Sigfrido Battaini (head of the Milanese branch), DC politician Massimo De Carolis (also a P2 lodge member and co-founder of the Maggioranza Silenziosa movement), journalist and MSI member Giorgio Pisanò, Franciscan friar Enrico Zucca (abbot of the convent of Sant'Angelo in Milan, who had been involved in the famous theft of Mussolini's corpse), shady private investigator Tom Ponzi, neo-fascist bomber Gianni Nardi, and MAR leader Carol Fumagalli. According to the aforementioned materials from the UAR archives, which were later supplemented by the firsthand testimony of reported members and operatives of this secret group, the "Anello" entity was involved in a number of important covert activities, including both "Plan Solo" and the Borghese Coup, In connection with the latter operation, "Anello" operatives reportedly arranged for Borghese's flight to escape judicial punishment; the Black Prince was supposedly sheltered in Battaini's villa before being exfiltrated and accompanied to Spain. The same organization was also implicated in facilitating the August 1977 flight and exfiltration from Italy of wanted Nazi war criminal Herbert Kappler; identifying (perhaps with the help of Brigate Rosse informants) the location of Aldo Moro's secret BR prison, which certain higher government officials intentionally did not act upon; and negotiating (with the help of *mafiosi*) the release of DC politician Ciro Cirillo (who had been kidnapped by the BR on 27 April 1981). Some have speculated that the apparent Mafia-sponsored assassinations of well-informed *OP* journalist Mino Pecorelli and General Carlo Dalla Chiesa may have been linked, at least in part, to their worrisome discovery of the existence of "Anello."

What can be said with certainty, however, is that Miceli and D'Amato, both of whom were explicitly identified as "supporters" of the Borghese coup by key FN insiders, stood at the apex of secret, parallel apparatuses in Italy that were organically linked to the NATO and American security establishments. Given the context, this fact alone is of great potential significance. But there is additional testimony which suggests that these apparatuses, or at least certain elements of them, were activated and deployed on the night of 7–8 December 1970. In November 1983, Spiazzi told members of the parliamentary commission investigating P2 that his artillery unit had received orders to move on the evening of the coup. He claimed that he recalled that particular night very well, both because he was acting as unit commander in the absence of Colonel Re and because the entire 67th Infantry regiment, to which his unit was attached, was celebrating the anniversary of the battle of Montelungo. Spiazzi then described the precise sequence of events.

Sometime between 4:30 PM and 6 PM he received a phone call from his close friend, ON bigwig Elio Massagrande, who warned him that the FN would be carrying out a "demonstration" in Rome that very evening, at the behest of an important government leader (*personaggio*). Massagrande claimed that the Fronte was chosen because it was not a regular political party and because its members were notoriously right-wing, and further indicated that ON would not participate in the operation and had dissociated itself from it. Spiazzi had heard nothing about this beforehand and found it rather odd, but less than one hour later he received a second call from yet another friend, retired General Umberto Corniani, who also happened to be the FN's Veneto "delegate" and a key figure in the Gruppi Savoia (Savoy Groups), a militant monarchist organization with its own paramilitary squads.[279] Corniani told Spiazzi that Borghese had phoned him and ordered him to make everything ready, because a major action would be launched in the capital that same night. Spiazzi remained perplexed and noncommittal, but around 9 PM he received a coded phone telegram – transmitted by Comiliter headquarters in Padua through his regiment's Ufficio I operations channel in Cremona – ordering him to activate the "Triangle" emergency plan, which supposedly mandated that the entire "parallel SID" apparatus be immediately set in motion toward preselected objectives. Trustworthy elements within his own artillery unit were to march westward, meet up with the "Lancieri di Milano" unit in Monza, and then move on to invest the Sesto San Giovanni neighborhood in Milan, a hotbed of left-wing radicalism. Due to a fortuitous transfer of munitions that was in the process of being carried out that very day, which meant that two armored personnel carriers full of artillery shells were already loaded and ready to go, Spiazzi's unit was prepared to move almost immediately. By the time it reached the Agrate train station, however, a counterorder was issued via the same communications channels, and his forces thence returned to base.[280]

In addition to buttressing other allegations about the mobilization and deployment of military and Carabinieri units on the night of the Borghese coup, Spiazzi's testimony explicitly linked such actions to a top secret operational plan to be carried out by the parallel networks headed by Miceli and D'Amato, among others. As one would expect, his superiors within the military hierarchy subsequently denied knowing anything about the "Triangle" plan. Among those who made this claim were Admiral Henke, Armed Forces chief of staff in December 1970, and General Siro Rosseti, at that time head of SIOS-Esercito in the Lazio region. Other officers testified that they had no recollections of that evening, including Captain Pirro, head of the Ufficio I communications center at Cremona.[281] Once again, we are confronted with the problem of which witness or witnesses to believe, and in the absence of material evidence there is no way to be certain. Although it is obvious that Spiazzi, who was then seeking to defend himself against charges of subversion and political conspiracy, had very good reasons to attribute the responsibility for some of these illegal actions to his superiors, it is also true that the latter had equally strong motives for denying that these unconstitutional deployments took place and for covering up "parallel SID"'s possible involvement in them. By doing so, after all, they would have been protecting their own careers and reputations. Spiazzi's credibility in some other areas was attacked by the judges investigating the Borghese coup, perhaps with good reason, but much of the information he provided to Judge Tamburino and the P2 commission dovetailed very well with testimony and evidence that emerged in later years.

Even if some of the details can be said to be erroneous, it seems probable that there was considerably more than a kernel of truth in the revelations made by Spiazzi and others concerning the actions taken by certain parallel networks on the night of the "Tora Tora" operation. The existence of the "Triangle" plan and its activation that evening were both accepted without hesitation by MSI Senator and P2 commission member Giorgio Pisanò, who may well have received additional information about it from one of his contacts in the military intelligence service. In his account, however, no mention is made of the role allegedly played by "parallel SID." Pisanò characterizes "Triangle" as an emergency intervention plan that was based exclusively upon the mobilization and deployment of trustworthy anticommunist elements from each participating military unit. The actions justifying their seizure of key objectives and crackdown on "subversives" were to be carried out unwittingly by Borghese's men, not consciously by elements of parallel civilian-military structures referred to as "parallel SID."[282] Spiazzi, on the other hand, gives the distinct impression that both the FN and these parallel apparatuses had important, although different, roles to play that night. In any event, the extensive efforts made by Miceli to cover up Borghese's "coup" and protect the plotters should alone engender a certain amount of suspicion, because as SID chief he stood at the summit of one such network – perhaps the most important of them all – within the Defense Ministry.

Not coincidentally, apparent "parallel SID" leader Miceli also happened to be a member of the P2 masonic lodge, which served as another important but indirect conduit between the Atlantic security establishment and the Black Prince's men. The parliamentary commission investigating P2 uncovered evidence that Gelli had close links to a number of Western secret services and was probably a top-level operative for one or more of them, that he was connected to leading Republican Party circles in the United States, and that many key figures who had a "significant involvement" in the Borghese coup were members of his secretive, restricted, and highly selective organization.[283] This group not only included FN activists like Orlandini and Saccucci, secret service and parallel network personnel like Miceli and D'Amato, and military officers like Fanali and Ricci, but also one of Nixon's chief liaisons in Italy, Sicilian financier Sindona, through whose banking network the American government first laundered and then disseminated considerable sums of money which had been earmarked for anti-communist political groups.[284] It should also be pointed out that Miceli began to strengthen his contacts with Borghese and Orlandini in mid-1969, during the very period when he was recruited into the P2 lodge, and that one year later Gelli worked behind the scenes to support Miceli's successful bid to become head of SID by lobbying Defense Minister Tanassi through the latter's secretary, Bruno Palmiotti, another P2 member.[285] However, in discussing the interaction between P2 and the Borghese coup, it is not necessary to limit oneself to highlighting this overlapping network of personal connections.

Miceli's active role in covering up the "Tora Tora" operation has already been discussed in detail. In carrying out this series of obstructive maneuvers, he seems to have worked in tandem with the Venerable Master of the P2 lodge.[286] A good deal of information about Gelli's alleged efforts to protect the "Tora Tora" plotters was later recounted by neo-fascist militant Paolo Aleandri, whom Fabio and Alfredo De Felice had taken into their confidence.[287] In 1974, the two De Felice brothers were warned by a sympathetic Guardia di Finanza official that an arrest warrant was about to be issued for various FN leaders suspected of having been involved in the Borghese coup. This ominous news prompted them to flee to London for safety, whereas Filippo De Jorio, one of their closest co-conspirators, opted to take refuge elsewhere, first in Paris and then in Montecarlo. After charges against the two siblings were dropped at the first trial, both De Felices returned to Italy, Fabio to Poggio Catino and Alfredo to Rome. At this point, having already developed a good deal of trust in Aleandri, his former high school pupil, Fabio De Felice asked him to collaborate on their journal, *Politica e Strategia*, and sought to involve him in other projects that they were sponsoring. It was in this context that the De Felice brothers began openly discussing a rightist seizure of power and revealing details about the role played by Gelli in the Borghese operation.

Aleandri subsequently claimed that Alfredo had been in regular contact with Gelli, and that the latter had personally introduced the two of them. Then, prior to departing for a job at Alfa Romeo in South Africa, Alfredo specifically requested that Aleandri serve as the intermediary between De Jorio, who had not been absolved in the first trial, and the head of P2. Because both De Felice telephones were tapped, Alfredo told Aleandri that De Jorio would phone his house from Montecarlo, using the pseudonym "Marcelli," and asked the young radical to personally convey De Jorio's messages to Gelli. Thereafter Aleandri received several anxious phone calls from De Jorio, who implored him to visit Gelli in his luxurious suite at the Hotel Excelsior, remind him of his plight, and get updates on the status of the defendants in the second "Tora Tora" trial. These contacts were undertaken during the 1977–1978 period. The Venerable Master was apparently already working behind the scenes to improve the plotters' legal position, both by applying covert pressure on the relevant political and judicial authorities and by conditioning press coverage, and on one occasion he told Aleandri to reassure De Jorio that a general political solution was being arranged.[288] Although it will probably never be possible to determine exactly how much influence Gelli's multifaceted personal interventions exerted on this process, all the serious charges against the key Fronte Nazionale conspirators ended up being dropped.

Several years later, Fabio De Felice sent a letter to the president of the P2 commission, DC Deputy Tina Anselmi, in which he denied that he had ever met or seen Gelli, attacked the credibility of Aleandri, and criticized the tactics employed by the commission, especially its failure to solicit testimony from those it was accusing of involvement in illegal rightist subversion.[289] Nevertheless, there are several specific pieces of evidence which indicate that Gelli and other leading P2 figures went out of their way to impede the progress of the judicial investigations and otherwise provide assistance to the plotters. For example, when he was questioned about the Borghese coup by Colonel Antonio Viezzer of SID in the fall of 1973 or the spring of 1974, the Venerable Master himself sought to discredit Orlandini's damaging testimony by referring to the shipbuilder as an unreliable "teller of tall tales."[290] Much earlier, in March 1971, when the judges sought to question Miceli in person about the information his service had accumulated concerning the recently exposed FN coup, Attorney General Carmelo Spagnuolo – an important P2 member and a close associate of Gelli's – intervened personally and arranged it so that the general would not have to testify.[291] Four years later another key P2 "brother," General Raffaele Giudice of the Guardia di Finanza, prevailed upon his friend Achille Gallucci, head of the Rome Ufficio Istruzione, to intervene with the investigating magistrates so that Miceli would be freed on bail, a goal which was duly accomplished.[292]

Nor was the P2 lodge the only group within Italian freemasonry to be implicated in the coup, although all evidence of possible masonic involvement was excised from the three judicial sentences. The FN's "delegate" for Milan was Gavino Matta, a former Italian Fascist volunteer in Spain and a member of a "covered" Milanese lodge that was associated with the Grand Lodge (Piazza del Gesù) headed by Giovanni Ghinazzi. In the fall of 1970 Matta had written a letter to Gelli, informing him that his own lodge did not intend to support the P2 chief's initiatives because it was opposed in principle to violent methods, and that herewith he had been authorized to annul "every previous agreement" between the two lodges. But shortly thereafter he sent another letter to Gelli, this time indicating that he was available for action.[293] He was apparently as good as his word, for on the night of 7–8 December

1970 Matta had been in the midst of giving a lecture on coup techniques to the conspirators who had gathered at Orlandini's shipyard, but was interrupted just after midnight by the phone call instructing Orlandini to leave at once for Rosa's office.[294] Three months later, after receiving advance warning that the plotters were about to be arrested, he fled to Spain together with the Black Prince.[295] In this connection, it should be noted that Ghinazzi was himself implicated in later plots, and was therefore questioned by the judges investigating the Rosa dei Venti and the Sogno group.

To this incriminating information about the actions taken by influential freemasons must be added insider revelations about two planned neo-fascist thefts of compromising masonic documents. The first of these occurred in the spring of 1971, when MPON bigwig Paolo Signorelli asked Sergio Calore to help steal sensitive masonic materials from a villa outside Rome that was owned by Edoardo Formisano, regional MSI counselor for Lazio and Arturo Michelini's personal secretary. These materials, which supposedly contained information about the behind-the-scenes political backers of the Borghese coup, were successfully purloined and thence consigned to Rauti. Delle Chiaie was also apparently interested in this venture, because AN leader Adriano Tilgher kept Calore under surveillance until he was temporarily kidnapped and warned not to concern himself with the affair. Later on, right-wing killer Pierluigi Concutelli confided to Calore that the MPON had also planned to steal a cache of documents from Gelli's Villa Wanda in Arezzo, but that this project was then nixed by the organization's military leader, Giuseppe ("Beppino") Pugliese, who made it clear that the Venerable Master was untouchable.[296] The ultimate sponsors of these particular "black bag" jobs remain to be identified, as do the precise reasons for planning or carrying them out. It may be that members of the two main neo-fascist groups wished to obtain documentary evidence against the powerful political circles that secretly made instrumental use of violence and subversion, evidence which could then, if necessary, be utilized either to protect themselves or blackmail their manipulators. Alternatively, they may have been put up to it by elements linked to one or more of those very circles, who wanted to be certain that such evidence would not fall into the wrong hands. In either case, it is clear that these initiatives were both by-products of a complex pattern of internecine rivalries between shifting factions of freemasons, neo-fascists, secret service personnel, and politicians.

Perhaps most importantly, certain witnesses have testified that Gelli himself played a key role in determining the outcome of the coup. This matter is best considered in connection with the source of the counterorder that led to the much disputed recall of the conspirators in the wee hours of 8 December 1970.

The counterorder

To this day, the last-minute issuance of the counterorder by Borghese remains something of a mystery, largely because the Black Prince never provided a complete explanation of his reasons for issuing it. Yet few things could be more important in assessing the historical significance of the coup. Solving this mystery would not only help to clarify the aims pursued by leading FN plotters; it would also shed more light on the often divergent motives of the powerful political forces, both national and international, which may have tacitly sponsored the action and/or sought to exploit it for their own purposes.

Shortly after midnight on the evening of 8 December 1970, Borghese received a phone call that prompted him to cancel the operation and interrupt the maneuvers that were already underway. He told his assembled lieutenants at "command post A" that the external support which the plotters had counted on had failed to materialize, but did not reveal the name of the caller or provide further specifics. When Orlandini and Ciabatti arrived a few minutes later from "command post B," he explained that the projected plan to seize control of the Defense Ministry had been rendered impossible because military accomplices inside the building had failed to carry out their assigned tasks. Later, in the face of open hostility and bitter recriminations from several of his closest associates, he justified his issuance of the counterorder by saying that he himself had "obeyed superior orders,"[297] an explanation that was far too vague and laconic to satisfy the disappointed ultras, many of whom believed that they had been personally betrayed by their former hero. No further details seem to have been proffered about this matter by the Black Prince prior to his August 1974 death in Spain, which has only served to fuel subsequent speculation about the ultimate source of those orders and the identity of the caller.

It is of course possible that Borghese was telling the truth when he claimed that he called the operation off because he had learned that Defense Ministry insiders were not positioned to fulfill their allotted tasks. If the plotters counted upon the support of sympathetic elements within the armed forces, as indeed they apparently did, they would surely have recognized the importance of having a high-ranking military conspirator like General Fanali issue orders via normal communications channels located inside Palazzo Barracchini. Such orders would not only have served to "officially" authorize the provision of this hoped-for operational support, but would also have helped to deter non-participating military units from trying to interfere with the "legitimate" movements being carried out by both civilian and military participants. This projected scenario seems all the more credible given the fact that some of Delle Chiaie's men, with insider help, had supposedly taken control of the Interior Ministry's communications networks for a few hours that very same night. It also jibes with Saccucci's bitter lament that certain "groups of buffoons," together with "other little clowns, more or less in uniform," had been responsible for the failure of the coup.[298] If the Black Prince's explanation is accepted at face value, it can then be assumed that one of his loyal co-conspirators phoned to inform him about the unforeseen problems which had arisen in connection with the FN's plan to take control of the Defense Ministry. Yet this relatively straightforward scenario is problematic in other ways. It does not conform to other testimony concerning the alleged source(s) of the call(s) received by Borghese that evening, and it neither explains why the former war hero said he was obeying "superior orders," nor why he refused to provide further specifics when he was later subjected to aggressive questioning and harsh criticism by his key FN subordinates.

The first desideratum, then, is to try to identify which so-called superior may have transmitted the orders instructing the Black Prince to call off the operation. Several well-known candidates have been nominated for this dubious honor. Not surprisingly, one of them is General Miceli. As noted earlier, the information provided by Franco Antico to Lieutenant Colonel Genovesi had been transmitted up through the chain of command to the head of military intelligence service shortly after midnight. Some observers have suggested that Miceli, being a friend of Borghese's and a secret promoter of coup plots, then contacted the Black Prince by phone to warn him that the Fronte's subversive actions that evening had already been disclosed to SID.[299] Spiazzi offered a variation on this scenario. He identified Lieutenant Colonel Giuseppe Condò, one of Miceli's loyalists within SIOS-Esercito, as the person who actually conveyed the counterorder to Borghese.[300] But these particular claims were countered by other witnesses with indirect or direct insider knowledge. For example, a neo-fascist and SID informant involved in the operation, Torquato Nicoli, claimed that it was UAR chief D'Amato who called Borghese and transmitted the counterorder.[301] According to Paolo Aleandri, another neo-fascist, Fabio De Felice was convinced that Gelli had personally played a role in contacting the Black Prince and persuading him to terminate the operation.[302] For his part, Remo Orlandini insisted that the operation was called off because the call made by Fenwich to Nixon did not go through. He implied that Fenwich, or some other intermediary between the plotters and the American government, then transmitted this disappointing news to "command post A." Because anticipated American support for the coup was not forthcoming, Borghese was reluctantly compelled to abort the "Tora Tora" plan.

In short, many of the purported *sub rosa* backers of the operation have been accused of being ultimately responsible for calling it off by transmitting the infamous counterorder. These conflicting claims make it all the more difficult to identify the specific individual(s) who actually made phone call(s) to the Black Prince or one of his key henchmen that evening. Yet there is no necessary contradiction between the apparently divergent claims that Miceli, Condò, D'Amato, Gelli, or someone close to Fenwich had made calls that exerted some influence on Borghese's actions. Miceli was linked at least indirectly to Fenwich through his primary liaisons at the American embassy, among whom were hard-liners like Ambassador Graham Martin, Clavio, and certain unidentified CIA officials, and in spite of a dearth of tangible evidence the same may also have been true of Gelli, his P2 "brother" and lodgemaster. For his part, Condò was one of the key operatives in the SID chief's 1974 efforts to expose Edgardo Sogno's potentially embarrassing connections to Andreotti's wife's aunt, the *Marchesa* Maria Antonietta Nicastro.[303] Moreover, all five of the aforementioned individuals played important roles in clandestine, parallel networks that worked in tandem with NATO and U.S. security agencies. Indeed, given the partially overlapping goals of various national and international circles that sought to covertly condition Italian political developments, in the long run it may not really matter exactly *who* transmitted the counterorder to Borghese. The more important question is *why* such a message was conveyed, which can only be answered when the real goals of these backers have been further clarified.

The aims of the forces involved

The "Tora Tora" operation has up to now been depicted in one of two fundamentally incompatible ways. The first portrays Borghese and his followers as pathetic nostalgics who were acting entirely on their own initiative, and characterizes the operation as an amateur affair that was called off for some sort of trivial reason. Gelli later claimed, for instance, that a torrential downpour was all it took to derail the action, and others have suggested that key FN leaders had second thoughts at the last minute and went home to bed.[304] However reassuring such contemptuous dismissals of the seriousness of the affair may sound, they do not conform at all to Fiore's detailed judicial reconstruction, and they completely ignore both the overall political context and the close links that had been forged between the plotters and key elements within the security forces of the Italian state. For these and other reasons, this particular interpretation should not be taken seriously. In marked contrast, the second depicts the "coup" in a far more significant and sinister light. It characterizes Borghese and his ultras as the point men for, or the unwitting dupes of, far more powerful forces that sought, respectively, either to promote or make instrumental use of their anti-democratic plotting. There is scarcely any doubt that this second basic characterization is closer to the truth, but more attention has to be focused on what these forces operating behind the scenes were really up to.

Despite the attempts of certain mainstream and conservative commentators to dismiss "Tora Tora" as a farcical or chimerical affair, it is now generally accepted that the actions taken by Borghese's men on the night of 7–8 December were not meant to be carried out independently of other military and political operations. Neither the Black Prince nor any of his key subordinates, many of whom had had previous military experience, could honestly have believed that the limited paramilitary forces at their disposal would alone be sufficient to bring down the existing political system.[305] Most of them later admitted that they had counted on the intervention of elements of the Italian security forces for ultimate success, and several added, without equivocation, that they had anticipated the provision of American or NATO logistical support. These plausible claims cannot be dismissed as mere post-facto rationalizations for incompetence and failure, because they fit the known facts like a hand fits a glove. From the outset, the FN had both expressed its public solidarity with the armed forces and undertaken extensive covert efforts to recruit high-ranking military personnel, especially those in sensitive operational posts. Moreover, these complementary activities seem to have borne considerable fruit. Borghese's expressions of soldierly esteem were reciprocated by important circles within the military establishment, and certain active-duty officers apparently both encouraged the Black Prince to take action and promised to support the plotters if and when such an action was initiated. Despite their systematic efforts to limit the political damage stemming from their investigation, Judge Fiore and his colleagues were forced to admit that these officers, who they claimed it was impossible to identify with greater precision, had reneged on their promises at the crucial moment.[306] In any event, it is clear that the Black Prince did not authorize the "Tora Tora" action until he had satisfied himself that the promised military support would be forthcoming.

Once the idea that a completely autonomous or independent military action by the FN and its neo-fascist allies has been ruled out, there remain three more or less plausible scenarios. The first is that anti-democratic rightists within the ranks of the military and various security agencies had really been persuaded to join forces with the extraparliamentary bands led by Borghese. Like the Black Prince and his civilian followers, and perhaps in part prompted by the Fronte's secret but extensive proselytization and recruitment efforts, certain of these officials may well have come to believe that a communist seizure of power was imminent, either through legal or illegal means; that the degenerate *partitocrazia* was offering no effective resistance to this threat; that dramatic, even violent solutions were called for before it was too late; and that the former naval hero was the only figure with enough prestige to rally the public in support of an overtly authoritarian anti-communist regime. In this case the goal of all those involved, whether or not they were formally affiliated with the security apparatus of the state, would have been essentially the same – to launch a full-scale military coup similar, in its general outlines, to those that were successfully carried out by the Greek Colonels and countless Latin American praetorians.

It seems clear that the bulk of the FN's operational leaders honestly believed that sympathetic elements of the armed forces would support an outright Borghese-led attempt to overthrow the existing political class. However naïve such a notion may seem in retrospect, there is considerable evidence suggesting that this was precisely what they were counting on. The first is the proclamation that the Black Prince had personally prepared, in advance, to read over RAI-TV's airwaves (and perhaps also transmit via certain restricted military channels). As noted earlier, this consisted of an emotional public appeal for support aimed at "patriotic" Italians and members of the armed forces, coupled with an effort to reassure the United States and its NATO allies that the new government his followers intended to set up would not only maintain, but increase, its commitment to the Atlantic Alliance. It should also be recalled that Borghese's close associate Guadagni unabashedly promoted the Black Prince as an Italian version of De Gaulle, who alone would be able to establish a cisalpine "public safety" regime on the French model.[307] A similar belief that the coup would usher in a new government and that leading FN figures would then assume key positions in it was expressed by Orlandini, who told Fenwich that he himself would be appointed as chief of the armed forces general staff in the wake of a successful coup.[308] There is no doubt that equally grandiose ideas were shared by many other plotters, who mistakenly placed faith in the expressions of sympathy and promises of assistance reportedly proffered by various military and secret service personnel.

Although it is practically certain that Borghese and his men had some genuine admirers and active supporters within the ranks of the Italian security forces, the assistance of such avid loyalists was apparently provided on an *individual* rather than an official or institutional basis. Those who secretly represented formal or parallel institutional interests seem to have operated in accordance with very different agendas. Indeed, the majority of the observers who are familiar with the details of the "Tora Tora" affair, whether former participants or serious external investigators, have concluded that the FN plotters were duped and manipulated by elements of various military and intelligence organizations which they had mistakenly trusted and relied upon for the success of their venture. The proponents of this interpretation include knowledgeable individuals on all sides of the political spectrum, ranging from leading Fronte Nazionale protagonists and neo-fascist ultras to radical left-wing analysts and some relative "moderates." There are, however, serious differences of opinion about which personnel honestly supported the Black Prince's goals and which ones sought to sabotage or otherwise subvert those goals. There is probably no way to provide a definitive answer to these questions given the current lacunae in the available documentation, but it should be possible to make some educated guesses and rule out some of the more implausible scenarios.

There are two contrasting variants of the theory that the rightist ultras who were participating in what they thought was a coup had been secretly manipulated and instrumentalized by powerful political, military, and intelligence factions with divergent aims. Both of these variants share one common postulate: that the actions carried out by Borghese's forces would provide the pretext and the catalyst for the launching of a top secret anti-insurrectional plan by elements of the security forces of the Italian state. The plotters would thus undertake only the initial "provocation" phases of a far more complex and extensive operation. In this sense, they would perform the same function that right-wing extremists have often performed elsewhere, both before and after 1970. The key question is whether the FN conspirators were ultimately to benefit from, or be victimized by, their pro-coup provocation efforts that evening. In other national contexts, one can find examples of both these possible outcomes. Many of the rightist paramilitary groups whose violence provided a pretext for the 1967 military coup in Greece were later disbanded when they had outlived their usefulness or threatened to become too autonomous, and after helping to precipitate the 1980 military coup in Turkey, leading figures of the neo-fascist Milliyetçi Hareket Partisi (MHP: Nationalist Action [or Movement] Party) were first marginalized and then arrested and placed on trial for terrorist activities. In marked contrast, in Chile members of rightist paramilitary squads like Patria y Libertad were incorporated into DINA, the junta's secret police, and other security or propaganda agencies after the 1973 coup.

The first and more straightforward variant of the "state manipulation" theory is perhaps best referred to as the "anti-leftist" variant. This plan was apparently designed to unfold in the following way. Borghese's forces were to seize various key objectives with inside help, including the Interior Ministry, the Defense Ministry, the Foreign Affairs Ministry, the central headquarters of RAI-TV, and possibly the Quirinale presidential palace and the palaces housing the Senate and Chamber of Deputies. At the same time, contingents from AN, the ANPDI, and other rightist youth groups would foment disorders at strategic locations throughout Rome. Even if the PCI and extraparliamentary left were not provoked into some sort of overreaction, the goal was to create the impression that radical left-wing groups had taken to the streets in an insurrection attempt. In either case, the suppression of these violent disorders would have appeared to require the immediate intervention of the security forces. In short, carefully planned disturbances would produce a crisis of public order that would in turn precipitate the activation of emergency anti-insurrection plans by special cadres of the Carabinieri, selected units of the armed forces, and certain parallel apparatuses linked to the secret services. Once these official forces had moved into position and relieved the plotters who had seized control of the aforementioned objectives, the paramilitary civilian forces would then, no doubt to the chagrin of their leading militants, be consigned to a purely auxiliary and marginal status. They would be allowed to assist regular units in their efforts to arrest "subversive" leftist politicians and union leaders, and perhaps be assigned to carry out other "dirty" jobs. But their overall operational role would be severely circumscribed and their political influence would be practically nil, thus dashing the overinflated expectations of the Black Prince and his chief lieutenants.

A number of informed observers have argued, however, that Borghese and his plotters were themselves among the forces that were to be suppressed in the wake of the intervention by the security forces. Far from benefiting from their crucial provocateur role in the operation, they were intended to be its initial victims. This particular variant can be referred to as the "anti-extremism" variant. As in the "anti-leftist" variant, the actions taken by the Fronte and its allies were again supposed to provide the spark that catalyzed the activation of various emergency anti-insurrectional plans. It is therefore likely that some of these plans governed the reactions of the Carabinieri, others the response of regular military units, and still others the actions to be taken by clandestine structures and paramilitary networks linked to NATO or the United States. But in this case, along with radical leftists, "expendable" right-wingers like the Black Prince's followers were also primary targets of the crackdown. The action would have been publicly justified by the need to carry out a major strike against the dangerous "opposing extremisms" that were then posing a threat to the existence of the Italian state. But the real purpose was to make instrumental use of "black" terrorism and subversion in order to strengthen the political positions of certain factions affiliated in one way or another with the political establishment, factions that had supporters and referents in a number of other Western countries. By cracking down on both right- and left-wing ultras, certain of these ambitious and opportunistic politicians, government officials, and well-connected "outsiders" were apparently hoping to pose as the "saviors" of Italian democracy. Who were these unscrupulous men, and how did they possibly make use of the Borghese coup?

Two shifting factional groupings seem to have been behind the "state manipulation" scenarios outlined earlier, because both were at odds with the proponents of an outright coup. The first of these was the so-called presidentialist group. It consisted of a number of highly influential political figures, both within and outside government, who believed that the postwar First Republic was too unstable, corrupt, and inefficient to resolve Italy's profound economic, political, and social crises or increase her international role and stature. The chief problem they identified was the weakness of the executive branch in relation to the power and privileges enjoyed by representatives of the disputatious parties, both inside the corridors of Parliament and throughout the administrative apparatus of the entire country. After all, in spite of the political dominance of DC-led coalitions and the general continuity of fundamental policies and decision-making processes in the period after 1948, Italy was a country where particular cabinets had fallen on an average of more than once per year. Indeed, the whole party system, rooted as it was in patronage, corruption, and influence-peddling, presented a target of opportunity for unscrupulous forces of all types, including the communists, who could easily exploit its many weaknesses with their own well-organized and highly disciplined party apparatus. The presidentialists wanted to replace this "soft," inefficient, and easily conditioned system, which in their view was ripe for an eventual communist takeover, with a brand-new Second Republic. To accomplish this goal, they advocated the formation of a temporary "emergency government" and the carrying out of constitutional reforms. These reforms would be designed, among other things, to greatly expand the powers of the president at the expense of Parliament, and to alter the nature of the latter by eliminating proportional representation and instituting a more stable two-party arrangement that was loosely modeled on the American system.[309]

The second of the two manipulative factional groupings consisted of influential elements within the existing political establishment that sought to make use of political violence and subversion in order to buttress their own personal and clientelistic power base and thereby gain advantages in the covert infighting that has always characterized Italian parliamentary and bureaucratic politics. These "establishment manipulators," who can perhaps be usefully subdivided into cynical opportunists and those who were firmly convinced that their own career advancement was in the higher interests of the country, were generally affiliated with leading factions of the DC. It should be pointed out that the DC exhibited certain unique characteristics that distinguished it from most other modern European parties. As a politically dominant interclass Catholic party, it encompassed an unusually broad variety of social groups and sectional lobbies whose specific interests could not always be easily reconciled. These included, among others, the reformist, left-leaning economic agenda of Catholic workers, the moderately conservative interests of the middle class forces that constituted the party's majority, the anti-reformist policies generally advocated by large landowners and certain groups of industrialists, and the far right "social" concerns of its integralist elements. This aggregation of conflicting intraparty interests was further complicated by the external pressure periodically applied by powerful but internally divided Vatican circles. As an outgrowth of these extraordinary countervailing forces, the party developed into a vast, sprawling apparatus that was composed of loosely connected clientelistic networks and, consequently, riven by intense factional disputes.[310] Indeed, it could be argued that the internal struggles between various DC factions were as important as the DC's rivalries with other parties in determining the constellation of forces at the apex of the Italian state. It would, however, be wrong to associate all these DC *correnti* with specific ideological and programmatic agendas, for many evolved into self-interested patronage networks that revolved around particular leaders whose own policies shifted over time.

Given the divergent political aims of the "presidentialists" and the "establishment manipulators," it would be natural to associate the former with the "anti-leftist" variant and the latter with the "anti-extremism" variant. On the surface, the presidentialists seemingly intended to marginalize the more disreputable elements of the far right after using them to take control of the government, whereas the establishment manipulators aimed to utilize them in a dual way, first to provide the pretext for a military intervention and then to serve as the sacrificial rightist victims of subsequent official crackdowns on the "opposing extremisms." But such a simplified bifurcation between their respective plans for Borghese and his men may not fully correspond to reality. Note, for example, that the so-called white coup sponsored three years later by Sogno, a leading and indefatigable presidentialist conspirator, specifically provided for the "burning" of violent neo-fascist groups and the promotion of a "progressive" social agenda. It was hoped that these actions would help to garner public support for their attempts to form a temporary "emergency" regime.[311] This suggests that the presidentialists may have earlier envisioned a similar action against the radical right, despite their ostensible attempts to forge "alliances" with some neo-fascist leaders, and it has even been argued that they intended to "burn" the ultras in order to clear the way for the carrying out of their own plans.[312] On the other hand, it may be that certain establishment manipulators did not really want to eradicate the entire paramilitary right, but only certain "disposable" factions of it. Because they presumably intended to base a considerable portion of their own popularity on their continued attempts to control the scourge of violence perpetrated by the "opposing extremisms," they may well have wished to exploit future acts of right-wing terrorism in order to periodically renew this source of public support. In that case, it would have been in their long-term interest to ensure the survival of certain neo-fascist networks, if not to covertly foster occasional acts of violence by their members. Exploiting fears of genuine or artificially manufactured "threats" to the existing state has long been an effective technique employed by political leaders, whatever their ideologies, who sought to fortify their own positions of power.

The fundamental differences between the attitudes of the presidentialists and the establishment manipulators toward the existing political class can be boiled down to a single declaratory sentence. The former wanted to replace or radically reorganize that class, whereas the latter, being important members of it, sought to preserve it even as they worked to improve their own positions within it. But this divergence should not obscure some important underlying similarities between the two groups. Both were resolutely pro-Atlanticist in their geopolitical orientation and uncompromisingly anti-communist on the home front, and in this sense their views did not differ greatly from those of Borghese and his chief lieutenants. These attitudes alone made such conspiratorial groups acceptable, at least as a last resort, to influential circles within the governments and secret services of the United States and other Western nations. Under normal circumstances many of those circles clearly preferred to avoid undertaking risky political ventures that might backfire, but faced with the prospect of a possible communist assumption of power, even via legal means, they would probably not have hesitated to have had recourse to groups of this type. Only some of the more radical neo-fascists who collaborated on some level with the Black Prince were considered wholly beyond the pale, because they were genuinely hostile to Atlanticism and opposed to American "imperialism."

With this background, the roles played by the various quasi-official forces that secretly encouraged Borghese to launch the provocative "Tora Tora" operation can perhaps be further clarified. The best place to begin is with the "political" figures associated with the leadership group of the Fronte Nazionale, specifically Filippo De Jorio and the two De Felice brothers, who were nicknamed the "brothers Karamasov" by their co-conspirators. De Jorio was a high-profile lawyer who had developed close links with "vast sectors of the parliamentary right," above all influential conservative factions of the DC.[313] According to his own 1975 admission, he had served as one of Prime Minister Mariano Rumor's political counselors in 1969, and had then been elected as a DC deputy for the Lazio region. By age thirty-seven he had acquired so much prestige, "both within governmental circles and inside the party structure," that he was regularly invited to participate in top-level meetings with DC leaders such as Rumor, DC Secretary Flaminio Piccoli, and Giulio Orlando.[314] During this period, moreover, he apparently became one of Giulio Andreotti's right-hand men. He later revealed that he had played an active role in the planning and organizing work which took place prior to the May 1972 elections, and that in connection with this and other duties he had occupied an office near Prime Minister Andreotti's on the third floor of Palazzo Chigi. The following year he acted as a political counselor for Andreotti, at whose request he advocated a rejection of the center-left formula at the June DC congress. In October of that same year, after Andreotti's government had fallen, the former prime minister and members of his faction held a meeting at Rome's Cinema Antares. At this gathering De Jorio was the only speaker seated on the stage next to Andreotti, along with the coterie of government officials and bureaucrats who backed the latter's political return.[315]

De Jorio was thus in regular and direct contact with some of the most powerful figures in the Italian political establishment throughout the entire period when he was actively involved in FN plots, because his involvement in such plotting by no means ceased after the abrupt termination of the "Tora Tora" operation. Among other things, he played an active role during the top-level FN meetings held in January and February of 1971, as well as at the December 1971 meeting in Genoa between industrialist Andrea Piaggio and Admiral Roselli Lorenzini. He also openly supported the FN leaders who were originally arrested for participating in the Borghese coup, first by serving as Orlandini's lawyer and then by speaking at a 13 February 1972 public rally held in support of the arrestees at the Cinema Adriano in Rome.[316] But where did his real loyalties lie, to the right-wing *golpistas* commanded by the Black Prince, to the presidentialists operating behind the scenes, or to certain opportunistic politicians? In his sentence Judge Fiore highlighted De Jorio's importance by noting his close relations with Orlandini, his presence at crucial FN meetings before and after the coup, and his projected appointment to an important post within the post-coup government, but implied that he was a Fronte loyalist who was using his connections with powerful political figures on behalf of the plotters.[317]

There are, however, reasons to doubt this politically convenient interpretation. It is true that De Jorio served as the main intermediary between the FN plotters and various influential politicians who claimed to be sympathetic to their cause, but it may well be that he was working at the behest of the latter, whose interests were in reality quite different than – if not antithetical to – those of Borghese. Among other things, De Jorio's links to various secret or parallel structures need to be kept in mind. Around the time of the coup, for example, he was president of the Ufficio Alti Studi Strategici, located inside the Defense Ministry, and was therefore in close contact with the leaders of the Italian armed forces.[318] His name also appeared prominently on the P2 membership list, and as noted earlier he later managed, using Aleandri as his liaison, to solicit Gelli's intervention in support of his legal defense. Beyond that, he was connected to a vast network of "private" intelligence-linked organizations and personnel, many of them indefatigable advocates of unconventional warfare and/or unconstitutional action. On 14 March 1971 – only three days before the initial arrest of Orlandini and other leading plotters – De Jorio attended the premier meeting of the rightist Associazione Amici delle Forze Armate (Friends of the Armed Forces Association), along with the Black Prince himself and retired General Giovanni De Lorenzo, of "Plan Solo" notoriety. He was also among those present at the infamous 24 June 1971 conference on "Guerra Non Ortodossa e Difesa," which was sponsored by the Istituto di Studi Militari (ISM: Military Studies Institute), an advocacy group headed by Paolo Possenti that had been created in the 1960s by a far right DC parliamentary association. Later still, De Jorio provided the seed money for the establishment of the *Politica e Strategia* journal, which consistently promoted various forms of military intervention – short of an outright coup d'etat – in response to leftist subversion and violence. In October 1974, moreover, he publicly criticized the judges who had issued a search warrant for presidentialist proponent Sogno.[319] Thus De Jorio operated right in the midst of that shadowy right-wing milieu where elements of the state, the parallel state, and ostensibly anti-state forces intermingled, plotted, and sought to exploit and manipulate each other.

Alfredo and Fabio De Felice were the FN figures who collaborated most intimately with De Jorio, albeit in a subordinate capacity, and they frequently appeared at the DC official's side during the most significant Fronte gatherings, including a November 1970 meeting with Orlandini and the first two post-coup meetings in 1971. Although both actively participated in the operational planning and coordination work that preceded the Borghese coup, as well as in subsequent plotting, the focus of their efforts lay in somewhat different areas. Alfredo concerned himself above all with "political" matters, and was in large part responsible for maintaining contacts between the plotters and various political and military circles, whereas Fabio concentrated on "organizational" matters, in particular on strengthening FN links with the entire spectrum of ultra-rightist groups.[320] Fewer details have surfaced about Alfredo's role, because key right-wing *pentiti* were not as close to him as they were to Fabio. It seems certain, however, that Alfredo graduated from a university with a degree in chemistry, and according to Aleandri he subsequently obtained a job as an industrial counselor in De Jorio's office. And although De Jorio initially financed and was nominally the editor of *Politica e Strategia*, it may be that Alfredo was really in charge of the publication.[321]

As for Fabio, the elder of the two De Felice brothers, he had had a long history of activism in Italian and European neo-fascist circles. On 8 March 1953, in the course of an action organized by the MSI to protest Allied policy toward Trieste, he lost the lower part of his left leg when a bomb exploded outside the Fronte Sloveno's (Slovene Front) Contrada del Corso headquarters in that city. He then became an MSI Deputy, but was expelled from the party in October 1955, presumably for expressing views critical of the leadership. After promoting a short-lived MSI dissident movement called the Movimento Antifascista Italiano (Italian Anti-Fascist Movement [!]), he joined an international anti-Marxist center created by the Fronte per la Rinascita Nazionale (Front for National Revival). In 1963, he and MSI ultra Giulio Caradonna formed the Centro di Europa Unità (Center for European Unity), with financial assistance from unspecified sponsors in Spain and France. Four years later, he became chief of propaganda for Pacciardi's "presidentialist" Nuova Repubblica movement. Aleandri later confirmed that Fabio was closely linked to Caradonna, and added that he had similar relations with ON leaders Rauti and Clemente Graziani.[322] And if Aleandri's radical neo-fascist associate Sergio Calore is to be believed, Fabio was also one of the founders, along with Delle Chiaie (AN), Graziani (MPON), Paolo Signorelli (MPON), and Enzo Maria Dantini, of the "Nazi-Maoist" Organizzazione Lotta di Popolo (OLP: People's Struggle Organization) in early 1970.[323] Fabio's myriad associations with such extremists by no means ended after Borghese's venture failed. SID informant Francesco Primicino aptly characterized the situation that obtained throughout the 1970s and right up into the early 1980s when he noted that Fabio was linked to the whole of the extraparliamentary right.[324]

As in the case of De Jorio, the problem here is to determine whose interests the De Felices were in fact serving. Several clues are provided by the testimony of Aleandri, Calore, and other neo-fascist *pentiti*, but certain ambiguities unfortunately remain. A good deal of evidence suggests that Fabio De Felice was a genuine proponent of radical rightist ideas and violent strategies for conditioning Italy's political environment. According to Aleandri, who was a student in his secondary school philosophy class and thence developed a close political relationship with his former teacher, Fabio was heavily influenced by the philosophical and political views of esoteric "traditionalists" like Julius Evola and René Guénon, two idols of the Italian far right. As such, he expressed a fundamental antagonism toward the materialistic cultural values and the leveling massification process associated with modern democratic states, and in their place promoted the ideal of an "organic," hierarchical society of the medieval type. Because it was no longer possible to reestablish such a society, the next best thing would be the creation of a "national-socialist" society purged of its plebeian and pseudo-democratic elements.[325] He recognized, like Evola, that this was an uncompromisingly elitist and anti-democratic view which would never appeal to the mainstream bourgeois and leftist forces in Italy, and thus advocated the assumption of power by a dedicated minority, even if this required – but only as a last resort – an outright coup d'etat. In the meantime, he felt that the one existing group that embodied "traditionalist" values and could attract sufficient support among alienated anti-leftist youths was Ordine Nuovo, so much so that he and his brother apparently wrote anonymous articles for various ON publications.[326] On the surface, all this would lead one to conclude that Fabio was a genuine Evolan militant, and that in the period leading up to and following the "Tora Tora" operation he and his brother were interacting with De Jorio and other political and military officials on behalf of Borghese and the FN. It may even be true.

Other information exists, however, which complicates and casts considerable doubt on this relatively straightforward scenario. First, both De Felice brothers had connections to a number of parastate or parallel intelligence structures that will by now be familiar to the reader. Alfredo was apparently a close friend of the UAR's Federico Umberto D'Amato, and Fabio admitted monitoring developments alongside the latter from within the Interior Ministry during the heavy-handed police repression of the 5 July 1960 Porta San Paolo demonstration against Fernando Tambroni's government.[327] The pair were also closely associated with Gelli, if the testimony of a host of neo-fascist insiders can be taken seriously. For example, Walter Sordi explicitly testified that right-wing terrorist Gilberto Cavallini had told him Fabio was a member of P2 who had personal contacts with Gelli. And, as noted earlier, the Venerable Master of the P2 lodge helped to facilitate the mid-1970s flight of the two De Felice brothers, and then sought to lessen their legal problems stemming from various FN plots. Moreover, in his efforts to establish and maintain regular contact with supposed pro-coup sympathizers within the Carabinieri, Alfredo had always relied upon Gelli as his exclusive intermediary. Thus it is not surprising to learn that Fabio later met with Carabinieri Colonel Michele Santoro on several occasions at the Castel San Pietro villa of right-wing criminologist Aldo Semerari. Santoro was one of the key subordinates of General Giovanbattista Palumbo, commander of the "Pastrengo" Carabinieri division in Milan, who after 1972 lay at the apex of a powerful P2-linked cell within that division.[328] Perhaps most importantly, Aleandri testified that at the time of the Borghese coup Fabio De Felice had some contacts with CIA operative Fenwich through a certain Maria Francini of Forano Sabino, who bragged openly of her links to influential Vatican circles and her special relations with the American and Israeli intelligence services. Although Fabio found her personally disagreeable, she later helped the brothers to escape and arranged for them to stay at some sort of "Jewish" establishment in Geneva before they found refuge in the London home of Fenwich's wife. Both De Felices were also said to have relied upon the behind-the-scenes support of conservative networks inside the Vatican, not to mention particular sections of the DC.[329]

Second, Fabio De Felice's relationship to the radical right was a very complex and ambiguous one, both before and after the Borghese coup. His possible involvement with the OLP, a murky and possible provocateur organization that propagated Franco Freda's ideas about combining the forces of the radical right and left in a joint attack on the "bourgeois" system, has already been alluded to. At around the same time, if not earlier, Fabio established close working relations with MPON leaders Signorelli and Massimiliano Fachini. These three, along with the OLP's Dantini, later organized themselves into a clandestine directorate or leadership group that began to secretly control the activities of ON itself and the front groups with which it was integrally linked. According to Aleandri, Fabio De Felice was the key figure within that invisible collegial body.[330] From the fall of 1976 on, a series of meetings were held at the homes of Fabio himself, Signorelli, and Aldo Semerari. The purpose of these gatherings, which were typically attended by this trio and a number of younger neo-fascist militants, was to formulate a new political plan designed to consolidate the remnants of various extremist groups that had been disrupted and fragmented by the exposure of a series of rightist "coup" plots and terrorist bombings in 1973 and 1974, the 1975 trial of the "Tora Tora" plotters, and an official crackdown on the paramilitary right in the wake of Pierluigi Concutelli's assassination of Judge Vittorio Occorsio. The flight of several key neo-fascist leaders (like Delle Chiaie and ON's Clemente Graziani) to safer havens abroad, coupled with the breakdown of the sometimes acrimonious attempts to unite ON and AN into a single organization, had only exacerbated this tendency toward disaggregation.[331]

In any event, it was at the aforementioned meetings that the adoption of a new decentralized and self-financing terrorist strategy, modeled in large part on the one employed by left-wing terrorist groups like the Brigate Rosse (Red Brigades), was first proposed and then agreed upon. This particular strategy, which depended upon the compartmentalization of relatively autonomous and "spontaneous" terrorist cells that were to operate behind a variety of organizational facades, ultimately passed through four successive stages. These ranged from a trial phase in which minor attacks were made and claimed by non-existent groups, to a phase of "demonstrative" assaults geared toward providing specialized training to young terrorists, to a phase of more serious violence in which human casualties were intentionally generated, to the final phase in which outright bomb massacres were contemplated and then carried out. Fabio himself was later implicated in the sponsorship of a number of these terrorist actions, including the failed bombing outside the Consiglio Superiore della Magistratura headquarters in Rome's Piazza Independenza, the 23 June 1980 assassination of Judge Mario Amato, and the Bologna train station bombing a little over one month later. Although he was later acquitted of the charges brought against him in connection with the most serious of these acts of violence, it seems fair to conclude, as neo-fascist Walter Sordi in fact did, that he had no qualms about perpetrating public bombings to achieve his political goals.[332]

Fabio's actions, as described up to this point, could still be viewed as consistent with genuine neo-fascist subversion. But the situation was more opaque than it may seem at first glance. To carry out their strategy, he and the other members of the secret ON directorate made extensive efforts to recruit and indoctrinate younger right-wing extremists. Not all of these lads fully shared the political ideas of their self-appointed mentors. The militants associated with ON, Terza Posizione (Third Position), and Costruiamo l'Azione (Let's Take Action) who participated in aspects of this strategy were in fact divided into three main factions, the most "traditional" of which was the one led by Fabio and Semerari. In contrast to the faction headed by Signorelli and Elio Massagrande, which ostensibly sought to establish a national socialist state after a violent seizure of power and claimed to be more open to the novel ideas associated with the newer generation of neo-fascist ultras, and the faction headed by Aleandri and Calore, which honestly adopted a left-leaning "social" strategy and proposed a link-up with certain elements of the extraparliamentary left, Fabio and Semerari preferred to eschew direct revolutionary action. Instead, they worked to establish a logistical base that could serve as a hub for linking various institutional and non-institutional forces. In order to facilitate an eventual assumption of power, Fabio further recommended the formation of a clandestine (*non pubblica*) structure which would penetrate and make instrumental use of anti-communist organizations that operated in public. Exploiting the cover provided by these organizations, he ultimately aimed to infiltrate and covertly control key centers of official and quasi-official power, ostensibly in the interests of a future revolutionary transformation of society.[333]

However, a number of developments led Calore and Aleandri to suspect that Fabio and his brother were playing a complex double game. By the late 1970s the two younger radicals had undergone a political transformation of their own, one which had led them to borrow ideas associated with the New Left and conjoin them with the more revolutionary aspects of the original fascist worldview. Their first clear indication that the elder De Felice brother's role might be other than what it seemed occurred when they decided to establish a journal of their own and diverge from the "reactionary" line promoted by Fabio. At first the latter pretended to go along with the idea. But he subsequently antagonized his former protégés when he sought to exert personal control over their new project, an intrusive effort which provoked fisticuffs and ended up precipitating a complete schism, both organizationally and ideologically. After the break, Aleandri and Calore began to reflect on the role that Fabio may have played as a "force of intoxication" in certain developments.[334] They later concluded, for example, that Fabio had not simply tried to reorganize the paramilitary right after 1975, but also to assume personal control over the entire reorganization process. More specifically, he sought to develop a hegemonic political "line" that would undergird the actions taken by all the decentralized operational cells, and to control those cells covertly by infiltrating his own loyalists into them.[335]

Were it not for other factors, it might be possible to write even this off as a simple reflection of rampant egotism, misdirected authoritarianism, or the development of some sort of *Führer* complex. But Fabio's intention of making instrumental use of terrorism paralleled all too closely the uses to which the secret services and unscrupulous politicians regularly made of subversion and violence. Indeed, he repeatedly emphasized the role terrorism played in the context of a far more elaborate political scheme. On one occasion he told Aleandri that "a massacre makes no sense if no one exploits its political effects," and on another occasion he admitted openly that armed bands were only one, and perhaps the least important, aspect of a much vaster political design.[336] In his scheme the primary function of such armed bands, it would seem, was to commit acts of terrorism that would (1) prepare the public psychologically for an authoritarian crackdown and (2) provide a tangible pretext for the intervention of the security forces of the state. According to convicted terrorist Vinciguerra, the *sub rosa* institutional backers of pseudo-revolutionary rightists – including those who, in his view, made up the secret ON directorate – would not only authorize the carrying out of terrorist actions by the paramilitary groups under their control, but would also attempt to "cover" and otherwise exploit autonomous terrorist actions carried out by genuine revolutionaries who were not under their control. Fabio's insistence that planned public bombings should not be openly sponsored likewise placed him firmly within the older neo-fascist tradition of not claiming responsibility for perpetrating massacres, massacres in which personnel from the secret services were consistently implicated. Perhaps most significantly, he admitted to Aleandri that the political design he was carrying out had been set in motion "on a level far superior to our own."[337]

Who, then, occupied this higher level? Some of Fabio's closest erstwhile comrades and protégés later became convinced that their would-be mentor was manipulating them in the interests of reactionary forces associated with the very political establishment they were seeking to overthrow. This cadre of serious revolutionaries in groups such as Costruiamo l'Azione and Terza Posizione had belatedly recognized that the long succession of would-be "coups" and terrorist massacres had only served to stabilize the corrupt bourgeois system and strengthen the position of certain unscrupulous elements within the existing political class. After reflecting further upon their own firsthand experiences, they concluded that the strategy being carried out by the De Felices had been developed by those in charge of various parallel security apparatuses. As per usual, they identified the culprits as members of the political and military circles with which Fabio and Alfredo were in regular contact, in particular certain elements of the Carabinieri, along with secret service personnel from the UAR and the military intelligence service, all of which were in turn linked in some way to Gelli and the P2 lodge.[338] These reasonable but unverifiable inferences naturally engendered a good deal of bitterness, so much so that at a certain point Calore and Aleandri seriously considered assassinating the P2 chief, who for them embodied in his person the *poteri occulti* which had systematically manipulated, exploited, and betrayed the aspirations of the revolutionary right.[339]

Based on the testimony of several of these neo-fascist insiders and on other indications, the two PCI-affiliated judges who investigated the Bologna train station bombing concluded that Fabio De Felice and other members of the clandestine ON directorate had functioned as de facto agents of these secret and parallel services, as well as the intermediaries ("cut-outs," in intelligence parlance) between those services and the paramilitary right. Although Fabio seems to have been the key operative within that group, he was not the only one among them who had connections to said services. Signorelli was not only linked personally to Gelli, but apparently also to officials in SID, the Carabinieri, and the Army. For his part, Fachini had been implicated in the Piazza Fontana massacre and also had links to the secret services. The same is true of Semerari, who in addition had developed a close association with key figures in the Camorra, by whom he was apparently later murdered in an unusually brutal fashion. Last but not least, Fabio apparently participated in several joint political projects with Dantini, whose name was later discovered on a list of individuals that were considered for recruitment into the top secret "stay/behind" paramilitary networks. In short, as the judges themselves emphasized, practically everyone involved in the Bologna bombing and related crimes can be suspected of having some sort of relationship to the Italian intelligence agencies, however obscure or ill-defined it may have been. This conclusion, although undoubtedly exaggerated for political effect, received some indirect confirmation from, of all sources, the military intelligence service itself, which had been "reorganized" and renamed the Servizio Informazioni per la Sicurezza Militare (SISMI: Intelligence Service for Military Security) in 1978.[340] Both SID and its successor SISMI repeatedly acted to obstruct efforts to identify and prosecute the perpetrators of right-wing violence. After initially feigning ignorance about the criminal activities of ON-derived groups like Costruiamo l'Azione and the Movimento Rivoluzionario Populare (MRP: Popular Revolutionary Movement), even though they were keeping track of them all along, they then went out of their way to derail the judicial investigation by systematically spreading disinformation, planting false clues, and suggesting unproductive leads.[341] Although this was nothing new in cases involving "black" terrorism, such behavior is in and of itself a significant indication that something was going on behind the scenes.

There seems to be little doubt, then, that at the time of the Borghese coup both De Felice brothers were actively colluding with elements within the security forces of the state, both official and parallel. It may be objected that the preceding account of Fabio's apparently duplicitous behavior dealt in part with the era after 1976, which leaves open the possibility that something had changed between 1970 and the second half of the decade. Given the fact that during this interval arrest warrants were issued for him and his brother based on their purported involvement in the "Tora Tora" operation, it is possible that the initial failure of various quasi-official forces to prevent them from being brought to trial prompted Fabio to seek a measure of revenge by actively assisting subversive and anti-state elements within the neo-fascist milieu. But if he was in fact colluding with D'Amato as early as 1960, it is more likely that the thread which tied together all of his later political activities was a covert association with the UAR and/or other parallel apparatuses. His involvement with a new generation of ultras after 1975 should thus probably be seen as a continuation of his earlier manipulation of the radical right on behalf of those apparatuses.

There are two possible explanations for this behavior. One is that Fabio was merely pretending to be an Evolan enthusiast in order to penetrate neo-fascist circles and thence make instrumental use of them. The second, which is perhaps even more disturbing, is that there was no real contradiction between holding radical Evolan views and assisting the security services of the state to buttress the position of conservative forces within the political establishment. Although Evola's visceral rejection of the modern bourgeois world appealed to alienated youths who found it satisfying to rebel against authority figures and social conventions, some of his specific viewpoints – for example, the idea that communism represented the more immediate threat even though the materialistic values associated with the United States would ultimately prove more damaging to the spiritual vitality of traditional European civilization – could be translated in practice into a naïve and counterproductive collaboration with pro-Atlantic and anti-communist hard-liners inside the government bureaucracy. And Evola's glorification of the ascetic "warrior elites" who offered a forlorn resistance, both existential and physical, amid the ruins of the modern world could be seen as applicable to the "lost soldiers" who filled the ranks of the OAS. As was suggested in articles previously cited, such an identification probably helped to prepare the way for the adoption of *guerre révolutionnaire* concepts and techniques by an entire generation of neo-fascist extremists. In this sense it is possible that Fabio, like many other opportunistic Evolans (including Rauti of ON and Delle Chiaie of AN), foolishly hitched his wagon to bourgeois forces that happily exploited him to promote long-term interests which, beyond the common ground of anti-communism, were fundamentally antithetical to his own.

Regardless of what the exact motives of Fabio De Felice and his brother were, along with De Jorio they were almost certainly working in conjunction with elements of the political establishment at the time of the Borghese coup. De Jorio was their immediate superior within the FN hierarchy, and as noted he was closely associated with DC leader Giulio Andreotti, who has been a key figure in that establishment since the late 1940s. Andreotti has long been recognized as one of the most sophisticated and Machiavellian politicians in postwar Italy, if not all of Europe. He is a member of the second leadership generation within the DC, that which emerged in the immediate aftermath of World War II.[342] Between 1941 and 1944, he was president of the Federazione Universitaria Cattolici Italiani (FUCI: University Federation of Italian Catholics). He thence began his postwar political career by serving as undersecretary of the Council of Ministers under Alcide De Gasperi, who had become prime minister in December 1945 after the collapse of the government headed by Resistance leader Ferruccio Parri. Since then, he held innumerable cabinet posts himself, ranging from defense minister to finance minister to minister of foreign affairs, and served as prime minister seven times between 1972 and 1992. He long remained an immensely powerful figure within both the dominant political party and the *partitocrazia*, that corrupt, immobile system of "rule by parties" which serious reformers and radicals of all stripes have incessantly but ineffectively denounced. And unlike most of his peers, he managed – up until the 1990s, at least – to weather all the storms of controversy that surrounded him during the last five decades.[343] These facts are generally known. What is less well-understood, however, is that since 1944 he has reportedly been affiliated with various clandestine networks, both domestic and foreign, which have covertly but actively sought to condition the Italian political environment. In part, this is a natural process that everyone who holds high public office will be enmeshed in to some degree. Yet not all politicians have courted and worked to exploit such networks as avidly, assiduously, or effectively as Andreotti.

It would be impractical and enormously time-consuming to try to delineate all of the secret "parapolitical" activities Andreotti has purportedly engaged in over the years, especially given the current dearth of solid evidence. A few suggestive examples will therefore have to suffice. To begin with, Andreotti's close association with De Gasperi may have led to his direct or indirect involvement in covert influence operations. De Gasperi himself was a distinguished political figure with a firm commitment to formal democracy and a principled opposition to right- and left-wing authoritarianism, and his role in the establishment of a postwar democratic structure uncontaminated by anti-constitutional elements was in general a salutary one. Even so, like all great statesmen, he was not entirely immune to the seductions of power and the forbidden, vicarious pleasures associated with covert action. Toward the end of World War II, with the secret assistance of powerful Vatican circles, he had actively promoted a scheme to set up a bloc of East European states that would serve as a bulwark against Soviet expansionism. Among the clerics who backed this chimerical project was Austrian bishop Alois Hudal, a key figure in the initial establishment of exfiltration networks for wanted Nazis and East European collaborators who were trying to escape punishment for war crimes. In 1947, De Gasperi personally guaranteed the safety of Ferenc Vajta, a wanted Hungarian fascist who worked for French and British intelligence. He also agreed to assist, albeit unofficially, the Krizari (Crusaders) anti-Tito paramilitary group, which was made up largely of former Ustaše.[344] Shortly thereafter, De Gasperi actively collaborated in American efforts to influence the April 1948 elections, through both overt and covert means, and he became the chief beneficiary of these efforts when he was duly confirmed as prime minister.[345] Finally, he was invited to meet on 25 September 1952 with a number of high-ranking political figures, including Prince Bernhard of the Netherlands, CIA chief Walter Bedell Smith, French social democrat Guy Mollet, Belgian Foreign Minister Paul Van Zeeland, and French Prime Minister Antoine Pinay, in order to lay the groundwork for the creation of the so-called Bilderberg Group. This now notorious association, which was named after the Hotel de Bilderberg in Oosterbeek where the members held their first formal conference in May of 1954, was apparently the brainchild of a pro-Atlantic Polish refugee and former Special Operations Executive (SOE) agent named Joseph Retinger. Ever since its foundation, the Bilderberg Group has unfortunately attracted the obsessive attention of legions of conspiracy theorists, most but not all of whom have been associated with the far right. Although there is nothing necessarily sinister about the holding of secret, heavily guarded meetings between representatives of the Atlantic ruling elites, and the more extravagant claims about the alleged plotting of the "Bilderbergers" can easily be dismissed, it would nonetheless be unwise to presume that the private discussions regularly held at these exclusive gatherings attended by top-level American and European officials were wholly devoid of broader political significance.[346] In any event, the topics under discussion and the precise role played by De Gasperi cannot be further clarified until more information has been made available by insiders.

As for Andreotti, his assumption of a variety of influential posts in successive cabinets, particularly his stint as defense minister from 1959 to 1966, brought him into regular and sustained contact with a host of American and NATO military officers who were responsible for European defense matters. Among these officers was a self-described "friend," Army Colonel Vernon Walters, who served as military attaché in Rome from 1960 to 1962 and in that capacity often acted as an interpreter during meetings between high-ranking Italian and American officials. Walters, who was later appointed lieutenant general and then deputy director of the CIA (1972–1976), was a well-known rightist who in 1961 was said to have promoted direct American military intervention to prevent the PSI from entering the government coalition in Italy.[347] Andreotti also established close relations with Henry Kissinger, Nixon's national security advisor, so much so that Kissinger wrote a glowing foreword to the English translation of the Italian politician's observations about the United States.[348] Moreover, he was on friendly terms with General Alexander Haig, "an old acquaintance as NATO commander," who together with Kissinger was later accused of having authorized Gelli to recruit four hundred top-ranking Italian and NATO military officers into P2 in the fall of 1969.[349] One concrete example of the close relations that Andreotti maintained with influential elements of the American political and security establishments may have had a considerable impact on his subsequent relations with Miceli. The latter had apparently provided some highly negative assessments of Andreotti in intelligence reports that he dutifully passed on to his American counterparts. These assessments were later shown to the Italian politician by his friends within those agencies, a breach of secrecy and propriety that fanned Andreotti's rancor toward Miceli and perhaps contributed to his decision to make the SID chief the "fall guy" in connection with the "Tora Tora" affair.[350]

Beyond these official contacts with personnel entrusted with planning military, paramilitary, and covert political operations, Andreotti was apparently linked to a number of international networks which have been implicated in a variety of behind-the-scenes activities. The first of these was an international anti-communist intelligence service called Pro Deo (For God). According to one PCI-linked source, in 1945 a young Andreotti served as the private secretary for a right-wing Belgian priest named Felix Morlion, who with the help of the Office of Strategic Services (OSS) had created Pro Deo during the war and had then transferred its headquarters to Rome in 1944. However that may be, there is no doubt whatsoever that Morlion's Pro Deo organization was linked to several Western secret services, or that it has since been involved in a number of important covert operations.[351]

Andreotti's association with Pro Deo is not a certainty, but in 1948 the shrewd Roman politician undoubtedly became a "knight" in an authentic chivalric order, the Sovereign Military and Hospitaller Order of Saint John of Jerusalem, Cyprus, Rhodes, and Malta, better known today as the Sovereign Military Order of Malta (SMOM) or, simply, the Knights of Malta. There is no need to recount the long and illustrious history of the SMOM from the time of its foundation as a Christian philanthropic and military order in the eleventh and twelfth centuries to its reestablishment as a sovereign state with papal assistance in the late nineteenth century. What needs to be emphasized here is that it has since become a powerful and rather secretive organization whose ranks are filled with the Catholic elite of Europe and the Americas, including a large number of major statesmen, international financiers, and top-ranking intelligence officials. Although it remains unclear whether the order has acted on its own initiative to promote anti-communist "crusades" and establish secret cells within various Western secret services, whether it has been infiltrated by personnel from these latter who have sought to manipulate and exploit it for such purposes, or whether – as seems most likely – some intricate combination of these two processes was at work, there is no doubt that the SMOM has been involved in innumerable covert political and financial operations during the postwar period.[352] In connection with this study, it is worth noting that "Organizzazione X"/NDS member Roberto Cavallaro testified that SID was compelled by statute to provide information, via the Carabinieri, to the SMOM, a claim that was later contested by Spiazzi.[353]

Moreover, Andreotti later became a member of the so-called Cercle Pinay (Pinay Circle), as well as a "lifetime member" of one of the main associations linked to that group, the Brussels-based Académie Européenne de Sciences Politiques (AESP: European Academy of Political Sciences). Established in 1969, the Cercle Pinay was an informal and unofficial pan-European network of conservative pro-Atlantic political and business leaders whose titular head was the aforementioned "Bilderberger," Antoine Pinay, who was also an SMOM "knight." But the actual operational control of the Cercle was in the hands of Pinay's deputy, the lawyer Jean Violet, a prewar activist in the terrorist Cagoule ("Hooded Ones") organization who became a paid operative of both SDECE and the BND during the 1950s. Violet and other members of the Cercle were also linked, typically via intermediaries like Aginter Presse and affiliated groups such as the AESP, to an extensive array of other Western intelligence and security agencies, including the CIA, MI6, the Spanish Dirección General de Seguridad (DGS), the Portuguese PIDE, and the Swiss intelligence service. The AESP itself was headed by a kingpin of the postwar Belgian right, Florimond Damman, and counted among its leading members Pinay, Violet, Archduke Otto von Habsburg (head of the Paneuropa-Union [PEU: Pan-European Union]), Manuel Fraga (a leader of the right-wing Alianza Popular [People's Alliance] party in Spain), Father Yves-Marc Dubois (a Dominican priest who worked for SDECE and the Vatican intelligence service), Paul Vanden Boeynants (a hardline Belgian defense minister implicated in many scandals), Alfredo Sanchez-Bella (a top Opus Dei official and operative of the Spanish intelligence service under Franco), Jacques Soustelle (ex-OAS), Giancarlo Valori (a key figure in P2 before his falling-out with Gelli), and C. C. van den Heuvel (formerly an official of the Dutch Binnenlandse Veiligheidsdienst [BVD: Domestic Security Service] and thence head of the "private" Internationaal Documentatie en Informatie Centrum [Interdoc] in the Hague), to name only a few.[354] Although there is no evidence that Andreotti was personally involved in the various criminal and subversive activities in which groups linked to Cercle Pinay and AESP were periodically implicated, such as the alleged fostering of coup plots in Belgium in the 1970s and early 1980s, his close association with powerful Atlanticist political, financial, and secret service circles may have some bearing on the behind-the-scenes role he is said to have played in the Borghese affair.

Of more direct relevance, however, was the close relationship between Andreotti and the P2 lodge. The former prime minister's name was almost entirely absent from the majority report of the parliamentary commission investigating the P2 affair. This diplomatic omission may lead the ill-informed reader to conclude that he played no role in the activities of the lodge and had no connections with Gelli, but such an assumption is not necessarily warranted. Indeed, the evidence suggests that Andreotti went out of his way to aid Gelli and certain other key members of P2 from the early 1960s on. In the first half of that decade, while serving as defense minister, he awarded a contract for producing forty thousand mattresses for NATO's armed forces to the Frosinone factory of Giovanni Pofferi's Permaflex firm, where Gelli was employed as head of the sales department. This turned out to be the beginning of the latter's rise to economic prominence.[355] Although Andreotti later claimed that he first met Gelli in 1977, at a ceremony celebrating Juan Perón's second return to power in Argentina, a 19 March 1973 Guardia di Finanza report prepared by Major Di Salvo suggested that the relationship between the two men may have dated back to the 1962 period.[356] Andreotti also pretended that he took no interest in P2 until the scandal exploded onto the front pages, an assertion that is scarcely believable given the nature of his relationship to P2 "brother" Sindona, both before and after the September 1974 collapse of the latter's vast but unstable financial empire.

Michele Sindona's meteoric rise and scandalous career would have been inconceivable if de facto alliances between Allied intelligence agencies, organized crime, influential Vatican circles, and a wide variety of ultraconservative political groups had not been formed during World War II and then extended into the postwar era. There is no need to describe Sindona's extraordinary life history in detail, because entire books have been devoted to that subject, but in the current context his close working relationship with elements of Western intelligence deserves further emphasis. These connections seem to have dated back to the period of the Allied invasion of Sicily, at which time he admitted befriending a number of American soldiers. The latter provided him with additional provisions at a time when he was engaging in black market foodstuff exchanges authorized by Sicilian-American Mafia leader Vito Genovese, who along with "Lucky" Luciano had been recruited by the American government to help pave the way for the invasion and occupation of the island. It may be that Max Corvo, a member of Earl Brennan's OSS team who landed in Sicily just after the Allied landing, was among those Americans. This probability is strengthened by the fact that Sindona later turned to Corvo for assistance after he got into serious trouble with the American authorities following the failure of New York's Franklin National Bank, which he had purchased a controlling interest of in 1972.[357]

Sindona's associations with Western intelligence networks took a qualitative leap in the early 1950s, after he moved to Milan and established a brilliant career as a tax lawyer and financial advisor. Following the bishop of Messina's recommendation, he met with Monsignor Amleto Tondini, an official of the Curia whose sister was married to one of of Sindona's cousins. After their meeting, Tondini wrote a letter of introduction for him to Prince Massimo Spada, who was both an SMOM "knight" and an important financial advisor to the Vatican. Spada immediately took the young lawyer under his wing, and thence introduced him to several important people, including Cardinal Giovanni Battista Montini, the future Pope Paul VI.[358] Montini was a key figure in the Vatican's intelligence apparatus who had worked closely with the OSS during World War II and had subsequently maintained his connections with leading U.S. intelligence personnel, especially James Jesus Angleton, who had in the meantime been placed in charge of the CIA's Vatican Desk.[359] This association with Montini, who as pope would later appoint Sindona as the Vatican's financial advisor, drew the unscrupulous Sicilian directly into a complex web of covert anti-communist operations being carried out by the Vatican and its Western intelligence allies.

The first documented example of Sindona's personal involvement in such operations occurred in early 1955. At that time Montini, who had recently been appointed archbishop of Milan, was seeking to counteract growing communist labor influence by making personal visits to several factories and celebrating masses on the premises. This plan was vehemently opposed by powerful PCI union officials, so Montini turned to Sindona for help. The young financier pressured his clients who owned factories to help overcome this communist opposition, and then personally accompanied Montini on his factory visits, during which the latter warned workers about the dangers of leftist policies and appealed to them to support the Church. After months of such proselytization, many workers ended up voting to replace communist union leaders. Four years later, Sindona raised over two million dollars in a single day after Montini appealed to him for assistance in funding the construction of a home for the elderly, the Casa della Madonnina. It was later suggested that much of this money may have been provided to Sindona by the CIA or the Mafia.[360] Whether or not this particular suggestion is warranted, the use of Sindona's banks and financial companies to funnel secret U.S. or Vatican funds to anti-communist political groups was apparently not an uncommon occurrence, and the practice later assumed a far more sinister dimension.

In April 1967, for example, the Continental Bank of Illinois transferred four million dollars to Sindona's Banca Privata Finanziaria. After receiving these funds, Sindona immediately wired the money – ostensibly a "loan" that was guaranteed by the Central Bank of Greece – to Colonel George Papadopoulos through a bank account of the Helleniki Tecniki construction company, which was in fact controlled by the Greek Army. Shortly afterwards, Papadopoulos and other right-wing military officers launched the coup that overthrew parliamentary democracy and ushered in a seven-year period of military dictatorship. In 1970, Sindona bought a two million dollar bond issue from the National Bank of Yugoslavia, supposedly at the request of the CIA, which then placed the bonds in "friendly" Yugoslav hands. A couple of years later, Sindona's banks were used as a conduit for some of the millions of dollars allocated by Nixon for the funding of right-wing groups in Italy. The bulk of this money, as noted earlier, was then passed on by Ambassador Martin to Miceli for distribution. At around the same time Sindona purchased the *Rome Daily American*, a financially strapped English-language newspaper published in the Eternal City which had earlier received secret subsidies from the CIA. He later claimed that he did so at the specific request of Martin, who wanted to ensure that the paper remained in trustworthy, pro-Atlantic hands.[361]

Nor were these the only connections between Sindona and personnel associated with the security and intelligence establishments of the Western Alliance. In early 1976 Gelli enlisted the aid of Edgardo Sogno and Luigi Cavallo, Sogno's right-hand man, in his efforts to protect Sindona from the American and Italian judicial authorities. In exchange for a payment of 100,000 dollars by Sindona, Sogno and Cavallo orchestrated a campaign – with the unwitting assistance of genuine leftist groups – to make it appear as though the Italian left despised and wished to assassinate the notorious financier. What makes this operation noteworthy is the fact that these two veteran anti-communists had worked for elements of NATO intelligence since the mid-1950s, if not earlier.[362] Furthermore, the shareholders in Sindona's various banks not only included the Vatican, but also Britain's Hambros Bank, Ltd., one of the world's leading merchant banks. The postwar representative of the Hambros Bank in Italy was none other than John McCaffery, who had been head of SOE's station in Berne during the latter phases of World War II and had worked very closely with both Allen Dulles of the OSS and with Sogno's "Franchi" partisan organization. McCaffery was a hard-line anti-communist who sympathized with Sindona's increasingly right-wing views, so much so that the Sicilian felt safe in approaching him in 1972 with his plan to sponsor a political coup. Sindona claimed that his goal was to "secure the backing of the armed forces for orthodox democratic politicians who wanted a proper Parliamentary government and not a branch office of the Kremlin." After being falsely reassured that neo-fascists were to be excluded from participation in the coup, McCaffery presented the financier with "a detailed plan for the take-over of the government and for the new administration's first year in office." The Scotsman added that he was "sure to a moral certainty that Sindona spoke about the proposed coup with important figures in the American Central Intelligence Agency and with top-level officials in the American Embassy in Rome," including Ambassador Martin, and that "there exist numerous documents in America which reflect the benevolence on the part of the United States towards the coup organized by Sindona."[363] These latter claims certainly seem plausible, but in any case it appears that McCaffery, whether acting on his own initiative or as a representative of certain factions of British intelligence, actively supported Sindona's plans to alter the constellation of political forces in Italy by initiating a military action.

The behind-the-scenes role played by another major shareholder in Sindona's acquisitions, the Continental Bank of Illinois, is perhaps even more suggestive. It has already been noted that the bank was used to transfer four million dollars to the Greek Colonels just prior to the launching of the 21 April 1967 coup. This action, which occurred prior to Nixon's assumption of the presidency, suggests that the bank already served as a respectable financial "front" which was used to disguise the real sources of U.S. government subsidies to "friendly" political groups abroad. The chairman of the Continental Bank during this period was David M. Kennedy, a devout Mormon and Republican Party stalwart who helped raise money for Nixon's 1968 election campaign. By way of thanks, Nixon appointed Kennedy as treasury secretary between 1969 and 1971, after which the latter served as U.S. ambassador to NATO. There is no doubt, then, that Sindona's financial dealings with American business circles, many of whose members were in turn linked to the Mafia, brought him into direct contact with key members of Nixon's entourage. It should therefore come as no surprise to learn that when Sindona got into hot water with Securities and Exchange Commission regulators and the U.S. Justice Department in the wake of the tumultuous 1974 collapse of his Franklin National Bank, the law firm which defended him was Mudge, Rose, Guthrie, and Alexander, where Nixon had previously been a partner and where his ex–Attorney General John Mitchell found employment after his period of government service.[364]

All of this constituted an important backdrop to the mutually supportive relationship that seems to have existed between Andreotti and the Sicilian banker for nearly thirty years. Sometime around 1960, then Defense Minister Andreotti was introduced to Sindona, perhaps by Monsignor Montini himself. According to the politician's own admission, he subsequently developed a great deal of respect for Sindona's undeniable abilities as a financial manipulator.[365] In part, this was undoubtedly due to the fact that Sindona had funneled millions of dollars into the coffers of the DC's center-right factions. Although it is probable that Sindona began dispensing funds to the DC in the 1960s, some of which may have originally been passed on to him by the Vatican, the Mafia, or U.S. intelligence, financial documents reveal that he provided the party with a total of eleven billion to twelve billion lire in the period between 1972 and the May 1974 divorce referendum. This was accomplished not only through direct subsidies disguised as "short-term loans," but also through monthly stipends and the establishment of "no-risk" DC-affiliated accounts at Sindona's banks.[366] In any case, in December 1973 Andreotti publicly hailed the businessman as the "savior of the lira" at an Italian-American dinner held at the Hotel Saint Regis in New York City. At that time, he must have already known about Sindona's role in laundering the proceeds from the Mafia's heroin trafficking, his attempts to drive down the value of the lira and profit from the resulting exchange rates, and his increasingly elaborate fiscal con games, something which became obvious to everyone when the latter's financial house of cards collapsed the following year.

Even more suggestively, Andreotti was later accused of working behind the scenes after the *crack* (collapse) to help Sindona, at least to avoid being extradited to Italy, if not to save his failing banks and companies. This is an enormously complex story, and most of the evidence concerning Andreotti's role stems from the testimony of various protagonists in the affair.[367] On the basis of the contrasting analyses presented by partisan members of the commission investigating the Sindona case, it would appear that Andreotti expressed sympathy for the financier and acted as if he intended to help him, but that in the end he decided not to jeopardize his own political influence by providing too much tangible aid to Sindona. Such behavior would be entirely in character for Andreotti, who was seemingly willing to let others pay the penalty for illicit activities in which he himself was deeply involved. He was, after all, the quintessential "establishment manipulator." Because he was utterly convinced that his own accretion of power would benefit his party, his Church, and his country, he felt that the use of any and all means was justified to bring about this end. There is no doubt, however, that between 1975 and 1979 Andreotti was in regular contact with Sindona and his lawyers (typically via intermediaries like Banco di Roma manager Fortunato Federici), that Sindona looked to him for help and expected that he would provide it, that he may well have applied some *sub rosa* pressure to ameliorate the position of "St. Peter's banker," and that he might have done a good deal more if the Sicilian's judicial and financial situation had not become so hopeless and potentially compromising. Whatever the extent of Andreotti's intervention, many people directly involved in aspects of these secret negotiations explicitly identified him as Sindona's key referent or ally within the Italian political establishment, a claim that seems plausible.[368]

At the same time that Sindona was allegedly being helped by Andreotti, he was undoubtedly receiving substantial behind-the-scenes assistance from Gelli and other members of P2. Among these latter were international businessman Umberto Ortolani, banker Roberto Calvi, Supreme Court president Carmelo Spagnuolo, Italian-American financier Robert Memmo (a close associate of Texas oilman and Nixon ally John Connally), Public Works Minister Gaetano Stammati, Società Condotte dell'Acqua president Loris Corbi, MSI Senator Mario Tedeschi, *OP* editor Mino Pecorelli, DC leader Massimo De Carolis, Federici, Sogno, Cavallo, and Guarino. Together these influential masonic "brethren" played a key role, directly or indirectly, in every aspect of the multifaceted operations designed to "salvage" the Sicilian's financial affairs and prevent his extradition from the United States to Italy. Among other things, these efforts involved applying pressure on the Banca d'Italia to prevent the liquidation of the Banca Privata Finanziaria's holdings, influencing the actions of the Italian Supreme Court, mediating the conflict between Sindona and Calvi, slandering Sindona's enemies in the press, terminating the investigations of officials who were uncovering Sindona's illegal financial dealings, delaying the extradition process, and indirectly assisting the staged 1979 "kidnapping" of the Sicilian by the Gruppo Proletario Eversivo (Destructive Proletarian Group), a non-existent far left organization.[369] In short, from 1974 on Gelli utilized portions of his vast network of national and international connections – a network that reportedly included Andreotti – in order to mount a sustained covert lobbying campaign on behalf of Sindona.

Several informed observers have thus emphasized that the Venerable Master's systematic efforts to save the financier moved in tandem with those allegedly undertaken by Andreotti, even though the latter was in a more exposed public position and was apparently unwilling to risk or sacrifice his political career in the process. This general convergence of activities on behalf of Sindona, together with the initiatives taken by Andreotti over the years in support of Gelli – and vice versa – suggests that the Machiavellian pair had overlapping and interrelated political agendas. It is almost certainly an oversimplification and an exaggeration to claim, as Roberto Calvi's widow Clara and the banker Carlo Bordoni both later did, that Andreotti was the real leader of P2. After all, there is no documentary evidence indicating that he was even a formal member of the lodge. But Partito Radicale (Radical Party) deputy Massimo Teodori was entirely justified in concluding that P2, far from being a subversive group in opposition to the existing system, was an organic (albeit clandestine) element of the very *partitocrazia* that Andreotti had so ably exploited to acquire and maintain his political influence.[370] Nevertheless, Teodori errs in focusing so much attention on Italian domestic politics, because it causes him to minimize the significance of the pro-Atlantic international stance adopted by both the P2 lodge and the DC political establishment with which Andreotti was associated. Indeed, it was precisely their covert support of the interests of NATO and their active opposition to the advances made by the European left which tied Gelli and Andreotti not only to each other, but also to various Western intelligence and security networks. Although they also began to build bridges to the PCI in anticipation of the probable formation of a "national unity" government in 1976, both were manipulative opportunists who had shrewdly capitalized on postwar geopolitical realities by hitching their wagons securely to the Atlantic Alliance.

With this background, it may at last be possible to elucidate Andreotti's role in the Borghese coup. There is some circumstantial evidence suggesting that he was the primary "promoter" of the operation within the political establishment. In the early evening of 7 December 1970, ON leader Massagrande had warned Spiazzi that the FN would be carrying out a "demonstration" later that night at the behest of an important government official. When members of the P2 parliamentary commission later asked Spiazzi to speculate about who that official might be, the artillery officer indicated that the answer could most likely be found in an October 1974 article that Filippo De Jorio had written for the philo-fascist weekly *Il Borghese*, "Il Giuda è tra noi." In this article, which was then reprinted in the 16 October 1974 issue of *Secolo d'Italia*, De Jorio criticized Andreotti for having cynically abandoned his earlier support for the center-right coalition formula, and for betraying De Jorio and other opponents of the center-left by transmitting SID's reports to the judges investigating the "Tora Tora" plot. De Jorio was undoubtedly motivated to make this charge because Andreotti's actions had led to his own arrest in connection with that plot, and he was clearly hinting that this very same "Judas" had himself encouraged Borghese to carry out his projected coup on the eve of Tito's scheduled visit to Rome. Although Spiazzi did not mention Andreotti by name, he acknowledged that a former defense minister was probably the secret political sponsor of Borghese's action. In doing so, he implied that the same person had given the order to activate the "Triangle" operation, an action which he claimed was directly connected to the "coup." These claims seem quite plausible, although there is, understandably, no hard evidence to substantiate them.[371] If it is assumed, for argument's sake, that they are true, it then becomes possible to speculate about Andreotti's probable motives. In such a case, it is self-evident that his aim would neither have been to sponsor a military coup nor to establish a "presidentialist" regime, but rather to exploit the resulting disorder politically in order to buttress certain factions of the DC and extend his own influence within the party. De Jorio's later defense of his own actions – why would he have sought to overthrow the political system which he himself was an integral part of? – is even more applicable to Andreotti, a far more powerful figure.[372] By a process of elimination, then, it can be concluded that if the latter gave some sort of "green light" to Borghese and his men, his goal was to use the Black Prince's action to justify a crackdown on the so-called opposing extremisms, including the FN and its neo-fascist allies.[373]

Regardless of whether Andreotti or someone else was behind it, this apparent attempt to make instrumental use of and eliminate "disposable" elements of the far right was sabotaged at the last minute when someone warned Borghese either that the promised official support would not be forthcoming or that he and his men were themselves going to be the likely victims of their own provocation. Those who have been variously identified as having issued that warning were Miceli, Condò (Miceli's subordinate at SIOS-Esercito), D'Amato, Gelli (who was closely linked to both Miceli and Andreotti), and Fenwich (who was associated with supposed pro-coup circles within the Nixon administration). But the motives of these particular individuals, or of the groups secretly backing them, may have been rather different.

Although both Miceli and Gelli were self-professed admirers and friends of Borghese who had no qualms about promoting right-wing violence in order to prevent the left from gaining strength or coming to power, this does not necessarily mean that they were in total agreement about short- or long-term political goals. It seems certain that Miceli acted to prevent the FN plotters from being entrapped and "burned," as well as to protect them from judicial reprisals in the years after the coup, but the reasons for this are not as clear as one might suppose. The SID chief has generally been portrayed as a far right sympathizer, in which case he must in part have shared Borghese's antipathy toward the political class, as well as his desire to supplant or at least overhaul it. This alone could have provided the general with sufficient personal motivation to come to the Black Prince's assistance. Other secret service officials have claimed, however improbably, that Miceli had been a firm supporter of the DC's more centrist Doroteo faction until he was ousted from SID in disgrace, and that it was only afterwards that he embraced the hard right and joined the MSI.[374] If so, in warning Borghese he may have been acting in accordance with the designs of factions within the political class which sought to stymie their rivals bent on launching an "anti-extremism" action. Finally, he may have been following directives issued by international and national security personnel who oversaw the official and parallel apparatuses he headed. These personnel may have originally decided to promote Borghese's operation for one reason or another, and then had second thoughts about the wisdom of carrying it out. The same range of possibilities could also apply to Miceli's P2 lodgemaster. Gelli and his secret society were almost certainly the instruments of other centers of power, both national and international, but it remains unclear whether he was operating in the interests of those who sought to condition but preserve the status quo, the "presidentialists" (as his "Piano di Rinascita Democratica" would lead one to believe), or the hard-liners who promoted far more drastic solutions. He may have mediated between all three factions, or played each off against the others for his own gain, an interpretation that is strengthened by the contemporaneous presence of members of each rival faction within his lodge.

The same problems beset the outside observer who is seeking to clarify the role played by various military and security forces in Borghese's operation. There is no doubt whatsoever that individuals associated with all of these forces – the three branches of the armed services, the Carabinieri, the Pubblica Sicurezza corps, the UAR, SID, and the parallel networks affiliated with these groups – had actively encouraged Borghese to launch a coup and had promised to provide him with tangible support if he did so. Some of these officers may have honestly favored and actually backed this course of action, but those on the highest levels were either unwilling to risk their careers when the time came or had purposely misled the Black Prince about their real operational and political objectives. Most of the personnel who filled the ranks of the military and police units that were mobilized and deployed on the night of the "coup" undoubtedly believed that they were engaging in maneuvers. The bulk of those with some insider knowledge about Borghese's plans probably expected that they would be employed in a crackdown on the far left. Only a very few could have been informed that armed elements of the extraparliamentary right were also going to be arrested or otherwise suppressed – if indeed that was the goal of certain factions within the state apparatus and the political class.

Of all the security forces implicated in the affair, the UAR was the organization that was most directly compromised. It is impossible to believe that Delle Chiaie and his men could have taken control of the armory within the Interior Ministry in the absence of high-level collusion. Major Capanna alone could not have effectuated such a complex and risky operation without the knowledge and consent of D'Amato or some other top official. If UAR personnel were willing to place themselves in such an exposed position, however, it is doubtful that they were participating in an "anti-extremism" operation targeting the right along with the left. After all, there would have been too many neo-fascist eyewitnesses who could have provided details about the assistance they received inside the Viminale. MSI senator Giorgio Pisanò has suggested that AN and its official backers were operating autonomously, if not in accordance with a different agenda than the other FN plotters, even though they were ostensibly following Borghese's orders.[375] This is certainly possible, given Delle Chiaie's seeming unscrupulousness and willingness to sacrifice associates and abstract principles for his own personal advantage. But it is hard to believe that AN's paramilitary squads were going to be deployed in an operation directed *against* the forces of Borghese and Orlandini. What seems more probable is that the UAR was acting in support of an "anti-leftist" provocation or, much less likely, an outright American-backed coup, and that D'Amato and his associates were unaware of the fact that elements from other parallel networks were secretly working at cross-purposes to sponsor the "anti-extremism" variant. Whatever D'Amato's game was, the theft of the Beretta machine pistol by members of AN served to prevent the immediate exposure of the operation and the later betrayal of the plotters under Delle Chiaie's command.

The role played by various international forces, in particular the Nixon administration and U.S. and NATO security agencies, is equally difficult to elucidate. Once again, there is little doubt that certain individuals who acted as intermediaries between the plotters and the Americans, whether those in Nixon's entourage or those affiliated with the embassy in Rome, had persuaded Borghese that the U.S. government secretly backed his projected coup. But it is impossible to determine whether these liaison men were acting in good faith, knowingly manipulating Orlandini, or being misled themselves by their American contacts. The actions taken by Fenwich and Talenti offer no real clue to this mystery. Given the current state of the evidence, it is also unclear whether Nixon and Kissinger ever seriously considered sponsoring a rightist coup in Italy, although their unconstitutional policies elsewhere make it unwise to categorically reject such a scenario. It is in any case apparent that there were deep divisions within the American policy-making establishment about what course of action to follow in Italy. Nixon had many enemies within the diplomatic and intelligence communities who sought to delay the implementation or sabotage some of his national security initiatives. This subterranean struggle between the president and his opponents within various U.S. government bureaucracies led directly to the Watergate affair and ultimately destroyed Nixon's political career.

What can be said with apodictic certainty, however, is that there were intense factional rivalries within the ranks of all the forces implicated in the Borghese coup. It is not yet possible to identify the exact composition of the competing factions, which in any case shifted over time, but the course and outcome of that coup reflected the intense and largely covert factional struggles between national and international proponents of a military coup, a "presidentialist" solution, and a strengthening of the existing political system. There are some noteworthy ironies in all this. Although the individuals suspected of giving the counterorder were severely criticized later by the plotters, whoever actually did so may have saved some of the more unsavory elements of the extraparliamentary right from being massacred or arrested *en masse*. These latter survived to be exploited anew by rival secret service factions, which continued to utilize them to condition the Italian political environment by encouraging them to commit terrorist acts and foment anti-democratic coups. Moreover, all of the official and quasi-official groups involved initially sought to cover up the "Tora Tora" affair and protect the FN conspirators, in part because they were themselves implicated in it. But beneath the surface of this mutually beneficial phase of cooperation, each of the factions was manuevering to exploit the situation for its own political advantage. This process came to a head in the middle of 1974, when Andreotti acted to weaken his political rivals by publicly exposing various FN-linked plots.

One last point deserves to be emphasized before this account can be brought to a close. The chief danger presented by the Borghese coup did not lie in the actions carried out by retired military veterans or neo-fascist paramilitary squads, but rather in the political exploitation of those actions by elements of the state apparatus and their international referents.[376] It would be a serious mistake, then, to regard the operation as an abject failure simply because the Black Prince called off the paramilitary phases of the action at the last minute. Indeed, on a political level the "coup" proved to be a great success. As FN leader Lunetta later put it, the "political result[s] that those who organized the attack sought to attain w[ere] achieved: the deep-freezing (*congelamento*) of the [center-left] policies of Aldo Moro, the removal of the PCI from the government arena, [and] the assurance of [Italy's] total pro-Atlantic and pro-American loyalty." He then summed up the situation as follows: "[t]he truth is that there was a coup and that it succeeded."[377] Note that these general results were considered desirable and actively pursued by each of the factions identified earlier, and from that point of view they *all* benefited from the "Tora Tora" operation even though they may not have attained their more specific operational objectives. In this sense, the Borghese coup was merely a microcosm of the entire history of right-wing terrorism and subversion in Italy, for in practically every case the most serious and threatening aspect of such criminal activities had to do with the way they were politically exploited by the powers that be. These violent destabilization tactics were generally put to authoritarian uses, and they invariably resulted in a stabilization of the existing political structure, much to the chagrin of many of the radical neo-fascists who genuinely sought to overthrow the hated "bourgeois" state.

Addendum

An additional issue that has surfaced explicitly since this chapter was originally written is whether there was an operational linkage between the 12 December 1969 neo-fascist bombings, including the massacre at the Banca Nazionale dell'Agricoltura in Milan's Piazza Fontana, and the "Borghese coup." Indeed, based on the testimony of certain neo-fascist *pentiti* (such as Sergio Calore), Judge Salvini argued that the actions taken by the FN in December 1970 may have originally been scheduled for December 1969, in conjunction with an anti-insurrectional operation launched by the military and the Carabinieri, as a response to the official police attribution of the bombings to "anarchists" and the resultant likelihood of left-wing street disorders.[378] As Marcella Bianco has suggested, "[w]e are therefore confronted with two strategies, one involving a massacre and the other a coup, which, at least at the higher levels, ran on parallel tracks."[379] However, this interpretation has been criticized, in my opinion not altogether convincingly, by both Massimiliano Griner and Vladimiro Satta.[380] Nevertheless, one major argument against this thesis is that, as was suggested earlier, the FN was not yet ready in late 1969 to carry out an effective operation of this type, because it lacked sufficient manpower and was still in the process of forging relations with both official and unofficial groups. Hence it seems more probable that the 12 December 1969 bombings were designed to precipitate a pre-planned anti-insurrectional operation against the left carried out exclusively by military and Carabinieri components, not a "coup" launched by the FN. When the hoped-for military crackdown and political shift did not occur in 1969, many of the neo-fascists involved in that year's terrorist actions then participated in Borghese's "coup" in 1970. And when that too did not achieve the desired results because it was called off at the last minute, certain ultras from ON and AN went on to support other "coup" plots in 1973 and 1974 associated with the MAR and the Compass Rose network.

Notes

1 For this "naval" phase of the Decima MAS's operations, see Borghese's own account in *Sea Devils* (Chicago: Regnery, 1954), a translation of *Decima Flottiglia MAS*. For the advice and assistance he reportedly provided to his German counterparts in Berlin in exchange for some technical information and plastic explosives, and his friendly relations with Dönitz at the German submarine headquarters in Paris, see ibid., pp. 191–8. Note also that Borghese had commanded a submarine during the Spanish Civil War and had served briefly in Franco's Navy. See ibid., p. 201.
2 For the history of the Decima MAS between September 1943 and May 1945, see Ricciotti Lazzero, *La Decima MAS: La Compagna di ventura del "principe nero"* (Milan: Rizzoli, 1984).
3 Compare ibid., pp. 20, 23, 59–60, 62–4, 70–3, 123, 168–217; and Zara Algardy, *Processi ai fascisti: Anfuso, Caruso, Graziani e Borghese di fronte alla giustizia* (Florence: Parenti, 1958), pp. 222–4.
4 See Lazzero, *Decima MAS*, pp. 11, 49–54, 57–8, 69–70; and Algardy, *Processi ai fascisti*, pp. 224–5.
5 Compare Lazzero, *Decima MAS*, pp. 29–30, 53, 60–1, 71; Algardy, *Processi ai fascisti*, pp. 189, 221–2; and especially Timothy J. Naftali, "ARTIFICE: James Angleton and X-2 Operations in Italy," in *The Secrets War: The Office of Strategic Services in World War II*, ed. by George C. Chalou (Washington, DC: National Archives and Records Administration, 1992), p. 226. For more details about Borghese's stay/behind network, see Stato Maggiore della Regia Marina, "Organizzazione segreta della X M.A.S.," 11 August 1945, Box 128, Entry 174, Records Group 226, National Archives.
6 Compare Lazzero, *Decima MAS*, pp. 61–2, 109–10, 122–4, 140–51, 226–8; and Algardy, *Processi ai fascisti*, pp. 220–1.
7 Ibid., pp. 236–45; Naftali, "ARTIFICE," p. 226 (quote); and the interview with Angleton in "Valerio Borghese ci serviva," *Epoca* 27:1323 (11 February 1976), pp. 26–7. One person who seems to have collaborated with Angleton on this sensitive mission was Commander Carlo Resio, code-named SALTY, one of the X-2 chief's agents within the Servizio Informazioni Segreta (SIS: Secret Intelligence Service), the Italian Navy's wartime intelligence service.

8 For further details about the trial, see Algardy, *Processi ai fascisti*, pp. 201–41. The great leniency shown to Borghese was in part the result of the sympathetic attitude of the judicial authorities in Rome, a stronghold of pro-fascist sentiment, as well as his status as one of the few *bona fide* war heroes in the Italian armed forces during World War II. He had been awarded a number of prestigious medals, including the Cross of Savoy and the German Iron Cross.
9 For a general description of the course of some of the more famous trials, see ibid., passim.
10 Pier Giuseppe Murgia, *Ritorneremo! Storia e cronaca del fascismo dopo la Resistenza, 1950–1953* (Milan: Sugar, 1976), p. 165, note 76.
11 For Borghese's low profile, see Giampaolo Pansa, *Borghese mi ha detto* (Milan: Palazzi, 1971), pp. 39–40. For his post-release legal actions, see Pier Giuseppe Murgia, *Il vento del nord: Storia e cronaca del fascismo dopo la Resistenza, 1945–1950* (Milan: Sugar, 1975), p. 191; and Algardy, *Processi ai fascisti*, pp. 246–7. The only one of Borghese's claims the court accepted was his acquittal for the murder charges.
12 Interestingly enough, even before Borghese was released from prison, an intelligence report compiled by James Jesus Angleton in 1947 indicated that members of his old military unit, the Decima MAS, had commenced activities again. Its most active member at this time was the Fascist journalist Ezio Maria Gray, who later became a moderate MSI leader, and it received financing from *Marchese* Patrizzi, *Commendatore* Luce, and the architectural engineers Tudini and Valenti. See Roberto Faenza and Marco Fini, *Gli Americani in Italia* (Milan: Feltrinelli, 1976), pp. 263–4.
13 These early postwar covert projects initiated by the right to condition the Italian political system have yet to be thoroughly examined by historians, largely because many of the key official records have not yet been placed at the disposal of researchers. Preliminary attempts to describe these activities have been made by various left-wing Italian journalists, in part on the basis of previously classified documentary materials. See, for example, Murgia, *Ritorneremo!*, especially pp. 177–317; Faenza and Fini, *Americani in Italia*, passim. For a somewhat later period, see Roberto Faenza, *Il malaffare: Dall'America di Kennedy all'Italia, a Cuba, al Vietnam* (Milan: Mondadori, 1978), pp. 264–376. In addition, there are a few specialized works that deal with certain aspects of these projects.
14 For details on the involvement of U.S. intelligence personnel in these efforts to draw Italian rightists into the Atlanticist camp, see Murgia, *Ritorneremo!*, p. 213. The two works of Murgia contain an extraordinary wealth of detail about little-known aspects of rightist anti-communist operations in Italy up through 1953. Unfortunately, it is often impossible to identify or evaluate the specific sources he used in his reconstruction, especially regarding the more sensitive covert operations. Although some of the details he provides have been confirmed by other sources, others cannot be verified given the current state of the documentation. Because much of the following account of Borghese's activities up to and including his adhesion to the MSI is based on that of Murgia, the reader should keep in mind that many of his claims remain difficult to substantiate.
15 Ibid., p. 206.
16 For more on the role played by the Comitati Civici in this "national front" project, see ibid., pp. 236–43. In general, see Carlo Falconi, *Gedda e l'Azione cattolica* (Florence: Parenti, 1958), pp. 125–40, etc.; and Gianni Baget Bozzo, *Il partito cristiano al potere: La DC di De Gasperi e di Dossetti, 1945–1954* (Florence: Vallecchi, 1974), volume 1, pp. 220–6, and volume 2, pp. 389–95. Information that later surfaced in the course of the Congressional investigations headed by Senator Frank Church (D.-Id.) and Representative Otis Pike (D.-N.Y.) into U.S. intelligence activities, as well as official material subsequently released in response to Freedom of Information Act (FOIA) requests, confirms that the CIA provided financing and organizational assistance to Gedda and the Comitati Civici, and that Angleton was personally involved in the anti-communist propaganda projects that resulted. See, for example, Faenza and Fini, *Americani in Italia*, pp. 276–8, 318–24.
17 Murgia, *Ritorneremo!*, pp. 214, 238. Note that Angleton himself denied ever seeing or contacting Borghese again after helping him to escape from the clutches of vengeful partisans in 1945. See the interview with the former CIA counterintelligence chief published as "Valerio Borghese ci serviva," p. 27. Although such a self-serving denial should not be

accepted at face value, actual evidence of subsequent Angleton encounters with Borghese has yet to be produced. A meeting of this type would have certainly fallen within the purview of Angleton's responsibilities in Italy, however, and his involvement in various postwar anti-communist projects in that country is now a matter of public record.
18 Ibid., p. 214. This conclusion is overly simplistic if not downright misleading, and in any case the CIA's involvement in the 1968 creation of Borghese's Fronte Nazionale remains to be demonstrated. If there was any late 1960's counterpart of this earlier "national front" coalition project, it was probably the Lega Italiana Unità (United League of Italy), not Borghese's Fronte Nazionale. Nevertheless, it appears that the U.S.-backed project of the early 1950s was also formally known as the Fronte Nazionale. Murgia always uses lowercase letters when using the phrase, but in a 26 June 1951 letter to Umberto II of Savoy (Vittorio Emanuelle III's son and unlucky would-be successor), Prince Gianfranco Alliata di Montereale, an influential monarchist leader in Sicily and future Propaganda Due (P2) masonic lodge member, used initial capitals whenever he referred to this earlier national front. See the portions quoted in the detailed historical study of Domenico De Napoli, *Il movimento monarchico in Italia dal 1946 al 1954* (Naples: Loffredo, 1980), pp. 131–2, who himself adopts Alliata's orthography.
19 Murgia, *Ritorneremo!*, pp. 214–15, 240.
20 Ibid., pp. 215–16; Giorgio Almirante and Francesco Palamenghi-Crispi, *Il Movimento sociale italiano* (Milan: Nuova Accademia, 1958), p. 55; and Petra Rosenbaum, *Il nuovo fascismo da Salò ad Almirante: Storia del MSI* (Milan: Feltrinelli, 1975), p. 83.
21 Murgia, *Ritorneremo!*, p. 216, citing the 8 December 1951 issue of *Lotta Politica*.
22 For Borghese's introduction, see Julius Evola, *Gli uomini e le rovine* (Rome: Settimo Sigillo, 1990), pp. 9–11. The original version of this work, which included that introduction, was published in 1953.
23 Piero Ignazi, *Il polo escluso: Profilo del Movimento sociale italiano* (Bologna: Mulino, 1989), p. 71, note 54.
24 Murgia, *Ritorneremo!*, pp. 216, 240.
25 Stefano Finotti, "Difesa occidentale e Patto atlantico: La scelta internazionale del MSI, 1947–1954," *Storia delle Relazioni Internazionali* 4:1 (1988), p. 118. For an edited version of the text of the De Marsanich's speech, see Massimo Magliaro, ed., *Guida al MSI-DN: L'alternativa in movimento* (no place: Nuove Prospettive, 1984), pp. 151–3. There are some minor errors in the account of Murgia, *Ritorneremo!*, pp. 216–17.
26 Murgia, *Ritorneremo!*, p. 217. One of the sources he cites for this mission is the 1–31 December 1951 issue of the independent left fascist publication *Il Pensiero Nazionale*, which was edited by national syndicalist Stanis Ruinas.
27 Borghese's public show of support for the conservative, pro-American line of De Marsanich and Michelini engendered a great deal of resentment within the MSI left, which felt spurned and betrayed. Thus Ferruccio Ferrini, former RSI Undersecretary of the Navy, published some harsh articles in *Pensiero Nazionale*. In them he accused Borghese of plotting against Mussolini, trying to seize power for himself, and escaping Mussolini's retribution only due to the intervention of some German generals who had already begun negotiating with the Anglo-Americans, then suggested that the Black Prince himself may have already made contact and secret agreements with the latter. See his "Pagine inedite della RSI," *Pensiero Nazionale* 5:23–29 (1–31 December 1951); compare ibid., 6:3 (16–29 February 1952). Cited in Murgia, *Ritorneremo!*, p. 231, note 92. As has been shown earlier, these assumptions were largely justified.
28 Ibid., pp. 218–19.
29 Ibid., p. 219; Almirante and Palmarenghi-Crispi, *Movimento sociale italiano*, p. 61.
30 It is interesting that Murgia attributes the origin of *Secolo* to a conservative, U.S.-backed manuever to promote an Atlanticist line within MSI circles. On the surface, this does not jibe with certain other accounts, particularly some in the ambit of the party, which identify *Secolo* as an expression of the internal MSI left from 1952 to 1956. See, e.g., Gianni S. Rossi, *Alternativa e doppiopetto: Il MSI dalla contestazione alla destra nazionale, 1968–1973* (Rome: Istituto di Studi Corporativi, 1992), p. 25, note 23. This apparent discrepancy can be explained

by the fact that the ideological orientation of *Secolo* shifted several times in the course of its checkered history, and that there was not always complete agreement or uniformity between the paper's domestic and foreign policy positions. At the outset *Secolo* seems to have been designed to promote a pro-Atlantic geopolitical stance, but it then moved leftwards in the "social" sphere after Almirante assumed more control over its direction. In 1958, Michelini established another official party organ, *Il Popolo Italiano*, to contest the influence of *Secolo* and promote the leadership's moderate line. Although this latter venture was not a success, the moderates subsequently assumed control over *Secolo*, which thence began to adopt more conservative positions. To untangle these complexities and fully trace the newspaper's various ideological fluctuations, one would have to do a detailed content analysis and relate its positions to MSI factional struggles in different periods.

31 Almirante and Palamenghi-Crispi, *Movimento sociale italiano*, p. 57.
32 Murgia, *Ritorneremo!*, p. 219.
33 Ibid., pp. 373–5; Pansa, *Borghese mi ha detto*, pp. 40–1; and Almirante and Palamenghi-Crispi, *Movimento sociale italiano*, pp. 62–3. Compare Rosenbaum, *Nuovo fascismo*, p. 83; and Giulio Caradonna, *Diario di battaglie* (Rome: Europa, [1968]), p. 108 (Rovigo).
34 Ignazi, *Polo escluso*, p. 89, note 50.
35 Pansa, *Borghese mi ha detto*, p. 41.
36 Murgia, *Ritorneremo!*, p. 112. On 3 November of the previous year, Borghese had been among the speakers at a Lega Nazionale (National League) rally held at the Cinema Rossetti in Trieste, during which a group of neo-fascists attacked a young DC supporter. The rally was followed by a march toward San Giusto. The procession was led by some MSI militants carrying a tricolor wreath shaped like an X, to which were attached two blue ribbons with the slogan "To Valerio Borghese – Trieste Italiana." See Claudio Tonel, ed., *Dossier sul neofascismo a Trieste, 1945–1983* (Trieste: Dedolibri, 1991), p. 86.
37 Extraparliamentary Left Research Group, *La strage di stato: Vent'anni dopo*, ed. Giancarlo De Palo and Aldo Giannuli (Rome: Associate, 1989), p. 254. For the delicate negotiations over Trieste and their political ramifications, see Diego De Castro, *La questione di Trieste: L'azione politica e diplomatica italiana dal 1943 al 1954* (Trieste: LINT, 1981), 2 volumes; Roberto G. Rabel, *Between East and West: Trieste, the United States, and the Cold War, 1941–1954* (Durham and London: Duke University, 1988); and Giampaolo Valdevit, *La questione di Trieste, 1941–1954: Politica internazionale e contesto locale* (Milan: Angeli, 1986).
38 Rosenbaum, *Nuovo fascismo*, p. 201.
39 Ibid., p. 202. It should be emphasized that Romualdi was far from being a radical Evolan. Like other moderates among the party's rightist opposition, including Gray, Ernesto De Marzio, and Nicola Foschini, he lent his support to Michelini at the crucial 1956 Milan Congress. For the rapprochement between this "soft" right and the moderate center on the eve of that Congress, see Almirante and Palamenghi-Crispi, *Movimento sociale italiano*, p. 73.
40 Pansa, *Borghese mi ha detto*, p. 41.
41 Ignazi, *Polo escluso*, pp. 87–8, note 44; and Almirante and Palamenghi-Crispi, *Movimento sociale italiano*, pp. 75–6.
42 As Borghese himself admitted in a 1970 interview. See Pansa, *Borghese mi ha detto*, p. 124: "I am, by nature, rather intolerant of any form of party discipline."
43 For Borghese's deep-seated resentment toward the postwar regime and consequent receptivity to coup plots, see Eggardo Beltrametti, *Il colpo di stato militare in Italia* (Rome: Volpe, 1975), pp. 98–9. It should be recalled that Beltrametti was a key organizer of the 1965 *guerre révolutionnaire* conference at the Parco dei Principi Hotel, funded by SIFAR, and a leading proponent of military-backed actions in a total war against communist subversion in Italy. According to investigative journalist Gianni Flamini, Beltrametti provided a copy of the published conference proceedings (*La guerra rivoluzionaria*) to Borghese. See Flamini, *Il partito del golpe: Le strategie della tensione e del terrore dal primo centrosinistra organico al sequestro Moro* (Ferrara: Bovolenta, 1981), volume 1, p. 94.
44 The accounts in the various secondary sources about Borghese's role in the FNCR split are contradictory. According to the Extraparliamentary Left Research Group, Borghese helped precipitate the schism and then aligned himself with the UNCRSI, which backed

the official MSI line and was organically linked to the party. See *Strage di stato: Vent'anni dopo*, p. 254. In contrast, Rosenbaum claims that the split was engineered by Michelini loyalists after FNCR head Borghese had broken with the MSI's moderate line. See *Nuovo fascismo*, p. 71. Rossi also links Borghese to the more radical FNCRSI, which vociferously criticized the MSI for being "bourgeois and reactionary." See *Alternativa e doppiopetto*, p. 62. The latter interpretation seems far more credible, since after 1956 the Black Prince became a fierce opponent of the MSI's leadership group, at least publicly.

45 Rossi, *Alternativa e doppiopetto*, p. 74; and Ignazi, *Polo escluso*, p. 89, note 50.

46 Paolo Guzzanti, *Il neofascismo e le sue organizzazioni paramilitari* (Rome: Partito Socialista Italiana, 1972), p. 23. Borghese's contacts with Luigi Turchi were also noted by the Extra-parliamentary Left Research Group, which added that his father Franz, the editor of *Piazza d'Italia*, was later an active promoter of Nixon's election among groups of Italian immigrants in America. See *Strage di stato: Vent'anni dopo*, p. 257. According to the latter source, Borghese, Luigi Turchi, and Caradonna were all among the right-hand men (*uomini di fiducia*) of Kostas Plevris, the Greek secret service operative entrusted by the Colonels with organizing their covert activities in Italy.

47 The suggestion that Borghese may have had contacts with Italian political leaders in exclusive Roman salons is that of Rosario Minna, "Il terrorismo di destra," *Terrorismi in Italia*, ed. by Donatella della Porta (Bologna: Mulino/Istituto Cattaneo, 1984), p. 47. Minna, then a judge at the Turin Tribunal, has had considerable experience investigating cases of right-wing subversion.

48 The most detailed account I have been able to find about Borghese's financial shenanigans is that of Flamini, *Partito del golpe*, volume 1, p. 168. Compare also Guzzanti, *Neofascismo e le sue organizzazioni paramilitari*, p. 24; Minna, "Terrorismo di destra," p. 47; and Norberto Valentini, *La notte della Madonna: L'Italia tragicomica del golpe nei documenti inediti dei servizi segreti* . . . (Rome: Le Monde, 1978), pp. 27–8. The ambiguity about whether Sindona simply resigned or intentionally transferred his position as president of the bank to Borghese derives from the ambiguity of the phrasing in Flamini's account ("*ceduta da Sindona*"). According to Renzo Vanni, in 1962 Borghese received ten billion lire from Trujillo through the Finanziaria Italiana company. See *Trent'anni di regime bianco* (Pisa: Giardini, 1976), p. 141. It is also worth noting that Ovidio Lefebvre D'Ovidio and his younger brother Antonio, the more powerful and brilliant of the two, were among the key Italians later implicated in the Lockheed Corporation's bribery scandal, for which see Flamini, *Partito del golpe*, volume 2, pp. 19–20; Giuseppe D'Avanzo, *Dossier Lockheed: Contributo alla ricerca di una verità* (Rome: B&C, 1976); Giorgio Galli, *L'Italia sotterranea: Storia, politica e scandali* (Bari: Laterza, 1983), pp. 177–80; David Boulton, *The Lockheed Papers* (London: J. Cape, 1978), pp. 135–58; Maurizio De Luca et al., *Tutti gli uomini dell'Antilope* (Milan: Mondadori, 1977), especially pp. 39–45; and a number of press reports dating from 1976, for example, Paolo Ojetti, "Le duecento società dell'avvocato [Antonio] Lefebvre," *L'Europeo* 32:21 (21 May 1976), pp. 118–19. Perhaps it is no coincidence that both Ovidio and Borghese were among those linked to the earlier bank collapse, since during that period the enterprises of the Lefebvre brothers seem to have been utilized by the secret services to "cover" certain highly secretive political operations. Thus in 1961, Ettore De Martino, a stockholder in many of Antonio's (dummy) firms, liquidated the front company – Torre Marina – which had previously been used by the Servizio Informazioni Forze Armate (SIFAR: Armed Forces Intelligence Service) to purchase the land at Alghero in Sardinia, land that thenceforth functioned as a training base for special warfare personnel, including recruits for the clandestine "Gladio" network. See Paolo Ojetti, "Il SIFAR comprava terreni in Sardegna," *L'Europeo* 32:22 (28 May 1976), p. 40. Compare Parlamento, Commissione parlamentare d'inchiesta sul terrorismo in Italia e sulle cause della mancata individuazione dei responsabili delle stragi [hereinafter CPI/Stragi], *[22 Aprile 1992] Relazione sull'inchiesta condotta sulle vicende connesse all'Operazione Gladio* (Rome: Camera dei Deputati, 1992), p. 41, note 2. Among Torre Marina's shareholders (*soci*) were originally General Ettore Musco (at the time head of SIFAR), Colonel Felice Santini (then head of Servizio Informazioni Operative e

Situazione [SIOS]-Aeronautica and later Air Force attaché in Washington), and Colonel Antonio Lanfalone (a top official in SIFAR's administrative section); on 5 January 1956 these three sold their shares to General De Lorenzo, Colonel Luigi Tagliamonte (chief of SIFAR's administrative section), and Colonel Giulio Fettarappa Sandri (head of Ufficio R). The only civilian among the stockholders was the engineer Aurelio Rossi.

49 For details on aspects of Sindona's career, see Parlamento, Commissione parlamentare d'inchiesta sul caso Sindona e sulle responsabilità politiche ed amministrative ad esso eventualmente connesse [hereinafter CPI/Sindona], *Relazione conclusiva [e le] relazioni di minoranza* (Rome: Camera dei Deputati, 1982). Compare Maurizio De Luca, ed., *Sindona: Gli atti d'accusa dei giudici di Milano* (Rome: Riuniti, 1986); Nick Tosches, *Power on Earth: Michele Sindona's Explosive Story* (New York: Arbor House, 1986); and Mario Tedeschi, *Ambrosiano: Il contro processo* (Rome: Serarcangeli, 1988). More will be said later about Sindona's intelligence links.

50 General information on Gil Robles and CEDA can be found in any serious book that deals with the political history of twentieth-century Spain. A good introduction to the Spanish right, with much information about CEDA, can be found in Paul Preston, *The Politics of Revenge: Fascism and the Military in Twentieth-Century Spain* (London: Unwin Hyman, 1990). For CEDA itself, see the two-volume work of José R. Montero, *La CEDA: El catolicismo social y politico en la II República* (Madrid: Ministerio de Trabajo y Seguridad Social, 1988). For specific accounts of Gil Robles' political career, see José María Garcia Escudero, *Vista a la derecha: Canovas, Maura, Cambo, Gil Robles, Lopez Rodo, Fraga* (Madrid: RIALP, 1988), pp. 179–226; and José Gutierrez-Rave Montero, *Gil Robles, caudillo frustrado* (Madrid: ERSA/Prensa Española, 1967). Many of Gil Robles' own writings have also been published, for example, *No fue posible la paz* (Barcelona: Ariel, 1968), and *Marginalia política* (Barcelona: Ariel, 1975).

51 There is an enormous bibliography on Opus Dei. Some useful studies include Giancarlo Rocca, *L'Opus Dei: Appunti e documenti per una storia* (Rome: Paoline, 1985); Daniel Artegues, *El Opus Dei en España, 1828–1962: Su evolución ideologica y política de los origenes al intento de dominio* (Paris: Ruedo Iberico, 1971); Yvon Le Vaillant, *Sainte Maffia: Le dossier de l'Opus Dei* (Paris: Mercure de France, 1971); Michael J. Walsh, *Opus Dei: An Investigation into the Secret Society Struggling for Power within the Roman Catholic Church* (San Francisco: Harper, 1992); and Jesus Ynfante, *La prodigiosa aventura del Opus Dei: Genesis y desarollo de la Santa Mafia* (Paris: Ruedo Iberico, 1970).

52 Cited by Valentini, *Notte della Madonna*, pp. 83–4.

53 For Rocca's recruitment of former Decima MAS members, see Parlamento, Commissione parlamentare d'inchiesta sugli eventi del giugno-luglio 1964 [hereinafter CPI/De Lorenzo], *Relazione di maggioranza* (Rome: Camera dei Deputati, 1971), p. 554; and CPI/De Lorenzo, *Relazioni di minoranza: Terracini et al* (Rome: Camera dei Duputati, 1971), pp. 162–3. Although the testimony of Senator Jannuzzi was then contested by the Carabinieri officers who he claimed had told him about this illegal recruitment, and was thus rejected as unconfirmable hearsay by conservative members who formed the majority of the parliamentary commission, this claim has now been confirmed by the publication of Cerica's testimony to the Lombardi Commission investigating the 1964 "coup." See CPI/Stragi, *Relazione sulla documentazione concernente gli "omissis" dell'inchiesta SIFAR* (Rome: Camera dei Deputati, 1991), volume 4, pp. 260–1, 298–9. Most of the journalists and academicians, who have examined the matter had already accepted that Rocca did indeed make efforts to recruit former RSI soldiers, especially from the Decima MAS. See, for example, Giuseppe De Lutiis, *Storia dei servizi segreti in Italia* (Rome: Riuniti, 1984), p. 72.

54 Faenza, *Malaffare*, p. 369.

55 See especially the testimony of Colonel Cerica – not coincidentally one of the same officers who denied Jannuzzi's version of their discussion about the illegal recruitment activities of Rocca – before the Lombardi Commission investigating De Lorenzo's "deviations." See CPI/Stragi, *Relazione . . . concernante gli "omissis" dell'inchiesta SIFAR*, volume 4, pp. 262–97. Compare the converging testimony provided by Lieutenant Colonel

Roberto Podestà to a journalist from the newsweekly *ABC* in November of 1967, cited in Extraparliamentary Left Research Group, *Strage di stato:Vent'anni dopo*, pp. 191–2.
56 Flamini, *Partito del golpe*, volume 1, pp. 121–2. Compare the brief descriptions of the Comitato Tricolore in Pansa, *Borghese mi ha detto*, p. 163; Guzzanti, *Neofascismo e le sue organizzazioni paramilitari*, p. 27.
57 Pansa, *Borghese mi ha detto*, p. 69. But Guadagni also claimed that the Black Prince did not suddenly decide to form the FN one day after having thought about it for a long time. Instead, influential people from all over Italy had been approaching Borghese and asking him why he taking was doing nothing to impede the spreading degeneracy and chaos. It was these entreaties from sympathetic patriots that supposedly prompted him to respond and take concrete action. See ibid., pp. 117–18.
58 Flamini, *Partito del golpe*, volume 2, p. 3. According to the Extraparliamentary Left Research Group, the Circolo dei Selvatici originally served as a cultural "front" for an earlier RSI veterans association headed by Borghese, the Fronte Grigioverde (Grey-Green Front [a reference to the color of Italian military uniforms]). It was then later used to "cover" the early gatherings of the FN. See *Strage di stato:Vent'anni dopo*, pp. 191, 254–5.
59 This promotion of a united Europe freed from Western as well as Eastern domination, and for a State that transcended traditional political categories has been taken by some to mean that Borghese himself supported some radical fascist ideological positions characteristic of the RSI. Although he may have found some of this rhetoric congenial, it seems clear that he employed it primarily for tactical reasons – to appeal to the RSI veterans and youthful neo-fascist activists who had always idolized him and whom he was then seeking to recruit into the FN. He resented the "humiliating" provisions of the postwar peace treaty and often claimed to be opposed on a philosophical level to the materialistic cultural values associated with the United States, but prior to 1971 his de facto support for an Atlanticist military alliance against communism never wavered. In this context, it should be pointed out that in 1973 Edgardo Sogno – who no one could possibly accuse of supporting radical neo-fascist positions – also planned to combine an authoritarian rightist political stance with an ostensibly progressive social agenda so as to defuse opposition to his "white coup," a subtler sort of anti-communist strategy characteristic of the more enlightened sectors of the American government with whom he had often collaborated. It is even possible that the Black Prince's appeals to transcend ideological boundaries reflected the new strategy of manipulation then being initiated by the radical right to compromise leftist forces. Finally, on a number of occasions Borghese insisted that attempts to revitalize classical fascism or recreate the Partito Nazionale Fascista (PNF: National Fascist Party) would be foolish and counterproductive.
60 Pansa, *Borghese mi ha detto*, pp. 134–5.
61 Ibid., pp. 135–8.
62 As noted earlier. See Lazzero, *Decima MAS*, pp. 141–52.
63 Pansa, *Borghese mi ha detto*, pp. 93, 102–4, 139.
64 Ibid., pp. 67–8.
65 Ibid., pp. 47–8, 92–3, 137.
66 Ibid., pp. 63–7, 91, 139–40.
67 Ibid., pp. 80–1, 89–95, 100–2, 104–10, 117–19, 121–2. Note that *colpetto* can mean either "little blow" or "little coup," and it is possible that Borghese was being purposely ambiguous with his language in this instance.
68 Ibid., pp. 93, 101–3.
69 Tribunale di Roma, Giudice Istruttore Filippo Fiore, *Sentenza-ordinanza n. 1054/71 del 5 novembre 1975 nel procedimento penale contro Borghese, Junio Valerio + 140* [hereinafter *Sentenza 5 XI 75 contro Borghese*], pp. 69–70.
70 Cited by Flamini, *Partito del golpe*, volume 2, p. 5.
71 Pansa, *Borghese mi ha detto*, pp. 67–71.
72 Extraparliamentary Left Research Group, *Strage di stato:Vent'anni dopo*, p. 254.
73 Flamini, *Partito del golpe*, volume 1, p. 94.

74 Ibid., volume 2, pp. 5–6. For Orlandini's background, see Valentini, *Notte della Madonna*, pp. 26–7. For Guadagni's, see Pansa, *Borghese mi ha detto*, p. 43. Orlandini later told SID man Labruna that he personally set up the first FN cell, after which others were slowly developed throughout the peninsula. See Valentini, *Notte della Madonna*, p. 39.
75 For details concerning the FN's organizational structure and its purposes, see Pansa, *Borghese mi ha detto*, pp. 43, 88–9; *Sentenza 5 XI 75 contro Borghese*, pp. 71–2; Guzzanti, *Neofascismo e le sue organizzazioni paramilitari*, p. 23.
76 For the general nature of the "A" and "B" groups, see *Sentenza 5 XI 75 contro Borghese*, pp. 71–2. Compare Flamini, *Partito del golpe*, volume 2, p. 5; and Ferraresi, "Destra eversiva," p. 60. Tomasso Adami Rook, a Pisan engineer and assistant manager of the Galileo firm in Florence, was the national leader of the FN's "B groups." Although he later denied that there was any division of labor between the "B" and "A" groups, this claim was disproved by numerous other sources of information. See *Sentenza 5 XI 75 contro Borghese*, p. 227.
77 For brief accounts of the FN's activities in the first half of 1969, see *Sentenza 5 XI 76 contro Borghese*, pp. 71–2, 76; and Flamini, *Partito del Golpe*, volume 2, pp. 8–9, 29–31, 58–9. These accounts are based primarily on the information collected in various SID reports concerning the Borghese coup, which were later published in Parlamento, Commissione parlamentare d'inchiesta sulla loggia massonica P2 [hereinafter CPI/P2], *Allegati alla relazione, Serie II: Documentazione raccolti dalla commissione*, volume 7, tome 16, pp. 147–329.
78 Pansa, *Borghese mi ha detto*, p. 43; Flamini, *Partito del golpe*, volume 2, p. 8; and Rosenbaum, *Nuovo fascismo*, p. 84.
79 For characterizations of the FN's adherents, see Pansa, *Borghese mi ha detto*, pp. 42–3; Ferraresi, "Destra eversiva," pp. 60–1; Minna, "Terrorismo di Destra," p. 47; and Adalberto Baldoni, *Noi rivoluzionari. La destra e il "caso italiano": Appunti per una storia, 1960–1986* (Rome: Settimo Segillo, 1986), p. 188. Guzzanti specifically notes the presence of some rightist ex-partisans disposed to follow Borghese's obscure "aristocratic" line. See his *Neofascismo e le sue organizzazioni paramilitari*, p. 23.
80 For FN financing, see *Sentenza 5 XI 75 contro Borghese*, pp. 69, 72; and Minna, "Terrorismo di destra," p. 47. Specifics about the industrialists and other wealthy supporters of the FN can be found throughout Fiore's sentence and volume 2 of Flamini's *Partito del golpe*. As will become clear later, support from financial circles in northern Italy, especially Liguria, did not cease following the FN's aborted December 1970 coup.
81 Estimates of the number of FN supporters are widely divergent. For example, Guadagni claimed that there were "hundreds of thousands" of such supporters. Borghese, more prudently and realistically, numbered them at "several thousand," including "a fairly large number of youths." See Pansa, *Borghese mi ha detto*, pp. 79–80. Various secondary sources estimate the total number at between one thousand and three thousand members. Compare ibid., p. 43, citing the Interior Ministry report; Guzzanti, *Neofascismo e le sue organizzazioni paramilitari*, p. 24; and Rosenbaum, *Nuovo fascismo*, p. 84. These latter estimates jibe with Judge Fiore's conclusions that the results of Borghese's recruiting efforts were "unexpectedly meagre." See *Sentenza 5 XI 75 contro Borghese*, p. 72.
82 Pansa, *Borghese mi ha detto*, pp. 99–100. The CNR was founded in November 1967, and within two years it claimed to have established forty-eight provincial committees and to number nine thousand to ten thousand militants. In August 1969 it began publishing a monthly journal, *Forza, Uomo*. According to De Sario, formerly National Secretary of the Partito Socialdemocratico Italiano's (PSDI: Italian Social Democratic Party) national youth federation, the members of the CNR were "fascist protesters" inspired by Giuseppe Mazzini, Niccolò Bombacci, Vilfredo Pareto, Filippo Corridoni, the Futurists, and the Mussolini of 1919, among others. Although the CNR publicly repudiated violence and sought to appeal, like Pierre Poujade in France, to the small shopkeepers, in its journal its members were characterized as "men ready for an arduous revolutionary struggle" against a "democracy that [was] suffocating freedom." The CNR's activities were mainly concentrated in Milan and Varese during 1970. See ibid., pp. 164–5.

83 Flamini, *Partito del golpe*, volume 2, pp. 95–7. For more on the Lega itself, which was officially established in Milan on 8 March 1970, see Pansa, *Borghese mi ha detto*, pp. 173–4.
84 For Monti as the FN's intermediary to Sogno, see Flamini, *Partito del golpe*, volume 2, p. 196.
85 Cited by ibid., volume 2, p. 8. Unfortunately, he fails to note the date of this report.
86 Pansa, *Borghese mi ha detto*, pp. 98–9. Borghese referred to ON militants as "very fine youths." Interestingly, Rauti, Sermonti, and Maceratini were all appointed to the MSI's Central Committee after rejoining the party, and the latter was put in charge of the party's "civil emergencies" section. See Rossi, *Alternativa e doppiopetto*, p. 108.
87 For the appointment of Saccucci, see Flamini, *Partito del golpe*, volume 2, p. 141. Saccucci brought a number of other ON and AN members into the FN at the time he joined. See ibid., p. 8.
88 Marco Sassano, *La politica della strage* (Padua: Marsilio, 1972), p. 100.
89 Extraparliamentary Left Research Group, *Strage di stato: Vent'anni dopo*, p. 257.
90 Cited by Flamini, *Partito del golpe*, volume 2, p. 102. For discussions about a future coup, see Valentini, *Notte della Madonna*, p. 14, citing an account written after the coup by a journalist closely linked to rightist circles, who then provided it to SID man Labruna. The same source notes that Campo, Delle Chiaie's number two man in AN, was responsible for organizing and executing clandestine plans, and that Perri was put in charge of maintaining relations between AN and the FN. Compare also *Sentenza 5 XI 75 contro Borghese*, p. 454, for confirmation of Perri's role. Both Campo and Perri were apparently members of the AN's own national directorate. See the later trial against AN (for reconstituting the fascist party): Tribunale di Roma, Presidente Pasquale Iapichino, *Sentenza n. 6961 del 5 giugno 1976 nel procedimento penale contro Agnellini, Roberto + 63* [hereinafter *Sentenza 5VI 76 contro Agnellini*], pp. 1–2.
91 *Sentenza 5 XI 75 contro Borghese*, pp. 114–15, 280, 454–5; and Vitalone's *Requisitoria*, p. 113, cited by Pietro Calderoni, ed., *Servizi segreti. Tutte le deviazioni: Dal piano "Solo" al golpe Borghese, dalla P2 alla strage di Bologna, dal caso Cirillo al Super SISMI* (Naples: Tullio Pironti, 1986), p. 44; and Baldoni, *Noi rivoluzionari*, p. 188.
92 See "Che cosa hanno detto i neofascisti all'*Europeo*?," *L'Europeo* 30:33 (15 August 1974), p. 26. Leroy insisted, however, that during that NOE/ENO Congress there was no talk of placing bombs, and that his close associate Yves Guérin-Sérac [Guillou] could neither "be linked to bombs" nor "have inspired homicidal ideas." As the account of Aginter Presse in the previous chapter has indicated, the latter claim is clearly not true. For the close association between Leroy, Borghese, and the other Italians mentioned, see Flamini, *Partito del golpe*, volume 1, pp. 143–4.
93 Extraparliamentary Left Research Group, *Strage di stato: Vent'anni dopo*, pp. 251–2, 257. Borghese himself denied having any meetings with Greek plotters prior to the December 1969 Piazza Fontana bombing, and insisted that these and other bogus claims were part and parcel of a Partito Socialista Italiano (PSI: Italian Socialist Party) propaganda campaign aimed at discrediting him. See Pansa, *Borghese mi ha detto*, pp. 121–3.
94 Various details of Borghese's efforts to recruit Mafia aid for his projected coup can be found, to provide only a few examples, in Pietro Calderoni, "Golpe di mafia," *L'Espresso* 34:11 (20 March 1988), pp. 7–8, citing Antonino Calderone's testimony. Compare the remarks by FN leader Gaetano Lunetta in Mario Scialoja, "Fu vero golpe," *L'Espresso* 35:4 (29 January 1989), p. 39, who claimed that it was a contingent of *mafiosi* from Sicily (rather than AN members) who carried out the failed mission to capture Vicari. See also Philip Willan, *Puppetmasters: The Political Use of Terrorism in Italy* (London: Constable, 1991), pp. 96–8, citing the testimony of Buscetta and Liggio. This was later confirmed in interviews with journalists by General Gianadelio Maletti, later head of SID's Ufficio D. See Andrea Sceresini, Nicola Palma, and Maria Elena Scandaliato, *Piazza Fontana, noi sapevano: Golpe e stragi di Stato. La verità del generale Maletti* (Rome: Alberti, 2010), p. 150. Therein Maletti claimed that a DC parliamentarian, Giovanni Gioia, had endeavored to enroll *mafiosi* in the coup, and that they were operating in Rome, and agreed that their assigned task may have been to seize the TV transmitters on Monte Mario.

95 *Sentenza 5 XI 75 contro Borghese*, p. 74.
96 Pansa, *Borghese mi ha detto*, pp. 54–7, 96–8, 130. In Borghese's view, a sense of higher patriotic duty and a spirit of self-sacrifice were required of a military man. If someone in the service believed that the concept of the fatherland had become outdated, he should take off his uniform at once, go home, and get another job, because he would not be able to discharge his duties properly.
97 Ibid., pp. 96–7.
98 Ibid., p. 98.
99 Valentini, *Notte della Madonna*, p. 54. In an April 1969 "intelligence report" he wrote on the Italian right, neo-fascist journalist and SID operative Guido Giannettini indicated that the FN sought to make use of veterans groups and other contacts to strengthen its links with the armed forces. See Roberto Pesenti, ed., *Le stragi del SID: I generali sotto accusa* (Milan: Mazzotta, 1974), p. 76.
100 Flamini, *Partito del golpe*, volume 2, p. 103.
101 Compare Guzzanti, *Neofascismo e le sue organizzazioni paramilitari*, p. 23; and Extraparliamentary Left Research Group, *Strage di stato:Vent'anni dopo*, p. 257.
102 Cited by Valentini, *Notte della Madonna*, pp. 39–40, 45. Compare ibid., p. 14, citing the report on the coup prepared for Labruna by right-wing journalist Guido Paglia, which was itself based on information provided by both Orlandini and Adriano Monti. Many other people were named as FN supporters in the period after the 1970 coup. Although it is sometimes difficult to be certain just what time frame Orlandini is referring to, the alleged FN supporters listed here apparently backed the Fronte prior to the launching of that coup.
103 Ibid., pp. 64–5, for some of Orlandini's allusions to the important role played by freemasonry in the 1970 coup. Further details were later provided by Andrea Barberi and Nazareno Pagani, "Un'ombra da Piazza Fontana a Pecorelli," in *L'Italia della P2* (Milan: Mondadori, 1981), pp. 63–4. Note that there is some discrepancy between the Orlandini quotes cited in the latter source, which refer simply to *ufficiali iscritti* in the context of a discussion of the FN's military supporters, and the summary of his testimony by Valentini, who refers to three thousand official masonic adepts rather than military officers per se. In the text I have interpreted these "three thousand" as military officers who were affiliated with masonry, although this may not have been what Orlandini meant. In any event, it is interesting that the normally tenacious Labruna did not investigate this masonic connection further, and that his superiors failed to mention these particular Orlandini revelations in the reports they sent to the judicial authorities. More detailed information about the involvement of P2 in the Borghese coup did not surface until the activities of the lodge were accidentally uncovered in the early 1980s, at which point it was discovered that Miceli and other high-ranking SID officials were themselves members of the organization. See further later.
104 For the Carabinieri's general conservative legalist orientation, see Richard Collin, *The De Lorenzo Gambit: The Italian Coup Manqué of 1964* (Beverly Hills and London: Sage, 1976), pp. 21, 27–8. However, as with almost all state security forces, the Carabinieri corps was riven with factionalism, and within it there were influential elements with extremist, anti-democratic sentiments. It was surely no accident, for example, that General De Lorenzo placed his reliance almost exclusively on the Carabinieri, specifically the powerful legions in Milan and Rome, in designing his "anti-subversive" Plan Solo. For details concerning the politicization of the corps and the infighting among various Carabinieri factions, see Giorgio Boatti, *L'Arma: I Carabinieri da De Lorenzo a Mino, 1962–1977* (Milan: Feltrinelli, 1978), passim. For a recent study of the 1964 coup, see Mimmo Franzinelli, *Il piano Solo: I servizi segreti, il centro-sinistra e il "golpe" del 1964* (Milan: Mondadori, 2010).
105 For general accounts of the Italian police since the end of World War II, most of which focus (perhaps unfairly) on their politicization and abuses, see Romano Canosa, *La polizia in Italia dal 1945 ad oggi* (Bologna: Mulino, 1976); and Angelo D'Orsi, *La polizia: Le forze dell'ordine italiano* (Milan: Feltrinelli, 1972).

106 Indeed, Orlandini became increasingly upset because these officials kept making excuses to avoid taking action, so much so that at a certain point he felt that this inaction would doom the plans of the conspirators. See Valentini, *Notte della Madonna*, pp. 41, 77–8, 85.
107 For their testimony, see Valentini, *Notte della Madonna*, pp. 85–6, 141–3, 164; Flamini, *Partito del golpe*, volume 2, pp. 31–2, 102–3. Among the revelations Orlandini made to SID men Labruna and Romagnoli in Lugano were that prior to their 1969 meetings, the shipbuilder had made contact with Miceli in 1968 through a civilian intermediary, then had met with him several times at a hotel in the Roman neighborhood of Prati, near Piazza Cola Di Rienzo. Orlandini also confirmed Romagnoli's query about whether their initial contact grew out of earlier contacts between Borghese and Miceli in 1954 and 1955, in connection with a plan to launch an anti-communist crusade in Sicily. If true, this links the events of 1970 explicitly to those of the earlier rightist plots, and demonstrates a continuity, hitherto only suspected, between some of the personnel involved.
108 *Sentenza 5 XI 75 contro Borghese*, p. 347. Compare Valentini, *Notte della Madonna*, p. 15, citing Guido Paglia's report about the coup.
109 Cited by Antonio Cipriani and Gianni Cipriani, *Sovranità limitata: Storia dell'eversione atlantica in Italia* (Rome: Associate, 1991), p. 157, note 21. Compare Giacomo Pacini, *Il cuore occulto del potere: Storia dell'Ufficio Affari Riservati del Viminale, 1919–1984* (Rome: Nutrimenti, 2010), pp. 204–9; and Willan, *Puppetmasters*, p. 92, who note that the close links between these two men later caused many neo-fascist participants to suspect that Drago was a double agent who had acted to sabotage the coup.
110 For the training of FN, AN, and ON members at the base, see Corrado Incerti and Sandro Ottolenghi, "Il campo di Alghero," *L'Europeo* 32:21 (21 May 1976), p. 39. According to their unnamed informant, the Alghero base was ostensibly administered by the Defense Ministry, but was in fact run by the secret services, specifically Ufficio D of SID. The commander of the base was reportedly Colonel Fernando Pastore Stocchi, who had previously been Miceli's personal secretary at SIOS-Esercito. This informant also claimed that select groups of *left-wing* terrorists and Arab guerrillas were likewise trained there. Some of this eye-opening information turned out to be incorrect. For example, it was Ufficio R within SIFAR, SID, and SISMI, not Ufficio D, that was responsible for administering the activities of "Gladio," and it was the 5th section (Studi e Addestramento [Studies and Training]) of Ufficio R that was in charge of the Capo Marrargiu base near Alghero, which in August 1956 was denominated the Centro Addestramento Guastatori (CAD: Demolition Training Center). For the key role of the Sardinia base in training "Gladio" personnel, see CPI/Stragi, *Prerelazione sull . . . Operazione Gladio*, pp. 27–9. There is now a large and ever-growing literature on the Italian component, code-named "Gladio," of the stay/behind networks established throughout Western Europe after World War II. See, for example, [General] Gerardo Serravalle, *Gladio* (Rome: Associate, 1993), head of Ufficio R's 5th section from 1971 to 1974; [General] Paolo Inzerilli, *Gladio: La verità negata* (Bologna: Analisi, 1995), chief of the 5th section from 1974 to 1980; idem, *La vittoria dei gladiatori: Da Malga Porzus all'assoluzione di Rebbibia* (Brescia: Bietti, 2009); Emanuele Bettini, *Gladio: La Repubblica parallela* (Rome: Ediesse, 1996); Giacomo Piacini, *Le organizzazioni paramilitari nell'Italia repubblicana, 1945–1991* (Rome: Prospettive, 2008); and Andrea Pannocchia and Franco Tosolini, *Gladio: Storia di finti complotti e di veri patrioti* (Valdagno: G. Rossato, 2010), which endeavors to debunk some of the more conspiratorial interpretations; Sergio Flamigni, ed. *Dossier Gladio: Documenti sulla organizzazione paramilitare sègrete di matrice statunitense, attiva in Italia dagli anni Cinquanta al 1990, in violazione della Costituzione* (Milan: Kaos, 2012); and Giacomo Pacini, *Le altre Gladio: La lotta segreta anticomunista in Italia, 1943–1991* (Turin: Einaudi, 2014). A study that may be particularly relevant to aspects of the topic of this chapter is Giorgio Cavalleri, *La Gladio del lago: Il gruppo "Vega" fra J. V. Borghese, RSI, servizi segreti americani, e l'Italia del dopoguerra* (Varese: Essezeta-Arterigere, 2006). For discussions of "Gladio" within the broader ambit of covert activities in postwar Italy, compare Davide Cammarone, ed., *La malaitalia, ovvero la strategia del crimine impunito dai misteri di Gladio*

ai delitti politici (Palermo: Zisa, 1991); Alessandro Silj, *Malpaese: Criminalità, corruzione e politica nell'Italia della prima Repubblica, 1943–1994* (Rome: Donzelli, 1994); and Giovanni Fasanella, Claudio Sestieri, and Giovanni Pellegrino, *Segreto di Stato: La verità da Gladio al caso Moro* (Turin: Einaudi, 2000). See also various studies focused on the secret postwar paramilitary apparatuses set up by the PCI and other components of the radical left, including Gianni Donno, *La gladio rossa del PCI, 1945–1967: Con 180 documenti inediti* (Catanzaro: Rubbetino, 2001); and Rocco Turi, *Gladio rossa: Una catena di complotti e delitti, dal dopoguerra al caso Moro* (Venice: Marsilio, 2004), actions that may well have justified the U.S. and NATO's parallel creation of stay/behind networks in Italy.

111 CPI/Stragi, *Prerelazione sull . . . Operazione Gladio*, pp. 27–9.
112 Cited in Valentini, *Notte della Madonna*, pp. 55, 136–8. More information on Selenia can be found, in the context of the Lockheed scandal, in De Luca et al., *Tutti gli uomini dell'Antilope*, pp. 69–70. Therein Selenia is described as a "veritable den of generals," eleven of whom, drawn from the Italian Army, Navy, and Air Force, served as its expert advisors. Many other ex-officers and relatives of military notables were among the firm's employees. Indeed, Selenia did not even hesitate to hire a retiring Air Force general who had earlier been officially responsible for monitoring the activities of the company! It was in fact very common for high-ranking military officials to work for defense contractors after they retired.
113 Valentini, *Notte della Madonna*, pp. 58–9.
114 For more on Plevris' background and activities, both in Greece and Italy, see Andreas Lentakes, *Parakratikes Organoseis kai eikoste prôte Apriliou* (Athens: Kastaniotes, 1975), pp. 358–9; and Vassilis Kapetanyannis, "Neo-Fascism in Modern Greece," *Neo-Fascism in Europe*, ed. by Luciano Cheles et al. (London and New York: Longman, 1991), pp. 199, 209, note 33; the 20 March 1975 Bologna Questura report cited by Flamini, *Partito del golpe*, volume 1, p. 150; Cesare De Simone, *La pista nera: Tattica dell'infiltrazione e strategia delle bombe. Il complotto fascista contro la Repubblica* (Rome: Riuniti, 1972), pp. 18–19; and "Patrice Chairoff" [Dominique Yvan Calzi], *Dossier néo-nazisme* (Paris: Ramsay, 1977), pp. 291–301. For further discussion, see the two preceding chapters.
115 The complete lists can be found in CPI/P2, *Allegati alla relazione, Serie II: Documentazione raccolti dalla commissione, vol. I: Le carte sequestrate a Castiglion Fibocchi*, tomes 1–4. Evaluations of their reliability can be found in idem, *vol. II: Riscontri sull'attendibilità delle liste*, tomes 1–9. Somewhat more accessible for those not working in Italy is the main list at the end of Martín Berger, *Historia de la lógia masonica P-2* (Buenos Aires: El Cid/Fundación para la Democracia en Argentina, 1983), Appendix 2, pp. 125–51. There are a number of errors and omissions in the latter, especially concerning the Italian "brethren," but it provides more useful information regarding the Argentine members of P2. Some of the P2 members implicated in the Borghese coup are listed by De Lutiis, *Storia dei servizi segreti in Italia*, p. 182.
116 Flamini, *Partito del golpe*, volume 2, pp. 159–60.
117 Ibid., pp. 177–8, citing an SID report.
118 *Sentenza 5 XI 75 contro Borghese*, p. 77.
119 Flamini, *Partito del golpe*, volume 2, pp. 176–7, 180. Compare *Sentenza 5 XI 75 contro Borghese*, p. 348, for Frattini's testimony about the role played by Drago.
120 Guzzanti, *Neofascismo e le sue organizzazioni paramilitari*, pp. 23–4. Compare Vanni, *Trent'anni di regime bianco*, p. 355. For the information about the Army's provision of trainers and material for these exercises, see Ferruccio Albanese, "Parasoccorso per l'Italia," *Lo Specchio* (13 September 1970), cited by De Lutiis, *Storia dei servizi segreti in Italia*, pp. 132, 144, note 80.
121 Flamini, *Partito del golpe*, volume 2, pp. 178–9, citing SID reports. Note that the first two training courses listed, when combined together, were identical to the title of the published proceedings of the 1965 (SIFAR-funded) Istituto Pollio conference on *guerra rivoluzionaria*. This was hardly coincidental, since the ideas expressed at that conference profoundly influenced the subsequent strategies and tactics employed by the Italian

extraparliamentary right. Convicted right-wing terrorist Vincenzo Vinciguerra later claimed that ON leaders made little effort to disguise their organization of such paramilitary camps because they were doing so with the connivance of the police, Carabinieri, and military. See his *Ergastolo per la libertà: Verso la verità sulla strategia della tensione* (Florence: Arnaud, 1989), p. 7.

122 Vanni, *Trent'anni di regime bianco*, p. 355.
123 For descriptions of the meetings, see Extraparliamentary Left Research Group, *Strage di stato: Vent'anni dopo*, p. 134; and Sassano, *Politica della strage*, p. 107. Among the participants at the 15 November meeting — according to the former source — were Calzolari; paratroop General Michele Caforio; "Commander" Guido Bianchini, a former Decima MAS man and later Borghese loyalist in the FN; a group of paratroopers, including some from the RSI's "Nembo" unit; and a number of extraparliamentary rightists, including members of AN and Europa Civiltà. Note that Caforio and Stelio Frattini later sued the publishers of *Strage di Stato*. Caforio claimed that he was in Reggio Calabria on that date, after having arrived there on a military aircraft. See Extraparliamentary Left Research Group, *Strage di stato: Vent'anni dopo*, pp. 118–19. The plaintiffs were apparently unable to prove their cases, however, since the same information appears in later editions of the book. The same source indicates that Borghese himself may have attended the 6 December meeting.
124 Extraparliamentary Left Research Group, *Strage di stato: Vent'anni dopo*, p. 120; Sassano, *Politica della strage*, p. 106. Among those who attended these dinners, according to Calzolari's wife, was Cardinal Eugène Tisserant. Prior to taking his sacerdotal vows, Tisserant was an Army colonel who had been sent on an important mission to the Middle East by the French secret service. Later, he became a member of the Roman Curia and aligned himself with its integralist faction. Along with Cardinal Alfredo Ottaviani, Tisserant was allegedly one of the chief Vatican protectors of Organisation de l'Armée Secrète (OAS: Secret Army Organization) leaders who took refuge in Italy following the failed Algerian putsch in 1961, including *guerre révolutionnaire* theorist Colonel Charles Lacheroy. See Extraparliamentary Left Research Group, *Strage di stato: Vent'anni dopo*, pp. 123–4 (including note). Tisserant was also in contact with Aginter Presse. In November 1966 his former secretary, Monsignor Georges Roche, wrote as follows to Aginter chief Yves Guillou: "You know that I share your sentiments as well as those of your group. It is with all my heart that I wish for the success of your efforts and pray that your works will be blessed." See Frédéric Laurent, *L'Orchestre noir* (Paris: Stock, 1978), p. 132.
125 Pansa, *Borghese mi ha detto*, pp. 122–3. It is simply untrue that Calzolari was too young to have been in the Decima MAS. Although he was too young to have participated in Borghese's earlier naval exploits, he would have been seventeen in 1943 and hence could have been among the many youths who joined the ranks of Borghese's infantry units during the RSI period.
126 All of these details can be found in the account of Sassano, *Politica della strage*, pp. 106–7. The untrustworthy source of the revelations about the post-*strage* meeting was Evelino Loi, about whom see immediately later.
127 Ibid., pp. 108–9.
128 Extraparliamentary Left Research Group, *Strage di stato: Vent'anni dopo*, p. 117 (and note).
129 Ibid., pp. 121–3; and Sassano, *Politica della strage*, pp. 109–10, 111–2.
130 Extraparliamentary Left Research Group, *Strage di stato: Vent'anni dopo*, pp. 121–2. Compare Sassano, *Politica della strage*, p. 109.
131 Sassano, *Politica della strage*, pp. 110–11; and Flamini, *Partito del golpe*, volume 2, p. 143.
132 For Pirina's testimony, see Flamini, *Partito del golpe*, volume 2, p. 144, quoting directly from Vitalone's *Requisitoria*. Luberti was a likely murder suspect, since he was a genuine psychopath. During the Nazi retreat in the Salò period, Luberti and his paramilitary band were singlehandedly responsible for the murder of over two hundred people, the brutal torture of many others, and the rapes of dozens of women, crimes for which he was nicknamed the "hangman of Albenga." In a book titled *I camerati*, Luberti later

claimed that he was "fiercer than the SS" and that "murder will always be the most stimulating of human activities." Although he was condemned to death by firing squad at a 1946 trial in Savona, the sentence was repeatedly reduced until he was released from prison in 1953. After his release, he soon reestablished contact with Borghese, and involved himself in various right-wing political activities prior to becoming an FN money-handler. On 18 January 1970, at around the same time that Calzolari died, Luberti shot his German girlfriend Carla Grüber in the head with a 7.65 caliber pistol. Her decomposing body was discovered in their apartment on 3 April, but it was not until 10 July 1972 that the police captured him in Portici after a firefight. For Luberti's background, see Sassano, *Politica della strage*, pp. 113–16.
133 Extraparliamentary Left Research Group, *Strage di stato:Vent'anni dopo*, pp. 135–8. Here it is worth recalling that Improta was one of the police officials who unceasingly promoted the "anarchist trail" in the Piazza Fontana investigation, an attempt to cover the footsteps of the real perpetrators for which he was later sanctioned. See, for example, Flamini, *Partito del golpe*, volume 3:2, p. 522.
134 Loi was born into a Sardinian family with communist sympathies. Shortly after moving to Rome in the mid-1960s, he had climbed to the top of the Colosseum and threatened to jump off if he was not provided with employment, a bizarre act that netted him a housecleaning job at a monsignor's residence. Within a few days he quit and began frequenting Stazione Termini, the main train station in Rome, in the company of a group of unemployed southern Italians and Sardinians who eked out a precarious living from day to day. When elements of the leftist student movement occupied Rome University's Faculty of Law in Piazza Esedra during the winter of 1968, Loi managed to persuade the occupying students to let him participate in their struggle, thereby obtaining a place to stay at night. In that locale, he organized a contingent of his southern Italian friends and helped repel a series of neo-fascist attacks. The law school was cleared out by the police in early February 1969, at which point the students occupied the main campus. Three thousand police and Carabinieri then made a dawn attack on the campus, arresting seven people in the process. Since one of Loi's friends was among those arrested, Loi himself was provided with 400,000 lire gathered via a student collection on behalf of the arrestees, but was immediately kicked out of the movement after student leaders discovered that he had pocketed these donations. He then began associating with radical rightists. These actions help to illuminate his character, or lack thereof.
135 Extraparliamentary Left Research Group, *Strage di stato: Vent'anni dopo*, pp. 138–42. According to Loi, Carabinieri Captain Servolino was a regular visitor to MSI headquarters, whereas Servolino's colleague Captain Nobili (commander of the Piazza Venezia Carabinieri company), Lieutenant Colonels Giordano (from the Army) and Lilli, and General Dalla Chiesa supposedly frequented FN headquarters. If the latter reference is to Carabinieri General Carlo Alberto Dalla Chiesa, this claim is scarcely believable.
136 All of these details are found in the preliminary sentence of Judge Occorsio, which was excerpted by neo-fascist journalist Mario Tedeschi, *La strage contro lo stato* (Milan: Borghese, 1973), pp. 126–30.
137 Extraparliamentary Left Research Group, *Strage di stato:Vent'anni dopo*, p. 141.
138 Ibid.
139 For these details, see *Reggio 1970: Una rivolta tra cronaca e storia* (Reggio Calabria: n.p., n.d.), pp. 6–7, 31–6, and passim; the Ciccio Franco interview published in Gianni Rossi, ed., *La rivolta. Reggio Calabria: Le ragioni di ieri e la realtà di oggi* (Rome: Isituto di Studi Corporativi, 1991), pp. 217–29; and Rossi, *Alternativa e doppiopetto*, pp. 156–67. All of these are neo-fascist sources – the first radical, the last two moderate.
140 For Borghese's visits to Reggio, see *Reggio 1970*, pp. 24–8; and Rossi, *Alternativa e doppiopetto*, p. 157. The former source provides a number of interesting details. For example, after discovering that his rally had been banned, Borghese went with Genoese Zerbi to the Questura to talk to Police Commissioner Emilio Santillo. When the Black Prince entered the police station, all the policemen present snapped to attention. Santillo then

indicated, as if to apologize, that he was ordered to interdict the rally by the political establishment. Despite this show of respect, a four-hour pitched battle later broke out between Borghese's supporters and the police.

141 See Rossi, *Alternativa e doppiopetto*, pp. 157–8; Pansa, *Borghese mi ha detto*, pp. 81–6; and *Reggio 1970*, p. 77 (reprint of an FN leaflet).
142 The details provided in the next two paragraphs are based on the account of Flamini, *Partito del golpe*, volume 2, pp. 111–15, who bases his on police reports and the trial testimony.
143 Ibid., p. 143.
144 *Sentenza 5 XI 75 contro Borghese*, pp. 74–5. Compare the assessment of public prosecutor Claudio Vitalone in his 1974 *Requisitoria*, p. 77, wherein Borghese's strategy was identified as the carrying out of provocations, specifically public disturbances, in order to precipitate and justify the launching of repressive counterblows by the forces of order. Cited by Claudio Nunziata, " 'Golpe Borghese' e 'Rosa dei Venti': Come si svuota un processo," in *Eversione di destra, terrorismo, stragi: I fatti e intervento giudiziario*, ed. by Vittorio Borraccetti (Milan: Angeli, 1986), p. 80.
145 Cited in *Sentenza 5 XI 75 contro Borghese*, p. 81, note 7.
146 For Borghese's operational plans, see ibid., pp. 78–82; and Valentini, *Notte della Madonna*, Part I, passim.
147 Valentini, *Notte della Madonna*, pp. 15–16, 25; and Flamini, *Partito del golpe*, volume 2, p. 225. Talenti was a key Nixon supporter in Italy who served as some sort of intermediary between Miceli and various FN leaders, including Orlandini.
148 Cited in Valentini, *Notte della Madonna*, pp. 15–17. Labruna's source for this information was almost certainly Guido Paglia, who was not only closely linked to Delle Chiaie and AN, but was also an Aginter Presse "correspondent" and one of the eighty-one journalists allegedly on SID's payroll. See Vinciguerra, *Ergastolo per la libertà*, p. 24. For the latter information, see the 5 December 1976 edition of the rightist weekly *Il Tempo*, cited by De Lutiis, *Storia dei servizi segreti in Italia*, pp. 177, 189–90, note 99.
149 Vitalone's *Requisitoria*, p. 95, cited by Nunziata, " 'Golpe Borghese' e 'Rosa dei Venti'," p. 88. Additional information about Fanali's background will be provided later.
150 *Sentenza 5 XI 75 contro Borghese*, pp. 85–8. Compare Flamini, *Partito del golpe*, volume 2, pp. 222–4. For the designations "command post A" and "command post B," see Orlandini's testimony cited in Valentini, *Notte della Madonna*, p. 139. For the acquisition of the arms, see *Sentenza 5 XI 75 contro Borghese*, pp. 246–7, 299–302, 343–5, 457–8, 473–5, 479–80. According to various witnesses, the money to purchase these weapons was provided by a so-called Comitato Ristretto Genovese (Select Genoese Committee) consisting of Pietro Catanoso, Ernesto Grosso, and Leopoldo Zunino, although no proof was ever found to substantiate this. In any event, it is certain that on 2 December 1970 Benvenuto persuaded Gabriele Di Nardo, Paolo Pinacci, Federico Ratti, and Renato Ridella to accompany Frattini and him to the Armeria Galli on Via Moscova in Milan, from where a handful of Winchester carbines and Heckler & Koch repeater rifles were directly purchased. The latter three then "loaned" Frattini and Benvenuto their permits to carry arms.
151 Valentini, *Notte della Madonna*, p. 17. Compare *Sentenza 5 XI 75 contro Borghese*, p. 116, citing an SID report.
152 *Sentenza 5 XI 75 contro Borghese*, pp. 122–6, 460–4, 488–90.
153 Ibid., pp. 118–21. Serpieri had played a key role as an informant in connection with the Piazza Fontana bombing. Antico's provision of information to SID on the night of the coup will be discussed later.
154 For these events, see ibid., pp. 89–90; Valentini, *Notte della Madonna*, pp. 17, 51–2, 135; and Flamini, *Partito del golpe*, volume 2, pp. 222–3. Lunetta's illuminating testimony can be found in Scialoja, "Fu vero golpe." Note also that Orlandini later told Labruna that some of the AN members who first entered the Viminale on the afternoon of 7 December were of particular utility because they already "had knowledge of certain things." See

Sentenza 5 XI 75 contro Borghese, p. 116. This cryptic remark may simply refer to the fact that Drago had provided a detailed hand-drawn map of the interior of the Viminale to AN leaders, but it may also have been some sort of allusion to inside information previously obtained by Delle Chiaie, perhaps owing to his alleged relationship with UAR official D'Amato.
155 Valentini, *Notte della Madonna*, pp. 17–18, 133–4.
156 For the gross incompetence of the investigators – no officials and none of those on guard duty that night at the Viminale were even questioned – see the account in Fiore's *Sentenza 5 XI 75 contro Borghese*, pp. 94–5, where it is implied that this may have been the result of something worse than negligence, that is, complicity in a cover-up.
157 *Sentenza 5 XI 75 contro Borghese*, pp. 90–5. In a later appellate sentence, it was argued that this composite weapon may have been in the armory long before the coup took place. However, this absurd explanation does not explain how Orlandini and other plotters knew of its existence. See Nunziata, " 'Golpe Borghese' e 'Rosa dei Venti'," p. 75.
158 For the unsuccessful Vicari operation, see *Sentenza 5 XI 75 contro Borghese*, pp. 127–9. The alleged FN-Mafia links have been noted earlier.
159 *Sentenza 5 XI 75 contro Borghese*, pp. 105–7. Berti's background is worth noting. During World War II he had fought with the "Littorio" Division on the French front, and after the war had been condemned by the Rome Court of Appeals for promoting collaboration with the invading Germans. Yet this background did not prevent him – along with thousands of others who were compromised in similar ways – from resuming a career in "the most delicate ganglia of the bureaucratic structure." See Flamini, *Partito del golpe*, volume 2, p. 225, citing trial documents.
160 *Sentenza 5 XI 75 contro Borghese*, pp. 107–13, 249–56.
161 Ibid., pp. 96–8.
162 Ibid., pp. 98–101.
163 For these dramatic details, many of which remain unconfirmed, see the verbatim testimony of Orlandini published in Valentini, *Notte della Madonna*, pp. 139–40. Compare *Sentenza 5 XI 75 contro Borghese*, pp. 130, 132–3.
164 See *Sentenza 5 XI 75 contro Borghese*, pp. 363–4, for Lombardi's probable role in this task.
165 Ibid., pp. 101–103, 131.
166 Ibid., p. 93, citing Orlandini's testimony.
167 Ibid., pp. 131–2.
168 Ibid., pp. 131–9; Flamini, *Partito del golpe*, volume 3:1, pp. 3–6.
169 *Sentenza 5 XI 75 contro Borghese*, pp. 41–3.
170 De Lutiis, *Storia dei servizi segreti in Italia*, p. 102; and Willan, *Puppetmasters*, p. 90.
171 *Sentenza 5 XI 75 contro Borghese*, pp. 45–50.
172 Ibid., pp. 92–3.
173 See the summary of the 1978 sentence in Nunziata, " 'Golpe Borghese' e 'Rosa dei Venti'," pp. 74–8. Compare Vitalone's *Requisitoria*, p. 126, cited ibid., p. 86, for the overly simplistic suggestion that only a few disloyal officers sympathized with or supported Borghese's action. By criticizing this reductionist approach, I do not mean to indict the Italian armed forces as a whole, but rather to suggest that certain influential but minoritarian *factions* within the military establishment promoted such an authoritarian involution.
174 See Corte d'Assise di Roma, Presidente Giuseppe Giuffrida e Giudice Estensore Antonio Germano Abate, *Sentenza n. 29/78 del 14 luglio 1984 nel procedimento penale contro Orlandino, Remo + 77* [hereinafter *Sentenza 14 VII 84 contro Orlandini*], pp. 649–50, where various charges against Orlandini, Delle Chiaie, Berti, and other leading conspirators (for armed insurrection against the state, the theft of arms from the Interior Ministry, the illegal transport of weapons, and the attempted kidnapping of Police Chief Vicari) were dropped "because the event[s] did not occur (*non sussiste*)." [!!!]
175 See Cecchi, *Storia della P2*, p. 141.
176 *Sentenza 5 XI 75 contro Borghese*, pp. 389–90.

177 SID reports were prepared about various aspects of FN plotting on 25 November 1968, 11 May 1969, 22 May 1970, 6 August 1970, 28–29 August 1970, 19 September 1970 (two), and 7 December 1970. See Nunziata, " 'Golpe Borghese' e 'Rosa dei Venti'," pp. 93–4. Most of these were later published in CPI/P2, *Allegati alla relazione, Serie II: Documentazione*, volume 7, tome 16, pp. 147–329. Miceli should have familiarized himself with the general information contained in these reports after he became head of the service in October 1970, since such intelligence reports were regularly transmitted to the office of the chief of SID.

178 *Sentenza 5 XI 75 contro Borghese*, pp. 156–7.

179 Ibid., pp. 157–60. Nunziata is particularly critical of this inadequate initial effort by SID to verify Antico's information. As he points out, an external examination of the Viminale palace from the plaza side made it impossible for Genovesi and his partner to observe the side entrances to the building, one of which members of Delle Chiaie's group had made use of to carry out their assigned tasks. See " 'Golpe Borghese' e 'Rosa dei Venti'," p. 94.

180 For Miceli's inaction, see *Sentenza 5 XI 75 contro Borghese*, pp. 160–1, 391–2. Compare Nunziata, " 'Golpe Borghese' e 'Rosa dei Venti'," p. 94; and De Lutiis, *Storia dei servizi segreti in Italia*, p. 101. Several secondary sources, basing their accounts on prosecutor Vitalone's *Requisitoria*, as well as other documentary materials, claim that Miceli was informed of Antico's tip shortly after midnight. But Gasca Queirazza subsequently testified that he provided preliminary details regarding the coup to Miceli at 1:10 AM on 8 December. See *Sentenza 5 XI 75 contro Borghese*, p. 392.

181 However, a strange anomaly surfaced in connection with this conversation. Although Miceli did his best to muddy the waters, he accidentally told Marchesi about the meeting at the gym on Via Eleniana, even though Gasca Queirazza had not mentioned any such meeting when he had earlier spoken to Miceli. Although Marchesi later admitted that this talk with Miceli may have occurred the next day, by which time Miceli may have been officially informed about the ANPDI meeting, suspicions remained that the head of SID may have had another inside source of information about what transpired on the evening of 7–8 December. See *Sentenza 5 XI 75 contro Borghese*, pp. 390, 392.

182 These testimonies are cited by Valentini, *Notte della Madonna*, pp. 199–202.

183 De Lutiis, *Storia dei servizi segreti in Italia*, p. 101; and Laurent, *Orchestre noir*, p. 247.

184 *Sentenza 5 XI 75 contro Borghese*, pp. 161–3.

185 Ibid., pp. 404–5.

186 Ibid., pp. 163–5. The key passages of this report, taken from Vitalone's *Requisitoria*, are cited by Nunziata in " 'Golpe Borghese' e 'Rosa dei Venti'," pp. 92–3.

187 *Sentenza 5 XI 75 contro Borghese*, pp. 165–7. The details of Labruna's investigation and Orlandini's testimony form the basis of Valentini's important book, *Notte della Madonna*. Much of the information provided by Orlandini has been used in the preceding reconstruction, and more will be referred to in the narrative later. For more on the NOD, see ibid., pp. 11–13; and De Lutiis, *Storia dei servizi segreti in Italia*, pp. 191–2. Further details on Maletti's investigation of the coup have since been revealed by the general himself. See Sceresini et al., *Piazza Fontana*, pp. 136, 142–4.

188 *Sentenza 5 XI 75 contro Borghese*, pp. 167–8.

189 Ibid., pp. 179–80. Miceli's testimony about his reaction to the "big" Labruna report can be found in Flamini, *Partito del golpe*, volume 3:2, p. 600. However, Maletti claimed that Miceli maintained a poker face when he first provided a copy of the report to the latter. See Sceresini et al., *Piazza Fontana*, p. 145. Maletti also indicated (ibid., p. 144) that the "Mallopone" consisted of several dozen pages.

190 For these details, see Valentini, *Notte della Madonna*, pp. 151–3.

191 Ibid., pp. 153, 158–68.

192 Ibid., pp. 198–9, 203. For more on Sogno's "white coup" activities, see Pietro Di Muccio de Quattro, *Il golpe bianco di Edgardo Sogno* (Macerata: Liberilibri, 2013). For his entire

career, compare Edgardo Sogno and Aldo Cazzullo, *Testamento di un anticomunista. Dalla Resistenzia al golpe bianco: Storia di un italiano* (Milan: Sperling & Kupfer, 2010).
193 Valentini, *Notte della Madonna*, pp. 203–4.
194 For these quotes, see Cipriani and Cipriani, *Sovranità limitata*, p. 159; and De Lutiis, *Storia dei servizi segreti in Italia*, pp. 106–7.
195 *Sentenza 5 XI 75 contro Borghese*, pp. 181–2, 388–91, 407–8, 411–13.
196 Antonio De Falco, in a 21 June 1974 *Il Giorno* article cited by Boatti, *L'Arma*, p. 186, note 23.
197 9 February 1984 Aleandri testimony, quoted verbatim in CPI/P2, *Allegati alla relazione, Serie I: Resoconti stenografici delle sedute della commissione*, volume 14, pp. 368–70. Therein he confirmed his prior 23 September and 16 October 1982 testimony before various judges, which was published in CPI/P2, *Serie II: Documentazione*, volume 3, tome 4, part 1, pp. 47, 55. Compare also Cipriani and Cipriani, *Sovranità limitata*, p. 156.
198 *Sentenza 5 XI 75 contro Borghese*, pp. 316–18. Unfortunately, the crucial role of De Jorio was glossed over in the sentence. See ibid., pp. 323–8.
199 Scialoja, "Fu vero golpe," pp. 38–9. Note that there may be some problems with Lunetta's testimony. It is perhaps more reasonable to assume, for example, that the guards assigned to protect the Viminale were from the Pubblica Sicurezza corps instead of the Carabinieri. The former are under the administrative control of the Interior Ministry, whereas the latter, as a part of the army, are organizationally dependent upon the Defense Ministry. Capanna, the key "inside" man at the Viminale, was a member of the Celere, the anti-riot squad of the national police. Even so, it is possible that certain Carabinieri were seconded to guard the Interior Ministry that night.
200 Quoted by Flamini, *Partito del golpe*, volume 3:1, p. 27.
201 Cipriani and Cipriani, *Sovranità limitata*, pp. 156–7. Compare Orlandini's testimony to Labruna, cited in Valentini, *Notte della Madonna*, p. 140. Here it is worth noting that Mingarelli was earlier implicated in De Lorenzo's 1964 "coup," and was later accused by judges of attempting to derail the investigation of the 1972 Peteano bombing.
202 See CPI/P2, *Relazione di Minoranza: Giorgio Pisanò [MSI]* (Rome: Camera dei Deputati, 1984), p. 137.
203 Boatti, *L'Arma*, p. 138, note 16, citing a 29 November 1973 article in the Italian newsweekly *Panorama*.
204 Valentini, *Notte della Madonna*, p. 209.
205 Ibid., pp. 46–7. These detachments had allegedly been sent by Armed Forces chief of staff Henke, who had supposedly established a Mafia-like clique within the service that carried out illegal shakedowns and accepted payoffs. In this case, bribes had been paid to ensure that no weapons would be found.
206 Compare the analyses in ibid., p. 153; and De Lutiis, *Storia dei servizi segreti in Italia*, pp. 104–5.
207 16 October 1982 Aleandri testimony, published in CPI/P2, *Allegati alla relazione, Serie II: Documentazione*, volume 3, tome 4, part 1, p. 55.
208 Cited by Flamini, *Partito del golpe*, volume 3:1, p. 27, and – more fully – by Cipriani and Cipriani, *Sovranità limitata*, p. 157, note 2. Compare Sassano, *SID e partito americano*, p. 86.
209 Cited in Scialoja, "Fu vero golpe," pp. 38–9.
210 See Sassano, *SID e partito americano*, p. 88, for the latter claim.
211 *Sentenza 5 XI 75 contro Borghese*, pp. 241–2.
212 De Lutiis, *Storia dei servizi segreti in Italia*, p. 99.
213 *Sentenza 5 XI 75 contro Borghese*, pp. 90–1. Compare Vitalone's *Requisitoria*, pp. 76–7, cited by Calderoni, ed., *Servizi segreti*, p. 46.
214 Valentini, *Notte della Madonna*, pp. 9–10. As Valentini rightly notes, this so-called thanks also served as a warning, specifically a reminder to SID that certain of its own officials were complicit in the coup.
215 See Valentini, *Notte della Madonna*, pp. 39–64, 69–87, and passim for Orlandini's testimony; Scialoja, "Fu vero golpe," pp. 38–9, for Lunetta's.

216 Compare Sassano, *SID e partito americano*, p. 86; and Laurent, *Orchestre noir*, p. 248.
217 *Sentenza 5 XI 75 contro Borghese*, pp. 297–8, 365–7. It was apparently Lo Vecchio, an especially active plotter, who recruited Casero into the FN and convinced him to support the operation.
218 Nunziata, " 'Golpe Borghese' e 'Rosa dei Venti'," p. 87. Compare Calderoni, ed., *Servizi segreti*, p. 53.
219 Cited by De Lutiis, *Storia dei servizi segreti in Italia*, p. 104. Note that this could help to explain why Saccucci's efforts to train FN members in guerrilla warfare may have been tangibly supported by the Army General Staff.
220 See CPI/P2, *Relazione di Minoranza: Pisanò*, pp. 135–40, for further details about this plan. Senator Pisanò's basic source for this was Lieutenant Colonel Amos Spiazzi, who claimed that his artillery unit was activated, in accordance with the stipulations of the "Triangle" plan, on the night of the Borghese coup. The implications of this will be discussed at greater length later, in connection with the alleged involvement of "parallel SID" in the "Tora Tora" operation.
221 Virgilio Ilari, *Le Forze Armate tra politica e potere, 1943–1976* (Florence: Vallecchi, 1979), p. 105.
222 For background information on Fanali's career, see ibid., pp. 37, 97, 105; Flamini, *Partito del golpe*, volume 1, p. 185; and De Luca et al., *Tutti gli uomini dell'Antilope*, p. 35.
223 Ilari, *Forze Armate tra politica e potere*, p. 156.
224 See the passage cited verbatim by Flamini, *Partito del golpe*, volume 3:1, p. 73. Lucertini had been appointed as Fanali's successor as Air Force chief of staff.
225 On ISSED and *Politica e Strategia*, see ibid., volume 3:1, p. 212. Among the articles written by Fanali for the journal were "Come è possibile oggi la difesa dell'Europa" in 1 (December 1972), pp. 43–7, and "Il fianco meridionale della NATO," in 2 (March 1973), pp. 88–94.
226 See Valentini, *Notte della Madonna*, pp. 176–7, citing the report prepared by one of the attendees, Lieutenant Colonel Giuseppe Condò, who had been ordered by Miceli and General Salvatore Coniglio, chief of SIOS-Esercito, to obtain further information about Sogno's activities. Compare Flamini, *Partito del golpe*, volume 3:2, pp. 511–2.
227 Flamini, *Partito del golpe*, volume 4:1, pp. 36–7, citing the 10 February 1975 issue of *Il Tempo*.
228 On CIDAS and its first two conferences, see ibid., volume 3:1, pp. 266–7, 662. Among the more famous academic attendees were Raymond Aron, Thomas Molnar, and Paul Feyerabend. Of more relevance to this study is the fact that the participants included Gaetano Rasi, Armin Mohler, Alain de Benoist, and Hennig Eichberg, all leading thinkers associated with diverse intellectual currents of the postwar radical right. The latter two, in particular, helped lead that right out of the nostalgic, pro-fascist ideological ghetto and toward more unorthodox currents of thought (many of which borrowed elements from the left), and thence became leading figures in the *nouvelle droite* in France and Germany. In any event, the presentations at the first CIDAS conference were later published as *Intellettuali per la libertà* (Turin: CIDAS, 1973); those in the second as *Conoscenza per la libertà* (Turin: CIDAS, 1975). A list of well-wishers and participants at the latter can be found on pp. 345–52. Among the well-wishers were author Anthony Burgess, science fiction writer Arthur C. Clarke, geneticist Hans Eysenck, social scientist Ernest Gellner, natural scientist Konrad Lorenz, philosopher Karl Popper, physicist Werner Heisenberg, and historian Arnold Toynbee, along with French Front National (FN: National Front) leader Jean-François Chiappe, who identified himself as a "historian," and others with less distinguished pedigrees.
229 See Flamini, *Partito del golpe*, volume 4:1, pp. 91–3, for details about this CIDAS conference.
230 Ibid., volume 4:2, pp. 469–70. For more on Dell'Amico, see De Lutiis, *Storia dei servizi segreti in Italia*, pp. 156–60.
231 See Flamini, *Partito del golpe*, volume 2, p. 203; and Ilari, *Forze Armate tra politica e potere*, p. 155.

232 Valentini, *Notte della Madonna*, pp. 39, 78. Note that Orlandini indicated that he himself had last met with Roselli Lorenzini *before* his arrest in March 1971, but that afterwards it had been too dangerous since both of their names had been linked to conspiratorial plotting. Moreover, in contrast to Lercari, Orlandini named Air Force General Giulio Cesare Graziani – rather than Fanali and Lucertini – as Roselli Lorenzini's chief operational subordinate. At that time, Graziani was commander of the Second Air Region. Ibid., p. 78.

233 Flamini, *Partito del golpe*, volume 3:1, p. 93, citing the Lercari memorandum.

234 See ibid., volume 2, p. 204, and volume 3:1, pp. 282–3. Supposedly, Lercari and other FN members contacted the Greek junta with the help of a very close associate of Papadopoulos, and then asked the latter to provide the plotters with financial help and, once the operation was launched, to send two cruisers into the Adriatric in order to interdict arms trafficking networks that could supply anti-coup forces.

235 Ibid., volume 2, p. 203.

236 See ibid., pp. 114, 185, for the incident in Paris, etc. Fanali's stint as headmaster of the NATO Defense College is revealed by De Luca et al., *Tutti gli uomini dell'Antilope*, p. 35.

237 See, for example, De Luca et al., *Tutti gli uomini dell'Antilope*, pp. 37–8, 106–10, 118–25. Apparently, Fanali bought a luxurious villa in Sassolini, about sixty miles outside Rome near the sea, and stock in a number of companies, including SIP and Montedison, with the bribes he obtained from Lockheed.

238 Ilari, *Forze Armate tra politica e potere*, p. 150.

239 See Vitalone's *Requisitoria*, p. 94, cited by Calderoni, ed., *Servizi segreti*, pp. 49–50; and Willan, *Puppetmasters*, p. 96. It is not known how Orlandini obtained these documents.

240 Cited in Scialoja, "Fu vero golpe," p. 39. On the surface, this claim seems hard to believe. Verona is a considerable distance from Rome, and major troop movements of this type would surely have been difficult to disguise.

241 Cited in Valentini, *Notte della Madonna*, p. 135. For his entire testimony regarding American involvement, see ibid., pp. 55–6, 82, 135–9.

242 This document is fully cited in *Sentenza 5 XI 75 contro Borghese*, pp. 81–2, note 7.

243 Sceresini et al., *Piazza Fontana*, pp. 139–42.

244 Cited by Nunziata, "'Golpe Borghese' e 'Rosa dei Venti'," p. 85.

245 For Patria y Libertad's use of "false flag" terrorist provocations, see Poul Jensen, *The Garotte: The United States and Chile, 1970–1973* (Aarhus: Aarhus University, 1988), pp. 232–5, as well as Taylor Branch and Eugene M. Propper, *Labyrinth: The Sensational Story of International Intrigue in the Search for the Assassins of Orlando Letelier* (New York: Penguin, 1983), p. 62. Propper was the U.S. prosecutor who investigated the 21 September 1976 murder of exiled Chilean leftist Orlando Letelier, which occurred in broad daylight on Washington, DC's embassy row. Propper soon discovered that the "hit" had been ordered by General Juan Manuel Contreras, the head of the post-coup Chilean secret police, the Dirección de Inteligencia Nacional (DINA: National Intelligence Directorate), and that it had been carried out by Cuban and American contract agents affiliated with that agency's 5th (External Operations) Department. For the organization of DINA, see the diagram in Ascanio Cavallo Castro et al., *Chile, 1973–1988: La historia oculta del regimen militar* (Santiago de Chile: Antártica, 1988), p. 50.

246 See, for example, Luis Vega, *Anatomia de un golpe de estado: La caída de Allende* (Jerusalem: La Semana, 1983), p. 168, citing the example of the Vanguardia Obrera Popular (Popular Workers' Vanguard).

247 On the activities, connections, and funding of Patria y Libertad, see U.S. Congress, Senate, Committee to Study Governmental Operations with Respect to Intelligence Activities, *Covert Action in Chile, 1963–1973*, Report, 94th Congress, 1st Session (Washington, DC: Government Printing Office, 1975), pp. 24, 31; Donald Freed, with Fred Landis, *Death in Washington: The Murder of Orlando Letelier* (Westport, CT: Lawrence Hill, 1980), pp. 51, 55–6, 66–7; Branch and Propper, *Labyrinth*, pp. 62–3, 349–50, 378–80, 494–500; and John Dinges and Saul Landau, *Assassination on Embassy Row* (New York: Pantheon,

1980), pp. 41, 54, 56, 69, 103, 106–18, etc. Further information can be found in general histories of the coup and its precursors. Some of the more "noteworthy" aspects of Patria y Libertad deserve to be highlighted here. Among other things, it possessed both a legal organizational facade and a clandestine cell structure, which was subdivided into training squads, "death squads," and shock troops; its cadres were trained by former military officers, many of whom were graduates of the CIA's International Police Academy or the U.S. Army's School of the Americas in Panama; its leaders reportedly had frequent contacts with officials at the American embassy; it was regularly engaged in anti-democratic terrorist actions and psychological warfare operations, both before and after the 1973 coup; it was directly involved in the murder of pro-constitutionalist military officers, including Generals René Schneider and Carlos Prats; it promoted anti-Semitism and professed to have a national syndicalist ideology; it had links to ultra rightist groups and drug trafficking networks throughout Latin America, including those established by anti-Castro Cuban exiles who had worked for the CIA; and many of its members were incorporated into Chilean security agencies after the coup, including the newly formed DINA. For a remarkably thorough and detailed analysis of American policy toward the Allende regime, with a particular consideration for the characteristics and limitations of the available sources concerning that policy, see Jensen, *The Garotte*, passim.

248 See, for example, the account by Robinson Rojas Sandford, *The Murder of Allende and the End of the Chilean Way to Socialism* (New York: Harper & Row, 1976), p. 7. This claim was disputed by Robert J. Alexander, *The Tragedy of Chile* (Westport, CT: Greenwood, 1978), p. 281, who noted that by that time many radical right terrorists had already been imprisoned or forced into exile by the Allende regime. In any event, among the many far right paramilitary groups which constituted these "independent units" were the Comando de Ex-Cadetes (Commando of Former Cadets), PROTECO (Protección contra el Comunismo [Protection Against Communism]), Soberanía, Orden y Libertad (Sovereignty, Order, and Freedom), and the Comando Rolando Matus (Roland Matus Commando), which was linked to the rightist Partido Nacional (National Party). Rojas, a radical Chilean leftist who blamed Allende for being overly cautious and making too many compromises with the forces of reaction, also claimed that the Americans stationed two destroyers off the coast of Valparaíso and one destroyer and a submarine off the coast of Talcahuano on the day of the coup. This small task force had originally been assigned to participate in the annual "Operation Unitas" maneuvers alongside ships from the Chilean navy. See *Murder of Allende*, pp. 185, 188. If these naval forces were really meant to support the military *golpistas* in Chile, even as a last resort, Orlandini's claims about abortive American naval support for "Tora Tora" do not seem quite so far-fetched. No actual evidence has been produced to support this contention in connection with the Chilean coup, however.

249 For Nixon's special hostility toward the liberal CIA and State Department snobs from Ivy League schools, particularly the former, see Henry A. Kissinger, *White House Years* (Boston: Little Brown, 1979), p. 36. The "clowns" phrase can be found in R[ichard] N[ixon], *The Memoirs of Richard Nixon* (New York: Grosset & Dunlap, 1978), p. 447. It may not be wise to attach too much weight to this contemptuous outburst, which was prompted by Nixon's frustration over the CIA's failure to provide him with advance warning about Lon Nol's 1970 coup against Prince Norodom Sihanouk in Cambodia. Nevertheless, British historian Rhodri Jeffreys-Jones aptly sums up Nixon's overall attitude as follows: "There can be little question concerning Nixon's continuing doubts about the competence and loyalty of CIA personnel." See *The CIA and American Democracy* (New Haven and London: Yale University, 1989), p. 177.

250 The literature on the Watergate scandal is enormous, and need not be cited here. However, it should be pointed out that Nixon's efforts were perhaps sabotaged from the outset by some of the "loyalists" recruited into his special investigative units. It may well be the case, for example, that "former" CIA men E. Howard Hunt and James W.

McCord, two of the key Plumbers, had been infiltrated into the unit by the Agency itself, possibly with the aim of neutralizing Nixon's efforts to set up a special power base. See, for example, Jim Hougan, *Secret Agenda: Watergate, Deep Throat, and the CIA* (New York: Ballantine, 1984), pp. 3–31 and passim; [former Watergate burglar] Eugenio Martinez, "Mission Impossible," *Harper's Magazine* (October 1974), p. 52.

251 Jensen, *The Garotte*, p. 127. An interesting parallel can be found in Nixon's attempts to create a new anti-drug agency under direct White House control, in the process circumventing normal bureaucratic channels and controls. See Edward J. Epstein, *Agency of Fear: Opiates and Political Power in America* (New York: Putnam, 1977).

252 For an account of these delicate State Department and CIA initiatives, see Mario Margiocco, *Stati Uniti e PCI, 1943–1980* (Bari: Laterza, 1981), pp. 122–8; and Claudio Gatti, *Rimanga tra noi: L'America, l'Italia, la "questione comunista." I segreti di 50 anni di storia* (Milan: Leonardo, 1991), pp. 88–90.

253 See Alan A. Platt and Robert Leonardi, "American Foreign Policy and the Postwar Italian Left," *Political Science Quarterly* 93:2 (Summer 1978), p. 212.

254 See Gatti, *Rimanga tra noi*: pp. 79–81, 85–7, 95–107, 110–2.

255 Cited by Willan, *Puppetmasters*, pp. 98–9. Compare Gatti, *Rimanga tra noi*, pp. 100, 103–4.

256 See U.S. Congress, House of Representatives, Select Committee on Intelligence, published unofficially as *CIA: The Pike Report* (Nottingham: Spokesman, 1977), pp. 194–5. For evidence that Miceli controlled the distribution of a much greater percentage of the ten million dollar total, see Gatti, *Rimanga tra noi*, pp. 119–21. A good deal of this money went to the MSI and DC, but 3.4 million dollars was provided to an unspecified "political organization created and supported by the CIA."

257 For Clavio as a CIA officer operating under cover, see Cipriani and Cipriani, *Sovranità limitata*, p. 170. This was also strongly implied by Spanish secret service operative Luis González-Mata (in the reference cited immediately later). Yet I have seen no evidence to indicate that he was affiliated with the CIA station in Rome, something that appears even less likely given the hostility displayed by both Nixon and Martin toward agency personnel. Like many Americans, foreigners have a tendency to attribute all American clandestine intelligence activities to the CIA. As a result, the actions undertaken overseas by the three U.S. military intelligence services, the Defense Intelligence Agency (DIA), and the FBI are often completely ignored, despite the fact that these organizations were, during the Cold War era, stuffed to the gills with hard-liners who had a very narrow conception of the national interest. By comparison, CIA personnel were generally more moderate and cosmopolitan, especially in the analytical branches. There is, however, no doubt that Clavio was a covert operations specialist. Among other things, he was the organizer of a false coup plot against General Alfredo Stroessner, dictator of Paraguay. This was arranged so that it would implicate the notorious French drug trafficker Auguste Ricord, who had taken refuge in Paraguay after the 1955 overthrow of Perón, and thereby prompt Stroessner to extradite him to the United States so that he could be brought to trial. The architect of the plan to have Ricord turned over to the Americans was Kissinger himself, and the instrument to be used by Clavio was the Vanguardia Latino-Américana (VLA: Latin American Vanguard), a phony pro-Castro revolutionary group which González-Mata claims to have created many years before. American economic pressure ended up achieving the desired result before this provocation was actually launched, but it provides an excellent example of the kinds of operations Clavio specialized in. For further details, see Luis Gonzalez-Mata, *Cygne: Mémoires d'un agent secret* (Paris: Grasset, 1976), pp. 311–23.

258 Scialoja, "Fu vero golpe," p. 38.

259 Former DCI William Colby specifically noted that in the 1950s the CIA station in Rome always tried to use "outside officers" – those who, like Fenwich, operated under a private cover and had no visible connections to official American agencies – as intermediaries when making unofficial contacts with Italian nationals. The only times that exceptions were made was when the missions were so important that "inside officers"

could alone be trusted to handle them. See Colby and Peter Forbath, *Honorable Men: My Life in the CIA* (New York: Simon & Schuster, 1978), p. 120. Perhaps this was one such exception.
260 See Laurent, *Orchestre noir*, p. 255, quoting an issue of *L'Espresso* without citing the date.
261 See Serravalle, *Gladio*, pp. 94–7. Compare CPI/Stragi, *[22 Aprile 1992] Relazione sull' . . . Operazione Gladio*, pp. 22–3; and Jonathan Kwitney, "The CIA's Secret Armies in Europe," *The Nation* 254:13 (6 April 1992), pp. 444–5. That this was not merely a case of selective memory is confirmed by the fact that Serravalle had prepared a report for his superiors, dated 22 December 1972, about what transpired at this meeting. For more information on the career backgrounds of Stone and Sednaoui, see [CIA defector and communist sympathizer] Philip Agee and Louis Wolf, eds., *Dirty Work [1]: The CIA in Western Europe* (Secaucus, NJ: Lyle Stuart, 1978), pp. 670–2 (Stone), 645–6 (Sednaoui). Compare East German propagandist Julius Mader, *Who's Who in the CIA: A Biographical Reference Work on 3000 Officers of the Civil and Military Branches of the Secret Services of the USA in 120 Countries* ([East] Berlin: Mader, 1968), p. 501 (Stone). Stone was born in Ohio in 1925, served in the U.S. Army in World War II, obtained a B.A. degree from the University of Southern California, spent a year at the School of Advanced International Studies (SAIS), and served at CIA stations in Iran, the Sudan, Syria (from which he was expelled in 1957 for trying to organize a military coup to overthrow the Ba'thist Party), Pakistan, Nepal, and Vietnam before arriving in Italy. Sednaoui was born in Egypt in 1925, attended the American University in Beirut and Columbia University, served overseas in the U.S. Army, and worked for the CIA in Morocco before being assigned to the Italian station. Note, however, that Gatti's informants told him that Stone had become disillusioned about the employment of covert operations after his experiences in Syria.
262 CPI/Stragi, *[22 Aprile 1992] Relazione sull' . . . Operazione Gladio*, pp. 18–19.
263 Ibid., p. 23; Serravalle, *Gladio*, pp. 94–7. The General's reaction to this proposal, if recounted accurately, was equally bizarre. He felt that he had only two options, since he was temporarily unable to consult his superior Fortunato. Either he should refer the matter to Miceli for consideration, in which case he feared that the proposal would be accepted and he would be compelled to engage in illegal policing activities [!!]. Or he could simply reply – naïvely or falsely – that such internal security operations were not part of the organization's formal mandate. He chose the latter approach, adding that he no longer felt that the PCI represented a threat to the system, that he suspected that 70% of the communists would take up arms against the invaders if the Russians sought to occupy Italy, and that (jokingly) if such an event transpired he would have no hesitation about enrolling communist resistance fighters into the secret organization! Not surprisingly, this response annoyed the humorless Stone, and from that point on – if not earlier, as seems obvious from some of his own rather naïve observations – Serravalle was kept out of the information loop concerning covert anti-PCI measures. More significantly, these and other incidents led the latter to suspect that the official "stay/behind" network in fact served as a cover for an even more secret and unconstitutional organization, perhaps identifiable with "parallel SID." See Serravalle, *Gladio*, pp. 98, 38–41, etc. This is probably much closer to the truth.
264 Compare Gatti, *Rimanga tra noi*, pp. 88–90. It is, of course, possible that the more liberal CIA and State Department personnel at the embassy genuinely opposed Martin's plan to support "suspect" groups on the far right, whether for principled or purely tactical reasons. They may have wished to pursue the "opening to the left" policy in a more aggressive way, or simply been concerned about the likelihood that American support for the right, if exposed, would seriously damage efforts to promote pro-Atlantic centrists. Given the current state of the documentation, it is impossible to identify the precise factional divisions within the embassy staff.
265 Tamburino accusations, cited by Flamini, *Partito del golpe*, volume 3:2, p. 698; and Cipriani and Cipriani, *Sovranità limitata*, p. 167.

266 De Lorenzo's direct testimony is cited in CPI/De Lorenzo, *Relazione di minoranza*, p. 69.
267 See De Lutiis, *Storia dei servizi segreti in Italia*, pp. 127–8.
268 See the interview with Cavallaro in Corrado Incerti, "Clamorose rivelazioni," *L'Europeo* 30:42 (17 October 1974), pp. 26–9. However, Cavallaro admitted decades later that what he had denominated as Organizzazione X in 1974 was in fact a reference to the Nuclei di Difesa dello Stato, about which see more infra, note 276. See Pacini, *Le altre Gladio*, p. 266, citing Cavallaro's 1994 and 2010 testimony in separate trials.
269 For summaries of this testimony, see De Lutiis, *Storia dei servizi segreti in Italy*, pp. 111–12. Note that Spiazzi's testimony about the coded message from Venturi was disputed by the latter, who claimed that such codes were never used. Since this chapter was written, two books have appeared about Spiazzi's activities. Compare Sandro Neri, *Segreti di stato: Le verità di Amos Spiazzi* (Reggio Emilia: Aliberti, 2008); and a book by the protagonist himself, Amos Spiazzi Di Corte Regia, *Il mistero della Rosa dei Venti* (no place: Centro Studi Carlomagno, 2011).
270 Quoted verbatim by De Lutiis, *Storia dei servizi segreti in Italia*, p. 142, note 46.
271 Cited by Valentini, *Notte della Madonna*, p. 204.
272 Quoted in De Lutiis, *Storia dei servizi segreti in Italia*, p. 129.
273 See Vinciguerra's testimony, cited in *La strategia delle stragi, dalla sentenza della Corte d'Assise di Venezia per la strage di Peteano* (Rome: Riuniti, 1989), pp. 316–24. This book consists of an edited version of the judicial sentence concerning the Peteano bombing and its background. Further details about this parallel apparatus can be found throughout his extraordinary revealing book, *Ergastolo per la libertà*. Compare also Vinciguerra, *La strategia del depistaggio: Peteano, 1972–1992* (Sasso Marconi: Fenicottero, 1993).
274 This conflation of two distinct secret organizations operating on different levels by Andreotti (and also by Spiazzi) was clearly an attempt to muddy the waters and make it more difficult for the authorities and the public to uncover the actual structure of the entire secret anti-communist apparatus. See Pacini, *Le altre Gladio*, pp. 258–9.
275 See, for example, the analysis in Rita di Giovacchino, *Il libro nero della Prima Repubblica* (Rome: Fazi, 2005), at 19% (ebook).
276 See Pacini, *Le altre Gladio*, pp. 255–73.
277 For the information on "Anello" and/or the Noto Servizio in this paragraph and the next, compare Di Giovacchino, *Libro nero della Prima Repubblica*, at 20%; Pacini, *Cuore occulto del potere*, pp. 154–64; Paolo Barbieri and Paolo Cucchiarelli, *La strage con I capelli bianchi: La sentenze per Piazza Fontana* (Rome: Riuniti, 2003), pp. 19–21; Aldo Giannuli, *Il Noto servizio, Giulio Andreotti e il caso Moro: La clamorosa scoperta di un servizio segreto che riscrive la recente storia d'Italia* (Milan: Tropea, 2011); and Stefania Limiti, *L'Anello della Repubblica: La scoperta di un nuovo servizio segreto, dal Fascismo alle Brigate Rosse* (Milan: Chiarelettere, 2014), in addition to the detailed material in several recent judicial sentences. See also the brief interview with former P2 lodge head Licio Gelli, "Licio Gelli: 'Berlusconi un debole, Andreotti a capo dell'Anello e Fini è senza carattere," *Oggi* (15 February 2011), available at www.oggi.it/people/vip-e-star/2011/02/15/licio-gelli-berlusconi-un-debole-andreotti-a-capo-dellanello-e-fini-e-senza-carattere/?refresh_ce-cp. Therein Gelli stated, without equivocation, that "I had P2, Cossiga had Gladio, and Andreotti had Anello."
278 Limiti, *Anello della Repubblica*, p. 25.
279 For Corniani's links to the Gruppi Savoia, Edgardo Sogno, and the MNOP, see Flamini, *Partito del golpe*, volume 3:1, pp. 87–9, citing Spiazzi's testimony before Judge Tamburino.
280 For a transcript of Spiazzi's testimony, see CPI/P2, *Allegati alla relazione, Serie I: Resoconti*, volume 13, pp. 272–5, 280. General Maletti confirmed that Spiazzi's unit had headed toward Milan on the night of the coup to carry out a strike, and that it was not a mere exercise. See Sceresini et al., *Piazza Fontana*, p. 135.
281 Ibid., pp. 246 (Rosseti), 321–2 (Henke), 280 (Spiazzi concerning Pirro).
282 CPI/P2, *Relazione di minoranza: Pisanò*, pp. 135–40.
283 For the "significant involvement" of P2 figures in the Borghese coup, see CPI/P2, *Relazione di maggioranza* (Rome: Camera dei Deputati, 1984), p. 87.

284 The role played by Sindona in financing rightist groups in the early 1970s was first revealed by Roberto Cavallaro. See further later for some examples of this.
285 See CPI/P2, *Relazione di minoranza: Massimo Teodori [PR]* (Rome: Camera dei Deputati, 1984), p. 24. This was later admitted to Judge Pier Luigi Vigna by Gelli himself. See CPI/P2, *Relazione di maggioranza*, p. 80. Not coincidentally, Gelli also worked behind the scenes to secure the promotion of high-ranking P2 members to the apex of other key security apparatuses, for example, Generals Raffaele Giudice (1974–1978), Marcello Floriani (1978–1980), and Orazio Giannini (1980–1981) to head the GdF; General Enrico Mino (1973–1977) to head the Carabinieri; and – *after* the secret service "reform" of 1977 – General Giulio Grassini to head SISDE, General Giuseppe Santovito to head SISMI, and Prefect Walter Pelosi to head CESIS. See ibid., pp. 80–1.
286 Compare Calderoni, ed., *Servizi segreti*, p. 64, who concludes that Gelli's activities moved in "perfect harmony" with the "documented inertia" of Miceli.
287 For the details found in the next two paragraphs, see Aleandri's testimony in CPI/P2, *Allegati alla relazione, Serie II: Documentazione*, volume 3, tome 4, part 1, especially pp. 35–6, 43–8, 51–4, 56–9. Aleandri had first developed a friendship with Fabio De Felice while he was a student at the "Gregorio da Catino" scientific high school in Poggio Mirteto, where De Felice taught philosophy. The teenager sympathized with De Felice's critiques of the economism and "positivist myths" of modern bourgeois society, as well as with the ideas of esoteric "traditionalist" intellectuals like Evola and René Guenon, whose works his teacher had recommended. After graduating in 1973, Aleandri kept in regular contact with De Felice and Franco Celletti, a mutual friend, and in the course of a series of subsequent gatherings De Felice came to trust his former student so much that he began to make a series of important revelations to him about clandestine right-wing activities. Among other things, Fabio claimed that he and his brother now acted as the behind-the-scenes leaders of Ordine Nuovo, whose ostensible chiefs were Clemente Graziani and Paolo Signorelli.
288 See Willan, *Puppetmasters*, p. 95, citing a 22 June 1989 interview he conducted with Aleandri. Compare the latter's 16 October 1982 testimony before Judge Ferdinando Imposimato, published in CPI/P2, *Allegati alla relazione, Serie II: Documentazione*, volume 3, tome 4, part 1, pp. 57–8.
289 Excerpts from De Felice's letter were published in CPI/P2, *Relazione di Minoranza: Pisanò*, pp. 133–5. Note, however, that Aleandri never claimed that Fabio had met Gelli, only that Alfredo was in contact with him. See, for example, his 23 September 1982 testimony before Judge Rosario Minna, cited in CPI/P2, *Allegati alla relazione, Serie II: Documentazione*, volume 3, tome 4, part 1, p. 48.
290 See Viezzer's 30 November 1982 testimony at the Bologna court, published in CPI/P2, *Allegati alla relazione, Serie II: Documentazione*, volume 3, tome 4, part 1, p. 121; and his 13 October 1982 testimony before the P2 commission, reproduced in CPI/P2, *Allegati alla relazione, Serie I: Resoconti*, volume 6, p. 127. Compare Willan, *Puppetmasters*, p. 95. In the end, Viezzer was himself recruited into P2 by Gelli.
291 De Lutiis, *Storia dei servizi segreti in Italia*, pp. 101–2.
292 This information first appeared in the infamous MI.FO.BIALI file (p. 169), wherein it was indicated that a phone tap revealed that Giudice told Miceli on 12 May 1975 that he had personally intervened with Gallucci to have the former SID chief released from prison. See Calderoni, ed., *Servizi segreti*, p. 67. Miceli initially denied this in his 29 June 1982 testimony to the P2 commission, but when confronted with the evidence was forced to admit that Giudice may have mentioned it to him. See CPI/P2, *Allegati alla relazione, Serie I: Resoconti*, volume 4, pp. 541–2. The MI.FO.BIALI file concerns, among other things, a vast and illicit scheme to purchase petroleum by General Giudice, SID-linked journalist Mino Pecorelli, and Maurizio Foligni.
293 Flamini, *Partito del golpe*, volume 2, pp. 193–4. The contrast between these two letters is perhaps to be explained by the fact that the first was written on behalf of Matta's lodge, whereas the second may have referred to Matta's personal decision. But Flamini implies, perhaps justifiably, that the second letter reflected a change in the lodge's policy toward P2.

294 Calderoni, ed., *Servizi segreti*, pp. 52, 63.
295 De Lutiis, *Storia dei servizi segreti in Italia*, p. 103; Cecchi, *Storia della P2*, p. 145.
296 See Calderoni, ed., *Servizi segreti*, pp. 64–6. The sources for this information were Calore (13 December 1984 testimony to the public prosecutor in Bologna) and Pietro Casasanta (21 March 1985 testimony to same), a safecracker who refused to participate in the first theft because he was a friend of Formisano's. Concutelli was the neo-fascist who, using a special American-made MAC-10 machine pistol that had originally been consigned to the Spanish intelligence service, assassinated Judge Vittorio Occorsio in the streets of Rome on 10 July 1976. For the details of this crime, to which elements of the "Black International" made important contributions, see Corte d'Assise di Firenze, Presidente Pietro Cassano, Giudice Estensore Francesco Carvisiglia, *Sentenza n. 1/85 del 21 marzo 1985 nel procedimento penale contro Graziani, Clemente + 18*, passim. After his arrest, Concutelli personally strangled two talkative neo-fascist *pentiti* inside Italian prisons.
297 See *Sentenza 5 XI 75 contro Borghese*, pp. 131–3, for Borghese's justifications for issuing the counterorder.
298 These remarks were made by Saccucci in the course of a tapped 20 January 1971 phone call to Costantino Massimo Bozzini, one of the "group leaders" mentioned in his address book and his liaison man with FN leader Rosa. See *Sentenza 5 XI 75 contro Borghese*, pp. 268–70, 500. The two also discussed the need to administer an "exemplary lesson" to the person responsible for the last-minute interruption of the operation, but Bozzini replied that the FN could not get a hold of/lay a hand on (*dargli in mano*) that particular individual. See ibid., p. 132. The person in question was not further identified, but it could have been a reference to Borghese himself, although some have suspected Gelli.
299 See, for example, Sassano, *SID e partito americano*, pp. 86–8. This particular left-wing journalist also argues that the operation was prematurely exposed because Antico accidentally informed Genovesi, who was not his regular SID handler and was not among the coup backers within the service. This then made it impossible for Genovesi's complicit superiors to cover the action up, and they thus had no choice but to warn and delay taking action against the *golpistas*. Unfortunately, Sassano cites no real evidence in support of either of these claims, although they are certainly not implausible.
300 See CPI/P2, *Allegati alla relazione, Serie I: Resoconti*, volume 13, p. 276. Compare CPI/P2, *Relazione di minoranza: Pisanò*, p. 139. Note that in late 1974 Condò died of heart disease, at age 42, another of the "providential" deaths of key protagonists which many observers found suspicious. See Flamini, *Partito del golpe*, volume 3:2, p. 722, for his death.
301 Sceresini et al., *Piazza Fontana*, p. 139. Maletti responded to Nicoli's claim, however, by saying that if it was D'Amato, he was merely acting as an intermediary in a long chain leading to the Ministry of Defense or the military high command, if not "higher."
302 See his testimony in CPI/P2, *Allegati alla relazione, Serie I: Resoconti*, volume 14, p. 370; and CPI/P2, *Allegati alla relazione, Serie II: Documentazione*, volume 3, tome 4, part 1, p. 47. Note, however, that in the latter Aleandri emphasized that De Felice did not present any concrete details in support of his conviction.
303 Flamini, *Partito del golpe*, volume 3:2, pp. 511–12, 519–20. Miceli's primary goal was to try and implicate Nicastro in Sogno's anti-democratic activities, thereby damaging Andreotti's prestige and political image. Another target in this operation to gather intelligence about Sogno's subversive plotting – in connection with which the former Resistance hero was seeking allies in both the "black" circles of the Roman nobility and the hierarchy of the armed forces – was Miceli's main rival Maletti, an ally of these so-called presidentialists. Regarding this matter, compare also the note found on 11 November 1980 in the home of Maletti, reproduced in CPI/P2, *Allegati alla relazione, Serie II: Documentazione*, volume 3, tome 4, part 1, pp. 828–31.
304 See Willan, *Puppetmasters*, p. 95, for Gelli's claim that the plotters all returned home because it started to rain! He made this patently ridiculous assertion during a 27 June 1989 interview with Willan.

305 Compare *Sentenza 14 VII 84 contro Orlandini*, p. 97.
306 *Sentenza 5 XI 75 contro Borghese*, pp. 132–4.
307 The sources for these details have already been cited. It should be noted, however, that Delle Chiaie later claimed that Borghese had never seriously believed in the possibility of carrying out a coup, despite the crafty efforts of secret service personnel to fuel such hopes. See his testimony, following his arrest in Venezuela and extradition to Italy, summarized in Sandro Acciari and Pietro Calderoni, "Parola di golpista," *L'Espresso* 33:16 (26 April 1987), p. 15. But Delle Chiaie also insisted that his own involvement in the coup was totally fabricated by Maletti and Labruna of SID, which is scarcely believable given the reluctant but damning testimony of other plotters. Everything the self-serving "black bombardier" says must be treated with great caution, despite the fact that he undoubtedly has a vast amount of firsthand knowledge concerning neo-fascist links to various intelligence and security services.
308 Cited in Gatti, *Rimanga tra noi*, p. 102. Unbeknownst to Orlandini, Fenwich taped this June 1970 conversation and then consigned the recording to Ambassador Martin.
309 For more on the specific views of the "presidentialists," see especially Edgardo Sogno, *La Seconda Repubblica* (Florence: Sansoni, 1974), passim.
310 For the historical development and main characteristics of the DC, see especially Baget Bozzo, *Partito cristiano al potere*; Gianni Baget Bozzo, *Il partito cristiano e l'apertura a sinistra: La DC di Fanfani e di Moro, 1954–1962* (Florence: Vallecchi, 1977); and Francesco Malgeri, ed., *Storia della Democrazia cristiana* (Rome: Cinque Lune, 1987–88), of which five volumes have so far appeared, covering the period from 1943 to 1989; Paolo Possenti, *Storia della D.C., dalle origini al centro-sinistra* (Rome: Ciarrapico, 1978); Giorgio Galli, *Storia della Democrazia cristiana* (Bari: Laterza, 1978); and Manlio Di Lalla, *Storia della Democrazia cristiana* (Turin: Marietti, 1979–82), 3 volumes, which cover the period up till May 1968. For the importance and role of the DC factions, see Alan S. Zuckerman, *The Politics of Faction: Christian Democratic Rule in Italy* (New Haven: Yale University, 1979).
311 See Tribunale di Torino, Giudice Istruttore Luciano Violante, *Sentenza n. 665/75 del 5 maggio 1976 nel procedimento penale contro Sogno, Edgardo + altri*, pp. 31–2, 35.
312 See Cipriani and Cipriani, *Sovranità limitata*, p. 154.
313 *Sentenza 5 XI 75 contro Borghese*, p. 328. Compare Flamini, *Partito del golpe*, volume 2, p. 7.
314 See Flamini, *Partito del golpe*, volume 2, p. 68, citing De Jorio's own claims in an article that appeared in the 29 August 1975 issue of *Secolo d'Italia*. Note that he prepared this account of his background in order to defend himself against charges of political conspiracy in connection with the Borghese coup.
315 Ibid., volume 3:1, pp. 162–3, and volume 3:2, pp. 369–70, 419–20.
316 Ibid., volume 3:1, pp. 3–5, 28, 93, 116–17. Among the other speakers at the public rally were MSI theorist Armando Plebe, right-wing journalist Gino Ragno, MSI Senator Mario Tedeschi, and ON bigwig Giulio Maceratini.
317 *Sentenza 5 XI 75 contro Borghese*, pp. 323–8.
318 CPI/P2, *Relazione di minoranza: Pisanò*, p. 136.
319 For details, see Flamini, *Partito del golpe*, volume 3:1, pp. 22–3, 60–2, 212, and volume 3:2, p. 641. The president of the Amici delle Forze Armate was former RSI official Elios Toschi; the Secretary General was Gino Ragno, who also headed the reactionary Associazione per l'Amicizia Italo-Tedesca (Association for Italian-German Friendship). Among the other attendees at the organization's first meeting were MSI ultras like Giulio Caradonna, Luigi Turchi, and Massimo Anderson; monarchist extremists like Alfredo Covelli; DC rightists such as Possenti; leading "presidentialists" like Randolfo Pacciardi; and *guerre révolutionnaire* proponents like retired General Giorgio Liuzzi, formerly armed forces Chief of Staff, and Marino Bon Valsassina, who had given a presentation at the 1965 Istituto Pollio conference. Immediately after the meeting, a march was organized in the direction of Piazza Venezia, toward the tomb of the unknown soldier. With De Lorenzo at their head, many of the overexcited participants yelled pro-coup slogans such

as "We've had it with the bordellos, we want the Colonels" and "Ankara, Athens, now it's Rome's turn." See ibid., volume 3:1, pp. 22–3. Note further that De Jorio, General Fanali, and Ivan Matteo Lombardo all promoted greater cooperation between the United States and Europe for the defense of the Mediterranean in the September 1974 issue of *Politica e Strategia*, and that De Jorio published a special issue of that journal concerning leftist infiltration into the armed forces, which contained articles by secret service-linked "political warfare" specialists like Brian Crozier, Michel Garder, and Carabinieri commander Corrado San Giorgio. See ibid., volume 3:2, pp. 598, 660–1. According to Aleandri, De Jorio financed the journal, which was sold in kiosks and distributed free to high-ranking members of the armed forces. See his testimony in CPI/P2, *Allegati alla relazione, Serie II: Documentazione*, volume 3, tome 4, part 1, pp. 44, 54.
320 For the general responsibilities of the De Felice brothers, see *Sentenza 5 XI 75 contro Borghese*, pp. 316–18. Compare Aleandri's testimony in CPI/P2, *Allegati alla relazione, Serie II: Documentazione*, volume 3, tome 4, part 1, pp. 35, 46–7, 53.
321 See Aleandri's testimony in CPI/P2, *Allegati alla relazione, Serie II: Documentazione*, volume 3, tome 4, part 1, pp. 35, 47–8.
322 For Fabio's injuries during the Trieste action, see Caradonna, *Diario di battaglie*, pp. 104–5. For his subsequent associations, see the 26 June 1974 SID report reproduced in CPI/P2, *Allegati alla relazione, Serie II: Documentazione*, volume 3, tome 4, part 1, p. 238. I have been unable to obtain further information about the Fronte per la Rinascita Nazionale. The "Centro di Europa Unità" mentioned in the SID report should not be confused with the 1950's publication produced by the MSI's Centro Studi Europei (European Study Center), *Europa Unità*, or the center itself. The 1963 date indicates that the reference was to another organization altogether. If so, it must have been too ephemeral to have left an imprint in the sources dealing with the Italian radical right.
323 See Giuseppe De Lutiis, ed., *La strage: L'atto d'accusa dei giudici di Bologna* (Rome: Riuniti, 1986), p. 192. (This book contains an edited version of the actual sentence concerning the 2 August 1980 bombing of the central train station in Bologna, the bloodiest terrorist massacre in the history of postwar Europe. Officially, the title should be listed as follows: Tribunale di Bologna, Giudici Istruttore Vito Zincani e Sergio Castaldo, *Sentenza-Ordinanza nel procedimento penale del 14 giugno 1986 contro Adinolfi, Gabriele + 56*. Herein the title of the book will be cited to avoid confusion, since the pagination is different.) For more on the OLP, see Flamini, *Partito del golpe*, volume 2, p. 156. The latter author cites a Rome Questura report that lists the organization's founders as "Nazi-Maoists" like Dantini, Ugo Gaudenzi, and Ugo Cascella. No mention is made therein of Fabio De Felice or the other OLP "founders" named by Calore. Note that the initials OLP were the same as those used in the Italian acronym for the Palestine Liberation Organization, causing several leftists to suspect that they were purposely chosen in order to mislead outsiders about the right-wing origins of the group.
324 For the role played by Fabio De Felice in the new "anti-state" strategy adopted by the radical right after 1974, see Aleandri's testimony in CPI/P2, *Allegati alla relazione, Serie II: Documentazione*, volume 3, tome 4, part 1, pp. 38–41, 58–9, 61–8. Compare Sergio Calore's views in ibid., pp. 102–5. For Primicino's remarks, see ibid., p. 113. There is considerable controversy about whether this strategy represented a significant break with the previous pattern of collaboration and collusion between extremist neo-fascist groups and elements of the state apparatus, and a proper assessment of the activities of Fabio (and other ambiguous figures such as ON leader Paolo Signorelli and criminologist Aldo Semerari) could go a long way toward resolving this controversy. For a general discussion of this "new" rightist terrorism, and the view that it was a genuinely new development (with which I concur), see Vittorio Borraccetti, "Introduzione," in *Eversione di destra*, especially pp. 21–4; and Giancarlo Capaldo et al., "L'eversione di destra a Roma dal 1977 al 1983: Spunti per una ricostruzione del fenomeno," in ibid., pp. 198–244.
325 Compare the critique of fascism, from the right, offered by Evola in *Il Fascismo: Saggio di una analisi dal punto di vista della destra* (Rome: Volpe, 1970). This interpretation

has always struck me as odd, to say the least, since without these plebeian, pseudo-democratic, and populist features there can be no genuine fascism.

326 For these details, see Aleandri's testimony in CPI/P2, *Allegati alla relazione, Serie II: Documentazione*, volume 3, tome 4, part 1, pp. 43–4, 52–4, 65–6. Fabio's interaction with Aleandri took place during the period from 1974 to 1979, so it remains possible that these ideas germinated subsequent to the launching of the coup. This seems unlikely, however, given his association with various far right groups from the early 1950s on.

327 Ibid., pp. 55–6 (Aleandri). For further details of the police assault on the demonstrators at Porta San Paolo, which was led by mounted Carabinieri, see Canosa, *Polizia in Italia*, p. 218.

328 For Gelli as the link between Alfredo and the Carabinieri and his assistance in helping both De Felices to avoid arrest, see CPI/P2, *Allegati alla relazione, Serie II: Documentazione*, volume 3, tome 4, part 1, pp. 35, 47–8, 56. Compare Flamini, *Partito del golpe*, volume 4:1, p. 117. For Cavallini's revelations to Sordi regarding Fabio's association with P2 and Gelli, see De Lutiis, ed., *La strage*, p. 132. For the meetings between Fabio, Semerari, and Colonel Santoro, see Aleandri's testimony cited in Salvi, ed., *Strategia delle stragi*, pp. 113–14. Santoro claimed that he did not recall whether he ever met Fabio, but other witnesses confirmed many of Aleandri's claims. Palumbo's background and activities are themselves worth noting. After 8 September 1943, he had been a member of the so-called Fiamme Bianche (White Flames), an RSI anti-partisan formation. Moreover, his anti-democratic sympathies apparently did not diminish in the postwar period. According to Nicolò Bozzi, another Carabinieri officer at the "Pastrengo" division, it was not unusual to encounter prominent right-wingers – for example, MSI Senators Gastone Nencioni and Giorgio Pisanò, and Adamo Degli Occhi of the Maggioranza Silenziosa movement – conferring with Palumbo at division headquarters. Note also that on several occasions Palumbo and his right-hand men in the corps were directly implicated in misleading judicial authorities about the source of various terrorist actions. Among other things, they helped to lay the false "anarchist trail" after the December 1969 Piazza Fontana bombing and then sought to impede and derail the search for the Peteano bomber, Vincenzo Vinciguerra. Santoro played an important personal role in the latter effort. See ibid., p. 110 (Bozzi testimony) and passim (for evidence of Carabinieri interference with the Peteano investigation). For information on Palumbo's affiliation with P2 and the meetings between three high-ranking "Pastrengo" officials (including Palumbo) and Gelli at the latter's villa, see CPI/P2, *Relazione di maggioranza*, pp. 79, 81–2, 90–1; CPI/P2, *Relazione di minoranza: Teodori*, p. 31. Finally, it should be pointed out that the "Pastrengo" division had been assigned a key role in De Lorenzo's projected "Plan Solo" operation, and that thereafter it became a veritable den of *delorenziani*.

329 See CPI/P2, *Allegati alla relazione, Serie II: Documentazione*, volume 3, tome 4, part 1, pp. 36, 55, 71–2; CPI/P2, *Serie I: Resoconti*, volume 14, p. 379.

330 For the formation of a "secret leadership group" within ON by Fabio De Felice, Signorelli, Fachini, and possibly Alfredo De Felice, see CPI/P2, *Serie II: Documentazione*, volume 3, tome 4, part 1, p. 53; and De Lutiis, ed., *La strage*, pp. 193, 200. For Fabio as the key referent within that group, see the latter source, p. 195; for the early 1970 origins of Fabio's association with Fachini and Signorelli, see ibid., p. 130.

331 See CPI/P2, *Allegati alla relazione, Serie II: Documentazione*, volume 3, tome 4, part 1, p. 58 (Aleandri), for these meetings and Fabio's goal of consolidating and reorganizing the paramilitary right. Aleandri said Calore confided to him that one of the chief reasons for the breakdown of AN-ON unification plans, which formed the backdrop for these gatherings, was that members of ON had discovered that members of AN were secretly collecting dossiers on them. See ibid., p. 40. If so, this was presumably being done for the UAR or some other intelligence agency.

332 For the outlines of this new "decentralized spontaneism" terrorist strategy, see ibid., pp. 61–3; De Lutiis, ed., *La strage*, pp. 190–1, 196–7. For Fabio's willingness to employ violence and his involvement in promoting various terrorist attacks, see the former

source, pp. 63 and 65 (Aleandri), and 99 (Sordi), as well as the latter source, pp. 132, 205, 208, 274. Note also that Fabio often allowed wanted right-wing terrorists, such as Roberto Fiore of Terza Posizione, to stay at his villa. See Aleandri's testimony cited in the former source, p. 68. As for the dismissal of the most serious charges against him, it should be pointed out that the evidence against him was primarily circumstantial rather than material. For these and other reasons, many of which were far less justifiable and explicable, he ended up getting off scot-free, like almost everyone else who had been accused of secretly sponsoring right-wing terrorism in the period between 1968 and 1984.

333 See Aleandri testimony in CPI/P2, *Allegati alla relazione, Serie II: Documentazione*, volume 3, tome 4, part 1, pp. 43–4, 65–6.
334 See Aleandri's testimony in CPI/P2, *Serie I: Resoconti*, volume 14, p. 384.
335 For Fabio's efforts to exert practical control over the splintered remnants of the paramilitary right, see CPI/P2, *Serie II: Documentazione*, volume 3, tome 4, part 1, pp. 38, 58–9, 61–4, 68.
336 De Lutiis, ed., *La strage*, pp. 27, 89, 196.
337 Ibid., pp. 87, 96, 196 (quote), 207 (Vinciguerra). For Fabio's goal of provoking a military intervention, see Primicino's testimony in CPI/P2, *Allegati alla relazione, Serie II: Documentazione*, volume 3, tome 4, part 1, pp. 112–13.
338 See, for example, De Lutiis, ed., *La strage*, pp. 190–1, 199–200, 203, and passim.
339 Compare ibid., pp. 382–4, 386–8, 395, 397–8 (Aleandri); and CPI/P2, *Serie II: Documentazione*, volume 3, tome 4, part 1, pp. 102–3, 109–10 (Calore). Calore specifically claimed that Fabio secretly sought to promote P2 goals in the pages of the radical neo-fascist journal, *Costruiamo l'Azione*. For a general history of the post-1976 neo-fascist groups that operated in accordance with the "armed spontaneism" strategy, see Ferraresi, "Destra eversiva," pp. 74–96.
340 See De Lutiis, ed., *La strage*, pp. 77, 123, 132, 193, 200–1, 207, 212, 216–17, 287–301.
341 Ibid., pp. 54–5, 227–83.
342 See Robert Leonardi and Douglas A. Wertman, *Italian Christian Democracy: The Politics of Dominance* (London: MacMillan, 1989), p. 106.
343 For a general outline of Andreotti's political career, see his own account in *Governare con la crisi* (Milan: Rizzoli, 1991), passim. Like all self-serving political autobiographies, this one is highly selective in its coverage, and needs to be supplemented by external sources.
344 For De Gasperi's involvement in efforts to foster anti-communist projects in Eastern Europe and, however peripherally, to protect wanted Nazis, see Mark Aarons and John Loftus, *Unholy Trinity: How the Vatican's Nazi Networks betrayed Western Intelligence to the Soviets* (New York: St. Martin's, 1991), pp. 17–18, 65, 133–4, 237. Along with Hudal, De Gasperi's circle of influential supporters at the Vatican included Monsignor Giovanni Battista Montini, who later became Pope Paul VI. More will soon be said about the latter's clandestine activities.
345 On the active role played by De Gasperi in the American-backed anti-communist campaign preceding the 1948 election, see James E. Miller, "Taking Off the Gloves: The United States and the Italian Elections of 1948," *Diplomatic History* 7:1 (Winter 1983), pp. 35–55. His involvement in some of the more covert aspects, such as arranging for the secret provision of twenty-five thousand American firearms to his government, is described by Faenza and Fini, *Americani in Italia*, pp. 256–9.
346 For the establishment and nature of the Bilderberg Group, see Thomas J. Gijswijt, "Uniting the West: The Bilderberg Group, the Cold War and European Integration, 1952–1966" (Unpublished Ph.D. Dissertation: Heidelberg University, 2007); [former Spanish intelligence operative] Luis González-Mata, *Les vraies maîtres du monde* (Paris: Grasset, 1979), pp. 19–92, which, despite the lurid title, contains some very useful information along with a number of suspect claims; Wim Klinkenberg, *Prins Bernhard: Een politieke biografie* (Amsterdam: Onze Tijd, 1979), pp. 305–22, who characterizes the group in the title of the relevant chapter as "an Atlantic general staff"; and Alden Hatch, *Bernhard: Prince of the*

Netherlands (Garden City, NY: Doubleday, 1962), pp. 235–51, an unabashed sympathizer who argues that the group's meetings have had a "great but indefinable impact on the history of our times" (p. 235). Note that Retinger played a key role in establishing and directing a plethora of early postwar organizations that worked actively to strengthen the political, economic, military, and cultural connections between the United States and the nations of Europe, including the Council of Europe. Some of these organizations, such as the European Movement, were later discovered to have been the recipients of covert funding from the CIA and other American intelligence agencies. See, for example, Steve Weissman et al., "The CIA Backs the Common Market," in *Dirty Work [1]*, ed. by Agee and Wolf, pp. 201–3; and González-Mata, *Vraies maîtres du monde*, p. 20. Compare Retinger's own account in *Joseph Retinger: Memoirs of an Eminence Grise*, ed. by John Pomian (London: Sussex University, 1972), pp. 203–60. He claims that in the end De Gasperi could not actually make it to the 1952 prepatory meeting of the Bilderberg Group, but that the Italian leader was an active supporter of the European Movement who frequently met with Retinger from 1948 on. See ibid., pp. 232, 251. For more on the activities of Bedell Smith as CIA director, see the internal CIA study by Ludwell Lee Montague, *General Walter Bedell Smith as Director of Central Intelligence, October 1950–February 1953* (University Park and London: Pennsylvania State University, 1992). Note, however, that the published version omits most of the more sensitive covert and paramilitary operations undertaken by the CIA during his tenure as DCI.

347 For Andreotti's connections to the American and NATO security establishments, see his own observations in *The U.S.A. Up Close: From the Atlantic Pact to Bush* (New York and London: New York University, 1992), pp. 32–46 and passim. For his relationship with his "friend" Walters, see ibid., pp. 32–3, 169, 181–2, 186–7, 196; compare Vernon A. Walters, *Silent Missions* (Garden City: Doubleday, 1978), pp. 359–67, 567. For Walters' advocacy of an anti-PSI military intervention, see Platt and Leonardi, "American Foreign Policy and the Postwar Italian Left," p. 208. Some sources have sought to rebut this eyewitness testimony, including former CIA director Richard Helms, who claimed, rather ambiguously, that Walters would not have advocated a political project contrary to that of the White House because he was a "loyal man who always did what was asked of him." Quoted by Gatti in *Rimanga tra noi*, p. 57. But when Walters' frequent involvement – indirect or otherwise – in right-wing military coups in various Third World countries is taken into consideration, this testimony seems far less improbable. See, for example, Ellen Ray and William Schaap, "Vernon Walters: Crypto-Diplomat and Terrorist," *Covert Action Information Bulletin* 26 (Summer 1986), especially pp. 4–6. For a specific instance in connection with the 1964 military coup in Brazil, see Jan Knippers Black, *United States Penetration of Brazil* (Philadelphia: University of Pennsylvania, 1977), pp. 43–9, 69–72, 220–1. For a brief listing of Walters' official appointments, which included a stint as a member of NATO's Standing Group in Washington from 1955 to 1960, see John Ranelagh, *The Agency: The Rise and Decline of the CIA* (New York: Simon & Schuster, 1987), p. 757. Once again, however, there was nothing necessarily sinister about the fact that Andreotti entertained close relations with Walters, who was then serving as military attaché in Rome, as it was part and parcel of his duties as defense minister.

348 For the foreward, see Andreotti, *U.S.A. Up Close*, pp. vii–x.

349 See ibid., p. 79, for the Haig reference. For Gelli's links to Kissinger and Haig, to whom the P2 chief was supposedly introduced by CIA Clandestine Services chief Theodore ("Ted") Shackley, see the 1983 SISMI report quoted in Cipriani and Cipriani, *Sovranità limitata*, p. 156. This claim was later reiterated by self-described CIA contract agent Richard Brennecke, a generally unreliable source. See Frank Snepp, "Brennecke Exposed," *Village Voice* 36:37 (10 September 1991), pp. 27–31.

350 See CPI/Stragi, *Relazione sulla documentazione rinvenuta il 9 ottobre 1990 in via Monte Nevoso, a Milano* (Rome: Camera dei Deputati, 1991), pp. 160–1. This particular volume contains transcriptions of the handwritten notes written by Aldo Moro while he was

a prisoner of the Brigate Rosse, notes that were mysteriously found in the same apartment where he was imprisoned twelve years after his 1978 murder. Thus the evidence concerning this aspect of the feud between Miceli and Andreotti was provided by Moro himself, who was Andreotti's chief rival within the DC during the early 1970s. Compare Cipriani and Cipriani, *Sovranità limitata*, p. 159. In this connection, it should be emphasized that the covert infighting between Miceli and Maletti reflected the subterranean political struggle between their respective political allies, Moro and Andreotti.

351 For Andreotti as Morlion's secretary, see Cipriani and Cipriani, *Sovranità limitata*, p. 17. For more on Morlion and Pro Deo, see Valérie Aubourg, "'A Philosophy of Democracy under God': C. D. Jackson, Henry Luce et le mouvement Pro Deo, 1941–1964," *Revue Française d'Études Américaines* 107 (March 2006), pp. 29–46; Walter De Bock, *Les plus belles années d'une génération: L'Ordre Nouveau en Belgique avant, pendant et après la Seconde Guerre Mondiale* (Berchem: EPO, no date), pp. 45–53; and Morlion, "Ik en de CIA: Gewoon belachelijk!," *De Standaard* (12 February 1976). For confirmation of the OSS-Pro Deo connection, see Anthony Cave Brown, *The Last Hero: Wild Bill Donovan* (New York: New York Times, 1982), p. 684. Others have sought to link Andreotti to a bizarre pseudo-chivalric order based in France known as the Prieuré de Sion (Priory of Sion), about which a great deal of fanciful and conspiratorial nonsense has been written (some of which was later incorporated into Dan Brown's conspiracy thriller, *The Da Vinci Code*). For Andreotti's alleged connections to the Prieuré, see Michael Baigent et al., *The Messianic Legacy: Startling Evidence about Jesus Christ and a Society Still Influential Today!* (New York: Dell, 1986), p. 353. For a good short overview of the actual history of, and bogus mythology surrounding, the Prieuré, see Massimo Introvigne, "Beyond *The Da Vinci Code*: History and Myth of the Priory of Sion," CESNUR [Centro Studi sulle Nuove Religioni: Center for the Study of New Religions] website, based on a paper the author delivered at a CESNUR conference in Palermo, 2–5 June 2005, available at www.cesnur.org/2005/pa_introvigne.htm. For more details, see Massimo Introvigne, *Gli Illuminati e il Priorato di Sion: La verità sulle due società segrete del Codice Da Vinci e di Angeli e Demoni* (Milan: Piemme, 2005), pp. 99–172.

352 For Andreotti as a "knight" of the SMOM, see Alessandro De Feo, "Ortolani cavalleria, carica!," *L'Espresso* 27:25 (28 June 1981), p. 25. Compare André Van Bosbeke, *Opus Dei en Belgique* (Anvers: EPO, 1986), p. 148. For more on the lesser-known political activities of the SMOM, see Martin A. Lee, "Their Will Be Done," *Mother Jones* 8:6 (July 1983), especially pp. 22–5; "Françoise Hervet" (pseudonym), "Knights of Darkness: The Sovereign Military Order of Malta," in *Covert Action Information Bulletin* 25 (Winter 1986), pp. 27–38; Kevin Coogan, "The Friends of Michele Sindona," *Parapolitics U.S.A.* 3 (August 1981), pp. 71–103; André van Bosbeke, *Chevaliers du vingtième siècle: Enqûete sur les sociétés occultes et les ordres de chevalerie contemporaine* (Berchem: EPO, 1988), pp. 119–29, 195–227; and Penny Lernoux, *People of God: The Struggle for World Catholicism* (New York: Penguin, 1989), pp. 283–301. Compare the barely fictionalized book by Roger Peyrefitte, *Knights of Malta* (New York: Criterion, 1959), passim, for some juicy tidbits about Vatican and SMOM infighting. Among the many influential SMOM "knights" outside Italy in recent times were Otto von Habsburg (head of several pro-Atlantic pan-European organizations), General Reinhard Gehlen (the former Nazi intelligence official who later headed the BND), Alexandre De Marenches (ex-chief of SDECE), William J. Casey (ex-OSS, Reagan's CIA director until his death in early 1987), James Jesus Angleton (ex-OSS and former head of CIA counterintelligence), George Raymond Rocca (Angleton's chief counterintelligence assistant at CIA), John A. McCone (former CIA director), Clare Booth Luce (U.S. ambassador to Italy), retired General Alexander Haig (ex–secretary of state), J. Peter Grace (an American businessman closely linked to the intelligence community, who helped recruit wanted Nazi war criminals after World War II), William Simon (former U.S. treasury secretary), William F. Buckley (ex-CIA) and his brother James (who headed Radio Free Europe/Radio Liberty after the war), King Baudouin of Belgium, Robert Gayre (a British intelligence officer who

later edited the hereditarian *Mankind Quarterly*), King Juan Carlos of Spain, Valéry Giscard d'Estaing (formerly prime minister of France), and Argentine dictator Juan Perón. Key Italians who were affiliated with the SMOM included Baron Luigi Parrilli (who acted as a liaison between SS Gruppenführer Karl Wolff and Allen Dulles of the OSS at the end of the war), Monsignor Fiorenzo Angelini (an intermediary between the Vatican and Gedda's Comitati Civici), General Giovanni De Lorenzo (former head of SIFAR), General Giovanni Allavena (De Lorenzo's assistant at SIFAR, who later joined P2 and secretly provided Gelli with copies of the confidential secret service files which were supposedly destroyed), Admiral Eugenio Henke (ex-head of SID), General Giuseppe Aloja (Armed Forces chief of staff and De Lorenzo's right-wing rival within the military), Admiral Giovanni Torrisi (a former commander of NATO's central Mediterranean sector, then Armed Forces chief of staff and P2 "brother"), General Giulio Grassini (head of SISDE and P2 member), General Giuseppe Santovito (head of SISMI and a member of P2), Umberto Ortolani (Gelli's second-in-command in the P2 lodge), and a host of influential Italian politicians other than Andreotti (including Giovanni Gronchi, Antonio Segni, Giovanni Leone, Amintore Fanfani, Arnaldo Forlani, Paolo Emilio Taviani, etc.). This list reads like a veritable "who's who" of the Italian political and security establishment.

353 See CPI/P2, *Allegati alla relazione, Serie I: Resoconti*, volume 13, p. 299. Elsewhere, however, Spiazzi acknowledged that Cavallaro was a member of a top-secret parallel apparatus who knew details about the "stay/behind" networks that no military officer had yet revealed to the public. He also described him as an able, intelligent person whose testimony was largely accurate, even though he sometimes mixed the truth with falsehoods. See ibid., p. 278.

354 Andreotti himself noted his affiliation with the Cercle Pinay, which he described as a "small and entirely informal group of Europeans and Americans set up to discuss current world affairs." He added that the Cercle met once or twice a year, usually in Washington at the home of Nelson Rockefeller, but sometimes in Europe; one of these latter meetings was held in Bavaria, where the host was CSU chief Franz Josef Strauss. Pinay, Father Dubois, David Rockefeller, and Italian construction magnate Carlo Pesenti were regular attendees, and Henry Kissinger also sometimes participated. See Andreotti, *U.S.A. Up Close*, p. 61. For more information on the Cercle Pinay and its vast network of connections, both overt and clandestine, see the important study by "David Allan" (pseudonym), *Le Cercle Pinay: Service de renseignement privé de la droite paneuropéenne* (Brussels: unpublished manuscript, 1992); and Adrian Hänni, "A Global Crusade against Communism: The Cercle in the 'Second Cold War'," in *Transnational Anti-Communism and the Cold War: Agents, Activities and Networks*, ed. by Luc van Dongen, Stéphanie Roulin, and Giles Scott-Smith (New York: Palgrave Macmillan, 2014), pp. 161–74. Compare also Pierre Péan, *V: Enquête sur l'affaire des "avions renifleurs" et ses ramifications proches ou lointaines* (Paris: Fayard, 1984), especially pp. 33–54 (for Violet's background) and 55–95 (for the Cercle Pinay). For Andreotti as a "lifetime member" of the AESP, which was founded in 1969, see the organization's 1978 membership list published by Hugo Gijsels, *Netwerk Gladio* (Louvain: Kritak, 1991), p. 152. His name does not appear on the AESP's 1975 list, however, which suggests that he only became a formal member later. For Pinay's SMOM affiliation, see Hervet, "Knights of Darkness," p. 38. For more on Pinay, see Christiane Rimbaud, *Pinay* (Paris: Perrin, 1990); and Sylvie Guillaume, *Antoine Pinay ou la confiance en politique* (Paris: Fondation Nationale des Sciences Politiques, 1984). For more on Otto von Habsburg and the PEU, see the critical work by Knut Erdmann et al., *Mobilmachung: Die Habsburger Front* (Bonn and Berlin: Bundesvorstand der Jungen Europäischen Föderalisten, 1979). Compare the laudatory overview by Erich Feigl, *Otto von Habsburg: Profil eines Lebens* (Vienna: Amalthea, 1992). For the archduke's political and geopolitical ideas, see Otto von Habsburg, *Europa, Garant der Freiheit* (Munich and Vienna: Herold, 1980); Otto von Habsburg, *Idee Europa: Angebot der Freiheit* (Munich: Herold, 1976); and Otto von Habsburg, *Europe, champ de bataille ou grande puissance* (Paris:

Hachette, 1966), among many other works. For more on Fraga, see José María Bernáldez, *El patron de la derecha: Biografía de Fraga* (Barcelona: Plaza & Janes, 1985); Manuel Martinez Ferrol, *Radiografía política del profesor Manuel Fraga Iribarne* (Madrid: Crespo, 1978); Manuel F. Quintanilla, *El pensamiento de Fraga* (Guadalajara: Ocejon, 1976); and Fernando Jáuregui, *La derecha después de Fraga* (Madrid: El País, 1987). Compare Fraga's own accounts of his career in *Memoria breve de una vida pública* (Barcelona: Planeta, 1980); and Fraga, *En busca del tiempo servido* (Barcelona: Planeta, 1987). For Alianza Popular, see Lourdes López Nieto, *Alianza Popular: Estructura y evolución electoral de un partido conservador, 1976–1982* (Madrid: Centro de Investigaciónes Sociologicas/Siglo XXI de España, 1988); and Carlos Davila, *De Fraga a Fraga: Crónica secreta de Alianza Popular* (Barcelona: Plaza & Janes, 1989). Interdoc was an ostensibly "private" organization founded in October 1961 and funded by the BVD that systematically collected information about leftist groups in Europe which were considered a threat to the NATO alliance. See Laurent, *Orchestre noir*, pp. 303–4 (citing a 28 October 1963 SIFAR report, which reveals that Luigi Gedda had participated at the founding meeting). See further Giles Scott-Smith, *Western Anti-Communism and the Interdoc Network: Cold War Internationale* (New York: Palgrave Macmillan, 2012); and Peter Klerks, *Terreurbestrijding in Nederland, 1970–1988* (Amsterdam: Ravijn, 1989), pp. 282–3, note 11. Not coincidentally, van den Heuvel was also the Dutch representative of the World Anti-Communist League (WACL), another intelligence-linked international network with a right-wing political coloration.

355 For the circumstances surrounding the awarding of this contract to Permaflex, see Antonio Caminati, *Il materasso dalle molle d'oro: La Permaflex, l'Italbed e le altre imprese di Giovanni Pofferi* (Rome: Ediesse, 1984), pp. 33–40. Compare also CPI/P2, *Relazione di minoranza: Teodori*, pp. 153–4.

356 Cited in CPI/P2, *Relazione di minoranza: Teodori*, p. 154.

357 For the Corvo link, see Luigi DiFonzo, *St. Peter's Banker* (New York: Watts, 1983), p. 237; "Lombard," *Soldi truccati: I segreti del sistema Sindona* (Milan: Feltrinelli, 1980), pp. 39–41; and De Luca, ed., *Sindona: Gli atti d'accusa dei giudici di Milano*, pp. xii–xiv. In his memoirs Corvo not only makes no mention of Sindona, but also falsely denies that his OSS team established close contacts with the Mafia. See *The OSS in Italy: A Personal Memoir* (New York: Praeger, 1990), pp. 22–3. For documentary evidence to the contrary, see Rodney Campbell, *The Luciano Project: The Secret Wartime Collaboration of the Mafia and the U.S. Navy* (New York: McGraw-Hill, 1977), pp. 180–2. For Sindona's Mafia-authorized foodstuff exchanges in Sicily, see DiFonzo, *St. Peter's Banker*, pp. 24–5; "Lombard," *Soldi truccati*, pp. 37–41; Paolo Panerai and Maurizio De Luca, *Il crack: Sindona, la DC, il Vaticano e gli altri amici* (Milan: Mondadori, 1975), pp. 17–18; and David A. Yallop, *In God's Name: An Investigation into the Murder of Pope John Paul I* (New York: Bantam, 1984), p. 106. The latter work should be used with special caution. For further details about the collapse of the Franklin National Bank, see especially Joan Edelman Spero, *The Failure of the Franklin National Bank* (New York: Columbia University, 1980).

358 DiFonzo, *St. Peter's Banker*, pp. 13–32; Panerai and De Luca, *Il Crack*, pp. 77–85; and "Lombard," *Soldi truccati*, pp. 43–6, although the latter focuses on Spada (and, in later years, American archbishop Paul Marcinkus) and completely ignores the role of Montini.

359 Montini was no ordinary official within the Vatican secretariat, since Pope Pius XII regularly assigned him "particularly delicate and difficult tasks" to perform. Among other things, the pope placed Montini in charge of supervising the Vatican's efforts to resettle displaced persons and refugees in western and central Europe, a task that fell under the bureaucratic authority of the Amministrazione del Patrimonio della Sede Apostolica (APSA: Administration of the Patrimony of the Holy See). As head of APSA, Montini was responsible for overseeing the establishment of "ratlines" – exfiltration routes – and providing passports and other identification documents to tens of thousands of refugees. In this capacity, he facilitated the activities of fascist sympathizers like Bishop Alois Hudal and Father Krunoslav Draganović, who focused their efforts on

protecting wanted Nazi war criminals and collaborators by helping them to escape and avoid punishment. See Mark Aarons and John Loftus, *Unholy Trinity: How the Vatican's Nazi Networks betrayed Western Intelligence to the Soviets* (New York: St. Martin's, 1991), pp. 18–19, 34–6, 58, 85, 116. Moreover, some evidence exists which suggests that Montini was one of X-2 chief Angleton's main informants inside the Vatican during World War II. See ibid., pp. 235–7; and Robin W. Winks, *Cloak and Gown: Scholars in the Secret War* (New York: Morrow, 1987), p. 354.

360 See, for example, the interview with former CIA officer Victor Marchetti, who testified that a large number of bishops and monsignors – including Montini – were the recipients of secret CIA funding. He speculates that Montini may not have been aware of the ultimate source of those funds, but this scarcely seems believable given the latter's extensive experience in covert operations and his close relationship with Angleton and other U.S. intelligence officials. Compare DiFonzo, *St. Peter's Banker*, pp. 34–5; and David A. Yallop, *In God's Name: An Investigation into the Murder of Pope John Paul I* (Toronto and New York: Bantam, 1984), p. 108.

361 For Sindona's participation in these CIA-linked affairs, see DiFonzo, *St. Peter's Banker*, p. 93, 99–101, 102–4; Panerai and De Luca, *Il Crack*, pp. 151–2; and Yallop, *In God's Name*, p. 130–1. Note that Martin called Sindona a "liar" and denied that the Sicilian had purchased the *Rome Daily American* at his request. For confirmation of the CIA's funding of the publication, see John M. Crewdson and Joseph B. Treaster, "Worldwide Propaganda Network Built by CIA," *New York Times* (26 December 1977), p. 37. Compare "Lombard," *Soldi truccati*, pp. 44–5.

362 See DiFonzo, *St. Peter's Banker*, pp. 227–30, for more details about the involvement of Sogno and Cavallo in these particular covert operations. Among other affiliations, the latter two men were both key figures in the Italian branch of the transnational CIA-funded Paix et Liberté organization.

363 This information was contained in a 3 February 1981 affidavit that McCaffery prepared in support of Sindona, at a time when the financier was facing serious criminal charges in the United States and Italy, as well as extradition to the latter country. His goal was to portray Sindona as a patriotic anti-communist and friend of America who would be persecuted for political reasons if he were sent back to Italy. The affidavit is quoted in full in ibid., pp. 104–6. For more on Hambros Bank's involvement in Sindona's business affairs, see Panerai and De Luca, *Il Crack*, pp. 38–41.

364 For Sindona's links to the American political establishment, in particular top Republican Party circles, see Panerai and De Luca, *Il Crack*, pp. 149–57; Penny Lernoux, *In Banks We Trust: Money-Making, Lending, and Laundering from Boardrooms to Back Alleys* (New York: Penguin, 1986), pp. 180–1; CPI/Sindona, *Relazione di minoranza: Giuseppe D'Alema et al [PCI]*, especially pp. 498–501. Roberto Gaja, Italy's ambassador in Washington, DC, from July 1975 to March 1978, later testified that Sindona had originally felt "absolutely secure" in conducting his less than licit financial activities within the United States due to the support he felt he had from the Nixon administration, the State Department, and certain congressional circles. See the latter source, p. 498. Among the other Nixon men linked to Sindona were Harold Gleason, president of the Franklin National Bank, who handled the sales of Nixon's Park Avenue apartment in 1969 and later introduced Sindona to Maurice Stans, the treasurer of Nixon's Committee to Re-Elect the President (CRP) who was implicated in illegal payoffs in connection with the Watergate scandal. Gleason's son, it should be added, worked at Mudge, Rose, Guthrie, and Alexander. Other powerful figures involved with the Sicilian banker were Philip Guarino, chairman of the Italian-American division of the Republican National Committee and an honorary P2 member, and Paul Rao Jr., an attorney for the Gambino "family." Both were leaders of the ultraconservative, Sindona-funded Americans for a Democratic Italy organization, and both provided affidavits to the Justice Department in support of Sindona (along with McCaffery, Sogno, and Gelli, among others). Finally, it should be pointed out that David Kennedy had developed excellent personal relations with the future head of the

Vatican Bank, Monsignor Paul Marcinkus of Cicero, the previously Mafia-saturated Chicago suburb where Continental Bank was headquartered. For more on Marcinkus's role in Sindona's schemes and the resulting loss of millions of dollars invested by the Vatican, see Leonardo Coen and Leo Sisti, *Il Caso Marcinkus: Le vie del denaro sono infinite* (Milan: Mondadori, 1991); and Rossend Domenech Matillo, *Marcinkus: L'Avventura delle finanze vaticane* (Naples: Tullio Pironti, 1988).

365 See CPI/Sindona, *Relazione di maggioranza*, p. 160; and CPI/Sindona, *Relazione di minoranza: D'Alema et al*, p. 368. For Montini's personal role in introducing the two men, see Lernoux, *In Banks We Trust*, p. 181, although not all of her information is accurate, especially about European (as opposed to Latin American) matters.

366 For Sindona's funding of the DC, see CPI/Sindona, *Relazione di maggioranza*, pp. 60–74; CPI/Sindona, *Relazione di minoranza: Teodori*, pp. 543–9. Compare DiFonzo, *St. Peter's Banker*, pp. 93, 101–2; and "Lombard," *Soldi truccati*, pp. 131–49.

367 For the role of Andreotti in the Sindona affair, including his alleged efforts to "save" the latter, compare CPI/Sindona, *Relazione di maggioranza*, pp. 117–20, 141–61; CPI/Sindona, *Relazione di minoranza: D'Alema et al*, pp. 367–73; and CPI/Sindona, *Relazione di minoranza: Teodori*, pp. 524–6, 547–9, 566–73. Compare also CPI/P2, *Relazione di minoranza: Teodori*, pp. 37–40. The majority report, not surprisingly, tends to minimize Andreotti's role, whereas the aforementioned minority reports reflect PCI and PR attempts to indict the entire *partitocrazia*, of which Andreotti has long been a key representative. The latter therefore tend to focus on important but lesser known issues that the political establishment would prefer to sweep under the carpet.

368 See, in particular, the remarks of Claudio Pontello, an influential DC deputy, and Michele Strina, one of Sindona's defense attorneys, cited in CPI/P2, *Relazione di minoranza: D'Alema et al*, p. 367. Compare also Federici's remarks, cited by Flamini, *Partito del golpe*, volume 4:1, pp. 117–18. Note, however, that Sindona also had links to Amintore Fanfani during the late 1960s and early 1970s.

369 For the full range of P2 actions in support of Sindona, see CPI/Sindona, *Relazione di minoranza: D'Alema et al*, especially pp. 378–9, 480–3; and CPI/Sindona, *Relazione di minoranza: Teodori*, pp. 574–87, 592–3. Compare De Luca, ed., *Sindona*, pp. 211–22.

370 See especially CPI/P2, *Relazione di minoranza: Teodori*, pp. 161–2.

371 For Spiazzi's testimony, see CPI/P2, *Allegati alla relazione, Serie I: Resoconti*, volume 13, pp. 292, 294, 286. I have not been able to obtain a copy of De Jorio's article, for which see Flamini, *Partito del golpe*, volume 3:2, p. 686. For his part, Maletti insisted that "Andreotti knew everything, of that there is no doubt." He reportedly had informants everywhere, including in the Vatican, SID, and SIOS. See Sceresini et al., *Piazza Fontana*, p. 142. However, having intuited that the "Borghese coup" would be a "flop" or knowing in advance that it would be called off, Andreotti either held himself apart or was secretly involved in instrumentalizing it for his own ends.

372 De Jorio's argument can be found in another article that appeared in the 29 July 1975 edition of *Secolo d'Italia*: "Today it is asserted that I conspired and even organized an armed insurrection. A conspiracy and insurrection against whom? Against the [state] power in which I myself took part?" Quoted in Flamini, *Partito del golpe*, volume 2, p. 68.

373 Compare the testimony of Spiazzi, who concluded that Andreotti intended to eliminate Borghese and carry out a "center extremist" countercoup. See CPI/P2, *Allegati alla relazione, Serie I: Resoconti*, volume 13, p. 294.

374 See CPI/P2, *Relazione di minoranza: Teodori*, p. 27.

375 See CPI/P2, *Relazione di minoranza: Pisanò*, p. 137. It should be recalled, however, that Pisanò not only had a personal grudge against Delle Chiaie, but also that the MSI senator was himself working for factions of SID. All of his claims regarding Delle Chiaie therefore need to be carefully evaluated.

376 Compare CPI/P2, *Relazione di minoranza: Teodori*, pp. 26–7; and General Rosseti's testimony in CPI/P2, *Allegati alla relazione, Serie I: Resoconti*, volume 13, pp. 240–1, 255.

377 Quoted in Scialoja, "Fu vero golpe," p. 37. Compare Nicola Tonietto, "Un colpo di stato mancato? Il golpe Borghese e l'eversione nera in Italia," *Diacronie: Studi di Storia Contemporanea* 27:3 (2016), pp. 24–5, whose views also parallel my own.

378 See Tribunale di Milano, Giudice Istruttore Guido Salvini, *Sentenza-ordinanza n. 2643/84A del 18 marzo 1995 nel procedimento penale control Azzi, Nico + 25* [hereinafter *Sentenza 18 III 95 contro Azzi*], pp. 290–6. The key excerpt from Calore's testimony appears in ibid., p. 295. Compare the brief summary of Salvini's hypothesis in Anna Cento Bull, *Italian Neofascism: The Strategy of Tension and the Politics of Nonreconciliation* (New York and Oxford: Berghahn, 2007), pp. 40–1.

379 See Marcella Bianco, "Il legame tra Piazza Fontana e il 'Golpe Borghese' nelle recenti indagini giudiziarie," *Studi Storici* 41:1 (January–March 2000), p. 47. Compare the similar wording by Salvini himself in *Sentenza 18 III 95 contro Azzi*, p. 295.

380 Compare Massimiliano Griner, *Piazza Fontana e il mito della strategia della tensione* (Turin: Lindau, 2011), pp. 99–108, 277; and Vladimiro Satta, *I nemici delle Repubblica: Storia degli anni di piombo* (Milan: Rizzoli, 2016), pp. 348–51.

6

THE MAY 1973 TERRORIST ATTACK AT MILAN POLICE HQ

Anarchist 'propaganda of the deed' or 'false-flag' provocation?[1]

Between the late 1960s and the mid-1970s Italy was subjected to one of the most sustained campaigns of right-wing terrorism and subversion in the history of postwar Europe. This campaign, which has been dubbed the 'strategy of tension', was planned and carried out by a diverse assortment of clandestine national and international networks. The glue which bound these disparate groups together was a mutual desire to resist the spread of communist influence, but in other ways their political agendas differed quite markedly. Within this heterogeneous, unstable, and protean coalition, a direct outgrowth of Cold War political tensions, three major factions can be identified.

The most subversive faction was composed of radical neo-fascists, who actually carried out most of the provocations and acts of political violence and claimed, more or less honestly, to be seeking to overthrow the hated 'bourgeois' democratic state and replace it with a new revolutionary regime that would not be beholden to either 'imperialist' superpower. The radicals were in turn manipulated or co-opted by two rival and far more powerful conservative factions, both of which sought to make instrumental use of terrorist violence to strengthen the pro-Atlantic orientation of the Italian state. These differed, however, in their attitudes toward the existing governmental system. The 'presidentialists', who were inspired by Charles de Gaulle's example in France, wanted to transform the Italian political system in an authoritarian direction by reinforcing the powers of the executive branch at the expense of the fractious, corrupt parliament – even if it became necessary to instigate a 'temporary' military takeover and forcibly dissolve the current Senate and Chamber of Deputies in order to accomplish these objectives. In contrast, the 'establishment manipulators' sought to exploit disorder and political violence so as to strengthen their own personal positions within the *partitocrazia*. Yet despite their often bitter internecine quarrels, which not infrequently resulted in mutual betrayals and behind-the-scenes efforts to expose or otherwise sabotage each other's carefully laid plans, all three factions were determined to prevent the left from coming to power in Italy, whether through violent and subversive or legal and democratic means. To accomplish this central objective, the sponsors and perpetrators of the 'strategy of tension' covertly conditioned the political environment by means of a combination of public bombings, assassinations, coup plots, infiltrations of left-wing groups, provocations, and psychological warfare operations.

Initially, this elaborate *sub rosa* campaign was designed to derail the highly controversial and bitterly contested 'center-left' experiment, a wary policy of coalition between Democrazia Cristiana (DC) and the Partito Socialista Italiano (PSI) which was promoted, with varying degrees of enthusiasm, by certain powerful factions within both parties. Following the outbreak and spread of student protests in 1968 and the dramatic increase of worker agitation and militancy during the so-called hot autumn of 1969, this anti-constitutional plotting took on a new urgency and was marked by a series of sensational and often deadly acts of violence, including the terrorist campaign culminating in the 12 December 1969 bombing of a bank in Milan's Piazza Fontana, the popular uprising manipulated by neo-fascists in Reggio Calabria, the 7 December 1970 coup attempt launched in Rome by Prince Junio Valerio Borghese, the car bombing that killed three Carabinieri officers near Peteano in 1972, and the 1973 attack outside Milan police headquarters which is the subject of this study. Other serious actions were thereafter undertaken to forestall an even more terrifying prospect, the possibility that the Partito Comunista Italiano (PCI) might join the ruling governmental coalition on the national level. The most noteworthy of these were a series of abortive coup plots during 1973 and 1974, the 28 May 1974 bomb massacre in Brescia's Piazza della Loggia, the 4 August 1974 conflagration on the 'Italicus' express train, and the 2 August 1980 bombing of the train station in communist-run Bologna, one of the bloodiest single incidents of political terrorism in Europe since the end of World War II.[2]

These violent actions were designed to achieve several overlapping objectives, among which were (1) to terrorize the public into demanding (or at least accepting) the introduction of repressive security measures; (2) to frighten the moderate left into abandoning or scaling back plans for social, economic, and political reforms; (3) to provoke violent overreactions by the PCI's base and the extraparliamentary left; and, in this way, (4) to precipitate an intervention and crackdown, temporary or otherwise, by the armed forces. In short, the goal was to heighten the levels of fear and tension so much that the security forces, buoyed by large-scale support from a psychologically traumatized public concerned about its own physical safety, would be compelled to intervene directly in political affairs, ostensibly to deal with the threat posed by 'left-wing' subversives. The seriousness of the situation was reflected in Italian police records, which attributed 83 per cent of the 4,384 officially registered acts of political violence between 1969 and 1975 to the extreme right.[3]

There were three main factors which lent this 'strategy of tension' a heightened degree of historical and political importance. First of all, the Italian neo-fascists who carried it out were linked in various ways to the so-called Black International, a loosely interconnected network of far right groups throughout Europe and other parts of the world. Second, through elements of this network they became acquainted with the full gamut of sophisticated countersubversive techniques that had been developed by French military experts and were subsumed under the term *guerre révolutionnaire*, which they thenceforth applied more or less systematically. Third, they received technical assistance, logistical aid, 'cover', and other sorts of protection from hard-line factions within various Western intelligence services, as well as from the dictatorial regimes that then held power in Greece, Portugal, Spain, and various Latin American countries.[4]

Two salient characteristics of the 'strategy of tension' unfortunately present acute problems for historical researchers. For one thing, like all clandestine and covert activities this strategy was characterized by secrecy and deception, which makes it exceptionally difficult for an outsider to penetrate the layers of artfully manufactured falsehoods and get at the truth, especially in the absence of comprehensive documentation. For another, one of the most noteworthy features of the organized right-wing terrorist campaigns carried out in postwar Europe was the extent to which they made use of 'false flag' operations. These were covert operations which were not only designed to conceal the identity of the real sponsors and perpetrators, thus ensuring 'plausible deniability', but also to incriminate radical left-wing groups that could legitimately be suspected of having carried them out, thereby stirring up public hostility against opposing political extremists.[5] There were several ways to accomplish this objective. The least sophisticated method was launching a terrorist attack and then publicly claiming responsibility for it on behalf of, or otherwise implicating, an opposing political group that the actual culprits hoped to discredit. Another was forming a bogus 'left-wing' organization, inducing some naïve leftists to join, and then using it as a 'cover' to carry out counterproductive violent actions. Even more effective was infiltrating a genuine leftist group and encouraging its more hotheaded members to initiate direct confrontations with the authorities and other acts of violence. The most sophisticated variant of all involved successfully infiltrating a *bona fide* left-wing organization, rising through its ranks and achieving a position of influence within the leadership cadre, and then directing it – from the inside – to carry out barbaric actions which would generate widespread public revulsion and alienate its less committed base of supporters. All of these methods, except perhaps the last-named, were employed in Italy by neo-fascist ultras, albeit with varying degrees of effectiveness.[6] This article will be the first of many historical case studies aimed at reconstructing key episodes of the 'strategy of tension' in detail, making use of judicial sentences, parliamentary inquests, and numerous other primary and secondary sources.

Gianfranco Bertoli and the grenade attack

The period between the so-called Borghese coup in December 1970, which marked the end of the first phase of the 'strategy of tension', and the May 1973 grenade attack in front of Milan police headquarters was an era of spiraling social, economic, and political crises. Although student and worker protests had subsided considerably since 1969, continued agitation had compelled the government and big business to initiate some long overdue reforms. Traditional social mores were themselves under siege, as the bitter controversy over the legalization of divorce demonstrated, and many Italian citizens not surprisingly found such rapid cultural changes disconcerting. As if to compound these domestic difficulties, international market forces fueled a recession which threatened the livelihood of members of a broad range of social groups, and as usual the disputatious Italian parliament failed to take decisive ameliorative action. These troubling developments precipitated a shift to the right in the 1972 elections, in which the neo-fascist Movimento Sociale Italiano (MSI) doubled its previous percentage of the vote. On the extraparliamentary level, militant demonstrations and violent confrontations were regularly staged by both the right and the left. When PCI Secretary Enrico Berlinguer began promoting an 'historic compromise' between his party and the other leading parties, the DC and the PSI, intransigent anti-communists of all stripes began to feel that their worst nightmare, the entry of the 'reds' into the corridors of national power, was becoming a reality. Their subversive plotting therefore reached a crescendo during this period, and took concrete form in a series of seditious schemes in which neo-fascist radicals, promoters of a greatly strengthened executive branch (the 'presidentialists'), and elements within the political 'establishment' who sought to exploit disorder for their own opportunistic reasons, comingled and colluded in an effort to translate their sometimes irreconcilable plans into reality. The primary organizations involved in these anti-constitutional activities were Carlo Fumagalli's Movimento di Azione Rivoluzionaria (MAR), Edgardo Sogno's 'white' coup apparatus, the Rosa dei Venti group in the Veneto, the Propaganda Due (P2) masonic lodge headed by Venerable Master Licio Gelli, and neo-fascist 'front' groups such as Ordine Nero.[7]

On 17 May 1973, right in the midst of this increasingly suffocating atmosphere of psychological tension, clandestine plotting, and politically motivated violence, there was yet another traumatic act of terrorism, one which is perhaps emblematic of the entire 'strategy of tension'.[8] At 10:57 AM, toward the end of a ceremony at the main Milan police station in memory of Luigi Calabresi, the former police commissioner in that city who had been assassinated one year before by terrorists,[9] a man named Gianfranco Bertoli hurled an Israeli-made fragmentation grenade toward the building from the opposite side of Via Fatebenefratelli. Although falling well short of the entrance to the Questura, the detonation of the grenade nevertheless resulted in the death of four bystanders and the wounding of more than forty. In the midst of the chaos and confusion caused by this carnage, Bertoli tried to melt into the crowd, but he had been observed tossing the explosive and was quickly surrounded and immobilized by a group of outraged citizens. At that point he yelled 'viva Pinelli, viva anarchism'. It was soon discovered that he had an anarchist symbol, a circled A, tattooed on his arm, and in statements made to the police and magistrates after his arrest he claimed to be an individualist anarchist inspired by Max Stirner who had acted alone to try and kill Interior Minister Mariano Rumor, in attendance at the ceremony, in order to avenge the suspicious 15 December 1969 death of the anarchist Giuseppe Pinelli during an interrogation by Calabresi's men.[10] This politically convenient testimony, however perplexing it might appear to anyone familiar with Stirner's writings, was at once seized upon by the press to buttress favored theories about the source of terrorism. Thus right-wing newspapers immediately characterized Bertoli's attack as yet another example of uncontrolled leftist violence and subversion, centrist papers presented it as further evidence of the dangers posed by 'opposing extremisms' to Italian democracy, and the leftist press, mindful of past provocations, did not hesitate to label Bertoli a Fascist provocateur. It is fair to say that the general public, influenced by the popular media, initially considered the perpetrator to be an unbalanced anarchist, and this interpretation can still be found in books by mainstream academics on terrorism in Italy.[11]

However, the picture that emerged during several judicial investigations is considerably more complex, if not altogether different. In order to clarify this, it is necessary to detail Bertoli's background and movements prior to the attack. According to his own account, by the age of twenty Bertoli had become an ideological Bolshevik and had forged links to the PCI federation in Venice. His alleged conversion to individualistic anarchism occurred later, 'first as a visceral reaction' and then on the basis of a more serious examination of various anarchist texts.[12] But the evidence indicates that prior to this supposed adoption of leftist ideas he had already embarked upon a life of petty crime, during which he was arrested and imprisoned several times, became associated with local elements of organized crime, and established connections to some figures linked to the extreme right and secret services in the Veneto.[13]

Among these right-wingers was Rodolfo Mersi, a refugee from Yugoslav-occupied Venezia Giulia who had immediately adhered to the MSI after settling in Venice. In 1953 or 1954 Mersi became a police informant in that city, supposedly on his own initiative. His primary assignment was to discover hidden arms caches, and it was in this capacity that he crossed paths with Bertoli, who was involved in local underworld-linked arms trafficking by 1955 and had tried to sell Mersi some weapons from a deposit in Asiago.[14] Mersi informed the police, and shortly thereafter Bertoli himself was recruited as a police informant and became a collaborator of the Servizio Informazioni Forze Armate (SIFAR) and various unidentified 'international secret services'. This judicial conclusion was confirmed by Admiral Mario Casardi, a former Servizio Informazioni Difesa (SID) chief who testified in May 1975 that Bertoli had been a SIFAR informant from 1954 to 1960.[15] Bertoli thence began to furnish machine guns and pistols to the Fronte Anticomunista Italiano, a right-wing group led by a former Repubblica Sociale Italiano (RSI) supporter which received support from Giuseppe Togni and the chemical industrialist Franco Marinotti, and along with his friend and fellow SIFAR collaborator Giorgio Sorteni – one of the key witnesses for much of this phase of Bertoli's past – he made efforts to locate hidden communist arms deposits. Bertoli did not deny Sorteni's assertions, but put another gloss on these actions by claiming that he had undertaken them to help the local PCI federation keep tabs on its enemies.[16]

This latter claim is scarcely believable, both because it would suggest that SIFAR was so inept that it would unknowingly recruit an amateur PCI double agent as a collaborator and because it does not jibe with the overall pattern of Bertoli's associations and subsequent activities. According to right-wing 'political soldier' and self-confessed Peteano bomber Vincenzo Vinciguerra, for example, Bertoli fell in with Ordine Nuovo circles in Mestre, an industrial town on the mainland across from Venice.[17] Moreover, he allegedly displayed a membership card from the anti-communist organization Pace e Libertà while employed at the Montecatini chemical plant in Porto Marghera in 1964 and 1965,[18] and at some point during the 1960s he shared a jail cell together with his friend from Dolo, Sandro Sedona, a future member of the Veneto group affiliated with the Rosa dei Venti organization.[19] This is certainly a peculiar curriculum vitae for a self-proclaimed leftist sympathizer. Nevertheless, even with his connections to certain segments of the state security apparatus, Bertoli was often in trouble with local authorities. He drank heavily, and continued to engage in acts of petty theft, some of which involved gratuitous violence. He also may have participated in acts of neo-fascist *squadrismo*. Thus, according to information provided to MSI secretary Giorgio Almirante by one of that party's Padua leaders a week after the 17 May attack, Bertoli had taken part in the notorious 16 April 1969 neo-fascist assault on the Paduan city hall, for which MSI provincial leader Lionello Luci and thirty-six others were charged by the public prosecutor's office.[20]

Bertoli's activities before the attack

Despite this previous history of rightist militancy and secret service collaboration – or more likely because of it – toward the end of the 1960s Bertoli began to frequent various anarchist groups, including the Circolo Nestor Machno in Venice.[21] Although his drunkenness, links with organized crime, and occasional admissions of friendly relations with fascists made the members of that group suspect that he was a provocateur, Bertoli was able to obtain the assistance of various anarchists and leftists in 1970–1971, when he sought to leave Italy after being charged with armed robbery in Padua.[22] He was helped in his efforts to expatriate by various members of the Circolo Anarchico Ponte della Ghisolfa in Milan, including Amedeo Bertolo and Umberto Del Grande, who furnished him with the passport of Massimo Magri, which they had obtained from Aldo Bonomi and to which they affixed Bertoli's picture. A post-*strage* investigation by members of the Partito Comunista d'Italia/Marxista-Leninista (PCdI/M-L), a Maoist group to which Magri belonged, revealed that Magri's passport had been stolen in 1969 and added to a stock of other stolen passports gathered by members of the leftist student movement in order to help Greeks who were being persecuted by the Colonels' regime to emigrate.[23] Files discovered in an apartment linked to the terrorist Brigate Rosse (BR) in 1974, presumably deriving from an internal BR investigation prompted by Bonomi's temporary affiliation with that organization, revealed that Bertoli had found refuge at a certain Bevilacqua's house at Saint Moritz in Switzerland after crossing the border in the Sondrio zone with Bonomi's help, a reconstruction which was subsequently confirmed by the court testimony of the individuals involved.[24]

At this point Bertoli's travel itinerary becomes somewhat unclear. Although the roughly forged passport he was using did not match his age or height at all, such obvious discrepancies did not impede his ability to pass through ID checkpoints in several European countries.[25] He apparently went to Germany and Holland before heading to Avignon, France, where Bertolo had instructed him to meet with a Spanish political refugee named Martín Armand.[26] Bertoli then went on to Marseilles, where he seems to have made friends or contacts who have not yet been identified.[27] While in Marseilles he obtained a visa from the Israeli consulate without any difficulty or delays, and then travelled on to Tel Aviv in early 1971. After marking time for a few days in a hotel, he moved to the Karmiyah kibbutz, where he remained for the next twenty-seven months. During this sojourn in Israel, at least three suggestive things transpired. First of all, he shared a room there for some time with Jacques Jemmi, and also often socialized with Jemmi's brother Jean-Michel, both of whom were associated with two neo-fascist organizations in France, the Mouvement Jeune Révolution (MJR) and Ordre Nouveau, and who were then in transit to the Colonels' Greece.[28] Given the nature of those organizations, which will be discussed later, and the destination of the Jemmis, their intensive interaction with Bertoli could be important. Second, prior to his departure from Israel on 8 May 1973, he received several letters from Italy, and one which arrived between February and April that year visibly worried him. According to the testimony of various residents at the kibbutz, Bertoli indicated that this letter provided him with a departure date and travel itinerary, and that it was necessary that he arrive in Marseilles by 15 May in order to meet a friend.[29] Third, Bertoli claimed to have obtained the Israeli-made hand grenade he used in the attack from the armory of the kibbutz where he stayed, hidden it in his room, smuggled it onto the ship *Dan* through two checkpoints in Israel and then through others in Europe, and brought it all the way to Milan with him, but this reconstruction of events conflicts with other testimony and is problematic for various reasons. The Israeli government denied that any bombs were stored in or stolen from the armory of the Karmiyah kibbutz, Jacques Jemmi denied having seen the grenade in the room he shared with Bertoli, and it is unlikely that prior to boarding the vessel the latter could have fooled the Israeli authorities by distracting their attention and shifting it from one hand to the other, as he claimed.[30] For this reason, the investigating magistrates concluded that he probably acquired the bomb in Marseilles, or possibly in Milan itself.[31]

Further mysteries surround Bertoli's stay in Marseilles, which according to the judges 'is one of the most troubling pages of the story because it probably contains the key to explaining the real preparation of the massacre'.[32] Bertoli claimed he went to Marseilles to avoid both passport checks at Genoa, where the *Dan* made a stop, and remaining in Italy any longer than necessary, since there was an arrest warrant out for him, but this account is hardly credible. While in Israel he had probably already learned that the arrest warrant had been rescinded, since he had received several letters from Italy, and after passing through ID checkpoints all over Europe without difficulty it is doubtful that he suddenly felt it necessary to go on to Marseilles because he became worried about a passport check at Genoa.[33] Moreover, as noted earlier, he had already indicated to acquaintances in Israel that his initial destination was Marseilles. Upon his arrival in that port city, he took a room at the Hôtel du Rhône for three days, but actually slept there only the first night, if at all, and behaved in an ostentatious manner seemingly designed to ensure that he was remembered, according to the proprietress.[34] Unfortunately, Bertoli's movements and activities during his stay in Marseilles remain obscure. According to the investigating magistrates, there are vague indications that he met with the person or persons who had summoned him to the city, but the French and Italian police were unable to obtain tangible evidence of such encounters.

At 6 AM on 16 May Bertoli took a train to Milan, where he arrived at 4 PM. According to his own account, he left his baggage (with the grenade) and changed money at the train station, took the subway to the Piazza Duomo stop to 'pass the time' by touring the city center, rented a room at the Pensione Italia on Via Vetruvio, and phoned the home of his old friend Mersi,[35] who had moved to Milan from Venice several years earlier, become a member of the MSI's Confederazione Italiana Sindacato Nazionale Lavoratori (CISNAL), and gotten a job as a waiter at the Ristorante Alfio, located a few meters from police headquarters on Via Senato. That same afternoon, however, he also made an attempt to contact Amedeo Bertolo, the anarchist acquaintance who had previously helped him elude the police by facilitating his departure from Italy. Although he initially denied doing so, at around 4:30 PM Bertoli introduced himself to Seja Anneli at her newsstand in Via Orefici and asked to speak to Augusta Farvo, Anneli's aunt, whose home was known in political circles as the 'anarchist salon' of Milan. Anneli told him she would relay the message, and when Bertoli returned to the newstand two hours later she accompanied him to Farvo's house. After ringing the bell, Bertoli spoke to Farvo on the intercom, telling her that he was an anarchist from Venice who wanted to speak to Bertolo and asking for the latter's address. When he failed to explain adequately why he needed that address, Farvo became suspicious and told him to look it up in the phone book.[36] Bertoli then gave up, although he may have spoken to Bertolo later on the phone, and visited Mersi's house. Although Mersi himself was not yet there, Bertoli stayed and talked to his wife, Antonietta Di Lalla, until Mersi returned home some time before midnight. He spent the time trying to impress Di Lalla and did not reveal the specific reasons for his visit to Milan even after Mersi arrived, but let it be known that he was forced to leave Israel, that he feared he was being followed and watched, and that he felt he was mixed up in things from which he could not escape, at one point even blurting out that he hoped he would be stopped.[37] At around 1:30 AM Bertoli returned to his boarding house for the night.

The next day, according to his own account, Bertoli got up at 7:30 AM, bought a copy of *Corriere della Sera* (supposedly to learn the location of the ceremony for Calabresi), took the subway to Piazza Duomo, went to a nearby bar for a cognac, arrived at Via Fatebenefratelli at 10:40, a little after the departure of Interior Minister Rumor and Police Chief Efisio Zanda Loy, and tossed the bomb.[38] This reconstruction did not satisfy the judges at all, since several witnesses claimed to have seen him in the area of the Questura at an earlier hour. Two employees at the

Bar Annunciata – a different bar than the one where he said he bought a cognac – testified that they served him at 9:30 and 9:45, and again at 10:30, whereas a certain Gemelli of the Polizia Scientifica said he observed Bertoli with two other people on the sidewalk across from the Questura at around 9:50. Bertoli himself was hard to miss, and one of his two companions had long blonde hair and a beard *à la* Jesus. This not only indicated that he had accomplices present in Milan, which he repeatedly denied, but also suggested to the investigating magistrates that Rumor or other representatives of the state may not have been the real targets, as Bertoli insisted. This latter suggestion received indirect support from other eyewitnesses at the scene, who claimed that Bertoli did not actually wind up and hurl the grenade toward the police station entrance, but simply aimed it at the sidewalk and tossed it, thus provoking a massacre of innocent citizens. It was not until he was cornered by members of the crowd afterwards that he yelled 'viva Pinelli', thereby associating himself with and incriminating the anarchists.[39]

Bertoli and the anarchists

These then are the basic facts about the crime and the background of the perpetrator, but as usual there are enough gaps and contradictions in the judicial records to generate confusion and permit different interpretations of the events. There are two main possibilities. The first is that Bertoli really did act alone, that he was an unbalanced 'lone nut' with anarchist sympathies. After all, Bertoli himself never abandoned his claim to have acted alone and in conformity with the historical tradition of anarchist 'propaganda of the deed' gestures.[40] When confronted by evidence that he had long had contacts with or received assistance from the security services and diverse political extremists, he attempted to justify this by saying that as an individualist anarchist he had no problems carrying out an act of revolt using means and opportunities provided to him by totally divergent political circles, including 'forces of the right [and] the police'.[41] He cited as an example the 1893 attack on the French parliament by the anarchist Auguste Vaillant, who he asserted had been armed and assisted by the police, obviously for their own reasons.[42] He also argued, apropos of his association with both radical rightists and some leftists, that '[a]t the root of every extreme position of the right or the left there is always a feeling of revolt against the existing society',[43] the implication being that this feeling provides them with a common psychological bond which transcends ideological differences, a view which has much to recommend it and is nowadays shared by many political analysts and psychological researchers. These explanations are superficially plausible, and perhaps receive some indirect support from the conclusions of the examining psychiatrists, who determined that Bertoli, though very bright and knowledgeable about political and philosophical texts, was a person with an 'absolute incapacity' to find a place for himself in normal society, which caused him to revolt against it, commit crimes, and develop associations with criminal elements and diverse political extremists.[44] This post-facto psychiatric analysis, however simplistic, is certainly not belied by his previous history of violence and criminality.

However, Bertoli's politically convenient account of his own motivations, which despite his assumption of full responsibility had the practical effect of implicating the left in general and anarchist circles in particular, was decisively rejected by the judges at both trials. They assumed, not without good cause, that Bertoli's probable reason for providing misleading and often vague testimony – about the provenance of the bomb, his activities in Marseilles, his efforts to contact Bertolo, his movements on the day of the attack, and so forth – was to protect his sponsors and accomplices, since if he had acted alone it would not have been necessary to engage in such obfuscation. Moreover, instead of viewing his failure to attack Rumor and Zanda Loy as the result of incompetence, they interpreted it to mean that he was not really attempting to harm the highest-ranking members of the government, which in turn proved his act did not reflect the 'solitary revolt of an anarchist', since anarchists invariably aimed to strike a blow against the symbols and representatives of state power.[45] Furthermore, they rightly emphasized that a person with Bertoli's unstable emotional makeup was ideally suited to be manipulated and used instrumentally, and believed there was a 'strong probability' that this was indeed the case.[46] That notion was indirectly buttressed by the testimony of a Paduan mobster with pro-Nazi ideas named Coser, who had previously worked together on illegal capers with Bertoli and viewed him as a 'follower' who was incapable of following through on plans without the support of others.[47] Thus on the basis of both logic and the considerable corpus of evidence at their disposal, the investigating magistrates concluded that there were unknown people behind Bertoli who 'pulled the strings' and that the attack itself was 'inspired by an organized group and linked to a vast and obscure criminal design'.[48] At the time, however, they did not explicitly identify the group they suspected of secretly sponsoring the crime.

This conclusion clearly adds weight to the second main possibility, that there was a larger group of conspirators involved and that Bertoli was merely the individual selected by that group to make the attack. Considering the nature of Bertoli's past associations, that group could in theory be identified as either a loose network of anarchists or groups on the extreme right linked to elements of various Western secret services. The former interpretation was promoted by the right-wing press in a histrionic anti-anarchist campaign similar to those it had previously employed with success in 1969. It was based upon the incontestable evidence that Bertoli had established contacts with anarchist groups in Venice and Milan, a feat he accomplished by claiming to be an ideological sympathizer and attending some of their meetings, and that certain members of those groups, along with one would-be BR adherent, later helped him avoid being arrested by facilitating his expatriation. In addition, Bertoli's ostentatious expression of negative opinions about Calabresi, both at the kibbutz in Israel (where he also lauded Pinelli) and to Mersi's wife, on the surface conformed to his image as an anarchist.[49] It is also possible that Bertoli spoke on the phone to the anarchist Bertolo the day before the attack, as noted earlier, and afterwards Bertolo definitely lied about not previously meeting Bertoli, whom he had earlier helped to obtain the falsified Magri passport.[50] Finally, since the people with whom he met in Marseilles and those with whom he was seen in Milan have not yet been identified, it remains possible that he had obtained some logistical assistance from a clandestine network of leftists, who certainly would have had a motive to try and avenge Pinelli's death, purportedly at the hands of Calabresi, by attacking state representatives attending a dedication ceremony on the anniversary of the former police commissioner's murder.[51]

However, this possibility was also firmly rejected by the investigating magistrates, who found no evidence that any of the leftists who crossed Bertoli's path – neither those who had helped arrange his escape in 1970 nor those whom he tried to contact in Milan in 1973 – were in any way involved in the attack on the Questura.[52] They argued instead that, given his past associations with the extreme right and the secret services, his proclaimed ideology was an 'artificially adopted cover' which enabled him to pursue other goals, that his attempt to contact Bertolo the day before the attack may have been an act of provocation, and that his movements and leftist associations were probably arranged by others in order to 'confound the matrix of the criminal design'.[53] This hypothesized effort to create a leftist 'legend' for Bertoli not only corresponds to the specific reconstruction of events in this case, but also perfectly conforms to the long-established pattern of far right and secret service attempts to infiltrate, manipulate, and implicate the left in terrorist actions. For this reason, it is this latter possibility that must be further explored, though as usual the judges stopped well short of trying to retrace such a politically explosive trail back to its ultimate sponsors.

Bertoli's secret service links

Many witnesses testified that Bertoli began to serve as a police informant and SIFAR collaborator in the mid-1950s, and the reasons are scarcely difficult to imagine. He was then in a very vulnerable legal position, having already established a long arrest record for petty crimes and having just been accused of arms trafficking by police informant Mersi. Like the majority of common criminals who end up collaborating with the forces of order, he was scarcely able to refuse to accede to their demands for cooperation, since the alternative was going to jail. It can also be assumed that a social outcast with an uncertain income would find it difficult to resist an offer to collaborate with powerful elements of the state apparatus in return for even a modest stipend. And, like most other people associated with organized crime, it is likely that Bertoli had rightist sympathies or, at least, vaguely regressive social views which would have provided no obstacle to his being employed in operations against the left. To these general considerations still another can be added. Once people are drawn into a collaborative but dependent relationship with the security services, it is difficult if not impossible for them to unilaterally end that relationship because those agencies have over time collected even more 'dirt' with which to blackmail them. And if blackmail alone fails to yield the desired results, force or the threat of force can always be used to coerce consent. In short, once having fallen into their clutches, Bertoli probably never fully escaped from the control of elements of the secret services. This factor would certainly account for the hints he dropped to the

Mersis in 1973 about being trapped in circumstances from which he could not escape.

His continued association with Mersi, an ambiguous figure, is itself suggestive. There is reason to believe that Mersi may have served as Bertoli's 'handler' at various crucial points, including on the eve of the actual attack. According to some of his co-workers, Mersi made some rather mysterious remarks during this period. On the night of 16 May, after his wife called to inform him that Bertoli had arrived at their home for a visit, Mersi at once called another number and made the following brief declaration before hanging up the receiver: 'Doctor, the train has already arrived, and I will be home in 35 to 40 minutes'. Whom was he notifying about Bertoli's arrival in Milan, and why was he informing anyone at all about his friend's appearance? Nor was this the only disquieting aspect of Mersi's behavior. Shortly after learning about the attack he made a couple of other phone calls from the restaurant where he worked, told his boss that he had to inform the police that an anarchist had thrown the bomb instead of a neo-fascist, then ran out the door and rushed down to the Questura to provide information.[54] How could he have divined who was responsible so soon after the attack, unless he knew in advance that Bertoli was going to commit the crime? Thus the most likely explanation would seem to be that Mersi was himself working on behalf of the covert sponsors of the attack, first by serving as their intermediary to his friend Bertoli and then by helping to lend credence to a false 'anarchist' trail. Given his past history as a police informant, it is not hard to believe that these sponsors included elements of the Italian security services. Unfortunately, the judges did not fully investigate Mersi's curious behavior, an action that might have helped to uncover the identity of those sponsors.

Be that as it may, Bertoli's direct and indirect associations with the intelligence services probably provide the key to illuminating many features of his activities which are otherwise difficult to explain. For example, since he had previously been employed by SIFAR to locate secret communist arms caches, and in that capacity may have infiltrated the PCI federation in Venice in the mid-1950s, it is very likely that his later attempts to join anarchist circles were carried out at the behest of military intelligence for the purposes of collecting information and/or facilitating future provocations. It is even possible that some of the criminal activities he subsequently engaged in were encouraged or sponsored by SIFAR in order to provide him with a legitimate cover as a fugitive, thereby enabling him to obtain, via anarchist circles, the assistance of clandestine, leftist, exfiltration networks, which if necessary could then be dismantled, manipulated, or implicated in criminal activity. Furthermore, if his handlers had decided to send him abroad for a while before reactivating him for future operations, the assistance of friendly foreign secret services may well have been enlisted. Although this suggestion is based upon informed speculation rather than hard evidence, it would certainly help to explain such peculiar things as Bertoli's uncanny ability to pass through several ID checks in Europe and Israel using the poorly falsified passport he had acquired with anarchist help. It also receives a certain amount of circumstantial confirmation in the judges' reconstruction of events.

Traces of possible contact with, or assistance from, the French security services can be found in at least two stages of the bomber's career. Thus when Bertoli went to Milan in 1971, shortly before his successful expatriation, he visited Mersi and told him that he already possessed a fake French passport.[55] This is significant because, if true, it would demonstrate that Bertoli did not really need to obtain a falsified Italian passport from the anarchists, which would strengthen the case for provocation. Then too, the use of a less obviously forged French passport might have accounted for his easy passage through ID checks prior to entering Germany, Holland, and France. Even more suspicious was the failure of the French authorities to produce a list of the calls made from Marseilles to Milan on the days Bertoli was in the French seaport, despite receiving a request to do so from their Italian counterparts.[56] On the surface, this was an unusually uncooperative act. Yet given the specific context, it is certainly possible that their obstructionist behavior was the result — if not of national chauvinism, petty bureaucratic disputes over jurisdiction, or outright incompetence — of some sort of effort to cover up incriminating evidence that Bertoli had made contact during that period with persons compromised in acts of subversion or linked to friendly secret services. One can only speculate, however, since the French authorities will probably never reveal the real reasons for their failure to assist Italian investigators.

Finally, Bertoli's close association with the Jemmi brothers in Israel also may have brought him into contact with French intelligence and parallel police networks. As noted earlier, the Jemmis were affiliated with two neo-fascist organizations in France, both of which had been infiltrated by the secret services or their front groups and thence used to carry out information gathering, acts of terrorism, or provocations.[57] For example, Yves Guillou's (Guérin-Sérac's) international Aginter Presse network recruited most of its French 'correspondents' from the Mouvement Jeune Révolution (MSR) and, to a lesser extent, Occident. According to Aginter and Ordre et Tradition files, it appears that Ordre et Tradition exercised a hidden influence over the MJR, and several documents found at Aginter's offices indicate not only that certain MJR leaders spent time in Lisbon but that several MJR militants received training from Aginter unconventional warfare specialists. These Aginter records, which illustrate the 'privileged relations' between Aginter and the MJR, are substantiated by other sources. A former MJR student leader testified that '*Jeune Révolution* [the MJR's newspaper] regularly published the articles of Aginter Presse', and added that the contacts between the two organizations were 'very compartmentalized and passed through the Ordre et Tradition center, which was the clandestine political organization of the MJR'.[58] And a French police report revealed that former Organisation de l'Armée Secrète (OAS)-Métro chief and MJR leader Pierre Sergent, following his return from exile after the amnesty law of 24 July 1968 took effect, immediately began solidifying his network of international supporters, and had 'very frequent contacts with ex-Captain Guillou, director of the Aginter Presse agency in Lisbon, whom he met with in Switzerland and who appears to guide him in his enterprise [to forge a movement throughout Europe on the organizational foundation of the MJR]'.[59] Given this connection and Sergent's own OAS background, it is surely no accident that the MJR created a clandestine organizational structure and provided counterrevolutionary warfare (*guerre révolutionnaire*) training to its militants. Moreover, within the context of *rapprochement* between the Gaullists and their former far right/OAS enemies which occurred in the wake of the leftist revolts of May 1968, the *barbouzes* of the Service d'Action Civique (SAC) incorporated several MJR members into their units of counterrevolutionary shock troops.[60]

Later, Ordre Nouveau developed even more extensive links to secret service networks. According to Gilbert Lecavelier, a former SAC member who himself handled the operation, the utilization of Ordre Nouveau was among the most successful of the efforts undertaken by the French security services to make use of the extreme right. This particular operation was mounted by Lecavelier through an SAC front group known as Etudes Techniques et Commerciales (ETEC), at the behest of both the Renseignement Générale (RG) of the Paris Prefecture of Police's 2nd Section, which was responsible for 'special operations', and SAC leader Charly Lascorz. After convincing two Ordre Nouveau leaders about the potential advantages of collusion with the RG, Lecavelier was appointed as a 'technical counselor' to the neo-fascist organization's security service and given a free hand to set up a special group of militants to collect intelligence, by means of infiltrations and the theft of files, on the radical left. The information this group gathered soon began to flow into dossiers at ETEC's office, whence copies were disseminated to the RG's 2nd Section and Lascorz, who in turn made them available to the West German Bundesnachrichtendienst (BND) through an intermediary, a former Abwehr operative named Dr Scheuermann. In exchange, Lecavelier managed, with the help of the RG, to get official bans of Ordre Nouveau's meetings lifted and to 'obtain the benevolent neutrality of the police' in various circumstances, ranging from non-interference in the organization's leafletting campaigns to having arrested Ordre Nouveau members released from jail without being charged.[61]

Although it is possible that Bertoli's close association with the Jemmi brothers at the Karmiyah kibbutz was purely coincidental, this seems rather unlikely in view of Bertoli's own links to the Italian far right and security services and the documented collusion between the French neo-fascist organizations with which the Jemmis were affiliated and various intelligence networks.[62] These facts suggest that the Israeli authorities may also have been involved in a broader secret service operation to exfiltrate Bertoli from Europe and shelter him abroad, which would go a long way toward explaining how he managed, allegedly with a badly forged passport, first to obtain a visa from the Israeli consulate in Marseilles with no delays and then to renew it every three months once he arrived in Israel. As the investigating judges pointed out, the Israelis normally check visa applications – and presumably the documents upon which those applications are based – with special thoroughness.[63] Any form of *sub rosa* Israeli participation in such an operation in turn strengthens the possibility that Bertoli was telling the truth when he claimed to have obtained the bomb from the kibbutz where he was staying and then brought it through Israeli checkpoints at the time of his departure for Marseilles in May 1973. In this event official Israeli denials regarding the provenance of the device would be entirely predictable, and should not be accepted at face value any more than similar denials made by other governments which are trying to hide their participation in sensitive covert operations. Nevertheless, Bertoli could have obtained an Israeli-made hand grenade from anyone able to acquire international arms, and there is absolutely no evidence either that organs of the Israeli government furnished Bertoli with that particular grenade or that they were aware of what the final objective of his mission was. If the Israeli secret service was involved at all in the Bertoli operation, which is far from certain, it was probably in exchange for reciprocal favors provided by one or more of its European counterparts and involved nothing more than arranging for Bertoli to stay in Israel and make contact with the Jemmis.

Bertoli and parallel 'action' networks in Italy

Throughout most of his adult life, then, Bertoli maintained contacts with elements linked to various secret services and the extreme right, most of which had at some point, if not regularly, been involved in acts of violence, terrorism, and provocation. Although attempts to clarify the precise role played by foreign intelligence agencies and neo-fascists in Bertoli's activities must remain speculative given the absence of documentary proof, the direct or indirect involvement of their Italian counterparts is scarcely in doubt. The final piece of the puzzle concerning the identity of Bertoli's sponsors seems to have been provided by Padua magistrate Giovanni Tamburino, who in 1973 and 1974 conducted a painstaking judicial investigation into the activities of the Rosa dei Venti network, a quasi-official clandestine umbrella organization that apparently consisted of over twenty right-wing civilian paramilitary groups. The two main elements of this network were a group of Ligurian financiers associated with the remnants of Prince Borghese's Fronte Nazionale and various neo-fascist elements, the most important of which seem to have operated in the Veneto region. Among the leading figures in the Rosa dei Venti were retired Bersaglieri general and Movimento Nazionale di Opinione Pubblica (MNOP) co-founder Francesco Nardella, his successor as head of NATO's Ufficio Guerra Psicologica headquarters in Verona, Colonel Rolando Dominioni, Carabinieri informant and alleged international intelligence operative Dario Zagolin, and two high-ranking Fascist officials from the Repubblica Sociale Italiano (RSI) era, ex-paratrooper Sandro Rampazzo and amnestied Brigate Nere 'war criminal' Eugenio Rizzato.

Documents found in various police searches revealed that the members of the organization were employing a top secret military code system that was no longer in official use (FARILC 59), that they had prepared a detailed insurrectional plan, a stock of blank death sentences, and a list of over 1,700 individuals slated for 'neutralization', that they had accumulated significant quantities of weapons, and that they were engaging in a variety of intelligence-gathering activities.[64]

Still more significantly, Tamburino soon discovered that a key coordinator of these anti-constitutional Rosa forces was Major Amos Spiazzi, an artillery and intelligence officer who was also a member of an even more secretive, higher level group which journalists referred to somewhat imprecisely as 'parallel SID'. According to the testimony of certain key members of this latter organization who had been arrested and charged with political conspiracy, including Spiazzi himself, former CISNAL activist Roberto Cavallaro, and SID chief Vito Miceli, 'parallel SID' was a clandestine structure operating outside of but parallel to the official chain of command of the Italian military intelligence services. More unsettling details were soon forthcoming – that this structure was directed by a mixed civilian and military leadership group consisting of high-ranking European and American intelligence officials, politicians, and industrialists, that it held regular meetings in Brussels, that it was composed exclusively of pro-Atlantic loyalists who were dedicated to preventing a communist takeover in Italy, that it was financed in part by Italian and foreign multinational corporations, and that it was secretly backed by NATO's security apparatus. Although Spiazzi and Miceli sought to emphasize its legitimate defensive functions, if not its strict constitutional legality, Cavallaro acknowledged that its actual methods were anything but defensive or democratic. He claimed that from the mid-1960s on it had covertly manipulated, financed, and directed right- and left-wing terrorist groups, via intermediaries, to undertake a strategy of destabilization. The immediate objective was to provoke the security forces into activating emergency contingency plans designed to re-establish public order, an intervention which the plotters felt was necessary to ensure their long-term goal of maintaining the Atlanticist orientation of the Italian government. Such attempts to 'destabilize in order to stabilize' constituted the very essence of the terrorist 'strategy of tension'.[65]

Unfortunately, Judge Tamburino's investigation was derailed just as he was about to expose some of the Rosa organization's primary behind-the-scenes sponsors. Two months after he issued a 31 October 1974 arrest warrant for Miceli, whom he accused of organizing a 'secret association of military personnel and civilians in order to provoke an armed insurrection and . . . an illegal transformation of the constitution of the State and the form of government by means of the intervention of the armed forces', the Rome Court of Appeals transferred the responsibility for handling that investigation to the more politically responsive judicial organs of the capital.[66] Furthermore, the materials accumulated by Tamburino, as well as his preliminary reconstruction of the facts, were then rendered inaccessible to the public by the authorities. However, from the citations found in the invaluable study by investigative journalist Gianni Flamini, the leading specialist on the 'strategy of tension' in Italy, it appears that he at least was able to examine some of this documentation before it was covered by state secrecy laws. The following summary is therefore based upon his reconstruction, the accuracy of which cannot be confirmed in all of its details without access to the evidence gathered by Tamburino.

According to Flamini, it was a letter Bertoli received in Israel from Mestre sometime around the beginning of May 1973 which provided him with instructions about the mission he was to carry out, a mission for which Rizzato, the civilian leader of the Rosa dei Venti group in the Veneto, was to provide technical assistance and monetary compensation. Due to delays in receiving funds from the Rosa's

Genoan financial backers, Rizzato began to have second thoughts about the operation, but a bomb detonated outside the window of his home in Padua on 14 May 1973 persuaded him to follow through with his agreed upon contribution to the mission. Having already supposedly missed a scheduled appointment with Bertoli, Rizzato hastily visited his co-conspirator Spiazzi, who was then participating in military exercises in Calabria, in an effort to contact Cavallaro, Spiazzi's intermediary to the financiers. After meeting with Cavallaro in Verona and pressuring him to make contact with the Genoese, within two days Rizzato managed to obtain a portion of the one million lire Giancarlo De Marchi consigned to Cavallaro, then allegedly provided it to Bertoli in accordance with Spiazzi's instructions. Flamini hence concluded that 'parallel SID', the cell-like intelligence apparatus that covertly directed the activities of the Rosa dei Venti structure and was also linked to the 'Gladio' stay/behind paramilitary networks, was the organization which covertly sponsored the 'anarchist' Bertoli's attack on the Milan Questura. According to this reconstruction, the latter's bloody provocation was meant to spark civil disturbances which would in turn precipitate the long-planned intervention of certain military units.[67]

In support of this interpretation, Flamini provided details that point to Veneto links in the attack, which would in any case be logical to expect given Bertoli's prior interactions with extreme rightists and secret service personnel in that area. First of all, Flamini postulates that at some point during his previous stays in Padua Bertoli had been in contact with Franco Freda, a key figure in the 'strategy of tension' and one of those accused of material involvement in the 1969 Piazza Fontana bombing. After all, Padua was the place where Bertoli committed the robbery that resulted in the issuance of an arrest warrant in his name, as well as the site where he allegedly participated in neo-fascist attacks in 1969. In this connection, it should be remembered that Freda had close contacts with members of MSI youth groups, Ordine Nuovo, and Avanguardia Nazionale, and that his Ezzelino bookstore on Via Patriarcato in Padua was a well-known hangout for local right-wing extremists. It is thus all the more interesting to learn that the Italian-language copy of Max Stirner's *Der Einzige und sein Eigentum* which was found in Bertoli's baggage at the Milan train station turned out to have been published by the Casa Editrice Ennesse, one of the publishing houses owned by Freda's long-term collaborator, Giovanni Ventura.[68] Furthermore, there was a certain neo-fascist and secret service operative nicknamed 'Jesus Christ' who was involved in arms trafficking in the Veneto and had links to the Rosa plotters. Flamini speculates that this could have been the long-haired, bearded figure seen with Bertoli on the morning of the massacre, and that he could have provided the latter with the grenade.[69] Although this is certainly possible, especially considering that various radical rightists were then posing as leftists by growing their hair long and adopting a countercultural image (as the case of neo-fascist provocateur Mario Merlino perfectly illustrates), there is no proof that 'Jesus Christ' was the person with Bertoli. Flamini further claimed that a car awaited Bertoli near the Questura, perhaps to drive him to the train station to pick up his baggage, and that he received radio instructions before tossing the grenade.[70] All of this fits in with the supposition of a Veneto source for that device.

These suggestive details, which presumably derive from material gathered in Tamburino's investigation, are at present impossible for outsiders to verify. Nevertheless the judge himself, who had access to a vast corpus of now inaccessible material, concluded that 'Bertoli appears indubitably linked to some Rosa dei Venti bigwigs [*personaggi*]' and that 'profound connections' existed between his own investigation and the one concerning the massacre in Milan, an opinion shared at least in part by Judge Antonio Lombardi, who was conducting the latter.[71] Lombardi made it a point to question some key Rosa dei Venti protagonists, including Cavallaro and Giampaolo Porta Casucci, and ended up accusing Rizzato of participating in the attack. Bertoli also came under investigation in the Movimento d'Azione Rivoluzionaria/Carlo Fumagalli inquest. In the end, however, due to the artificial jurisdictional separation of all these interrelated inquiries and the usual docility of the Rome magistrates in the face of political pressure, the charges against Rizzato were dropped for lack of evidence at the Bertoli trial, and Bertoli's name was extracted from both the MAR and the Rome Borghese/Rosa trials. Once again, the most fruitful but elusive trails were sabotaged and prematurely abandoned by those charged with getting to the bottom of an important terrorist incident.

If it is assumed that Bertoli was manipulated or controlled by someone connected to the Rosa dei Venti or 'parallel SID', the question then becomes what faction within that organizational complex was directing him and what was the real purpose of his attack. Was his act really meant to provoke an outright military intervention, as Flamini assumed, or was it intended to derail the plans of those military and civilian extremists who genuinely sought to instigate such a coup? Cavallaro later testified that the projected 2 June 1973 date of the plotters' planned military response was shipwrecked because someone committed a 'false move' and failed to carry out his task. Although this remark could refer to Fumagalli's inaction in the Valtellina, it may be even more applicable to Bertoli's bungled attack on Rumor, a regular target of the radical right in those years.[72] However, it seems more probable that Bertoli's action was sponsored by more 'moderate' Atlanticist groups connected with the political establishment, which sought to exploit fears of a coup so as to promote either a 'presidentialist' takeover or to preserve and extend their own base of power within the existing system, precisely in order to sabotage the coup the ultras had scheduled for summer. On the basis of the currently available evidence, it is impossible to be certain.

In either case, there was an embarrassing postscript to the Bertoli affair for the powerful domestic and international political circles which had fomented anti-constitutional actions and sought to derail various judicial inquiries during the 1970s. At the end of 1990, an almost empty file with the name Gianfranco Bertoli was found by Judge Felice Casson among the classified records of civilians recruited into the top secret 'Gladio' organization, which were stored just outside Rome at the Servizio Informazioni per la Sicurezza Militare's (SISMI) archive in Fort Braschi. The secret services immediately claimed that this was not the same Bertoli who had made the 1973 attack, and that it was a case of a simple homonym. Their hurried rebuttal came as no surprise to anyone, since if they had admitted that this was the same Bertoli it would have confirmed the disquieting suspicion that the names of various perpetrators of terrorist violence would be included if the lists of 'gladiators' were all made public, a suspicion which later proved to be entirely justified. Although it is true that Bertoli is a fairly common Italian surname, in the end the authorities were unable to provide solid evidence that Bertoli the gladiator was someone other than Bertoli the terrorist, something that would have been easy enough to do had they really been two separate people. In lieu of such proof, one is certainly entitled to doubt these official claims given the strong possibility that the attack was covertly sponsored by elements of those very same secret services. Indeed, SISMI's botched post-facto attempt to demonstrate that there were two different Bertolis only increases the suspicion that the man who carried out the May 1973 massacre was the very same person who had earlier been recruited into the 'Gladio' stay/behind paramilitary network.[73] Regardless of this question of identity, it is absolutely certain that there are many obscure features of the Bertoli case which, if fully clarified, might help illuminate important aspects of the history of Italian terrorism and subversion during the early 1970s.

Conclusion

The preceding reconstruction has provided various indications that Gianfranco Bertoli's 1973 terrorist attack in Milan represented more than a simple case of oppositional left-wing violence or anarchist-inspired 'propaganda of the deed'. This does not mean, however, that Bertoli was not a highly alienated, psychologically unbalanced, and rather pathetic individual who seems to have found solace in anarchist or egoist doctrines, which provided him with a moral and political justification for taking out his frustration against the world by committing brutal acts of violence. His entire personal history demonstrated that he was a person with violent propensities and few scruples, and as such he was temperamentally well-suited to carry out the grenade attack for which he was arrested and later sentenced to life imprisonment. In that sense, he conveniently conformed to the distorted but nonetheless widespread public perception of 'anarchists' as squalid, immoral individuals capable of anything and everything. Yet this same sordid background as an oft-imprisoned petty criminal and informant made him particularly vulnerable to blackmail and threats, as well as ideally suited to be used instrumentally and set up as a 'fall guy' or 'patsy', by agents of the state or various clandestine political groups with whom he came into contact. He himself seems to have been painfully aware of the hopelessness of his overall position, as his anxious remarks to Mersi on the eve of the attack imply, and it is perhaps this fatalistic conviction that has been responsible for his otherwise inexplicable silence from the time of his arrest until the present day.[74]

Therefore, although many aspects of the crime and its background remain murky, the investigating magistrates were apparently justified in concluding that Bertoli was secretly manuevered by elements of particular parallel apparatuses operating within the bosom of the Italian secret services, perhaps in collusion with their counterparts in other countries. If this was in fact the case, it can scarcely be doubted that his violent deed was specifically choreographed for political exploitation by one of the three rival factions engaged in manipulating and making instrumental use of both rightist and leftist terrorism in Italy. It is not yet possible to personally identify the covert sponsors of the attack, but given the political context and the current state of the evidence it would certainly be unwise to assume that Bertoli was an 'individualist anarchist' who acted alone and of his own free will. His lengthy background as a SIFAR operative, his continual contacts with neo-fascist militants, the many strange 'coincidences' that abound in the case, and his own inability to provide a satisfactory explanation for his actions all make it difficult to accept such a reassuring scenario at face value. The May 1973 attack at the Milan police headquarters may not constitute the most representative example of the lengthy campaign of terror and political conditioning that has come to be known as the 'strategy of tension', as right-wing bomber Vincenzo Vinciguerra has implied – surely that dubious honor belongs to the 12 December 1969 Piazza Fontana massacre – but it does lend additional circumstantial support to the case of those who postulate the existence of covert state sponsorship or state manipulation of key incidents of Italian terrorism during the so-called years of lead.

Addendum

Since this article was first published, new revelations have been made concerning this 17 May 1973 attack against Milan police headquarters, revelations that only strengthen the conclusions therein that the self-proclaimed anarchist Gianfranco Bertoli had – knowingly or unwittingly – carried out the attack with the assistance of other political forces operating behind the scenes. For reasons that are not entirely clear, Bertoli himself has continued to insist that he was a bona fide anarchist who acted alone, even though he also acknowledged that, like other anarchists in the past, he would have had no qualms about accepting aid provided by rival or opposed political forces.[75] However, the evidence now clearly indicates that, whatever his own personal ideological beliefs, he did not carry out the attack entirely on his own initiative. In his 1998 sentence against members of La Fenice and Ordine Nuovo (ON), Investigating Magistrate Guido Salvini devoted two chapters to the Bertoli case. The first analyzed the testimony of neo-fascist *pentiti* Carlo Digilio and Martino Siciliano, who provided evidence that Bertoli, prior to carrying out the attack, was in contact with, and being aided and manipulated by, key members of the ON cells in Venice/Mestre and Trieste. The second provided indications that Bertoli's attack on Interior Minister Mariano Rumor in Via Fatebenefratelli was related to Rumor's prior unwillingness to declare a 'state of emergency' in the wake of the 12 December 1969 Piazza Fontana massacre, which therefore linked the two attacks to a single 'destabilization' strategy.[76]

To make a long and complicated story short, it now seems that Bertoli had served as an informant (code-named 'Negro') for SIFAR and SID for a longer period than was originally thought. Although his activities as an informant for SIFAR were temporarily terminated in 1960, he was later apparently hired by its successor SID to provide further information during the period between 1966 and 1971.[77] Moreover, according to the testimony of Digilio, (1) the Venice/Mestre ON cell headed by Carlo Maria Maggi was trying to organize an attack to 'wipe out' (*spazzare via*) Rumor, an enemy of the right, but that after Vincenzo Vinciguerra refused to carry out such an attack, Maggi sought to use Bertoli, an impoverished, attention- and respect-seeking individualist anarchist based in Mestre who was ready for anything and wanted to 'avenge' the anarchist Giuseppe Pinelli, to do so; (2) Maggi and, in particular, ex-mercenary and fellow ON member Giorgio Boffelli knew Bertoli personally; (3) Digilio encountered Bertoli in person in early May 1973 at a residence in Verona on Via Stella, along with Francesco Neami and Marcello Soffiati, who had transported the anarchist there; (4) those ON militants, along with Maggi, were training Bertoli to carry out such an attack and 'brainwashing' him to help him convince the police that he acted alone, in exchange for beer, food, and a small amount of money; (5) Digilio saw two or three hand grenades on those premises; (6) Bertoli told him he had spent some time in Israel; and (7) after the attack failed to kill Rumor, Maggi was angry and demanded to know what had happened.[78] For his part, Siciliano testified that (1) Bertoli knew ON's Paolo Morin as well as Maggi, and that he kept in touch with Morin during his sojourn in Israel; and (2) after the 1973 attack in Milan, Delfo Zorzi indicated that it was connected to ON's strategy. Digilio was told that Sergio Minetto had procured the money to pay Bertoli from the Americans, but testified that his contact, Captain David Carret from U.S. Army intelligence, was previously unaware of and in fact unhappy about Bertoli's risky failed attack. Others claimed that Israeli intelligence operatives knew about and were favorably disposed to an attack on Rumor, and that there was a pro-Israeli 'defense of the West' orientation amongst some ON militants in the Veneto, twenty of whom were allegedly brought to Israel to receive paramilitary training.[79] Judge Salvini therefore concluded that Bertoli, although motivated to carry out the Milan attack for his own idiosyncratic personal and ideological reasons, received material aid and a 'decisive' psychological push to do so from the ON ultras rather than the anarchist milieu.[80]

The second major finding is that Rumor was personally blamed by the neo-fascist perpetrators of the 12 December 1969 bombings in Milan and Rome, which were intended to implicate the anarchist milieu in terrorism, for not authorizing the declaration of a 'state of emergency' or the activation of anti-insurrection military contingency plans directed against the far left. Thereafter neo-fascist circles bore a tremendous animosity towards Rumor, which they reportedly sought to translate into action by periodically hatching assassination plots against the DC leader, who was favorably disposed towards collaborating and forming governments with the PSI.[81] Moreover, in refusing to declare a 'state of emergency' and authorize military action, Rumor allegedly blocked a far more serious scheme promoted by conservative factions of the DC (and their American backers?) to temporarily dissolve the Parliament and sabotage the formation or continuation of any government coalition that included the PSI. According to the testimony of 'Walter Rubini' (pseudonym for PCI-affiliated researcher Fulvio Bellini), the author of an important 1978 book titled *Il segreto della Repubblica* who later testified before the court authorities on 2 April 1997, there was a tremendous institutional conflict in 1969 within the DC between the pro-American *corrente* headed by Giuseppe Saragat and the left-leaning *corrente* headed by Aldo Moro. Rumor was originally aligned with the Saragat faction, but after witnessing the overwhelming popular response to the Piazza Fontana *strage*, he allied himself with Moro and refused to facilitate an authoritarian involution of the Italian government. In an effort to compromise, however, Rumor did sanction the official promotion of the so-called red trail in the wake of the 12 December bombings, rather than an in-depth investigation of the 'black trail' that would have led to exposing the involvement of the Freda cell, the secret compartmentalized cellular structure of ON, and Avanguardia Nazionale (AN) in the provocation. Bellini attributed this eye-opening information, which was elaborated in chapters 6 and 7 of his book, to an English journalist affiliated with Reuters, who was actually an intelligence operative – information that later seemed to be confirmed in the 'Moro memorial' found in 1978 in Via Monte Nevoso in Milan, wherein Bertoli's attack on Rumor was also alluded to four times in connection with the Piazza Fontana bombing.[82] In sum, a terrorist 'false flag' operation that failed to achieve its objectives in 1969 laid the groundwork for Bertoli's 1973 hand grenade attack at Milan's police headquarters.

Acknowledgements

The author would like to thank the Inst. on Global Conflict and Cooperation for providing the necessary funding for archival research in various European countries; Profs Richard A. Webster and Gerald D. Feldman (U. of California at Berkeley), for their encouragement and overall guidance; Prof. Leonard B. Weinberg (U. of Nevada at Reno), for information about the treasure trove of judicial sentences at the Istituto di Studi e Ricerche 'Carlo Cattaneo' in Bologna; the researchers and staff members at the Istituto Cattaneo, for the provision of access to these materials as well as their gracious hospitality; Senator Gianfranco Pasquino, Prof. Franco Ferraresi (U. di Torino), Prof. Piero Ignazi (U. di Bologna), and journalist Gianni Flamini, all of whom provided useful research leads; Frau Gitta Grossmann at the Institut für Zeitgeschichte in Munich, for personal assistance in the closed stacks; the staffs of the Biblioteca della Camera dei Deputati, Rome, the Biblioteca Nazionale, Rome, the Bibliothéque Nationale, Paris, the Hoover Inst. library, Stanford U., and the interlibrary loan staffs at both the U. of California at Berkeley and Columbia U.

Notes

1 Reprinted with permission from Jeffrey M. Bale, "The May 1973 Terrorist Attack at Milan Police HQ: Anarchist 'propaganda of the deed' or 'false-flag' provocation?," *Terrorism and Political Violence* 8:1 (1996), 132–166, www.tandfonline.com/10.1080/09546559608427337.
2 For the general historical context within which the 'strategy of tension' was carried out, see Paul Ginsborg, *A History of Contemporary Italy: Society and Politics, 1943–1988* (New York: Penguin, 1990). For particularly insightful attempts to place right-wing terrorism

and various other sorts of postwar Italian subversion, corruption, and misrule in their proper historical and political context, see Alessandro Silj, *Malpaese: Criminalità, corruzione e politica nell'Italia della prima Repubblica, 1943–1994* (Rome: Donzelli, 1994); Massimo Teodori, *Misteri, Montecitorio, malaffare* (no place: Fenicottero, 1991); Giorgio Galli, *La crisi italiana e la destra internazionale* (Milan: Mondadori, 1974) [the essential portions of which were later repr. as *La destra in Italia* (Milan: Gammalibri, 1983)]; Giorgio Galli, *Affari di stato, L'Italia sotteranea, 1943–1990: Storia politica, partiti, corruzione, misteri, scandali* (Milan: Kaos, 1991); and Angelo Ventura, "I poteri occulti nella Repubblica italiana: Il problema storico," in *I 'poteri occulti' nella Repubblica: Mafia, camorra, P2, stragi impunite*, ed. by Comune di Venezia, Ufficio Affari Istituzionali (Venice: Marsilio, 1984) pp. 17–52. Less sophisticated and nuanced analytically but nevertheless filled with valuable details is the overview of subversion and terrorism provided by Antonio Cipriani and Gianni Cipriani, *Sovranità limitata: Storia dell'eversione atlantica in Italia* (Rome: Associate, 1991). Of more historical and theoretical interest, though overly convoluted, is Franco De Felice, "Doppia lealtà e doppio Stato," *Studi Storici* 30:3 (July–September 1989), especially pp. 525–63.

It should also be pointed out that the 'strategy of tension', despite its unusual intensity and high cost in human lives, was only a relatively recent phase in a much longer history of clandestine anti-communist initiatives in postwar Italy, one which included such anti-constitutional operations as the formation of the top secret 'Gladio' stay/behind networks and General Giovanni De Lorenzo's abortive plan to launch a 'pre-emptive' coup in 1964. For the latter, see esp. Parlamento, V Legislatura, Commissione d'inchiesta parlamentare sugli eventi del giugno-luglio 1964, *Relazione di minoranza* (Rome: Camera dei Deputati, 1971); and Parlamento, X Legislatura, Commissione d'inchiesta parlamentare sul terrorismo in Italia e sulle cause della mancata individuazione dei responsabili delle stragi [hereinafter CPI/Stragi], *Relazione sulla documentazione concernente gli 'omissis' dell'inchiesta SIFAR* (Rome: Camera dei Deputati, 1991), 4 volumes. For sources on 'Gladio', see *infra*, note 72.

3 For a detailed reconstruction of the entire 'strategy of tension', see esp. Gianni Flamini, *Il partito del golpe: Le strategie della tensione e del terrore dal primo centrosinistra organico al sequestro Moro* (Ferrara: Bovolenta, 1981–5), four volumes in six parts, an extremely rich motherlode of information whose value is undermined only by its rigidly chronological approach to the topic. The only book-length study in English which deals at any length with this campaign of rightist terrorism is by British journalist Philip Willan, *Puppetmasters: The Political Use of Terrorism in Italy* (London: Constable, 1991), but compare also the general academic histories of Italian terrorism by Richard Drake, *The Revolutionary Mystique and Terrorism in Contemporary Italy* (Bloomington and Indianapolis: Indiana University Press, 1989); and Leonard Weinberg and William Lee Eubank, *The Rise and Fall of Italian Terrorism* (Boulder and London: Westview, 1987), both of which deftly survey and analyze some of its key aspects.

Forthcoming scholarly studies of the 'strategy of tension' will include a new book by a leading Italian expert on the radical right, Franco Ferraresi (ed. and co-author of an outstanding earlier study, *La destra radicale* [Milan: Feltrinelli, 1984]), and an expanded version of my own doctoral dissertation, which focuses especially on the international dimensions of neo-fascist terrorism in Italy. For the original version, see Jeffrey M. Bale, "The 'Black' Terrorist International: Neo-Fascist Paramilitary Networks and the 'Strategy of Tension' in Italy, 1968–1974" (Unpublished Ph.D. Dissertation: History Dept., University of California at Berkeley, 1994). For the statistics cited regarding the high percentage of terrorist attacks attributable to the far right between 1968 and 1974, see Ugo Pecchioli, "Prefazione," in *Rapporto sul terrorismo: Le stragi, gli agguati, i sequestri, le sigle, 1969–1980*, ed. by Mauro Galleni (Milan: Rizzoli, 1981), p. 19. Pecchioli was the PCI's primary specialist on terrorism and security issues, but his calculations can be verified by comparing them with the data found elsewhere in this volume. Compare Donatella della Porta and Maurizio Rossi, *Cifre crudeli: Bilancio dei terrorismi italiani* (Bologna: Istituto Cattaneo, 1984), for slightly different figures.

4 These three distinguishing characteristics of the 'strategy of tension' have been thoroughly documented by Flamini (note 2) and Bale (note 2), both passim. For the complex

anti-constitutional actions undertaken by the Italian intelligence agencies, see Giuseppe De Lutiis, *Storia dei servizi segreti in Italia* (Rome: Riuniti, 1984). For the crucial impact of French counterrevolutionary warfare specialists on the subsequent development of neo-fascist terrorism, see Frédéric Laurent, *L'Orchestre noir* (Paris: Stock, 1978).

5 Among the few academic specialists on terrorism who have paid sufficient attention to the rightist use of 'false flag' operations in postwar Europe is Philip Jenkins, "Under Two Flags: Provocation and Deception in European Terrorism," *Terrorism* 11:4 (1988), pp. 275–87; and "Strategy of Tension: The Belgian Terrorist Crisis, 1982–1986," *Terrorism* 13:4–5 (1990), pp. 299–309. For a more general perspective on undercover infiltration and provocation operations, see Gary Marx, "Thoughts on a Neglected Category of Social Movement Participant: The Agent Provocateur and the Informant," *American Journal of Sociology* 80:2 (September 1974), pp. 402–42. For detailed discussions of the mechanics of such operations, in cases where they were generally conducted directly by the state rather than indirectly through ostensibly autonomous right-wing organizations, see Nurit Schleifman, *Undercover Agents in the Russian Revolutionary Movement: The SR Party, 1902–1914* (Basingstoke: Macmillan/St Antony's Coll., 1988); and Ward Churchill and Jim Vander Wall, *Agents of Repression: The FBI's Secret War against the Black Panther Party and the American Indian Movement* (Boston: South End, 1990).

6 The most clearcut examples of these sorts of operations in Italy occurred in the period between April 1968 and December 1969, in connection with the provocations and bombings which led up to the Piazza Fontana massacre. For further details about these operations, see Extraparliamentary Left Research Group, *La strage di stato: Vent'anni dopo*, ed. by Giancarlo De Palo and Aldo Giannuli (Rome: Associate, 1989 [1970]), pp. 148–96, 223–4; Flamini (note 2) Vols 1 and 2; Renzo Vanni, *Trent'anni di regime bianco* (Pisa: Giardini, 1976), pp. 219–21, 241–5; and esp. Cesare De Simone, *La pista nera. Tattica dell'infiltrazione e strategia delle bombe: Il complotto fascista contro la Repubblica* (Rome: Riuniti, 1972), as well as documentary materials and testimony cited and summarized in the various judicial sentences concerning the wave of terrorist attacks in 1969. Examples of the first three of these four methods are easy to provide, and it is possible that the fourth was also successfully employed.

An example of the first was the commission of several bombings in front of police stations and schools in November 1968 by members of the neo-fascist group Avanguardia Nazionale, which were specifically designed to cast suspicion on the extraparliamentary left. Examples of the creation of various pseudo-leftist groups by neo-fascist militants included the Circolo XXII Marzo, the Movimento Studentesco Operaia d'Avanguardia, the Gruppo Primavera, the Banda XXII Ottobre, and so forth.

An example of the third technique was AN activist Mario Merlino's successful infiltration of a succession of anarchist circles (including the Circolo Bakunin and its more radical 22 Marzo offshoot), which among other things involved growing his hair long and ostentatiously employing extremist left-wing rhetoric. Once inside, he consistently advocated carrying out acts of violence and personally sought to precipitate confrontations with the police at demonstrations. As for the fourth, there is some circumstantial evidence suggesting – though by no means proving – that the Mario Moretti faction of the leftist Brigate Rosse was in fact infiltrated, manipulated, and possibly even covertly directed from inside by agents of one or more Italian security organizations (perhaps in part through the intermediary of the mysterious Hyperion language school in France). For this complex subject, see Giuseppe Zupo and Vincenzo Marini Recchia, *Operazione Moro: I fili ancora coperti di una trama politica criminale* (Milan: Angeli, 1984), pp. 202–74; Sergio Flamini, *La tela del ragno: Il delitto Moro* (Rome: Associate, 1988), passim; Mimmo Scarano and Maurizio De Luca, *Il mandarino è marcio: Terrorismo e cospirazione nel caso Moro* (Rome: Riuniti, 1985), passim; and Willan (note 2) pp. 179–356.

In this connection, it should be recalled that it was precisely this faction that was responsible for the 1978 kidnapping and assassination of Prime Minister Aldo Moro. Note that these sorts of infiltration and provocation techniques were specifically alluded to in a 1968 document prepared by Italian 'correspondents' linked to Aginter Presse, a

Lisbon-based international press agency set up in 1966 by former French Army and Organisation de l'Armée Secréte [OAS] veteran Yves Guillou, which was 'covered' and partially financed by the Portuguese secret police and used as a front by right-wing counterrevolutionary warfare specialists and terrorists. The essential portions of the document, titled 'Notre action politique', are quoted in Laurent (note 3) pp. 169–71. For more on Aginter, its personnel, and its operations, see three reports prepared by the post-1974 Portuguese government, Serviço do Descobrimento e da Coordenaçao de Informaçoes, *ELP Relatório, Número 1* [29 March 1975]; *ELP Relatório, Número 2: Aginter Presse*; and *Número 3*; Laurent (note 3), passim; 'Patrice Chairoff' (pseudonym for intelligence operative Ivan-Dominique Calzi), *Dossier néo-nazisme* (Paris: Ramsay, 1977), pp. 157–62; and former Spanish secret service officer Luis González-Mata, *Terrorismo internacional: La extrema derecha, la extrema izquierda, y los crimenes de estado* (Barcelona: Argos, 1978), pp. 153–64. The last two 'insider' sources need to be utilized with special caution, because they contain many undocumented and perhaps spurious claims.

7 For this particularly complex phase of the 'strategy of tension', see Flamini (note 2) 3/1 and 3/2. For Fumagalli and the MAR, see esp. Procura della Repubblica di Brescia, Pubblico Ministro Francesco Trovato, *Requisitoria del 13 marzo 1976 nel procedimento penale contro Agnellini, Roberto + 80*; Achille Lega and Giorgio Santerini, *Strage a Brescia, potere a Roma: Trame nere e trame bianche* (Milan: Mazzotta, 1976), pp. 127–237; Cipriani and Cipriani (note 1) pp. 129–32, 182–5.

For more on Sogno's background and his 'presidentialist' coup plotting, see Luciano Garibaldi, *L'altro italiano. Edgardo Sogno: Sessant'anni di antifascismo e di anticomunismo* (Milan: Ares, 1992); Franco Fucci, *Spie per la libertà: I servizi segreti della Resistenza italiana* (Milan: Mursia, 1983), especially pp. 142–56; Tribunale di Torino, Giudice Istruttore Luciano Violante, *Sentenza n. 665/75 del 5 maggio 1976 nel procedimento penale contro Sogno, Edgardo + altri*; Alberto Papuzzi, *Il provocatore: Il caso Cavallo e la FIAT* (Turin: Einaudi, 1976); De Lutiis (note 3) pp. 145–55; and Norberto Valentini, *La notte della Madonna: L'Italia tragicomica del golpe . . .* (Rome: Monde, 1978), pp. 171–87. Compare Edgardo Sogno, *Il golpe bianco* (Milan: Scorpione, 1978); Edgardo Sogno, *La Seconda Repubblica* (Florence: Sansoni, 1974). See *infra*, note 17, for more on the international Paix et Liberté network with which his Pace e Libertà organization was affiliated.

For Gelli and P2, see esp. the materials gathered during extensive parliamentary investigation, including the majority or Anselmi report (Parlamento, IX Legislatura, Commissione parlamentare d'inchiesta sulla loggia massonica P2 [hereinafter CP1/P2], *Relazione di maggioranza* [Rome: Camera dei Deputati, 1984]), five dissenting minority reports, and over one hundred thick volumes containing testimony and documents. Compare also the various secondary sources, including Martín Berger, *Historia de la lógia masonica P2* (Buenos Aires: El Cid, 1983); Andrea Barbieri and others, *L'Italia della P2* (Milan: Mondadori, 1981); Alberto Cecchi, *Storia della P2* (Rome: Riuniti, 1985); Roberto Fabiani, *I massoni in Italia* (Milan: L'Espresso, 1978); Gianfranco Piazzesi, *Gelli: La carriera di un eroe di questa Italia* (Milan: Garzanti, 1983); Marco Ramat and others, *La resistabile ascesa della P2: Poteri occulti e stato democratico* (Bari: De Donato, 1983); Renato Risaliti, *Licio Gelli, a carte scoperte* (Florence: Fernando Brancato, 1991); and Gianni Rossi and Francesco Lombrassa, *In nome della 'loggia': Le prove di come la massoneria segreta ha tentato di impadronarsi dello stato italiano. I retroscena della P2* (Rome: Napoleone, 1981). Defenders of P2 include Pier Carpi, *Il caso Gelli: La verità sulla loggia P2* (Bologna: INEI, 1982); and Gelli himself in *La verità* (Lugano: Demetra, 1989). For the Rosa dei Venti, see infra, note 63.

For Ordine Nero, see the lengthy series of judicial sentences, the most detailed of which are Tribunale di Bologna, Giudice Istruttore Vito Zincani, *Sentenza-ordinanza n. 270/74 del 25 giugno 1976 nel procedimento contro Balistrieri, Umberto + 37*; Corte d'Assise di Bologna, Presidente Mario Negri, and Giudice Estensore Giovanni Romeo, *Sentenza del 20 luglio 1983 nel procedimento penale contro Tuti, Mario + 3*; Corte d'Assise d'Apello di Bologna, Presidente Enrico Carfagnini, *Sentenza n. 1/845 del 14 febbraio nel procedimento penale contro Batani, Massimo +16*; and the huge 'file' on secret service operative and infiltrator Claudia Ajello.

8 According to right-wing ultra Vincenzo Vinciguerra, the confessed perpetrator of the 31 May 1972 Peteano car bombing which resulted in the deaths of three Carabinieri, the attack on the Milan Questura might be the 'key episode' in comprehending the strategy of tension, since it revealed 'in an exemplary fashion' the union between political power, the state apparatus, and elements of the neo-fascist group Ordine Nuovo. See his testimony to the public prosecutor and investigating magistrate in Brescia, cited in Giovanni Salvi, ed., *La strategia delle stragi, dalla sentenza della Corte d'Assize di Venezia per la strage di Peteano: Dal tentato golpe del 1964 alla P2, i depistaggi, il ruolo dei generali, l'operato dei servizi segreti* (Rome: Riuniti, 1989), p. 321.

9 Calabresi was assassinated on 17 May 1972 just as he was leaving his home. The investigation was initially oriented toward far left circles, in particular the organization Lotta Continua, but nothing tangible emerged in the way of evidence. Following the arrest of a wanted neo-fascist named Gianni Nardi in Sept. 1972, an investigation into possible rightist links to Calabresi's murder was undertaken, but again without definitive results. This stalled inquiry was later renewed, since in early 1974 Servizio Informazioni Difesa (SID) operative Guido Giannettini told a reporter from *L'Espresso* that the Bundesnachrichtendienst (BND) had arranged for Calabresi's assassination when they learned that he had discovered that the West German service was furnishing concrete assistance to certain extreme right groups in Italy, and in June 1974 right-wing militant Marcello Bergamaschi testified that his MAR chief, Carlo Fumagalli, knew many things about Calabresi's death. Even so, this investigation also petered out. Then, in 1979, a document was discovered at a secret base of the left-wing terrorist group Prima Linea that termed Calabresi's execution an 'act of proletarian justice', reactivating the investigation of Lotta Continua. Within a year certain Prima Linea *pentiti,* including Roberto Sandalo, confirmed that this was the correct trail. Finally, in July 1988 a former Lotta Continua militant, Leonardo Marino, turned himself in to the Carabinieri and testified that he and Ovidio Bompressi, acting on the orders of Adriano Sofri and Giorgio Pietrostefani, committed the assassination, and as a result he and the others were arrested and brought to trial. In spite of a lack of any material evidence supporting Marino's sometimes contradictory testimony, they were found guilty in both the initial trial and by the Court of Appeals. However, various observers have raised serious doubts about both the guilt of some of the accused and the judicial methods used to convict them. See e.g. the work of the well-known historian Carlo Ginzburg, *Il giudice e lo storico: Considerazioni in margine al processo Sofri* (Turin: Einaudi, 1991), a personal friend of Sofri's. In 1992 the appellate sentence was annulled by the Court of Cassation, which ordered a new trial. One year later, these judges found all three defendants not guilty. Compare Sandro Provvisionato, *Misteri d'Italia: Cinquant'anni di trame e delitti senza colpevoli* (Bari: Laterza, 1993), pp. 102–23; and Silj (note 1) p. 126 and note 3.

10 For basic descriptions of the attack and Bertoli's proclaimed motives, see Corte d'Assize di Milano, Presidente Mario del Rio and Giudice Estensore Antonio Stella, *Sentenza n. 12/75 del 1 marzo 1975 nel procedimento penale contro Bertoli, Gianfranco* [hereinafter *Sentenza 1 III 75 contro Bertoli*], pp. 1, 3, 32–4, 36; and Tribunale di Milano, Giudice Istruttore Antonio Lombardi, *Sentenza del 30 luglio 1976 nel procedimento penale contro Bertoli, Gianfranco* [hereinafter *Sentenza 30 VII 76 contro Bertoli*], p. 29, 36. Compare also newspaper accounts on 18 May 1973. For the controversial circumstances surrounding Pinelli's death, see the partisan journalistic accounts of Camilla Cederna, *Pinelli: Una finestra sulla strage* (Milan: Feltrinelli, 1971); Comitato di Controinformazione, *Pinelli: Un omicidio politico* (Padua: Galilei, 1970); and Marco Sassano, *Pinelli: Un suicidio di stato* (Padua: Marsilio, 1971).

11 See e.g. Weinberg and Eubank (note 2) p. 58. Their interpretation appears to be based solely on the account in *La Stampa* the day after the attack. An 'Arab terrorist' trail was also pursued for a time. In response to an anonymous telephone call on 18 May 1973, which claimed that a member of al-Fatah was staying at the Albergo Luna, that this person gave Bertoli the grenade he used, and that during the attack this same individual was making a phone call to Beirut from Piazza Rialto di Venezia, a Yemeni named Muhammad

Mansur was arrested both for using a false passport and because he was suspected of having been involved in some way in Bertoli's crime. However, after an investigation, no evidence was found linking Mansur to Bertoli, nor was any connection established between the Bertoli affair and the 22 May death, in Italy, of Israeli student Moshe Katz. See *Sentenza 30 VII 76 contro Bertoli* (note 9), pp. 29–30.
12 This account of his shifting political orientation is based on the testimony of a court-appointed psychological expert, which was in turn presumably based on an analysis of Bertoli's own accounts of his background. See *Sentenza 1 III 75 contro Bertoli*, p. 36. There is no mention in the sentence of any tangible, corroborative evidence of his earlier Bolshevism, links to the PCI, or conversion to anarchism.
13 For his criminal background, see *Sentenza 1 III 75 contro Bertoli* (note 9), pp. 18, 34–7; *Sentenza 30 VII 76 contro Bertoli* (note 9), pp. 31, 42–3. Compare Provvisionato (note 8), pp. 129–30, who notes that his rap sheet filled up two and a half of paper. Bertoli was born in Venice in 1933. His father was a tailor and owner of a clothing store that later went out of business, and he had two brothers, Pierantonio, a DC sympathizer, and Guglielmo, an MSI labor official. After his family disowned and refused to continue supporting him, the young troublemaker developed into a full-fledged criminal.
14 For Mersi's background and earliest links to Bertoli, see *Sentenza 1 III 75 contro Bertoli* (note 9), pp. 19, 36; and *Sentenza 30 VII 76 contro Bertoli* (note 9), pp. 31, 41.
15 For Bertoli's collaboration with the police and secret services, see *Sentenza 1 III 75 contro Bertoli*, pp. 36–7. Although no effort was made by the judges to identify precisely which 'international secret services' Bertoli may have been collaborating with, a reference to one or more Western secret services is implicit. For Casardi's admission that Bertoli was working with the Italian counterespionage service, see Giuseppe Nicotri and Leo Sisti, "L'Enigma Bertoli," *L'Espresso* 36:47 (25 November 1990), p. 13; Flamini (note 2), volume 4:1, p. 44. It is very doubtful that Bertoli's employment by this service was actually terminated in 1960, as Casardi claimed, since there is much circumstantial evidence suggesting that Bertoli maintained links to various secret services up until 17 May 1973, the day of his attack. Note further that due to its involvement in political scandals, including both abortive 'coups' and acts of terrorism, the Italian military intelligence service underwent three reorganizations and name changes in a little over a decade, from SIFAR to SID in 1966 and from SID to the Servizio Informazioni per la Sicurezza Militare (SISMI) in 1978. Unfortunately, none of these 'reforms' succeeded in ridding the service of corrupt and anti-constitutional elements.
16 For Bertoli's arms trafficking, the Fronte Anticomunista Italiano, and the mission to discover PCI arms deposits, see *Sentenza 1 III 75 contro Bertoli* (note 9), pp. 36–7; *Sentenza 30 VII 76 contro Bertoli* (note 9), p. 31; Flamini, *Partito del golpe* (note 2), volume 3:2, p. 345, and 4:1, p. 43; and Provvisionato (note 8), p. 131. According to the latter source, Sorteni testified that he and Bertoli had procured arms for the Fronte on behalf of Carabinieri Captain Aurelio Bonetti, who then headed SIFAR's Centro Controspionaggio (CS) in Padua, and added that Bertoli had been in contact with three other Carabinieri officers seconded to SIFAR, from whom he received money. Admiral Casardi later claimed that these subsidies were soon terminated because the information provided by Bertoli was of little value, but this remains to be demonstrated. See Gianni Barbacetto, ed., *Il Grande Vecchio: Dodici giudici raccontano le loro inchieste sui grandi misteri d'Italia da Piazza Fontana a Gladio* (Milan: Baldini & Castoldi, 1993), p. 96.

The backgrounds of Togni and Marinotti are also worth noting. Togni was a former minister of industry who helped facilitate Luigi Gedda's 7 Sept. 1947 'Catholic March on Rome' by urging the police and transportation authorities to permit the free circulation of vehicles utilized by the nearly seventy thousand participants, this at a time when there were severe restrictions placed on Sunday vehicular traffic. See Pier Giuseppe Murgia, *Il vento del nord: Storia e cronaca del Fascismo dopo la Resistenza, 1945–1950* (Milan: Sugar, 1975) p. 355. Gedda, then head of Azione Cattolica, would soon after organize the anti-communist Comitati Civici, a vast network of lay Catholics funded covertly by

Confindustria and, via the Vatican Bank, elements of the American national security establishment. For the Comitati Civici, see Carlo Falconi, *Gedda e l'Azione cattolica* (Florence: Parenti, 1958) pp. 125–40; and Roberto Faenza and Marco Fini, *Gli Americani in Italia* (Milan: Feltrinelli, 1976), pp. 276–8, 318–24.

Marinotti was the owner of the giant SNIA Viscosa chemical company. From autumn 1944 on, he served as a mediator between SS Brigadeführer Wilhelm Harster, head of the Nazi Sicherheitsdienst in northern Italy, and the British Intelligence Service. He then made contact, through Msgr. Bernardini (the papal nuncio in Switzerland), with local OSS leader Allen Dulles. Marinotti sought to persuade Dulles, apparently with the backing of some influential members of the Curia, to allow twenty-five German divisions to withdraw from the peninsula so that they could be sent to fight the Russians. In return, the Germans would abandon northern Italy to the Anglo-Americans. This proposal was rejected, and in early 1945 Riccardo Lombardi, the new Socialist prefect of Milan, ordered the arrest of Marinotti and several other industrialists who had prospered under Fascism. See Murgia *supra* pp. 36–7, note 11, 60, 110. Nevertheless, he and other compromised chemical industrialists were thence protected and courted by the British, who sought to use their firms as points of penetration into the Italian economy. Perhaps more importantly, Marinotti and Francesco Odasso, chairman of the board at SNIA Viscosa, were accused in an internal PCI intelligence report of being among the promoters of an anti-communist movement designed 'to eliminate all the philo-communists from the Italian political sphere'. This was to be done through the financing of squads of killers recruited from among professional gangsters and former Fascists. Using false designations, these squads were to make attacks on government officials and perpetrate public massacres that would then be blamed on the communists. The relationship between this supposed movement and the later Fronte Anticomunista Italiano is unclear. See Faenza and Fini *supra* pp. 69 (citing an OSS report from 24 Oct. 1944 [1945?]), 152, note 2.

17 See Salvi (note 7), p. 330. Along with Stefano Delle Chiaie's Avanguardia Nazionale and Franco Freda's cell in Padua, Ordine Nuovo was among the most active and violent neo-fascist formations in postwar Italy. For general information about these groups, see Franco Ferraresi, "La destra eversiva," in *La destra radicale*, ed. by Ferraresi (Milan: Feltrinelli, 1984), pp. 62–71; and Rosario Minna, "Il terrorismo di destra," in *Terrorismi in Italia*, ed. by Donatella della Porta (Bologna: Mulino, 1984), pp. 33–5.

18 Flamini (note 2), volume 3:2, p. 345. Although he cites no source for this specific claim, it probably derives from Judge Giovanni Tamburino's investigation of the Rosa dei Venti group. For the origins of Pace e Libertà, an international CIA-funded organization first established in France (as the Union Démocratique pour la Paix et la Liberté) in March 1949, see Irwin M. Wall, *The United States and the Making of Postwar France, 1945–1954* (Cambridge: Cambridge University Press, 1991), pp. 150–1, 293; and René Sommer, "Paix et Liberté? La Quatrième République contre le PC[F]," *L'Histoire* 40 (December 1981), pp. 26–35. Under the leadership of Jean-Paul David, it engaged in both extensive propaganda against communist 'peace' initiatives and various covert intelligence operations until 1954, when it was compromised in the so-called leakages scandal. Some of its operatives later participated in anti-communist labor union activities, and – according to journalists linked to the Parti Communiste Français – did not hesitate to resort to violence. E.g., see Marcel Caille, *Les truands du patronat* (Paris: Sociales, 1977), pp. 57–8. Branches were subsequently established in several other European countries, including Belgium, the Netherlands, and West Germany. The leader of the Italian branch was Edgardo Sogno, a former 'white' partisan with close links to the British and American secret services who was subsequently implicated in intelligence-linked covert operations against the left, including 'presidentialist' coup plots. For more on Sogno, see *supra*, note 6.

19 Flamini (note 2), volume 2, p. 58, and volume 3:2, pp. 344–5.

20 Ibid., volume 3/2, p. 357. For an account of this attack, see Flamini, volume 2, pp. 34–6. Due to the notorious laxity of the Paduan authorities toward acts of right-wing violence, the charges against the accused were all later dropped.

21 *Sentenza 30 VII 76 contro Bertoli* (note 9), pp. 39–40.
22 The crime for which Bertoli and another man, Gastone Faccin, were accused was the attempted armed robbery of an elderly couple in Padua. Faccin was arrested by the Carabinieri, but Bertoli managed to flee and escape arrest. Flamini (note 2), volume 2, p. 200.
23 For the details of Bertoli's expatriation and the subsequent internal leftist investigations of the Bertoli case, see Tribunale di Milano, Giudice Istruttore Antonio Lombardi, *Sentenza del 15 marzo 1980 nel procedimento penale contro Del Grande, Umberto + 2* [hereinafter *Sentenza 15 III 80 contro Del Grande*], pp. 46–9. Interestingly, Calabresi had begun a file on Bertoli in connection with this expatriation operation, which contained a picture identical to the one affixed to Bertoli's falsified passport. It was Enrico Rovelli, another member of the Circolo Ponte della Ghisolfa, not coincidentally the same group to which Pinelli had belonged, who provided a copy of this photo to Calabresi. See ibid., p. 47; *Sentenza 30 VII 76 contro Bertoli* (note 9), pp. 32–3. According to other sources, Calabresi had received additional information about Bertoli's movements from Veneto neo-fascist informant Gianfranco Belloni. See Flamini (note 2), volume 3:2, p. 345; and Provvisionato (note 8), p. 133. In 1972 Magri was a PCdI/M-L candidate for the Chamber of Deputies. See Nicotri and Sisti (note 14), p. 14.
24 *Sentenza 15 III 80 contro Del Grande* (note 22), pp. 47–8. Compare Provvisionato (note 8), pp. 132–3. Although the rightist press emphasized this BR link to Bertoli in order to discredit the left, the indirect involvement of BR member Bonomi in the expatriation of Bertoli has been viewed by some leftist journalists as further evidence of secret service penetration and manipulation of the BR. See Flamini (note 2), volume 4:1, p. 43; and Cipriani and Cipriani (note 1), pp. 140–2. In this connection, it should be noted that Bonomi was an ambiguous character whose suspicious attempts to develop an ongoing association with the BR were eventually rebuffed, and that documents later found in the secret 'anti-infiltration' archives of Avanguardia Operaia claimed that he worked for SID. See Barbacetto (note 15), p. 96.
25 *Sentenza 30 VII 76 contro Bertoli*, pp. 32–3.
26 Or perhaps Armand Martín. See *Sentenza 15 III 80 contro Del Grande* (note 22), p. 49. Because I have not been able to obtain further information about this person from Spanish or French sources, I suspect that the name was a pseudonym used to cover his real identity.
27 *Sentenza 30 VII 76 contro Bertoli* (note 9), p. 31.
28 *Sentenza 1 III 75 contro Bertoli* (note 9), pp. 6–7, 37; *Sentenza 30 VII 76 contro Bertoli* (note 9), pp. 38–42. For the Jemmis being in transit to Greece, see Flamini (note 2), volume 3:2, p. 345; and Laurent (note 3), p. 265. The spelling 'Jemmi' may be nothing more than an Italianized version corresponding to the pronunciation of the French original Yemmi, but I have not been able to find any further reference to the brothers – under either spelling – in the corpus of French sources dealing with neo-fascism. For more on the MJR, Ordre Nouveau, and closely interrelated French neo-fascist organizations, see Joseph Algazy, *L'Extrême droite en France de 1965 à 1984* (Paris: Harmattan, 1989), pp. 45–64, 76–115; Francis Bergeron and Philippe Vilgier, *De Le Pen à Le Pen: Une histoire des nationaux et des nationalistes sous la Cinquième République* (Bouere: Dominique Martin Morin, 1985), pp. 70–5, 79–91, 98–104; François Duprat, *Les mouvements d'extrême droite en France depuis 1944* (Paris: Albatros, 1972), pp. 167–70, 177–82, 192–207. The last two sources are of extreme right provenance, and Duprat was himself very active in numerous neo-fascist movements from the 1950s until his assassination by car bomb on 18 March 1978. Compare also Serge Dumont, *Les brigades noires: L'Extrême droite en France et en Belgique francophone de 1944 à nos jours* (Berchem: EPO, 1983), pp. 124–37; and Gregory Pons, *Les rats noirs* (Paris: Simoën, 1977), pp. 7–29.
29 *Sentenza 1 III 75 contro Bertoli* (note 9), pp. 13–15.
30 Ibid., pp. 5–10. The judicial sentences do not specifically identify the type of explosive device used by Bertoli, but according to various secondary sources it was a SIPE Mk2 hand grenade, the standard make issued to the Israeli Army. See "Bertoli: Un "anarchico"

di fedeltà atlantica," *Maquis Dossier* 2 (June 1985), p. 72; and Provvisionato (note 8), p. 128; Barbacetto (note 15), p. 95.
31 *Sentenza 30 VII 76 contro Bertoli* (note 9), pp. 30–1.
32 *Sentenza 1 III 75 contro Bertoli* (note 9), p. 11.
33 Ibid., pp. 10–12. However, this sudden reluctance would be understandable if he was in fact carrying the grenade from Israel.
34 Ibid., pp. 12–13; *Sentenza 30 VII 76 contro Bertoli*, p. 38. There is a disagreement between the two sentences about whether Bertoli even slept at the hotel one night; according to the former he did not, whereas the latter claims he did sleep there his first night in Marseilles.
35 *Sentenza 1 III 75 contro Bertoli*, p. 15.
36 Ibid., pp. 16–17; *Sentenza 30 VII 76 contro Bertoli* (note 9), pp. 39–40.
37 *Sentenza 1 III 75 contro Bertoli* (note 9), pp. 20–1; *Sentenza 30 VII 76 contro Bertoli* (note 9), p. 41.
38 *Sentenza 1 III 75 contro Bertoli* (note 9), p. 24.
39 For judicial reconstructions of the sequence of events, based on the testimony of eyewitnesses, see ibid., pp. 24–30. The detail about Bertoli's Jesus-like companion is based on the account in Flamini (note 2), volume 3:2, p. 51.
40 *Sentenza 1 III 75 contro Bertoli* (note 9), p. 3.
41 *Sentenza 30 VII 76 contro Bertoli* (note 9), p. 43.
42 Ibid. This is an interesting example, since the French police have long been accused or suspected of supplying Vaillant with the bomb he used, though there are disputes about whether the latter was a willing provocateur or a genuine anarchist who was unwittingly manipulated by the state. See, e.g., Jean Maîtron, *Le mouvement anarchiste en France, 1880–1914* (Paris: Maspero, 1975 [1951]), volume 1, pp. 230–3; and Bernard Thomas, *Les provocations policières: Quand la politique devient un roman* (Paris: Fayard, 1972), pp. 55–70. However, Jean-Paul Brunet has recently argued that the police were probably not involved in fomenting or facilitating Vaillant's attack, since the bomb design was too unstable to give any assurance that the intended targets would be hit and since carrying out the operation would have required the cooperation of ten or fifteen officials, including the interior minister, all of whom would have had to have been willing to risk their entire careers and then remain silent to preserve their secret. See *La police de l'ombre: Indicateurs et provocateurs dans la France contemporaine* (Paris: Seuil, 1990), pp. 263–74. Although the first argument may well have some merit, Brunet's psychological reasoning escapes me. Since the end of the nineteenth century, there have been numerous successful provocations and 'false flag' operations carried out by fifteen or more government officials and agents willing to take such risks. There is absolutely no reason to think that similar actions could not have been successful in Vaillant's time, as indeed they often were.
43 *Sentenza 30 VII 76 contro Bertoli* (note 9), pp. 42–3.
44 Ibid., p. 42.
45 *Sentenza 1 III 75 contro Bertoli* (note 9), pp. 27–30, 32–4. Here, I think the judges may be reading too much into Bertoli's failure to attack the two high-ranking officials. But compare Provvisionato (note 8), pp. 128–9, who claims that Rumor and his entourage had already departed, with considerable journalistic fanfare, from the opposite side of the Questura.
46 Ibid., p. 38; *Sentenza 30 VII 76 contro Bertoli* (note 9), pp. 43–4.
47 Ibid., p. 43.
48 Ibid., p. 44 ('unknown persons . . . pulled the strings'); and *Sentenza 1 III 75 contro Bertoli* (note 9) p. 1 (' . . . linked to a vast and obscure criminal design').
49 *Sentenza 1 III 75 contro Bertoli*, p. 20; and *Sentenza 30 VII 76 contro Bertoli*, p. 38.
50 *Sentenza 15 III 80 contro Del Grande* (note 22), pp. 48–9. Although he would have also been motivated to lie if he had been involved in the massacre, the most probable explanations for Bertolo's provision of false testimony in this context are that he did not want to

be charged with helping a wanted criminal elude the police, and wished to avoid being implicated in a terrorist attack in which he had taken no part.

51 In this connection, it is interesting to note that many apparently bona fide anarchist organizations continue to maintain that Bertoli was a genuine anarchist and that those who have labelled him as a rightist provocateur are participating in a 'squalid manuever', specifically a campaign of disinformation and defamation, sponsored by the bourgeois power structure. See e.g. Centro di Iniziativa Luca Rossi, ed., *Gladio, stragi, riforme istituzionali* (Milan: Cento Fiori, 1991), p. 46. Curiously, among the organizations later found defending Bertoli was the Circolo Anarchico Ponte della Ghisolfa in Milan, one of the groups which Bertoli's actions implicated, and seemingly were designed to implicate. Although further efforts should be made to definitively determine Bertoli's true allegiances and sponsors, as these younger generations of anarchists have demanded, it is hardly logical in this context to suggest that persons connected to the Italian state would have had any rational motive to label a genuine anarchist as a rightist provocateur with links to the secret services. This approach would only have been politically useful if Bertoli was a genuine anarchist who was very influential in anarchist circles, in which case the goal would have been to 'snitch-jacket' him, that is, to smear his reputation and discredit his image among his comrades. There was clearly no reason to do this in Bertoli's case. On the contrary, in this instance government functionaries would have had every reason to claim that a state-sponsored provocateur was really a left-wing extremist, as in fact they regularly attempted to do throughout the period when Bertoli perpetrated his massacre.

52 *Sentenza 15 III 80 contro Del Grande* (note 22), pp. 49–50; and *Sentenza 1 III 75 contro Bertoli* (note 9), pp. 17–18.

53 Ibid., pp. 18, 41–2.

54 Compare the slightly contradictory accounts in *Sentenza 1 III 75 contro Bertoli* (note 9), pp. 22–4; *Sentenza 30 VII 76 contro Bertoli* (note 9), pp. 41–2; and *Provvisionato* (note 8), pp. 136–7.

55 *Sentenza*, ibid., p. 32.

56 Ibid., p. 33.

57 For the extreme right as a privileged and especially fruitful source of recruitment for the French security services, see Serge Ferrand and Gilbert Lecavelier, *Aux ordres du SAC* (Paris: Albin Michel, 1982), pp. 75–6, wherein the intense rivalry between the various services for rightist recruits is emphasized. Compare 'Patrice Chairoff' (pseudonym for Calzi), *Dossier B . . . comme barbouzes* (Paris: Alain Moreau, 1975), p. 45, who specifically notes that extreme right groups were used by SAC and the Ministry of the Interior to detonate 'a confrontation between extremists of both sides', which then provided a pretext for, and was soon followed by, a wave of anti-revolutionary repression. This was directed primarily against the left, but was also used to smash the revolutionary right when the latter became too independent or its services were no longer needed. Chairoff also correctly points out that such 'infiltration/repression' methods had become the 'classical system' for state crackdowns in France, and their analogies with the 'strategy of tension' and the use of the 'opposing extremisms' theory by Italian authorities is certainly no coincidence.

58 See Laurent (note 3), p. 131. As noted in note 5, *supra*, Aginter Presse was a Lisbon-based center for countersubversive warfare. In exchange for funding, logistical support, and 'cover' provided by the Portuguese secret police, the agency carried out 'plausibly deniable' terrorist and provocation operations at the behest of various Western secret services, most of which were aimed at suppressing independence movements in Africa or neutralizing far left groups in Europe. Ordre et Tradition was Aginter's international 'action' branch, which had a clandestine paramilitary wing known as the Organisation d'Action contre le Communisme International (OACI).

59 Algazy (note 27), p. 81, quoting direct from a 24 March 1969 report on MJR activities by the Direction Centrale of the Renseignements Généraux.

60 Chairoff (note 56), p. 162. Nor is it a fluke that Occident, the MJR's chief rival and the parent organization of many later Ordre Nouveau militants, was also approached

by various persons on behalf of the French services. At least one notorious mercenary with close links to the Service de Documentation Extérieure et de Contre-Espionnage (SDECE), Bob Denard, made attempts to recruit members of Occident, while a parallel effort was made by mercenary Jacques Depret to recruit them for use in rival Polícia Internacional e de Defesa do Estado (PIDE) and Aginter Presse operations in Africa on behalf of the Portuguese government, a circumstance which greatly annoyed SDECE and temporarily strained the normally good relations between the two services. See Laurent (note 3), p. 370, who cites a 10 January 1968 SDECE report on the activities of Depret and his associates which was sent to PIDE (the Portuguese secret police). Therein SDECE claimed, apparently in an effort to discourage PIDE contacts with Occident, that the movement was 'filled [*truffé*] with police informants and provocateurs'. For Depret's own account of his exploits in Africa, see 'Jacques Debreton' (pseudonym for Depret), *Coup d'état à Brazzaville* (Brussels: Espace, 1966), the preface of which was co-authored by Jean-Marie Laurent, a key Aginter Presse operative. For an excellent introduction to the French Army's *guerre révolutionnaire* doctrine, see Peter Paret, *French Revolutionary Warfare from Indochina to Algeria: The Analysis of a Political and Military Doctrine* (New York: Praeger, 1964).

61 For these details, and several examples of collaborative actions between Ordre Nouveau and the SAC, RG, or the riot police, see Ferrand and Lecavelier (note 56), pp. 76–85. Other instances of such collaboration involving the SAC, the Sûreté Militaire, and an Ordre Nouveau front group, the Groupe d'Intervention Nationaliste (GIN), are described by Pons, *Rats noirs* (note 27), pp. 226–32. Compare Chairoff (note 56), pp. 47–9.

62 After consulting Israeli sources – and making a serious but ultimately vain attempt to obtain a response from Israeli officials concerning Bertoli's sojourn in Israel – Richard A. Webster discovered that the Karmiyah kibbutz, located a couple of miles from the coast to the north of the Gaza strip, had been established in 1950 by French and Tunisian Jews who were members of an extreme left-wing Zionist organization. He therefore suggested that the real reason why the Jemmis and Bertoli stayed at Karmiyah was because French-speakers would logically have been placed there by the Israeli authorities. Personal communication with Webster, 2 Oct. 1992. This innocuous interpretation is certainly plausible, but in order to consider it the most likely explanation a couple of additional questions would have to be answered. First of all, how many Israeli kibbutzim have been established by, and thus serve as magnets for, French-speakers? If the number is very small, perhaps it was only a coincidence that all three of these men resided there. If not, what is the statistical probability that their joint sojourn at Karmiyah was random? Second, there is no indication in the sources I have consulted that Bertoli speaks French. His stay in Marseilles may seem suggestive, but there are, after all, many visitors to foreign countries who manage to get around and conduct affairs without knowing the language of their hosts. Moreover, the original left-wing orientation of Karmiyah only adds to the possible confusion about Bertoli's political orientation. Was he sent to this particular kibbutz by genuine leftists or by rightist elements who wanted to strengthen his leftist 'legend'? There is no way to know, given the current state of the documentation. The Israeli authorities have remained tight-lipped, and according to one source the Israeli secret services obstructed Italian efforts to obtain more information about Bertoli's stay at the kibbutz. See Provvisionato (note 8), p. 135.

63 *Sentenza 30 VII 76 contro Bertoli* (note 9), p. 32.

64 For general information on the Rosa dei Venti organization and its secret sponsors, see Tribunale di Roma, Giudice Istruttore Filippo Fiore, *Sentenza n. 1051/71 del 5 novembre 1975 nel procedimento penale contro Borghese, Junio Valerio + 140*, especially pp. 137–52; Silj (note 1), pp. 159–67; Cipriani and Cipriani (note 1), pp. 163–74; the section concerning Judge Tamburino's findings in Barbacetto (note 15), pp. 61–84; and Jeffrey M. Bale, "Compass Rose Plot," *Europe since 1945: An Encyclopedia*, forthcoming from Garland. For further details, see Flamini (note 2), volume 3:1 and 3:2, passim. For more on the ultraconservative MNOP, see the latter source, volume 2, pp. 197–9; and volume 3:1,

pp. 86–9. The other MNOP co-founder was Sicilian prince and P2 'brother' Gianfranco Alliata di Montereale, a cultured but nonetheless shadowy figure who was implicated in other covert rightist initiatives. The name of the Rosa organization technically means 'compass rose', the term for the directional symbol that appears on a compass. Perhaps not coincidentally, this is also the symbol for NATO. However, the name apparently had multiple meanings, since it could be taken more literally to mean 'rose of twenty', possibly a reference to the twenty or so groups it encompassed, or 'rose of the winds', which metaphorically implied that the organization could strike anywhere, from every direction.

65 For this sometimes conflicting insider testimony regarding the nature of 'parallel SID', compare CP1/P2, *Allegati alla relazione, I Serie: Resoconti stenografici della commissione*, volume 13, especially pp. 267–71, 276–82 (Spiazzi testimony); the interview with Spiazzi in Sergio Zavoli, *La notte della Repubblica* (Rome and Milan: Nuova Eri/Mondadori, 1992), pp. 150–1; De Lutiis (note 3), pp. 111–12, 129; the interview with Cavallaro in Corrado Incerti, "Clamorose rivelazioni," *L'Europeo* 30:42 (17 October 1974), pp. 26–9; and Flamini (note 2), volume 3:1, pp. 307–8; volume 3:2, pp. 334–8. In general, Spiazzi downplayed the significance of the Rosa dei Venti organization and sought to minimize the subversive aspects of 'parallel SID' by contesting and undermining Cavallaro's more sensationalistic revelations. In order to determine whose version is closer to the truth, their specific testimony should be placed within the more general context of insider allegations about the systematic secret service manipulation of right-wing terrorism. According to at least five knowledgeable neo-fascist radicals, including Vinciguerra, Marco Affatigato, Sergio Calore, Paolo Aleandri, and Marcello Soffiati, Atlanticist factions within the political establishment and security services covertly manipulated, made instrumental use of, and otherwise sabotaged or exploited every major anti-system operation carried out by the Italian revolutionary right from the 1960s on through the 1980s. Neither Judge Tamburino nor the more astute members of the parliamentary committee investigating P2, such as Partito Radicale deputy Massimo Teodori, found Spiazzi's sanitized accounts convincing.

66 For the specific charges, see the quotes in Flamini (note 2), volume 3:2, p. 698; and Cipriani and Cipriani (note 1), p. 167.

67 Flamini, ibid., pp. 344–7.

68 Ibid., pp. 347–50. Ventura was himself accused of material involvement in the Freda group's 1969 bombing campaign, which culminated in the 12 December Piazza Fontana massacre. For a recent general introduction to this inordinately complicated case, see Giorgio Boatti, *Piazza Fontana. 12 dicembre 1969: Il giorno dell'innocenza perduta* (Milan: Feltrinelli, 1993).

69 Ibid., pp. 351–2.

70 Ibid., p. 352. Compare Barbacetto (note 15), pp. 97–8, who suggests that Bertoli's failure to harm Rumor caused his accomplices to abandon him instead of covering his escape. In this connection, several witnesses noticed a white Fiat 125 speeding away from the scene shortly after the explosion. See Provvisionato (note 8), p. 138. In my opinion, however, Bertoli was always meant to serve as a sacrificial lamb, and there was never any intention of helping him to escape afterwards. If the aim all along was not to have an 'anarchist' arrested and accused of carrying out a brutal act of terrorism, why would Bertoli have gone to the trouble of getting an anarchy symbol tattoo and spent so much time creating a false anarchist 'legend'? But he was probably assured, falsely as it turned out, that something would be done to acquit him in court, or at least to lessen the severity of his sentence.

71 Quoted in Flamini (note 2), volume 3:2, pp. 352–3. More recently, Lombardi has confirmed that the vast international organization which he suspected was behind Bertoli's act of terrorism was the Rosa dei Venti (and, by extension, its secret service sponsors). In his sentence he had already noted Bertoli's links to Sandro Sedona, and he subsequently became convinced that the Rosa group had in fact sponsored the failed attack on Rumor. See Barbacetto (note 15), p. 98. Moreover, it may be significant that elements linked to the Rosa dei Venti structure operated in Marseilles. See Provvisionato (note 8), p. 134.

72 Quoted from Tamburino sentence in ibid., p. 354. An earlier 'false move' was the botched 7 April 1973 attempt by neo-fascist Nico Azzi, a member of the Milanese La Fenice group, to place a bomb on the Turin – Rome express train. For more on this action, which resulted in the premature detonation of the bomb in Azzi's hands, see Procura della Repubblica di Genoa, Pubblico Ministero Carlo Barile, *Requisitoria del 22 gennaio 1974 nel procedimento penale contro Azzi, Nico Gianni + 3*; and Tribunale di Genoa, Giudice Istruttore Giovanni Grillo, *Sentenza-ordinanza n. 831/73 del 6 marzo 1974 contro Azzi, Nico Gianni + 3*. The ultras in La Fenice were closely linked to Ordine Nuovo and the Rosa dei Venti organization, and just prior to his accident Azzi had ostentatiously displayed materials produced by the far left Lotta Continua group, suggesting that this action was a provocation designed to implicate the latter in a major terrorist crime. See Flamini (note 2), volume 3:2, pp. 318–21.

73 For the presence of Bertoli's name on the list of 'gladiators', see Nicotri and Sisti (note 14), p. 12; Giovanni Maria Bellu and Giuseppe D'Avanzo, *I giorni di Gladio: Come morì la Prima Repubblica* (Milan: Sperling & Kupfer, 1991), pp. 153, 243; Provvisionato (note 8), pp. 138–9; and Barbacetto (note 15), pp. 207–8. These same sources reveal that Bertoli was not the only worrisome 'homonym' found among the names in the files and lists of gladiators.

Among the others were Enzo Maria Dantini (previously a leader of the 'Nazi-Maoist' Organizzazione Lotta di Popolo), neo-fascist activist Gianni Nardi (a close associate of MAR terrorist Giancarlo Esposti), Manlio Portolan (a Freda associate from Trieste investigated for his involvement in the *attentat* at Grumolo delle Abbadesse), and Marco Morin (the ballistics expert from Venice who was accused of helping to lay a false trail during the judicial investigation of the Peteano bombing and was later assigned to analyze the weaponry used in the Aldo Moro kidnapping and assassination case).

For the ham-fisted effort of SISMI to demonstrate that another perfectly respectable but utterly clueless individual named Giancarlo Bertoli was the actual gladiator listed in the file, see the last-named source, pp. 207–8. Note also that Bertoli the gladiator was supposedly decommissioned on 20 January 1971 – only about one month before Bertoli the terrorist's arrival in Israel. See Provvisionato (note 8), p. 139.

For more on the web of 'Gladio' stay/behind networks, which were established by the US and its NATO allies in most western and southern European countries, see the report of the parliamentary investigative committee in Italy, CPI/Stragi, *[9 luglio 1991] Pre-relazione sull'inchiesta condotta dalla Commissione in ordine alle vicende connesse all'operazione Gladio, con annessi gli atti del dibattito svoltosi sul documento stesso* (Rome: Camera dei Deputati, 1991). Similar reports were issued by parliamentary commissions in Belgium and Switzerland. Also available are journalistic publications, including Jean-François Brozzu-Gentile, *L'Affaire Gladio: Les réseaux secrets américaine au coeur du terrorisme en Europe* (Paris: Albin Michel, 1994); Ronald Bye and Finn Sjue, *Norges hemmeligehær Historien om Stay Behind* (Oslo: Tiden Norsk, 1995); Hugo Gijsels, *Netwerk Gladio* (Louvain: Kritak, 1991); Leo A. Müller, *Gladio–das Erbe des Kalten Krieges: Der NATO-Geheimbund und sein deutscher Vorläufer* (Reinbek: Rowohlt, 1991); and Jan Willems, ed., *Gladio* (Brussels: EPO/Reflex, 1991); one detailed historical study by Bob de Graaf and Cees Wiebes, *Gladio, der vrije jongens: Een particuliere geheime dienst in Koude Oorlogstijd* (The Hague: Koninginnegracht, 1992) concerning a similar anti-communist network in the Netherlands; and the first-hand accounts of two high-ranking secret service officials who were responsible for overseeing the Italian 'Gladio' organization, [Gen.] Gerardo Serravalle, *Gladio* (Rome: Associate, 1991); and Gen. Paolo Inzerilli, *Gladio: la verità negata* (Bologna: Analisi, 1995).

74 Bertoli's continued silence is one of the major facts which needs to be explained by those who postulate that he had accomplices and/or was covertly controlled and manipulated by other forces. In other words, why would anyone willingly accept a life sentence if they could provide information or evidence demonstrating that they were compelled to commit a serious crime by others operating behind the scenes? The only explanation is that Bertoli feared, not without justification, that he might suffer a worse fate if he told the entire truth, since the examples of the punishment meted out in prison to *mafiosi* and

political terrorists who had decided to 'spill the beans' could scarcely have been overlooked by him.

75 Gianfranco Bertoli, *Storia di un terrorista: Un mistero italiano* (Milan: Emotion/Tracce, 1995). Compare the illuminating testimony of Bertoli from another judicial process, cited by Massimiliano Griner, *Piazza Fontana e il mito della strategia della tensione* (Turin: Lindau, 2011), p. 174: 'I am an individualist anarchist and would not have any difficulty, so as to effectuate an act of revolt, in using means and occasions offered to me by totally different ideological milieus (right-wing forces, the police)'. Note, however, that Griner is a rightist author who portrays Bertoli as a genuine anarchist who was not carrying out a 'false flag' attack on behalf of Ordine Nuovo, other right-wing groups, or elements of the secret services.

76 See Tribunale di Milano, Guidice Istruttore Guido Salvino, *Sentenza-ordinanza n. 9/92A del 3 febraio 1998 nel procedimento penale contro Rognoni, Giancarlo + 32* [hereinafter *Sentenza 3 II 98 contro Rognoni*], pp. 252–68.

77 See the discussion in Andrea Sceresini, Nicola Palma, and Maria Elena Scandaliato, *Piazza Fontana, noi sapevano! Golpe e stragi di Stato: La verità del generale Maletti* (Rome: Aliberti, 2010), pp. 218–20. More updated details about Bertoli's activities can be found in Tribunale di Milano, Giudice Istruttore Antonio Lombardi, *Sentenza-ordinanza del 18 luglio 1998 nel procedimento penale contro Maggi, Carlo Maria ed altri*. Unfortunately, I have thus far been unable to obtain a copy of this sentence.

78 *Sentenza 3 II 98 contro Rognoni*, pp. 252–6.

79 Ibid., pp. 256–9.

80 Ibid., p. 256.

81 Ibid., pp. 260–2. Compare also Vincenzo Vinciguerra, *Stato d'emergenza: Raccolta di scritti sulla strage di piazza Fontana* (no place: Lulu, no date), pp. 34–48.

82 *Sentenza 3 II 98 contro Rognoni*, pp. 262–8. Compare also the book by "Walter Rubini," *Il segreto della Repubblica* (Milan: FLAN, 1978). This work was republished in 2005 by Selene with a new introduction.

7
CONCLUDING THOUGHTS ON THE TERRORIST "STRATEGY OF TENSION" IN ITALY

The campaign of right-wing terrorism and subversion that falls under the rubric of the "strategy of tension" continued, in one form or another, up through the early 1980s. However, it took novel and distinctive forms in the period after 1976. As the previously cited testimony of neo-fascist *pentiti* like Paolo Aleandri and Sergio Calore suggests, during the late 1970s a number of new clandestine neo-fascist groups emerged which adopted a more decentralized organizational structure and advocated an operational approach based upon "armed spontaneism." In part this represented an attempt to create new organizational forms that would be less subject to monitoring and penetration, but in part it also reflected the realization by some older neo-fascist leaders that a new radicalism and revolutionary spirit was infecting the younger generation of neo-fascist militants, many of whom admired the apparent efficiency of the Brigate Rosse (BR: Red Brigades) and had been influenced more generally by the critiques of "bourgeois" society and the fashions and modes of cultural expression associated with the extraparliamentary left.[1] However, although these young ultras may have believed that they were in this way avoiding the errors of the older generation, which, as was becoming increasingly apparent, had been systematically compromised and manipulated by the security services, what they failed to realize was the extent to which the second generation organizations, such as Terza Posizione (TP: Third Position) and Costruiamo l'Azione (Let's Take Action), were also corrupted and used instrumentally by elements collaborating with those services. When this later became clearer, and the radicals made an effort to break away from their controllers and carry out independent actions against the state, they were quickly suppressed by the security forces. Only those activists who were wittingly or unwittingly carrying out provocations for the benefit of the state, such as some of those affiliated with the Nuclei Armati Rivoluzionari (NAR: Armed Revolutionary Cells), were allowed to conduct their activities undisturbed. Among the key figures in the latter organization was Giuseppe Valerio ("Giusva")

Fioravanti, who together with his girlfriend Francesca Mambro was later formally charged with carrying out the 1980 bombing of the Bologna train station.[2]

These remarks are not intended as the prologue to a detailed discussion of the later phases of the "strategy of tension," but rather to suggest why the 1973–1974 period constitutes a watershed beyond which these particular chapters should not proceed. By the end of 1974, the "classical" phase of that strategy had exhausted itself, in part because Giulio Andreotti had helped, for entirely instrumental motives, to rip asunder strands of the web of quasi-official protection that had until then been extended to cover terrorists associated with historic neo-fascist groups such as Ordine Nuovo (ON: New Order) and Avanguardia Nazionale (AN: National Vanguard). A new historical phase in the development of right-wing terrorism in Italy then began. There was a two-year transitional phase during which leaders of the two organizations, often from sanctuaries abroad, sought to forge a joint operational alliance. With the collapse of those initiatives, the new "spontaneous" organizations mentioned earlier began to emerge. In short, right-wing violence in the period between 1975 and 1980 deserves to be the subject of another study altogether.

At this juncture the chief desideratum is to make some general observations, by way of conclusion, about the wider significance of the "strategy of tension." A number of issues are involved here that need to be addressed briefly. The first is whether what occurred in Italy was reflective primarily of Italian traditions and conditions, or whether it constituted merely one example of a far broader political pattern in the postwar era. The second has to do with the motives of the parties involved in this terrorist strategy. What induced radical neo-fascists, who professed a revolutionary ideology which was virulently anti-capitalist and anti-American, to make common cause with the conservative guardians of Atlanticism, both in Europe and across the Atlantic? And what induced elements of ostensibly democratic and humanitarian regimes, like those in Western Europe and the United States, to collude with political extremists who professed a worldview that millions of people from their own countries had died opposing in the first half of the 1940s? In short, what does this operational alliance reveal about the larger political context, and the methods by which the various groups involved pursued their own interests? Finally, what methodological relevance does this study have for future political and historical research?

There are a number of ways to interpret the terrorist and anti-constitutional activities recounted in the preceding chapters. One can, of course, ascribe them primarily to domestic factors, as many have sought to do. There are in fact some good reasons for taking this approach. A long historical tradition of political disunity and foreign domination seems to have prompted significant numbers of Italians to have recourse to deception, manipulation, and conspiratorial politics, which in turn may have lent the praxis of *furberia* – the skillful maneuvering of others, largely through trickery, for one's own advantage – a degree of cultural importance it might not otherwise have had. Moreover, the failure of Italian statesmen to develop a powerful, efficient, and centralized state capable of resolving basic social problems and thereby inspiring a broader civic loyalty that transcended traditional familial and regional loyalties, both in the wake of the political unification of the peninsula and after the fall of Fascism, allowed these ingrained traits which had earlier facilitated survival and compensated for political weakness to flourish and become institutionalized in the form of clientelistic patronage networks and party factions. Hence there are indigenous historical and structural reasons for the development and extension of the so-called *sottogoverno*, the great influence of the *poteri occulti*, and the salience of conspiratorial and clandestine politics in postwar Italy. On the surface, at least, it would appear that this sort of political activity reached a scale and intensity there that was unusual, if not unique.[3]

There are, however, two objections that can be made to this thesis, despite its general plausibility and at least partial validity. For one thing, it is debatable whether this sort of behind-the-scenes maneuvering and plotting was more common in Italy than elsewhere. An argument can be made that such activity constitutes politics-as-usual almost everywhere. Certainly, the list of scandals that have afflicted other influential countries in the postwar era is scarcely less noteworthy.[4] It may also be that one hears more about conspiratorial politics in Italy simply because Italians tend to interpret politics in that way due to the historical factors identified earlier. Given that background, it would be natural – albeit somewhat paradoxical – for there to be a greater amount of open and public discussion about such secret machinations. Yet there were certain other features that also seem to have made the Italian case unique. For example, a higher proportion of these activities in Italy involved the use of political violence, as opposed to being limited to economic corruption and the illicit behavior typically associated with political elites. Moreover, the scandals in Italy were frequently related to one another in a convoluted but nonetheless organic fashion, which again may reflect the peculiarities of the Italian context, particularly its high degree of political polarization.[5]

Even so, without minimizing the undeniable importance of these domestic influences, national factors alone cannot account for the omnipresence of subversion and terrorism in postwar Italy. The strategic position of the Italian peninsula, which dominates the central Mediterranean basin, the existence of the largest communist party in Western Europe, and the apparent political instability of the government have inevitably prompted powerful international forces to intervene regularly in Italian domestic politics. It has already been noted that this type of intervention began on a large scale even before the elections of 1948, and it has since continued in different forms on numerous other occasions, especially in periods of acute international crisis and bipolar hostility. The importance of such interventions, many of which were carried out covertly in order to ensure "plausible deniability," should therefore not be underestimated or overlooked. This is all the more true given that indications of the involvement of one or more secret services in Italian terrorism, particularly right-wing terrorism, have repeatedly surfaced. It can in fact be argued that a good deal of the serious "neo-fascist" violence that afflicted the Italian people for over a decade can be laid at the doorstep, whether directly or indirectly, of factions within those services which were most closely affiliated with the security apparatus of the Atlantic Alliance. Such an interpretation receives additional corroboration when an explicitly comparative perspective is adopted. After all, a similar pattern of intervention has occurred in many other countries that have, often despite themselves, found themselves on the "front lines" in the secret wars waged by the superpowers and their client states.

One relevant example, in this context, is provided by the network of paramilitary "stay/behind" organizations that were created throughout Europe by the United States and its allies within the security forces of various nations during the height of the Cold War. Such organizations were briefly discussed earlier in connection with acts of subversion and terrorism in Italy, but only a more holistic view is capable of illuminating the role that they occasionally seem to have played in acts of political violence or other sorts of anti-constitutional activities. The purpose here is not to reconstruct the history of these networks, either in Italy or elsewhere, but rather to provide a few illustrative examples of the activities they have been involved in that to one degree or another exemplify the issues under consideration here. These networks were originally formed in order to serve as behind-the-lines resistance organizations in the event of a Soviet invasion of Europe. Although some observers have since claimed that their real purpose all along was to control the domestic left-wing opposition, that view is a short-sighted one reflecting either blatant political partisanship or an overly cynical post facto interpretation that fails to take account of the historical context at the time when those networks were created. The truth is that during the late 1940s and the first half of the 1950s, leading elements of the security establishments of the United States and most Western European countries were genuinely and justifiably concerned about hostile Soviet intentions. Some believed that outright war with the Soviets was imminent, and therefore felt it necessary to prepare actively for such a war without further delay. Although in retrospect such an assessment can be recognized as having been overly pessimistic if not alarmist, this was by no means apparent in 1948 and 1949, when truculent Soviet behavior made it seem all too plausible.

On the other hand, recent critics are quite right to point out that, whatever their original purpose, elements of some of these networks did later become involved in internal security functions. Before providing some examples of this, however, it would be wise to note another important characteristic of these organizations. In every country the personnel recruited into these groups were drawn, as one might expect, from a mixture of liberal anti-communist, moderately conservative, ultraconservative, or right-wing forces. Sometimes these stemmed from conservative anti-Nazi groups, as in Holland, but in certain countries they were drawn in part from ex-fascist or neo-fascist formations.[6] In West Germany, for example, the stay/behind network was made up primarily of activists from the postwar Bund Deutscher Jugend (BDJ: German Youth League), many of whom were reportedly unreconstructed Nazis. In Sweden, the original cadres for the network were recruited from the ranks of the wartime Sveaborg organization, a pro-Nazi collaborationist group. Elsewhere they tended to include members of both categories, former anti-fascists and former fascists who had decided to bury their past differences in the interests of the anti-communist cause.[7] Given the personnel involved, their apparent periodic involvement in anti-constitutional actions should not be a cause for surprise, although it is also increasingly clear that some leftist (and also radical neo-fascist) observers have retrospectively exaggerated the role played by these particular networks in perpetrating serious acts of terrorism.

There are three noteworthy examples of the involvement of personnel from the stay/behind networks in internal repression that may well have a bearing on the situation in Italy. In Greece the stay/behind organization, known by the code name "Red Sheepskin," consisted of specially trained commandos from the Lochoi Oreinon Katadromon (LOK: Mountain Pursuit Companies), which had been placed under the operational control of the Kentrike Yperesia Plerophorion (KYP: Central Intelligence Service). A good deal has been said about the KYP's subversive and anti-democratic activities in the preceding chapters, but the important point to note here is that the LOK and its commander not only participated in the 21 April 1967 right-wing military coup, but also in the brutal 16–17 November 1973 repression of protesting students at the Polytechnic University in Athens, apparently in accordance with the prearranged "Keravnos (Thunderbolt) Plan."[8] Perhaps even more revealing was the reportedly systematic involvement of elements of the Turkish stay/behind group, the Kontr-Gerilla (KG: Counter-Guerrilla) organization, which was attached to the Özel Harp Dairesi (ÖHD: Special Warfare Department) of the Armed Forces General Staff, in various terrorist and pro-coup actions. The KG, whose civilian personnel were recruited in part from the ranks of neo-fascists affiliated with the Milliyetçi Hareket Partisi (MHP: Nationalist Action Party), allegedly specialized in carrying out terrorist provocations designed to provide a pretext for a military intervention, as well as other sorts of covert operations in conjunction with the Army and the Milli İstihbarat Teşkilati (MIT: National Intelligence Agency).[9] A final example of this type is perhaps provided by the Belgian stay/behind networks, the 8th Section of the Service de Renseignements et d'Action (SDRA-8: Intelligence and Action Service), which was under the control of the military intelligence service, the Service Général de Renseignement (SGR: General Intelligence Service), and the Section Training, Communication et Mobilisation (S.T.C./Mob.: Training, Communications, and Mobilization Section, renamed D. 15 on 1 November 1990), which was under the authority of the Sûreté de l'État (State Security Service). Elements of this complex network were later implicated – justly or not – in certain actions designed to promote a mini-"strategy of tension" in Belgium during the early 1980s, as well as in earlier covert anti-communist operations, including the 18 August 1950 assassination of Parti Communiste de Belgique (Communist Party of Belgium) leader Julien Lahaut.[10]

What these examples suggest is that the Americans and their North Atlantic Treaty Organization (NATO) allies set up organizations that, whatever their original purpose, sometimes later engaged directly and, in some cases, perhaps more systematically in anti-constitutional "countersubversive" operations. The rank-and-file of several of these organizations consisted, to one degree or other, of civilian right-wing extremists with openly anti-democratic sentiments. Viewed from this perspective, especially in light of the documented Allied recruitment of Nazi unconventional warfare specialists after World War II and the undeniable existence of many other parallel networks set up by the Americans or NATO to fight communism in postwar Europe, it is hard to view the events associated with the "strategy of tension" as a strictly Italian phenomenon. Furthermore, when account is taken of United States covert operations in Latin America and other parts of the Third World, which too often involved the creation of paramilitary apparatuses that subsequently carried out brutal campaigns designed to terrorize the general population – which, as per Mao Zedong, constituted the "water" within which the "fish" (guerrillas) swam – there can scarcely be any doubt that similar operations might have been secretly set in motion in Europe if the situation appeared threatening enough.

A number of qualifications need to be made, however. First, it seems certain that elements of these networks operated autonomously or independently in certain instances. To put it another way, it is not always clear that they were following orders, either those issued by their nominal superiors within their own nation's command structure or those issued indirectly by their more distant international referents. They may have been pursuing their own anti-democratic agendas under the "cover" provided by these official but clandestine security organizations. Second, even if they were instructed to take action by officials linked to NATO or the Atlantic Alliance, this may only mean that personnel associated with hardline factions within certain security bureaucracies were interested in pursuing such actions, perhaps even unbeknownst to or against the express wishes of other factions within their own agencies or home governments. Third, it is clear that such drastic measures were only adopted in circumstances that were perceived as particularly threatening. In marked contrast to their behavior in many Third World countries, the governments of the United States' NATO allies did not wish to set up authoritarian right-wing regimes in place of formal parliamentary democracies on the European continent. Indeed, they often preferred to support moderate social democratic parties, especially in the early postwar period, because they felt that such political forces were better able to neutralize the appeal of the communists, who had emerged from World War II with greatly increased prestige. Finally, as noted earlier, such extreme measures were restricted to strategically important countries that were considered especially unstable, untrustworthy, or vulnerable. There is no evidence, for example, that the stay/behind networks established in Norway, Denmark, and Sweden engaged in political subversion of this type. The political situation in those nations simply did not warrant it. Italy, unfortunately, was not blessed with the same degree of stability. In any event, it should be obvious that ignoring the international context within which the "strategy of tension" was carried out would be a serious oversight.

A second major problem that requires some explanation is the reason why radical neo-fascists, conservative intelligence officers, and ostensibly democratic statesmen made common cause. This was only possible due to the presence of certain crosscutting issues that they all could agree upon. The most important of these was undoubtedly anti-communism, which provided the glue that held this disparate coalition together in the face of profoundly different and often antithetical values and political goals. There were a number of reasons why certain groups of neo-fascists participated in these operations, which in the end strengthened the very same "reactionary" and "bourgeois" forces that they professed to detest. In the Italian context, one reason was that the ideas of Julius Evola, the esoteric traditionalist who exerted a major influence on the thinking of postwar neo-fascist ultras, provided a justification for doing whatever it took to oppose communism. Although Evola believed that the values embodied by the United States represented a greater long-term threat to European civilization, he recognized that the communists represented the chief danger in the short run, for if they were able to seize power the very survival of "eternal" European values would be placed in jeopardy. Hence the communists had to be dealt with first.

Moreover, as right-wing terrorist Vincenzo Vinciguerra has made clear, Evola had so emptied fascist ideas of their genuinely revolutionary content that this had the effect of encouraging "neo-fascists" who did not even understand the essence of fascism to believe that elements of the Italian military and police were their chief allies. In his view, the naïve ultras who promoted an alliance between neo-fascist "soldiers without uniforms" and "militants in the service" had utterly failed to understand the Army's shameful betrayal of the Fascist regime and its subsequent collaboration with elements of the Resistance.[11] Unfortunately, this disastrous misconception was further reinforced by the dramatic rebellion of the seditious French Army officers, whose exploits fired right-wing civilians throughout Europe with enthusiasm and thus came to constitute a model for the latter's own actions. The subsequent direct interaction between neo-fascists and these *guerre révolutionnaire* specialists only compounded this tendency, and it was in part this identification that led radical fascists to mistake backwards-looking dictatorships like that of the Greek Colonels for genuine revolutionary regimes, with all the practical consequences that this entailed.

Finally, there were a number of practical and emotional benefits that neo-fascists could obtain by collaborating with factions within the armed forces and the security services. These included all the forms of tangible "assistance" discussed at length earlier, including the provision of technical aid, logistical support, "cover," and other sorts of protection that enabled these ultras to carry out acts of violence and terrorism with impunity – at least until such time as their services were no longer needed. Another important benefit, at least from the psychological point of view, was the thrill of engaging in clandestine and covert operations under the direction of real professionals, which is just the sort of thing that can easily appeal to youthful political activists searching for both meaning and a place in the world. Such intangible emotional factors should not be overlooked in this context. Finally, working for the secret services enabled certain neo-fascist leaders either to benefit themselves or devote their full attention to the far from dull tasks associated with covert action and subversion. In short, they were able to profit tangibly by doing the kinds of exciting "work" they enjoyed most. This was certainly true of Delle Chiaie.

For the secret services, there were likewise benefits to be had by associating with right-wing extremists. The most important of these was the ability to contract out especially compromising jobs to seemingly autonomous forces, thereby covering up their own behind-the-scenes involvement in them. Maintaining this sort of "plausible deniability" was absolutely essential, for otherwise the entire purpose for conducting covert operations would have been defeated. After all, if governments were not anxious to conceal their involvement in delicate anti-democratic and anti-constitutional activities, they could simply carry them out directly and then openly claim responsibility for them. This is why the utilization and manipulation of intermediaries was so crucial to the ultimate success and effectiveness of such operations. At the opportune moment, of course, such intermediaries could be and often were "burned," either by being physically eliminated or publicly compromised in some way. For both parties, then, there were generally finite limits to the utility and durability of these sorts of arrangements, but it was the secret services that often had the upper hand, at least in their collaborative arrangements with domestic extremists (as opposed to foreign extremists). They normally had the resources, expertise, and institutional power to be able to discard their local agents when these became more of a liability than an asset. Domestic ultras were thus usually the junior partners in these temporary working relationships, partners whose positions were only assured as long as they served the interests of the services. At the same time, however, those extremists would periodically turn on their former state "benefactors" when their agendas diverged too much, making such relationships dangerous for all parties, who were trying to manipulate each other.

Nevertheless, the neo-fascists who colluded with the Italian security forces were more or less systematically manipulated from the very beginning. They were encouraged to carry out a series of violent actions whose ultimate effects, far from laying the groundwork for a coup d'etat and a revolutionary transformation of society, served only to strengthen the U.S.-dominated Atlantic Alliance and the corrupt *partitocrazia* in Italy that they themselves had hoped to overthrow. What the international and national sponsors of the "strategy of tension" were actually conducting was a complex strategy designed to keep the socialist left and the communists from entering the corridors of power on a national level and, in the process, assure Italy's continued fidelity to the Atlantic Alliance. As noted earlier, these sponsors were themselves divided into two main factional groupings, those who sought to preserve the current political structure from which they derived tangible benefits, and those who sought to replace that dysfunctional system with a "presidentialist" arrangement that would strengthen the executive branch at the expense of Parliament. To accomplish these tasks, however, these rival factions both employed the *tactics* of destabilization by making instrumental use of right-wing radicals, with or without the latters' assent. What they were really engaged in all along was "destabilizing in order to stabilize," as Vinciguerra and many other knowledgeable insiders and observers have emphasized. In that sense, the participating neo-fascists were also political victims, at least to the extent that one can refer to those who intentionally place bombs in public places as "victims." In the end, with some noteworthy exceptions, they did not benefit any more from the "strategy of tension" than their counterparts on the extraparliamentary left. The beneficiaries were almost invariably their *sub rosa* sponsors.

Alas, this pattern of manipulation dated back to the nineteenth century, if not much earlier. According to former Office of Strategic Services (OSS) and Central Intelligence Agency (CIA) operative Paul W. Blackstock, "the myopia and political fanaticism of extremist groups makes them especially vulnerable to manipulation in political warfare operations."[12] This is all the more true when the extremists in question glorify authority and idealize state power, as is typical of both fascists and Marxist-Leninists. A rather more cynical version of the same idea was expressed in 1870 by a French police inspector, who noted that "[i]n a group of ten secret society members there are always three stool pigeons working for the police (*mouchards*), six well-meaning imbeciles, and one dangerous man."[13] If one extends the point about *mouchards* to include *agents provocateurs* as well as simple informants, this statement appears to have a good deal of validity. Unfortunately, this phenomenon has rarely been the subject of systematic historical study, despite its great potential importance in the development of social and political movements, rightist and leftist. In the Italian context, Philip Willan has made an important distinction between the type of secret service manipulation to which neo-fascist and far left terrorists in Italy were subjected. He argues that neo-fascists, due to their generally favorable view of state authority and the military, were manipulated in the fashion of a glove puppet, whereas left-wing ultras, given their hostility to the existing state, were manipulated in the fashion of a marionette that was held secretly by an unknown party.[14] There is much truth to this, particularly if one restricts it to the "historic" neo-fascist groups like Ordine Nuovo and Avanguardia Nazionale. However, in the later, "spontaneous" phase of neo-fascist terrorism, state manipulation of the revolutionary right often assumed a form more similar to that employed against the revolutionary left.

In any event, in order to understand the wave of neo-fascist terrorism that Italy was subjected to between 1968 and 1980, one needs to go beyond the conventional approaches to the phenomenon. Given the often tendentious nature of the sources and the overall complexity of conspiratorial politics, it would be rash to assume that every single detail in the preceding historical reconstructions will end up being corroborated if and when additional sources of information become available. Yet the overall pattern seems unmistakable. The unpalatable truth is that elements within various Western security and intelligence services have all too often played a considerable covert role in the sponsorship and political manipulation of terrorism in postwar Europe. The same may well prove to be true of some of their erstwhile East Bloc counterparts. It would seem, then, that far more attention needs to be paid to the activities of these and other powerful, behind-the-scenes forces. To ignore the clandestine and covert dimensions of Cold War political violence is to miss a good deal of the picture.

Notes

1 For the radicalization of the neo-fascist milieu, the split between the older and younger generations, and the later phases of right-wing terrorism, see Franco Ferraresi, "La destra eversiva," in *La destra radicale*, ed. by Franco Ferraresi (Milan: Feltrinelli, 1984), pp. 74–96; Vittorio Borracetti, "Introduzione," in *Eversione di destra, terrorismo, stragi: I fatti e l'intervento*

giudiziario, ed. by Vittorio Borracetti (Milan: Angeli, 1986), pp. 21–4; Giancarlo Capaldi et al., "L'eversione di destra a Roma dal 1977 al 1983: Spunti per una ricostruzione del fenomeno," in *Eversione di destra, terrorismo, stragi: I fatti e l'intervento giudiziario*, ed. by Vittorio Borracetti (Milan: Angeli, 1986), pp. 198–244; Nicola Rao, *Neofascisti! La Destra italiana da Salò a Fiuggi nel ricordo dei protagonisti* (Rome: Settimo Segillo, 1999), pp. 195–210; Gabriele Adinolfi and Roberto Fiore, *Noi, Terza Posizione* (Rome: Settimo Segillo, 2000); and Ugo Maria Tassinari, *Guerrieri, 1975–1982: Storie di una generazione in nero* (Pozzuoli: Immaginapoli, 2005). For the cultural and intellectual background of this dramatic shift, see Marco Revelli, "La nuova destra," in *Destra radicale*, especially pp. 119–37; Monica Zucchinali, *A destra in Italia oggi: Destra missina, moderata o reaganiana, destra radicale e nuova destra* (Milan: Sugar, 1986), pp. 113–97; Rao, *Neofascisti!*, pp. 185–93; and Enzo Raisi, *Storia ed idee della nuova destra italiana* (Rome: Settimo Segillo, 1990).

2 For the sordid but nonetheless tragic story of Fioravanti and Mambro, compare Giovanni Bianconi, *A mano armata: Vita violenta di Giusva Fioravanti* (Milan: Baldini & Castoldi, 1992); and Piero Corsini, *I terroristi della porta accanto. Storie del terrorismo nero: Valerio Fioravanti, Francesca Mambro e la militanza nei NAR* (Naples: Tullio Pironti, 2007). Compare also Gianluca Semprini, *La strage di Bologna e il terrorista sconosciuto: Il caso Ciavardini* (Milan: Bietti, 2003). It should be pointed out, however, that many aspects of this 1980 *strage* remain to be clarified, and that some authors attribute the responsibility to other terrorist groups altogether. See, e.g., Gabriele Paradisi, Gian Paolo Pelizzaro, and François de Quengo de Tonquédec, *Dossier strage di Bologna: La pista segreta* (Bologna: Giraldi, 2010), who argue, based on the views and information provided by some judges and military officers, that the real perpetrators may have been operatives linked to Jūrj Habash's Jabhat al-Shaʻbiyya li-Tahrīr Filastīn (PFLP: Popular Front for the Liberation of Palestine). Compare Valerio Cutonilli and Rosario Priore, *I segreti di Bologna: La verità sull'atto terroristico più grave della storia italiana* (Milan: Chiarelettere, 2016).

3 On the Italian context within which these traits flourished and an excellent evaluation of the *poteri occulti*, see Angelo Ventura, "I poteri occulti nella Repubblica italiana: Il problema storico," in *I "poteri occulti" nella Repubblica: Mafia, camorra, P2, stragi impunite*, ed. by Comune di Venezia and Ufficio Affari Istituzionale (Venice: Marsilio, 1984), pp. 17–52. In my opinion, Ventura is one of the shrewdest analysts of recent Italian politics, particularly those with a clandestine dimension.

4 Compare, for example, the German scandals enumerated in Rudiger Liedtke, *Skandal-Chronik: Das Lexikon der Affären und Skandale in Wildwest-Deutschland* (Frankfurt: Eichborn, 1987); Fritz Lietsch, *Bananenrepublik: Skandale und Affären in der Bundesrepublik* (Munich: Heyne, 1989); and Georg M. Hafner and Edmund Jacoby, *Die Skandale der Republik* (Hamburg: Hoffmann & Campe, 1990). For overviews of the postwar Italian scandals, see Sergio Turone, *Partiti e Mafia: Dalla P2 alla droga* (Rome: Laterza, 1985); Giorgio Galli, *Affari di stato. L'Italia sotteranea, 1943–1990: Storia politica, partiti, corruzione, misteri, scandali* (Milan: Kaos, 1991); and Sandro Provvisionato, *Misteri d'Italia: Cinquant'anni di trame e delitti senza colpevoli* (Rome and Bari: Laterza, 1993). For a general introductory reference to some of the major postwar scandals in various parts of the world, see *Political Scandals and Causes Celebres since 1945: An International Reference Compendium* (Harlow: Longman, 1991).

5 For more on Italian scandals, see the excellent article by Judith Chubb and Maurizio Vannicelli, "Italy: A Web of Scandals," in *The Politics of Scandal: Power and Process in Liberal Democracies*, ed. by Andrei S. Markovits and Mark Silverstein (New York and London: Holmes and Meier, 1988), pp. 122–50. This entire volume is a very useful anthology of articles on recent scandals in various countries, although the editors' thesis that "scandals" can only occur in liberal democratic regimes is debatable.

6 For the Dutch underground networks, a series of overlapping organizations that revolved largely around the indefatigable anti-communist Louis Einthoven, see Hugo Gijsels, *Netwerk Gladio* (Louvain: Kritak, 1991), pp. 49–64; Bob de Graaff and Cees Wiebes, *Gladio, der vrije jongens: Een particuliere geheime dienst in Koude Oorlogstijd* (The Hague:

Koninginnegracht, 1992); Dick Engelen, *De Nederlandse stay-behind-organisatie in de koude oorlog, 1945–1992: Een institutioneel onerzoek* (The Hague: Rijksarchiefdienst/PIVOT, 2005); and Dick Engelen, "Lessons Learned: The Dutch 'Stay-Behind' Organization, 1945–1992," *Journal of Strategic Studies* 30:6 (December 2007), pp. 981–96. Compare also Paul Krijnen, *"Zonodig met behulp van wapens": Geschiedenis van rechtse paramilitaire organisaties in Nederland* (Amsterdam: SUA, 1983), especially pp. 67–90; and Giles Scott-Smith, *Western Anti-Communism and the Interdoc Network: Cold War Internationale* (New York: Palgrave Macmillan, 2012), pp. 56–64.

7 For the constituent groups affiliated with these stay/behind networks in Europe, see Daniele Ganser, *NATO's Secret Armies: Operation Gladio and Terrorism in Western Europe* (London and New York: Frank Cass, 2005); Jean-François Brozzu-Gentile, *L'Affaire Gladio: Les réseaux secrets américains au coeur du terrorisme en Europe* (Paris: Albin Michel, 1994); Leo A. Müller, *Gladio – das Erbe des Kalten Krieges: Der NATO-Geheimbund und sein deutscher Vorläufer* (Reinbek: Rowohlt, 1991), pp. 51–60; Gerald Desmaretz, *Stay-Behind: Les réseaux secrets de la Guerre froide* (Paris: Jourdan, 2015); and Olav Riste, " 'Stay Behind': A Clandestine Cold War Phenomenon," *Journal of Cold War Studies* 16:4 (Fall 2014), pp. 35–59. For the BDJ, see ibid., pp. 71–153; Kurt Hirsch, *Rechts von der Union: Personen, Organisationen, Parteien seit 1945. Ein Lexikon* (Munich: Knesebeck & Schuler, 1989), pp. 202–5; Erich Schmidt-Eenboom, *Schnüffler ohne Nase. Der BND – die unheimliche Macht im Staate* (Dusseldorf: ECON, 1993), pp. 365–78; Erich Schmidt-Eenboom and Ulrich Stoll, *Die Partisanen der NATO: Stay-Behind-Organisationen in Deutschland, 1946–1991* (Berlin: Ch. Links, 2015), pp. 23–79; and Peter Dudek and Hans-Gerd Jaschke, *Entstehung und Entwicklung des Rechtsextremismus in der Bundesrepublik: Zur Tradition einer besonderen politischen Kultur* (Opladen: Westdeutscher, 1984), volume 1, pp. 356–88, and volume 2, pp. 163–94 (documentation). For the Sveaborg affiliation with these networks, see Müller, *Gladio*, pp. 59–60. For more on the background and personnel of the Sveaborg organization, see Armas Sastamoinen, *Hitlers svenska förtrupper* (Stockholm: Federativs, 1947), pp. 43–70.

8 For the Greek stay/behind group, see Ganser, *NATO's Secret Armies*, pp. 212–3; and Müller, *Gladio*, pp. 54–5. For the LOK's involvement in the coup plot and the attack on the Polytechnic, see C. M. Woodhouse, *The Rise and Fall of the Greek Colonels* (New York: Franklin Watts, 1985), pp. 21, 135.

9 For the identification of the KG organization as the stay/behind group in Turkey, see Ganser, *NATO's Secret Armies*, pp. 224–44; and Müller, *Gladio*, pp. 56–7. For more on the KG and its activities, see Süleyman Genç, *Biçagin Sirtindaki Türkiye: CIA/MIT/Kontr-Gerilla* (Istanbul: Der, 1978); and Emin Değer, *CIA, Kontr-Gerilla ve Türkiye* (Ankara: Caglar, 1977); and *Kontr-Gerilla ve MHP: CIA'nin Türkiye'deki Kontrgerilla Teorisi ve Uygulamasi* (Istanbul: Aydinlik, 1978). As the preceding titles indicate, it is generally believed that there were close links between the KG and the CIA. These sources are, however, products of the far left. Compare also Ertugrul Mavioglu and Ahmet Sik, *Kirk katir kirk satir: Kontrgerilla ve Ergenekon'u anlama kilavuzu* (Istanbul: Ithaki, 2010).

10 For the Belgian stay/behind groups, see especially Part I of Jan Willems, ed., *Gladio* (Brussels: EPO/Reflex, 1991), pp. 5–60 (articles by Willems and Michel Bouffioux); and Gijsels, *Netwerk Gladio*, pp. 27–48, 65–148. Compare Ganser, *NATO's Secret Armies*, pp. 125–47; and Müller, *Gladio*, p. 53. For the assassination of Lahaut, see Rudy Van Doorslaer and Etienne Verhoeyen, *L'Assassinat de Julien Lahaut: Une histoire de l'anticommunisme en Belgique* (Anvers: EPO, 1987). For the violent and subversive activities afflicting Belgium from the 1960s to the 1980s, see René Haquin, *Des taupes dans l'extrême droite: La Sûreté de l'État et le WNP* (Anvers: EPO, no date); Walter De Bock et al., *L'Extrême droite et l'état* (Berchem: EPO, no date); Hugo Gijsels, *L'Enquête: 20 années de déstabilisation en Belgique* (Paris and Brussels: Longue Vue, 1989); Danny Ilegems, Raf Sauviller, and Jan Willems, *De Bende-Tapes* (Louvain: Kritak, 1990); Els Cleemput and Alain Guillaume, *La rançon d'une vie: Paul Vanden Boeynants, 30 jours aux mains de Patrick Haemers* (Zonhoven: Boek, 1990); Philippe Brewaeys and Jean-Frédérick Deliège, *De Bonvoisin et Cie: De Liège à Bruxelles, les prédateurs et l'état* (Brussels: EPO, 1992); Gilbert Dupont and Paul Ponsaers, *Les tueurs:*

Six années d'enquête (Anvers: EPO, 1988); and Christian Carpentier and Frédérick Moser, *La Sûreté de l'État: Histoire d'une déstabilisation* (Ottignies: Quorum, 1993). This is an immensely complex matter that I had hoped to study further before I was diverted by the growing jihadist threat. For a critique of overly conspiratorial interpretations concerning the Belgian stay/behind network by an historian, compare Hervé Hasquin, *Le soi-disant "Gladio belge": Aux origines d'un désamour d'un pays et de ses services secrets* (Brussels: Académie Royale de Belgique, 2016).

11 Vinciguerra, *Ergastolo per la libertà: Verso la verità sulla strategia della tensione* (Florence: Arnaud, 1989), pp. 3–6.

12 See his fascinating work *The Strategy of Subversion: Manipulating the Politics of Other Nations* (Chicago: Quadrangle, 1964), p. 54.

13 Quoted in Howard C. Payne, *The Police State of Louis Napoleon Bonaparte, 1851–1860* (Seattle: University of Washington, 1966), p. 265.

14 See *Puppetmasters: The Political Use of Terrorism in Italy* (London: Constable, 1991), pp. 179–80.

8
THE ULTRANATIONALIST RIGHT IN TURKEY AND THE ATTEMPTED ASSASSINATION OF POPE JOHN PAUL II

Introduction

Like most dramatic and unsettling political events, the attempted assassination of Pope John Paul II by Turkish gunman Mehmet Ali Ağca temporarily captured the imagination of the world's media and political pundits. Although the initial public outrage and concern generally faded once it became clear that the pope would survive and be able to resume his manifold duties as head of the Roman Catholic Church, certain individuals and groups have pursued the issue for a much longer time, usually for political reasons of one sort or another. As a result, a considerable literature about the crime has already appeared, most of which focuses on tracing its background, reconstructing its successive phases, and determining its ultimate sponsorship and purposes. Yet no consensus has been reached about many of the key elements in the unfolding plot, which is perhaps not surprising given its potentially explosive political ramifications. Indeed, these very ramifications have encouraged the type of politically motivated speculation that has in the main only served to obscure the actual events behind layers of falsehood. Before these layers become too dense to penetrate, more serious research needs to be undertaken so that various contentious issues can be clarified and certain spurious claims exposed.

Among the major controversies that still rage, two that have particular importance are the inter-related questions of Ağca's organizational affiliations and motives for trying to kill the pope. Since these are complicated subjects that cannot possibly be dealt with in their entirety herein, I will focus my attention on two narrower issues. First, with what elements of the Turkish extreme right was Ağca affiliated? And second, could this affiliation *in and of itself* have provided him with a strong motive to try to murder the pope? Although these particular questions are not terribly difficult to answer if one is familiar with the historical background of various Turkish political groupings and ideological currents, most of those who have sought to analyze the "plot to kill the pope" lack precisely this familiarity.[1] One result is that both those who accept and those who deny the possibility of an indigenous Turkish sponsorship of the papal assassination attempt have usually made fundamental interpretive errors or, at the very least, oversimplified assessments. The purpose of this article is to shed light on the Turkish political milieu from which Ağca emerged, a milieu which clearly provided him with both a motive *and* the wherewithal to shoot the pope. Even so, this does not necessarily prove that indigenous Turkish forces were solely or even primarily responsible for planning and executing that attempt, and given the limitations of the currently available data, it would be foolish to foreclose other possibilities or reach definitive conclusions about its ultimate sponsorship.

The secondary literature on the papal assassination plot is already extensive and continues to proliferate, but the bulk of it is highly problematic, albeit for diverse reasons. For simplicity's sake, it can be divided into three major categories, each of which is dominated by publications with clear rightist or leftist political biases. However, these categories are not entirely discrete, and it is often quite difficult to be certain to which category a given work belongs.[2]

The first such category is literature which seems to be *consciously* produced and/or disseminated for propaganda purposes, often by people with direct or indirect links to the intelligence services of countries that are members of either the North Atlantic Treaty Organization (NATO) or the Warsaw Pact. These works, being designed primarily to manipulate public perceptions and thereby generate support for the adoption of certain desired policies, contain a considerable amount of disinformation and sometimes appear to constitute components of more extensive psychological operations.[3] This type of literature is by now quite common on both sides. On the Western side,[4] it includes the highly influential books by Paul B. Henze[5] and Claire Sterling[6], lesser known works by Vendelín Slugenov[7] and Giovanni Bensi,[8] and a host of articles and TV commentaries by other terrorism television "experts" like Alexandre de Marenches,[9] Michael A. Ledeen,[10] and Ray S. Cline.[11] Much of this material reflects the interests of hawkish, right-wing factions within various Western intelligence agencies, not necessarily the views of those agencies as a whole.[12] On the Eastern side, one can cite a number of official Bulgarian and Soviet publications, as well as those produced by pro-Soviet Western communists, whether or not they are actually members of official communist parties or front groups.[13] To say that all of these works seem designed mainly to exploit propaganda themes is not to say that all of the information contained in them is false, since propaganda is most effective when it judiciously mixes truth and falsehood.[14] Although there is some useful material in virtually all of these works, one should never accept them at face value or forget that they were produced to lend support to certain policy agendas or for propagandistic purposes.

The second major category consists of literature that naïvely and uncritically incorporates propaganda or disinformation themes, and thereby both obscures their sources and aids in their dissemination to a wider audience. This constitutes by far the largest category on the Western side, ranging from superficial journalistic treatments and commentaries to quasi-scholarly articles.[15] On the Eastern side it is hard to tell just how extensive this category is, despite the exaggerated claims that are frequently made about the effectiveness of Soviet disinformation campaigns and other "active measures."[16] Although Soviet propaganda is certainly recycled in a large number of relatively orthodox far left publications, it is often difficult to determine if this is done consciously by Soviet-controlled agents – which would place it within the first category – or unwittingly by communist sympathizers with an idealized view about the nature of the Soviet Union. Either way, such propaganda is rarely picked up by mainstream conservative and liberal publications in the West which, if anything, tend to gullibly accept or intentionally promote the propaganda lines of their *own* governments.[17] In any event, the literature in this category usually adds little in the way of new information and – like that in the first category – is generally produced by people who are clearly sympathetic to the cause of one side or the other, which causes them to apply critical reasoning only to the arguments of the opposition – if they do so at all.

The third and final category, literature produced by researchers with relatively independent and critical minds, is by far the smallest in terms of volume. On the right side of the political spectrum, only one work specifically dealing with the papal plot comes to mind,[18] although there are some fine academic studies of terrorism *per se* with abroadly conservative or rightist bias.[19] On the left, this category is dominated by the works of Edward S. Herman and Frank Brodhead, the most recent of which is, despite its authors' excessive reluctance to credit accounts of alleged East Bloc criminality, the single most thorough and intelligent analysis of the subject to have appeared so far.[20]

Here too can be found some excellent articles, and two important book-length studies by Turkish journalist Uğur Mumcu.[21] Also in this category are several fine articles by political moderates, especially Michael Dobbs of the *Washington Post*.[22] Predictably, this type of literature has often been studiously ignored or viciously smeared by the dogmatic partisans on both sides, with the result that the latter's widely disseminated propaganda and disinformation has generally had an impact disproportionate to its actual value.

The major theories that have been proffered concerning the alleged sponsorship of the "plot to kill the pope" are also three in number, although each can be found in somewhat different variants. In most cases, they grow logically out of the particular political biases of their proponents, but as I hope to demonstrate later only one of them is thoroughly based on reliable evidentiary support rather than speculation.

The first is the theory that the Soviet Komitet Gosudarst'vennoy Bezopasnosti (KGB: Committee for State Security), acting through a chain of intermediaries, including the surrogate Bulgarian Komitet za Darzhavna Sigur'nost (KDS [later DS]: Committee for State Security), a branch of the Turkish mafia headquartered in Sofia, and elements of an extreme *right-wing* Turkish paramilitary organization, the Bozkurtlar (Gray Wolves), recruited Ağca and arranged the assassination attempt.[23] The motive is plausibly ascribed to Politburo fears that Pope John Paul II, a former

Polish cardinal named Karol Józef Wojtyła, would fuel popular opposition to the Soviet-backed regime in Poland, and perhaps also in other eastern European countries.[24] Proponents of this "Bulgarian connection" differ on certain important details, such as the precise point at which Ağca was supposedly recruited by East Bloc intelligence,[25] but all agree that the Soviets had both a strong motive and the technical means to plan and direct such an operation. Although no fair-minded observer could legitimately quibble with these latter notions, Soviet and Bulgarian writers have predictably denied that such a motive existed, and even otherwise perceptive researchers have downplayed it.[26] The chief problem with this "KGB plot" thesis is that almost all of the evidence is contaminated or otherwise unreliable, consisting as it does of Ağca's often fantastic and contradictory statements,[27] information intentionally "leaked" by various unnamed intelligence sources that can neither be traced nor independently verified,[28] the problematic testimony of several Soviet Bloc defectors,[29] and the many unsupported assertions and suppositions of intelligence-linked disinformationists.[30]

To these evidentiary problems must also be added others of a logical nature. First of all, would the Russian leadership, however paranoid and ruthless, be foolish enough to initiate an operation that millions of people – especially Poles – would *automatically* assume they were behind and which would thus probably serve to catalyze the very unrest and opposition they hoped to defuse in eastern Europe?[31] More importantly, is it likely that the KGB and DS, professional intelligence organizations whose efficiency is usually touted by Western "experts," would *systematically* violate virtually all of the most elementary rules of tradecraft and agent-handling by, among other things, hiring an emotionally unstable person as the triggerman, employing an unusually large number of support personnel (which could adversely affect the maintenance of secrecy), bringing Ağca to Sofia for sixty days and allowing him to stay at the highly visible Hotel Vitosha, sending a notorious Turkish assassin, whose activities were well-known to Western police and security forces, to several European countries for a lengthy stay prior to the actual assassination attempt, and arranging for Bulgarian case officers to meet with him personally (instead of through intermediaries) to plan the attack?[32] Human error makes such a scenario possible, but all of these factors together make it seem rather implausible.

The second theory is a mirror image of the first, in that the alleged sponsor of the attack on the pope was the U.S. Central Intelligence Agency (CIA), acting through *its* intermediaries, which are variously identified as one or more Western intelligence services and the networks of right-wing (including fascist) extremists in Turkey and Europe that they are said to control.[33] Among these purported intermediaries were the Turkish Millî İstihbarat Teşkilâtı (MİT: National Intelligence Agency),[34] Alparslan Türkeş' Milliyetçi Hareket Partisi (MHP: Nationalist Action [or Movement] Party) and its affiliated Bozkurt commandos (including Ağca himself), Licio Gelli's "covered" right-wing Masonic lodge Propaganda Due (P2),[35] the secret "Super S" faction within the Italian Servizio Informazioni Sicurezza Militare (SISMI),[36] certain European neo-fascist organizations, fanatical Catholic "integralist" circles,[37] the West German Bundesnachrichtendienst (BND), the Israeli Mossad Letafkidim Meyouchadim (Mossad: Central Institute for Intelligence and Special Duties), the Vatican's intelligence apparatus, the NATO secret service, and assorted reactionary politicians.[38] This is a scenario that has been promoted almost exclusively by propaganda and disinformation specialists from East Bloc countries and pro-communist authors in the West. A number of distinct motives for this Western plot have been enumerated, some of which are rather fanciful,[39] but there is virtually unanimous agreement that one of its major purposes was to provide a pretext for launching a fresh propaganda campaign designed to discredit the Soviet Union and its allies and thereby prevent any thaw in the so-called New Cold War then being waged by the Reagan administration.[40] However, although the CIA has demonstrated links to most of the aforementioned organizations, and some of its factions have made post-facto covert efforts to attribute the attempted assassination to the KGB, it seems unlikely that even the most hawkish American officials would sanction or embark upon such an extreme and risky measure in connection with John Paul II, a conservative on most religious and many political issues.[41] More importantly, even if the case for CIA sponsorship were as compelling as that for KGB sponsorship, which is doubtful given the absence of a clear motive, the available evidence is insufficient to support the thesis that U.S. intelligence orchestrated Ağca's attack on the pope.[42]

Nevertheless, this skepticism about the theories of KGB or CIA sponsorship should not be misinterpreted. No one should entertain any illusions about the "morality" or "innocence" of the world's secret services, which systematically and extensively employ a plethora of "black" techniques, including political assassinations and the manipulation of terrorist groups. Reliable information has recently surfaced concerning the protection offered by various East Bloc intelligence services to fugitive left-wing terrorists,[43] and the available evidence *does* suggest that the three Bulgarian officials who were eventually indicted by Italian prosecutors in the Ağca case were up to something — even if it had nothing to do with the attack on the pope.[44] Likewise, there is plenty of evidence indicating that Western intelligence services have secretly created and/or supported parallel police apparatuses, and that factions within these services have covertly promoted terrorist operations and manipulated terrorist groups on all sides of the political spectrum, examples of which will be noted later.[45]

The third and final theory is that the assassination attempt was actually what it initially appeared to be — the effort of a rather unstable and megalomaniacal Turkish ultranationalist, with the help of some of his comrades and their criminal allies, to eliminate a figure who they perceived, not entirely without justification, to be the symbol of Western and Christian "imperialism." This interpretation is entirely consistent with both the ideological milieu from which Ağca emerged in Turkey and the bulk of the reliable evidence concerning the plot. In addition to supporting the validity of this initial or main conspiracy, one that was rooted in indigenous Turkish politics, the evidence also suggests that there was a "second conspiracy" launched by Cold War hawks within various Western governments and intelligence services to pin the crime on the Bulgarians and Soviets by manipulating Ağca's testimony,[46] although this will not be covered in any detail herein.

Ağca's political and ideological background

The issue of Ağca's links to political groups in Turkey is obviously of great importance in any attempt to determine his sources of organizational support and probable motives in connection with the shooting of Pope John Paul II. Considering the overwhelming amount of evidence linking the young gunman to the Turkish extreme right, the controversy that has arisen about his affiliations and views would be inexplicable if not for the efforts of various influential polemicists and propagandists to obscure the issue for political reasons. This is all the more unfortunate in that the initial media reports on Ağca's background were reasonably accurate.

Shortly after the assassination attempt in St. Peter's Square on 13 May 1981, it was reported in newspapers of record throughout the world that Mehmet Ali Ağca was associated with the Turkish ultranationalist right, specifically the Bozkurt paramilitary terrorist organization affiliated with the MHP.[47] Indeed, Ağca was one of the most notorious right-wing terrorists in Turkey, since he had previously participated in the 1 February 1979 assassination of the highly respected editor of the liberal daily *Milliyet*, Abdi İpekçi. In late November 1979, with the help of extreme rightists within the Turkish security forces, he escaped from the maximum security Kartal-Maltepe military prison, on the eve of the pope's scheduled visit to Turkey. One day after his escape, he wrote a letter to *Milliyet* threatening to kill the "Crusader Commander" (*Haçlı Kumandanı*) if this visit was not cancelled. He did not make good on this threat at the time, but with the assistance provided by other Bozkurt comrades he eluded Turkish authorities, acquired financing and weapons, and eventually made his way to St. Peter's Square for the assassination attempt. In short, the information acquired shortly after the crime clearly revealed Ağca's rightist political background and suggested his likely motives for shooting the pope, and most of the additional details that have since been uncovered have tended to confirm these early assessments.

However, a number of Eastern and Western regimes had a vested political interest in exploiting the incident for propaganda purposes, so it was probably inevitable that these relatively cogent initial analyses would come under attack by disinformationists in both camps.[48] Within the Soviet Bloc, Ağca's links to the Turkish far right were eagerly seized upon, and quickly led to the elaboration of the aforementioned thesis of ultimate CIA sponsorship. On the Western side, the existence of these same links initially posed problems for the propagandists. However, their task was facilitated by a general public awareness that the Soviets were not favorably disposed toward the pope, whom they perceived as a troublesome, reactionary meddler in internal eastern European and especially Polish affairs.[49] Ağca himself provided further grist for the Western disinformation mills immediately after his arrest by admitting that he spent nearly two months in Bulgaria and claiming to have undergone training at a left-wing Palestinian guerrilla camp in Lebanon.[50] These two statements originally formed the *sole* basis of Western attempts to portray Ağca as a Soviet Bloc assassin, for it was not until May 1982 – *after* he had apparently been pressured by members of the Camorra and coached by Italian secret service agents in Ascoli Piceno prison – that he began to identify the Bulgarians as sponsors of the attack on the pope.[51] The "Bulgarian connection" thesis has since been widely propagated in the non-communist media.

But Western opinion-shapers were still faced with the difficulty of reconciling Ağca's well-publicized status as a right-wing killer with the notion that he acted in the service of an orthodox pro-Soviet regime. The only way that this could be done was to portray Ağca's attack on the pope as a "false flag" terrorist operation, that is, one that was designed to look as though it had been committed by the *other* side. Although some pro-communist commentators have disparaged this suggestion by falsely claiming that it would be "unthinkable" for a socialist state to collude with "fascists,"[52] this well-known operational technique has regularly been employed by various Western *and* Eastern intelligence and security agencies. Among the numerous Western examples that could be provided, one may mention the creation of pseudo–Mau Mau "counter-gangs" controlled by the British army in Kenya, the establishment of false "national liberation" movements by the Portuguese secret police in Mozambique and elsewhere in Africa, the setting off of bombs in Cairo by an Israeli special operations unit (Unit 131) which was then attributed to anti-Western Egyptians,[53] the directing of a supposed "Libyan" terrorist group – al Da'wa al-Masīh (The Call of the Messiah [i.e., Jesus, who is regarded as an Islamic rather than a Christian prophet by Muslims]) – by a French secret service agent,[54] the systematic utilization of bogus *and* real left-wing organizations as a cover by Italian neo-fascist terrorists in the late 1960s and early 1970s, and the possible creation or manipulation of an ostensibly leftist terrorist organization (the Grupo de Resisténcia Antifascista Primero de Octubre, or GRAPO) by the Spanish intelligence agency.[55] The evidence is harder to come by for similar activities by communist bloc intelligence services, but one may note the sending of pro-Nazi literature (and, in one case, a bomb) to Western politicians and diplomats, purportedly from the nonexistent Kampfverband für Unabhängiges Deutschland, by Czech intelligence agents, and the likely infiltration and manipulation of right-wing Croatian terrorist groups by the KGB or the Yugoslav secret service.[56]

Nevertheless, although only a fanatic or a fool could believe that the Soviets would never resort to using such effective provocation techniques to accomplish particular political objectives, it would be equally absurd to claim that they had done so in a given case unless there was at least *some* reliable evidence to suggest it.[57] Since such evidence was not immediately forthcoming in Ağca's case, Western disinformation peddlers like Henze and Sterling were forced to distort the facts about the Turk's background in order to make it seem as though he was acting under Bulgarian and ultimately Soviet control. This involved promoting two interrelated theses. The first was that Ağca was not really a rightist militant, an argument that appears in different variants, including some that are mutually contradictory. The second, favored by Henze and some pro-Soviet sources, was that Ağca was not a Muslim religious extremist and hence would not have attempted to kill the "Crusader Commander" for the reasons stated in his letter to *Milliyet*, which must therefore have been designed as a smokescreen to conceal the actual motives. To get at the real story, it is necessary to describe Ağca's political background in some detail.

Ağca's links to the Turkish ultranationalist right

In order to demonstrate that Ağca's attempt to shoot the pope was the result of a leftist rather than a rightist plot, Henze and Sterling had to try to show that Ağca's rightist affiliations served primarily as a cover to disguise behind-the-scenes Soviet Bloc control or manipulation. Thus, although Sterling acknowledged that Ağca "had long moved in right-wing circles,"[58] she and Henze put forth a number of arguments to minimize the significance of this fact. Most of them not only contradict the available evidence, but also suffer from logical inconsistencies.

Thus, in an effort to make it appear that Ağca was not a "typical" Turkish rightist – whatever that means – Henze and Sterling variously characterize him as a "megalomaniac," an "international terrorist" who transcended or conjoined rightist and leftist ideologies, an "apolitical" individual who operated mainly on the basis of greed, a well-trained Soviet "hit man" or secret agent, a leftist sympathizer, and a "mentally normal person."[59] Other proponents of the "Bulgarian connection" portray him as a shrewd but unstable psychopath.[60] Aside from the difficulties inherent in describing any individual's complex psychological makeup and motivations, it is *a priori* unlikely that Ağca could be all of these contradictory characters rolled into one.

The depictions of Ağca's organizational links and activities by said authors are likewise filled with unresolved contradictions. On the one hand, both Henze and Sterling repeatedly emphasize that Ağca was not officially on the membership rolls of the MHP or Bozkurtlar and that there were no confirmed links between Ağca and high-ranking MHP officials, including Türkeş himself,[61] and Sterling goes so far as to say that "all the evidence showed him to be a minor figure on the fringes of [the rightist] movement."[62] On the other hand, Ağca's many demonstrable connections to the right are ascribed, at least in part, to an elaborate cover operation devised by his alleged Bulgarian or Soviet handlers.[63] As Herman and Brodhead have correctly pointed out, if these communist intelligence services were in fact engaged in carefully creating a covert rightist "legend" for Ağca, they would have made certain that he formally joined one or more extreme right organizations to help strengthen it.[64] After all, "false flag" operations depend for their success on the preservation of such façades.

Henze and Sterling also insist that Ağca did not involve himself in the usual sort of rightist political actions, including agitation and violent confrontations with the left.[65] Their clear implication is that his secret communist sponsors did not want to compromise his cover or operational flexibility by allowing him to engage in activities that might lead to his arrest and interrogation. But if this is so, why did they permit him to participate in the dramatic assassination of İpekçi, which was certain to generate extraordinary publicity? Even if we assume that the Soviets had a compelling motive for killing İpekçi as well as a need to test Ağca's resourcefulness and loyalty, this is not compatible with the notion of holding Ağca in reserve for an especially sensitive future operation. In any case, to have distanced Ağca from his militant right-wing comrades by having him avoid daily scuffles would have been to cast undue suspicion on his bona fides. These unsubstantial hypotheses are already difficult enough to reconcile, but Sterling tries to have it both ways by claiming that it does not even matter whether Ağca was on the "outer fringe or inner core of the Gray Wolf movement," since his "mysterious connections led to the right and left alike."[66] As we shall see, this latter assertion remains unproven. At this point, it would be better to present an overview of Ağca's manifold rightist affiliations, taking note of controversies and spurious argumentation when they arise, than to continue highlighting the many inconsistencies and illogicalities in the accounts of Henze and Sterling.

Mehmet Ali Ağca was born in 1958 and grew up on the outskirts of Malatya in a shantytown (*gecekondu*) known as Yeşiltepe. The death of his father when he was eight years old made it particularly difficult for him and his family to eke out a decent existence, but despite this adversity he became a voracious reader and an excellent student.[67] He seems to have met some of his later right-wing comrades (including Yavuz Çaylan) at Yeşiltepe junior high school, and it is known that Yeşiltepe was at that time under rightist control.[68] This latter circumstance, when combined with his Sunni religious beliefs, may well help to explain his early attraction to the right,[69] yet it was not until he transferred to senior high school, a former teacher-training facility near the center of Malatya, that one can discern his first clear connections to the ultranationalist right. The MHP had seized control over that school shortly before Ağca arrived, and had begun offering seminars on fascism and Türkeş' ideological principles.[70] This institution thence served as a meeting place for a local Bozkurt subgroup, which was led by Oral Çelik and included within its ranks Çaylan, Mehmet and Hasan Şener, and Yalçın Özbey.[71] Since all of these figures later played important roles in Ağca's terrorist escapades, there can be little doubt that Ağca fell in with this group in senior high school. This was confirmed later, for when Turkish police raided Ağca's family home following his arrest for the murder of İpekçi, they found photographs of Ağca together with local Bozkurt and Idealist (*ülkücü*) leaders, posters of Türkeş, and MHP literature.[72]

However, Ağca may have also become involved with local elements of Abuzer Uğurlu's Turkish mafia at this time. Uğurlu came from the same town in Malatya province – Pötürge – as the Şener brothers, made use of several key customs posts infiltrated by the MHP to conduct his business, and seems to have hired Çelik and other Malatyalı Bozkurtlar for various smuggling operations.[73] This alliance between organized crime and the extreme right conforms to a pattern common throughout the world,[74] and in Turkey it served the interests of both Uğurlu, who needed political protection to cover his smuggling activities, and the MHP, which needed funding for both its overt and subversive political actions.[75] According to one generally unreliable source, Ağca occasionally drove Uğurlu's trucks along heroin smuggling routes while still in school at Malatya,[76] but whether or not this is true Uğurlu was at least indirectly involved in many of the later phases of Ağca's career.

In the fall of 1976, Ağca registered as a student in the University of Ankara's History and Geography program and moved into the school's rightist-controlled Beşevler dormitory, although he may not have attended classes regularly.[77] Little is known about his extracurricular activities, including those of a political nature.[78] Henze argues, based on Ağca's own confession and Ankara police records, that he "avoided entanglements in agitation," whereas Feroz Ahmad suggests that he participated in political violence since he "apparently was [already] an experienced hit-man" by the time he moved to İstanbul in 1978.[79] Although his latter claim remains to be substantiated, Ağca must have been engaged in *some* sort of illicit activities during his stay in Ankara, for on 13 December 1977 1,600 dollars in Turkish lira was deposited in the Beyazıt (University) branch of the Türkiye İş Bankası in İstanbul, several months *before* he actually arrived there, ostensibly to attend school.[80] This was the first of many deposits made in his or his mother's name at several Turkish banks in the next few months, the source of which has yet to be clarified. Ağca himself claimed to have accompanied pro-communist Türkiye Halk Kurtuluş Ordusu (THKO: People's Liberation Army of Turkey) leader Teslim Töre and Sedat Sirri Kadem, a Malatya schoolchum and alleged Devrimçi Sol (DEV-SOL: Revolutionary Left) militant, to train at a Palestinian guerrilla camp in Lebanon from the spring to the fall of 1977,[81] but there is no corroborating evidence to support this statement and many of the details seem improbable.

In the fall of 1978 Ağca enrolled in the Economics program at İstanbul University, one of the country's most prestigious academic institutions. There is some question about whether he actually took the examination that qualified him for entrance there, and he seems to have spent little time going to or studying for classes since school records indicate he never completed those for which he registered.[82] While in İstanbul he lived in a rightist youth hostel,[83] but again there is controversy over whether he involved himself in right-wing political violence. Sterling insists that he laid low and avoided such sordid activities, but Ahmad says that students in the hostel where he lived remembered him as a rightist militant who was allegedly seen shooting two leftists in the legs and concludes that "[h]is notoriety was such that leftists tried to kill him on several occasions."[84] Although proponents of the "Bulgarian connection" imply that the many bank deposits in Ağca's name – which together totalled 15,000–18,000 dollars, a huge sum for a poor Turkish student – were provided by his supposed communist sponsors, more compelling circumstantial evidence suggests that Ağca received this money for participating in black market (*kara borsa*) smuggling operations undertaken by a network of rightist Malatya comrades who had likewise moved to İstanbul.[85] Perhaps part of it also constituted an advance payment for the planned assassination of İpekçi.[86] Whatever the exact case, "one gets the impression that by this time Ağca's student status may have been mostly a cover for other activity which was absorbing most of his time."[87]

The 1 February 1979 murder of İpekçi was the first high-profile crime in which Ağca was involved, and it soon earned him widespread notoriety within Turkey and brought him to the attention of police and security agencies in several other countries. Much still remains unclarified about İpekçi's murder, including the precise motive, but it is certain that the actual perpetrators of the crime were almost all Malatyalı Bozkurtlar with whom Ağca had long been associated.[88] First of all, the driver of the killers' car was Ağca's friend Çaylan, a fact which the latter subsequently admitted.[89] Second, Ağca claimed to have gotten the gun used to kill İpekçi from Mehmet Şener and – perhaps more importantly – to have returned it to him at the Aksaray district office of the MHP when the job was completed.[90] Third, a mass of circumstantial evidence suggests that *another* rightist participated in the attack along with Ağca. Most informed observers believe Malatya Bozkurt leader Çelik was that person, and some go so far as to claim that he was the actual triggerman, not Ağca.[91] Others have implicated still another right-wing militant, Ömer Ay, who was head of the Ülkücü Teknik Elemanlar Derneği (ÜTED: Idealist Technical Worker's Association) in Nevşehir prior to his flight and attempt to obtain political asylum in West Germany.[92] Ağca later said that his old Malatya friend Özbey actually fired the gun in the İpekçi murder, even though he had personally taken the blame.[93] The important point for our purposes is not to determine who actually pulled the trigger, but to recognize that *whoever* did so was a right-wing militant linked to the MHP and probably a member of the Bozkurt chapter from Ağca's hometown.

The ultimate sponsors and planners of the attack have not yet been identified with certainty. In 1983, long after Ağca had been pressured to implicate the Bulgarians, he identified Uğurlu as the culprit. However, Mumcu presents a strong case that it was Çelik who masterminded the İpekçi assassination, as well as most of Ağca's other illegal actions.[94] Çelik was at that time the "main lieutenant" of Abdullah Çatlı, who had headed the Ankara branch of the Bozkurtlar and had become the "second in command" of the national Ülkücü Gençlik Derneği (ÜGD: Idealist Youth Association) during the 1970s as a result of his skills as an "enforcer" for Türkeş.[95] In my view the most logical explanation is that İpekçi was killed by these rightist militants due to MHP opposition to what he symbolized, a moderate opposed to political extremism and terrorism to the point of advocating martial law to protect the social democratic Ecevit government.[96] He was also favorably disposed toward Western civilization and was engaged in promoting a reconciliation between Turkey and Greece, aims that were anathema to the radical segments of the ultranationalist right.[97] Perhaps this crime also served the MHP's long-term strategy of provocation, which was apparently designed to lead to a coup by rightist supporters within the Turkish military.

In any case, after the assassination Ağca seems to have made no significant changes in either his lifestyle or his activities. During this period he may even have been involved in other political violence, and he continued to frequent various right-wing haunts in İstanbul. On 25 June 1979 he was arrested by Turkish police at one such place, a Bozkurt hangout known as the Café Marmara.[98] Ağca immediately confessed to murdering İpekçi and after fingering Çaylan and Şener – presumably to make his story more credible, since others were known to have been involved – he began insisting that he was an independent terrorist without organizational support, who was "not the servant of any political ideas or ideology."[99] At his October trial, Ağca further attempted to distance himself from his right-wing political associates by claiming that pro-Ecevit Turkish Interior Minister Hasan Fehmi Güneş had offered to help him escape from jail if he claimed that a high official of the MHP had ordered him to kill İpekçi, a charge Güneş vehemently denied.[100] Nevertheless, Turkish authorities rightly concluded that Ağca was a Bozkurt militant.

On 25 September 1979, even before the trial had begun, Ağca was shifted to the Kartal-Maltepe military prison, the highest security facility in the country, and was placed in its maximum security section.[101] On the night of 23 November 1979, several days after proclaiming that he was innocent in the İpekçi shooting and would name the real killers at his next court appearance, he was sprung from prison with the help of several guards that were affiliated with the MHP, some of whom also received bribes from Uğurlu.[102] After walking through eight checkpoints dressed in a military uniform, an "escape [which] would have been impossible without help from high quarters,"[103] Ağca joined Çelik, who Mumcu and others believe was the planner of the escape along with Çatlı.[104] However, Uğurlu was also probably involved in the process, not only financially but through his Bozkurt contacts inside Kartal-Maltepe.[105] Ağca was then safehoused in İstanbul by Çatlı's Bozkurt underground for over twenty days, during which time he wrote the anti-pope letter to *Milliyet* and murdered two people, including lottery ticket salesman Ramazan Gündüz, whom he suspected of tipping off the police as to his whereabouts.[106]

Sometime around the beginning of 1980, Çelik organized Ağca's escape route across Turkey and his border crossing into Iran, which occurred on 1 February.[107] There are contradictory reports about Ağca's exact itinerary,[108] but the feature that stands out in each of them is that all of the people involved in aiding him were Idealists. Çelik seems to have accompanied him, Mehmet Şener's brother Hasan drove him from İstanbul to Ankara, several other rightists provided him with temporary shelter or assistance (including Mustafa Dikici, Mehmet Kurşun, Hasan Murat Pale, and Hamit Gökenç, who gave Ağca a passport), ÜGD leader Muhsin Yazıcıoğlu helped arrange for him to get this passport, and rightist militant Timur Selçuk received payment from Mehmet Şandir, an MHP member, *Hergün* journalist, and partner in the Tümpaş trading firm – along with the leader of the Avrupa Demokratik Ülkücü Türk Dernekleri Federasyonu (ADÜTDF: European Federation of Democratic Turkish Idealist Clubs), Musa Serdar Çelebi – to smuggle him across the border to Erzurum.[109] Meanwhile, Çatlı, from his new base of operations in Varna, instructed Ömer Ay to procure another passport for Ağca to use in the future. Ay borrowed two IDs collected by İbrahim Kurt (a former head of the Nevşehir ÜGD), substituted other photos on them (including one of Erkan Ender, a former Idealist policeman), and used them to obtain two "perfectly forged" passports from a passport office where the security director was a religious rightist named Haydar Tek.[110] The one for Ağca was in the name of Faruk Özgün, and it was later delivered to him in Bulgaria.

No one knows why Ağca crossed the border into Iran or what he did between February and July of 1980, when he appeared in Sofia. Western propagandists like Henze argue that he secretly met with Turkish leftist leader Töre and perhaps entered the Soviet Union to undergo training at a KGB camp, whereas some East Bloc propagandists claim that he joined up with CIA-backed supporters of the recently deposed Shāh and played some role in the U.S. attempt to rescue Americans held hostage by Iranian militants in Tehran![111] There is absolutely no evidence to support either contention, and I suspect that the main reason for smuggling Ağca into Iran was simply to throw Turkish authorities off his trail.

Ağca next appeared in Sofia. In the second week of July 1980, he had a meeting in the deluxe Vitosha Hotel with an Uğurlu underling, Ömer Mersan, who paid him 800 dollars and apparently made arrangements with Çatlı to secure the false Özgün passport for him.[112] Mersan was not a committed rightist, but rather an underworld operator whose Munich-based Vardar Company served as a conduit for drug and arms trafficking by the Uğurlu family.[113] This trafficking involved the extensive use of MHP-affiliated organizations and personnel in Western Europe, who received safehousing, weapons, and large influxes of cash in return for their participation. It also depended upon the cooperation of the Bulgarian authorities, who obtained hard currency and intelligence information in exchange for allowing the use of Bulgaria as a staging area for smuggling operations. Eventually, Ağca also claimed to have met with a mysterious Bulgarian named "Mustafaeff," with Çelik, with Uğurlu's subordinate partner Bekir Çelenk, and with another Bulgarian named "Kolev," that is, Todor Aivazov, one of the three later charged in Italy for their alleged role in the papal plot.[114] But aside from Ağca's unreliable and manipulative testimony, information about his doings in Bulgaria is practically nonexistent.

The situation becomes somewhat clearer after Ağca left Bulgaria on 31 August 1980. Although his precise movements are obscure at times, it is certain that he spent the next several months traveling throughout Western Europe, although he did make short jaunts to Tunisia and Majorca during this period. There is unanimous agreement that he did so with the help of a number of Turkish rightists who were affiliated with branches of the MHP's external support organization.[115] Even Henze admits that a "case could be made that Ağca had been sheltered and prepared for action against the pope inside a Gray Wolf network in Germany."[116] Among the people involved were his old Malatyalı comrades Çelik, Özbey, and Şener, some of whom had fled Turkey along with thousands of other ultra-rightists after the military coup on 12 September 1980, when the new junta began to make mass arrests of MHP members and Bozkurtlar, including Türkeş and other party leaders.[117] But the most important assistance of all was provided by ADÜTDF chief Musa Serdar Çelebi, the second most powerful Idealist in Europe after Türkeş' friend and MHP ideologue Enver Altaylı.

The ADÜTDF was originally established in 1978, ostensibly as a "coordinating body for cultural, religious, and welfare organizations set up by Turks in

Germany,"[118] but beneath this benign exterior it represented nothing more than the reorganization of the MHP's overseas branches that had been banned by the Turkish government in 1976.[119] Indeed, this "cultural" organization performed the very same functions as the old one had – recruiting Turkish *Gastarbeiter* into the MHP, indoctrinating them in Türkeş' fascist-inspired ideology, and helping to finance MHP and Bozkurt subversion inside Turkey, in part with profits derived from arms and drug trafficking.[120] By the time of the 1980 coup, the ADÜTDF claimed to have fifty thousand members organized into 129 branches, eighty-seven of which were in West Germany, and German police estimated that at least twenty-six thousand Turkish workers were members of extreme right groups.[121] Nor were these organizations reluctant to use violence. There are a number of examples of rightist assaults on Turkish workers and left-wing activists in Germany and elsewhere, some of which resulted in deaths. Ağca himself may have committed two murders in return for ADÜTDF logistical support.[122]

As evidence of Ağca's links to these overseas MHP affiliates, it should be noted that the young assassin contacted Çelebi himself on several occasions. He called him from Bulgaria in the summer of 1980 and again from Majorca in late April 1981, in the latter case exclaiming "I have received the money . . . [and] will now go to Rome and finish the job."[123] Equally importantly, he met Çelebi twice: once in Milan on 15 December 1980 to talk things over and obtain 500 dollars from him, the second time in Zurich on 3 March 1981, at which time Çelenk reportedly paid out 1.5 million dollars to be divided three ways between Çelebi, Çelik, and Ağca.[124] Çelebi's innocent version of these events has not held up under serious scrutiny, and it can therefore be said that he was the highest ranking member of the Turkish far right to be unequivocably linked to the papal assassination plot.

Other connections between Ağca and this Europe-based right-wing milieu have also been discovered. First of all, Çelik purchased the 9mm Browning pistol used to shoot the pope from an Austrian gunrunner with Nazi sympathies, Horst Grillmayer, and then passed it on to a Bozkurt leader in Olten, Switzerland, named Ömer Bağcı for safekeeping. Ağca later called Bağcı from Majorca and arranged to meet him in Milan on 9 May 1981, where the gun was finally transferred.[125] Furthermore, he made a twenty-minute call from Rome on 13 April 1981 to Hasan Taşkın, "one of the top ten Gray Wolves" in West Germany. Taşkın implausibly claimed under interrogation that it must have been a wrong number, and German police were content not to press the issue![126]

At long last we have arrived at St. Peter's Square on the fateful day, and here too other members of the Turkish extreme right made their appearance. It is now known that Ağca had two accomplices with him on that occasion. In October 1982, he tried to mislead Italian investigators by claiming that the Bulgarian "Kolev" (Aivazov) was the man photographed while running away across the square after the shooting, but shortly thereafter admitted that it was actually his close friend Çelik.[127] The other accomplice is thought to have been Ömer Ay, the Nevşehir Idealist who had earlier helped Ağca obtain the Özgün passport, although this is not a certainty.[128]

There is also an interesting postscript to the crime that may be of importance to our topic. A letter postmarked Munich and dated 20 July 1981 that was purportedly written by Ağca to Türkeş was sent anonymously to *Milliyet*. The letter reads as follows:

> Illustrious Leader (*Sayın Başbuğum*), First, I kiss your hands with my deep respects, and I want to express my debt of infinite thanks for your paternal interest. I am in no difficulties, with help of all kinds from my brother Idealists who have taken me into their hearts. I find myself in the happy condition of doing my duty with honor, with the pride of being a Turk . . . the duty of grand Ideals. May God (*Tanrı*) protect the Turks and make them Great.[129]

The circumstances under which this letter was found were highly suspicious, as was its method of arrival at the *Milliyet* offices, both of which lend credence to the belief of Henze and Sterling that it was a clumsy forgery. Nevertheless, others have argued that the letter was subjected to a battery of tests by Turkish authorities that confirmed its authenticity, and it *was* thence officially accepted as evidence by the Ankara military court presiding over the huge MHP-Türkeş trial.[130] If it is in fact genuine, the case for an indigenous Turkish plot to kill the pope would be further strengthened.

In short, there is no doubt that Ağca's links to the Turkish ultranationalist right dated back to his high school days in Malatya and continued *uninterrupted* right up until the moment that he wounded Pope John Paul II.[131] However, this seemingly straightforward picture has been complicated by Ağca's claims to have had links to the PLO and the Bulgarian secret police, which has allowed Western propagandists to insist that the rightist Turkish networks involved were either covertly controlled or cleverly manipulated by the Bulgarians, with the help of Turkish mafiosi who had been recruited, co-opted, or coerced into participating. This is certainly possible, but too many unresolved evidentiary and logical problems remain to justify accepting such a thesis without further investigation.

First and foremost, Ağca's statements cannot be accepted at face value. It has already been pointed out that he repeatedly lied and altered his testimony, and even Judge Ilario Martella, the Italian magistrate who singlemindedly pursued a "Bulgarian connection" he had already accepted as fact, acknowledged Ağca's "devilish ability, displayed many times, to produce well-constructed, fantastic and incredible stories."[132] Yet Martella and various disinformation peddlers have nonetheless accepted his statements as accurate whenever it suited their purposes,[133] despite the fact that Ağca had clear motives for implicating the left in his crime. For one thing, as a confirmed Turkish ultranationalist he would have been virulently hostile to both Soviet Russia and the left-wing opposition in general, whether domestic or foreign. For another, as a prisoner facing a life term or death, he would have been motivated to tell Italian authorities what he thought they wanted to hear – or confirm what they were pressuring him to say – in order to obtain a more lenient sentence. The adoption of such a strategem also served to protect his probable rightist sponsors and known accomplices, including his friends Oral Çelik and Yalçın Özbey.[134] Given Ağca's record of telling outright lies and his obvious political and personal motives for promoting – however belatedly – a "Bulgarian connection," Mumcu and others are right to insist that *nothing* he says should be believed in the absence of independent confirmation.[135] Is there any such confirmation of his claims to have been trained in a Palestinian guerrilla camp or directed by Bulgarian secret agents?

According to Ağca's testimony, in 1977 he accompanied Töre and Sırrî Kadem to a Palestinian camp south of Beirut, where he received forty days of training in guerrilla tactics. While there, he supposedly encountered other Turks from the "most disparate of Turkey's subversive groups" and, upon his return to Turkey, "established clandestine relations with six underground organizations," four on the radical left and two on the radical right.[136]

Unfortunately, there is no evidence to support Ağca's contention, nor is it even plausible. Although it is certain that factions of the PLO trained Turkish left-wing guerrillas and that they also periodically trained European neo-Nazis,[137] it is rather difficult to believe that Turkish leftists, Turkish ultranationalists, Turkish religious rightists, Kurdish separatists, and anti-Turkish Armenian terrorists were all being trained simultaneously in the same camp or that they were subsequently colluding with one another on a regular basis.[138] Efforts to forge a temporary anti-government alliance between Turkish ultranationalists and extreme leftists might possibly have been made *after* the military's 1980 crackdown on (and betrayal of) the MHP, but such collaborative efforts would have been much less likely beforehand – unless they involved provocations – since the MHP was at that time apparently working in conjunction with rightist factions of the armed forces and the MİT to crush the left and provoke an authoritarian right-wing coup. It is much more probable that Turkish rightists were trained in paramilitary camps set up by the right-wing Katā'ib al-Lubnānīyah (Lebanese Phalange).[139] In any event, there is no independent confirmation of Ağca's claim to have been trained by Palestinians.

The situation regarding Ağca's Bulgarian links is more complicated. Although again there is no outside evidence to corroborate Ağca's claims to have had meetings with various Bulgarian officials, either in Bulgaria or in Italy, it cannot be denied that Ağca spent time in Bulgaria or that he periodically received financial and logistical aid from Turkish mobster Abuzer Uğurlu, who helped direct smuggling operations out of Sofia. But the nature of the relationship between Uğurlu and the Bulgarian authorities remains a disputed topic.

Elements of the Bulgarian government certainly established a direct working relationship with the Uğurlu mob through KINTEX, the official state import-export agency. Apparently, KINTEX was founded in 1968, following the merger of three smaller commercial import-export firms,[140] and it has since overseen "the international trade of such legitimate commodities as arms, textiles, appliances and cigarettes."[141] Moreover, despite the predictable East Bloc denials and the doubts expressed by Herman and Brodhead,[142] there is sufficient reliable evidence to indicate that KINTEX has also participated in the illicit trafficking of narcotics and weapons from and through Bulgarian territory, in conjunction with other state agencies that serve as distribution outlets.[143] To facilitate these activities, "Bulgarian officials, through KINTEX, designate [non-Bulgarian] 'representatives' to operate as brokers who [then] establish arrangements with smugglers for bartered contraband."[144] According to the U.S. Drug Enforcement Administration (DEA), Uğurlu, Çelenk, and Mustafa Kisaçik were among the "more notable" Turkish traffickers linked to KINTEX, and along with representatives of KINTEX some of these traffickers "have also been named as associates of members of the right-wing Baskurtlar [sic] . . . in Istanbul and Frankfurt, Western Germany."[145] Since some sources have claimed that "top ranking members of the Bulgarian intelligence service [DS]" serve as the directors of KINTEX,[146] one may well wonder just what Uğurlu's motives were in dealing with Ağca.

One interpretation has been offered by hard-liners like Henze and Nathan M. Adams, Senior Editor for *Reader's Digest*, a popular international magazine with a long history of apparent participation in CIA disinformation campaigns.[147] In their conspiratorial reconstruction, there is a clear chain of command linking the alleged puppeteers of the Soviet KGB to their DS lackies at KINTEX, then to KINTEX-linked smugglers and possible DS agents Uğurlu and Çelenk, and finally to right-wing dupe Ağca. This argument begins with the idea that the Bulgarian regime has been the most subservient of all the regimes established by the Soviets in eastern Europe, which may be true even today, in 1991. But Henze goes so far as to claim that "nothing Bulgaria does can be regarded separately from the larger framework of pernicious and destructive *Soviet* operations directed against the Free World," and that "there is no aspect of Soviet-sponsored subversion in which the communist government of Bulgaria has not taken part – and continues to take part."[148] Based on this *a priori* assumption, he and Adams enthusiastically accept the problematic testimony of Stefan Sverdlov, a colonel in the DS prior to his defection to the West in 1971, who claims that the heads of the Warsaw Pact security services met in Moscow in 1967 to plan actions to "exploit and hasten the inherent 'corruption' of Western society."[149] As a result, the DS supposedly issued a directive on 16 July 1970 (#M-120/00–0500) which promoted the destabilization of Western society through, among other means, the narcotics trade.[150] Acting through the newly formed KINTEX, the DS has since then engaged in the systematic trading of Middle Eastern drugs for European guns, which have then been supplied to terrorist groups to further Soviet destabilization efforts in Turkey and elsewhere. To accomplish this they made use of selected non-Bulgarian smugglers, especially Turks, as intermediaries. Some of these latter were purportedly also recruited as DS agents, including Uğurlu himself, who according to various anonymous or unreliable sources had served in such a capacity for many years prior to Ağca's assassination attempt.[151] If all of the preceding are accepted without reservations, a circumstantial case can be made that Uğurlu recruited Ağca to kill the pope and provided him with assistance at the behest of his DS and Soviet handlers.

There are, however, innumerable problems with this scenario which, when evaluated together, suggest a far more plausible alternative. In the first place, perhaps not all the illicit activities occurring in Bulgaria were under government control, nor can they necessarily be ascribed to government policy.[152] According to Jack R. Perry, former U.S. ambassador to Bulgaria, "the impression was inescapable to those living in Sofia that Bulgaria was like a Mafia operation on a grand scale."[153] Graft was widespread, and some of the smuggling attributed to the Bulgarian government may have been carried out by corrupt "individuals – often with friends and relatives in the highest places – who were out to make money" for themselves.[154] This does not absolve the Bulgarian regime from its documented participation in international arms and drug smuggling, but it does suggest that some of this smuggling has been organized for private gain rather than in accordance with official policy, even though the two motives are not necessarily mutually exclusive.[155] Moreover, according to the acting Deputy Administrator of the DEA in 1984, Bulgarian involvement in this activity cannot be linked to the Soviets and the DEA lacks sufficient evidence to indict any high Bulgarian officials for participation in it.[156]

Second, there are logical shortcomings in the theory that KINTEX smuggling was part of a master anti-Western plot. KINTEX apparently arranged to sell weapons secretly to several *anti*-communist states and groups, including the South African government, right-wing Christian Phalangists in Lebanon, the Nicaraguan *contra* forces, and Turkish rightists.[157] Even if the latter can be said to support Soviet destabilization operations merely by facilitating internal violence in Turkey,[158] sales to the others definitely do not square with East Bloc political interests. This suggests an *economic* rather than a political motivation for Bulgarian participation in illegal trafficking in guns and drugs. Indeed, several of the representatives from U.S. agencies called upon to testify on this subject before congressional committees listed Bulgarian objectives as (1) the acquisition of hard Western currency, which is in short supply in that country, (2) the supplying of various left-wing insurgent groups with arms, "in support of communist revolutionary aims," and (3) the gathering of intelligence from international smuggling networks that are allowed to operate in or through Bulgarian territory.[159] In short, the DS trafficked in arms and drugs for the same reasons as many Western intelligence agencies – to obtain untraceable currency that could be used to fund secret operations, to help arm governments or insurgent groups supporting their own political aims, and to acquire useful intelligence information from widely traveled and well-connected smugglers.[160]

Third, there are serious problems with some of the sources supporting the claims of Henze, Sterling, and Adams concerning the Bulgarians. Thus, Sverdlov's testimony about the supposed Soviet-sponsored master plan to destabilize the West is impossible to verify, as is his claim about the contents of the 1970 DS document. Aside from various inherent problems with the *public* testimony of defectors, which is invariably manipulated and sometimes manufactured out as a whole cloth by their new handlers,[161] in this case there is no way to examine the document in question to determine whether or not it is genuine, or even if it actually exists.[162] One is certainly entitled to be suspicious here, since on another occasion documentation about Bulgarian involvement in illicit trafficking was shown to be forged.[163] It is therefore not surprising that U.S. government agencies concerned with this issue have admitted that they have "no information by which to corroborate the existence of Warsaw Pact meetings with destabilization directives," or of the purported DS document.[164] According to the testimony of R. M. Palmer, Deputy Assistant Secretary of State for European and Canadian Affairs, many of the allegations about Bulgarian use of the drug trade to finance terrorism and undermine the West "come from confidential sources, and have understandably proved difficult to substantiate."[165] The same is true of allegations that Uğurlu and Çelenk had been recruited into the DS, although these latter allegations are plausible.

In sum, the conspirational scenario can only remain a hypothesis – and not a very convincing one – in the absence of more concrete evidence. It is one thing to acknowledge that the Bulgarian regime and Turkish smugglers had entered into a mutually beneficial economic arrangement, which is supported by a good deal of evidence from diverse sources, and altogether something else to assert that this constitutes proof that the DS, acting on behalf of the KGB, *controlled* the far-flung activities of the Sofia-based Turkish mafia. Moreover, it seems highly unlikely that the virulently anticommunist *and* anti-Russian Turkish right would enter into anything more than a temporary marriage of convenience with one of the Soviet Union's closest allies. And to suggest, as Henze does, that Çelebi's huge ADÜTDF organization had fallen under the control of the Bulgarian secret police is *a priori* illogical.[166]

Using similar kinds of arguments, one could make an even stronger case for Western sponsorship of the papal plot. There are a number of suggestive bits of information, including the testimony of MİT informant and *agent provocateur* Hoca Koçyiğit to the effect that the MİT had paid Ağca *not* to implicate his [rightist] accomplices in the İpekçi murder and had promised to organize his escape if he was arrested.[167] Even Sterling has raised the question of whether Ağca was manipulated by a faction within the MİT, and Mumcu has argued that Uğurlu also had links to that agency.[168] Then there is the infamous inaction of West German authorities in response to Turkish government appeals to search for and arrest Ağca, as well as their extraordinarily inept questioning of Turkish rightists and others involved in some way with Ağca, including Şener, Mersan, Çelebi, the Taşkın brothers, and Çatlı.[169] It also turned out that Grillmayer had a BND "control" officer named Paul Saalbach, as Austrian police soon discovered to their dismay after arresting him in 1983 for trying to smuggle a huge truckload of automatic weapons across their border from Bulgaria.[170] There is also a clear BND link to Türkeş' lieutenant Altaylı, who listed his BND contacts (including a former Azerbaijani SS officer) in a letter he wrote to the MHP *başbuğ*.[171] Finally, there are numerous connections between the CIA and MHP, both in Turkey and Europe. It seems clear that the CIA and U.S. military intelligence recruited civilian Idealists into the Kontr-Gerilla organization, and former Turkoman SS man Ruzi Nazar has been identified by several investigators as the liaison between CIA personnel, including Henze himself, and the MHP leadership in West Germany.[172]

However, another interpretation of the Bulgarian-Uğurlu-Ağca relationship is entirely consistent with the verifiable facts, without any reliance upon jumps in logic or guilt-by-association arguments. Although acknowledging that the

Bulgarian authorities have "established a policy of encouraging and facilitating" the smuggling of narcotics, as well as weapons, and that they "tolerate, if not shield" certain Turkish dealers, it is not based on the unsubstantiated and implausible claim that the Bulgarians *guided* or *controlled* the smugglers and their associates.[173] The fact that Uğurlu and Çelenk used Bozkurt members as transporters and handlers in their smuggling infrastructure proves nothing about Bozkurt relations with the Bulgarian government, and indeed John C. Lawn, the aforementioned DEA official, reports that "no direct association between Kintex and the . . . 'Gray Wolves' has been established, according to our information."[174] And although Henze and Sterling imply that the MHP acted as a mere instrument of the Turkish mafia, the relationship between the two groups was far more complex than they indicate.[175] If anything, the MHP seems to have been the dominant partner. In the opinion of Örsan Öymen, the leading Turkish journalist specializing on the Ağca case, "it was the Gray Wolves who were in a position to ask favors from the Mafia" due to their political influence and control over the Turkish customs ministry, especially prior to the 1980 military coup.[176] Establishing good relations with the MHP and its affiliates was thus necessary if Uğurlu wished to engage in large-scale smuggling across the Turkish border. For its part, the MHP depended upon Uğurlu's smuggling networks to facilitate its extensive drugs-for-guns trafficking in western Europe,[177] and also to help wanted Bozkurt terrorists elude Turkish justice and eventually reach "safe houses" established by the ADÜTDF in West Germany and elsewhere.

Ağca himself obviously made use of these networks to escape from the Turkish authorities. The main question is whether he subsequently shot the pope on his own initiative or on the orders of his MHP superiors. Since the former view would make it difficult to explain why he was assisted in his personal vendetta by Çelik and Ay, it seems likely that a larger group within the MHP sponsored the attack. This scenario would not only account for the extensive logistical support Ağca received from both Sofia-based Turkish mobsters and high-ranking MHP officials in Europe, but also would be consonant with the MHP's – and, by extension, Ağca's – anti-Western and anti-Christian ideology.

The MHP and its aversion to the pope

Although it has now been established that Ağca was closely linked to ultranationalist organizations since at least his senior high school days, it is not possible to discern his probable motives for attempting to assassinate the pope without sketching the historical development of the MHP and clarifying certain features of its ideology. The party is generally perceived as an heir to both the pan-Turkist stream of Turkish nationalism and secularist traditions institutionalized by Kemal Atatürk. This characterization of the MHP's orientation is largely accurate, at least in terms of its original political program and the views of its early leadership cadres. But changing political conditions in the late 1960s prompted important shifts in the party's political imagery and rhetoric, shifts which rapidly expanded and thereby transformed its original composition, especially at the base.

Turkism (*Türkçülük* or *Türklük*) is a variety of Turkish nationalism in which the object of primary political loyalty and main source of collective pride is some notion of Turkish identity or "Turkishness," defined variously in linguistic, historical, cultural, racial, and/or geographical terms.[178] Its irredentist variant is known as pan-Turkism, the guiding objective of which is the establishment of some sort of cultural or political union among "all peoples of proven or alleged Turkic origins," the majority of whom live outside of Anatolia.[179] Like most other varieties of Turkish nationalism, pan-Turkism was influenced first by Western European conceptions of liberal nationalism, then by Central and Eastern European conceptions of integral or illiberal nationalism, which soon superceded the more humanitarian and cosmopolitan liberal type. Integral nationalism is characterized by "a particularly excessive, exaggerated, and exclusive emphasis on the nation at the expense of other values," an emphasis which typically results in the promotion of jingoism and imperialism and the subordination of personal liberties and all other loyalties to the alleged interests of the nation.[180]

The development of such an intolerant, chauvinistic version of Turkism and pan-Turkism occurred primarily during the period of acute crisis between 1900 and the establishment of the Turkish Republic in 1923, a period in which the continued existence of a Turkish state in Anatolia was challenged by European aggression and internal ethnic revolts. Atatürk met this challenge by initiating a series of fundamental political reforms, one aspect of which was the forcible redirection of Turkish nationalism toward the more pragmatic and less threatening Anatolianism (*Anadoluculuk or Türkiyecilik*), a form of patriotism in the narrow, territorial sense of the term. Once he embarked upon this policy, expansionist and racist forms of pan-Turkism could no longer be openly promoted. Pan-Turkist groups in early Republican Turkey were thus compelled to confine themselves to organizing cultural activities and helping Turkic refugees from Russian-occupied territories,[181] though bands of Turkic émigrés in Europe continued to agitate for the liberation of their kinsmen, the "Captive Turks" under Soviet control.[182] But relations soured between the Turkish and Russian revolutionary regimes after 1925, and Nazi racial doctrines soon after began to exert an influence upon many pan-Turkist thinkers, since when modified this type of biological racism reinforced the already existing racist tendencies of integral Turkish nationalism and pan-Turkist irredentism. Therefore, in the period leading up to Atatürk's death, cultural-historical concerns rapidly gave way to virulent expressions of militarism and "racial pan-Turkism" (*ırkçı Türkçülük*) in most of the influential pan-Turkist publications, and rival pan-Turkist leaders like Hüseyin Nihal Atsız and Reza Oğuz Türkkan outdid each other in trading racist insults, aggressively promoting military and political schemes designed to liberate and unify the numerous Turkic peoples enslaved by the Soviet Union, and organizing clandestine cells to foment subversion.[183] Pan-Turkist militancy reached a crescendo following the German invasion of Russia, as did the flirtation of some officials with the Nazi regime, but after the tide of battle turned in 1943 the Turkish government increasingly shifted from an official position of neutrality toward support for the Allied cause. In this new political and military environment, the open promotion of expansionist pan-Turkism and racism became a dangerous embarrassment, and the government decided to make a symbolic statement by cracking down on pan-Turkist agitation.

The mass anti-government demonstrations organized by Türkkan and Atsız in the wake of the official closing of the latter's journal *Orhun* provided the pretext, and on 9 May 1944 over thirty leading pan-Turkists – including a young army captain, Alparslan Türkeş – were arrested and charged with subversion. The government and the press then launched a massive campaign against pan-Turkism and racism, which were held to be "diseased" ideologies inimicable to the well-being of the Turkish state. The formation of pan-Turkist secret societies with "sinister" anti-government agendas was also roundly criticized.[184] All of this ended with the banning of pan-Turkist organizations and the prosecution of twenty-three pan-Turkist leaders in a trial lasting from September 1944 to March 1945. In October 1945, however, the sentences imposed on ten of these leaders were overturned by the Military Court of Cassation, and at a new trial held between August 1946 and March 1947, all charges against the accused were dropped.[185]

The chief cause of this turnabout was the changed nature of the postwar political climate. Imperious Soviet demands exacerbated anti-Russian feelings among the Turks, and heightened fears of Soviet-sponsored domestic subversion in the new Cold War environment led to a change in official attitudes toward Turkish ultranationalists, including pan-Turkists, whose militant anti-communist sentiments would – it was hoped – make them reliable allies in the event of civil disturbances.[186] These concerns resulted in the lifting of many of the governmental restrictions on pan-Turkist organizations, a policy which was (with some notable exceptions) continued by the conservative and generally pro-Western Demokrat Parti (DP: Democrat Party) regime that came to power in the elections of 1950. Despite Soviet diplomatic concessions in the years after 1953, DP leader Adnan Menderes promoted "a violent, almost irrational anti-communist and anti-Soviet stand" until shortly before his ouster in the 27 May 1960 coup.[187]

As a result of their acquittal and vindication at their second trial, pan-Turkist leaders emerged with increased prestige, and their movement managed to obtain the type of extensive publicity it had been unable to generate for itself. Older activists resumed their activities and propaganda, and new pan-Turkist organizations and publications proliferated, both in Turkey and abroad.[188] Although many of the groups inside Turkey emphasized "cultural" pan-Turkism and anti-communism (since the latter had an unusually high appeal at that time), and admitted "religious or nationalist [that is, Kemalist] right-wingers close to the administration" into their ranks (to give themselves added respectability and forestall renewed "official censure"),[189] Nazi-inspired "scientific" racism and maximalist political pan-Turkism were also present, whether visible or lying just beneath the surface.[190] Among the most important of the new ultranationalist organizations with pan-Turkist leanings were the anti-communist Türkiye Komünizmle Mücadele Derneği (TKMD: Association for Fighting Communism in Turkey) and the Türk Gençlik Teşkilâtı (TGT: Organization of Turkish Youth), which was particularly active in expressing its irredentist concerns. Especially influential journals were the predominantly anti-communist *Toprak*, which appeared from 1954 to 1976, and Atsız's *Orkun* (1950–1952), which promoted both racial pan-Turkism and virulent anti-communism.[191] This then was the situation that obtained in the ultranationalist camp prior to the rapid socio-economic transformation of Turkey in the wake of the 1960 military coup, which resulted in the development of disruptive conditions that were conducive to the growth of political extremism, both rightist and leftist, and the organization of ultranationalists into a fascist political party like the MHP.[192]

The key figure involved in the formation of the MHP and the creation of its ultranationalist program was Alparslan Türkeş.[193] Türkeş was born in Cyprus in 1917, and moved with his family to İstanbul when he was fifteen years old. After studying Turkish history, literature, and philosophy, he graduated from the military academy in 1938 and joined the army. In 1944 he was one of those arrested, tried, and sentenced by the authorities for his participation in the aforementioned pan-Turkist demonstrations.[194] After his acquittal, he spent "some time" in Germany, was assigned to the office of the Turkish Military Attaché in Washington, D.C. in 1957 and 1958, was attached to the NATO Land Forces command in Ankara just prior to the 1960 coup, and also seems to have been among a group of colonels who had planned an abortive coup even earlier.[195] He was one of the more active and important plotters behind the 1960 Revolution, and indeed it was his voice that first announced the coup over the radio to an astounded Turkish public. However, the military junta which took power and formed the Millî Birlik Komitesi (MBK: Committee of National Unity) was divided into several factions, and Türkeş soon emerged as the leader of both the "radicals" and, within that group, the "proto-fascists." The essential aim of these military radicals was to institute drastic social reforms from above and delay returning power to new civilian authorities, whom they felt would be corrupt and lacking in real vision.[196] For a time Türkeş was regarded as the real power behind the MBK's titular head, General Cemal Gürsel, but he and his supporters – the so-called Fourteen – were eventually expelled from the Komite and exiled to distant Turkish embassies abroad.

But the Fourteen kept in contact even during their period of exile, and met together in Brussels in July 1962 to plan their future actions. Shortly thereafter they were allowed to return to Turkey, and Türkeş at once attempted to re-enter politics.[197] After being rebuffed by the Adalet Partisi (AP: Justice Party) and temporarily flirting with the idea of forming a new political party, he decided to seize control of the small, conservative Cumhuriyetçi Köylü Millî Partisi (CKMP: Republican Peasant Nation Party).[198] He and a group of his supporters (including several of the Fourteen) then joined the CKMP, and after a short struggle with its conservative leadership, Türkeş managed to get himself elected as party chairman on 1 August 1965. At that point there was a split in the party, and several of the older members left after criticizing Türkeş for subverting its principles by giving it a "national-socialist bent." Their departure facilitated the latter's efforts to transform the CKMP into a vehicle to promote his own ultranationalist political agenda, and after doing so he officially renamed the party the MHP in 1969.[199]

The MHP's program, developed primarily by Türkeş, was conceived as a revolutionary "third way" (*üçüncü yol*) independent of – and opposed to – both capitalism and communism. In this sense it was analogous to fascism as well as other types of revolutionary nationalism, despite Türkeş' public claims that his party's nationalist ideology was anti-fascist and anti-Nazi. Its purpose was rapidly to strengthen the Turkish nation by adopting the principle that "everything is for the Turkish nation, toward the Turk, and according to the Turk" (*Herşey Türk milleti için, Türk'e doğru ve Türk'e göre*).[200] Two years before his takeover of the CKMP, Türkeş had elaborated a set of nine principles, and these were then codified in his 1965 pamphlet, *Dokuz Işık*.[201] In order, these "nine lights" were nationalism (*milliyetçilik*), which was portrayed in progressive and non-chauvinistic terms; idealism (*ülkücülük*), which was defined as service and loyalty to the nation and the desire to raise Turkey to the highest level of civilization; moralism (*ahâkçilik*), which was related to Turkish traditions and customs;[202] "socialism" or social-mindedness (*toplumculuk* – not *sosyalizm*), which – like fascist socialism – urged the establishment of state control over key economic affairs and the promotion of social welfare, but not the expropriation of private property; scientism (*ilimcilik*), which was described in purely secular terms;[203] "freedomism" or promotion of freedom (*hürriyetçilik*) in all spheres of public and private life, in accordance with the United Nations charter [!]; "peasantism" or being pro-peasant (*köycülük*), which meant promoting rural development and agricultural (including land) reforms; developmentalism and populism (*gelişmecilik ve halkçılık*), which referred to progress on behalf of the people and by the people; and industrialism and technologism (*endüstricilik ve teknikçilik*), which were fully supported. All of these seemed to fall squarely within the Kemalist tradition, a fact that Türkeş repeatedly stressed.[204] The emphasis throughout was on nationalism, to which all of the other principles were subordinate,[205] but Türkeş constantly claimed that it was a non-aggressive form of nationalism which eschewed pan-Turkism and racism.

Yet beneath this moderate image, which was reiterated in several subsequent publications designed for mass consumption,[206] lurked far more dangerous sentiments that were openly expressed in materials produced for members of the party and its satellite or parallel organizations. The nation was in fact viewed as an organic totality to which the individual and his rights were totally subordinated. The interests of that nation were to be guarded and promoted by an interventionist and authoritarian "national state" (*millî devlet*), at the head of which would stand a leader (*başbuğ*) who was "accountable to no class or group."[207] Economically, society was to be divided into six "sectors" and organized into corporate occupational groups directed from above, that is, a corporatist system was planned, and both workers' and capitalist interests were to be subordinated to the needs of a state-controlled and relatively autarchic national economic policy. The MHP was also elitist, since it sought to establish a "hierarchical and nonegalitarian social order" divided between enlightened managers and the masses. "Anti-national" (that is, communist and leftist) elements were to be harshly suppressed, and the Turkish state cleansed of all "subversive" ethnic minorities.[208] This latter emphasis suggests that racism was still an important undercurrent within the MHP, and indeed several writings by party members and supporters advocated blatant racism with biological overtones.[209] Moreover, maximalist political pan-Turkism and unabashed militarism were common features of internal and "unofficial" party publications, and they even seeped into public materials. One such publication spoke of the establishment of a "Great Turkish State that would once again dominate the entire world," while a party supporter exclaimed that a "Turkish nationalist can love peace only as a tool for new wars."[210] Finally, although the MHP presented itself to the public as "the most determined defender of the [existing] system," its militants were told that "nationalist-socialist" (*milliyetçi-toplumcu*) thought was revolutionary and constituted "the fiercist enemy of the present order."[211] Therefore, there can scarcely be any doubt that the MHP was a genuinely fascist party.

The same dichotomy is observable when one compares the formally "democratic" organizational structure of the MHP with its actual functioning and its parallel apparatuses. Like other Turkish political parties, the MHP had a hierarchical structure with centralized organs that oversaw the activities of regional and local branches, as well as standardized regulations and established procedures for conducting its affairs.[212] But that is where the similarity ends, for the MHP's "vertical pattern of authority" resembled that of a military organization, and the authority and control exercised by the party chairman (Türkeş) exceeded that exercised by his counterpart in the socialist Türkiye İşçi Partisi (TİP: Worker's [or Labor] Party of Turkey) and was equaled only by the heads of clandestine and illegal Marxist-Leninist groups, including the Türkiye Komünist Partisi (TKP: Communist Party of Turkey).[213] Even more significant was the MHP's creation of parallel Idealist (*Ülkücü*) associations – in both Turkey and Europe – that were organically linked to the party despite their ostensible independence. These were analogous to the "parallel hierarchies" commonly set up by totalitarian revolutionary movements, both communist and fascist. Such organizations were created for various sectors in Turkish society, including youth, professional, and regional groupings,[214] and recruited much of their personnel from preexisting ultranationalist and pan-Turkist organizations. As a result, by the end of the 1960s the MHP dominated the secular right-wing portion of the Turkish political spectrum.

The most serious development of all was Türkeş' establishment of paramilitary training camps (*komando kamplan*) from 1968 on, camps in which thousands of Turkish youths were subjected to physical training (including the handling of weapons) and ideological indoctrination.[215] Following their training, these cadres (who originally called themselves "nationalist-socialists," then Gray Wolves) were used to attack leftist groups with the sanctioning of the conservative AP and, even more ominously, recruited into the Kontr-Gerilla organization to perform various dirty jobs for the military, police, and MİT.[216] By the second half of the 1970s, the MHP had become the world's largest neo-fascist party.[217] It was able to participate in two rightist "nationalist front" (*Milliyetçi Cephe*) coalition governments, and in return for its crucial support in the creation of conservative electoral majorities the party was granted cabinet positions and control over various ministries, including (after

1977) the Ministry of Customs and Monopolies and that of Commerce.[218] From this position within sectors of the state apparatus the party's militants were ideally placed not only to help finance and arm themselves (in large part through illicit arms and drug smuggling in conjunction with the Turkish mafia), but also to initiate a strategy of terrorism, provocations, and destabilization seemingly geared toward precipitating a rightist military coup.[219] This they finally managed to accomplish in 1980, with the witless assistance of the terrorist left. However, the new military regime showed its "gratitude" by banning the MHP, arresting hundreds of its members and affiliated Idealist militants, and bringing the party's leaders (including Türkeş) to trial, although the treatment of the latter was relatively lenient compared to that metered out to radical leftists.[220]

It now remains only to demonstrate that the MHP's ideology incorporated strong anti-Western attitudes, attitudes which were undoubtedly transmitted to the party's militant followers, including the Bozkurtlar. This is necessary because Henze falsely claims that "Türkeş and his party were never really anti-Western," and then suggests that the MHP was a fully secularized ultranationalist party whose supporters lacked the anti-Christian feelings characteristic of religious rightists associated with the Millî Selâmet Partisi (MSP: National Salvation Party) or various fundamentalist religious brotherhoods.[221] In short, Henze denies that the extreme right-wing circles Ağca was linked to had any motives to kill the pope, which by default means that the radical left were the real culprits.

Henze is wrong on both counts, however. Even if it is assumed for a moment that he is correct in portraying the MHP as being devoid of religious elements, the fact is that the party was strongly opposed to Western "imperialism" in general, and especially to Western cultural and economic domination of Turkey. As Herman and Brodhead rightly point out, Türkeş' brand of pan-Turkism appealed to right-wing radicals who believed that their nation was being humiliated and exploited by both the Soviet Union *and* the capitalist powers of the West.[222] Fear of foreign economic control and subversion of indigenous national values is characteristic of integral nationalist movements, and in fascist movements this attitude is by definition conjoined with vehement anti-capitalism.[223] Thus, it should come as no surprise to find the following diatribe attributed to an MHP spokesman:

> Finance capital is by its nature and purpose not national. Banks, insurance companies and financial trust that are attached to it are the mortal enemies of the national economy. In fact there is a contradiction between finance capital and all the elements of the national economy. Finance capital is concerned with the weakening and destroying [of] the national economy in all its aspects by robbing the banks, manipulating the stock exchange and by various other swindles. It exploits all the possibilities in Turkey through puppet enterprises which speed up the productive economy. It makes the national wealth its own property by setting up plants which encourage luxury and waste (Coca-Cola, Fanta, etc.) and exploits the national wealth (the plunder of minerals). There is also a class of compradors which participates in these activities of this

anti-national capital, reaping large profits and sharing in the crime. They are virtually traitors. Thus the struggle between the national and the anti-national economy is one between international capital and its accomplices against the nation. What is needed now is to establish the effect of these accomplices of the anti-national economy on our social groups and then to attack.[224]

If nothing else, this indicates that the anti-imperialist note penned by Ağca, which Henze grossly misinterprets and claims to find perplexing, clearly conformed to the MHP's fascist outlook.[225] Yet the party's hostility toward the West has always been tempered by its even greater hostility toward the Soviet Union and its recognition that Turkey requires external economic assistance to finance its development into a world power. Therefore, despite Türkeş' resentment about the "Coca-Colaization" of Turkish society, he has continued to advocate Turkish participation in the NATO alliance, U.S. military assistance programs, and the European Economic Community (EEC) so as to enable Turkey to offset the threat posed by Soviet power.[226]

The MHP's secular anti-Western sentiments were further reinforced when Türkeş adopted an Islamist veneer for his party. Türkeş himself is by no means religious. He remains a committed pan-Turkist and probably also a secularist at heart, and was so openly in the past. Thus, the MBK faction he led sought to "substitute a[n ultra]nationalist ideology for Islam . . . through education and propaganda."[227] To this end he and his supporters established an organization known as the Ülkü ve Kültür Birliği (Union of Ideals and Culture) in June 1960, but it collapsed following their expulsion from the junta. Nor was there any emphasis on Islam in the wake of his 1965 takeover of the CKMP, as both the party's program and his theoretical treatise of that year make apparent.[228] Further support for this contention can be found in certain publications by orthodox Muslim activists, who doubted the sincerity of Türkeş' conversion to Islam and referred the reader to his earlier anti-religious and extreme secularist pronouncements.[229] By 1969, however, he was consistently expressing favorable views about Islam and indeed began depicting the MHP as a defender of Islam in Turkey.[230] He even added three crescents to the MHP's Bozkurt banner.[231] Since the ideas of racial pan-Turkism and a supranational Islamic *Ümmet* are fundamentally incompatible, some of Türkeş' oldest and most extreme pan-Turkist comrades – who were known as the "Shamanists" – left the MHP in disgust as a result of the party's new "nationalist-Islamist" orientation.[232] What is it that accounted for Türkeş' sudden turn toward Islam?

To understand this shift, it must be recognized that Islam continues to be a powerful force in modern Turkey. Despite Atatürk's forcible disestablishment of religion in several areas of Turkish life, popular support for Islam was never eradicated, especially in rural areas.[233] Although during the Kemalist period devout Muslims did not generally dare to resist anti-religious policies imposed on them, when the period of authoritarian monoparty rule gave way to a liberalized multiparty political system, Islam underwent a tremendous resurgence and in fact became an important political factor in electoral contests.[234] All opposition parties soon discovered that they could obtain large numbers of votes by promising to ease the restrictions Atatürk had placed on Islam, and did so in the name of freedom and democracy. This in part accounted for the victories of the DP and, later, the AP.[235] Islam again made itself felt in educational affairs, and small religious parties appeared on the scene openly to contest for public support. As Ahmad indicates, the result was that parties such as Necmettin Erbakan's Millî Nizam Partisi (National Order Party) – the forerunner of his later MSP – threatened to take votes away from other conservative and rightist parties.[236]

It is therefore clear that Türkeş adopted Islam for entirely pragmatic reasons – in order to obtain a mass political base.[237] By the late 1960s it had become apparent to him that a pure pan-Turkist ideology could not attract sufficiently broad support to enable the MHP to attain power, either through electoral or subversive means. He thence publicly embraced Islam, though not at the expense of the ultranationalism and racial pan-Turkism that still underlay his political agenda. After 1968 he made more appeals to Islamic sentiment, went on a pilgrimage to Mecca, established good relations with some prominent religious figures, established close links to the extremist Süleymancı religious brotherhood, and instituted compulsory religious instruction for party-linked Idealist militants, including the Bozkurtlar.[238] Yet his manipulation of religious themes was often quite cynical, and the expressions of anti-Christian hostility in MHP publications were probably designed chiefly to prevent rival parties from monopolizing them. The terrorist provocations he organized to precipitate vicious and bloody sectarian religious clashes demonstrated his lack of genuine concern for the faithful.[239] The nature of the role Islam played in the MHP, as opposed to the MSP, is perhaps best summarized by P. Xavier Jacob:

> Each of the two parties included the Muslim religion in its program . . . but for [the MSP] Islam is the first and most fundamental element, and nationalism should be placed at the service of religion or completely muted, indeed totally denied, in the name of the *umma*, whereas for [the MHP] religion is secondary and should be placed at the service of nationalism, to cement it, consecrate it, and give it an intangible, absolute, and holy value.[240]

Despite these important differences in emphasis, the MHP acquired "the image of a religious party in terms of both its militants and its electorate" and "increasingly resembled" the MSP as time wore on.[241] One indication of this is the intense struggle that developed between the two parties to obtain the support of the religious vote. Indeed, by the autumn of 1979 Idealist militants were having skirmishes with the MSP-linked Akıncılar, not because the former were unbelievers but because both of their parent parties sought to monopolize control over *religious* education in Turkey.[242] Henze's image of the MHP as a completely secularized party is thus inaccurate.

Far from demonstrating that the Soviets laid a false trail, the Ağca case actually reveals the extent to which religious themes had permeated the MHP's parallel organizations and, when fused with ultranationalism and racism, provided the type of potent ideological brew that could easily motivate members of those organizations to try to kill a figure they viewed as an agent of Western and Christian imperialism. Despite Henze's obfuscation of the situation, strong religious sentiments have been attributed to Ağca by many people, including his brother Adnan and Italian prosecutor Antonio Albano who, in his report, characterized Ağca as "deeply Islamic by culture and mentality."[243] That he was unexceptional in this respect within the milieu of the MHP is suggested by the hostile polemics against the pope found in the official party newspaper *Hergün*. In several issues of *Hergün* that were published around the time of the pope's November 1979 visit to Turkey, for example, John Paul II was accused of coming to İstanbul with a hidden political agenda – to unite Christendom and initiate a crusade against Islam with the aim of restoring the Byzantine empire! In these articles the pope was repeatedly referred to as the "Crusader Commander" (*Haçlı Komutanı*), and in its 20 November issue *Hergün* employed a phraseology almost identical to that used a few days later by Ağca in his letter to *Milliyet*.[244] This does not prove that Ağca was a genuine rightist, for if he wanted to pose as a Bozkurt he would have adopted language appropriate to the Turkish ultranationalist right. It does demonstrate, however, that the attitudes he expressed in his two notes were fully consonant with the MHP's political propaganda.

In sum, there is no justification for assuming that the Bozkurtlar lacked motives to kill the pope or, by extension, that they must have acted as the agents of some other political entity. The fact that Henze continues to advocate such an erroneous interpretation would be perplexing unless due consideration is given to his long career as a government-linked propagandist and high-level CIA case officer in Turkey.[245] It is therefore unfortunate that this interpretation has been uncritically accepted and disseminated by much of the mainstream media in the West.

Conclusion

In the preceding study a case has been made that the paramilitary organizations affiliated with the MHP, or factions within those organizations, were behind the attempted assassination of Pope John Paul II. But given the impossibility of gaining access to certain hidden or classified sources (including documents in the files of various Western and Eastern security and intelligence agencies), which alone might enable a historian to fully reconstruct the crime, this cannot be conclusively demonstrated. All reconstructions must be regarded as tentative at this point, and considering what is now known about the sordid activities of the world's intelligence organizations, it may indeed turn out that those who argue for KGB or Western intelligence sponsorship are correct.

Nevertheless, currently available primary and secondary sources suggest that neither of the conspiratorial theses that have received a wide exposure within their repective spheres stand up under close scrutiny. Although both the "KGB plot" and "CIA plot" theories rest upon suspect sources, circumstantial evidence, and strained logic, this has not prevented eager polemicists on both sides from generating propaganda campaigns to promote them. In the West, influential opinion shapers have cynically or unwittingly disseminated disinformation supporting the "Bulgarian connection" thesis, which has clearly affected public perceptions about the events in St. Peter's Square. Nevertheless, the bulk of the evidence currently available points to an indigenous Turkish plot launched by the ultranationalist right. Ağca undoubtedly operated within this milieu for several years, and until someone demonstrates otherwise it must be assumed that he was what he appeared to be – a Turkish and Islamic extremist. It is also undeniable that the ideology of the MHP's commandos was infused with anti-Western and anti-Christian sentiments, which provided them with as strong a motive for trying to kill the pope as any police detective could ask for.

Acknowledgements

The author would like to thank Professors Rudi P. Lindner (University of Michigan) and John Masson Smith (University of California, Berkeley), as well as Dr. Grace Smith (University of California, Berkeley), for their instruction in matters Turkish and, even more importantly, for their friendship and consistent support over the years; the members of my dissertation commitee at Berkeley, Professors Richard A. Webster, Gerald D. Feldman, and Peter Dale Scott, for their informed feedback; Robin Ramsay, Stephen Dorril, and David Teacher from the excellent British parapolitics publication, *Lobster;* the Turkish Studies Association, for presenting me with their annual award and prize for the Best Student Research Paper in 1988; Bernard Fensterwald from the Assassinations Archive and Research Center in Washington, D.C., for some tangible, unsolicited support; and the University of California's Institute on Global Conflict and Cooperation, for offering me a two-year dissertation fellowship that enabled me to travel overseas to Europe and gather further primary and secondary source materials for this and other research projects.

Notes

1 The exceptions are Uğur Mumcu, Örsan Öymen, and Paul Henze, although Henze distorts the Turkish background, perhaps in order to mislead the unsophisticated reader into accepting his thesis of Soviet culpability.
2 A good example is provided by the recent book by Michael Parenti, *Inventing Reality: The Politics of the Mass Media* (New York: St. Martin's, 1986). Despite his blatant pro-Soviet biases and uncritical repetition of certain arguments about the papal plot, some of which parallel those found in East Bloc sources (see pp. 130–47 and 161–66), it is unclear whether Parenti is a willing propagandist or a misguided left-wing idealist. Similar problems are posed by certain works by rightist authors who, knowingly or not, disseminate various Western intelligence disinformation themes about the papal plot. See, for example, Francisco Chao Hermida, *Terrorismo y drogas: Hijos mellizos de la subversión* (Caracas: Arte, 1984), pp. 17–40; and Vittorfranco N. Pisano, *The Dynamics of Subversion and Violence in Contemporary Italy* (Stanford: Hoover Institution, 1987), pp. 128–30.
3 *Disinformation* is false, distorted or otherwise misleading information that is *consciously* generated and disseminated in order to manipulate the perceptions and behavior of targeted audiences (as opposed to *misinformation*, which is the product of honest error). Compare the CIA's own definition, cited in Richard H. Shultz and Roy Godson, *Dezinformatsia: Active Measures in Soviet Strategy* (Washington, DC: Pergamon/Brassey's, 1984), p. 37. See also the useful description of the disinformation dissemination process by Czech intelligence defector Ladislav Bittman, *The KGB and Soviet Disinformation: An*

Insider's View (Washington, DC: Pergamon/Brassey's, 1985), pp. 48–55. "Psychological Operations" is a more general term for influence operations in support of larger politico-military campaigns and objectives. See, for example, Alfred H. Paddock Jr., "Military Psychological Operations and U.S. Strategy," in *Psychological Operations: The Soviet Challenge*, ed. by Joseph S. Gordon (Boulder & London: Westview, 1988), p. 145.

4 For more on Western disinformation themes and sources on the subject of terrorism, see Philip Paull, "International Terrorism: The Propaganda War" (Unpublished M.A. Thesis: San Francisco State University, 1982); Edward S. Herman, *The Real Terror Network: Terrorism in Fact and Propaganda* (Boston: South End, 1982), esp. pp. 47–62; and Edward S. Herman and Gerry O'Sullivan, *The "Terrorism" Industry: The Experts and Institutions that Shape Our View of Terror* (New York: Pantheon, 1989). This last work should be required reading for everyone concerned with contemporary terrorism. However, I do not share its authors' apparent assumption that all the claims made by members of the intelligence-linked "terrorism industry," especially those concerning alleged Soviet Bloc atrocities or misdeeds, are false – though they are suspect and certainly need to be independently verified before being accepted as accurate.

5 Henze, author of *The Plot to Kill the Pope* (New York: Scribner's, 1985) and numerous articles, as well as a consultant for various television shows on the papal plot, is a "former" CIA official with extensive operational experience in Turkey, first as a case officer in 1957–58, then as Chief of Station (COS) in Ankara from 1973 to 1977. See Ellen Ray and others, eds., *Dirty Work 2: The CIA in Africa* (Seacaucus, NJ: Lyle Stuart, 1979), pp. 382–3; Uğur Mumcu, *Papa, Mafya, Ağca* (İstanbul: Tekin, 1984), pp. 24–5 and passim; and Edward S. Herman and Frank Brodhead, *The Rise and Fall of the Bulgarian Connection* (New York: Sheridan Square, 1986), esp. pp. 146–8 and 157–9. For confirmation of his function as COS, see Philip Taubman and Leslie Gelb, "U.S. Aides Cautious on Pope Shooting," *New York Times* (27 January 1983), p. A12. Perhaps more importantly, inside Turkey he is widely suspected of having been the covert orchestrator of various terrorist and pro-coup actions undertaken by the so-called Kontr-Gerilla (KG; Counter-Guerrilla) organization attached to the Özel Harp Dairesi (ÖHD; Special Warfare Department) of the General Staff of the Turkish armed forces. See, for example, "Dietro tutti i golpe," *Panorama* [Milan] 23.997 (26 May 1985), p. 107, although I have seen no actual evidence of this.

6 Sterling is the author of *The Time of the Assassins: Anatomy of an Investigation* (New York: Holt, Rinehart & Winston, 1985) and several articles, as well as being – like Henze – a consultant for various television documentaries. While it would be rash to claim unequivocally that she is a U.S. intelligence asset, her background strongly suggests that possibility. In the first place, she contributed for many years to a conservative Italian publication that was in part covertly funded by the CIA – the English-language *Rome Daily American*. For this CIA funding, see John M. Crewdson and Joseph B. Treaster, "Worldwide Propaganda Network Built by CIA," *New York Times* (26 December 1977), p. 37. Subsequently, she wrote articles for Milan's *Il Giornale Nuovo*, another conservative paper that some people also claim is used by the CIA to disseminate disinformation. See Fred Landis, "Robert Moss, Arnaud de Borchgrave, and Right-Wing Disinformation," *Covert Action Information Bulletin* 10 (August–September 1980), p. 43. Much more significantly, conservative Italian criminologist Franco Ferracuti, testifying before the Italian parliamentary commission investigating the secret rightist Masonic lodge P2, said that Michael Ledeen – himself a hawkish right-wing analyst and occasional alleged operative for U.S. and Italian intelligence – had told him in the late 1970s that Sterling was a "courier" between the Italian internal security agency (the Servizio Informazioni Sicurezza Democratica, or SISDE) and the Center for Strategic and International Studies (CSIS), a conservative think tank formerly affiliated with Georgetown University that employs numerous former CIA and military intelligence officers and seems to disseminate, inadvertently or intentionally, certain Western disinformation themes. See Pietro Calderoni, "E cosi'CIA," *L'Espresso* 32:21 (1 June 1986), p. 23. For CSIS, see Fred Landis, "Georgetown's Ivory Tower for Old Spooks," *Inquiry* 2:16 (30 September 1979), pp. 7–9. Note also that Sterling was the popularizer of the "Soviet terror network" thesis in her sensationalistic work, *The Terror*

Network: The Secret War of International Terrorism (New York: Holt, Rinehart, 1981), which had a considerable impact on public perceptions of terrorism in spite of its exaggerated claims and factual distortions. Even if Sterling is not herself a paid intelligence asset, her works reveal her to be a journalist who relies heavily and uncritically on information supplied to her by confidential Western intelligence sources. See Conor Cruise O'Brien, "The Roots of Terrorism," *New Republic* 185:4 (25 July 1981), pp. 29–30; and Philip Jenkins, "The Assassins Revisited: Claire Sterling and the Politics of Intelligence," *Intelligence and National Security* 1:3 (September 1986), p. 460. Indeed, various U.S. intelligence analysts assigned to examine her sources concluded that she was essentially recycling old CIA media disinformation in her publications. See Gregory Treverton, *Covert Action: The Limits of Intervention in the Postwar World* (New York: Basic, 1987), p. 165; Bob Woodward, *Veil: The Secret Wars of the CIA, 1981–1987* (New York: Simon & Schuster, 1987), p. 129; and Joseph E. Persico, *Casey: From the OSS to the CIA* (New York: Viking, 1990), p. 288. Compare also James Adams, *The Financing of Terror: Behind the PLO, IRA, Red Brigades and M-19 Stand the Paymasters* (New York: Simon & Schuster, 1986), p. 3.

7 Slugenov is a right-wing Vatican priest who published the first full-length book on the papal assassination attempt, *Das Drama auf der Piazza San Pietro vom 13. Mai 1981 und die Ereignisse in der Cova da Iria vom 13. Mai bis 13. Oktober 1917* (Rome and Coblenz: Pro Fratribus, 1982). In that work he partly based his conspiratological argument, that the KGB trained Ağca and ordered the papal shooting, on an Italian military intelligence (SISMI) document dated 19 May 1981, which seems to have been a forgery since it was rejected as evidence by conservative Italian judge Ilario Martella at Ağca's trial. See Herman and Brodhead, *Rise and Fall*, pp. 98 (incl. n. 104) and 102, n. 2. The publisher of Slugenov's work, Pro Fratribus, is a secretive anti-communist Catholic organization which devotes most of its efforts to surreptitiously aiding persecuted Christians *behind* the Iron Curtain. Although headquartered in Rome, from where it has been directed since 1968 by Slovakian bishop Pavel Hnilica, it has branches throughout western Europe, as well as in Argentina and the United States. See Sandro Magister, "Tutto Papa, chiesa e banca," *L'Espresso* 35:44 (5 November 1989), p. 8. Compare also the organization's entry in the *Annuario cattolico d'Italia 1981/1982* (Rome: Italiana, 1981), p. 1457. Like other anti-communist émigré organizations from eastern European and Asian "Captive Nations" (see *infra*, note 188), it may receive funding from, and provide a front for, Western intelligence agencies. Note also that elements of SISMI and its organizational predecessors have often been involved in rightist coup plots and neo-fascist terrorist incidents, as well as efforts to obstruct investigations into those activities, and thus the agency cannot necessarily be viewed as an unbiased source of information even under the best of circumstances. For these subversive activities, see the multi-volume study of Gianni Flamini, *Il partito del golpe: Le strategie della tensione e del terrore dal primo centrosinistra organico al sequestro moro* (Ferrara: Bovolenta, 1981–85); Giuseppe De Lutiis, *Storia dei servizi segreti in Italia* (Rome: Riuniti, 1984), both passim. The latter book is published by the official publishing house of the Partito Comunista Italiano (PCI), but is a well-researched work based almost entirely on information derived from either the mainstream Italian media or the reports and documents made public in the course of several parliamentary and judicial investigations into Italian secret service "deviations."

8 Bensi, a Sovietologist and Radio Free Europe/Radio Liberty (RFE/RL) commentator, is the author of *La pista sovietica: Terrorismo, violenza, guerra e propaganda nella teoria e nella prassi di Mosca* (Milan: Sugar, 1983). The main value of the book is that the author provides extensive translated selections from the official East Bloc press which clearly demonstrate the manipulative and hypocritical character of pro-Soviet accounts of both the pope's character and the assassination attempt.

9 De Marenches is the former head of the French foreign intelligence service, at that time known as SDECE. He is not only a rightist and a devout Catholic, but also an extremely pro-American intelligence officer who was appointed Directeur Général in 1970 by Georges Pompidou and thence went on to purge some anti-American Gaullist

elements within SDECE so as to "reconcile" relations between that agency and the CIA. See esp. Roger Faligot and Pascal Krop, *La Piscine: Les services secrets français, 1944–1984* (Paris: Seuil, 1985), pp. 310–17; and an article reprinted from *Le Nouvel Observateur* by Réné Backmann and others, "What the CIA Is Looking for in France," in *Dirty Work [1]: The CIA in Western Europe*, ed. by Philip Agree and Louis Wolf (Seacaucus, NJ: Lyle Stuart, 1978), pp. 180–2. His views on the papal assassination attempt can be found in a recent book containing a series of interviews with him conducted by television journalist Christine Ockrent, *Dans le secret des princes* (Paris: Stock, 1986), excerpted by Yves Cuau, "Services secrets: Révélations explosives," *L'Express* 1834 (5 September 1986), pp. 21–2. Therein he claims to have received "credible" evidence from unknown sources that there was going to be a Soviet Bloc attempt on the pope's life, which caused him to send two trusted lieutenants to Italy to warn the pope in January 1980, after making contact with the Vatican through an "important French ecclesiastic." It should also be pointed out that de Marenches was a friend of Francesco Pazienza, who was a member of the conspiratorial right-wing "Super S" faction within SISMI and a collaborator of Ledeen's. And as Herman and Brodhead rightly emphasize (*Rise and Fall*, pp. 118–19, n. 41), de Marenches "was himself an important disinformationist and recycler of the disinformation of other intelligence agencies." Note, for example, the "cooked" intelligence report he provided to another right-wing disinformationist with intelligence connections, Arnaud de Borchgrave – at that time later editor of Sun-Myung Moon's *Washington Times* – about an alleged Soviet plan to "undermine the structures of the Western world" through terrorism, which was supposedly launched at the Tricontinental Conference held in Havana in 1968. See de Borchgrave, "Unspiking Soviet Terrorism," *International Security Review* 7:1 (Spring 1982), pp. 5–16. This journal was published by a Unification Church front group.

10 Ledeen began his public career as a historian of Italian fascism, but after working in Italy for several years he became involved in a number of apparent intelligence-connected ventures, including *Il Giornale Nuovo*, CSIS, and an international group organized to "study" terrorism in Italy. According to his erstwhile friend Pazienza, he was later recruited as agent Z-3 by SISMI (in which capacity he became involved in a number of scandals), and subsequently he became the "international terrorism" and Italy expert attached to Secretary of State Alexander Haig's staff. More recently, in addition to promoting disinformation themes in a variety of conservative or rightist publications, including *Commentary* and *Human Events*, he reportedly served as an intermediary between the U.S. National Security Council (NSC) and ex-Iranian secret police (Sāzmān-i Ittilāʿāt va Amnīyat-i Kishvar, or SAVAK; National Intelligence and Security Organization) officer Manūchahr Qurbānīfar during the early phases of the illegal Iran-Contra operation. For more details, see Herman and Brodhead, *Rise and Fall*, pp. 94–99, 159–62, and passim; Jonathan Marshall and others, *The Iran-Contra Connection: Secret Teams and Covert Operations in the Reagan Era* (Boston: South End, 1987), pp. 41–2, 71–3, and 174–81; U.S. Government, President's Special Review Board, [*The Tower Commission*] *Report*, 26 February 1987 (Washington, DC: GPO, 1987), esp. appendix 2, pp. 4–6; U.S. Congress, Joint Committee, *Report of the Congressional Committees Investigating the Iran-Contra Affair, with Supplemental, Minority, and Additional Views*, 100th Congress, 1st Session, 13 November 1987 (Washington, DC: GPO, 1987), pp. 165–70; Diana Johnstone, "The Ledeen Connections," *In These Times* (8–14 September 1982), pp. 4–5; and several articles in the mainstream Italian press. Philip Jenkins thinks Pazienza's testimony regarding Ledeen's recruitment by SISMI is "impossible to believe" ("Assassins Revisited," p. 468), but provides neither contrary evidence nor opposing arguments. Although Pazienza is a smooth operator and a skilled dissimulator whose shifting testimonies warrant skepticism, in this case his claims dovetail nicely with what is known about Ledeen's activities in other contexts.

11 Cline was a career CIA officer who worked for many years in the clandestine services. Among other things, he served as COS in Taiwan from 1958 to 1962 (during which time he may have helped organize and fund the Asian People's Anti-Communist League [APACL], the forerunner of the World Anti-Communist League [WACL], a far right

umbrella organization that later encompassed several neo-fascist groups), and as Deputy Director of Intelligence (DDI) from 1962 to 1966. Since his formal retirement from the agency, he has worked in other capacities for the U.S. government and is now on the staff of CSIS. He has also been actively involved in numerous other extreme right political ventures, including WACL and the Moon-sponsored U.S. Global Strategy Council. For his predictably conspiratorial view of the papal assassination plot, see "Soviet Footprints in St. Peter's Square," *Terrorism* 7:1 (1984), pp. 53–5. For more on Cline's background, see his own book, *The CIA: Reality vs. Myth* (Washington, DC: Acropolis, 1982); the biographical information provided about him, in his capacity as one of the "chief advisors," in a promotional book on the CIA by John Patrick Quirk, *The Central Intelligence Agency: A Photographic History* (Guilford, CT: Foreign Intelligence Press, 1986), p. 5; and Scott Anderson and Jon Lee Anderson, *Inside the League: The Shocking Exposé of How Terrorists, Nazis, and Latin American Death Squads have Infiltrated the World Anti-Communist League* (New York: Dodd, Mead, 1986), pp. 555–6, 126, and 259–60 (WACL links).

12 It is important to recognize that intelligence organizations are not political monoliths, and that within most Western intelligence agencies political views run the gamut from liberal to ultrarightist, although conservative or right-of-center views clearly predominate, especially in the operational branches. For an example of the views of intelligence community moderates on the papal plot, see the critical review of the Henze and Sterling books by ex-OSS and CIA officer William Hood, "Unlikely Conspiracy," *Problems of Communism* 33 (March–April 1984), pp. 67–70. Their views on "KGB terrorism" in general are reflected in the editorial by former CIA official Harry Rositzke, "If There Were No KGB, Would the Scale and Intensity of Terrorism Be Diminished," *New York Times* (20 July 1981), p. A17, a question to which he responds in the negative.

13 The official government publications include *The Anatomy of a Slander Campaign* (Sofia: Sofia Press, 1983); Iona Andronov, *On the Wolf's Track* (Sofia: Sofia Press, 1983); Iona Andronov, *The Triple Plot* (Sofia: Sofia Press, 1984); *"The Bulgarian Connection": Accusation without Proofs. Verbatim Report from the International Meeting of Journalists held in Sofia on February 7, 1985* (Sofia: Sofia Press, 1985); *"The Bulgarian Connection": The End of a Provocation* (Sofia: Sofia Press, 1983); Eduard Kovalyov and Igor Seydkh, *"Bulgarian Connection": CIA & Co. On the Outcome of the Antonov Trial* (Moscow: Novosti, 1986); Ivan Palchev, *The Assassination Attempt against the Pope and the Roots of Terrorism* (Sofia: Sofia Press, 1985); and Boyan Traikov, *Mystification, Dr. Martella!: Letters to Rome Addressed to Dr. Ilario Martella* (Sofia: Sofia Press, 1984). Most of the preceding have been translated into several Western languages. Compare also the Polish work by Eugeniusz Guz, *Zamach na Papieza* (Warsaw: KAW, 1983). Pro-Soviet Western works include Christian Roulette, *Jean-Paul II, Antonov, Agca: La filière* (Paris: Sorbier, 1984); Christian Roulette, *Jean-Paul II, Antonov, Agca: Le procès* (Paris: Halles de Paris, 1985); Maria Rosa Calderoni and Carlo Fido, *Processo del secolo: L'attentato al Papa e la Bulgarian Connection* (Palermo: Mazzone/ILA Palma, 1985); David Eisenhower and John Murray, *Warwords: U.S. Militarism, the Catholic Right and the "Bulgarian Connection"* (New York: International, 1986), pp. 69–123; and Hubert Reichel, *Die Russen kommen-pünktlich: Eine Geschichte des Antikommunismus von der 20er Jahren bis zu Reagan und Strauss* (Frankfurt am Main: Marxistische Blätter, 1983), pp. 63–8, as well as many articles in the left-wing press.

14 See, for example, Jacques Ellul, *Propaganda: The Formation of Men's Attitudes* (New York: Vintage, 1965), pp. 53–61.

15 The best examples are probably the unreliable works by Gordon Thomas and Max Morgan-Witts, *Pontiff* (New York: Doubleday, 1983); and *The Year of Armageddon: The Pope and the Bomb* (London: Granada, 1984), both of which are characterized by an extraordinarily naïve reliance on Western intelligence informants, who manipulate the authors mercilessly. For other examples of uncritical disinformation recycling, see the articles by Thomas P. Melady and John F. Kikoski, "The Attempted Assassination of the Pope," *Orbis* 28:4 (Winter 1985), pp. 775–801; and John L. Scherer, "The Plot to Kill the Pope," *Terrorism* 7:4 (1985), pp. 351–65. It would be impossible to list the innumerable journalistic

commentators in mainstream newspapers who have rushed to adopt the "KGB plot" thesis. For more on this, see Herman and Brodhead, *Rise and Fall*, pp. 174–205 and passim.

16 See, for example, Chapman Pincher (a right-wing British journalist with close links to British intelligence), *The Secret Offensive* (New York: St. Martin's, 1985), pp. 1–6, 259–60, and passim; and Arnaud de Borchgrave, "Terrorism in Relation to Disinformation," in *State Terrorism and the International System*, ed. by [Moon Front Group] the International Security Council (New York: CAUSA International, 1986), pp. 31–9, as well as the latter's editorial "Bum Tips and Spies," *New York Times* (12 August 1981), p. A27. For a contrary view, see the editorial by ex-CIA officer Rositzke, "KGB Disinformation," *New York Times* (21 July 1981), p. A15.

17 For examples, see the many studies by Noam Chomsky, including two recent works that focus on this type of media subservience in connection with terrorism, *The Culture of Terrorism* (Boston: South End, 1988); and *Pirates and Emperors: International Terrorism in the Real World* (New York: Claremont, 1986). Compare also Herman, *Real Terror Network*; and Herman and O'Sullivan, *"Terrorism" Industry*. However, in their foreign policy analyses, these three authors all display pronounced and indeed vituperative anti-American and anti-Western biases.

18 Robert A. Friedlander, *An Infinity of Mirrors: Mehmet Ali Agca and the "Plot to Kill the Pope"* (Gaithersburg, MD: International Association of Chiefs of Police, 1983). Although this brief study relies heavily on rightist and disinformation sources, it is clearly an honest attempt to reconstruct the crime and its conclusions are properly cautious.

19 For intelligent, broadly conservative analyses of terrorism, see the earliest publications by Paul Wilkinson, esp. the first edition of *Political Terrorism* (London: MacMillan, 1974); the maverick J. Bowyer Bell's, *A Time of Terror: How Democratic Societies Respond to Revolutionary Violence* (New York: Basic, 1978); and particularly the excellent study by Grant Wardlaw, *Political Terrorism: Theory, Tactics, and Counter-Measures* (Cambridge: Cambridge University, 1982). Many of the works by Brian Jenkins of the RAND Corporation, a former military intelligence officer and certainly no "dove," are also very interesting and thought-provoking, for example, *International Terrorism: A New Mode of Conflict* (Los Angeles: Crescent, 1975). Yet in comparison with the many hard-liners in the field of "terrorology," the preceding specialists seem extraordinarily reasonable and, indeed, almost liberal in inspiration (although over time Wilkinson has arguably moved steadily to the right and perhaps closer to the disinformation crowd).

20 This is the aforementioned *Rise and Fall of the Bulgarian Connection*. For an earlier version, see the special issue of *Covert Action Information Bulletin* titled "Disconnecting the Bulgarian Connection," 23 (Spring 1985). *Covert Action* is a controversial left-wing publication that exposes Western intelligence misdeeds. Although many of the contributors to the magazine are good journalistic or academic researchers who produce solid and informative articles, its chief editors are uncritical communist sympathizers who have occasionally floated East Bloc disinformation (about, for example, the origins of AIDS), regularly censored articles or passages critical of leftist regimes, and apparently exchanged information with the Cuban intelligence service.

21 Among the articles are several written by Diana Johnstone for *In These Times*, including the aforementioned "Ledeen Connections"; "The Sources of the Bulgarian Connection," *ITT* (26 June–9 July 1985), pp. 12–13; "Finger-Pointing in the Pontif [sic] Plot Labyrinth," *ITT* (29 January–4 February 1986), pp. 11 and 22; "Rome's Verdict: A Qualified Acquittal," *ITT* (16–22 April 1986), p. 9, and Örsan Öymen, "Behind the Scenes of the Ağca Investigation," a seven-part article in *Milliyet* from 18 to 25 November 1984. The two Mumcu works concerned specifically with the papal plot are the aforementioned *Papa, Mafya, Ağca* and *Ağca dosyası* (İstanbul: Tekin, 1982). In addition to these valuable but not entirely problem-free works, Mumcu has also written at least three other books dealing with aspects of terrorism in Turkey, including *Silâh kaçakçılığı ve terör* (İstanbul: Tekin, 1981); *Terörsüz özgürlük* (İstanbul: Tekin, 1982); and *Tüfek icad oldu . . .* (İstanbul: Tekin, 1980).

22 Among Dobbs's numerous excellent articles are "A Communist Plot to Kill the Pope – or a Liar's Fantasy," *Washington Post* (18 May 1984), pp. C1–C2; and his four-part "Man Who Shot the Pope" series in the *Washington Post* from 14 to 17 October 1984.
23 The most succinct statement of this thesis is offered by Sterling in "Unravelling the Riddle," in *Terrorism: How the West Can Win*, ed. by Benjamin Netanyahu (New York: Farrar Straus & Giraud, 1986), pp. 103–4. Compare Henze, *Plot to Kill the Pope*, pp. 128, 161–3, 194–200, and 210–16; and Edouard Sablier, *Le fil rouge: Histoire secrète du terrorisme international* (Paris: Plon, 1983), pp. 243–57. Thomas and Morgan-Witts not only indict the KGB and Bulgarians, but also the Libyans, Syrians, and Palestinians! See *Pontiff*, pp. 17, 210–11, 292, 294, 408–11, and 457–58, n. 1.
24 Henze, *Plot to Kill the Pope*, pp. 124–5 and 153–9; Sterling, *Time of the Assassins*, pp. 115–29; and Dobbs, "A Communist Plot . . . ?," p. C1.
25 Thus, for example, Henze thinks it may have occurred in the spring of 1979 (*Plot to Kill the Pope*, pp. 203–4), whereas Sterling suggests that he was a "sleeper" recruited earlier on, which would explain his alleged training in Palestinian or Syrian guerrilla camps and the bank accounts opened in his name before he arrived in İstanbul in 1978 (*Time of the Assassins*, pp. 49–50, 101–3). Thomas and Morgan-Witts claim that Ağca first made contact with the extreme left in Malatya, through his schoolmate and Devrimci Sol (DEV-SOL: Revolutionary Left) militant Sedat Sirri Kadem (*Pontiff*, pp. 290–1). There is no evidence to support *any* of these theories other than Ağca's shifting testimony.
26 Although the relations between Pope John Paul II and the Soviet authorities are certainly more complicated than Henze and Sterling portray them, I find the efforts of those who try to minimize East Bloc hostility toward the Pontiff entirely unconvincing. See, for example, Herman and Brodhead, *Rise and Fall*, pp. 14–15 and 210. Soviet antipathy toward John Paul II long predated the actual establishment of Solidarnosc, as their official press clearly indicates. East Bloc authors try to obscure this situation by arguing that the pope incurred the wrath of Western regimes by promoting disarmament, meeting with PLO representatives, and criticizing US foreign policy in Central America and other places. See Kovalyov and Sedykh, "*Bulgarian Connection*," pp. 19–25.
27 Ağca contradicted himself and/or changed testimony over one-hundred times, and made a number of outlandish statements, including a claim to be Jesus Christ. For an overview of Ağca's main contradictions and retractions, see Herman and Brodhead, *Rise and Fall*, pp. 18–41. Compare Dobbs, "A Communist Plot . . . ?," p. C2, on the frequency of Ağca's lying.
28 Sterling, and Thomas and Morgan-Witts rely heavily on information provided by anonymous intelligence sources, often for their most crucial arguments. See, for example, Sterling, *Time of the Assassins*, pp. 44–45, 72–75, and 90–96; Thomas and Morgan-Witts, *Pontiff*, pp. 449 (n. 19), 452 (n. 5), and 453–44 (n. 5); and Thomas and Morgan-Witts, *Year of Armageddon*, pp. 128–35, 277–84, 386 (n. 8), and 405 (n. 25).
29 For a good discussion of some of the problems involved in defector testimony, see Herman and Brodhead, *Rise and Fall*, pp. 234–40 (appendix C). However, I feel that they ignored one of the single most problematic factors – the high degree of control exercised over defectors by their new handlers. Although most defectors from the Soviet Bloc have good personal and/or moral reasons for their antipathy to communism and probably need little prompting to implicate their former masters in the most sordid deeds, it is important to emphasize that from the moment a potential defector makes contact with an enemy intelligence officer, assuming he is not a "dangle" or a "double" – he loses most of his independence and bargaining leverage. Later on, if he does not cooperate fully with his debriefers and handlers, they can always threaten to publicize his treachery or return him to his country of origin or embassy. In other words, even if a defector was unwilling to lie or disseminate disinformation about his former country's activities, which is probably a rare circumstance, he would not have much choice in the matter. This is a factor which must always be weighed when attempting to evaluate the reliability of defector testimony, and one that often tends to offset the benefits deriving from the fact that defectors may

well have detailed firsthand knowledge of communist intelligence techniques and operations. The preceding remarks obviously apply to the belated public "revelations" recently made by Viktor Sheymov concerning Andropov's responsibility for ordering the papal assassination attempt. This assertion is scarcely rendered more credible by Sheymov's implausible claim (which echoes those of Henze and Sterling) that the CIA under Casey refused to publicize such explosive information in the interests of preserving détente – this at a time when Reagan was publicly characterizing the Soviet Union as the "Evil Empire," and when Casey himself was rejecting intelligence reports from the field that did not conform to his and his boss's exaggerated claims about Soviet sponsorship of both international terrorism and subversion in Central America. See, for example, Woodward, *Veil*, pp. 124–9; and Persico, *Casey*, pp. 220–1 and 286–7. However, since the reliability of defector testimony varies greatly, ranging as it does from the relatively sober accounts and analyses of Bittman to the incredible assertions of opportunists (like Jan Šejna) or paranoids (like Anatoliy Golitsyn – see his *New Lies for Old: The Communist Strategy of Deception and Disinformation* [Brighton: Wheatsheaf, 1986], wherein it is claimed that the Sino-Soviet split was an elaborate deception operation), such testimony requires careful assessment on a case-by-case basis rather than uncritical acceptance or curt dismissal *in toto*.

30 Thus, for example, the work of Henze is filled with politically motivated speculations and hypotheses. Practically every paragraph contains verbs in the subjunctive or conditional tenses, innuendos followed by question marks, or – worst of all – baseless presumptions stated as if they had already been proven. See, for example, *Plot to Kill the Pope*, pp. 135 (second paragraph), 137 (third paragraph), 161–62 (third paragraph on), 177–80 (whole section), 194 (second paragraph), and so forth.

31 This is corroborated in a survey taken by *Paris Match* in mid-1983, which revealed that two out of three Poles in Poland believed that Soviet leaders were behind the papal assassination attempt. Cited by Paul B. Henze, "Misinformation and Disinformation: The Plot to Kill the Pope," *Survey* 27:118/199 (Autumn–Winter 1983), p. 14, n. 24. I have no idea whether this survey is representative. Compare also Herman and Brodhead, *Rise and Fall*, p. 14; and Dobbs, "A Communist Plot . . . ?," p. C2. However, I think they underestimate the propensity of regimes – especially those as paranoid as the Soviet regime – to initiate actions which end up being counterproductive to the attainment of desired goals. Hubris and shortsightedness can never be factored out of supposedly rational decision-making processes.

32 Herman and Brodhead, *Rise and Fall*, pp. 15–17; Hood, "Unlikely Conspiracy," pp. 68–70; Palchev, *Attempted Assassination*, pp. 63–65; and Parenti, *Inventing Reality*, p. 162. Note that even Sterling initially cast doubts on the theory of Soviet involvement in the attack, saying that it was "crazy" since "there would have been a better getaway plot." See the interview with her in "An Authority on Terrorism Offers a Chilling New Theory on the Shooting of the Pope," *People Magazine* 15:21 (1 June 1981), p. 34.

33 Kovalyov and Sedykh, *"Bulgarian Connection,"* pp. 79–80; and Antonov, *Wolf's Track*, pp. 21–46.

34 I know of no published work devoted entirely to the organization and operations of the MİT, although a number of works touch upon it in connection with the KG. One example is Süleyman Genç, *Bıçağın sırtındaki Türkiye: CIA-MİT kontr-gerilla* (İstanbul: Der, 1978).

35 For more on P2, see esp. the many volumes of materials published by the Italian parliamentary commission investigating the organization – Camera dei Deputati, *Commissione parlamentare d'inchiesta sulla Loggia massonica P2* (Rome: Camera dei Deputati, 1984–90) – which is divided into the majority (Anselmi) report, five dissenting minority reports, and over one-hundred thick volumes of attached documents and testimony. Compare also Martin Berger, *Historia de la Lógia Masonica P2* (Buenos Aires: El Cid, 1983); Andrea Barbieri and others, *L'Italia della P2* (Milan: Mondadori, 1981); Alberto Cecchi, *Storia della P2* (Rome: Riuniti, 1985); Roberto Fabiani, *I massoni in Italia* (Milan: L'Espresso, 1978);

Gianfranco Piazzesi, *Gelli: La carriere di un eroe di questa Italia* (Milan: Garzanti, 1983); Marco Ramat and others, *La resistibile ascesa della P2: Poteri occulti e Stato democratico* (Bari: De Donato, 1983); and Gianni Rossi and Francesco Lombrassa, *In nome della 'Loggia': Le prove di come la massoneria segreta ha tentato di impadronirsi dello Stato italiano. I retroscenda della P2* (Rome: Napoleone, 1981). Pro-P2 works include those of Gelli supporter Pier Carpi, *Il caso Gelli: La verità sulla Loggia P2* ... (Bologna: INEI, 1982), and the truly Orwellian work of Gelli himself, *La verità* (Lugnano: Demetra, 1989), which in spite of its title bears little resemblance to the truth.

36 For more on Super SISMI, see "[Sezione] Speciale: Servizi segreti e strutture clandestine. La riconstruzione giudiziaria del supersismi," *Questione Giustizia* 6:1 (1987), pp. 121–92.

37 Integralists are Catholic ultra-traditionalists who believe that the Church's doctrine is eternal and unchanging, and who seek to infuse it – by force if necessary – into all facets of modern life. As such, they are opposed to the process of secularization and to all attempts to reform or adapt Church policies in accordance with changing social conditions. See for example, Emile Poulat, *Modernistica: Horizons, physionomies, débats* (Paris: Nouvelles Editions Latines, 1982), pp. 46–57; and Father Charles Antoine, *O Integrismo brasileiro* (Rio de Janeiro: Civilização Brasileira, 1980), pp. 11–15. This view has often led to their adoption of rightist political policies and totalitarian methods, as for example in the case of France, where integralists colluded with military elites and neo-fascists in promoting coups and terrorism during the late 1950s and 1960s. See for example, Jacques Maîtres, "Le Catholicisme d'extrême droite et la croisade antisubversive," *Revue Française de Sociologie* 2:2 (April–June 1961), pp. 106–17.

38 An excellent general introduction to the BND (and other West German intelligence agencies) is provided by Thomas Walde, *ND-Report: Die Rolle der Geheimen Nachrichtendienste im Regierungssystem der Bundesrepublik Deutschland* (Munich: Piper, 1971), pp. 79–105. The best sketch of Mossad's structure and functioning is probably the CIA's own leaked 1979 analysis, *Israel: Foreign Intelligence and Security Services*, which was published in *Counterspy* 6:3 (May–June 1982), pp. 34–54. Most of the other works on the Israeli intelligence services are "hagiographic." There is as yet no study that adequately delineates the organization and manifold operations of the Vatican's intelligence apparatus. Not surprisingly, covert activities carried out by components of the NATO secret services are often difficult to discern and reconstruct, but some of its purported operations in the Italian sphere are sketched by Flamini, *Partito del golpe*, passim.

39 Thus, for example, Kovalyov and Sedykh argue (*"Bulgarian Connection,"* pp. 28–30) that Mossad may have been behind the papal attack since John Paul II had recently angered the Israeli government by meeting with PLO representatives, and the incident served Israeli interests to heighten U.S.-Soviet hostility. Strangely enough, an Austrian Security Service file leaked to Thomas and Morgan-Witts also implicated Mossad in Ağca's mission. See *Pontiff*, p. 454, n. 4.

40 Andronov, *Wolf's Track*, pp. 9 and 45–46; Palchev, *Assassination Attempt*, pp. 11–13; Kovalyov and Sedykh, *"Bulgarian Connection,"* p. 80; and Eisenhower and Murray, *Warwords*, pp. 2–4.

41 For more on John Paul II's policies, see Paul Johnson, *Pope John Paul II and the Catholic Restoration* (New York: St. Martin's, 1981); Giancarlo Zizola, *La restaurazione di papa Wojtyla* (Rome: Laterza, 1985); and the highly controversial (and apparently falsified) work by Antoni Gronowicz, *God's Broker: The Life and Times of John Paul II* (New York: Richardson & Snyder, 1984). For his activities in Poland, see J. F. Brown, ed., *The Pope in Poland* (Washington, DC: RFE/RL, 1979); and Eric O. Hanson, *The Catholic Church in World Politics* (Princeton: Princeton University, 1987), pp. 197–233.

42 Herman and Brodhead argue (*Rise and Fall*, pp. 241–4) that as strong a case can be made for CIA sponsorship as for KGB sponsorship, but also recognize that the former consists, like its "Bulgarian connection" counterpart, mainly of suppositions, hypothesized linkages, and circumstantial evidence.

43 For the East German Ministerium für Staatssicherheit's (MfS, or Stasi) provision of support for fugitive Rote Armee Fraktion (RAF) terrorists, see the recent revelations published

in *Der Spiegel*, esp. "Oma im Altkader," 44:24 (11 June 1990), pp. 86–9; "Stasi & RAF," 44:25 (18 June 1990), pp. 97–105; and "Hier bleibt jeder für sich," 44:26 (25 June 1990), pp. 82–7. These revelations are based not only on the testimony of wanted RAF terrorists arrested in East Germany, but also on Stasi documents recently made public. And according to formerly classified Hungarian documents, Carlos and other terrorists received shelter in that country and had close links to the Hungarian secret service. See Serge Raffy, "Carlos et l'armée rouge du crime," *Nouvel Observateur* 1343 (2–8 August 1990), pp. 20–4, although the article draws conclusions that are not supported by the currently available evidence. The only thing that is certain is that some leftist terrorists were sheltered by various East Bloc secret services *after* committing independently planned acts of violence. There is as yet no evidence that these services actually planned or directed those terrorist acts, though it would not surprise me if this were sometimes the case.
44 A number of anomalies and errors were discovered in the testimonies proffered by Antonov and his two co-defendants being tried *in absentia*, which should certainly give rise to suspicion even though there is as yet no corroborating evidence of their alleged meetings with Ağca. Also, it seems probable that Antonov at least *was* a DS operative, as his job – head of the local official Bulgarian airline – is typically a position staffed by intelligence officers. Thus, whether or not he was involved in the papal plot, he was probably never the "innocent" political prisoner portrayed by East Bloc and Western pro-communist sources. Indeed, I suspect that the attack on the pope provided an excellent pretext to enable the Italian government to decapitate networks of Bulgarian agents controlled by Antonov and his associates.
45 Anyone who carefully examines the recent history of right-wing terrorist groups will soon stumble upon evidence of their links to elements of various Western secret services, although the precise nature of these links varies from case to case. The spate of recent revelations about clandestine paramilitary "stay behind" networks in Europe (including Turkey) which were set up in the 1940s and 1950s by U.S. and NATO intelligence personnel, tends to confirm the existence of such links. Although these anti-communist networks were ostensibly created to serve as behind-the-lines resistance organizations in the event of a Soviet military invasion of western and/or southern Europe, they were at times employed to covertly condition the domestic political environment through various undemocratic means, including the use of violence and the manipulation of terrorism. This was certainly the case in Turkey.
46 This notion of a "dual conspiracy" derives from the analysis of Herman and Brodhead, *Rise and Fall*, pp. 3–8 and 206–9. Confirmation of the "coaching" of Ağca by Italian secret service personnel can be found in the court testimony of Camorra *pentito* Giovanni Pàndico. See Pietro Calderoni, "Cella con servizi," *L'Espresso* 31:25 (26 June 1985), pp. 22–4; and Bruno Rubino, "Pazienza? La pista bulgara è idea sua," *Epoca* 36:1813 (5 July 1985), pp. 30–3. Compare also Pietro Calderoni and Mario Scialoja, "Colpevole! No, innocente! No . . . ," *L'Espresso* 26:51 (25 December 1983), p. 19, for the converging testimony of Giuseppe Cilleri, former right-hand man of Nuova Camorra sub-boss Vincenzo Casillo.
47 See, for example, Howe, "Rightist Web of Intrigue," pp. A1 and A8; R. W. Apple Jr., "Mehmet Ali Agca: 6 Years of Neofascist Ties," *New York Times* (25 May 1981), pp. A1 and A6; Metin Münir, "The Gray Wolf: Man Arrested in Rome Attempt Thought to be Turkish Assassin," *Washington Post* (14 May 1981), pp. A1 and A11; amd Feroz Ahmad, "Agca: The Making of a Terrorist," *Boston Globe* (7 June 1981), p. A4.
48 Compare Michael Dobbs, "Child of Turkish Slum Finds Way in Crime," *Washington Post* (14 October 1984), p. A20.
49 For an example of hostile Soviet attitudes toward John Paul II, see the 30 December 1982 TASS statement cited by Henze, *Plot to Kill the Pope*, pp. 184–5. Numerous other examples are provided by Bensi, *Pista sovietica*, pp. 9–26, who demonstrates how East Bloc opinions on the pope have been cynically shifted for different audiences.
50 Sterling, *Time of the Assassins*, pp. 18–19.

51 Herman and Brodhead, *Rise and Fall*, pp. 102–12; Johnstone, "Finger-Pointing," pp. 11 and 22; and many articles in the mainstream Italian press. Obviously, Soviet Bloc authors also emphasize this, for example, Palchev, *Assassination Attempt*, pp. 19–22; and Antonov, *Wolf's Track*, pp. 9–10.
52 Eisenhower and Murray, *Warwords*, pp. 100–1; and Parenti, *Inventing Reality*, p. 162. Even if one excludes the Nazi-Soviet pact, this is a ridiculously naïve and historically inaccurate claim. One need only mention the Soviet recruitment of Nazi scientists and security specialists in the aftermath of World War II, for which see Christopher Simpson, *Blowback: America's Recruitment of Nazis and Its Effects on the Cold War* (New York: Weidenfeld & Nicolson, 1988), pp. 78–9. For the East German employment of ex-Nazis, including former Schutzstaffel (SS) and Sicherheitsdienst (SD) personnel, see Olaf Kappelt, *Braunbuch DDR: Nazis in der DDR* (Berlin: Reichmann, 1981), passim. This book was produced by West Germany in response to an East German "brown book" regarding the presence of ex-Nazis in the West German government, and in both cases it is easy enough to confirm the claims on the basis of extant Nazi records.
53 For the pseudo-Mau Mau, see Frank Kitson, *Gangs and Counter-Gangs* (London: Barrie & Rockliff, 1960), pp. 72–211. For examples of Portuguese anti-resistance operations in Africa, see Frédéric Laurent, *Orchestre noir* (Paris: Stock, 1978), pp. 148–56. For Unit 131, see Yoram Peri, *Battles and Ballots: Israeli Military in Politics* (Cambridge, UK: Cambridge University, 1983), pp. 237–8.
54 See the fascinating articles by Pepe Díaz Herrero and others, "French Connection: El jefe de los terroristas libios es un agente francés," *Cambio 16* 755 (19 May 1986), pp. 36–9; and Miguel Angel Liso, "París confirma su infiltración en el terrorismo libio," *Cambi 16* 756 (26 May 1986), pp. 38–9 [incorrect heading]. Note that al-Da'wa was a multinational terrorist organization consisting of Lebanese, Syrian, Spanish, and Portuguese members. It was formed in Lebanon in 1978, propounded an eclectic ideology combining Islamic and Libyan "socialist" elements, and apparently received funds, logistical support, and mission orders from the Libyan embassy – the People's Bureau – in Madrid. In 1985 its military leader was recruited by French intelligence, which subsequently helped finance it and direct its operations, including a bombing at the Air France office in Lisbon. The goal of both French intelligence and the Spanish Centro Superior de Información de la Defensa (CESID) – the post-Franco Spanish intelligence apparatus – was ostensibly to penetrate the Libyan embassy itself and thereby learn of Libyan terrorist plans, but their real purpose was apparently to provide a pretext for closing the Libyan embassy in Madrid and expelling Libyan diplomats, which did in fact occur following the arrest of several al-Da'wa members and the dissolution of the organization. In short, French intelligence helped initiate terrorist operations that were designed to further discredit the Libyan regime.
55 For rightist manipulations in Italy, see Flamini, *Partito del golpe*, passim vols. 1–3; and Jeffrey M. Bale, "Right-Wing Terrorists and the Extraparliamentary Left in Post–World War II Europe: Collusion or Manipulation?," *Berkeley Journal of Sociology* 32 (1987), pp. 207–12. For more on the "strategy of tension," see also the other articles in this volume. For GRAPO, see Luís González-Mata, *Terrorismo internacional: La estrema derecha, la estrema izquierda, y los crimenes de estado* (Barcelona: Argos, 1978), pp. 266–74. However, the reliability of Gonzalez-Mata and the extent to which GRAPO was manipulated by the Spanish right both remain open issues. See further Alejandro Muñoz Alonso, *El terrorismo en España: El terror frente a la convivencia pluralista en libertad* (Barcelona: Planeta/Instituto de Estudios Económicos, 1982), pp. 77–87; and "GRAPO y CIA," *Cambio 16* 271 (20 February 1977), pp. 8–13.
56 For Czech "neo-Nazis," see Ladislav Bittman, *The Deception Game* (New York: Ballantine, 1972), pp. 1–3. The author goes on to claim that this was far from an exceptional case. For an unconfirmed allegation about the manipulation of Croatian rightists, see Stephen Clissold, *Croat Separatism: Nationalism, Dissidence and Terrorism* (London: Institute for the Study of Conflict, 1979), pp. 10–11. However, the source for this is none other than the infamous Czech defector and disinformation peddler, former Major-General Jan Šejna, who implausibly links a cross-border foray into Yugoslavia by émigré saboteurs to an

alleged Warsaw Pack military plan (code-named "Polarka": Pole Star) that was designed to provide a pretext for a Soviet invasion of both Yugoslavia and the eastern half of Austria! Although Clissold's study is in general quite fair, Šejna is notoriously unreliable. See, for example, Herman and Brodhead, *Rise and Fall*, pp. 135–6, and 237–8. Note also that the ISC, the publisher of the Clissold piece, is a research center headed by Brian Crozier, a specialist on insurgency who has reportedly long been an asset of various Western intelligence agencies. To give only one example, he formerly played a leading role in the London-based Forum World Features "news service," which was subsequently exposed in the mainstream American and British press as a propaganda agency for the CIA and MI6, the British foreign intelligence organization. For excellent summaries of the histories of Crozier and the ISC, see "Background Paper: The ISC," *State Research Bulletin* 1 (October 1977), pp. 13–17; and appendices 1 and 8 in *Lobster* 11 (1986), pp. 34–9 and 51–2, a special issue of this journal devoted entirely to the domestic covert operations of British intelligence. Nevertheless, many monographs in the ISC's "Conflict Studies" series are informative and reliable.

57 This does not seem to discourage Henze, who argues that "we are past the point where it serves the interest of any party except the Soviets to adopt the minimalist, legalistic approach which argues that if there is no 'documentary evidence' or some other form of incontrovertible proof that the Government of the USSR is behind something, we must assume that it is not." See "The Long Effort to Destabilize Turkey," *Atlantic Community Quarterly* 19:4 (Winter 1981–82), p. 468. Compare also Sterling (*Time of the Assassins*, p. 137), who denies the need to find a "smoking gun." Not surprisingly, when it comes to assertions of Western political misdeeds, these two demand the type of conclusive documentation that they deny the need for in the case of hostile communist regimes. And while I agree with them that it is often difficult if not impossible to obtain such clear evidence of clandestine and covert operations, one surely needs more than they have provided to warrant accusing another superpower of such a serious crime.

58 Sterling, *Time of the Assassins*, p. 70.

59 Henze, *Plot to Kill the Pope*, pp. 129–30, 134–5, 198–200, and 204; and Sterling, *Time of the Assassins*, pp. 12–13, 43–4, 50, 71, 101–2, 206, 232, and 246.

60 Thomas and Morgan-Witts, *Pontiff*, passim. Much of their psychological analysis is amateurish and therefore unconvincing.

61 Henze, *Plot to Kill the Pope*, pp. 27, 131–2, 139, 150, 198–9, and 201; and Sterling, *Time of the Assassins*, pp. 25, 47, 70, 75, and 247. Ağca did in fact have connections to several high-ranking MHP officials, although the evidence for his links to Türkeş himself remains controversial.

62 Sterling, *Time of the Assassins*, p. 70.

63 Ibid., p. 102; and Henze, *Plot to Kill the Pope*, pp. 152, 176, and 199.

64 Herman and Brodhead, *Rise and Fall*, pp. 55–6.

65 Henze, *Plot to Kill the Pope*, pp. 27, 38–39, and 136; Sterling, *Time of the Assassins*, pp. 40 and 45; and Thomas and Morgan-Witts, *Pontiff*, p. 332. This is a disputed matter, not a certainty.

66 Sterling, *Time of the Assassins*, p. 71.

67 Ibid., pp. 40–1; and Henze, *Plot to Kill the Pope*, pp. 30–2.

68 Henze, *Plot to Kill the Pope*, p. 39. Dobbs dates Ağca's association with the right from his junior high school days. See "Child of Turkish Slum," p. A20. For Yeşiltepe junior high as a rightist institution, see Sterling, *Time of the Assassins*, p. 39.

69 Compare Dobbs, "Child of Turkish Slum," p. A20. Right- and left-wing terrorists in Turkey often had similar personality types, and their initial decision to become affiliated with one of these political extremes was frequently the result of circumstantial factors rather than firm ideological commitments. See Bruce Hoffman, "The Prevention of Terrorism and the Rehabilitation of Terrorists: Some Preliminary Thoughts," *RAND Paper* 7059 (February 1985), pp. 1–2; and Dobbs, "Child of Turkish Slum," citing Halûk Şahin of *Nokta* magazine. The fact that Ağca was a Sunni probably also predisposed him to become a rightist, since rival Turkish Shi'ites (Alevis) were often leftists. Compare the testimony of Çaylan, cited by Henze, *Plot to Kill the Pope*, p. 39.

70 Apple, "6 Years of Neofascist Ties," p. A1.
71 Dobbs, "Child of Turkish Slum," p. A20.
72 Apple, "6 Years of Neofascist Ties," p. A1; and Marvine Howe, "Turk's Hometown Puzzled by His Climb to Notoriety," *New York Times* (23 May 1981), p. 2. According to Thomas and Morgan-Witts, who seem to have acquired part of Ağca's personal library – the one Henze claimed Ağca's mother said she had burned (*Plot to Kill the Pope*, pp. 31–32) – it included Frederick Forsyth's novel about a right-wing plot to assassinate De Gaulle, *The Day of the Jackal*, and they assert that Ağca read it several times. See *Pontiff*, pp. 9–10 and 445.
73 Dobbs, "Child of Turkish Slum," p. A20. Çelik seems to have worked for Uğurlu's co-Godfather Bekir Çelenk. See Sterling, *Time of the Assassins*, p. 92.
74 See, for example, Henrik Krüger, *The Great Heroin Coup: Drugs, Intelligence, and International Fascism* (Boston: South End, 1980).
75 Dobbs, "Child of Turkish Slum," p. A20. The MHP was in a position to provide this in the mid- to late 1970s by virtue of its participation in coalition governments and consequent assumption of control over the Customs Ministry. Indeed, an MHP member was appointed to head the Ministry of State Monopolies and Customs, and many other rightists were then recruited to fill lower-level customs posts. See further later.
76 Thomas and Morgan-Witts, *Pontiff*, p. 12.
77 Henze, *Plot to Kill the Pope*, pp. 36–7 and 131; Dobbs, "Child of Turkish Slum," p. A20; and Sterling, *Time of the Assassins*, p. 45.
78 According to Dobbs ("Child of Turkish Slum," p. A20), it is not known whether Ağca participated in rightist student clashes with the left.
79 Henze, *Plot to Kill the Pope*, p. 131. Compare Sterling, *Time of the Assassins*, p. 45. For Ahmad's view, see "Making of a Terrorist," p. A4. Thomas and Morgan-Witts claim – as usual without providing any evidence – that Türkeş was preparing him for a "hit" during the time he resided in Ankara. See *Pontiff*, pp. 209–10.
80 Henze, *Plot to Kill the Pope*, p. 136.
81 Sterling, *Time of the Assassins*, pp. 18–19; Henze, *Plot to Kill the Pope*, pp. 132–3; Thomas and Morgan-Witts, *Pontiff*, p. 288; and Sablier, *Fil Rouge*, pp. 246–7.
82 Henze, *Plot to Kill the Pope*, pp. 133 and 136; and Sterling, *Time of the Assassins*, p. 45.
83 Howe, "Turks in Disagreement," p. A4.
84 Sterling, *Time of the Assassins*, p. 45; Thomas and Morgan-Witts, *Pontiff*, p. 332; and Ahmad, "Making of a Terrorist," p. A4.
85 For alleged communist sources of this money, see Henze, *Plot to Kill the Pope*, pp. 137–8; Sterling, *Time of the Assassins*, pp. 49–50; and Thomas and Morgan-Witts, *Pontiff*, pp. 293–4 and 331. On Ağca's involvement in smuggling, see Apple, "6 Years of Neofascist Ties," p. A6; Dobbs, "Child of Turkish Slum," p. A20; and Henze, *Plot to Kill the Pope*, p. 137. Thomas and Morgan-Witts claim (*Pontiff*, pp. 209–10) that Türkeş got Ağca involved in such activities while Ağca was still in Ankara.
86 Henze, *Plot to Kill the Pope*, pp. 137–8; and Apple, "6 Years of Neofascist Ties.," p. A6.
87 Henze, *Plot to Kill the Pope*, p. 137.
88 Mumcu, *Papa, Mafya, Ağca*, pp. 34–42.
89 Sterling, *Time of the Assassins*, pp. 48–9. Compare Henze, *Plot to Kill the Pope*, p. 146.
90 Ahmad, "Making of a Terrorist," p. A4; Apple, "6 Years of Neofascist Ties," p. A6; Howe, "Turks in Disagreement," p. 4; Mumcu, *Papa, Mafya, Ağca*, pp. 40–2; Sterling, *Time of the Assassins*, p. 49; and Henze, *Plot to Kill the Pope*, p. 146. If so, this corresponded to standard MHP practice. See Mehmet Ali Ağaoğulları, "The Ultranationalist Right," in *Turkey in Transition: New Perspectives*, ed. by Irvin C. Schick and Ertuğrul Ahmet Tonak (New York: Oxford University, 1987), p. 205. However, Çaylan claimed at the trial that the gun was wrapped in cloth and thrown out of the window of the car. Unfortunately, Şener himself eluded authorities and fled the country before he could be arrested.
91 Örsan Öymen, cited by Martin A. Lee and Kevin Coogan, "The Agca Con," *Village Voice* (24 December 1985), p. 21.

The ultranationalist right in Turkey **453**

92 Henze, *Plot to Kill the Pope*, pp. 164–5. See Mumcu, *Papa, Mafya, Ağca*, p. 46, for Ay's organizational affiliation.
93 Henze, *Plot to Kill the Pope*, pp. 201–2. This is quite possible, since it was shortly after Ağca announced that he would tell who the real shooter was that he was sprung from prison, which leads one to suspect that he was withholding important information.
94 For Uğurlu as the villain, see Henze, *Plot to Kill the Pope*. For the case against Çelik, see Mumcu, *Ağca Dosyası*, pp. 57–61. Henze (*Plot to Kill the Pope*, p. 198) tries to transform the significance of this by pointing to Çelik's links to Uğurlu, which supposedly proved that he was a Soviet agent!
95 Lee and Coogan, "Agca Con," p. 21. See Mumcu, *Papa, Mafya, Ağca*, pp. 45 and 363, for Çatlı's organizational affiliations.
96 Although Henze unconvincingly tries to absolve the MHP and implicate the Soviets in this crime (*Plot to Kill the Pope*, pp. 139–45), most knowledgeable people attribute the killing of İpekçi to the Turkish far right. It is well known in Turkey that İpekçi was a consistent critic of both the MHP and the religious right Millî Selâmet Partisi (MSP) of Necmettin Erbakan, as well as all types of political terrorism and smuggling. See, for example, Mumcu, *Papa, Mafya, Ağca*, pp. 154–73; and Mumcu, *Ağca dosyası*, pp. 51–7. Moreover, the 945-page indictment (*İddianame*) prepared by the Ankara military court against Türkeş and other MHP leaders – which I have not been able to obtain a copy of as of this writing – listed the İpekçi killing as one of the cases for which they were being prosecuted. See Marvine Howe, "Turkey Charges Fascist Party Sought Dictatorship by Force," *New York Times* (20 May 1981), p. A8. However, a 1984 Turkish prosecutor's report suggested that the real motive was not so much political as economic. In that report, it was concluded that Uğurlu had hired Ağca to kill İpekçi in order to forestall the latter's publication of a series on the Turkish mafia. See David Ignatius, "Turks Closer to Linking Pope's Assailant with Bulgaria," *Wall Street Journal* (17 July 1984), p. 26. Much of that report's analysis seems to me to be problematic, however.
97 The MHP's ambivalent attitude toward the West will be discussed later. Türkeş' hostility toward Greece is clearly manifested in his own words in *Dış politikamız ve Kıbrıs* (İstanbul: Kutluğ, 1974), as well as many MHP-linked publications.
98 Apple, "6 Years of Neofascist Ties," p. A6; and Dobbs, "Child of Turkish Slum," p. A1. There is some controversy over how the Turkish police were tipped off. Henze (*Plot to Kill the Pope*, p. 148) and Sterling (*Time of the Assassins*, p. 48) claim that the tip was anonymous and that the caller never picked up the reward money, which leads the former to suggest that someone purposely tried to make it look like Ağca was a rightist. Yet even if this is true, there are other possible explanations. For example, it could be that the informant became fearful and decided not to risk collecting his reward. See Roulette, *Filiére*, pp. 140–1. And others claim that lottery ticket salesman Ramazan Gündüz notified the police in person, which would explain how Ağca later learned who he was and murdered him. See Thomas and Morgan-Witts, *Pontiff*, pp. 376–7.
99 Henze, *Plot to Kill the Pope*, pp. 149–50.
100 Ibid., p. 149. MIT informant Hoca Koçyiğit also claimed that Güneş had pressured Ağca to implicate the MHP in the İpekçi assassination. See Sterling, *Time of the Assassins*, pp. 77 and 239, n. 5 (in chap. 6 section). However, the testimony of such informants, especially those with rightist sympathies, is far from conclusive in this context.
101 Henze, *Plot to Kill the Pope*, p. 150; Sterling, *Time of the Assassins*, p. 77; and Thomas and Morgan-Witts, *Pontiff*, p. 378.
102 Apple, "6 Years of Neofascist Ties," p. A6; Dobbs, "Child of Turkish Slum," p. A21; Mumcu, *Papa, Mafya, Ağca*, p. 44; and Henze, *Plot to Kill the Pope*, pp. 151–2 (although he fails to mention their rightist affiliation). Ağca had already made an unsuccessful attempt to escape on 5 November 1979 with Attila Serpil, another rightist militant. See Mumcu, *Papa, Mafya, Ağca*, p. 44. For Uğurlu's bribes, see Dobbs, "Child of Turkish Slum," p. A20.
103 Sterling, *Time of the Assassins*, p. 51.

104 Mumcu, *Papa, Mafya, Ağca*, pp. 44–5; and Lee and Coogan, "Agca Con," p. 21.
105 Dobbs, "Child of Turkish Slum," p. A20. Indeed, Uğurlu actually visited a Bozkurt named Doğan Yıldırım at Kartal-Maltepe at the same time Ağca was there. See Dobbs, "From Sofia to St. Peter's," *Washington Post* (15 October 1984), p. A18.
106 Lee and Coogan, "Agca Con," p. 21; and Apple, "6 Years of Neofascist Ties," p. A6.
107 Dobbs, "Child of Turkish Slum," p. A21.
108 Henze, *Plot to Kill the Pope*, pp. 159–60.
109 Mumcu, *Papa, Mafya, Ağca*, pp. 45–7 and 370; Sterling, *Time of the Assassins*, p. 92; and Henze, *Plot to Kill the Pope*, pp. 159–60. Henze fails to note the rightist affiliations of Dikici, Kurşun, Murat Pale, and Gökenç. *Hergün* was an official MHP publication.
110 Mumcu, *Papa, Mafya, Ağca*, p. 46; Howe, "Rightist Web of Intrigue," p. A8; and Sterling, *Time of the Assassins*, pp. 44–55 and 67.
111 Henze, *Plot to Kill the Pope*, pp. 161–3; and Andronov, *Triple Plot*, pp. 29–35.
112 Mersan later admitted meeting someone named "Metin" at the Vitosha, but claimed that he learned this was Ağca only *after* the latter's arrest in Rome; he also denied any involvement in the passport scheme. Henze, *Plot to Kill the Pope*, p. 164; and Sterling, *Time of the Assassins*, pp. 34–5. Uğurlu also acknowledged paying "Metin" 800 dollars, but said he did so at the request of Yıldırım. See Dobbs, "From Sofia to St. Peter's," p. A18.
113 Sterling, *Time of the Assassins*, pp. 34–5, 58–60, 84, and 223–5; and Henze, *Plot to Kill the Pope*, p. 164.
114 At first, no one could identify anyone named Mustafaeff, but in May 1982 Ağca claimed that he was the director of Bulgar-Tabac, a state tobacco monopoly manufacturing Marlboros under license. See Sterling, *Time of the Assassins*, p. 111. This has not been confirmed, to my knowledge. For Aivazov and Çelenk, see Dobbs, "From Sofia to St. Peter's," p. A18. Naturally, they deny ever meeting Ağca, which of course proves nothing.
115 Compare Dobbs, "From Sofia to St. Peter's," pp. A18–A19; Apple, "6 Years of Neofascist Ties," p. A6; Mumcu, *Papa, Mafya, Ağca*, passim; Howe, "Rightist Web of Intrigue," pp. A1 and A8; Herman and Brodhead, *Rise and Fall*, pp. 53–4; and all pro-communist sources. Ahmad argues ("Making of a Terrorist," p. A4) that European neo-fascists aided Ağca because it would have been too difficult for the MIT-infiltrated Turkish right in Europe to do so; but he presents no evidence of this. However, former MHP member Ali Yurtaslan indicates that the MHP in general received support from French and German fascist parties. See his *MHP merkezindeki adam Ali Yurtaslan'ın itirafı* (İstanbul: Aydınlık, 1980), p. 113.
116 *Plot to Kill the Pope*, p. 11. Compare Sterling, *Time of the Assassins*, p. 231, where she notes that Ağca "moved from one Gray Wolf safe house to another in Europe."
117 Dobbs, "From Sofia to St. Peter's," p. A18. For more on the Turkish military's crackdown on the MHP, see Ağaoğulları, "Ultranationalist Right," pp. 205–6.
118 Henze, *Plot to Kill the Pope*, p. 169.
119 Herman and Brodhead, *Rise and Fall*, p. 53; and Barbara Hoffman and others, *Graue Wölfe, Koranschulen, Idealistenvereine: Türkische Faschisten in der Bundesrepublik* (Cologne: Pahl-Rugenstein, 1981), pp. 71–2. It should be noted that the publisher of the latter work – Pahl-Rugenstein – has strong links to the Soviet-backed Deutsche Kommunistische Partei (DKP), despite its public image as an independent left outfit. See, for example, Wilhelm Mensing, *Maulwürfe im Kulturbeet: DKP-Einfluss in Presse, Literatur und Kunst* (Zurich: Interfrom, 1983), pp. 124–8.
120 Hoffman, *Graue Wölfe*, pp. 69–89; Ağaoğulları, "Ultranationalist Right," pp. 199–200; and also Yurtaslan, *MHP merkezindeki adam*, passim.
121 Kevin Klose, "Probe of Turkish Right Links Pope Suspect," *Washington Post* (19 May 1981), p. A10; John Tagliabue, "Militant Views among Turks Trouble Bonn," *New York Times* (21 May 1981), p. A6; Howe, "Rightist Web of Intrigue," p. A8; and Herman and Brodhead, *Rise and Fall*, p. 53. The twenty-six thousand figure, subdivided into twenty-three thousand MHP supporters and three thousand MSP supporters, is based on Bundesministerium des Innern, *Verfassungsschutz[bericht] 1980* (Bonn: BMI, 1981),

p. 143. This is the 1980 version of an annual report produced by the Bundesamt für Verfassungsschutz on extremist political groups operating in West Germany.
122 For violence perpetrated by Turkish rightists in Europe, see Hoffman, *Graue Wölfe*, pp. 74 and 101–4; and "Graue Wölfe: Jede Mark ist eine Kugel," *Spiegel* 34:37 (8 September 1980), pp. 58–61. Ağca's two victims were Idealist Necati Uygur and Turkish journalist Halil Tireli. See Apple, "6 Years of Neofascist Ties," p. A6; and Mumcu, *Papa, Mafya, Ağca*, p. 143.
123 Henze, *Plot to Kill the Pope*, p. 170.
124 Henze, *Plot to Kill the Pope*, pp. 168–70. Compare Sterling, *Time of the Assassins*, p. 147; and Dobbs, "From Sofia to St. Peter's," p. A18.
125 Sterling, *Time of the Assassins*, pp. 33–4. Compare Henze, *Plot to Kill the Pope*, pp. 175 and 177; and Dobbs, "From Sofia to St. Peter's," p. A18.
126 Sterling, *Time of the Assassins*, pp. 33 and 54. Compare Henze, *Plot to Kill the Pope*, pp. 176–7; and Apple, "6 Years of Neofascist Ties," p. A6.
127 Dobbs, "Agca's Changing Testimony," *Washington Post* (17 October 1984), pp. A1 and A21.
128 Sterling, *Time of the Assassins*, pp. 44–5.
129 Cited in Mumcu, *Ağca dosyası*, p. 107; and (in English translation) in Sterling, *Time of the Assassins*, p. 69. Note that *Tanrı* is the pre-Islamic Turkish sky deity, and that the phrase used by Ağca – *Tanrı Türkü Korusun* – is a standard pan-Turkist exclamation. See Jacob M. Landau, *Pan-Turkism in Turkey: A Study of Irredentism* (London: Hurst, 1981), pp. 147 and 150.
130 Compare Sterling, *Time of the Assassins*, pp. 69–70; Henze, *Plot to Kill the Pope*, pp. 188–9; and Mumcu, *Ağca dosyası*, pp. 106–10. However, its acceptance as evidence does *not* prove it was genuine, for the Turkish authorities (like their counterparts elsewhere) are certainly not above accepting bogus evidence – or even manufacturing it – if they think it will serve their purposes.
131 Compare Herman and Brodhead, *Rise and Fall*, pp. 54–5.
132 Martella's investigative process exhibited considerable biases and in some cases involved the use of improper judicial procedures. For a general critique, see Herman and Brodhead, *Rise and Fall*, pp. 112–21. They also rightly emphasize the highly polarized political context within which the Italian judicial system operates (see pp. 66–100). The Martella quote about Ağca's storytelling ability is cited by Dobbs, "A Communist Plot . . . ?," p. C2. Ağca's extraordinary skill at dissimulation has been emphasized by almost every researcher into the papal assassination plot. The only issue is whether this was a product of psychosis, careful training, a combination of the two, or other factors.
133 Their general argument is that although Ağca lied frequently, he mixed truth in with those lies and provided a wealth of details that he could only have learned if the events he described had actually taken place. See, for example, Sterling, *Time of the Assassins*, pp. 147–8 and passim. While I agree that Ağca cleverly mixed truth and falsehood, I am not at all convinced that the elements regarded as true by "Bulgarian connection" proponents are in fact the ones that are true. Many of them later turned out to be false, and other details that were accurate seem to have been gleaned by Ağca from media accounts and books or provided to him by his secret service "coaches." See Herman and Brodhead, *Rise and Fall*, pp. 102–12 and 121–2; Dobbs, "Agca Makes Bulgarian Connection Official," p. A25; and a number of articles in the Italian press.
134 Herman and Brodhead, *Rise and Fall*, pp. 55–108. Elsewhere in his report, Martella acknowledged that Ağca's hostility towards communism was a factor that influenced his testimony. See Dobbs, "A Communist Plot . . . ?," p. C2. For Ağca's close personal relationship with Çelik, see Dobbs, "From Sofia to St. Peter's," p. A18; and Henze, *Plot to Kill the Pope*, p. 198.
135 Cited by Dobbs, "Child of Turkish Slum," p. A21.
136 See Sterling, *Time of the Assassins*, p. 18, citing Italian judge Antonio Abate's Statement of Motivation. These included the THKO, the Türkiye Halk Kurtuluş Partisi-Cephe

(THKP-C: People's Liberation Party-Front of Turkey), Emeğin Birliği (Association of Labor), and Halkın Kurtuluşu (People's Liberation) on the left, and the ultranationalist Ülkücüler (Idealists affiliated with the MHP) and religious rightist Akıncılar or "Raiders" (affiliated with the MSP) on the right. For more on the THKO and THKP-C, see Jacob Landau, *Radical Politics in Modern Turkey* (Leiden: Brill, 1974), pp. 41–4; and Ahmet Samim, "The Left," in *Turkey in Transition*, pp. 159–60. For Halkın Kurtuluşu, see the latter, pp. 165 and 147. For the Akıncılar, see Otmar Oehring, *Die Türkei im Spannungsfeld extremer Ideologien, 1973–1980: Eine Untersuchung der politischen Verhältnisse* (Berlin: Klaus Schwarz, 1984), pp. 164–7. The *ülkücüler* will be dealt with at length later.

137 For PLO training of left-wing guerrillas from Turkey, see Yılmaz Çetiner, *El-Fateh* (İstanbul: May, 1970); Robert W. Olson, "Al-Fatah in Turkey: Its Influence on the 12 March Coup," *Middle Eastern Studies* 9:2 (May 1973), pp. 197–205; and Landau, *Radical Politics*, p. 41. And it is now known that members of the neo-Nazi Wehrsportgruppe Hoffmann received guerrilla warfare training at PLO camps. See Bundesministerium des Innern, *Verfassungsschutz[bericht] 1980*, p. 26; and Bundesministerium des Innern, *Verfassungsschutz[bericht] 1982* (Bonn: BMI, 1983), p. 126. This has been played up in the Western press in order to discredit the PLO, as well as by Lebanese Phalangist spokesmen in an effort to divert attention from their own training of European neo-Nazis and neo-fascists. See Giuseppe De Lutiis, ed., *La strage: L'atto d'accusa dei giudici di Bologna* (Rome: Riuniti, 1986), pp. 235–6.

138 This is not so much due to their psychological dissimilarities or even – at least in the case of the fascist MHP and anti-Soviet radical leftists – to their entirely incompatible ideologies, but rather to the historic enmities between some of these groups. Thus, for example, such enmities would have made it practically impossible for Kurdish separatists and Idealists to train together, despite their mutual hostility toward the Turkish regime.

139 See the testimony of Girgin, cited by Sterling, *Time of the Assassins*, p. 73. He claims that both Idealists and religious rightists were being trained at a Phalange camp in the Ketai region. Another possible source of Bozkurt training is recounted by Frank Terpil, a former CIA officer involved in the Edwin Wilson scandal. According to Terpil, Bozkurtlar received training in assassination techniques and explosive from an active-duty CIA officer vacationing in İstanbul, in karate from North Korean experts, and in "clandestine eavesdropping" from some West Germans. See Jim Hougan's interview of Terpil in *Penthouse Magazine* (December 1983), p. 190 (I am indebted to Scott Van Wynsberghe for bringing this reference to my attention). It is at present impossible to evaluate the accuracy of Terpil's claim, but even if he is telling the truth this doesn't prove that Ağca was himself among these Bozkurt trainees. For more on Terpil and Wilson, see Joseph C. Goulden, *The Death Merchant: The Rise and Fall of Edwin P. Wilson* (New York: Simon & Schuster, 1984); and Peter Maas, *Manhunt: The Incredible Pursuit of a CIA Agent Turned Terrorist* (New York: Random House, 1986), which displays more skepticism about the official portrayal of Wilson as a "rogue agent."

140 See Drug Enforcement Agency (DEA), "The Involvement of the People's Republic of Bulgaria in International Narcotics Trafficking," in U.S. Congress, Senate, Committee on Labor and Human Resources, *Drugs and Terrorism: Hearing before the Subcommittee on Alcohol and Drug Abuse*, 98th Congress, 2nd Session, 2 August 1984 (Washington, DC: GPO, 1984), p. 58; and "Prepared Statement of John C. Lawn, Acting Deputy Administrator of the Drug Enforcement Agency," in U.S. Congress, House, Committee on Foreign Relations, *Bulgarian-Turkish Narcotics Connection: United States-Bulgarian Relations and International Drug Trafficking. Hearings and Markup before the Committee on Foreign Affairs and its Subcommittee on Europe and the Middle East*, 98th Congress, 2nd Session, 7 and 24 June, and 26 September 1984 (Washington, DC: GPO, 1984), p. 7. Henze claims that it was in 1965, without providing any evidence. See his prepared statement in the latter, p. 26. Likewise Mumcu, *Silâh Kaçakçılığı*, p. 114.

141 "Lawn Statement," *Bulgarian-Turkish Narcotics Connection*, p. 5.

142 *Rise and Fall*, pp. 225–33. Note, however, that these doubts are supported by the U.S. Customs Service. In response to a congressional questionnaire, that agency stated that it

had "no hard evidence that the Government of Bulgaria has conducted illicit narcotics trafficking" and concluded that it was "doubtful that any concrete, tangible violations exists [sic] at this time, only allegations exist." See *Bulgarian-Turkish Narcotics Connection*, p. 115. However, I do not believe that the Customs Service is as well equipped with intelligence sources or analysts as the DEA, and there may also be bureaucratic or political factors involved in this assessment.

143 DEA, "Involvement," *Drugs and Terrorism*, p. 62. Bulgarian involvement has now been thoroughly documented in the recent trial of a massive Trento-based arms- and drug-smuggling ring. See Tribunale di Trento, Giudice Istruttore Carlo Palermo, *Sentenza-ordinanza nel procedimento penale contro Renato Gamba + 26*, 15 November 1984. Sections of this 5,989-page report (!) are excerpted in *Armi e droga: L'atto d'accusa del giudice Carlo Palermo* (Rome: Riuniti, 1988). Therein portions of Ağca's testimony concerning Bulgarian involvement (pp. 57–64) are corroborated by international trafficker Wākkaş Ṣalaḥ al-Dīn (pp. 48–50 and 54–57) (note, however, that the report also contains plenty of evidence of the involvement of Western intelligence personnel in the activities of this trafficking network). Compare also Nathan Adams, "Prepared Statement," in *Bulgarian-Turkish Narcotics Connection*, pp. 72–3; and Sterling, *Time of the Assassins*, pp. 94–5. MHP arms-smuggling operations in Varna are verified by Yurtaslan, *MHP merkezindeki adam*, p. 99. For confirmation of KINTEX's role in the drugs-for-guns trade by other sources, see Newsday Staff, *The Heroin Trail: The First Journalistic Investigation into the Heroin Traffic from Turkey to France to Its Ultimate Customer – the Young American Addict* (New York: Signet, 1973–74), pp. 50–8; Mumcu, *Silâh kaçakçılığı*, pp. 114–18; and Fabrizio Calvi and Olivier Schmidt, *Intelligence secrètes: Annales de l'espionnage* (Paris: Hachette, 1988), pp. 66–7. Note also that the *Newsday* team provides a list of "Istanbul patrons" who were "expected, when asked, to supply intelligence information to the Bulgarian secret police." See *Heroin Trial*, pp. 53–4.

144 DEA, "Involvement," *Drugs and Terrorism*, p. 60; "Lawn Statement," *Bulgarian-Turkish Narcotics Connection*, pp. 9–10; and "Statement of R. M. Palmer, Deputy Assistant Secretary of State for European and Canadian Affairs," in *Bulgarian-Turkish Narcotics Connection*, pp. 16–17.

145 DEA, "Involvement," *Drugs and Terrorism*, p. 61.

146 Ibid., p. 58; and "Lawn Statement," *Bulgarian-Turkish Narcotics Connection*, p. 7. Note, however, that the veracity (or even the existence) of the anonymous source they cite is impossible to determine.

147 On this, see Fred Landis, "The CIA and Reader's Digest," *Covert Action Information Bulletin* 29 (Winter 1988), pp. 41–7. For an example, see Edward Jay Epstein, *Deception: The Invisible War between the KGB and the CIA* (New York: Simon & Schuster, 1989), pp. 12–20.

148 "Prepared Statement," *Bulgarian-Turkish Narcotics Connection*, p. 25 (emphasis in original). Of course, these remarks were made prior to the recent upheavals in eastern Europe.

149 DEA, "Involvement," *Drugs and Terrorism*, p. 58; and Nathan M. Adams, "Drugs for Guns: The Bulgarian Connection," *Reader's Digest* 123:739 (November 1983), p. 88.

150 DEA, "Involvement," *Drugs and Terrorism*, p. 58; Adams, "Drugs for Guns," p. 87; and "Henze Statement," *Bulgarian-Turkish Narcotics Connection*, p. 30.

151 For KINTEX's trafficking and alleged subversion, see Adams, "Drugs for Guns," pp. 91–8; and "Henze Statement," *Bulgarian-Turkish Narcotics Connection*, pp. 26–8. For Uğurlu as a DS operative, see Sterling, *Time of the Assassins*, p. 96, citing information leaked to her by an anonymous source at a "major U.S. intelligence agency" (p. 93). According to said source, Uğurlu started smuggling in Bulgaria in 1969 and "was recruited as an agent of the Bulgarian secret service" in 1974. Later, a committee of anonymous Turkish generals "confirmed" that both Uğurlu *and* Çelenk had been recruited by the DS (pp. 225–6).

152 "Prepared Statement of Jack R. Perry, Retired Foreign Service Officer and Former U.S. Ambassador to Bulgaria," *Bulgarian-Turkish Narcotics Connection*, p. 64. Unlike Adams, Perry has great experience in Bulgarian affairs and is fluent in both Russian

and Bulgarian. But contrast the testimony of the Bulgarian defector, "Colonel X," who claims that "nothing, absolutely nothing, can escape the notice of the [Bulgarian] state security organization." See "Henze Statement," *Bulgarian-Turkish Narcotics Connection*, p. 30, citing the 24 January 1983 issue of *Le Quotidien de Paris*.
153 "Perry Statement," *Bulgarian-Turkish Narcotics Connection*, p. 64.
154 Ibid. Compare his verbal testimony on p. 61. *Contra* Lawn's testimony on p. 92.
155 Thus, Adams claims that working for KINTEX was especially appealing to DS officers, since they were allowed to pocket their KINTEX wages in addition to their normal pay. See his "Prepared Statement," *Bulgarian-Turkish Narcotics Connection*, p. 72.
156 See Lawn's testimony in *Bulgarian-Turkish Narcotics Connection*, pp. 92–3.
157 See Henze's testimony in *Bulgarian-Turkish Narcotics Connection*, p. 42 (citing *London Observer*); "Henze Statement," p. 27; Henze, *Drugs and Terrorism*, p. 116; Anthony Sampson, *The Arms Bazaar: From Lebanon to Lockheed* (New York: Bantam, 1978), p. 10; and Adams, "Drugs for Guns," p. 97. Compare Mumcu, *Silâh kaçakçılığı*, pp. 114–16, who also points out that the Bulgarian government formed commercial partnerships with "anti-communist" Turks.
158 As Henze naturally claims. See *Plot to Kill the Pope*, p. 55.
159 "Lawn Statement," *Bulgarian-Turkish Narcotics Connection*, pp. 8–9; "Statement of Francis M. Mullen, Jr., Administrator, DEA," *Drugs and Terrorism*, p. 22; and DEA, "Involvement," *Drugs and Terrorism*, p. 60.
160 For Western intelligence involvement in the drug trade, see esp. Krüger, *Great Heroin Coup*; Jonathan Kwitney, *The Crimes of Patriots: A True Tale of Dope, Crime, and the CIA* (New York: Simon & Schuster, 1987); and Alfred W. McCoy, *The Politics of Heroin in Southeast Asia* (New York: Harper, 1972), all passim. The recent involvement of CIA-connected Cuban exiles and Nicaraguan *contras* in the smuggling of cocaine into the United States to financially support the war against the Sandinistas is only the latest in a long series of such drug-funded operations. For this see U.S. Congress, Senate, Committee on Foreign Relations, Subcommittee on Terrorism, Narcotics, and International Operations, *Drugs, Law Enforcement and Foreign Policy; A Report*, 100th Congress, 2nd Session, December 1988 (Washington, DC: GPO, 1989), esp. pp. 36–62; and Leslie Cockburn, *Out of Control: The Story of the Reagan Administration's Secret War in Nicaragua, the Illegal Arms Pipeline, and the Contra Drug Connection* (New York: Atlantic Monthly, 1987), pp. 100–4 and 152–88.
161 For confirmation of the manipulation of defector testimony by a neoconservative investigative journalist, see Epstein, *Deception*, pp. 19–20: "This program of surreptitious authorship had disturbing implications. It meant that much of the material in the public record on the history of the spy war that come from first-hand witnesses – that is, defectors – had been authorized and selected, if not written, by an interested party: the CIA."
162 This is quite convenient for Henze and Adams, since it absolves them from having to prove that the document was genuine, which seems unlikely. Adams tries to blame the document's unavailability on the current leftist Greek regime – see his testimony in *Bulgarian-Turkish Narcotics Connection*, pp. 98–9 – but in his earlier article he reported that Sverdlov worked for Greek intelligence for eight years *after* his defection, that is, from 1971 to 1979 ("Drugs for Guns," pp. 87–8). Since the first three of those years corresponded to the last three of the brutal right-wing regime of the Colonels, whose leaders had close links to the CIA, it is doubtful that such incriminating documents would not have been made available to U.S. intelligence, and then subsequently been leaked to the press – *if* they were genuine. Compare Herman and Brodhead, *Rise and Fall*, p. 239.
163 See the DEA response to a congressional questionnaire in *Bulgarian-Turkish Narcotics Connection*, pp. 113–14. Here I will not even belabor the fact that the alleged communist subversion of the West with narcotics is a thirty-year-old propaganda and disinformation theme of the American right. Although there is some evidence indicating that certain communist regimes and guerrilla groups have participated in the drug trade as middlemen, there is no substantive evidence that supports the theory that this participation was part of a "master plan" to destabilize the West.

164 "Lawn Statement," *Bulgarian-Turkish Narcotics Connection*, pp. 6–7; and DEA, "Involvement," *Drugs and Terrorism*, p. 58.
165 See his testimony in *Bulgarian-Turkish Narcotics Connection*, p. 14.
166 *Plot to Kill the Pope*, p. 169; and Henze, "Misinformation and Disinformation," p. 15 and n. 26.
167 Roulette, *Filière*, pp. 147–8, citing *Milliyet* (10 February 1981). Compare also Andronov, *Triple Plot*, pp. 28–9.
168 For Ağca's possible links to the MİT, see *Time of the Assassins*, p. 102: "The state of affairs in [Turkey] between 1977 and 1979 suggested that [Ağca] was *on the payroll of some covert 'operational' faction in* MİT, Turkey's CIA, divided then into factions using tactics of infiltration and provocation on both extreme right and left" (italics mine). This is an extraordinary admission for Sterling to make, even though she tries to deny its significance by arguing that the MİT was divided into rightist and leftist factions (p. 47) – a doubtful assertion, if by "left" she means anything beyond supporting Ecevit's shaky coalition government – and then insisting that it did not really matter whether the MİT faction manipulating Ağca was rightist or leftist, since Uğurlu "was on the best of terms with both." Although it is *known* that Uğurlu had established good relations with the Turkish far right, I have run across nothing to corroborate Sterling's claim that the "Godfather" had established any relations with MİT leftists, assuming that the latter even existed. When one recalls that the MİT was in part organized by U.S. intelligence after World War II, it must be assumed that its personnel were carefully screened to make sure that they did not have leftist sympathies. It is of course possible that leftists later infiltrated the organization, but I have seen little evidence of this, and in any case such "leftist" elements could hardly have posed a serious challenge to the overwhelming strength of the rightist bloc within the MİT. Mumcu's claims about Uğurlu are cited by Dobbs, "From Sofia to St. Peter's," p. A18.
169 This inaction is noted by almost everyone. For some interesting charges and excuses, see "Turks Assail Allies in Pope's Shooting," *New York Times* (24 May 1981), p. 8; the pair of articles in *New York Times* (16 May 1981), p. 5, which deal with West German and Interpol defenses of their actions; and John Tagliabue, "Germany Finds No Evidence Accused Turk Lived There," *New York Times* (19 May 1981), p. A8. For the inept questioning see, for example, Sterling, *Time of the Assassins*, pp. 106–7 (Mehmet Şener and Çatlı), 33 and 54 (Taşkın), 55–57 (Mersan), and so forth.
170 Thomas and Morgan-Witts, *Pontiff*, p. 457, n. 4. Note that Henze omits this significant detail in his account of Grillmayer's arrest. See *Plot to Kill the Pope*, pp. 175–6.
171 Mumcu, *Papa, Mafya, Ağca*, pp. 143–5, and passim. Compare Howe, "Rightist Web of Intrigue," p. A8; and Tagliabue, "Germany Finds No Evidence," p. A8.
172 For CIA-MHP links, see Emin Değer, *CIA kontr-gerilla ve Türkiye* (Ankara: Çağlar, 1977), pp. 109–15; *Kontr-gerilla ve MHP: CIA'nin Türkiye'deki kontrgerilla teorisi ve uygulaması* (Istanbul: Aydınlık, 1978), pp. 130–3 and passim; and Jürgen Roth and Kamil Taylan, *Die Türkei: Republik unter Wölfen* (Bornheim: Lamuv, 1981), pp. 90–4, 116–20 and 130–7. The preceding are all leftist or far left sources, but Mehmet Ali Birand also notes that the KG organization was made up of "patriotic citizens," that is, Idealists and other rightists. See *12 Eylül saat 04.00* (n.p.: Karacan, 1984), p. 89. According to Doğan Özgüden, the Kontr-Gerilla organization provided facilities for Bozkurt terrorists being sought by the Turkish authorities after the proclamation of martial law in 1979. See his *Extreme-Right in Turkey: Grey Wolves' Pan-Turkism, Islamic Fundamentalism, Turco-Islamic Synthesis* (Brussels: Info-Türk, 1988), p. 38. The latter author is a former editor of the extreme left Turkish weekly, *Ant*. See Landau, *Radical Politics*, pp. 65 and 70–2. For the role played by Nazar, see Mumcu, *Tüfek icad oldu . . .*, pp. 28–30; Mumcu, *Papa, Mafya, Ağca*, pp. 145–7, 195–7 and 368; Mumcu, *Ağca dosyası*, pp. 24–31; and Herman and Brodhead, *Rise and Fall*, pp. 63–4. This is also stressed by communist authors, including Andronov, *Wolf's Track*, pp. 34–41; and Kovalyov and Sedykh, "Bulgarian Connection," p. 10.
173 For Bulgarian encouragement and facilitation of smuggling, see "Lawn Statement," *Bulgarian-Turkish Narcotics Connection*, p. 5. Compare also Henze's testimony in

Bulgarian-Turkish Narcotics Connection, p. 42. Note that this is not the same thing as asserting that Bulgaria orchestrates and fully controls this trafficking, which does not generally seem to be the case. Compare Herman and Brodhead, *Rise and Fall*, p. 59. Thus, for example, Lawn has admitted that not all of the illicit drugs transmitting Bulgaria go through KINTEX (*Bulgarian-Turkish Narcotics Connection*, p. 93), which implies that some go through without the Bulgarian government's knowledge, or at least without its active participation. Compare also the testimony of Perry in *Bulgarian-Turkish Narcotics Connection*, p. 100. Henze nevertheless claims (*Drugs and Terrorism*, p. 119) that many of the narcotics being smuggled through networks operating out of Bulgaria do not even pass through Bulgaria, which is also quite likely. For Bulgarian shielding of drug dealers, see "Palmer Statement," *Bulgarian-Turkish Narcotics Connection*, pp. 16–17.

174 "Lawn Statement," *Bulgarian-Turkish Narcotics Connection*, p. 10. This of course does not rule out the possibility of an *indirect* association.

175 Herman and Brodhead, *Rise and Fall*, p. 60.

176 Cited by Dobbs in "Child of Turkish Slum," p. A21.

177 See, for example, "The Heroin Trail and Gray Wolves Guns," *Searchlight* [U.K.] 65 (November 1980), p. 7; and Mumcu, *Tüfek icad oldu . . .*, pp. 128–30.

178 The original version of this article included a lengthy discussion of the development of Turkish nationalism, most of which was excised due to space limitations. For the best general accounts of the development of Turkism, which in the second half of the nineteenth century began competing with other notions of solidarity based on dynastic, tribal, religious, familial, or strictly territorial criteria, see David Kushner, *The Rise of Turkish Nationalism, 1876–1908* (London: Cass, 1977), passim; and the relevant sections of the rich narratives of Bernard Lewis, *The Emergence of Modern Turkey* (London: Oxford University/RiIA, 1968); and Niyazi Berkes, *The Development of Secularism in Turkey* (Princeton, NJ: Princeton University, 1964). Excellent analyses of the ideas of some early proponents of Turkism can be found in François Georgeon, *Aux origines du nationalisme turc: Yusuf Akçura, 1876–1935* (Paris: ADPF, 1980); Taha Parla, *The Social and Political Thought of Ziya Gökalp, 1876–1924* (Leiden: Brill, 1985); and Jacob M. Landau, *Tekinalp, Turkish Patriot, 1883–1961* (Leiden: NINO, 1984).

179 For pan-Turkism, see esp. Jacob M. Landau, *Pan-Turkism in Turkey: A Study of Irredentism* (London: Hurst, 1981); Col. Charles Warren Hostler, *Turkism and the Soviets: The Turks of the World and Their Political Objectives* (London and New York: George Allen & Unwin/Praeger, 1957); and Serge A. Zenkovsky, *Pan-Turkism and Islam in Russia* (Cambridge, MA: Harvard University, 1960). Note that pan-Turkism should not be confused with pan-Turanism, an even more extensive pan-concept developed by neo-Magyar nationalists in Hungary that embraced not only the Turkic peoples, but all other peoples thought to be related to them, such as the Magyars, Finns, Estonians, Mongols, and, according to some, the Koreans and Japanese. See the fine study by Joseph A. Kessler, "Turanism and Pan-Turanism in Hungary, 1890–1944" (Ph.D. Dissertation: University of California at Berkeley, 1967).

180 Louis L. Snyder, *The Meaning of Nationalism* (New Brunswick, NJ: Rutgers University, 1954), pp. 77 (following Max Boehm), and 117. Compare Carlton J. Hayes, *Historical Evolution of Modern Nationalism* (New York: Macmillan, 1931), pp. 165–6. The term "integral nationalism" was first coined by Charles Maurras, leader of the extreme right monarchist organization, Action Française, which had certain proto- or quasi-fascist features.

181 Landau, *Pan-Turkism in Turkey*, pp. 72–3 and 77–8; and Hostler, *Turkism and the Soviets*, pp. 168–9.

182 The most important of these émigré groups were affiliated with the Promethean League, a semi-clandestine anti-Soviet umbrella organization set up by the Polish intelligence service and actively sponsored by high-ranking figures within the Polish government, including President Józef Piłsudski himself. On this organization, see Landau, *Pan-Turkism in Turkey*, pp. 78–80; Hostler, *Turkism and the Soviets*, pp. 157–60; Wlodzimierz

Backowski, *Prometeizm Polski* (Warsaw: Polityka, 1939); Stephen Dorril, *MI6: Inside the Covert World of Her Majesty's Secret Intelligence Service* (New York: Free Press, 2000), chapter 12; and Roman Smal-Stocki, *The Nationality Problem in the Soviet Union and Russian Communist Imperialism* (Milwaukee, WI: Bruce, 1952), pp. 158–63. Thus the Promethean League was a sort of forerunner of the abovementioned World Anti-Communist League, for which see Anderson and Anderson, *Inside the League*, passim.

183 See, for example, Landau, *Pan-Turkism in Turkey*, pp. 115–16, 74–5, and 85–90; Hostler, *Turkism and the Soviets*, pp. 119 and 181–2; and Kemal H. Karpat, *Turkey's Politics: The Transition to a Multi-Party System* (Princeton: Princeton University, 1959), pp. 263–5, n. 40. For the views of Atsız and Türkkan, see Atsız, *Türk Tarihinde Meseleler* (Ankara: Afşin, 1966); Atsız, *Türk ülküsü* (Ankara: Afşin, 1973 [1956]); and Türkkan, *Milliyetçilik Yolunda. Ergenekon-Bozkurt-Gök Börü: yeni ve eski yazılar* (n.p.: Müftüoğlu, 1944).

184 See, for example, the anthology *Irkçılık-Turancılık* (Ankara: TITE, 1944).

185 For the arrests and trials, see the accounts in Landau, *Pan-Turkism in Turkey*, pp. 112–15; and Edward Weisband, *Turkish Foreign Policy, 1943–1945: Small State Diplomacy and Great Power Politics* (Princeton: Princeton University, 1973), pp. 244–6.

186 Hostler, *Turkism and the Soviets*, pp. 185–7; and Ağaoğulları, "Ultranationalist Right," p. 188. For the general situation, see Kemal H. Karpat, "Turkish-Soviet Relations," in *Turkey's Foreign Policy in Transition, 1950–1974* (Leiden: Brill, 1975), pp. 83–4.

187 For the lifting of restrictions on pan-Turkism, see Landau, *Pan-Turkism in Turkey*, p. 122; and Hostler, *Turkism and the Soviets*, pp. 185 and 187–8. But compare Ağaoğulları, "Ultranationalist Right," p. 189. For Menderes, see Karpat, "Turkish-Soviet Relations," pp. 85–7.

188 Landau, *Pan-Turkism in Turkey*, pp. 115–22; Hostler, *Turkism and Soviets*, pp. 189–91; and Ağaoğulları, "Ultranationalist Right," pp. 189–90. I suspect that many of the pan-Turkist groups and publications that were based in Europe received secret funding from various Western intelligence agencies, since at that time the latter were heavily funding other anti-communist émigré organizations from areas behind the Iron Curtain. See, for example, Faligot and Krop, *Piscine*, pp. 98–104; Simpson, *Blowback*, pp. 222–8, 266–9 and passim; and John Loftus, *The Belarus Secret* (New York: Knopf, 1982), pp. 118–19 and passim.

189 Ağaoğulları, "Ultranationalist Right," p. 190.

190 Landau, *Pan-Turkism in Turkey*, pp. 115–17 and passim.

191 Landau, *Pan-Turkish in Turkey*, pp. 130–1; Landau, *Radical Politics*, pp. 203–4; and İlhan E. Derendelioğlu, *Türkiyede milliyetçilik hareketleri: Toplantılar, mitingler, nümayişler, bildiriler, cemiyetler, basın* (n.p.: Toker, 1968), pp. 161–2 and 353–60.

192 Ağaoğulları, "Ultranationalist Right," p. 192.

193 The following biographical information is taken from Landau, *Radical Politics*, p. 206; and Walter F. Weiker, *The Turkish Revolution, 1960–1961: Aspects of Military Politics* (Washington, DC: Brookings Institute, 1963), pp. 125–7.

194 For his own account of these events, see *1944 milliyetçilik olayı* (İstanbul: Yaylacık, 1968). According to various leftist analysts, a secret Nazi document also listed Türkeş as one of the Turks with whom the Germans had established "good connections." See, for example, Hoffman, *Graue Wölfe*, pp. 49–50. I do not know whether or not this document is genuine.

195 These assignments in Washington and links to NATO should raise suspicions about Türkeş' possible links to Western intelligence and military circles, since these types of positions usually involve close interaction with the latter. Many of the "Third World" officers who held such positions later participated in pro-Western coups and/or other sorts of political warfare. Hoffman asserts that this was the case, but does not provide any evidence. See *Graue Wölfe*, p. 50. For Türkeş' possible participation in an earlier coup plot, see Ali Fuad Başgil, *La révolution militaire de 1960 en Turquie (ses origines): Contribution à l'etude de l'histoire politique intérieure de la Turquie contemporaine* (Geneva: Perret-Gentil, 1963), p. 172.

196 Weiker, *Turkish Revolution*, pp. 125–7 and 132; Semih Vaner, "The Army," in *Turkey in Transition*, pp. 240, 242, and 249–50; and Feroz Ahmad, *The Turkish Experiment in Democracy, 1950–1975* (Boulder and London: Westview/RIIA, 1977), pp. 165–6. Friedrich-Wilhelm Fernau merges Vaner's "proto-fascists" with the "nationalists of the right" and distinguishes between them and the "socialists" among the radicals. See his "Le retour des 'quatorze' en Turquie," *Orient* 7:1 (1963), p. 20. I prefer Vaner's scheme.

197 For the return of the Fourteen, see Fernau, "Retour des 'quatorze'," pp. 17–24; and Landau, *Radical Politics*, p. 207. Apparently, no concrete plans of a collaborative nature resulted from the Brussels meeting.

198 Landau, *Radical Politics*, pp. 208–9; and Ağaoğulları, "Ultranationalist Right," p. 193.

199 For the ideological split in and reorientation of the CKMP, see Ağaoğulları, "Ultranationalist Right," p. 193. According to Ağaoğulları (pp. 193 and 212, n. 77), the new name was inspired by Türkeş' preoccupation with Franco's Falange party, which had earlier been called the Partido de Movimiento Nacional.

200 For Türkeş' conception of the MHP's program as a "third way" between capitalism and communism, see Türkeş, *Temel görüşler* (İstanbul: Dergah, 1975), pp. 37–8. Compare Ağaoğulları, "Ultranationalist Right," p. 194. For the anti-fascist claims, see Türkeş, *Temel görüşler*, pp. 48 and 53–8. The quoted principle appears in Türkeş, *Temel görüşler*, p. 38.

201 See Fernau, "Retour des 'quatorze'," p. 22; and Türkeş, *Dokuz ışık; Milliyetçilik, ülkücülük, ahlâkçılık, toplumculuk, ilimcilik, hürriyetçilik, köycülük, gelismecilik ve halkçılık, endüstricilik ve teknikçilik* (İstanbul: Çınar, 1965).

202 But note that Islam was not explicitly mentioned in this early work. See Türkeş, *Dokuz Işık*, p. 4.

203 Note, however, that this term was also used by religious reactionaries to describe "Islamic" science.

204 Landau, *Radical Politics*, p. 220. Indeed, Weiker described Türkeş as an "ardent" Kemalist (*Turkish Revolution*, p. 126).

205 Landau, *Radical Politics*, pp. 226–7. This is, as noted earlier, the defining characteristic of integral nationalism.

206 These included, among many others, *Milliyetçi Hareket Partisi tüzüğü* (Ankara: Emel, 1973); *Kudretli, müreffeh ve büyük bir Türkiye için MHP programı* (Ankara: Ari, 1973); *MHP el kitabı* (Ankara: MHP, 1977); and the party's various election communiques, as well as later works by Türkeş, such as *Temel görüşler* and *Millî doktrin dokuz ışık* (İstanbul: Dokuz Işık, 1978). The last of these is analyzed briefly by Oehring, *Türkei im Spannungsfeld*, pp. 168–9. However, it needs to be pointed out that there are important shifts of emphasis between the short 1965 version of the "nine lights" and the much longer 1978 version (for example, a new emphasis on religion in the latter), and that extremist views can be found even in some of the more "moderate" MHP publications. For some examples, see, for example, Oehring, *Türkei im Spannungsfeld*, pp. 177–9; and Hoffman, *Graue Wölfe*, pp. 49–68.

207 Ağaoğulları, "Ultranationalist Right," pp. 195–6. The term *başbuğ* is an old Central-Asian term for "leader." See the same work, p. 213, n. 100. This distant origin provides Türkeş with an argument for denying its equation with *Duce* or *Führer*. See *Milliyetçi Hareket Partisi ve Ülkücü Kuruluşlar Davası: Sorgu-Alparslan Türkeş* (Ankara: Mayaş, 1982), pp. 62–4.

208 Ağaoğulları, "Ultranationalist Right," pp. 195–7 and 214, n. 107.

209 Cited in Ağaoğulları, "Ultranationalist Right," p. 214, n. 107.

210 See, for example, *MHP el kitabı*, p. 4, and other publications cited by Ağaoğulları, "Ultranationalist Right," pp. 197 and 213, n. 104.

211 Ağaoğulları, "Ultranationalist Right," p. 197.

212 See, esp. Landau, *Radical Politics*, pp. 210–13, based on the *MHP Tüzüğü*.

213 Landau, *Radical Politics*, pp. 214 and 107; and Ağaoğulları, "Ultranationalist Right," pp. 193 and 198 (citing the *MHP iddianamesi*, p. 256).

214 For a general description of the MHP's parallel organizations, see Ağaoğulları, "Ultranationalist Right," pp. 198–200, again citing the *MHP iddianamesi*, pp. 270–3 and 291–313;

Yurtaslan, *MHP merkezindeki adam*, pp. 65–84; and Landau, *Radical Politics*, p. 214. The most important of these was the aforementioned ÜGD and its successor, the Ülkü Yolu Derneği (ÜYD: Path of Ideal Association). In addition to these MHP-linked organizations with a "light cover," "deep cover" MHP fronts with no visible link to their parent organization were also created after Ecevit's declaration of martial law in 1978, including the Esir Türkleri Kurtarma Ordusu (ETKO: Captive Turks Liberation Army) and the Türk İntikam Tugayı (TİT: Turkish Revenge Brigade). See Ağaoğulları, "Ultranationalist Right," p. 205; and Yurtaslan, *MHP merkezindeki adam*, pp. 79–80. Despite these organizational characteristics, the totalitarian nature of the MHP was initially denied by C. H. Dodd, *Democracy and Development in Turkey* (Walkington, UK; Eothen, 1979), p. 121. This conclusion was based more on the MHP's ideological pronouncements than on a close observation of its actual practices, and Dodd later acknowledged the MHP's totalitarian nature. See *The Crisis of Turkish Democracy* (Walkington, UK; Eothen, 1983), p. 45.

215 Dodd, *Crisis of Turkish Democracy*, pp. 199 and 215–16, n. 125, citing a secret report prepared by the Ministry of the Interior and the Directorate of Security, which was presented to Prime Minister Süleyman Demirel in 1970. Compare Landau, *Radical Politics*, pp. 214–17, and esp. the relevant sections of the *MHP iddianamesi*. Note that prayers were introduced into the daily camp schedules for the religious participants. See, for example, Landau, *Radical Politics*, p. 215.

216 Ağaoğulları, "Ultranationalist Right," pp. 192–3 and 200–1. He cites (pp. 216–17, n. 42) a *Cumhuriyet* article wherein Türkeş himself declared that the "idealist youths are assisting the security forces of the state." See pp. 42–44 above for the idealist-KG-MİT nexus.

217 Charles Patmore, "Türkes: The Right's Chosen Leader," *New Statesman* 97:2507 (6 April 1979), p. 478.

218 Ağaoğulları, "Ultranationalist Right," pp. 200–2; and *Black Book on the Militarist "Democracy" in Turkey* (Brussels: Info-Türk, 1986), p. 331. Compare Henze, *Plot to Kill the Pope*, p. 169, who reveals that ADÜTDF leader Çelebi had joined the Customs Ministry in 1976 and thence become involved with Bulgarian smuggling. Others claim that the MHP also infiltrated police and security services during the period that it controlled the Ministry of State Security. See for example, Lucille W. Pevsner, *Turkey's Political Crisis: Background, Perspectives, Prospects* (New York and Washington, D C: Praeger/CSIS, 1984), p. 65; Patmore, "Türkes," p. 478; and Howe, "Fascist Party Sought Dictatorship by Force," p. A8 (based on the *MHP iddianamesi*).

219 Ağaoğulları, "Ultranationalist Right," pp. 203–6; and Roth and Taylan, *Republik unter Wölfen*, pp. 91–4. Compare the *MHP iddianamesi*, which indicates that Ağca said his motive for killing İpekçi was "to create circumstances that would induce the masses to accept a regime that was based on force and destroys [sic] all freedoms through intimidation by terror" (cited by Howe, "Fascist Party Sought Dictatorship by Force," p. A8). By and large this indictment gives the impression that the party sought to overthrow the Turkish government and seize power on its own, but this reflects a conscious effort to isolate the MHP politically and down-play the fact that influential factions within the army, police, and MİT were colluding in – if not actually planning and directing – some of the party's terrorist and propaganda activities. Compare Özgüden, *Extreme-Right in Turkey*, p. 72. But see issue n. 193 of the MHP publication *Devlet*, wherein a three-stage MHP strategy for the seizure of power was outlined: (1) conquest of the streets, (2) conquest of the state [apparatus], and (3) conquest of the Parliament. Cited by Hoffman, *Graue Wölfe*, p. 68. In the long run, these goals may not have been mutually exclusive.

220 Hoffman, *Graue Wölfe*, pp. 205–6. For an exaggerated view of the junta's lenient treatment of the MHP after the coup, see Özgüden, *Extreme-Right in Turkey*, pp. 70–5.

221 Henze, *Plot to Kill the Pope*, p. 142. He does not baldly state that MHP supporters were fully secularized or lacked anti-Christian sentiments, but rather claims that the Turkish secular and religious right had little in common (see pp. 6, 8, and passim). For more on the MSP, see Jacob M. Landau, *Politics and Islam, the National Salvation Party in Turkey* (Salt Lake City, UT: University of Utah, 1976); Binnaz Toprak, "Politicization of Islam in a

Secular State: The National Salvation Party," in *From Nationalism to Revolutionary Islam: Essays on Social Movements in the Contemporary Near and Middle East*, ed. by Said Amer Arjomand (Albany, NY: SUNY, 1984), pp. 119–33; Türker Alkan, "The National Salvation Party in Turkey," in *Islam and Politics in the Modern Middle East*, ed. by Metin Heper and Raphael Israeli (London and Sydney: Croom Helm, 1984), pp. 79–102; Mehmet Ali Ağaoğulları, *L'Islam dans la vie politique de la Turquie* (Ankara: AuSBF, 1982); and Ali Yaşar Sarıbay, *Türkiye'de modernleşme, din, ve parti politikası: "Milli Selâmet Partisi örnekolayı"* (İstanbul: Alan, 1985), esp. pp. 108–215. For more on its leader Erbakan's views, which in places overlap Türkeş', see the former's *Millî gazete* (İstanbul: Dergâh, 1975).
222 Herman and Brodhead, *Rise and Fall*, p. 48.
223 Contrary to Marxist claims, all genuinely fascist movements are virulently anti-capitalist, even though in practice they have often been compelled to make temporary tactical alliances with powerful business interests in order to achieve specific goals (for example, the seizure of power itself, or the subsequent maintenance of high levels of military production). Had the fascists actually won the war, however, it is likely that many of these business leaders, who had already been politically subordinated by the Nazis, would have been targeted as enemies by the party hierarchs.
224 Cited by Ahmad, *Turkish Experiment in Democracy*, pp. 263–4, n. 40. The passage cited appeared in an MSP-linked publication – *Yeniden Millî Mücadele*. See Landau, *Radical Politics*, pp. 182 and 192. Note that the MSP was also violently opposed to capitalism and communism, both of which it viewed as facets of a Zionist plot to rule the world. See, for example, Alkan, "National Salvation Party," pp. 94 and 96–7, citing *Millî Gazete* articles, including some by Erbakan himself. Compare *Millî görüş*, pp. 248–54, regarding alleged Zionist control of the Common Market.
225 Henze, *Plot to Kill the Pope*, pp. 8–9; and Henze, "Misinformation and Disinformation," pp. 8–9, n. 17, where he ascribes Ağca's remarks about El Salvador and Afghanistan to Bulgarian "urging or direction," apparently not realizing that such statements, if they really could only be made by a Turkish "leftist loyal to the Soviet Union," would not be consistent with presumed East Bloc efforts to create a rightist "legend" for the young gunman. Moreover – intentionally or not – Henze seriously misinterprets the significance of Ağca's remarks, which correspond to the Turkish far right's hostility toward both Western and Soviet imperialism, and reflect its paranoia about the supposed "anti-Muslim crusade" led by the pope. See Herman and Brodhead, *Rise and Fall*, p. 48.
226 See, for example, Türkeş, *Temel görüşler*, pp. 169–209 and 263–84. Compare also his *Türkiye ve dünya* (Ankara: Emel, 1979), pp. 24–40.
227 For MBK goals, see Ahmad, *Turkish Experiment in Democracy*, p. 373. For the UKB, see the same work, pp. 373–4; and Weiker, *Turkish Revolution*, pp. 133–4.
228 See *Müreffeh ve kuvvetli Türkiye için C.K.M.P. programı* (Ankara: CKMP, 1965). For the transformation of the CKMP into the MHP, and the development of the latter, see Hakan Akpınar, *Kurtların kardeşliği: CKMP'den MHP'ye 1965-2005* (İstanbul: Bir Harf, 2005).
229 Landau, *Radical Politics*, pp. 231–2, citing in particular a published dialogue between the Islamist journalist N. M. Polat and Nurcular leader Bekir Berk, *İslamî Hareket ve Türkeş* (İstanbul: İttihad, 1969).
230 Landau, *Radical Politics*, p. 231; and Özgüden, *Extreme-Right in Turkey*, p. 27.
231 Landau, *Radical Politics*, p. 29; and Howe, "Fascist Party Sought Dictatorship by Force," p. A8.
232 For the incompatibility of pan-Turkism and pan-Islamism, see Özgüden, *Extreme-Right in Turkey*, p. 27. For the departure of the "Shamanists," including Atsız, see Ağaoğulları, "Ultranationalist Right," p. 198. Moreover, the anti-religious sentiments they embodied persisted among some Turkist MHP elements into the mid-1970s. In 1976, for example, some young MHP members were accused of burning Qur'āns and proclaiming "we are Turks first, and Muslims second." See Maxime Rodinson, "Complexe islamo-turc et mythes occidentaux," *Le Monde* (23 May 1981), p. 2.

233 For a listing of Atatürk's anti-religious measures, see Binnaz Toprak, "The Religious Right," in *Turkey in Transition*, pp. 223–4. For the survival of popular support for Islam, see the same work, p. 225; and Landau, *Radical Politics*, pp. 171–2.

234 The literature on this subject is quite large. See, for example, Uriel Heyd, *The Revival of Islam in Turkey* (Jerusalem: Magnes/Hebrew University, 1968); Bernard Lewis, "Islamic Revival in Turkey," *International Affairs* 28:1 (January 1952), pp. 38–48; Howard A. Reed, "Revival of Islam in Secular Turkey," *Middle East Journal* 8:3 (Summer 1954), pp. 267–82; and P. Xavier Jacob, *L'enseignement religieux dans la Turquie modern* (Berlin: Klaus Schwarz, 1982), pp. 155–80.

235 Landau, *Radical Politics*, pp. 172–4; Toprak, "Religious Right," pp. 225–7; and Binnaz Toprak, *Islam and Political Development in Turkey* (Leiden: Brill, 1981), pp. 71–94.

236 For the impact of Islam on education, see esp. Jacob, *Enseignement religieux*, passim. For the MNP and MSP, see Ahmad, *Turkish Experiment in Democracy*, p. 317. Compare Alkan, "National Salvation Party," p. 83, who notes that the strongest verbal attacks against the MSP came not from leftists, but from other rightist and conservative parties competing for the same electorate.

237 Dodd, *Democracy and Development*, p. 119; Ağaoğulları, "Ultranationalist Right," p. 198; Landau, *Radical Politics*, p. 231; Pevsner, *Turkey's Political Crisis*, p. 65; Oehring, *Türkei im Spannungsfeld*, pp. 173–5; and Patmore, "Türkeş," p. 478.

238 Ağaoğulları, "Ultranationist Right," p. 198. For the religious indoctrination of the Idealists, see Yurtaslan, *MHP merkezindeki adam*, p. 88 (inside prison); and Hoffman, *Graue Wölfe*, pp. 77–85. See also *supra*, note 215.

239 Özgüden, *Extreme-Right in Turkey*, pp. 33–7.

240 See his "Phénomènes de scission interne en Turquie," *L'Afrique et l'Asie Modernes* 121 (1979), p. 44.

241 Ağaoğulları, "Ultranationalist Right," p. 198.

242 Jacob, *Enseignement religieux*, p. 205.

243 See, for example, Henze, *Plot to Kill the Pope*, pp. 5–6 and 9–10, who cites some examples in the Western media; Thomas and Morgan-Witts, *Pontiff*, pp. 11, 15–16; and Albano as excerpted by Dobbs, "Child of Turkish Slum," p. A20.

244 See Mumcu, *Papa, Mafya, Ağca*, pp. 213–17, citing *Hergün* articles from 19, 20, and 29 November 1979. For a brief overview of the historical background that engendered these attitudes among the Turks, see Rodinson, "Complexe islamo-turc," p. 2. The similar quotes are cited by Rodinson, p. 217 (Ağca: "Dini lider, maskalı haçlı Kumandanı," *Hergün*: "Dini lider olmaktan çok, Bizans hayalı ile yaşayan bir haçlı komutanı"). Compare Thomas and Morgan-Witts, *Pontiff*, pp. 15–16, on Ağca's attitudes toward the pope(s). Sterling herself initially acknowledged this in her *People Magazine* interview, "Authority on Terrorism," p. 32.

245 Note that Henze's attempt to portray everyone who does not agree with his interpretation as a Soviet sympathizer or, at least, a dupe of East Bloc propaganda campaigns – *without* ever responding to their substantive critiques, much less providing evidence for these assertions – is standard operating procedure among Western disinformationists, and is analogous to the efforts of Soviet propagandists to label all critics of the official line as "agents of imperialism" or "bourgeois counterrevolutionaries." For the use of this technique by Henze, see "Misinformation and Disinformation," where he refers to Mumcu as a "purveyor of Soviet-originated disinformation" (p. 15, n. 25.) – based in part on the so-called Tunçkanat documents controversy – and to Herman and Brodhead as "two Soviet apologists in the US" (p. 16). Given that Henze is himself a consistent font of propaganda and disinformation, as well as a frequent apologist for authoritarian rightist regimes, one can only marvel at the audacity of his efforts to attribute these characteristics to so many others.

9

'NATIONAL REVOLUTIONARY' GROUPUSCULES AND THE RESURGENCE OF 'LEFT-WING' FASCISM

The case of France's Nouvelle Résistance[1]

> *The five years I spent in Troisième Voie were formative. A youth in a groupuscule can learn one hundred times more than one who remains in the youth organization of a large party.*[2]

> *We must begin with thousands of tiny revolutions so that one day the great revolution which will change the face of the world will come.*[3]

The French word 'groupuscule', like its closest English counterpart 'grouplet', is generally used to refer to organizations of different types whose most obvious characteristic is their small size. Since small size is in turn all too often equated with insignificance, scholars have tended to ignore the study of political groupuscules, which they view as unpopular fringe elements within the overall constellation of a given nation's political forces, and to focus their attention instead on larger and higher profile organizations such as electoral parties.[4] While perhaps understandable, this widespread neglect of groupuscules operating on the margins of conventional politics is not always warranted, especially in the case of self-styled revolutionary vanguards. Although outright seizures of power by such vanguard groups appear to be increasingly unlikely in both Western Europe and North America, groupuscules that are nowadays being overlooked may nonetheless turn out to be very important in other ways. One need only mention 'Usāma b. Lādin's diffuse terrorist network, al-Qā'ida (The Base), to illustrate this crucial point. Moreover, since the overwhelming majority of European neo-fascist organizations – including the most important clandestine terrorist cells, ideological 'think tanks', counter-cultural youth groups and transnational networks – fall into this 'groupuscular' category, ignoring such groupuscules can only result in a total failure to appreciate the historical significance of the post-war radical right.

A few preliminary theoretical observations are therefore in order. There exist several means by which apparently weak political groupuscules may, given the right circumstances, become much more historically significant. First, the formation of groupuscules not only enables fringe groups to maintain internal social solidarity and sustain ideological purity in a hostile social environment but, once created, such structures can become important incubators of, and transmission belts for, unconventional political ideas that eventually spread beyond their own boundaries. This is all the more likely with the advent of the Internet, which today makes it possible for any computer-literate person to disseminate political messages, no matter how unpopular, to a much larger audience. Second, there is often a greater degree of overlap between the personnel of fringe groupuscules and more respectable cultural circles or political institutions than is visible to the untutored eye, a sort of 'grey zone' where extremists and moderates, knowingly or not, rub shoulders with one another.[5] This is generally the product of two distinct but interrelated processes. On the one hand, members of groupuscules often seek to infiltrate and covertly influence the attitudes and actions of larger, more conventional political parties and other relatively mainstream socio-cultural bodies. On the other, elements from the so-called establishment periodically seek to make use of fringe groupuscules in various ways. To mention only two of many possible examples, factions of the secret services have often infiltrated, manipulated and made instrumental use of political groupuscules in order to carry out covert, 'plausibly deniable' operations,[6] and more mainstream political parties have at times intentionally recruited members of such groupuscules for various purposes, ranging from low-level campaigning and bodyguard duties to serving as intellectual spokespersons or even political candidates. Third, like-minded groupuscules very often join together to form much more extensive transnational networks, both in the real world and, increasingly, in cyberspace. Fourth, in times of acute social, political or economic crisis, such groupuscules, even if previously perceived as extremist, can rapidly attract a larger base of disenfranchised supporters who now suddenly find their radical perspectives appealing. Finally, if necessary groupuscules can, given their small and often secretive organizational structure, more easily be transformed into fully clandestine and highly compartmentalized terrorist cells than can larger, more public organizations.

The (changing) nature of neo-fascist groupuscules

There are two salient characteristics of post-war fascism that at first glance may seem paradoxical. On the one hand, there has been an extraordinary proliferation of small neo-fascist groups – that is, groupuscules – within every country of Western and Southern Europe since the end of World War II. On the national level, however, the omnipresence of divisive ideological conflicts, profound differences over political tactics, and contentious personal disputes between competing would-be *Führers* has made it very difficult for these sectarian and often insular groups to co-ordinate their activities in any meaningful way. The history of neo-fascism is therefore replete with a kaleidoscopic array and bewildering variety of organizations, personalities and doctrines, many of which have been the direct or indirect outgrowths of a complex process of fission and fusion precipitated by bitter internal struggles and rivalries.[7] On the other hand, some of the very same groups that could not manage to find a basis for co-operation with similarly minded organizations inside their own countries have made strenuous efforts to 'internationalize' and link up with their counterparts in other nations, both throughout Europe and elsewhere in the world.[8] In spite of all the transformations that have taken place within this milieu, both ideological and organizational, this peculiar combination of fragmentation within national boundaries and transnational alliance formation has remained a constant pattern between 1945 and the present day.

Groupuscules, neo-fascist or otherwise, can be analysed in both functional and historical terms. From a functional standpoint, one of the most acute observers of the radical-right youth subculture in France during the 1980s and 1990s has characterized recent neo-fascist groupuscules as hybrid organizations incorporating some of the traits associated with four different types of groups: mass parties (in terms of their emphasis on ideology, their use of militants, their concern for the popular factor and their claim to represent excluded political and social elements); pressure groups (as regards their overt and covert lobbying activities, their infiltration of other organizations and exploitation of dual membership and their application of pressure by means of violence); terrorist organizations (with respect to their insularity and their semi-clandestine and sectarian nature); and armies (in terms of their emphasis on discipline, maintenance of hierarchies and their penchant for training and paramilitary activities).[9] Although the suggestion that all neo-fascist groupuscules share every one of these characteristics is problematic, if not erroneous, there is no doubt that such groupuscules often are hybrid formations that do not fall neatly within standard, well-delimited political or organizational categories. Moreover, despite displaying certain common traits by virtue of their participation in the same political milieu and their small size, all neo-fascist groupuscules develop a number of unique features that serve, on closer inspection, to distinguish them from their temporal counterparts. Furthermore these features are not frozen in time.

On the contrary, groupuscules with some degree of longevity almost invariably evolve over time in response to new conditions and circumstances. Even the animators of more ephemeral groups – those that fail to survive the aforementioned processes of fission and fusion – often try to make up for their prior mistakes by organizing new formations capable of overcoming the perceived shortcomings of earlier and still-existing groups. It would therefore be a serious mistake to adopt an overly schematic, ahistorical model, as social scientists are wont to do, since neo-fascist groupuscules of, say, the 1990s are by no means identical to those of the 1960s. Very significant ideological, organizational and cultural shifts occurred during that tumultuous thirty-year period, shifts that not only reflected broader historical trends but also internal processes of evolution within the neo-fascist milieu. Indeed, by comparing and contrasting characteristic features of the more recent organizations discussed later with those of representative groupuscules operating in the 1960s, one can learn a great deal about the historical evolution of neo-fascism.

Occident: a typical 1960s neo-fascist groupuscule

One of the most representative French neo-fascist groupuscules during the 1960s was the Mouvement Occident, which was officially founded in April 1964 by former Jeune Nation leader Pierre Sidos and others after their rival Dominique Venner assumed control of Europe-Action. Occident was a sectarian, semi-clandestine vanguard organization with a hierarchical structure based on the leadership principle; it provided ideological and paramilitary training to its members, infiltrated other (mainly student) organizations and soon became notorious for carrying out extremely violent commando actions against its left-wing counterparts. Occident's leaders promoted a 'nationalist revolution' against the Gaullist regime, a cult of youth, intransigent anti-communism, the all-out defence of Western Civilization and its colonial outposts, a corporatist regime, anti-capitalism, anti-materialism and antisemitism.[10] In short, Occident was in most respects a characteristic mid-1960s neo-fascist groupuscule.

For our purposes, Occident's geopolitical and cultural predilections are of particular importance. It should first be pointed out that, in the period between the onset of the Cold War and the collapse of Communism, the European radical right adopted three distinct – and in many ways incompatible – geopolitical perspectives, one Western-oriented, one Eurocentric and one Russophilic. Double-breasted-suit-wearing 'fascist' moderates and elements of numerous non-fascist far-right currents, including Catholic integralists, monarchists and certain ultranationalists, were politically wedded to the Atlantic Alliance and its major sponsor, the United States. This was because these latter entities, despite their manifest shortcomings, were viewed as the bulwarks of a Western civilization that was locked in a life-or-death struggle with an implacable communist adversary. In contrast to the relatively pro-American orientation of this numerically dominant 'Atlanticist' faction, several revolutionary neo-fascist elements advocated the establishment of a unified, militarized Europe, a Nation Europa, that would constitute a 'third force' capable of 'liberating' Europe and resisting the twin 'imperialisms' of international communism and U.S.-controlled international capitalism, both of which were perceived as being anti-national, anti-European, materialistic, exploitative, dehumanizing and – according to pro-Nazi elements – controlled by parasitic Jews. An even smaller number of fascist radicals, such as the European Liberation Front, the 'nationalist neutralists' in Germany, some 'national communists' and the national Bolsheviks, instead promoted a *de facto* alliance with the Soviet Bloc in order to rid Europe of its American 'occupiers'.[11]

During the height of the Cold War, however, even most neo-fascist radicals were reluctantly compelled, despite their incessant rhetorical attacks on capitalism and their genuine hostility to U.S. cultural hegemony, to make common cause with pro-American elements within their own countries in order to fight communism.

After all, the intransigent defence of Western civilization was a strategy whose success ultimately rested on American military and economic power. In this sense, too, Occident was rather typical of mid-1960s neo-fascist groupuscules. Having adopted the Manichaean worldview of their Organisation de l'Armée Secrète (OAS) heroes – that all anti-colonial struggles in the Third World were secretly sponsored and directed by the communists – it should come as no surprise to find that Occident openly lauded the reactionary, authoritarian regimes in South Vietnam, Portugal and Greece (after 1967) simply because they were virulently anti-communist, that the organization joined Roger Holeindre's Front Uni de Soutien au Sud-Vietnam in early 1968, that it urged the U.S. military to attack North Vietnam and that one of its principal slogans was 'defend the West wherever it is attacked'.[12]

A second characteristic of Occident was its cultural 'squareness'. Precisely because its members viewed all domestic leftists as witting or unwitting communist agents, they were not particularly open to new counter-cultural trends in art, fashion or protest-oriented rock music, since these developments were increasingly associated with 'pacifist' hippies and the 'anti-national' New Left. Thus, positive commentaries on contemporary youth culture and music do not appear in the group's flyers or its chief publication, *Occident Université*. In that sense, despite their never-ending paeans to the dynamism and vitality of youth, their publicly displayed attitudes towards this profusion of new cultural trends tended to mirror those of reactionary social conservatives and their own 'square' parents.

It was largely due to these peculiar geopolitical and cultural factors that, following the dramatic outbreak in France of an open student and workers' revolt in May 1968, Occident ended up aligning itself and actively collaborating with the hated Gaullist forces of law and order and reactionary conservatives in an effort to suppress the radical left. Only such a traumatic series of violent events, which seemingly threatened to precipitate a civil war in France, could have led to the rapid burying of hatchets between the Gaullist regime and its bitter OAS enemies or between fascist radicals and reformist 'bourgeois' conservatives. That is precisely what occurred. Although Occident's leaders were at first divided over how to respond, and a few of its youthful militants actually chose to join left-wing student protesters on the barricades because of their hatred for the Gaullists and feelings of generational solidarity, when push came to shove the overwhelming majority ended up marching under Cross of Lorraine banners at the huge Gaullist-sponsored rally on 30 May, alongside those with whom they had previously been at odds. It was symptomatic of this newly formed marriage of convenience that representatives of the secret services soon after made discreet overtures to Occident's leaders and offered to support covertly their efforts to wrest control of the University of Paris law school on rue Assas from student protesters, an offer that was accepted.[13] Once the crisis was over, however, the government forcibly dissolved Occident along with dozens of radical-left groupuscules, which were now all depicted as threats to public order. The differences between earlier, 'nostalgic' neo-fascist groups such as Occident and the more radical, left-leaning formations that proliferated from the mid-1970s on should therefore become obvious as soon as the chief characteristics of Nouvelle Résistance (NR) are highlighted. Before turning to its organizational history, however, the background of its founder Christian Bouchet needs to be elucidated.

Who is Christian Bouchet?

Christian Bouchet was born in Angers in 1955 into what he himself has described as a 'petit-bourgeois' provincial family. All of his close family members were associated with the political right in the pre-war, wartime and post-war eras, which created severe hardships for them in the immediate aftermath of World War II; he freely admits that growing up in this milieu had a profound effect on his own political worldview.[14] Bouchet initiated his long career as a political activist by briefly joining the Action Française's successor organization, Restauration Nationale, and in 1969 he formed a small anti-leftist group while attending Catholic high school. In 1970 he rejoined Restauration Nationale, but a year later he moved on to a breakaway group known as the Nouvelle Action Française.[15] In 1973 he abandoned the monarchist movement altogether and joined a left-fascist national revolutionary group known as the Organisation Lutte du Peuple (OLP), which among other things advocated solidarity with revolutionary nationalist movements in the Third World, especially radical Arab regimes that openly opposed both 'Zionism' and 'American imperialism'.[16] At first glance this may appear to be a rather strange political itinerary, since intransigent monarchism scarcely seems compatible with left-wing currents of fascism. But it should be recalled that Action Française 'study groups' such as the Cercle Proudhon originally brought pro-royalist ultranationalists, anarchists and revolutionary syndicalists together in the early twentieth century to discuss both 'national' and 'social' questions, and that as such it constituted one of the very first proto-fascist groups. This same point has likewise been emphasized by Bouchet, and when viewed in this light it is not at all hard to see how a dissident, non-conformist Action Française supporter could end up in a left-leaning national revolutionary group such as Lutte du Peuple.[17] From that point on, Bouchet developed into an increasingly important leader within this particular political current of the French far right.[18] Although he has at times left the fold and, for ideological or tactical reasons, joined more mainstream rightist organizations – such as the *nouvelle droite*'s Groupement de Recherches et d'Études pour la Civilisation Européenne (GRECE) in the early 1980s, Bruno Mégret's Comité d'Action Républicaine (CAR) in 1982, and Mégret's later Front National breakaway group, the Mouvement National Républicaine in 1999 – he has nonetheless continued to play a leading role in a succession of national revolutionary groupuscules, including the Mouvement Nationaliste Révolutionnaire, Troisième Voie (TV), Nouvelle Résistance and Unité Radicale (UR). During the past two decades he has also been more or less active in the occult and counter-cultural undergrounds, although as will soon become clear the precise nature and extent of his involvement in these spheres remains a matter of controversy.

The organizational history and ideology of Nouvelle Résistance

In February 1979 elements from Lutte du Peuple (including Bouchet), the Groupe Action-Jeunesse (GAJ) and the Groupes Nationalistes Révolutionnaires de Base (GNR) joined together to form the Mouvement Nationaliste Révolutionnaire (MNR) under the leadership of ex-GAJ chief Jean-Gilles Malliarakis, one of the most prominent and interesting French neo-fascist militants. Ideologically speaking, the MNR was a left-leaning neo-fascist group which promoted a second French Revolution, a 'Europe independent of the blocs', the struggle against 'American imperialism', the 'expropriation' of multinational corporations, the nationalization of big monopolies, the 'abolition of bourgeois privileges', the taxation of capital, and syndicalism, as well as the defence of French and European civilization, a Mediterranean-based foreign policy, economic corporatism, the termination of unskilled immigration, and the establishment of a strong but decentralized state.[19] Given its self-proclaimed revolutionary agenda, the MNR originally avoided any participation in electoral politics, focusing instead on disseminating propaganda, engaging in high-profile street actions, and recruiting, training and organizing youth cadres for political action, which in turn provoked ongoing government surveillance and several police interrogations of Malliarakis. However, it remained a numerically small vanguard group whose attempts to forge alliances with other groupuscules and establish broader umbrella organizations (like the Regroupement Nationaliste) met with failure.[20]

In 1985, however, the cadres of the MNR were suddenly reinforced by elements from the Parti des Forces Nouvelles (PFN) and its student group at the time, the Groupe Union Défense (GUD). To attract additional new members and systematize its organization, the group decided to change its name to Troisième Voie (TV), although its ideological tenets remained the same. In a 1988 tract prepared by Bouchet, at that time the group's secretary-general, TV claimed to be the 'only national revolutionary movement in France' and set forth a political programme outlining its primary objectives: the independence and unity of Europe, which required the eradication of 'Yankee imperialism' in all of its forms; the replacement of the existing U.S.-dominated system with a direct or semi-direct 'organic democracy', which entailed the nationalization of multinational corporations and the 'abolition of bourgeois privileges'; the 'rediscovery of our doctrinal roots', which meant breaking once and for all with the folkloric and reactionary features of the traditional radical right (both electoral and groupuscular) and reaffirming their ideological debt to non-conformist revolutionary romantics, ranging from French 'socialists' like Auguste Blanqui and Pierre Proudhon to national Bolsheviks like Ernst Niekisch and Karl-Otto Paetel to left-wing fascists like Ramiro Ledesmas Ramos; and, finally, the forging of operational alliances with Third World revolutionaries, radical ecologists and anti-superpower neutralists.[21] Although TV's syncretic ideology, which borrowed from both radical-right and radical-left sources, was far from unique in national revolutionary circles, the group also launched various practical initiatives designed to appeal to youthful elements of various counter-cultural undergrounds. To this end TV, a small cadre organization with only a few hundred militants, created a number of satellite formations (and publications) aimed not only at students (Jeune Garde) and workers (the Colectif Syndical Nationaliste), which was standard practice for neo-fascist groups, but also at activist circles of skinheads, such as the Jeunesses Nationalistes-Révolutionnaires (JNR), headed by the infamous 'bootboy' Serge Ayoub, better known as 'Batskin', and other underground rock 'n' roll and industrial music fans.[22] Although TV has justly been characterized as 'one of the most active and dynamic' of French radical-right movements of the 1980s, bitter internal debates about whether its militants should join (that is, infiltrate) rightist political parties and/or participate in electoral campaigns led to increasing dissension and factionalism.[23]

It was just such a dispute over strategy and tactics that, in August 1991, caused Christian Bouchet – who was at that time the leader of TV's most left-leaning faction, the Tercéristes Radicaux – to break with the parent body and form Nouvelle Résistance.[24] Bouchet had been advocating a 'Trotskyist' strategy whereby TV would enter the 'bourgeois' Front National (FN) as an organized faction, obtain positions on the party's national council, and thence begin subverting and transforming it from within. Malliarakis initially opposed any sort of entrism strategy, but later changed his mind and urged TV's activists to join the FN on an individual basis. In the end, these tactical differences could not be reconciled. Bouchet had also begun promoting the creation of a 'united anti-system front' composed of disparate revolutionary forces, domestic and foreign, that were uncompromisingly opposed to American imperialism and global capitalism, a task that he felt would be better served by forming a new combat organization. These factors led directly to the establishment of his own groupuscule, NR, to which most of the members of TV's provincial sections and even some leading figures from its central committee immediately adhered. The new formation quickly set up 'base groups' and 'contact points' in several French towns and began publishing its own journal, which was originally titled *Lutte du peuple*. NR subsequently founded a cadre training school and developed a more elaborate organizational structure consisting of an executive council, the movement's 'parliament' and strategic directorate, and an executive bureau divided into four sections, each with nine subsections.[25] Despite Bouchet's own emphasis on the quasi-democratic features of NR, such as consensual decision-making and the election of subsection chiefs, there can be little doubt that as secretary-general he and the other members of the group's political bureau effectively determined its ideological orientation, political strategy and operational tactics. In the final analysis, NR militants who refused to support the group's evolving 'line' seem to have had few options other than to break away and join or form other groupuscules.[26]

Although astute observers have alternately characterized it as 'national leftist', 'national Bolshevik' or 'national communist', and its enemies on the left and right have falsely branded it as a 'neo-Nazi' or 'communist' group, NR in fact promoted a left-fascist national revolutionary ideology with a Eurasian 'Nation Europa' and

Third World solidarity orientation. Like all left-wing fascists, NR's leaders strongly emphasized socialist, anti-capitalist and anti-imperialist themes along with revolutionary nationalism – in this case in the form of pan-European ethnic nationalism ('from Galway to Vladivostok') and micro-nationalist self-determination rather than that based on the traditional nation-state – and identified an eclectic array of unconventional radical-right and radical-left personages and groups as their ideological forebears, the most important of whom were a trio of deceased but increasingly influential 'anti-Western Europeanists': Ernst Niekisch, Francis Parker Yockey and Jean Thiriart.[27] Since Soviet-style Communism was then in the process of collapsing in Eastern Europe, NR purposely abandoned the 'third position' designation used by previous left-fascist groups opposed to both superpowers; in these new geopolitical conditions, its sole remaining enemy was the liberal capitalist system of the West, which NR believed was on the verge of attaining political, military, economic and cultural hegemony over the entire planet, in the process mercilessly exploiting people, ravaging the environment, eradicating historic ethno-cultural groups and defusing potential resistance by means of economic co-optation and the propagation of a debilitating bourgeois consumer ethos. The principal animator and chief beneficiary of this homogenizing, totalitarian New World Order was said to be the United States, whose power allegedly rested not only on its own military and economic might, but also on various instruments of 'neo-colonial' control, including international organizations, subordinate foreign governments, multinational corporations and the mainstream media.[28]

The political strategy and tactics of Nouvelle Résistance

What, then, was to be done? NR believed that it was necessary to lay the organizational and cultural groundwork for an anti-system revolution, both in Europe and elsewhere. Given the unfavourable nature of the existing balance of power, however, it was premature to try to organize and launch a 'protracted people's war', much less a violent *putsch* against the political establishment. The initiation of armed struggle depended on the existence of what Bouchet referred to as an 'external lung' (a non-European country that could provide assistance) or a 'Piedmont' (a European region that could serve as a logistical and operational base). In the meantime, the task of revolutionary groups like NR was to pursue an arduous, long-term 'counterpower' strategy designed, slowly but surely, to undermine the authority and legitimacy of the system. To help accomplish this, NR advocated the creation of 'liberated zones' and 'concrete utopias' inside the belly of the beast: a veritable 'counter-society' consisting of a decentralized network of alternative institutions operating within the interstices of mainstream society (small businesses, co-operatives, agricultural communes, media outlets, artisanal enterprises, etc.) that would not only contribute to economic self-sufficiency but also showcase NR's anti-establishment values.[29] NR claimed that there was already widespread popular dissatisfaction with the bourgeois system and that many other oppositional groups, whether or not they realized it, held views close to its own. Even so, such an ambitious strategic objective appears rather grandiose for an 'ultra-minoritarian' groupuscule with perhaps 150–300 committed activists – and the ability to mobilize a few hundred more on special occasions – and a press that at most reached a few thousand.[30] This seemingly insurmountable problem of numerical weakness, together with NR's own ideological proclivities, caused the organization to lay special emphasis on, first, the provision of 'active support to all anti-system resistances abroad' and, second, the utilization of a complex infiltration/entrism strategy *vis-à-vis* other political, social and cultural groups. Both require further clarification.

Since the threat posed by the American-dominated capitalist New World Order was perceived as global, resistance to this system also had to be organized on a global scale. As a result, NR sought to forge a 'united anti-system front' on a quadri-continental level. This could not be accomplished until the 'false' right/left dichotomy and other 'sterile' ideological cleavages, which had long divided revolutionaries into rival camps and thereby only benefited the system, were abandoned and replaced by a new and supposedly more apt pro-system 'centre'/anti-system 'periphery' dichotomy. Since the traditional extreme right and orthodox far left had allegedly been co-opted and integrated into the system, it was necessary to rally all of the marginalized, non-conformist, 'peripheral' forces that remained steadfastly opposed to the *status quo*, wherever they could be found.[31] In order to achieve this objective, NR committed itself to providing active (though not necessarily uncritical) support to all the movements, organizations and regimes that were openly resisting American imperialism and globalization, ranging from left-wing guerrillas to the extraparliamentary right, from radical ecologists to ethno-cultural separatists, from 'patriotic socialists' to non-reactionary nationalists, from indigenous peoples struggling for self-determination to Muslim fundamentalists resisting modernization, from anti-bourgeois youth movements to protesting workers and students, and from anti-Western Third World regimes to the fossilized remnants of Stalinism. Such support was manifested in several ways.

First of all, NR lauded an extraordinary assortment of revolutionary groups and anti-American regimes in its various publications, and sometimes even organized public demonstrations in support of their causes. To provide only a few examples, one can find paeans to fascist intellectuals, the Zapatistas in Mexico, Che Guevara, Earth First!, former left-wing Euroterrorists, Muʻammar al-Qadhdhāfī's Libya, neo-Peronist Argentina, North Korea, Fidel Castro's Cuba, contemporary Russian Communists, Palestinian groups of both the Marxist and Islamist persuasions, Basque and Corsican separatists, pan-African organizations, and fallen nineteenth-century Communards, all within the pages of *Lutte du peuple*.[32] Second, leading NR militants have repeatedly initiated contacts with their counterparts in other radical groups in order to foster mutual co-operation, if not to form outright alliances, and have likewise travelled overseas to meet with representatives of several anti-American regimes, including Libya, Iraq, Iran and North Korea, as well as politicians in post-Communist Russia.[33] Finally, NR was one of the driving forces in the creation of a new Front Européen de Libération (FEL), an international umbrella organization inspired by Yockey's original version and modelled after Thiriart's Jeune Europe network, which was intended to strengthen the collaboration between left-fascist, ecology, regionalist and unorthodox left movements in different parts of the world. Its founders sought to emulate the Comintern by laying the basis for a European party with a national directorate on the continental level and regional directorates in each nation. The FEL's membership has fluctuated somewhat since its establishment in the autumn of 1991, but it has so far been confined almost exclusively to left-fascist and national-Bolshevik groups. Among these have been Juan Llopart's Alternativa Europea from Spain, Patrick Harrington's Third Way (initially) and then Troy Southgate's National Revolutionary Faction from Britain, Eduard Limonov and Aleksandr Dugin's Natsionalno-Bolshevistskaia Partiia from Russia, and – in the extra-European, FEL-sponsored Liaison Committee for Revolutionary Nationalists – the Arkansas-based American Front from the United States and Kerry Bolton's National Destiny from New Zealand.[34] In short, NR assiduously sought to compensate for its own numerical weakness by linking up with anti-system forces throughout the world.

In France, the group instead endeavoured to augment its influence by pursuing an elaborate and perhaps incompatible coalition and entrism strategy. On the one hand, it sought to link up with a diverse array of radical extraparliamentary groups, join the coalitions they had formed and participate in their anti-system agitation and propaganda activities. For example, NR was actively involved in the campaigns against McDonald's and Eurodisney, the protests against NATO intervention in the Balkans and the World Trade Organization, demonstrations in support of the renewal of the Palestinian *intifada* and the lifting of sanctions on Iraq, and local ecological activism.[35] On the other hand, it periodically collaborated with 'national populist' political parties and participated in electoral campaigns. Although the group's manifesto went to great trouble to provide a theoretical justification for future interaction with both anti-system forces and rightist electoral parties, in actual practice this seemingly contradictory course of action was viewed with great suspicion by militants within NR itself.[36] Inevitably, such overtures to 'reactionaries' provoked dissension and organizational schisms. One such instance occurred in the latter half of 1996 – after Bouchet's adoption of a policy encouraging NR activists also to become members of the Front National – when the self-proclaimed 'progressive wing' openly broke with Bouchet, sought to expel his faction from NR and thence adhered to Luc Michel's Belgian-based Parti Communautaire National-Européen, a group of 'national communist' ultras who considered themselves the true heirs of Jean Thiriart.[37] Despite these costly defections, Bouchet was now determined to expand his organization's influence far beyond what was typical for an insular, sectarian groupuscule, and as such he continued to advocate an entrism strategy in the group's meetings and publications, as well as to woo elements of the electoral right that he felt could be further radicalized.

In the summer of 1997, having taken cognizance of the increasingly blue-collar social composition of the FN and the growing influence of *nouvelle droite* thinkers within its ranks, Bouchet 'decided to dissolve NR and work as a faction both in and out of the FN using the names Résistance and Jeune Résistance'. As he later put it, 'we now try to have an influence on [the FN's] youth group and on its more radical wing . . . [and] work as *Militant* has done in the [British] Labour Party'.[38] Since then, Bouchet claims that his group has continued to gain adherents and influence in nationalist circles. In NR's place, the Union des Cercles Résistance (UCR) and Jeune Résistance (JR) were created. Unité Radicale was officially founded in June 1998, when the GUD formed an alliance with the UCR and JR, and it has since become the main vehicle for Bouchet's political activism.[39] According to its own statement of purpose, UR's aim was to serve as a pole or pivot for rallying and organizing the radical, extraparliamentary elements of the 'national movement' in France so that they could exert a much greater ideological influence and thereby counter the attempts by rightist moderates and careerists to compromise with the system. As NR had ended up doing, UR urged its members and sympathizers to join rightist electoral parties, help strengthen the influence of their radical rank-and-file members, attain positions of responsibility within the host organizations, and work to get its preferred candidates elected to political office. The aim was not to seize political power on its own, but to create a national revolutionary organization capable of conditioning the entire national movement, in the same way that the Gauche Socialiste group was able to condition the French Socialist Party. Such an aggressive entrism strategy would thus allow UR to become 'more than a groupuscule'.[40]

Within UR, the UCR was the section made up of working professionals, Jeune Résistance of high school students and young workers, and the GUD of university students. Like NR, UR formed 'base groups' everywhere it was active. These groups were in turn linked to the organization's Collectif National de Coordination, the body responsible for co-ordinating and directing UR's political activities, campaigns and press by means of regular national conferences and internal bulletins.[41] In 1999, when Bruno Mégret abandoned the FN and formed the Mouvement National Républicaine, UR hastened to offer the latter its 'total' support. Although UR has retained full organizational autonomy to this day, in accordance with their proclaimed strategy Bouchet and many of his organization's members at once joined Mégret's new group, 'deeply penetrated' it, obtained positions on its national council and actively participated in its electoral campaigns. UR's support for Mégret was neither uncritical nor unconditional, though, since it was to be immediately withdrawn if the new party softened its anti-immigration stance. Furthermore, the immigration issue was not the only potential bone of contention between the two organizations, as Bouchet recently criticized Mégret's 'Islamists out of France' platform for being too pro-American.[42]

Nor did its links to Mégret's party mean that electoral politics had become an end in itself for UR. On the contrary, in September 2000 Bouchet was among the signatories of a petition in which the formation of a 'trans-movement organization' called La CoordiNation was announced: 'For us the important thing is not [one's] party membership card', but one's willingness to take action in defence of nationalist principles. At this juncture, the petition continued, the most pressing need was to reverse the nation's growing social fragmentation, itself fuelled primarily by state-sanctioned ethnic integration.[43]

Combat on the (counter)cultural front

Bouchet's various groupuscules, however, did not confine their actions exclusively to political matters. Indeed, one of the most noteworthy features of NR (and later UR) was its efforts to operate and exert influence in the cultural sphere, particularly in various counter-cultural youth undergrounds. As Bouchet himself put it: 'I think that the cultural fight must be as important as the political fight . . . [a] grassroots cultural fight and not one of the university variety', a sentiment echoed in UR's own statement of purpose:

> [Cultural combat] is indispensable for us. We are aware that one can gain more sympathizers with a CD than with a newspaper, with a song or a comic book than with a tract . . . For us it's not a matter of influencing the culture of the elite but the culture of the people. Thus our cultural combat is being conducted on the level of record labels, comic book publishing houses and the promotion of musical groups. We have a weakness for thinking that a good CD that is listened to by working-class youth [*la jeunesse populaire*] and that can spread our ideas to them has more importance than a GRECE colloquium that does nothing but reinforce the ideas of those already convinced.[44]

Elsewhere in *Questions et réponses*, the importance of targeting and 're-nationalizing' young people was likewise clearly emphasized.[45] This recognition of the importance of cultural struggle helps to explain the extensive coverage of underground music in NR and UR publications, as well as the publication of underground music fanzines by circles close to Bouchet.

As has been noted, Troisième Voie (TV) had previously pursued an 'opening to youth counter-cultures' strategy by creating a skinhead front group and giving some coverage to underground rock 'n' roll and industrial music. At first glance the musical coverage in *Révolution européenne* does not seem altogether atypical of that found in 'hip' alternative culture publications – Johnny Cash rated a good review, whereas U.S. corporate pop acts like Madonna and Michael Jackson did not – but a closer perusal clearly reveals TV's political biases. For example, the increasingly commercial left-wing punk band Bérurier Noir was criticized, among other things, for displaying a phony, hypocritical anti-system stance, given that some of its concerts were sponsored by government cultural agencies, whereas pile-driving 1977-era French synth punk group Métal Urbaine was praised for exhibiting a nihilistic and allegedly Nietzschean worldview.[46] Meanwhile, Batskin's skinhead followers established close links with certain neo-fascist Oi labels, such as ex-TV militant Gaël Bodilis's Rebelles Européennes record label and distribution company in Brest. Coverage of underground music was also quite common in NR's succession of publications, although in this case the blatantly political nature of the articles and interviews was impossible to miss. In their 'Bruits Européens' section, one can find promotional pieces on a host of far-right musical groups that span the stylistic spectrum, including Britain's Death in June (industrial) and Sol Invictus ('apocalyptic folk'), Italy's Londinium SPQR (Oi), Austria's Allerseelen (experimental), North America's RAHOWA (metallic hardcore), Sweden's Unleashed (death metal), and France's Frakass (Oi), Animae Mortalitas (black metal), Kayserbund (electronic) and Brixia (Celtic pop). Even more astonishingly, the sort of techno music favoured by ravers was lauded as 'European' and anti-liberal, and Breton rap band Basic Celtos was enthusiastically promoted despite the black American origins of the particular style of music they embraced. Other articles exhibited naiveté regarding the 'spirituality' of heavy metal, foolishness concerning the cultural rootedness of the Turbo-Folk music peddled by right-wing Serbian paramilitary leader 'Arkan' and his gangster associates, and wishful thinking about the growing 'fascist' character of contemporary music.[47]

Perhaps more importantly, Bouchet and other NR leaders also tacitly supported – or possibly even secretly sponsored – the publication of several counter-cultural fanzines that had no official links to his various political groupuscules. According to French journalists, anti-fascist 'watchdog' groups and his political enemies inside the nationalist camp, NR had close connections to the Rouge et Noir distribution company and underground music magazines such as *Raven's Chat, Requiem gothique* and above all *Napalm Rock*, the successor to an earlier hard rock magazine called *Métal Assaut*. These claims have been confirmed by Bouchet himself and by Michael Moynihan, a source friendly to Bouchet and co-author of *Lords of Chaos*, the most detailed work that has yet appeared on the violent, right-wing fringes of the black metal counter-culture, who quoted the remarks of 'Gungnir', the editor of *Napalm Rock*, to the effect that the magazine was 'issued regularly under the auspices of Nouvelle Résistance'.[48] This is rather illuminating not only because the contents of *Napalm Rock* were very extreme in their support for anti-Christian violence, but also because a scandal erupted when copies of this black metal fanzine and NR's internal bulletin *Rune* were later found by police in the possession of the four youths who had desecrated the Toulon cemetery on the evening of 8–9 June 1996. As examples of *Napalm Rock*'s anti-mainstream views, one can cite the 'wanted poster' accusing Jesus Christ of 'crimes against humanity' that appeared in issue number 4, as well as the thirty-page dossier in issue 3 devoted to black metal that described convicted Swedish church-burner and murderer Varg Vikernes as a 'proud and valiant Viking warrior' who was imprisoned after committing acts of violence 'for the political and spiritual liberation of his country'.[49] Although subsequent left-wing media campaigns linking rightist political organizations like NR, the neo-pagan GRECE and the FN (through NR leader Beck, at the time an assistant to the FN mayor of Orange) to the wave of cemetery 'profanations' then being carried out in southern France appear to be politically motivated 'guilt-by-association' polemics, there is no doubt that publications like *Napalm Rock* openly applauded the extreme actions of black metal musicians like Burzum's Vikernes, thereby indirectly encouraging other disaffected youths to emulate them. It may be, then, that for a time these semi-independent fanzines played an integral role in NR's strategy of rallying and mobilizing 'anti-system' forces, in this instance those on the cultural fringes.[50]

The crucial question here is whether Bouchet's extensive efforts to penetrate and influence various youth counter-cultures were basically manipulative political ploys or whether certain youthful militants within his succession of movements had a genuine counter-cultural sensibility and were thus true fans of the different types of underground music they promoted. Although this question is perhaps impossible for an outsider to answer, there is some evidence to suggest that both processes were at work simultaneously. It seems clear, for example, that despite his political non-conformity and interest in the occult, Bouchet himself is something of a 'square', at least in the context of youth counter-cultures. After all, in a 1998 article, one of his principal complaints about the ' '68 generation' was that they had institutionalized 'slovenly dress'. On the other hand, a certain Bertrand, an activist in Troisième Voie who was interviewed by journalist Christophe Bourseiller, was clearly a 'hip' character with a real love for, and knowledge of, fringe culture and alternative rock.[51] Even if one adopts the most cynical interpretation possible, namely that Bouchet and his comrades were feigning interest in youth counter-cultures in order to manipulate and exploit them for their own partisan purposes, the fact remains that they at least recognized the importance of these movements in the ongoing struggle for cultural hegemony, whereas the most nostalgic, reactionary and 'square' elements within the firmament of the radical right have until very recently tended to remain unambiguously hostile to them.[52]

Fascism: beyond right and left

The preceding case study of Nouvelle Résistance helps to illustrate many of the characteristic features of neo-fascist groupuscules in the post-war era. First, it demonstrates that such grouplets were flexible, hybrid formations capable of serving a wide variety of purposes depending on the specific political and ideological context. Among other things, for example, NR served as an activist cadre organization, a publishing house, a radical current inside more mainstream political parties, a liaison organization between other national revolutionary and national-Bolshevik groups, a transmission belt for anti-American and anti-Israeli propaganda, a mechanism for covert infiltration and a bridge into the counter-cultural underground. Second, its organizational history was marked throughout by the complex fission and fusion processes typical of the groupuscular milieu, in which contentious activists come together for a time before breaking away from one another and moving off in new directions, much like unstable particles on the molecular and subatomic levels. One of the chief reasons for this was that NR's infiltration/entrism strategy was inherently contradictory: how, after all, can one simultaneously appeal both to nationalist moderates *and* anti-system revolutionaries, to 'bourgeois squares' *and* counter-cultural rebels? Third, it suggests that such groupuscules may at times exert a degree of political or intellectual influence out of proportion to their limited numerical strength, in the sense that NR militants, in order to achieve their goal of forging a united front of anti-system forces, simultaneously operated and disseminated their radical notions in diverse spheres, both inside France and beyond, ranging from rightist political parties to other far-right groupuscules to circles of radical ecologists to non-conformist ultra-leftists to key figures within the occult, neo-pagan and music undergrounds. Finally, NR is in certain respects emblematic of the crucially important ideological and cultural shifts that have taken place within the neo-fascist milieu between the early 1970s and the present, particularly its increasing openness to left-wing ideological conceptions and unconventional counter-cultural lifestyles.

Indeed, NR was itself a product, directly or indirectly, of the dramatic post-1968 resurgence of left-fascist intellectual currents. As noted earlier, the bulk of the European right, whether moderate or extreme, responded to the traumatic worker and student revolts that broke out in the late 1960s with undisguised fear and hostility, and hence many right-wing ultras ended up actively colluding with the forces of order to repress the left. As early as 1968, however, certain small groups of neo-fascist radicals began expressing open sympathy for the student protesters, to the point where a few even joined them on the barricades in an effort to bring down the hated 'bourgeois' system. Most of these fascist radicals were either members of left-fascist groupuscules inspired by Thiriart's geopolitical conceptions or individual fascist non-conformists who were seduced by diverse aspects of the 1960s youth counter-culture, such as Hartwig Singer and Ugo Gaudenzi. By the mid-1970s, several new left-leaning 'national revolutionary' groups had appeared on the scene, including the Nationalrevolutionäre Aufbauorganisation in Germany, the Organisation Lutte du Peuple in France and Terza Posizione in Italy, and a new rightist youth counter-culture began to be forged, a process exemplified by the sudden appearance of the youth-oriented 'Hobbit Camps' in Italy.[53] Since then, this fledgling underground radical-right youth culture has rapidly evolved and increasingly adopted counter-cultural trappings previously associated with the student left (including the wearing of long or spikey hair, earrings and jeans). For some time it has been in the process of building its own transnational infrastructure, to the point where, despite periodic government censorship, scores of Oi, metal, experimental and industrial bands nowadays have the opportunity to release records thanks to the existence of a chameleon-like network of small independent labels and distributors. At the same time, more and more left-fascist groupuscules have appeared, both in Western and in Eastern Europe. In short, despite the continued existence of a handful of small, nostalgic, Hitler-worshipping cult groups in Western Europe, the 'Nazification' of significant portions of the skinhead counter-culture, and the post-Communist resurgence of neo-Nazism in Eastern Europe, the stereotypical media image of fascists as uniform-wearing, goose-stepping thugs with buzzcuts who listen to Wagner and oppose all cultural innovation has not been applicable to influential segments of the neo-fascist milieu for decades. Once these dramatic ideological and cultural transformations have been fully appreciated, one is prompted to question many other conventional interpretations of fascism.

During the past three decades, an intense scholarly debate about the nature of fascism has been raging. Thanks to the pioneering work of a number of leading scholars – most notably Eugen Weber, Renzo De Felice and Zeev Sternhell – older characterizations of fascism as an inherently conservative, wholly reactionary and entirely right-wing political phenomenon have given way to much more sophisticated and nuanced understandings. It now seems evident, as Sternhell especially has argued, that fascism was originally the product of *fin-de-siècle* attempts by dissidents from diverse intellectual traditions to conjoin currents of radical, 'anti-bourgeois' nationalism and 'anti-materialist', non-Marxist variants of socialism. In practice, these previously distinct and seemingly antithetical political currents proved difficult to integrate, and for this very reason all proto-fascist and fascist movements consisted of a myriad of competing right- and left-wing factions – namely those that emphasized the importance of the 'national question' (or, in the case of the Nazis, the 'racial question') and those that emphasized the importance of the 'social question' – that struggled fiercely with one another for dominance and control. Given the peculiar constellation of political forces characteristic of inter-war Europe, where there was little or no 'political space' available on the left side of the spectrum for the growth of a new revolutionary movement, the rightist elements within European fascist movements were almost invariably able to outmanoeuvre and then marginalize, suppress or exterminate their left-leaning rivals. This does not rule out the possibility, however, that in other political circumstances, left-fascist currents might come to the fore and fascist-style movements might end up moving to the left instead of the right. In Argentina, for example, the Peronist movement, which may have created the only post-World War II regime with a genuinely fascist ideological stamp, lurched sharply to the left, established a strong social base within the workers' movement and promoted a radical third-positionist 'line' *vis-à-vis* the two superpower blocs.[54]

Similar shifts to the left are also frequently observable among neo-fascists in post-war Europe. The earliest left-fascist groupuscules, most notably Jeune Europe, were established even before the student and worker revolts of 1968. In the wake of those dramatic events, newer, 'hipper' generations of left fascists emerged during the 1970s and have since continued to expand their intellectual and cultural influence. Since the collapse of the 'really existing' Communist states in Eastern Europe and the further discrediting of the entire Marxist revolutionary project, conditions have become even more propitious for the proliferation of left-fascist groupuscules. After all, there is now only one remaining 'imperialist' superpower, the United States, and 'capitalist globalization' has largely replaced 'international communism' as the chief 'threat' to European independence. Under these circumstances, it is hardly surprising to discover that new generations of fascist radicals are actively participating in the 'anti-globalization' campaign, supporting all sorts of anti-American regimes and movements in the Third World, retrospectively praising the causes and actions of left-wing Euroterrorist groups and making 'red-brown' political alliances with ex-Communists, ecologists and anti-Western left-wing nationalists. In that sense, case-studies of left-leaning neo-fascist groupuscules like Nouvelle Résistance not only help to shed light on the nature of fascism as a political phenomenon, but also lend further to Sternhell's provocative thesis that fascism brought together diffuse currents of cultural criticism from both the extreme right and the far left in order to forge a new revolutionary ideology that would go 'beyond right and left'.

Acknowledgements

The author wishes to thank, first, the Office of Scholarly Programs at the Library of Congress for funding and research support, and, second, Christian Bouchet for his generosity in providing copies of Nouvelle Résistance publications and other primary source materials, as well as his willingness to answer questions about his personal background and political activities. Both Kevin Coogan and Roger Griffin offered useful feedback on the content.

Notes

1 Reprinted with permission from Jeffrey M. Bale, " 'National Revolutionary' Groupuscules and the Resurgence of 'Left-Wing' Fascism: The Case of France's Nouvelle Résistance," *Patterns of Prejudice* 36:3 (2002), 24–49, www.tandfonline.com/10.1080/003132202128811475.
2 André-Yves Beck, former Nouvelle Résistance leader and current Front National official, quoted in Christian Bouchet (ed.), *Les Nouveaux Nationalistes* (Paris: Déterna, 2001), p. 24. Foreign-language translations, unless otherwise stated, are by the author.
3 Christian Bouchet, former Nouvelle Résistance leader, quoted in Jean-Paul Bourre, *Les Profanateurs: La Nébuleuse de tous les périls. Nouvelle Droite, skinheads, rock metal, néonazis* (n.p.: Le Comptoir, 1997), p. 68, citing Philippe Hertens, *Le Nationalisme radicale en France: Enquête* (Paris: Magrie, 1994).
4 A large and ever-growing number of academic studies dealing with 'neo-fascist' electoral parties such as the Front National, the Freiheitliche Partei Österreichs, Alleanza Nazionale, Fuerza Nueva and the Republikaner have been published in recent years, whereas only a handful have been devoted to individual neo-fascist groupuscules, even when the latter have had considerable operational and/or ideological significance. Among the rare exceptions are Roger Griffin, "Net Gains and GUD Reactions: Patterns of Prejudice in a Neo-Fascist *groupuscule*," *Patterns of Prejudice* 33:2 (April 1999), pp. 31–50; and Xavier Casals, *Neonazis en España: De los audiciones wagnerianas a los skinheads* (Barcelona: Grijalbo, 1995), pp. 37–194, which focuses on the neo-Nazi Circulo Español de Amigos de Europa (CEDADE); and those appearing in this special issue of *Patterns of Prejudice*. Perhaps not surprisingly, neo-fascists themselves have published the bulk of the serious works on lesser-known groupuscules within their own milieu: see e.g. Colectivo 'Karl-Otto Paetel', *Fascismo rojo* (Valencia: Colectivo 'Karl-Otto Paetel', 1998); Gabriele Adinolfi and Roberto Fiore, *Noi, Terza posizione* (Rome: Settimo Segillo, 2000); and Yannick Sauveur, "Jean Thiriart et le national communautarisme européen" (Unpublished thesis, Université de Paris, 1978), later reprinted and distributed by Thiriart's supporters.
5 The term 'grey zone' has sometimes been employed by German left-wing commentators to refer to the allegedly cosy, behind-the-scenes relationships between the conservative right and neo-Nazis: see e.g. Michael Venner, *Nationale Identität: Die neue Rechte und die Grauzone zwischen Konservatismus und Rechtsextremismus* (Cologne: PapyRossa, 1994).
6 See e.g. Gianni Flamini, *Il partito del golpe: Le strategie della tensione e del terrore dal primo centrosinistra organico al sequestro Moro, 1964–1978*, 4 vols in 6 parts (Ferrara: Bovolenta, 1981–5); and Frédéric Laurent, *L'Orchestre noir* (Paris: Stock, 1978).
7 Compare the astute observations of fascist theorist Maurice Bardèche, *Qu'est-ce que le fascisme?* (Paris: Sept Couleurs, 1961), pp. 97–8, 101.

8 For the seeming paradox between these two characteristics of European neo-fascism, see Joseph Algazy, *La tentation néo-fasciste en France, 1944–1965* (Paris: Fayard, 1984), pp. 289–91.
9 See Eric Rossi, *Jeunesse française des années 80–90: La tentation néo-fasciste* (Paris: Université Pantheon-Arras, 1995), p. 157.
10 For Occident, see Joseph Algazy, *L'Extrême-Droite en France de 1965 à 1984* (Paris: Harmattan, 1989), pp. 45–64; François Duprat, *Les Mouvements d'extrême droite en France depuis 1944* (Paris: Albatros, 1972), especially 126–79; and Francis Bergeron and Philippe Vilgier, *De Le Pen à Le Pen: Une Histoire des nationaux et des nationalistes sous la Vème république* (Bouère: Dominique Martin Morin, 1985), especially 70–5. The last two sources are of far-right provenance.
11 On the pro-Western v. pan-European geopolitical orientations, see Giorgio Galli, *La crisi italiana e la destra internazionale* (Milan: Mondadori, 1974), p. 60. For the pro-Soviet (or pro-Russian) groups, see especially Kurt P. Tauber, *Beyond Eagle and Swastika: German Nationalism since 1945* (Middletown, CT: Wesleyan University Press, 1967), volume 1, pp. 147–203. See also Kevin Coogan, *Dreamer of the Day: Francis Parker Yockey and the Postwar Fascist International* (New York: Autonomedia, 1999).
12 See Algazy, *L'Extrême-Droite*, pp. 45, 60; Duprat, *Les Mouvements d'extrême droite en France depuis 1944*, pp. 150, 152–8; and Bergeron and Vilgier, *De Le Pen à Le Pen*, pp. 70–1, 76.
13 Compare Philippe Vilgier and Pascal Gauchon, *La Droite en mouvements, nationaux et nationalistes, 1962–1981* (Paris: Vastra, 1981), p. 48, and Duprat, *Les Mouvements d'extrême droite en France depuis 1944*, pp. 158–63. Many other European neo-fascist groupuscules collaborated covertly but tangibly with elements of various state security forces, including Ordine Nuovo and Avanguardia Nazionale in Italy, the Mouvement Jeune Révolution and Ordre Nouveau in France, Jovem Portugal, the Kinema tes 4 Augoustou (4th of August Movement) in Greece, Westland New Post in Belgium and the Milliyetçi Hareket Partisi (Nationalist Action Party) in Turkey.
14 This biographical information was provided by Christian Bouchet himself, both in questionnaires that I sent to him (hereinafter Bouchet Questionnaire I and II) and in a series of interviews he gave to others: in the recently published book *Nouveaux Nationalistes* (see note 1); to Kerry Bolton for the New Zealand magazine *The Nexus*; and to Troy Southgate for *The English Alternative* (no. 9, summer 1998), the British National Revolutionary Faction's chief publication. According to Bouchet, one of his uncles was a member of the Camelots du Roi (the shock troops of the royalist, proto-fascist Action Française) and a Vichy Milicien who was later killed by rebels in Algeria; his maternal grandfather was a collaborator who was condemned to death by the Resistance, and who only escaped being executed when a jeep full of GIs placed him under arrest; and most other members of his mother's family were imprisoned after World War II. All of his family members and their close friends later supported the violent OAS campaigns to maintain French control over Algeria.
15 For more on Restauration Nationale and the Nouvelle Action Française splinter group, see François-Marin Fleutot and Patrick Louis, *Les Royalistes: Enquête sur les amis du roi aujourd'hui* (Paris: Albin Michel, 1989), pp. 19–20; and Patrick Louis, *Histoire des royalistes: De la Libération à nos jours* (Paris: Grancher, 1994).
16 Lutte du Peuple was the French counterpart of a left-fascist organization originally founded in Italy in May 1969 by Ugo Gaudenzi and others, the Organizzazione Lotta di Popolo. Among the activists who later became associated with the latter were Enzo Maria Dantini (whose name later appeared on a list of 'Gladio' members) and two notorious 'Nazi-Maoists', Claudio Mutti and Franco Freda. For the French branch, see Algazy, *L'Extrême-Droite*, 150–1, and Bergeron and Vilgier, *De Le Pen à Le Pen*, pp. 97–8.
17 For more on Action Française, 'royalist syndicalism' and the Cercle Proudhon, see especially Zeev Sternhell, *La Droite révolutionnaire, 1885–1914: Les Origines françaises du fascisme* (Paris: Seuil, 1978), pp. 364–72, 385–400; and Paul Mazgaj, *The Action Française and Revolutionary Syndicalism* (Chapel Hill: University of North Carolina Press, 1979), pp. 170–93

and passim. For Bouchet's own analysis of this transition, see Bouchet interview in Boucher (ed.), *Nouveaux Nationalistes*, pp. 50–1.
18 A brief description of the 'national revolutionary' current within the French radical right can be found in Christophe Bourseiller, *Extrême Droite: L'Enquête* (Paris: François Bourin, 1991), pp. 107–11.
19 See the MNR's 'platform' and nineteen-point programme, reprinted in Jean-Gilles Malliarakis, *Ni trusts, ni soviets* (Paris: Trident, 1985), pp. 63–74. This ideological agenda, marked as it was by revolutionary romanticism, has been justly characterized by Algazy as 'half-fascist, half-Communard' (*L'Extrême-Droite*, 176).
20 See Alain Rollat, *Les Hommes de l'extrême droite: Le Pen, Marie, Ortiz et les autres* (Paris: Calmann-Lévy, 1985), pp. 176–9.
21 Cited by Christophe Bourseiller, *Les Ennemis du système: Enquête sur les mouvements extrémistes en France* (Paris: Robert Laffont, 1989), pp. 189–91.
22 Ibid., p. 192. Bouchet himself claims to have played a key role in transforming TV from an informal group into a structured cadre organization (see Bouchet (ed.), *Nouveaux Nationalistes*, p. 54). Aside from the creation of the JNR, another sign of TV's 'opening to youth countercultures' was the appearance of underground music reviews in *Révolution européenne*, the organization's monthly journal (see *infra*, note 45). As for 'Batskin', he broke with TV in 1990 and formed a series of new organizations to rally skins and 'hooligans' for political action (e.g. see Jean-Yves Camus and René Monzat, *Les Droites nationales et radicales en France: Répertoire critique* (Lyon: Presses Universitaires de Lyon, 1992), pp. 324–5).
23 Quoted in Bourseiller, *Les ennemis du système*, p. 193.
24 Very little has so far been published on NR, other than a handful of hard-to-obtain academic theses, one scholarly article on NR's ideological concepts and scattered references in journalistic sources. The following brief account of the schism within TV and the establishment and organization of NR is based on the following materials: Camus and Monzat, *Les Droites nationales et radicales en France*, pp. 336, 341; the interview with Bouchet in Bouchet (ed.), *Nouveaux Nationalistes*, especially 54–7; and Bouchet Questionnaires I and II.
25 For the group's organizational structure, see NR's manifesto, *Pour la cause du peuple* (Nantes: Ars, 1992), pp. 25–6. Within the executive bureau, section I was responsible for administration and finance, section II for press and media relations, section III for agitation and propaganda, and section IV for security, intelligence, counterintelligence (*contre-infiltration*) and 'infiltration'. In this context, 'infiltration' can only refer to the penetration and manipulation of other parties and groups. NR's cadre school was named after Blanqui. It should also be noted that NR's principal publication, *Lutte du peuple*, was later renamed *La Voix du peuple*, and subsequently rechristened *Résistance*.
26 NR's ostensibly democratic features are highlighted in *Pour la cause du peuple*, pp. 25–6, and by Bouchet personally in a 1 July 2001 e-mail to the author, in which he claimed that he was often out-voted by other members of the political bureau. In a subsequent (7 July 2001) e-mail, Bouchet identified the members of NR's original political bureau as himself, André-Yves Beck (an ex-TV leader and future member of the FN's central committee), Jean-Marc Vivenza (an ex-TV militant, experimental musician and expert on René Guénon and Buddhism) and Thierry Mudry (an ex-member of GRECE and the Thiriart-inspired Partisans Européens group); later, a new bureau was formed consisting of Bouchet, Beck, Laurent Baudoux (an ex-TV member who later fell out with Bouchet and joined a 'national communist' groupuscule headed by Thiriart enthusiast Luc Michel), Bruno Gayot (a former member of the GAJ, MNR and TV who also later broke with Bouchet and joined Michel) and Fabrice Robert (an ex-TV militant and future member of Unité Radical).
27 See *Pour la cause du peuple*, pp. 10–16. Among the other figures and movements listed as sources of ideological inspiration in NR's manifesto are revolutionary *putschist* Blanqui; anarchist Proudhon; integral nationalist Maurice Barrès; French fascist Georges Valois;

left-leaning Spanish Falangists Ledesmas and Manuel Hedilla; the Futurists; radical Italian 'fascists of the first hour'; inter-war German national Bolsheviks; anti-Nazi Strasserites; and revolutionary nationalist Third World dictators like Juan Perón of Argentina and Jamāl 'Abd al-Nāsir of Egypt. The symbols adopted by NR were likewise borrowed from disparate political sources: the five-pointed star used by post-war left-wing guerrillas and terrorists; the black-and-red flags employed by Ledesmas's movement; the eagle associated with the national-Bolshevik group Widerstand; and the sword and hammer employed by Otto Strasser's Schwarze Front. An excellent analysis of certain features of NR's ideology can be found in Jean-Yves Camus, "Une avant-garde populiste: *peuple* et *nation* dans le discours de Nouvelle Résistance," *Mots* 55 (June 1998), pp. 128–38.

28 For NR's virulent critique of 'Yankee imperialism' in all of its alleged guises, see *Pour la cause du peuple*, pp. 9–10, 13–14, 16–21. For its shift of focus from a previously 'double' enemy to a present 'single' enemy, see Camus and Monzat, *Les Droites nationales et radicales en France*, p. 341.

29 *Pour la cause du peuple*, pp. 22–4. See also Troy Southgate's interview with Bouchet in *The English Alternative*.

30 *Pour la cause du peuple*, pp. 8, 13, 23. For estimates of NR's numerical strength, see Jean-Yves Camus (ed.), *Extrémismes en Europe* (Paris: L'Aube/Luc Pire/Centre Européen de Recherche et d'Action sur le Racisme et l'Antisémitisme (CERA), 1997), p. 181; Jean-Yves Camus (ed.), *Les Extrémismes en Europe: État des lieux en 1998* (Paris: L'Aube/Luc Pire/CERA, 1998), p. 185; and especially the 3 August 1994 Bouchet letter reproduced in Rossi, *Jeunesse française des années 80–90*, p. 345.

31 *Pour la cause du peuple*, pp. 17–18, 21–2. NR's scheme for forging an anti-system operational alliance between right- and left-wing revolutionaries was heavily indebted to the provocative ideas first expounded by 'Nazi-Maoist' Franco Freda, *La disintegrazione del sistema* (Padua: Ar, 1969), whereas the 'centre/periphery' division was borrowed from *nouvelle droite* theorist Alain de Benoist. Obviously, NR would have found it impossible to embark on an 'opening to the left' and 'solidarity with the Third World' strategy had it not explicitly defended all struggles for national self-determination, including those within former European and French colonies. Needless to say, such a view was diametrically opposed to the rabidly pro-colonial attitudes of 1960s neo-fascist groups like Occident. Even NR's anti-immigration views were couched in pseudo-leftist, non-racist terms.

32 It would take up too much space to document this fully. Representative examples from *Lutte du peuple* include: "25 anniversaire du Front populaire pour la libération de la Palestine," no. 13, February–March 1993, 8–11; "Dossier panafricanisme," no. 22, May–June 1994, 4–7; "Verts et régionalistes, l'espoir du rénouveau," no. 23, September–October 1994, 12–15; "Kim Il Sung, 15 avril 1912–8 juillet 1994," no. 24, November–December 1994, 9; "Chiapas, un an après," no. 25, January–February 1995, 5–7; "Entretien avec un militant d'Earth First!," no. 28, September–October 1995, 8; and "Che, un héros nationaliste révolutionnaire," no. 30, February–March 1996, 5. As Bouchet himself later put it, when asked where he located himself on the political spectrum: 'I am much closer to a Carlos [the Jackal] or a Horst Mahler [ex-Rote Armee Fraktion], both of whom are from the extreme left, than I am to a Romain Marie [né Bernard Anthony, head of the Catholic integralist wing of the FN]' (quoted in Bouchet (ed.), *Nouveaux Nationalistes*, p. 88). Indeed, one finds laudatory articles and/or interviews with both Carlos and Mahler in NR's publications: Daniel Milan, "Notre ami Carlos," *Résistance* 3 (March 1998), p. 25; Kai-Uwe Zwetschke, "Nouvelles convergences en Allemagne: Horst Mahler, un itineraire rouge-brun," *Résistance* 8, date illegible, which was followed by an interview with the former left-wing terrorist, who (along with several other German New Leftists) has since moved far to the right.

33 Bouchet interview in Bouchet (ed.), *Nouveaux Nationalistes*, pp. 58–9. For actual examples, see "Le Front européen de libération à Teheran," *Lutte du peuple* 22 (May–June 1994), p. 11; "15 jours en Libye," *Lutte du peuple* 25 (January–February 1995), pp. 8–12;

and "Quand Guenadi Zuganov soutenait la Front européen de libération," *Lutte du peuple* 31 (April–May 1996), p. 8.
34 For the FEL, see Georges Kergon, "Le Front européen de Libération," in *Rapport 1995: Panorama des actes racistes et de l'extrémisme de droite en Europe* (Paris: Centre de Recherche d'Information et de Documentation Antiraciste, 1996), pp. 219–26. See also Bouchet's interview in *The English Alternative*. For the group's own manifesto, see Troy Southgate, "The manifesto of the European Liberation Front," 1999, www.obsidian-blade.com/synthesis/articles/elf.htm (as of 29 May 2002). According to Bouchet, the FEL was designed in part to replace the Groupe du 12 Mars, an earlier international co-ordinating body that TV, the Italian group Terza Posizione, and Belgian *nouvelle droite* activist Robert Steuckers had founded in March 1988 (compare Bouchet (ed.), *Nouveaux Nationalistes*, p. 57, and Camus and Monzat, *Les Droites nationales et radicales en France*, p. 91). Note that the FEL was named after an earlier transnational fascist network called the European Liberation Front, the brainchild of one of NR's mentors, Francis Parker Yockey (see Coogan).
35 Some NR activists had earlier gone to Croatia and Bosnia to resist Serb aggression but, after NATO got militarily involved in Balkan affairs, NR began portraying Serbia as a victim of Western imperialism (see Bouchet (ed.), *Nouveaux Nationalistes*, pp. 58–9, 87; and Emma Patissier, "Aggression contre la Serbie: Crapuscule de l'Occident," *Résistance* 8, date illegible).
36 NR's manifesto stressed that revolutionary organizations could not afford to adopt a rigid structure, since they had to remain flexible enough to adapt quickly to sudden changes in the political environment. According to the circumstances, then, NR sometimes needed to act under its own name, whereas on other occasions it was necessary for it to carry out actions using the cover provided by a wide array of specialized structures or publications whose links with NR may or may not have been apparent. If the situation warranted it, NR must even be able to 'dissolve' inside larger and more influential political organizations. Moreover, NR actively encouraged its militants to join a multiplicity of other groups and parties and, once they had become members, to attain positions of responsibility inside those entities. At no time, however, were NR militants to abandon their core values or lose sight of their political objectives (see *Pour la cause du peuple*, 24–5). This clearly provided a theoretical rationale for the launching of penetration and infiltration operations against other groups, which could then, depending upon the situation, enable NR to recruit members of other groups, openly advocate certain 'lines' from inside their ranks or – in Trojan Horse fashion – covertly undermine and subvert their agendas. This last possibility must be taken seriously given the existence of a special NR section responsible for 'infiltration' and Bouchet's own later admissions: 'In order to give [the united anti-system front] substance, we were reduced to infiltrating anarchistic, ecological and regionalist groups or creating them ourselves'. As examples of NR's exercise of covert control over infiltrated organizations, he has cited the French section of Earth First!, Ecolo-J (the youth organization of the French Greens) and the French section of the Trotskyist Socialist Worker's Party (see Bouchet (ed.), *Nouveaux Nationalistes*, p. 61, and Bouchet's interview in *The English Alternative*). It is difficult for an outsider to determine just how successful this infiltration strategy actually was.
37 For this schism, see "Néo-nazisme: Les Militants nationaux-révolutionnaires rejoignent les nationaux-bolshéviques," *Réseau Voltaire*, 11 November 1996; and various materials prepared by the 'progressive wing' itself, including a 10 August 2001 e-mail sent to the author, to which were appended two documents: Bruno Gayot, 'Right of reply of the Nouvelle Résistance Association (Law of 1901) to the magazine "Résistances" (Brussels), 5 February 1999', and Laurent Baudoux, 'Right of reply of the "Front Européen de Libération" Association (Law of 1910) to the magazine "Résistances" (Brussels), 5 February 1999'. These latter sources reveal that there is an ongoing dispute between Bouchet and his rivals concerning who is legally entitled to use the names NR and FEL, even though most outside observers associate both monikers exclusively with the organizations created

by Bouchet and his faction. The 'progressives' confirm, however, that their break with Bouchet was motivated primarily by his decision to join the 'fascists' in the FN, but also note their opposition to his 'sectarian' and 'anti-Christian' activities, i.e. 'underground music, satanism and so on'.
38 Bouchet interview in *The English Alternative*, and Bouchet Questionnaire II.
39 This account is based on Bouchet Questionnaire II and several key UR publications, including: *Questions et réponses: Qu'est-ce qu'Unité Radicale* (Nantes: Ars Magna, n.d.); *Notre programme* (n.d.); *Front politique* (n.d.); and *Front international* (n.d.), all of which can be found on UR's website (www.unite-radicale.com) (as of 14 May 2002).
40 See especially *Questions et réponses*, pp. 2–6. The rest of this document discusses UR's ideological sources and international orientation, which are very similar to those of TV and NR (7–14). For UR's programme, see *Notre programme*. The group constituted, like its predecessor NR, the French section of the FEL (see *Front international*, p. 2).
41 *Questions et réponses*, pp. 6–7; *Front politique*, p. 1.
42 *Questions et réponses*, pp. 2–4; Bouchet 16 July 2001 e-mail. Bouchet himself obtained nearly 7 per cent of the vote in the most recent French district elections. For his open criticism of Mégret's anti-Islamist stance after 11 September 2001, see Esbé, "French Fascists Declare War on the Enemy Within," *Searchlight* 317 (November 2001), p. 11.
43 See *Appel aux militants des forces nationales* (Paris: CoordiNation, 2000).
44 Compare Bouchet interview in *The English Alternative* (first quote), and *Questions et réponses*, 12 (second quote).
45 *Questions et réponses*, p. 5.
46 See e.g. Christian Villa, "The Long Black Man," *Révolution européenne* 15–16 (June 1989), p. 10; "Michael Jackson: Made in USA," *Révolution européenne* 7 (June–July 1988), p. 9; Cédric Martin, "Bérurier Noir: Assis à la gauche de Goldman," *Révolution européenne* 17–18 (July–August 1989), p. 8; and Pierre Denghien, "Métal Urbaine: Les Nietzschéens du No Future," *Révolution européenne* 19 (September 1989), p. 9.
47 See e.g. "Revolte contre le monde musique: Entretien avec Tony Wakeford de Sol Invictus," *Résistance* 2 (December 1997–January 1998), pp. 31–3; Fabrice Robert, "Londinium SPQR: Un Groupe au service de l'idéal NR," *Résistance* 3 (March 1998), pp. 33–4; "Rencontre avec Kadmon du groupe Allerseelen," *Lutte du peuple* 31 (April–May 1996), p. 15; "Entretien avec Animae Mortalitas, groupe de black metal nationaliste," *Jeune Résistance* 10 (April–May 1998), pp. 10–11; "Entretien avec le groupe Frakass," *Jeune Résistance* 11 (June–July 1998), p. 10; "Entretien avec Basic Celtos," *Jeune Résistance* 15, date illegible; "Raves et techno: Un phénomène néo-européen?," *Lutte du peuple* 29 (November–December 1995), pp. 11–14; and Karl Hauffen, "Nous vivons une époque formidable: La Musique est-elle fasciste?," *Jeune Résistance* 14 (December 1998). Note, however, that, in his 3 August 1994 letter cited earlier, Bouchet emphasized that NR was linked much more closely, culturally speaking, with 'post-industrial and industrial music' circles than with skinhead Oi music fans, who 'are incapable of being organized according to Leninist principles' (reproduced in Rossi, *Jeunesse française des années 80–90*, p. 345).
48 For the links between NR and these underground music fanzines, see especially Bouchet Questionnaire II, wherein he reveals that *Napalm Rock* was an unofficial publication put out by a member of NR; that *Raven's Chat* was published by a NR sympathizer; and that *Requiem gothique* was published by another NR member; on the other hand, that NR had no connection at all to *Combat* (a fanzine put out by students in Aix-en-Provence who were mostly FN members) or *Deo Occidi* (a music zine published by neo-Nazis). Compare the journalistic accounts of Romain Rosso, "Les Profanations sont d'extrême droite," *L'Express* 2350 (18 June 1996), p. 43 (which conveniently displays a reproduction of the 'Wanted for Crimes against Humanity' poster about Jesus Christ from *Napalm Rock*, no. 4); Bourre, *Les Profanateurs*, pp. 49–50, 57–8, 64–9, 185–8; Paul Ariés, *Le Retour du diable: Satanisme, exorcisme, extrême droite* (Brussels: Golias, 1997), pp. 8, 86–7, 235–6; and Michael Moynihan and Didrik Søderlind, *Lords of Chaos: The Bloody Rise of the Satanic Metal Underground* (Venice, CA: Feral House, 1998), pp. 274, 309 ('Gungnir' quote). Moynihan's own involvement in the countercultural right-wing underground has been

documented by Kevin Coogan, "How 'Black' Is Black Metal?," *Hit List* 1:1 (February–March 1999), pp. 32–53. Not surprisingly, Moynihan's experimental band Blood Axis has frequently been promoted in Bouchet's publications (see e.g. "Rencontre avec Michael Moynihan du groupe Blood Axis," *Lutte du peuple* 32 (Spring 1996), p. 15). The most hostile accounts can be found in far-left and far-right sources, e.g. International Third Position (ITP), *Satanism and Its Allies: The Nationalist Movement under Attack* (London: Final Conflict, 1998), pp. 61–4, 73–5. The ITP was a new groupuscule created by former third-positionist Irish fascist Derek Holland after he converted to Catholic traditionalism. The aforementioned pamphlet, though chock full of vulgar Jew-baiting and gay-baiting, not to mention acute paranoia about real and imagined manifestations of satanism, nonetheless contains lots of 'inside' information that helps to shed light on important factional rifts within the radical-right milieu.

49 For a brief account of the so-called profanation of Toulon, see Ariés, *Le Retour du diable: Satanisme, exorcisme, extrême droite*, pp. 7–9. For an illuminating overview of various occult dimensions of the post-war radical right, see Nicholas Goodrick-Clarke, *Black Sun: Aryan Cults, Esoteric Nazism and the Politics of Identity* (New York: New York University Press, 2002).

50 Jean-Paul Bourre has argued that both NR's leaders and black metal extremists detested the Judaeo-Christian ethos and shared a mutual desire to 'destabilize the system, in noise and fury, like the pagan bands of ancient times' (62). This raises the thorny issue of Bouchet's longstanding personal interest in paganism, esotericism and occultism, as well as his previous association with practising occultist organizations like the Crowleyite Ordo Templi Orientis (OTO) and occult 'study groups' like the Groupe de Thèbes. Note that his doctoral thesis in ethnology (from the University of Paris VII) concerned the 'scandalous' English hedonist and magician Aleister Crowley, and was later self-published as *Aleister Crowley et le mouvement Thélèmite* (Château-Thébaud: Chaos, n.d.). Bouchet has always insisted that NR and its predecessors and successors were completely secular and included Christians, Muslims, pagans, atheists and agnostics, and that his occult and political activities were completely distinct. This does not seem to have always been true, however. While giving a lecture in Moscow to the Russian branch of the OTO, e.g., he reportedly stressed the close links between Nazism and secret societies and downplayed accounts of Nazi atrocities: see Frater Marsyas, 'Mega Therion and his books in the Russian tradition', accessible on the Pan's Asylum Camp OTO website, http://oto.ru/cgi/texteng.pl/article/texts/2 (as of 14 May 2002). While this claim cannot be independently confirmed, and has in fact been denied outright by Bouchet in a 4 September 2001 e-mail to the author, there are indications that Bouchet sometimes used his political formations as a vehicle to promote neo-pagan and anti-Christian themes. One can, e.g., find anti-Catholic attitudes in NR's publications, and not only in the music section: "Non à la secte papale! Exigeons notre retrait des registres de baptêmes!," *Lutte du peuple* 28 (September–October 1995), p. 7; and "Dehors Popaul!," *Lutte du peuple* 31 (April–May 1996), p. 10. In the same 4 September e-mail, Bouchet claimed that his harsh criticisms of Catholic traditionalist penetration of the 'national movement' were attributable not to neo-pagan animus, but rather to the longstanding French tradition of political secularism. He added that it would have been politically counterproductive for NR to have promoted neo-paganism; domestically, it would have cut the movement off from the popular masses, consigned it to a political ghetto and turned it into a political-religious sect, and, internationally, it would have interfered with NR's efforts to establish useful contacts with Arab and other Muslim groups. Yet, even though it may have been unwise for NR to promote radical neo-paganism openly or officially, this does not rule out the possibility that the organization's leaders secretly sought to make use of other, seemingly unaffiliated, groups and publications – including countercultural fanzines – to disseminate neo-pagan, anti-Christian themes.

51 Compare and contrast the attitudes expressed by Christian Bouchet, "Mai 68 et après," *Résistance* 5 (July–August 1998), pp. 6–7, and those of Bertrand, quoted in Bourseiller, *Les ennemis du système*, pp. 187–9.

52 Note the complaints by the founder of the Spanish national revolutionary rock 'n' roll label Ra-Ta-Ta-Ta, who bemoaned the fact that 'petit-bourgeois' Francoists, such as the members of Blas Piñar's party Fuerza Nueva, still condemned rock (see 'Entretien avec la label Ra-Ta-Ta-Ta', *Résistance*, no. 8, date illegible). This lament was echoed by Gregory Ombrouck (alias 'Gungnir'), the editor of *Napalm Rock*: 'In France nationalist movements (with the exception of Nouvelle Résistance) ignore rock music and culture in general' (quoted in Moynihan and Søderlind, 310). This statement was not entirely true, since long before the mid-1990s various neo-fascist groupuscules were seeking to promote and exploit Oi music for their own political purposes, and it is even less true today, now that elements within the 'bourgeois' FN are busily promoting Rock Identitaire Français.

53 For the (sometimes violent) disputes between minority pro-protester and majority anti-protester elements within the neo-fascist milieu following the outbreak of left-wing student protests in 1968, see note 12, *supra*, and the accounts of Adalberto Baldoni, *La destra in Italia, 1945–1969* (Rome: Pantheon, 2000), pp. 587–602; and Nicola Rao, *Neofascisti! La destra italiana da Salò a Fiuggi nel ricordo dei protagonisti* (Rome: Settimo Segillo, 1999), pp. 115–26. These same sources also discuss the emergence of early left-fascist groupuscules in the 1960s and/or 1970s, as do Orazio Ferrara, *Il mito negato da Giovane Europa ad Avanguardia di popolo: La destra eretica negli anni settanta* (Sarno: Centro Studi I Diòscuri, 1996); Giorgio Cingolani, *La destra in armi: Neofascisti italiani tra ribellismo ed eversione, 1977–1982* (Rome: Riuniti, 1996); Günter Bartsch, *Revolution von rechts? Ideologie und Organisation der Neuen Rechten* (Freiburg: Herder, 1975); Karl-Heinz Pröhuber, *Die nationalrevolutionäre Bewegung in Westdeutschland* (Hamburg: Deutsch-Europäischer Studien, 1980); and Marco Revelli, "La nuova destra," in *La destra radicale*, ed. by Franco Ferraresi (Milan: Feltrinelli, 1984), pp. 119–214. For the 'Hobbit Camps' in Italy, see 'Giuseppe Bessarione' [pseud.] (ed.), *Lambro/Hobbit: La cultura giovanile di destra in Italia e in Europa* (Rome: Arcana, 1979); and Apiù Mani, *Hobbit/Hobbit* (Rome: LEDE, 1982). In Spain, this cultural shift began somewhat later, in the 1980s (see Colectivo Karl-Otto Paetel). Ironically, Bouchet was rather atypical for a left fascist in as much as he was politically and culturally hostile to the New Left from the outset and has remained so until the present day. This antithetical attitude was also reflected in NR's publications (e.g. see M.A., "Un contre mai 68," *Jeune Résistance*, no. 12 [between July and December 1998], wherein the events of that era are characterized as 'a vast buffoonery led by overly spoiled rich kids').

54 For the thesis that fascism was a political 'latecomer' in a European context in which the 'political space' on the left side of the spectrum had already been 'pre-empted' by other movements and parties, see Juan J. Linz, "Some Notes toward a Comparative Study of Fascism in Sociological-Historical Perspective," in *Fascism: A Reader's Guide*, ed. by Walter Laqueur (Berkeley: University of California Press, 1978), especially 4–8. In post-war Argentina, on the other hand, there was no 'political space' available on the right side of the spectrum, so Perón moved to the left. Although he never sought to establish a regime of the fascist type, his *justicialismo* doctrine closely resembled fascism from a purely ideological standpoint. A. James Gregor has gone further and argued that many post-war Third World regimes were more akin to fascism than communism, despite their leftist veneer: see his provocative work, *The Fascist Persuasion in Radical Politics* (Princeton: Princeton University Press, 1974).

CONTENTS OF VOLUME II

The Darkest Sides of Politics, II: State Terrorism, "Weapons of Mass Destruction," Religious Extremism, and Organized Crime

Jeffrey M. Bale

1 Terrorists as state "Proxies": separating fact from fiction
2 South Africa's Project Coast: "Death Squads," covert state-sponsored poisonings, and the dangers of CBE proliferation
3 Cults and external social control: The covert political operations of Sun Myung-Moon's Unification church
4 Apocalyptic Millenarian Groups: Assessing the Threat of Biological Terrorism
5 Jihādist ideology and strategy and the possible employment of WMD
6 Islamism and totalitarianism
7 Denying the link between Islamist ideology and Jihādist terrorism: "Political Correctness" and the undermining of counterterrorism
8 "Nothing to Do with Islam"?: The terrorism and atrocities of the Islamic State in Iraq and Greater Syria are inspired and justified by its interpretations of Islam
9 Ahmad Rassam and the December 1999 "Millennium Plot"
10 Some problems with the notion of a "Nexus" between ideological terrorists and criminals

INDEX

Abate, Antonio 289
Absil, Jean-Claude 97
academicians, mirror imaging and 6–7
Académie Européenne de Sciences Politiques (AESP: European Academy of Political Sciences) 316–17
Accame, Giano 143, 277
Action Committee to Keep Reggio the Capital (Comitato d'Azione per Reggio Capoluogo) 249
Action Française (French Action) 141, 471
action psychologique 137, 139, 144
action squads 225
Adams, Nathan M. 427–8
ADÜTDF *see* Avrupa Demokratik Ülkücü Türk Dernekleri Federasyonu (ADÜTDF: European Federation of Democratic Turkish Idealist Clubs)
Afrikaner Broederbond (AB) 53
Ağca, Mehmet Ali 411, 437; ADÜTDF links of 423–4; arrest/trial of 421–2; birth of 419; Bozkurt subgroup of 419; Bulgaria meetings/activities of 423; Bulgarian links of 426–30; higher education of 420; high school influences on 419; introduction to 411–12, 415–16; İpekçi murder and 421; KINTEX links to 426–8; letter to *Milliyet* 425; lifestyle/activities of, post İpekçi assassination 421–2; political/ideological background of 416–18; prison escape of 422; statements by, truthfulness of 425–6; Turkey escape into Iran by 422–3; Turkey ultranationalist right links of 418–30; Uğurlu and 419–20
Agence Internationale de Presse (International Press Agency) 140; *see also* Aginter Presse
Agencia Internacional de la Prensa (AIP: International Press Agency) 162
Agenzia Oltremare (Overseas Agency) 143
Aginter Presse 136–45, 236, 376; Black International and 150–1; components of 141; correspondents, network of 142–3; *guerre révolutionnaire* methods and 136–9, 144; Guillou and 139–41, 143–4; history of 143–5; MFA and 140; neo-fascist groups associated with 142; overview of 139–45; PCS/ML and 144–5; personnel recruited for 141–2; strategy of tension 143–4
Ahmad, Feroz 420, 438
Aide Mutuelle Européenne (European Mutual Aid) 98
Aid Organization for War Wounded (Hjelpeorganisasjonen for Krigsskadede) 85
Aissiou, Akli 98
Aivazov, Todor 423
Aktion Neue Rechte (ANR: New Right Action) 83
Albano, Antonio 439
Albertini, Georges 86
"Alberto Pollio" Institute for Historical and Military Studies (Istituto di Studi Storici e Militari "Alberto Pollio") 153

Aleandri, Paolo 270–1, 294, 298, 310, 399
Alemanno, Antonio 287
Alemany, Alfredo Blas 161
Algérie Française 138
Allavena, Giovanni 270
Allende, Salvador 163, 281
Allerseelen 479
Almirante, Giorgio 146, 369
Almirón, Eduardo 163
al-Nāsir, Jamāl 77
Aloja, Giuseppe 153
Alparslan Türkeş' Milliyetçi Hareket Partisi (MHP: Nationalist Action Party) 414, 416, 429–39; anti-Western sentiments 437; Atatürk and 430–1; CKMP and 433; as defender of Islam 437–8; historical development of 430–6; ideologies of 436–9; organizational structure of 435; pan-Turkism and 431–3; paramilitary training camps of 435–6; Türkeş and formation of 433–6; Turkism, described 431
al-Qāʻida 466
Altalyı, Enver 423, 429
Altamirano, Carlos 162
Alternativa Europea 476
Althusser, Louis 18
Amato, Mario 309
Amaudruz, Gaston-Armand 69, 236
Amaudruz, Guy 86, 89–91, 93–4
American Front 476
American Nazi Party (ANP) 151
American Sociological Association (ASA) 8
Amis du Grand Reich Allemand (AGRA: Friends of the Great German Empire) 95
Amitiés Belgo-Katangaises (Belgian-Katangan Friendship) 96
anarchists, Bertoli and 372–4
Anders, Władysław 291
Anderson, Massimo 248
Andreotti, Giulio 168, 305, 314–17, 320–2, 400
Anello 290–2
Anfuso, Filippo 219
Angleton, James Jesus 214–15, 217, 285, 318
Animae Mortalitas 479
Anneli, Seja 371
Anselmi, Tina 295
Anti-Bolshevik Bloc of Nations (ABN) 98
anti-Bolshevik internationals 63
Antico, Franco 255, 264, 298
anti-extremism variant, Borghese Coup and 302–3
Anti-Komintern (Anti-Comintern) 63

anti-leftist variant, Borghese Coup and 301–2
Antiterrorismo ETA (ETA Anti-Terrorism) 143
Anti-Terrorist Liberation Groups (Grupos Antiterroristas de Liberación (GAL)) 158
Appareil Mondial Secret d'Action Révolutionnaire (AMSAR: Secret World Apparatus for Revolutionary Action) 168
Apter, David E. 20
Arbeitsgemeinschaft Nationaler Gruppen (ANG: Syndicate of National Groups) 69
Arendt, Hannah 20–1
Argentine Secretaría de Inteligencia de Estado (SIDE: State Intelligence Secretariat) 163
Argoud, Antoine 96
Arista, Gino 253
Arkan 479
Armand, Martín 370
Armed Forces Intelligence Service (Servizio Informazioni Forze Armate (SIFAR)) 153
Armed Forces Movement (Movimento das Forças Armadas (MFA)) 140
Armed Revolutionary Cells (Nuclei Armati Rivoluzionari (NAR)) 399
Aron, Raymond 22, 25
Aschenauer, Rudolf 67
Asociación Argentina-Europea 87
Association for Fighting Communism in Turkey (Türkiye Komünizmle Mücadele Derneği(TKMD)) 432
Association of National Socialist Confederates (Verband Nationalsozialistischer Eidgenossen) 86
Association of Volunteers for the Crusade 85
Associazione Amici delle Forze Armate (Friends of the Armed Forces Association) 306
Associazione Nazionale Arditi d'Italia (National Special Forces Association of Italy) 217
Associazione Nazionale Combattenti Italiani di Spagna (ANCIS: National Association of Italian Veterans in Spain) 217
Associazione Paracadutisti Italiani (API: Italian Paratrooper Association) 217
Atatürk, Kemal 430–1, 437–8
Atlantic Alliance 64, 288–9, 300
Atlanticism 217, 219, 305, 400
Atlantic Pact Security Office (Ufficio Sicurezza Patto Atlantico (USPA)) 287
Atsız, Hüseyin Nihal 431–3

Auslandsorganisation (AO: Foreign Organization) 69
Austrian Freedom Party (Freiheitliche Partei Österreich (FPÖ)) 83
Austrian Social Movement (Österreichische Soziale Bewegung) 87
authoritarianism 29
authoritarian states 3
Avanguardia Nazionale (AN: National Vanguard) 142, 145, 147, 151, 161, 234, 380, 400; Fronte Nazionale and 235–6
Avrupa Demokratik Ülkücü Türk Dernekleri Federasyonu (ADÜTDF: European Federation of Democratic Turkish Idealist Clubs) 422–4
Ay, Ömer 421–2, 424
Ayoub, Serge 473
Azores Liberation Front (Frente de Libertaçao das Açores (FLA)) 143
Azzi, Nico 175

Babenberg Fellowship (Kameradschaft Babenberg) 83
Bağcı, Ömer 424
Ballesteros, Manuel 87
Bánzer Suárez, Hugo 164
"Barbarigo" battalion 214
Barbasetti, Giuseppe 238
Barbie, Klaus 71, 79, 164–5
Barbieri, Domenico 255
Bardèche, Maurice 69, 86–9
Bartoli, Andrea 9
Bar-Zohar, Michael 67
Basic Celtos 479
Batskin 473, 478
Battaini, Sigfrido 291
Baugé-Prévost, Jacques 94
Baumann, Jean 90
Bauverd, Jean-Maurice 69, 94
Bauwens, Raoul 96, 100
Bavarian Illuminati 49
Beck-Broichsitter, Helmut 68
Belgian Fascist Revolutionary Movement (Mouvement Révolutionnaire Fasciste Belge) 93
Belgian-Katangan Friendship (Amitiés Belgo-Katangaises) 96
Belgian National Party (Parti National Belge) 96
Belgique-Congo (CADBA publication) 95–6
Bell, Daniel 8, 21–2
Beltrametti, Eggardo 153, 170, 231, 276
Benelli, Giovanni 277
Benet, Miguel Gómez 148
Bensi, Giovanni 412

Benvenuto, Pietro 254
Bergermayer, Anton 83
Berkenkruis (SMF publication) 84
Berlinguer, Enrico 367
Bernard, Henri 86
Bernardini, Armand 140
Berti, Luciano 253
Bertoli, Gianfranco 366–85; activities prior to grenade attack 369–72; anarchists and 372–4; grenade attack May 1973, Milan police headquarters 366–9; as informant 383–4; overview of 364–6; parallel 'action' networks in Italy and 378–82; secret service links 374–8
Bertolo, Amedeo 369, 371
Bérurier Noir 478
Biamonte, Thomas 283
Bianchini, Guido 247
Bianco, Marcella 327
Biazzo, Corrado 258
Bidault, Georges 139
Bilderberg Group 314–15
Binet, René 69, 86, 89–93
black bombardier 156, 161, 164–5
Black International 365–6
Black International, Italian components of 145–75; Aloja and 153–4; Avanguardia Nazionale and 145, 147; characteristics of 149; Delle Chiaie and 147–8, 151–2, 156–66; Freda and 145, 148–9, 152, 166–7; Giannettini and 167–70; *guerre révolutionnaire* doctrine and 170–4; OAS connections to 150–1; Ordine Nuovo and 145–7; overview of 145–6; Rauti and 145–7, 149–51, 153–6; Signor P affair 155–6; strategy of tension and 174–5; Townley and 161–2; Western security/intelligence service collaboration by 152–3
Black Prince *see* Borghese, Junio Valerio
Blackstock, Paul W. 407
Blanco, Luis Carrero 157
Blanqui, Auguste 472
Bodilis, Gaël 478
Boeynants, Paul Vanden 317
Boffelli, Giorgio 384
Bolton, Kerry 476
Bonaparte, Napoleon 17
Bonifacio, Henri 86
Bonnet, Gabriel 97
Bonomi, Aldo 369
Bordes, Gérard 98
Bordoni, Carlo 322
Borghese, Junio Valerio 148, 157, 212–13, 365; *see also* Borghese Coup, December

1970 Rome; Fronte Nazionale (FN: National Front); CIA and 217–18; Decima MAS and 213–15; financial scheme involvement of 223–4; military background of 213–14; MSI career of 218–23; prison release of 216–17; subversive plot involvement of 224–5; war crimes trial 215–16
Borghese Coup, December 1970 Rome 212–327; American support for 280–1; Andreotti and 314–17, 320–2; anti-democratic rightists and 300–1; background to 213–25; counterorder, Borghese issuance of 296–9; De Felice brothers and 306–14; De Jorio and 305–6, 322–3; establishment manipulation theory and 303–5; exposure/investigation of 261–3; forces involved in, aims of 299–326; National Front 225–51; NATO involvement in 279–80; Nixon and 281–4, 325–6; operational linkages with 326–7; overview of 212–13; Piazza Fontana bombings and 326–7; security forces investigations of 263–96; Sindona and 317–22; state manipulation theory and 301–3; "Tora Tora" operation 251–61, 299–300; Triangle plan and 292–3
Bormann, Martin 65, 73
Borsi di Parma, Vittorio Emmanuele 267–8, 275
Bottari, Mario 256
Botto, Ernesto 219
Bouchet, Christian 471, 473; *see also* Nouvelle Résistance (NR)
Boudon, Raymond 22–3
bourgeois ideologies 18–19
Bourseiller, Christophe 480
Boussart, René 98
Bozkurtlar (Gray Wolves) 413, 421, 430
Bozzini, Massimo 258
Brennan, Earl 318
British National Socialist Movement (NSM) 151
Brixia 479
Brockdorff, Werner 72
Brodhead, Frank 413, 418, 426, 436; *see also* Ağca, Mehmet Ali
Brosio, Manlio 277
the Brotherhood (Die Bruderschaft) 66–70
Die Bruderschaft (the Brotherhood) 66–70
Brune, Jean 142
Brunner, Alois 71, 79
Brzezinski, Zbigniew 13, 21
Bulgarian Komitet za Darzhavna Sigur'nost (KDS: Committee for State Security) 413

Bund Heimattreuer Deutscher (BHD: Federation of Patriotic Germans) 68
Bürger-und Bauerninitiative (BBI: Townsman and Countryman Initiative) 68
Buscaroli, Piero 277
Buscetta, Tomasso 236

Cacciuttolo, Antonio 264
Cagnoni, Angelo 243, 254
Calabresi, Luigi 367
Calcaterra, Francesco 254
Calderone, Antonino 236
Calderone, Giuseppe "Pippo" 236
Calle de Atocha massacre 161
Callejas, Inés Mariana 162
Calore, Sergio 160, 296, 307, 310, 399
Calvi, Clara 322
Calvi, Roberto 321–2
Calzolari, Armando 244–7
Calzolari, Maria Pia 245–6
Calzona, Giuseppe 158
Campo, Flavio 235, 255
Candía, Alfredo Ovando 164
Capanna, Enzo 255
Cappellini, Esperio 242
Cardellini, Sergio 256
Cardoso, Rua António Maria 140
Carmassi, Pietro 256
Carrasco, Jorge 161
Carret, David 384
Casardi, Mario 267–8, 368
Casero, Giuseppe 253
Cash, Johnny 478
Casson, Felice 381
Çatlı, Abdullah 421–2
Cauchi, Augusto 158–9
Cavallaro, Roberto 287, 316, 379–81
Cavallo, Luigi 276, 319, 321
Çaylan, Yavuz 419, 421
Çelebi, Musa Serdar 422–4, 429
Çelenk, Bekir 423, 427, 430
Çelik, Oral 419, 422–4, 426
Cellules Communistes Combattantes (CCC) 103
Central Documentation Service of the President of the Government (Servicio Central de Documentación de la Presidencia de Gobierno (SECED)) 157–8
Central Institute for Intelligence and Special Duties (Israeli Mossad Letafkidim Meyouchadim (Mossad)) 415
Central Intelligence Agency (CIA) 46, 54, 71, 217–18, 319, 414–15, 429

Centre d'Études et de Formation Contre-Révolutionnaire (Counter-Revolutionary Studies and Training Center) 97
Centre d'Études Supérieures de Psychologie Sociale (CESPS: Social Psychology Higher Studies Center) 97, 138
Centro Italiano Documentazione Azione Studi (CIDAS: Italian Documentation Center for Studies of Action) 277
Centro Studi Ordine Nuovo (CSON: New Order Study Center) 145–6, 221
Cercle Pinay 316–17
Cercle Proudhon 471
Cerica, Guglielmo 224
Cesarsky, Jorge 159
Chairoff, Patrice 85
Chamberlain, Houston Stewart 94
Château-Jobert, Pierre 138–9
Chilean Dirección de Inteligencia Nacional (DINA: National Intelligence Directorate) 161–3
Christiansen, Rolf 85
Christophersen, Thies 68
CIA *see* Central Intelligence Agency (CIA)
Ciabatti, Dante 254, 297
Ciammarucconi, Giuseppe 86
Cicuttini, Carlo 158, 175
Ciolfi, Gennaro 254
Circolo Anarchico Ponte della Ghisolfa 369
Circolo Nestor Machno (anarchist group) 369
Círculo Español de Amigos de Europa (CEDADE: Spanish Circle of Friends of Europe) 142, 151–2, 161
Cirillo, Ciro 291–2
Cité Catholique 138
Civic Action Movement (Mouvement d'Action Civique (MAC)) 95–9
Clavero, Antonio 161
Clavio, James D. 283–4
Cline, Ray S. 412
Codreanu, Corneliu 71
Cohn, Norman 52
Coleman, Peter T. 9
Collectif National de Coordination 477
collectivism 28
Coltellacci, Roman 157
Comitati Civici (Civic Committees) network 217
Comitato d'Azione per Reggio Capoluogo (Action Committee to Keep Reggio the Capital) 249
Comité d'Action et de Défense des Belges en Afrique (CADBA: Committee for Action and Defense of the Belgians in Africa) 95
Comité d'Action Républicaine (CAR) 471
Comité Français National (CNF: French National Committee) 86–7
Comité Tixier-Vignancourt (Tixier-Vignancourt Committee) 142
Committee for Action and Defense of the Belgians in Africa (Comité d'Action et de Défense des Belges en Afrique (CADBA)) 95
Committee for State Security (Bulgarian Komitet za Darzhavna Sigur'nost (KDS)) 413
Committee for State Security (Soviet Komitet Gosudarst'vennoy Bezopasnosti (KGB)) 413–14
Committee of National Unity (Millî Birlik Komitesi (MKB)) 433
communist ideologies 18
Communist Party of Turkey (Türkiye Komünist Partisi (TKP)) 435
Communitarian Action Front (Front d'Action Communautaire) 86
Comrades' Alliance (Das Kameradenwerk) 66–7
Concutelli, Pierluigi 153, 158, 160, 162, 296, 309
Condò, Giuseppe 298, 323
Conesa, Roberto 160
Confederacion Española de Derechas Autónomas (CEDA: Spanish Confederation of Autonomous Right-Wing Groups) 223–4
Confederación Nacional de Ex-Combatientes (National Federation of Former Soldiers) 85
Confederation of European Communitarian Labor Unions (Union des Syndicats Communautaires Européens) 100
Confederazione Italiana Sindacato Nazionale Lavoratori (CISNAL) 371
Conscience Européenne (Thiriart-inspired publication) 102–3
Conseil National de la Résistance (National Resistance Council) 139
conspiracies: *vs.* conspiracy theories 51–2; defined 50
conspiracy theories/theorists 46–7; *vs.* actual conspiracies 51–2; beliefs of 48–50, 53–4; characteristics of 48, 50; Grand Conspiracies of 52–3; Kossy on 50; scholarly publications related to 47–8; umbrella man and 50

conspiratorial groups: as Evil Incarnate 48–9; as monolithic and unerring 49; as motive force of historical change and development 50; as omnipotent 49; as omnipresent 49
conspiratorial paranoia 29–30
conspiratorial politics 50–1
containment strategy 61
Contreras, Juan Manuel 161–2
Corbi, Loris 321
Corniani, Umberto 292
Correia, Costa 140
Corriere della Sera 290
Cortivo, Paolo 268
Corvo, Max 318
Cossu, Giulio 248
Costituente Nazionale Rivoluzionaria (CNR: Revolutionary National Constituent Assembly) 234
Costruiamo l'Azione (Let's Take Action) 399
Cosyns-Verhaegen, Roger 98
Cot, Georges 142
Counterrevolutionary Combat Movement (Mouvement de Combat Contre-Révolutionnaire) 139
Counter-Revolutionary Studies and Training Center (Centre d'Études et de Formation Contre-Révolutionnaire) 97
Covisa, Mariano Sánchez 148, 157
Crescenzi, Giulio 255
critical conceptions of ideology 16, 22
critical theorists 16
Crozier, Brian 276
Cuartero, Miguel 277
Cuesta, Raimundo Fernández 157
Cumhuriyetçi Köylü Millî Partisi (CKMP: Republican Peasant Nation Party) 433
Curutchet, Jean-Marie 96

Dalla Chiesa, Carlo 292
D'Amato, Federico Umberto 156, 240, 272–3, 298, 308, 323, 325
D'Ambrosio, Vincenzo 254
Damman, Florimond 142, 316
Danish Front Fighters' Association (Dansk Frontkämpfer Forbund) 85
Danish Reform Movement (Dansk Reform Bewegelse) 86–7
D'Annunzio, Gabriele 221
Dansk Frontkämpfer Forbund (Danish Front Fighters' Association) 85
Dansk Reform Bewegelse (Danish Reform Movement) 86–7

Dantini, Enzo Maria 307
Dastier, René 99
D'Aubuisson, Roberto 164
De Angelis, Alessandro 258
de Barcellos, José 142
Debbaudt, Jean-Robert 90
de Bergard, Hubert 94
de Boccard, Enrico 170
De Capei, Alessandro Uboldi 277
De Carolis, Massimo 291, 321
de Carvalho, Armando Marques 142
de Castera, Guy d'Avezac 142
Decima Flottiglia MAS (10th Assault Vehicle Flotilla) 213–14; unique aspects of 214–15
De Felice, Alfredo 276, 294–5, 306–7
De Felice, Fabio 271, 294–5, 298, 306–13
De Felice, Renzo 481
de Figueirede, José Valle 142
De Gasperi, Alcide 215–16, 313–14
de Gaulle, Charles 230–1, 364
de Gobineau, Joseph Arthur 94
Degrelle, Léon 71, 74
dehumanization of designated enemies 29
De Jorio, Filippo 271, 276, 278, 294–5, 305–6, 322–3
de Lapouge, Georges Vacher 94
Del Grande, Umberto 369
De Lillo, Marcello 265
Dell'Amico, Lando 277
Delle Chiaie, Stefano 147–8, 151–2, 156–66, 235–6, 255, 307
De Lorenzo, Giovanni 153, 212, 270, 272, 287, 306
Delplace, José 97
Delta Front (Fronte Delta) 234
Del Valle, Pedro 168
de Maistre, Joseph 97
De Marchi, Giancarlo 261, 380
De Marco, Franco 248
de Marenches, Alexandre 412
De Marsanich, Augusto 87, 218
democratic states 3
Democrazia Cristiana (DC) 365
Demokrat Parti (DP: Democrat Party) 432
demonization of designated enemies 29
Depret, Jacques 142
Der Einzige und sein Eigentum (Stirner) 380
Der Freiwillige (HAIG publications) 82
de Rivera, José Antonio Primo 98
De Rosa, Giovanni 253, 274
De Roux, Dominique 168
Der Wiking-Ruf (HAIG publications) 82
De Sario, Giacomo 234

designated enemies, dehumanization/
  demonization of 29
de Spínola, António 77–8
Destructive Proletarian Group (Gruppo
  Proletario Eversivo) 322
Destutt de Tracy, Antoine 16–17, 22
Deutsche Bank 65
Deutsche Gemeinschaft (DG: German
  Association) 68
Deutsche Reichspartei (DRP: German
  Reich Party) 68
Deutsches Kulturwerk Europäischen Geistes
  (DKEG: German Cultural Association
  for the European Spirit) 68
Deutsche Soziale Bewegung (DSB) 87
Deutsche Union (DU: German Union) 68
Deutsche Volksunion (DVU: German
  Peoples' Union) 68
Devrimçi Sol (DEV-SOL: Revolutionary
  Left) 420
de Vuyst, Peter 84
Die Kameradschaft (newsletter) 83
Die Organisation der ehemaligen
  SS-Angehörigen (ODESSA:
  Organization of Former SS Members)
  66–7
Die Wochenzeitung (National Democratic
  Party publication) 83
Digilio, Carlo 383
Dikici, Mustafa 422
Di Lalla, Antonietta 371
Dillen, Karel 87
Di Luia, Serafino 151
Di Martino, Fabio 258
di Montereale, Alliata 277
Directed Operational Cell (Nucleo
  Operativo Diretto (NOD)) 266
disinformation campaigns 412–13
Dobbs, Michael 413
Dokuz Işık (Türkeş pamphlet) 434
Dominici, Carmelo 250
Dominioni, Rolando 378
Dönitz, Karl 213
Dörner, Hermann 73
D'Orsi, Agostino 267
Drago, Salvatore 239–40, 254
Dresdner Bank 65
Drug Enforcement Administration (DEA)
  165–6, 427
Dubois, Yves-Marc 316–17
Dugin, Aleksandr 476
Dulles, Allen 71, 77, 217, 319
Dumont, Claude 97
Dumont, Serge 98
Durkheim, Émile 20
Dutch Social Movement (Nederlandse
  Sociale Beweging) 87

Eatwell, Roger 12–13, 15
École Internationale de Cadres Anti-
  Communistes (International School for
  Anti-Communist Cadres) 97
Eichmann, Adolph 68, 71, 73, 79
Eisele, Hans 67
Eisenhower, Dwight D. 73
Elisabeth, "Mother" Helene 67
Engdahl, Per 86–7
Engels, Friedrich 17–18
Enlai, Zhou 102
Erbakan, Necmettin 438
Erra, Enzo 146
Escrivá de Balaguer, José María 224
establishment manipulators 303–4, 364
Establishment of Social Peace (Soziale
  Friedenswerk) 67
ETA Anti-Terrorism (Antiterrorismo ETA)
  143
Ethnike Stratiotike Astinomia (ESA:
  National Military Police) 157
Ethnikos Syndesmos Ellenon Spudaston
  Italias (ESESI: League of Greek
  Nationalist Students in Italy) 151, 250
Etudes Techniques et Commerciales
  (ETEC) 377
Étudiants Nationalistes Français (National
  French Students) 96
Europa Civiltà (European Civilization) 234
Europäische Verbindungstelle (EVS:
  European Liaison Office) 89
European Academy of Political Sciences
  (Académie Européenne de Sciences
  Politiques (AESP)) 316–17
European Civilization (Europa Civiltà) 234
European Communitarian Party (Parti
  Communautaire Européen (PCE)) 101
European Federation of Democratic
  Turkish Idealist Clubs (Avrupa
  Demokratik Ülkücü Türk Dernekleri
  Federasyonu (ADÜTDF)) 422–4
European Liaison Office (Europäische
  Verbindungstelle (EVS)) 89
European Mutual Aid (Aide Mutuelle
  Européenne) 98
European *Ordnungsmacht* 63
European Revolution (Révolution
  Européenne) 100
European Social Democratic Party (Partito
  Socialdemocratico Europeo (PSDE)) 277

European Social Movement (Mouvement Social Européen/Europäische Sozialbewegung (MSE/ESB)) 84–90
European Working Group in the Low Countries (Werkgemeenschap Europa in de Lage Landen) 87
Evil Incarnate, conspirators as 48–9
Evola, Giulio Cesare ("Julius") 145–6, 308, 405
Exército de Libertação Português (ELP: Portuguese Liberation Army) 143
external lung 474
extremism: authoritarianism and 29; Coleman and Bartoli definition of 9; collectivism and 28; conspiratorial paranoia and 29–30; defining characteristics of 9–10; dehumanization/demonization of designated enemies and 29; vs. extremist 8–9; of goals 10; hyper-moralism and 28; ideological, characteristics of 27–30; Manicheanism and 27; of means 10–11; monism and 27; Taylor on 10; totalitarianism and 29; utopianism and 27–8
extremist: characteristics of 8–9; vs. extremism 8–9; Himmelstein on 8–9; Hoffer on 9–10; as relational term 9; Wilcox on 10; Wintrobe on 10
extremophile 2

Fabruzzi, Fausto 151
Fachini, Massimiliano 175, 309, 312
Faedrelandet 86
Faenza, Roberto 225
Falange Española 161
false consciousness 18
false flag operations 149, 154, 366, 417–18
Fanali, Duilio 238, 259, 275–9
fanaticism, descriptive characteristics of 10
Farago, Ladislas 67
Farvo, Augusta 371
Fasci di Azione Rivoluzionaria (FAR: Revolutionary Action Fasci) 146
fascism, characterizations of 480–3
fascist internationals 63
Fatherland and Freedom National Front (Frente Nacional Patria y Libertad) 281
Fédération des Étudiants Nationalistes (FEN) 142
Fédération Général des Étudiants Européens (General Federation of European Students) 100
Federation of Austrian Fellowships (Verband Österreichischer Kameradschaften) 83
Federation of Patriotic Germans (Bund Heimattreuer Deutscher (BHD)) 68
Federation of Republican National Veterans (Federazione Nazionale Combattenti Repubblicani (FNCR)) 217
Federazione Nazionale Combattenti della Repubblica Sociale Italiana (FNCRSI: National Federation of RSI Veterans) 223
Federazione Nazionale Combattenti Repubblicani (FNCR: Federation of Republican National Veterans) 217
Federazione Universitaria Cattolici Italiani (FUCI: University Federation of Italian Catholics) 313
Federlini, Luigi 233
Feldmühle paper company 74
Fenwich, Hugh 241, 283–4, 323, 325
Ferrari, Dorrello 171
Ferreira, Moniz 94
Ferreira, Zarco Moniz 90, 142, 149, 152
Feuer, Lewis S. 20, 22
Fiebelkorn, Joachim 165
Finaldi, Gianfranco 170
Finer, Leslie 155
Finnish Social Movement (Suomen Sociallinen Liike (SSL)) 87
Fiorani, Guido 254
Fioravanti, Giuseppe Valerio ("Giusva") 399–400
Fiore, Filippo 230
Fischer, David Hackett 54
Fischer, Theodor 86
Flamini, Gianni 379–80
Fleckenstein, Edward A. 87
Flemish Association of Former East Front Fighters (Vlaams Verbond van Oud-Oostfrontstrijders) 84
Flemish Bloc (Vlaams Blok (VB)) 87
Flemish Militant Order (Vlaamse Militanten Orde (VMO)) 84
Fonjallaz, Arthur 91
Foreign Documentation and Counter-Espionage Service (Service de Documentation Extérieure et de Contre-Espionnage (SDECE)) 139
forensic ideologies 12
Forlenza, Luigi 272
Formazione Nazionale Giovanile (National Youth Training) 167
Formisano, Edoardo 296
Forsyth, Frederick 66
Fortunato, Fausto 285
Foster, Richard 277

Foundation for Former Political
Delinquents (Stichting Oud Politieke
Delinquenten (SOPD)) 84
Fraga, Manuel 159, 163, 316
Francia, Salvatore 158
Franco, Francesco ("Ciccio") 249
Franke-Gricksch, Alfred 68–9
Frankfurt School philosophers 19
Frattini, Stelio 243, 254
Freda, Giorgio ("Franco") 145, 148–9, 152,
166–7, 309, 380
Free Africa Organization (Organisation de
l'Afrique Libre) 143
Free Corps Denmark (Frikorps Danmarks)
85
Free Corps Germany (Freikorps
Deutschland) 69
Freeden, Michael 11
freedom fighting *vs.* terrorism 4–5
"Freedom for Rudolf Hess" Support
Association (Hilfsgemeinschaft Freiheit
für Rudolf Hess) 68
Freiheitliche Partei Österreich (FPÖ:
Austrian Freedom Party) 83
Freikorps Deutschland (Free Corps
Germany) 69
French Action (Action Française) 141, 471
French Cercle International de Relations
Culturelles (International Circle for
Cultural Relations) 86
French National Committee (Comité
Français National (CNF)) 86–7
Frente de Libertaçao das Açores (FLA:
Azores Liberation Front) 143
Frente de Libertaçao de Moçambique
(FRELIMO: Mozambique Liberation
Front) 145
Frente Nacional de Juventud (FNJ:
National Youth Front) 151
Frente Nacional Patria y Libertad
(Fatherland and Freedom National
Front) 281
Frey, Gerhard 68
Friedrich, Carl J. 13, 21
Friends of the Armed Forces Association
(Associazione Amici delle Forze Armate)
306
Friends of the Great German Empire
(Amis du Grand Reich Allemand
(AGRA)) 95
Frikorps Danmarks (Free Corps Denmark)
85
Front d'Action Communautaire
(Communitarian Action Front) 86

Front de Libération Nationale (FLN:
National Liberation Front) 138
Fronte Delta (Delta Front) 234
Fronte Nazionale (FN: National Front)
213, 225–51, 473; American intelligence
officials and 240–2; armed forces of
237–41; Avanguardia Nazionale and
235–6; Borghese establishment of 225–6;
Borghese use of, to launch coup 229–31;
Calzolari and 244–7; Comitato Tricolore
as 226, 230–1; coup operational plans
242–3; developmental history of 231–2;
groups linked to 234–5; ideologies of
226–8; Loi and 247–9; Mafia recruitment
into 236–7; Ordine Nuovo and 234–5;
Orientamenti Programmatici definition of
227, 229; Reggian activists of 249–51;
right-wing extremist contacts of 236–7;
secret supporters of 229–30, 233–4;
stated goals of 228–9, 233; structure of
232–3
Fronte Universitario di Azione Nazionale
(FUAN: University Front for National
Action) 86, 148
Front Européen de Libération (FEL) 475–6
Front National-Européen du Travail
(National European Labor Front) 100
Front National pour l'Algérie Français in
France (National Front for Algeria in
France) 96
Front Uni de Soutien au Sud-Vietnam 470
Fuerza Nueva (New Force) 142, 161
Fukuyama, Francis 22
Fulchignoni, Felice 291
Fumagalli, Carlo 234, 291, 367
furtive fallacy 54

Gaddi, Giuseppe 62
Gallucci, Achille 295
García, Arturo Ruiz 159
García-Rodríguez, Luis Antonio 148
Garder, Michel 276
Gardes, Jean 77
Gardy, Paul 77
Garibaldi, Giuseppe 254
Gasca Queirazza, Federico 264, 266
Gattai, Giuseppe 234
Gaudenzi, Ugo 481
Gauleiter Circle (Gauleiter-Kreis) 70
Gauleiter-Kreis (Gauleiter Circle) 70
Gauthier, Alain 142
Gayre, Robert 87
GCR 161
Gedda, Luigi 217

Gehlen, Reinhard 75, 77
Gehret, Gottlob 69
Gelli, Licio 53, 242, 308, 317, 321, 323–4, 367, 414
General Federation of European Students (Fédération Général des Étudiants Européens) 100
Geneste, Marc 276
Genoese Zerbi, Felice 249–51
Genoud, François 94
Genovese, Vito 318
Genovesi, Giorgio 264
Gerd Spindler 70
German Association (Deutsche Gemeinschaft (DG)) 68
German Cultural Association for the European Spirit (Deutsches Kulturwerk Europäischen Geistes (DKEG)) 68
German Peoples' Union (Deutsche Volksunion (DVU)) 68
German Reich Party (Deutsche Reichspartei (DRP)) 68
German Union (Deutsche Union (DU)) 68
Gherbetz, Karl 83
Ghiacci, Salvatore 255
Ghinazzi, Giovanni 295
Gianfranceschi, Fausto 146
Giannettini, Guido 152–3, 167–70, 267
Giannuli, Aldo 61
Gille, Herbert O. 68, 82
Gil Robles, José María 223
Giovane Europa 152
Girón, José Antonio 85, 148
Giudice, Raffaele 295
Giudici, Gian Maria 272
Gladio network 285
goals, extremism of 10
Godeau, Willy 96–7
Goebbel, Joseph 70
Gökenç, Hamit 422
Gómez, Arce 165
Gramsci, Antonio 18–19
Grand Conspiracies 52–3
Grandes, Agustín Muñoz 152
Gray Wolf movement 419, 423, 430
Graziani, Clemente 146, 150, 158, 172, 235, 307
Graziani, Rodolfo 220
Grillmayer, Horst 424, 429
Griner, Massimiliano 327
Gringoire 86
Grisolia, Alberto 290
Groupe Action-Jeunesse (GAJ) 472
Groupement de Recherche et d'Études sur la Civilisation Européenne (GRECE: Research and Study Group for European Civilization) 84, 471, 479
Groupes Nationalistes Révolutionnaires de Base (GNR) 472
Groupe Union Défense (GUD) 472
groupuscules: defined 466; examples of 466; fascism and 480–3; functional analysis of 468; historical analysis of 468–9; Mouvement Occident as 469–71; neglect of 466; neo-fascist, changing nature of 467–9; theoretical observations of 466–7
Grupos Antiterroristas de Liberación (GAL: Anti-Terrorist Liberation Groups) 158
Gruppi di Azione Rivoluzionaria (Revolutionary Action Groups) 147
Gruppo di Ar (Ar[yan] Group) 148–9
Gruppo Proletario Eversivo (Destructive Proletarian Group) 322
Guadagni, Benito 226, 232
Guaza, José Ignacio Fernández 159
Guderian, Heinz 68
Gueiler, Lidya 164
Guénon, René 308
Guérin-Sérac, Yves (Ralf) 139, 376; *see also* Guillou, Yves-Felix Marie
guerra rivoluzionaria 171
guerre révolutionnaire methods 136–9, 143–4, 276, 366; in Algeria 138–9; described 137; Giannettini and 169–70; Greek Army officers interest in 154–5; key characteristic of 178–9; OAS and 136, 139; as right-wing terrorism 138–9; as subversive warfare 137
Gui, Luigi 279
Guillou, Jean-Marie 142
Guillou, Yves-Felix Marie 139–41, 143–4, 150
Gündüz, Ramazan 422
Güne, Hasan Fehmi 422
Gürsel, Cemal 433
Guzzanti, Paolo 243

Haig, Alexander 315
Hamsun, Knut 85
Harrington, Patrick 476
Harvey, William 225
Hausser, Paul 68
Haussleiter, August 68
Hélie, Hugues Stéphane 142
Help for Invalid Former East Front Fighters, Next of Kin, and Political Prisoners (Hulp aan Invalide Oud-Oostfrontstrijders, Nabestaanden, Politieke Gevangenen (HINAG)) 84
Henke, Eugenio 267

Henze, Paul B. 412, 418, 420, 423, 425, 427–30, 436, 438–9; *see also* Ağca, Mehmet Ali
Hergün (MHP newspaper) 422, 439
Herman, Edward S. 413, 418, 426, 436; *see also* Ağca, Mehmet Ali
Hertog Jan Van Brabant 84
Heydrich, Reinhard 72
Heywood, Andrew 13
Higher Institute of Psychosomatic, Biological, and Racial Sciences (Institut Supérieur des Sciences Psychosomatiques, Biologiques et Raciales) 94
Hilfsgemeinschaft auf Gegenseitigkeit der ehemaligen Soldaten der Waffen-SS (HIAG: Mutual Aid Support Group for Former Waffen SS Soldiers) 81–5; in Austria 83–4; in Belgium 84; in Denmark 85; in Netherlands 84; in Spain 85
Hilfsgemeinschaft Freiheit für Rudolf Hess ("Freedom for Rudolf Hess" Support Association) 68
Himmelstein, Jerome L. 8–9
Himmler, Heinrich 63
hit teams 158
Hjelpeorganisasjonen for Krigsskadede (Aid Organization for War Wounded) 85
Hobbit Camps 481
Hoffer, Eric 9–10
Hofstadter, Richard 52
Hogard, Jacques 97
Holeindre, Roger 470
hot autumn of 1969 365
Hovden, Hroar 86
H. S. Lucht company 74, 80
Hudal, Alois 69, 314
Hulp aan Invalide Oud-Oostfrontstrijders, Nabestaanden, Politieke Gevangenen (HINAG: Help for Invalid Former East Front Fighters, Next of Kin, and Political Prisoners) 84
human behavior, social scientists and 14–16
hyper-moralism 28

Idealist Technical Worker's Association (Ülkücü Teknik Elemanlar Derneği (ÜTED)) 421
Idealist Youth Association (Ülkücü Gençlik Derneği (ÜGD)) 421
ideocracy 30
ideocrats 30
ideological extremism *see* extremism
ideological extremists: described 2–3; Smelser on 10

ideological method 20
idéologie 16
ideologies: Althusser on 18; Apter on 20; Bell on 8; bourgeois 18–19; categorizing 22–3; characteristics of 8; communist 18–19; conceptions of 16–23; definition of 11–12; Durkheim on 20; Eagleton on 8, 15; Eatwell on 12; Engels on 17–18; explanations and 23; Feuer on 20; forensic 12; Freeden on 11; Gramsci on 18–19; Kardiner on 20; latent 12; Lenin on 18; Lukács on 18; Marx on 17–18; McLellan on 8, 11; modern definitions of 23; negative characterizations of 20–1; political 13–16, 23–6; religious 25–6; Sargent on 12; Seliger on 16; Smelser on 24, 26; Solzhenitsyn on 8; termed 16–17; Thompson on 12, 16; totalitarian 20–1; traditional definitions of 23
Ideology and Politics (Seliger) 16
I. G. Farben 65
Ignazi, Piero 219
Il Borghese (rightist weekly) 233
Il Noto Servizio (the Known Service) 291
Il segreto della Repubblica (Rubini) 385
Il Tempo (Roman daily) 143, 153
Improta, Umberto 247
inclusive conceptions of ideology 16, 22
Institute for Norwegian Occupation History (Institutt for Norsk Okkupasjonhistorie) 85
Institute of Strategic and Defense Studies (Istituto di Studi Strategici e per la Difesa (ISSED)) 276
Institut Supérieur des Sciences Psychosomatiques, Biologiques et Raciales (Higher Institute of Psychosomatic, Biological, and Racial Sciences) 94
Institutt for Norsk Okkupasjonhistorie (Institute for Norwegian Occupation History) 85
International Circle for Cultural Relations (French Cercle International de Relations Culturelles) 86
International Freedom League (Ligue Internationale de la Liberté (LIL)) 98
international neo-fascist networks, postwar 60–105; Black International, Italian components of; beliefs of 62–3; characteristics of 61–2; European Social Movement (Mouvement Social Européenne) 85–90; internationals, described 60–1; Jeune Europe 94–105; Nazi escape/action organizations,

underground 64–80; New European Order (Europäische Neu-Ordnung) 90–4; overview of 60–4; state-private networks, described 61; Waffen-SS support network 80–5
International Police and Defense of the State/General Security Directorate (Polícia Internacional e de Defesa do Estado/Direcção Géral de Segurança (PIDE/DGS)) 139–40, 143
International Press Agency (Agence Internationale de Presse) 140
International Press Agency (Agencia Internacional de la Prensa (AIP)) 162
internationals, described 60–1
International School for Anti-Communist Cadres (École Internationale de Cadres Anti-Communistes) 97
Ioannides, Dimitrios 157
İpekçi, Abdi 416, 418–21; see also Ağca, Mehmet Ali
Iron Guard (Rumanian Garda de Fier) 86
Israeli Mossad Letafkidim Meyouchadim (Mossad: Central Institute for Intelligence and Special Duties) 415
Istituto di Studi Strategici e per la Difesa (ISSED: Institute of Strategic and Defense Studies) 276
Italian Communist Party (Partito Comunista Italiano (PCI)) 175, 229
Italian Documentation Center for Studies of Action (Centro Italiano Documentazione Azione Studi (CIDAS)) 277
Italian Paratrooper Association (Associazione Paracadutisti Italiani (API)) 217
Italian Servizio Informazioni Sicurezza Militare (SISMI) 414
Italian Socialist Party (Partito Socialista Italiano (PSI)) 175, 216
Italian Social Movement (Movimento Sociale Italiano (MSI)) 69, 85–6

Jackson, Michael 478
Jacob, P. Xavier 438
Jannuzzi, Raffaele 224
Janssens, Émile 97
Jemmi, Jacques 370, 376
Jemmi, Jean-Michel 370
Jeune Europe (JE: Young Europe) 89, 94–105, 142, 152, 482
Jeune Garde Socialiste (Young Socialist Guard) 95

Jeune Nation 469
Jeune Résistance (JR) 477
Jeunesses Nationales (National Youth) 96–7
Jeunesses Nationalistes-Révolutionnaires (JNR) 473
jihadist terrorist attacks 1
John Birch Society 52, 96
Johnson, William R. 46
Joly, Pierre 96–8
Jonge Wacht (Young Guard) 84
Jöntvedt, Einar 86
Jordan, Colin 151
Jordan, Frede 86
Junge Europäische Legion (JEL: Young European Legion) 93–4
Justin, Jean Emmanuel 142

Kaltefleiter, Werner 277
Kaltenbrunner, Ernst 65, 72–3
Das Kameradenwerk (Comrades' Alliance) 66–7
Kameradschaft Babenberg (Babenberg Fellowship) 83
Kameradschaft IV (Fellowship IV) 83
Kappler, Herbert 291
Kardiner, Abram 20
Kaufmann, Karl 68
Kayserbund 479
Kennedy, David M. 320
Kennedy, John F. 50, 95–6
Kernmayer, Erich 69, 82–3
KGB see Soviet Komitet Gosudarst'vennoy Bezopasnosti (KGB: Committee for State Security)
Khrushchev, Nikita 96
Kiefer, Wilhelm 69
Kielsen, Arthur 86
Kinema tes 4 Augoustou (K4A: 4th of August Movement) 142, 236
KINTEX 426–8
Kisaçik, Mustafa 427
Kissinger, Henry 282, 315, 325
Kitson, Frank 144
Klöckner AG 74
Knudsen, Franklin 86
Koçyiğit, Hoca 429
Koehl, Robert 81
Komitet Gosudarst'vennoi Bezopasnosti (KGB) 54, 103
Komma tes 4 Augoustou (K4A: 4th of August Party) 236
Kossy, Donna 50
Kottakis, Michael 155
Krause, Franz 85

Krogh, Egil ("Bud") 282
Krupp 65, 74
Kudsk, Jens 86
Kumm, Otto 68, 81
Kurşun, Mehmet 422
Kurt, İbrahim 422

Labin, Eduard 142
Labin, Suzanne 98, 142
Labruna, Antonio 156–7, 224
Lacheroy, Charles 97
La CoordiNation 477
Ladas, Ioannis 157
La disintegrazione del sistema (Freda) 152
Lagaillarde, Pierre 97, 167
La guerra non ortodossa (SIFAR manual) 169
La Morte, Gaetano 254
La Nation Européenne (PCE publication) 101
Landig, Wilhelm 87, 90
Lane, Robert E. 12, 14
Laperches, René-Georges 98
Lascorz, Charly 377
latent ideologies 12
Laurent, Frédéric 141
Laurent, Jean-Marie 142, 145, 151
La Victoire 86
Lawn, John C. 430
League of Greek Nationalist Students in Italy (Ethnikos Syndesmos Ellenon Spudaston Italias (ESESI)) 151, 250
Lecavelier, Gilbert 377
Lecerf, Émile 95, 100
Ledeen, Michael A. 412
Lefebvre d'Ovidio, Ovidio 223
Lega Italia Unità (United League of Italy) 234
Legione Nera (the Black Legion) 146
Légion Nationale (National Legion) 95
Leighton, Bernardo 162
Le mani rosse sulle Forze armate (Aloja) 153–4
Lemonnier, Guy 86
Lenin, Vladimir 18, 171
Le Pen, Jean-Marie 96
Lercari, Attilio 275, 288
Lerner, Max 15
Le Rouxel, Henri 142
Leroy, Robert 77, 236
Leroy, Robert-Henri 141–2, 145
Letelier, Orlando 163
L'Étincelle (PCS/ML paper) 145
Liaison Committee for Revolutionary Nationalists 476
Liggio, Luciano 236–7

Ligini, Marco 248
Ligue Internationale Anticommuniste (International Anti-Communist League) 63
Ligue Internationale de la Liberté (LIL: International Freedom League) 98
Lillo, Ramón 161
Limonov, Eduard 476
Lipset, Seymour Martin 21
Ljungberg, Bengt Olov 86
Llopart, Juan 476
Lockheed Aircraft Corporation 279
Loggia Massonica Propaganda Due (P2) 53
Loi, Evelino 247–9
Lombardi, Antonio 381
Lombardi, Francesco 253, 260
Lombardo, Ivan Matteo 276
Lonciari, Fabio 86
Londinium SPQR 479
London Observer 155
Lopes, Gomes 168
López Rega, José 163
Lords of Chaos 479
Lo Vecchio, Giuseppe 253, 259
Lucas, Scott 61
Luce, Clare Booth 283
Luci, Lionello 369
Luciano, "Lucky" 318
Lukács, György 18
Lunetta, Gaetano 242–3, 255, 271, 273, 279, 284, 326
Lutte du Peuple 472
Lutte du peuple (NR journal) 473

Maceratini, Giulio 235
Macridis, Roy C. 14
Madonna 478
Maggi, Carlo Maria 175, 384
Maggioranza Silenziosa (Silent Majority) 234
Magnino, Leo 276
Magri, Massimo 369
Main Rouge (Red Hand) 98, 139
Maletti, Gianadelio 156–7, 242, 266–7
Malliarakis, Jean-Gilles 472
"Malloppone" report 267
Mambro, Francesca 400
Mānī 27
Manicheanism 27
"Manifeste à la Nation Européenne" (Thiriart) 99–100
Mannheim, Karl 19
Mao Zedong 136, 171, 228, 404
Marchesi, Enzo 265

Marcianò, Paolo 250
Marcinkus, Paul 283
Marcuse, Herbert 19
Mariantoni, Alberto 255
Marinotti, Franco 368
Martel, Robert 96
Martella, Ilario 425
Martin, Graham A. 282–4, 286
Marx, Karl 17–18
Marxists 13, 16, 19–20
Massagrande, Elio 153, 157–8, 160–1, 164, 175, 292, 310
Massi, Ernesto 87, 221
materialistic societies, mirror imaging and 6
Mathieu, Guy 142
Matta, Gavino 295–6
Maurras, Charles 141
May 13th Popular Movement (Mouvement Populaire du 13 Mai (MP13)) 96–8
Mazzari, Ugo 242
McCaffery, John 319
McCloy, John J. 67
McLellan, David 8
means, extremism of 10–11
Meany, George 277
Mégret, Bruno 471, 477
Mellinthin, Heinz 84
Melsen, Konrad 85
Memmo, Robert 321
Menderes, Adnan 432
Mengele, Josef 71, 79
Mereu, Francesco 264
Merlino, Mario 151, 170
Mersan, Ömer 423
Mersi, Rodolfo 368, 375–6
Mertins, Gerhard 78
Mesa, Luis García 164
Messerschmidt 65
Messerschmidt-Werke 74
Métal Assaut (music magazine) 479
Métal Urbaine 478
Meyer, Kurt ("Panzer") 82–3
Meza, García 165–6
MFA *see* Movimento das Forças Armadas (MFA: Armed Forces Movement)
Micalizio, Giacomo 256
Miceli, Vito 239, 264–70, 274, 286, 288–9, 293–4, 298, 323, 379
Michel, Luc 476
Michelini, Arturo 86, 221
Mieville, Roberto 216
Milá, Ernesto 151
Millî Birlik Komitesi (MBK: Committee of National Unity) 433

Millî Nizam Partisi (National Order Party) 438
Millî Selâmet Partisi (MSP: National Salvation Party) 436
Milliyet (liberal daily) 416, 422
Minetto, Sergio 384
Mingarelli, Dino 271
Mino, Enrico 267
Minogue, Kenneth 12, 22
Miori, Hugo Raúl 164
mirror imaging 6–8; academicians from different disciplines and 6–7; defined 6; examples of 7; materialistic societies and 6; problems with, factors contributing to 6–7; social scientists and 6–7, 14
Missions spéciales (Guillou mini-manual) 143–4
Mitchell, John 282, 320
Modafferi, Demetrio 250
moderate Cold War-era anti-communist networks 61
Mondlane, Eduardo 145
monism 27
Montandon, Georges 94
Monterey Terrorism Research and Education Program (MonTREP) 55
Monti, Adalberto 254
Monti, Adriano 234, 241, 255
Montini, Giovanni Battista 318
Monzat, René 103
More, Thomas 27
Moreau, Alain 142
Moreau, Henri 99–100
Moreau, Odette 86
Morente, Federico Quintero 160
Morin, Paolo 384
Morlion, Felix 315
Moro, Aldo 275, 288, 291, 326, 385
Mortilla, Armando 150–1
Mosley, Oswald 86, 96, 99
Mota, Jorge 151–2
Mouvement d'Action Civique (MAC: Civic Action Movement) 95–9
Mouvement de Combat Contre-Révolutionnaire (Counterrevolutionary Combat Movement) 139
Mouvement Jeune Nation (Young Nation Movement) 95–6, 138
Mouvement Jeune Révolution (MJR) 370, 376
Mouvement Nationaliste Révolutionnaire (MNR) 471–2
Mouvement National Républicaine 471, 477

Mouvement Occident 469–71
Mouvement Révolutionnaire Fasciste Belge (Belgian Fascist Revolutionary Movement) 93
Mouvement Social Européen/Europäische Sozialbewegung (MSE/ESB: European Social Movement) 84–90
Mouvement Social pour les Provinces Romanes en Belgique (Social Movement for the Roman Provinces in Belgium) 87
Movimento das Forças Armadas (MFA: Armed Forces Movement) 140
Movimento d'Azione Rivoluzionaria (MAR: Revolutionary Action Movement) 234, 367
Movimento Politico Ordine Nuovo (MPON: New Order Political Movement) 146, 235
Movimento Sociale Italiano (MSI: Italian Social Movement) 69, 85–6, 145, 367
Moynihan, Michael 479
Mozambique Liberation Front (Frente de Libertaçao de Moçambique (FRELIMO)) 145
Mumcu, Uğur 413, 421–2, 426
Murgia, Pier Giuseppe 218
Mussolini, Anna Maria 86
Mussolini, Benito 86, 214
mutual aid societies 61
Mutual Aid Support Group for Former Waffen SS Soldiers (Hilfsgemeinschaft auf Gegenseitigkeit der ehemaligen Soldaten der Waffen-SS (HIAG)) 81–5; in Austria 83–4; in Belgium 84; in Denmark 85; in Netherlands 84; in Spain 85

Nanni, Roberto 158
Napalm Rock (music magazine) 479
Nardella, Francesco 278, 288, 378
Nardi, Gianni 291
Nationaal Europese Sociale Beweging (NESB: National-European Social Movement) 84, 87
National Association of Italian Veterans in Spain (Associazione Nazionale Combattenti Italiani di Spagna (ANCIS)) 217
"national Catholicism" (doctrine) 138
national chauvinism 62
"national communism" (neo-fascist doctrine) 138
National Democratic Party of Germany (Nationaldemokratische Partei Deutschlands (NDP)) 68

Nationaldemokratische Partei Deutschlands (NPD: National Democratic Party of Germany) 68
National Destiny 476
National European Labor Front (Front National-Européen du Travail) 100
National-European Social Movement (Nationaal Europese Sociale Beweging (NESB)) 84, 87
National Federation of Former Soldiers (Confederación Nacional de Ex-Combatientes) 85
National Federation of RSI Veterans (Federazione Nazionale Combattenti della Repubblica Sociale Italiana (FNCRSI)) 223
National French Students (Étudiants Nationalistes Français) 96
National Front (Fronte Nazionale (FN)) 213, 225–51, 473; American intelligence officials and 240–2; armed forces of 237–41; Avanguardia Nazionale and 235–6; Borghese establishment of 225–6; Borghese use of, to launch coup 229–31; Calzolari and 244–7; Comitato Tricolore as 226, 230–1; coup operational plans 242–3; developmental history of 231–2; groups linked to 234–5; ideologies of 226–8; Loi and 247–9; Mafia recruitment into 236–7; Ordine Nuovo and 234–5; *Orientamenti Programmatici* definition of 227, 229; Reggian activists of 249–51; right-wing extremist contacts of 236–7; secret supporters of 229–30, 233–4; stated goals of 228–9, 233; structure of 232–3
National Front for Algeria in France (Front National pour l'Algérie Français in France) 96
National Intelligence Agency (Turkish Millî İstihbarat Teşkilâtı (MİT)) 414, 429
National Intelligence Directorate (Chilean Dirección de Inteligencia Nacional (DINA)) 161–3
Nationalist Action Party (Alparslan Türkeş' Milliyetçi Hareket Partisi (MHP)) 414, 416, 429, 430–9; anti-Western sentiments 437; Atatürk and 430–1; CKMP and 433; as defender of Islam 437–8; historical development of 430–6; ideologies of 436–9; organizational structure of 435; pan-Turkism and 431–3; paramilitary training camps of 435–6; Türkeş and formation of 433–6; Turkism, described 431

National Labor Party (Partito Nazionale del Lavoro) 221
National Legion (Légion Nationale) 95
National Liberation Front (Front de Libération Nationale (FLN)) 138
National Military Police (Ethnike Stratiotike Astinomia (ESA)) 157
National Order Party (Millî Nizam Partisi) 438
National Rally (Rassemblement National) 96
National Resistance Council (Conseil National de la Résistance) 139
Nationalrevolutionäre Aufbauorganisation 481
National Revolutionary Faction 476
National Salvation Party (Millî Selâmet Partisi (MSP)) 436
National Security Council 282
Nationalsozialistische Deutsche Arbeiterpartei (NSDAP: National-Socialist German Workers' Party) 65
National Special Forces Association of Italy (Associazione Nazionale Arditi d'Italia) 217
National Vanguard (Avanguardia Nazionale (AN)) 142, 145, 147, 151, 161, 234, 380, 400
National Youth (Jeunesses Nationales) 96–7
National Youth Front (Frente Nacional de Juventud (FNJ)) 151
National Youth Training (Formazione Nazionale Giovanile) 167
Nation-Belgique (MAC journal) 96, 99
Nation Europa (journal) 150
Nation Europa concept 63–4
Nation Européenne 98
Natsionalno-Bolshevistskaia Partiia 476
Naumann, Werner 70, 74
Naumann Circle (Naumann-Kreis) 69–70
Naumann-Kreis (Naumann Circle) 69–70
Nazar, Ruzi 429
Nazi escape/action organizations, underground 60–1, 64–80; Allied powers involvement in 79–80; Die Bruderschaft (the Brotherhood) 66–70; Catholic Church and 80; clandestine political/paramilitary operations of 72–3; elsewhere in Europe 69; escape routes for war criminals 70–2, 78–9; financing of 65–6; Das Kameradenwerk (Comrades' Alliance) 66, 67; Naumann-Kreis (Naumann Circle) 69–70; ODESSA: Organization of Former SS Members (Die Organisation der ehemaligen SS-Angehörigen) 66–7; published works addressing 64–5; reach and power of 72; Die Schleuse (the Lock-Gate) 66–7; Skorzeny and 72–8; Die Spinne (the Spider) 66–7; Die Stille Hilfe für Kriegsgefangene und Internierte (Silent Help for Prisoners-of-War and Internees) 66–8; von Schubert and 78
Nazi Nordiska Rikspartiet (NRP: Nordic Empire Party) 85
Neami, Francesco 175, 384
Nederlandse Sociale Beweging (Dutch Social Movement) 87
Nehring, Joachim 69
neo-fascist groupuscules: changing nature of 467–9; characteristic features of 480–3; Mouvement Occident as 469–71
neo-fascist paramilitary/terrorist groups, 1960s/1970s Europe and Latin America 3
Neumann, Raúl Eduardo Iturriaga 162
neutral conceptions of ideology 16, 22
New European Order (Nouvelle Ordre Européen/Europäische Neu-Ordnung (NOE/ENO)) 89–94, 149–50, 236
New Left(s) 22
New Order (Ordine Nuovo (ON)) 234–5
New Order Political Movement (Movimento Politico Ordine Nuovo (MPON)) 146, 235
New Order Study Center (Centro Studi Ordine Nuovo (CSON)) 145–6, 221
New Right Action (Aktion Neue Rechte (ANR)) 83
New Swedish Movement (Nysvenska Rörelsen (NSR)) 86
New World Order 474–5
Nicastro, Maria Antonietta 298
Nicoli, Torquato 254, 298
Niekisch, Ernst 472, 474
nine lights principles 434
Nixon, Richard 241, 281–4, 320, 325
Nordborg, Yngve 86
Nordic Empire Party (Nazi Nordiska Rikspartiet (NRP)) 85
Norsk Reform Bevaegelse (Norwegian Reform Movement) 87
North Atlantic Treaty Organization (NATO) 217, 403–4, 412
Norwegian Reform Movement (Norsk Reform Bevaegelse) 87
Nouvelle Action Française 471
Nouvelle École 161

Nouvelle Ordre Européen/Europäische Neu-Ordnung (NOE/ENO: New European Order) 89–94, 149–50, 236
Nouvelle Résistance (NR) 471; Bouchet and 471; counter-cultural actions of 478–80; ideology of 473–4; organizational history of 472–3; political strategy/tactics of 474–7
Nuclei Armati Rivoluzionari (NAR: Armed Revolutionary Cells) 399
Nucleo Operativo Diretto (NOD: Directed Operational Cell) 266
Nysvenska Rörelsen (NSR: New Swedish Movement) 86

Oakeshott, Michael 22
OAS *see* Organisation de l'Armée Secrète (OAS: Secret Army Organization)
Occhi, Adamo Degli 234
Occident *see* Mouvement Occident
Occorsio, Vittorio 160, 248, 309
ODESSA: Organization of Former SS Members (Die Organisation der ehemaligen SS-Angehörigen) 66–7
Oerlikon 69
Office of Special Operations (OSO) 46
Offie, Carmel 217
Olino, Renato 271
Operación Cóndor 164
Operation Triangle 274–5
Opus Dei 223–4
Ordine Nero 367
Ordine Nuovo (New Order (ON)) 161, 234–5, 380, 400
Ordine Nuovo (bimonthly journal) 146, 150
Ordine Nuovo (ON) 142, 145–7; assaults carried out by 176; foreign intelligence of NATO/CIA and 177–8; ideological views of 145–6; membership levels of 146; OAS and 150; right-wing extremist links with 149, 176–7; structure of 175–6
Ordre Nouveau 142, 370
Organisation de l'Afrique Libre (Free Africa Organization) 143
Organisation de l'Armée Secrète (OAS: Secret Army Organization) 96, 136, 139, 470
Organisation de Salut Public (Public Salvation Organization) 96
Organisation Lutte du Peuple (OLP) 471, 481
Organization of Turkish Youth (Türk Gençlik Teşkilâtı (TGT)) 432
Orientamenti Programmatici 227, 229

Orlandini, Remo 224, 232, 255–7, 260–1, 266, 271–2, 279–80, 297–8
Orlando, Gaetano 234
Orlando, Giulio 305
Orsi, Claudio 152
Ortiz, Joseph 97
Ortolani, Umberto 321
OSO *see* Office of Special Operations (OSO)
Österreichische Soziale Bewegung (Austrian Social Movement) 87
Ousset, Jean 97
Overseas Agency (Agenzia Oltremare) 143
Öymen, Örsan 430
Özbey, Yalçın 419, 421, 426
Özgün, Faruk 423

Pabst, Waldemar 69
Pacciardi, Randolfo 225, 276
Pace, Cosimo 239, 265
Paetel, Karl-Otto 472
Paglia, Guido 155, 255
Pagliai, Pierluigi 163–5, 175
Paladin Group 78
Pale, Hasan Murat 422
Palladino, Carmine 255
Pallara, Salvatore 247
Pallavicini, Elvina 276
Pallotto, Roberto 255
Palmer, R. M. 429
Palumbo, Giovanbattista 308
Pansa, Giampaolo 228
pan-Turkism 431–3
Paoletti, Pietro 233
Papadopoulos, George 319
Papadopoulos, Giorgios 155
papal assassination plot: Bulgarian sponsorship, theory of 426–30; CIA plot thesis concerning 414–15; as false flag terrorist operation 417; introduction to 411–16; KGB plot thesis concerning 413–14; literature on, for propaganda purposes 412; literature on, incorporating propaganda or disinformation themes 412–13; literature on, produced by researchers of independent/critical minds 413; MHP and 430–9; sponsorship of, theories concerning 413–16; by Turkish ultranationalist theory 415–16; Western sponsorship, theory of 429
parallel SID 286–90, 292–4, 379–80
Pardo, Aldo 250–1
Parri, Ferruccio 216, 313
Parsons, Talcott 21

Parti Communautaire Européen (PCE: European Communitarian Party) 101
Parti Communautaire National-Européen 476
Parti Communiste Suisse/Marxiste-Leniniste (PCS/ML: Swiss Communist Party/Marxist-Leninist) 144–5
particular conceptions of ideology 19
Parti des Forces Nouvelles (PFN) 472
Parti National Belge (Belgian National Party) 96
Partito Comunista d'Italia/Marxista-Leninista (PCdI/M-L) 369
Partito Comunista Italiano (PCI: Italian Communist Party) 175, 229, 365
Partito Nazionale del Lavoro (National Labor Party) 221
Partito Socialdemocratico Europeo (PSDE: European Social Democratic Party) 277
Partito Socialista Italiano (PSI: Italian Socialist Party) 175, 216, 365
Parvulesco, Jean 168
Pattakos, Stylianos 154
Pavelić, Ante 71
Paz, Virgilio 161–2
PCS/ML see Parti Communiste Suisse/Marxiste-Leniniste (PCS/ML: Swiss Communist Party/Marxist-Leninist)
Peace and Freedom Democratic Union (Union Démocratique pour la Paix et la Liberté) 97
Péan, Pierre 86
Pecorelli, Mino 292, 321
Peeters, Piet 84
Penn, Alfred Wayne 27
People's League for Peace and Freedom (Volksbund für Frieden und Freiheit (VFF)) 70
People's Liberation Army of Turkey (Türkiye Halk Kurtuluş Ordusu (THKO)) 420
Pepper, José Vicente 142
Perón, Eva 77
Perón, Juan 77, 317
Perri, Cesare 235
Perry, Jack R. 428
Piaggio, Andrea 278, 305
Piazza della Loggia bomb massacre 365
Piazza Fontana bomb massacre 147–9, 155, 170, 312, 365
Piccoli, Flaminio 305
Piedmont 474
Piekalkiewicz, Jaroslaw 27
Pignatelli, Valerio 219

Pike, Otis 284
Piñar, Blas 157
Pinay, Antoine 316
Pinelli, Giuseppe 367, 384
Pinochet, Augusto 161
Pirina, Marco 247, 251, 254
Pisanò, Giorgio 156, 271, 291, 293, 325
Pisano, Sandro 235
Pius XII, Pope 80
Placidi, Ruggero 268
plausible deniability 76, 366, 401, 406
Plebe, Armando 277
Plevris, Kostas 236
Ploncard, Jacques 139, 142
Plumbers Unit 281–2
Pofferi, Giovanni 317
Polícia Internacional e de Defesa do Estado/Direcção Géral de Segurança (PIDE/DGS: International Police and Defense of the State/General Security Directorate) 139–40, 143
Politica e Strategia (ISSED journal) 276
political ideologies 13–16, 23–6; affective dimension of 25; Brzezinski on 13; divisions of 25; Eatwell on 13, 15; elements of 26; Friedrich on 13; Lane on 14; Lerner on 15; Macridis on 14; Rejai on 24; Smelser on 24, 26; Vincent on 14; Weigel on 15; Wright on 15
Political Man (Lipset) 21
political paranoia *vs.* political realism 46–55; conspiratorial politics and 50–1; elements of 48; historical importance/efficacy of 46–7; scholarly publications related to 47–8; source materials for research of 54–5
political terrorist attacks, Italy 364–6; characteristics of 366; factions identified in 364–5; false flag operations and 366; historical/political importance of 365–6; objectives of 365; overview of 364–6
Poltronieri, Umberto 257
Pomar, Eliodoro 158, 254
Pompei, Alberto 254
Pompidou, Georges 78
Ponzi, Tom 291
Porta Casucci, Giampaolo 381
Portolan, Manlio 175
Portuguese Liberation Army (Exército de Libertação Português (ELP)) 143
Possenti, Paolo 306
postmodernists 16
Poulantzas, Michael 154
Poumpouras, Antoine 155

Prantl, Max 69
presidentialist group, of state manipulation 302–3, 325–6
presidentialists 364, 367
Priester, Karl-Heinz 70, 86–7
Primicino, Francesco 307
private anti-communist organizations 61
Pro Deo 315–16
Propaganda Due (P2) 414; masonic lodge 367
Proudhon, Pierre 472
Public Salvation Organization (Organisation de Salut Public) 96
Pugliese, Giuseppe ("Beppino") 296

Qadhdhāfī, Mu'ammar al- 103
Quisling, Vidkun 63, 85

radical Cold War-era anti-communist networks 61
radical neo-fascists 364
RAHOWA 479
Raingeard de la Bletière, Jean Denis 142
Ramos, Ramiro Ledesmas 472
Rampazzo, Sandro 378
Rasi, Gaetano 276
Rassemblement National (National Rally) 96
Rauff, Walther 71, 79
Rauti, Giuseppe ("Pino") 90, 94
Rauti, Pino 145–7, 149–51, 153–6, 175, 234–5, 307
Raven's Chat (music magazine) 479
Reader's Digest 427
Reazione (journal) 149
Rebelles Européennes (record label) 478
Rebull, Tomás García 161
reform ideologies 25
Reitano, Antonio 254
Rejai, Mostafa 24–5
religious ideologies 25–6
Repubblica Sociale Italiana (RSI: Italian Social Republic) 213
Republican Peasant Nation Party (Cumhuriyetçi Köylü Millî Partisi (CKMP)) 433
Requiem gothique (music magazine) 479
Research and Study Group for European Civilization (Groupement de Recherche et d'Études sur la Civilisation Européenne (GRECE)) 84
Restauration Nationale 471
Restivo, Franco 265
restrictive conceptions of ideology 16, 22–3
Retinger, Joseph 314

Revilla, Tomás Perez 159
Revolutionary Action Fasci (Fasci di Azione Rivoluzionaria (FAR)) 146
Revolutionary Action Movement (Movimento d'Azione Rivoluzionaria (MAR)) 234
revolutionary ideologies 25
Revolutionary Left (Devrimçi Sol (DEV-SOL)) 420
Revolutionary National Constituent Assembly (Costituente Nazionale Rivoluzionaria (CNR)) 234
Révolution européenne 478
Révolution Européenne (European Revolution) 100
Rheinmetall 65
Ribacchi, Alberto 255
Ricci, Mario 158
Ricci, Ugo 278
Rimi, Filippo 237
Rimi, Natale 237
Rinner, Felix 83
Ristuccia, Michele 291
Rivista Militare (journal) 153
Rizzato, Eugenio 288, 378, 380
Roatta, Mario 291
Robison, John 49
Rocca, Renzo 153, 224–5
Rockwell, George Lincoln 151
Rodríguez, Pablo 281
Rogers, William P. 282
Rognoni, Giancarlo 158, 175
rollback strategy 61
Roma (right-wing publication) 167
Romagnoli, Sandro 266
Romano, Maria Piera 244, 246
Romualdi, Pino 167, 221
Ronconi, Pio Filippani 171–2
Rook, Tommaso Adami 233, 242, 271
Rosa, Dalmazio 259
Rosa, Mario 227, 232, 247, 254
Rosa dei Venti 286–8, 290, 296, 367, 369, 378, 381
Roselli Lorenzini, Giuseppe 238, 268, 275, 278, 305
Rosenberg, Alfred 94
Rosseti, Siro 293
Rossi, Alessandro 255
Rössler, Fritz 86, 90
Rotilio, Pierino 248
Royuela, Alberto 148
RSI National Veterans' Union (Unione Nazionale Combattenti della Repubblica Sociale Italiana (UNCRSI)) 222–3

Rubini, Walter 384–5
Rudel, Hans-Ulrich 67, 70, 79, 87, 96, 99
Rumanian Garda de Fier (Iron Guard) 86
Rumor, Mariano 279, 305, 367, 384–5
Russell, Seymour 284–5

Saalbach, Paul 429
Sablonsky, Jay S. 142
Saccucci, Sandro 235, 257–8, 260, 265
Saint Martin's Fund (Sint-Maartensfonds (SMF)) 84
Salan, Raoul 97
Salvini, Guido 141, 383
Sanchez-Bella, Alfredo 317
Şandir, Mehmet 422
San Giorgio, Corrado 276
San Martín, José Ignacio 157
Santoro, Michele 308
Saragat, Giuseppe 224, 252, 385
Sargent, Lyman Tower 12
Sassen, Willem ("Alfons") 79
Satta, Vladimiro 327
Sauge, Georges 97
Scelba, Mario 220
Scelba Law 146, 219
Schacht, Hjalmar 74
Scheel, Gustav Adolf 68
Scheinwerfer publishing circle 68–9
Schellenberg, Walter 72
Schirinzi, Giuseppe 250–1
Die Schleuse (the Lock-Gate) 66–7
Schutzstaffel (SS: Protection Squadron) 65
Schweizerische Faschistische Bewegung (Swiss Fascist Movement) 91
Schwend, Friedrich 71, 79
scientific racist treatises 94
Secolo d'Italia (right-wing publication) 167
Secret Army Organization (Organisation de l'Armée Secrète (OAS)) 136, 139
Secret World Apparatus for Revolutionary Action (Appareil Mondial Secret d'Action Révolutionnaire (AMSAR)) 168
security forces, Borghese Coup investigations by 263–96; Anello and 290–2; Carabinieri officers and 270–2; Casardi and 267–8; CIA and 281–6; D'Amato and 272–3; Fanali and 275–9; Genovesi and 264; Maletti and 266–7; Miceli and 264–70, 286, 288–9, 293–4; military officers involvement 274–5; NATO involvement 279–80; parallel SID and 286–90, 292–4; Pubblica Sicurezza involvement 273–4; Roselli Lorenzini and 275, 278; SID and 263–4

Sednaoui, Michael 285
Segni, Antonio 224
Selçuk, Timur 422
Seliger, Martin 16
Sembianza, Benito 250
Semerari, Aldo 308–9
Şener, Hasan 419, 422
Şener, Mehmet 419–20, 422
Sergent, Pierre 96, 142, 376–7
Sermonti, Rutilio 235
Serpieri, Stefano 236, 255
Serra, Abrantes 140
Serranò, Ugo 250
Serravalle, Gerardo 285–6
Service de Documentation Extérieure et de Contre-Espionnage (SDECE: Foreign Documentation and Counter-Espionage Service) 139
Servicio Central de Documentación de la Presidencia de Gobierno (SECED: Central Documentation Service of the President of the Government) 157–8
Servizio Informazioni Difesa (SID) 368
Servizio Informazioni Forze Armate (SIFAR: Armed Forces Intelligence Service) 153, 368, 375
Servizio Informazioni Operative e Situazione (SIOS)-Esercito (Army Intelligence Service for Situational and Operational Intelligence) 169
Servizio Informazioni per la Sicurezza Militare's (SISMI) 381
Shils, Edward 22
Sibert, Edwin 75
Siciliano, Martino 383
Sidos, Pierre 469
Sierra, Angel 159
Signorelli, Paolo 175, 296, 307, 309–10
Signor P affair 155–6
Silent Help for Prisoners-of-War and Internees (Die Stille Hilfe für Kriegsgefangene und Internierte) 66–8
Silent Majority (Maggioranza Silenziosa) 234
Sima, Horia 71, 86
Sindona, Michele 223, 283, 317–22
Singer, Hartwig 481
Sint-Maartensfonds (SMF: Saint Martin's Fund) 84
Siotto, Elio 268
Sirri Kadem, Sedat 420, 426
Skinner, B. F. 14
Skorzeny, Otto 70, 72–8, 96, 141, 148, 167
Slugěnov, Vendelín 412
Smelser, Neil 10, 24–6

Socialist Reich Party (Sozialistische Reichspartei (SRP)) 68
Social Movement for the Roman Provinces in Belgium (Mouvement Social pour les Provinces Romanes en Belgique) 87
Social Psychology Higher Studies Center (Centre d'Études Supérieures de Psychologie Sociale (CESPS)) 97, 138
social scientists: human behavior and 14–16; mirror imaging and 6–7
social solidarity 25–6
Soffiati, Marcello 384
Sogno, Edgardo 234, 269, 276, 298, 319, 321, 367
Soldat de l'Opposition Algérienne (SOA: Soldiers of the Algerian Opposition) 143
Soldiers of the Algerian Opposition (Soldat de l'Opposition Algérienne (SOA)) 143
Sol Invictus 478
"Solo" counterinsurgency plan 212
Solzhenitsyn, Aleksandr 8
Sordi, Walter 308, 310
Sorteni, Giorgio 368
Soustelle, Jacques 317
Southgate, Troy 476
Soutre, Jean-René 167
Sovereign Military Order of Malta (SMOM) 316
Soviet Komitet Gosudarst'vennoy Bezopasnosti (KGB: Committee for State Security) 413–14
Soziale Friedenswerk (Establishment of Social Peace) 67
Sozialistische Reichspartei (SRP: Socialist Reich Party) 68
Spada, Massimo 318
Spaggiari, Albert 161
Spagnuolo, Carmelo 295, 321
Spampanato, Bruno 220
Spanish Circle of Friends of Europe (Círculo Español de Amigos de Europa (CEDADE)) 142, 151–2, 161
Spanish Confederation of Autonomous Right-Wing Groups (Confederacion Española de Derechas Autónomas (CEDA)) 223–4
Spiazzi, Amos 175, 287–8, 292–3, 298, 322–3, 378–80
Spigai, Virgilio 278
Die Spinne (the Spider) 66–7
Stammati, Gaetano 321
Stangl, Franz 71

State Intelligence Secretariat (Argentine Secretaría de Inteligencia de Estado (SIDE)) 163
state manipulation theory, Borghese Coup and 301–3
state-private network 61
status quo ideologies 25
stay/behind networks 402–3
Stefàno, Bruno Luciano 158, 258, 260
Steiner, Felix 68
Sterling, Claire 412, 418, 420, 425, 428, 430; see also Ağca, Mehmet Ali
Sternhell, Zeev 481–2
Stichting Oud Politieke Delinquenten (SOPD: Foundation for Former Political Delinquents) 84
Die Stille Hilfe für Kriegsgefangene und Internierte (Silent Help for Prisoners-of-War and Internees) 66–8
Stirner, Max 367–8, 380
Stone, Howard ("Rocky") 283, 286
strategy of tension 149, 169, 171, 174, 176, 236, 364–5, 399–407
Strauss, Franz Josef 277
Stroessner, Alfredo 164
Student, Kurt 68
Studies in Intelligence (OSO journal) 46
Sturlese, Remo 256
Suárez, Roberto 165
Suomen Sociallinen Liike (SSL: Finnish Social Movement) 87
SuperS faction 414
Supreme Headquarters Allied Powers Europe (SHAPE) 102, 219
Surgeon, Pierre-Jean 142
Sverdlov, Stefan 427
Swiss Communist Party/Marxist-Leninist (Parti Communiste Suisse/Marxiste-Leniniste (PCS/ML)) 144–5
Swiss Fascist Movement (Schweizerische Faschistische Bewegung) 91
Swiss People's Party (Volkspartei der Schweiz/Parti Populaire Suisse (VPS/PPS)) 86, 93
Syndicate of National Groups (Arbeitsgemeinschaft Nationaler Gruppen (ANG)) 69

Taddei, Ezio 224
Talenti, Pier Francesco 253, 283, 325
Tamburino, Giovanni 378
Tanassi, Mario 279
Taşkın, Hasan 424
Taubert, Eberhard 70

Taylor, Maxwell 10
Tè, Sergio 246
Tecniche della guerra rivoluzionaria (Giannettini) 169–70
Tedeschi, Mario 321
Teichmann, Paul 95–6, 100
Tek, Haydar 423
Teodori, Massimo 322
Tercéristes Radicaux 473
terrorism: defined 4; definitional problems with 3–5; *vs.* freedom fighting 4–5; use of 4; as violent technique of psychological manipulation 4–5
terrorism analysis 3–30; definitional problems with 3–5; ideologies/extremist ideologies and 8–30; methodological problems with 5–6; mirror imaging problems with 6–8
terrorism studies, methodological problems in 5–6
terrorist acts: components of 4; triadic nature of 4
Terza Posizione (TP: Third Position) 399, 481
Third Way 476
Third World revolutionary movements 22
Thiriart, Jean-François 94–105, 474–6
Thompson, John B. 12, 16
Thyssen 65
Tilgher, Adriano 251, 296
Timmel, Roland 87
Tisei, Aldo 165
Titta, Adalberto 291
Tixier-Vignancourt Committee (Comité Tixier-Vignancourt) 142
Togni, Giuseppe 368
Tondini, Amleto 318
"Tora Tora" operation 251–61; ANPDI gym and 258–9; cancellation of 259–60; headquarters/command post strategies 253–5; missions, allocation of 253; Orlandini and 255–7; overview of 251–2; projected arrestees following 252–3; RAI-TV transmitter objective 256–7; Saccucci and 257–8; Vicari kidnapping and 256; Viminale armory and, taking control of 255–6
Torchia, Giorgio 143
Töre, Teslim 420, 423
total conceptions of ideology 19
Totalitarian Dictatorship and Autocracy (Friedrich and Brzezinski) 21
totalitarian ideologies 20–1; defined 21
totalitarianism 29; theorists 13, 20

Townley, Michael 161–2
Townsman and Countryman Initiative (Bürger-und Bauerninitiative (BBI)) 68
Trinquier, Roger 97
Troisième Voie (TV) 471–3, 478, 480
Trujillo, Rafael ("Ramfis") 142, 223
Tshombé, Moise 96
Tubino, Giacomo 288
Turchi, Franz 220
Türkeş, Alparslan 432–8
Turkey ultranationalist right 411–40
Türk Gençlik Teşkilâtı (TGT: Organization of Turkish Youth) 432
Turkish Millî İstihbarat Teşkilâtı (MİT: National Intelligence Agency) 414, 429
Turkism, described 431
Türkiye Halk Kurtuluş Ordusu (THKO: People's Liberation Army of Turkey) 420
Türkiye İşçi Partisi (TİP: Worker's/Labor Party of Turkey) 435
Türkiye Komünist Partisi (TKP: Communist Party of Turkey) 435
Türkiye Komünizmle Mücadele Derneği (TKMD: Association for Fighting Communism in Turkey) 432
Türkkan, Reza Oğuz 431–2

Ufficio Sicurezza Patto Atlantico (USPA: Atlantic Pact Security Office) 287
Uğurlu, Abuzer 419–22, 426–7, 430
Ülkücü Gençlik Derneği (ÜGD: Idealist Youth Association) 421
Ülkücü Teknik Elemanlar Derneği (ÜTED: Idealist Technical Worker's Association) 421
Ülkü ve Kültür Birliği (Union of Ideals and Culture) 437
Ulrichsberg Community (Ulrichsberggemeinschaft) 83
Ulrichsberggemeinschaft (Ulrichsberg Community) 83
umbrella man 50
underground neo-fascist networks, post-World War II 3
Union Démocratique pour la Paix et la Liberté (Peace and Freedom Democratic Union) 97
Union des Cercles Résistance (UCR) 477
Union des Syndicats Communautaires Européens (Confederation of European Communitarian Labor Unions) 100
Unione Nazionale Combattenti della Repubblica Sociale Italiana (UNCRSI: RSI National Veterans' Union) 222–3

Index **515**

Union for the Defense of Oppressed Peoples (Union pour la Défense des Peuples Opprimés) 98
Union of Ideals and Culture (Ülkü ve Kültür Birliği) 437
Union pour la Défense des Peuples Opprimés (Union for the Defense of Oppressed Peoples) 98
United League of Italy (Lega Italia Unità) 234
United States: Counter-Intelligence Corps (CIC) 75; Friends of Germany group in 68; New Left(s) in 22
Unité Radicale (UR) 471, 477
University Federation of Italian Catholics (Federazione Universitaria Cattolici Italiani (FUCI)) 313
University Front for National Action (Fronte Universitario di Azione Nazionale (FUAN)) 86, 148
Unleashed 479
utopia 27
utopianism 27–8

Vaillant, Auguste 372
Vajta, Ferenc 314
Valín, Alberto 164
Vallentin, Jean 142
Valori, Giancarlo 317
Van den Broeck, Jean 100
van den Heuvel, C. C. 317
van Dyck, Johann 87
Vannier, Jean 140
van Overstraeten, Toon 84
van Tienen, Paul 84, 90
Venner, Dominique 469
Ventura, Giovanni 149, 175, 380
Venturi, Mauro 288
Verband Deutscher Soldaten (VdS) 81
Verband Nationalsozialistischer Eidgenossen (Association of National Socialist Confederates) 86
Verband Österreichischer Kameradschaften (Federation of Austrian Fellowships) 83
Vereinigte Österreichische Eisen-und Stahlwerke (VÖESt) 74
Veritas Ubique (bimonthly bulletin) 140
Versluis, Arthur 30
Vessichelli, Raffaele 272
Viaggio, Santino 247–8
Vicari, Angelo 252, 256, 265
Viezzer, Antonio 295
Viggiani, Egidio 270
Vikernes, Varg 479

Viking Youth (Wiking-Jugend) 68
Vincent, Andrew 14, 19
Vinciguerra, Vincenzo 174, 289, 369, 383–4, 405
Viola, Roberto 163
Violante, Luciano 269
Violet, Jean 316
Vitalone, Claudio 247, 269, 272
Vito Pace 258
Vitozzi, Aldo 246
Vlaams Blok (VB: Flemish Bloc) 87
Vlaamse Militanten Orde (VMO: Flemish Militant Order) 84
Vlaams Verbond van Oud-Oostfrontstrijders (Flemish Association of Former East Front Fighters) 84
Volksbund für Frieden und Freiheit (VFF: People's League for Peace and Freedom) 70
Volkspartei der Schweiz/Parti Populaire Suisse (VPS/PPS: Swiss People's Party) 86, 93
Volkswagenwerk 65
Vollenweider, Erwin 86, 90, 93
von Arnswaldt, Wolf 162
von Habsburg, Otto 316
von Leers, Johannes 78
von Manteuffel, Hasso 68
von Metternich, Clemens 49
von Oven, Wilfred 70
von Schalburg, Christian Frederick 85
von Schubert, Gerhard Hartmut 78
von Thadden, Adolf 99
Voter's Alliance for Americans of German Ancestry 87

Waffen-SS support network 80–5; campaigns of 82; HIAG and 81–5; Meyer and 82–3
Walters, Vernon 315
Wang Yujiang 102
Warsaw Pact 412, 429
Washington Post 413
Weber, Eugen 481
Weigel, George 15
WerBell, Mitchell, III 160
Werkgemeenschap Europa in de Lage Landen (European Working Group in the Low Countries) 87
Western Europe, New Left(s) in 22
West German Bundesnachrichtendienst (BND) 415
white coup apparatus 367
Wiking-Jugend (Viking Youth) 68

Wilcox, Laird 10
Willan, Philip 407
Wintrobe, Ronald 10
Wojtyła, Karol Józef 414; *see also* John Paul II, Pope
Wolff, Karl 71, 213–14
Wolff-Trust 74
Wolthius, Jan A. 84
Worker's/Labor Party of Turkey (Türkiye İşçi Partisi (TIP)) 435
World Anti-Communist League (WACL) 98, 164
World Union of National Socialists (WUNS) 142, 151
Wright, Anthony 15

Yang Xiaonong 102
Yazıcıoğlu, Muhsin 422

Yeo-Thomas, Forest 76
Yockey, Francis Parker 474–5
Young Europe (Jeune Europe (JE)) 89, 94–105, 142, 152, 482
Young European Legion (Junge Europäische Legion (JEL)) 93–4
Young Nation Movement (Mouvement Jeune Nation) 95–6
Young Socialist Guard (Jeune Garde Socialiste) 95

Zagolin, Dario 378
Zappulla, Benito 166
Zellerbach, James David 283
Zoccoli, Giovandomenico 250
Zoratti, Bruno 277
Zorzi, Delfo 175, 384
Zucca, Enrico 291